CODE OF CANON LAW

LATIN-ENGLISH EDITION

NEW ENGLISH TRANSLATION

CANON LAW SOCIETY OF AMERICA

CODEX IURIS CANONICI

AUCTORITATE

IOANNIS PAULI PP. II

PROMULGATUS

LIBRERIA EDITRICE VATICANA

1989

CODE OF CANON LAW

LATIN-ENGLISH EDITION

NEW ENGLISH TRANSLATION

Prepared under the auspices of the
Canon Law Society of America

CANON LAW SOCIETY OF AMERICA
Washington, DC 20064

CONTENTS

OUTLINE OF THE
CODE OF CANON LAW

FOREWORD TO THE TRANSLATION

Under the auspices of the Canon Law Society of America, the first English translation in the United States of the 1983 *Codex iuris canonici* was completed and published before the *vacatio legis* of the code had expired. The translation project was initiated in 1980, and a litany of canonical experts had the occasion to offer recommendations on the English rendering of the individual canons. The task of translation was an *arduum sane munus,* a difficult task indeed.

Since its appearance, the 1983 CLSA translation of the revised code provided a solid basis for canonical ministry and scholarship in the English-speaking world. The Church is properly grateful for the scholarly care evidenced in the translation.

HISTORY OF THE NEW TRANSLATION PROJECT

Subsequent to the first CLSA translation, several modifications and corrections to the translation were proposed. Also, corrections were made in the Latin text by the Supreme Legislator (see *AAS* 75 (1983) [22 September 1983] Pars II, Appendix). Furthermore, the lived experience of the code sometimes clarified the meaning of canons, as did the various authentic interpretations.

Therefore, in December, 1992, the CLSA Board of Governors established the *COMMITTEE FOR THE NEW CLSA TRANSLATION OF THE CODE OF CANON LAW.* Its members were: Robert P. Deeley, J.C.D. (Archdiocese of Boston), Michael Moodie, S.J., J.C.D. (California Province of the Society of Jesus), and John A. Renken, S.T.D., J.C.D., chairperson (Diocese of Springfield in Illinois).

Staff assistance and editorial direction were provided throughout this project by Patrick Cogan, S.A., S.T.L., J.C.D., Ph.D. (CLSA Executive Coordinator).

Soon after the Translation Committee began its work, it became very evident that a simple *revision* of the CLSA translation would not be beneficial, but that only a completely *new* translation would assure accuracy and consistency of language and style.

The Translation Committee received from the Office of the CLSA Executive Coordinator the numerous recommended translation modifications which this office had received since the first translation appeared. The committee also had the advantage of consulting other vernacular translations of the CIC and also the CLSA translation of the CCEO (1992). The CLSA membership was also invited to forward any recommended modifications, most of which were received by June, 1993.

The *first draft translation* was completed in September, 1994. After this review process was completed, it became evident that additional work was still needed to created a more easily readable English text.

The *second draft translation* was completed in December, 1995. Ten canonists were invited to review the translation.

The *third draft translation* was completed in August, 1996. The draft text was presented to the CLSA Board of Governors and, subsequently, to the NCCB Committee on Canonical Affairs. The committee chairperson met with the NCCB committee on February 27, 1997, to explain the background of the translation project and to answer questions about the third draft translation. Thereafter, the members of the NCCB committee, personally or with the assistance of their own canonical experts, offered helpful comments about the translation and proposed some possible alternative renderings. The members of the NCCB Committee were: Archbishop Thomas C. Kelly, O.P. (Louisville), Bishops Raymond L. Burke (La Crosse), Michael R. Coté (auxiliary, Portland), Thomas G. Doran (Rockford), David E. Fellhauer, chairperson (Victoria), Raymond E. Goedert (auxiliary, Chicago), John J. Myers (Peoria).

Following this review by the NCCB committee, The Most Reverend Anthony M. Pilla (Cleveland), President of the NCCB, communicated on August 8, 1997 to the President of the CLSA: "Upon the recommendations of the NCCB Committee on Canonical Affairs, I hereby grant the requisite *nihil obstat* to the Canon Law Society of America for the publication of the CLSA new English Translation of the Code of Canon Law."

PRINCIPLES GUIDING THE NEW TRANSLATION

The following principles were adopted to guide the labors of this translation project:

1. The Latin text is and remains the only official version of the code. Only this text has public force and effectiveness. The English translation does not and cannot replace the Latin. Indeed, the Latin must be consulted for clarification of meaning and complete accuracy. (Cf. *Norms* from the Papal Secretariat of State, January 28, 1983).

2. The English translation intends to be as accurate and faithful to the Latin original as reasonably possible. Although to translate is in some way to interpret, the meaning of the Latin has been conveyed carefully, with every intention to avoid distortions and to be loyal to the *mens ecclesiae*.

3. Generally, terms (words and phrases) are consistently translated throughout the code unless there are canonical reasons to vary a translated term in a given context.

4. The translation intends to be intelligible to educated American readers. Where appropriate, the language is gender inclusive, as is Latin. Appropriate grammatical principles are employed to provide a readable text consonant with contemporary American English usage. The active voice is employed when possible. Serial commas are used. Lengthy Latin sentences are rendered into brief English sentences for the sake of clarity. Subjunctive verb forms are normally rendered by straightforward imperative or obligatory language rather than by shades of exhortation or recommendation (e.g., *is to appoint* rather than *should appoint*). The strongest Latin command is the passive periphrastic: it is rendered in English by *must*.

5. Some very technical canonical words are translated into English with the Latin following in parenthesis in the text.

PERSONS WHO ASSISTED IN THE TRANSLATION PROJECT

Comments suggesting modifications in the first CLSA translation were received from the following persons by the Office of the CLSA Executive Coordinator prior to the establishment of the Translation Committee:

Alvey, Leonard
Brockhaus, Thomas A., O.S.B.
Garcia, Otto L.
Gemuend, David
Green, Thomas J.
Hill, Richard A., S.J.
Kneal, Ellsworth
Morrisey, Francis G., O.M.I.

Myers, John J.
O'Brien, Thomas C.
Plans, John F.
Richardson, James W., C.M.
Richstatter, Thomas, O.F.M.
Robertson, John
Smith, Rosemary, S.C.
Wellens, S.C., M.Afr.

The committee received suggested modifications to the CLSA translation from the following members of the CLSA. Most of these suggestions were received by June, 1993.

Bailey, David P.
Bartchak, Mark L.
Bettwy, Barbara
Blyskal, Lucy, C.S.J.
Bogdan, Leonard A.
Burke, Raymond L.
Cafardi, Nicholas P.
Cogan, Patrick J., S.A.
Coriden, James A.
Cox, Craig A.
Cunningham, Richard
DiGirolamo, Paul
Dolciamore, John V.

Doran, Thomas G.
Doyle, Jerald A.
Duarte, J. Scott
Easton, Frederick C.
Faris, John D.
Glavin, Edward R.
Graham, James
Green, Thomas J.
Griffin, Bertram F.
Gutgsell, Michael F.
Hack, Michael
Hennessey, Joseph M.
Holland, Sharon, I.H.M.

Huels, John, O.S.M.
Hynous, David M., O.P.
Ingels, Gregory
Kaucheck, Kenneth R.
Kennedy, Robert T.
Kretschmer, Albert S., S.V.D.
Laird, William F.
Mallett, James K.
McDermott, Rose, S.S.J.
McManus, Frederick R.
Montero, Eduardo G.
Moran, Thomas A.
Mullin, Joseph P., S.M.
Örsy, Ladislas, S.J.
Pfaller, Benedict, O.S.B.
Pfnausch, Edward G.

Pokusa, Joseph W.
Provost, James H.
Punderson, Joseph R.
Redmann, Esther, O.S.U.
Smilanic, Daniel A.
Soule, W. Becket, O.P.
Steffen, Kenneth C.
Stetson, William H.
Thériault, Michel
Vincent, Amos J.
Walsh, Maurice B., S.J.
Walters, Ronald F., O.F.M.
Wellens, S.C., M.Afr.
Woestman, William, O.M.I.
Wrenn, Lawrence G.

The Translation Committee invited 41 CLSA members to review a section of its *first draft translation;* the sections were distributed in November, 1994, and comments were received by mid-January, 1995. Replies came from the following 22 canonists:

Bailey, David P.
Conn, James, S.J.
Coriden, James A.
Easton, Frederick C.
Graham, James
Green, Thomas J.
Griffin, Bertram F.
Holland, Sharon, I.H.M.
Huels, John, O.S.M.
Hynous, David M., O.P.
Ingels, Gregory

Kennedy, Robert T.
Laird, William
McDermott, Rose, S.S.J.
McManus, Frederick R.
Örsy, Ladislas, S.J.
Seasoltz, R. Kevin, O.S.B.
Smilanic, Daniel A.
Soule, W. Becket, O.P.
Stetson, William
Verbrugge, Albert
Wrenn, Lawrence

The following canonists reviewed the *second draft translation:*

Beal, John P.
Green, Thomas J.

Holland, Sharon, I.H.M.
McDermott, Rose, S.S.J.

The Index was prepared by John A. Renken, S.T.D., J.C.D. (chairperson of the Translation Committee, Diocese of Springfield in Illinois). The following persons also contributed to and/or reviewed it:

Brennan, Dominica, O.P.
Cogan, Patrick, S.A.

Counce, Paul
Steffen, Kenneth

ABBREVIATIONS AND SIGLA

AA	Decr. *Apostolicam actuositatem*, 18 nov. 1965 (AAS 59 [1966] 837–864)
AAS	*Acta Apostolicae Sedis, Commentarium officiale*
Adh.	Adhortatio
AG	Decr. *Ad gentes*, 7 dec. 1965 (AAS 58 [1966] 947–990)
AIE	SCRIS Decr. *Ad instituenda experimenta*, 4 iun. 1970 (AAS 62 [1970] 549–550)
All.	Allocutio
AP	Paulus PP. VI, m.p. *Ad pascendum*, 15 aug. 1972 (AAS 64 [1972] 534–540)
Ap.	Apostolica
art.	Articulus
AS	Paulus PP. VI, m.p. *Apostolica sollicitudo*, 15 sept. 1965 (AAS 57 [1965] 775–780)
c./cc.	Canon / canones, *Codex Iuris Canonici*, 1917
CA	Sec Rescr. *Cum admotae*, 6 nov. 1964 (AAS 59 [1967] 374–378)
CAl	Pius PP. XII, m.p. *Crebrae allatae*, 22 febr. 1949 (AAS 31 [1949] 89–117)
can. / cann.	Canon / canones, *Codex Iuris Canonici Orientalis*
cap.	Caput
CC	Pius PP. XI, Enc. *Casti connubii*, 31 dec. 1930 (AAS 22 [1930] 539–592)
CD	Decr. *Christus Dominus*, 28 oct. 1965 (AAS 58 [1966] 673–696)
CE	Paulus PP. VI, m.p. *Catholica Ecclesia*, 23 oct. 1976 (AAS 68 [1976] 694–696)
CEM	*De Sacra Communione et de Cultu Mysterii Eucharistici extra Missam*, 1973
circ.	Circulares
CI	Pontificia Commissio ad Codicis Canones Authentice Interpretandos
CICS	Pontificium Consilium Instrumentis Communicationis Socialis Praepositum
CIP	Pontificia Commissio a Iustitia et Pace
CIV	Pontificia Commissio Decretis Concilii Vaticani II interpretandis
CM	Paulus PP. VI, m.p. *Causas matrimoniales*, 28 mar. 1971 (AAS 63 [1971] 441–446)
CMat	Paulus PP. VI, m.p. *Cum matrimonialium*, 8 sep. 1973 (AAS 65 [1973] 577–581)
Const.	Constitutio
CPEN	Consilium a Publicis Ecclesiae Negotiis (a 1-I-1968)

CS	Pius PP. XII, m.p. *Cleri sanctitati*, 2 iun. 1957 (AAS 49 [1957] 433–600)
CSan	SCR Instr. *Cum Sanctissimus*, 19 mar. 1948 (AAS 40 [1948] 293–297)
CT	Ioannes Paulus PP. II, Litt. *Catechesi Tradendae*, 16 oct. 1979 (AAS 71 [1979] 1277–1340)
DCG	SCpC *Directorium catechisticum generale*, 11 apr. 1971 (AAS 64 [1972] 97–176)
Decl.	Declaratio
Decr.	Decretum
DH	Decl. *Dignitatis humanae*, 7 dec. 1965 (AAS 58 [1966] 929–946)
DO	SCUF *Directorium Oecumenicum*, I: 14 maii 1967 (AAS 59 [1967] 574–592); II: 16 apr. 1970 (AAS 62 [1970] 705–724)
DPME	SCE *Directorium de pastorali ministerio Episcoporum*, 22 feb. 1973
DS	Denzinger-Schönmetzer, *Enchiridion Symbolorum Definitionum et Declarationum de rebus fidei et morum*, ed. 33, 1965
DSD	Pius PP. XI, Const. Ap. *Deus scientiarum Dominus*, 24 maii 1931 (AAS 23 [1931] 241–262)
DV	Const. Dogmatica *Dei Verbum*, 18 nov. 1965 (AAS 58 [1966] 817–835)
EcS	Paulus PP. VI, Enc. *Ecclesiam Suam*, 6 aug. 1964 (AAS 56 [1964] 609–659)
EM	Paulus PP. VI, m.p. *De Episcoporum muneribus*, 15 iun. 1966 (AAS 58 [1966] 467–472)
Emys	SRC Instr. *Eucharisticum mysterium*, 25 maii 1967 (AAS 59 [1967] 539–573)
EN	Paulus PP. VI, Adh. Ap. *Evangelii nuntiandi*, 8 dec. 1975 (AAS 68 [1976] 5–76)
Enc.	Encyclica
Ep.	Epistula
EP	SCDF Decr. *Ecclesiae Pastorum*, 19 mar. 1975 (AAS 67 [1975] 281–284)
ES	Paulus PP. VI, m.p. *Ecclesiae Sanctae*, 6 aug. 1966 (AAS 58 [1966] 757–787)
ET	Paulus PP. VI, Adh. Ap. *Evangelica testificatio*, 29 iun. 1971 (AAS 63 [1971] 497–526)
facul.	Facultas, facultates
FC	Ioannes Paulus PP. II, Adh. Ap. *Familiaris Consortio*, 22 nov. 1981 (AAS 74 1982] 81–191)
GE	Decl. *Gravissimum Educationis*, 28 oct. 1965 (AAS 58 [1966] 728–739)
gen.	Generalis
GS	Const. pastoralis *Gaudium et Spes*, 7 dec. 1966 (AAS 58 [1966] 1025–1115)
Hom.	Homilia
HV	Paulus PP. VI, Enc. *Humanae vitae*, 25 iul. 1968 (AAS 60 [1968] 481–503)
IC	SCDS Instr. *Immensae caritatis*, 29 ian. 1973 (AAS 65 [1973] 264–271)
ID	SCSCD Instr. *Inaestimabile donum*, 3 apr. 1980 (AAS 72 [1980] 331–343)
IOe	SRC Instr. *Inter Oecumenici*, 26 sept. 1964 (AAS 56 [1964] 877–900)
IGLH	*Institutio Generalis de Liturgia Horarum*, 11 apr. 1971

IGMR	*Institutio Generalis Missalis Romani,* 26 mar. 1970
IM	Decr. *Inter mirifica,* 4 dec. 1963 (AAS 56 [1964] 145–157)
Ind.	Indultum
Instr.	Instructio
LG	Const. dogmatica *Lumen gentium,* 21 nov. 1964 (AAS 57 [1965] 5–75)
Litt.	Litterae
LMR	SCRIS *Life and Mission of Religious in the Church* (Plenaria of SCRIS) 20 aug. 1980
l.s.	Latae sententiae
MC	Pius PP. XII, Enc. *Mystici Corporis,* 29 iun. 1943 (AAS 35 [1943] 193–248)
MD	Pius PP. XII, Enc. *Mediator Dei,* 20 nov. 1947 (AAS 39 [1947] 521–600)
MF	Paulus PP. VI, Enc. *Mysterium fidei,* 3 sep. 1965 (AAS 57 [1965] 753–774)
MG	Paulus PP. VI, All. *Magno gaudio,* 23 maii 1964 (AAS 56 [1964] 565–571)
MM	Paulus PP. VI, m.p. *Matrimonia mixta,* 31 mar. 1970 (AAS 62 [1970] 257–263)
m.p.	Litt. Ap. *Motu proprio* datae
MQ	Paulus PP. VI, m.p. *Ministeria quaedam,* 15 aug. 1972 (AAS 64 [1972] 529–534)
MR	SCRIS et SCE, Normae *Mutuae Relationes,* 14 maii 1978 (AAS 70 [1978] 473–506)
MS	SCDF Instr. *Matrimonii sacramentum,* 18 mar. 1966 (AAS 58 [1966] 235–239)
nep	LG nota explicativa praevia
Notif.	Notificatio
NPEM	CPEN *Normae de promovendis ad Episcopale ministerium in Ecclesia Latina,* 25 mar. 1972 (AAS 64 [1972] 386–391)
NSRR	Pius PP. XI, *Normae Sacrae Romanae Rotae Tribunalis,* 29 iun. 1934 (AAS 26 [1934] 449–491)
NSSA	*Normae speciales in Supremo Tribunali Signaturae Apsotolicae ad experimentum servandae,* 23 mar. 1968
OBP	*Ordo Baptismi parvulorum,* 10 iun 1969
OC	*Ordo Confirmationis,* 22 aug. 1971
OChr	SCpC Litt. circ. *Omnes christifideles,* 25 ian. 1973
OCM	*Ordo Celebrandi Matrimonium,* 19 mar. 1969
ODE	*Ordo Dedicationis Ecclesiae et Altaris,* 29 maii 1977
OE	Decr. *Orientalium Ecclesiarum,* 21 nov. 1964 (AAS 57 [1965] 76–89)
OEx	*Ordo Exequiarum,* 15 aug. 1969
OICA	*Ordo Initiationis Christianae Adultorum,* 1 iun. 1974
OP	*Ordo Paenitentiae,* 2 dec. 1973
Ord.	Ordinarius
OS (1966)	*Sec. Ordo Synodi Episcoporum celebrandae promulgatur a Summo Pontifice approbatus,* 8 dec. 1966 (AAS 59 [1967] 91–103)

OS (1969)	CPEN *Ordo Synodi Episcoporum celebrandae recognitus et auctus,* 24 iun. 1969 (AAS 61 [1969] 525–539)
OS (1971)	CPEN *Ordo Synodi Episcoporum celebrandae recognitus et auctus nonnullis additamentis perficitur,* 20 aug. 1971 (AAS 63 [1971] 702–704)
OT	Decr. *Optatam totius,* 28 oct. 1965 (AAS 58 [1966] 713–727)
OUI	*Ordo Unctionis infirmorum eorumque Pastoralis Curae,* 7 dec. 1972
PA	SCpC Notae directivae *Postquam Apostoli,* 25 mar. 1980 (AAS 72 [1980] 343–364)
Paen.	Paulus PP. VI, Const. Ap. *Paenitemini,* 17 feb. 1966 (AAS 58 [1966] 177–185)
part.	Particularis
PC	Decr. *Perfectae caritatis,* 28 oct. 1965 (AAS 58 [1966] 702–712)
PCCICOR	Pontificia Commissio Codici Iuris Canonici Orientalis Recognoscendo
PCCICR	Pontificia Commissio Codici Iuris Canonici Recognoscendo
PF	Pius PP. XII, m.p. *Primo feliciter,* 12 mar. 1948 (AAS 450 [1948] 283–286)
PL	Migne, *Patrologia latina*
PM	Paulus PP. VI, m.p. *Pastorale Munus,* 30 nov. 1963 (AAS 56 [1964] 5–12)
PME	Pius PP. XII, Const. Ap. *Provida Mater Ecclesia,* 2 feb. 1947 (AAS 39 [1947] 114–124)
PO	Decr. *Presbyterorum Ordinis,* 7 dec. 1965 (AAS 58 [1966] 991–1024)
p. / pp.	Pagella / pagellae
PR	*Pontificale Romanum*
Prae.	Praenotanda
Principia	SE Normae, *Principia quae Codicis Iuris Canonici recognitionem dirigant* (*Communicationes* 1 [1969] 77–86)
PrM	SCDS Instr. *Provida Mater,* 15 aug. 1936 (AAS 28 [1936] 313–361)
PS	SCpC Litt. circ. *Presbyteri sacra,* 11 apr. 1970 (AAS 62 [1970] 459–465)
RC	SCRIS Instr. *Renovationis causam,* 6 ian. 1969 (AAS 61 [1969] 103–120)
Rescr.	Rescriptum
Resol.	Resolutio
Resp.	Responsum
REU	Paulus PP. VI, Const. Ap. *Regimini Ecclesiae Universae,* 15 aug. 1967 (AAS 59 [1967] 885–928)
RFS	SCIC *Ratio fundamentalis institutionis sacerdotalis,* 6 ian. 1970 (AAS 62 [1970] 321–384)
RH	Ioannes Paulus PP. II, Enc. *Redemptor hominis,* 4 mar. 1979 (AAS 71 [1979] 257–324)
RPE	Paulus PP. VI, Const. Ap. *Romano Pontifici eligendo,* 1 oct. 1975 (AAS 67 [1975] 609–645)
SA	Supremum Tribunal Signaturae Apostolicae
SAr	SCSO Instr. *Sacrae artis,* 30 iun. 1952 (AAS 44 [1952] 542–546)

SC	Const. *Sacrosanctum Concilium*, 4 dec. 1963 (AAS 56 [1964] 97–138)
SCC	Sacra Congregatio Concistorialis (usque ad 31-XII-1967)
SCConc	Sacra Congregatio Concilii (usque ad 31-XII-1967)
SCCD	Sacra Congregatio pro Cultu Divino (a 8-V-1969 usque ad 11-VII-1975)
SCDF	Sacra Congregatio pro Doctrina Fidei (a 7-XII-1965)
SCDS	Sacra Congregatio de Disciplina Sacramentorum (usque ad 11-VII-1975)
SCE	Sacra Congregatio pro Episcopis (a 1-1-1968)
SCEO	Sacra Congregatio pro Ecclesia Orientali (usque ad 31-XII-1967) / pro Ecclesiis Orientalibus (a 1-1-1968)
SCGE	Sacra Congregatio pro Gentium Evangelizatione seu de Propraganda Fide (a 1-1-1968)
SCh	IOANNES PAULUS PP. II. Const. Ap. *Sapientia christiana*, 15 apr. 1979 (AAS 71 [1979] 469–499)
SCIC	Sacra Congregatio pro Institutione Catholica (a 1-1-1968)
SCNE	Sacra Congregatio pro Negotiis Ecclesiasticis Extraordinariis (usque ad 31-XII-1967)
SCong	SCR Normae *Sacra Congregatio*, 7 iul. 1956
SCpC	Sacra Congregatio pro Clericis (a 1-1-1968)
SCPF	Sacra Congregatio de Propaganda Fide (usque ad 31-XII-1967)
SCR	Sacra Congregatio de Religiosis (usque ad 31-XII-1967)
SCRIS	Sacra Congregatio pro Religiosis et Institutis Saecularibus (a 1-1-1968)
SCSCD	Sacra Congregatio pro Sacramentis et Cultu Divino (a 11-VII-1975)
SCSO	Sacra Congregatio Sancti Officii (usque ad 7-XII-1965)
SCSSU	Sacra Congregatio de Seminariis et de Studiorum Universitatibus (usque ad 31-XII-1967)
SCUF	Secretariatus ad Christianorum Unitatem Fovendam
SDO	PAULUS PP. VI, m.p. *Sacrum diaconatus ordinem*, 18 iun. 1967 (AAS 59 [1967] 697–704)
SFS	SCIC Litt. circ. *Spiritual formation in seminaries*, 6 ian. 1980
SE	Synodus Episcoporum
Sec	Secretaria Status
SN	PIUS PP. XII, m.p. *Sollicitudinem nostram*, 6 ian. 1950 (AAS 42 [1950] 5–120)
SOE	PAULUS PP. VI, m.p. *Sollicitudo omnium Ecclesiarum*, 24 iun. 1969 (AAS 61 [1969] 473–484)
SPA	Sacra Paenitentiaria Apostolica
SpC	PIUS PP. XII, Const. Ap. *Sponsa Christi*, 21 nov. 1950 (AAS 43 [1951] 5–24)
SPNC	Secretariatus pro non credentibus
SRC	Sacra Congregatio Rituum (usque ad 8-V-1969)
SRR	Sacra Romana Rota

SRRD	*Sacrae Romanae Rotae Decisiones seu Sententiae*
Ssap	PIUS PP. XII, Const. Ap. *Sedes sapientiae*, 31 maii 1956 (AAS 48 [1956] 334–345)
tit.	Titulus
UR	Decr. *Unitatis redintegratio*, 21 nov. 1964 (AAS 57 [1965] 90–112)
UT	SE *Ultimis temporibus*, 30 nov. 1971 (AAS 63 [1971] 898–922)
VS	SCRIS Instr. *Venite seorsum*, 15 aug. 1969 (AAS 61 [1969] 674–690)

APOSTOLIC CONSTITUTION

SACRAE DISCIPLINAE LEGES

To our venerable brothers, cardinals, archbishops,
bishops, priests, deacons
and to the other members of the people of God,
John Paul, bishop,
servant of the servants of God
as a perpetual record.

During the course of the centuries the Catholic Church has been accustomed to reform and renew the laws of canonical discipline so that in constant fidelity to its divine founder, they may be better adapted to the saving mission entrusted to it. Prompted by this same purpose and fulfilling at last the expectations of the whole Catholic world, I order today, January 25, 1983, the promulgation of the revised Code of Canon Law. In so doing, my thoughts go back to the same day of the year 1959 when my predecessor of happy memory, John XXIII, announced for the first time his decision to reform the existing *corpus* of canonical legislation which had been promulgated on the feast of Pentecost in the year 1917.

Such a decision to reform the Code was taken together with two other decisions of which the Pontiff spoke on that same day: the intention to hold a synod of the Diocese of Rome and to convoke an ecumenical council. Of these two events, the first was not closely connected with the reform of the Code; but the second, the council, is of supreme importance in regard to the present matter and is closely connected with it.

If we ask why John XXIII considered it necessary to reform the existing Code, the answer can perhaps be found in the Code itself which was promulgated in the year 1917. But there exists also another answer and it is the decisive one: namely, that the reform of the Code of Canon Law appeared to be definitely desired and requested by the same council which devoted such great attention to the Church.

As is obvious, when the revision of the Code was first announced the council was an event of the future. Moreover, the acts of its magisterium and especially its doctrine on the Church would be decided in the years 1962–1965; however, it is clear to everyone that John XXIII's intuition was very true, and with good reason it must be said that his decision was for the long-term good of the Church.

Therefore the new Code which is promulgated today necessarily required the previous work of the council. Although it was announced together with the ecumenical council, nevertheless it follows it chronologically because the work undertaken in its preparation, which had to be based upon the council, could not begin until after the latter's completion.

Turning our minds today to the beginning of this long journey, to that January 25, 1959 and to John XXIII himself who initiated the revision of the Code, I must recognize that this Code derives from one and the same intention, the renewal of Christian living. From such an intention, in fact, the entire work of the council drew its norms and its direction.

If we now pass on to consider the nature of the work which preceded the promulgation of the Code and also the manner in which it was carried out, especially during the pontificates of Paul VI and John Paul I, and from then until the present day, it must be clearly pointed out that this work was brought to completion in an outstandingly *collegial* spirit. This applies not only in regard to the material drafting of the work, but also to the very substance of the laws enacted.

This note of collegiality eminently characterizes and distinguishes the process of developing the present Code; it corresponds perfectly with the teaching and the character of the Second Vatican Council. Therefore not only because of its content but also because of its very origin, the Code manifests the spirit of this council in whose documents the Church, the universal "sacrament of salvation" (dogmatic constitution on the Church *Lumen gentium,* nn. 1, 9, 48), is presented as the people of God and its hierarchical constitution appears based on the college of bishops united with its head.

For this reason, therefore, the bishops individually and as episcopates were invited to collaborate in the preparation of the new Code so that by means of such a long process, by as collegial a method as possible, juridical formulae would gradually mature which would later serve for the use of the entire Church. *Experts* chosen from all over the world also took part in all these phases of the work, specialists in theology, history and especially canon law.

To one and all of them I wish to express today my sentiments of deep gratitude.

In the first place there come before my eyes the figures of the deceased cardinals who presided over the preparatory commission: Cardinal Pietro Ciriaci who began the work, and Cardinal Pericle Felici who, for many years, guided the course of the work almost to its end. I think then of the secretaries of the same commission: Monsignor Giacomo Violardo, later cardinal, and Father Raimondo Bidagor, S.J., both of whom in carrying out this task poured out the treasures of their doctrine and wisdom. Together with them I recall the cardinals, archbishops, bishops and all those who were members of that commission, as well as the consultors of the individual study groups engaged during these years in such a difficult work, and whom God in the meantime has called to their eternal reward. I pray to God for all of them.

I am pleased to remember also the living, beginning with the present pro-president of the commission, our venerable brother Archbishop Rosalio Castillo Lara. For a very long time he has done excellent work in a task of such great responsibility. I pass then to our beloved son, Monsignor William Onclin, whose devotion and diligence have greatly contributed to the happy outcome of the work. I finally mention all the others in the commission itself, whether as cardinal members or as officials, consultors and collaborators in the various study groups, or in other offices who have given their appreciated contribution to the drafting and the completion of such a weighty and complex work.

Therefore, in promulgating the Code today, I am fully aware that this act is an expression of pontifical authority and therefore is invested with a *primatial character*. But I am also aware that this Code in its objective content reflects the *collegial solicitude* of all my brothers in the episcopate for the Church. Indeed, by a certain analogy with the council, it should be considered as the fruit of a *collegial collaboration* because of the united efforts on the part of specialized persons and institutions throughout the whole Church.

A second question arises concerning the very nature of the Code of Canon Law. To reply adequately to this question one must mentally recall the distant patrimony of law contained in the books of the Old and New Testament from which is derived the whole juridical-legislative tradition of the Church, as from its first source.

Christ the Lord, indeed, did not in the least wish to destroy the very rich heritage of the law and the prophets which was gradually formed from the history and experience of the people of God in the Old Testament, but he brought it to completion (cf. Mt. 5:17) such that in a new and higher way it became part of the heritage of the New Testament. Therefore, although in expounding the paschal mystery St. Paul teaches that justification is not obtained by the works of the law but by means of faith (cf. Rom. 3:28; Gal. 2:16), he does not thereby exclude the binding force of the Decalogue (cf. Rom. 13:28; Gal. 5:13–25, 6:2), nor does he deny the importance of discipline in the Church of God (cf. I Cor. 5 and 6). Thus the writings of the New Testament enable us to understand even better the importance of discipline and make us see better how it is more closely connected with the saving character of the evangelical message itself.

This being so, it appears sufficiently clear that the Code is in no way intended as a substitute for faith, grace, charisms, and especially charity in the life of the Church and of the faithful. On the contrary, its purpose is rather to create such an order in the ecclesial society that, while assigning the primacy to love, grace and charisms, it at the same time renders their organic development easier in the life of both the ecclesial society and the individual persons who belong to it.

As the Church's principal legislative document founded on the juridical-legislative heritage of revelation and tradition, the Code is to be regarded as an indispensable instrument to ensure order both in individual and social life, and also in the Church's own activity. Therefore, besides containing the fundamental elements of the hierarchical and organic structure of the Church as willed by her divine founder or as based upon apostolic, or in any case most ancient, tradition, and besides the fundamental principles which govern the exercise of the threefold office entrusted to the Church itself, the Code must also lay down certain rules and norms of behavior.

The instrument which the Code is fully corresponds to the nature of the Church, especially as it is proposed by the teaching of the Second Vatican Council in general and in a particular way by its ecclesiological teaching. Indeed, in a certain sense this new Code could be understood as a great effort to translate this same conciliar doctrine and ecclesiology into *canonical* language. If, however, it is impossible to translate perfectly into *canonical* language the conciliar image of the Church, nevertheless the Code must always be referred to this image as the primary pattern whose outline the Code ought to express insofar as it can by its very nature.

From this, certain fundamental criteria are derived which should govern the entire new Code within the limits of its specific matter and of the language appropriate to that material.

It could indeed be said that from this there is derived that note of complementarity which the Code presents in relation to the teaching of the Second Vatican Council, in particular with reference to the two constitutions, the dogmatic constitution *Lumen gentium* and the pastoral constitution *Gaudium et spes.*

Hence it follows that what constitutes the substantial *newness* of the Second Vatican Council, in line with the legislative tradition of the Church, especially in regard to ecclesiology, constitutes likewise the *newness* of the new Code.

Among the elements which characterize the true and genuine image of the Church we should emphasize especially the following: the doctrine in which the Church is presented as the people of God (cf. dogmatic constitution *Lumen gentium,* chapter 2) and hierarchical authority as service (cf. ibid., chapter 3); the doctrine in which the Church is seen as a *communion* and which therefore determines the relations which are to exist between the particular churches and the universal Church, and between collegiality and the primacy; likewise the doctrine according to which all the members of the people of God, in the way suited to each of them, participate in the threefold priestly, prophetic and kingly office of Christ, to which doctrine is also linked that which concerns the duties and rights of the faithful and particularly of the laity; and finally, the Church's commitment to ecumenism.

If, therefore, the Second Vatican Council has drawn both new and old from the treasury of tradition, and the new consists precisely in the elements which I have enumerated, then it is clear that the Code should also reflect the same note of fidelity in newness and of newness in fidelity, and conform itself to this in its own subject matter and in its own particular manner of expression.

The new Code of Canon Law appears at a moment when the bishops of the whole Church not only are asking for its promulgation, but are crying out for it insistently and almost with impatience.

As a matter of fact, the Code of Canon Law is extremely necessary for the Church. Since the Church is organized as a social and visible structure, it must also have norms: in order that its hierarchical and organic structure be visible; in order that the exercise of the functions divinely entrusted to it, especially that of sacred power and of the administration of the sacraments, may be adequately organized; in order that the mutual relations of the faithful may be regulated according to justice based upon charity, with the rights of individuals guaranteed and well-defined; in order, finally, that common initiatives undertaken to live a Christian life ever more perfectly may be sustained, strengthened and fostered by canonical norms.

Finally, by their very nature canonical laws are to be observed. The greatest care has therefore been taken to ensure that in the lengthy preparation of the Code the wording of the norms should be accurate, and that they should be based on a solid juridical, canonical and theological foundation.

After all these considerations it is naturally to be hoped that the new canonical legislation will prove to be an efficacious means in order that the Church may progress in conformity with the spirit of the Second Vatican Council and may every day be ever more suited to carry out its office of salvation in this world.

With a confident spirit I am pleased to entrust these considerations of mine to all as I promulgate this fundamental body of ecclesiastical laws for the Latin Church.

May God grant that joy and peace with justice and obedience obtain favor for this Code, and that what has been ordered by the head be observed by the body.

Trusting therefore in the help of divine grace, sustained by the authority of the blessed apostles Peter and Paul, with certain knowledge, in response to the wishes of the bishops of the whole world who have collaborated with me in a collegial spirit, and with the supreme authority with which I am vested, by means of this Constitution, to be valid forever in the future, I promulgate the present Code as it has been set in order and revised. I command that for the future it is to have the force of law for the whole Latin Church, and I entrust it to the watchful care of all those concerned in order that it may be observed. So that all may more easily be informed and have a thorough knowledge of these norms before they have juridical binding force, I declare and order that they will have the force of law beginning from the first day of Advent of this year 1983, and this notwithstanding any contrary ordinances, constitutions, privileges (even worthy of special or individual mention), or customs.

I therefore exhort all the faithful to observe the proposed legislation with a sincere spirit and good will in the hope, that there may flower again in the Church a renewed discipline and that consequently the salvation of souls may be rendered ever more easy under the protection of the Blessed Virgin Mary, Mother of the Church.

Given at Rome, January 25, 1983, from the Vatican Palace, the fifth year of my pontificate.

John Paul II

PREFACE TO THE LATIN EDITION

From the time of the primitive Church it has been customary to collect the sacred canons into one book to facilitate a knowledge of them as well as their use and observance especially by sacred ministers, since "no priest is permitted to be ignorant of the sacred canons" as Pope Celestine warned in a letter to the bishops of Apulia and Calabria (July 21, 429: cf. Jaffe,[2] n. 371; Mansi IV, col. 469). His words are echoed by the Fourth Council of Toledo (633), which prescribed the following after the restoration of ecclesiastical discipline in the kingdom of the Visigoths once the Church had been freed from Arianism: "Priests are to know the sacred scripture and the canons" because "ignorance, the mother of all errors, is especially to be avoided by priests of God" (can. 25: Mansi X, col. 627).

In fact during the first ten centuries nearly everywhere there flourished countless collections of ecclesiastical laws. These private collections contained norms issued especially by the councils and the Roman Pontiffs as well as other norms taken from lesser sources. In the middle of the twelfth century, this mass of collections and norms, not infrequently contradicting one another, was put in order again through the private initiative of the monk Gratian. This concordance of laws and collections, later called the *Decretum Gratiani,* constituted the first part of that significant collection of laws of the Church which, in imitation of the *Corpus Iuris Civilis* of the Emperor Justinian, was called the *Corpus Iuris Canonici* and contained the laws which had been passed during two centuries by the supreme authority of the Roman pontiffs with the assistance of experts in canon law called glossators. Besides the Decree of Gratian, in which the earlier norms were contained, the *Corpus* consists of the *Liber Extra* of Gregory IX, the *Liber Sextus* of Boniface VIII, *the Clementinae,* i.e. the collection of Clement V promulgated by John XXII, to which are added the *Extravagantes* of this pope and the *Extravagantes communes,* decretals of various Roman pontiffs never gathered in an authentic collection. The ecclesiastical law which this *Corpus* embraces constitutes the classical law of the Catholic Church and is commonly called by this name.

To this corpus of law of the Latin Church corresponds to some extent the *Syntagma canonum* or oriental corpus of canons of the Greek Church.

Subsequent laws, especially those enacted by the Council of Trent during the time of the Catholic Reformation and those issued later by various dicasteries of the Roman Curia, were never digested into one collection. This was the reason why during the course of time legislation outside the *Corpus Iuris Canonici* constituted "an immense pile of laws piled on top of other laws." The lack of a systematic arrangement of the laws and the lack of legal certainty along with the obsolescence of and *lacunae* in many laws led to a situation where church discipline was increasingly imperiled and jeopardized.

Therefore during the preparatory period prior to the First Vatican Council, many bishops asked that a new and sole collection laws be prepared to expedite the pastoral care of the people of God in a more certain and secure fashion. Although this task could not be implemented through conciliar action, the Apostolic See subsequently addressed certain more urgent disciplinary issues through a new organization of laws. Finally, Pope Pius X, at the very beginning of his pontificate, undertook this task when he proposed to collect and reform all ecclesiastical laws and determined that the enterprise be carried out under the leadership of Cardinal Pietro Gasparri.

The first issue to be resolved in such a significant and difficult undertaking was the internal and external form of the new collection. It was decided to forego the method of compilations of laws whereby individual laws would have been expressed in the extensiveness of the original text; rather the modern method of codification was chosen. Hence texts containing and proposing a precept were expressed in a new and briefer form. However, all of the material was organized in five books which substantially imitated the system of Roman law institutes on persons, things and actions. The work took twelve years with the collaboration of experts, consultors and bishops throughout the Church. The character of the new Code was clearly enunciated in the beginning of canon 6: "The Code generally retains the existing discipline although it introduces appropriate changes." Therefore it was not a case of enacting a new law but rather a matter of arranging in a new fashion the operative legislation at that time. After the death of Pius X, this universal, exclusive, and authentic collection was promulgated on May 27, 1917 by his successor Benedict XV; it took effect on May 19, 1918.

Everyone hailed the universal law of this Pio-Benedictine Code, which made a significant contribution to the effective promotion of pastoral ministry throughout the Church, which in the meantime was experiencing new growth. Nevertheless, both the external situation of the Church in a world which had experienced sweeping changes and significant shifts in customs within a few decades as well as progressive internal factors within the ecclesiastical community necessarily brought it about that a new reform of canon law was increasingly more imperative and was requested. The Supreme Pontiff John XXIII clearly recognized the signs of the times, for when he first announced the Roman Synod and the Second Vatican Council, he also announced that these events would be a necessary preparation for undertaking the desired renewal of the Code.

Shortly after the Ecumenical Council had begun, the Commission for the Revision of the Code of Canon Law was established on March 28, 1963 with Cardinal Pietro Ciriaci as president and Monsignor Giacomo Violardo as secretary. However, the cardinal members of the Commission in a meeting with the president on November 12 of that same year agreed that the true and proper efforts of the Commission should be deferred and should commence only at the conclusion of the Council. The reform was to be carried out according to the decisions and principles to be determined by that same Council. Meanwhile on April 17, 1964 Paul VI added seventy consultors to the Commission established by his predecessor John XXIII; he subsequently named other cardinal members and consultors from all over the world to participate in the expediting of the project. On February 24, 1965 the Supreme Pontiff named Rev. Raimondo Bidagor, S.J. the new secretary of the Commission since Monsignor Violardo had been promoted to the office of secretary of the Congregation for the Discipline of the Sacraments; on November 17 of the same year the pope appointed Monsignor William Onclin as adjunct secretary of the Commission. After the death of Cardinal Ciriaci, Archbishop Pericle Felici, former general secretary of Vatican Council II, was named pro-president on February 21, 1967. On June 26 of that same year he became a member of the Sacred College of Cardinals and subsequently assumed the office of president of the Commission. Since Father Bidagor ceased functioning as secretary of the Commission on November 1, 1973 on the occasion of his eightieth birthday, Most Reverend Rosalio Castillo Lara, S.D.B., titular bishop of Praecausa and coadjutor bishop of Trujillo, Venezuela, was named the new secretary of the Commission. On May 17, 1982 he was appointed pro-president of the Commission upon the premature death of Cardinal Felici.

On November 20, 1965, just before the closing of the Second Vatican Council, there was a solemn session of the Commission in the presence of the Supreme Pontiff Paul VI, at which were present the cardinal members of the Commission, the secretaries, consultors and officials of the Secretariat appointed in the meantime. This session publicly inaugurated the work of the Code Commission. The allocution of the Supreme Pontiff laid the foundations of the whole enterprise to a certain extent. It was recalled that canon law flows from the nature of the Church, that it is rooted in the power of jurisdiction entrusted to the Church by Christ, and that its purpose is to be viewed in terms of the care of souls in view of external salvation. Furthermore, the character of church law was illustrated; its necessity was vindicated against the more common objections; the history of the progress of law and its collections was alluded to; and especially there was highlighted the urgent need of a new reform of the law to respond to the ongoing need of appropriately adapting church discipline to changing circumstances.

The Supreme Pontiff further indicated to the Commission two elements which should underly the whole revision effort. First of all it was not simply a matter of a new organization of the laws as had occurred at the time of the Pio-Benedictine

Code; but rather it was also and especially a matter of reforming the norms to accommodate them to a new mentality and new needs even if the old law was to supply the foundation for the work of revision. Careful attention was to be paid to all the decrees and acts of the Second Vatican Council since they contain the main lines of legislative renewal either because norms were issued which directly affected new institutes and ecclesiastical discipline, or because it was necessary that the doctrinal riches of the Council, which contributed so much to pastoral life, have their consequences and necessary impact on canonical legislation.

Repeatedly in allocutions, precepts and decisions during the following years, the two above mentioned elements were recalled to the minds of the Commission members by the Supreme Pontiff, who continued to oversee the whole enterprise from on high and assiduously pursue it.

If the subcommissions or study groups were to carry on their work in a methodical fashion, it was necessary above all that there be identified and approved certain principles which would serve as guidelines during the process of revising the whole Code. The central committee of consultors prepared the text of a document, which, at the request of the Supreme Pontiff, was submitted to the examination of a general session of the synod of bishops in October 1967. The following principles were approved nearly unanimously.

1. In renewing the law the juridic character of the new Code, which the social nature of the Church requires, is to be retained. Therefore the Code is to furnish norms so that the members of the Christian faithful in living the Christian life may share in the goods offered by the Church to lead them to eternal salvation. Hence, in view of this end, the Code must define and protect the rights and obligations of each person towards others and towards the ecclesiastical society to the extent that these rights and obligations pertain to divine worship and the salvation of souls.

2. There is to be a coordination between the external forum and the internal forum, which is proper to the Church and has been operative for centuries, so as to preclude any conflict between the two.

3. To foster the pastoral care of souls as much as possible, the new law, besides the virtue of justice, is to take cognizance of charity, temperance, humaneness and moderation, whereby equity is to be pursued not only in the application of the laws by pastors of souls but also in the legislation itself. Hence unduly rigid norms are to be set aside and rather recourse is to be taken to exhortations and persuasions where there is no need of a strict observance of the law on account of the public good and general ecclesiastical discipline.

4. In order that the Supreme Legislator and the bishops may collaborate in the care of souls and may exercise the pastoral office in a more positive fashion, those faculties to dispense from general laws which until now have been extraordinary are to become ordinary with reservations to the supreme power of the universal

Church or other higher authorities only in those areas which require an exception on account of the common good.

5. Careful attention is to be given to the greater application of the so-called principle of subsidiarity within the Church. It is a principle which is rooted in a higher one because the office of bishops with its attached powers is a reality of divine law. In virtue of this principle one may defend the appropriateness and even the necessity of providing for the welfare especially of individual institutes through particular laws and the recognition of a healthy autonomy for particular executive power while legislative unity and universal and general law are observed. On the basis of the same principle, the new Code entrusts either to particular laws or to executive power whatever is not necessary for the unity of the discipline of the universal Church so that appropriate provision is made for a healthy "decentralization" while avoiding the danger of division into or the establishment of national churches.

6. On account of the fundamental equality of all members of the Christian faithful and the diversity of offices and functions rooted in the hierarchical order of the Church, it is expedient that the rights of persons be appropriately defined and safeguarded. This brings it about that the exercise of authority appears more clearly as service, that its use is more clearly reinforced, and that abuses are removed.

7. In order that such objectives may be appropriately implemented, it is necessary that particular attention be given to the organization of a procedure which envisions the protection of subjective rights. Therefore in renewing the law attention should be paid to those elements which are most especially lacking in this area, i.e. administrative recourses and the administration of justice. To achieve this it is necessary that the various functions of ecclesiastical power be clearly distinguished, i.e. the legislative, administrative, and judicial functions. What individual functions are to be exercised by which governmental organs is also to be defined.

8. The principle of territoriality in the exercise of ecclesiastical government is to be revised somewhat, for contemporary apostolic factors seem to recommend personal jurisdictional units. Therefore the new Code is to affirm the following principle: generally speaking the portions of the people of God to be governed are to be determined territorially; however, if it is advantageous, other factors can be admitted as criteria for determining a community of the faithful, at least along with territoriality.

9. As an external, visible and independent society, the Church cannot renounce penal law. However, penalties are generally to be *ferendae sententiae* and are to be inflicted and remitted only in the external forum. *Latae sententiae* penalties are to be reduced to a few cases and are to be inflicted only for the most serious offenses.

10. Finally, as is admitted by all, the new systematic arrangement of the Code required by the revision process can only be sketched at the outset but cannot be defined and determined precisely. Therefore the new organization of the Code will

have to be pursued only after a sufficient revision of its individual parts, in fact only after nearly the whole work has been completed.

From these principles which ought to guide the process of revising the Code, it is quite clear that there is a need to apply everywhere the doctrine of the Church expressed by the Second Vatican Council, especially its determination that attention is to be paid not only to the external social dimensions of the Mystical Body of Christ but also and especially to its internal life.

And in point of fact the consultors were guided by these principles in drafting the new text of the Code.

Meanwhile a January 15, 1966 letter of the cardinal president of the Commission to the presidents of the conferences of bishops asked the bishops of the whole Catholic world to express their concerns and advice regarding the law to be drafted and the best way of structuring relationships between the conferences of bishops and the Commission so as to maximize their cooperation for the good of the Church. Furthermore, the bishops were also asked to send to the Secretariat of the Commission the names of canonical experts in their respective regions who in the judgment of the bishops were the most distinguished in terms of canonical expertise; the special competence of these experts was also to be indicated. The consultors and their collaborators could be selected and named from these individuals. Actually, at the very beginning and throughout the working of the Commission, besides its cardinal members the following collaborated in the drafting of the new Code of Canon Law: bishops, priests, religious, laity, experts in canon law, theology, pastoral practice, and civil law from all over the Catholic world. During the whole revision process 105 cardinals, 77 archbishops and bishops, 73 secular presbyters, 47 religious presbyters, 3 religious women and 12 lay persons from 5 continents and 31 countries served as members, consultors and other types of collaborators with the Commission.

Even before the last session of the Second Vatican Council, the consultors of the Commission were gathered in a private session on May 6, 1965, in which, with the consent of the Holy Father, the Commission president submitted three fundamental questions for their study. It was asked first whether one or two codes, i.e. Latin and Oriental, were to be drafted; it was also asked what methodology was to be followed in the drafting process or how the Commission and its organs were to proceed; finally, it was asked what would be an appropriate division of labor among the various subcommissions, which would be functioning simultaneously. Reports prepared by three groups established to deal with these questions were forwarded to all the Commission members.

The cardinal members of the Commission met for the second time on November 25, 1965 to discuss these same questions and respond to certain proposals *(dubia)* formulated concerning them.

A principle regarding the systematic organization of the new Code to be proposed to the synod of bishops was drawn up from a *votum* of the central committee of consultors, which had met on April 3–7, 1967. After the meeting of the synod, it was deemed appropriate to establish in November, 1967 a special committee of consultors to study the systematic organization of the Code. At a meeting of this committee at the beginning of April, 1968, all agreed on not incorporating in the Code properly liturgical laws, norms on beatification and canonization processes, and norms on the external relations of the Church. All agreed as well that in the part on the people of God there would be placed norms on the juridic status of all members of the Christian faithful and a distinct treatment of the powers and faculties which pertain to the exercise of the different functions and offices. Finally all agreed that the structure of the books of the Pio-Benedictine Code could not be maintained in its integrity.

During the third meeting of the cardinal members of the Commission on May 28, 1968, they substantially approved a temporary arrangement according to which the study groups already established were organized in a new way: "the systematic organization of the Code," "general norms," "the sacred hierarchy," "institutes of perfection," "laity," "physical and moral persons in general," "marriage," "sacraments other than marriage," "the ecclesiastical magisterium," "the patrimonial law of the Church," "processes," "penal law."

The issues dealt with by the study group on "physical and juridic persons" (it was subsequently called this) were later incorporated in the book on "general norms." Furthermore it was deemed appropriate to establish a study group on "sacred places and times and divine worship." In view of their broader competence, the names of some other study groups were changed: the group on "the laity" was later called the group on "the rights and associations of the faithful and the laity"; the group on "religious" was later called the group on "institutes of perfection" and finally the group on "institutes of life consecrated through the profession of the evangelical counsels."

The principal features of the method followed during the more than sixteen year revision process are to be briefly recalled. The consultors of the individual groups fulfilled their significant duties with the greatest dedication, considering only the good of the Church either in preparing written observations on the parts of their own schemata, or in discussing various issues at meetings in Rome at determined times, or in examining the animadversions, observations and opinions on their schemata which were forwarded to the Commission. The procedure was as follows. To each of the consultors, who numbered from eight to fourteen on the individual study groups, was assigned a certain issue which was to be studied in view of the revision process, with the present Code as the point of departure. After an examination of the questions, each consultor was to transmit a written opinion to the Secretariat of the Commission as well as a copy to the *relator* and, if time permitted, to all the members of the study group. The consultors of the study group met in Rome according to a predetermined schedule. With the *relator* leading the discussions, all the questions and opinions were considered until a text of canons was approved, at times after a process of voting on individual parts, and drafted in schema form. During the session the *relator* was aided by an official who functioned as an actuary.

The number of meetings for each study group was greater or lesser depending on the concrete issues, and the work was carried on for years.

Especially during the latter stages of the process, certain mixed study groups were established so that consultors from different groups could meet and discuss issues which directly pertained to several groups and had to be resolved through common counsel.

After the drafting of some schemata was completed by the study groups, the Supreme Legislator was asked to give some concrete indications of the subsequent steps to be taken in continuing the work. According to the norms handed down at the time, those steps were as follows.

The schemata together with an explanatory report were sent to the Supreme Pontiff, who determined whether they were to be forwarded for consultation purposes. After this permission was obtained, the printed schemata were submitted to the examination of the universal episcopate and other consultative organs (namely, the dicasteries of the Roman Curia, ecclesiastical universities and faculties, and the Union of Superiors General) in order that they might express their opinion within a prudently determined time frame—not less than six months. At the same time, the schemata were also forwarded to the cardinal members of the Commission so as to enable them to make their general or particular observations at this stage of the process.

The order in which the schemata were sent is as follows:

1972—the schema on administrative procedure;
1973—the schema on sanctions in the Church;
1975—the schema on the sacraments;
1976—the schema on the procedure for the protection of rights or processes;
1977—the schema on institutes of life consecrated by the profession of the evangelical counsels, the schema on general norms, the schema on the people of God, the schema on the Church's teaching office, the schema on sacred times and places and divine worship, and the schema on the patrimonial law of the Church.

Undoubtedly the revised Code could not have been appropriately prepared without the inestimable and continuous cooperation afforded the Commission by numerous very valid animadversions especially of a pastoral character offered by bishops and conferences of bishops. The bishops submitted very many written animadversions, either general ones on the schemata considered as a whole or particular ones on individual canons.

Of great benefit also were those general and particular animadversions submitted by the sacred congregations, tribunals and other institutes of the Roman Curia, based on their experience in the central government of the Church. This was also true for the scientific and technical proposals and suggestions offered by ecclesiastical universities and faculties reflecting different schools and ways of thinking.

The study, examination and collegial discussion of all the animadversions, general and particular, which were forwarded to the Commission constituted a weighty and veritably immense burden which lasted seven years. The Secretariat of the Commission took pains carefully to organize and synthesize all the animadversions, proposals and suggestions which, after they had been forwarded to the consultors and carefully examined by them, were subsequently collegially discussed in working sessions conducted by the ten study groups.

Every animadversion was considered with the utmost care and diligence. This was true even in the case of animadversions contradicting one another (which frequently happened). Due consideration was given not only to their sociological importance (namely, the number of consultative organs and persons who proposed them), but especially to their doctrinal and pastoral value, their coherence with the doctrine and implementing norms of the Second Vatican Council, the pontifical magisterium, and their necessary coherence with the juridic canonical system when examined from a specifically technical and scientific standpoint. In fact, as often as it was a case of a doubtful matter or when questions of special importance were debated, the opinion of the cardinal members of the Commission was sought during one of their plenary sessions. In other cases in view of the specific matter under discussion, the Congregation for the Doctrine of the Faith and other dicasteries of the Roman Curia were consulted. Finally, many corrections and changes were incorporated in the canons of the early schemata at the request or suggestion of the bishops and other consultative organs, so that some schemata were entirely renewed or changed.

After all the schemata had been reworked, the Secretariat of the Commission and the consultors undertook a further weighty task. It was a matter of seeing to an internal coordination of all the schemata, of ensuring a uniform terminology throughout especially from a technical-juridic standpoint, of drafting canons in brief and elegant formulations, and finally of definitively determining a systematic organization so that all of the schemata, prepared by distinct study groups, could be integrated into one completely harmonious Code.

The new systematic organization which, as it were, spontaneously emerged slowly during the revision process, is based on two principles, one of which is fidelity to the more general principles already determined by the central committee, the other of which is its practical usefulness so that the new Code can be easily understood and used not only by experts but also by pastors and indeed by all members of the Christian faithful.

The new Code therefore consists of seven books which are entitled: General Norms, The People of God, The Teaching Function of the Church, The Sanctifying Function of the Church, The Temporal Goods of the Church, Sanctions in the Church, and Processes. Even if the different rubrics which precede the individual books of the old and new Code appear to indicate sufficiently the differences between the two systems, nonetheless the systematic innovations of the new Code are much more evident in light of its parts, sections, titles and rubrics. But it is certain that the new organization not only corresponds better to the proper matter and character of canon law than the old organization, but also, and what is of greater importance, the new is more in keeping with the ecclesiology of the Second Vatican Council and those principles flowing from it which were proposed at the very outset of the revision process.

On June 29, 1980, the solemnity of the blessed Apostles Peter and Paul, the printed schema of the whole Code was presented to the Supreme Pontiff, who decided it was to be forwarded to the cardinal members of the Commission for their definitive examination and judgment. In order to highlight even more the participation of the whole Church in the last phase of the revision process, the Supreme Pontiff determined that other members be added to the Commission, cardinals and even bishops selected from the whole Church, conferences of bishops or councils or groups of conferences of bishops proposing candidates. Thus the expanded Commission numbered seventy-four members. At the beginning of 1981 they forwarded many animadversions which subsequently were subjected to a careful examination, diligent study and collegial discussion by the Secretariat of the Commission, with the help of consultors endowed with special expertise in the individual issues being discussed. A synthesis of all the animadversions together with the responses given by the Secretariat and the consultors was forwarded to the members of the Commission in August, 1981.

A plenary session was convoked by order of the Supreme Pontiff to deliberate on the entire text of the new Code and to cast a definitive vote on it. The session took place October 20–28, 1981 in the aula of the synod of bishops. There was a discussion of six questions of particular weight and importance as well as of other questions proposed at the request of at least ten Fathers. At the end of the plenary session, the Fathers unanimously responded *placet* (affirmatively) to the following question: whether it pleased the Fathers that, after the examination during the plenary session of the schema of the Code and the emendations already introduced, the same schema along with the changes which had received a majority vote during the plenary session was worthy of being presented as soon as possible to the Supreme Pontiff, who would issue the Code at a time and in a way which seemed best. Consideration was also to be given to other animadversions which had been presented as well as to a certain polishing of the text regarding its style and Latinity (which tasks were entrusted to the president and the Secretariat).

The entire text of the Code thereby reworked and approved was enlarged by the addition of canons from the schema on the Fundamental Law of the Church which had to be inserted in the Code in light of the material with which they dealt. After the Latin style of the text was further polished, it was printed and given to the Supreme Pontiff on April 22, 1982 with a view toward promulgation.

The Supreme Pontiff, however, personally reviewed this latest schema with the help of certain experts and in consultation with the pro-president of the Pontifical Commission for the Revision of the Code of Canon Law. After mature consideration the Supreme Pontiff decreed that the new Code was to be promulgated on January 25, 1983, i.e., the anniversary of the first announcement by Pope John XXIII of the undertaking of the Code's revision.

Since after nearly twenty years the pontifical commission established for this purpose has felicitously completed the difficult task entrusted to it, there is now available to pastors and other members of the Christian faithful the most recent law of the Church, which is characterized by simplicity, precision, elegance and true legal science. Furthermore, since it is fully pervaded by charity, equity, humanity and a true Christian spirit, it attempts to correspond to the divinely given external and internal characteristics of the Church. It also seeks to take cognizance of the conditions and needs of the contemporary world. But if on account of the excessively swift changes in contemporary human society certain elements of the new law become less perfect and require a new review, the Church is endowed with such a wealth of resources that, not unlike prior centuries, it will be able to undertake the task of renewing the laws of its life.

Now, however, the law can no longer be unknown. Pastors have at their disposal secure norms by which they may correctly direct the exercise of the sacred ministry. To each person is given a source of knowing his or her own proper rights and duties. Arbitrariness in acting can be precluded. Abuses which perhaps have crept into ecclesiastical discipline because of a lack of legislation can be more easily rooted out and prevented. Finally, all the works, institutes and initiatives of the apostolate may progress expeditiously and may be promoted since a healthy juridic organization is quite necessary for the ecclesiastical community to live, grow and flourish. May our most gracious God grant this through the intercession of the Blessed Virgin Mary, the Mother of the Church, her spouse St. Joseph, Patron of the Church, and Saints Peter and Paul.

CODE OF CANON LAW

LATIN-ENGLISH EDITION

NEW ENGLISH TRANSLATION

BOOK I. GENERAL NORMS

LIBER I. DE NORMIS GENERALIBUS

CAN. 1 The canons of this Code regard only the Latin Church.

CAN. 2 For the most part the Code does not define the rites which must be observed in celebrating liturgical actions. Therefore, liturgical laws in force until now retain their force unless one of them is contrary to the canons of the Code.

CAN. 3 The canons of the Code neither abrogate nor derogate from the agreements entered into by the Apostolic See with nations or other political societies. These agreements therefore continue in force exactly as at present, notwithstanding contrary prescripts of this Code.

CAN. 4 Acquired rights and privileges granted to physical or juridic persons up to this time by the Apostolic See remain intact if they are in use and have not been revoked, unless the canons of this Code expressly revoke them.

CAN. 5 §1. Universal or particular customs presently in force which are contrary to the prescripts of these canons and are reprobated by the canons of this Code are absolutely sup-

CAN. 1 Canones huius Codicis unam Ecclesiam latinam respiciunt.

CAN. 2 Codex plerumque non definit ritus, qui in actionibus liturgicis celebrandis sunt servandi; quare leges liturgicae hucusque vigentes vim suam retinent, nisi earum aliqua Codicis canonibus sit contraria.

CAN. 3 Codicis canones initas ab Apostolica Sede cum nationibus aliisve societatibus politicis conventiones non abrogant neque iis derogant; eaedem idcirco perinde ac in praesens vigere pergent, contrariis huius Codicis praescriptis minime obstantibus.

CAN. 4 Iura quaesita, itemque privilegia quae, ab Apostolica Sede ad haec usque tempora personis sive physicis sive iuridicis concessa, in usu sunt nec revocata, integra manent, nisi huius Codicis canonibus expresse revocentur.

CAN. 5 §1. Vigentes in praesens contra horum praescripta canonum consuetudines sive universales sive particulares, quae ipsis canonibus huius Codicis reprobantur, pror-

1: c. 1

2: c. 2; SRC Resp., 8 mar. 1919 (AAS 11 [1919] 145); SCConc Resol., 14 feb. 1920 (AAS 12 [1920] 117–119); SCConc Resol., 10 iun. 1922 (AAS 15 [1923] 224–227)

3: c. 3; BENEDICTUS PP. XV, All., 21 nov. 1921 (AAS 13 [1921] 521–524): CI Resp. ad c. 404, 26 nov. 1922 (AAS 15 [1923] 128); CD 20; ES I, 18 §2

4: c. 4; CI Resp., 29 maii 1918; CI Resp. IV: 6, 2–3 iun. 1918 (AAS 10 [1918] 346); CI Resp. 2, 16 oct. 1919 (AAS 11 [1919] 476); SCSO Resp., 26 nov. 1919; CI Resp. IV, 14 iul. 1922 (AAS 14 [1922] 527); CI Resp. IV, 12 nov. 1922 (AAS 14 [1922] 662); CI Resp., 26 nov. 1922 (AAS 15 [1923] 128); CI Resp. I, 30 dec. 1937 (AAS 30 [1938] 73): PIUS PP. XII, Litt. *Ap. Litteris suis*, 11 nov. 1939 (AAS 32 [1940] 41); PAULUS PP. VI: All., 14

ian. 1964 (AAS 56 [1964] 193–197); PAULUS PP. VI, m.p. *Romanae dioecesis*, 30 iun. 1968, 10 (AAS 60 [1968] 379)

5 §1: c. 5; SCConc Resol., 8 feb. 1919 (AAS 11 [1919] 280–284); CI Resp. 6. 16 oct. 1919 (AAS 11 [1919] 477); SCConc Resol., 14 feb. 1920 (AAS 12 [1920] 163–166); SCConc Resol., 13 nov. 1920 (AAS 13 [1921] 43–46); SCConc Resol., 11 dec. 1920 (AAS 13 [1921] 262–268); SCConc Resol., 11 dec. 1920 (AAS 14 [1922] 42–46); SCR Resp., 18–20 mar. 1922 (AAS 14 [1922] 352–353); CI Resp., 26 nov. 1922 (AAS 15 [1923] 128); SCConc Resol., 13 iun. 1925, III (AAS 17 [1925] 538–540); SCDS Instr. *Plures petitiones*, 30 iun. 1932 (AAS 24 [1932] 271–272)

pressed and are not permitted to revive in the future. Other contrary customs are also considered suppressed unless the Code expressly provides otherwise or unless they are centenary or immemorial customs which can be tolerated if, in the judgment of the ordinary, they cannot be removed due to the circumstances of places and persons.

§2. Universal or particular customs beyond the law *(praeter ius)* which are in force until now are preserved.

CAN. 6   §1. When this Code takes force, the following are abrogated:

1° the Code of Canon Law promulgated in 1917;

2° other universal or particular laws contrary to the prescripts of this Code unless other provision is expressly made for particular laws;

3° any universal or particular penal laws whatsoever issued by the Apostolic See unless they are contained in this Code;

4° other universal disciplinary laws regarding matter which this Code completely reorders.

§2. Insofar as they repeat former law, the canons of this Code must be assessed also in accord with canonical tradition.

sus suppressae sunt, nec in posterum revivis-cere sinantur; ceterae quoque suppressae habeantur, nisi expresse Codice aliud caveatur, aut centenariae sint vel immemorabiles, quae quidem, si de iudicio Ordinarii pro locorum ac personarum adiunctis submoveri nequeant, tolerari possunt.

§2. Consuetudines praeter ius hucusque vigentes, sive universales sive particulares, servantur.

CAN. 6   §1. Hoc Codice vim obtinente, abrogantur:

1° Codex Iuris Canonici anno 1917 promulgatus;

2° aliae quoque leges, sive universales sive particulares, praescriptis huius Codicis contrariae, nisi de particularibus aliud expresse caveatur;

3° leges poenales quaelibet, sive universales sive particulares a Sede Apostolica latae, nisi in ipso hoc Codice recipiantur;

4° ceterae quoque leges disciplinares universales materiam respicientes, quae hoc Codice ex integro ordinatur.

§2. Canones huius Codicis, quatenus ius vetus referunt, aestimandi sunt ratione etiam canonicae traditionis habita.

---

5 §2: cc. 106, 5° et 6°, 136 §1, 171 §2, 346, 417 §3, 441, 1°, 462, 6°, 463 §1, 471 §4, 476 §5, 547 §1, 730, 740, 831 §§2 et 3, 1041, 1100, 1234 §1, 1251 §1, 1290 §2, 1410, 1444 §1, 1455, 3°, 1482, 1502, 1519 §2, 1535, 1555 §1, 1805, 2080; SCConc Resol., 14 feb. 1920 (AAS 12 [1920] 163–165)

6 §1: cc. 6, 1°, 5° et 6°, 489; CI Resp. II, 3 ian. 1918; CI Resp. III, 17 feb. 1918 (AAS 10 [1918] 170); SCSO Decr. *Cum in Codice,* 22 mar. 1918 (AAS 10 [1918] 136); CI Resp., 30 mar. 1918; SCC Decr. *Proxima sacra,* 25 apr. 1918 (AAS 10 [1918] 190–192); SCR Decr.

Ad normam canonis, 26 iun. 1918 (AAS 10 [1918] 290); SCC Resp., 22 feb. 1919 (AAS 11 [1919] 75–76); SCSO Resp., 26 nov. 1919; CI Resp. II, 24 nov. 1920 (AAS 12 [1920] 573); SCR Decl., 26 oct. 1921, III (AAS 13 [1921] 538); CI Resp., 26 nov. 1922 (AAS 15 [1923] 128); SCConc Resol., 9 iun. 1923 (AAS 17 [1925] 508–510); CI Resp., 13 dec. 1923 (AAS 16 [1924] 609); SCSO Decr. *Supremae Sacrae,* 13 iul. 1930 (AAS 22 [1930] 344); Princ. prooemium

6 §2: c. 6, 2°–4°

TITLE I.
Ecclesiastical Laws

CAN. 7 A law is established when it is promulgated.

CAN. 8 §1. Universal ecclesiastical laws are promulgated by publication in the official commentary, *Acta Apostolicae Sedis*, unless another manner of promulgation has been prescribed in particular cases. They take force only after three months have elapsed from the date of that issue of the *Acta* unless they bind immediately from the very nature of the matter, or the law itself has specifically and expressly established a shorter or longer suspensive period *(vacatio)*.

§2. Particular laws are promulgated in the manner determined by the legislator and begin to oblige a month after the day of promulgation unless the law itself establishes another time period.

CAN. 9 Laws regard the future, not the past, unless they expressly provide for the past.

CAN. 10 Only those laws must be considered invalidating or disqualifying which expressly establish that an act is null or that a person is unqualified.

CAN. 11 Merely ecclesiastical laws bind those who have been baptized in the Catholic Church or received into it, possess the sufficient use of reason, and, unless the law expressly provides otherwise, have completed seven years of age.

TITULUS I. De Legibus
Ecclesiastics

CAN. 7 Lex instituitur cum promulgatur.

CAN. 8 §1. Leges ecclesiasticae universales promulgantur per editionem in *Actorum Apostolicae Sedis commentario officiali*, nisi in casibus particularibus alius promulgandi modus fuerit praescriptus, et vim suam exserunt tantum expletis tribus mensibus a die qui *Actorum* numero appositus est, nisi ex natura rei illico ligent aut in ipsa lege brevior aut longior vacatio specialiter et expresse fuerit statuta.

§2. Leges particulares promulgantur modo a legislatore determinato et obligare incipiunt post mensem a die promulgationis, nisi alius terminus in ipsa lege statuatur.

CAN. 9 Leges respiciunt futura, non praeterita, nisi nominatim in eis de praeteritis caveatur.

CAN. 10 Irritantes aut inhabilitantes eae tantum leges habendae sunt, quibus actum esse nullum aut inhabilem esse personam expresse statuitur.

CAN. 11 Legibus mere ecclesiasticis tenentur baptizati in Ecclesia catholica vel in eandem recepti, quique sufficienti rationis usu gaudent et, nisi aliud iure expresse caveatur, septimum aetatis annum expleverunt.

7: c. 8 §1

8 §1: c. 9; SE Relatio *Pastor aeternus*, 27 oct. 1969, II/5, 2b

8 §2: cc. 291 §1, 335 §2, 362

9: c. 10; CI Resp. IV: 6–8, 2–3 iun. 1918 (AAS 10 [1918] 346); SCConc 17 maii 1919 (AAS 11 [1919] 349–354); SCC Decl., 1 aug. 1919, I (AAS 11 [1919] 346); SCR Resp., 6 oct. 1919 (AAS 11 [1919] 420); CI Resp. 2, 16 oct. 1919 (AAS 11 [1919] 476); CI Resp., 3 dec. 1919; CI Resp. V, 24 nov. 1920 (AAS 12 [1920] 575); CI Resp. IV, 14 iul. 1922 (AAS 14 [1922] 527); SCSO Decr. *Post editam*, 15 nov. 1966 (AAS 58 [1966] 1186)

10: c. 11

11: c. 12; CI Resp. I, 3 ian. 1918; SCConc Instr. *Saepenumero*, 14 iul. 1941, 2 (AAS 33 [1941] 390); DCG Addendum *Inter alia*, 11 apr. 1971, 1 (AAS 64 [1972] 173); SCSCD et SCpC Litt. circ., 31 mar. 1977

CAN. 12 §1. Universal laws bind everywhere all those for whom they were issued.

§2. All who are actually present in a certain territory, however, are exempted from universal laws which are not in force in that territory.

§3. Laws established for a particular territory bind those for whom they were issued as well as those who have a domicile or quasi-domicile there and who at the same time are actually residing there, without prejudice to the prescript of can. 13.

CAN. 13 §1. Particular laws are not presumed to be personal but territorial unless it is otherwise evident.

§2. Travelers are not bound:

1° by the particular laws of their own territory as long as they are absent from it unless either the transgression of those laws causes harm in their own territory or the laws are personal;

2° by the laws of the territory in which they are present, with the exception of those laws which provide for public order, which determine the formalities of acts, or which regard immovable goods located in the territory.

§3. Transients are bound by both universal and particular laws which are in force in the place where they are present.

CAN. 14 Laws, even invalidating and disqualifying ones, do not oblige when there is a doubt about the law. When there is a doubt about a fact, however, ordinaries can dispense from laws provided that, if it concerns a reserved dispensation, the authority to whom it is reserved usually grants it.

CAN. 12 §1. Legibus universalibus tenentur ubique terrarum omnes pro quibus latae sunt.

§2. A legibus autem universalibus, quae in certo territorio non vigent, eximuntur omnes qui in eo territorio actu versantur.

§3. Legibus conditis pro peculiari territorio ii subiciuntur pro quibus latae sunt, quique ibidem domicilium vel quasi-domicilium habent et simul actu commorantur, firmo praescripto can. 13.

CAN. 13 §1. Leges particulares non praesumuntur personales, sed territoriales, nisi aliud constet.

§2. Peregrini non adstringuntur:

1° legibus particularibus sui territorii quamdiu ab eo absunt, nisi aut earum transgressio in proprio territorio noceat, aut leges sint personales;

2° neque legibus territorii in quo versantur, iis exceptis quae ordini publico consulunt, aut actuum sollemnia determinant, aut res immobiles in territorio sitas respiciunt.

§3. Vagi obligantur legibus tam universalibus quam particularibus quae vigent in loco in quo versantur.

CAN. 14 Leges, etiam irritantes et inhabilitantes, in dubio iuris non urgent; in dubio autem facti Ordinarii ab eis dispensare possunt, dummodo, si agatur de dispensatione reservata, concedi soleat ab auctoritate cui reservatur.

12 §1: c. 13 §1; EM V
12 §2: c. 14 §1, 3°
12 §3: c. 13 §2
13 §1: c. 8 §2
13 §2: c. 14 §1, 1° et 2°; CI Resp. 4, 17 aug. 1919; CI Resp., 24 nov. 1920 (AAS 12 [1920] 575); SCConc Resol., 9 feb. 1924 (AAS 16 [1922] 94–95); SCConc Resol., 15 nov. 1924; SCConc Litt. circ., 1 iul. 1926 (AAS 18 [1926] 312–313); SCR Litt. circ., 15 iul. 1926; SCConc Decr. *Prudentissimo*, 28 iul. 1931 (AAS 23 [1931] 336–337)
13 §3: c. 14 §2
14: c. 15; CA I, 13

CAN. 15 §1. Ignorance or error about invalidating or disqualifying laws does not impede their effect unless it is expressly established otherwise.

§2. Ignorance or error about a law, a penalty, a fact concerning oneself, or a notorious fact concerning another is not presumed; it is presumed about a fact concerning another which is not notorious until the contrary is proven.

CAN. 16 §1. The legislator authentically interprets laws as does the one to whom the same legislator has entrusted the power of authentically interpreting.

§2. An authentic interpretation put forth in the form of law has the same force as the law itself and must be promulgated. If it only declares the words of the law which are certain in themselves, it is retroactive; if it restricts or extends the law, or if it explains a doubtful law, it is not retroactive.

§3. An interpretation in the form of a judicial sentence or of an administrative act in a particular matter, however, does not have the force of law and only binds the persons for whom and affects the matters for which it was given.

CAN. 17 Ecclesiastical laws must be understood in accord with the proper meaning of the words considered in their text and context. If the meaning remains doubtful and obscure, recourse must be made to parallel places, if there are such, to the purpose and circumstances of the law, and to the mind of the legislator.

CAN. 18 Laws which establish a penalty, restrict the free exercise of rights, or contain an

CAN. 15 §1. Ignorantia vel error circa leges irritantes vel inhabilitantes earundem effectum non impediunt, nisi aliud expresse statuatur.

§2. Ignorantia vel error circa legem aut poenam aut circa factum proprium aut circa factum alienum notorium non praesumitur; circa factum alienum non notorium praesumitur, donec contrarium probetur.

CAN. 16 §1. Leges authentice interpretatur legislator et is cui potestas authentice interpretandi fuerit ab eodem commissa.

§2. Interpretatio authentica per modum legis exhibita eandem vim habet ac lex ipsa et promulgari debet; si verba legis in se certa declaret tantum, valet retrorsum; si legem coarctet vel extendat aut dubiam explicet, non retrotrahitur.

§3. Interpretatio autem per modum sententiae iudicialis aut actus administrativi in re peculiari, vim legis non habet et ligat tantum personas atque afficit res pro quibus data est.

CAN. 17 Leges ecclesiasticae intellegendae sunt secundum propriam verborum significationem in textu et contextu consideratam; quae si dubia et obscura manserit, ad locos parallelos, si qui sint, ad legis finem ac circumstantias et ad mentem legislatoris est recurrendum.

CAN. 18 Leges quae poenam statuunt aut liberum iurium exercitium coarctant aut

15 §1: c. 16 §I
15 §2: c. 16 §2
16 §1: c. 17 §1; BENEDICTUS PP. XV, m. p. *Cum iuris canonici,* 15 sep. 1917 (AAS 9 [1917] 483–484); CI Resp., 9 dec. 1917 (AAS 10 [1918] 77); CI Resp., 9 dec. 1917 (AAS 11 [1919] 480); PAULUS PP. VI, m. p. *Finis Concilio,* 3 ian. 1966, 5 (AAS 58 [1966] 37–40); Sec No-tif., 99766, 11 iul. 1967; Sec Litt. circ., 115121, 25 mar. 1968; Sec Litt., 134634, 14 apr. 1969
16 §2: c.17 §2
16 §3: c. 17 §3
17: c. 18
18: c. 19

exception from the law are subject to strict interpretation.

CAN. 19   If a custom or an express prescript of universal or particular law is lacking in a certain matter, a case, unless it is penal, must be resolved in light of laws issued in similar matters, general principles of law applied with canonical equity, the jurisprudence and practice of the Roman Curia, and the common and constant opinion of learned persons.

CAN. 20   A later law abrogates, or derogates from, an earlier law if it states so expressly, is directly contrary to it, or completely reorders the entire matter of the earlier law. A universal law, however, in no way derogates from a particular or special law unless the law expressly provides otherwise.

CAN. 21   In a case of doubt, the revocation of a pre-existing law is not presumed, but later laws must be related to the earlier ones and, insofar as possible, must be harmonized with them.

CAN. 22   Civil laws to which the law of the Church yields are to be observed in canon law with the same effects, insofar as they are not contrary to divine law and unless canon law provides otherwise.

exceptionem a lege continent, strictae subsunt interpretationi.

CAN. 19   Si certa de re desit expressum legis sive universalis sive particularis praescriptum aut consuetudo, causa, nisi sit poenalis, dirimenda est attentis legibus latis in similibus, generalibus iuris principiis cum aequitate canonica servatis, iurisprudentia et praxi Curiae Romanae, communi constantique doctorum sententia.

CAN. 20   Lex posterior abrogat priorem aut eidem derogat, si id expresse edicat aut illi sit directe contraria, aut totam de integro ordinet legis prioris materiam; sed lex universalis minime derogat iuri particulari aut speciali, nisi aliud in iure expresse caveatur.

CAN. 21   In dubio revocatio legis praeexsistentis non praesumitur, sed leges posteriores ad priores trahendae sunt et his, quantum fieri potest, conciliandae.

CAN. 22   Leges civiles ad quas ius Ecclesiae remittit, in iure canonico iisdem cum effectibus serventur, quatenus iuri divino non sint contrariae et nisi aliud iure canonico caveatur.

19: c. 20; BENEDICTUS PP. XV, Const. Ap. *Providentissima Mater Ecclesia*, 27 maii 1917 (AAS 9/2 [1917] 5); SCConc Resol. 10 ian. 1920 (AAS 12 [1920] 43–47); SCR Resp. 20 iul. 1923 (AAS 15 [1923] 457–458); REU 1 §1; PAULUS PP. VI, All., 8 feb. 1973 (AAS 65 [1973] 95–103)

20: c. 22

21: c. 23

22: cc. 255, 547 §2, 581 §2, 987, 5°, 1016, 1059, 1063 §3, 1080, 1186, 1301 §1, 1508, 1529, 1553 §2, 1770 §2, 1°, 1813 §2, 1926, 1933 §3, 1961, 2191 §3, 3°, 2198, 2223 §3, 2° et 3°; SCDS Resp., 2 iul. 1917; CI Resp., 23 mar. 1919; SCDS Resp., 20 iun. 1919; SCR Rescr., 3 feb. 1921; SCDS Ind., 16 iun. 1922; SCDS Resol., 25 ian. 1927; SCConc Litt. circ., 20 iun. 1929 (AAS 21 [1929] 384–399); SCR Instr. *Questa Sacra Congregazione*, 6 feb. 1930 (AAS 22 [1930] 138–144); Sec Litt. circ., 5 sep. 1935; SCSO Resp., 28 iun. 1938; Sec. Litt. circ., 10 aug. 1941; SCC Instr. *Solemne semper*, 23 apr. 1951, XIV (AAS 43 [1951] 564); SCR Rescr., 1 apr. 1955; SCR Resp., 26 mar. 1957; SCR Resp., 1 mar. 1958; SCR Rescr., 22 aug. 1959; SCSO Resp., 1 mar. 1961; CD 19; GS 74; Sec Notif., 22 aug. 1966; Sec Notif., 16 feb. 1967; CM II

TITLE II.
Custom

CAN. 23 Only that custom introduced by a community of the faithful and approved by the legislator according to the norm of the following canons has the force of law.

CAN. 24 §1. No custom which is contrary to divine law can obtain the force of law.

§2. A custom contrary to or beyond canon law *(praeter ius canonicum)* cannot obtain the force of law unless it is reasonable; a custom which is expressly reprobated in the law, however, is not reasonable.

CAN. 25 No custom obtains the force of law unless it has been observed with the intention of introducing a law by a community capable at least of receiving law.

CAN. 26 Unless the competent legislator has specifically approved it, a custom contrary to the canon law now in force or one beyond a canonical law *(praeter legem canonicam)* obtains the force of law only if it has been legitimately observed for thirty continuous and complete years. Only a centenary or immemorial custom, however, can prevail against a canonical law which contains a clause prohibiting future customs.

CAN. 27 Custom is the best interpreter of laws.

CAN. 28 Without prejudice to the prescript of can. 5, a contrary custom or law revokes a custom which is contrary to or beyond

TITULUS II.
De Consuetudine

CAN. 23 Ea tantum consuetudo a communitate fidelium introducta vim legis habet, quae a legislatore approbata fuerit, ad normam canonum qui sequuntur.

CAN. 24 §1. Nulla consuetudo vim legis obtinere potest, quae sit iuri divino contraria.

§2. Nec vim legis obtinere potest consuetudo contra aut praeter ius canonicum, nisi sit rationabilis; consuetudo autem, quae in iure expresse reprobatur, non est rationabilis.

CAN. 25 Nulla consuetudo vim legis obtinet, nisi a communitate legis saltem recipiendae capaci cum animo iuris inducendi servata fuerit.

CAN. 26 Nisi a competenti legislatore specialiter fuerit probata, consuetudo vigenti iuri canonico contraria aut quae est praeter legem canonicam, vim legis obtinet tantum, si legitime per annos triginta continuos et completos servata fuerit; contra legem vero canonicam, quae clausulam contineat futuras consuetudines prohibentem, sola praevalere potest consuetudo centenaria aut immemorabilis.

CAN. 27 Consuetudo est optima legum interpres.

CAN. 28 Firmo praescripto can. 5, consuetudo, sive contra sive praeter legem, per contrariam consuetudinem aut legen revo-

---

23: c. 25; SCConc 14 dec. 1918 (AAS 11 [1919] 128–133); SCConc 11 dec. 1920 (AAS 13 [1921] 262–268)

24 §1: c. 27 §1

24 §2: cc. 27, 28; SCConc 14 dec. 1918 (AAS 11 [1919] 128–133); CI Resp. 15, 16 oct. 1919 (AAS 11 [1919] 479); SCConc Resol., 11 dec. 1920 (AAS 14 [1922] 42–46); CI Resp., 26 nov. 1922 (AAS 15 [1923] 128); SCDS Resol., 24 iul. 1925 (AAS 18 [1926] 43–44);

SCDS Instr. *Ex responsionibus*, 25 nov. 1925 (AAS 18 [1926] 44–47); SCConc 23 apr. 1927 (AAS 19 [1927] 415)

25: c. 26

26: cc. 27 §1, 28; SCConc Resol., 11 dec. 1920 (AAS 14 [1922] 42–46)

27: c. 29

28: c. 30; ES I, 18 §1

the law *(praeter legem)*. Unless it makes express mention of them, however, a law does not revoke centenary or immemorial customs, nor does a universal law revoke particular customs.

catur; sed, nisi expressam de iis mentionem faciat, lex non revocat consuetudines centenarias aut immemorabiles, nec lex universalis consuetudines particulares.

TITLE III. General Decrees and Instructions

TITULUS III. De Decretis Generalibus et de Instructionibus

CAN. 29   General decrees, by which a competent legislator issues common prescripts for a community capable of receiving law, are laws properly speaking and are governed by the prescripts of the canons on laws.

CAN. 30   A person who possesses only executive power is not able to issue the general decree mentioned in can. 29 unless, in particular cases, it has been expressly granted to that person by a competent legislator according to the norm of law and the conditions stated in the act of the grant have been observed.

CAN. 31   §1. Those who possess executive power are able to issue, within the limits of their competence, general executory decrees, namely, those which more precisely determine the methods to be observed in applying the law or which urge the observance of laws.

§2. With respect to the promulgation and suspensive period *(vacatio)* of the decrees mentioned in §1, the prescripts of can. 8 are to be observed.

CAN. 32   General executory decrees oblige those who are bound by the laws whose methods of application the same decrees determine or whose observance they urge.

CAN. 29   Decreta generalia, quibus a legislatore competenti pro communitate legis recipiendae capaci communia feruntur praescripta, proprie sunt leges et reguntur praescriptis canonum de legibus.

CAN. 30   Qui potestate exsecutiva tantum gaudet, decretum generale, de quo in can. 29, ferre non valet, nisi in casibus particularibus ad normam iuris id ipsi a legislatore competenti expresse fuerit concessum et servatis condicionibus in actu concessionis statutis.

CAN. 31   §1. Decreta generalia exsecutoria, quibus nempe pressius determinantur modi in lege applicanda servandi aut legum observantia urgetur, ferre valent, intra fines suae competentiae, qui potestate gaudent exsecutiva.

§2. Ad decretorum promulgationem et vacationem quod attinet, de quibus in §1, serventur praescripta can. 8.

CAN. 32   Decreta generalia exsecutoria eos obligant qui tenentur legibus, quarum eadem decreta modos applicationis determinant aut observantiam urgent.

29: BENEDICTUS PP. XV, m.p. *Cum iuris canonici*, 15 sep. 1917, II–III (AAS 9 [1917] 484)
31 §1: BENEDICTUS PP. XV, m.p. *Cum iuris* *canonici*, 15 sep. 1917, II (AAS 9 [1917] 484); PAULUS PP. VI, m.p. *Munus Apostolicum*, 10 iun. 1966 (AAS 58 [1966] 465–466)

CAN. 33 §1. General executory decrees, even if they are issued in directories or in documents of another name, do not derogate from laws, and their prescripts which are contrary to laws lack all force.

§2. Such decrees cease to have force by explicit or implicit revocation made by competent authority as well as by cessation of the law for whose execution they were given. They do not, however, cease when the authority of the one who established them expires unless the contrary is expressly provided.

CAN. 34 §1. Instructions clarify the prescripts of laws and elaborate on and determine the methods to be observed in fulfilling them. They are given for the use of those whose duty it is to see that laws are executed and oblige them in the execution of the laws. Those who possess executive power legitimately issue such instructions within the limits of their competence.

§2. The ordinances of instructions do not derogate from laws. If these ordinances cannot be reconciled with the prescripts of laws, they lack all force.

§3. Instructions cease to have force not only by explicit or implicit revocation of the competent authority who issued them or of the superior of that authority but also by the cessation of the law for whose clarification or execution they were given.

CAN. 33 §1. Decreta generalia exsecutoria, etiamsi edantur in directoriis aliusve nominis documentis, non derogant legibus, et eorum praescripta quae legibus sint contraria omni vi carent.

§2. Eadem vim habere desinunt revocatione explicita aut implicita ab auctoritate competenti facta, necnon cessante lege ad cuius exsecutionem data sunt; non autem cessant resoluto iure statuentis, nisi contrarium expresse caveatur.

CAN. 34 §1. Instructiones, quae nempe legum praescripta declarant atque rationes in iisdem exsequendis servandas evolvunt et determinant, ad usum eorum dantur quorum est curare ut leges exsecutioni mandentur, eosque in legum exsecutione obligant; eas legitime edunt, intra fines suae competentiae, qui potestate exsecutiva gaudent.

§2. Instructionum ordinationes legibus non derogant, et si quae cum legum praescriptis componi nequeant, omni vi carent.

§3. Vim habere desinunt instructiones non tantum revocatione explicita aut implicita auctoritatis competentis, quae eas edidt, eiusve superioris, sed etiam cessante lege ad quam declarandam vel exsecutioni mandandam datae sunt.

34 §1: BENEDICTUS PP. XV, m.p. *Cum iuris canonici*, 15 sep. 1917, II (AAS 9 [1917] 484); SCDS Instr. *Questa Sacra Congregazione*, 20 iun. 1919; SCPF Instr. *Cum a pluribus*, 25 iul. 1920 (AAS 12 [1920] 331–333); SCR Instr. *Doceatur*, 25 mar. 1922 (AAS 14 [1922] 278)

TITLE IV. Singular Administrative Acts

CHAPTER I. Common Norms

CAN. 35 A singular administrative act, whether it is a decree, a precept, or a rescript, can be issued by one who possesses executive power within the limits of that person's competence, without prejudice to the prescript of can. 76, §1.

CAN. 36 §1. An administrative act must be understood according to the proper meaning of the words and the common manner of speaking. In a case of doubt, those which refer to litigation, pertain to threatening or inflicting penalties, restrict the rights of a person, injure the acquired rights of others, or are contrary to a law which benefits private persons are subject to a strict interpretation; all others are subject to a broad interpretation.

§2. An administrative act must not be extended to other cases besides those expressed.

CAN. 37 An administrative act which regards the external forum must be put in writing. Furthermore, if it is given in commissorial form, the act of its execution must be put in writing.

CAN. 38 An administrative act, even if it is a rescript given *motu proprio*, lacks effect insofar as it injures the acquired right of another or is contrary to a law or approved custom, unless the competent authority has expressly added a derogating clause.

CAN. 39 Conditions in an administrative act are considered added for validity only when

TITULUS IV. De Actibus Administrativis Singularibus

CAPUT I. Normae Communes

CAN. 35 Actus administrativus singularis, sive est decretum aut praeceptum sive est rescriptum, elici potest, intra fines suae competentiae, ab eo qui potestate exsecutiva gaudet, firmo praescripto can. 76, §1.

CAN. 36 §1. Actus administrativus intellegendus est secundum propriam verborum significationem et communem loquendi usum; in dubio, qui ad lites referuntur aut ad poenas comminandas infligendasve attinent aut personae iura coarctant aut iura aliis quaesita laedunt aut adversantur legi in commodum privatorum, strictae subsunt interpretationi; ceteri omnes, latae.

§2. Actus administrativus non debet ad alios casus praeter expressos extendi.

CAN. 37 Actus administrativus, qui forum externum respicit, scripto est consignandus; item, si fit in forma commissoria, actus huius exsecutionis.

CAN. 38 Actus administrativus, etiam si agatur de rescripto *Motu proprio* dato, effectu caret quatenus ius alteri quaesitum laedit aut legi consuetudinive probatae contrarius est, nisi auctoritas competens expresse clausulam derogatoriam addiderit.

CAN. 39 Condiciones in actu administrativo tunc tantum ad validitatem censentur

---

36 §1: cc. 49, 50; SCSO Resp., 6 dec. 1966
36 §2: c. 49
37: c. 56; SACRA CONGREGATIO PRO CAUSIS SANCTORUM, Decr. *Ne ob diuturnum*, 3 apr. 1970

(AAS 62 [1970] 554–555)
38: c. 46
39: c. 39; SCSO Resp., 14 ian. 1960

they are expressed by the particles if *(si)*, unless *(nisi)*, or provided that *(dummodo)*.

CAN. 40 The executor of any administrative act invalidly carries out his or her function before receiving the relevant letter and verifying its authenticity and integrity, unless previous notice of the letter had been communicated to the executor by authority of the one who issued the act.

CAN. 41 The executor of an administrative act to whom is entrusted merely the task of execution cannot refuse the execution of this act unless it clearly appears that the act itself is null or cannot be upheld for another grave cause, or the conditions attached to the administrative act itself have not been fulfilled. Nevertheless, if the execution of the administrative act seems inopportune due to the circumstances of person or place, the executor is to suspend the execution. In such cases the executor is to inform immediately the authority who issued the act.

CAN. 42 The executor of an administrative act must proceed according to the norm of the mandate. If, however, the executor did not fulfill the essential conditions attached to the relevant letter and did not observe the substantial form of proceeding, the execution is invalid.

CAN. 43 The executor of an administrative act can, according to his or her prudent judgment, substitute another as executor unless substitution has been forbidden, the executor has been chosen for personal qualifications, or a substitute has been predetermined. In these cases, however, the executor may entrust the preparatory acts to another.

CAN. 44 The executor's successor in office

adiectae, cum per particulas *si, nisi, dummodo* exprimuntur.

CAN. 40 Exsecutor alicuius actus administrativi invalide suo munere fungitur, antequam litteras receperit earumque authenticitatem et integritatem recognoverit, nisi praevia earundem notitia ad ipsum auctoritate eundem actum edentis transmissa fuerit.

CAN. 41 Exsecutor actus administrativi cui committitur merum exsecutionis ministerium, exsecutionem huius actus denegare non potest, nisi manifesto appareat eundem actum esse nullum aut alia ex gravi causa sustineri non posse aut condiciones in ipso actu administrativo appositas non esse adimpletas; si tamen actus administrativi exsecutio adiunctorum personae aut loci ratione videatur inopportuna, exsecutor exsecutionem intermittat; quibus in casibus statim certiorem faciat auctoritatem quae actum edidit.

CAN. 42 Exsecutor actus administrativi procedere debet ad mandati normam; si autem condiciones essentiales in litteris appositas non impleverit ac substantialem procedendi formam non servaverit, irrita est exsecutio.

CAN. 43 Actus administrativi exsecutor potest alium pro suo prudenti arbitrio sibi substituere, nisi substitutio prohibita fuerit, aut electa industria personae, aut substituti persona praefinita; hisce autem in casibus exsecutori licet alteri committere actus praeparatorios.

CAN. 44 Actus administrativus exsecu-

40: c. 53; SCR Ind., 2 maii 1955
41: c. 54 §1
42: c. 55

43: c. 57
44: c. 58

can also execute an administrative act unless the executor was chosen for personal qualifications.

CAN. 45 If the executor has erred in any way in the execution of an administrative act, the executor is permitted to execute the same act again.

CAN. 46 An administrative act does not cease when the authority of the one who established it expires unless the law expressly provides otherwise.

CAN. 47 The revocation of an administrative act by another administrative act of a competent authority takes effect only from the moment at which the revocation is legitimately made known to the person for whom it has been given.

CHAPTER II. **Singular Decrees and Precepts**

CAN. 48 A singular decree is an administrative act issued by a competent executive authority in which a decision is given or a provision is made for a particular case according to the norms of law. Of their nature, these decisions or provisions do not presuppose a petition made by someone.

CAN. 49 A singular precept is a decree which directly and legitimately enjoins a specific person or persons to do or omit something, especially in order to urge the observance of law.

CAN. 50 Before issuing a singular decree, an authority is to seek out the necessary information and proofs and, insofar as possible, to hear those whose rights can be injured.

CAN. 51 A decree is to be issued in writing,

tioni mandari potest etiam ab exsecutoris successore in officio, nisi fuerit electa industria personae.

CAN. 45 Exsecutori fas est, si quoquo modo in actus administrativi exsecutione erraverit, eundem actum iterum exsecutioni mandare.

CAN. 46 Actus administrativus non cessat resoluto iure statuentis, nisi aliud iure expresse caveatur.

CAN. 47 Revocatio actus administrativi per alium actum administrativum auctoritatis competentis effectum tantummodo obtinet a momento, quo legitime notificatur personae pro qua datus est.

CAPUT II. **De Decretis et Praeceptis Singularibus**

CAN. 48 Decretum singulare intellegitur actus administrativus a competenti auctoritate exsecutiva editus, quo secundum iuris normas pro casu particulari datur decisio aut fit provisio, quae natura sua petitionem ab aliquo factam non supponunt.

CAN. 49 Praeceptum singulare est decretum quo personae aut personis determinatis aliquid faciendum aut omittendum directe et legitime imponitur, praesertim ad legis observantiam urgendam.

CAN. 50 Antequam decretum singulare ferat, auctoritas necessarias notitias et probationes exquirat, atque, quantum fieri potest, eos audiat quorum iura laedi possint.

CAN. 51 Decretum scripto feratur ex-

with the reasons at least summarily expressed if it is a decision.

CAN. 52 A singular decree has force only in respect to the matters which it decides and for the persons for whom it was given. It obliges these persons everywhere, however, unless it is otherwise evident.

CAN. 53 If decrees are contrary to one another, a particular decree prevails over a general in those matters which are specifically expressed. If they are equally particular or equally general, the decree later in time modifies the earlier to the extent that the later one is contrary to it.

CAN. 54 §1. A singular decree whose application is entrusted to an executor takes effect from the moment of execution; otherwise, from the moment it is made known to the person by the authority of the one who issued it.

§2. To be enforced, a singular decree must be made known by a legitimate document according to the norm of law.

CAN. 55 Without prejudice to the prescripts of cann. 37 and 51, when a very grave reason prevents the handing over of the written text of a decree, the decree is considered to have been made known if it is read to the person to whom it is destined in the presence of a notary or two witnesses. After a written record of what has occurred has been prepared, all those present must sign it.

CAN. 56 A decree is considered to have been made known if the one for whom it is destined has been properly summoned to receive or hear the decree but, without a just cause, did not appear or refused to sign.

CAN. 57 §1. Whenever the law orders a de-

pressis, saltem summarie, si agatur de decisione, motivis.

CAN. 52 Decretum singulare vim habet tantum quoad res de quibus decernit et pro personis quibus datum est; eas vero ubique obligat, nisi aliud constet.

CAN. 53 Si decreta inter se sint contraria, peculiare, in iis quae peculiariter exprimuntur, praevalet generali; si aeque sint peculiaria aut generalia, posterius tempore obrogat priori, quatenus ei contrarium est.

CAN. 54 §1. Decretum singulare, cuius applicatio committitur exsecutori, effectum habet a momento exsecutionis; secus a momento quo personae auctoritate ipsius decernentis intimatur.

§2. Decretum singulare, ut urgeri possit, legitimo documento ad normam iuris intimandum est.

CAN. 55 Firmo praescripto cann. 37 et 51, cum gravissima ratio obstet ne scriptus decreti textus tradatur, decretum intimatum habetur si ei, cui destinatur, coram notario vel duobus testibus legatur, actis redactis, ab omnibus praesentibus subscribendis.

CAN. 56 Decretum pro intimato habetur, si is cui destinatur, rite vocatus ad decretum accipiendum vel audiendum, sine iusta causa non comparuerit vel subscribere recusaverit.

CAN. 57 §1. Quoties lex iubeat decre-

cree to be issued or an interested party legitimately proposes a petition or recourse to obtain a decree, the competent authority is to provide for the matter within three months from the receipt of the petition or recourse unless the law prescribes some other time period.

§2. When this time period has passed, if the decree has not yet been given, the response is presumed to be negative with respect to the presentation of further recourse.

§3. A presumed negative response does not exempt the competent authority from the obligation of issuing the decree and even of repairing the damage possibly incurred, according to the norm of can. 128.

CAN. 58 §1. A singular decree ceases to have force through legitimate revocation by competent authority as well as through cessation of the law for whose execution it was given.

§2. A singular precept not imposed by a legitimate document ceases when the authority of the one who issued it expires.

CHAPTER III. **Rescripts**

CAN. 59 §1. A rescript is an administrative act issued in writing by competent executive authority; of its very nature, a rescript grants a privilege, dispensation, or other favor at someone's request.

§2. The prescripts established for rescripts are valid also for the oral granting of a permission or favors unless it is otherwise evident.

CAN. 60 Any rescript can be requested by all those who are not expressly prohibited from doing so.

tum ferri vel ab eo, cuius interest, petitio vel recursus ad decretum obtinendum legitime proponatur, auctoritas competens intra tres menses a recepta petitione vel recursu provideat, nisi alius terminus lege praescribatur.

§2. Hoc termino transacto, si decretum nondum datum fuerit, responsum praesumitur negativum, ad propositionem ulterioris recursus quod attinet.

§3. Responsum negativum praesumptum non eximit competentem auctoritatem ab obligatione decretum ferendi, immo et damnum forte illatum, ad normam can. 128, reparandi.

CAN. 58 §1. Decretum singulare vim habere desinit legitima revocatione ab auctoritate competenti facta necnon cessante lege ad cuius exsecutionem datum est.

§2. Praeceptum singulare, legitimo documento non impositum, cessat resoluto iure praecipientis.

CAPUT III. **De Rescriptis**

CAN. 59 §1. Rescriptum intelligitur actus administrativus a competenti auctoritate exsecutiva in scripts elicitus, quo suapte natura, ad petitionem alicuius, conceditur privilegium, dispensatio aliave gratia.

§2. Quae de rescriptis statuuntur praescripta, etiam de licentiae concessione necnon de concessionibus gratiarum vivae vocis oraculo valent, nisi aliud constet.

CAN. 60 Rescriptum quodlibet impetrari potest ab omnibus qui expresse non prohibentur.

58 §2: c.24
60: c. 36 §1; SCSO Resp. I, 27 ian. 1928 (AAS 20 [1928] 75)

CAN. 61 Unless it is otherwise evident, a rescript can be requested for another even without the person's assent and has force before the person's acceptance, without prejudice to contrary clauses.

CAN. 62 A rescript in which no executor is given has effect at the moment the letter is given; other rescripts, at the moment of execution.

CAN. 63 §1. Subreption, or concealment of the truth, prevents the validity of a rescript if in the request those things were not expressed which according to law, style, and canonical practice must be expressed for validity, unless it is a rescript of favor which is given *motu proprio*.

§2. Obreption, or a statement of falsehood, also prevents the validity of a rescript if not even one proposed motivating reason is true.

§3. The motivating reason in rescripts for which there is no executor must be true at the time when the rescript is given; in others, at the time of execution.

CAN. 64 Without prejudice to the authority of the Penitentiary for the internal forum, a favor denied by any dicastery of the Roman Curia cannot be granted validly by any other dicastery of the same Curia or by another competent authority below the Roman Pontiff without the assent of the dicastery before which the matter was initiated.

CAN. 65 §1. Without prejudice to the prescripts of §§2 and 3, no one is to petition from another ordinary a favor denied by one's own

CAN. 61 Nisi aliud constet, rescriptum impetrari potest pro alio, etiam praeter eius assensum, et valet ante eiusdem acceptationem, salvis clausulis contrariis.

CAN. 62 Rescriptum in quo nullus datur exsecutor, effectum habet a momento quo datae sunt litterae; cetera, a momento exsecutionis.

CAN. 63 §1. Validitati rescripti obstat subreptio seu reticentia veri, si in precibus expressa non fuerint quae secundum legem, stilum et praxim canonicam ad validitatem sunt exprimenda, nisi agatur de rescripto gratiae, quod *Motu proprio* datum sit.

§2. Item validitati rescripti obstat obreptio seu expositio falsi, si ne una quidem causa motiva proposita sit vera.

§3. Causa motiva in rescriptis quorum nullus est exsecutor, vera sit oportet tempore quo rescriptum datum est; in ceteris, tempore exsecutionis.

CAN. 64 Salvo iure Paenitentiariae pro foro interno, gratia a quovis dicasterio Romanae Curiae denegata, valide ab alio eiusdem Curiae dicasterio aliave competenti auctoritate infra Romanum Pontificem concedi nequit, sine assensu dicasterii quocum agi coeptum est.

CAN. 65 §1. Salvis praescriptis §§2 et 3, nemo gratiam a proprio Ordinario denegatam ab alio Ordinario petat, nisi facta

---

61: c 37; SCR Resp., 1 aug. 1922 (AAS 14 [1922] 501)

62: c. 38; SCDS Normae, 7 maii 1923, 103 (AAS 15 [1923] 413); SCDF Normae, 13 ian. 1971, V/1 (AAS 63 [1971] 306); SCDF Decl., 26 iun. 1972, IV (AAS 64 [1972] 642)

63 §1: cc. 42 §1, 45; SPA Monitum *Quo magis,* dec. 1941

63 §2: cc. 40, 42 §2; SCDS Decr. *Catholica doctri-*

na, 7 maii 1923 (AAS 15 [1923] 390); SCDF Normae, 13 ian. 1971, II/1 (AAS 63 [1971] 303); SCDS Instr. *Dispensationis matrimonii rati,* 7 mar. 1972, I/f (AAS 64 [1972] 247–248)

63 §3: c. 41; SCDS Normae, 7 maii 1923, 103 (AAS 15 [1923] 413)

64: c. 43

65 §1: c. 44 §1

ordinary unless mention of the denial has been made. When this mention has been made, however, the ordinary is not to grant the favor unless he has obtained the reasons for the denial from the prior ordinary.

§2. A favor denied by a vicar general or by an episcopal vicar cannot be granted validly by another vicar of the same bishop even if the reasons for the denial have been obtained from the vicar who denied it.

§3. A favor denied by a vicar general or by an episcopal vicar and afterwards obtained from the diocesan bishop without any mention made of this denial is invalid. A favor denied by a diocesan bishop, however, even if mention is made of the denial, cannot be obtained validly from his vicar general or episcopal vicar without the consent of the bishop.

CAN. 66   A rescript does not become invalid due to an error in the name of the person to whom it is given or by whom it is issued, or of the place where the person resides, or in the matter concerned, provided that, in the judgment of the ordinary, there is no doubt about the person or the matter.

CAN. 67   §1. If it happens that two contrary rescripts are obtained for one and the same thing, the particular prevails over the general in those matters which are particularly expressed.

§2. If they are equally particular or equally general, the earlier in time prevails over the later unless there is express mention of the earlier one in the later one or unless the person who obtained the earlier one has not used the rescript out of malice or notable negligence.

denegationis mentione; facta autem mentione, Ordinarius gratiam ne concedat, nisi habitis a priore Ordinario denegationis rationibus.

§2. Gratia a Vicario generali vel Vicario episcopali denegata, ab alio Vicario eiusdem Episcopi, etiam habitis a Vicario denegante denegationis rationibus, valide concedi nequit.

§3. Gratia a Vicario generali vel a Vicario episcopali denegata et postea, nulla facta huius denegationis mentione, ab Episcopo dioecesano impetrata, invalida est; gratia autem ab Episcopo dioecesano denegata nequit valide, etiam facta denegationis mentione, ab eius Vicario generali vel Vicario episcopali, non consentiente Episcopo, impetrari.

CAN. 66   Rescriptum non fit irritum ob errorem in nomine personae cui datur vel a qua editur, aut loci in quo ipsa residet, aut rei de qua agitur, dummodo iudicio Ordinarii nulla sit de ipsa persona vel de re dubitatio.

CAN. 67   §1. Si contingat ut de una eademque re duo rescripta inter se contraria impetrentur, peculiare, in iis quae peculiariter exprimuntur, praevalet generali.

§2. Si sint aeque peculiaria aut generalia, prius tempore praevalet posteriori, nisi in altero fiat mentio expressa de priore, aut nisi prior impetrator dolo vel notabili neglegentia sua rescripto usus non fuerit.

65 §2: ES I, 14 §4
65 §3: c. 44 §2; ES I, 14 §4
66: c. 47

67 §1: c. 48 §1
67 §2: c. 48 §2

§3. In a case of doubt whether a rescript is invalid or not, recourse is to be made to the one who issued it.

CAN. 68 A rescript of the Apostolic See in which no executor is given must be presented to the ordinary of the one who obtained it only when it is prescribed in the same letter, or it concerns public matters, or it is necessary that conditions be verified.

CAN. 69 A rescript for whose presentation no time is specified can be shown to the executor at any time, provided that there is neither fraud nor malice.

CAN. 70 If in a rescript the granting of a favor is entrusted to an executor, it is up to the prudent judgment and conscience of the executor to grant or deny the favor.

CAN. 71 No one is bound to use a rescript given only in his or her favor unless bound to do so by a canonical obligation from another source.

CAN. 72 Rescripts granted by the Apostolic See which have expired can be extended once by the diocesan bishop for a just cause, but not beyond three months.

CAN. 73 Rescripts are not revoked by a contrary law unless the law itself provides otherwise.

CAN. 74 Although one can use in the internal forum a favor granted orally, the person is bound to prove the favor in the external forum whenever someone legitimately requests it.

CAN. 75 If a rescript contains a privilege or dispensation, the prescripts of the following canons are also to be observed.

§3. In dubio num rescriptum irritum sit necne, recurratur ad rescribentem.

CAN. 68 Rescriptum Sedis Apostolicae in quo nullus datur exsecutor, tunc tantum debet Ordinario impetrantis praesentari, cum id in iisdem litteris praecipitur, aut de rebus agitur publicis, aut comprobari condiciones oportet.

CAN. 69 Rescriptum, cuius praesentationi nullum est definitum tempus, potest exsecutori exhiberi quovis tempore, modo absit fraus et dolus.

CAN. 70 Si in rescripto ipsa concessio exsecutori committatur, ipsius est pro suo prudenti arbitrio et conscientia gratiam concedere vel denegare.

CAN. 71 Nemo uti tenetur rescripto in sui dumtaxat favorem concesso, nisi aliunde obligatione canonica ad hoc teneatur.

CAN. 72 Rescripta ab Apostolica Sede concessa, quae exspiraverint, ab Episcopo dioecesano iusta de causa semel prorogari possunt, non tamen ultra tres menses.

CAN. 73 Per legem contrariam nulla rescripta revocantur, nisi aliud in ipsa lege caveatur.

CAN. 74 Quamvis gratia oretenus sibi concessa quis in foro interno uti possit, tenetur illam pro foro externo probare, quoties id legitime ab eo petatur.

CAN. 75 Si rescriptum contineat privilegium vel dispensationem, serventur insuper praescripta canonum qui sequuntur.

67 §3: c. 48 §3
68: c. 51; SCDS Normae, 7 maii 1923, 105 (AAS 15 [1923] 413)
69: c. 52
70: c. 54 §2
71: c. 69

72: PM 1; SCE Facul., 1 ian. 1968, 13: SCGE Facul., 1 ian. 1971, 9
73: c. 60 §2
74: c. 79
75: c. 62

CHAPTER IV. **Privileges**

CAN. 76 §1. A privilege is a favor given through a particular act to the benefit of certain physical or juridic persons; it can be granted by the legislator as well as by an executive authority to whom the legislator has granted this power.

§2. Centenary or immemorial possession induces the presumption that a privilege has been granted.

CAN. 77 A privilege must be interpreted according to the norm of can. 36, §1, but that interpretation must always be used by which the beneficiaries of a privilege actually obtain some favor.

CAN. 78 §1. A privilege is presumed to be perpetual unless the contrary is proved.

§2. A personal privilege, namely one which follows the person, is extinguished with that person's death.

§3. A real privilege ceases through the complete destruction of the thing or place; a local privilege, however, revives if the place is restored within fifty years.

CAN. 79 A privilege ceases through revocation by the competent authority according to the norm of can. 47, without prejudice to the prescript of can. 81.

CAN. 80 §1. No privilege ceases through renunciation unless the competent authority has accepted the renunciation.

§2. Any physical person can renounce a privilege granted only in that person's favor.

§3. Individual persons cannot renounce a

CAPUT IV. **De Privilegiis**

CAN. 76 §1. Privilegium, seu gratia in favorem certarum personarum sive physicarum sive iuridicarum per peculiarem actum facta, concedi potest a legislatore necnon ab auctoritate exsecutiva cui legislator hanc potestatem concesserit.

§2. Possessio centenaria vel immemorabilis praesumptionem inducit concessi privilegii.

CAN. 77 Privilegium interpretandum est ad normam can. 36, §1; sed ea semper adhibenda est interpretatio, qua privilegio aucti aliquam revera gratiam consequantur.

CAN. 78 §1. Privilegium praesumitur perpetuum, nisi contrarium probetur.

§2. Privilegium personale, quod scilicet personam sequitur, cum ipsa extinguitur.

§3. Privilegium reale cessat per absolutum rei vel loci interitum; privilegium vero locale, si locus intra quinquaginta annos restituatur, reviviscit.

CAN. 79 Privilegium cessat per revocationem competentis auctoritatis ad normam can. 47, firmo praescripto can. 81.

CAN. 80 §1. Nullum privilegium per renuntiationem cessat, nisi haec a competenti auctoriate fuerit acceptata.

§2. Privilegio in sui dumtaxat favorem concesso quaevis persona physica renuntiare potest.

§3. Privilegio concesso alicui personae

---

76 §2: c. 63 §2
77: cc. 49, 50, 67, 68
78 §1: c. 70
78 §2: c. 74
78 §3: c. 75

79: cc. 60 §1, 71; CD 28; Paen. V; ES I, 18 §1
80 §1: c. 72 §1
80 §2: c. 72 §2
80 §3: c. 72 §§3 et 4

privilege granted to some juridic person or granted in consideration of the dignity of a place or of a thing, nor is a juridic person free to renounce a privilege granted to it if the renunciation brings disadvantage to the Church or to others.

CAN. 81 A privilege is not extinguished when the authority of the one who granted it expires unless it has been given with the clause, at our good pleasure *(ad beneplacitum nostrum)*, or some other equivalent expression.

CAN. 82 A privilege which is not burdensome to others does not cease through non-use or contrary use. If it is to the disadvantage of others, however, it is lost if legitimate prescription takes place.

CAN. 83 §1. A privilege ceases through the lapse of the time period or through the completion of the number of cases for which it had been granted, without prejudice to the prescript of can. 142, §2.

§2. It also ceases if, in the judgment of the competent authority, circumstances are so changed in the course of time that it becomes harmful or its use illicit.

CAN. 84 One who abuses the power given by a privilege deserves to be deprived of that privilege. Therefore, when the holder of a privilege has been warned in vain, an ordinary is to deprive the one who gravely abuses it of a privilege which he himself has granted. If the privilege was granted by the Apostolic See, however, an ordinary is bound to notify the Apostolic See.

iuridicae, aut ratione dignitatis loci vel rei, singulae personae renuntiare nequeunt; nec ipsi personae iuridicae integrum est privilegio sibi concesso renuntiare, si renuntiatio cedat in Ecclesiae aliorumve praeiudicium.

CAN. 81 Resoluto iure concedentis, privilegium non extinguitur, nisi datum fuerit cum clausula *ad beneplacitum nostrum* vel alia aequipollenti.

CAN. 82 Per non usum vel per usum contrarium privilegium aliis haud onerosum non cessat; quod vero in aliorum gravamen cedit, amittitur, si accedat legitima praescriptio.

CAN. 83 §1. Cessat privilegium elapso tempore vel expleto numero casuum pro quibus concessum fuit, firmo praescripto can. 142, §2.

§2. Cessat quoque, si temporis progressu rerum adiuncta ita iudicio auctoritatis competentis immutata sint, ut noxium evaserit aut eius usus illicitus fiat.

CAN. 84 Qui abutitur potestate sibi ex privilegio data, privilegio ipso privari meretur; quare, Ordinarius, frustra monito privilegiario, graviter abutentem privet privilegio quod ipse concessit; quod si privilegium concessum fuerit ab Apostolica Sede, eandem Ordinarius certiorem facere tenetur.

81: c. 73
82: c. 76
83 §1: c. 77

83 §2: c. 77
84: c. 78

CHAPTER V. **Dispensations**

CAN. 85   A dispensation, or the relaxation of a merely ecclesiastical law in a particular case, can be granted by those who possess executive power within the limits of their competence, as well as by those who have the power to dispense explicitly or implicitly either by the law itself or by legitimate delegation.

CAN. 86   Laws are not subject to dispensation to the extent that they define those things which are essentially constitutive of juridic institutes or acts.

CAN. 87   §1. A diocesan bishop, whenever he judges that it contributes to their spiritual good, is able to dispense the faithful from universal and particular disciplinary laws issued for his territory or his subjects by the supreme authority of the Church. He is not able to dispense, however, from procedural or penal laws nor from those whose dispensation is specially reserved to the Apostolic See or some other authority.

§2. If recourse to the Holy See is difficult and, at the same time, there is danger of grave harm in delay, any ordinary is able to dispense from these same laws even if dispensation is reserved to the Holy See, provided that it concerns a dispensation which the Holy See is accustomed to grant under the same circumstances, without prejudice to the prescript of can. 291.

CAN. 88   A local ordinary is able to dispense from diocesan laws and, whenever he judges that it contributes to the good of the

CAPUT V. **De Dispensationibus**

CAN. 85 Dispensatio, seu legis mere ecclesiasticae in casu particulari relaxatio, concedi potest ab iis qui potestate gaudent exsecutiva intra limites suae competentiae, necnon ab illis quibus potestas dispensandi explicite vel implicite competit sive ipso iure sive vi legitmae delegationis.

CAN. 86 Dispensationi obnoxiae non sunt leges quatenus ea definiunt, quae institutorum aut actuum iuridicorum essentialiter sunt constitutiva.

CAN. 87 §1. Episcopus dioecesanus fideles, quoties id ad eorundem spirituale bonum conferre iudicet, dispensare valet in legibus disciplinaribus tam universalibus quam particularibus pro suo territorio vel suis subditis a suprema Ecclesiae auctoritate latis, non tamen in legibus processualibus aut poenalibus, nec in iis quarum dispensatio Apostolicae Sedi aliive auctoritati specialiter reservatur.

§2. Si difficilis sit recursus ad Sanctam Sedem et simul in mora sit periculum gravis damni, Ordinarius quicumque dispensare valet in iisdem legibus, etiam si dispensatio reservatur Sanctae Sedi, dummodo agatur de dispensatione quam ipsa in iisdem adiunctis concedere solet, firmo praescripto can. 291.

CAN. 88 Ordinarius loci in legibus dioecesanis atque, quoties id ad fidelium bonum conferre iudicet, in legibus a Concilio

85: c. 80; SCSO Normae, 1 iul. 1931, 3; EM IV; SCGE Facul., 1 ian. 1971, 23

86: EM IV

87 §1: CD 8b; EM II–IX; Princ. 4

87 §2: c. 81; Cl Resp. V, 12 nov. 1922; SCNE Ind., 19 nov. 1941 (AAS 33 [1941] 516–517); Sec Notif., 1 ian.

1942; CI Resp. 1, 27 iul. 1942 (AAS 34 [1942] 241); CI Resp. B/I, 26 iun. 1947 (AAS 39 [1947] 374); CI Resp. 1, 26 ian. 1949 (AAS 41 [1949] 158); CA I, 13; SCDF Decl., 26 iun. 1972, IV (AAS 64 [1972] 642); SCDF Normae, 14 oct. 1980, art. 1 §2

88: c. 82

faithful, from laws issued by a plenary or provincial council or by the conference of bishops.

CAN. 89 A pastor and other presbyters or deacons are not able to dispense from universal and particular law unless this power has been expressly granted to them.

CAN. 90 §1. One is not to be dispensed from an ecclesiastical law without a just and reasonable cause, after taking into account the circumstances of the case and the gravity of the law from which dispensation is given; otherwise the dispensation is illicit and, unless it is given by the legislator himself or his superior, also invalid.

§2. In a case of doubt concerning the sufficiency of the cause, a dispensation is granted validly and licitly.

CAN. 91 Even when outside his territory, one who possesses the power to dispense is able to exercise it with respect to his subjects even though they are absent from the territory, and, unless the contrary is expressly established, also with respect to travelers actually present in the territory, as well as with respect to himself.

CAN. 92 A dispensation is subject to a strict interpretation according to the norm of can. 36, §1, as is the very power to dispense granted for a particular case.

CAN. 93 A dispensation which has successive application ceases in the same ways as a privilege as well as by the certain and total cessation of the motivating cause.

plenario vel provinciali aut ab Episcoporum conferentia latis dispensare valet.

CAN. 89 Parochus aliique presbyteri aut diaconi a lege universali et particulari dispensare non valent, nisi haec potestas ipsis expresse concessa sit.

CAN. 90 §1. A lege ecclesiastica ne dispensetur sine iusta et rationabili causa, habita ratione adiunctorum casus et gravitatis legis a qua dispensatur; alias dispensatio illicita est et, nisi ab ipso legislatore eiusve superiore data sit, etiam invalida.

§2. Dispensatio in dubio de sufficientia causae valide et licite conceditur.

CAN. 91 Qui gaudet potestate dispensandi eam exercere valet, etiam extra territorium exsistens, in subditos, licet e territorio absentes, atque, nisi contrarium expresse statuatur, in peregrinos quoque in territorio actu degentes, necnon erga seipsum.

CAN. 92 Strictae subest interpretationi non solum dispensatio ad normam can. 36, §1, sed ipsamet potestas dispensandi ad certum casum concessa.

CAN. 93 Dispensatio quae tractum habet successivum cessat iisdem modis quibus privilegium, necnon certa ac totali cessatione causae motivae.

89: c. 83

90 §1: c. 84 §1; SCSO Normae, 1 iul. 1931, 3; CD 8b; EM VII; SCDF Normae, 13 ian. 1971, II/3b (AAS 63 [1971] 304); SCDF Decl., 26 iun. 1972, II (AAS 64 [1972] 642); SCDF Litt. circ., 14 oct. 1980, 5 (AAS 72 [1980] 1134); SCDF Normae, 14 oct. 1980, 2 et 3

90 §2: c. 84 §2

91: c. 201 §§1 et 3; SCEO Resp. I–IV, 24 iul. 1948

92: c. 85

93: c. 86

TITLE V. **Statutes and Rules of Order**

CAN. 94 §1. Statutes in the proper sense are ordinances which are established according to the norm of law in aggregates of persons *(universitates personarum)* or of things *(universitates rerum)* and which define their purpose, constitution, government, and methods of operation.

§2. The statutes of an aggregate of persons *(universitas personarum)* bind only the persons who are its legitimate members; the statutes of an aggregate of things *(universitas rerum)*, those who direct it.

§3. Those prescripts of statutes established and promulgated by virtue of legislative power are governed by the prescripts of the canons on laws.

CAN. 95 §1. Rules of order *(ordines)* are rules or norms, which must be observed in meetings, whether convened by ecclesiastical authority or freely convoked by the Christian faithful, as well as in other celebrations. They define those things which pertain to the constitution, direction, and ways of proceeding.

§2. These rules of order bind those who participate in these assemblies or celebrations.

TITULUS V. **De Statutis et Ordinibus**

CAN. 94 §1. Statuta, sensu proprio, sunt ordinationes quae in universitatibus sive personarum sive rerum ad normam iuris conduntur, et quibus definiuntur earundem finis, consititutio, regimen atque agendi rationes.

§2. Statutis universitatis personarum obligantur solae personae quae legitime eiusdem membra sunt; statutis rerum universitatis, ii qui eiusdem moderamen curant.

§3. Quae statutorum praescripta vi potestatis legislativae condita et promulgata sunt, reguntur praescriptis canonum de legibus.

CAN. 95 §1. Ordines sunt regulae seu normae quae servari debent in personarum conventibus, sive ab auctoritate ecclesiastica indictis sive a christifidelibus libere convocatis, necnon aliis in celebrationibus, et quibus definiuntur quae ad constitutionem, moderamen et rerum agendarum rationes pertinent.

§2. In conventibus celebrationibusve, ii regulis ordinis tenentur, qui in iisdem partem habent.

94 §1: cc. 101 §2, 395 §4, 397, 410, 411 §2, 416, 417 §2, 418 §1, 422 §2, 1376 §2; DSD 5, 56; SCSSU Instr. *Sacra Congregatio,* 12 iun. 1931, 1: 3°a; 3, *Appendix II,* (AAS 23 [1931] 264, 283–284); UR 8; CD 38: 2, 3; GE 11; SCIC Normae 20 maii 1968, Introductio; SCh 7; SCIC Ordinationes, 29 apr. 1979, art. 6, *Appendix I* ad art. 6 (AAS 71 [1979] 501, 518–519)
94 §2: c. 410 §1
95 §1: IOANNES PP. XXIII, m. p. *Appropinquante*

Concilio, 6 aug. 1962 (AAS 54 [1962] 609–631); Sec Normae, 13 sep. 1963; PAULUS PP. VI, Normae, 2 iul. 1964; Sec Rescr., 8 dec. 1966 (AAS 59 [1967] 91–103); CPEN Rescr., 24 iun. 1969 (AAS 61 [1969] 525–539); CPEN Rescr., 20 aug. 1971 (AAS 63 [1971] 702–704)
95 §2: IOANNES PP. XXIII. m.p. *Appropinquante Concilio,* 6 aug. 1962 (AAS 54 [1962] 611)

TITLE VI. Physical and Juridic Persons

CHAPTER I. The Canonical Condition of Physical Persons

CAN. 96 By baptism one is incorporated into the Church of Christ and is constituted a person in it with the duties and rights which are proper to Christians in keeping with their condition, insofar as they are in ecclesiastical communion and unless a legitimately issued sanction stands in the way.

CAN. 97 §1. A person who has completed the eighteenth year of age has reached majority; below this age, a person is a minor.

§2. A minor before the completion of the seventh year is called an infant and is considered not responsible for oneself (*non sui compos*). With the completion of the seventh year, however, a minor is presumed to have the use of reason.

CAN. 98 §1. A person who has reached majority has the full exercise of his or her rights.

§2. A minor, in the exercise of his or her rights, remains subject to the authority of parents or guardians except in those matters in which minors are exempted from their authority by divine law or canon law. In what pertains to the appointment of guardians and their authority, the prescripts of civil law are to be observed unless canon law provides otherwise or unless in certain cases the diocesan bishop, for a just cause, has decided to provide for the matter through the appointment of another guardian.

TITULUS VI. De Personis Physicis et Iuridicis

CAPUT I. De Personarum Physicarum Condicione Canonica

CAN. 96 Baptismo homo Ecclesiae Christi incorporatur et in eadem constituitur persona, cum officiis et iuribus quae christianis, attenta quidem eorum condicione, sunt propria, quatenus in ecclesiastica sunt communione et nisi obstet lata legitime sanctio.

CAN. 97 §1. Persona quae duodevigesimum aetatis annum explevit, maior est; infra hanc aetatem, minor.

§2. Minor, ante plenum septennium, dicitur infans et censetur non sui compos, expleto autem septennio, usum rationis habere praesumitur.

CAN. 98 §1. Persona maior plenum habet suorum iurium exercitium.

§2. Persona minor in exercitio suorum iurium potestati obnoxia manet parentum vel tutorum, iis exceptis in quibus minores lege divina aut iure canonico ab eorum potestate exempti sunt; ad constitutionem tutorum eorumque potestatem quod attinet, serventur praescripta iuris civilis, nisi iure canonico aliud caveatur, aut Episcopus dioecesanus in certis casibus iusta de causa per nominationem alius tutoris providendum aestimaverit.

96: c. 87; SCSO Resp. 1, 27 ian. 1928 (AAS 20 [1928] 75); SCSO Decr. *In generali consessu*, 15 ian. 1940 (AAS 32 [1940] 52); MC pp. 203–204; LG 11, 14; UR 3, 4; AG 7; OBP 4

97 §1: c.88 §1
97 §2: c. 88 §3; OBP 1
98 §1: c. 89
98 §2: cc. 89, 1648, 1650, 1651

CAN. 99   Whoever habitually lacks the use of reason is considered not responsible for oneself *(non sui compos)* and is equated with infants.

CAN. 100   A person is said to be: a resident *(incola)* in the place where the person has a domicile; a temporary resident *(advena)* in the place where the person has a quasi-domicile; a traveler *(peregrinus)* if the person is outside the place of a domicile or quasi-domicile which is still retained; a transient *(vagus)* if the person does not have a domicile or quasi- domicile anywhere.

CAN. 101   §1. The place of origin of a child, even of a neophyte, is that in which the parents had a domicile or, lacking that, a quasi-domicile when the child was born or, if the parents did not have the same domicile or quasi-domicile, that of the mother.

§2. In the case of a child of transients, the place of origin is the actual place of birth; in the case of an abandoned child, it is the place where the child was found.

CAN. 102   §1. Domicile is acquired by that residence within the territory of a certain parish or at least of a diocese, which either is joined with the intention of remaining there permanently unless called away or has been protracted for five complete years.

§2. Quasi-domicile is acquired by residence within the territory of a certain parish or at least of a diocese, which either is joined with the intention of remaining there for at least three months unless called away or has in fact been protracted for three months.

§3. A domicile or quasi-domicile within the

CAN. 99   Quicumque usu rationis habitu caret, censetur non sui compos et infantibus assimilatur.

CAN. 100   Persona dicitur: *incola*, in loco ubi est eius domicilium; *advena*, in loco ubi quasi-domicilium habet; *peregrinus*, si versetur extra domicilium et quasi-domicilium quod adhuc retinet; *vagus*, si nullibi domicilium habeat vel quasi-domicilium.

CAN. 101   §1. Locus originis filii, etiam neophyti, est ille in quo cum filius natus est, domicilium, aut, eo deficiente, quasi-domicilium habuerunt parentes vel, si parentes non habuerint idem domicilium vel quasi-domicilium, mater.

§2. Si agatur de filio vagorum, locus originis est ipsemet nativitatis locus; si de exposito, est locus in quo inventus est.

CAN. 102   §1. Domicilium acquiritur ea in territorio alicuius paroeciae aut saltem dioecesis commoratione, quae aut coniuncta sit cum animo ibi perpetuo manendi si nihil inde avocet, aut ad quinquennium completum sit protracta.

§2. Quasi-domicilium acquiritur ea commoratione in territorio alicuius paroeciae aut saltem dioecesis, quae aut coniuncta sit cum animo ibi manendi saltem per tres menses si nihil inde avocet, aut ad tres menses reapse sit protracta.

§3. Domicilium vel quasi-domicilium in

99: c. 88 §3
100: c. 91
101 §1: c. 90 §1; CI Resp., 26 nov. 1922 (AAS 15 [1923] 128)
101 §2: c. 90 §2

102 §1: c. 92 §1
102 §2: c. 92 §2
102 §3: c. 92 §3; SCC Instr. *Sollemne semper,* 23 apr. 1951, III (AAS 43 [1951] 563)

territory of a parish is called parochial; within the territory of a diocese, even though not within a parish, diocesan.

CAN. 103 Members of religious institutes and societies of apostolic life acquire a domicile in the place where the house to which they are attached is located; they acquire a quasi-domicile in the house where they are residing, according to the norm of can. 102, §2.

CAN. 104 Spouses are to have a common domicile or quasi-domicile; by reason of legitimate separation or some other just cause, both can have their own domicile or quasi-domicile.

CAN. 105 §1. A minor necessarily retains the domicile and quasi-domicile of the one to whose power the minor is subject. A minor who is no longer an infant can also acquire a quasi-domicile of one's own; a minor who is legitimately emancipated according to the norm of civil law can also acquire a domicile of one's own.

§2. Whoever for some other reason than minority has been placed legitimately under the guardianship or care of another has the domicile and quasi-domicile of the guardian or curator.

CAN. 106 Domicile and quasi-domicile are lost by departure from a place with the intention of not returning, without prejudice to the prescript of can. 105.

CAN. 107 §1. Through both domicile and quasi-domicile, each person acquires his or her pastor and ordinary.

§2. The proper pastor or ordinary of a transient is the pastor or local ordinary where the transient is actually residing.

territorio paroeciae dicitur paroeciale; in territorio dioecesis, etsi non in paroecia, dioecesanum.

CAN. 103 Sodales institutorum religiosorum et societatum vitae apostolicae domicilium acquirunt in loco ubi sita est domus cui abscribuntur; quasi-domicilium in domo ubi, ad normam can. 102, §2, commorantur.

CAN. 104 Coniuges commune habeant domicilium vel quasi-domicilium; legitimae separationis ratione vel alia iusta de causa, uterque habere potest proprium domicilium vel quasi-domicilium.

CAN. 105 §1. Minor necessario retinet domicilium et quasi-domicilium illius, cuius potestati subicitur. Infantia egressus potest etiam quasi-domicilium proprium acquirere; atque legitime ad normam iuris civilis emancipatus, etiam proprium domicilium.

§2. Quicumque alia ratione quam minoritate, in tutelam vel curatelam legitime traditus est alterius, domicilium et quasi-domicilium habet tutoris vel curatoris.

CAN. 106 Domicilium et quasi-domicilium amittitur discessione a loco cum animo non revertendi, salvo praescripto can. 105.

CAN. 107 §1. Tum per domicilium tum per quasi-domicilium suum quisque parochum et Ordinarium sortitur.

§2. Proprius vagi parochus vel Ordinarius est parochus vel Ordinarius loci in quo vagus actu commoratur.

104: c. 93; CI Resp. I, 14 iul. 1922 (AAS 14 [1922] 526); PrM 6 §2
    105 §1: c. 93
    105 §2: c. 93 §1

106: c. 95
107 §1: c. 94 §1; SCC 9 iun. 1923 (AAS 17 [1923] 508–510); EM VII
    107 §2: c. 94 §2

§3. The proper pastor of one who has only a diocesan domicile or quasi-domicile is the pastor of the place where the person is actually residing.

CAN. 108 §1. Consanguinity is computed through lines and degrees.

§2. In the direct line there are as many degrees as there are generations or persons, not counting the common ancestor.

§3. In the collateral line there are as many degrees as there are persons in both the lines together, not counting the common ancestor.

CAN. 109 §1. Affinity arises from a valid marriage, even if not consummated, and exists between a man and the blood relatives of the woman and between the woman and the blood relatives of the man.

§2. It is so computed that those who are blood relatives of the man are related in the same line and degree by affinity to the woman, and vice versa.

CAN. 110 Children who have been adopted according to the norm of civil law are considered the children of the person or persons who have adopted them.

CAN. 111 §1. Through the reception of baptism, the child of parents who belong to the Latin Church is enrolled in it, or, if one or the other does not belong to it, both parents have chosen by mutual agreement to have the offspring baptized in the Latin Church. If there is no mutual agreement, however, the child is enrolled in the ritual Church to which the father belongs.

§3. Illius quoque qui non habet nisi domicilium vel quasi-domicilium dioecesanum, parochus proprius est parochus loci in quo actu commoratur.

CAN. 108 §1. Consanguinitas computatur per lineas et gradus.

§2. In linea recta tot sunt gradus quot generationes, seu quot personae, stipite dempto.

§3. In linea obliqua tot sunt gradus quot personae in utraque simul linea, stipite dempto.

CAN. 109 §1. Affinitas oritur ex matrimonio valido, etsi non consummato, atque viget inter virum et mulieris consanguineos, itemque mulierem inter et viri consanguineos.

§2. Ita computatur ut qui sunt consanguinei viri, iidem in eadem linea et gradu sint affines mulieris, et vice versa.

CAN. 110 Filii, qui ad normam legis civilis adoptati sint, habentur ut filii eius vel eorum qui eos adoptaverint.

CAN. 111 §1. Ecclesiae latinae per receptum baptismum adscribitur filius parentum, qui ad eam pertineant vel, si alteruter ad eam non pertineat, ambo concordi voluntate optaverint ut proles in Ecclesia latina baptizaretur; quodsi concors voluntas desit, Ecclesiae rituali ad quam pater pertinet adscribitur.

---

107 §3: c. 94 §3
108 §1: c. 96 §1
108 §2: c. 96 §2
109 §1: c. 97 §§1 et 2; SCSO Resp., 31 ian 1957 (AAS 49 [1957] 77)
109 §2: c. 97 §3
110: cc. 1059, 1080

111 §1: cc. 98 §1, 756 §§1 et 2; CI Resp. 11, 16 oct. 1919 (AAS 11 [1919] 478); SCEO Decr. *Cum data fuerit,* 1 mar. 1929, art. 43 (AAS 21 [1929] 159); SCEO Decr. *Graeci-rutheni ritus,* 24 maii 1930 art. 48 (AAS 22 [1930] 353); SCEO Decr. *Per Decretum,* 23 nov. 1940 (AAS 33 [1941] 27–28)

§2. Anyone to be baptized who has completed the fourteenth year of age can freely choose to be baptized in the Latin Church or in another ritual Church *sui iuris*; in that case, the person belongs to the Church which he or she has chosen.

CAN. 112 §1. After the reception of baptism, the following are enrolled in another ritual Church *sui iuris*:

1° a person who has obtained permission from the Apostolic See;

2° a spouse who, at the time of or during marriage, has declared that he or she is transferring to the ritual Church *sui iuris* of the other spouse; when the marriage has ended, however, the person can freely return to the Latin Church;

3° before the completion of the fourteenth year of age, the children of those mentioned in nn. 1 and 2 as well as, in a mixed marriage, the children of the Catholic party who has legitimately transferred to another ritual Church; on completion of their fourteenth year, however, they can return to the Latin Church.

§2. The practice, however prolonged, of receiving the sacraments according to the rite of another ritual Church *sui iuris* does not entail enrollment in that Church.

CHAPTER II. Juridic Persons

CAN. 113 §1. The Catholic Church and the Apostolic See have the character of a moral person by divine ordinance itself.

§2. Quilibet baptizandus qui quartum decimum aetatis annum expleverit, libere potest eligere ut in Ecclesia latina vel in alia Ecclesia rituali sui iuris baptizetur; quo in casu, ipse ad eam Ecclesiam pertinet quam elegerit.

CAN. 112 §1. Post receptum baptismum, alii Ecclesiae rituali sui iuris adscribuntur:

1° qui licentiam ab Apostolica Sede obtinuerit;

2° coniux qui, in matrimonio ineundo vel eo durante, ad Ecclesiam ritualem sui iuris alterius coniugis se transire declaraverit; matrimonio autem soluto, libere potest ad latinam Ecclesiam redire;

3° filii eorum, de quibus in nn. 1 et 2, ante decimum quartum aetatis annum completum itemque, in matrimonio mixto, filii partis catholicae quae ad aliam Ecclesiam ritualem legitime transierit; adepta vero hac aetate, iidem possunt ad latinam Ecclesiam redire.

§2. Mos, quamvis diuturnus, sacramenta secundum ritum alicuius Ecclesiae ritualis sui iuris recipiendi, non secumfert adscriptionem eidem Ecclesiae.

CAPUT II. De Personis Iuridicis

CAN. 113 §1. Catholica Ecclesia et Apostolica Sedes moralis personae rationem habent ex ipsa ordinatione divina.

111 §2: Pius PP. XII, m. p. *Postquam Apostolicis Litteris,* 9 feb. 1952, c. 303 §1, 1° (AAS 44 [1952] 144)

112 §1: c. 98 §§3 et 4; CI Resp. VI, 10 nov. 1925 (AAS 17 [1925] 583); SCEO Decr. *Nemini licere,* 6 dec. 1928 (AAS 20 [1928] 416–417); Pontificia Commissio pro Russia, Instr. *Edito in Actis,* 26 aug. 1929, I (AAS 21 [1929] 609); SCEO Decr. *Graeci-rutheni rit-*

us, 24 maii 1930, art. 44 (AAS 22 [1930] 353); CI Resp. I, 29 apr. 1940 (AAS 32 [1940] 212); SCEO Decr. *Quo firmior,* 23 nov. 1940 (AAS 33 [1941] 28); CS 11 §1; OE 4; OICA Appendix, 2

112 §2: c. 98 §5

113 §1: c. 100 §1

§2. In the Church, besides physical persons, there are also juridic persons, that is, subjects in canon law of obligations and rights which correspond to their nature.

CAN. 114 §1. Juridic persons are constituted either by the prescript of law or by special grant of competent authority given through a decree. They are aggregates of persons *(universitates personarum)* or of things *(universitates rerum)* ordered for a purpose which is in keeping with the mission of the Church and which transcends the purpose of the individuals.

§2. The purposes mentioned in §1 are understood as those which pertain to works of piety, of the apostolate, or of charity, whether spiritual or temporal.

§3. The competent authority of the Church is not to confer juridic personality except on those aggregates of persons *(universitates personarum)* or things *(universitates rerum)* which pursue a truly useful purpose and, all things considered, possess the means which are foreseen to be sufficient to achieve their designated purpose.

CAN. 115 §1. Juridic persons in the Church are either aggregates of persons *(universitates personarum)* or aggregates of things *(universitates rerum).*

§2. An aggregate of persons *(universitas personarum),* which can be constituted only with at least three persons, is collegial if the members determine its action through participation in rendering decisions, whether by equal right or

§2. Sunt etiam in Ecclesia, praeter personas physicas, personae iuridicae, subiecta scilicet in iure canonico obligationum et iurium quae ipsarum indoli congruunt.

CAN. 114 §1. Personae iuridicae constituuntur aut ex ipso iuris praescripto aut ex speciali competentis auctoritatis concessione per decretum data, universitates sive personarum sive rerum in finem missioni Ecclesiae congruentem, qui singulorum finem transcendit, ordinatae.

§2. Fines, de quibus in §1, intelleguntur qui ad opera pietatis, apostolatus vel caritatis sive spiritualis sive temporalis attinent.

§3. Auctoritas Ecclesiae competens personalitatem iuridicam ne conferat nisi iis personarum aut rerum universitatibus, quae finem persequuntur reapse utilem atque, omnibus perpensis, mediis gaudent quae sufficere posse praevidentur ad finem praestitutum assequendum.

CAN. 115 §1. Personae iuridicae in Ecclesia sunt aut universitates personarum aut universitates rerum.

§2. Universitas personarum, quae quidem nonnisi ex tribus saltem personis consitui potest, est collegialis, si eius actionem determinant membra, in decisionibus ferendis concurrentia, sive aequali iure sive

113 §2: c. 99
114 §1: c. 100 §1; SCConc Resol., 13 nov. 1920 (AAS 13 [1921] 135–144); CI Resp., 26 sep. 1921; SCR Decr. *Quod iam,* 30 nov. 1922 (AAS 14 [1922] 644); SCConc Resol., 5 mar. 1932 (AAS 25 [1933] 436–438); Pius PP. XII, Litt. Ap. *Quam Romani Pontifices,* 14 sep. 1949 (AAS 43 [1951] 722–724); Sec Notif., 15 iun. 1953 (AAS 45 [1953] 570); SCR Decr. *Sacra Congrega-*

tio, 9 dec. 1957; Sec Notif., 16 nov. 1959 (AAS 51 [1959] 875)
114 §2: c. 100 §1; SCR Decr. *Sacra Congregatio,* 9 dec. 1957
114 §3: c. 1489 §2
115 §1: c. 99
115 §2: c. 100 §2

not, according to the norm of law and the statutes; otherwise it is non-collegial.

§3. An aggregate of things *(universitas rerum)*, or an autonomous foundation, consists of goods or things, whether spiritual or material, and either one or more physical persons or a college directs it according to the norm of law and the statutes.

CAN. 116 §1. Public juridic persons are aggregates of persons *(universitates personarum)* or of things *(universitates rerum)* which are constituted by competent ecclesiastical authority so that, within the purposes set out for them, they fulfill in the name of the Church, according to the norm of the prescripts of the law, the proper function entrusted to them in view of the public good; other juridic persons are private.

§2. Public juridic persons are given this personality either by the law itself or by a special decree of competent authority expressly granting it. Private juridic persons are given this personality only through a special decree of competent authority expressly granting it.

CAN. 117 No aggregate of persons *(universitas personarum)* or of things *(universitas rerum)*, intending to obtain juridic personality, is able to acquire it unless competent authority has approved its statutes.

CAN. 118 Representing a public juridic person and acting in its name are those whose competence is acknowledged by universal or particular law or by its own statutes. Representing a private juridic person are those whose competence is granted by statute.

non, ad normam iuris et statutorum; secus est non collegialis.

§3. Universitas rerum seu fundatio autonoma constat bonis seu rebus, sive spiritualibus sive materialibus, eamque, ad normam iuris et statutorum, moderantur sive una vel plures personae physicae sive collegium.

CAN. 116 §1. Personae iuridicae publicae sunt universitates personarum aut rerum, quae ab ecclesiastica auctoritate competenti constituuntur ut intra fines sibi praestitutos nomine Ecclesiae, ad normam praescriptorum iuris, munus proprium intuitu boni publici ipsis commissum expleant; ceterae personae iuridicae sunt privatae.

§2. Personae iuridicae publicae hac personalitate donantur sive ipso iure sive speciali competentis auctoritatis decreto eandem expresse concedenti; personae iuridicae privatae hac personalitate donantur tantum per speciale competentis auctoritatis decretum eandem personalitatem expresse concedens.

CAN. 117 Nulla personarum vel rerum universitas personalitatem iuridicam obtinere intendens, eandem consequi valet nisi ipsius statuta a competenti auctoritate sint probata.

CAN. 118 Personam iuridicam publicam repraesentant, eius nomine agentes, ii quibus iure universali vel particulari aut propriis statutis haec competentia agnoscitur; personam iuridicam privatam, ii quibus eadem competentia per statuta tribuitur.

117: Pius PP. XII, Litt. Ap. *Quam Romani Pontifices*, 14 sep. 1949 (AAS 43 [1951] 722–724); Sec Notif., 15 iun. 1953 (AAS 45 [1953] 570); Sec Notif., 26 oct. 1953 (AAS 45 [1953] 821); Sec Notif., 16 nov. 1959 (AAS 51 [1959] 875); Ioannes PP. XXIII, Litt. Ap. *Religiosissimo*, 8 dec. 1962 (AAS 55 [1963] 444–446)

CAN. 119 With regard to collegial acts, unless the law or statutes provide otherwise:

1° if it concerns elections, when the majority of those who must be convoked are present, that which is approved by the absolute majority of those present has the force of law; after two indecisive ballots, a vote is to be taken on the two candidates who have obtained the greater number of votes or, if there are several, on the two senior in age; after the third ballot, if a tie remains, the one who is senior in age is considered elected;

2° if it concerns other affairs, when an absolute majority of those who must be convoked are present, that which is approved by the absolute majority of those present has the force of law; if after two ballots the votes are equal, the one presiding can break the tie by his or her vote;

3° what touches all as individuals, however, must be approved by all.

CAN. 120 §1. A juridic person is perpetual by its nature; nevertheless, it is extinguished if it is legitimately suppressed by competent authority or has ceased to act for a hundred years. A private juridic person, furthermore, is extinguished if the association is dissolved according to the norm of its statutes or if, in the judgment of competent authority, the foundation has ceased to exist according to the norm of its statutes.

§2. If even one of the members of a collegial juridic person survives, and the aggregate of

CAN. 119 Ad actus collegiales quod attinet, nisi iure vel statutis aliud caveatur:

1° si agatur de electionibus, id vim habet iuris, quod, praesente quidem maiore parte eorum qui convocari debent, placuerit parti absolute maiori eorum qui sunt praesentes; post duo inefficacia scrutinia, suffragatio fiat super duobus candidatis qui maiorem suffragiorum partem obtinuerint, vel, si sunt plures, super duobus aetate senioribus; post tertium scrutinium, si paritas maneat, ille electus habeatur qui senior sit aetate;

2° si agatur de aliis negotiis, id vim habet iuris, quod, praesente quidem maiore parte eorum qui convocari debent, placuerit parti absolute maiori eorum qui sunt praesentes; quod si post duo scrutinia suffragia aequalia fuerint, praeses suo voto paritatem dirimere potest;

3° quod autem omnes uti singulos tangit, ab omnibus approbari debet.

CAN. 120 §1. Persona iuridica natura sua perpetua est; extinguitur tamen si a competenti auctoritate legitime supprimatur aut per centum annorum spatium agere desierit; persona iuridica privata insuper extinguitur, si ipsa consociatio ad normam statutorum dissolvatur, aut si, de iudicio auctoritatis competentis, ipsa fundatio ad normam statutorum desierit.

§2. Si vel unum ex personae iuridicae collegialis membris supersit, et personarum

119: cc. 100 §1, 180 §1, 321, 329 §3, 433 §2, 526; SCR Litt. circ., 9 mar. 1920 (AAS 12 [1920] 366); SCR Ind., 18 oct. 1928; SCR Ind., 4 iul. 1929; SCR Ind., 6 dec. 1940; Pius PP. XII, Const. Ap. *Vacantis Apostolicae Sedis*, 8 dec. 1945, 68 (AAS 38 [1946] 87); Ioannes PP. XXIII, m.p. *Appropinquante Concilio*, 6 aug. 1962, art. 39 (AAS 54 [1962] 624); Ioannes PP. XXIII, m.p. *Summi Pontificis electio* 5 sep. 1962, XV (AAS 54

[1962] 638–639); Sec Normae, 13 sep. 1963, art. 39; Sec Rescr., 8 dec. 1966, art. 24 (AAS 59 [1967] 99–100); CPEN Rescr., 24 iun. 1969, art. 26 (AAS 61 [1969] 535); Paulus PP. VI, Const. Ap. *Romano Pontifici eligendo*, 1 oct. 1975, 65 (AAS 67 [1975] 634)
   120 §1: c. 102 §1; ES I, 34 §1
   120 §2: c. 102 §2

persons *(universitas personarum)* has not ceased to exist according to its statutes, that member has the exercise of all the rights of the aggregate *(universitas)*.

CAN. 121 If aggregates of persons *(universitates personarum)* or of things *(universitates rerum)*, which are public juridic persons, are so joined that from them one aggregate *(universitas)* is constituted which also possesses juridic personality, this new juridic person obtains the goods and patrimonial rights proper to the prior ones and assumes the obligations with which they were burdened. With regard to the allocation of goods in particular and to the fulfillment of obligations, however, the intention of the founders and donors as well as acquired rights must be respected.

CAN. 122 If an aggregate *(universitas)* which possesses public juridic personality is so divided either that a part of it is united with another juridic person or that a distinct public juridic person is erected from the separated part, the ecclesiastical authority competent to make the division, having observed before all else the intention of the founders and donors, the acquired rights, and the approved statutes, must take care personally or through an executor:

1° that common, divisible, patrimonial goods and rights as well as debts and other obligations are divided among the juridic persons concerned, with due proportion in equity and justice, after all the circumstances and needs of each have been taken into account;

2° that the use and usufruct of common goods which are not divisible accrue to each juridic person and that the obligations proper to them are imposed upon each, in due proportion determined in equity and justice.

122: c. 1500; SCConc Resol., 16 iul. 1932 (AAS 25 [1933] 470–472)

universitas secundum statuta esse non desierit, exercitium omnium iurium universitatis illi membro competit.

CAN. 121 Si universitates sive personarum sive rerum, quae sunt personae iuridicae publicae, ita coniungantur ut ex iisdem una constituatur universitas personalitate iuridica et ipsa pollens, nova haec persona iuridica bona iuraque patrimonialia prioribus propria obtinet atque onera suscipit, quibus eaedem gravabantur; ad destinationem autem praesertim bonorum et ad onerum adimpletionem quod attinet, fundatorum oblatorumque voluntas atque iura quaesita salva esse debent.

CAN. 122 Si universitas, quae gaudet personalitate iuridica publica, ita dividatur ut aut illius pars alii personae iuridicae uniatur aut ex parte dismembrata distincta persona iuridica publica erigatur, auctoritas ecclesiastica, cui divisio competat, curare debet per se vel per exsecutorem, servatis quidem in primis tum fundatorum ac oblatorum voluntate tum iuribus quaesitis tum probatis statutis:

1° ut communia, quae dividi possunt, bona atque iura patrimonialia necnon aes alienum aliaque onera dividantur inter personas iuridicas, de quibus agitur, debita cum proportione ex aequo et bono, ratione habita omnium adiunctorum et necessitatum utriusque;

2° ut usus et ususfructus communium bonorum, quae divisioni obnoxia non sunt, utrique personae iuridicae cedant, oneraque iisdem propria utrique imponantur, servata item debita proportione ex aequo et bono definienda.

CAN. 123   Upon the extinction of a public juridic person, the allocation of its goods, patrimonial rights, and obligations is governed by law and its statutes; if these give no indication, they go to the juridic person immediately superior, always without prejudice to the intention of the founders and donors and acquired rights. Upon the extinction of a private juridic person, the allocation of its goods and obligations is governed by its own statutes.

CAN. 123   Extincta persona iuridica publica, destinatio eiusdem bonorum iuriumque patrimonialium itemque onerum regitur iure et statutis, quae, si sileant, obveniunt personae iuridicae immediate superiori, salvis semper fundatorum vel oblatorum voluntate necnon iuribus quaesitis; extincta persona iuridica privata, eiusdem bonorum et onerum destinatio propriis statutis regitur.

TITLE VII. Juridic Acts

CAN. 124   §1. For the validity of a juridic act it is required that the act is placed by a qualified person and includes those things which essentially constitute the act itself as well as the formalities and requirements imposed by law for the validity of the act.

§2. A juridic act placed correctly with respect to its external elements is presumed valid.

CAN. 125   §1. An act placed out of force inflicted on a person from without, which the person was not able to resist in any way, is considered as never to have taken place.

§2. An act placed out of grave fear, unjustly inflicted, or out of malice is valid unless the law provides otherwise. It can be rescinded, however, through the sentence of a judge, either at the instance of the injured party or of the party's successors in law, or *ex officio.*

CAN. 126   An act placed out of ignorance or out of error concerning something which constitutes its substance or which amounts to a

TITULUS VII. De Actibus Iuridicis

CAN. 124   §1. Ad validitatem actus iuridici requiritur ut a persona habili sit positus, atque in eodem adsint quae actum ipsum essentialiter constituunt, necnon sollemnia et requisita iure ad validitatem actus imposita.

§2. Actus iuridicus quoad sua elementa externa rite positus praesumitur validus.

CAN. 125   §1. Actus positus ex vi ab extrinseco personae illata, cui ipsa nequaquam resistere potuit, pro infecto habetur.

§2. Actus positus ex metu gravi, iniuste incusso, aut ex dolo, valet, nisi aliud iure caveatur; sed potest per sententiam iudicis rescindi, sive ad instantiam partis laesae eiusve in iure successorum sive ex officio.

CAN. 126   Actus positus ex ignorantia aut ex errore, qui versetur circa id quod eius substantiam constituit, aut qui recidit in

---

123: c. 1501
124 §1: c. 1680 §1; SCConc Resol., 17 maii 1919 (AAS 11 [1919] 382–387)

125 §1: c. 103 §1
125 §2: c. 103 §2
126: c. 104

condition *sine qua non* is invalid. Otherwise it is valid unless the law makes other provision. An act entered into out of ignorance or error, however, can give rise to a rescissory action according to the norm of law.

CAN. 127 §1. When it is established by law that in order to place acts a superior needs the consent or counsel of some college or group of persons, the college or group must be convoked according to the norm of can. 166 unless, when it concerns seeking counsel only, particular or proper law provides otherwise. For such acts to be valid, however, it is required that the consent of an absolute majority of those present is obtained or that the counsel of all is sought.

§2. When it is established by law that in order to place acts a superior needs the consent or counsel of certain persons as individuals:

1° if consent is required, the act of a superior who does not seek the consent of those persons or who acts contrary to the opinion of all or any of them is invalid;

2° if counsel is required, the act of a superior who does not hear those persons is invalid; although not obliged to accept their opinion even if unanimous, a superior is nonetheless not to act contrary to that opinion, especially if unanimous, without a reason which is overriding in the superior's judgment.

§3. All whose consent or counsel is required are obliged to offer their opinion sincerely and, if the gravity of the affair requires it, to observe secrecy diligently; moreover, the superior can insist upon this obligation.

CAN. 128 Whoever illegitimately inflicts damage upon someone by a juridic act or by

condicionem *sine qua non*, irritus est; secus valet, nisi aliud iure caveatur, sed actus ex ignorantia aut ex errore initus locum dare potest actioni rescissoriae ad normam iuris.

CAN. 127 §1. Cum iure statuatur ad actus ponendos Superiorem indigere consensu aut consilio alicuius collegii vel personarum coetus, convocari debet collegium vel coetus ad normam can. 166, nisi, cum agatur de consilio tantum exquirendo, aliter iure particulari aut proprio cautum sit; ut autem actus valeant requiritur ut obtineatur consensus partis absolute maioris eorum qui sunt praesentes aut omnium exquiratur consilium.

§2. Cum iure statuatur ad actus ponendos Superiorem indigere consensu aut consilio aliquarum personarum, uti singularum:

1° si consensus exigatur, invalidus est actus Superioris consensum earum personarum non exquirentis aut contra earum vel alicuius votum agentis;

2° si consilium exigatur, invalidus est actus Superioris easdem personas non audientis; Superior, licet nulla obligatione teneatur accedendi ad earundem votum, etsi concors, tamen sine praevalenti ratione, suo iudicio aestimanda, ab earundem voto, praesertim concordi, ne discedat.

§3. Omnes quorum consensus aut consilium requiritur, obligatione tenentur sententiam suam sincere proferendi atque, si negotiorum gravitas id postulat, secretum sedulo servandi; quae quidem obligatio a Superiore urgeri potest.

CAN. 128 Quicumque illegitime actu iuridico, immo quovis alio actu dolo vel cul-

---

127 §1: c. 105, 2°
127 §2: c. 105, 1°; SCConc Resol., 13 nov. 1920 (AAS 13 [1921] 43–46); SCpC Litt. circ., 25 ian. 1973, 8

127 §3: c. 105, 3°
128: c. 1681

any other act placed with malice or negligence is obliged to repair the damage inflicted.

pa posito, alteri damnum infert, obligatione tenetur damnum illatum reparandi.

TITLE VIII. The Power of Governance

TITULUS VIII. De Potestate Regiminis

CAN. 129 §1. Those who have received sacred orders are qualified, according to the norm of the prescripts of the law, for the power of governance, which exists in the Church by divine institution and is also called the power of jurisdiction.

CAN. 129 §1. Potestatis regiminis, quae quidem ex divina institutione est in Ecclesia et etiam potestas iurisdictionis vocatur, ad normam praescriptorum iuris, habiles sunt qui ordine sacro sunt insigniti.

§2. Lay members of the Christian faithful can cooperate in the exercise of this same power according to the norm of law.

§2. In exercitio eiusdem potestatis, christifideles laici ad normam iuris cooperari possunt.

CAN. 130 Of itself, the power of governance is exercised for the external forum; sometimes, however, it is exercised for the internal forum alone, so that the effects which its exercise is meant to have for the external forum are not recognized there, except insofar as the law establishes it in determined cases.

CAN. 130 Potestas regiminis de se exercetur pro foro externo, quandoque tamen pro solo foro interno, ita quidem ut effectus quos eius exercitium natum est habere pro foro externo, in hoc foro non recognoscantur, nisi quatenus id determinatis pro casibus iure statuatur.

CAN. 131 §1. The ordinary power of governance is that which is joined to a certain office by the law itself; delegated, that which is granted to a person but not by means of an office.

CAN. 131 §1. Potestas regiminis ordinaria ea est, quae ipso iure alicui officio adnectitur; delegata, quae ipsi personae non mediante officio conceditur.

§2. The ordinary power of governance can be either proper or vicarious.

§2. Potestas regiminis ordinaria potest esse sive propria sive vicaria.

§3. The burden of proving delegation rests on the one who claims to have been delegated.

§3. Ei qui delegatum se asserit, onus probandae delegationis incumbit.

129 §1: c. 196

129 §2: SCConc Resol., 14 dec. 1918 (AAS 11 [1919] 128–133); Pontificia Commissio pro Russia, Ind., 20 ian. 1930; SA Resp. 19 nov. 1947 ; Pius PP. XII, All., 5 oct. 1957 (AAS 49 [1957] 927); LG 33; AA 24; SA Decisio, 11 iun. 1968; SCRIS Rescr., 7 feb. 1969; SCRIS Decr. *Clericalia instituta*, 27 nov. 1969 (AAS 61 [1969] 739–740), Sec Facul., 1 oct. 1974; EN 73a; SCRIS Rescr., 26 iun. 1978, 3; SCRIS Resp., 21 aug. 1978; PA 7, 17

130: cc. 196, 202; SPA Ind., 4 nov. 1927; SPA Ind., dec. 1927; SPA Rescr., 11 apr. 1962; Princ. 2; SPA Rescr., 19 iun. 1970

131 §1: c. 197 §1; SCDS Decr. *Catholica doctrina*, 7 maii 1923, 4 (AAS 15 [1923] 392); CI Resp. IV, 26 mar. 1952 (AAS 44 [1952] 497)

131 §2: c. 197 §2; CI Resp. IV, 26 mar. 1952 (AAS 44 [1952] 497)

131 §3: c. 200 §2

CAN. 132 §1. Habitual faculties are governed by the prescripts for delegated power.

§2. Nevertheless, unless the grant expressly provides otherwise or the ordinary was chosen for personal qualifications, a habitual faculty granted to an ordinary is not withdrawn when the authority of the ordinary to whom it was granted expires, even if he has begun to execute it, but the faculty transfers to any ordinary who succeeds him in governance.

CAN. 133 §1. A delegate who exceeds the limits of the mandate with respect to either matters or persons does not act at all.

§2. A delegate who carries out those things for which the person was delegated in some manner other than that determined in the mandate is not considered to exceed the limits of the mandate unless the manner was prescribed for validity by the one delegating.

CAN. 134 §1. In addition to the Roman Pontiff, by the title of ordinary are understood in the law diocesan bishops and others who, even if only temporarily, are placed over some particular church or a community equivalent to it according to the norm of can. 368 as well as those who possess general ordinary executive power in them, namely, vicars general and episcopal vicars; likewise, for their own members, major superiors of clerical religious institutes of pontifical right and of clerical societies of apostolic life of pontifical right who at least possess ordinary executive power.

§2. By the title of local ordinary are understood all those mentioned in §1 except the su-

CAN. 132 §1. Facultates habituales reguntur praescriptis de potestate delegata.

§2. Attamen nisi in eius concessione aliud expresse caveatur aut electa sit industria personae, facultas habitualis Ordinario concessa non perimitur resoluto iure Ordinarii cui concessa est, etiamsi ipse eam exsequi coeperit, sed transit ad quemvis Ordinarium qui ipsi in regimine succedit.

CAN. 133 §1. Delegatus qui sive circa res sive circa personas mandati sui fines excedit, nihil agit.

§2. Fines sui mandati excedere non intellegitur delegatus, qui alio modo ac in mandato determinatur, ea peragit ad quae delegatus est, nisi modus ab ipso delegante ad validitatem fuerit praescriptus.

CAN. 134 §1. Nomine Ordinarii in iure intelleguntur, praeter Romanum Pontificem, Episcopi dioecesani aliique qui, etsi ad interim tantum, praepositi sunt alicui Ecclesiae particulari vel communitati eidem aequiparatae ad normam can. 368, necnon qui in iisdem generali gaudent potestate exsecutiva ordinaria, nempe Vicarii generales et episcopales; itemque, pro suis sodalibus, Superiores maiores clericalium institutorum religiosorum iuris pontificii et clericalium societatum vitae apostolicae iuris pontificii, qui ordinaria saltem potestate exsecutiva pollent.

§2. Nomine Ordinarii loci intelleguntur omnes qui in §1 recensentur, exceptis Supe-

132 §2: c. 66 §2; SCC Decr. *Proxima sacra*, 25 apr. 1918 (AAS 10 [1918] 190–192); SCC Resp., 1 iul. 1918 (AAS 10 [1918] 325); Pius PP. XI, m.p. *Post datam*, 20 apr. 1923 (AAS 15 [1923] 193–194)
133 §1: c. 203 §1
133 §2: c. 203 §2

134 §1: c. 198 §1; SCC Decl., 20 ian. 1919 (AAS 12 [1920] 43); SCPF Ep., 8 dec. 1919 (AAS 12 [1920] 120); SCC Decr. *Ad Sacra Limina*, 28 feb. 1959 (AAS 43 [1959] 272–274)
134 §2: c. 198 §2

periors of religious institutes and of societies of apostolic life.

§3. Within the context of executive power, those things which in the canons are attributed by name to the diocesan bishop are understood to belong only to a diocesan bishop and to the others made equivalent to him in can. 381, §2, excluding the vicar general and episcopal vicar except by special mandate.

CAN. 135 §1. The power of governance is distinguished as legislative, executive, and judicial.

§2. Legislative power must be exercised in the manner prescribed by law; that which a legislator below the supreme authority possesses in the Church cannot be validly delegated unless the law explicitly provides otherwise. A lower legislator cannot validly issue a law contrary to higher law.

§3. Judicial power, which judges or judicial colleges possess, must be exercised in the manner prescribed by law and cannot be delegated except to perform acts preparatory to some decree or sentence.

§4. In what pertains to the exercise of executive power, the prescripts of the following canons are to be observed.

CAN. 136 Unless the nature of the matter or a prescript of law establishes otherwise, a person is able to exercise executive power over his subjects, even when he or they are outside his territory; he is also able to exercise this power over travelers actually present in the territory if it concerns granting favors or executing universal laws or particular laws which bind them according to the norm of can. 13, §2, n. 2.

rioribus institutorum religiosorum et societatum vitae apostolicae.

§3. Quae in canonibus nominatim Episcopo dioecesano, in ambitu potestatis exsecutivae tribuuntur, intelleguntur competere dumtaxat Episcopo dioecesano aliisque ipsi in can. 381, §2 aequiparatis, exclusis Vicario generali et episcopali, nisi de speciali mandato.

CAN. 135 §1. Potestas regiminis distinguitur in legislativam, exsecutivam et iudicialem.

§2. Potestas legislativa exercenda est modo iure praescripto, et ea, qua in Ecclesia gaudet legislator infra auctoritatem supremam, valide delegari nequit, nisi aliud iure explicite caveatur; a legislatore inferiore lex iuri superiori contraria valide ferri nequit.

§3. Potestas iudicialis, qua gaudent iudices aut collegia iudicialia, exercenda est modo iure praescripto, et delegari nequit, nisi ad actus cuivis decreto aut sententiae praeparatorios perficiendos.

§4. Ad potestatis exsecutivae exercitium quod attinet, serventur praescripta canonum qui sequuntur.

CAN. 136 Potestatem exsecutivam aliquis, licet extra territorium existens, exercere valet in subditos, etiam a territorio absentes, nisi aliud ex rei natura aut ex iuris praescripto constet; in peregrinos in territorio actu degentes, si agatur de favoribus concedendis aut de exsecutioni mandandis sive legibus universalibus sive legibus particularibus, quibus ipsi ad normam can. 13, §2, n. 2 tenentur.

135 §1: cc. 201 §§2 et 3, 335 §1, 2220 §1, 2221; Pius PP. XI, Enc. *Quas primas*, 11 dec. 1925 (AAS 17 [1925] 599); SCDS Litt. circ., 15 iun. 1952; CS 399 §1; LG 27, REU 106, 107; Princ. 7
136: c. 201 §§1 et 3

CAN. 137 §1. Ordinary executive power can be delegated both for a single act and for all cases unless the law expressly provides otherwise.

§2. Executive power delegated by the Apostolic See can be subdelegated for a single act or for all cases unless the delegate was chosen for personal qualifications or subdelegation was expressly forbidden.

§3. Executive power delegated by another authority who has ordinary power can be subdelegated only for individual cases if it was delegated for all cases. If it was delegated for a single act or for determined acts, however, it cannot be subdelegated except by express grant of the one delegating.

§4. No subdelegated power can be subdelegated again unless the one delegating has expressly granted this.

CAN. 138 Ordinary executive power as well as power delegated for all cases must be interpreted broadly; any other, however, must be interpreted strictly. Nevertheless, one who has delegated power is understood to have been granted also those things without which the delegate cannot exercise this power.

CAN. 139 §1. Unless the law determines otherwise, the fact that a person approaches some competent authority, even a higher one, does not suspend the executive power, whether ordinary or delegated, of another competent authority.

§2. Nevertheless, a lower authority is not to become involved in cases submitted to a higher

CAN. 137 §1. Potestas exsecutiva ordinaria delegari potest tum ad actum tum ad universitatem casuum, nisi aliud iure expresse caveatur.

§2. Potestas exsecutiva ab Apostolica Sede delegata subdelegari potest sive ad actum sive ad universitatem casuum, nisi electa fuerit industria personae aut subdelegatio fuerit expresse prohibita.

§3. Potestas exsecutiva delegata ab alia auctoritate potestatem ordinariam habente, si ad universitatem casuum delegata sit, in singulis tantum casibus subdelegari potest; si vero ad actum aut ad actus determinatos delegata sit, subdelegari nequit, nisi de expressa delegantis concessione.

§4. Nulla potestas subdelegata iterum subdelegari potest, nisi id expresse a delegante concessum fuerit.

CAN. 138 Potestas exsecutiva ordinaria necnon potestas ad universitatem casuum delegata late interpretanda est, alia vero quaelibet stricte; cui tamen delegata potestas est, ea quoque intelleguntur concessa sine quibus eadem potestas exerceri nequit.

CAN. 139 §1. Nisi aliud iure statuatur, eo quod quis aliquam auctoritatem, etiam superiorem, competentem adeat, non suspenditur alius auctoritatis competentis exsecutiva potestas, sive haec ordinaria est sive delegata.

§2. Causae tamen ad superiorem auctoritatem delatae ne se immisceat inferior,

137 §1: c. 199 §1; CI Resp. 3, 16 oct. 1919 (AAS 11 [1919] 477); CI Resp. VI, 26 mar. 1952 (AAS 44 [1952] 497)

137 §2: c. 199 §2; CI Resp. VI, 26 mar. 1952 (AAS 44 [1952] 497)

137 §3: c. 199 §§3 et 4; CI Resp. V, 20 maii 1923 (AAS 16 [1924] 114–115); CI Resp. IV, 28 dec. 1927

(AAS 20 [1928] 61–62); CI Resp. VI, 26 mar. 1952 (AAS 44 [1952] 497)

137 §4: c. 199 §5; CI Resp. VI, 26 mar. 1952 (AAS 44 [1952] 497)

138: c. 200 §1

139 §1: c. 204 §1

139 §2: c. 204 §2

authority except for a grave and urgent cause; in this case, the lower authority is immediately to notify the higher concerning the matter.

CAN. 140 §1. When several persons have been delegated *in solidum* to transact the same affair, the one who first begins to deal with it excludes the others from doing so unless that person subsequently was impeded or did not wish to proceed further in carrying it out.

§2. When several persons have been delegated collegially to transact an affair, all must proceed according to the norm of can. 119 unless the mandate has provided otherwise.

§3. Executive power delegated to several persons is presumed to be delegated to them *in solidum.*

CAN. 141 When several persons have been delegated successively, that person is to take care of the affair whose mandate is the earlier and has not been subsequently revoked.

CAN. 142 §1. Delegated power ceases: by fulfillment of the mandate; by expiration of the time or completion of the number of cases for which it was granted; by cessation of the purpose for the delegation; by revocation of the one delegating directly communicated to the delegate as well as by resignation of the delegate made known to and accepted by the one delegating. It does not cease, however, when the authority of the one delegating expires unless this appears in attached clauses.

§2. Nevertheless, an act of delegated power which is exercised for the internal forum alone and is placed inadvertently after the lapse of the time limit of the grant is valid.

nisi ex gravi urgentique causa; quo in casu statim superiorem de re moneat.

CAN. 140 §1. Pluribus in solidum ad idem negotium agendum delegatis, qui prius negotium tractare inchoaverit alios ab eodem agendo excludit, nisi postea impeditus fuerit aut in negotio peragendo ulterius procedere noluerit.

§2. Pluribus collegialiter ad negotium agendum delegatis, omnes procedere debent ad normam can. 119, nisi in mandato aliud cautum sit.

§3. Potestas exsecutiva pluribus delegata, praesumitur iisdem delegata in solidum.

CAN. 141 Pluribus successive delegatis, ille negotium expediat, cuius mandatum anterius est, nec postea revocatum fuit.

CAN. 142 §1. Potestas delegata extinguitur: expleto mandato; elapso tempore vel exhausto numero casuum pro quibus concessa fuit; cessante causa finali delegationis; revocatione delegantis delegato directe intimata necnon renuntiatione delegati deleganti significata et ab eo acceptata; non autem resoluto iure delegantis, nisi id ex appositis clausulis appareat.

§2. Actus tamen ex potestate delegata, quae exercetur pro solo foro interno, per inadvertentiam positus, elapso concessionis tempore, validus est.

140 §1: c. 205 §2
140 §2: c. 205 §3
140 §3: c. 205 §1
141: c. 206; CT Resp. VI, 26 mar. 1952 (AAS 44 [1952] 497)

142 §1: c. 207 §1; CT Resp. VI, 26 mar. 1952 (AAS 44 [1952] 497)
142 §2: c. 207 §2; CT Resp. VI, 26 mar. 1952 (AAS 44 [1952] 497)

CAN. 143 §1. Ordinary power ceases by loss of the office to which it is connected.

§2. Unless the law provides otherwise, ordinary power is suspended if, legitimately, an appeal is made or a recourse is lodged against privation of or removal from office.

CAN. 144 §1. In factual or legal common error and in positive and probable doubt of law or of fact, the Church supplies executive power of governance for both the external and internal forum.

§2. The same norm is applied to the faculties mentioned in cann. 882, 883, 966, and 1111, §1.

CAN. 143 §1. Potestas ordinaria extinguitur amisso officio cui adnectitur.

§2. Nisi aliud iure caveatur, suspenditur potestas ordinaria, si contra privationem vel amotionem ab officio legitime appellatur vel recursus interponitur.

CAN. 144 §1. In errore communi de facto aut de iure, itemque in dubio positivo et probabili sive iuris sive facti, supplet Ecclesia, pro foro tam externo quam interno, potestatem regiminis exsecutivam.

§2. Eadem norma applicatur facultatibus de quibus in cann. 882, 883, 966, et 1111, §1.

TITLE IX. Ecclesiastical Offices

CAN. 145 §1. An ecclesiastical office is any function constituted in a stable manner by divine or ecclesiastical ordinance to be exercised for a spiritual purpose.

§2. The obligations and rights proper to individual ecclesiastical offices are defined either in the law by which the office is constituted or in the decree of the competent authority by which the office is at the same time constituted and conferred.

TITULUS IX. De Officiis Ecclesiasticis

CAN. 145 §1. Officium ecclesiasticum est quodlibet munus ordinatione sive divina sive ecclesiastica stabiliter constitutum in finem spiritualem exercendum.

§2. Obligationes et iura singulis officiis ecclesiasticis propria definiuntur sive ipso iure quo officium constituitur, sive decreto auctoritatis competentis quo constituitur simul et confertur.

---

143 §1: c. 208; CI Resp. VI, 26 mar. 1952 (AAS 44 [1952] 497)

143 §2: c. 208; CI Resp. VI, 26 mar. 1952 (AAS 44 [1952] 497)

144 §1: c. 209; CI Resp. VI, 26 mar. 1952 (AAS 44 [1952] 497)

144 §2: SCDS Instr. *Sacerdos,* 14 sep. 1946, 13 (AAS 38 [1946] 356); CI Resp. V et VI, 26 mar. 1952 (AAS 44 [1952] 497)

145 §1: c. 145 §1; PO 20

CHAPTER I. **Provision of Ecclesiastical Office**

CAN. 146   An ecclesiastical office cannot be acquired validly without canonical provision.

CAN. 147   The provision of an ecclesiastical office is made: through free conferral by a competent ecclesiastical authority; through installation by the same authority if presentation preceded it; through confirmation or admission granted by the same authority if election or postulation preceded it; finally, through simple election and acceptance by the one elected if the election does not require confirmation.

CAN. 148   The provision of offices is also the competence of the authority to whom it belongs to erect, change, and suppress them unless the law establishes otherwise.

CAN. 149   §1. To be promoted to an ecclesiastical office, a person must be in the communion of the Church as well as suitable, that is, endowed with those qualities which are required for that office by universal or particular law or by the law of the foundation.

§2. Provision of an ecclesiastical office made to one who lacks the requisite qualities is invalid only if the qualities are expressly required for the validity of the provision by universal or particular law or by the law of the foundation. Otherwise it is valid but can be rescinded by decree of competent authority or by sentence of an administrative tribunal.

§3. Provision of an office made as a result of simony is invalid by the law itself.

CAN. 150   An office which entails the full care of souls and for whose fulfillment the ex-

CAPUT I. **De Provisione Officii Ecclesiastici**

CAN. 146   Officium ecclesiasticum sine provisione canonica valide obtineri nequit.

CAN. 147   Provisio officii ecclesiastici fit: per liberam collationem ab auctoritate ecclesiastica competenti; per institutionem ab eadem datam, si praecesserit praesentatio; per confirmationem vel admissionem ab eadem factam, si praecesserit electio vel postulatio; tandem per simplicem electionem et electi acceptationem, si electio non egeat confirmatione.

CAN. 148   Auctoritati, cuius est officia erigere, innovare et supprimere, eorundem provisio quoque competit, nisi aliud iure statuatur.

CAN. 149   §1. Ut ad officium ecclesiasticum quis promoveatur, debet esse in Ecclesiae communione necnon idoneus, scilicet iis qualitatibus praeditus, quae iure universali vel particulari aut lege fundationis ad idem officium requiruntur.

§2. Provisio officii ecclesiastici facta illi qui caret qualitatibus requisitis, irrita tantum est, si qualitates iure universali vel particulari aut lege fundationis ad validitatem provisionis expresse exigantur; secus valida est, sed rescindi potest per decretum auctoritatis competentis aut per sententiam tribunalis administrativi.

§3. Provisio officii simoniace facta ipso iure irrita est.

CAN. 150   Officium secumferens plenam animarum curam, ad quam adimplendam or-

146: c. 147 §1; SCConc Decr. *Catholica Ecclesia*, 29 iun. 1950 (AAS 42 [1950] 601–602); SCC Decl., 17 mar. 1951 (AAS 43 [1951] 174)

147: c. 148 §1; SCConc Decr. *Cum ob belli*, 26 feb. 1919 (AAS 11 [1919] 77)

149 §1: cc. 149, 153 §1
149 §2: c. 153 §3
149 §3: c. 729
150: c. 154

ercise of the priestly order is required cannot be conferred validly on one who is not yet a priest.

CAN. 151 The provision of an office which entails the care of souls is not to be deferred without a grave cause.

CAN. 152 Two or more incompatible offices, that is, offices which together cannot be fulfilled at the same time by the same person, are not to be conferred upon one person.

CAN. 153 §1. The provision of an office which by law is not vacant is by that fact invalid and is not validated by subsequent vacancy.

§2. Nevertheless, if it concerns an office which by law is conferred for a determined period of time, provision can be made within six months before the expiration of this time and takes effect from the day of the vacancy of the office.

§3. A promise of some office, no matter by whom it is made, produces no juridic effect.

CAN. 154 An office vacant by law, which may still be possessed illegitimately by someone, can be conferred provided that it has been declared properly that the possession is not legitimate and mention of this declaration is made in the letter of conferral.

CAN. 155 A person who confers an office in the place of another who is negligent or impeded acquires no power thereafter over the person upon whom the office was conferred. The juridic condition of that person, however, is established just as if the provision had been completed according to the ordinary norm of law.

CAN. 156 The provision of any office is to be put in writing.

dinis sacerdotalis exercitium requiritur, ei qui sacerdotio nondum auctus est valide conferri nequit.

CAN. 151 Provisio officii animarum curam secumferentis, sine gravi causa ne differatur.

CAN. 152 Nemini conferantur duo vel plura officia incompatibilia, videlicet quae una simul ab eodem adimpleri nequeunt.

CAN. 153 §1. Provisio officii de iure non vacantis est ipso facto irrita, nec subsequenti vacatione convalescit.

§2. Si tamen agatur de officio quod de iure ad tempus determinatum confertur, provisio intra sex menses ante expletum hoc tempus fieri potest, et effectum habet a die officii vacationis.

§3. Promissio alicuius officii, a quocumque est facta, nullum parit iuridicum effectum.

CAN. 154 Officium de iure vacans, quod forte adhuc ab aliquo illegitime possidetur, conferri potest, dummodo rite declaratum fuerit eam possessionem non esse legitimam, et de hac declaratione mentio fiat in litteris collationis.

CAN. 155 Qui, vicem alterius neglegentis vel impediti supplens, officium confert, nullam inde potestatem acquirit in personam cui collatum est, sed huius condicio iuridica perinde constituitur, ac si provisio ad ordinariam iuris normam peracta fuisset.

CAN. 156 Cuiuslibet officii provisio scripto consignetur.

151: cc. 155, 458
152: c. 156 §§1 et 2
153 §1: c. 150 §1
153 §3: c. 150 §2

154: c. 151
155: c. 158
156: c. 159

ART. 1. *Free Conferral*

CAN. 157 Unless the law explicitly establishes otherwise, it is for the diocesan bishop to provide for ecclesiastical offices in his own particular church by free conferral.

ART. 2. *Presentation*

CAN. 158 §1. Presentation for an ecclesiastical office by a person who has the right of presentation must be made to the authority to whom it belongs to install in that office. Moreover, this must be done within three months from notice of the vacancy of the office unless other provision has been made legitimately.

§2. If some college or group of persons has the right of presentation, the person to be presented is to be designated according to the prescripts of cann. 165-179.

CAN. 159 No one is to be presented unwillingly; therefore, a person who is proposed for presentation and questioned about his or her intention can be presented unless the person declines within eight useful days.

CAN. 160 §1. The person who possesses the right of presentation can present one or even several persons, either at the same time or successively.

§2. No one can present oneself; a college or group of persons, however, can present one of its own members.

CAN. 161 §1. Unless the law establishes otherwise, a person who has presented one found unsuitable can present another candidate within a month, but once more only.

§2. If the person presented renounces or dies

ART. 1. *De Libera Collatione*

CAN. 157 Nisi aliud explicite iure statuatur, Episcopi dioecesani est libera collatione providere officiis ecclesiasticis in propria Ecclesia particulari.

ART. 2. *De Praesentatione*

CAN. 158 §1. Praesentatio ad officium ecclesiasticum ab eo, cui ius praesentandi competit, fieri debet auctoritati cuius est ad officium de quo agitur institutionem dare, et quidem, nisi aliud legitime cautum sit, intra tres menses ab habita vacationis officii notitia.

§2. Si ius praesentationis cuidam collegio aut coetui personarum competat, praesentandus designetur servatis cann. 165–179 praescriptis.

CAN. 159 Nemo invitus praesentetur; quare qui praesentandus proponitur, mentem suam rogatus, nisi intra octiduum utile recuset, praesentari potest.

CAN. 160 §1. Qui iure praesentationis gaudet, unum aut etiam plures, et quidem tum una simul tum successive, praesentare potest.

§2. Nemo potest seipsum praesentare; potest autem collegium aut coetus personarum aliquem suum sodalem praesentare.

CAN. 161 §1. Nisi aliud iure statuatur, potest qui aliquem praesentaverit non idoneum repertum, altera tantum vice, intra mensem, alium candidatum praesentare.

§2. Si praesentatus ante institutionem

157: c. 152; CD 28; ES I, 18 §1
158 §1: c. 1457
158 §2: c. 1460 §1
159: c. 1436

160 §1: c. 1460 §4
160 §2: c. 1461
161 §1: c. 1465 §1
161 §2: c. 1468

before the installation, the one who has the right of presentation can exercise this right again within a month from the notice of the renunciation or death.

CAN. 162 A person who has not made presentation within the useful time according to the norm of can. 158, §1 and can. 161 as well as one who has twice presented an unsuitable person loses the right of presentation for that case. The authority to whom it belongs to install freely provides for the vacant office, with the assent, however, of the proper ordinary of the person appointed.

CAN. 163 The authority competent to install the person presented according to the norm of law is to install the one legitimately presented whom the authority has found suitable and who has accepted. If several persons legitimately presented have been found suitable, the authority must install one of them.

ART. 3. *Election*

CAN. 164 Unless the law has provided otherwise, the prescripts of the following canons are to be observed in canonical elections.

CAN. 165 Unless the law or the legitimate statutes of a college or group have provided otherwise, if a college or group of persons has the right of election to office, the election is not to be delayed beyond three months of useful time computed from the notice of the vacancy of the office. If this limit has passed without action, the ecclesiastical authority who has the right of confirming the election or the right of providing for the office successively is to make provision freely for the vacant office.

CAN. 166 §1. The person presiding over a

factam renuntiaverit aut de vita decesserit, potest qui iure praesentandi pollet, intra mensem ab habita renuntiationis aut mortis notitia, ius suum rursus exercere.

CAN. 162 Qui intra tempus utile, ad normam can. 158, §1 et can. 161, praesentationem non fecerit, itemque qui bis praesentaverit non idoneum repertum, pro eo casu ius praesentationis amittit, atque auctoritati, cuius est institutionem dare, competit libere providere officio vacanti, assentiente tamen proprio provisi Ordinario.

CAN. 163 Auctoritas, cui ad normam iuris competit praesentatum instituere, instituat legitime praesentatum quem idoneum reppererit et qui acceptaverit; quod si plures legitime praesentati idonei reperti sint, eorundem unum instituere debet.

ART. 3. *De Electione*

CAN. 164 Nisi aliud iure provisum fuerit, in electionibus canonicis serventur praescripta canonum qui sequuntur.

CAN. 165 Nisi aliud iure aut legitimis collegii vel coetus statutis cautum sit, si cui collegio aut coetui personarum sit ius eligendi ad officium, electio ne differatur ultra trimestre utile computandum ab habita notitia vacationis officii; quo termino inutiliter elapso, auctoritas ecclesiastica, cui ius confirmandae electionis vel ius providendi successive competit, officio vacanti libere provideat.

CAN. 166 §1. Collegii aut coetus prae-

162: c. 1465 §1
163: c. 1466 §§1 et 3
164: c. 160

165: c. 161
166 §1: c. 162 §1; SCR Resp. I, 2 iul. 1921 (AAS 13 [1921] 481–482)

college or group is to convoke all those belonging to the college or group; the notice of convocation, however, when it must be personal, is valid if it is given in the place of domicile or quasi-domicile or in the place of residence.

§2. If anyone of those to be convoked was overlooked and for that reason was absent, the election is valid. Nevertheless, at the instance of that same person and when the oversight and absence have been proved, the election must be rescinded by the competent authority even if it has been confirmed, provided that it is evident juridically that recourse had been made at least within three days from the notice of the election.

§3. If more than one-third of the electors were overlooked, however, the election is null by the law itself unless all those overlooked were in fact present.

CAN. 167 §1. When the notice of the convocation has been given legitimately, those present on the day and at the place determined in the same notice have the right to vote. The faculty of voting by letter or proxy is excluded unless the statutes legitimately provide otherwise.

§2. If one of the electors is present in the house where the election occurs but cannot be present at the election due to ill health, his or her written vote is to be sought by the tellers.

CAN. 168 Even if a person has the right to vote in his or her own name under several titles, the person can vote only once.

CAN. 169 For an election to be valid, no one can be admitted to vote who does not belong to the college or group.

CAN. 170 An election whose freedom ac-

ses convocet omnes ad collegium aut ad coetum pertinentes; convocatio autem, quando personalis esse debet, valet, si fiat in loco domicilii vel quasi-domicilii aut in loco commorationis.

§2. Si quis ex vocandis neglectus et ideo absens fuerit, electio valet; attamen ad eiusdem instantiam, probata quidem praeteritione et absentia, electio, etiam si confirmata fuerit, a competenti auctoritate rescindi debet, dummodo iuridice constet recursum saltem intra triduum ab habita notitia electionis fuisse transmissum.

§3. Quod si plures quam tertia pars electorum neglecti fuerint, electio est ipso iure nulla, nisi omnes neglecti reapse interfuerint.

CAN. 167 §1. Convocatione legitime facta, suffragium ferendi ius habent praesentes die et loco in eadem convocatione determinatis, exclusa, nisi aliud statutis legitime caveatur, facultate ferendi suffragia sive per epistolam sive per procuratorem.

§2. Si quis ex electoribus praesens in ea domo sit, in qua fit electio, sed electioni ob infirmam valetudinem interesse nequeat, suffragium eius scriptum a scrutatoribus exquiratur.

CAN. 168 Etsi quis plures ob titulos ius habeat ferendi nomine proprio suffragii, non potest nisi unicum suffragium ferre.

CAN. 169 Ut valida sit electio, nemo ad suffragium admitti potest, qui ad collegium vel coetum non pertineat.

CAN. 170 Electio, cuius libertas quoquo

166 §2: c. 162 §2
166 §3: c. 162 §§3 et 4
167 §1: c. 163
167 §2: c. 168

168: c. 164
169: c. 165
170: c. 166

tually has been impeded in any way is invalid by the law itself.

CAN. 171 §1. The following are unqualified to vote:

1° a person incapable of a human act;

2° a person who lacks active voice;

3° a person under a penalty of excommunication whether through a judicial sentence or through a decree by which a penalty is imposed or declared;

4° a person who has defected notoriously from the communion of the Church.

§2. If one of the above is admitted, the person's vote is null, but the election is valid unless it is evident that, with that vote subtracted, the one elected did not receive the required number of votes.

CAN. 172 §1. To be valid, a vote must be:

1° free; therefore the vote of a person who has been coerced directly or indirectly by grave fear or malice to vote for a certain person or different persons separately is invalid;

2° secret, certain, absolute, determined.

§2. Conditions attached to a vote before the election are to be considered as not having been added.

CAN. 173 §1. Before an election begins, at least two tellers are to be designated from the membership of the college or group.

§2. The tellers are to collect the votes, to examine in the presence of the one presiding over the election whether the number of ballots corresponds to the number of electors, to count the votes themselves, and to announce openly how many votes each person has received.

modo reapse impedita fuerit, ipso iure invalida est.

CAN. 171 §1. Inhabiles sunt ad suffragium ferendum:

1° incapex actus humani;

2° carens voce activa;

3° poena excommunicationis innodatus sive per sententiam iudicialem sive per decretum quo poena irrogatur vel declaratur;

4° qui ab Ecclesiae communione notorie defecit.

§2. Si quis ex praedictis admittatur, eius suffragium est nullum, sed electio valet, nisi constet, eo dempto, electum non rettulisse requisitum suffragiorum numerum.

CAN. 172 §1. Suffragium, ut validum sit, esse debet:

1° liberum; ideoque invalidum est suffragium eius, qui metu gravi aut dolo, directe vel indirecte, adactus fuerit ad eligendam certam personam aut diveras personas disiunctive;

2° secretum, certum, absolutum, determinatum.

§2. Condiciones ante electionem suffragio appositae tamquam non adiectae habeantur.

CAN. 173 §1. Antequam incipiat electio, deputentur e gremio collegii aut coetus duo saltem scrutatores.

§2. Scrutatores suffragia colligant et coram praeside electionis inspiciant an schedularum numerus respondeat numero electorum, suffragia ipsa scrutentur palamque faciant quot quisque rettulerit.

171 §1: c. 167 §1, 1° et 3°–5°

171 §2: c. 167 §2

172 §1: c. 169 §1

172 §2: c. 169 §2

173 §1: c. 171 §1

173 §2: c. 171 §2

§3. If the number of votes exceeds the number of electors, the voting is without effect.

§4. All the acts of an election are to be transcribed accurately by the secretary and are to be preserved carefully in the archive of the college after they have been signed at least by the same secretary, the one presiding, and the tellers.

CAN. 174 §1. Unless the law or the statutes provide otherwise, an election can also be done by compromise, provided that the electors, by unanimous and written consent, transfer the right to elect on that occasion to one or more suitable persons, whether from among the membership or outside it, who are to elect in the name of all by virtue of the faculty received.

§2. If it concerns a college or group composed of clerics alone, those commissioned must be ordained; otherwise the election is invalid.

§3. Those commissioned must observe the prescripts of the law concerning elections and, for the validity of the election, the conditions attached to the compromise agreement which are not contrary to the law; conditions contrary to the law, however, are to be considered as not having been attached.

CAN. 175 The compromise ceases and the right to vote returns to those authorizing the compromise:

1° by revocation by the college or group before any action was taken;

2° if some condition attached to the compromise agreement was not fulfilled;

3° if the election had been completed but was null.

CAN. 176 Unless the law or the statutes provide otherwise, the person who has received

§3. Si numerus suffragiorum superet numerum eligentium, nihil est actum.

§4. Omnia electionis acta ab eo qui actuarii munere fungitur accurate describantur, et saltem ab eodem actuario, praeside ac scrutatoribus subscripta, in collegii tabulario diligenter asserventur.

CAN. 174 §1. Electio, nisi aliud iure aut statutis caveatur, fieri etiam potest per compromissum, dummodo nempe electores, unanimi et scripto consensu, in unum vel plures idoneos sive de gremio sive extraneos ius eligendi pro ea vice transferant, qui nomine omnium ex recepta facultate eligant.

§2. Si agatur de collegio aut coetu ex solis clericis constanti, compromissarii in sacris debent esse constituti; secus electio est invalida.

§3. Compromissarii debent iuris praescripta de electione servare atque, ad validitatem electionis, condiciones compromisso appositas, iuri non contrarias, observare; condiciones autem iuri contrariae pro non appositis habeantur.

CAN. 175 Cessat compromissum et ius suffragium ferendi redit ad compromittentes:

1° revocatione a collegio aut coetu facta, re integra;

2° non impleta aliqua condicione compromisso apposita;

3° electione absoluta, si fuerit nulla.

CAN. 176 Nisi aliud iure aut statutis caveatur, is electus habeatur et a collegii aut

173 §3: c. 171 §3
173 §4: c. 171 §5
174 §1: c. 172 §1
174 §2: c. 172 §2

174 §3: c. 172 §3
175: c. 173
176: c. 174

the required number of votes according to the norm of can. 119, n. 1 is considered elected and is to be announced as such by the one presiding over the college or group.

CAN. 177 §1. An election must be communicated immediately to the person elected who must inform the one presiding over the college or group whether or not he or she accepts the election within eight useful days after receiving the notification; otherwise, the election has no effect.

§2. If the one elected has not accepted, the person loses every right deriving from the election and does not regain any right by subsequent acceptance but can be elected again. A college or group, however, must proceed to a new election within a month from notification of non-acceptance.

CAN. 178 The person elected who has accepted an election which does not need confirmation obtains the office in full right immediately; otherwise, the person acquires only the right to the office.

CAN. 179 §1. If the election requires confirmation, the person elected must personally or through another seek confirmation from the competent authority within eight useful days from the day of acceptance of election; otherwise, the person is deprived of every right unless it has been proved that the person was prevented from seeking confirmation by a just impediment.

§2. The competent authority cannot deny confirmation if the person elected has been found suitable according to the norm of can. 149, §1, and the election was conducted according to the norm of law.

coetus praeside proclametur, qui requisitum suffragiorum numerum rettulerit, ad normam can. 119, n. 1.

CAN. 177 §1. Electio illico intimanda est electo, qui debet intra octiduum utile a recepta intimatione significare collegii aut coetus praesidi utrum electionem acceptet necne; secus electio effectum non habet.

§2. Si electus non acceptaverit, omne ius ex electione amittit nec subsequenti acceptatione convalescit, sed rursus eligi potest; collegium autem aut coetus intra mensem a cognita non-acceptatione ad novam electionem procedere debet.

CAN. 178 Electus, acceptata electione, quae confirmatione non egeat, officium pleno iure statim obtinet; secus non acquirit nisi ius ad rem.

CAN. 179 §1. Electus, si electio confirmatione indigeat, intra octiduum utile a die acceptatae electionis confirmationem ab auctoritate competenti petere per se vel per alium debet; secus omni iure privatur, nisi probaverit se a petenda confirmatione iusto impedimento detentum fuisse.

§2. Competens auctoritas, si electum reppererit idoneum ad normam can. 149, §1, et electio ad normam iuris fuerit peracta, confirmationem denegare nequit.

177 §1: c. 175; CI Resp. 1 et 2, 4 nov. 1919
177 §2: c. 176 §1; CI Resp. 1 et 2, 4 nov. 1919
178: c. 176 §2; CI Resp. 4, 4 nov. 1919

179 §1: c. 177 §1
179 §2: c. 177 §2; CI Resp. 3, 4 nov. 1919

§3. Confirmation must be given in writing.

§4. Before being notified of confirmation, the person elected is not permitted to become involved in the administration of the office, whether in matters spiritual or temporal, and acts possibly placed by the person are null.

§5. Once notified of the confirmation, the one elected obtains the office in full right unless the law provides otherwise.

ART. 4. *Postulation*

CAN. 180 §1. If a canonical impediment from which a dispensation can be and customarily is granted prevents the election of a person whom the electors believe to be more suitable and whom they prefer, by their votes they can postulate that person from the competent authority unless the law provides otherwise.

§2. Those commissioned to elect in virtue of a compromise cannot postulate unless this was expressed in the compromise.

CAN. 181 §1. At least two-thirds of the votes are required for a postulation to have force.

§2. A vote for postulation must be expressed by the words, *I postulate*, or the equivalent. The formula, *I elect or I postulate*, or the equivalent is valid for election if there is no impediment; otherwise it is valid for postulation.

CAN. 182 §1. A postulation must be sent within eight useful days by the one presiding to the authority competent to confirm the election, to whom it pertains to grant the dispensation from the impediment, or, if the authority does not have this power, to petition the dispensation from a higher authority. If confirmation is not

§3. Confirmatio in scriptis dari debet.

§4. Ante intimatam confirmationem, electo non licet sese immiscere administrationi officii sive in spiritualibus sive in temporalibus, et actus ab eo forte positi nulli sunt.

§5. Intimata confirmatione, electus pleno iure officium obtinet, nisi aliud iure caveatur.

ART. 4. *De Postulatione*

CAN. 180 §1. Si electioni illius, quem electores aptiorem putent ac praeferant, impedimentum canonicum obstet, super quo dispensatio concedi possit ac soleat, suis ipsi suffragiis eum possunt, nisi aliud iure caveatur, a competenti auctoritate postulare.

§2. Compromissarii postulare nequeunt, nisi id in compromisso fuerit expressum.

CAN. 181 §1. Ut postulatio vim habeat, requiruntur saltem duae tertiae partes suffragiorum.

§2. Suffragium pro postulatione exprimi debet per verbum: *postulo*, aut aequivalens; formula: *eligo vel postulo*, aut aequipollens, valet pro electione, si impedimentum non exsistat, secus pro postulatione.

CAN. 182 §1. Postulatio a praeside intra octiduum utile mitti debet ad auctoritatem competentem ad quam pertinet electionem confirmare, cuius est dispensationem de impedimento concedere, aut, si hanc potestatem non habeat, eandem ab auctoritate superiore petere; si non requiritur confir-

179 §3: c. 177 §3
179 §4: c. 176 §3; CI Resp., 15 aug. 1918
179 §5: c. 177 §4
180 §1: c. 179 §1
180 §2: c. 179 §2

181 §1: c. 180 §1; CI Resp. 5–7, 4 nov. 1919; CI Resp. 1 et 2, 1 iul. 1922 (AAS 14 [1922] 406)
181 §2: c. 180 §2
182 §1: c. 181 §1; CI Resp. 8, 4 nov. 1919

required, a postulation must be sent to the authority competent to grant the dispensation.

§2. If a postulation has not been sent within the prescribed time, by that fact it is null, and the college or group is deprived of the right of electing or postulating for that occasion unless it is proved that the one presiding had been prevented from sending the postulation by a just impediment or had refrained from sending it at the opportune time by malice or negligence.

§3. The person postulated acquires no right by postulation; the competent authority is not obliged to admit the postulation.

§4. Electors cannot revoke a postulation made to a competent authority unless the authority consents.

CAN. 183 §1. If a postulation has not been admitted by the competent authority, the right of electing reverts to the college or group.

§2. If a postulation has been admitted, however, this is to be made known to the person postulated, who must respond according to the norm of can. 177, §1.

§3. A person who accepts a postulation which has been admitted acquires the office in full right immediately.

CHAPTER II. Loss of Ecclesiastical Office

CAN. 184 §1. An ecclesiastical office is lost by the lapse of a predetermined time, by reaching the age determined by law, by resignation, by transfer, by removal, and by privation.

§2. An ecclesiastical office is not lost by the expiration in any way of the authority of the one who conferred it unless the law provides otherwise.

matio, postulatio mitti debet ad auctoritatem competentem ut dispensatio concedatur.

§2. Si intra praescriptum tempus postulatio missa non fuerit, ipso facto nulla est, et collegium vel coetus pro ea vice privatur iure eligendi aut postulandi, nisi probetur praesidem a mittenda postulatione iusto fuisse detentum impedimento aut dolo vel neglegentia ab eadem tempore opportuno mittenda abstinuisse.

§3. Postulato nullum ius acquiritur ex postulatione; eam admittendi auctoritas competens obligatione non tenetur.

§4. Factam auctoritati competenti postulationem electores revocare non possunt, nisi auctoritate consentiente.

CAN. 183 §1. Non admissa ab auctoritate competenti postulatione, ius eligendi ad collegium vel coetum redit.

§2. Quod si postulatio admissa fuerit, id significetur postulato, qui respondere debet ad normam can. 177, §1.

§3. Qui admissam postulationem acceptat, pleno iure statim officium obtinet.

CAPUT II. De Amissione Officii Ecclesiastici

CAN. 184 §1. Amittitur officium ecclesiasticum lapsu temporis praefiniti, expleta aetate iure definita, renuntiatione, translatione, amotione necnon privatione.

§2. Resoluto quovis modo iure auctoritatis a qua fuit collatum, officium ecclesiasticum non amittitur, nisi aliud iure caveatur.

182 §2: c. 181 §2
182 §3: c. 181 §3
182 §4: c. 181 §4
183 §1: c. 182 §1

183 §2: c. 182 §2
183 §3: c. 182 §3
184 §1: c. 183 §1
184 §2: c. 183 §2

§3. Loss of an office which has taken effect is to be made known as soon as possible to all those who have some right over the provision of the office.

CAN. 185 The title of emeritus can be conferred upon a person who loses an office by reason of age or of resignation which has been accepted.

CAN. 186 Loss of an office by the lapse of a predetermined time or by the reaching of a certain age takes effect only from the moment when the competent authority communicates it in writing.

ART. 1. *Resignation*

CAN. 187 Anyone responsible for oneself (*sui compos*) can resign from an ecclesiastical office for a just cause.

CAN. 188 A resignation made out of grave fear that is inflicted unjustly or out of malice, substantial error, or simony is invalid by the law itself.

CAN. 189 §1. To be valid, a resignation, whether it requires acceptance or not, must be made to the authority to whom it pertains to make provision of the office in question; this must be done either in writing, or orally in the presence of two witnesses.

§2. The authority is not to accept a resignation which is not based on a just and proportionate cause.

§3. A resignation which requires acceptance lacks all force if it is not accepted within three months; one which does not require acceptance takes effect when it has been communicated by the one resigning according to the norm of law.

§3. Officii amissio, quae effectum sortita est, quam primum omnibus nota fiat, quibus aliquod ius in officii provisionem competit.

CAN. 185 Ei, qui ob impletam aetatem aut renuntiationem acceptatam officium amittit, titulus emeriti conferri potest.

CAN. 186 Lapsu temporis praefiniti vel adimpleta aetate, amissio officii effectum habet tantum a momento, quo a competenti auctoritate scripto intimatur.

ART. 1. *De Renuntiatione*

CAN. 187 Quisquis sui compos potest officio ecclesiastico iusta de causa renuntiare.

CAN. 188 Renuntiatio ex metu gravi, iniuste incusso, dolo vel errore substantiali aut simoniace facta, ipso iure irrita est.

CAN. 189 §1. Renuntiatio, ut valeat, sive acceptatione eget sive non, auctoritati fieri debet cui provisio ad officium de quo agitur pertinet, et quidem scripto vel oretenus coram duobus testibus.

§2. Auctoritas renuntiationem iusta et proportionata causa non innixam ne acceptet.

§3. Renuntiatio quae acceptatione indiget, nisi intra tres menses acceptetur, omni vi caret; quae acceptatione non indiget effectum sortitur communicatione renuntiantis ad normam iuris facta.

184 §3: c. 191 §2
187: c. 184
188: c. 185
189 §1: cc. 186, 187

189 §2: c. 189 §1
189 §3: c. 189 §2; CI Resp. III/1, 14 iul. 1922 (AAS 14 [1922] 526–527)

§4. A resignation can be revoked by the one resigning as long as it has not taken effect; once it has taken effect it cannot be revoked, but the one who resigned can obtain the office by some other title.

ART. 2. *Transfer*

CAN. 190 §1. A transfer can be made only by a person who has the right of providing for the office which is lost as well as for the office which is conferred.

§2. If a transfer is made when the officeholder is unwilling, a grave cause is required and the manner of proceeding prescribed by law is to be observed, always without prejudice to the right of proposing contrary arguments.

§3. To take effect a transfer must be communicated in writing.

CAN. 191 §1. In a transfer, the prior office becomes vacant through the canonical possession of the other office unless the law provides otherwise or competent authority has prescribed otherwise.

§2. The person transferred receives the remuneration assigned to the prior office until the person has taken canonical possession of the other office.

ART. 3. *Removal*

CAN. 192 A person is removed from office either by a decree issued legitimately by competent authority, without prejudice to rights possibly acquired by contract, or by the law itself according to the norm of can. 194.

CAN. 193 §1. A person cannot be removed from an office conferred for an indefinite peri-

§4. Renuntiatio, quamdiu effectum sortita non fuerit, a renuntiante revocari potest; effectu secuto revocari nequit, sed qui renuntiavit, officium alio ex titulo consequi potest.

ART. 2. *De Translatione*

CAN. 190 §1. Translatio ab eo tantum fieri potest, qui ius habet providendi officio quod amittitur et simul officio quod committitur.

§2. Si translatio fiat invito officii titulari, gravis requiritur causa et, firmo semper iure rationes contrarias exponendi, servetur modus procedendi iure praescriptus.

§3. Translatio, ut effectum sortiatur, scripto intimanda est.

CAN. 191 §1. In translatione, prius officium vacat per possessionem alterius officii canonice habitam, nisi aliud iure cautum aut a competenti auctoritate praescriptum fuerit.

§2. Remunerationem cum priore officio conexam translatus percipit, donec alterius possessionem canonice obtinuerit.

ART. 3. *De Amotione*

CAN. 192 Ab officio quis amovetur sive decreto ab auctoritate competenti legitime edito, servatis quidem iuribus forte ex contractu quaesitis, sive ipso iure ad normam can. 194.

CAN. 193 §1. Ab officio quod alicui confertur ad tempus indefinitum, non potest

---

189 §4: c. 191 §1; CI Resp. III/2, 14 iul. 1922 (AAS 14 [1922] 526–527)
  190 §1: c. 193 §1
  190 §2: c. 193 §2

191 §1: c. 194 §1
191 §2: c. 194 §2
192: c. 192 §1
193 §1: c. 192 §2

od of time except for grave causes and according to the manner of proceeding defined by law.

§2. The same is valid for the removal of a person from an office conferred for a definite period of time before this time has elapsed, without prejudice to the prescript of can. 624, §3.

§3. A person upon whom an office is conferred at the prudent discretion of a competent authority according to the prescripts of the law can, upon the judgment of the same authority, be removed from that office for a just cause.

§4. To take effect, the decree of removal must be communicated in writing.

CAN. 194 §1. The following are removed from an ecclesiastical office by the law itself:

1° a person who has lost the clerical state;

2° a person who has publicly defected from the Catholic faith or from the communion of the Church;

3° a cleric who has attempted marriage even if only civilly.

§2. The removal mentioned in nn. 2 and 3 can be enforced only if it is established by the declaration of a competent authority.

CAN. 195 If a person is removed not by the law itself but by a decree of competent authority from an office which provides the person's support, the same authority is to take care that the support is provided for a suitable period, unless other provision is made.

ART. 4. *Privation*

CAN. 196 §1. Privation from office, namely, a penalty for a delict, can be done only according to the norm of law.

§2. Privation takes effect according to the prescripts of the canons on penal law.

quis amoveri nisi ob graves causa atque servato procedendi modo iure definito.

§2. Idem valet, ut quis ab officio, quod alicui ad tempus determinatum confertur, ante hoc tempus elapsum amoveri possit, firmo praescripto can. 624, §3.

§3. Ab officio quod, secundum iuris praescripta, alicui confertur ad prudentem discretionem auctoritatis competentis, potest quis iusta ex causa, de iudicio eiusdem auctoritatis, amoveri.

§4. Decretum amotionis, ut effectum sortiatur, scripto intimandum est.

CAN. 194 §1. Ipso iure officio ecclesiastico amovetur:

1° qui statum clericalem amiserit;

2° qui a fide catholica aut a communione Ecclesiae publice defecerit;

3° clericus qui matrimonium etiam civile tantum attentaverit.

§2. Amotio, de qua in nn. 2 et 3, urgeri tantum potest, si de eadem auctoritatis competentis declaratione constet.

CAN. 195 Si quis, non quidem ipso iure, sed per decretum auctoritatis competentis ab officio amoveatur quo eiusdem subsistentiae providetur, eadem auctoritas curet ut ipsius subsistentiae per congruum tempus prospiciatur, nisi aliter provisum sit.

ART. 4. *De Privatione*

CAN. 196 §1. Privatio ab officio, in poenam scilicet delicti, ad normam iuris tantummodo fieri potest.

§2. Privatio effectum sortitur secundum praescripta canonum de iure poenali.

TITLE X. Prescription

CAN. 197 The Church receives prescription as it is in the civil legislation of the nation in question, without prejudice to the exceptions which are established in the canons of this Code; prescription is a means of acquiring or losing a subjective right as well as of freeing oneself from obligations.

CAN. 198 No prescription is valid unless it is based in good faith not only at the beginning but through the entire course of time required for prescription, without prejudice to the prescript of can. 1362.

CAN. 199 The following are not subject to prescription:

1° rights and obligations which are of the divine natural or positive law;

2° rights which can be obtained from apostolic privilege alone;

3° rights and obligations which directly regard the spiritual life of the Christian faithful;

4° the certain and undoubted boundaries of ecclesiastical territories;

5° Mass offerings and obligations;

6° provision of an ecclesiastical office which, according to the norm of law, requires the exercise of a sacred order;

7° the right of visitation and the obligation of obedience, in such a way that the Christian faithful cannot be visited by any ecclesiastical authority or are no longer subject to any authority.

TITULUS X. De Praescriptione

CAN. 197 Praescriptionem, tamquam modum iuris subiectivi acquirendi vel amittendi necnon ab obligationibus sese liberandi, Ecclesia recipit prout est in legislatione civili respectivae nationis, salvis exceptionibus quae in canonibus huius Codicis statuuntur.

CAN. 198 Nulla valet praescriptio, nisi bona fide nitatur, non solum initio, sed toto decursu temporis ad praescriptionem requisiti, salvo praescripto can. 1362.

CAN. 199 Praescriptioni obnoxia non sunt:

1° iura et obligationes quae sunt legis divinae naturalis aut positivae;

2° iura quae obtineri possunt ex solo privilegio apostolico;

3° iura et obligationes quae spiritualem christifidelium vitam directe respiciunt;

4° fines certi et indubii circumscriptionum ecclesiasticarum;

5° stipes et onera Missarum;

6° provisio officii ecclesiastici quod ad normam iuris exercitium ordinis sacri requirit;

7° ius visitationis et obligatio oboedientiae, ita ut christifideles a nulla auctoritate ecclesiastica visitari possint et nulli auctoritati iam subsint.

197: c. 1508; SA Sententia, 12 dec. 1972   199: c. 1509. 1°–5° et 7°
198: c. 1512

TITLE XI. Computation of Time

CAN. 200   Unless the law expressly provides otherwise, time is to be computed according to the norm of the following canons.

CAN. 201   §1. Continuous time is understood as that which undergoes no interruption.

§2. Useful time is understood as that which a person has to exercise or to pursue a right, so that it does not run for a person who is unaware or unable to act.

CAN. 202   §1. In law, a day is understood as a period consisting of 24 continuous hours and begins at midnight unless other provision is expressly made; a week is a period of 7 days; a month is a period of 30 days, and a year is a period of 365 days unless a month and a year are said to be taken as they are in the calendar.

§2. If time is continuous, a month and a year must always be taken as they are in the calendar.

CAN. 203   §1. The initial day *(a quo)* is not computed in the total unless its beginning coincides with the beginning of the day or the law expressly provides otherwise.

§2. Unless the contrary is established, the final day *(ad quem)* is computed in the total which, if the time consists of one or more months or years, or one or more weeks, is reached at the end of the last day of the same number or, if a month lacks a day of the same number, at the end of the last day of the month.

TITULUS XI. De Temporis Supputatione

CAN. 200   Nisi aliud expresse iure caveatur, tempus supputetur ad normam canonum qui sequuntur.

CAN. 201   §1. Tempus continuum intellegitur quod nullam patitur interruptionem.

§2. Tempus utile intellegitur quod ita ius suum exercenti aut persequenti competit, ut ignoranti aut agere non valenti non currat.

CAN. 202   §1. In iure, dies intellegitur spatium constans 24 horis continuo supputandis, et incipit a media nocte, nisi aliud expresse caveatur; hebdomada spatium 7 dierum; mensis spatium 30 et annus spatium 365 dierum, nisi mensis et annus dicantur sumendi prout sunt in calendario.

§2. Prout sunt in calendario semper sumendi sunt mensis et annus, si tempus est continuum.

CAN. 203   §1. Dies *a quo* non computatur in termino, nisi huius initium coincidat cum initio diei aut aliud expresse in iure caveatur.

§2. Nisi contrarium statuatur, dies *ad quem* computatur in termino, qui, si tempus constet uno vel pluribus mensibus aut annis, una vel pluribus hebdomadis, finitur expleto ultimo die eiusdem numeri aut, si mensis die eiusdem numeri careat, expleto ultimo die mensis.

200: c. 31; Pius PP. XI, Const. *Infinita Dei misericordia,* 29 maii 1924 (AAS 16 [1924] 212)
   201 §1: c. 35
   201 §2: c. 35
   202 §1: c. 32

202 §2: c. 34 §§1 et 2
203 §1: c. 34 §3, 2° et 3°; CI Resp. II, 12 nov. 1922 (AAS 14 [1922] 661)
   203 §2: c. 34 §3, 3° et 4°; CI Resp. II, 12 nov. 1922 (AAS 14 [1922] 661)

BOOK II. THE PEOPLE OF GOD

LIBER II. DE POPULO DEI

PART I. THE CHRISTIAN FAITHFUL

PARS I. DE CHRISTIFIDELIBUS

CAN. 204 §1. The Christian faithful are those who, inasmuch as they have been incorporated in Christ through baptism, have been constituted as the people of God. For this reason, made sharers in their own way in Christ's priestly, prophetic, and royal function, they are called to exercise the mission which God has entrusted to the Church to fulfill in the world, in accord with the condition proper to each.

§2. This Church, constituted and organized in this world as a society, subsists in the Catholic Church governed by the successor of Peter and the bishops in communion with him.

CAN. 205 Those baptized are fully in the communion of the Catholic Church on this earth who are joined with Christ in its visible structure by the bonds of the profession of faith, the sacraments, and ecclesiastical governance.

CAN. 206 §1. Catechumens, that is, those who ask by explicit choice under the influence of the Holy Spirit to be incorporated into the Church, are joined to it in a special way. By this same desire, just as by the life of faith, hope, and charity which they lead, they are united with the Church which already cherishes them as its own.

§2. The Church has a special care for catechumens; while it invites them to lead a life of the gospel and introduces them to the celebra-

CAN. 204 §1. Christifideles sunt qui, utpote per baptismum Christo incorporati, in populum Dei sunt constituti, atque hac ratione muneris Christi sacerdotalis, prophetici et regalis suo modo participes facti, secundum propriam cuiusque condicionem, ad missionem exercendam vocantur, quam Deus Ecclesiae in mundo adimplendam concredidit.

§2. Haec Ecclesia, in hoc mundo ut societas constituta et ordinata, subsistit in Ecclesia catholica, a successore Petri et Episcopis in eius communione gubernata.

CAN. 205 Plene in communione Ecclesiae catholicae his in terris sunt illi baptizati, qui in eius compage visibili cum Christo iunguntur, vinculis nempe professionis fidei, sacramentorum et ecclesiastici regiminis.

CAN. 206 §1. Speciali ratione cum Ecclesia conectuntur catechumeni, qui nempe, Spiritu Sancto movente, explicita voluntate ut eidem incorporentur expetunt, ideoque hoc ipso voto, sicut et vita fidei, spei et caritatis quam agunt, coniunguntur cum Ecclesia, quae eos iam ut suos fovet.

§2. Catechumenorum specialem curam habet Ecclesia quae, dum eos ad vitam ducendam evangelicam invitat eosque ad

---

204 §1: LG 9–17, 31, 34–36; AA 2, 6, 7, 9, 10
204 §2: LG 8, 9, 14, 22, 38; GS 40
205: LG 14

206 §1: LG 14
206 §2: SC 64; AG 14

tion of sacred rites, it already grants them various prerogatives which are proper to Christians.

CAN. 207   §1. By divine institution, there are among the Christian faithful in the Church sacred ministers who in law are also called clerics; the other members of the Christian faithful are called lay persons.

§2. There are members of the Christian faithful from both these groups who, through the profession of the evangelical counsels by means of vows or other sacred bonds recognized and sanctioned by the Church, are consecrated to God in their own special way and contribute to the salvific mission of the Church; although their state does not belong to the hierarchical structure of the Church, it nevertheless belongs to its life and holiness.

sacros ritus celebrandos introducit, eisdem varias iam largitur praerogativas, quae christianorum sunt propriae.

CAN. 207 §1. Ex divina institutione, inter christifideles sunt in Ecclesia ministri sacri, qui in iure et clerici vocantur; ceteri autem et laici nuncupantur.

§2. Ex utraque hac parte habentur christifideles, qui professione consiliorum evangelicorum per vota aut alia sacra ligamina, ab Ecclesia agnita et sancita, suo peculiari modo Deo consecrantur et Ecclesiae missioni salvificae prosunt; quorum status, licet ad hierarchicam Ecclesiae structuram non spectet, ad eius tamen vitam et sanctitatem pertinet.

TITLE I. The Obligations and Rights of All the Christian Faithful

TITULUS I. De Omnium Christifidelium Obligationibus et Iuribus

CAN. 208   From their rebirth in Christ, there exists among all the Christian faithful a true equality regarding dignity and action by which they all cooperate in the building up of the Body of Christ according to each one's own condition and function.

CAN. 209   §1. The Christian faithful, even in their own manner of acting, are always obliged to maintain communion with the Church.

§2. With great diligence they are to fulfill the duties which they owe to the universal Church

CAN. 208 Inter christifideles omnes, ex eorum quidem in Christo regeneratione, vera viget quoad dignitatem et actionem aequalitas, qua cuncti, secundum propriam cuiusque condicionem et munus, ad aedificationem Corporis Christi cooperantur.

CAN. 209 §1. Christifideles obligatione adstringuntur, sua quoque ipsorum agendi ratione, ad communionem semper servandam cum Ecclesia.

§2. Magna cum diligentia officia adimpleant, quibus tenentur erga Ecclesiam tum

207 §1: c. 107; LG 10, 20, 30–33
207 §2: c. 107; LG 43–47
208: LG 32; GS 49, 61

209 §1: LG 11–13, 23, 32; GS 1; SE *Elapso Oecumenico,* 22 oct. 1969
209 §2: LG 30; AA 10

and the particular church to which they belong according to the prescripts of the law.

CAN. 210 All the Christian faithful must direct their efforts to lead a holy life and to promote the growth of the Church and its continual sanctification, according to their own condition.

CAN. 211 All the Christian faithful have the duty and right to work so that the divine message of salvation more and more reaches all people in every age and in every land.

CAN. 212 §1. Conscious of their own responsibility, the Christian faithful are bound to follow with Christian obedience those things which the sacred pastors, inasmuch as they represent Christ, declare as teachers of the faith or establish as rulers of the Church.

§2. The Christian faithful are free to make known to the pastors of the Church their needs, especially spiritual ones, and their desires.

§3. According to the knowledge, competence, and prestige which they possess, they have the right and even at times the duty to manifest to the sacred pastors their opinion on matters which pertain to the good of the Church and to make their opinion known to the rest of the Christian faithful, without prejudice to the integrity of faith and morals, with reverence toward their pastors, and attentive to common advantage and the dignity of persons.

CAN. 213 The Christian faithful have the right to receive assistance from the sacred pastors out of the spiritual goods of the Church, especially the word of God and the sacraments.

CAN. 214 The Christian faithful have the

universam, tum particularem ad quam, secundum iuris praescripta, pertinent.

CAN. 210 Omnes christifideles, secundum propriam condicionem, ad sanctam vitam ducendam atque ad Ecclesiae incrementum eiusque iugem sanctificationem promovendam vires suas conferre debent.

CAN. 211 Omnes christifideles officium habent et ius allaborandi ut divinum salutis nuntium ad universos homines omnium temporum ac totius orbis magis magisque perveniat.

CAN. 212 §1. Quae sacri Pastores, utpote Christum repraesentantes, tamquam fidei magistri declarant aut tamquam Ecclesiae rectores statuunt, christifideles, propriae responsabilitatis conscii, christiana oboedientia prosequi tenentur.

§2. Christifidelibus integrum est, ut necessitates suas, praesertim spirituales, suaque optata Ecclesiae Pastoribus patefaciant.

§3. Pro scientia, competentia et praestantia quibus pollent, ipsis ius est, immo et aliquando officium, ut sententiam suam de his quae ad bonum Ecclesiae pertinent sacris Pastoribus manifestent eamque, salva fidei morumque integritate ac reverentia erga Pastores, attentisque communi utilitate et personarum dignitate, ceteris christifidelibus notam faciant.

CAN. 213 Ius est christifidelibus ut ex spiritualibus Ecclesiae bonis, praesertim ex verbo Dei et sacramentis, adiumenta a sacris Pastoribus accipiant.

CAN. 214 Ius est christifidelibus, ut cul-

210: LG 39–12; AA 6
211: LG 17; AG 1, 2, 5, 35–37
212 §1: c. 1323; LG 25, 37; PO 9
212 §2: c. 682; IM 8; LG 37; AA 6; PO 9; GS 92

212 §3: IM 8; LG 37; AA 6; PO 9; GS 92
213: c. 682; SC 19; LG 37; PO 9
214: SC 4; OE 2, 3, 5

right to worship God according to the prescripts of their own rite approved by the legitimate pastors of the Church and to follow their own form of spiritual life so long as it is consonant with the doctrine of the Church.

CAN. 215 The Christian faithful are at liberty freely to found and direct associations for purposes of charity or piety or for the promotion of the Christian vocation in the world and to hold meetings for the common pursuit of these purposes.

CAN. 216 Since they participate in the mission of the Church, all the Christian faithful have the right to promote or sustain apostolic action even by their own undertakings, according to their own state and condition. Nevertheless, no undertaking is to claim the name *Catholic* without the consent of competent ecclesiastical authority.

CAN. 217 Since they are called by baptism to lead a life in keeping with the teaching of the gospel, the Christian faithful have the right to a Christian education by which they are to be instructed properly to strive for the maturity of the human person and at the same time to know and live the mystery of salvation.

CAN. 218 Those engaged in the sacred disciplines have a just freedom of inquiry and of expressing their opinion prudently on those matters in which they possess expertise, while observing the submission due to the magisterium of the Church.

CAN. 219 All the Christian faithful have the right to be free from any kind of coercion in choosing a state of life.

tum Deo persolvant iuxta praescripta proprii ritus a legitimis Ecclesiae Pastoribus approbati, utque propriam vitae spiritualis formam sequantur, doctrinae quidem Ecclesiae consentaneam.

CAN. 215 Integrum est christifidelibus, ut libere condant atque moderentur consociationes ad fines caritatis vel pietatis, aut ad vocationem christianam in mundo fovendam, utque conventus habeant ad eosdem fines in communi persequendos.

CAN. 216 Christifideles cuncti, quippe qui Ecclesiae missionem participent, ius habent ut propriis quoque inceptis, secundum suum quisque statum et condicionem, apostolicam actionem promoveant vel sustineant; nullum tamen inceptum nomen catholicum sibi vindicet, nisi consensus accesserit competentis auctoritatis ecclesiasticae.

CAN. 217 Christifideles, quippe qui baptismo ad vitam doctrinae evangelicae congruentem ducendam vocentur, ius habent ad educationem christianam, qua ad maturitatem humanae personae prosequendam atque simul ad mysterium salutis cognoscendum et vivendum rite instruantur.

CAN. 218 Qui disciplinis sacris incumbunt iusta libertate fruuntur inquirendi necnon mentem suam prudenter in iis aperiendi, in quibus peritia gaudent, servato debito erga Ecclesiae magisterium obsequio.

CAN. 219 Christifideles omnes iure gaudent ut a quacumque coactione sint immunes in statu vitae eligendo.

215: c. 685; Pius PP. XI, Enc. *Quadragesimo Anno,* 15 maii 1931 (AAS 23 [1931] 177–178); IOANNES PP. XXIII, Enc. *Pacem in terris,* 11 apr. 1963 (AAS 55 [1963] 263); AA 18–21; PO 8; GS 68

216: LG 37; AA 24, 25; PO 9

217: c. 1372 §1; GE 2

218: GE 10; GS 62; SCh 39

219: cc. 214, 542, 1°, 971, 1087 §§1 et 2, 2352; IOANNES PP. XXIII, Enc. *Pacem in terris,* 11 apr. 1963 (AAS 55 [1963] 261); GS 26, 29, 52

CAN. 220 No one is permitted to harm illegitimately the good reputation which a person possesses nor to injure the right of any person to protect his or her own privacy.

CAN. 221 §1. The Christian faithful can legitimately vindicate and defend the rights which they possess in the Church in the competent ecclesiastical forum according to the norm of law.

§2. If they are summoned to a trial by a competent authority, the Christian faithful also have the right to be judged according to the prescripts of the law applied with equity.

§3. The Christian faithful have the right not to be punished with canonical penalties except according to the norm of law.

CAN. 222 §1. The Christian faithful are obliged to assist with the needs of the Church so that the Church has what is necessary for divine worship, for the works of the apostolate and of charity, and for the decent support of ministers.

§2. They are also obliged to promote social justice and, mindful of the precept of the Lord, to assist the poor from their own resources.

CAN. 223 §1. In exercising their rights, the Christian faithful, both as individuals and gathered together in associations, must take into account the common good of the Church, the rights of others, and their own duties toward others.

§2. In view of the common good, ecclesiastical authority can direct the exercise of rights which are proper to the Christian faithful.

CAN. 220 Nemini licet bonam famam, qua quis gaudet, illegitime laedere, nec ius cuiusque personae ad propriam intimitatem tuendam violare.

CAN. 221 §1. Christifidelibus competit ut iura, quibus in Ecclesia gaudent, legitime vindicent atque defendant in foro competenti ecclesiastico ad normam iuris.

§2. Christifidelibus ius quoque est ut, si ad iudicium ab auctoritate competenti vocentur, iudicentur servatis iuris praescriptis, cum aequitate applicandis.

§3. Christifidelibus ius est, ne poenis canonicis nisi ad normam legis plectantur.

CAN. 222 §1. Christifideles obligatione tenentur necessitatibus subveniendi Ecclesiae, ut eidem praesto sint quae ad cultum divinum, ad opera apostolatus et caritatis atque ad honestam ministrorum sustentationem necessaria sunt.

§2. Obligatione quoque tenentur iustitiam socialem promovendi necnon, praecepti Domini memores, ex propriis reditibus pauperibus subveniendi.

CAN. 223 §1. In iuribus suis exercendis christifideles tum singuli tum in consociationibus adunati rationem habere debent boni communis Ecclesiae necnon iurium aliorum atque suorum erga alios officiorum.

§2. Ecclesiasticae auctoritati competit, intuitu boni communis, exercitium iurium, quae christifidelibus sunt propria, moderari.

220: c. 2355; GS 26, 27; Ioannes PP. XXIII, Enc. *Pacem in terris,* 11 apr. 1963 (AAS 55 [1963] 260)

221 §1: c. 1646

221 §2: c. 2214 §2

221 §3: cc. 2195, 2222

222 §1: c. 1496; AA 21; AG 36; PO 20, 21; Paulus PP. VI, Adh. Ap. *Nobis in animo,* 25 mar. 1974 (AAS 66 [1974] 185)

222 §2: AA 8; DH 1, 6, 14; GS 26, 29, 42, 65, 68, 69, 72, 75, 88

TITLE II. The Obligations and Rights of the Lay Christian Faithful

CAN. 224 In addition to those obligations and rights which are common to all the Christian faithful and those which are established in other canons, the lay Christian faithful are bound by the obligations and possess the rights which are enumerated in the canons of this title.

CAN. 225 §1. Since, like all the Christian faithful, lay persons are designated by God for the apostolate through baptism and confirmation, they are bound by the general obligation and possess the right as individuals, or joined in associations, to work so that the divine message of salvation is made known and accepted by all persons everywhere in the world. This obligation is even more compelling in those circumstances in which only through them can people hear the gospel and know Christ.

§2. According to each one's own condition, they are also bound by a particular duty to imbue and perfect the order of temporal affairs with the spirit of the gospel and thus to give witness to Christ, especially in carrying out these same affairs and in exercising secular functions.

CAN. 226 §1. According to their own vocation, those who live in the marital state are bound by a special duty to work through marriage and the family to build up the people of God.

§2. Since they have given life to their children, parents have a most grave obligation and possess the right to educate them. Therefore, it

TITULUS II. De Obligationibus et Iuribus Christifidelium Laicorum

CAN. 224 Christifideles laici, praeter eas obligationes et iura, quae cunctis christifidelibus sunt communia et ea quae in aliis canonibus statuuntur, obligationibus tenentur et iuribus gaudent quae in canonibus huius tituli recensentur.

CAN. 225 §1. Laici, quippe qui uti omnes christifideles ad apostolatum a Deo per baptismum et confirmationem deputentur, generali obligatione tenentur et iure gaudent, sive singuli sive in consociationibus coniuncti, allaborandi ut divinum salutis nuntium ab universis hominibus ubique terrarum cognoscatur et accipiatur; quae obligatio eo vel magis urget iis in adiunctis, in quibus nonnisi per ipsos Evangelium audire et Christum cognoscere homines possunt.

§2. Hoc etiam peculiari adstringuntur officio, unusquisque quidem secundum propriam condicionem, ut rerum temporalium ordinem spiritu evangelico imbuant atque perficiant, et ita specialiter in iisdem rebus gerendis atque in muneribus saecularibus exercendis Christi testimonium reddant.

CAN. 226 §1. Qui in statu coniugali vivunt, iuxta propriam vocationem, peculiari officio tenentur per matrimonium et familiam ad aedificationem populi Dei allaborandi.

§2. Parentes, cum vitam filiis contulerint, gravissima obligatione tenentur et iure gaudent eos educandi; ideo parentum chris-

225 §1: Pius PP. XII, All., 14 oct. 1951 (AAS 43 [1951] 784–792); Pius PP. XII, All., 5 oct. 1957 (AAS 49 [1957] 922–939); LG 33; AA 2, 3, 17; AG 21, 36

225 §2: LG 31; AA 2–4, 7; GS 43
226 §1: AA 11; GS 52
226 §2: c. 1372 §2; GE 3

is for Christian parents particularly to take care of the Christian education of their children according to the doctrine handed on by the Church.

CAN. 227 The lay Christian faithful have the right to have recognized that freedom which all citizens have in the affairs of the earthly city. When using that same freedom, however, they are to take care that their actions are imbued with the spirit of the gospel and are to heed the doctrine set forth by the magisterium of the Church. In matters of opinion, moreover, they are to avoid setting forth their own opinion as the doctrine of the Church.

CAN. 228 §1. Lay persons who are found suitable are qualified to be admitted by the sacred pastors to those ecclesiastical offices and functions which they are able to exercise according to the precepts of the law.

§2. Lay persons who excel in necessary knowledge, prudence, and integrity are qualified to assist the pastors of the Church as experts and advisors, even in councils according to the norm of law.

CAN. 229 §1. Lay persons are bound by the obligation and possess the right to acquire knowledge of Christian doctrine appropriate to the capacity and condition of each in order for them to be able to live according to this doctrine, announce it themselves, defend it if necessary, and take their part in exercising the apostolate.

§2. They also possess the right to acquire that fuller knowledge of the sacred sciences which are taught in ecclesiastical universities and faculties or in institutes of religious sciences, by at-

tianorum imprimis est christianam filiorum educationem secundum doctrinam ab Ecclesia traditam curare.

CAN. 227 Ius est christifidelibus laicis, ut ipsis agnoscatur ea in rebus civitatis terrenae libertas, quae omnibus civibus competit; eadem tamen libertate utentes, curent ut suae actiones spiritu evangelico imbuantur, et ad doctrinam attendant ab Ecclesiae magisterio propositam, caventes tamen ne in quaestionibus opinabilibus propriam sententiam uti doctrinam Ecclesiae proponant.

CAN. 228 §1. Laici, qui idonei reperiantur, sunt habiles ut a sacris Pastoribus ad illa officia ecclesiastica et munera assumantur, quibus ipsi secundum iuris praescripta fungi valent.

§2. Laici debita scientia, prudentia et honestate praestantes, habiles sunt tamquam periti aut consiliarii, etiam in consiliis ad normam iuris, ad Ecclesiae Pastoribus adiutorium praebendum.

CAN. 229 §1. Laici, ut secundum doctrinam christianam vivere valeant, eandemque et ipsi enuntiare atque, si opus sit, defendere possint, utque in apostolatu exercendo partem suam habere queant, obligatione tenentur et iure gaudent acquirendi eiusdem doctrinae cognitionem, propriae uniuscuiusque capacitati et condicioni aptatam.

§2. Iure quoque gaudent pleniorem illam in scientiis sacris acquirendi cognitionem, quae in ecclesiasticis universitatibus facultatibusve aut in institutis scientiarum reli-

227: LG 37; AA 24; PO 9; GS 43
228 §1: LG 33; CD 10; AA 24
228 §2: LG 33, 37; CD 27; AA 20, 26; AG 30; PO 17

229 §1: LG 35; DH 14; AA 29; AG 26; GS 43
229 §2: GE 10; GS 62; SCh 31

tending classes there and pursuing academic degrees.

§3. If the prescripts regarding the requisite suitability have been observed, they are also qualified to receive from legitimate ecclesiastical authority a mandate to teach the sacred sciences.

CAN. 230 §1. Lay men who possess the age and qualifications established by decree of the conference of bishops can be admitted on a stable basis through the prescribed liturgical rite to the ministries of lector and acolyte. Nevertheless, the conferral of these ministries does not grant them the right to obtain support or remuneration from the Church.

§2. Lay persons can fulfill the function of lector in liturgical actions by temporary designation. All lay persons can also perform the functions of commentator or cantor, or other functions, according to the norm of law.

§3. When the need of the Church warrants it and ministers are lacking, lay persons, even if they are not lectors or acolytes, can also supply certain of their duties, namely, to exercise the ministry of the word, to preside over liturgical prayers, to confer baptism, and to distribute Holy Communion, according to the prescripts of the law.

CAN. 231 §1. Lay persons who permanently or temporarily devote themselves to special service of the Church are obliged to acquire the appropriate formation required to fulfill their function properly and to carry out this function conscientiously, eagerly, and diligently.

§2. Without prejudice to the prescript of can.

giosarum traduntur, ibidem lectiones frequentando et gradus academicos consequendo.

§3. Item, servatis praescriptis quoad idoneitatem requisitam statutis, habiles sunt ad mandatum docendi scientias sacras a legitima auctoritate ecclesiastica recipiendum.

CAN. 230 §1. Viri laici, qui aetate dotibusque pollent Episcoporum conferentiae decreto statutis, per ritum liturgicum praescriptum ad ministeria lectoris et acolythi stabiliter assumi possunt; quae tamen ministeriorum collatio eisdem ius non confert ad sustentationem remunerationemve ab Ecclesia praestandam.

§2. Laici ex temporanea deputatione in actionibus liturgicis munus lectoris implere possunt; item omnes laici muneribus commentatoris, cantoris aliisve ad normam iuris fungi possunt.

§3. Ubi Ecclesiae necessitas id suadeat, deficientibus ministris, possunt etiam laici, etsi non sint lectores vel acolythi, quaedam eorundem officia supplere, videlicet ministerium verbi exercere, precibus liturgicis praeesse, baptismum conferre atque sacram communionem distribuere, iuxta iuris praescripta.

CAN. 231 §1. Laici, qui permanenter aut ad tempus speciali Ecclesiae servitio addicuntur, obligatione tenentur ut aptam acquirant formationem ad munus suum debite implendum requisitam, utque hoc munus conscie, impense et diligenter adimpleant.

§2. Firmo praescripto can. 230, §1, ius

229 §3: AG 41; GS 63; SCh 22
230 §1: MQ III, VII, XII
230 §2: MQ V
230 §3:IOe 37; AA 24; SCDS Instr. *Fidei custos*, 30

apr. 1969; SCpC Resp., 20 nov. 1973
231 §1: AA 12, 28–32; AG 17
231 §2: AA 22; AG 17

230, §1 and with the prescripts of civil law having been observed, lay persons have the right to decent remuneration appropriate to their condition so that they are able to provide decently for their own needs and those of their family. They also have a right for their social provision, social security, and health benefits to be duly provided.

habent ad honestam remunerationem suae condicioni aptatam, qua decenter, servatis quoque iuris civilis praescriptis, necessitatibus propriis ac familiae providere valeant; itemque iis ius competit ut ipsorum praevidentiae et securitati sociali et assistentiae sanitariae, quam dicunt, debite prospiciatur.

TITLE III. Sacred Ministers or Clerics

CHAPTER I. The Formation of Clerics

CAN. 232 The Church has the duty and the proper and exclusive right to form those who are designated for the sacred ministries.

CAN. 233 §1. The duty of fostering vocations rests with the entire Christian community so that the needs of the sacred ministry in the universal Church are provided for sufficiently. This duty especially binds Christian families, educators, and, in a special way, priests, particularly pastors. Diocesan bishops, who most especially are to be concerned for promoting vocations, are to teach the people entrusted to them of the importance of the sacred ministry and of the need for ministers in the Church and are to encourage and support endeavors to foster vocations, especially by means of projects established for that purpose.

TITULUS III. De Ministris Sacris Seu de Clericis

CAPUT I. De Clericorum Institutione

CAN. 232 Ecclesiae officium est atque ius proprium et exclusivum eos instituendi, qui ad ministeria sacra deputantur.

CAN. 233 §1. Universae communitati christianae officium incumbit fovendarum vocationum, ut necessitatibus ministerii sacri in tota Ecclesia sufficienter provideatur; speciatim hoc officio tenentur familiae christianae, educatores atque peculiari ratione sacerdotes, praesertim parochi. Episcopi dioecesani, quorum maxime est de vocationibus provehendis curam habere, populum sibi commissum de momento ministerii sacri deque ministrorum in Ecclesia necessitate edoceant, atque incepta ad vocationes fovendes, operibus praesertim ad hoc institutis, suscitent ac sustentent.

232: c. 1352; OT passim; SCSSU Ep., 14 mai 1963
233 §1: c. 1353; Pius PP. XI, Ep. *Officiorum omnium*, 1 aug. 1922 (AAS 14 [1922] 449–458); Pius PP. XI, Enc. *Ad catholici sacerdotii*, 20 dec. 1935 (AAS 28 [1936] 44); Pius PP. XII, m. p. *Cum nobis*, 4 nov. 1941, (AAS 33 [1941] 479); SCSSU Normae, 8 sep. 1943 (AAS 35 [1943] 369–370); Pius PP. XII, Adh. Ap. *Menti nostrae*, 23 sep. 1950, III (AAS 42 [1950]

681–694); Sec Ep., 13 iul. 1952; Ioannes PP. XXIII, All., 16 dec. 1961 (AAS 54 [1962] 32–36); Sec Ep., 2 feb. 1962; SCSSU Litt. circ., 20 feb. 1962; Paulus PP. VI, Ep. *Summi Dei*, 4 nov. 1963 (AAS 55 [1963] 979–995); Sec et SCR Notif., 23 ian. 1964; SCR Litt. circ., 2 feb. 1964; SCR Litt. circ., 15 ian. 1965; CD 15; OT 2; AA 11; PO 11; RFS 5–10; DPME 197; SCIC Litt. circ., 2 ian. 1978

§2. Moreover, priests, and especially diocesan bishops, are to have concern that men of a more mature age who consider themselves called to the sacred ministries are prudently assisted in word and deed and duly prepared.

CAN. 234 §1. Minor seminaries and other similar institutions are to be preserved, where they exist, and fostered; for the sake of fostering vocations, these institutions provide special religious formation together with instruction in the humanities and science. Where the diocesan bishop judges it expedient, he is to erect a minor seminary or similar institution.

§2. Unless in certain cases circumstances indicate otherwise, young men disposed to the priesthood are to be provided with that formation in the humanities and science by which the youth in their own region are prepared to pursue higher studies.

CAN. 235 §1. Young men who intend to enter the priesthood are to be provided with a suitable spiritual formation and prepared for their proper duties in a major seminary throughout the entire time of formation or, if in the judgment of the diocesan bishop circumstances demand it, for at least four years.

§2. The diocesan bishop is to entrust those who legitimately reside outside a seminary to a devout and suitable priest who is to be watchful

§2. Solliciti sint insuper sacerdotes, praesertim vero Episcopi dioecesani, ut qui maturioris aetatis viri ad ministeria sacra sese vocatos aestiment, prudenter verbo opereque adiuventur ac debite praeparentur.

CAN. 234 §1. Serventur, ubi exsistunt, atque foveantur seminaria minora aliave instituta id genus, in quibus nempe, vocationum fovendarum gratia, provideatur ut peculiaris formatio religiosa una cum institutione humanistica et scientifica tradatur; immo, ubi id expedire iudicaverit Episcopus dioecesanus, seminarii minoris similisve instituti erectioni prospiciat.

§2. Nisi certis in casibus adiuncta aliud suadeant, iuvenes quibus animus est ad sacerdotium ascendere, ea ornentur humanistica et scientifica formatione, qua iuvenes in sua quisque regione ad studia superiora peragenda praeparantur.

CAN. 235 §1. Iuvenes, qui ad sacerdotium accedere intendunt, ad formationem spiritualem convenientem et ad officia propria instituantur in seminario maiore per totum formationis tempus, aut, si adiuncta de iudicio Episcopi dioecesani id postulent, per quattuor saltem annos.

§2. Qui extra seminarium legitime morantur, ab Episcopo dioecesano commendentur pio et idoneo sacerdoti, qui invig-

233 §2: Pius PP. XII, Adh. Ap. *Menti nostrae*, 23 sep. 1950, III (AAS 42 [1950] 684); OT 3; RFS 19; DPME 196; SCIC Litt. circ., 14 iul. 1976

234 §1: c. 1354 §§1 et 2; Pius PP. XI, Ep. Ap. *Officiorum omnium*, 1 aug. 1922 (AAS 14 [1922] 451–452); SCSSU Ep., 26 maii 1928; Pius PP. XII, All., 6 sep. 1957 (AAS 49 [1957] 845–849); SCSSU Litt. circ., 22 feb. 1963; Paulus PP. VI, Ep. *Summi Dei*, 4 nov. 1963 (AAS 55 [1963] 979–995); OT 3; SCIC Litt. circ., 23 maii 1968; RFS 11–19; DPME 194

234 §2: SCSSU Ep., 3 maii 1947, II; Pius PP. XII,

Adh. Ap. *Menti nostrae*, 23 sep. 1950, III (AAS 42 [1950] 687); Ssap IV; OT 13; RFS 16

235 §1: cc. 972 §1, 1354 §§1 et 2; Benedictus PP. XV, Ep. *Saepe Nobis*, 30 nov. 1921 (AAS 13 [1921] 556); Paulus PP. VI, Ep. *Summi Dei*, 4 nov. 1963 (AAS 55 [1963] 979–995); OT 4; RFS Introductio, 1, 20; Ioannes Paulus PP. II, Ep. *Magnus dies*, 8 apr. 1979 (AAS 71 [1979] 392)

235 §2: cc. 972 §1, 1370; Sec Normae, 14 apr. 1946; OT 12; Paulus PP. VI, Enc. *Sacerdotalis caelibatus*, 24 iun. 1967, 71 (AAS 59 [1967] 685); RFS 42

that they are carefully formed in the spiritual life and in discipline.

CAN. 236 According to the prescripts of the conference of bishops, those aspiring to the permanent diaconate are to be formed to nourish a spiritual life and instructed to fulfill correctly the duties proper to that order:

1° young men are to live at least three years in some special house unless the diocesan bishop has established otherwise for grave reasons;

2° men of a more mature age, whether celibate or married, are to spend three years in a program defined by the conference of bishops.

CAN. 237 §1. Where it is possible and expedient, there is to be a major seminary in every diocese; otherwise, the students who are preparing for the sacred ministries are to be entrusted to another seminary, or an interdiocesan seminary is to be erected.

§2. An interdiocesan seminary is not to be erected unless the conference of bishops, if the seminary is for its entire territory, or the bishops involved have obtained the prior approval of the Apostolic See for both the erection of the seminary and its statutes.

CAN. 238 §1. Seminaries legitimately erected possess juridic personality in the Church by the law itself.

§2. In the handling of all affairs, the rector of

ilet ut ad vitam spiritualem et ad disciplinam sedulo efformentur.

CAN. 236 Aspirantes ad diaconatum permanentem secundum Episcoporum conferentiae praescripta ad vitam spiritualem alendam informentur atque ad officia eidem ordini propria rite adimplenda instruantur:

1° iuvenes per tres saltem annos in aliqua domo peculiari degentes, nisi graves ob rationes Episcopus dioecesanus aliter statuerit;

2° maturioris aetatis viri, sive caelibes sive coniugati, ratione ad tres annos protracta et ab eadem Episcoporum conferentia definita.

CAN. 237 §1. In singulis dioecesibus sit seminarium maius, ubi id fieri possit atque expediat; secus concredantur alumni, qui ad sacra ministeria sese praeparent, alieno seminario aut erigatur seminarium interdioecesanum.

§2. Seminarium interdioecesanum ne erigatur nisi prius approbatio Apostolicae Sedis, tum ipsius seminarii erectionis tum eiusdem statutorum, obtenta fuerit, et quidem ab Episcoporum conferentia, si agatur de seminario pro universo eius territorio, secus ab Episcopis quorum interest.

CAN. 238 §1. Seminaria legitime erecta ipso iure personalitate iuridica in Ecclesia gaudent.

§2. In omnibus negotiis pertractandis

236, 1°: LG 29; AG 16; SDO 6–10; SCIC Litt. circ., 16 iul. 1969; AP VII; DPME 196

236, 2°: LG 29; AG 16; SDO 14, 15; SCIC Litt. circ., 16 iul. 1969; AP VII; DPME 196

237 §1: cc. 1354 §§2 et 3, 1357 §3; BENEDICTUS PP. XV, Ep. *Saepe Nobis*, 30 nov. 1921 (AAS 13 [1921] 555–556); PIUS PP. XI, Ep. *Officiorum omnium*, 1 aug. 1922 (AAS 14 [1922] 449–458); PIUS PP. XI, Enc. *Ad catholici sacerdotii*, 20 dec. 1935 (AAS 28 [1936] 44); SCSSU Litt. circ., 22 feb. 1963, I; PAULUS PP. VI, Ep.

Summi Dei, 4 nov. 1963 (AAS 55 [1963] 979–995); OT 4, 7; RFS 20, 21; DPME 193; IOANNES PAULUS PP. II, Ep. *Magnus dies*, 8 apr. 1979 (AAS 71 [1979] 392)

237 §2: cc. 1354 §3, 1357 §4; SCPF Normae, 27 apr. 1934; SCSSU Normae, 25 ian. 1945; SCPF Normae, 1962; OT 7; RFS 21; CIV Resp. II, 11 feb. 1972 (AAS 64 [1972] 397); DPME 193

238 §1: c. 99

238 §2: c. 1368

the seminary represents it unless competent authority has established otherwise for certain affairs.

CAN. 239 §1. Every seminary is to have a rector who presides over it, a vice-rector if one is needed, a finance officer, and, if the students pursue their studies in the seminary itself, teachers who give instruction in various disciplines coordinated in an appropriate manner.

§2. Every seminary is to have at least one spiritual director, though the students remain free to approach other priests who have been designated for this function by the bishop.

§3. The statutes of a seminary are to provide ways through which the other moderators, the teachers, and even the students themselves participate in the responsibility of the rector, especially in maintaining discipline.

CAN. 240 §1. In addition to ordinary confessors, other confessors are to come regularly to the seminary. Without prejudice to the discipline of the seminary, students are always free to approach any confessor, whether in the seminary or outside it.

§2. When decisions are made about admitting students to orders or dismissing them from the seminary, the opinion of the spiritual director and confessors can never be sought.

CAN. 241 §1. A diocesan bishop is to admit

personam seminarii gerit eius rector, nisi de certis negotiis auctoritas competens aliud statuerit.

CAN. 239 §1. In quolibet seminario habeantur rector, qui ei praesit, et si casus ferat vice-rector, oeconomus, atque si alumni in ipso seminario studiis se dedant, etiam magistri, qui varias disciplinas tradant apta ratione inter se compositas.

§2. In quolibet seminario unus saltem adsit spiritus director, relicta libertate alumnis adeundi alios sacerdotes, qui ad hoc munus ab Episcopo deputati sint.

§3. Seminarii statutis provideantur rationes, quibus curam rectoris, in disciplina praesertim servanda, participent ceteri moderatores, magistri, immo et ipsi alumni.

CAN. 240 §1. Praeter confessarios ordinarios, alii regulariter ad seminarium accedant confessarii, atque, salva quidem seminarii disciplina, integrum semper sit alumnis quemlibet confessarium sive in seminario sive extra illud adire.

§2. In decisionibus ferendis de alumnis ad ordines admittendis aut e seminario dimittendis, numquam directoris spiritus et confessariorum votum exquiri potest.

CAN. 241 §1. Ad seminarium maius ab

239 §1: c. 1358; SCSSU Ep., 8 oct. 1921, II; SCSSU Ep., 26 maii 1928; OT 5; RFS 27–31

239 §2: c. 1358; SCSSU Ep., 8 oct. 1921, II; SCSSU Ep., 26 maii 1928; SCSSU Ep., 3 maii 1947, I; RFS 27, 55; DPME 192

239 §3: c. 1359; PIUS PP. XII, Adh. Ap. *Menti nostrae*, 23 sep. 1950 (AAS 42 [1950] 686); SCIC Litt. circ., 7 mar. 1967; SCIC Litt. circ., 23 maii 1968; PAULUS PP. VI, All., 27 mar. 1969 (AAS 61 [1969] 253–256); RFS Introductio 2, 24, 29, 38

240 §1: c. 1361 §§1 et 2; RFS 55; DPME 192; SCIC Instr. *In ecclesiasticam*, 3 iun. 1979, 35, 36

240 §2: c. 1363 §2; PIUS PP. XI, Enc. *Ad catholici*

sacerdotii, 20 dec. 1935 (AAS 28 [1936] 41); SCSSU Ep., 3 maii 1947; SCDS Litt. circ., 27 dec. 1955, 1

241 §1: c. 1363 §1; PIUS PP. XI, Enc. *Ad catholici sacerdotii*, 20 dec. 1935 (AAS 28 [1936] 39, 40); PIUS PP. XII, Adh. Ap. *Menti nostrae*, 23 sep. 1950, II (AAS 42 [1950] 684–685); SCSSU Litt. circ., 27 sep. 1960, I, 1–5; SCSO Monitum *Cum comperto*, 15 iul. 1961, 4 (AAS 53 [1961] 571); PAULUS PP. VI, Ep. *Summi Dei*, 4 nov. 1963 (AAS 55 [1963] 987–988); OT 6; PAULUS PP. VI, Enc. *Sacerdotalis caelibatus*, 24 iun. 1967, 62–72 (AAS 59 [1967] 682–686); RFS 11, 39; SCIC Normae, 11 apr. 1974, 38

to a major seminary only those who are judged qualified to dedicate themselves permanently to the sacred ministries; he is to consider their human, moral, spiritual, and intellectual qualities, their physical and psychic health, and their correct intention.

§2. Before they are accepted, they must submit documents of the reception of baptism and confirmation and any other things required by the prescripts of the program of priestly formation.

§3. If it concerns admitting those who were dismissed from another seminary or religious institute, testimony of the respective superior is also required, especially concerning the cause for their dismissal or departure.

CAN. 242 §1. Each nation is to have a program of priestly formation which is to be established by the conference of bishops, attentive to the norms issued by the supreme authority of the Church, and which is to be approved by the Holy See. This program is to be adapted to new circumstances, also with the approval of the Holy See, and is to define the main principles of the instruction to be given in the seminary and general norms adapted to the pastoral needs of each region or province.

§2. All seminaries, both diocesan and interdiocesan, are to observe the norms of the program mentioned in §1.

CAN. 243 In addition, each seminary is to have its own rule, approved by the diocesan

Episcopo dioecesano admittantur tantummodo ii qui, attentis eorum dotibus humanis et moralibus, spiritualibus et intellectualibus, eorum valetudine physica et psychica necnon recta voluntate, habiles aestimantur qui ministeriis sacris perpetuo sese dedicent.

§2. Antequam recipiantur, documenta exhibere debent de susceptis baptismo et confirmatione aliaque quae secundum praescripta institutionis sacerdotalis Rationis requiruntur.

§3. Si agatur de iis admittendis, qui ex alieno seminario vel instituto religioso dimissi fuerint, requiritur insuper testimonium respectivi superioris praesertim de causa eorum dimissionis vel discessus.

CAN. 242 §1. In singulis nationibus habeatur institutionis sacerdotalis Ratio, ab Episcoporum conferentia, attentis quidem normis a suprema Ecclesiae auctoritate latis, statuenda et a Sancta Sede approbanda, novis quoque adiunctis, approbante item Sancta Sede, accommodanda, qua institutionis in seminario tradendae definiantur summa principia atque normae generales necessitatibus pastoralibus uniuscuiusque regionis vel provinciae, aptatae.

§2. Normae Rationis, de qua in §1, serventur in omnibus seminariis, tum dioecesanis tum interdioecesanis.

CAN. 243 Habeat insuper unumquodque seminarium ordinationem

241 §2: c. 1363 §2

241 §3: c. 1363 §3; SCR et SCSSU Decr. *Consiliis initis*, 25 iul. 1941 (AAS 33 [1941] 371); SCSSU Resp., 8 mar. 1945; SCSSU Litt. circ., 12 ian. 1950; SCSSU Decr. *Sollemne habet*, 12 iul. 1957 (AAS 49 [1957] 640); SCPF Resp., 28 oct. 1957; SCPF Resp., 11 ian. 1958; SCSSU Resp., 6 feb. 1958; SCSSU Resp., 19 mar. 1963; Scssu Resp., 12 apr. 1967

242 §1: OT 1; PAULUS PP. VI, All., 27 mar. 1969

(AAS 61 [1969] 253–256); SCIC Litt. circ., 12 oct. 1966; RFS 1; DPME 191

242 §2: OT 1; RFS 2

243: c. 1357 §3; SCSSU Litt. circ., 27 sep. 1960, II, 4; OT 7–11; PAULUS PP. VI, Enc. *Sacerdotalis caelibatus*, 24 iun. 1967, 66 (AAS 59 [1967] 683); SCIC Litt. circ., 23 maii 1968; RFS 2, 25; DPME 191; SCIC Normae, 11 apr. 1974, 74; SCIC Litt. circ., 6 ian. 1980, p. 20

bishop, or, if it is an interdiocesan seminary, by the bishops involved, which is to adapt the norms of the program of priestly formation to particular circumstances and especially to determine more precisely the points of discipline which pertain to the daily life of the students and the order of the entire seminary.

CAN. 244 The spiritual formation and doctrinal instruction of the students in a seminary are to be arranged harmoniously and so organized that each student, according to his character, acquires the spirit of the gospel and a close relationship with Christ along with appropriate human maturity.

CAN. 245 §1. Through their spiritual formation, students are to become equipped to exercise the pastoral ministry fruitfully and are to be formed in a missionary spirit; they are to learn that ministry always carried out in living faith and charity fosters their own sanctification. They also are to learn to cultivate those virtues which are valued highly in human relations so that they are able to achieve an appropriate integration between human and supernatural goods.

§2. Students are so to be formed that, imbued with love of the Church of Christ, they are

propriam, ab Episcopo dioecesano aut, si de seminario interdioecesano agatur, ab Episcopis quorum interest, probatam, qua normae institutionis sacerdotalis Rationis adiunctis particularibus accommodentur, ac pressius determinentur praesertim disciplinae capita quae ad alumnorum cotidianam vitam et totius seminarii ordinem spectant.

CAN. 244 Alumnorum in seminario formatio spiritualis et institutio doctrinalis harmonice componantur, atque ad id ordinentur, ut iidem iuxta uniuscuiusque indolem una cum debita maturitate humana spiritum Evangelii et arctam cum Christo necessitudinem acquirant.

CAN. 245 §1. Per formationem spiritualem alumni idonei fiant ad ministerium pastorale fructuose exercendum et ad spiritum missionalem efformentur, discentes ministerium expletum semper in fide viva et in caritate ad propriam sanctificationem conferre; itemque illas excolere discant virtutes quae in hominum consortione pluris fiunt, ita quidem ut ad aptam conciliationem inter bona humana et supernaturalia pervenire valeant.

§2. Ita formentur alumni ut, amore Ecclesiae Christi imbuti, Pontifici Romano Petri

244: Pius PP. XI, Enc. *Ad catholici sacerdotii*, 20 dec. 1935 (AAS 28 [1936] 23–33); SCSSU Litt. circ., 2 feb. 1945; SCSSU Ep., 7 mar. 1950 (AAS 42 [1950] 836–840); Pius PP. XII, Adh. Ap. *Menti nostrae*, 23 sep. 1950, III (AAS 42 [1950] 689–691); SCSSU Litt. circ., 5 iun. 1959; Ioannes PP. XXIII, All., 29 iul. 1961 (AAS 53 [1961] 559–565); OT 4, 8, 11; RFS 14, 44, 45, 51, 76, 91; DPME 195; SCIC Litt. circ., 22 feb. 1976, 22, 25, 38, 73; SCIC Litt. circ., 6 ian. 1980

245 §1: Pius PP. XII, Adh. Ap. *Menti nostrae*, 23 sep. 1950, III (AAS 42 [1950] 689–690); SCSSU Litt. circ., 27 sep. 1960; Ioannes PP. XXIII, All., 29 iul. 1961 (AAS 53 [1961] 559–565); Paulus PP. VI, Ep.

Summi Dei, 4 nov. 1963 (AAS 55 [1963] 979–995); OT 8, 9, 11; PO 3, 14; Paulus PP. VI, Enc. *Sacerdotalis caelibatus*, 24 iun. 1967, 70, 71 (AAS 59 [1967] 684–686); RFS 14, 44, 45, 51, 58, 96; SCGE Litt. circ., 17 maii 1970; SCIC Normae, 11 apr. 1974, 81; SCIC Instr. *In ecclesiasticam*, 3 iun. 1979; SCIC Litt. circ., 6 ian. 1980

245 §2: c. 127; Pius PP. XII, All., 24 iun. 1939 (AAS 31 [1939] 250–251); Pius PP. XII, Exhortatio *In auspicando*, 28 iun. 1948 (AAS 40 [1948] 374–376); Pius PP. XII, Adh. Ap. *Menti nostrae*, 23 sep. 1950 (AAS 42 [1950] 690); OT 9, 11; PO 7, 8, 15; RFS 46, 47, 49; SCIC Normae, 11 apr. 1974, 71; SCIC Litt. circ., 6 ian. 1980

bound by humble and filial charity to the Roman Pontiff, the successor of Peter, are attached to their own bishop as faithful co-workers, and work together with their brothers. Through common life in the seminary and through relationships of friendship and of association cultivated with others, they are to be prepared for fraternal union with the diocesan *presbyterium* whose partners they will be in the service of the Church.

CAN. 246 §1. The eucharistic celebration is to be the center of the entire life of a seminary in such a way that, sharing in the very love of Christ, the students daily draw strength of spirit for apostolic work and for their spiritual life especially from this richest of sources.

§2. They are to be formed in the celebration of the liturgy of the hours by which the ministers of God pray to God in the name of the Church for all the people entrusted to them, and indeed, for the whole world.

§3. The veneration of the Blessed Virgin Mary, including the marian rosary, mental prayer, and other exercises of piety are to be fostered; through these, students are to acquire a spirit of prayer and gain strength in their vocation.

§4. Students are to become accustomed to

successori humili et filiali caritate devinciantur, proprio Episcopo tamquam fidi cooperatores adhaereant et sociam cum fratribus operam praestent; per vitam in seminario communem atque per amicitiae coniunctionisque necessitudinem cum aliis excultam praeparentur ad fraternam unionem cum dioecesano presbyterio, cuius in Ecclesiae servitio erunt consortes.

CAN. 246 §1. Celebratio Eucharistica centrum sit totius vitae seminarii, ita ut cotidie alumni, ipsam Christi caritatem participantes, animi robur pro apostolico labore et pro vita sua spirituali praesertim ex hoc ditissimo fonte hauriant.

§2. Efformentur ad celebrationem liturgiae horarum, qua Dei ministri, nomine Ecclesiae pro toto populo sibi commisso, immo pro universo mundo, Deum deprecantur.

§3. Foveantur cultus Beatae Mariae Virginis etiam per mariale rosarium, oratio mentalis aliaque pietatis exercitia, quibus alumni spiritum orationis acquirant atque vocationis suae robur consequantur.

§4. Ad sacramentum paenitentiae fre-

246 §1: c. 1367, 1° et 2°; SCSSU Instr. *Postquam Pius,* 8 dec. 1938; Pius PP. XII, All., 24 iun. 1939 (AAS 31 [1939] 249); Pius PP. XII, Adh. Ap. *Menti nostrae,* 23 sep. 1950, III (AAS 42 [1950] 666); Ioannes PP. XXIII, All., 29 iul. 1961 (AAS 53 [1961] 563); IOe 14, 15; SCSSU Instr. *Doctrina et exemplo,* 25 dec. 1965, 23–25; OT 8; RFS 52; SCIC Instr. *In ecclesiasticam,* 3 iun. 1979, 22–27; SCIC Litt. circ., 6 iun. 1980, II, 2

246 §2: SCSSU Litt. circ., 2 feb. 1945; Pius PP. XII, Adh. Ap. *Menti Nostrae,* 23 sep. 1950, I (AAS 42 [1950] 669–671); IOe 16; SCSSU Instr. *Doctrina et exemplo,* 25 dec. 1965, 26–31; OT 8; RFS 53; SCIC Instr. *In ecclesiasticam,* 3 iun. 1979, 28–31; SCIC Litt. circ., 6 ian. 1980, II, 1

246 §3: c. 1367, 1°; Pius PP. XII, Adh. Ap. *Menti*

Nostrae, 23 sep. 1950 (AAS 42 [1950] 672–673, 689); Ioannes PP. XXIII, All., 29 iul. 1961, 2 (AAS 53 [1961] 563–564); LG 67; OT 8; RFS 54; Paulus PP. VI, Adh. Ap. *Marialis cultus,* 2 feb. 1974, 42–55 (AAS 66 [1974] 152–162); SCIC Normae, 11 apr. 1974, 75–78; SCIC Instr. *In ecclesiasticam,* 3 iun. 1979, 10–11; SCIC Litt. circ., 6 ian. 1980

246 §4: c. 1367, 2°; SCSSU Litt., 8 oct. 1921, II; SCSSU Litt., 26 maii 1928; Pius PP. XII, Enc. *Mystici Corporis,* 29 iun. 1943 (AAS 35 [1943] 235); Pius PP. XII, Adh. Ap. *Menti Nostrae,* 23 sep. 1950 (AAS 42 [1950] 674); Ioannes PP. XXIII, All., 29 iul. 1961 (AAS 53 [1961] 559–565); RFS 45, 55; SCIC Instr. *In ecclesiasticam,* 3 iun. 1979, 35–36; SCIC Litt. circ., 6 ian. 1980

approach the sacrament of penance frequently; it is also recommended that each have a director of his spiritual life whom he has freely chosen and to whom he can confidently open his conscience.

§5. Each year students are to make a spiritual retreat.

CAN. 247 §1. Students are to be prepared through suitable education to observe the state of celibacy and are to learn to honor it as a special gift of God.

§2. They are duly to be informed of the duties and burdens which are proper to sacred ministers of the Church; no difficulty of the priestly life is to be omitted.

CAN. 248 The doctrinal instruction given is to be directed so that students acquire an extensive and solid learning in the sacred disciplines along with a general culture appropriate to the necessities of place and time, in such way that, grounded in their own faith and nourished thereby, they are able to announce in a suitable way the teaching of the gospel to the people of their own time in a manner adapted to their understanding.

CAN. 249 The program of priestly formation is to provide that students not only are carefully taught their native language but also

quenter accedere assuescant alumni, et commendatur ut unusquisque habeat moderatorem suae vitae spiritualis libere quidem electum, cui confidenter conscientiam aperire possit.

§5. Singulis annis alumni exercitiis spiritualibus vacent.

CAN. 247 §1. Ad servandum statum caelibatus congrua educatione praeparentur, eumque ut peculiare Dei donum in honore habere discant.

§2. De officiis et oneribus, quae ministris sacris Ecclesiae propria sunt, alumni debite reddantur certiores, nulla vitae sacerdotalis difficultate reticita.

CAN. 248 Institutio doctrinalis tradenda eo spectat, ut alumni, una cum cultura generali necessitatibus loci ac temporis consentanea, amplam atque solidam acquirant in disciplinis sacris doctrinam, ita ut, propria fide ibi fundata et inde nutrita, Evangelii doctrinam hominibus sui temporis apte, ratione eorundem ingenio accommodata, nuntiare valeant.

CAN. 249 Institutionis sacerdotalis Ratione provideatur ut alumni non tantum accurate linguam patriam edoceantur, sed eti-

246 §5: c. 1367, 4°; Pius PP. XII, Adh. Ap. *Menti Nostrae*, 23 sep. 1950 (AAS 42 [1950] 674–675); RFS 56

247 §1: Pius PP. XII, All., 24 iun. 1939 (AAS 31 [1939] 249–250); Pius PP. XII, Adh. Ap. *Menti nostrae*, 23 sep. 1950 (AAS 42 [1950] 690–691); Pius PP. XII, Enc. *Sacra virginitas*, 25 mar. 1954 (AAS 46 [1954] 161–191); Ioannes PP. XXIII, All., 26 iun. 1960 (AAS 52 [1960] 226); OT 10; PO 16; Paulus PP. VI, Enc. *Sacerdotalis caelibatus*, 24 iun. 1967 (AAS 59 [1967] 657–697); Sec Litt. circ., 2 feb. 1969; RFS 48; Paulus PP. VI, Ep. *Le dichiarazioni*, 2 feb. 1970 (AAS 62 [1970] 98–103); UT 915–918; SCIC Normae, 11 apr. 1974; Ioannes Paulus PP. II, Litt. Ap. *Novo incipiente*, 8 apr. 1979, 8, 9 (AAS 71 [1979] 405–409)

247 §2: OT 9; Paulus PP. VI, Enc. *Sacerdotalis*

caelibatus, 24 iun. 1967, 69 (AAS 59 [1967] 684); RFS Introductio, 4; SCIC Normae, 11 apr. 1974, 83

248: Pius PP. XII, All., 24 iun. 1939 (AAS 31 [1939] 247); SCSSU Ep., 7 mar. 1950 (AAS 42 [1950] 836–840); Pius PP. XII, Adh. Ap. *Menti nostrae*, 23 sep. 1950, III (AAS 42 [1950] 681–694); Pius PP. XII, All., 17 oct. 1953 (AAS 45 [1953] 682–689); Ioannes PP. XXIII, All., 29 iul. 1961 (AAS 53 [1961] 559–565); Paulus PP. VI, Ep. *Summi Dei*, 4 nov. 1963 (AAS 55 [1963] 979–995); OT 13–18; AG 1–6; GS 58, 62; DPME 195; RFS 59; SPNC Nota, 10 iul. 1970; SCIC Litt. circ., 22 feb. 1976, 4–16, 117

249: c. 1364, 2°; Pius PP. XI, Ep. *Officiorum omnium*, 1 aug. 1922 (AAS 14 [1922] 449–458); Pius PP. XI, m. p. *Latinarum litterarum*, 20 oct. 1924 (AAS 16

understand Latin well and have a suitable understanding of those foreign languages which seem necessary or useful for their formation or for the exercise of pastoral ministry.

CAN. 250 The philosophical and theological studies which are organized in the seminary itself can be pursued either successively or conjointly, in accord with the program of priestly formation. These studies are to encompass at least six full years in such a way that the time dedicated to philosophical disciplines equals two full years and to theological studies four full years.

CAN. 251 Philosophical instruction must be grounded in the perennially valid philosophical heritage and also take into account philosophical investigation over the course of time. It is to be taught in such a way that it perfects the human development of the students, sharpens their minds, and makes them better able to pursue theological studies.

CAN. 252 §1. Theological instruction is to be imparted in the light of faith and under the

am linguam latinam bene calleant necnon congruam habeant cognitionem alienarum linguarum, quarum scientia ad eorum formationem aut ad ministerium pastorale exercendum necessaria vel utilis videatur.

CAN. 250 Quae in ipso seminario philosophica et theologica studia ordinantur, aut successive aut coniuncte peragi possunt, iuxta institutionis sacerdotalis Rationem; eadem completum saltem sexennium complectantur, ita quidem ut tempus philosophicis disciplinis dedicandum integrum biennium, studiis vero theologicis integrum quadriennium adaequet.

CAN. 251 Philosophica institutio, quae innixa sit oportet patrimonio philosophico perenniter valido, et rationem etiam habeat philosophicae investigationis progredientis aetatis, ita tradatur, ut alumnorum formationem humanam perficiat, mentis aciem provehat, eosque ad studia theologica peragenda aptiores reddat.

CAN. 252 §1. Institutio theologica, in lumine fidei, sub Magisterii ductu, ita imper-

[1924] 417–420); Pius PP. XII, Enc. *Divino afflante Spiritu*, 30 sep. 1943 (AAS 35 [1943] 306–307); SCSSU Ep., 27 oct. 1957 (AAS 50 [1958] 292–297); Ioannes PP. XXIII, Const. Ap. *Veterum sapientia*, 22 feb. 1962 (AAS 54 [1962] 129–135); SCSSU Instr. *Sacrum latinae linguae*, 22 apr. 1962, cap. III, art. I–II, cap. V (AAS 54 [1962] 339–368); Paulus PP. VI, Ep. *Summi Dei*, 4 nov. 1963 (AAS 55 [1963] 979–995); Paulus PP. VI, m.p. *Studia latinitatis*, 22 feb. 1964 (AAS 56 [1964] 225–231); OT 13; ES I, 3; RFS 66, 67

250: c. 1365 §§1 et 2; SCSSU Ep., 26 apr. 1920; SCSSU Ep., 2 oct. 1921, III; Benedictus PP. XV, Ep. *Saepe Nobis*, 30 nov. 1921 (AAS 13 [1921] 554–559); Pius PP. XI, Ep. Ap. *Officiorum omnium*, 1 aug. 1922 (AAS 14 [1922] 449–451); RFS 60, 61, 70, 76; SCIC Litt. circ., 22 feb. 1976, 129, 132

251: SCSSU Ep., 26 apr. 1920, VIII; SCSSU Ep., 2 oct. 1921, III B; SCSSU Litt. circ., 1 iul. 1958; Pius PP. XI, Ep. Ap. *Officiorum omnium*, 1 aug. 1922 (AAS 14 [1922] 454); Pius PP. XI, Enc. *Studiorum Ducem*, 29 iun. 1923 (AAS 15 [1923] 307–329); Pius PP. XII, Enc.

Humani generis, 12 aug. 1950 (AAS 42 [1950] 561–578); Pius PP. XII, All., 17 oct. 1953 (AAS 45 [1953] 682–690); SCSSU Litt. circ., 1 iul. 1958; Paulus PP. VI, Ep. *Summi Dei*, 4 nov. 1963 (AAS 55 [1963] 979–995); OT 15; GE 10; SCSSU Resp., 20 dec. 1965; Paulus PP. VI, All., 10 sep. 1965 (AAS 57 [1965] 788–792); RFS 70–75; SCIC Litt. circ., 20 ian. 1972; Paulus PP. VI, Ep. Ap. *Lumen Ecclesiae*, 20 nov. 1974 (AAS 66 [1974] 673–702); SCIC Litt. circ., 22 feb. 1976, 48–53; SCh 79, 80; Ioannes Paulus PP. II, All., 17 nov. 1979 (AAS 71 [1979] 1472–1483); Ioannes Paulus PP. II, All., 15 dec. 1979 (AAS 71 [1979] 1538–1549)

252 §1: SCSSU Ep., 26 apr. 1920, IX; SCSSU Ep., 2 oct. 1921, III C; Pius PP. XII, All., 24 iun. 1939 (AAS 31 [1939] 247–248); Pius PP. XII, Adh. Ap. *Menti nostrae*, 23 sep. 1950 (AAS 42 [1950] 688); OT 16; DV 2–4; 14–17; 25; SCIC Normae, 20 maii 1968, 30 notula 12; RFS 76; SCIC Instr. *Tra i molteplici*, 22 feb. 1976; SCh 66–68

leadership of the magisterium in such a way that the students understand the entire Catholic doctrine grounded in divine revelation, gain nourishment for their own spiritual life, and are able properly to announce and safeguard it in the exercise of the ministry.

§2. Students are to be instructed in sacred scripture with special diligence in such a way that they acquire a comprehensive view of the whole of sacred scripture.

§3. There are to be classes in dogmatic theology, always grounded in the written word of God together with sacred tradition; through these, students are to learn to penetrate more intimately the mysteries of salvation, especially with St. Thomas as a teacher. There are also to be classes in moral and pastoral theology, canon law, liturgy, ecclesiastical history, and other auxiliary and special disciplines, according to the norm of the prescripts of the program of priestly formation.

CAN. 253 §1. The bishop or bishops concerned are to appoint to the function of teacher in philosophical, theological, and juridic disciplines only those who are outstanding in virtue

tiatur, ut alumni integram doctrinam catholicam, divina Revelatione innixam, cognoscant, propriae vitae spiritualis reddant alimentum eamque, in ministerio exercendo, rite annuntiare ac tueri valeant.

§2. In sacra Scriptura peculiari diligentia erudiantur alumni, ita ut totius sacrae Scripturae conspectum acquirant.

§3. Lectiones habeantur theologiae dogmaticae, verbo Dei scripto una cum sacra Traditione semper innixae, quarum ope alumni mysteria salutis, s. Thoma praesertim magistro, intimius penetrare addiscant, itemque lectiones theologiae moralis et pastoralis, iuris canonici, liturgiae, historiae ecclesiasticae, necnon aliarum disciplinarum, auxiliarium atque specialium, ad normam praescriptorum institutionis sacerdotalis Rationis.

CAN. 253 §1. Ad magistri munus in disciplinis philosophicis, theologicis et iuridicis, ab Episcopo aut ab Episcopis, quorum interest, ii tantum nominentur qui, virtutibus

---

252 §2: c. 1365 §2; SCSSU Ep., 26 apr. 1920, IX b; SCSSU Ep., 25 ian. 1924; Pius PP. XI, m. p. *Bibliorum scientiam,* 27 apr. 1924 (AAS 16 [1924] 180–182); Pius PP. XII, Enc. *Divino afflante Spiritu,* 30 sep. 1943 (AAS 35 [1943] 301, 321–322); Pontificia Commissio Biblica Instr. *Sanctissimus Dominus,* 13 maii 1950 (AAS 42 [1950] 495–505); SCSO Monitum *Biblicarum disciplinarum,* 20 iun. 1961 (AAS 53 [1961] 507); Pontificia Commissio Biblica Instr. *Sancta Mater Ecclesia,* 21 apr. 1964 (AAS 56 [1964] 712–718); OT 16; RFS 78; SCIC Litt. circ., 22 feb. 1976, 79–84

252 §3: c. 1365 §§2 et 3; SCSSU Decr. *Cum novum iuris,* 7 aug. 1917 (AAS 9 [1917] 439); SCSSU Ep., 26 apr. 1920, IX; SCSSU Ep., 2 oct. 1921, III C; Pius PP. XI, Ep. *Officiorum omnium,* 1 aug. 1922 (AAS 14 [1922] 449–458); SCSSU Ep., 8 sep. 1926 (AAS 18 [1926] 453–455); Pius PP. XI, Const. Ap. *Divini cultus,* 20 dec. 1928 (AAS 21 [1929] 33–41); SCSSU Litt.,

28 aug. 1929 (AAS 22 [1930] 146–148); SCSSU Litt., 21 dec. 1944 (AAS 37 [1945] 173–176); SCSSU Ep., 15 aug. 1949 (AAS 41 [1949] 618–619); Pius PP. XII, Enc. *Musicae sacrae,* 25 dec. 1955, IV (AAS 48 [1956] 5–25); SCSO Instr. *Contra doctrinam,* 2 feb. 1956 (AAS 48 [1956] 144–145); SCSSU Litt. circ., 25 maii 1961; Ioannes PP. XXIII, Ep. *Iucunda laudatio,* 8 dec. 1961 (AAS 53 [1961] 810–813); Paulus PP. VI, Ep. *Summi Dei,* 4 nov. 1963 (AAS 55 [1963] 979–995); SC passim; IOe 11, 12, 14; OT 16; DV 24; SCSSU Instr. *Doctrina et exemplo,* 25 dec. 1965; SCIC Litt. circ., 2 apr. 1975; SCIC Instr. *Tra i molteplici,* 22 feb. 1976, 85–115; SCIC Instr. *In ecclesiasticam,* 3 iun. 1979, 1, 43–60, Appendix

253 §1: c. 1366 § 3; Pius PP. XI, m. p. *Bibliorum scientiam,* 27 apr. 1924 (AAS 16 [1924] 180–182); Ssap 362; OT 5; RFS 32–35; DPME 192; SCIC Instr. *Tra i molteplici,* 22 feb. 1976, 118–119

and have obtained a doctorate or licentiate from a university or faculty recognized by the Holy See.

§2. Care is to be taken that different teachers are appointed to teach sacred scripture, dogmatic theology, moral theology, liturgy, philosophy, canon law, ecclesiastical history, and other disciplines which must be taught according to their proper methodology.

§3. The authority mentioned in §1 is to remove a teacher who is gravely deficient in his or her function.

CAN. 254 §1. In giving instruction in their disciplines, teachers are to have a constant concern for the intimate unity and harmony of the entire doctrine of the faith so that students find that they learn one science. For this to be realized more suitably, there is to be someone in the seminary who directs the entire curriculum of studies.

§2. Students are to be instructed in such a way that they also become qualified to examine questions by their own appropriate research and with scientific methodology; therefore, there are to be assignments in which the students learn to pursue certain studies through their own efforts under the direction of the teachers.

CAN. 255 Although the entire formation of students in the seminary has a pastoral purpose, strictly pastoral instruction is to be organized through which students learn the principles and skills which, attentive also to the needs of place and time, pertain to the exercise of the

praestantes, laurea doctorali aut licentia potiti sunt in universitate studiorum aut facultate a Sancta Sede recognita.

§2. Curetur ut distincti totidem nominentur magistri qui doceant sacram Scripturam, theologiam dogmaticam, theologiam moralem, liturgiam, philosophiam, ius canonicum, historiam ecclesiasticam, aliasque, quae propria methodo tradendae sunt, disciplinas.

§3. Magister qui a munere suo graviter deficiat, ab auctoritate, de qua in §1, amoveatur.

CAN. 254 §1. Magistri in disciplinis tradendis de intima universae doctrinae fidei unitate et harmonia iugiter solliciti sint, ut unam scientiam alumni se discere experiantur; quo aptius id obtineatur, adsit in seminario qui integram studiorum ordinationem moderetur.

§2. Ita alumni edoceantur, ut et ipsi habiles fiant ad quaestiones aptis investigationibus propriis et scientifica methodo examinandas; habeantur igitur exercitationes, in quibus, sub moderamine magistrorum, alumni proprio labore studia quaedem persolvere discant.

CAN. 255 Licet universa alumnorum in seminario formatio pastoralem finem persequatur, institutio stricte pastoralis in eodem ordinetur, qua alumni principia et artes addiscant quae, attentis quoque loci ac temporis necessitatibus, ad ministerium Dei popu-

253 §2: c. 1366 §3; RFS 32
253 §3: RFS 33
254 §1: Ssap 363; SC 16; OT 5, 17; RFS 27, 63, 77, 90; SCIC Instr. *Tra i molteplici,* 22 feb. 1976, 121–127
254 §2: OT 17; RFS 38, 91; SCIC Instr. *Tra i*

molteplici, 22 feb. 1976, 71
255: c. 1365 §3; SCSSU Ep., 26 apr. 1920, IX D; Ssap 363; OT 4, 19; RFS 79, 94; SCIC Instr. *Tra i molteplici,* 22 feb. 1976, 102–106

ministry of teaching, sanctifying, and governing the people of God.

CAN. 256 §1. Students are to be instructed diligently in those things which in a particular manner pertain to the sacred ministry, especially in catechetical and homiletic skills, in divine worship and particularly the celebration of the sacraments, in relationships with people, even non-Catholics or non-believers, in the administration of a parish, and in the fulfillment of other functions.

§2. Students are to be instructed about the needs of the universal Church in such a way that they have solicitude for the promotion of vocations and for missionary, ecumenical, and other more urgent questions, including social ones.

CAN. 257 §1. The instruction of students is to provide that they have solicitude not only for the particular church in whose service they are to be incardinated but also for the universal Church, and that they show themselves

lum docendi, sanctificandi et regendi exercendum pertineant.

CAN. 256 §1. Diligenter instruantur alumni in iis quae peculiari ratione ad sacrum ministerium spectant, praesertim in arte cathechetica et homiletica exercenda, in cultu divino peculiarique modo in sacramentis celebrandis, in commercio cum hominibus, etiam non catholicis vel non credentibus, habendo, in paroecia administranda atque in ceteris muneribus adimplendis.

§2. Edoceantur alumni de universae Ecclesiae necessitatibus, ita ut sollicitudinem habeant de vocationibus promovendis, de quaestionibus missionalibus, oecumenicis necnon de aliis, socialibus quoque, urgentioribus.

CAN. 257 §1. Alumnorum institutioni ita provideatur, ut non tantum Ecclesiae particularis in cuius servitio incardinentur, sed universae quoque Ecclesiae sollicitudinem habeant, atque paratos se exhibeant Ecclesi-

256 §1: SCC Normae, 28 iun. 1917 34–37 (AAS 9 [1917] 328–334); SCSSU Ep., 8 sep. 1926 (AAS 18 [1926] 453–455); SCSSU Litt., 28 aug. 1929 (AAS 22 [1930] 146–148); SCSSU Instr. *La formazione*, 21 dec. 1944 (AAS 37 [1945] 173–176); SCSSU Ep., 15 aug. 1949 (AAS 41 [1949] 618–619); SCSSU Litt. circ., 3 sep. 1963; Ssap 364; OT 20; SCSSU Instr. *Doctrina et exemplo*, 25 dec. 1965, 44–69; SPNC Instr. *Documentum quod*, 28 aug. 1968, II/1, 1 (AAS 60 [1968] 701–702); SCpC Instr. *Peregrinans in terra*, 30 apr. 1969, II, 3, B, a (AAS 61 [1969] 373–374); RFS 518, 94, 95; SCIC Instr. *In ecclesiasticam*, 3 iun. 1979, 59

256 §2: PIUS PP. XI, Enc. *Rerum Orientalium*, 8 sep. 1928 (AAS 20 [1928] 284–285); SCSSU Litt., 28 aug. 1929 (AAS 22 [1930] 146–148); SCSSU Ep., 10 mar. 1932; SCSSU Litt. circ., 27 ian. 1935; PIUS PP. XI, Enc. *Divini Redemptoris*, 19 mar. 1937 (AAS 29 [1937] 97–99); SCPF Decr. *Piae Unionis*, 14 apr. 1937 (AAS 29 [1937] 437, 440); PIUS PP. XII, Adh. Ap. *Menti nostrae*, 23 sep. 1950 (AAS 42 [1950] 696–697); IOANNES PP. XXIII, Enc. *Mater et Magistra*, 15 maii 1961 (AAS 53 [1961] 453–454); SCSSU Litt. circ., 25 maii 1961; CD

6; OT 20; AG 39; PAULUS PP. VI, Enc. *Populorum progressio*, 26 mar. 1967 (AAS 59 [1967] 257–299); RFS 69, 80, 96; SCUF Directorium, 16 apr. 1970 (AAS 62 [1970] 705–724); SCGE Litt. circ., 17 maii 1970; PAULUS PP. VI, Litt. Ap. *Octogesima adveniens*, 14 maii 1971 (AAS 63 [1971] 401–403); SE *Convenientes ex universo*, 30 nov. 1971 (AAS 63 [1971] 923–926); PONTIFICIA COMMISSIO DE SPIRITUALI MIGRATORUM ATQUE ITINERANTIUM CURA Litt. circ., 26 maii 1978 (AAS 70 [1978] 357–359); IOANNES PAULUS PP. II, Enc. *Redemptor hominis*, 4 mar. 1979 (AAS 71 [1979] 282–285)

257 §1: SCC Litt. circ., 24 oct. 1951 (AAS 44 [1952] 231–232); PIUS PP. XII, Ep. *Ad Ecclesiam Christi*, 29 iun. 1955 (AAS 47 [1955] 540–543); PAULUS PP. VI, All., 9 iul. 1963 (AAS 55 [1963] 684–685); CD 6; OT 20; PO 10; PAULUS PP. VI, All., 3 iul. 1966 (AAS 58 [1966] 636–639); ES I, 3 §1; RFS 96; SCGE Litt. circ., 17 maii 1970; PONTIFICIA COMMISSIO DE SPIRITUALI MIGRATORUM ATQUE ITINERANTIUM CURA Normae, 29 iun. 1974; PA 23

prepared to devote themselves to particular churches which are in grave need.

§2. The diocesan bishop is to take care that clerics intending to move from their own particular church to a particular church of another region are suitably prepared to exercise the sacred ministry there, that is, that they learn the language of the region and understand its institutions, social conditions, usages, and customs.

CAN. 258 In order that students also learn the art of exercising the apostolate in practice, during the course of studies and especially during times of vacation they are to be initiated into pastoral practice by means of appropriate activities, determined by judgment of the ordinary, adapted to the age of the students and the conditions of the places, and always under the direction of a skilled priest.

CAN. 259 §1. The diocesan bishop or, for an interdiocesan seminary, the bishops involved are competent to decide those things which pertain to the above-mentioned governance and administration of the seminary.

§2. The diocesan bishop or, for an interdiocesan seminary, the bishops involved are to visit the seminary frequently, to watch over the formation of their own students as well as the philosophical and theological instruction taught in the seminary, and to keep themselves informed about the vocation, character, piety, and progress of the students, especially

is particularibus, quarum gravis urgeat necessitas, sese devovere.

§2. Curet Episcopus dioecesanus ut clerici, a propria Ecclesia particulari ad Ecclesiam particularem alterius regionis transmigrare intendentes, apte praeparentur ad ibidem sacrum ministerium exercendum, ut scilicet et linguam regionis addiscant, et eiusdem institutorum, condicionum socialium, usuum et consuetudinum intellegentiam habeant.

CAN. 258 Ut apostolatus exercendi artem in opere ipso etiam addiscant, alumni, studiorum curriculo decurrente, praesertim vero feriarum tempore, praxi pastorali initientur per opportunas, sub moderamine semper sacerdotis periti, exercitationes, alumnorum aetati et locorum condicioni aptatas, de iudicio Ordinarii determinandas.

CAN. 259 §1. Episcopo dioecesano aut, si de seminario interdioecesano agatur, Episcopis quorum interest, competit, quae ad seminarii superius regimen et administrationem spectant, decernere.

§2. Episcopus dioecesanus aut, si de seminario interdioecesano agatur, Episcopi, quorum interest, frequenter seminarium ipsi visitent, in formationem suorum alumnorum necnon in institutionem, quae in eodem tradatur, philosophicam et theologicam invigilent, et de alumnorum vocatione, indole, pietate ac profectu cognitionem sibi compar-

---

257 §2: PIUS PP. XII, Exhortatio *In auspicando*, 28 iun. 1948 (AAS 40 [1948] 375); PIUS PP. XII, Enc. *Evangelii praecones*, 2 iun. 1951 (AAS 43 [1951] 507); SCC Litt. circ., 24 oct. 1951 (AAS 44 [1952] 231–232); CD 6; OT 20; AG 38; PO 10; ES I, 3 §§1 et 3; RFS 67; PA 23

258: Ssap 364; OT 21; RFS 97–99; DPME 195; SCIC Normae, 11 apr. 1974, 88

259 §1: c. 1357 §1; SCSSU Litt., 9 oct. 1921; BENEDICTUS PP. XV, Ep. *Saepe Nobis*, 30 nov. 1921 (AAS 13 [1921] 557); SCSSU Normae, 7 mar. 1929; SCSSU Litt. circ., 6 iul. 1966; DPME 191

259 §2: c. 1357 §2; SCSSU Ep., 26 apr. 1920, II; BENEDICTUS PP. XV, Ep. *Saepe Nobis*, 30 nov. 1921 (AAS 13 [1921] 557); SCSSU Litt. circ., 25 iul. 1928; SCSSU Litt. circ., 6 iul. 1966; RFS 22; DPME 191, 195

with a view to the conferral of sacred ordination.

CAN. 260 In carrying out their proper functions, all must obey the rector, to whom it belongs to care for the daily supervision of the seminary according to the norm of the program of priestly formation and of the rule of the seminary.

CAN. 261 §1. The rector of a seminary and, under his authority, the moderators and teachers for their part are to take care that the students observe exactly the norms prescribed by the program of priestly formation and by the rule of the seminary.

§2. The rector of a seminary and the director of studies are carefully to provide that the teachers properly perform their function according to the prescripts of the program of priestly formation and of the rule of the seminary.

CAN. 262 A seminary is to be exempt from parochial governance. The rector of the seminary or his delegate fulfills the office of pastor for all those who are in the seminary, except for matrimonial matters and without prejudice to the prescript of can. 985.

CAN. 263 The diocesan bishop or, for an interdiocesan seminary, the bishops involved in a way determined by them through common counsel must take care that provision is made for the establishment and maintenance of the seminary, the support of the students, the remuneration of the teachers, and the other needs of the seminary.

CAN. 264 §1. In addition to the offering mentioned in can. 1266, a bishop can impose a

ent, maxime intuitu sacrarum ordinationum conferendarum.

CAN. 260 Rectori, cuius est cotidianum moderamen curare seminarii, ad normam quidem institutionis sacerdotalis Rationis ac seminarii ordinationis, omnes in propriis muneribus adimplendis obtemperare debent.

CAN. 261 §1. Seminarii rector itemque, sub eiusdem auctoritate, moderatores et magistri pro parte sua curent ut alumni normas Ratione institutionis sacerdotalis necnon seminarii ordinatione praescriptas adamussim servent.

§2. Sedulo provideant seminarii rector atque studiorum moderator ut magistri suo munere rite fungantur, secundum praescripta Rationis institutionis sacerdotalis ac seminarii ordinationis.

CAN. 262 Exemptum a regimine paroeciali seminarium esto: et pro omnibus qui in seminario sunt, parochi officium, exepta materia matrimoniali et firmo praescripto can. 985, obeat seminarii rector eiusve delegatus.

CAN. 263 Episcopus dioecesanus vel, si de seminario interdioecesano agatur, Episcopi quorum interest, pro parte ab eis communi consilio determinata, curare debent ut provideatur seminarii constitutioni et conservationi, alumnorum sustentationi necnon magistrorum remunerationi aliisque seminarii necessitatibus.

CAN. 264 §1. Ut seminarii necessitatibus provideatur, praeter stipem de qua in

---

260: cc. 1360 §2, 1369; SCSSU Ep., 9 oct. 1921, II; SCSSU Ep., 2 maii 1928; SCSSU Normae, 7 mar. 1929; RFS 29
261 §1: c. 1369 §1; SCSSU Ep., 9 oct. 1921, II; SCSSU Ep., 2 maii 1928; SCSSU Litt. circ., 25 iul. 1928

261 §2: c. 1369 §3; RFS 38, 90
262: c. 1368; SCPF Resp., 4 apr. 1952
263: c. 1357 §1
264 §1: c. 1355, 2°; SCC Ind., 25 ian. 1945

tax in the diocese to provide for the needs of the seminary.

§2. All ecclesiastical juridic persons, even private ones, which have a seat in the diocese are subject to the tax for the seminary unless they are sustained by alms alone or in fact have a college of students or teachers to promote the common good of the Church. A tax of this type must be general, in proportion to the revenues of those who are subject to it, and determined according to the needs of the seminary.

CHAPTER II. The Enrollment, or Incardination, of Clerics

CAN. 265 Every cleric must be incardinated either in a particular church or personal prelature, or in an institute of consecrated life or society endowed with this faculty, in such a way that unattached or transient clerics are not allowed at all.

CAN. 266 §1. Through the reception of the diaconate, a person becomes a cleric and is incardinated in the particular church or personal prelature for whose service he has been advanced.

§2. Through the reception of the diaconate, a perpetually professed religious or a definitively incorporated member of a clerical society of apostolic life is incardinated as a cleric in the same institute or society unless, in the case of societies, the constitutions establish otherwise.

§3. Through the reception of the diaconate, a member of a secular institute is incardinated

can. 1266, potest Episcopus in dioecesi tributum imponere.

§2. Tributo pro seminario obnoxiae sunt cunctae personae iuridicae ecclesiasticae etiam privatae, quae sedem in dioecesi habeant, nisi solis eleemosynis sustententur aut in eis collegium discentium vel docentium ad commune Ecclesiae bonum promovendum actu habeatur; huiusmodi tributum debet esse generale, reditibus eorum qui eidem obnoxii sunt proportionatum, atque iuxta necessitates seminarii determinatum.

CAPUT II. De Clericorum Adscriptione Seu Incardinatione

CAN. 265 Quemlibet clericum oportet esse incardinatum aut alicui Ecclesiae particulari vel praelaturae personali, aut alicui instituto vitae consecratae vel societati hac facultate praeditis, ita ut clerici acephali seu vagi minime admittantur.

CAN. 266 §1. Per receptum diaconatum aliquis fit clericus et incardinatur Ecclesiae particulari vel praelaturae personali pro cuius servitio promotus est.

§2. Sodalis in instituto religioso a votis perpetuis professus aut societati clericali vitae apostolicae definitive incorporatus, per receptum diaconatum incardinatur tamquam clericus eidem instituto aut societati, nisi ad societates quod attinet aliter ferant constitutiones.

§3. Sodalis instituti saecularis per receptum diaconatum incardinatur Ecclesiae par-

264 §2: c. 1356

265: c. 111; CI Resp. I, 1, 24 iul. 1939 (AAS 31 [1939] 321); PO 10

266 §1: SCConc Resol., 10 mar. 1923 (AAS 16 [1924] 51–55); SCConc Resol., 14 feb. et 11 iul. 1925

(AAS 18 [1926] 48–55); AP IX

266 §2: cc. 115, 585, 678; SCConc Resol., 15 jul. 1933 (AAS 26 [1934] 234–236); CI Resp., 24 iul. 1947

266 §3: SCR Resp., 1952

in the particular church for whose service he has been advanced unless he is incardinated in the institute itself by virtue of a grant of the Apostolic See.

CAN. 267 §1. For a cleric already incardinated to be incardinated validly in another particular church, he must obtain from the diocesan bishop a letter of excardination signed by the same bishop and a letter of incardination from the diocesan bishop of the particular church in which he desires to be incardinated signed by that bishop.

§2. Excardination thus granted does not take effect unless incardination in another particular church has been obtained.

CAN. 268 §1. A cleric who has legitimately moved from his own particular church to another is incardinated in the latter particular church by the law itself after five years if he has made such a desire known in writing both to the diocesan bishop of the host church and to his own diocesan bishop and neither of them has expressed opposition in writing to him within four months of receiving the letter.

§2. Through perpetual or definitive admission into an institute of consecrated life or into a society of apostolic life, a cleric who is incardinated in the same institute or society according to the norm of can. 266, §2 is excardinated from his own particular church.

CAN. 269 A diocesan bishop is not to allow the incardination of a cleric unless:

ticulari pro cuius servitio promotus est, nisi vi concessionis Sedis Apostolicae ipsi instituto incardinetur.

CAN. 267 §1. Ut clericus iam incardinatus alii Ecclesiae particulari valide incardinetur, ab Episcopo dioecesano obtinere debet litteras ab eodum subscriptas excardinationis; et pariter ab Episcopo dioecesano Ecclesiae particularis, cui se incardinari desiderat, litteras ab eodem subscriptas incardinationis.

§2. Excardinatio ita concessa effectum non sortitur nisi incardinatione obtenta in alia Ecclesia particulari.

CAN. 268 §1. Clericus qui a propria Ecclesia particulari in aliam legitime transmigraverit, huic Ecclesiae particulari, transacto quinquennio, ipso iure incardinatur, si talem voluntatem in scriptis manifestaverit tum Episcopo dioecesano Ecclesiae hospitis tum Episcopo dioecesano proprio, neque horum alteruter ipsi contrariam scripto mentem intra quattuor menses a receptis litteris significaverit.

§2. Per admissionem perpetuam aut definitivam in institutum vitae consecratae aut in societatem vitae apostolicae, clericus qui, ad normam can. 266, §2, eidem instituto aut societati incardinatur, a propria Ecclesia particulari excardinatur.

CAN. 269 Ad incardinationem clerici Episcopus dioecesanus ne deveniat nisi:

267 §1: c. 112; SCC Decr. *Magni semper,* 30 dec. 1918 (AAS 11 [1919] 39–43); SCPF Decr. *Ad tuendam,* 24 oct. 1948 (AAS 41 [1948] 34–35); Pius PP. XII, Const. Ap. *Exsul familia,* 1 aug. 1952 (AAS 44 [1952] 649–704)

267 §2: c. 116; SCC Decr. *Magni semper,* 30 dec. 1918 (AAS 11 [1919] 39–43); SCPF Decr. *Ad tuendam,* 24 oct. 1948 (AAS 41 [1948] 34–35); Pius PP. XII, Const. Ap. *Exsul familia,* 1 aug. 1952 (AAS 44 [1952] 649–704)

268 §1: ES I, 3 §5; PA 31

268 §2: cc. 115, 585; SCConc Resol., 15 iul. 1933 (AAS 26 [1934] 234–236)

269: c. 117

1° the necessity or advantage of his own particular church demands it, and without prejudice to the prescripts of the law concerning the decent support of clerics;

2° he is certain from a legitimate document that excardination has been granted and, in addition, has appropriate testimonials from the excardinating diocesan bishop, under secrecy if necessary, concerning the life, behavior, and studies of the cleric;

3° the cleric has declared in writing to the same diocesan bishop that he wishes to be dedicated to the service of the new particular church according to the norm of law.

CAN. 270 Excardination can be licitly granted only for just causes such as the advantage of the Church or the good of the cleric himself. It cannot be denied, however, except for evident, grave causes. A cleric who thinks he has been wronged and has found an accepting bishop, however, is permitted to make recourse against the decision.

CAN. 271 §1. Apart from the case of true necessity of his own particular church, a diocesan bishop is not to deny permission to clerics, whom he knows are prepared and considers suitable and who request it, to move to regions laboring under a grave lack of clergy where they will exercise the sacred ministry. He is also to make provision that the rights and duties of these clerics are determined through a written agreement with the diocesan bishop of the place they request.

§2. A diocesan bishop can grant permission for his clerics to move to another particular church for a predetermined time, which can even be renewed several times. Nevertheless,

1° necessitas aut utilitas suae Ecclesiae particularis id exigat, et salvis iuris praescriptis honestam sustentationem clericorum respicientibus;

2° ex legitimo documento sibi constiterit de concessa excardinatione, et habuerit praeterea ab Episcopo dioecesano excardinanti, sub secreto si opus sit, de clerici vita, moribus ac studiis opportuna testimonia;

3° clericus eidem Episcopo dioecesano scripto declaraverit se novae Ecclesiae particularis servitio velle addici ad normam iuris.

CAN. 270 Excardinatio licite concedi potest iustis tantum de causis, quales sunt Ecclesiae utilitas aut bonum ipsius clerici; denegari autem non potest nisi exstantibus gravibus causis; licet tamen clerico, qui se gravatum censuerit et Episcopum receptorem invenerit, contra decisionem recurrere.

CAN. 271 §1. Extra casum verae necessitatis Ecclesiae particularis propriae, Episcopus dioecesanus ne deneget licentiam transmigrandi clericis, quos paratos sciat atque aptos aestimet qui regiones petant gravi cleri inopia laborantes, ibidem sacrum ministerium peracturi; prospiciat vero ut per conventionem scriptam cum Episcopo dioecesano loci, quem petunt, iura et officia eorundem clericorum stabiliantur.

§2. Episcopus dioecesanus licentiam ad aliam Ecclesiam particularem transmigrandi concedere potest suis clericis ad tempus praefinitum, etiam pluries renovandum, ita

270: PO 10
271 §1: PO 10; ES I, 3 §2; PA 26, 27

271 §2: ES 1, 3 §4; PA 28, 30

this is to be done so that these clerics remain incardinated in their own particular church and, when they return to it, possess all the rights which they would have had if they had been dedicated to the sacred ministry there.

§3. For a just cause the diocesan bishop can recall a cleric who has moved legitimately to another particular church while remaining incardinated in his own church provided that the agreements entered into with the other bishop and natural equity are observed; the diocesan bishop of the other particular church, after having observed these same conditions and for a just cause, likewise can deny the same cleric permission for further residence in his territory.

CAN. 272 A diocesan administrator cannot grant excardination or incardination or even permission to move to another particular church unless the episcopal see has been vacant for a year and he has the consent of the college of consultors.

CHAPTER III. **The Obligations and Rights of Clerics**

CAN. 273 Clerics are bound by a special obligation to show reverence and obedience to the Supreme Pontiff and their own ordinary.

CAN. 274 §1. Only clerics can obtain offices for whose exercise the power of orders or the power of ecclesiastical governance is required.

§2. Unless a legitimate impediment excuses them, clerics are bound to undertake and fulfill faithfully a function which their ordinary has entrusted to them.

tamen ut iidem clerici propriae Ecclesiae particulari incardinati maneant, atque in eandem redeuntes omnibus gaudeant iuribus, quae haberent si in ea sacro ministerio addicti fuissent.

§3. Clericus qui legitime in aliam Ecclesiam particularem transierit propriae Ecclesiae manens incardinatus, a proprio Episcopo dioecesano iusta de causa revocari potest, dummodo serventur conventiones cum altero Episcopo initae atque naturalis aequitas; pariter, iisdem condicionibus servatis, Episcopus dioecesanus alterius Ecclesiae particularis iusta de causa poterit eidem clerico licentiam ulterioris commorationis in suo territorio denegare.

CAN. 272 Excardinationem et incardinationem, itemque licentiam ad aliam Ecclesiam particularem transmigrandi concedere nequit Administrator dioecesanus, nisi post annum a vacatione sedis episcopalis, et cum consensu collegii consultorum.

CAPUT III. **De Clericorum Obligationibus et Iuribus**

CAN. 273 Clerici speciali obligatione tenentur Summo Pontifici et suo quisque Ordinario reverentiam et oboedientiam exhibendi.

CAN. 274 §1. Soli clerici obtinere possunt officia ad quorum exercitium requiritur potestas ordinis aut potestas regiminis ecclesiastici.

§2. Clerici, nisi legitimo impedimento excusentur, munus, quod ipsis a suo Ordinario commissum fuerit, suscipere ac fideliter adimplere tenentur.

271 §3: c. 144
272: c. 113
273: c. 127; PO 7; PAULUS PP. VI, All., 1 mar. 1965

(AAS 57 [1965] 326)
274 §1: c. 118; SCDF Ep. (Prot. 151/76), 8 feb. 1977
274 §2: c. 128

CAN. 275 §1. Since clerics all work for the same purpose, namely, the building up of the Body of Christ, they are to be united among themselves by a bond of brotherhood and prayer and are to strive for cooperation among themselves according to the prescripts of particular law.

§2. Clerics are to acknowledge and promote the mission which the laity, each for his or her part, exercise in the Church and in the world.

CAN. 276 §1. In leading their lives, clerics are bound in a special way to pursue holiness since, having been consecrated to God by a new title in the reception of orders, they are dispensers of the mysteries of God in the service of His people.

§2. In order to be able to pursue this perfection:

1° they are first of all to fulfill faithfully and tirelessly the duties of the pastoral ministry;

2° they are to nourish their spiritual life from the two-fold table of sacred scripture and the Eucharist; therefore, priests are earnestly invited to offer the eucharistic sacrifice daily and deacons to participate in its offering daily;

3° priests and deacons aspiring to the presbyterate are obliged to carry out the liturgy of the hours daily according to the proper and approved liturgical books; permanent dea-

CAN. 275 §1. Clerici, quippe qui omnes ad unum conspirent opus, ad aedificationem nempe Corporis Christi, vinculo fraternitatis et orationis inter se uniti sint, et cooperationem inter se prosequantur, iuxta iuris particularis praescripta.

§2. Clerici missionem agnoscant et promoveant, quam pro sua quisque parte laici in Ecclesia et in mundo exercent.

CAN. 276 §1. In vita sua ducenda ad sanctitatem persequendam peculiari ratione tenentur clerici, quippe qui, Deo in ordinis receptione novo titulo consecrati, dispensatores sint mysteriorum Dei in servitium Eius populi.

§2. Ut hanc perfectionem persequi valeant:

1° imprimis ministerii pastoralis officia fideliter et indefesse adimpleant;

2° duplici mensa sacrae Scripturae et Eucharistiae vitam suam spiritualem nutriant; enixe igitur sacerdotes invitantur ut cotidie Sacrificium eucharisticum offerant, diaconi vero ut eiusdem oblationem cotidie participent;

3° obligatione tenentur sacerdotes necnon diaconi ad presbyteratum aspirantes cotidie liturgiam horarum persolvendi secundum proprios et probatos liturgicos libros; diaconi

275 §1: PO 8; Paulus PP. VI, Enc. *Sacerdotalis caelibatus,* 24 iun. 1967, 79 (AAS 59 [1967] 688–689); RFS 3, 6, 46, 47; UT 912–913

275 §2: Pius PP. XI, Enc. *Firmissimam constantiam,* 28 mar. 1937 (AAS 29 [1937] 190–199); AA 25; PO 9

276 §1: c. 124; Pius PP. XI, Enc. *Firmissimam constantiam,* 28 mar. 1937 (AAS 29 [1937] 190–199); LG 28, 41; PO 12, 13

276 §2, 1°: LG 41; PO 12, 14, 18, 19; UT 913–915; DPME 109

276 §2, 2°: Pius PP. XII, All., 24 iun. 1939 (AAS 31

[1939] 249); MD 562–566, 568–576; Pius PP. XII, Adh. Ap. *Menti nostrae,* 26 sep. 1950 (AAS 42 [1950] 666–673); Ioannes PP. XXIII, Enc. *Sacerdotii nostri primordia,* 1 aug. 1959 (AAS 51 [1959] 545–579); DV 25; PO 14, 18, 19; SDO 26; RFS 53; UT 913–915

276 §2, 3°: c. 135; MD 581–583; Pius PP. XII, Adh. Ap. *Menti nostrae,* 26 sep. 1950 (AAS 42 [1950] 669); SC 86–99; SDO 27; Paulus PP. VI, Enc. *Sacerdotalis caelibatus,* 24 iun. 1967, 28 (AAS 59 [1967] 668); Paulus PP. VI, Const. Ap. *Laudis canticum,* 1 nov. 1970 (AAS 63 [1970] 534); IGLH 17, 29; UT 913–915

cons, however, are to carry out the same to the extent defined by the conference of bishops;

4° they are equally bound to make time for spiritual retreats according to the prescripts of particular law;

5° they are urged to engage in mental prayer regularly, to approach the sacrament of penance frequently, to honor the Virgin Mother of God with particular veneration, and to use other common and particular means of sanctification.

CAN. 277 §1. Clerics are obliged to observe perfect and perpetual continence for the sake of the kingdom of heaven and therefore are bound to celibacy which is a special gift of God by which sacred ministers can adhere more easily to Christ with an undivided heart and are able to dedicate themselves more freely to the service of God and humanity.

§2. Clerics are to behave with due prudence towards persons whose company can endanger their obligation to observe continence or give rise to scandal among the faithful.

§3. The diocesan bishop is competent to establish more specific norms concerning this matter and to pass judgment in particular cases concerning the observance of this obligation.

CAN. 278 §1. Secular clerics have the right to associate with others to pursue purposes in keeping with the clerical state.

§2. Secular clerics are to hold in esteem especially those associations which, having statutes

autem permanentes eandem persolvant pro parte ab Episcoporum conferentia definita;

4° pariter tenentur ad vacandum recessibus spiritualibus, iuxta iuris particularis praescripta;

5° sollicitantur ut orationi mentali regulariter incumbant, frequenter ad paenitentiae sacramentum accedant, Deiparam Virginem peculiari veneratione colant, aliisque mediis sanctificationis utantur communibus et particularibus.

CAN. 277 §1. Clerici obligatione tenentur servandi perfectam perpetuamque propter Regnum coelorum continentiam, ideoque ad caelibatum adstringuntur, quod est peculiare Dei donum, quo quidem sacri ministri indiviso corde Christo facilius adhaerere possunt atque Dei hominumque servitio liberius sese dedicare valent.

§2. Debita cum prudentia clerici se gerant cum personis, quarum frequentatio ipsorum obligationem ad continentiam servandam in discrimen vocare aut in fidelium scandalum vertere possit.

§3. Competit Episcopo dioecesano ut hac de re normas statuat magis determinatas utque de huius obligationis observantia in casibus particularibus iudicium ferat.

CAN. 278 §1. Ius est clerics saecularibus sese consociandi cum aliis ad fines statui clericali congruentes prosequendos.

§2. Magni habeant clerici saeculares praesertim illas consociationes quae, statutis

276 §2, 4°: c. 127; PIUS PP. XI, Const. Ap. *Summorum Pontificum*, 25 iul. 1922 (AAS 14 [1922] 420–422); PIUS PP. XI, Enc. *Mens nostra*, 20 dec. 1929 (AAS 21 [1929] 689–706); CD 16; PO 10; SDO 28; UT 913–915; DPME 110

276 § 2, 5°: c. 125; PIUS PP. XII, Adh. Ap. *In auspicando*, 28 iun. 1948 (AAS 40 [1948] 374–375); LG 66; PO 18; SDO 26; UT 913–915; PAULUS PP. VI, Adh. Ap.

Marialis cultus, 2 feb. 1974, 43–51 (AAS 66 [1974] 153–160); IOANNES PAULUS PP. II, Ep. *Novo incipiente*, 8 apr. 1979 (AAS 71 [1979] 412, 415, 416)

277 §1: cc. 132, 133 §1; PO 16; UT 912–913

277 §2: c. 133 §3; PO 16

277 §3: c. 133 §3

278 §1: PO 8; DPME 109c

278 §2: PO 8; UT 920

recognized by competent authority, foster their holiness in the exercise of the ministry through a suitable and properly approved rule of life and through fraternal assistance and which promote the unity of clerics among themselves and with their own bishop.

§3. Clerics are to refrain from establishing or participating in associations whose purpose or activity cannot be reconciled with the obligations proper to the clerical state or can prevent the diligent fulfillment of the function entrusted to them by competent ecclesiastical authority.

CAN. 279 §1. Even after ordination to the priesthood, clerics are to pursue sacred studies and are to strive after that solid doctrine founded in sacred scripture, handed on by their predecessors, and commonly accepted by the Church, as set out especially in the documents of councils and of the Roman Pontiffs. They are to avoid profane novelties and pseudo-science.

§2. According to the prescripts of particular law, priests are to attend pastoral lectures held after priestly ordination and, at times established by the same law, are also to attend other lectures, theological meetings, and conferences which offer them the opportunity to acquire a fuller knowledge of the sacred sciences and pastoral methods.

§3. They are also to acquire knowledge of other sciences, especially of those which are connected with the sacred sciences, particularly insofar as such knowledge contributes to the exercise of pastoral ministry.

a competenti auctoritate recognitis, per aptam et convenienter approbatam vitae ordinationem et fraternum iuvamen, sanctitatem suam in ministerii exercitio fovent, quaeque clericorum inter se et cum proprio Episcopo unioni favent.

§3. Clerici abstineant a constituendis aut participandis consociationibus, quarum finis aut actio cum obligationibus statui clericali propriis componi nequeunt vel diligentem muneris ipsis ab auctoritate ecclesiastica competenti commissi adimpletionem praepedire possunt.

CAN. 279 §1. Clerici studia sacra, recepto etiam sacerdotio, prosequantur, et solidam illam doctrinam, in sacra Scriptura fundatam, a maioribus traditam et communiter ab Ecclesia receptam sectentur, uti documentis praesertim Conciliorum ac Romanorum Pontificum determinatur, devitantes profanas vocum novitates et falsi nominis scientiam.

§2. Sacerdotes, iuxta iuris particularis praescripta, praelectiones pastorales post ordinationem sacerdotalem instituendas frequentent atque, statutis eodem iure temporibus, aliis quoque intersint praelectionibus, conventibus theologicis aut conferentiis, quibus ipsis praebeatur occasio pleniorem scientiarum sacrarum et methodorum pastoralium cognitionem acquirendi.

§3. Aliarum quoque scientiarum, earum praesertim quae cum sacris conectuntur, cognitionem prosequantur, quatenus praecipue ad ministerium pastorale exercendum confert.

278 §3: SCSO Resp. 8 iul. 1927 (AAS 19 [1927] 278); SCC Resp., 4 feb. 1929 (AAS 21 [1929] 42); SCSO Resp., 11 ian. 1951 (AAS 43 [1951] 91); UT 912–913
  279 §1: c. 129; Pius PP. XII, Adh. Ap. *Menti nostrae,* 26 sep. 1950 (AAS 42 [1950] 692–693); CD 16, 28; PO 19; ES I, 7; SCpC Litt. circ., 4 nov. 1969, 5 (AAS 62 [1970] 125)
  279 §2: c. 131; SCpC Litt. circ., 4 nov. 1969, 16–25 (AAS 62 [1970] 130–134); DPME 114
  279 §3: PO 19; DPME 114

CAN. 280   Some practice of common life is highly recommended to clerics; where it exists, it must be preserved as far as possible.

CAN. 281   §1. Since clerics dedicate themselves to ecclesiastical ministry, they deserve remuneration which is consistent with their condition, taking into account the nature of their function and the conditions of places and times, and by which they can provide for the necessities of their life as well as for the equitable payment of those whose services they need.

§2. Provision must also be made so that they possess that social assistance which provides for their needs suitably if they suffer from illness, incapacity, or old age.

§3. Married deacons who devote themselves completely to ecclesiastical ministry deserve remuneration by which they are able to provide for the support of themselves and their families. Those who receive remuneration by reason of a civil profession which they exercise or have exercised, however, are to take care of the needs of themselves and their families from the income derived from it.

CAN. 282   §1. Clerics are to foster simplicity of life and are to refrain from all things that have a semblance of vanity.

§2. They are to wish to use for the good of the Church and works of charity those goods which have come to them on the occasion of the exercise of ecclesiastical office and which are left over after provision has been made for their decent support and for the fulfillment of all the duties of their own state.

CAN. 283   §1. Even if clerics do not have a

CAN. 280   Clerics valde commendatur quaedam vitae communis consuetudo; quae quidem, ubi viget, quantum fieri potest, servanda est.

CAN. 281   §1. Clerici, cum ministerio ecclesiastico se dedicant, remunerationem merentur quae suae condicioni congruat, ratione habita tum ipsius muneris naturae, tum locorum temporumque condicionum, quaque ipsi possint necessitatibus vitae suae necnon aequae retributioni eorum, quorum servitio egent, providere.

§2. Item providendum est ut gaudeant illa sociali assistentia, qua eorum necessitatibus, si infirmitate, invaliditate vel senectute laborent, apte prospiciatur.

§3. Diaconi uxorati, qui plene ministerio ecclesiastico sese devovent, remunerationem merentur qua sui suaeque familiae sustentationi providere valeant; qui vero ratione professionis civilis, quam exercent aut exercuerunt, remunerationem obtineant, ex perceptis inde reditibus sibi suaeque familiae necessitatibus consulant.

CAN. 282   §1. Clerici vitae simplicitatem colant et ab omnibus quae vanitatem sapiunt se abstineant.

§2. Bona, quae occasione exercitii ecclesiastici officii ipsis obveniunt, quaeque supersunt, provisa ex eis honesta sustentatione et omnium officiorum proprii status adimpletione, ad bonum Ecclesiae operaque caritatis impendere velint.

CAN. 283   §1. Clerici, licet officium resi-

280: c. 134; PO 8; DPME 112
281 §1: CD 16; PO 17, 20; ES I, 4, 8; UT 921; DPME 117
281 §2: CD 16; PO 21; ES I, 4, 8; UT 921
281 §3: SDO IV, 19–21

282 §1: c. 138; PO 16, 17; UT 914, 917
282 §2: c. 1473; PO 17
283 §1: c. 143; SCConc Litt. circ., 1 iul. 1926 (AAS 18 [1926] 312–313)

residential office, they nevertheless are not to be absent from their diocese for a notable period of time, to be determined by particular law, without at least the presumed permission of their proper ordinary.

§2. They are entitled, however, to a fitting and sufficient time of vacation each year as determined by universal or particular law.

CAN. 284 Clerics are to wear suitable ecclesiastical garb according to the norms issued by the conference of bishops and according to legitimate local customs.

CAN. 285 §1. Clerics are to refrain completely from all those things which are unbecoming to their state, according to the prescripts of particular law.

§2. Clerics are to avoid those things which, although not unbecoming, are nevertheless foreign to the clerical state.

§3. Clerics are forbidden to assume public offices which entail a participation in the exercise of civil power.

§4. Without the permission of their ordinary, they are not to take on the management of goods belonging to lay persons or secular offices which entail an obligation of rendering accounts. They are prohibited from giving surety even with their own goods without consultation with their proper ordinary. They also are to refrain from signing promissory notes, namely, those through which they assume an obligation to make payment on demand.

CAN. 286 Clerics are prohibited from con-

dentiale non habeant, a sua tamen dioecesi per notabile tempus, iure particulari determinandum, sine licentia saltem praesumpta Ordinarii proprii, ne discedant.

§2. Ipsis autem competit ut debito et sufficienti quotannis gaudeant feriarum tempore, iure universali vel particulari determinato.

CAN. 284 Clerici decentem habitum ecclesiasticum, iuxta normas ab Episcoporum conferentia editas atqui legitimas locorum consuetudines, deferant.

CAN. 285 §1. Clerici ab iis omnibus, quae statum suum dedecent, prorsus abstineant, iuxta iuris particularis praescripta.

§2. Ea quae, licet non indecora, a clericali tamen statu aliena sunt, clerici vitent.

§3. Officia publica, quae participationem in exercitio civilis potestatis secumferunt, clerici assumere vetantur.

§4. Sine licentia sui Ordinarii, ne ineant gestiones bonorum ad laicos pertinentium aut officia saecularia, quae secumferunt onus reddendarum rationum; a fideiubendo, etiam de bonis propriis, inconsulto proprio Ordinario, prohibentur; item a subscribendis syngraphis, quibus nempe obligatio solvendae pecuniae, nulla definita causa, suscipitur, abstineant.

CAN. 286 Prohibentur clerici per se vel

283 §2: PO 20
284: c. 136 §1; ES I, 25 §2d; SCConc Decr. *Prudentissimo sane*, 28 iul. 1931 (AAS 23 [1931] 336–337); SCSSU Monitum, 20 iul. 1949
285 §1: c. 140; SCConc Litt. circ., 1 iul. 1926 (AAS 18 [1926] 312–313); SCSO Decr. *Suprema Sacra Congregatio*, 26 mar. 1942 (AAS 34 [1942] 148)
285 §2: c. 139 §1

285 §3: c. 139 §2; SCConc Resp., 15 mar. 1927 (AAS 19 [1927] 138); SCConc Decr. *Cum activa*, 16 iul. 1957 (AAS 49 [1957] 635); SCConc Notif., 15 feb. 1958 (AAS 50 [1958] 116); UT passim; IOANNES PAULUS PP. II, Ep. *Magnus dies*, 8 apr. 1979, 7 (AAS 71 [1979] 404)
285 §4: c. 139 §3
286: c. 142; SCConc Decr. *Plurimis ex documentis*, 22 mar. 1950 (AAS 42 [1950] 330–331)

ducting business or trade personally or through others, for their own advantage or that of others, except with the permission of legitimate ecclesiastical authority.

CAN. 287 §1. Most especially, clerics are always to foster the peace and harmony based on justice which are to be observed among people.

§2. They are not to have an active part in political parties and in governing labor unions unless, in the judgment of competent ecclesiastical authority, the protection of the rights of the Church or the promotion of the common good requires it.

CAN. 288 The prescripts of cann. 284, 285, §§3 and 4, 286, and 287, §2 do not bind permanent deacons unless particular law establishes otherwise.

CAN. 289 §1. Since military service is hardly in keeping with the clerical state, clerics and candidates for sacred orders are not to volunteer for military service except with the permission of their ordinary.

§2. Clerics are to use exemptions from exercising functions and public civil offices foreign to the clerical state which laws and agreements or customs grant in their favor unless their proper ordinary has decided otherwise in particular cases.

per alios, sive in propriam sive in aliorum utilitatem, negotiationem aut mercaturam exercere, nisi de licentia legitimae auctoritatis ecclesiasticae.

CAN. 287 §1. Clerici pacem et concordiam iustitia innixam inter homines servandam quam maxime semper foveant.

§2. In factionibus politicis atque in regendis consociationibus syndicalibus activam partem ne habeant, nisi iudicio competentis auctoritatis ecclesiasticae, Ecclesiae iura tuenda aut bonum commune promovendum id requirant.

CAN. 288 Diaconi permanentes praescriptis canonum 284, 285, §§3 et 4, 286, 287, §2 non tenentur, nisi ius particulare aliud statuat.

CAN. 289 §1. Cum servitium militare statui clericali minus congruat, clerici itemque candidati ad sacros ordines militiam ne capessant voluntarii, nisi de sui Ordinarii licentia.

§2. Clerici utantur exemptionibus, quas ab exercendis muneribus et publicis civilibus officiis a statu clericali alienis, in eorum favorem leges et conventiones vel consuetudines concedunt, nisi in casibus particularibus aliter Ordinarius proprius decreverit.

287 §1: PO 6; GS 91–93; UT 912–913; SE *Convenientes ex universo,* 30 nov. 1971 (AAS 63 [1971] 932–937)

287 §2: CI Resp. I, 2–3 iun. 1918 (AAS 10 [1918] 344); BENEDICTUS PP. XV, Ep., 12 mar. 1919 (AAS 11 [1919] 122–123); Sec Ep., 2 oct. 1922; SCR Litt. circ., 10 feb. 1924; SCConc Resp., 15 mar. 1927 (AAS 19 [1927] 138); UT 912–913

288: SDO 17, 31

289 §1: cc.121, 141; SCC Decr. *Redeuntibus e militari,* 25 oct. 1918 (AAS 10 [1918] 481–486); SCC Decl., 21 dec. 1918 (AAS 11 [1919] 6–7); SCC Resp., 28 mar. 1919 (AAS 11 [1919] 177–178); SCR Decr. *Militare servitium,* 30 iul. 1957 (AAS 49 [1957] 871–874)

289 §2: c. 123

CHAPTER IV. Loss of the Clerical State

CAN. 290 Once validly received, sacred ordination never becomes invalid. A cleric, nevertheless, loses the clerical state:

1° by a judicial sentence or administrative decree, which declares the invalidity of sacred ordination;

2° by a penalty of dismissal legitimately imposed;

3° by rescript of the Apostolic See which grants it to deacons only for grave causes and to presbyters only for most grave causes.

CAN. 291 Apart from the case mentioned in can. 290, n. 1, loss of the clerical state does not entail a dispensation from the obligation of celibacy, which only the Roman Pontiff grants.

CAN. 292 A cleric who loses the clerical state according to the norm of law loses with it the rights proper to the clerical state and is no longer bound by any obligations of the clerical state, without prejudice to the prescript of can. 291. He is prohibited from exercising the power of orders, without prejudice to the prescript of can. 976. By the loss of the clerical state, he is deprived of all offices, functions, and any delegated power.

CAN. 293 A cleric who loses the clerical

CAPUT IV. De Amissione Status Clericalis

CAN. 290 Sacra ordinatio, semel valide recepta, numquam irrita fit. Clericus tamen statum clericalem amittit:

1° sententia iudiciali aut decreto administrativo, quo invaliditas sacrae ordinationis declaratur;

2° poena dimissionis legitime irrogata;

3° rescripto Apostolicae Sedis; quod vero rescriptum diaconis ob graves tantum causas, presbyteris ob gravissimas causas ab Apostolica Sede conceditur.

CAN. 291 Praeter casus de quibus in can. 290, n. 1, amissio status clericalis non secumfert dispensationem ab obligatione caelibatus, quae ab uno tantum Romano Pontifice conceditur.

CAN. 292 Clericus, qui statum clericalem ad normam iuris amittit, cum eo amittit iura statui clericali propria, nec ullis iam adstringitur obligationibus status clericalis, firmo praescripto can. 291; potestatem ordinis exercere prohibetur, salvo praescripto can. 976; eo ipso privatur omnibus officiis, muneribus et potestate qualibet delegata.

CAN. 293 Clericus, qui statum cleri-

290, 1°: cc. 211, 1993–1998; SCDS Decr. *Ut locorum Ordinarii,* 9 iun. 1931 (AAS 23 [1931] 457–492)

290, 2°: cc. 211 §1, 2198, 12°, 2305, 2314 §1, 3°, 2343 §1, 3°, 2354 §2, 2368 §1, 2388 §1

290, 3°: SCR Resp., 23 iun. 1954; EM IX, 1; PAULUS PP. VI, Enc. *Sacerdotalis caelibatus,* 24 iun. 1967 (AAS 59 [1967] 691); SCDF Normae, 13 ian. 1971 (AAS 63 [1971] 303–308); SCDF Litt. circ., 13 ian. 1971 (AAS 63 [1971] 309–310); SCDF Decl., 26 iun. 1972 (AAS 64 [1972] 641–643); SCDF Litt. circ., 14 oct. 1980 (AAS 72 [1980] 1132–1135); SCDF Normae, 14 oct. 1980 (AAS 72 [1980] 1136–1137)

291: c. 213 §2; IOANNES PAULUS PP. II, Ep. *Novo incipiente,* 8 apr. 1979, 9 (AAS 71 [1979] 409–411); SCDF Litt. circ., 14 oct. 1980, 3 (AAS 72 [1980] 1133–1134); SCDF Normae, 14 oct. 1980, 1 (AAS 72 [1980] 1136)

292: c. 213 §1; UT 917; SCDF Normae, 13 ian. 1971, VI, 4 (AAS 63 [1971] 308); SCIC Decl., 15 aug. 1975; SCIC Notif., 20 aug. 1976; SCDF Normae, 14 oct. 1980, 5 (AAS 72 [1980] 1134)

293: c. 212 §2; SCSO Litt. circ. et Normae, 2 feb. 1964; SCDF Normae, 14 oct. 1980, 6 (AAS 72 [1980] 1134–1135)

state cannot be enrolled among clerics again except through a rescript of the Apostolic See.

calem amisit, nequit denuo inter clericos adscribi, nisi per Apostolicae Sedis rescriptum.

TITLE IV. Personal Prelatures

CAN. 294   After the conferences of bishops involved have been heard, the Apostolic See can erect personal prelatures, which consist of presbyters and deacons of the secular clergy, to promote a suitable distribution of presbyters or to accomplish particular pastoral or missionary works for various regions or for different social groups.

CAN. 295   §1. The statutes established by the Apostolic See govern a personal prelature, and a prelate presides over it as the proper ordinary; he has the right to erect a national or international seminary and even to incardinate students and promote them to orders under title of service to the prelature.

§2. The prelate must see to both the spiritual formation and decent support of those whom he has promoted under the above-mentioned title.

CAN. 296   Lay persons can dedicate themselves to the apostolic works of a personal prelature by agreements entered into with the prelature. The statutes, however, are to determine suitably the manner of this organic cooperation and the principal duties and rights connected to it.

CAN. 297   The statutes likewise are to define the relations of the personal prelature with

TITULUS IV. De Praelaturis Personalibus

CAN. 294   Ad aptam presbyterorum distributionem promovendam aut ad peculiaria opera pastoralia vel missionalia pro variis regionibus aut diversis coetibus socialibus perficienda, praelaturae personales quae presbyteris et diaconis cleri saecularis constent, ab Apostolica Sede, auditis quarum interest Episcoporum conferentiis, erigi possunt.

CAN. 295   §1. Praelatura personalis regitur statutis ab Apostolica Sede conditis, eique praeficitur Praelatus ut Ordinarius proprius, cui ius est nationale vel internationale seminarium erigere necnon alumnos incardinare, eosque titulo servitii praelaturae ad ordines promovere.

§2. Praelatus prospicere debet sive spirituali institutioni illorum, quos titulo praedicto promoverit, sive eorundem decorae sustentationi.

CAN. 296   Conventionibus cum praelatura initis, laici operibus apostolicis praelaturae personalis sese dedicare possunt; modus vero huius organicae cooperationis atque praecipua officia et iura cum illa coniuncta in statutis apte determinentur.

CAN. 297   Statuta pariter definiant rationes praelaturae personalis cum Ordinariis

294: PO 10; ES I, 4; REU 49 §1; SCE Instr. *Nemo est*, 22 aug. 1969, 16 §3 (AAS [1969] 621); DPME 172
295 §1: ES I, 4; REU 49 §1; SCE Instr. *Nemo est*, 22 aug. 1969, 16 §3 (AAS [1969] 621)
295 §2: ES I, 4

296: ES I, 4
297: SCC Decr. *Ad consulendum*, 21 mar. 1964; PO 10; ES I, 4; SCE Decr. *Ad consulendum*, 11 mar. 1975

the local ordinaries in whose particular churches the prelature itself exercises or desires to exercise its pastoral or missionary works, with the previous consent of the diocesan bishop.

locorum, in quorum Ecclesiis particularibus ipsa praelatura sua opera pastoralia vel missionalia, praevio consensu Episcopi dioecesani, exercet vel exercere desiderat.

TITLE V. Associations of the Christian Faithful

CHAPTER I. Common Norms

CAN. 298 §1. In the Church there are associations distinct from institutes of consecrated life and societies of apostolic life; in these associations the Christian faithful, whether clerics, lay persons, or clerics and lay persons together, strive in a common endeavor to foster a more perfect life, to promote public worship or Christian doctrine, or to exercise other works of the apostolate such as initiatives of evangelization, works of piety or charity, and those which animate the temporal order with a Christian spirit.

§2. The Christian faithful are to join especially those associations which competent ecclesiastical authority has erected, praised, or commended.

CAN. 299 §1. By means of a private agreement made among themselves, the Christian faithful are free to establish associations to pursue the purposes mentioned in can. 298, §1, without prejudice to the prescript of can. 301, §1.

§2. Even if ecclesiastical authority praises or commends them, associations of this type are called private associations.

§3. No private association of the Christian

TITULUS V. De Christifidelium Consociationibus

CAPUT I. Normae Communes

CAN. 298 §1. In Ecclesia habentur consociationes distinctae ab institutis vitae consecratae et societatibus vitae apostolicae, in quibus christifideles, sive clerici sive laici sive clerici et laici simul, communi opera contendunt ad perfectiorem vitam fovendam, aut ad cultum publicum vel doctrinam christianam promovendam, aut ad alia apostolatus opera, scilicet ad evangelicationis incepta, ad pietatis vel caritatis opera exercenda et ad ordinem temporalem christiano spiritu animandum.

§2. Christifideles sua nomina dent iis praesertim consociationibus, quae a competenti auctoritate ecclesiastica aut erectae aut laudatae vel commendatae sint.

CAN. 299 §1. Integrum est cristifidelibus, privata inter se conventione inita, consociationes constituere ad fines de quibus in can. 298, §1 persequendos, firmo praescripto can. 301, §1.

§2. Huiusmodi consociationes, etiamsi ab auctoritate ecclesiastica laudentur vel commendentur, consociationes privatae vocantur.

§3. Nulla christifidelium consociatio pri-

298 §1: c. 685; Pius PP. XI, Enc. *Ubi arcano*, 23 dec. 1922 (AAS 14 [1922] 692–693); Pius PP. XI, Ep. *Dilecte fili*, 7 nov. 1929 (AAS 21 [1929] 664–668); *CD* 17; OT 2; GE 6, 8; AA 5–8, 11, 18, 19; PO 8
298 §2: c. 684; SCConc Resol., 13 nov. 1920 (AAS 13 [1921] 135–144); SCSO Resp., 8 iul. 1927 (AAS 19

[1927] 278); Pius PP. XII, Const. Ap. *Bis saeculari*, 27 sep. 1948 (AAS 40 [1948] 393–402); SCSO Monitum, 28 iul. 1950 (AAS 42 [1950] 553); AA 21
299 §1: SCConc Resol., 13 nov. 1920 (AAS 13 [1921] 135–144); AA 19, 24
299 §2: AA 24

faithful is recognized in the Church unless competent authority reviews its statutes.

CAN. 300   No association is to assume the name *Catholic* without the consent of competent ecclesiastical authority according to the norm of can. 312.

CAN. 301   §1. It is for the competent ecclesiastical authority alone to erect associations of the Christian faithful which propose to hand on Christian doctrine in the name of the Church or to promote public worship, or which intend other purposes whose pursuit is of its nature reserved to the same ecclesiastical authority.

§2. Competent ecclesiastical authority, if it has judged it expedient, can also erect associations of the Christian faithful to pursue directly or indirectly other spiritual purposes whose accomplishment has not been sufficiently provided for through the initiatives of private persons.

§3. Associations of the Christian faithful which are erected by competent ecclesiastical authority are called public associations.

CAN. 302   Those associations of the Christian faithful are called clerical which are under the direction of clerics, assume the exercise of sacred orders, and are recognized as such by competent authority.

CAN. 303   Associations whose members share in the spirit of some religious institute while in secular life, lead an apostolic life, and strive for Christian perfection under the higher direction of the same institute are called third orders or some other appropriate name.

vata in Ecclesia agnoscitur, nisi eius statuta ab auctoritate competenti recognoscantur.

CAN. 300   Nulla consociatio nomen «catholicae» sibi assumat, nisi de consensu competentis auctoritatis ecclesiasticae, ad normam can. 312.

CAN. 301   §1. Unius auctoritatis ecclesiasticae competentis est erigere christifidelium consociationes, quae sibi proponant doctrinam christianam nomine Ecclesiae tradere aut cultum publicum promovere, vel quae alios intendant fines, quorum prosecutio natura sua eidem auctoritati ecclesiasticae reservatur.

§2. Auctoritas ecclesiastica competens, si id expedire iudicaverit, christifidelium consociationes quoque erigere potest ad alios fines spirituales directe vel indirecte prosequendos, quorum consecutioni per privatorum incepta non satis provisum sit.

§3. Christifidelium consociationes quae a competenti auctoritate ecclesiastica eriguntur, consociationes publicae vocantur.

CAN. 302   Christifidelium consociationes clericales eae dicuntur, quae sub moderamine sunt clericorum, exercitium ordinis sacri assumunt atque uti tales a competenti auctoritate agnoscuntur.

CAN. 303   Consociationes, quarum sodales, in saeculo spiritum alicuius instituti religiosi participantes, sub altiore eiusdem instituti moderamine, vitam apostolicam ducunt et ad perfectionem christianam contendunt, tertii ordines dicuntur aliove congruenti nomine vocantur.

300: AA 24

301 §1: c. 686 §1; SCConc Resol., 13 nov. 1920 (AAS 13 [1921] 135–144); Pius PP. XI, Ep. *Dilecte fili,* 7 nov. 1929 (AAS 21 [1929] 664–668); Pius PP. XII, All., 4 sep. 1940 (AAS 32 [1940] 362–372); AA 24

301 §2: c. 686 §1; SCConc Resol., 13 nov. 1920 (AAS 13 [1921] 135–144); Pius PP. XI, Ep. *Dilecte fili,* 7 nov. 1929 (AAS 21 [1929] 664–668); AA 24

303: c. 702; ES I, 35; REU 73 §3

CAN. 304 §1. All public or private associations of the Christian faithful, by whatever title or name they are called, are to have their own statutes which define the purpose or social objective of the association, its seat, government, and conditions required for membership and which determine the manner of its acting, attentive, however, to the necessity or advantage of time and place.

§2. They are to choose a title or name for themselves adapted to the usage of time and place, selected above all with regard to their intended purpose.

CAN. 305 §1. All associations of the Christian faithful are subject to the vigilance of competent ecclesiastical authority which is to take care that the integrity of faith and morals is preserved in them and is to watch so that abuse does not creep into ecclesiastical discipline. This authority therefore has the duty and right to inspect them according to the norm of law and the statutes. These associations are also subject to the governance of this same authority according to the prescripts of the canons which follow.

§2. Associations of any kind are subject to the vigilance of the Holy See; diocesan associations and other associations to the extent that they work in the diocese are subject to the vigilance of the local ordinary.

CAN. 306 In order for a person to possess the rights and privileges of an association and the indulgences and other spiritual favors granted to the same association, it is necessary and sufficient that the person has been validly re-

CAN. 304 §1. Omnes christifidelium consociationes, sive publicae sive privatae, quocumque titulo seu nomine vocantur, sua habeant statuta, quibus definiantur consociationis finis seu obiectum sociale, sedes, regimen et condiciones ad partem in iisdem habendam requisitae, quibusque determinentur agendi rationes, attentis quidem temporis et loci necessitate vel utilitate.

§2. Titulum seu nomen sibi eligant, temporis et loci usibus accommodatum, maxime ab ipso fine, quem intendunt, selectum.

CAN. 305 §1. Omnes christifidelium consociationes subsunt vigilantiae auctoritatis ecclesiasticae competentis, cuius est curare ut in iisdem integritas fidei ac morum servetur, et invigilare ne in disciplinam ecclesiasticam abusus irrepant, cui itaque officium et ius competunt ad normam iuris et statutorum easdem invisendi; subsunt etiam eiusdem auctoritatis regimini secundum praescripta canonum, qui sequuntur.

§2. Vigilantiae Sanctae Sedis subsunt consociationes cuiuslibet generis; vigilantiae Ordinarii loci subsunt consociationes dioecesanae necnon aliae consociationes, quatenus in dioecesi operam exercent.

CAN. 306 Ut quis consociationis iuribus atque privilegiis, indulgentiis aliisque gratiis spiritualibus eidem consociationi concessis fruatur, necesse est et sufficit ut secundum iuris praescripta et propria consoci-

304 §1: cc. 689 §1, 697
304 §2: c. 688
305 §1: cc. 336 §2, 690 §1; SCConc Resol., 13 nov. 1920 (AAS 13 [1921] 135–144); Pius PP. XI, Enc. *Maximam gravissimamque*, 18 ian. 1924 (AAS 16 [1924] 5–11)

305 §2: cc. 394 §1, 690 §2; SCConc Resol., 13 nov. 1920 (AAS 13 [1921] 135–144); ES I, 35; SA Normae, nov. 1968
306: c. 692; CI Resp. I, 4 ian. 1946 (AAS 38 [1946] 162); SCConc Ind., 24 maii 1950

ceived into it and has not been legitimately dismissed from it according to the prescripts of law and the proper statutes of the association.

CAN. 307 §1. The reception of members is to be done according to the norm of law and the statutes of each association.

§2. The same person can be enrolled in several associations.

§3. Members of religious institutes can join associations according to the norm of their proper law with the consent of their superior.

CAN. 308 No one legitimately enrolled is to be dismissed from an association except for a just cause according to the norm of law and the statutes.

CAN. 309 According to the norm of law and the statutes, legitimately established associations have the right to issue particular norms respecting the association itself, to hold meetings, and to designate moderators, officials, other officers, and administrators of goods.

CAN. 310 A private association which has not been established as a juridic person cannot, as such, be a subject of obligations and rights. Nevertheless, the members of the Christian faithful associated together in it can jointly contract obligations and can acquire and possess rights and goods as co-owners and co-possessors; they are able to exercise these rights and obligations through an agent or a proxy.

CAN. 311 Members of institutes of consecrated life who preside over or assist associations in some way united to their institute are to take care that these associations give assistance to the works of the apostolate which already exist in a diocese, especially cooperating,

ationis statuta, in eandem valide receptus sit et ab eadem non sit legitime dimissus.

CAN. 307 §1. Membrorum receptio fiat ad normam iuris ac statutorum uniuscuiusque consociationis.

§2. Eadem persona adscribi potest pluribus consociationibus.

§3. Sodales institutorum religiosorum possunt consociationibus, ad normam iuris proprii, de consensu sui Superioris nomen dare.

CAN. 308 Nemo legitime adscriptus a consociatione dimittatur, nisi iusta de causa ad normam iuris et statutorum.

CAN. 309 Consociationibus legitime constitutis ius est, ad normam iuris et statutorum, edendi peculiares normas ipsam consociationem respicientes, celebrandi comitia, designandi moderatores, officiales, ministros atque bonorum administratores.

CAN. 310 Consociatio privata quae uti persona iuridica non fuerit constituta, qua talis subiectum esse non potest obligationum et iurium; christifideles tamen in ea consociati coniunctim obligationes contrahere atque uti condomini et compossessores iura et bona acquirere et possidere possunt; quae iura et obligationes per mandatarium seu procuratorem exercere valent.

CAN. 311 Sodales institutorum vitae consecratae qui consociationibus suo instituto aliquo modo unitis praesunt aut assistunt, curent ut eaedem consociationes operibus apostolatus in dioecesi exsistentibus adiutorium praebeant, cooperantes praesertim, sub

---

307 §1: c. 694 §1; SCConc Resp., 18 mar. 1941   **308:** c. 696 §1
307 §2: c. 693 §2   **309:** c. 697 §1
307 §3: c. 693 §4   **311:** ES I, 35

under the direction of the local ordinary, with associations which are ordered to the exercise of the apostolate in the diocese.

CHAPTER II. Public Associations of the Christian Faithful

CAN. 312 §1. The authority competent to erect public associations is:

1° the Holy See for universal and international associations;

2° the conference of bishops in its own territory for national associations, that is, those which from their founding are directed toward activity throughout the whole nation;

3° the diocesan bishop in his own territory, but not a diocesan administrator, for diocesan associations, except, however, for those associations whose right of erection has been reserved to others by apostolic privilege.

§2. Written consent of the diocesan bishop is required for the valid erection of an association or section of an association in a diocese even if it is done by virtue of apostolic privilege. Nevertheless, the consent given by a diocesan bishop for the erection of a house of a religious institute is also valid for the erection in the same house or church attached to it of an association which is proper to that institute.

CAN. 313 Through the same decree by which the competent ecclesiastical authority according to the norm of can. 312 erects it, a public association and even a confederation of public associations is constituted a juridic person and, to the extent it is required, receives a mis-

directione Ordinarii loci, cum consociationibus quae ad apostolatum in dioecesi exercendum ordinantur.

CAPUT II. De Christifidelium Consociationibus Publicis

CAN. 312 §1. Ad erigendas consociationes publicas auctoritas competens est:

1° pro consociationibus universalibus atque internationalibus, Sancta Sedes;

2° pro consociationibus nationalibus, quae scilicet ex ipsa erectione destinantur ad actionem in tota natione exercendam, Episcoporum conferentia in suo territorio;

3° pro consociationibus dioecesanis, Episcopus dioecesanus in suo cuiusque territorio, non vero Administrator dioecesanus, iis tamen consociationibus exceptis quarum erigendarum ius ex apostolico privilegio aliis reservatum est.

§2. Ad validam erectionem consociationis aut sectionis consociationis in dioecesi, etiamsi id vi privilegii apostolici fiat, requiritur consensus Episcopi dioecesani scripto datus; consensus tamen ab Episcopo dioecesano praestitus pro erectione domus instituti religiosi valet etiam ad erigendam in eadem domo vel ecclesia ei adnexa consociationem quae illius instituti sit propria.

CAN. 313 Consociatio publica itemque consociationum publicarum confoederatio, ipso decreto quo ab auctoritate ecclesiastica ad normam can. 312 competenti erigitur, persona iuridica constituitur et missionem recipit, quatenus requiritur, ad fines quos ipsa

312 §1, 1°: c. 686 §§1 et 2; COETUS SANCTAE ROMANAE ECCLESIAE CARDINALIUM Resp. III, 2 (AAS 15 [1923] 39–40); SA Normae, nov. 1968

312 §1, 2°: c. 686 §§1 et 2; SCE Rescr., 28 iun. 1969; SCGE Rescr., 26 nov. 1978

312 §1, 3°: c. 686 §§2 et 4

312 §2: c. 686 §3

313: c. 687; PIUS PP. XI, Ep. *Dilecte fili*, 6 nov. 1929 (AAS 21 [1929] 665); PIUS PP. XI, Ep. Ap. *Ex officiosis litteris*, 10 nov. 1933 (AAS 26 [1934] 628–633); PIUS PP. XI, Enc. *Firmissimam constantiam*, 28 mar. 1937 (AAS 29 [1937] 191–193); AA 20; ES I, 35

sion for the purposes which it proposes to pursue in the name of the Church.

CAN. 314 The statutes of each public association and their revision or change need the approval of the ecclesiastical authority competent to erect the association according to the norm of can. 312, §1.

CAN. 315 Public associations are able on their own initiative to undertake endeavors in keeping with their own character. These endeavors are governed according to the norm of the statutes, though under the higher direction of the ecclesiastical authority mentioned in can. 312, §1.

CAN. 316 §1. A person who has publicly rejected the Catholic faith, has defected from ecclesiastical communion, or has been punished by an imposed or declared excommunication cannot be received validly into public associations.

§2. Those enrolled legitimately who fall into the situation mentioned in §1, after being warned, are to be dismissed from the association, with due regard for its statutes and without prejudice to the right of recourse to the ecclesiastical authority mentioned in can. 312, §1.

CAN. 317 §1. Unless the statutes provide otherwise, it is for the ecclesiastical authority mentioned in can. 312, §1 to confirm the moderator of a public association elected by the public association itself, install the one presented, or appoint the moderator in his own right. The same ecclesiastical authority also appoints the chaplain or ecclesiastical assistant, after having heard the major officials of the association, when it is expedient.

sibi nomine Ecclesiae persequendos proponit.

CAN. 314 Cuiuslibet consociationis publicae statuta, eorumque recognitio vel mutatio, approbatione indigent auctoritatis ecclesiasticae cui competit consociationis erectio ad normam can. 312, §1.

CAN. 315 Consociationes publicae incepta propriae indoli congrua sua sponte suscipere valent, eaedemque reguntur ad normam statutorum, sub altiore tamen directione auctoritatis ecclesiasticae, de qua in can. 312, §1.

CAN. 316 §1. Qui publice fidem catholicam abiecerit vel a communione ecclesiastica defecerit vel excommunicatione irrogata aut declarata irretitus sit, valide in consociationes publicas recipi nequit.

§2. Qui legitime adscripti in casum inciderint de quo in §1, praemissa monitione, a consociatione dimittantur, servatis eius statutis et salvo iure recursus ad auctoritatem ecclesiasticam, de qua in can. 312, §1.

CAN. 317 §1. Nisi aliud in statutis praevideatur, auctoritatis ecclesiasticae, de qua in can. 312, §1, est consociationis publicae moderatorem ab ipsa consociatione publica electum confirmare aut praesentatum instituere aut iure proprio nominare; cappellanum vero seu assistentem ecclesiasticum, auditis ubi id expediat consociationis officialibus maioribus, nominat eadem auctoritas ecclesiastica.

314: c. 689

315: Pius PP. XI, Ep. *Dilecte fili,* 6 nov. 1929 (AAS 21 [1929] 665); Pius PP. XI, Ep. Ap. *Ex officiosis litteris,* 10 nov. 1933 (AAS 26 [1934] 628–633); Pius PP. XI, Enc. *Firmissimam constantiam,* 28 mar. 1937 (AAS

29 [1937] 191–193); AA 20; ES I, 35
316 §1: c. 693 §1
316 §2: c. 696 §2
317 §1: c. 698 §1

§2. The norm stated in §1 is also valid for associations which members of religious institutes erect outside their own churches or houses in virtue of apostolic privilege. In associations which members of religious institutes erect in their own church or house, however, the nomination or confirmation of the moderator and chaplain pertains to the superior of the institute, according to the norm of the statutes.

§3. In associations which are not clerical, lay persons are able to exercise the function of moderator. A chaplain or ecclesiastical assistant is not to assume that function unless the statutes provide otherwise.

§4. Those who exercise leadership in political parties are not to be moderators in public associations of the Christian faithful which are ordered directly to the exercise of the apostolate.

CAN. 318 §1. In special circumstances and where grave reasons require it, the ecclesiastical authority mentioned in can. 312, §1 can designate a trustee who is to direct the association for a time in its name.

§2. The person who appointed or confirmed the moderator of a public association can remove the moderator for a just cause, after the person has heard, however, the moderator and the major officials of the association according to the norm of the statutes. The person who appointed a chaplain can remove him according to the norm of cann. 192–195.

CAN. 319 §1. Unless other provision has been made, a legitimately erected public association administers the goods which it possesses according to the norm of the statutes under the higher direction of the ecclesiastical authority

§2. Norma in §1 statuta valet etiam pro consociationibus a sodalibus institutorum religiosorum vi apostolici privilegii extra proprias ecclesias vel domos erectis; in consociationibus vero a sodalibus institutorum religiosorum in propria ecclesia vel domo erectis, nominatio aut confirmatio moderatoris et cappellani pertinet ad Superiorem instituti, ad normam statutorum.

§3. In consociationibus quae non sunt clericales, laici exercere valent munus moderatoris; cappellanus seu assistens ecclesiasticus ad illud munus ne assumatur, nisi aliud in statutis caveatur.

§4. In publicis christifidelium consociationibus quae directe ad apostolatum exercendum ordinantur, moderatores ne ii sint, qui in factionibus politicis officium directionis adimplent.

CAN. 318 §1. In specialibus adiunctis, ubi graves rationes id requirant, potest ecclesiastica auctoritas, de qua in can. 312, §1, designare commissarium, qui eius nomine consociationem ad tempus moderetur.

§2. Moderatorem consociationis publicae iusta de causa removere potest qui eum nominavit aut confirmavit, auditis tamen tum ipso moderatore tum consociationis officialibus maioribus ad normam statutorum; cappellanum vero removere potest, ad normam cann. 192–195, qui eum nominavit.

CAN. 319 §1. Consociatio publica legitime erecta, nisi aliud cautum sit, bona quae possidet ad normam statutorum administrat sub superiore directione auctoritatis ecclesiasticae de qua in can. 312, §1, cui

317 §2: c. 698 §1
317 § 4: Pius PP. XI, Ep. *Dilecte fili*, 6 nov. 1929 (AAS 21 [1929] 665); Pius PP. XI, Ep. *Dobbiamo intrattenerLa*, 26 apr. 1931 (AAS 23 [1931] 148); Pius PP.

XI, Enc. *Non abbiamo bisogno*, 29 iun. 1931 (AAS 23 [1931] 294–296)
318 §2: c. 698 §3
319 §1: c. 691 §1

mentioned in can. 312, §1, to which it must render an account of administration each year.

§2. It must also render to the same authority a faithful account of the expenditure of the offerings and alms which it has collected.

CAN. 320   §1. Only the Holy See can suppress associations it has erected.

§2. For grave causes, a conference of bishops can suppress associations it has erected. A diocesan bishop can suppress associations he has erected and also associations which members of religious institutes have erected through apostolic indult with the consent of the diocesan bishop.

§3. The competent authority is not to suppress a public association unless the authority has heard its moderator and other major officials.

CHAPTER III. Private Associations of the Christian Faithful

CAN. 321   The Christian faithful guide and direct private associations according to the prescripts of the statutes.

CAN. 322   §1. A private association of the Christian faithful can acquire juridic personality through a formal decree of the competent ecclesiastical authority mentioned in can. 312.

§2. No private association of the Christian faithful can acquire juridic personality unless the ecclesiastical authority mentioned in can. 312, §1 has approved its statutes. Approval of the statutes, however, does not change the private nature of the association.

quotannis administrationis rationem reddere debet.

§2. Oblationum quoque et eleemosynarum, quas collegerit, eidem auctoritati fidelem erogationis rationem reddere debet.

CAN. 320   §1. Consociationes a Sancta Sede erectae nonnisi ab eadem supprimi possunt.

§2. Ob graves causas ab Episcoporum conferentia supprimi possunt consociationes ab eadem erectae; ab Episcopo dioecesano consociationes a se erectae, et etiam consociationes ex apostolico indulto a sodalibus institutorum religiosorum de consensu Episcopi dioecesani erectae.

§3. Consociatio publica ab auctoritate competenti ne supprimatur, nisi auditis eius moderatore aliisque officialibus maioribus.

CAPUT III. **De Christifidelium Consociationibus Privatis**

CAN. 321   Consociationes privatas christifideles secundum statutorum praescripta dirigunt et moderantur.

CAN. 322   §1. Consociatio christifidelium privata personalitatem iuridicam acquirere potest per decretum formale auctoritatis ecclesiasticae competentis, de qua in can. 312.

§2. Nulla christifidelium consociatio privata personalitatem iuridicam acquirere potest, nisi eius statuta ab auctoritate ecclesiastica, de qua in can. 312, §1, sint probata; statutorum vero probatio consociationis naturam privatam non immutat.

319 §2: c. 691 §5
320 §1: c. 699 §2
320 §2: c. 699 §1

321: SCConc Resol., 13 nov. 1920 (AAS 13 [1921] 135–144)
322 §1: c. 100 §1

CAN. 323 §1. Although private associations of the Christian faithful possess autonomy according to the norm of can. 321, they are subject to the vigilance of ecclesiastical authority according to the norm of can. 305 and even to the governance of the same authority.

§2. It also pertains to ecclesiastical authority, while respecting the autonomy proper to private associations, to be watchful and careful that dissipation of their energies is avoided and that their exercise of the apostolate is ordered to the common good.

CAN. 324 §1. A private association of the Christian faithful freely designates its moderator and officials according to the norm of the statutes.

§2. A private association of the Christian faithful can freely choose a spiritual advisor, if it desires one, from among the priests exercising ministry legitimately in the diocese; nevertheless, he needs the confirmation of the local ordinary.

CAN. 325 §1. A private association of the Christian faithful freely administers those goods it possesses according to the prescripts of the statutes, without prejudice to the right of competent ecclesiastical authority to exercise vigilance so that the goods are used for the purposes of the association.

§2. A private association is subject to the authority of the local ordinary according to the norm of can. 1301 in what pertains to the administration and distribution of goods which have been donated or left to it for pious causes.

CAN. 326 §1. A private association of the Christian faithful ceases to exist according to the norm of its statutes. The competent au-

CAN. 323 §1. Licet christifidelium consociationes privatae autonomia gaudeant ad normam can. 321, subsunt vigilantiae auctoritatis ecclesiasticae ad normam can. 305, itemque eiusdem auctoritatis regimini.

§2. Ad auctoritatem ecclesiasticam etiam spectat, servata quidem autonomia consociationibus privatis propria, invigilare et curare ut virium dispersio vitetur, earumque apostolatus exercitium ad bonum commune ordinetur.

CAN. 324 §1. Christifidelium consociatio privata libere sibi moderatorem et officiales designat, ad normam statutorum.

§2. Christifidelium consociatio privata consiliarium spiritualem, si quemdam exoptet, libere eligere potest inter sacerdotes ministerium legitime in dioecesi exercentes; qui tamen indiget confirmatione Ordinarii loci.

CAN. 325 §1. Christifidelium consociatio privata ea bona quae possidet libere administrat, iuxta statutorum praescripta, salvo iure auctoritatis ecclesiasticae competentis vigilandi ut bona in fines associationis adhibeantur.

§2. Eadem subest loci Ordinarii auctoritati ad normam can. 1301 quod attinet ad administrationem erogationemque bonorum, quae ipsi ad pias causas donata aut relicta sint.

CAN. 326 §1. Extinguitur christifidelium consociatio privata ad normam statutorum; supprimi etiam potest a competenti auctori-

323 §1: cc. 336 §2, 690 §1; SCConc Resol., 13 nov. 1920 (AAS 13 [1921] 135–144)
323 §2: CD 17; AA 19

324 §1: SCConc Resol., 13 nov. 1920 (AAS 13 [1921] 135–144); AA 19

thority can also suppress it if its activity causes grave harm to ecclesiastical doctrine or discipline or is a scandal to the faithful.

§2. The allocation of the goods of an association which has ceased to exist must be determined according to the norm of its statutes, without prejudice to acquired rights and the intention of the donors.

CHAPTER IV. Special Norms for Associations of the Laity

CAN. 327 Lay members of the Christian faithful are to hold in esteem associations established for the spiritual purposes mentioned in can. 298, especially those which propose to animate the temporal order with the Christian spirit and in this way greatly foster an intimate union between faith and life.

CAN. 328 Those who preside over associations of the laity, even those which have been erected by virtue of apostolic privilege, are to take care that their associations cooperate with other associations of the Christian faithful where it is expedient and willingly assist various Christian works, especially those in the same territory.

CAN. 329 Moderators of associations of the laity are to take care that the members of the association are duly formed to exercise the apostolate proper to the laity.

tate, si eius actio in grave damnum cedit doctrinae vel disciplinae ecclesiasticae, aut scandalo est fidelium.

§2. Destinatio bonorum consociationis extinctae ad normam statutorum determinanda est, salvis iuribus quaesitis atque oblatorum voluntate.

CAPUT IV. Normae Speciales de Laicorum Consociationibus

CAN. 327 Christifideles laici magni faciant consociationes ad spirituales fines, de quibus in can. 298, constitutas, eas speciatim quae rerum temporalium ordinem spiritu christiano animare sibi proponunt atque hoc modo intimam inter fidem et vitam magnopere fovent unionem.

CAN. 328 Qui praesunt consociationibus laicorum, iis etiam quae vi privilegii apostolici erectae sunt, curent ut suae cum aliis christifidelium consociationibus, ubi id expediat, cooperentur, utque variis operibus christianis, praesertim in eodem territorio existentibus, libenter auxilio sint.

CAN. 329 Moderatores consociationum laicorum curent, ut sodales consociationis ad apostolatum laicis proprium exercendum debite efformentur.

326 §2: c. 1515 §1
327: c. 686; Pius PP. XII, All., 5 oct. 1957 (AAS 49 [1957] 924–931); LG 31; AA 2, 7, 19
328: Pius PP. XII, All., 12 oct. 1952; Pius PP. XII,
All., 11 ian. 1953
329: IM 15; LG 35; AA 4, 28–32; DH 14; AG 26; GS 43, 72

PART II. THE HIERARCHICAL CONSTITUTION OF THE CHURCH

PARS II. DE ECCLESIAE CONSTITUTIONE HIERARCHICA

SECTION I. The Supreme Authority of the Church

SECTIO I. *De Suprema Ecclesiae Auctoritate*

CHAPTER I. The Roman Pontiff and the College of Bishops

CAPUT I. **De Romano Pontifice deque Collegio Episcoporum**

CAN. 330 Just as by the Lord's decision Saint Peter and the other Apostles constitute one college, so in a like manner the Roman Pontiff, the successor of Peter, and the bishops, the successors of the Apostles, are united among themselves.

CAN. 330 Sicut, statuente Domino, sanctus Petrus et ceteri Apostoli unum Collegium constituunt, pari ratione Romanus Pontifex, successor Petri, et Episcopi, successores Apostolorum, inter se coniuguntur.

ART. 1. *The Roman Pontiff*

ART. 1. *De Romano Pontifice*

CAN. 331 The bishop of the Roman Church, in whom continues the office given by the Lord uniquely to Peter, the first of the Apostles, and to be transmitted to his successors, is the head of the college of bishops, the Vicar of Christ, and the pastor of the universal Church on earth. By virtue of his office he possesses supreme, full, immediate, and universal ordinary power in the Church, which he is always able to exercise freely.

CAN. 331 Ecclesiae Romanae Episcopus, in quo permanet munus a Domino singulariter Petro, primo Apostolorum, concessum et successoribus eius transmittendum, Collegii Episcoporum est caput, Vicarius Christi atque universae Ecclesiae his in terris Pastor; qui ideo vi muneris sui suprema, plena, immediata et universali in Ecclesia gaudet ordinaria potestate, quam semper libere exercere valet.

CAN. 332 §1. The Roman Pontiff obtains full and supreme power in the Church by his acceptance of legitimate election together with episcopal consecration. Therefore, a person

CAN. 332 §1. Plenam et supremam in Ecclesia potestatem Romanus Pontifex obtinet legitima electione ab ipso acceptata una cum episcopali consecratione. Quare,

330: LG 22, nep

331: c. 218; Pius PP. XI, Enc. *Ecclesiam Dei,* 12 nov. 1923 (AAS 15 [1923] 573–574); Pius PP. XI, Enc. *Mortalium animos,* 6 ian. 1928 (AAS 20 [1928] 10); LG

18, 20, 22, 23, nep 3 et 4; OE 3; UR 2; CD 2

332 §1: c. 219; Pius PP. XII, Const. Ap. *Vacantis Apostolicae Sedis,* 8 dec. 1945, 101 (AAS 38 [1946] 97); CD 2; RPE 88

elected to the supreme pontificate who is marked with episcopal character obtains this power from the moment of acceptance. If the person elected lacks episcopal character, however, he is to be ordained a bishop immediately.

§2. If it happens that the Roman Pontiff resigns his office, it is required for validity that the resignation is made freely and properly manifested but not that it is accepted by anyone.

CAN. 333 §1. By virtue of his office, the Roman Pontiff not only possesses power over the universal Church but also obtains the primacy of ordinary power over all particular churches and groups of them. Moreover, this primacy strengthens and protects the proper, ordinary, and immediate power which bishops possess in the particular churches entrusted to their care.

§2. In fulfilling the office of supreme pastor of the Church, the Roman Pontiff is always joined in communion with the other bishops and with the universal Church. He nevertheless has the right, according to the needs of the Church, to determine the manner, whether personal or collegial, of exercising this office.

§3. No appeal or recourse is permitted against a sentence or decree of the Roman Pontiff.

CAN. 334 Bishops assist the Roman Pontiff in exercising his office. They are able to render him cooperative assistance in various ways, among which is the synod of bishops. The car-

eandem potestatem obtinet a momento acceptationis electus ad summum pontificatum, qui episcopali charactere insignitus est. Quod si charactere episcopali electus careat, statim ordinetur Episcopus.

§2. Si contingat ut Romanus Pontifex muneri suo renuntiet, ad validitatem requiritur ut renuntiatio libere fiat et rite manifestetur, non vero ut a quopiam acceptetur.

CAN. 333 §1. Romanus Pontifex, vi sui muneris, non modo in universam Ecclesiam potestate gaudet, sed et super omnes Ecclesias particulares earumque coetus ordinariae potestatis obtinet principatum, quo quidem insimul roboratur atque vindicatur potestas propria, ordinaria et immediata, qua in Ecclesias particulares suae curae commissas Episcopi pollent.

§2. Romanus Pontifex, in munere supremi Ecclesiae Pastoris explendo, communione cum ceteris Episcopis immo et universa Ecclesia semper est coniunctus; ipsi ius tamen est, iuxta Ecclesiae necessitates, determinare modum, sive personalem sive collegialem, huius muneris exercendi.

§3. Contra sententiam vel decretum Romani Pontificis non datur appellatio neque recursus.

CAN. 334 In eius munere exercendo, Romano Pontifici praesto sunt Episcopi, qui eidem cooperatricem operam navare valent variis rationibus, inter quas est synodus Epis-

332 §2: cc. 185, 186

333 §1: c. 218 §2; Pius PP. XI, Enc. *Mortalium animos,* 6 ian. 1928 (AAS 20 [1928] 15); Pius PP. XI, Enc. *Ad salutem,* 20 apr. 1930 (AAS 22 [1930] 211–212); Pius PP. XI, Enc. *Lux veritatis,* 25 dec. 1931 (AAS 23 [1931] 497–505); Pius PP. XII, Enc. *Mystici Corporis,* 29 iun. 1943 (AAS 35 [1943] 210–213, 227); Pius PP. XII, Enc. *Sempiternus rex,* 8 sep. 1951 (AAS 43 [1951] 633); LG 13, 18, 22, 27; CD 2, 8

333 §2: Pius PP. XII, Enc. *Mystici Corporis,* 29 iun. 1943 (AAS 35 [1943] 210–215); Pius PP. XII, Enc. *Fidei donum,* 21 apr. 1957 (AAS 49 [1957] 236–237); LG 13, 18, 22, 23, 27, nep 3 et 4; AG 22; SE *Nunc nobis,* 25 oct. 1969

333 §3: c. 228 §2

334: c. 230; CD 10; Paulus PP. VI, m. p. *Pro comperto sane,* 6 aug. 1967, I, II (AAS 59 [1967] 883); REU prooemium §1; SE *Nunc nobis,* 25 oct. 1969

dinals also assist him, as do other persons and various institutes according to the needs of the times. In his name and by his authority, all these persons and institutes fulfill the function entrusted to them for the good of all the churches, according to the norms defined by law.

CAN. 335 When the Roman See is vacant or entirely impeded, nothing is to be altered in the governance of the universal Church; the special laws issued for these circumstances, however, are to be observed.

ART. 2. *The College of Bishops*

CAN. 336 The college of bishops, whose head is the Supreme Pontiff and whose members are bishops by virtue of sacramental consecration and hierarchical communion with the head and members of the college and in which the apostolic body continues, together with its head and never without this head, is also the subject of supreme and full power over the universal Church.

CAN. 337 §1. The college of bishops exercises power over the universal Church in a solemn manner in an ecumenical council.

§2. It exercises the same power through the united action of the bishops dispersed in the world, which the Roman Pontiff has publicly declared or freely accepted as such so that it becomes a true collegial act.

§3. It is for the Roman Pontiff, according to the needs of the Church, to select and promote the ways by which the college of bishops is to exercise its function collegially regarding the universal Church.

coporum. Auxilio praeterea ei sunt Patres Cardinales, necnon aliae personae itemque varia secundum temporum necessitates instituta; quae personae omnes et instituta, nomine et auctoritate ipsius, munus sibi commissum explent in bonum omnium Ecclesiarum, iuxta normas iure definitas.

CAN. 335 Sede romana vacante aut prorsus impedita, nihil innovetur in Ecclesiae universae regimine; serventur autem leges speciales pro iisdem adiunctis latae.

ART. 2. *De Collegio Episcoporum*

CAN. 336 Collegium Episcoporum, cuius caput est Summus Pontifex cuiusque membra sunt Episcopi vi sacramentalis consecrationis et hierarchica communione cum Collegii capite et membris, et in quo corpus apostolicum continuo perseverat, una cum capite suo, et numquam sine hoc capite, subiectum quoque supremae et plenae potestatis in universam Ecclesiam exsistit.

CAN. 337 §1. Potestatem in universam Ecclesiam Collegium Episcoporum sollemni modo exercet in Concilio Oecumenico.

§2. Eandem potestatem exercet per unitam Episcoporum in mundo dispersorum actionem, quae uti talis a Romano Pontifice sit indicta aut libere recepta, ita ut verus actus collegialis efficiatur.

§3. Romani Pontificis est secundum necessitates Ecclesiae seligere et promovere modos, quibus Episcoporum Collegium munus suum quoad universam Ecclesiam collegialiter exerceat.

335: cc. 241, 436; Pius PP. XII, Const. Ap. *Vacantis Apostolicae Sedis,* 8 dec. 1945, 1–28 (AAS 38 [1946] 67–74); RPE 1–26; REU prooemium
336: c. 329 §1; Pius PP. XI, Enc. *Ecclesiam Dei,* 12 nov. 1923 (AAS 15 [1923] 573–574); LG 20, 22, 23, nep;

CD 4, 44, 49; AG 38; SE *Elapso Oecumenico,* 22 oct. 1969
337 §1: c. 228; LG 22, 25; CD 4
337 §2: LG 22; CD 4; DPME 50–53
337 §3: LG 22, nep 3

CAN. 338 §1. It is for the Roman Pontiff alone to convoke an ecumenical council, preside over it personally or through others, transfer, suspend, or dissolve a council, and to approve its decrees.

§2. It is for the Roman Pontiff to determine the matters to be treated in a council and establish the order to be observed in a council. To the questions proposed by the Roman Pontiff, the council fathers can add others which are to be approved by the Roman Pontiff.

CAN. 339 §1. All the bishops and only the bishops who are members of the college of bishops have the right and duty to take part in an ecumenical council with a deliberative vote.

§2. Moreover, some others who are not bishops can be called to an ecumenical council by the supreme authority of the Church, to whom it belongs to determine their roles in the council.

CAN. 340 If the Apostolic See becomes vacant during the celebration of a council, the council is interrupted by the law itself until the new Supreme Pontiff orders it to be continued or dissolves it.

CAN. 341 §1. The decrees of an ecumenical council do not have obligatory force unless they have been approved by the Roman Pontiff together with the council fathers, confirmed by him, and promulgated at his order.

§2. To have obligatory force, decrees which the college of bishops issues when it places a truly collegial action in another way initiated or freely accepted by the Roman Pon-

CAN. 338 §1. Unius Romani Pontificis est Concilium Oecumenicum convocare, eidem per se vel per alios praesidere, item Concilium transferre, suspendere vel dissolvere, eiusque decreta approbare.

§2. Eiusdem Romani Pontificis est res in Concilio tractandas determinare atque ordinem in Concilio servandum constituere; propositis a Romano Pontifice quaestionibus Patres Concilii alias addere possunt, ab eodem Romano Pontifice probandas.

CAN. 339 §1. Ius est et officium omnibus et solis Episcopis qui membra sint Collegii Episcoporum, ut Concilio Oecumenico cum suffragio deliberativo intersint.

§2. Ad Concilium Oecumenicum insuper alii aliqui, qui episcopali dignitate non sint insigniti, vocari possunt a suprema Ecclesiae auctoritate, cuius est eorum partes in Concilio determinare.

CAN. 340 Si contingat Apostolicam Sedem durante Concilii celebratione vacare, ipso iure hoc intermittitur, donec novus Summus Pontifex illud continuari iusserit aut dissolverit.

CAN. 341 §1. Concilii Oecumenici decreta vim obligandi non habent nisi una cum Concilii Patribus a Romano Pontifice approbata, ab eodem fuerint confirmata et eius iussu promulgata.

§2. Eadem confirmatione et promulgatione, vim obligandi ut habeant, egent decreta quae ferat Collegium Episcoporum, cum actionem proprie collegialem ponit iuxta ali-

338 §1: cc. 222 §1, 227; LG 22

338 §2: c. 226; IOANNES PP. XXIII, All., 11 oct. 1962 (AAS 54 [1962] 786–795); LG 22, nep 3

339 §1: c. 223 §1, 2° et §2; IOANNES PP. XXIII, Const. Ap. *Humanae salutis*, 25 dec. 1961 (AAS 54 [1962] 5–13)

339 §2: c. 223 §1, 4° et §§2 et 3; IOANNES PP.,

XXIII, m. p. *Appropinquante Concilio*, 6 aug. 1962 (AAS 54 [1962] 609–631); *Ordo Concilii Oecumenici Vaticani II celebrandi*, art. 1. (AAS 54 [1962] 612)

340: c. 229

341 §1: cc. 222 §2, 227; LG 22; FORMULA CONFIRMATIONIS IN CONCILIO VATICANO II ADHIBITA

341 §2: LG 22, nep 4

tiff need the same confirmation and promulgation.

CHAPTER II. **The Synod of Bishops**

CAN. 342   The synod of bishops is a group of bishops who have been chosen from different regions of the world and meet together at fixed times to foster closer unity between the Roman Pontiff and bishops, to assist the Roman Pontiff with their counsel in the preservation and growth of faith and morals and in the observance and strengthening of ecclesiastical discipline, and to consider questions pertaining to the activity of the Church in the world.

CAN. 343   It is for the synod of bishops to discuss the questions for consideration and express its wishes but not to resolve them or issue decrees about them unless in certain cases the Roman Pontiff has endowed it with deliberative power, in which case he ratifies the decisions of the synod.

CAN. 344   The synod of bishops is directly subject to the authority of the Roman Pontiff who:

1° convokes a synod as often as it seems opportune to him and designates the place where its sessions are to be held;

2° ratifies the election of members who must be elected according to the norm of special law and designates and appoints other members;

3° determines at an appropriate time before the celebration of a synod the contents of the questions to be treated, according to the norm of special law;

4° defines the agenda;

5° presides at the synod personally or through others;

um a Romano Pontifice inductum vel libere receptum modum.

CAPUT II. **De Synodo Episcoporum**

CAN. 342   Synodus Episcoporum coetus est Episcoporum qui, ex diversis orbis regionibus selecti, statutis temporibus una conveniunt ut arctam coniunctionem inter Romanum Pontificem et Episcopos foveant, utque eidem Romano Pontifici ad incolumitatem incrementumque fidei et morum, ad disciplinam ecclesiasticam servandam et firmandam consiliis adiutricem operam praestent, necnon quaestiones ad actionem Ecclesiae in mundo spectantes perpendant.

CAN. 343   Synodi Episcoporum est de quaestionibus pertractandis disceptare atque expromere optata, non vero easdem dirimere de iisque ferre decreta, nisi certis in casibus potestate deliberativa eandem instruxerit Romanus Pontifex, cuius est in hoc casu decisiones synodi ratas habere.

CAN. 344   Synodus Episcoporum directe subest auctoritati Romani Pontificis, cuius quidem est:

1° synodum convocare, quotiescumque id ipsi opportunum videatur, locumque designare ubi coetus habendi sint;

2° sodalium, qui ad normam iuris peculiaris eligendi sunt, electionem ratam habere aliosque sodales designare et nominare;

3° argumenta quaestionum pertractandarum statuere opportuno tempore ad normam iuris peculiaris ante synodi celebrationem;

4° rerum agendarum ordinem definire;

5° synodo per se aut per alios praeesse;

342: LG 23; CD 5; AS prooemium, I–II; OS (1969) 1

343: AS II

344: AS III; OS (1966) 1, 17; OS (1969) 1

6° concludes, transfers, suspends, and dissolves the synod.

CAN. 345   The synod of bishops can be assembled in a general session, that is, one which treats matters that directly pertain to the good of the universal Church; such a session is either ordinary or extraordinary. It can also be assembled in a special session, namely, one which considers affairs that directly pertain to a determinate region or regions.

CAN. 346   §1. A synod of bishops assembled in an ordinary general session consists of members of whom the greater part are bishops elected for each session by the conferences of bishops according to the method determined by the special law of the synod; others are designated by virtue of the same law; others are appointed directly by the Roman Pontiff; to these are added some members of clerical religious institutes elected according to the norm of the same special law.

§2. A synod of bishops gathered in an extraordinary general session to treat affairs which require a speedy solution consists of members of whom the greater part are bishops designated by the special law of the synod by reason of the office which they hold; others are appointed directly by the Roman Pontiff; to these are added some members of clerical religious institutes elected according to the norm of the same law.

§3. A synod of bishops gathered in a special session consists of members especially selected from those regions for which it was called, according to the norm of the special law which governs the synod.

6° synodum ipsam concludere, transferre, suspendere et dissolvere.

CAN. 345   Synodus Episcoporum congregari potest aut in coetum generalem, in quo scilicet res tractantur ad bonum Ecclesiae universae directe spectantes, qui quidem coetus est sive ordinarius sive extraordinarius, aut etiam in coetum specialem, in quo nempe aguntur negotia quae directe ad determinatam determinatasve regiones attinent.

CAN. 346   §1. Synodus Episcoporum quae in coetum generalem ordinarium congregatur, constat sodalibus quorum plerique sunt Episcopi, electi pro singulis coetibus ab Episcoporum conferentiis secundum rationem iure peculiari synodi determinatam; alii vi eiusdem iuris deputantur; alii a Romano Pontifice directe nominantur; quibus accedunt aliqui sodales institutorum religiosorum clericalium, qui ad normam eiusdem iuris peculiaris eliguntur.

§2. Synodus Episcoporum in coetum generalem extraordinarium congregata ad negotia tractanda quae expeditam requirant definitionem, constat sodalibus quorum plerique, Episcopi, a iure peculiari synodi deputantur ratione officii quod adimplent, alii vero a Romano Pontifice directe nominantur; quibus accedunt aliqui sodales institutorum religiosorum clericalium ad normam eiusdem iuris electi.

§3. Synodus Episcoporum, quae in coetum specialem congregatur, constat sodalibus delectis praecipue ex iis regionibus pro quibus convocata est, ad normam iuris peculiaris, quo synodus regitur.

345: AS IV; OS (1969) 4
346 §1: AS V, VII, X, XII; OS (1966) 2, 5 §§1 et 4; OS (1969) 1, 2, 5 §§1 et 4
346 §2: AS VI; OS (1966) 5 §§2 et 4; OS (1969) 5 §2
346 §3: AS VII; OS (1966) 5 §3; OS (1969) 5 §§3 et 4

CAN. 347 §1. When the Roman Pontiff concludes a session of the synod of bishops, the function entrusted in it to the bishops and other members ceases.

§2. If the Apostolic See becomes vacant after a synod is convoked or during its celebration, the session of the synod and the function entrusted to its members are suspended by the law itself until the new Pontiff has decided to dissolve or continue the session.

CAN. 348 §1. The synod of bishops has a permanent general secretariat presided over by a general secretary who is appointed by the Roman Pontiff and assisted by the council of the secretariat. This council consists of bishops, some of whom are elected by the synod of bishops itself according to the norm of special law while others are appointed by the Roman Pontiff. The function of all these ceases when a new general session begins.

§2. Furthermore, for each session of the synod of bishops one or more special secretaries are constituted who are appointed by the Roman Pontiff and remain in the office entrusted to them only until the session of the synod has been completed.

CHAPTER III. The Cardinals of the Holy Roman Church

CAN. 349 The cardinals of the Holy Roman Church constitute a special college which provides for the election of the Roman Pontiff according to the norm of special law. The cardinals assist the Roman Pontiff either collegially when they are convoked to deal with questions of major importance, or individually

CAN. 347 §1. Cum synodi Episcoporum coetus a Romano Pontifice concluditur, explicit munus in eadem Episcopis aliisque sodalibus commissum.

§2. Sede Apostolica post convocatam synodum aut inter eius celebrationem vacante, ipso iure suspenditur synodi coetus, itemque munus sodalibus in eodem commissum, donec novus Pontifex coetum aut dissolvendum aut continuandum decreverit.

CAN. 348 §1. Synodi Episcoporum habetur secretaria generalis permanens, cui praeest Secretarius generalis, a Romano Pontifice nominatus, cuique praesto est consilium secretariae, constans Episcopis, quorum alii, ad normam iuris peculiaris, ab ipsa synodo Episcoporum eliguntur, alii a Romano Pontifice nominantur, quorum vero omnium munus explicit, ineunte novo coetu generali.

§2. Pro quolibet synodi Episcoporum coetu praeterea unus aut plures secretarii speciales constituuntur qui a Romano Pontifice nominantur, atque in officio ipsis commisso permanent solum usque ad expletum synodi coetum.

CAPUT III. De Sanctae Romanae Ecclesiae Cardinalibus

CAN. 349 S.R.E. Cardinales peculiare Collegium constituunt, cui competit ut electioni Romani Pontificis provideat ad normam iuris peculiaris; Cardinales item Romano Pontifici adsunt sive collegialiter agendo, cum ad quaestiones maioris momenti tractandas in unum convocantur, sive ut singuli,

347 §1: AS XI
347 §2: OS (1969) 17 §4
348 §1: AS XII; OS (1971) 11–13

348 §2: AS XII; OS (1971) 13
349: c. 230; IOANNES PP. XXIII, m. p. *Cum gravissima*, 15 apr. 1962 (AAS 54 [1962] 256–258); RPE 33

when they help the Roman Pontiff through the various offices they perform, especially in the daily care of the universal Church.

CAN. 350 §1. The college of cardinals is divided into three orders: the episcopal order, to which belong cardinals to whom the Roman Pontiff assigns title of a suburbicarian church and Eastern patriarchs who have been brought into the college of cardinals; the presbyteral order and the diaconal order.

§2. The Roman Pontiff assigns each of the cardinals of the presbyteral or diaconal orders his own title or *diaconia* in Rome.

§3. Eastern patriarchs who have been made members of the college of cardinals have their own patriarchal see as a title.

§4. The cardinal dean holds as his title the Diocese of Ostia together with the other church he already has as a title.

§5. Through a choice made in consistory and approved by the Supreme Pontiff and with priority of order and promotion observed, cardinals from the presbyteral order can transfer to another title, and cardinals from the diaconal order to another *diaconia* and if they have been in the diaconal order for ten full years, even to the presbyteral order.

§6. A cardinal transferring through choice from the diaconal order to the presbyteral order takes precedence over all those cardinal presbyters who were brought into the cardinalate after him.

CAN. 351 §1. The Roman Pontiff freely se-

scilicet variis officiis, quibus funguntur, eidem Romano Pontifici operam praestando in cura praesertim cotidiana universae Ecclesiae.

CAN. 350 §1. Cardinalium Collegium in tres ordines distribuitur: episcopalem, ad quem pertinent Cardinales quibus a Romano Pontifice titulus assignatur Ecclesiae suburbicariae, necnon Patriarchae orientales qui in Cardinalium Collegium relati sunt; presbyteralem et diaconalem.

§2. Cardinalibus ordinis presbyteralis ac diaconalis suus cuique titulus aut diaconia in Urbe assignatur a Romano Pontifice.

§3. Patriarchae orientales in Cardinalium Collegium assumpti in titulum habent suam patriarchalem sedem.

§4. Cardinalis Decanus in titulum habet dioecesim Ostiensem, una cum alia Ecclesia quam in titulum iam habebat.

§5. Per optionem in Consistorio factam et a Summo Pontifice approbatam, possunt, servata prioritate ordinis et promotionis, Cardinales ex ordine presbyterali transire ad alium titulum et Cardinales ex ordine diaconali ad aliam diaconiam et, si per integrum decennium in ordine diaconali permanserint, etiam ad ordinem presbyteralem.

§6. Cardinalis ex ordine diaconali transiens per optionem ad ordinem presbyteralem, locum obtinet ante omnes illos Cardinales presbyteros, qui post ipsum ad Cardinalatum assumpti sunt.

CAN. 351 §1. Qui Cardinales pro-

350 §1: c. 231 §1; IOANNES PP. XXIII, m. p. *Ad suburbicarias*, 10 mar. 1961 (AAS 53 [1961] 198); IOANNES PP. XXIII, m. p. *Suburbicariis sedibus*, 11 apr. 1962, I (AAS 54 [1962] 253–256); PAULUS PP. VI, m. p. *Ad purpuratorum Patrum*, 11 feb. 1965, I (AAS 57 [1965] 295)

350 §2: c. 231 §2

350 §3: PAULUS PP. VI, m. p. *Ad purpuratorum*

Patrum, 11 feb. 1965 (AAS 57 [1965] 295–296)

350 §4: c. 236 §4

350 §5: c. 236 §1; CI Resp., 29 maii 1934 (AAS 26 [1934] 493)

350 §6: c. 236 §2; CI Resp., 29 maii 1934 (AAS 26 [1934] 493)

351 §1: c. 232 §1; IOANNES PP. XXIII, m. p. *Cum gravissima*, 15 apr. 1962 (AAS 54 [1962] 256–258)

lects men to be promoted as cardinals, who have been ordained at least into the order of the presbyterate and are especially outstanding in doctrine, morals, piety, and prudence in action; those who are not yet bishops must receive episcopal consecration.

§2. Cardinals are created by a decree of the Roman Pontiff which is made public in the presence of the college of cardinals. From the moment of the announcement they are bound by the duties and possess the rights defined by law.

§3. When the Roman Pontiff has announced the selection of a person to the dignity of cardinal but reserves the name of the person *in pectore*, the one promoted is not bound in the meantime by any of the duties of cardinals nor does he possess any of their rights. After the Roman Pontiff has made his name public, however, he is bound by the same duties and possesses the same rights; he possesses the right of precedence, though, from the day of reservation *in pectore*.

CAN. 352 §1. The dean presides over the college of cardinals; if he is impeded, the assistant dean takes his place. Neither the dean nor the assistant dean possesses any power of governance over the other cardinals but is considered as first among equals.

§2. When the office of dean is vacant, the cardinals who possess title to a suburbicarian church and they alone are to elect one from their own group who is to act as dean of the college; the assistant dean, if he is present, or else the oldest among them, presides at this election. They are to submit the name of the person elected to the Roman Pontiff who is competent to approve him.

moveantur, libere a Romano Pontifice seliguntur viri, saltem in ordine presbyteratus constituti, doctrina, moribus, pietate necnon rerum agendarum prudentia egregie praestantes; qui nondum sunt Episcopi, consecrationem episcopalem recipere debent.

§2. Cardinales creantur Romani Pontificis decreto, quod quidem coram Cardinalium Collegio publicatur; inde a publicatione facta officiis tenentur atque iuribus gaudent lege definitis.

§3. Promotus ad cardinalitiam dignitatem, cuius creationem Romanus Pontifex annuntiaverit, nomen autem in pectore sibi reservans, nullis interim tenetur Cardinalium officiis ullisque eorum gaudet iuribus; postquam autem a Romano Pontifice eius nomen publicatum fuerit, iisdem tenetur officiis fruiturque iuribus, sed iure praecedentiae gaudet a die reservationis in pectore.

CAN. 352 §1. Cardinalium Collegio praeest Decanus, eiusque impediti vices sustinet Subdecanus; Decanus, vel Subdecanus, nulla in ceteros Cardinales gaudet potestate regiminis, sed ut primus inter pares habetur.

§2. Officio Decani vacante, Cardinales titulo Ecclesiae suburbicariae decorati, iique soli, praesidente Subdecano si adsit, aut antiquiore ex ipsis, e coetus sui gremio unum eligant qui Decanum Collegii agat; eius nomen ad Romanum Pontificem deferant, cui competit electum probare.

351 §2: c. 233 §1
351 §3: c. 233 §2
352 §1: c. 237 §1; PAULUS PP. VI, m. p. *Sacro Car-*

dinalium Consilio, 26 feb. 1965, V (AAS 57 [1965] 297)
352 §2: PAULUS PP. VI, m. p. *Sacro Cardinalium Consilio*, 26 feb. 1965, II (AAS 57 [1965] 297)

§3. The assistant dean is elected in the same manner as that described in §2, with the dean himself presiding. The Roman Pontiff is also competent to approve the election of the assistant dean.

§4. If the dean and assistant dean do not have a domicile in Rome, they are to acquire one there.

CAN. 353 §1. The cardinals especially assist the supreme pastor of the Church through collegial action in consistories in which they are gathered by order of the Roman Pontiff who presides. Consistories are either ordinary or extraordinary.

§2. For an ordinary consistory, all the cardinals, at least those present in Rome, are called together to be consulted concerning certain grave matters which occur rather frequently or to carry out certain very solemn acts.

§3. For an extraordinary consistory, which is celebrated when particular needs of the Church or the treatment of more grave affairs suggests it, all the cardinals are called together.

§4. Only the ordinary consistory in which some solemnities are celebrated can be public, that is, when prelates, representatives of civil societies, and others who have been invited to it are admitted in addition to the cardinals.

CAN. 354 The cardinals who preside over dicasteries and other permanent institutes of the Roman Curia and Vatican City and who have completed the seventy-fifth year of age are asked to submit their resignation from office to the Roman Pontiff who will see to the matter after considering the circumstances.

§3. Eadem ratione de qua in §2, praesidente ipso Decano, eligitur Subdecanus; Subdecani quoque electionem probare Romano Pontifici competit.

§4. Decanus et Subdecanus, si in Urbe domicilium non habeant, illud ibidem acquirant.

CAN. 353 §1. Cardinales collegiali actione supremo Ecclesiae Pastori praecipue auxilio sunt in Consistoriis, in quibus iussu Romani Pontificis eoque praesidente congregantur; Consistoria habentur ordinaria aut extraordinaria.

§2. In Consistorium ordinarium, convocantur omnes Cardinales, saltem in Urbe versantes, ad consultationem de quibusdam negotiis gravibus, communius tamen contingentibus, aut ad actus quosdam maxime sollemnes peragendos.

§3. In Consistorium extraordinarium, quod celebratur cum peculiares Ecclesiae necessitates vel graviora negotia tractanda id suadeant, convocantur omnes Cardinales.

§4. Solum Consistorium ordinarium, in quo aliquae sollemnitates celebrantur, potest esse publicum, cum scilicet praeter Cardinales admittuntur Praelati, legati societatum civilium aliive ad illud invitati.

CAN. 354 Patres Cardinales dicasteriis aliisve institutis permanentibus Romanae Curiae et Civitatis Vaticanae praepositi, qui septuagesimum quintum aetatis annum expleverint, rogantur ut renuntiationem ab officio exhibeant Romano Pontifici qui, omnibus perpensis, providebit.

352 §3: PAULUS PP. VI, m. p. *Sacro Cardinalium Consilio*, 26 feb. 1965, III (AAS 57 [1965] 297)
352 §4: c. 238 §§1 et 2; PAULUS PP. VI, m. p. *Sacro Cardinalium Consilio*, 26 feb. 1965, I (AAS 57 [1965] 296–297)
354: PAULUS PP. VI, m. p. *Ingravescentem aetatem*, 21 ian. 1970, I (AAS 62 [1970] 811)

CAN. 355 §1. The cardinal dean is competent to ordain as a bishop the one elected as Roman Pontiff if he needs to be ordained; if the dean is impeded, the assistant dean has the same right, and if he is impeded, the oldest cardinal from the episcopal order.

§2. The senior cardinal deacon announces the name of the newly elected Supreme Pontiff to the people; likewise, in the place of the Roman Pontiff, he places the pallium upon metropolitans or hands it over to their proxies.

CAN. 356 Cardinals are obliged to cooperate assiduously with the Roman Pontiff; therefore, cardinals who exercise any office in the curia and who are not diocesan bishops are obliged to reside in Rome. Cardinals who have the care of some diocese as the diocesan bishop are to go to Rome whenever the Roman Pontiff calls them.

CAN. 357 §1. The cardinals who have been assigned title to a suburbicarian church or a church in Rome are to promote the good of these dioceses or churches by counsel and patronage after they have taken possession of them. Nevertheless, they possess no power of governance over them nor are they to intervene in any way in those matters which pertain to the administration of their goods, their discipline, or the service of the churches.

§2. In those matters which pertain to their own person, cardinals living outside of Rome and outside their own diocese are exempt from the power of governance of the bishop of the diocese in which they are residing.

CAN. 355 §1. Cardinali Decano competit electum Romanum Pontificem in Episcopum ordinare, si electus ordinatione indigeat; impedito Decano, idem ius competit Subdecano, eoque impedito, antiquiori Cardinali ex ordine episcopali.

§2. Cardinalis Proto-diaconus nomen novi electi Summi Pontificis populo annuntiat; item pallia Metropolitis imponit eorumve procuratoribus tradit, vice Romani Pontificis.

CAN. 356 Cardinales obligatione tenentur cum Romano Pontifice sedulo cooperandi; Cardinales itaque quovis officio in Curia fungentes, qui non sint Episcopi dioecesani, obligatione tenentur residendi in Urbe; Cardinales qui alicuius dioecesis curam habent ut Episcopi dioecesani, Urbem petant quoties a Romano Pontifice convocentur.

CAN. 357 §1. Cardinales, quibus Ecclesia suburbicaria aut ecclesia in Urbe in titulum est assignata, postquam in eiusdem venerunt possessionem, earundem dioecesium et ecclesiarum bonum consilio et patrocinio promoveant, nulla tamen in easdem potestate regiminis pollentes, ac nulla ratione sese in iis interponentes, quae ad earum bonorum administrationem, ad disciplinam aut ecclesiarum servitium spectant.

§2. Cardinales extra Urbem et extra propriam dioecesim degentes, in iis quae ad sui personam pertinent exempti sunt a potestate regiminis Episcopi dioecesis in qua commorantur.

355 §1: c. 239 §2; Pius PP. XII, Const. Ap. *Vacantis Apostolicae Sedis*, 8 dec. 1945, 107 (AAS 38 [1946] 98); RPE 90b
355 §2: c. 239 §3
356: c. 238; REU prooemium

357 §1: c. 240 §2; Ioannes PP. XXIII, m. p. *Suburbicariis sedibus*, 11 apr. 1962, (AAS 54 [1962] 253–256); Paulus PP. VI, m. p. *Ad hoc usque tempus*, 15 apr. 1969, I–III (AAS 61 [1969] 226–227)
357 §2: c. 239 §1

CAN. 358 A cardinal to whom the Roman Pontiff entrusts the function of representing him in some solemn celebration or among some group of persons as a *legatus a latere*, that is, as his alter ego, as well as one to whom the Roman Pontiff entrusts the fulfillment of a certain pastoral function as his special envoy *(missus specialis)* has competence only over those things which the Roman Pontiff commits to him.

CAN. 359 When the Apostolic See is vacant, the college of cardinals possesses only that power in the Church which is attributed to it in special law.

CHAPTER IV. The Roman Curia

CAN. 360 The Supreme Pontiff usually conducts the affairs of the universal Church through the Roman Curia which performs its function in his name and by his authority for the good and service of the churches. The Roman Curia consists of the Secretariat of State or the Papal Secretariat, the Council for the Public Affairs of the Church, congregations, tribunals, and other institutes; the constitution and competence of all these are defined in special law.

CAN. 361 In this Code, the term Apostolic See or Holy See refers not only to the Roman Pontiff but also to the Secretariat of State, the Council for the Public Affairs of the Church, and other institutes of the Roman Curia, unless it is otherwise apparent from the nature of the matter or the context of the words.

CAN. 358 Cardinali, cui a Romano Pontifice hoc munus committitur ut in aliqua sollemni celebratione vel personarum coetu eius personam sustineat, uti Legatus a latere, scilicet tamquam eius alter ego, sicuti et illi cui adimplendum concreditur tamquam ipsius *misso speciali* certum munus pastorale, ea tantum competunt quae ab ipso Romano Pontifice eidem demandantur.

CAN. 359 Sede Apostolica vacante, Cardinalium Collegium ea tantum in Ecclesia gaudet potestate, quae in peculiari lege eidem tribuitur.

CAPUT IV. De Curia Romana

CAN. 360 Curia Romana, qua negotia Ecclesiae universae Summus Pontifex expedire solet et quae nomine et auctoritate ipsius munus explet in bonum et in servitium Ecclesiarum, constat Secretaria Status seu Papali, Consilio pro publicis Ecclesiae negotiis, Congregationibus, Tribunalibus, aliisque Institutis, quorum omnium constitutio et competentia lege peculiari definiuntur.

CAN. 361 Nomine Sedis Apostolicae vel Sanctae Sedis in hoc Codice veniunt non solum Romanus Pontifex, sed etiam, nisi ex rei natura vel sermonis contextu aliud appareat, Secretaria Status, Consilium pro publicis Ecclesiae negotiis, aliaque Romanae Curiae Instituta.

358: c. 266; SOE I, 3

359: c. 241; Pius PP. XII, Const. Ap. *Vacantis Apostolicae Sedis,* 8 dec. 1945, 1–5 (AAS 38 [1946] 67–68); RPE 1–6

360: c. 242; Paulus PP. VI, All., 21 sep. 1963 (AAS 55 [1963] 793–800); CD 9; REU I §1; SE *Nunc nobis,* 25 oct. 1969

361: c. 7

CHAPTER V. **Legates of the Roman Pontiff**

CAN. 362 The Roman Pontiff has the innate and independent right to appoint, send, transfer, and recall his own legates either to particular churches in various nations or regions or to states and public authorities. The norms of international law are to be observed in what pertains to the mission and recall of legates appointed to states.

CAN. 363 §1. To the legates of the Roman Pontiff is entrusted the office of representing the Roman Pontiff in a stable manner to particular churches or also to the states and public authorities to which they are sent.

§2. Those who are designated as delegates or observers in a pontifical mission at international councils or at conferences and meetings also represent the Apostolic See.

CAN. 364 The principal function of a pontifical legate is daily to make stronger and more effective the bonds of unity which exist between the Apostolic See and particular churches. Therefore, it pertains to the pontifical legate for his own jurisdiction:

1° to send information to the Apostolic See concerning the conditions of particular churches and everything that touches the life of the Church and the good of souls;

2° to assist bishops by action and counsel while leaving intact the exercise of their legitimate power;

3° to foster close relations with the confer-

CAPUT V. **De Romani Pontificis Legatis**

CAN. 362 Romano Pontifici ius est nativum et independens Legatos suos nominandi ac mittendi sive ad Ecclesias particulares in variis nationibus vel regionibus, sive simul ad Civitates et ad publicas Auctoritates, itemque eos transferendi et revocandi, servatis quidem normis iuris internationalis, quod attinet ad missionem et revocationem Legatorum apud Res Publicas constitutorum.

CAN. 363 §1. Legatis Romani Pontificis officium committitur ipsius Romani Pontificis stabili modo gerendi personam apud Ecclesias particulares aut etiam apud Civitates et publicas Auctoritates, ad quas missi sunt.

§2. Personam gerunt Apostolicae Sedis ii quoque, qui in pontificiam Missionem ut Delegati aut Observatores deputantur apud Consilia internationalia aut apud Conferentias et Conventus.

CAN. 364 Praecipuum munus Legati pontificii est ut firmiora et efficaciora in dies reddantur unitatis vincula, quae inter Apostolicam Sedem et Ecclesias particulares intercedunt. Ad pontificium ergo Legatum pertinet pro sua dicione:

1° ad Apostolicam Sedem notitias mittere de condicionibus in quibus versantur Ecclesiae particulares, deque omnibus quae ipsam vitam Ecclesiae et bonum animarum attingant;

2° Episcopis actione et consilio adesse, integro quidem manente eorundem legitimae potestatis exercitio;

3° crebras fovere relationes cum Episco-

362: c. 265; SOE I, 2; III, 1
363 §1: SOE I, 1, 2
363 §2: SOE II, 1
364: cc. 267, 269; CD 8a; GS 77; SOE IV–VI, VIII;

SCE *Index facultatum nuntiis, internuntiis et delegatis apostolicis tributarum,* 1 ian. 1968; SCPF *Index facultatum . . . in territoriis missionum,* 1 ian. 1971; NPEM IX, XII

ence of bishops by offering it assistance in every way;

4° regarding the nomination of bishops, to transmit or propose to the Apostolic See the names of candidates and to instruct the informational process concerning those to be promoted, according to the norms given by the Apostolic See;

5° to strive to promote matters which pertain to the peace, progress, and cooperative effort of peoples;

6° to collaborate with bishops so that suitable relations are fostered between the Catholic Church and other Churches or ecclesial communities, and even non-Christian religions;

7° in associated action with bishops, to protect those things which pertain to the mission of the Church and the Apostolic See before the leaders of the state;

8° in addition, to exercise the faculties and to fulfill other mandates which the Apostolic See entrusts to him.

CAN. 365 §1. It is also the special function of a pontifical legate who at the same time acts as a legate to states according to the norms of international law:

1° to promote and foster relations between the Apostolic See and the authorities of the state;

2° to deal with questions which pertain to relations between Church and state and in a special way to deal with the drafting and implementation of concordats and other agreements of this type.

§2. In conducting the affairs mentioned in §1, a pontifical legate, as circumstances suggest, is not to neglect to seek the opinion and counsel of

porum conferentia, eidem omnimodam operam praebendo;

4° ad nominationem Episcoporum quod attinet, nomina candidatorum Apostolicae Sedi transmittere vel proponere necnon processum informativum de promovendis instruere, secundum normas ab Apostolica Sede datas;

5° anniti ut promoveantur res quae ad pacem, ad progressum et consociatam populorum operam spectant;

6° operam conferre cum Episcopis, ut opportuna foveantur commercia inter Ecclesiam catholicam et alias Ecclesias vel communitates ecclesiales, immo et religiones non christianas;

7° ea quae pertinent ad Ecclesiae et Apostolicae Sedis missionem, consociata cum Episcopis actione, apud moderatores Civitatis tueri;

8° exercere praeterea facultates et cetera explere mandata quae ipsi ab Apostolica Sede committantur.

CAN. 365 §1. Legati pontificii, qui simul legationem apud Civitates iuxta iuris internationalis normas exercet, munus quoque peculiare est:

1° promovere et fovere necessitudines inter Apostolicam Sedem et Auctoritates Rei Publicae;

2° quaestiones pertractare quae ad relationes inter Ecclesiam et Civitatem pertinent; et peculiari modo agere de concordatis aliisque huiusmodi conventionibus conficiendis et ad effectum deducendis.

§2. In negotiis, de quibus in §1, expediendis, prout adiuncta suadeant, Legatus pontificius sententiam et consilium Episcoporum

---

365 §1: c. 267 §1; GS 76; SOE X, I   **365 §2:** REU 28; SOE X, 2

the bishops of the ecclesiastical jurisdiction and is to inform them of the course of affairs.

CAN. 366 In view of the particular character of the function of a legate:

1° the seat of a pontifical legation is exempt from the power of governance of the local ordinary unless it is a question of celebrating marriages;

2° after he has notified in advance the local ordinaries insofar as possible, a pontifical legate is permitted to perform liturgical celebrations in all churches of his legation, even in pontificals.

CAN. 367 The function of a pontifical legate does not cease when the Apostolic See becomes vacant unless the pontifical letter establishes otherwise; it does cease, however, when the mandate has been fulfilled, when the legate has been notified of recall, or when the Roman Pontiff accepts the legate's resignation.

dicionis ecclesiasticae exquirere ne omittat, eosque de negotiorum cursu certiores faciat.

Can. 366 Attenta peculiari Legati muneris indole:

1° sedes Legationis pontificiae a potestate regiminis Ordinarii loci exempta est, nisi agatur de matrimoniis celebrandis;

2° Legato pontificio fas est, praemonitis, quantum fieri potest, locorum Ordinariis, in ominbus ecclesiis suae legationis liturgicas celebrationes, etiam in pontificalibus, peragere.

CAN. 367 Pontificii Legati munus non exspirat vacante Sede Apostolica, nisi aliud in litteris pontificiis statuatur; cessat autem expleto mandato, revocatione eidem intimata, renuntiatione a Romano Pontifice acceptata.

SECTION II. Particular Churches and Their Groupings

TITLE I. Particular Churches and the Authority Established in Them

CHAPTER I. Particular Churches

CAN. 368 Particular churches, in which and from which the one and only Catholic

SECTIO II. *De Ecclesiis Particularibus deque Earundem Coetibus*

TITULUS I. De Ecclesiis Particularibus et de Auctoritate in Iisdem Constituta

CAPUT I. DE ECCLESIIS PARTICULARIBUS

CAN. 368 Ecclesiae particulares, in quibus et ex quibus una et unica Ecclesia

366: c. 269 §3; SOE 1–5
367: c. 268; SOE III, 2; RPE 21
368: c. 215; SCPF Instr. *Antequam haec,* 21 iun.

1942 (AAS 34 [1942] 347–349); LG 13, 23, 26; CD 11; AG 19; SCGE Normae, 24 apr. 1971, Introduzione, B; CE 2, 4

Church exists, are first of all dioceses, to which, unless it is otherwise evident, are likened a territorial prelature and territorial abbacy, an apostolic vicariate and an apostolic prefecture, and an apostolic administration erected in a stable manner.

CAN. 369 A diocese is a portion of the people of God which is entrusted to a bishop for him to shepherd with the cooperation of the *presbyterium,* so that, adhering to its pastor and gathered by him in the Holy Spirit through the gospel and the Eucharist, it constitutes a particular church in which the one, holy, catholic, and apostolic Church of Christ is truly present and operative.

CAN. 370 A territorial prelature or territorial abbacy is a certain portion of the people of God which is defined territorially and whose care, due to special circumstances, is entrusted to some prelate or abbot who governs it as its proper pastor just like a diocesan bishop.

CAN. 371 §1. An apostolic vicariate or apostolic prefecture is a certain portion of the people of God which has not yet been established as a diocese due to special circumstances and which, to be shepherded, is entrusted to an apostolic vicar or apostolic prefect who governs it in the name of the Supreme Pontiff.

§2. An apostolic administration is a certain portion of the people of God which is not erected as a diocese by the Supreme Pontiff due to special and particularly grave reasons and whose pastoral care is entrusted to an apostolic administrator who governs it in the name of the Supreme Pontiff.

CAN. 372 §1. As a rule, a portion of the

CAN. 369 Dioecesis est populi Dei portio, quae Episcopo cum cooperatione presbyterii pascenda concreditur, ita ut, pastori suo adhaerens ab eoque per Evangelium et Eucharistiam in Spiritu Sancto congregata, Ecclesiam particularem constituat, in qua vere inest et operatur una sancta catholica et apostolica Christi Ecclesia.

CAN. 370 Praelatura territorialis aut abbatia territorialis est certa populi Dei portio, territorialiter quidem circumscripta, cuius cura, specialia ob adiuncta, committitur alicui Praelato aut Abbati, qui eam, ad instar Episcopi dioecesani, tamquam proprius eius pastor regat.

CAN. 371 §1. Vicariatus apostolicus vel praefectura apostolica est certa populi Dei portio quae, ob peculiaria adiuncta, in dioecesim nondum est constituta, quaeque pascenda committitur Vicario apostolico aut Praefecto apostolico, qui eam nomine Summi Pontificis regant.

§2. Administratio apostolica est certa populi Dei portio, quae ob speciales et graves omnino rationes a Summo Pontifice in dioecesim non erigitur, et cuius cura pastoralis committitur Administratori apostolico, qui eam nomine Summi Pontificis regat.

CAN. 372 §1. Pro regula habeatur ut

catholica exsistit, sunt imprimis dioeceses, quibus, nisi aliud constet, assimilantur praelatura territorialis et abbatia territorialis, vicariatus apostolicus et praefectura apostolica necnon administratio apostolica stabiliter erecta.

369: SC 41; LG 25, 26, 28; CD 11; PO 4, 5
370: cc. 215 §2, 319–327; CE 2, 4; SCE Notif., 17 oct. 1977

371 §1: c. 293 §1; SCPF Instr., 21 iun. 1942 (AAS 34 [1942] 347–348)
372 §1: c. 216; CD 22; ES I, 4; DPME 172

people of God which constitutes a diocese or other particular church is limited to a definite territory so that it includes all the faithful living in the territory.

§2. Nevertheless, where in the judgment of the supreme authority of the Church it seems advantageous after the conferences of bishops concerned have been heard, particular churches distinguished by the rite of the faithful or some other similar reason can be erected in the same territory.

CAN. 373 It is only for the supreme authority to erect particular churches; those legitimately erected possess juridic personality by the law itself.

CAN. 374 §1. Every diocese or other particular church is to be divided into distinct parts or parishes.

§2. To foster pastoral care through common action, several neighboring parishes can be joined into special groups, such as vicariates forane.

CHAPTER II. **Bishops**

ART. 1. *Bishops In General*

CAN. 375 §1. Bishops, who by divine institution succeed to the place of the Apostles through the Holy Spirit who has been given to them, are constituted pastors in the Church, so that they are teachers of doctrine, priests of sacred worship, and ministers of governance.

§2. Through episcopal consecration itself, bishops receive with the function of sanctifying

portio populi Dei quae dioecesim aliamve Ecclesiam particularem constituat, certo territorio circumscribatur, ita ut omnes comprehendat fideles in territorio habitantes.

§2. Attamen, ubi de iudicio supremae Ecclesiae auctoritatis, auditis Episcoporum conferentiis quarum interest, utilitas id suadeat, in eodem territorio erigi possunt Ecclesiae particulares ritu fidelium aliave simili ratione distinctae.

CAN. 373 Unius supremae auctoritatis est Ecclesias particulares erigere; quae, legitime erectae, ipso iure personalitate iuridica gaudent.

CAN. 374 §1. Quaelibet dioecesis aliave Ecclesia particularis dividatur in distinctas partes seu paroecias.

§2. Ad curam pastoralem per communem actionem fovendam plures paroeciae viciniores coniungi possunt in peculiares coetus, uti sunt vicariatus foranei.

CAPUT II. **De Episcopis**

ART. 1. *De Episcopis in Genere*

CAN. 375 §1. Episcopi, qui ex divina institutione in Apostolorum locum succedunt per Spiritum Sanctum qui datus est eis, in Ecclesia Pastores constituuntur, ut sint et ipsi doctrinae magistri, sacri cultus sacerdotes et gubernationis ministri.

§2. Episcopi ipsa consecratione episcopali recipiunt cum munere sanctificandi

---

372 §2: Pius PP. XII, Const. Ap. *Exsul familia,* 1 aug. 1952, Tit. alter, IV (AAS 44 [1952] 699–700); OE 4; CD 23, 43; Princ. 8

373: cc. 100 §1, 215 §1; Pius PP. XII, Enc. *Mystici Corporis,* 29 iun. 1943 (AAS 35 [1943] 211); CI Resp., 23 iun. 1953; LG 22; CD 2; REU 49 §1

374 §1: c. 216 §§1–3; SCPF Instr. *Cum a pluribus,*

25 iul. 1920 (AAS 12 [1920] 331–333); CD 32; ES 1, 21; DPME 174–177

374 §2: c. 217; DPME 184–188

375 §1: c. 329 §1; Pius PP. XII, Enc. *Mystici Corporis,* 29 iun. 1943 (AAS 35 [1943] 211–212); LG 19, 20; CD 2; DPME 32–38

375 §2: LG 21, nep 2; CD 11; DPME 39–43

also the functions of teaching and governing; by their nature, however, these can only be exercised in hierarchical communion with the head and members of the college.

CAN. 376 Bishops to whom the care of some diocese is entrusted are called *diocesan*; others are called *titular*.

CAN. 377 §1. The Supreme Pontiff freely appoints bishops or confirms those legitimately elected.

§2. At least every three years, bishops of an ecclesiastical province or, where circumstances suggest it, of a conference of bishops, are in common counsel and in secret to compose a list of presbyters, even including members of institutes of consecrated life, who are more suitable for the episcopate. They are to send it to the Apostolic See, without prejudice to the right of each bishop individually to make known to the Apostolic See the names of presbyters whom he considers worthy of and suited to the episcopal function.

§3. Unless it is legitimately established otherwise, whenever a diocesan or coadjutor bishop must be appointed, as regards what is called the *ternus* to be proposed to the Apostolic See, the pontifical legate is to seek individually and to communicate to the Apostolic See together with his own opinion the suggestions of the metropolitan and suffragans of the province to which the diocese to be provided for belongs or with which it is joined in some grouping, and the suggestions of the president of the conference of bishops. The pontifical legate, moreover, is to

munera quoque docendi et regendi, quae tamen natura sua nonnisi in hierarchica communione cum Collegii capite et membris exercere possunt.

CAN. 376 Episcopi vocantur *dioecesani*, quibus scilicet alicuius dioecesis cura commissa est; ceteri *titulares* appellantur.

CAN. 377 §1. Episcopos libere Summus Pontifex nominat, aut legitime electos confirmat.

§2. Singulis saltem trienniis Episcopi provinciae ecclesiasticae vel, ubi adiuncta id suadeant, Episcoporum conferentiae, communi consilio et secreto elenchum componant presbyterorum etiam sodalium institutorum vitae consecratae, ad episcopatum aptiorum, eumque Apostolicae Sedi transmittant, firmo manente iure uniuscuiusque Episcopi Apostolicae Sedi nomina presbyterorum, quos episcopali munere dignos et idoneos putet, seorsim patefaciendi.

§3. Nisi aliter legitime statutum fuerit, quoties nominandus est Episcopus dioecesanus aut Episcopus coadiutor, ad ternos, qui dicuntur, Apostolicae Sedi proponendos, pontificii Legati est singillatim requirere et cum ipsa Apostolica Sede communicare, una cum suo voto, quid suggerant Metropolita et Suffraganei provinciae, ad quam providenda dioecesis pertinet vel quacum in coetum convenit, necnon conferentiae Episcoporum praeses; pontificius Legatus, insuper, quosdam e collegio consultorum et capitulo

376: CD passim

377 §1: cc. 329 §§2 et 3, 332 §1; CD 20; ES I, 10

377 §2: SCC Decr. *Inter suprema*, 19 mar. 1919 (AAS 11 [1919] 124–128); SCC Decr. *Maximam semper*, 20 nov. 1921 (AAS 13 [1921] 13–16); SCC Decr. *Quae de eligendis*, 19 mar. 1921 (AAS 13 [1921] 222–225); SCC Decr. *Quo expeditiori*, 30 apr. 1921

(AAS 13 [1921] 379–382); SCC Decr. *Ad proponendos*, 20 aug. 1921 (AAS 13 [1921] 430–432); ES I, 10; NPEM II–X

377 §3: SCC Resp. 25 apr. 1917 (AAS 9 [1917] 232–233); SCC Decr. *Regulas apprime*, 29 feb. 1924 (AAS 16 [1924] 160–161); NPEM XIII–XV; Sec Instr. *Secreta continere*, 4 feb. 1974, I, 7 (AAS 66 [1974] 91)

hear some members of the college of consultors and cathedral chapter and, if he judges it expedient, is also to seek individually and in secret the opinion of others from both the secular and non-secular clergy and from laity outstanding in wisdom.

§4. Unless other provision has been legitimately made, a diocesan bishop who judges that an auxiliary should be given to his diocese is to propose to the Apostolic See a list of at least three presbyters more suitable for this office.

§5. In the future, no rights and privileges of election, nomination, presentation, or designation of bishops are granted to civil authorities.

CAN. 378 §1. In regard to the suitability of a candidate for the episcopacy, it is required that he is:

1° outstanding in solid faith, good morals, piety, zeal for souls, wisdom, prudence, and human virtues, and endowed with other qualities which make him suitable to fulfill the office in question;

2° of good reputation;

3° at least thirty-five years old;

4° ordained to the presbyterate for at least five years;

5° in possession of a doctorate or at least a licentiate in sacred scripture, theology, or canon law from an institute of higher studies approved by the Apostolic See, or at least truly expert in the same disciplines.

§2. The definitive judgment concerning the suitability of the one to be promoted pertains to the Apostolic See.

CAN. 379 Unless he is prevented by a legitimate impediment, whoever has been pro-

cathedrali audiat et, si id expedire iudicaverit, sententiam quoque aliorum ex utroque clero necnon laicorum sapientia praestantium singillatim et secreto exquirat.

§4. Nisi aliter legitime provisum fuerit, Episcopus dioecesanus, qui auxiliarem suae dioecesi dandum aestimet, elenchum trium saltem presbyterorum ad hoc officium aptiorum Apostolicae Sedi proponat.

§5. Nulla in posterum iura et privilegia electionis, nominationis, praesentationis vel designationis Episcoporum civilibus auctoritatibus conceduntur.

CAN. 378 §1. Ad idoneitatem candidatorum episcopatus requiritur ut quis sit:

1° firma fide, bonis moribus, pietate, animarum zelo, sapientia, prudentia et virtutibus humanis excellens, ceterisque dotibus praeditus quae ipsum aptum efficiant ad officium de quo agitur explendum;

2° bona exsistimatione gaudens;

3° annos natus saltem triginta quinque;

4° a quinquennio saltem in presbyteratus ordine constitutus;

5° laurea doctoris vel saltem licentia in sacra Scriptura, theologia aut iure canonico potitus in instituto studiorum superiorum a Sede Apostolica probato, vel saltem in iisdem disciplinis vere peritus.

§2. Iudicium definitivum de promovendi idoneitate ad Apostolicam Sedem pertinet.

CAN. 379 Nisi legitimo detineatur impedimento, quicumque ad Episcopatum pro-

377 §4: CD 26; NPEM XIII, 3
377 §5: CD 20; NPEM XV
378 §1: c. 331 §§1 et 2; LG 21, 23, 25; NPEM VI, 2;

DPME 21–31
378 §2: c. 331 §3; NPEM XI, 2
379: c. 333

moted to the episcopacy must receive episcopal consecration within three months from the receipt of the apostolic letter and before he takes possession of his office.

CAN. 380 Before he takes canonical possession of his office, the one promoted is to make the profession of faith and take the oath of fidelity to the Apostolic See according to the formula approved by the Apostolic See.

ART. 2. *Diocesan Bishops*

CAN. 381 §1. A diocesan bishop in the diocese entrusted to him has all ordinary, proper, and immediate power which is required for the exercise of his pastoral function except for cases which the law or a decree of the Supreme Pontiff reserves to the supreme authority or to another ecclesiastical authority.

§2. Those who preside over the other communities of the faithful mentioned in can. 368 are equivalent in law to a diocesan bishop unless it is otherwise apparent from the nature of the matter or from a prescript of law.

CAN. 382 §1. One promoted as bishop cannot assume the exercise of the office entrusted to him before he has taken canonical possession of the diocese. Nevertheless, he is able to exercise offices which he already had in the same diocese at the time of promotion, without prejudice to the prescript of can. 409, §2.

§2. Unless he is prevented by a legitimate impediment, one promoted to the office of diocesan bishop must take canonical possession of

motus debet intra tres menses ab acceptis apostolicis litteris consecrationem episcopalem recipere, et quidem antequam officii sui possessionem capiat.

CAN. 380 Antequam canonicam possessionem sui officii capiat, promotus fidei professionem emittat atque iusiurandum fidelitatis erga Apostolicam Sedem praestet secundum formulam ab eadem Apostolica Sede probatam.

ART. 2. *De Episcopis Dioecesanis*

CAN. 381 §1. Episcopo dioecesano in dioecesi ipsi commissa omnis competit potestas ordinaria, propria et immediata, quae ad exercitium eius muneris pastorialis requiritur, exceptis causis quae iure aut Summi Pontificis decreto supremae aut alii auctoritati ecclesiasticae reserventur.

§2. Qui praesunt aliis communitatibus fidelium, de quibus in can. 368, Episcopo dioecesano in iure aequiparantur, nisi ex rei natura aut iuris praescripto aliud appareat.

CAN. 382 §1. Episcopus promotus in exercitium officii sibi commissi sese ingerere nequit, ante captam dioecesis canonicam possessionem; exercere tamen valet officia, quae in eadem dioecesi tempore promotionis iam retinebat, firmo praescripto can. 409, §2.

§2. Nisi legitimo detineatur impedimento, promotus ad officium Episcopi dioecesani debet canonicam suae dioecesis posses-

---

380: c. 332 §2; FORMULA IURAMENTI FIDELITATIS, 1972

381 §1: c. 334 §1; PIUS PP. XII, Enc. *Mystici Corporis,* 29 iun. 1943 (AAS 35 [1943] 211–212); LG 27; CD 8, 11; EM Introducio; SCE-SCpC Ep., 12 iul. 1972;

DPME 42
381 §2: c. 215 §2; EM III
382 §1: c. 334 §2; CD 26; ES I, 13 §3
382 §2: c. 333

his diocese within four months of receipt of the apostolic letter if he has not already been consecrated a bishop; if he has already been consecrated, within two months from receipt of this letter.

§3. A bishop takes canonical possession of a diocese when he personally or through a proxy has shown the apostolic letter in the same diocese to the college of consultors in the presence of the chancellor of the curia, who records the event. In newly erected dioceses, he takes canonical possession when he has seen to the communication of the same letter to the clergy and people present in the cathedral church, with the senior presbyter among those present recording the event.

§4. It is strongly recommended that the taking of canonical possession be done within a liturgical act in the cathedral church with the clergy and people gathered together.

CAN. 383 §1. In exercising the function of a pastor, a diocesan bishop is to show himself concerned for all the Christian faithful entrusted to his care, of whatever age, condition, or nationality they are, whether living in the territory or staying there temporarily; he is also to extend an apostolic spirit to those who are not able to make sufficient use of ordinary pastoral care because of the condition of their life and to those who no longer practice their religion.

§2. If he has faithful of a different rite in his diocese, he is to provide for their spiritual needs either through priests or parishes of the same rite or through an episcopal vicar.

§3. He is to act with humanity and charity to-

sionem capere, si iam non sit consecratus Episcopus, intra quattuor menses a receptis apostolicis litteris; si iam sit consecratus, intra duos menses ab iisdem receptis.

§3. Canonicam dioecesis possessionem capit Episcopus simul ac in ipsa dioecesi, per se vel per procuratorem, apostolicas litteras collegio consultorum ostenderit, praesente curiae cancellario, qui rem in acta referat, aut, in dioecesibus noviter erectis, simul ac clero populoque in ecclesia cathedrali praesenti earundem litterarum communicationem procuraverit, presbytero inter praesentes seniore in acta referente.

§4. Valde commendatur ut captio canonicae possessionis cum actu liturgico in ecclesia cathedrali fiat, clero et populo adstantibus.

CAN. 383 §1. In exercendo munere pastoris, Episcopus dioecesanus sollicitum se praebeat erga omnes christifideles qui suae curae committuntur, cuiusvis sint aetatis, condicionis vel nationis, tum in territorio habitantes tum in eodem ad tempus versantes, animum intendens apostolicum ad eos etiam qui ob vitae suae condicionem ordinaria cura pastorali non satis frui valeant necnon ad eos qui a religionis praxi defecerint.

§2. Fideles diversi ritus in sua dioecesi si habeat, eorum spiritualibus necessitatibus provideat sive per sacerdotes aut paroecias eiusdem ritus, sive per Vicarium episcopalem.

§3. Erga fratres, qui in plena commu-

382 §3: c. 334 §3
382 §4: SC 41; PAULUS PP. VI Const. Ap. *Mirificus eventus,* 7 dec. 1965 (AAS 57 [1965] 948–949)

383 §1: CD 16, 18; DPME 153–157
383 §2: CD 23, 3
383 §3: LG 27; CD 16; DPME 48, 158

ward the brothers and sisters who are not in full communion with the Catholic Church and is to foster ecumenism as it is understood by the Church.

§4. He is to consider the non-baptized as committed to him in the Lord, so that there shines on them the charity of Christ whose witness a bishop must be before all people.

CAN. 384 With special solicitude, a diocesan bishop is to attend to presbyters and listen to them as assistants and counselors. He is to protect their rights and take care that they correctly fulfill the obligations proper to their state and that the means and institutions which they need to foster spiritual and intellectual life are available to them. He also is to take care that provision is made for their decent support and social assistance, according to the norm of law.

CAN. 385 As much as possible, a diocesan bishop is to foster vocations to different ministries and to consecrated life, with special care shown for priestly and missionary vocations.

CAN. 386 §1. A diocesan bishop, frequently preaching in person, is bound to propose and explain to the faithful the truths of the faith which are to be believed and applied to morals. He is also to take care that the prescripts of the canons on the ministry of the word, especially those on the homily and catechetical instruction, are carefully observed so that the whole Christian doctrine is handed on to all.

§2. Through more suitable means, he is firmly to protect the integrity and unity of the faith

nione cum Ecclesia catholica non sint, cum humanitate et caritate se gerat, oecumenismum quoque fovens prout ab Ecclesia intellegitur.

§4. Commendatos sibi in Domino habeat non baptizatos, ut et ipsis caritas eluceat Christi, cuius testis coram omnibus Episcopus esse debet.

CAN. 384 Episcopus dioecesanus peculiari sollicitudine prosequatur presbyteros, quos tamquam adiutores et consiliarios audiat, eorum iura tutetur et curet ut ipsi obligationes suo statui proprias rite adimpleant iisdemque praesto sint media et institutiones, quibus ad vitam spiritualem et intellectualem fovendam egeant; item curet ut eorum honestae sustentationi atque assistentiae sociali, ad normam iuris, prospiciatur.

CAN. 385 Episcopus dioecesanus vocationes ad diversa ministeria et ad vitam consecratam quam maxime foveat, speciali cura vocationibus sacerdotalibus et missionalibus adhibita.

CAN. 386 §1. Veritates fidei credendas et moribus applicandas Episcopus dioecesanus fidelibus proponere et illustrare tenetur, per se ipse frequenter praedicans; curet etiam ut praescripta canonum de ministerio verbi, de homilia praesertim et catechetica institutione sedulo serventur, ita ut universa doctrina christiana omnibus tradatur.

§2. Integritatem et unitatem fidei credendae mediis, quae aptiora videantur, firmiter

383 §4: CD 11, 16; DPME 159

384: LG 28; CD 16; PO 20, 21; Es I, Introductio, 7, 8; DPME 107–117

385: LG 27; CD 15; OT 2; AG 20; DPME 118–119, 197; MR 38–39

386 §1: cc. 336 §2, 1327 §1; BENEDICTUS PP. XV,

Enc. *Humani generis,* 15 iun. 1917 (AAS 9 [1917] 305–317); SCC Normae, 28 iun. 1917 (AAS 9 [1917] 328–334); PIUS PP. XII, All., 31 maii 1954 (AAS 46 [1954] 314–315; LG 25; CD 13, 14; DPME 55–65

386 §2: c. 336 §2; LG 23; GE 10; GS 62; DPME 63, 65, 75

to be believed, while nonetheless acknowledging a just freedom in further investigating its truths.

CAN. 387 Since the diocesan bishop is mindful of his obligation to show an example of holiness in charity, humility, and simplicity of life, he is to strive to promote in every way the holiness of the Christian faithful according to the proper vocation of each. Since he is the principal dispenser of the mysteries of God, he is to endeavor constantly that the Christian faithful entrusted to his care grow in grace through the celebration of the sacraments and that they understand and live the paschal mystery.

CAN. 388 §1. After the diocesan bishop has taken possession of the diocese, he must apply a Mass for the people entrusted to him each Sunday and on the other holy days of obligation in his region.

§2. The bishop himself must personally celebrate and apply a Mass for the people on the days mentioned in §1. If he is legitimately impeded from this celebration, however, he is to apply the Masses either on the same days through another or on other days himself.

§3. A bishop to whom other dioceses besides his own have been entrusted, even under title of administration, satisfies the obligation by applying one Mass for all the people entrusted to him.

§4. A bishop who has not satisfied the obligation mentioned in §§1–3 is to apply as soon as possible as many Masses for the people as he has omitted.

CAN. 389 He is frequently to preside at the

CAN. 387 Episcopus dioecesanus, cum memor sit se obligatione teneri exemplum sanctitatis praebendi in caritate, humilitate et vitae simplicitate, omni ope promovere studeat sanctitatem christifidelium secundum uniuscuiusque propriam vocationem atque, cum sit praecipuus mysteriorum Dei dispensator, iugiter annitatur ut christifideles suae curae commissi sacramentorum celebratione in gratia crescant utque paschale mysterium cognoscant et vivant.

CAN. 388 §1. Episcopus dioecesanus, post captam dioecesis possessionem, debet singulis diebus dominicis aliisque diebus festis de praecepto in sua regione Missam pro populo sibi commisso applicare.

§2. Episcopus Missam pro populo diebus, de quibus in §1, per se ipse celebrare et applicare debet; si vero ab hac celebratione legitime impediatur, iisdem diebus per alium, vel aliis diebus per se ipse applicet.

§3. Episcopus, cui praeter propriam dioecesim aliae, titulo etiam administrationis, sunt commissae, obligationi satisfacit unam Missam pro universo populo sibi commisso applicando.

§4. Episcopus, qui obligationi, de qua in §§1–3, non satisfecerit, quam primum pro populo tot Missas applicet quot omiserit.

CAN. 389 Frequenter praesit in ecclesia

387: LG 26, 27, 41; CD 15, 16; DPME 21–23, 28
388 §1: c. 339 §1; PAULUS PP. VI, m. p. *Mysterii Paschalis*, 14 feb. 1969 (AAS 61 [1969] 222–226); SCpC Decr. *Litteris Apostolicis*, 25 iul. 1970

388 §2: c. 339 §4
388 §3: c. 339 §5
388 §4: c. 339 §6
389: SC 41; LG 26; DPME 81; EMys 7, 42

celebration of the Most Holy Eucharist in the cathedral church or another church of his diocese, especially on holy days of obligation and other solemnities.

CAN. 390 A diocesan bishop can perform pontifical functions in his entire diocese but not outside his own diocese without the express, or at least reasonably presumed, consent of the local ordinary.

CAN. 391 §1. It is for the diocesan bishop to govern the particular church entrusted to him with legislative, executive, and judicial power according to the norm of law.

§2. The bishop exercises legislative power himself. He exercises executive power either personally or through vicars general or episcopal vicars according to the norm of law. He exercises judicial power either personally or through the judicial vicar and judges according to the norm of law.

CAN. 392 §1. Since he must protect the unity of the universal Church, a bishop is bound to promote the common discipline of the whole Church and therefore to urge the observance of all ecclesiastical laws.

§2. He is to exercise vigilance so that abuses do not creep into ecclesiastical discipline, especially regarding the ministry of the word, the celebration of the sacraments and sacramentals, the worship of God and the veneration of the saints, and the administration of goods.

cathedrali aliave ecclesia suae dioecesis sanctissimae Eucharistiae celebrationi, in festis praesertim de praecepto aliisque sollemnitatibus.

CAN. 390 Episcopus dioecesanus in universa sua dioecesi pontificalia exercere potest; non vero extra propriam dioecesim sine expresso vel saltem rationabiliter praesumpto Ordinarii loci consensu.

CAN. 391 §1. Episcopi dioecesani est Ecclesiam particularem sibi commissam cum potestate legislativa, exsecutiva et iudiciali regere, ad normam iuris.

§2. Potestatem legislativam exercet ipse Episcopus; potestatem exsecutivam exercet sive per se sive per Vicarios generales aut episcopales ad normam iuris; potestatem iudicialem sive per se sive per Vicarium iudicialem et iudices ad normam iuris.

CAN. 392 §1. Ecclesiae universae unitatem cum tueri debeat, Episcopus disciplinam cunctae Ecclesiae communem promovere et ideo observantiam omnium legum ecclesiasticarum urgere tenetur.

§2. Advigilet ne abusus in ecclesiasticam disciplinam irrepant, praesertim circa ministerium verbi, celebrationem sacramentorum et sacramentalium, cultum Dei et Sanctorum, necnon bonorum administrationem.

390: c. 337 §1; PAULUS PP. VI, Instr. *Pontificales ritus*, 21 iun. 1968 (AAS 60 [1968] 406–412); DPME 81

391 §1: c. 335 §1; SCConc Resol., 19 feb. 1921 (AAS 13 [1921] 228–230); SA Decisio, 15 dec. 1923 (AAS 16 [1924] 105–112); PIUS PP. XII, Enc. *Mystici Corporis*, 29 iun. 1943 (AAS 35 [1943] 211–212); LG 27; DPME 32–38

391 §2: cc. 362, 366 §1, 368, 369, 1572, 1573; CD 27; COMMISSIO CENTRALIS COORDINANDIS POST CONCILIUM LABORIBUS ET CONCILII DECRETIS INTER-

PRETANDIS Resp., 10 iun. 1966 (AAS 60 [1968] 361); ES I, 14 §2

392 §1: c. 336 §1; LG 23; CD 16; PAULUS PP. VI, Adh. Ap. *Quinque iam anni*, 8 dec. 1970, I (AAS 63 [1971] 100)

392 §2: c. 336 §2; BENEDICTUS PP. XV, Ep. *Venerabilis frater*, 15 oct. 1921 (AAS 14 [1922] 7–10); SCConc Litt. circ., 15 ian. 1927; SCSO Decr. *Iam olim*, 26 maii 1937 (AAS 29 [1937] 304–305); LG 27; DPME 65, 83, 87, 133–138

CAN. 393 The diocesan bishop represents his diocese in all its juridic affairs.

CAN. 394 §1. A bishop is to foster various forms of the apostolate in the diocese and is to take care that in the entire diocese or in its particular districts, all the works of the apostolate are coordinated under his direction, with due regard for the proper character of each.

§2. He is to insist upon the duty which binds the faithful to exercise the apostolate according to each one's condition and ability and is to exhort them to participate in and assist the various works of the apostolate according to the needs of place and time.

CAN. 395 §1. Even if a diocesan bishop has a coadjutor or auxiliary, he is bound by the law of personal residence in the diocese.

§2. Apart from *ad limina* visits, councils, synods of bishops, conferences of bishops which he must attend, or some other duty legitimately entrusted to him, he can be absent from his diocese for a reasonable cause but not beyond a month, whether continuous or interrupted, and provided that he makes provision so that the diocese will suffer no detriment from his absence.

§3. He is not to be absent from the diocese on Christmas, during Holy Week, and on Easter, Pentecost, and the Feast of the Body and Blood of Christ, except for a grave and urgent cause.

§4. If a bishop has been illegitimately absent from the diocese for more than six months, the metropolitan is to inform the Apostolic See of his absence; if it concerns the metropolitan, the senior suffragan is to do so.

CAN. 393 In omnibus negotiis iuridicis dioecesis, Episcopus dioecesanus eiusdem personam gerit.

CAN. 394 §1. Varias apostolatus rationes in dioecesi foveat Episcopus, atque curet ut in universa dioecesi, vel in eiusdem particularibus districtibus, omnia apostolatus opera, servata uniuscuiusque propria indole, sub suo moderamine coordinentur.

§2. Urgeat officium, quo tenentur fideles ad apostolatum pro sua cuiusque condicione et aptitudine exercendum, atque ipsos adhortetur ut varia opera apostolatus, secundum necessitates loci et temporis, participent et iuvent.

CAN. 395 §1. Episcopus dioecesanus, etiamsi coadiutorem aut auxiliarem habeat, tenetur lege personalis in dioecesi residentiae.

§2. Praeterquam causa visitationis Sacrorum Liminum, vel Conciliorum, Episcoporum synodi, Episcoporum conferentiae, quibus interesse debet, aliusve officii sibi legitime commissi, a dioecesi aequa de causa abesse potest non ultra mensem, sive continuum sive intermissum, dummodo cautum sit ne ex eius absentia dioecesis quidquam detrimenti capiat.

§3. A dioecesi ne absit diebus Nativitatis, Hebdomadae Sanctae et Resurrectionis Domini, Pentecostes et Corporis et Sanguinis Christi, nisi ex gravi urgentique causa.

§4. Si ultra sex menses Episcopus a dioecesi illegitime abfuerit, de eius absentia Metropolita Sedem Apostolicam certiorem faciat; quod si agatur de Metropolita, idem faciat antiquior suffraganeus.

394 §1: CD 17; DPME 139–161
394 §2: Pius PP. XII, All., 5 oct. 1957 (AAS 49 [1957] 922–939); CD 17; DPME 143–147
395 §1: c. 338 §1
395 §2: c. 338 §2
395 §3: c. 338 §3
395 §4: c. 338 §4

CAN. 396 §1. A bishop is obliged to visit the diocese annually either in whole or in part, so that he visits the entire diocese at least every five years either personally or, if he has been legitimately impeded, through the coadjutor bishop, an auxiliary, vicar general, episcopal vicar, or another presbyter.

§2. A bishop is permitted to choose the clerics he prefers as companions and assistants on a visitation; any contrary privilege or custom is reprobated.

CAN. 397 §1. Persons, Catholic institutions, and sacred things and places, which are located within the area of the diocese, are subject to ordinary episcopal visitation.

§2. A bishop can visit members of religious institutes of pontifical right and their houses only in the cases expressed in law.

CAN. 398 A bishop is to strive to complete the pastoral visitation with due diligence. He is to take care that he does not burden or impose a hardship on anyone through unnecessary expenses.

CAN. 399 §1. Every five years a diocesan bishop is bound to make a report to the Supreme Pontiff on the state of the diocese entrusted to him, according to the form and time determined by the Apostolic See.

§2. If the year determined for submitting a report falls entirely or in part within the first two years of his governance of a diocese, a bishop can refrain from making and submitting his report on this one occasion.

CAN. 396 §1. Tenetur Episcopus obligatione dioecesis vel ex toto vel ex parte quotannis visitandae, ita ut singulis saltem quinquenniis universam dioecesim, ipse per se vel, si legitime fuerit impeditus, per Episcopum coadiutorem, aut per auxiliarem, aut per Vicarium generalem vel episcopalem, aut per alium presbyterum visitet.

§2. Fas est Episcopo sibi eligere quos maluerit clericos in visitatione comites atque adiutores, reprobato quocumque contrario privilegio vel consuetudine.

CAN. 397 §1. Ordinariae episcopali visitationi obnoxiae sunt personae, instituta catholica, res et loca sacra, quae intra dioecesis ambitum continentur.

§2. Sodales institutorum religiosorum iuris pontificii eorumque domos Episcopus visitare potest in casibus tantum iure expressis.

CAN. 398 Studeat Episcopus debita cum diligentia pastoralem visitationem absolvere; caveat ne superfluis sumptibus cuiquam gravis onerosusve sit.

CAN. 399 §1. Episcopus dioecesanus tenetur singulis quinquenniis relationem Summo Pontifici exhibere super statu dioecesis sibi commissae, secundum formam et tempus ab Apostolica Sede definita.

§2. Si annus pro exhibenda relatione determinatus ex toto vel ex parte inciderit in primum biennium ab inito dioecesis regimine, Episcopus pro ea vice a conficienda et exhibenda relatione abstinere potest.

396 §1: c. 343 §1; PAULUS PP. VI, All., 9 apr. 1967 (AAS 59 [1967] 413–416); DPME 166–170
  396 §2: c. 343 §2
  397 §1: c. 344 §1; CI Resp., 8 apr. 1924; DPME 168
  397 §2: c. 342 §2; ES I, 38, 39; DPME 118, 119
  398: c. 346; DPME 170
  399 §1: c. 340 §1; SCC Decr. *Per decretum,* 4 nov. 1918 (AAS 10 [1918] 487–503); SCPF Ep., 16 apr. 1922 (AAS 14 [1922] 287–307); SCC Decr. *Ad Sacra Limina,* 28 feb. 1959, 5 (AAS 51 [1959] 274); SCE Decr. *Ad Romanam Ecclesiam,* 29 iun. 1975, 3 (AAS 67 [1975] 676)
  399 §2: c. 340 §3; SCC Decr. *Ad Sacra Limina,* 28 feb. 1959, 6 (AAS 51 [1959] 274)

CAN. 400 §1. Unless the Apostolic See has established otherwise, during the year in which he is bound to submit a report to the Supreme Pontiff, a diocesan bishop is to go to Rome to venerate the tombs of the Blessed Apostles Peter and Paul and to present himself to the Roman Pontiff.

§2. A bishop is to satisfy the above-mentioned obligation personally unless he is legitimately impeded. In that case, he is to satisfy it through his coadjutor, if he has one, or auxiliary, or a suitable priest of his *presbyterium* who resides in his diocese.

§3. An apostolic vicar can satisfy this obligation through a proxy, even one living in Rome. This obligation does not bind an apostolic prefect.

CAN. 401 §1. A diocesan bishop who has completed the seventy-fifth year of age is requested to present his resignation from office to the Supreme Pontiff, who will make provision after he has examined all the circumstances.

§2. A diocesan bishop who has become less able to fulfill his office because of ill health or some other grave cause is earnestly requested to present his resignation from office.

CAN. 402 §1. A bishop whose resignation from office has been accepted retains the title of emeritus of his diocese and can retain a place of residence in that diocese if he so desires, unless in certain cases the Apostolic See provides otherwise because of special circumstances.

§2. The conference of bishops must take care that suitable and decent support is provided for

CAN. 400 §1. Episcopus dioecesanus, eo anno quo relationem Summo Pontifici exhibere tenetur, nisi aliter ab Apostolica Sede statutum fuerit, ad Urbem, Beatorum Apostolorum Petri et Pauli sepulcra veneraturus, accedat et Romano Pontifici se sistat.

§2. Episcopus praedictae obligationi per se ipse satisfaciat, nisi legitime sit impeditus; quo in casu eidem satisfaciat per coadiutorem, si quem habeat, vel auxiliarem, aut per idoneum sacerdotem sui presbyterii, qui in sua dioecesi resideat.

§3. Vicarius apostolicus huic obligationi satisfacere potest per procuratorem etiam in Urbe degentem; Praefectus apostolicus hac obligatione non tenetur.

CAN. 401 §1. Episcopus dioecesanus, qui septuagesimum quintum aetatis annum expleverit, rogatur ut renuntiationem ab officio exhibeat Summo Pontifici, qui omnibus inspectis adiunctis providebit.

§2. Enixe rogatur Episcopus dioecesanus, qui ob infirmam valetudinem aliamve gravem causam officio suo adimplendo minus aptus evaserit, ut renuntiationem ab officio exhibeat.

CAN. 402 §1. Episcopus, cuius renuntiatio ab officio acceptata fuerit, titulum emeriti suae dioecesis retinet, atque habitationis sedem, si id exoptet, in ipsa dioecesi servare potest, nisi certis in casibus ob specialia adiuncta ab Apostolica Sede aliter provideatur.

§2. Episcoporum conferentia curare debet ut congruae et dignae Episcopi renun-

400 §1: c. 341 §1; SCC Decr. *Ad Sacra Limina,* 28 feb. 1959, 1–3 (AAS 51 [1959] 274); SCE Decr. *Ad Romanam Ecclesiam,* 29 iun. 1975, 2, 3, 5 (AAS 67 [1975] 676)
400 §2: c. 342; SCC Decr. *Ad Sacra Limina,* 28 feb. 1959, 4 (AAS 51 [1959] 274)

400 §3: c. 299
401 §1: CD 21; ES I, 11
401 §2: CD 21; ES I, 11
402 §1: CD 21; ES I, 11; SCE Ep. (Prot. 335/67), 7 nov. 1970; SCE Ep. (Prot. 335/67), 31 aug. 1976
402 §2: CD 21; ES I, 11

a retired bishop, with attention given to the primary obligation which binds the diocese he has served.

ART. 3. *Coadjutor and Auxiliary Bishops*

CAN. 403 §1. When the pastoral needs of a diocese suggest it, one or more auxiliary bishops are to be appointed at the request of the diocesan bishop. An auxiliary bishop does not possess the right of succession.

§2. In more serious circumstances, even of a personal nature, an auxiliary bishop provided with special faculties can be given to a diocesan bishop.

§3. If it appears more opportune to the Holy See, it can appoint *ex officio* a coadjutor bishop who also has special faculties. A coadjutor bishop possesses the right of succession.

CAN. 404 §1. A coadjutor bishop takes possession of his office when he, either personally or through a proxy, has shown the apostolic letter of appointment to the diocesan bishop and college of consultors in the presence of the chancellor of the curia, who records the event.

§2. An auxiliary bishop takes possession of his offiice when he has shown the apostolic letter of appointment to the diocesan bishop in the presence of the chancellor of the curia, who records the event.

§3. If the diocesan bishop is completely impeded, however, it suffices that both the coadjutor bishop and the auxiliary bishop show the apostolic letter of appointment to the college of

tiantis sustentationi provideatur, attenta quidem primaria obligatione, qua tenetur dioecesis cui ipse inservivit.

ART. 3. *De Episcopis Coadiutoribus et Auxiliaribus*

CAN. 403 §1. Cum pastorales dioecesis necessitates id suadeant, unus vel plures Episcopi auxiliares, petente Episcopo dioecesano, constituantur; Episcopus auxiliaris iure successionis non gaudet.

§2. Gravioribus in adiunctis, etiam indolis personalis, Episcopo dioecesano dari potest Episcopus auxiliaris specialibus instructus facultatibus

§3. Sancta Sedes, si magis opportunum id ipsi videatur, ex officio constituere potest Episcopum coadiutorem, qui et ipse specialibus instruitur facultatibus; Episcopus coadiutor iure successionis gaudet.

Can. 404 §1. Episcopus coadiutor officii sui possessionem capit, cum litteras apostolicas nominationis, per se vel per procuratorem, ostenderit Episcopo dioecesano atque collegio consultorum, praesente curiae cancellario, qui rem in acta referat.

§2. Episcopus auxiliaris officii sui possessionem capit, cum litteras apostolicas nominationis ostenderit Episcopo dioecesano, praesente curiae cancellario, qui rem in acta referat.

§3. Quod si Episcopus dioecesanus plene sit impeditus, sufficit ut tum Episcopus coadiutor, tum Episcopus auxiliaris litteras apostolicas nominationis

403 §1: c. 350 §3; SCC Resol., 10 ian. 1920 (AAS 12 [1920] 41–42); CD 25, 26; ES I, 13 §1; DPME 199

403 §3: c. 350 §§1 et 2; CD 25; ES I, 13 §1; DPME 199; SCE Ep. (Prot. 335/67), 31 aug. 1976

404 §1: c. 353 §§1et 2
404 §2: c. 353 §1
404 §3: c. 353 §3

consultors in the presence of the chancellor of the curia.

CAN. 405 §1. A coadjutor bishop and an auxiliary bishop have the obligations and rights which are determined in the prescripts of the following canons and are defined in the letter of their appointment.

§2. A coadjutor bishop and the auxiliary bishop mentioned in can. 403, §2 assist the diocesan bishop in the entire governance of the diocese and take his place if he is absent or impeded.

CAN. 406 §1. The diocesan bishop is to appoint a coadjutor bishop and the auxiliary bishop mentioned in can. 403, §2 as vicar general. Moreover, the diocesan bishop is to entrust to him before others those things which by law require a special mandate.

§2. Unless the apostolic letter has provided otherwise and without prejudice to the provision of §1, a diocesan bishop is to appoint his auxiliary or auxiliaries as vicars general or at least as episcopal vicars, dependent only on his authority or that of the coadjutor bishop or auxiliary bishop mentioned in can. 403, §2.

CAN. 407 §1. In order to foster the present and future good of the diocese as much as possible, a diocesan bishop, a coadjutor, and the auxiliary mentioned in can. 403, §2 are to consult one another on matters of major importance.

§2. In considering cases of major importance, especially of a pastoral character, a diocesan bishop is to wish to consult the auxiliary bishops before others.

ostendant collegio consultorum, praesente curiae cancellario.

CAN. 405 §1. Episcopus coadiutor, itemque Episcopus auxiliaris, obligationes et iura habent quae determinantur praescriptis canonum, qui sequuntur, atque in litteris suae nominationis definiuntur.

§2. Episcopus coadiutor et Episcopus auxiliaris, de quo in can. 403, §2, Episcopo dioecesano in universo dioecesis regimine adstant atque eiusdem absentis vel impediti vices supplent.

CAN. 406 §1. Episcopus coadiutor, itemque Episcopus auxiliaris, de quo in can. 403, §2, ab Episcopo dioecesano Vicarius generalis constituatur; insuper ipsi prae ceteris Episcopus dioecesanus committat quae ex iure mandatum speciale requirant.

§2. Nisi in litteris apostolicis aliud provisum fuerit et firmo praescripto §1, Episcopus dioecesanus auxiliarem vel auxiliares suos constituat Vicarios generales vel saltem Vicarios episcopales, ab auctoritate sua, aut Episcopi coadiutoris vel Episcopi auxiliaris de quo in can. 403, §2, dumtaxat dependentes.

CAN. 407 §1. Ut quam maxime praesenti et futuro dioecesis bono faveatur, Episcopus dioecesanus, coadiutor atque Episcopus auxiliaris de quo in can. 403, §2, in rebus maioris momenti sese invicem consulant.

§2. Episcopus dioecesanus in perpendendis causis maioris momenti, praesertim indolis pastoralis, Episcopos auxiliares prae ceteris consulere velit.

405 §1: c. 351 §§1 et 2; CD 25, 26; ES I, 13
405 §2: c. 351 §2; CD 25, 26; ES I, 13
406 §1: c. 351 §3; CD 26; ES I, 13 §2; DPME 199, 201

406 §2: CD 26; ES I, 13 §2; 14; DPME 199
407 §1: CD 26; DPME 199
407 §2: CD 26

§3. Since a coadjutor bishop and an auxiliary bishop are called to share in the solicitude of the diocesan bishop, they are to exercise their duties in such a way that they proceed in harmony with him in effort and intention.

CAN. 408 §1. A coadjutor bishop and an auxiliary bishop who are not prevented by a just impediment are obliged to perform pontificals and other functions to which the diocesan bishop is bound whenever the diocesan bishop requires it.

§2. A diocesan bishop is not to entrust habitually to another the episcopal rights and functions which a coadjutor or auxiliary bishop can exercise.

CAN. 409 §1. When the episcopal see is vacant, the coadjutor bishop immediately becomes the bishop of the diocese for which he had been appointed provided that he has legitimately taken possession of it.

§2. When the episcopal see is vacant and unless competent authority has established otherwise, an auxiliary bishop preserves all and only those powers and faculties which he possessed as vicar general or episcopal vicar while the see was filled until a new bishop has taken possession of the see. If he has not been designated to the function of diocesan administrator, he is to exercise this same power, conferred by law, under the authority of the diocesan administrator who presides over the governance of the diocese.

CAN. 410 Like the diocesan bishop, a coadjutor bishop and an auxiliary bishop are obliged to reside in the diocese. Except for a brief time, they are not to be absent from it oth-

§3. Episcopus coadiutor et Episcopus auxiliaris, quippe qui in partem sollicitudinis Episcopi dioecesani vocati sint, munia sua ita exerceant, ut concordi cum ipso opera et animo procedant.

CAN. 408 §1. Episcopus coadiutor et Episcopus auxiliaris, iusto impedimento non detenti, obligantur ut, quoties Episcopus dioecesanus id requirat, pontificalia et alias functiones obeant, ad quas Episcopus dioecesanus tenetur.

§2. Quae episcopalia iura et functiones Episcopus coadiutor aut auxiliaris potest exercere, Episcopus dioecesanus habitualiter alii ne committat.

CAN. 409 §1. Vacante sede episcopali, Episcopus coadiutor statim fit Episcopus dioecesis pro qua fuerat constitutus, dummodo possessionem legitime ceperit.

§2. Vacante sede episcopali, nisi aliud a competenti auctoritate statutum fuerit, Episcopus auxiliaris, donec novus Episcopus possessionem sedis ceperit, omnes et solas servat potestates et facultates quibus sede plena, tamquam Vicarius generalis vel tamquam Vicarius episcopalis, gaudebat; quod si ad munus Administratoris dioecesani non fuerit designatus, eandem suam potestatem, a iure quidem collatam, exerceat sub auctoritate Administratoris dioecesani, qui regimini dioecesis praeest.

CAN. 410 Episcopus coadiutor et Episcopus auxiliaris obligatione tenentur, sicut et ipse Episcopus dioecesanus, residendi in dioecesi; a qua, praeterquam ratione alicuius

407 §3: CD 25
408 §1: c. 351 §4
408 §2: c. 351 §3

409 §1: c. 355 §1
409 §2: c. 355 §2; ES I, 13 §3
410: c. 354

er than to fulfill some duty outside the diocese or for vacation, which is not to exceed one month.

CAN. 411 The prescripts of cann. 401 and 402, §2 on resignation from office apply to a coadjutor and auxiliary bishop.

CHAPTER III. **The Impeded See and the Vacant See**

ART. 1. *The Impeded See*

CAN. 412 An episcopal see is understood to be impeded if by reason of captivity, banishment, exile, or incapacity a diocesan bishop is clearly prevented from fulfilling his pastoral function in the diocese, so that he is not able to communicate with those in his diocese even by letter.

CAN. 413 §1. When a see is impeded, the coadjutor bishop, if there is one, has governance of the diocese unless the Holy See has provided otherwise. If there is none or he is impeded, governance passes to an auxiliary bishop, the vicar general, an episcopal vicar, or another priest, following the order of persons established in the list which the diocesan bishop is to draw up as soon as possible after taking possession of the diocese. The list, which must be communicated to the metropolitan, is to be renewed at least every three years and preserved in secret by the chancellor.

§2. If there is no coadjutor bishop or he is impeded and the list mentioned in §1 is not available, it is for the college of consultors to select a priest to govern the diocese.

officii extra dioecesim implendi aut feriarum causa, quae ultra mensem ne protrahantur, nonnisi ad breve tempus discedant.

CAN. 411 Episcopo coadiutori et auxiliari, ad renuntiationem ab officio quod attinet, applicantur praescripta cann. 401 et 402, §2.

CAPUT III. **De Sede Impedita et de Sede Vacante**

ART. 1. *De Sede Impedita*

CAN. 412 Sedes episcopalis impedita intellegitur, si captivitate, relegatione, exsilio aut inhabilitate Episcopus dioecesanus plane a munere pastorali in dioecesi procurando praepediatur, ne per litteras quidem valens cum dioecesanis communicare.

CAN. 413 §1. Sede impedita, regimen dioecesis, nisi aliter Sancta Sedes providerit, competit Episcopo coadiutori, si adsit; eo deficiente aut impedito, alicui Episcopo auxiliari aut Vicario generali vel episcopali aliive sacerdoti, servato personarum ordine statuto in elencho ab Episcopo dioecesano quam primum a capta dioecesis possessione compondendo; qui elenchus cum Metropolita communicandus singulis saltem trienniis renovetur atque a cancellario sub secreto servetur.

§2. Si deficiat aut impediatur Episcopus coadiutor atque elenchus, de quo in §1, non suppetat, collegii consultorum est sacerdotem eligere, qui dioecesim regat.

411: CD 21; ES I, 11; SCE Ep. (Prot. 355/67), 7 nov. 1970

412: c. 429 §1

413 §1: c. 429 §§1 et 2; SCPF Resp. 3, 25 ian. 1954
413 §2: cc. 427, 429 §3; CD 27

§3. The one who has assumed the governance of a diocese according to the norm of §§1 or 2 is to advise the Holy See as soon as possible of the impeded see and the function he has assumed.

CAN. 414 Whoever has been called according to the norm of can. 413 to exercise the pastoral care of a diocese temporarily and only for the period in which the see is impeded is bound by the obligations and possesses the power in the exercise of the pastoral care of the diocese which a diocesan administrator has by law.

CAN. 415 If an ecclesiastical penalty prevents a diocesan bishop from exercising his function, the metropolitan or, if there is none or it concerns him, the suffragan senior in promotion, is to have recourse immediately to the Holy See so that it will make provision.

ART. 2. *The Vacant See*

CAN. 416 An episcopal see is vacant upon the death of a diocesan bishop, resignation accepted by the Roman Pontiff, transfer, or privation made known to the bishop.

CAN. 417 Everything that a vicar general or episcopal vicar does has force until they have received certain notice of the death of the diocesan bishop. Likewise, everything that a diocesan bishop, a vicar general, or an episcopal vicar does has force until they have received certain notice of the above-mentioned pontifical acts.

CAN. 418 §1. Upon certain notice of transfer, a bishop must claim the diocese to which he has been transferred *(ad quam)* and take canon-

§3. Qui dioecesis regimen, ad normam §§1 vel 2, susceperit, quam primum Sanctam Sedem moneat de sede impedita ac de suscepto munere.

CAN. 414 Quilibet, ad normam can. 413 vocatus ut ad interim dioecesis curam pastoralem gerat pro tempore quo sedes impeditur tantum, in cura pastorali dioecesis exercenda tenetur obligationibus atque potestate gaudet, quae iure Administratori dioecesano competunt.

CAN. 415 Si Episcopus dioecesanus poena ecclesiastica a munere exercendo prohibeatur, Metropolita aut, si is deficiat vel de eodem agatur, suffraganeus antiquior promotione ad Sanctam Sedem statim recurrat, ut ipsa provideat.

ART. 2. *De Sede Vacante*

CAN. 416 Sedes episcopalis vacat Episcopi dioecesani morte, renuntiatione a Romano Pontifice acceptata, translatione ac privatione Episcopo intimata.

CAN. 417 Vim habent omnia quae gesta sunt a Vicario generali aut Vicario episcopali, donec certam de obitu Episcopi dioecesani notitiam iidem acceperint, itemque quae ab Episcopo dioecesano aut a Vicario generali vel episcopali gesta sunt, donec certam de memoratis actibus pontificiis notitiam receperint.

CAN. 418 §1. A certa translationis notitia, Episcopus intra duos menses debet dioecesim *ad quam* petere eiusque canonicam

413 §3: c. 429 §4
414: cc. 438–444
415: c. 429 §5

416: c. 430 §1
417: c. 430 §2; CD 27; ES I, 14 §2
418 §1: c. 430 §3

ical possession of it within two months. On the day that he takes possession of the new diocese, however, the diocese from which he has been transferred *(a qua)* is vacant.

§2. Upon certain notice of transfer until the canonical possession of the new diocese, a transferred bishop in the diocese from which he has been transferred:

1° obtains the power of a diocesan administrator and is bound by the obligations of the same; all power of the vicar general and episcopal vicar ceases, without prejudice to can. 409, §2;

2° receives the entire remuneration proper to this office.

CAN. 419 When a see is vacant and until the designation of a diocesan administrator, the governance of a diocese devolves upon the auxiliary bishop or, if there are several, upon the one who is senior in promotion. If there is no auxiliary bishop, however, it devolves upon the college of consultors unless the Holy See has provided otherwise. The one who so assumes governance of the diocese is to convoke without delay the college competent to designate a diocesan administrator.

CAN. 420 When the see is vacant in an apostolic vicariate or prefecture, the governance is assumed by the pro-vicar or pro-prefect, appointed only for this purpose by the vicar or prefect immediately after the vicar or prefect has taken possession of the vicariate or prefecture, unless the Holy See has established otherwise.

CAN. 421 §1. The college of consultors must elect a diocesan administrator, namely the

possessionem capere; die autem captae possessionis dioecesis novae, dioecesis *a qua* vacat.

§2. A certa translationis notitia usque ad canonicam novae dioecesis possessionem, Episcopus translatus in dioecesis *a qua:*

1° Administratoris dioecesani potestatem obtinet eiusdemque obligationibus tenetur, cessante qualibet Vicarii generalis et Vicarii episcopalis potestate, salvo tamen can. 409, §2;

2° integram percipit remunerationem officio propriam.

CAN. 419 Sede vacante, regimen dioecesis, usque ad constitutionem Administratoris dioecesani, ad Episcopum auxiliarem, et si plures sint, ad eum qui promotione sit antiquior devolvitur; deficiente autem Episcopo auxiliari, ad collegium consultorum, nisi a Sancta Sede aliter provisum fuerit. Qui ita regimen dioecesis assumit, sine mora convocet collegium competens ad deputandum Administratorem dioecesanum.

CAN. 420 In vicariatu vel praefectura apostolica, sede vacante, regimen assumit Pro-Vicarius vel Pro-Praefectus ad hunc tantum effectum a Vicario vel a Praefecto immediate post captam possessionem nominatus, nisi aliter a Sancta Sede statutum fuerit.

CAN. 421 §1. Intra octo dies ab accepta vacationis sedis episcopalis notitia, Ad-

418 §2: cc. 194 §2, 430 §3, 1° et 3°
419: cc. 427, 431 §1, CD 26; ES I, 13 §3
420: c. 309 §§1 et 2
421 §1: cc. 427, 432 §1; SCC Decr. *Quum Delega-*

tus, 22 feb. 1919 (AAS 11 [1919] 75–76); SCC Decr. *Cohaerenter ad ea,* 8 maii 1919 (AAS 11 [1919] 233); SCPF Resp. 3, 26 ian. 1954

one who is to govern the diocese temporarily, within eight days from receiving notice of the vacancy of an episcopal see and without prejudice to the prescript of can. 502, §3.

§2. If a diocesan administrator has not been elected legitimately within the prescribed time for whatever cause, his designation devolves upon the metropolitan, and if the metropolitan church itself is vacant or both the metropolitan and the suffragan churches are vacant, it devolves upon the suffragan bishop senior in promotion.

CAN. 422 An auxiliary bishop or, if there is none, the college of consultors is to inform the Apostolic See of the death of a bishop as soon as possible. The one elected as diocesan administrator is to do the same concerning his own election.

CAN. 423 §1. One diocesan administrator is to be designated; any contrary custom is reprobated. Otherwise, the election is invalid.

§2. A diocesan administrator is not to be the finance officer at the same time. Therefore, if the finance officer of the diocese has been elected as administrator, the finance council is to elect a temporary finance officer.

CAN. 424 A diocesan administrator is to be elected according to the norm of cann. 165–178.

CAN. 425 §1. Only a priest who has completed thirty-five years of age and has not already been elected, appointed, or presented for the same vacant see can be designated validly to the function of diocesan administrator.

§2. A priest who is outstanding in doctrine

ministrator dioecesanus, qui nempe dioecesim ad interim regat, eligendus est a collegio consultorum, firmo praescripto can. 502, §3.

§2. Si intra praescriptum tempus Administrator dioecesanus, quavis de causa, non fuerit legitime electus, eiusdem deputatio devolvitur ad Metropolitam, et si vacans sit ipsa Ecclesia metropolitana aut metropolitana simul et suffraganea, ad Episcopum suffraganeum promotione antiquiorem.

CAN. 422 Episcopus auxiliaris et, si is deficiat, collegium consultorum quantocius de morte Episcopi, itemque electus in Administratorem dioecesanum de sua electione Sedem Apostolicam certiorem faciant.

CAN. 423 §1. Unus deputetur Administrator dioecesanus, reprobata contraria consuetudine; secus electio irrita est.

§2. Administrator dioecesanus ne simul sit oeconomus; quare si oeconomus dioecesis in Administratorem electus fuerit, alium pro tempore oeconomum eligat consilium a rebus oeconomicis.

CAN. 424 Administrator dioecesanus eligatur ad normam cann. 165–178.

CAN. 425 §1. Valide ad munus Administratoris dioecesani deputari tantum potest sacerdos qui trigesimum quintum aetatis annum expleverit et ad eandem vacantem sedem non fuerit iam electus, nominatus vel praesentatus.

§2. In Administratorem dioecesanum eli-

---

421 §2: c. 432 §2
422: c. 432 §4
423 §1: c. 433 §1
423 §2: c. 433 §3

424: cc. 432 §2, 433 §2
425 §1: c. 434 §1
425 §2: c. 434 §2

and prudence is to be elected as diocesan administrator.

§3. If the conditions previously mentioned in §1 have been neglected, the metropolitan or, if the metropolitan church itself is vacant, the suffragan bishop senior in promotion, after he has ascertained the truth of the matter, is to designate an administrator in his place. The acts of the one who was elected contrary to the prescripts of §1, however, are null by the law itself.

CAN. 426 When a see is vacant, the person who is to govern the diocese before the designation of a diocesan administrator possesses the power which the law grants to a vicar general.

CAN. 427 §1. A diocesan administrator is bound by the obligations and possesses the power of a diocesan bishop, excluding those matters which are excepted by their nature or by the law itself.

§2. When he has accepted election, the diocesan administrator obtains power and no other confirmation is required, without prejudice to the obligation mentioned in can. 833, n. 4.

CAN. 428 §1. When a see is vacant, nothing is to be altered.

§2. Those who temporarily care for the governance of the diocese are forbidden to do anything which can be prejudicial in some way to the diocese or episcopal rights. They, and consequently all others, are specifically prohibited, whether personally or through another, from removing or destroying any documents of the diocesan curia or from changing anything in them.

CAN. 429 A diocesan administrator is

gatur sacerdos, qui sit doctrina et prudentia praestans.

§3. Si praescriptae in §1 condiciones posthabitae fuerint, Metropolita aut, si ipsa Ecclesia metropolitana vacans fuerit, Episcopus suffraganeus promotione antiquior, agnita rei veritate, Administratorem pro a vice deputet; actus autem illius, qui contra praescripta §1 sit electus, sunt ipso iure nulli.

CAN. 426 Qui, sede vacante, ante deputationem Administratoris dioecesani, dioecesim regat, potestate gaudet quam ius Vicario generali agnoscit.

CAN. 427 §1. Administrator dioecesanus tenetur obligationibus et gaudet potestate Episcopi dioecesani, iis exclusis quae ex rei natura aut ipso iure excipiuntur.

§2. Administrator dioecesanus, acceptata electione, potestatem obtinet, quin requiratur ullius confirmatio, firma obligatione de qua in can. 833, n. 4.

CAN. 428 §1. Sede vacante, nihil innovetur.

§2. Illi qui ad interim dioecesis regimen curant, vetantur quidpiam agere quod vel dioecesi vel episcopalibus iuribus praeiudicium aliquod afferre possit; speciatim prohibentur ipsi, ac proinde alii quicumque, quominus sive per se sive per alium curiae dioecesanae documenta quaelibet subtrahant vel destruant, aut in iis quidquam immutent.

CAN. 429 Administrator dioecesanus

425 §3: c. 434 §3
426: c. 435
427 §1: c. 435 §§1 et 2; SCConc Resp. III, 10 maii 1931 (AAS 23 [1931] 235); SCPF Resp. 3, 26 ian. 1954; Sec Ep., 26 nov. 1963

427 §2: c. 438
428 §1: c. 436
428 §2: c. 435 §3
429: c. 440

obliged to reside in the diocese and to apply Mass for the people according to the norm of can. 388.

CAN. 430 §1. The function of a diocesan administrator ceases when the new bishop has taken possession of the diocese.

§2. The removal of a diocesan administrator is reserved to the Holy See. If an administrator resigns, the resignation must be presented in authentic form to the college competent to elect, but it does not need acceptance. If a diocesan administrator has been removed, resigns, or dies, another diocesan administrator is to be elected according to the norm of can. 421.

TITLE II. **Groupings of Particular Churches**

CHAPTER I. **Ecclesiastical Provinces and Ecclesiastical Regions**

CAN. 431 §1. To promote the common pastoral action of different neighboring dioceses according to the circumstances of persons and places and to foster more suitably the relations of the diocesan bishops among themselves, neighboring particular churches are to be brought together into ecclesiastical provinces limited to a certain territory.

§2. As a rule, exempt dioceses are no longer to exist. Therefore, individual dioceses and other particular churches within the territory of some ecclesiastical province must be joined to this ecclesiastical province.

obligatione tenetur residendi in dioecesi et applicandi Missam pro populo ad normam can. 388.

CAN. 430 §1. Munus Administratoris dioecesani cessat per captam a novo Episcopo dioecesis possessionem.

§2. Administratoris dioecesani remotio Sanctae Sedi reservatur; renuntiatio, quae forte ab ipso fiat, authentica forma exhibenda est collegio ad electionem competenti, neque acceptatione eget; remoto aut renuntiante Administratore dioecesano, aut eodem defuncto, alius eligatur Administrator dioecesanus ad normam can. 421.

TITULUS II. **De Ecclesiarum Particularium Coetibus**

CAPUT I. **De Provinciis Ecclesiasticis et de Regionibus Ecclesiasticis**

CAN. 431 §1. Ut communis diversarum dioecesium vicinarum, iuxta personarum et locorum adiuncta, actio pastoralis promoveatur, utque Episcoporum dioecesanorum inter se relationes aptius foveantur, Ecclesiae particulares viciniores componantur in provincias ecclesiasticas certo territorio circumscriptas.

§2. Dioeceses exemptae deinceps pro regula ne habeantur; itaque singulae dioeceses aliaeque Ecclesiae particulares intra territorium alicuius provinciae ecclesiasticae exsistentes huic provinciae ecclesiasticae adscribi debent.

430 §1: c. 443 §2
430 §2: c. 443 §1

431 §1: CD 40, 1
431 §2: CD 40, 2

§3. It is only for the supreme authority of the Church to establish, suppress, or alter ecclesiastical provinces after having heard the bishops involved.

CAN. 432 §1. The provincial council and the metropolitan possess authority in an ecclesiastical province according to the norm of law.

§2. An ecclesiastical province possesses juridic personality by the law itself.

CAN. 433 §1. If it seems advantageous, especially in nations where particular churches are more numerous, the Holy See can unite neighboring ecclesiastical provinces into ecclesiastical regions at the request of the conference of bishops.

§2. An ecclesiastical region can be erected as a juridic person.

CAN. 434 It belongs to a meeting of the bishops of an ecclesiastical region to foster cooperation and common pastoral action in the region. Nevertheless, such a meeting does not have the powers attributed to a conference of bishops in the canons of this Code unless the Holy See has specifically granted it certain powers.

CHAPTER II. **Metropolitans**

CAN. 435 A metropolitan, who is the archbishop of his diocese, presides over an ecclesiastical province. The office of metropolitan is joined with an episcopal see determined or approved by the Roman Pontiff.

CAN. 436 §1. In the suffragan dioceses, a metropolitan is competent:

§3. Unius supremae Ecclesiae auctoritatis est, auditis quorum interest Episcopis, provincias ecclesiasticas constituere, supprimere aut innovare.

CAN. 432 §1. In provincia ecclesiastica auctoritate, ad normam iuris, gaudent concilium provinciale atque Metropolita.

§2. Provincia ecclesiastica ipso iure personalitate iuridica gaudet.

CAN. 433 §1. Si utilitas id suadeat, praesertim in nationibus ubi numerosiores adsunt Ecclesiae particulares, provinciae ecclesiasticae viciniores, proponente Episcoporum conferentia, a Sancta Sede in regiones ecclesiasticas coniungi possunt.

§2. Regio ecclesiastica in personam iuridicam erigi potest.

CAN. 434 Ad conventum Episcoporum regionis ecclesiasticae pertinet cooperationem et actionem pastoralem communem in regione fovere; quae tamen in canonibus huius Codicis conferentiae Episcoporum tribuuntur potestates, eidem conventui non competunt, nisi quaedam specialiter a Sancta Sede ei concessa fuerint.

CAPUT II. **De Metropolitis**

CAN. 435 Provinciae ecclesiasticae praeest Metropolita, qui est Archiepiscopus dioecesis cui praeficitur; quod officium cum sede episcopali, a Romano Pontifice determinata aut probata, coniunctum est.

CAN. 436 §1. In dioecesibus suffraganeis Metropolitae competit:

---

431 §3: c. 215 §1; CD 41; ES I, 42
432 §1: c. 272; CD 40, 2
432 §2: cc. 99, 100 §1
433 §1: c. 215 §1; SCC Decr.*Conciliorum provincialium*, 15 feb. 1919 (AAS 11 [1919] 72–74); SCC Litt. circ., 22 mar. 1919 (AAS 11 [1919] 175–177); CD 40, 3;

41; ES I, 42
433 §2: c. 100; ES I, 42
434: SCC Litt. circ., 22 mar. 1919 (AAS 11 [1919] 175–177); SCConc Decr. *Il Codice*, 21 iun. 1932 (AAS 24 [1932] 242–243); CD 41; ES I, 42
435: c. 272

1° to exercise vigilance so that the faith and ecclesiastical discipline are observed carefully and to inform the Roman Pontiff of abuses, if there are any;

2° to conduct a canonical visitation for a cause previously approved by the Apostolic See if a suffragan has neglected it;

3° to designate a diocesan administrator according to the norm of cann. 421, §2, and 425, §3.

§2. Where circumstances demand it, the Apostolic See can endow a metropolitan with special functions and power to be determined in particular law.

§3. The metropolitan has no other power of governance in the suffragan dioceses. He can perform sacred functions, however, as if he were a bishop in his own diocese in all churches, but he is first to inform the diocesan bishop if the church is the cathedral.

CAN. 437 §1. Within three months from the reception of episcopal consecration or if he has already been consecrated, from the canonical provision, a metropolitan is obliged to request the pallium from the Roman Pontiff either personally or through a proxy. The pallium signifies the power which the metropolitan, in communion with the Roman Church, has by law in his own province.

§2. A metropolitan can use the pallium according to the norm of liturgical laws within any church of the ecclesiastical province over which he presides, but not outside it, even if the diocesan bishop gives his assent.

§3. A metropolitan needs a new pallium if he is transferred to another metropolitan see.

1° vigilare ut fides et disciplina ecclesiastica accurate serventur, et de abusibus, si qui habeantur, Romanum Pontificem certiorem facere;

2° canonicam visitationem peragere, causa prius ab Apostolica Sede probata, si eam suffraganeus neglexerit;

3° deputare Administratorem dioecesanum, ad normam cann. 421, §2 et 425, §3.

§2. Ubi adiuncta id postulent, Metropolita ab Apostolica Sede instrui potest peculiaribus muneribus et potestate in iure particulari determinandis.

§3. Nulla alia in dioecesibus suffraganeis competit Metropolitis potestas regiminis; potest vero in omnibus ecclesiis, Episcopo dioecesano praemonito, si ecclesia sit cathedralis, sacras exercere functiones, uti Episcopus in propria dioecesi.

CAN. 437 §1. Metropolita obligatione tenetur, intra tres menses a recepta consecratione episcopali, aut, si iam consecratus fuerit, a provisione canonica, per se aut per procuratorem a Romano Pontifice petendi pallium, quod quidem significatur potestas qua, in communione cum Ecclesia Romana, Metropolita in propria provincia iure instruitur.

§2. Metropolita, ad normam legum liturgicarum, pallio uti potest intra quamlibet ecclesiam provinciae ecclesiasticae cui praeest, minime vero extra eandem, ne accedente quidem Episcopi dioecesani assensu.

§3. Metropolita, si ad aliam sedem metropolitanam transferatur, novo indiget pallio.

---

436 §1, 1°: c. 274, 4°
436 §1, 2°: c. 274, 5°
436 §1, 3°: cc. 274, 3°, 432 §2
436 §2: CD 40, 1
436 §3: c. 274, 6°; CI Resp. I, 5 aug. 1941 (AAS 33

[1941] 378)
437 §1: c. 275; PAULUS PP. VI, m. p. *Inter eximia*, 11 maii 1978 (AAS 70 [1978] 441–442)
437 §2: c. 277
437 §3: c. 278

CAN. 438 The titles of patriarch and primate entail no power of governance in the Latin Church apart from a prerogative of honor unless in some matters the contrary is clear from apostolic privilege or approved custom.

CHAPTER III.
Particular Councils

CAN. 439 §1. A plenary council, that is, one for all the particular churches of the same conference of bishops, is to be celebrated whenever it seems necessary or useful to the conference of bishops, with the approval of the Apostolic See.

§2. The norm established in §1 is valid also for the celebration of a provincial council in an ecclesiastical province whose boundaries coincide with the territory of a nation.

CAN. 440 §1. A provincial council for the different particular churches of the same ecclesiastical province is to be celebrated whenever it seems opportune in the judgment of the majority of the diocesan bishops of the province, without prejudice to can. 439, §2.

§2. When a metropolitan see is vacant, a provincial council is not to be convoked.

CAN. 441 It is for the conference of bishops:

1° to convoke a plenary council;

2° to select the place to celebrate the council within the territory of the conference of bishops;

3° to select from among the diocesan bishops a president of the plenary council whom the Apostolic See must approve;

4° to determine the agenda and questions to be treated, set the opening and duration of a

CAN. 438 Patriarchae et Primatis titulus, praeter praerogativam honoris, nullam in Ecclesia latina secumfert regiminis potestatem, nisi de aliquibus ex privilegio apostolico aut probata consuetudine aliud constet.

CAPUT III. **De Conciliis Particularibus**

CAN. 439 §1. Concilium plenarium, pro omnibus scilicet Ecclesiis particularibus eiusdem conferentiae Episcoporum, celebretur quoties id ipsi Episcoporum conferentiae, approbante Apostolica Sede, necessarium aut utile videatur.

§2. Norma in §1 statuta valet etiam de concilio provinciali celebrando in provincia ecclesiastica, cuius termini cum territorio nationis coincidunt.

CAN. 440 §1. Concilium provinciale, pro diversis Ecclesiis particularibus eiusdem provinciae ecclesiasticae, celebretur quoties id, de iudicio maioris partis Episcoporum dioecesanorum provinciae, opportunum videatur, salvo can. 439, §2.

§2. Sede metropolitana vacante, concilium provinciale ne convocetur.

CAN. 441 Episcoporum conferentiae est:

1° convocare concilium plenarium;

2° locum ad celebrandum concilium intra territorium conferentiae Episcoporum eligere;

3° inter Episcopos dioecesanos concilii plenarii eligere praesidem, ab Apostolica Sede approbandum;

4° ordinem agendi et quaestiones tractandas determinare, concilii plenarii initium

438: c. 271
439 §1: c. 281; CD 36
440 §1: c. 283; SCC Decr. *Conciliorum provincial-*

ium, 15 feb. 1919 (AAS 11 [1919] 72–74)
440 §2: c. 284
441: cc. 281, 288

plenary council, transfer, extend, and dissolve it.

CAN. 442 §1. It is for the metropolitan with the consent of the majority of the suffragan bishops:

1° to convoke a provincial council;

2° to select the place to celebrate the provincial council within the territory of the province;

3° to determine the agenda and questions to be treated, set the opening and duration of the provincial council, transfer, extend, and dissolve it.

§2. It is for the metropolitan or, if he is legitimately impeded, a suffragan bishop elected by the other suffragan bishops to preside over a provincial council.

CAN. 443 §1. The following must be called to particular councils and have the right of a deliberative vote in them:

1° diocesan bishops;

2° coadjutor and auxiliary bishops;

3° other titular bishops who perform in the territory a special function committed to them by the Apostolic See or the conference of bishops.

§2. Other titular bishops, even retired ones, living in the territory can be called to particular councils; they also have the right of a deliberative vote.

§3. The following must be called to particular councils but with only a consultative vote:

1° the vicars general and episcopal vicars of all the particular churches in the territory;

2° major superiors of religious institutes and societies of apostolic life in a number for both

ac periodum indicere, illud transferre, prorogare et absolvere.

CAN. 442 §1. Metropolitae, de consensu maioris partis Episcoporum suffraganeorum, est:

1° convocare concilium provinciale;

2° locum ad celebrandum concilium provinciale intra provinciae territorium eligere;

3° ordinem agendi et quaestiones tractandas determinare, concilii provincialis initium et periodum indicere, illud transferre, prorogare et absolvere.

§2. Metropolitae, eoque legitime impedito, Episcopi suffraganei ab aliis Episcopis suffraganeis electi est concilio provinciali praeesse.

CAN. 443 §1. Ad concilia particularia convocandi sunt atque in eisdem ius habent suffragii deliberativi:

1° Episcopi dioecesani;

2° Episcopi coadiutores et auxiliares;

3° alii Episcopi titulares qui peculiari munere sibi ab Apostolica Sede aut ab Episcoporum conferentia demandato in territorio funguntur.

§2. Ad concilia particularia vocari possunt alii Episcopi titulares etiam emeriti in territorio degentes; qui quidem ius habent suffragii deliberativi.

§3. Ad concilia particularia vocandi sunt cum suffragio tantum consultivo:

1° Vicarii generales et Vicarii episcopales omnium in territorio Ecclesiarum particularium;

2° Superiores maiores institutorum religiosorum et societatum vitae apostolicae nu-

---

442 §1: cc. 284, 288
442 §2: c. 284, 2°
443 §1: cc. 282 §§1 et 2, 286 §§1 et 2

443 §2: cc. 282 §2, 286 §2
443 §3: cc. 282 §3, 286 §4

men and women which the conference of bishops or the bishops of the province are to determine; these superiors are to be elected respectively by all the major superiors of the institutes and societies which have a seat in the territory;

3° rectors of ecclesiastical and Catholic universities and deans of faculties of theology and of canon law, which have a seat in the territory;

4° some rectors of major seminaries elected by the rectors of the seminaries which are located in the territory, in a number to be determined as in n. 2.

§4. Presbyters and other members of the Christian faithful can also be called to particular councils, but with only a consultative vote and in such a way that their number does not exceed half the number of those mentioned in §§1–3.

§5. Moreover, cathedral chapters and the presbyteral council and pastoral council of each particular church are to be invited to provincial councils in such a way that each of them sends two of their members designated collegially by them; however, they have only a consultative vote.

§6. Others can also be invited as guests to particular councils, if it is expedient in the judgment of the conference of bishops for a plenary council, or of the metropolitan together with the suffragan bishops for a provincial council.

CAN. 444 §1. All who are called to particular councils must attend them unless they are prevented by a just impediment, about which they are bound to inform the president of the council.

mero tum pro viris tum pro mulieribus ab Episcoporum conferentia aut a provinciae Episcopis determinando, respective electi ab omnibus Superioribus maioribus institutorum et societatum, quae in territorio sedem habent;

3° Rectores universitatum ecclesiasticarum et catholicarum atque decani facultatum theologiae et iuris canonici, quae in territorio sedem habent;

4° Rectores aliqui seminariorum maiorum, numero ut in n. 2 determinando, electi a rectoribus seminariorum quae in territorio sita sunt.

§4. Ad concilia particularia vocari etiam possunt, cum suffragio tantum consultivo, presbyteri aliique christifideles, ita tamen ut eorum numerus non excedat dimidiam partem eorum de quibus in §§1–3.

§5. Ad concilia provincialia praeterea invitentur capitula cathedralia, itemque consilium presbyterale et consilium pastorale uniuscuiusque Ecclesiae particularis, ita quidem ut eorum singula duos ex suis membris mittant, collegialiter ab iisdem designatos; qui tamen votum habent tantum consultivum.

§6. Ad concilia particularia, si id iudicio Episcoporum conferentiae pro concilio plenario aut Metropolitae una cum Episcopis suffraganeis pro concilio provinciali expediat, etiam alii ut hospites invitari poterunt.

CAN. 444 §1. Omnes qui ad concilia particularia convocantur, eisdem interesse debent, nisi iusto detineantur impedimento, de quo concilii praesidem certiorem facere tenentur.

443 §4: cc. 282 §3, 286 §4
443 §5: c. 286 §3

444 §1: cc. 282 §§1 et 2, 286 §§1, 3 et 4, 287 §1, 289

§2. Those who are called to particular councils and have a deliberative vote in them can send a proxy if they are prevented by a just impediment; the proxy has only a consultative vote.

CAN. 445 A particular council, for its own territory, takes care that provision is made for the pastoral needs of the people of God and possesses the power of governance, especially legislative power, so that, always without prejudice to the universal law of the Church, it is able to decide what seems opportune for the increase of the faith, the organization of common pastoral action, and the regulation of morals and of the common ecclesiastical discipline which is to be observed, promoted, and protected.

CAN. 446 When a particular council has ended, the president is to take care that all the acts of the council are sent to the Apostolic See. Decrees issued by a council are not to be promulgated until the Apostolic See has reviewed them. It is for the council itself to define the manner of promulgation of the decrees and the time when the promulgated decrees begin to oblige.

CHAPTER IV. Conferences of Bishops

CAN. 447 A conference of bishops, a permanent institution, is a group of bishops of some nation or certain territory who jointly exercise certain pastoral functions for the Christian faithful of their territory in order to promote the greater good which the Church offers to humanity, especially through forms and programs of the apostolate fittingly adapted to the

§2. Qui ad concilia particularia convocantur et in eis suffragium habent deliberativum, si iusto detineantur impedimento, procuratorem mittere possunt; qui procurator votum habet tantum consultivum.

CAN. 445 Concilium particulare pro suo territorio curat ut necessitatibus pastoralibus populi Dei provideatur atque potestate gaudet regiminis, praesertim legislativa, ita ut, salvo semper iure universali Ecclesiae, decernere valeat quae ad fidei incrementum, ad actionem pastoralem communem ordinandam et ad moderandos mores et disciplinam ecclesiasticam communem servandam, inducendam aut tuendam opportuna videantur.

CAN. 446 Absoluto concilio particulari, praeses curet ut omnia acta concilii ad Apostolicam Sedem transmittantur; decreta a concilio edicta ne promulgentur, nisi postquam ab Apostolica Sede recognita fuerint; ipsius concilii est definire modum promulgationis decretorum et tempus quo decreta promulgata obligare incipiant.

CAPUT IV. De Episcoporum Conferentiis

CAN. 447 Episcoporum conferentia, institutum quidem permanens, est coetus Episcoporum alicuius nationis vel certi territorii, munera quaedam pastoralia coniunctim pro christifidelibus sui territorii exercentium, ad maius bonum provehendum, quod hominibus praebet Ecclesia, praesertim per apostolatus formas et rationes temporis et

444 §2: c. 287
445: c. 290; CD 36; DPME 213

446: c. 291
447: LG 23; CD 3, 37, 38; DPME 210

circumstances of time and place, according to the norm of law.

CAN. 448 §1. As a general rule, a conference of bishops includes those who preside over all the particular churches of the same nation, according to the norm of can. 450.

§2. If, however, in the judgment of the Apostolic See, having heard the diocesan bishops concerned, the circumstances of persons or things suggest it, a conference of bishops can be erected for a territory of lesser or greater area, so that it only includes either bishops of some particular churches constituted in a certain territory or those who preside over particular churches in different nations. It is for the Apostolic See to establish special norms for each of them.

CAN. 449 §1. It is only for the supreme authority of the Church to erect, suppress, or alter conferences of bishops, after having heard the bishops concerned.

§2. A legitimately erected conference of bishops possesses juridic personality by the law itself.

CAN. 450 §1. To a conference of bishops belong by the law itself all diocesan bishops in the territory, those equivalent to them in law, coadjutor bishops, auxiliary bishops, and other titular bishops who perform in the same territory a special function entrusted to them by the Apostolic See or conference of bishops. Ordinaries of another rite can also be invited though in such a way that they have only a consultative vote unless the statutes of the conference of bishops decree otherwise.

loci adiunctis apte accommodatas, ad normam iuris.

CAN. 448 §1. Episcoporum conferentia regula generali comprehendit praesules omnium Ecclesiarum particularium eiusdem nationis, ad normam can. 450.

§2. Si vero, de iudicio Apostolicae Sedis, auditis quorum interest Episcopis dioecesanis, personarum aut rerum adiuncta id suadeant, Episcoporum conferentia erigi potest pro territorio minoris aut maioris amplitudinis, ita ut vel tantum comprehendat Episcopos aliquarum Ecclesiarum particularium in certo territorio constitutarum vel praesules Ecclesiarum particularium in diversis nationibus exstantium; eiusdem Apostolicae Sedis est pro earundem singulis peculiares normas statuere.

CAN. 449 §1. Unius supremae Ecclesiae auctoritatis est, auditis quorum interest Episcopis, Episcoporum conferentias erigere, supprimere aut innovare.

§2. Episcoporum conferentia legitime erecta ipso iure personalitate iuridica gaudet.

CAN. 450 §1. Ad Episcoporum conferentiam ipso iure pertinent omnes in territorio Episcopi dioecesani eisque iure aequiparati, itemque Episcopi coadiutores, Episcopi auxiliares atque ceteri Episcopi titulares peculiari munere, sibi ab Apostolica Sede vel ab Episcoporum conferentia demandato, in eodem territorio fungentes; invitari quoque possunt Ordinarii alterius ritus, ita tamen ut votum tantum consultivum habeant, nisi Episcoporum conferentiae statuta aliud decernant.

---

448 §1: CD 38, 1
448 §2: SCPF Resp., 26 feb. 1964; CD 38, 5; ES I, 41 §§3 et 4; DPME 211
449 §1: CD 38, 5

449 §2: c. 100 §1
450 §1: CD 38, 2; CIV Resp., 31 oct. 1970 (AAS 62 [1970] 793)

§2. Other titular bishops and the legate of the Roman Pontiff are not by law members of a conference of bishops.

CAN. 451 Each conference of bishops is to prepare its own statutes which must be reviewed by the Apostolic See and which are to organize, among other things, the plenary meetings of the conference which are to be held and to provide for a permanent council of bishops, a general secretariat of the conference, and also other offices and commissions which, in the judgment of the conference, more effectively help it to achieve its purpose.

CAN. 452 §1. Each conference of bishops is to elect a president for itself, is to determine who is to perform the function of pro-president when the president is legitimately impeded, and is to designate a general secretary, according to the norm of the statutes.

§2. The president of a conference, and, when he is legitimately impeded, the pro-president, presides not only over the general meetings of the conference of bishops but also over the permanent council.

CAN. 453 Plenary meetings of a conference of bishops are to be held at least once each year and, in addition, whenever particular circumstances require it, according to the prescripts of the statutes.

CAN. 454 §1. By the law itself, diocesan bishops, those who are equivalent to them in law, and coadjutor bishops have a deliberative vote in plenary meetings of a conference of bishops.

§2. Auxiliary bishops and other titular bishops who belong to a conference of bishops have a deliberative or consultative vote according to the prescripts of the statutes of the conference.

§2. Ceteri Episcopi titulares necnon Legatus Romani Pontificis non sunt de iure membra Episcoporum conferentiae.

CAN. 451 Quaelibet Episcoporum conferentia sua conficiat statuta, ab Apostolica Sede recognoscenda, in quibus, praeter alia, ordinentur conferentiae conventus plenarii habendi, et provideantur consilium Episcoporum permanens et secretaria generalis conferentiae, atque alia etiam officia et commissiones quae iudicio conferentiae fini consequendo efficacius consulant.

CAN. 452 §1. Quaelibet Episcoporum conferentia sibi eligat praesidem, determinet quisnam, praeside legitime impedito, munere propraesidis fungatur, atque secretarium generalem designet, ad normam statutorum.

§2. Praeses conferentiae, atque eo legitime impedito pro-praeses, non tantum Episcoporum conferentiae conventibus generalibus, sed etiam consilio permanenti praeest.

CAN. 453 Conventus plenarii Episcoporum conferentiae habeantur semel saltem singulis annis, et praeterea quoties postulent peculiaria adiuncta, secundum statutorum praescripta.

CAN. 454 §1. Suffragium deliberativum in conventibus plenariis Episcoporum conferentiae ipso iure competit Episcopis dioecesanis eisque qui iure ipsis aequiparantur, necnon Episcopis coadiutoribus.

§2. Episcopis auxiliaribus ceterisque Episcopis titularibus, qui ad Episcoporum conferentiam pertinent, suffragium competit deliberativum aut consultivum, iuxta statuto-

450 §2: CD 38, 2; SOE VII, 2
451: CD 38, 3; ES I, 41 §§1 et 2; DPME 211

454 §1: CD 38, 2
454 §2: CD 38, 2

Nonetheless, only those mentioned in §1 have a deliberative vote in drawing up or changing the statutes.

CAN. 455 §1. A conference of bishops can only issue general decrees in cases where universal law has prescribed it or a special mandate of the Apostolic See has established it either *motu proprio* or at the request of the conference itself.

§2. The decrees mentioned in §1, in order to be enacted validly in a plenary meeting, must be passed by at least a two thirds vote of the prelates who belong to the conference and possess a deliberative vote. They do not obtain binding force unless they have been legitimately promulgated after having been reviewed by the Apostolic See.

§3. The conference of bishops itself determines the manner of promulgation and the time when the decrees take effect.

§4. In cases in which neither universal law nor a special mandate of the Apostolic See has granted the power mentioned in §1 to a conference of bishops, the competence of each diocesan bishop remains intact, nor is a conference or its president able to act in the name of all the bishops unless each and every bishop has given consent.

CAN. 456 When a plenary meeting of a conference of bishops has ended, the president is to send a report of the acts of the conference and its decrees to the Apostolic See so that the acts are brought to its notice and it can review the decrees if there are any.

rum conferentiae praescripta; firmum tamen sit eis solis, de quibus in §1, competere suffragium deliberativum, cum agitur de statutis conficiendis aut immutandis.

CAN. 455 §1. Episcoporum conferentia decreta generalia ferre tantummodo potest in causis, in quibus ius universale id praescripserit aut peculiare Apostolicae Sedis mandatum sive motu proprio sive ad petitionem ipsius conferentiae id statuerit.

§2. Decreta de quibus in §1, ut valide ferantur in plenario conventu, per duas saltem ex tribus partibus suffragiorum Praesulum, qui voto deliberativo fruentes ad conferentiam pertinent, proferri debent, atque vim obligandi non obtinent, nisi ab Apostolica Sede recognita, legitime promulgata fuerint.

§3. Modus promulgationis et tempus, a quo decreta vim suam exserunt, ab ipsa Episcoporum conferentia determinantur.

§4. In casibus in quibus nec ius universale nec peculiare Apostolicae Sedis mandatum potestatem, de qua in §1, Episcoporum conferentiae concessit, singuli Episcopi dioecesani competentia integra manet, nec conferentia eiusve praeses nomine omnium Episcoporum agere valet, nisi omnes et singuli Episcopi consensum dederint.

CAN. 456 Absoluto conventu plenario Episcoporum conferentiae, relatio de actis conferentiae necnon eius decreta a praeside ad Apostolicam Sedem transmittantur, tum ut in eiusdem notitiam acta perferantur, tum ut decreta, si quae sint, ab eadem recognosci possint.

---

455 §1: CD 38, 4; PONTIFICIA COMMISSIO CENTRALIS COORDINANDIS POST CONCILIUM LABORIBUS ET CONCILII DECRETIS INTERPRETANDIS, Resp., 10 iun. 1966 (AAS 60 [1968] 361); CIV Resp. I, 5 feb. 1968

(AAS 60 [1968] 361–362)
455 §2: CD 38, 4; DPME 212
455 §4: c. 101 §1, 2°; LG 27; CD 38, 4; DPME 212
456: LG nep 2; CD 38, 4

CAN. 457 It is for the permanent council of bishops to take care that the agenda for a plenary session of a conference is prepared and that decisions made in plenary session are properly executed. It is also for the council to take care of other affairs which are entrusted to it according to the norm of the statutes.

CAN. 458 It is for the general secretariat:

1° to prepare a report of the acts and decrees of a plenary meeting of a conference and the acts of the permanent council of bishops, to communicate the same to all the members of the conference, and to draw up other acts whose preparation the president of the conference or the permanent council entrusts to the general secretary;

2° to communicate to neighboring conferences of bishops the acts and documents which the conference in plenary meeting or the permanent council of bishops decides to send to them.

CAN. 459 §1. Relations between conferences of bishops, especially neighboring ones, are to be fostered in order to promote and protect the greater good.

§2. Whenever conferences enter into actions or programs having an international character, however, the Apostolic See must be heard.

CAN. 457 Consilii Episcoporum permanentis est curare, ut res in plenario conventu conferentiae agendae praeparentur et decisiones in conventu plenario statutae debite exsecutioni mandentur; eiusdem etiam est alia negotia peragere, quae ipsi ad normam statutorum committuntur.

CAN. 458 Secretariae generalis est:

1° relationem componere actorum et decretorum conventus plenarii conferentiae necnon actorum consilii Episcoporum permanentis, et eadem cum omnibus conferentiae membris communicare itemque alia acta conscribere, quae ipsi a conferentiae praeside aut a consilio permanenti componenda committuntur;

2° communicare cum Episcoporum conferentiis finitimis acta et documenta quae a conferentia in plenario conventu aut a consilio Episcoporum permanenti ipsis transmitti statuuntur.

CAN. 459 §1. Foveantur relationes inter Episcoporum conferentias, praesertim viciniores, ad maius bonum promovendum ac tuendum.

§2. Quoties vero actiones aut rationes a conferentiis ineuntur formam internationalem praeseferentes, Apostolica Sedes audiatur oportet.

457: CD 38, 3
458, 1°: CD 38, 3; ES I, 41 §5
458, 2°: ES I, 41 §5

459 §1: CD 38, 5; ES I, 41 §5; SE *Nunc nobis,* 27 oct. 1969
459 §2: ES I, 41 §4

TITLE III. The Internal Ordering of Particular Churches

CHAPTER I. The Diocesan Synod

CAN. 460 A diocesan synod is a group of selected priests and other members of the Christian faithful of a particular church who offer assistance to the diocesan bishop for the good of the whole diocesan community according to the norm of the following canons.

CAN. 461 §1. A diocesan synod is to be celebrated in individual particular churches when circumstances suggest it in the judgment of the diocesan bishop after he has heard the presbyteral council.

§2. If a bishop has the care of several dioceses or has the care of one as the proper bishop but of another as administrator, he can convoke one diocesan synod for all the dioceses entrusted to him.

CAN. 462 §1. The diocesan bishop alone convokes a diocesan synod, but not one who temporarily presides over a diocese.

§2. The diocesan bishop presides over a diocesan synod. He can, however, delegate a vicar general or episcopal vicar to fulfill this responsibility for individual sessions of the synod.

CAN. 463 §1. The following must be called to a diocesan synod as members of the synod and are obliged to participate in it:

1° a coadjutor bishop and auxiliary bishops;

TITULUS III. **De Interna Ordinatione Ecclesiarum Particularum**

CAPUT I. **De Synodo Dioecesana**

CAN. 460 Synodus dioecesana est coetus delectorum sacerdotum aliorumque christifidelium Ecclesiae particularis, qui in bonum totius communitatis dioecesanae Episcopo dioecesano adiutricem operam praestant, ad normam canonum qui sequuntur.

CAN. 461 §1. Synodous dioecesana in singulis Ecclesiis particularibus celebretur cum, iudicio Episcopi dioecesani et audito consilio presbyterali, adiuncta id suadeant.

§2. Si Episcopus plurium dioecesium curam habet, aut unius curam habet uti Episcopus proprius, alterius vero uti Administrator, unam synodum dioecesanam ex omnibus dioecesibus sibi commissis convocare potest.

CAN. 462 §1. Synodum dioecesanam convocat solus Episcopus dioecesanus, non autem qui ad interim dioecesi praeest.

§2. Synodo dioecesanae praeest Episcopus dioecesanus, qui tamen Vicarium generalem aut Vicarium episcopalem pro singulis sessionibus synodi ad hoc officium implendum delegare potest.

CAN. 463 §1. Ad synodum dioecesanam vocandi sunt uti synodi sodales eamque participandi obligatione tenetur:

1° Episcopus coadiutor atque Episcopi auxiliares;

460: c. 356 §1; CD 28, 36; *ES* III, 20; DPME 163, 165

461 §1: c. 356 §1; SCPF *Direttive per Sinodi interdiocesani*, 27 ian. 1979

461 §2: c. 356 §2
462 §1: c. 357 §1; DPME 163
462 §2: c. 355 §1

2° vicars general, episcopal vicars, and the judicial vicar;

3° canons of the cathedral church;

4° members of the presbyteral council;

5° lay members of the Christian faithful, even members of institutes of consecrated life, chosen by the pastoral council in a manner and number to be determined by the diocesan bishop or, where this council does not exist, in a manner determined by the diocesan bishop;

6° the rector of the diocesan major seminary;

7° vicars forane;

8° at least one presbyter from each vicariate forane, chosen by all those who have the care of souls there; also another presbyter must be chosen who, if the first is impeded, is to take his place;

9° some superiors of religious institutes and of societies of apostolic life which have a house in the diocese, chosen in a number and manner determined by the diocesan bishop.

§2. The diocesan bishop can also call others to a diocesan synod as members of the synod; they can be clerics, members of institutes of consecrated life, or lay members of the Christian faithful.

§3. If the diocesan bishop has judged it opportune, he can invite as observers to the diocesan synod other ministers or members of Churches or ecclesial communities which are not in full communion with the Catholic Church.

CAN. 464   If a member of the synod is prevented by a legitimate impediment, the mem-

2° Vicarii generales et Vicarii episcopales, necnon Vicarius iudicialis;

3° canonici ecclesiae cathedralis;

4° membra consilii presbyteralis;

5° christifideles laici, etiam sodales institutorum vitae consecratae, a consilio pastorali eligendi, modo et numero ab Episcopo dioecesano determinandis, aut, ubi hoc consilium non exstet, ratione ab Episcopo dioecesano determinata;

6° rector seminarii dioecesani maioris;

7° vicarii foranei;

8° unus saltem presbyter ex unoquoque vicariatu foraneo eligendus ab omnibus qui curam animarum inibi habeant; item eligendus est alius presbyter qui, eodem impedito, in eius locum substituatur;

9° aliqui Superiores institutorum religiosorum et societatum vitae apostolicae, quae in dioecesi domum habent, eligendi numero et modo ab Episcopo dioecesano determinatis.

§2. Ad synodum dioecesanam ab Episcopo dioecesano vocari uti synodi sodales possunt alii quoque, sive clerici, sive institutorum vitae consecratae sodales, sive christifideles laici.

§3. Ad synodum dioecesanam Episcopus dioecesanus, si id opportunum duxerit, invitare potest uti observatores aliquos ministros aut sodales Ecclesiarum vel communitatum ecclesialium, quae non sunt in plena cum Ecclesia catholica communione.

CAN. 464   Synodi sodalis, si legitimo detineatur impedimento, non potest mittere

463 §1, 2°: c. 358 §1, 1°
463 §1, 3°: c. 358 §1, 2°
463 §1, 5°: SCE Rescr., 29 maii 1968
463 §1, 6°: c. 358 §1, 3°
463 §1, 7°: c. 358 §1, 4°
463 §1, 8°: c. 358 §1, 7°

463 §1, 9°: c. 358 §1, 8°
463 § 2: c. 358 §2
463 §3: SCUF Directorium, I, 14 maii 1967, 3–6; 25–63
464: c. 359 §1

ber cannot send a proxy to attend it in his or her name. The member, however, is to inform the diocesan bishop of this impediment.

CAN. 465 All proposed questions are subject to the free discussion of the members during sessions of the synod.

CAN. 466 The only legislator in a diocesan synod is the diocesan bishop; the other members of the synod possess only a consultative vote. Only he signs the synodal declarations and decrees, which can be published by his authority alone.

CAN. 467 The diocesan bishop is to communicate the texts of the synodal declarations and decrees to the metropolitan and the conference of bishops.

CAN. 468 §1. The diocesan bishop is competent to suspend or dissolve a diocesan synod according to his prudent judgment.

§2. When an episcopal see is vacant or impeded, a diocesan synod is interrupted by the law itself until the succeeding diocesan bishop has decided that it is to be continued or has declared it terminated.

CHAPTER II. The Diocesan Curia

CAN. 469 The diocesan curia consists of those institutions and persons which assist the bishop in the governance of the whole diocese, especially in guiding pastoral action, in caring for the administration of the diocese, and in exercising judicial power.

CAN. 470 The appointment of those who exercise offices in the diocesan curia pertains to the diocesan bishop.

CAN. 471 All those who are admitted to offices in the curia must:

procuratorem qui ipsius nomine eidem intersit; Episcopum vero dioecesanum de hoc impedimento certiorem faciat.

CAN. 465 Propositae quaestiones omnes liberae sodalium disceptationi in synodi sessionibus subiciantur.

CAN. 466 Unus in synodo dioecesana legislator est Episcopus dioecesanus, aliis synodi sodalibus voto tantummodo consultivo gaudentibus; unus ipse synodalibus declarationibus et decretis subscribit, quae eius auctoritate tantum publici iuris fieri possunt.

CAN. 467 Episcopus dioecesanus textus declarationum ac decretorum synodalium communicet cum Metropolita necnon cum Episcoporum conferentia.

CAN. 468 §1. Episcopo dioecesano competit pro suo prudenti iudicio synodum dioecesanam suspendere necnon dissolvere.

§2. Vacante vel impedita sede episcopali, synodus dioecesana ipso iure intermittitur, donec Episcopus dioecesanus, qui succedit, ipsam continuari decreverit aut eandem extinctam declaraverit.

CAPUT II. De Curia Dioecesana

CAN. 469 Curia dioecesana constat illis institutis et personis, quae Episcopo operam praestant in regimine universae dioecesis, praesertim in actione pastorali dirigenda, in administratione dioecesis curanda, necnon in potestate iudiciali exercenda.

CAN. 470 Nominatio eorum, qui officia in curia dioecesana exercent, spectat ad Episcopum dioecesanum.

CAN. 471 Omnes qui ad officia in curia admittuntur debent:

465: c. 361; DPME 165
466: c. 362; LG 27; CD 8
468 §1: cc. 222 §1, 357 §1

468 §2: c. 229
469: c. 363 §1; CD 27; DPME 200
470: cc. 152, 364 §1; DPME 200

1° promise to fulfill their function faithfully according to the manner determined by law or by the bishop;

2° observe secrecy within the limits and according to the manner determined by law or by the bishop.

CAN. 472 The prescripts of Book VII, *Processes*, are to be observed regarding cases and persons which belong to the exercise of judicial power in the curia. The prescripts of the following canons, however, are to be observed regarding those things which pertain to the administration of the diocese.

CAN. 473 §1. A diocesan bishop must take care that all the affairs which belong to the administration of the whole diocese are duly coordinated and are ordered to attain more suitably the good of the portion of the people of God entrusted to him.

§2. It is for the diocesan bishop himself to coordinate the pastoral action of the vicars general or episcopal vicars. Where it is expedient, a moderator of the curia can be appointed who must be a priest and who, under the authority of the bishop, is to coordinate those things which pertain to the treatment of administrative affairs and to take care that the other members of the curia properly fulfill the office entrusted to them.

§3. Unless in the judgment of the bishop local circumstances suggest otherwise, the vicar general or if there are several, one of the vicars general, is to be appointed moderator of the curia.

§4. Where the bishop has judged it expedient, he can establish an episcopal council, con-

1° promissionem emittere de munere fideliter adimplendo, secundum rationem iure vel ab Episcopo determinatam;

2° secretum servare intra fines et secundum modum iure aut ab Episcopo determinatos.

CAN. 472 Circa causas atque personas quae in curia ad exercitium potestatis iudicialis pertinent, serventur praescripta Libri VII *De processibus*; de iis autem quae ad administrationem dioecesis spectant, serventur praescripta canonum qui sequuntur.

CAN. 473 §1. Episcopus dioecesanus curare debet ut omnia negotia quae ad universae dioecesis administrationem pertinent, debite coordinentur et ad bonum portionis populi Dei sibi commissae aptius procurandum ordinentur.

§2. Ipsius Episcopi dioecesani est coordinare actionem pastoralem Vicariorum sive generalium sive episcopalium; ubi id expediat, nominari potest Moderator curiae, qui sacerdos sit oportet, cuius est sub Episcopi auctoritate ea coordinare quae ad negotia administrativa tractanda attinent, itemque curare ut ceteri curiae addicti officium sibi commissum rite adimpleant.

§3. Nisi locorum adiuncta iudicio Episcopi aliud suadeant, Moderator curiae nominetur Vicarius generalis aut, si plures sint, unus ex Vicariis generalibus.

§4. Ubi id expedire iudicaverit, Episcopus, ad actionem pastoralem aptius foven-

471, 1°: c. 364 §2, 1°
471, 2°: c. 364 §2, 3°
472: c. 365; DPME 200
473 §1: CD 17; SCE-SCpC Ep., 19 iul. 1972;

PAULUS PP. VI, Const. Ap. *Vicariae potestatis*, 6 ian. 1977, 1 §3 (AAS 69 [1977] 7)
473 §2: CD 25, 26

sisting of the vicars general and episcopal vicars, to foster pastoral action more suitably.

CAN. 474 For validity, acts of the curia which are to have juridic effect must be signed by the ordinary from whom they emanate; they must also be signed by the chancellor of the curia or a notary. The chancellor, moreover, is bound to inform the moderator of the curia concerning such acts.

ART. 1. *Vicars General and Episcopal Vicars*

CAN. 475 §1. In each diocese the diocesan bishop must appoint a vicar general who is provided with ordinary power according to the norm of the following canons and who is to assist him in the governance of the whole diocese.

§2. As a general rule, one vicar general is to be appointed unless the size of the diocese, the number of inhabitants, or other pastoral reasons suggest otherwise.

CAN. 476 Whenever the correct governance of a diocese requires it, the diocesan bishop can also appoint one or more episcopal vicars, namely, those who in a specific part of the diocese or in a certain type of affairs or over the faithful of a specific rite or over certain groups of persons possess the same ordinary power which a vicar general has by universal law, according to the norm of the following canons.

CAN. 477 §1. The diocesan bishop freely appoints a vicar general and an episcopal vicar and can freely remove them, without prejudice

dam, constituere potest consilium episcopale, constans scilicet Vicariis generalibus et Vicariis episcopalibus.

CAN. 474 Acta curiae, quae effectum iuridicum habere nata sunt, subscribi debent ab Ordinario a quo emanant, et quidem ad validitatem, ac simul a curiae cancellario vel notario; cancellarius vero Moderatorem curiae de actis certiorem facere tenetur.

ART. 1. *De Vicariis Generalibus et Episcopalibus*

CAN. 475 §1. In unaquaque dioecesi constituendus est ab Episcopo dioecesano Vicarius generalis, qui, potestate ordinaria ad normam canonum qui sequuntur instructus, ipsum in universae dioecesis regimine adiuvet.

§2. Pro regula generali habeatur ut unus constituatur Vicarius generalis, nisi dioecesis amplitudo vel incolarum numerus aut aliae rationes pastorales aliud suadeant.

Can. 476 Quoties rectum dioecesis regimen id requirat, constitui etiam possunt ab Episcopo dioecesano unus vel plures Vicarii episcopales, qui nempe aut in determinata dioecesis parte aut in certo negotiorum genere aut quoad fideles determinati ritus vel certi personarum coetus eadem gaudent potestate ordinaria, quae iure universali Vicario generali competit, ad normam canonum qui sequuntur.

CAN. 477 §1. Vicarius generalis et episcopalis libere ab Episcopo dioecesana nominantur et ab ipso libere removeri possunt, fir-

---

474: cc. 372 §3, 373 §1, 374 §1, 2°
475 §1: c. 366 §1; SCPF Rescr., 7 nov. 1929: CD 27; DPME 201
475 §2: c. 366 §3; ES I, 14 §1; DPME 161, 201

476: CD 23, 27; ES I, 14 §§1 et 2; DPME 119, 161, 202
477 §1: c. 366 §2; ES I, 14 §§2 et 5

to the prescript of can. 406. An episcopal vicar who is not an auxiliary bishop is to be appointed only for a time to be determined in the act of appointment.

§2. When a vicar general is absent or legitimately impeded, a diocesan bishop can appoint another to take his place; the same norm applies to an episcopal vicar.

CAN. 478 §1. A vicar general and an episcopal vicar are to be priests not less than thirty years old, doctors or licensed in canon law or theology or at least truly expert in these disciplines, and recommended by sound doctrine, integrity, prudence, and experience in handling matters.

§2. The function of vicar general and episcopal vicar can neither be coupled with the function of canon penitentiary nor be entrusted to blood relatives of the bishop up to the fourth degree.

CAN. 479 §1. By virtue of office, the vicar general has the executive power over the whole diocese which belongs to the diocesan bishop by law, namely, the power to place all administrative acts except those, however, which the bishop has reserved to himself or which require a special mandate of the bishop by law.

§2. By the law itself an episcopal vicar has the same power mentioned in §1 but only over the specific part of the territory or the type of affairs or the faithful of a specific rite or group for which he was appointed, except those cases which the bishop has reserved to himself or to a vicar general or which require a special mandate of the bishop by law.

§3. Within the limit of their competence, the habitual faculties granted by the Apostolic See

mo praescripto can. 406; Vicarius episcopalis, qui non sit Episcopus auxiliaris, nominetur tantum ad tempus, in ipso constitutionis actu determinandum.

§2. Vicario generali absente vel legitime impedito, Episcopus dioecesanus alium nominare potest, qui eius vices suppleat; eadem norma applicatur pro Vicario episcopali.

CAN. 478 §1. Vicarius generalis et episcopalis sint sacerdotes annos nati non minus triginta, in iure canonico aut theologia doctores vel licentiati vel saltem in iisdem disciplinis vere periti, sana doctrina, probitate, prudentia ac rerum gerendarum experientia commendati.

§2. Vicarii generalis et episcopalis munus componi non potest cum munere canonici paenitentiarii, neque committi consanguineis Episcopi usque ad quartum gradum.

CAN. 479 §1. Vicario generali, vi officii, in universa dioecesi competit potestas exsecutiva quae ad Episcopum dioecesanum iure pertinet, ad ponendos scilicet omnes actus administrativos, iis tamen exceptis quos Episcopus sibi reservaverit vel qui ex iure requirant speciale Episcopi mandatum.

§2. Vicario episcopali ipso iure eadem competit potestas de qua in §1, sed quoad determinatam territorii partem aut negotiorum genus aut fideles determinati ritus vel coetus tantum pro quibus constitutus est, iis causis exceptis quas Episcopus sibi aut Vicario generali reservaverit, aut quae ex iure requirunt speciale Episcopi mandatum.

§3. Ad Vicarium generalem atque ad Vicarium episcopalem, intra ambitum eorum

477 §2: c. 366 §3; ES I, 14 §2
478 §1: c. 367 §1; ES I, 14 §2; DPME 201
478 §2: c. 367 §3; ES I, 14 §2
479 §1: c. 368 §1
479 §2: ES I, 14 §2
479 §3: c. 368 §2; ES I, 14 §2

to the bishop and the execution of rescripts also pertain to a vicar general and an episcopal vicar, unless it has been expressly provided otherwise or the personal qualifications of the diocesan bishop were chosen.

CAN. 480 A vicar general and an episcopal vicar must report to the diocesan bishop concerning the more important affairs which are to be handled or have been handled, and they are never to act contrary to the intention and mind of the diocesan bishop.

CAN. 481 §1. The power of a vicar general and an episcopal vicar ceases at the expiration of the time of the mandate, by resignation, by removal made known to them by the diocesan bishop, without prejudice to cann. 406 and 409, and at the vacancy of the episcopal see.

§2. When the function of the diocesan bishop is suspended, the power of a vicar general and an episcopal vicar is suspended also unless they are bishops.

ART. 2. *The Chancellor, Other Notaries, and the Archives*

CAN. 482 §1. In every curia a chancellor is to be appointed whose principal function, unless particular law establishes otherwise, is to take care that acts of the curia are gathered, arranged, and safeguarded in the archive of the curia.

§2. If it seems necessary, the chancellor can be given an assistant whose title is to be vice-chancellor.

§3. By reason of being chancellor and vice-chancellor they are notaries and secretaries of the curia.

competentiae, pertinent etiam facultates habituales ab Apostolica Sede Episcopo concessae, necnon rescriptorum exsecutio, nisi aliud expresse cautum fuerit aut electa fuerit industria personae Episcopi dioecesani.

CAN. 480 Vicarius generalis et Vicarius episcopalis de praecipuis negotiis et gerendis et gestis Episcopo dioecesano referre debent, nec umquam contra voluntatem et mentem Episcopi dioecesani agant.

CAN. 481 §1. Expirat potestas Vicarii generalis et Vicarii episcopalis expleto tempore mandati, renuntiatione, itemque, salvis cann. 406 et 409, remotione eisdem ab Episcopo dioecesano intimata, atque sedis episcopalis vacatione.

§2. Suspenso munere Episcopi dioecesani, suspenditur potestas Vicarii generalis et Vicarii episcopalis, nisi episcopali dignitate aucti sint.

ART. 2. *De Cancellario Aliisque Notariis et de Archivis*

CAN. 482 §1. In qualibet curia constituatur cancellarius, cuius praecipuum munus, nisi aliter iure particulari statuatur, est curare ut acta curiae redigantur et expediantur, atque eadem in curiae archivo custodiantur.

§2. Si necesse videatur, cancellario dari potest adiutor, cui nomen sit vice-cancellarii.

§3. Cancellarius necnon vice-cancellarius sunt eo ipso notarii et secretarii curiae.

480: c. 369 §§1 et 2; ES I, 14 §3; DPME 202
481 §1: c. 371; ES I, 14 §§2 et 5
481 §2: c. 371; ES I, 14 §2

482 §1: c. 372 §1
482 §2: c. 372 §2
482 §3: c. 372 §3

CAN. 483 §1. Besides the chancellor, other notaries can be appointed whose writing or signature establishes authenticity for any acts, for judicial acts only, or for acts of a certain case or affair only.

§2. The chancellor and notaries must be of unimpaired reputation and above all suspicion. In cases in which the reputation of a priest can be called into question, the notary must be a priest.

CAN. 484 It is the duty of notaries:

1° to draw up the acts and instruments regarding decrees, dispositions, obligations, or other things which require their action;

2° to record faithfully in writing what has taken place and to sign it with a notation of the place, day, month, and year;

3° having observed what is required, to furnish acts or instruments to one who legitimately requests them from the records and to declare copies of them to be in conformity with the original.

CAN. 485 The chancellor and other notaries can be freely removed from office by the diocesan bishop, but not by a diocesan administrator except with the consent of the college of consultors.

CAN. 486 §1. All documents which regard the diocese or parishes must be protected with the greatest care.

§2. In every curia there is to be erected in a safe place a diocesan archive, or record storage area, in which instruments and written documents which pertain to the spiritual and tem-

CAN. 483 §1. Praeter cancellarium, constitui possunt alii notarii, quorum quidem scriptura seu subscriptio publicam fidem facit quod attinet sive ad quaelibet acta, sive ad acta iudicialia dumtaxat, sive ad acta certae causae aut negotii tantum.

§2. Cancellarius et notarii debent esse integrae famae et omni suspicione maiores; in causis, quibus fama sacerdotis in discrimen vocari possit, notarius debet esse sacerdos.

CAN. 484 Officium notariorum est:

1° conscribere acta et instrumenta circa decreta, dispositiones, obligationes vel alia quae eorum operam requirunt;

2° in scriptis fideliter redigere quae geruntur, eaque cum significatione loci, diei, mensis et anni subsignare;

3° acta vel instrumenta legitime petenti ex regesto, servatis servandis, exhibere et eorum exempla cum autographo conformia declarare.

CAN. 485 Cancellarius aliique notarii libere ab officio removeri possunt ab Episcopo dioecesano, non autem ab Administratore dioecesano, nisi de consensu collegii consultorum.

CAN. 486 §1. Documenta omnia, quae dioecesim vel paroecias respiciunt, maxima cura custodiri debent.

§2. In unaquaque curia erigatur, in loco tuto, archivum seu tabularium dioecesanum, in quo instrumenta et scripturae, quae ad negotia dioecesana tum spiritualia tum tempo-

483 §1: c. 373 §§1 et 2
483 §2: c. 373 §§3 et 4
484, 1°: c. 374 §1, 1°
484, 2°: c. 374 §1, 2°
484, 3°: c. 374 §1, 3°
485: c. 373 §5

486 §1: c. 375 §1; Sec Litt. circ., 15 apr. 1923; PAULUS PP. VI, All., 6 nov. 1964 (AAS 56 [1964] 999–1001)
486 §2: c. 375 §1; SCPF Resp. 2, 14 mar. 1922; Sec Litt. circ., 15 apr. 1923

poral affairs of the diocese are to be safeguarded after being properly filed and diligently secured.

§3. An inventory, or catalog, of the documents which are contained in the archive is to be kept with a brief synopsis of each written document.

CAN. 487 §1. The archive must be locked and only the bishop and chancellor are to have its key. No one is permitted to enter except with the permission either of the bishop or of both the moderator of the curia and the chancellor.

§2. Interested parties have the right to obtain personally or through a proxy an authentic written copy or photocopy of documents which by their nature are public and which pertain to their personal status.

CAN. 488 It is not permitted to remove documents from the archive except for a brief time only and with the consent either of the bishop or of both the moderator of the curia and the chancellor.

CAN. 489 §1. In the diocesan curia there is also to be a secret archive, or at least in the common archive there is to be a safe or cabinet, completely closed and locked, which cannot be removed; in it documents to be kept secret are to be protected most securely.

§2. Each year documents of criminal cases in matters of morals, in which the accused parties have died or ten years have elapsed from the condemnatory sentence, are to be destroyed. A brief summary of what occurred along with the text of the definitive sentence is to be retained.

CAN. 490 §1. Only the bishop is to have the key to the secret archive.

ralia spectant, certo ordine disposita et diligenter clausa custodiantur.

§3. Documentorum, quae in archivo continentur, conficiatur inventarium seu catalogus, cum brevi singularum scripturarum synopsi.

CAN. 487 §1. Archivum clausum sit oportet eiusque clavem habeant solum Episcopus et cancellarius; nemini licet illud ingredi nisi de Episcopi aut Moderatoris curiae simul et cancellarii licentia.

§2. Ius est iis quorum interest, documentorum, quae natura sua sunt publica quaeque ad statum suae personae pertinent, documentum authenticum scriptum vel photostaticum per se vel per procuratorem recipere.

CAN. 488 Ex archivo non licet efferre documenta, nisi ad breve tempus tantum atque de Episcopi aut insimul Moderatoris curiae et cancellarii consensu.

CAN. 489 §1. Sit in curia dioecesana archivum quoque secretum, aut saltem in communi archivo armarium seu scrinium, omnino clausum et obseratum, quod de loco amoveri nequeat, in quo scilicet documenta secreto servanda cautissime custodiantur.

§2. Singulis annis destruantur documenta causarum criminalium in materia morum, quarum rei vita cesserunt aut quae a decennio sententia condemnatoria absolutae sunt, retento facti brevi summario cum textu sententiae definitivae.

CAN. 490 §1. Archivi secreti clavem habeat tantummodo Episcopus.

486 §3: c. 375 §2
487 §1: c. 377 §§1 et 2
487 §2: c. 384 §§1 et 2
488: c. 378 §§1 et 2

489 §1: c. 379 §1
489 §2: c. 379 §1; CI Resp. II, 5 aug. 1941 (AAS 33 [1941] 378)
490 §1: c. 379 §3

§2. When a see is vacant, the secret archive or safe is not to be opened except in a case of true necessity by the diocesan administrator himself.

§3. Documents are not to be removed from the secret archive or safe.

CAN. 491 §1. A diocesan bishop is to take care that the acts and documents of the archives of cathedral, collegiate, parochial, and other churches in his territory are also diligently preserved and that inventories or catalogs are made in duplicate, one of which is to be preserved in the archive of the church and the other in the diocesan archive.

§2. A diocesan bishop is also to take care that there is an historical archive in the diocese and that documents having historical value are diligently protected and systematically ordered in it.

§3. In order to inspect or remove the acts and documents mentioned in §§1 and 2, the norms established by the diocesan bishop are to be observed.

ART. 3. *The Finance Council and the Finance Officer*

CAN. 492 §1. In every diocese a finance council is to be established, over which the diocesan bishop himself or his delegate presides and which consists of at least three members of the Christian faithful truly expert in financial affairs and civil law, outstanding in integrity, and appointed by the bishop.

§2. Sede vacante, archivum vel armarium secretum ne aperiatur, nisi in casu verae necessitatis, ab ipso Administratore dioecesano.

§3. Ex archivo vel armario secreto documenta ne efferantur.

CAN. 491 §1. Curet Episcopus dioecesanus ut acta et documenta archivorum quoque ecclesiarum cathedralium, collegiatarum, paroecialium, aliarumque in suo territorio exstantium diligenter serventur, atque inventaria seu catalogi conficiantur duobus exemplaribus, quorum alterum in proprio archivo, alterum in archivo dioecesano serventur.

§2. Curet etiam Episcopus dioecesanus ut in dioecesi habeatur archivum historicum atque documenta valorem historicum habentia in eodem diligenter custodiantur et systematice ordinentur.

§3. Acta et documenta, de quibus in §§1 et 2, ut inspiciantur aut efferantur, serventur normae ab Episcopo dioecesano statutae.

ART. 3. *De Consilio a Rebus Oeconomics et de Oeconomo*

CAN. 492 §1. In singulis dioecesibus constituatur consilium a rebus oeconomicis, cui praesidet ipse Episcopus dioecesanus eiusve delegatus, et quod constat tribus saltem christifidelibus, in re oeconomica necnon in iure civili vere peritis et integritate praestantibus, ab Episcopo nominatis.

490 §2: cc. 379 §4, 382 §1
490 §3: c. 382 §§1 et 2
491 §1: c. 383 §1
491 §2: Sec Litt. circ., 15 apr. 1923; SCConc Normae, 24 maii 1939 (AAS 31 [1939] 266–268); PONTIFICIUM CONSILIUM ECCLESIASTICIS ITALIAE TABU-

LARIIS CURANDIS Instr. *A seguito,* 5 dec. 1960 (AAS 52 [1960] 1022–1025)
491 §3: cc. 378 §§1 et 2, 382 §1, 383 §2, 384 §2
492 §1: cc. 1520 §1, 1521 §1; SCConc Litt. circ., 20 iun. 1929, 9 (AAS 21 [1929] 397)

§2. Members of the finance council are to be appointed for five years, but at the end of this period they can be appointed for other five year terms.

§3. Persons who are related to the bishop up to the fourth degree of consanguinity or affinity are excluded from the finance council.

CAN. 493 In addition to the functions entrusted to it in Book V, *The Temporal Goods of the Church*, the finance council prepares each year, according to the directions of the diocesan bishop, a budget of the income and expenditures which are foreseen for the entire governance of the diocese in the coming year and at the end of the year examines an account of the revenues and expenses.

CAN. 494 §1. In every diocese, after having heard the college of consultors and the finance council, the bishop is to appoint a finance officer who is truly expert in financial affairs and absolutely distinguished for honesty.

§2. The finance officer is to be appointed for a five year term but can be appointed for other five year terms at the end of this period. The finance officer is not to be removed while in this function except for a grave cause to be assessed by the bishop after he has heard the college of consultors and the finance council.

§3. It is for the finance officer to administer the goods of the diocese under the authority of the bishop in accord with the budget determined by the finance council and, from the income of the diocese, to meet expenses which the bishop or others designated by him have legitimately authorized.

§4. At the end of the year, the finance officer

§2. Membra consilii a rebus oeconomicis ad quinquennium nominentur, sed expleto hoc tempore ad alia quinquennia assumi possunt.

§3. A consilio a rebus oeconomicis excluduntur personae quae cum Episcopo usque ad quartum gradum consanguinitatis vel affinitatis coniunctae sunt.

CAN. 493 Praeter munera ipsi commissa in Libro V *De bonis Ecclesiae temporalibus*, consilii a rebus oeconomicis est quotannis, iuxta Episcopi dioecesani indicationes, rationem apparare quaestuum et erogationum quae pro universo dioecesis regimine anno venturo praevidentur, necnon, anno exeunte, rationem accepti expensi probare.

CAN. 494 §1. In singulis dioecesibus ab Episcopo, auditis collegio consultorum atque consilio a rebus oeconomicis, nominetur oeconomus, qui sit in re oeconomica vere peritus et probitate prorsus praestans.

§2. Oeconomus nominetur ad quinquennium, sed expleto hoc tempore ad alia quinquennia nominari potest; durante munere, ne amoveatur nisi ob gravem causam ab Episcopo aestimandam, auditis collegio consultorum atque consilio a rebus oeconomicis.

§3. Oeconomi est, secundum rationem a consilio a rebus oeconomicis definitam, bona dioecesis sub auctoritate Episcopi administrare atque ex quaestu dioecesis constituto expensas facere, quas Episcopus aliive ab ipso deputati legitime ordinaverint.

§4. Anno vertente, oeconomus consilio a

492 §2: c. 1521 §1
492 §3: c. 1520 §2

494 §4: c. 1525 §1

must render an account of receipts and expenditures to the finance council.

CHAPTER III. The Presbyteral Council and the College of Consultors

CAN. 495 §1. In each diocese a presbyteral council is to be established, that is, a group of priests which, representing the *presbyterium,* is to be like a senate of the bishop and which assists the bishop in the governance of the diocese according to the norm of law to promote as much as possible the pastoral good of the portion of the people of God entrusted to him.

§2. In apostolic vicariates and prefectures, the vicar or prefect is to establish a council of at least three missionary presbyters whose opinion, even by letter, he is to hear in more serious matters.

CAN. 496 The presbyteral council is to have its own statutes approved by the diocesan bishop, attentive to the norms issued by the conference of bishops.

CAN. 497 In what pertains to the designation of members of the presbyteral council:

1° the priests themselves are freely to elect about half, according to the norm of the following canons and of the statutes;

2° according to the norm of the statutes, some priests must be *ex officio* members, that is, members who are to belong to the council by reason of the office entrusted to them;

3° the diocesan bishop is freely entitled to appoint others.

CAN. 498 §1. The following have the right of election, both active and passive, in constituting a presbyteral council:

CAPUT III. De Consilio Presbyterali et de Collegio Consultorum

CAN. 495 §1. In unaquaque dioecesi constituatur consilium presbyterale, coetus scilicet sacerdotum, qui tamquam senatus sit Episcopi, presbyterium repraesentans, cuius est Episcopum in regimine dioecesis ad normam iuris adiuvare, ut bonum pastorale portionis populi Dei ipsi commissae quam maxime provehatur.

§2. In vicariatibus et praefecturis apostolicis Vicarius vel Praefectus constituant consilium ex tribus saltem presbyteris missionariis, quorum sententiam, etiam per epistolam, audiant in gravioribus negotiis.

CAN. 496 Consilium presbyterale habeat propria statuta ab Episcopo dioecesano approbata, attentis normis ab Episcoporum conferentia prolatis.

CAN. 497 Ad designationem quod attinet sodalium consilii presbyteralis:

1° dimidia circiter pars libere eligatur a sacerdotibus ipsis, ad normam canonum qui sequuntur, necnon statutorum;

2° aliqui sacerdotes, ad normam statutorum, esse debent membra nata, qui scilicet ratione officii ipsis demandati ad consilium pertineant;

3° Episcopo dioecesano integrum est aliquos libere nominare.

CAN. 498 §1. Ius electionis tum activum tum passivum ad consilium presbyterale constituendum habent:

---

495 §1: LG 28; CD 27, 28; PO 7, 8; ES I, 15 §1; PS 5, 8; DPME 203
495 §2: c. 302

496: ES I, 15 §1; PS conclusio I b, II; DPME 203
497: PS 7
498 §1: ES I, 15 §2; PS 6; MR 56

1° all secular priests incardinated in the diocese;

2° secular priests not incardinated in the diocese and priests who are members of some religious institute or society of apostolic life, who reside in the diocese and exercise some office for the good of the diocese.

§2. To the extent that the statutes provide for it, the same right of election can be conferred on other priests who have a domicile or quasi-domicile in the diocese.

CAN. 499 The manner of electing members of the presbyteral council must be determined in the statutes in such a way that, insofar as possible, the priests of the *presbyterium* are represented, taking into account especially the different ministries and various regions of the diocese.

CAN. 500 §1. It is for the diocesan bishop to convoke the presbyteral council, preside over it, and determine the questions to be treated by it or receive proposals from the members.

§2. The presbyteral council possesses only a consultative vote; the diocesan bishop is to hear it in affairs of greater importance but needs its consent only in cases expressly defined by law.

§3. The presbyteral council is not able to act without the diocesan bishop who alone has charge of making public those things which have been established according to the norm of §2.

CAN. 501 §1. Members of the presbyteral council are to be designated for a time determined in the statutes, in such a way, however, that the entire council or some part of it is renewed within five years.

1° omnes sacerdotes saeculares in dioecesi incardinati;

2° sacerdotes saeculares in dioecesi non incardinati, necnon sacerdotes sodales alicuius instituti religiosi aut societatis vitae apostolicae, qui in dioecesi commorantes, in eiusdem bonum aliquod officium exercent.

§2. Quatenus statuta id provideant, idem ius electionis conferri potest aliis sacerdotibus, qui domicilium aut quasi-domicilium in dioecesi habent.

CAN. 499 Modus eligendi membra consilii presbyteralis statutis determinandus est, ita quidem ut, quatenus id fieri possit, sacerdotes presbyterii repraesententur, ratione habita maxime diversorum ministeriorum variarumque dioecesis regionum.

CAN. 500 §1. Episcopi dioecesani est consilium presbyterale convocare, eidem praesidere atque quaestiones in eodem tractandas determinare aut a membris propositas recipere.

§2. Consilium presbyterale gaudet voto tantum consultivo; Episcopus dioecesanus illud audiat in negotiis maioris momenti, eius autem consensu eget solummodo in casibus iure expresse definitis.

§3. Consilium presbyterale numquam agere valet sine Episcopo dioecesano, ad quem solum etiam cura spectat ea divulgandi quae ad normam §2 statuta sunt.

CAN. 501 §1. Membra consilii presbyteralis designentur ad tempus, in statutis determinatum, ita tamen ut integrum consilium vel aliqua eius pars intra quinquennium renovetur.

498 §2: ES I, 15 §2; PS 6
499: ES I, 15 §2: PS 6, 7; DPME 203
500 §1: PS 8

500 §2: PO 7; ES I, 15 §§1 et 3; PS 9
500 §3: PS 9

§2. When a see is vacant, the presbyteral council ceases and the college of consultors fulfills its functions. Within a year of taking possession, a bishop must establish the presbyteral council anew.

§3. If the presbyteral council does not fulfill the function entrusted to it for the good of the diocese or gravely abuses it, the diocesan bishop, after having consulted with the metropolitan, or, if it concerns the metropolitan see itself, with the suffragan bishop senior in promotion, can dissolve it but must establish it anew within a year.

CAN. 502 §1. From among the members of the presbyteral council and in a number not less than six nor more than twelve, the diocesan bishop freely appoints some priests who are to constitute for five years a college of consultors, to which belongs the functions determined by law. When the five years elapse, however, it continues to exercise its proper functions until a new college is established.

§2. The diocesan bishop presides over the college of consultors. When a see is impeded or vacant, however, the one who temporarily takes the place of the bishop or, if he has not yet been appointed, the priest who is senior in ordination in the college of consultors presides.

§3. The conference of bishops can establish that the functions of the college of consultors are to be entrusted to the cathedral chapter.

§4. In an apostolic vicariate and prefecture, the council of the mission mentioned in can. 495, §2 has the functions of the college of consultors unless the law establishes otherwise.

§2. Vacante sede, consilium presbyterale cessat eiusque munera implentur a collegio consultorum; intra annum a capta possessione Episcopus debet consilium presbyterale noviter constituere.

§3. Si consilium presbyterale munus sibi in bonum dioecesis commissum non adimpleat aut eodem graviter abutatur, Episcopus dioecesanus, facta consultatione cum Metropolita, aut si de ipsa sede metropolitana agatur cum Episcopo suffraganeo promotione antiquiore, illud dissolvere potest, sed intra annum debet noviter constituere.

CAN. 502 §1. Inter membra consilii presbyteralis ab Episcopo dioecesano libere nominantur aliqui sacerdotes, numero non minore quam sex nec maiore quam duodecim, qui collegium consultorum ad quinquennium constituant, cui competunt munera iure determinata; expleto tamen quinquennio munera sua propria exercere pergit usquedum novum collegium constituatur.

§2. Collegio consultorum praeest Episcopus dioecesanus; sede autem impedita aut vacante, is qui ad interim Episcopi locum tenet aut, si constitutus nondum fuerit, sacerdos ordinatione antiquior in collegio consultorum.

§3. Episcoporum conferentia statuere potest ut munera collegii consultorum capitulo cathedrali committantur.

§4. In vicariatu et praefectura apostolica munera collegii consultorum competunt consilio missionis, de quo in can. 495, §2, nisi aliud iure statuatur.

501 §2: ES I, 15 §4; PS 10
502 §1: cc. 385 §2, 424, 425 §1, 426 §1; CD 27
502 §2: DPME 205

502 §3: cc. 423, 427
502 §4: c. 302

CHAPTER IV. Chapters of Canons

CAPUT IV. **De Canonicorum Capitulis**

CAN. 503 A chapter of canons, whether cathedral or collegial, is a college of priests which performs more solemn liturgical functions in a cathedral or collegial church. In addition, it is for the cathedral chapter to fulfill the functions which the law or the diocesan bishop entrusts to it.

CAN. 503 Capitulum canonicorum, sive cathedrale sive collegiale, est sacerdotum collegium, cuius est functiones liturgicas sollemniores in ecclesia cathedrali aut collegiali persolvere; capituli cathedralis praeterea est munera adimplere, quae iure aut ab Episcopo dioecesano ei committuntur.

CAN. 504 The erection, alteration, or suppression of a cathedral chapter is reserved to the Apostolic See.

CAN. 504 Capituli cathedralis erectio, innovatio aut suppressio Sedi Apostolicae reservantur.

CAN. 505 Each and every chapter, whether cathedral or collegial, is to have its own statutes, drawn up through a legitimate capitular act and approved by the diocesan bishop. These statutes are neither to be changed nor abrogated except with the approval of the same diocesan bishop.

CAN. 505 Unumquodque capitulum, sive cathedrale sive collegiale, sua habeat statuta, per legitimum actum capitularem condita atque ab Episcopo dioecesano probata; quae statuta ne immutentur neve abrogentur, nisi approbante eodem Episcopo dioecesano.

CAN. 506 §1. The statutes of a chapter are to determine the constitution of the chapter and the number of canons, always without prejudice to the laws of its foundation. They are to define those things which the chapter and individual canons are to do in the performance of divine worship and ministry. They are to determine the meetings in which the affairs of the chapter are handled and establish the conditions required for the validity and liceity of those affairs, without prejudice to the prescripts of universal law.

CAN. 506 §1. Statuta capituli, salvis semper fundationis legibus, ipsam capituli constitutionem et numerum canonicorum determinent; definiant quaenam a capitulo et a singulis canonicis ad cultum divinum necnon ad ministerium persolvendum sint peragenda; decernant conventus in quibus capituli negotia agantur atque, salvis quidem iuris universalis praescriptis, condiciones statuant ad validitatem liceitatemque negotiorum requisitas.

§2. The statutes are also to define the compensation, whether stable or to be given on the occasion of the performance of some function, and, attentive to the norms issued by the Holy See, the insignia of the canons.

§2. In statutis etiam definiantur emolumenta, tum stabilia tum occasione perfuncti muneris solvenda necnon, attentis normis a Sancta Sede latis, quaenam sint canonicorum insignia.

503: c. 391 §1; SCE-SCpC Ep., 19 iul. 1972; DPME 205

504: c. 392

505: c. 410 §§1 et 2; SCConc Litt. circ., 25 iul. 1923 (AAS 15 [1923] 453)

506 §1: cc. 411 §§1 et 2, 412–422

506 §2: cc. 409, 420, 421 §2, 422: SCpC Litt. circ., 30 oct. 1970 (AAS 63 [1971] 314–315); SA Decisio, 26 iun. 1971

CAN. 507 §1. One of the canons is to preside over the chapter; other offices are also to be constituted according to the norm of the statutes, after the practice prevailing in the region has been taken into consideration.

§2. Other offices can be entrusted to clerics who do not belong to the chapter; through these offices they assist the canons according to the norm of the statutes.

CAN. 508 §1. By virtue of office, the canon penitentiary of a cathedral church and of a collegial church has the ordinary faculty, which he cannot delegate to others, of absolving in the sacramental forum outsiders within the diocese and members of the diocese even outside the territory of the diocese from undeclared *latae sentential* censures not reserved to the Apostolic See.

§2. Where there is no chapter, the diocesan bishop is to appoint a priest to fulfill the same function.

CAN. 509 §1. After having heard the chapter, it is for the diocesan bishop, but not a diocesan administrator, to confer each and every canonry, both in a cathedral church and in a collegial church; every contrary privilege is revoked. It is for the same bishop to confirm the person elected by the chapter to preside over it.

§2. A diocesan bishop is to confer canonries only upon priests outstanding in doctrine and integrity of life, who have laudably exercised the ministry.

CAN. 510 §1. Parishes are no longer to be

CAN. 507 §1. Inter canonicos habeatur qui capitulo praesit, atque alia etiam constituantur officia ad normam statutorum, ratione quoque habita usus in regione vigentis.

§2. Clericis ad capitulum non pertinentibus, committi possunt alia officia, quibus ipsi, ad normam statutorum, canonicis auxilium praebeant.

CAN. 508 §1. Paenitentiarius canonicus tum ecclesiae cathedralis tum ecclesiae collegialis vi officii habet facultatem ordinariam, quam tamen aliis delegare non potest, absolvendi in foro sacramentali a censuris latae sententiae non declaratis, Apostolicae Sedi non reservatis, in dioecesi extraneos quoque, dioecesanos autem etiam extra territorium dioecesis.

§2. Ubi deficit capitulum, Episcopus dioecesanus sacerdotem constituat ad idem munus implendum.

CAN. 509 §1. Episcopi dioecesani, audito capitulo, non autem Administratoris dioecesani, est omnes et singulos conferre canonicatus, tum in ecclesia cathedrali tum in ecclesia collegiali, revocato quolibet contrario privilegio; eiusdem Episcopi est confirmare electum ab ipso capitulo, qui eidem praesit.

§2. Canonicatus Episcopus dioecesanus conferat tantum sacerdotibus doctrina vitaeque integritate praestantibus, qui laudabiliter ministerium exercuerunt.

CAN. 510 §1. Capitulo canonicorum ne

507 §1: c. 393 §1; PIUS PP. XI, m. p. *Bibliorum scientiam,* 27 apr. 1924 (AAS 16 [1924] 180)
507 §2: c. 393 §2
508 §1: c. 401 §1
509 §1: c. 403; CI Resp., 26 nov. 1922 (AAS 15 [1923] 128); CI Resp. III, 10 nov. 1925 (AAS 17 [1925] 582); SCConc Resol., 4 mar. 1933 (AAS 27 [1935] 341–344); SCConc Resol., 15 iun. 1940 (AAS 33 [1941] 333–334)
509 §2: c. 404 §§1 et 2
510 §1: ES I, 21 §2

joined to a chapter of canons; the diocesan bishop is to separate from a chapter those parishes which are united to it.

§2. In a church which is at the same time parochial and capitular, a pastor is to be designated, whether chosen from among the members of the chapter or not. This pastor is bound by all the duties and possesses the rights and faculties which are proper to a pastor according to the norm of law.

§3. It is for the diocesan bishop to establish definite norms which fittingly integrate the pastoral duties of the pastor and the functions proper to the chapter, taking care that the pastor is not a hindrance to capitular functions nor the chapter to parochial functions. The diocesan bishop, who above all is to take care that the pastoral needs of the faithful are aptly provided for, is to resolve conflicts if they occur.

§4. Alms given to a church which is at the same time parochial and capitular are presumed given to the parish unless it is otherwise evident.

CHAPTER V. **The Pastoral Council**

CAN. 511 In every diocese and to the extent that pastoral circumstances suggest it, a pastoral council is to be constituted which under the authority of the bishop investigates, considers, and proposes practical conclusions about those things which pertain to pastoral works in the diocese.

CAN. 512 §1. A pastoral council consists of members of the Christian faithful who are in full communion with the Catholic Church—clerics, members of institutes of consecrated

amplius uniantur paroeciae; quae unitae alicui capitulo exstent, ab Episcopo dioecesano a capitulo separentur.

§2. In ecclesia, quae simul sit paroecialis et capitularis, designetur parochus, sive inter capitulares delectus, sive non; qui parochus omnibus obstringitur officiis atque gaudet iuribus et facultatibus quae ad normam iuris propria sunt parochi.

§3. Episcopi dioecesani est certas statuere normas, quibus officia pastoralia parochi atque munera capitulo propria debite componantur, cavendo ne parochus capitularibus nec capitulum paroecialibus functionibus impedimento sit; conflictus, si quidam habeantur, dirimat Episcopus dioecesanus, qui imprimis curet ut fidelium necessitatibus pastoralibus apte prospiciatur.

§4. Quae ecclesiae, paroeciali simul et capitulari, conferantur eleemosynae, praesumuntur datae paroeciae, nisi aliud constet.

CAPUT V. **De Consilio Pastorali**

CAN. 511 In singulis dioecesibus, quatenus pastoralia adiuncta id suadeant, constituatur consilium pastorale, cuius est sub auctoritate Episcopi ea quae opera pastoralia in dioecesi spectant investigare, perpendere atque de eis conclusiones practicas proponere.

CAN. 512 §1. Consilium pastorale constat christifidelibus qui in plena communione sint cum Ecclesia catholica, tum clericis, tum membris institutorum vitae consecratae, tum

---

510 §2: c. 415 §1; SCConc Resol., 17 mar. 1917 (AAS 9 [1917] 384–394); SCConc Resol., 19 feb. 1921 (AAS 14 [1922] 551–554); ES I, 21 §2
510 §3: c. 415 §§1 et 4
510 §4: c. 415 §2, 5°

511: CD 27; AG 30; PO 7; ES I, 16 §1; III, 20; OChr 6, 12; DPME 204; UT 920–921
512 §1: CD 27; ES I, 16 §3; OChr 7, 8; DPME 204; SDO V, 25; MR 56

life, and especially laity—who are designated in a manner determined by the diocesan bishop.

§2. The Christian faithful who are designated to a pastoral council are to be selected in such a way that they truly reflect the entire portion of the people of God which constitutes the diocese, with consideration given to the different areas of the diocese, social conditions and professions, and the role which they have in the apostolate whether individually or joined with others.

§3. No one except members of the Christian faithful outstanding in firm faith, good morals, and prudence is to be designated to a pastoral council.

CAN. 513 §1. A pastoral council is constituted for a period of time according to the prescripts of the statutes which are issued by the bishop.

§2. When the see is vacant, a pastoral council ceases.

CAN. 514 §1. A pastoral council possesses only a consultative vote. It belongs to the diocesan bishop alone to convoke it according to the needs of the apostolate and to preside over it; it also belongs to him alone to make public what has been done in the council.

§2. The pastoral council is to be convoked at least once a year.

CHAPTER VI. Parishes, Pastors, and Parochial Vicars

CAN. 515 §1. A parish is a certain community of the Christian faithful stably constituted

praesertim laicis, quique designantur modo ab Episcopo dioecesano determinato.

§2. Christifideles, qui deputantur ad consilium pastorale, ita seligantur ut per eos universa populi Dei portio, quae dioecesim constituat, revera configuretur, ratione habita diversarum dioecesis regionum, condicionum socialium et professionum, necnon partis quam sive singuli sive cum aliis coniuncti in apostolatu habent.

§3. Ad consilium pastorale ne deputentur nisi christifideles certa fide, bonis moribus et prudentia praestantes.

CAN. 513 §1. Consilium pastorale constituitur ad tempus, iuxta praescripta statutorum, quae ab Episcopo dantur.

§2. Sede vacante, consilium pastorale cessat.

CAN. 514 §1. Consilium pastorale, quod voto gaudet tantum consultivo, iuxta necessitates apostolatus convocare eique praeesse ad solum Episcopum dioecesanum pertinet; ad quem etiam unice spectat, quae in consilio pertractata sunt publici iuris facere.

§2. Saltem semel in anno convocetur.

CAPUT VI. De Paroeciis, de Parochis et de Vicariis Paroecialibus

CAN. 515 §1. Paroecia est certa communitas christifidelium in Ecclesia particulari

512 §2: OChr 7
512 §3: OChr 7, 9
513 § 1: ES I, 16 §2; OChr 7
513 §2: OChr 11

514 §1: CD 27; ES I, 16 §2; OChr 8, 10; DPME 204
514 §2: ES I, 16 §2
515 §1: cc. 216 §§1–3, 451 §1; SC 42; LG 26; CD 30; AA 10; AG 37

in a particular church, whose pastoral care is entrusted to a pastor *(parochus)* as its proper pastor *(pastor)* under the authority of the diocesan bishop.

§2. It is only for the diocesan bishop to erect, suppress, or alter parishes. He is neither to erect, suppress, nor alter notably parishes, unless he has heard the presbyteral council.

§3. A legitimately erected parish possesses juridic personality by the law itself.

CAN. 516 §1. Unless the law provides otherwise, a quasi-parish is equivalent to a parish; a quasi-parish is a definite community of the Christian faithful in a particular church, entrusted to a priest as its proper pastor but not yet erected as a parish because of particular circumstances.

§2. When certain communities cannot be erected as parishes or quasi-parishes, the diocesan bishop is to provide for their pastoral care in another way.

CAN. 517 §1. When circumstances require it, the pastoral care of a parish or of different parishes together can be entrusted to several priests *in solidum*, with the requirement, however, that in exercising pastoral care one of them must be the moderator, namely, the one who is to direct the joint action and to answer for it to the bishop.

§2. If, because of a lack of priests, the diocesan bishop has decided that participation in the exercise of the pastoral care of a parish is to be entrusted to a deacon, to another person who is

stabiliter constituta, cuius cura pastoralis, sub auctoritate Episcopi dioecesani, committitur parocho, qua proprio eiusdem pastori.

§2. Paroecias erigere, supprimere aut eas innovare unius est Episcopi dioecesani, qui paroecias ne erigat aut supprimat, neve eas notabiliter innovet, nisi audito consilio presbyterali.

§3. Paroecia legitime erecta personalitate iuridica ipso iure gaudet.

CAN. 516 §1. Nisi aliud iure caveatur, paroeciae aequiparatur quasi-paroecia, quae est certa in Ecclesia particulari communitas christifidelium, sacerdoti uti pastori proprio commissa, ob peculiaria adiuncta in paroeciam nondum erecta.

§2. Ubi quaedam communitates in paroeciam vel quasi-paroeciam erigi non possint, Episcopus dioecesanus alio modo earundem pastorali curae prospiciat.

CAN. 517 §1. Ubi adiuncta id requirant, paroeciae aut diversarum simul paroeciarum cura pastoralis committi potest pluribus in solidum sacerdotibus, ea tamen lege, ut eorundem unus curae pastoralis exercendae sit moderator, qui nempe actionem coniunctam dirigat atque de eadem coram Episcopo respondeat.

§2. Si ob sacerdotum penuriam Episcopus dioecesanus aestimaverit participationem in exercitio curae pastoralis paroeciae concredendam esse diacono aliive per-

515 §2: c. 216 §1; CI Resp., 26 sep. 1921; SCConc Resol., 14 ian. 1922 (AAS 14 [1922] 229–233); Sec Decl., 10 nov. 1922; CD 32; ES I, 21 §3; CIV Resp., 3 iul. 1969 (AAS [1969] 551); DPME 206

515 §3: cc. 99, 100 §1

516 §1: c. 216 §3; SCC Decl., 1 aug. 1919 (AAS 11 [1919] 346–347); SCPF Instr. *Cum e pluribus*, 25 iul.

1920 (AAS 12 [1920] 331–333); SCPF Decr. *Ordinarii quarumdam,* 9 dec. 1920 (AAS 13 [1921] 17–18)

516 §2: DPME 174, 183; EN 58

517 §1: c. 460 §2; CI Resp. IV, 14 iul. 1922 (AAS 14 [1922] 527)

517 §2: SCGE Instr. *La fonction évangélisatrice,* 19 nov. 1976, V

not a priest, or to a community of persons, he is to appoint some priest who, provided with the powers and faculties of a pastor, is to direct the pastoral care.

CAN. 518 As a general rule a parish is to be territorial, that is, one which includes all the Christian faithful of a certain territory. When it is expedient, however, personal parishes are to be established determined by reason of the rite, language, or nationality of the Christian faithful of some territory, or even for some other reason.

CAN. 519 The pastor *(parochus)* is the proper pastor *(pastor)* of the parish entrusted to him, exercising the pastoral care of the community committed to him under the authority of the diocesan bishop in whose ministry of Christ he has been called to share, so that for that same community he carries out the functions of teaching, sanctifying, and governing, also with the cooperation of other presbyters or deacons and with the assistance of lay members of the Christian faithful, according to the norm of law.

CAN. 520 §1. A juridic person is not to be a pastor. With the consent of the competent superior, however, a diocesan bishop, but not a diocesan administrator, can entrust a parish to a clerical religious institute or clerical society of apostolic life, even by erecting it in a church of the institute or society, with the requirement, however, that one presbyter is to be the pastor of the parish or, if the pastoral care is entrusted to several *in solidum*, the moderator as mentioned in can. 517, §1.

sonae sacerdotali charactere non insignitae aut personarum communitati, sacerdotem constituat aliquem qui, potestatibus et facultatibus parochi instructus, curam pastoralem moderetur.

CAN. 518 Paroecia regula generali sit territorialis, quae scilicet omnes complectatur christifideles certi territorii; ubi vero id expediat, constituantur paroeciae personales, ratione ritus, linguae, nationis christifidelium alicuius territorii atque alia etiam ratione determinatae.

CAN. 519 Parochus est pastor proprius paroeciae sibi commissae, cura pastorali communitatis sibi concreditae fungens sub auctoritate Episcopi dioecesani, cuius in partem ministerii Christi vocatus est, ut pro eadem communitate munera exsequatur docendi, sanctificandi et regendi, cooperantibus etiam aliis presbyteris vel diaconis atque operam conferentibus christifidelibus laicis, ad normam iuris.

CAN. 520 §1. Persona iuridica ne sit parochus; Episcopus autem dioecesanus, non vero Administrator dioecesanus, de consensu competentis Superioris, potest paroeciam committere instituto religioso clericali vel societati clericali vitae apostolicae, eam erigendo etiam in ecclesia instituti aut societatis, hac tamen lege ut unus presbyter sit paroeciae parochus, aut, si cura pastoralis pluribus in solidum committatur, moderator, de quo in can. 517, §1.

518 c. 216 §§1, 2 et 4; CI Resp., 26 sep. 1921, 3; CI Resp. I, 20 maii 1923 (AAS 16 [1924] 113); Pius PP. XII, Const. Ap. *Exsul Familia*, 1 aug. 1952, 32 (AAS 44 [1952] 699–700); CD 23; ES I, 21, 13; SCE Decl., 21 nov. 1966; DPME 174
519: cc. 216 §1, 415 §1; CD 30; DPME 176
520 §1: c. 452 §1; SCConc Instr. *A chiarimento*, 23 ian. 1931; ES I, 33 §1

§2. The entrusting of a parish mentioned in §1 can be made either perpetually or for a specific, predetermined time. In either case it is to be made by means of a written agreement between the diocesan bishop and the competent superior of the institute or society, which expressly and accurately defines, among other things, the work to be accomplished, the persons to be assigned to the parish, and the financial arrangements.

CAN. 521 §1. To become a pastor validly, one must be in the sacred order of the presbyterate.

§2. Moreover, he is to be outstanding in sound doctrine and integrity of morals and endowed with zeal for souls and other virtues; he is also to possess those qualities which are required by universal or particular law to care for the parish in question.

§3. For the office of pastor to be conferred on someone, his suitability must be clearly evident by some means determined by the diocesan bishop, even by means of an examination.

CAN. 522 A pastor must possess stability and therefore is to be appointed for an indefinite period of time. The diocesan bishop can appoint him only for a specific period if the conference of bishops has permitted this by a decree.

CAN. 523 Without prejudice to the prescript of can. 682, §1, the provision of the office of pastor belongs to the diocesan bishop, and indeed by free conferral, unless someone has the right of presentation or election.

CAN. 524 A diocesan bishop is to entrust

§2. Paroeciae commissio, di qua in §1, fieri potest sive in perpetuum sive ad certum praefinitum tempus; in utroque casu fiat mediante conventione scripta inter Episcopum dioecesanum et competentem Superiorem instituti vel societatis inita, qua inter alia expresse et accurate definiantur, quae ad opus explendum, ad personas eidem addicendas et ad res oeconomicas spectent.

CAN. 521 §1. Ut quis valide in parochum assumatur, oportet sit in sacro presbyteratus ordine constitutus.

§2. Sit praeterea sana doctrina et morum probitate praestans, animarum zelo aliisque virtutibus praeditus, atque insuper qualitatibus gaudeat quae ad paroeciam, de qua agitur, curandam iure sive universali sive particulari requiruntur.

§3. Ad officium parochi alicui conferendum, oportet de eius idoneitate, modo ab Episcopo dioecesano determinato, etiam per examen, certo constet.

CAN. 522 Parochus stabilitate gaudeat oportet ideoque ad tempus indefinitum nominetur; ad certum tempus tantum ab Episcopo dioecesano nominari potest, si id ab Episcoporum conferentia per decretum admissum fuerit.

CAN. 523 Firmo praescripto can. 682, §1, parochi officii provisio Episcopo dioecesano competit et quidem libera collatione, nisi cuidam sit ius praesentationis aut electionis.

CAN. 524 Vacantem paroeciam Episco-

520 §2: SCConc Instr. *A chiarimento*, 23 ian. 1931; SCR Normae, 15 feb. 1949, ES I, 33 §1; SCRIS Normae, 1 mar. 1975
521 §1: c. 453 §1
521 § 2: c. 453 §2; CD 31
521 §3: c. 459 §§1 et 3, 3°; CI Resp. I, 25 iun. 1932 (AAS 24 [1932] 284); DPME 206

522: c. 454 §1; SCConc Decr. *Concilium Plenarium*, 24 iun. 1931; CD 31; ES I, 20 §§1 et 2; SCConc Rescr., 2 maii 1967
523: cc. 455–456; SCConc Resol., 19 feb. 1921 (AAS 14 [1922] 551–554); SCConc Resol., 21 iun. 1930 (AAS 25 [1933] 38–40); CD 28, 31
524: c. 459 §§1 et 3, 1°; ES I, 19 §2

a vacant parish to the one whom he considers suited to fulfill its parochial care, after weighing all the circumstances and without any favoritism. To make a judgment about suitability, he is to hear the vicar forane and conduct appropriate investigations, having heard certain presbyters and lay members of the Christian faithful, if it is warranted.

CAN. 525 When a see is vacant or impeded, it belongs to the diocesan administrator or another who governs the diocese temporarily:

1° to install or confirm presbyters who have been legitimately presented or elected for a parish;

2° to appoint pastors if the see has been vacant or impeded for a year.

CAN. 526 §1. A pastor is to have the parochial care of only one parish; nevertheless, because of a lack of priests or other circumstances, the care of several neighboring parishes can be entrusted to the same pastor.

§2. In the same parish there is to be only one pastor or moderator in accord with the norm of can. 517, §1; any contrary custom is reprobated and any contrary privilege whatsoever is revoked.

CAN. 527 §1. The person who has been promoted to carry out the pastoral care of a parish obtains this care and is bound to exercise it from the moment of taking possession.

§2. The local ordinary or a priest delegated by him places the pastor in possession; he is to observe the method accepted by particular law or legitimate custom. The same ordinary, however, can dispense from that method for a just cause; in this case, the notification of the dis-

pus dioecesanus conferat illi quem, omnibus perpensis adiunctis, aestimet idoneum ad paroecialem curam in eadem implendam, omni personarum acceptione remota; ut iudicium de idoneitate ferat, audiat vicarium foraneum aptasque investigationes peragat, auditis, si casus ferat, certis presbyteris necnon christifidelibus laicis.

CAN. 525 Sede vacante aut impedita, ad Administratorem dioecesanum aliumve dioecesim ad interim regentem pertinet:

1° institutionem vel confirmationem concedere presbyteris, qui ad paroeciam legitime praesentati aut electi fuerint;

2° parochos nominare, si sedes ab anno vacaverit aut impedita sit.

CAN. 526 §1. Parochus unius paroeciae tantum curam paroecialem habeat; ob penuriam tamen sacerdotum aut alia adiuncta, plurium vicinarum paroeciarum cura eidem parocho concredi potest.

§2. In eadem paroecia unus tantum habeatur parochus aut moderator ad normam can. 517, §1, reprobata contraria consuetudine et revocato quolibet contrario privilegio.

CAN. 527 §1. Qui ad curam pastoralem paroeciae gerendam promotus est, eandem obtinet et exercere tenetur a momento captae possessionis.

§2. Parochum in possessionem mittit loci Ordinarius aut sacerdos ab eodem delegatus, servato modo lege particulari aut legitima consuetudine recepto; iusta tamen de causa potest idem Ordinarius ab eo modo dispensare; quo in casu dispensatio paroeci-

525: c. 455 §2
526 §1: cc. 156 §§1 et 2, 460 §1
526 §2: c. 460 §2

527 §1: c. 461
527 §2: c. 1444 §1

pensation to the parish replaces the taking of possession.

§3. The local ordinary is to prescribe the time within which possession of a parish must be taken. When this has elapsed without action, he can declare the parish vacant unless there was a just impediment.

CAN. 528 §1. A pastor is obliged to make provision so that the word of God is proclaimed in its entirety to those living in the parish; for this reason, he is to take care that the lay members of the Christian faithful are instructed in the truths of the faith, especially by giving a homily on Sundays and holy days of obligation and by offering catechetical instruction. He is to foster works through which the spirit of the gospel is promoted, even in what pertains to social justice. He is to have particular care for the Catholic education of children and youth. He is to make every effort, even with the collaboration of the Christian faithful, so that the message of the gospel comes also to those who have ceased the practice of their religion or do not profess the true faith.

§2. The pastor is to see to it that the Most Holy Eucharist is the center of the parish assembly of the faithful. He is to work so that the Christian faithful are nourished through the devout celebration of the sacraments and, in a special way, that they frequently approach the sacraments of the Most Holy Eucharist and penance. He is also to endeavor that they are led to practice prayer even as families and take part consciously and actively in the sacred liturgy which, under the authority of the diocesan bishop, the pastor must direct in his own parish and is bound to watch over so that no abuses creep in.

ae notificata locum tenet captae possessionis.

§3. Loci Ordinarius praefiniat tempus intra quod paroeciae possessio capi debeat; quo inutiliter praeterlapso, nisi iustum obstiterit impedimentum, paroeciam vacare declarare potest.

CAN. 528 §1. Parochus obligatione tenetur providendi ut Dei verbum integre in paroecia degentibus annuntietur; quare curet ut christifideles laici in fidei veritatibus edoceantur, praesertim homilia diebus dominicis et festis de praecepto habenda necnon catechetica institutione tradenda, atque foveat opera quibus spiritus evangelicus, etiam ad iustitiam socialem quod attinet, promoveatur; peculiarem curam habeat de puerorum iuvenumque educatione catholica; omni ope satagat, associata etiam sibi christifidelium opera, ut nuntius evangelicus ad eos quoque perveniat, qui a religione colenda recesserint aut veram fidem non profiteantur.

§2. Consulat parochus ut sanctissima Eucharistia centrum sit congregationis fidelium paroecialis; allaboret ut christifideles, per devotam sacramentorum celebrationem, pascantur, peculiarique modo ut frequenter ad sanctissimae Eucharistiae et paenitentiae sacramenta accedant; annitatur item ut iidem ad orationem etiam in familiis peragendam ducantur atque conscie et actuose partem habeant in sacra liturgia, quam quidem, sub auctoritate Episcopi dioecesani, parochus in sua paroecia moderari debet et, ne abusus irrepant, invigilare tenetur.

527 §3: c. 1444 §2
528 §1: cc. 467 §1, 468, 469; SC 35, 52; UR 11; CD 30; PO 6, 9; Paulus PP. VI, m. p. *Sacram Liturgiam,* 25 ian. 1964, III (AAS 56 [1964] 139–144); IOe 53
528 §2: Pius PP. XII, All., 17 feb. 1945; SC 42, 59; CD 30; EMys 26

CAN. 529 §1. In order to fulfill his office diligently, a pastor is to strive to know the faithful entrusted to his care. Therefore he is to visit families, sharing especially in the cares, anxieties, and griefs of the faithful, strengthening them in the Lord, and prudently correcting them if they are failing in certain areas. With generous love he is to help the sick, particularly those close to death, by refreshing them solicitously with the sacraments and commending their souls to God; with particular diligence he is to seek out the poor, the afflicted, the lonely, those exiled from their country, and similarly those weighed down by special difficulties. He is to work so that spouses and parents are supported in fulfilling their proper duties and is to foster growth of Christian life in the family.

§2. A pastor is to recognize and promote the proper part which the lay members of the Christian faithful have in the mission of the Church, by fostering their associations for the purposes of religion. He is to cooperate with his own bishop and the *presbyterium* of the diocese, also working so that the faithful have concern for parochial communion, consider themselves members of the diocese and of the universal Church, and participate in and sustain efforts to promote this same communion.

CAN. 530 The following functions are especially entrusted to a pastor:

1° the administration of baptism;

2° the administration of the sacrament of confirmation to those who are in danger of death, according to the norm of can. 883, n. 3;

3° the administration of Viaticum and of the anointing of the sick, without prejudice to the prescript of can. 1003, §§2 and 3, and the imparting of the apostolic blessing;

CAN. 529 §1. Officium pastoris sedulo ut adimpleat, parochus fideles suae curae commissos cognoscere satagat; ideo familias visitet, fidelium sollicitudines, angores et luctus praesertim participans eosque in Domino confortans necnon, si in quibusdam defecerint, prudenter corrigens; aegrotos, praesertim morti proximos, effusa caritate adiuvet, eos sollicite sacramentis reficiendo eorumque animas Deo commendando; peculiari diligentia prosequatur pauperes, afflictos, solitarios, e patria exsules itemque peculiaribus difficultatibus gravatos; allaboret etiam ut coniuges et parentes ad officia propria implenda sustineantur et in familia vitae christianae incrementum foveat.

§2. Partem quam christifideles laici in missione Ecclesiae propriam habent, parochus agnoscat et promoveat, consociationes eorundem ad fines religionis fovendo. Cum proprio Episcopo et cum dioecesis presbyterio cooperetur, allaborans etiam ut fideles communionis paroecialis curam habeant, iidemque tum dioecesis tum Ecclesiae universae membra se sentiant operaque ad eandem communionem promovendam participent vel sustineant.

CAN. 530 Functiones specialiter parocho commissae sunt quae sequuntur:

1° administratio baptismi;

2° administratio sacramenti confirmationis iis qui in periculo mortis versantur, ad normam can. 883, n. 3;

3° administratio Viatici necnon unctionis infirmorum, firmo praescripto can. 1003, §§2 et 3, atque apostolicae benedictionis impertitio;

529 §1: cc. 467 §1, 468 §1; Pius PP. XII, All., 6 feb. 1940; CD 18, 30; PO 6
529 §2: CD 30; PO 7–9

530: cc. 462, 466 §1, 938 §2; SCConc Resol., 11 feb. 1928; SCDS Decr. *Spiritus Sancti Munera*, 14 sep. 1946, I (AAS 38 [1946] 352)

4° the assistance at marriages and the nuptial blessing;

5° the performance of funeral rites;

6° the blessing of the baptismal font at Easter time, the leading of processions outside the church, and solemn blessings outside the church;

7° the more solemn eucharistic celebration on Sundays and holy days of obligation.

CAN. 531 Although another person has performed a certain parochial function, that person is to put the offerings received from the Christian faithful on that occasion in the parochial account, unless in the case of voluntary offerings the contrary intention of the donor is certain. The diocesan bishop, after having heard the presbyteral council, is competent to establish prescripts which provide for the allocation of these offerings and the remuneration of clerics fulfilling the same function.

CAN. 532 In all juridic affairs the pastor represents the parish according to the norm of law. He is to take care that the goods of the parish are administered according to the norm of cann. 1281–1288.

CAN. 533 §1. A pastor is obliged to reside in a rectory near the church. Nevertheless, in particular cases and if there is a just cause, the local ordinary can permit him to reside elsewhere, especially in a house shared by several presbyters, provided that the performance of parochial functions is properly and suitably provided for.

§2. Unless there is a grave reason to the contrary, a pastor is permitted to be absent from the parish each year for vacation for at most one continuous or interrupted month; those days which the pastor spends once a year in spiritu-

4° assistentia matrimoniis et benedictio nuptiarum;

5° persolutio funerum;

6° fontis baptismalis tempore paschali benedictio, ductus processionum extra ecclesiam, necnon benedictiones extra ecclesiam sollemnes;

7° celebratio eucharistica sollemnior diebus dominicis et festis de praecepto.

CAN. 531 Licet paroeciale quoddam munus alius expleverit, oblationes quas hac occasione a christifidelibus recipit ad massam paroecialem deferat, nisi de contraria offerentis voluntate constet quoad oblationes voluntarias; Episcopo dioecesano, audito consilio presbyterali, competit statuere praescripta, quibus destinationi harum oblationum necnon remunerationi clericorum idem munus implentium provideatur.

CAN. 532 In omnibus negotiis iuridicis parochus personam gerit paroeciae, ad normam iuris; curet ut bona paroeciae administrentur ad normam cann. 1281–1288.

CAN. 533 §1. Parochus obligatione tenetur residendi in domo paroeciali prope ecclesiam; in casibus tamen particularibus, si iusta adsit causa, loci Ordinarius permittere potest ut alibi commoretur, praesertim in domo pluribus presbyteris communi, dummodo paroecialium perfunctioni munerum rite apteque sit provisum.

§2. Nisi gravis obstet ratio, parocho, feriarum gratia, licet quotannis a paroecia abesse ad summum per unum mensem continuum aut intermissum; quo in feriarum tempore dies non computantur, quibus semel in

531: c. 463 §3; PO 20, 21; ES I, 8
533 §1: c. 465 §1; CD 30, 1

533 §2: c. 465 §§2, 3 et 5

al retreat are not computed in the time of vacation. In order to be absent from the parish for more than a week, however, a pastor is bound to inform the local ordinary.

§3. It is for the diocesan bishop to establish norms which see to it that during the absence of the pastor, a priest endowed with the necessary faculties provides for the care of the parish.

CAN. 534 §1. After a pastor has taken possession of his parish, he is obliged to apply a Mass for the people entrusted to him on each Sunday and holy day of obligation in his diocese. If he is legitimately impeded from this celebration, however, he is to apply it on the same days through another or on other days himself.

§2. A pastor who has the care of several parishes is bound to apply only one Mass for the entire people entrusted to him on the days mentioned in §1.

§3. A pastor who has not satisfied the obligation mentioned in §§1 and 2 is to apply as soon as possible as many Masses for the people as he has omitted.

CAN. 535 §1. Each parish is to have parochial registers, that is, those of baptisms, marriages, deaths, and others as prescribed by the conference of bishops or the diocesan bishop. The pastor is to see to it that these registers are accurately inscribed and carefully preserved.

§2. In the baptismal register are also to be noted confirmation and those things which pertain to the canonical status of the Christian faithful by reason of marriage, without preju-

anno parochus spirituali recessui vacat; parochus autem, ut ultra hebdomadam a paroecia absit, tenetur de hoc loci Ordinarium monere.

§3. Episcopi dioecesani est normas statuere quibus prospiciatur ut, parochi absentia durante, curae provideatur paroeciae per sacerdotem debitis facultatibus instructum.

CAN. 534 §1. Parochus, post captam paroeciae possessionem, obligatione tenetur singulis diebus dominicis atque festis in sua dioecesi de praecepto Missam pro populo sibi commisso applicandi; qui vero ab hac celebratione legitime impediatur, iisdem diebus per alium aut aliis diebus per se ipse applicet.

§2. Parochus, qui plurium paroeciarum curam habet, diebus de quibus in §1, unam tantum Missam pro universo sibi commisso populo applicare tenetur.

§3. Parochus, qui obligationi de qua in §§1 et 2 non satisfecerit, quam primum pro populo tot Missas applicet, quot omiserit.

CAN. 535 §1. In unaquaque paroecia habeantur libri paroeciales, liber scilicet baptizatorum, matrimoniorum, defunctorum, aliique secundum Episcoporum conferentiae aut Episcopi dioecesani praescripta; prospiciat parochus ut iidem libri accurate conscribantur atque diligenter asserventur.

§2. In libro baptizatorum abnotentur quoque confirmatio, necnon quae pertinent ad statum canonicum christifidelium, ratione matrimonii, salvo quidem praescripto can.

533 §3: c. 465 §§4 et 5

534 §1: c. 466 §§1, 3 et 5; SCConc Resol., 5 mar. 1932 (AAS 25 [1933] 436–438); SCpC Decr. *Litteris Apostolicis*, 25 iul. 1970 (ASS 63 [1971] 943–944)

534 §2: c. 466 §2; CI Resp. VI, 14 iul. 1922 (AAS 14 [1922] 528); SCConc Resol., 12 nov. 1927 (AAS 20

[1928] 84–87)

534 §3: c. 339 §4

535 §1: c. 470 §1; SCPF Resp. 2, 14 mar. 1922; PIUS PP. XII, Const. AP. *Exsul Familia*, 1 aug. 1952, 35 §2 (AAS 44 [1952] 700)

535 §2: c. 470 §2

dice to the prescript of can. 1133, of adoption, of the reception of sacred orders, of perpetual profession made in a religious institute, and of change of rite. These notations are always to be noted on a baptismal certificate.

§3. Each parish is to have its own seal. Documents regarding the canonical status of the Christian faithful and all acts which can have juridic importance are to be signed by the pastor or his delegate and sealed with the parochial seal.

§4. In each parish there is to be a storage area, or archive, in which the parochial registers are protected along with letters of bishops and other documents which are to be preserved for reason of necessity or advantage. The pastor is to take care that all of these things, which are to be inspected by the diocesan bishop or his delegate at the time of visitation or at some other opportune time, do not come into the hands of outsiders.

§5. Older parochial registers are also to be carefully protected according to the prescripts of particular law.

CAN. 536 §1. If the diocesan bishop judges it opportune after he has heard the presbyteral council, a pastoral council is to be established in each parish, over which the pastor presides and in which the Christian faithful, together with those who share in pastoral care by virtue of their office in the parish, assist in fostering pastoral activity.

§2. A pastoral council possesses a consultative vote only and is governed by the norms established by the diocesan bishop.

1133, ratione adoptionis, itemque ratione suscepti ordinis sacri, professionis perpetuae in instituto religioso emissae necnon mutati ritus; eaeque adnotationes in documento accepti baptismi semper referantur.

§3. Unicuique paroeciae sit proprium sigillum; testimonia quae de statu canonico christifidelium dantur, sicut et acta omnia quae momentum iuridicum habere possunt, ab ipso parocho eiusve delegato subscribantur et sigillo paroeciali muniantur.

§4. In unaquaque paroecia habeatur tabularium seu archivum, in quo libri paroeciales custodiantur, una cum Episcoporum epistulis aliisque documentis, necessitatis utilitatisve causa servandis; quae omnia, ab Episcopo dioecesano eiusve delegato, visitationis vel alio opportuno tempore inspicienda, parochus caveat ne ad extraneorum manus perveniant.

§5. Libri paroeciales antiquiores quoque diligenter custodiantur, secundum praescripta iuris particularis.

CAN. 536 §1. Si, de iudicio Episcopi dioecesani, audito consilio presbyterali, opportunum sit, in unaquaque paroecia constituatur consilium pastorale, cui parochus praeest et in quo christifideles una cum illis qui curam pastoralem vi officii sui in paroecia participant, ad actionem pastoralem fovendam suum adiutorium praestent.

§2. Consilium pastorale voto gaudet tantum consultivo et regitur normis ab Episcopo dioecesano statutis.

535 §3: c. 470 §4
535 §4: c. 470 §4
535 §5: Sec Litt. circ., 15 apr. 1923; SCConc Normae, 24 maii 1939 (AAS 31 [1939] 266–268); PONTIFICIUM CONSILIUM ECCLESIASTICIS ITALIAE TABU-LARIIS CURANDIS Instr. *A seguito*, 5 dec. 1960 (AAS 52 [1960] 1022–1025)
536 §1: CD 27; ES I, 16 §§1–3; OChr 6–12; DPME 179, 204; SDO V, 25
536 §2: CD 27; ES I, 16 §2; OChr 8, 10; DPME 204

CAN. 537 In each parish there is to be a finance council which is governed, in addition to universal law, by norms issued by the diocesan bishop and in which the Christian faithful, selected according to these same norms, are to assist the pastor in the administration of the goods of the parish, without prejudice to the prescript of can. 532.

CAN. 538 §1. A pastor ceases from office by removal or transfer carried out by the diocesan bishop according to the norm of law, by resignation made by the pastor himself for a just cause and accepted by the same bishop for validity, and by lapse of time if he had been appointed for a definite period according to the prescripts of particular law mentioned in can. 522.

§2. A pastor who is a member of a religious institute or is incardinated in a society of apostolic life is removed according to the norm of can. 682, §2.

§3. When a pastor has completed seventy-five years of age, he is requested to submit his resignation from office to the diocesan bishop who is to decide to accept or defer it after he has considered all the circumstances of the person and place. Attentive to the norms established by the conference of bishops, the diocesan bishop must provide suitable support and housing for a retired pastor.

CAN. 539 When a parish becomes vacant or when a pastor is prevented from exercising his pastoral function in the parish by reason of captivity, exile or banishment, incapacity or ill health, or some other cause, the diocesan bish-

CAN. 537 In unaquaque paroecia habeatur consilium a rebus oeconomicis, quod praeterquam iure universali, regitur normis ab Episcopo dioecesano latis et in quo christifideles, secundum easdem normas selecti, parocho in administratione bonorum paroeciae adiutorio sint, firmo praescripto can. 532.

CAN. 538 §1. Parochus ab officio cessat amotione aut translatione ab Episcopo dioecesano ad normam iuris peracta, renuntiatione iusta de causa ab ipso parocho facta et, ut valeat, ab eodem Episcopo acceptata, necnon lapsu temporis si, iuxta iuris particularis de quo in can. 522 praescripta, ad tempus determinatum constitutus fuerit.

§2. Parochus, qui est sodalis instituti religiosi aut in societate vitae apostolicae incardinatus, ad normam can. 682, §2 amovetur.

§3. Parochus, expleto septuagesimo quinto aetatis anno, rogatur ut renuntiationem ab officio exhibeat Episcopo dioecesano, qui, omnibus personae et loci inspectis adiunctis, de eadem acceptanda aut differenda decernat; renuntiantis congruae sustentationi et habitationi ab Episcopo dioecesano providendum est, attentis normis ab Episcoporum conferentia statutis.

CAN. 539 Cum vacat paroecia aut cum parochus ratione captivitatis, exsilii vel relegationis, inhabilitatis vel infirmae valetudinis aliusve causae a munere pastorali in paroecia exercendo praepeditur, ab Episcopo

537: cc. 1183, 1184, 1520 §§1 et 2, 1521 §1, 1525 §1; PO 17, DPME 131

538 §1: SCConc Resol., 11 nov. 1922 (AAS 15 [1923] 454–456); CI Resp. IX, 20 maii 1923 (AAS 16 [1924] 116); CD 31; ES I, 20 §§1–3; CIV Resp., 7 iul. 1978 (AAS 70 [1978] 534)

538 §2: ES I, 20 §1; MR 58

538 §3: CD 31; ES I, 20 §3; CIV Resp., 7 iul. 1978 (AAS 70 [1978] 534)

539: c. 429 §1; 472, 1°

op is to designate as soon as possible a parochial administrator, that is, a priest who takes the
place of the pastor according to the norm of
can. 540.

CAN. 540 §1. A parochial administrator is
bound by the same duties and possesses the
same rights as a pastor unless the diocesan bishop establishes otherwise.

§2. A parochial administrator is not permitted to do anything which prejudices the rights
of the pastor or can harm parochial goods.

§3. After he has completed his function, a parochial administrator is to render an account to
the pastor.

CAN. 541 §1. When a parish becomes vacant or a pastor has been impeded from exercising his pastoral function and before the appointment of a parochial administrator, the parochial vicar is to assume the governance of the
parish temporarily. If there are several vicars,
the one who is senior in appointment or, if
there are no vicars, a pastor determined by particular law assumes this governance.

§2. The one who has assumed the governance of a parish according to the norm of §1 is
immediately to inform the local ordinary about
the vacancy of the parish.

CAN. 542 Priests to whom the pastoral
care of some parish or of different parishes together is entrusted *in solidum* according to the
norm of can. 517, §1:

1° must be endowed with the qualities mentioned in can. 521;

2° are to be appointed or installed according

dioecesano quam primum deputetur administrator paroecialis, sacerdos scilicet qui
parochi vicem suppleat ad normam can. 540.

CAN. 540 §1. Administrator paroecialis
iisdem adstringitur officiis iisdemque gaudet
iuribus ac parochus, nisi ab Episcopo dioecesano aliter statuatur.

§2. Administratori paroeciali nihil agere
licet, quod praeiudicium afferat iuribus
parochi aut damno esse possit bonis paroecialibus.

§3. Administrator paroecialis post expletum munus parocho rationem reddat.

CAN. 541 §1. Vacante paroecia
itemque parocho a munere pastorali exercendo impedito, ante administratoris
paroecialis constitutionem, paroeciae regimen interim assumat vicarius paroecialis; si
plures sint, is qui sit nominatione antiquior,
et si vicarii desint, parochus iure particulari
definitus.

§2. Qui paroeciae regimen ad normam
§1 assumpserit, loci Ordinarium de paroeciae
vacatione statim certiorem faciat.

CAN. 542 Sacerdotes quibus in
solidum, ad normam can. 517, §1, alicuius
paroeciae aut diversarum simul paroeciarum
cura pastoralis committitur:

1° praediti sint oportet qualitatibus, de
quibus in can. 521;

2° nominentur vel instituantur ad

540 §1: c. 473 §1; CI Resp. V, 14 iul. 1922 (AAS 14
[1922] 527–528)
  540 §2: c. 473 §1
  540 §3: c. 473 §2
  541 §1: c. 472, 2°

541 §2: c. 472, 3°
  542: cc. 216 §3, 453 §§1 et 2, 454 §1, 459 §§1 et 3,
461, 1444 §§1 et 2; CD 31; ES I, 19 §2; 20 §§1 et 2;
SCConc Rescr., 2 maii 1967; DPME 206

to the norm of the prescripts of cann. 522 and 524;

3° obtain pastoral care only from the moment of taking possession; their moderator is placed in possession according to the norm of the prescripts of can. 527, §2; for the other priests, however, a legitimately made profession of faith replaces taking possession.

CAN. 543 §1. If the pastoral care of some parish or of different parishes together is entrusted to priests *in solidum*, each of them is obliged to perform the tasks and functions of pastor mentioned in cann. 528, 529, and 530 according to the arrangement they establish. All of them have the faculty of assisting at marriages and all the powers to dispense granted to a pastor by law; these are to be exercised, however, under the direction of the moderator.

§2. All the priests who belong to the group:

1° are bound by the obligation of residence;

2° are to establish through common counsel an arrangement by which one of them is to celebrate a Mass for the people according to the norm of can. 534;

3° the moderator alone represents in juridic affairs the parish or parishes entrusted to the group.

CAN. 544 When a priest from the group mentioned in can. 517, §1 or its moderator ceases from office as well as when one of them becomes incapable of exercising his pastoral function, the parish or parishes whose care is entrusted to the group do not become vacant. It is

normam praescriptorum cann. 522 et 524;

3° curam pastoralem obtinent tantum a momento captae possesionis; eorundem moderator in possessionem mittitur ad normam praescriptorum can. 527, §2; pro ceteris vero sacerdotibus fidei professio legitime facta locum tenet captae possessionis.

CAN. 543 §1. Si sacerdotibus in solidum cura pastoralis alicuius paroeciae aut diversarum simul paroeciarum committatur, singuli eorum, iuxta ordinationem ab iisdem statutam, obligatione tenentur munera et functiones parochi persolvendi de quibus in cann. 528, 529 et 530; facultas matrimoniis assistendi, sicuti et potestates omnes dispensandi ipso iure parocho concessae, omnibus competunt, exercendae tamen sunt sub directione moderatoris.

§2. Sacerdotes omnes qui ad coetum pertinent:

1° obligatione tenentur residentiae;

2° communi consilio ordinationem statuant, qua eorum unus Missam pro populo celebret, ad normam can. 534;

3° solus moderator in negotiis iuridicis personam gerit paroeciae aut paroeciarum coetui commissarum.

CAN. 544 Cum cesset ab officio aliquis sacerdos e coetu, de quo in can. 517, §1, vel coetus moderator, itemque cum eorundem aliquis inhabilis fiat ad munus pastorale exercendum, non vacat paroecia vel paroeciae, quarum cura coetui committitur; Episcopi

543 §1: cc. 462, 466 §1, 467 §1, 468, 469, 938 §2; SCDS Decr. *Spiritus Sancti Munera*, 14 sep. 1946, I (AAS 38 [1946] 352); PAULUS PP. VI, m. p. *Sacram Liturgiam*, 25 ian. 1964, III (AAS 56 [1964] 139–144); SC 35, 42, 52, 59; IOe 53; UR 11; CD 18, 30; PO 6–9;

EMys 26

543 §2: cc. 339 §4, 465 §§1–3 et 5, 466 §§1–3 et 5; CD 30, 1

544: c. 460 §2

for the diocesan bishop, however, to appoint another moderator; before someone is appointed by the bishop, the priest in the group who is senior in appointment is to fulfill this function.

CAN. 545 §1. Whenever it is necessary or opportune in order to carry out the pastoral care of a parish fittingly, one or more parochial vicars can be associated with the pastor. As co-workers with the pastor and sharers in his solicitude, they are to offer service in the pastoral ministry by common counsel and effort with the pastor and under his authority.

§2. A parochial vicar can be assigned either to assist in exercising the entire pastoral ministry for the whole parish, a determined part of the parish, or a certain group of the Christian faithful of the parish, or even to assist in fulfilling a specific ministry in different parishes together.

CAN. 546 To be appointed a parochial vicar validly, one must be in the sacred order of the presbyterate.

CAN. 547 The diocesan bishop freely appoints a parochial vicar, after he has heard, if he has judged it opportune, the pastor or pastors of the parishes for which the parochial vicar is appointed and the vicar forane, without prejudice to the prescript of can. 682, §1.

CAN. 548 §1. The obligations and rights of a parochial vicar, besides being defined in the canons of this chapter, diocesan statutes, and the letter of the diocesan bishop, are more

autem dioecesani est alium nominare moderatorem; antequam vero ab Episcopo alius nominetur, hoc munus adimpleat sacerdos eiusdem coetus nominatione antiquior.

CAN. 545 §1. Quoties ad pastoralem paroeciae curam debite adimplendam necesse aut opportunum sit, parocho adiungi possunt unus aut plures vicarii paroeciales, qui, tamquam parochi cooperatores eiusque sollicitudinis participes, communi cum parocho consilio et studio, atque sub eiusdem auctoritate operam in ministerio pastorali praestent.

§2. Vicarius paroecialis constitui potest sive ut opem ferat in universo ministerio pastorali explendo, et quidem aut pro tota paroecia aut pro determinata paroeciae parte aut pro certo paroeciae christifidelium coetu, sive etiam ut operam impendat in certum ministerium in diversis simul paroeciis persolvendum.

CAN. 546 Ut quis valide vicarius paroecialis nominetur, oportet sit in sacro presbyteratus ordine constitutus.

CAN. 547 Vicarium paroecialem libere nominat Episcopus dioecesanus, auditis, si opportunum id iudicaverit, parocho aut parochis paroeciarum pro quibus constituitur, necnon vicario foraneo, firmo praescripto can. 682, §1.

CAN. 548 §1. Vicarii paroecialis obligationes et iura, praeterquam canonibus huius capitis, statutis dioecesanis necnon litteris Episcopi dioecesani definiuntur, spe-

---

545 §1: cc. 475 §1, 476 §1; CD 30, 3
545 §2: c. 476 §§2 et 7
546: c. 453 §1
547: c. 476 §3; SCConc Resol., 13 nov. 1920 (AAS

13 [1921] 43–46); ES I, 19 §2; 30 §2; CIV Resp., 13 iun. 1960 (AAS 72 [1980] 767)
548 §1: c. 476 §6

specifically determined in the mandate of the pastor.

§2. Unless the letter of the diocesan bishop expressly provides otherwise, a parochial vicar is obliged to assist the pastor in the entire parochial ministry by reason of office, except for the application of the Mass for the people, and to substitute for the pastor if the situation arises according to the norm of law.

§3. A parochial vicar is to report to the pastor regularly concerning proposed and existing pastoral endeavors in such a way that the pastor and the vicar or vicars, through common efforts, are able to provide for the pastoral care of the parish for which they are together responsible.

CAN. 549 Unless the diocesan bishop has provided otherwise according to the norm of can. 533, §3 and unless a parochial administrator has been appointed, the prescripts of can. 541, §1 are to be observed when the pastor is absent. In this case, the vicar is also bound by all the obligations of the pastor, except the obligation of applying Mass for the people.

CAN. 550 §1. A parochial vicar is obliged to reside in the parish or, if he has been appointed for different parishes jointly, in one of them. Nevertheless, for a just cause the local ordinary can allow him to reside elsewhere, especially in a house shared by several presbyters, provided that this is not detrimental to the performance of his pastoral functions.

§2. The local ordinary is to take care that some manner of common life in the rectory is fostered between the pastor and the vicars where this can be done.

§3. A parochial vicar possesses the same right as a pastor concerning the time of vacation.

cialius autem mandato parochi determinantur.

§2. Nisi aliud expresse litteris Episcopi dioecesani caveatur, vicarius paroecialis ratione officii obligatione tenetur parochum in universo paroeciali ministerio adiuvandi, excepta quidem applicatione Missae pro populo, itemque, si res ferat ad normam iuris, parochi vicem supplendi.

§3. Vicarius paroecialis regulariter de inceptis pastoralibus prospectis et susceptis ad parochum referat, ita ut parochus et vicarius aut vicarii, coniunctis viribus, pastorali curae providere valeant paroeciae, cuius simul sunt sponsores.

CAN. 549 Absente parocho, nisi aliter Episcopus dioecesanus providerit ad normam can. 533, §3, et nisi Administrator paroecialis constitutus fuerit, serventur praescripta can. 541, §1; vicarius hoc in casu omnibus etiam obligationibus tenetur parochi, excepta obligatione applicandi Missam pro populo.

CAN. 550 §1. Vicarius paroecialis obligatione tenetur residendi in paroecia aut, si pro diversis simul paroeciis constitutus est, in earum aliqua; loci tamen Ordinarius, iusta de causa, permittere potest ut alibi resideat, praesertim in domo pluribus presbyteris communi, dummodo pastoralium perfunctio munerum nullum exinde detrimentum capiat.

§2. Curet loci Ordinarius ut inter parochum et vicarios aliqua vitae communis consuetudo in domo paroeciali, ubi id fieri possit, provehatur.

§3. Ad tempus feriarum quod attinet, vicarius paroecialis eodem gaudet iure ac parochus.

548 §2: c. 476 §6
548 §3: c. 476 §7; CD 30, 3
549: cc. 465 §§2, 3 et 5, 472, 2°, 475 §2

550 §1: c. 476 §5; CD 30, 1c
550 §2: c. 134; CD 30, 1c
550 §3: c. 465 §§2, 3 et 5

CAN. 551 The prescripts of can. 531 are to be observed in regards to offerings which the Christian faithful give to a vicar on the occasion of the performance of pastoral ministry.

CAN. 552 The diocesan bishop or diocesan administrator can remove a parochial vicar for a just cause, without prejudice to the prescript of can. 682, §2.

CHAPTER VII. Vicars Forane

CAN. 553 §1. A vicar forane, who is also called a dean, an archpriest, or some other name, is a priest who is placed over a vicariate forane.

§2. Unless particular law establishes otherwise, the diocesan bishop appoints the vicar forane, after he has heard the priests who exercise ministry in the vicariate in question according to his own prudent judgment.

CAN. 554 §1. For the office of vicar forane, which is not tied to the office of pastor of a certain parish, the bishop is to select a priest whom he has judged suitable, after he has considered the circumstances of place and time.

§2. A vicar forane is to be appointed for a certain period of time determined by particular law.

§3. The diocesan bishop can freely remove a vicar forane from office for a just cause in accord with his own prudent judgment.

CAN. 555 §1. In addition to the faculties legitimately given to him by particular law, the vicar forane has the duty and right:

1° of promoting and coordinating common pastoral activity in the vicariate;

CAN. 551 Ad oblationes quod attinet, quas occasione perfuncti ministerii pastoralis christifideles vicario faciunt, serventur praescripta can. 531.

CAN. 552 Vicarius paroecialis ab Episcopo dioecesano aut ab Administratore dioecesano amoveri potest, iusta de causa, firmo praescripto can. 682, §2.

CAPUT VII. De Vicariis Foraneis

CAN. 553 §1. Vicarius foraneus, qui etiam decanus vel archipresbyter vel alio nomine vocatur, est sacerdos qui vicariatui foraneo praeficitur.

§2. Nisi aliud iure particulari statuatur, vicarius foraneus nominatur ab Episcopo dioecesano, auditis pro suo prudenti iudicio sacerdotibus qui in vicariatu de quo agitur ministerium exercent.

CAN. 554 §1. Ad officium vicarii foranei, quod cum officio parochi certae paroeciae non ligatur, Episcopus seligat sacerdotem quem, inspectis loci ac temporis adiunctis, idoneum iudicaverit.

§2. Vicarius foraneus nominetur ad certum tempus, iure particulari determinatum.

§3. Vicarium foraneum iusta de causa, pro suo prudenti arbitrio, Episcopus dioecesanus ab officio libere amovere potest.

CAN. 555 §1. Vicario foraneo, praeter facultates iure particulari ei legitime tributas, officium et ius est:

1° actionem pastoralem in vicariatu communem promovendi et coordinandi;

551: c. 463 §3; PO 20, 21; ES I, 8
552: c. 477 §1; ES I, 32
553 §1: c. 445; ES I, 19 §1
553 §2: c. 446; DPME 187
554 §1: c. 446 §1; ES I, 19 §1; DPME 187

554 §2: ES I, 19 §2; DPME 187
554 §3: c. 446 §2; ES I, 19 §2; DPME 187
555 §1: c. 447 §1
555 §1, 1°: ES I, 19 §1

2° of seeing to it that the clerics of his district lead a life in keeping with their state and perform their duties diligently;

3° of seeing to it that religious functions are celebrated according to the prescripts of the sacred liturgy, that the beauty and elegance of churches and sacred furnishings are maintained carefully, especially in the eucharistic celebration and custody of the Most Blessed Sacrament, that the parochial registers are inscribed correctly and protected appropriately, that ecclesiastical goods are administered carefully, and finally that the rectory is cared for with proper diligence.

§2. In the vicariate entrusted to him, the vicar forane:

1° is to see to it that, according to the prescripts of particular law and at the times stated, the clerics attend lectures, theological meetings, or conferences according to the norm of can. 279, §2;

2° is to take care that spiritual supports are available to the presbyters of his district, and likewise to be concerned especially for those who find themselves in more difficult circumstances or are beset by problems.

§3. The vicar forane is to take care that the pastors of his district whom he knows to be gravely ill do not lack spiritual and material aids and that the funeral rites of those who have died are celebrated worthily. He is also to make provision so that, on the occasion of illness or death, the registers, documents, sacred furnishings, and other things which belong to the Church are not lost or removed.

§4. A vicar forane is obliged to visit the

2° prospiciendi ut clerici sui districtus vitam ducant proprio statui congruam atque officiis suis diligenter satisfaciant;

3° providendi ut religiosae functiones secundum sacrae liturgiae praescripta celebrentur, ut decor et nitor ecclesiarum sacraeque supellectilis, maxime in celebratione eucharistica et custodia sanctissimi Sacramenti, accurate serventur, ut recte conscribantur et debite custodiantur libri paroeciales, ut bona ecclesiastica sedulo administrentur; denique ut domus paroecialis debita diligentia curetur.

§2. In vicariatu sibi concredito vicarius foraneus:

1° operam det ut clerici, iuxta iuris particularis praescripta, statutis temporibus intersint praelectionibus, conventibus theologicis aut conferentiis, ad normam can. 279, §2;

2° curet ut presbyteris sui districtus subsidia spiritualia praesto sint, itemque maxime sollicitus sit de iis, qui in difficilioribus versantur circumstantiis aut problematibus anguntur.

§3. Curet vicarius foraneus ut parochi sui districtus, quos graviter aegrotantes noverit, spiritualibus ac materialibus auxiliis ne careant, utque eorum qui decesserint, funera digne celebrentur; provideat quoque ne, occasione aegrotationis vel mortis, libri, documenta, sacra supellex aliaque, quae ad Ecclesiam pertinent, depereant aut asportentur.

§4. Vicarius foraneus obligatione tenetur

555 §1, 2°: c. 447 §1, 1°; CD 30, 1
555 §1, 3°: c. 447 §1, 3° et 4°; DPME 187
555 §2, 1°: c. 448 §1

555 §2, 2°: CD 16
555 §3: c. 447 §3
555 §4: c. 447 §2

parishes of his district according to the determination made by the diocesan bishop.

secundum determinationem ab Episcopo dioecesano factam, sui districtus paroecias visitare.

CHAPTER VIII. Rectors of Churches and Chaplains

CAPUT VIII. **De Ecclesiarum Rectoribus et de Cappellanis**

ART. 1. *Rectors of Churches*

ART. 1. *De Ecclesiarum Rectoribus*

CAN. 556 Rectors of churches are understood here as priests to whom is committed the care of some church which is neither parochial nor capitular nor connected to a house of a religious community or society of apostolic life which celebrates services in it.

CAN. 556 Ecclesiarum rectores hic intelleguntur sacerdotes, quibus cura demandatur alicuius ecclesiae, quae nec sit paroecialis nec capitularis, nec adnexa domui communitatis religiosae aut societatis vitae apostolicae, quae in eadem officia celebret.

CAN. 557 §1. The diocesan bishop freely appoints the rector of a church, without prejudice to the right of election or presentation if someone legitimately has it; in that case, it is for the diocesan bishop to confirm or install the rector.

CAN. 557 §1. Ecclesiae rector libere nominatur ab Episcopo dioecesano, salvo iure eligendi aut praesentandi, si cui legitime competat; quo in casu Episcopi dioecesani est rectorem confirmare vel instituere.

§2. Even if a church belongs to some clerical religious institute of pontifical right, the diocesan bishop is competent to install the rector presented by the superior.

§2. Etiam si ecclesia pertineat ad aliquod clericale institutum religiosum iuris pontificii, Episcopo dioecesano competit rectorem a Superiore praesentatum instituere.

§3. The rector of a church which is connected with a seminary or other college which is governed by clerics is the rector of the seminary or college unless the diocesan bishop has determined otherwise.

§3. Rector ecclesiae, quae coniuncta sit cum seminario aliove collegio quod a clericis regitur, est rector seminarii vel collegii, nisi aliter Episcopus dioecesanus constituerit.

CAN. 558 Without prejudice to the prescript of can. 262, a rector is not permitted to perform the parochial functions mentioned in can. 530, nn. 1–6 in the church entrusted to him unless the pastor consents or, if the matter warrants it, delegates.

CAN. 558 Salvo praescripto can. 262, rectori non licet functiones paroeciales de quibus in can. 530, nn. 1–6, in ecclesia sibi commissa peragere, nisi consentiente aut, si res ferat, delegante parocho.

CAN. 559 A rector can perform liturgical

CAN. 559 Potest rector in ecclesia sibi

556: c. 479
557 §1: c. 480 §1
557 §2: c. 480 §2
557 §3: c. 480 §3

558: cc. 462, 466 §1, 481, 938 §2, 1368; SCDS Decr. *Spiritus Sancti Munera*, 14 sep. 1946, I (AAS 38 [1946] 352); SCPF Resp., 4 apr. 1952
559: c. 482

celebrations, even solemn ones, in the church entrusted to him, without prejudice to the legitimate laws of the foundation, and provided that, in the judgment of the local ordinary, they do not harm parochial ministry in any way.

CAN. 560 When the local ordinary considers it opportune, he can order a rector to celebrate in his church particular functions, even parochial ones, for the people and to make the church available for certain groups of the Christian faithful to conduct liturgical celebrations there.

CAN. 561 No one is permitted to celebrate the Eucharist, administer the sacraments, or perform other sacred functions in the church without the permission of the rector or another legitimate superior; this permission must be granted or denied according to the norm of law.

CAN. 562 The rector of a church, under the authority of the local ordinary and observing the legitimate statutes and acquired rights, is obliged to see to it that sacred functions are celebrated worthily in the church according to the liturgical norms and prescripts of the canons, that obligations are fulfilled faithfully, that goods are administered diligently, that the maintenance and beauty of sacred furnishings and buildings are provided for, and that nothing whatever occurs which is in any way unfitting to the holiness of the place and the reverence due to a house of God.

CAN. 563 Without prejudice to the prescript of can. 682, §2, the local ordinary, for a just cause and according to his own prudent judgment, can remove the rector of a church from office, even if he had been elected or presented by others.

commissa liturgicas celebrationes etiam sollemnes peragere, salvis legitimis fundationis legibus, atque dummodo de iudicio loci Ordinarii nullo modo ministerio paroeciali noceant.

CAN. 560 Loci Ordinarius, ubi id opportunum censeat, potest rectori praecipere ut determinatas in ecclesia sua pro populo celebret functiones etiam paroeciales, necnon ut ecclesia pateat certis christifidelium coetibus ibidem liturgicas celebrationes peracturis.

CAN. 561 Sine rectoris aliusve legitimi superioris licentia, nemini licet in ecclesia Eucharistiam celebrare, sacramenta administrare aliasve sacras functiones peragere; quae licentia danda aut deneganda est ad normam iuris.

CAN. 562 Ecclesiae rector, sub auctoritate loci Ordinarii servatisque legitimis statutis et iuribus quaesitis, obligatione tenetur prospiciendi ut sacrae functiones secundum normas liturgicas et canonum praescripta digne in ecclesia celebrentur, onera fideliter adimpleantur, bona diligenter administrentur, sacrae supellectilis atque aedium sacrarum conservationi et decori provideatur, neve quidpiam fiat quod sanctitati loci ac reverentiae domui Dei debitae quoquo modo non congruat.

CAN. 563 Retorem ecclesiae, etsi ab aliis electum aut praesentatum, loci Ordinarius ex iusta causa, pro suo prudenti arbitrio ab officio amovere potest, firmo praescripto can. 682, §2.

560: c. 483, 1°
561: c. 484 §1

562: c. 485
563: c. 486; ES I, 32

ART. 2. *Chaplains*

CAN. 564 A chaplain is a priest to whom is entrusted in a stable manner the pastoral care, at least in part, of some community or particular group of the Christian faithful, which is to be exercised according to the norm of universal and particular law.

CAN. 565 Unless the law provides otherwise or someone legitimately has special rights, a chaplain is appointed by the local ordinary to whom it also belongs to install the one presented or to confirm the one elected.

CAN. 566 §1. A chaplain must be provided with all the faculties which proper pastoral care requires. In addition to those which are granted by particular law or special delegation, a chaplain possesses by virtue of office the faculty of hearing the confessions of the faithful entrusted to his care, of preaching the word of God to them, of administering Viaticum and the anointing of the sick, and of conferring the sacrament of confirmation on those who are in danger of death.

§2. In hospitals, prisons, and on sea journeys, a chaplain, moreover, has the faculty, to be exercised only in those places, of absolving from *latae sententiae* censures which are neither reserved nor declared, without prejudice, however, to the prescript of can. 976.

CAN. 567 §1. The local ordinary is not to proceed to the appointment of a chaplain to a

ART. 2. *De Cappellanis*

CAN. 564 Cappellanus est sacerdos, cui stabili modo committitur cura pastoralis, saltem ex parte, alicuius communitatis aut peculiaris coetus christifidelium, ad normam iuris universalis et particularis exercenda.

CAN. 565 Nisi iure aliud caveatur aut cuidam specialia iura legitime competant, cappellanus nominatur ab Ordinario loci, cui etiam pertinet praesentatum instituere aut electum confirmare.

CAN. 566 §1. Cappellanus omnibus facultatibus instructus sit oportet quas recta cura pastoralis requirit. Praeter eas quae iure particulari aut speciali delegatione conceduntur, cappellanus vi officii facultate gaudet audiendi confessiones fidelium suae curae commissorum, verbi Dei eis praedicandi, Viaticum et unctionem infirmorum administrandi necnon sacramentum confirmationis eis conferendi, qui in periculo mortis versentur.

§2. In valetudinariis, carceribus et itineribus maritimis, cappellanus praeterea facultatem habet, his tantum in locis exercendam, a censuris latae sententiae non reservatis neque declaratis absolvendi, firmo tamen praescripto can. 976.

CAN. 567 §1. Ad nominationem cappellani domus instituti religiosi laicalis, Ordinar-

564: c. 698; SCC Instr. *Sollemne semper,* 23 apr. 1951 (AAS 43 [1951] 564); SCE Instr. *Nemo est,* 22 aug. 1969, 35–36 (AAS 61 [1969] 632–633); DPME 180, 183; SCE Decr. *Apostolatus maris,* 24 sep. 1977 (AAS 69 [1977] 737–746)

565: c. 698 §1; SCC Instr. *Sollemne semper,* 23 apr. 1951, X (AAS 43 [1951] 564); SCE Instr. *Nemo est,* 22 aug. 1969, 36 §2; 37 §2 (AAS 61 [1969] 632–633); SCE Decr. *Apostolatus maris,* 24 sep. 1977, I, art. 5 (AAS 69 [1977] 737–746)

566 §1: SCDS Decr. *Spiritus Sancti Munera,* 14 sep. 1946, I (AAS 38 [1946] 349); SCDS Resp., 30 dec. 1946; SCC Ind., 31 aug. 1953; SCC Facul., 19 mar. 1954 (AAS 46 [1954] 415–418); SCC Resp., 7 iul. 1956; SCE Instr. *Nemo est,* 22 aug. 1969, V (AAS 61 [1969] 632–633); SCE Decr. *Apostolatus maris,* 24 sep. 1977, II (AAS 69 [1977] 737–746)

566 §2: SCE Decr. *Apostolatus maris,* 24 sep. 1977, II, art. 1, 9 (AAS 69 [1977] 737–746)

567 §1: cc. 479 §2, 529

house of a lay religious institute without consulting the superior, who has the right to propose a specific priest after the superior has heard the community.

§2. It is for the chaplain to celebrate or direct liturgical functions; nevertheless, he is not permitted to involve himself in the internal governance of the institute.

CAN. 568   As far as possible, chaplains are to be appointed for those who are not able to avail themselves of the ordinary care of pastors because of the condition of their lives, such as migrants, exiles, refugees, nomads, sailors.

CAN. 569   Military chaplains are governed by special laws.

CAN. 570   If a non-parochial church is connected to the seat of a community or group, the chaplain is to be the rector of that church, unless the care of the community or of the church requires otherwise.

CAN. 571   In the exercise of his pastoral function, a chaplain is to preserve a fitting relationship with the pastor.

CAN. 572   In what pertains to the removal of a chaplain, the prescript of can. 563 is to be observed.

ius loci ne procedat, nisi consulto Superiore, cui ius est, audita communitate, quemdam sacerdotem proponere.

§2. Cappellani est liturgicas functiones celebrare aut moderari; ipsi tamen non licet regimine interno instituti sese immiscere.

CAN. 568   Pro iis qui ob vitae condicionem ordinaria parochorum cura frui non valent, uti sunt migrantes, exsules, profugi, nomades, navigantes, constituantur, quatenus fieri possit, cappellani.

CAN. 569   Cappellani militum legibus specialibus reguntur.

CAN. 570   Si communitatis aut coetus sedi adnexa est ecclesia non paroecialis, cappellanus sit rector ipsius ecclesiae, nisi cura communitatis aut ecclesiae aliud exigat.

CAN. 571   In exercitio sui pastoralis muneris, cappellanus debitam cum parocho servet coniunctionem.

CAN. 572   Quod attinet ad amotionem cappellani, servetur praescriptum can. 563.

568: SCDS Decr. *Spiritus Sancti Munera,* 14 sep. 1946, I (AAS 38 [1946] 349); SCDS Resp., 30 dec. 1946; SCC Ind., 31 aug. 1953; SCC Facul., 19 mar. 1954 (AAS 46 [1954] 415–418); SCC Resp., 7 iul. 1956; CD 18; ES I, 9; SCE Instr. *Nemo est,* 22 aug. 1969, V (AAS 61 [1969] 632–633); SCE Decr. *Apostolatus maris,* 24 sep. 1977, II (AAS 69 [1977] 737–746)

569: c. 451 §3; SCDS Resp., 8 oct. 1943; SCC Instr. *Sollemne semper,* 23 apr. 1951 (AAS 43 [1951] 564); SCC Instr. *Divinum persequens,* 2 iun. 1951 (AAS 43 [1951] 565–566); SCR Instr. *Sacrorum Administri,* 2

feb. 1955 (AAS 47 [1955] 93–97); SCC Instr. *Per instructionem,* 20 oct. 1956 (AAS 49 [1957] 150–163); SCC Decr. *Ad Sacra Limina,* 28 feb. 1959 (AAS 51 [1959] 274); SCC Decr. *Sacramentum Poenitentiae,* 27 nov. 1960 (AAS 53 [1961] 49–50)

571: SCDS Resp., 8 oct. 1943; SCC Instr. *Sollemne semper,* 23 apr. 1951, X (AAS 43 [1951] 564); CD 43; SCE Decr. *Apostolatus maris,* 24 sep. 1977, I, art. 5 (AAS 69 [1977] 737–746)

572: c. 486; ES I, 32

PART III.

INSTITUTES OF CONSECRATED LIFE AND SOCIETIES OF APOSTOLIC LIFE

PARS III. DE

INSTITUTIS VITAE CONSECRATAE ET DE SOCIETATIBUS VITAE APOSTOLICAE

SECTION I. Institutes of Consecrated Life

TITLE I. Norms Common to All Institutes of Consecrated Life

SECTIO I. *De Institutis Vitae Consecratae*

TITULUS I. **Normae Communes Omnibus Institutis Vitae Consecratae**

CAN. 573 §1. The life consecrated through the profession of the evangelical counsels is a stable form of living by which the faithful, following Christ more closely under the action of the Holy Spirit, are totally dedicated to God who is loved most of all, so that, having been dedicated by a new and special title to His honor, to the building up of the Church, and to the salvation of the world, they strive for the perfection of charity in the service of the kingdom of God and, having been made an outstanding sign in the Church, foretell the heavenly glory.

§2. The Christian faithful freely assume this form of living in institutes of consecrated life canonically erected by competent authority of the Church. Through vows or other sacred bonds according to the proper laws of the institutes, they profess the evangelical counsels of

CAN. 573 §1. Vita consecrata per consiliorum evangelicorum professionem est stabilis vivendi forma qua fideles, Christum sub actione Spiritus Sancti pressius sequentes, Deo summe dilecto totaliter dedicantur, ut, in Eius honorem atque Ecclesiae aedificationem mundique salutem novo et peculiari titulo dediti, caritatis perfectionem in servitio Regni Dei consequantur et, praeclarum in Ecclesia signum effecti, caelestem gloriam praenuntient.

§2. Quam vivendi formam in institutis vitae consecratae, a competenti Ecclesiae auctoritate canonice erectis, libere assumunt christifideles, qui per vota aut alia sacra ligamina iuxta proprias institutorum leges, consilia evangelica castitatis, paupertatis et

---

573 §1: c. 487; LG 42–44; CD 33; PC 1; RC 1; ET 7; MG: 567–568

573 §2: cc. 487, 488, 1°; LG 43–45; PC 5; AG 18

chastity, poverty, and obedience and, through the charity to which the counsels lead, are joined in a special way to the Church and its mystery.

CAN. 574 §1. The state of those who profess the evangelical counsels in institutes of this type belongs to the life and holiness of the Church and must be fostered and promoted by all in the Church.

§2. Certain Christian faithful are specially called by God to this state so that they possess a special gift in the life of the Church and contribute to its salvific mission, according to the purpose and spirit of the institute.

CAN. 575 The evangelical counsels, based on the teaching and examples of Christ the Teacher, are a divine gift which the Church has received from the Lord and preserves always through His grace.

CAN. 576 It is for the competent authority of the Church to interpret the evangelical counsels, to direct their practice by laws, and by canonical approbation to establish the stable forms of living deriving from them, and also, for its part, to take care that the institutes grow and flourish according to the spirit of the founders and sound traditions.

CAN. 577 In the Church there are a great many institutes of consecrated life which have different gifts according to the grace which has been given them: they more closely follow Christ who prays, or announces the kingdom of God, or does good to people, or lives with people in the world, yet who always does the will of the Father.

CAN. 578 All must observe faithfully the mind and designs of the founders regarding the

oboedientiae profitentur et per caritatem, ad quam ducunt, Ecclesiae eiusque mysterio speciali modo coniunguntur.

CAN. 574 §1. Status eorum, qui in huiusmodi institutis consilia evangelica profitentur, ad vitam et sanctitatem Ecclesiae pertinet, et ideo ab omnibus in Ecclesia fovendus et promovendus est.

§2. Ad hunc statum quidam christifideles specialiter a Deo vocantur, ut in vita Ecclesiae peculiari dono fruantur et, secundum finem et spiritum instituti, eiusdem missioni salvificae prosint.

CAN. 575 Consilia evangelica in Christi Magistri doctrina et exemplis fundata, donum sunt divinum, quod Ecclesia a Domino accepit Eiusque gratia semper conservat.

CAN. 576 Competentis Ecclesiae auctoritatis est consilia evangelica interpretari, eorundem praxim legibus moderari atqui stabiles inde vivendi formas canonica approbatione constituere itemque, pro parte sua, curare ut instituta secundum spiritum fundatorum et sanas traditiones crescant et floreant.

CAN. 577 Permulta in Ecclesia sunt instituta vitae consecratae, quae donationes habent differentes secundum gratiam quae data est eis: Christum, enim, pressius sequuntur sive orantem, sive Regnum Dei annuntiantem, sive hominibus benefacientem, sive cum eis in saeculo conversantem, semper autem voluntatem Patris facientem.

CAN. 578 Fundatorum mens atque proposita a competenti auctoritate ecclesias-

---

574 §1: c. 487; LG 44; MR 8; MG: 566
574 §2: LG 43; PC 2
575: LG 43; PC 1

576: LG 43–45
577: c. 488, 1°–4°, 7°; PME I; LG 36, 46; PC 8a, 11
578: LG 45; PC 2b; ES II: 16 §3

nature, purpose, spirit, and character of an institute, which have been sanctioned by competent ecclesiastical authority, and its sound traditions, all of which constitute the patrimony of the same institute.

CAN. 579   Diocesan bishops, each in his own territory, can erect institutes of consecrated life by formal decree, provided that the Apostolic See has been consulted.

CAN. 580   The aggregation of one institute of consecrated life to another is reserved to the competent authority of the aggregating institute; the canonical autonomy of the aggregated institute is always to be preserved.

CAN. 581   To divide an institute into parts, by whatever name they are called, to erect new parts, to join those erected, or to redefine their boundaries belongs to the competent authority of the institute, according to the norm of the constitutions.

CAN. 582   Mergers and unions of institutes of consecrated life are reserved to the Apostolic See only; confederations and federations are also reserved to it.

CAN. 583   Changes in institutes of consecrated life affecting those things which had been approved by the Apostolic See cannot be made without its permission.

CAN. 584   The suppression of an institute pertains only to the Apostolic See; a decision regarding the temporal goods of the institute is also reserved to the Apostolic See.

CAN. 585   It belongs to the competent authority of an institute to suppress its parts.

tica sancita circa naturam, finem, spiritum et indolem instituti, necnon eius sanae traditiones, quae omnia patrimonium eiusdem instituti constituunt, ab omnibus fideliter servanda sunt.

CAN. 579   Episcopi dioecesani, in suo quisque territorio, instituta vitae consecratae formali decreto erigere possunt, dummodo Sedes Apostolica consulta fuerit.

CAN. 580   Aggregatio alicuius instituti vitae consecratae ad aliud reservatur competenti auctoritati instituti aggregantis, salva semper canonica autonomia instituti aggregati.

CAN. 581   Dividere institutum in partes, quocumque nomine veniant, novas erigere, erectas coniungere vel aliter circumscribere ad competentem instituti auctoritatem pertinet, ad normam constitutionum.

CAN. 582   Fusiones et uniones institutorum vitae consecratae uni Sedi Apostolicae reservantur; eidem quoque reservantur confoederationes et foederationes.

CAN. 583   Immutationes in institutis vitae consecratae ea afficientes, quae a Sede Apostolica approbata fuerunt, absque eiusdem licentia fieri nequeunt.

CAN. 584   Institutum supprimere ad unam Sedem Apostolicam spectat, cui etiam reservatur de eius bonis temporalibus statuere.

CAN. 585   Instituti partes supprimere ad auctoritatem competentem eiusdem instituti pertinet.

579: cc. 488, 3°, 492 §1; SCR Normae, 6 mar. 1921, 3 (AAS 13 [1921] 313); SCR Decr. *Quod iam*, 30 nov. 1977 (AAS 14 [1922] 644–646); SCGE Normae, 10 iun. 1967

580: c. 492 §1; ES II: 39–41

581: cc. 494, 1500; AIE 1°

582: Pius PP. XII, Hom. *Exsultent hodie*, 18 sep. 1947 (AAS 39 [1947] 454–455); SpC VII; PC 21, 22; ES II: 39–41.

583: c. 495 §2

584: cc. 493, 1501; PC 21, 22; ES II: 39–41

585: cc. 494, 1500, 1501; AIE 1°

CAN. 586 §1. A just autonomy of life, especially of governance, is acknowledged for individual institutes, by which they possess their own discipline in the Church and are able to preserve their own patrimony intact, as mentioned in can. 578.

§2. It is for local ordinaries to preserve and safeguard this autonomy.

CAN. 587 §1. To protect more faithfully the proper vocation and identity of each institute, the fundamental code or constitutions of every institute must contain, besides those things which are to be observed as stated in can. 578, fundamental norms regarding governance of the institute, the discipline of members, incorporation and formation of members, and the proper object of the sacred bonds.

§2. A code of this type is approved by competent authority of the Church and can be changed only with its consent.

§3. In this code spiritual and juridic elements are to be joined together suitably; nevertheless, norms are not to be multiplied without necessity.

§4. Other norms established by competent authority of an institute are to be collected suitably in other codes and, moreover, can be reviewed appropriately and adapted according to the needs of places and times.

CAN. 588 §1. By its very nature, the state of consecrated life is neither clerical nor lay.

§2. That institute is called clerical which, by reason of the purpose or design intended by the

CAN. 586 §1. Singulis institutis iusta autonomia vitae, praesertim regiminis, agnoscitur, qua gaudeant in Ecclesia propria disciplina atque integrum servare valeant suum patrimonium, de quo in can. 578.

§2. Ordinariorum locorum est hanc autonomiam servare ac tueri.

CAN. 587 §1. Ad propriam singulorum institutorum vocationem et identitatem fidelius tuendam, in cuiusvis instituti codice fundamentali seu constitutionibus contineri debent, praeter ea quae in can. 578 servanda statuuntur, normae fundamentales circa instituti regimen et sodalium disciplinam, membrorum incorporationem atque institutionem, necnon proprium sacrorum ligaminum obiectum.

§2. Codex huiusmodi a competenti auctoritate Ecclesiae approbatur et tantummodo cum eiusdem consensu mutari potest.

§3. In hoc codice elementa spiritualia et iuridica apte componantur; normae tamen absque necessitate ne multiplicentur.

§4. Ceterae normae a competenti instituti auctoritate statutae apte in aliis codicibus colligantur, quae tamen iuxta exigentias locorum et temporum congrue recognosci et aptari possunt.

CAN. 588 §1. Status vitae consecratae, suapte natura, non est nec clericalis nec laicalis.

§2. Institutum clericale illud dicitur quod, ratione finis seu propositi a fundatore intenti

586 §1: CD 35: 3–4; MR 13c, 34
586 §2: LG 45; CD 35: 2; MR 9c et d, 28, 52
587 §1: LG 45; ES II: 12
587 §2: ES II: 8, 11
587 §3: MG: 569; PC 4; ES II: 4d, 12b, 13

587 §4: PC 3; ES II: 14
588 §1: cc. 107, 488, 4°; LG 43; PC 10, 15; CIV
Resp., 10 feb. 1966 (AAS 60 [1968] 360); ES II: 27
588 §2: c. 488, 4°; Ssap I

founder or by virtue of legitimate tradition, is under the direction of clerics, assumes the exercise of sacred orders, and is recognized as such by the authority of the Church.

§3. That institute is called lay which, recognized as such by the authority of the Church, has by virtue of its nature, character, and purpose a proper function defined by the founder or by legitimate tradition, which does not include the exercise of sacred orders.

CAN. 589 An institute of consecrated life is said to be of pontifical right if the Apostolic See has erected it or approved it through a formal decree. It is said to be of diocesan right, however, if it has been erected by a diocesan bishop but has not obtained a decree of approval from the Apostolic See.

CAN. 590 §1. Inasmuch as institutes of consecrated life are dedicated in a special way to the service of God and of the whole Church, they are subject to the supreme authority of the Church in a special way.

§2. Individual members are also bound to obey the Supreme Pontiff as their highest superior by reason of the sacred bond of obedience.

CAN. 591 In order to provide better for the good of institutes and the needs of the apostolate, the Supreme Pontiff, by reason of his primacy in the universal Church and with a view to common advantage, can exempt institutes of consecrated life from the governance of local ordinaries and subject them to himself alone or to another ecclesiastical authority.

CAN. 592 §1. In order better to foster the

vel vi legitimae traditionis, sub moderamine est clericorum, exercitium ordinis sacri assumit, et qua tale ab Ecclesiae auctoritate agnoscitur.

§3. Institutum vero laicale illud appellatur quod, ab Ecclesiae auctoritate qua tale agnitum, vi eius naturae, indolis et finis munus habet proprium, a fundatore vel legitima traditione definitum, exercitium ordinis sacri non includens.

CAN. 589 Institutum vitae consecratae dicitur iuris pontificii, si a Sede Apostolica erectum aut per eiusdem formale decretum approbatum est; iuris vero dioecesani, si ab Episcopo dioecesano erectum, approbationis decretum a Sede Apostolica non est consecutum.

CAN. 590 §1. Instituta vitae consecratae, utpote ad Dei totiusque Ecclesiae servitium speciali modo dicata, supremae eiusdem auctoritati peculiari ratione subduntur.

§2. Singuli sodales Summo Pontifici, tamquam supremo eorum Superiori, etiam ratione sacri vinculi oboedientiae parere tenentur.

CAN. 591 Quo melius institutorum bono atque apostolatus necessitatibus provideatur, Summus Pontifex, ratione sui in universam Ecclesiam primatus, intuitu utilitatis communis, instituta vitae consecratae ab Ordinariorum loci regimine eximere potest sibique soli vel alii ecclesiasticae auctoritati subicere.

CAN. 592 §1. Quo melius institutorum

588 §3: c. 488, 4°; CIV Resp., 10 feb. 1966 (AAS 60 [1968] 360); PC 10

589: c. 488, 3°; SCR Decr. *Quod iam,* 30 nov. 1922 (AAS 14 [1922] 644); SCRIS Normae, 20 iun. 1975

590 §1: LG 44; PC 5; RC 2

590 §2: c. 499 §1; MR 22

591: cc. 488, 2°, 615, 618 §1; SCR Decr. *Religiosae Sanctimonialium,* 23 iun. 1923 (AAS 15 [1923] 357–358); LG 45; CD 35, 3; MR 8, 22

592 §1: c. 510; SCR Decr. *Sancitum est,* 8 mar. 1922

communion of institutes with the Apostolic See, each supreme moderator is to send a brief report of the state and life of the institute to the Apostolic See, in a manner and at a time established by the latter.

§2. The moderators of every institute are to promote knowledge of documents of the Holy See which regard the members entrusted to them and are to take care about their observance.

CAN. 593 Without prejudice to the prescript of can. 586, institutes of pontifical right are immediately and exclusively subject to the power of the Apostolic See in regards to internal governance and discipline.

CAN. 594 Without prejudice to can. 586, an institute of diocesan right remains under the special care of the diocesan bishop.

CAN. 595 §1. It is for the bishop of the principal seat to approve the constitutions and confirm changes legitimately introduced into them, without prejudice to those things which the Apostolic See has taken in hand, and also to treat affairs of greater importance affecting the whole institute which exceed the power of internal authority, after he has consulted the other diocesan bishops, however, if the institute has spread to several dioceses.

§2. A diocesan bishop can grant dispensations from the constitutions in particular cases.

CAN. 596 §1. Superiors and chapters of institutes possess that power over members which is defined in universal law and the constitutions.

communio cum Sede Apostolica foveatur, modo et tempore ab eadem statutis, quilibet supremus Moderator brevem conspectum status et vitae instituti eidem Apostolicae Sedi mittat.

§2. Cuiuslibet instituti Moderatores promoveant notitiam documentorum Sanctae Sedis, quae sodales sibi concreditos respiciunt, eorumque observantiam curent.

CAN. 593 Firmo praescripto can. 586, instituta iuris pontificii quoad regimen internum et disciplinam immediate et exclusive potestati Sedis Apostolicae subiciuntur.

CAN. 594 Institutum iuris dioecesani, firmo can. 586, permanet sub speciali cura Episcopi dioecesani.

CAN. 595 §1. Episcopi sedis principis est constitutiones approbare et immutationes in eas legitime introductas confirmare, salvis iis in quibus Apostolica Sedes manus apposuerit, necnon negotia maiora totum institutum respicientia tractare, quae potestatem internae auctoritatis superent, consultis tamen ceteris Episcopis dioecesanis, si institutum ad plures dioeceses propagatum fuerit.

§2. Episcopus dioecesanus potest dispensationes a constitutionibus concedere in casibus particularibus.

CAN. 596 §1. Institutorum Superiores et capitula in sodales ea gaudent potestate, quae iure universali et constitutionibus definitur.

(AAS 14 [1922] 161–163); SCR Instr. *Doceatur quae decreta*, 25 mar. 1922 (AAS 14 [1922] 278–286); SCR Decr. *Cum, transactis*, 9 iul. 1947 (AAS 40 [1948] 378–381); SCR Normae, 9 dec. 1948

592 §2: c. 509 §1; LG 25; MR 29, 33
593: c. 618 §2

594: c. 492 §2
595 §1: cc. 492 §1, 495 §2
595 §2: CI Resp. III: II, 12 feb. 1935 (AAS 27 [1935] 93)
596 §1: c. 501 §1; SCRIS Decr. *Experimenta*, 2 feb. 1972, 1 (AAS 64 [1972] 393)

§2. In clerical religious institutes of pontifical right, however, they also possess ecclesiastical power of governance for both the external and internal forum.

§3. The prescripts of cann. 131, 133, and 137–144 apply to the power mentioned in §1.

CAN. 597 §1. Any Catholic endowed with a right intention who has the qualities required by universal and proper law and who is not prevented by any impediment can be admitted into an institute of consecrated life.

§2. No one can be admitted without suitable preparation.

CAN. 598 §1. Each institute, attentive to its own character and purposes, is to define in its constitutions the manner in which the evangelical counsels of chastity, poverty, and obedience must be observed for its way of living.

§2. Moreover, all members must not only observe the evangelical counsels faithfully and fully but also arrange their life according to the proper law of the institute and thereby strive for the perfection of their state.

CAN. 599 The evangelical counsel of chastity assumed for the sake of the kingdom of heaven, which is a sign of the world to come and a source of more abundant fruitfulness in an undivided heart, entails the obligation of perfect continence in celibacy.

CAN. 600 The evangelical counsel of poverty in imitation of Christ who, although he was rich, was made poor for us, entails, besides a life which is poor in fact and in spirit and is to be led productively in moderation and foreign to earthly riches, a dependence and limitation

§2. In institutis autem religionis clericalibus iuris pontificii pollent insuper potestate ecclesiastica regiminis pro foro tam externo quam interno.

§3. Potestati de qua in §1 applicantur praescripta cann. 131, 133 et 137–144.

CAN. 597 §1. In vitae consecratae institutum admitti potest quilibet catholicus, recta intentione praeditus, qui qualitates habeat iure universali et proprio requisitas nulloque detineatur impedimento.

§2. Nemo admitti potest sine congrua praeparatione.

CAN. 598 §1. Unumquodque institutum, attentis indole et finibus propriis, in suis constitutionibus definiat modum quo consilia evangelica castitatis, paupertatis et oboedientiae, pro sua vivendi ratione, servanda sunt.

§2. Sodales vero omnes debent non solum consilia evangelica fideliter integreque servare, sed etiam secundum ius proprium instituti vitam componere atque ita ad perfectionem sui status contendere.

CAN. 599 Evangelicum castitatis consilium propter Regnum coelorum assumptum, quod signum est mundi futuri et fons uberioris fecunditatis in indiviso corde, obligationem secumfert continentiae perfectae in caelibatu.

CAN. 600 Evangelicum consilium paupertatis ad imitationem Christi, qui propter nos egenus factus est cum esset dives, praeter vitam re et spiritu pauperem, operose in sobrietate ducendam et a terrenis divitiis alienam, secumfert dependentiam et limita-

---

596 §2: cc. 501 §1, 503
596 §3: CI Resp. VI, 26 mar. 1952 (AAS 44 [1952] 497)
597 §1: c. 538; Ssap II; OT 3; RC 4, 10: II
597 §2: RC 4, 11: I

598 §1: PC 12–14
598 §2: c. 593; Ssap III; LG 42, 43, 47; PC 2b
599: LG 42; PC 12; PO 16; ET 15
600: LG 42; PC 13; PO 17; ES II: 23, 24; ET 20, 21; RFS 50

in the use and disposition of goods according to the norm of the proper law of each institute.

CAN. 601 The evangelical counsel of obedience, undertaken in a spirit of faith and love in the following of Christ obedient unto death, requires the submission of the will to legitimate superiors, who stand in the place of God, when they command according to the proper constitutions.

CAN. 602 The life of brothers or sisters proper to each institute, by which all the members are united together as a special family in Christ, is to be defined in such a way that it becomes a mutual support for all in fulfilling the vocation of each. Moreover, by their communion as brothers or sisters rooted and founded in charity, members are to be an example of universal reconciliation in Christ.

CAN. 603 §1. In addition to institutes of consecrated life, the Church recognizes the eremitic or anchoritic life by which the Christian faithful devote their life to the praise of God and the salvation of the world through a stricter withdrawal from the world, the silence of solitude, and assiduous prayer and penance.

§2. A hermit is recognized by law as one dedicated to God in consecrated life if he or she publicly professes in the hands of the diocesan bishop the three evangelical counsels, confirmed by vow or other sacred bond, and observes a proper program of living under his direction.

CAN. 604 §1. Similar to these forms of consecrated life is the order of virgins who, expressing the holy resolution of following Christ

tionem in usu et dispositione bonorum ad normam iuris proprii singulorum institutorum.

CAN. 601 Evangelicum oboedientiae consilium, spiritu fidei et amoris in sequela Christi usque ad mortem oboedientis susceptum, obligat ad submissionem voluntatis erga legitimos Superiores, vices Dei gerentes, cum secundum proprias constitutiones praecipiunt.

CAN. 602 Vita fraterna, unicuique instituto propria, qua sodales omnes in peculiarem veluti familiam in Christo coadunantur, ita definiatur ut cunctis mutuo adiutorio evadat ad suam cuiusque vocationem adimplendam. Fraterna autem communione, in caritate radicata et fundata, sodales exemplo sint universalis in Christo reconciliationis.

CAN. 603 §1. Praeter vitae consecratae instituta, Ecclesia agnoscit vitam eremiticam seu anachoreticam, qua christifideles arctiore a mundo secessu, solitudinis silentio, assidua prece et paenitentia, suam in laudem Dei et mundi salutem vitam devovent.

§2. Eremita, uti Deo deditus in vita consecrata, iure agnoscitur si tria evangelica consilia, vota vel alio sacro ligamine firmata, publice profiteatur in manu Episcopi dioecesani et propriam vivendi rationem sub ductu eiusdem servet.

CAN. 604 §1. Hisce vitae consecratae formis accedit ordo virginum quae, sanctum propositum emittentes Christum pressius se-

601: LG 42; PC 14; PO 15; ET 23–28

602: PC 15; ES II: 25–29; ET 26, 32, 34, 39–41; VS V

603 §1: PAULUS PP. VI, Litt. Ap. *Optimam partem*, 18 apr. 1971 (AAS 63 [1971] 447–450); LG 43;

PC 1; AG 18, 40

603 §2: c. 487; LG 44

604 §1: SCR Resp., 25 mar. 1927 (AAS 19 [1927] 138–139); SC 80; *Ordo consecrationis virginum*, 31 maii 1970

more closely, are consecrated to God by the diocesan bishop according to the approved liturgical rite, are mystically betrothed to Christ, the Son of God, and are dedicated to the service of the Church.

§2. In order to observe their own resolution more faithfully and to perform by mutual assistance service to the Church in harmony with their proper state, virgins can be associated together.

CAN. 605 The approval of new forms of consecrated life is reserved only to the Apostolic See. Diocesan bishops, however, are to strive to discern new gifts of consecrated life granted to the Church by the Holy Spirit and are to assist promoters so that these can express their proposals as well as possible and protect them by appropriate statutes; the general norms contained in this section are especially to be utilized.

CAN. 606 Those things which are established for institutes of consecrated life and their members are equally valid in law for either sex, unless it is otherwise evident from the context of the wording or the nature of the matter.

quendi, ab Episcopo dioecesano iuxta probatum ritum liturgicum Deo consecrantur, Christo Dei Filio mystice desponsantur et Ecclesiae servitio dedicantur.

§2. Ad suum propositum fidelius servandum et ad servitium Ecclesiae, proprio statui consonum, mutuo adiutorio perficiendum, virgines consociari possunt.

CAN. 605 Novas formas vitae consecratae approbare uni Sedi Apostolicae reservatur. Episcopi dioecesani autem nova vitae consecratae dona a Spiritu Sancto Ecclesiae concredita discernere satagant iidemque adiuvent promotores ut proposita meliore quo fieri potest modo exprimant aptisque statutis protegant, adhibitis praesertim generalibus normis in hac parte contentis.

CAN. 606 Quae de institutis vitae consecratae eorumque sodalibus statuuntur, pari iure de utroque sexu valent, nisi ex contextu sermonis vel ex rei natura aliud constet.

TITLE II. **Religious Institutes**

TITULUS II. **De Institutis Religiosis**

CAN. 607 §1. As a consecration of the whole person, religious life manifests in the Church a wonderful marriage brought about by God, a sign of the future age. Thus the religious brings to perfection a total self-giving as a sacrifice offered to God, through which his or her whole existence becomes a continuous worship of God in charity.

Can. 607 §1. Vita religiosa, utpote totius personae consecratio, mirabile in Ecclesia manifestat conubium a Deo conditum, futuri saeculi signum. Ita religiosus plenam suam consummat donationem veluti sacrificium Deo oblatum, quo tota ipsius exsistentia fit continuus Dei cultus in caritate.

604 §2: AA 19
605: LG 45; PC 1, 19; AG 18; RC prooemium; MR 9c, 51

606: c. 490
607 §1: LG 44, 45; PC 1, 5, 12, 25; AG 18; ET 13; RC 2

§2. A religious institute is a society in which members, according to proper law, pronounce public vows, either perpetual or temporary which are to be renewed, however, when the period of time has elapsed, and lead a life of brothers or sisters in common.

§3. The public witness to be rendered by religious to Christ and the Church entails a separation from the world proper to the character and purpose of each institute.

CHAPTER I. **Religious Houses and Their Erection and Suppression**

CAN. 608 A religious community must live in a legitimately established house under the authority of a superior designated according to the norm of law. Each house is to have at least an oratory in which the Eucharist is to be celebrated and reserved so that it is truly the center of the community.

CAN. 609 §1. Houses of a religious institute are erected by the authority competent according to the constitutions, with the previous written consent of the diocesan bishop.

§2. In addition, the permission of the Apostolic See is required to erect a monastery of nuns.

CAN. 610 §1. The erection of houses takes place with consideration for their advantage to the Church and the institute and with suitable safeguards for those things which are required to carry out properly the religious life of the members according to the proper purposes and spirit of the institute.

§2. Institutum religiosum est societas in qua sodales secundum ius proprium vota publica perpetua vel temporaria, elapso tamen tempore renovanda, nuncupant atque vitam fraternam in communi ducunt.

§3. Testimonium publicum a religiosis Christo et Ecclesiae reddendum illam secumfert a mundo separationem, quae indoli et fini uniuscuiusque instituti est propria.

CAPUT I. **De Domibus Religiosis Earumque Erectione et Suppressione**

CAN. 608 Communitas religiosa habitare debet in domo legitime constituta sub auctoritate Superioris ad normam iuris designati; singulae domus habeant saltem oratorium, in quo Eucharistia celebretur et asservetur ut vere sit centrum communitatis.

CAN. 609 §1. Instituti religiosi domus eriguntur ab auctoritate competenti iuxta constitutiones, praevio Episcopi dioecesani consensu in scriptis dato.

§2. Ad erigendum monasterium monialium requiritur insuper licentia Apostolicae Sedis.

CAN. 610 §1. Domorum erectio fit prae oculis habita utilitate Ecclesiae et instituti atque in tuto positis iis quae ad vitam religiosam sodalium rite agendam requiruntur, iuxta proprios instituti fines et spiritum.

607 §2: cc. 487, 488, 1°, 577 §1, 594 §1; PC 15; ES II: 25; MR 10

607 §3: LG 44; PC 5; ES II: 31; ET 35

608: cc. 488, 5°, 497 §2, 516 §1, 610 §2, 1265 §1, 1274 §1; CI Resp. X, 14 iul. 1922 (AAS 14 [1922] 529); CI Resp. III et VII, 20 maii 1923 (AAS 16 [1924] 113–115);

ET 25, 48; SCRIS Decr. *Experimenta*, 2 feb. 1972, 1 (AAS 64 [1972] 393)

609 §1: c. 497 §1; AIE 2°

609 §2: c. 497 §1; AIE 2°

610 §1: c. 496; LG 45

§2. No house is to be erected unless it can be judged prudently that the needs of the members will be provided for suitably.

CAN. 611 The consent of the diocesan bishop to erect a religious house of any institute entails the right:

1° to lead a life according to the character and proper purposes of the institute;

2° to exercise the works proper to the institute according to the norm of law and without prejudice to the conditions attached to the consent;

3° for clerical institutes to have a church, without prejudice to the prescript of can. 1215, §3 and to perform sacred ministries, after the requirements of the law have been observed.

CAN. 612 For a religious house to be converted to apostolic works different from those for which it was established, the consent of the diocesan bishop is required, but not if it concerns a change which refers only to internal governance and discipline, without prejudice to the laws of the foundation.

CAN. 613 §1. A religious house of canons regular or of monks under the governance and care of its own moderator is autonomous unless the constitutions state otherwise.

§2. The moderator of an autonomous house is a major superior by law.

CAN. 614 Monasteries of nuns associated to an institute of men maintain their own way of life and governance according to the constitutions. Mutual rights and obligations are to be defined in such a way that spiritual good can come from the association.

§2. Nulla domus erigatur nisi iudicari prudenter possit fore ut congrue sodalium necessitatibus provideatur.

CAN. 611 Consensus Episcopi dioecesani ad erigendam domum religiosam alicuius instituti secumfert ius:

1° vitam ducendi secundum indolem et fines proprios instituti;

2° opera instituto propria exercendi ad normam iuris, salvis condicionibus in consensu appositis;

3° pro institutis clericalibus habendi ecclesiam, salvo praescripto can. 1215, §3, et sacra ministeria peragendi, servatis de iure servandis.

CAN. 612 Ut domus religiosa ad opera apostolica destinetur diversa ab illis pro quibus constituta est, requiritur consensus Episcopi dioecesani; non vero, si agatur de conversione, quae, salvis fundationis legibus, ad internum regimen et disciplinam dumtaxat referatur.

CAN. 613 §1. Domus religiosa canonicorum regularium et monachorum sub proprii Moderatoris regimine et cura sui iuris est, nisi constitutiones aliter ferant.

§2. Moderator domus sui iuris est de iure Superior maior.

CAN. 614 Monasteria monialium cuidam virorum instituto consociata propriam vitae rationem et regimen iuxta constitutiones obtinent. Mutua iura et obligationes ita definiantur ut ex consociatione spirituale bonum proficere possit.

610 §2: c. 496
611, 1°: CD 35: 2; MR 9c, 28, 52
611, 2°: c. 497 §2
611, 3°: cc. 497 §2, 1162 §4
612: c. 497 §4
613 §1: c. 488, 8°; SpC VI §1, 1° et §2, 1°

613 §2: c. 488, 8°; SpC VI §1, 2°
614: cc. 500 §2, 506 §2, 525, 527, 529, 533 §1, 1°, 534 §1, 549, 580 §3, 603 §2, 611, 645 §2, 647 §1, 652 §2, 1338 §2; SpC VI §2, 2°, et 3°; §3; CI Resp. I, II, IV, 24 nov. 1920 (AAS 12 [1920] 574–575)

CAN. 615 An autonomous monastery which does not have another major superior besides its own moderator and is not associated to another institute of religious in such a way that the superior of the latter possesses true power over such a monastery as determined by the constitutions is entrusted to the special vigilance of the diocesan bishop according to the norm of law.

CAN. 616 §1. The supreme moderator can suppress a legitimately erected religious house according to the norm of the constitutions, after the diocesan bishop has been consulted. The proper law of the institute is to make provision for the goods of the suppressed house, without prejudice to the intentions of the founders or donors or to legitimately acquired rights.

§2. The suppression of the only house of an institute belongs to the Holy See, to which the decision regarding the goods in that case is also reserved.

§3. To suppress the autonomous house mentioned in can. 613 belongs to the general chapter, unless the constitutions state otherwise.

§4. To suppress an autonomous monastery of nuns belongs to the Apostolic See, with due regard to the prescripts of the constitutions concerning its goods.

CHAPTER II. The Governance of Institutes

ART. 1. *Superiors and Councils*

CAN. 617 Superiors are to fulfill their function and exercise their power according to the norm of universal and proper law.

CAN. 615 Monasterium sui iuris, quod praeter proprium Moderatorem alium Superiorem maiorem non habet, neque alicui religiosorum instituto ita consociatum est ut eiusdem Superior vera potestate constitutionibus determinata in tale monasterium gaudeat, ad normam iuris peculiari vigilantiae Episcopi dioecesani committitur.

CAN. 616 §1. Domus religiosa legitime erecta supprimi potest a supremo Moderatore ad normam constitutionum, consulto Episcopo dioecesano. De bonis domus suppressae provideat ius proprium institutis, salvis fundatorum vel offerentium voluntatibus et iuribus legitime quaesitis.

§2. Suppressio unicae domus instituti ad Sanctam Sedem pertinet, cui etiam reservatur de bonis in casu statuere.

§3. Supprimere domum sui iuris, de qua in can. 613, est capituli generalis, nisi constitutiones aliter ferant.

§4. Monialium monasterium sui iuris supprimere ad Sedem Apostolicam pertinet, servatis ad bona quod attinet praescriptis constitutionum.

CAPUT II. De Institutorum Regimine

ART. 1. *De Superioribus et Consiliis*

CAN. 617 Superiores suum munus adimpleant suamque potestatem exerceant ad normam iuris universalis et proprii.

615: cc. 500 §2, 506 §2, 512 §1, 1°, 525, 534 §1, 535 §1, 549, 580 §3, 603 §1, 615, 645 §2, 647 §1, 652 §2
616 §1: cc. 498, 1501; ES I: 34; AIE 2°
616 §2: cc. 493, 498, 1501; PC 21

616 §3: ES II: 41
616 §4: PC 21; ES II: 41; AIE 2°
617: cc. 501 §1, 502

CAN. 618 Superiors are to exercise their power, received from God through the ministry of the Church, in a spirit of service. Therefore, docile to the will of God in fulfilling their function, they are to govern their subjects as sons or daughters of God and, promoting the voluntary obedience of their subjects with reverence for the human person, they are to listen to them willingly and foster their common endeavor for the good of the institute and the Church, but without prejudice to the authority of superiors to decide and prescribe what must be done.

CAN. 619 Superiors are to devote themselves diligently to their office and together with the members entrusted to them are to strive to build a community of brothers or sisters in Christ, in which God is sought and loved before all things. Therefore, they are to nourish the members regularly with the food of the word of God and are to draw them to the celebration of the sacred liturgy. They are to be an example to them in cultivating virtues and in the observance of the laws and traditions of their own institute; they are to meet the personal needs of the members appropriately, solicitously to care for and visit the sick, to correct the restless, to console the faint of heart, and to be patient toward all.

CAN. 620 Those who govern an entire institute, a province of an institute or part equivalent to a province, or an autonomous house, as well as their vicars, are major superiors. Comparable to these are an abbot primate and a superior of a monastic congregation, who nonetheless do not have all the power which universal law grants to major superiors.

CAN. 618 Superiores in spiritu servitii suam potestatem a Deo per ministerium Ecclesiae receptam exerceant. Voluntati igitur Dei in munere explendo dociles, ipsi subditos regant uti filios Dei, ac promoventes cum reverentia personae humanae illorum voluntariam oboedientiam, libenter eos audiant necnon eorum conspirationem in bonum instituti et Ecclesiae foveant, firma tamen ipsorum auctoritate decernendi et praecipiendi quae agenda sunt.

CAN. 619 Superiores suo officio sedulo incumbant et una cum sodalibus sibi commissis studeant aedificare fraternam in Christo communitatem, in qua Deus ante omnia quaeratur et diligatur. Ipsi igitur nutriant sodales frequenti verbi Dei pabulo eosque adducant ad sacrae liturgiae celebrationem. Eis exemplo sint in virtutibus colendis et in observantia legum et traditionum proprii instituti; eorum necessitatibus personalibus convenienter subveniant, infirmos sollicite curent ac visitent, corripiant inquietos, consolentur pusillanimes, patientes sint erga omnes.

CAN. 620 Superiores maiores sunt, qui totum regunt institutum, vel eius provinciam, vel partem eidem aequiparatam, vel domum sui iuris, itemque eorum vicarii. His accedunt Abbas Primas et Superior congregationis monasticae, qui tamen non habent omnem potestatem, quam ius universale Superioribus maioribus tribuit.

618: LG 43, 45; PC 14; ET 25; MR 13; SFS 3
619: SC 19; LG 44; CD 15, 16; PC 4, 6, 14, 15; DV 25; PO 7; ES II: 16; IOANNES PAULUS PP. II, Ep. Ap.

Sanctorum altrix, 11 iul. 1980, VI (AAS 72 [1980] 788–790)
620: cc. 488, 8°, 501 §3

CAN. 621 A grouping of several houses which constitutes an immediate part of the same institute under the same superior and has been canonically erected by legitimate authority is called a province.

CAN. 622 The supreme moderator holds power over all the provinces, houses, and members of an institute; this power is to be exercised according to proper law. Other superiors possess power within the limits of their function.

CAN. 623 In order for members to be appointed or elected validly to the function of superior, a suitable time is required after perpetual or definitive profession, to be determined by proper law, or if it concerns major superiors, by the constitutions.

CAN. 624 §1. Superiors are to be constituted for a certain and appropriate period of time according to the nature and need of the institute, unless the constitutions determine otherwise for the supreme moderator and for superiors of an autonomous house.

§2. Proper law is to provide suitable norms so that superiors, constituted for a definite time, do not remain too long in offices of governance without interruption.

§3. Nevertheless, they can be removed from office during their function or be transferred to another for reasons established in proper law.

CAN. 625 §1. The supreme moderator of an institute is to be designated by canonical election according to the norm of the constitutions.

§2. The bishop of the principal seat presides at the elections of a superior of the autonomous

CAN. 621 Plurium domorum coniunctio, quae sub eodem Superiore partem immediatam eiusdem instituti constituat et ab auctoritate legitima canonice erecta sit, nomine venit provinciae.

CAN. 622 Supremus Moderator potestatem obtinet in omnes instituti provincias, domos et sodales, exercendam secundum ius proprium; ceteri Superiores ea gaudent intra fines sui muneris.

CAN. 623 Ut sodales ad munus Superioris valide nominentur aut eligantur, requiritur congruum tempus post professionem perpetuam vel definitivam, a iure proprio vel, si agatur de Superioribus maioribus, a constitutionibus determinandum.

CAN. 624 §1. Superiores ad certum et conveniens temporis spatium iuxta naturam et necessitatem instituti constituantur, nisi pro supremo Moderatore et pro Superioribus domus sui iuris constitutiones aliter ferant.

§2. Ius proprium aptis normis provideat, ne Superiores, ad tempus definitum constituti, diutius sine intermissione in regiminis officis versentur.

§3. Possunt tamen durante munere ab officio amoveri vel in aliud transferri ob causas iure proprio statutas.

CAN. 625 §1. Supremus instituti Moderator electione canonica designetur ad normam constitutionum.

§2. Electionibus Superioris monasterii sui iuris, de quo in can. 615, et supremi Modera-

---

621: cc. 488, 6°, 494 §1; AIE 1°
622: c. 502
623: c. 504; AIE 3°
624 §§1 et 2: c. 505; CI Resp. II, 2–3 iun. 1918 (AAS 10 [1918] 344); SCR Resp., 6 mar. 1922 (AAS 14 [1922] 163–164); SCR Decr. *Religionum laicalium,* 31 maii

1966, 8 (AAS 59 [1967] 362–364); CA 19
624 §3: cc. 192 §1, 193
625 §1: c. 507
625 §2: c. 506 §§2 et 4; SCR Resp., 2 iul. 1921 (AAS 13 [1921] 481–482); CI Resp. II, 30 iul. 1934 (AAS 26 [1934] 494)

monastery mentioned in can. 615 and of the supreme moderator of an institute of diocesan right.

§3. Other superiors are to be constituted according to the norm of the constitutions, but in such a way that, if they are elected, they need the confirmation of a competent major superior; if they are appointed by a superior, however, a suitable consultation is to precede.

CAN. 626 Superiors in the conferral of offices and members in elections are to observe the norms of universal and proper law, are to abstain from any abuse or partiality, and are to appoint or elect those whom they know in the Lord to be truly worthy and suitable, having nothing before their eyes but God and the good of the institute. Moreover, in elections they are to avoid any procurement of votes, either directly or indirectly, whether for themselves or for others.

CAN. 627 §1. According to the norm of the constitutions, superiors are to have their own council, whose assistance they must use in carrying out their function.

§2. In addition to the cases prescribed in universal law, proper law is to determine the cases which require consent or counsel to act validly; such consent or counsel must be obtained according to the norm of can. 127.

CAN. 628 §1. The superiors whom the proper law of the institute designates for this function are to visit the houses and members entrusted to them at stated times according to the norms of this same proper law.

§2. It is the right and duty of a diocesan bishop to visit even with respect to religious discipline:

toris instituti iuris dioecesani praeest Episcopus sedis principis.

§3. Ceteri Superiores ad normam constitutionum constituantur; ita tamen ut, si eligantur, confirmatione Superioris maioris competentis indigeant; si vero a Superiore nominentur, apta consultatio praecedat.

CAN. 626 Superiores in collatione officiorum et sodales in electionibus normas iuris universalis et proprii servent, abstineant a quovis abusu et acceptione personarum, et, nihil praeter Deum et bonum instituti prae oculis habentes, nominent aut eligant quos in Domino vere dignos et aptos sciant. Caveant praeterea in electionibus a suffragiorum procuratione sive directe sive indirecte, tam pro seipsis quam pro aliis.

CAN. 627 §1. Ad normam constitutionum, Superiores proprium habeant consilium, cuius opera in munere exercendo utantur oportet.

§2. Praeter casus in iure universali praescriptos, ius proprium determinet casus in quibus consensus vel consilium ad valide agendum requiratur ad normam can. 127 exquirendum.

CAN. 628 §1. Superiores, qui iure proprio instituti ad hoc munus designantur, statis temporibus domos et sodales sibi commissos iuxta normas eiusdem iuris proprii visitent.

§2. Episcopi dioecesani ius et officium est visitare etiam quoad disciplinam religiosam:

625 §3: PC 14; ES II: 18
626: cc. 153 §2, 506 §1, 507 §§1 et 2
627 §1: c. 516 §1; PC 14

627 §2: c. 105
628 §1: c. 511

1° the autonomous monasteries mentioned in can. 615;

2° individual houses of an institute of diocesan right located in his own territory.

§3. Members are to act with trust toward a visitator, to whose legitimate questioning they are bound to respond according to the truth in charity. Moreover, it is not permitted for anyone in any way to divert members from this obligation or otherwise to impede the scope of the visitation.

CAN. 629 Superiors are to reside in their respective houses, and are not to absent themselves from their house except according to the norm of proper law.

CAN. 630 §1. Superiors are to recognize the due freedom of their members regarding the sacrament of penance and direction of conscience, without prejudice, however, to the discipline of the institute.

§2. According to the norm of proper law, superiors are to be concerned that suitable confessors are available to the members, to whom the members can confess frequently.

§3. In monasteries of nuns, in houses of formation, and in more numerous lay communities, there are to be ordinary confessors approved by the local ordinary after consultation with the community; nevertheless, there is no obligation to approach them.

§4. Superiors are not to hear the confessions of subjects unless the members request it on their own initiative.

§5. Members are to approach superiors with

1° monasteria sui iuris de quibus in can. 615;

2° singulas domos instituti iuris dioecesani in proprio territorio sitas.

§3. Sodales fiducialiter agant cum visitatore, cui legitime interroganti respondere tenentur secundum veritatem in caritate; nemini vero fas est quoquo modo sodales ab hac obligatione avertere, aut visitationis scopum aliter impedire.

CAN. 629 In sua quisque domo Superiores commorentur, nec ab eadem discedant, nisi ad normam iuris proprii.

CAN. 630 §1. Superiores sodalibus debitam agnoscant libertatem circa paenitentiae sacramentum et conscientiae moderamen, salva tamen instituti disciplina.

§2. Solliciti sint Superiores ad normam iuris proprii, ut sodalibus idonei confessarii praesto sint, apud quos frequenter confiteri possint.

§3. In monasteriis monialium, in domibus formationis et in communitatibus numerosioribus laicalibus habeantur confessarii ordinarii ab Ordinario loci probati, collatis consiliis cum communitate, nulla tamen facta obligatione ad illos accedendi.

§4. Subditorum confessiones Superiores ne audiant, nisi sponte sua sodales id petant.

§5. Sodales cum fiducia Superiores

628 §2, 1°: c. 512 §1, 1°
628 §2, 2°: c. 512 §1, 2°
628 §3: c. 513 §1, ET 25
629: c. 508
630 §1: cc. 521 §3, 522; CI Resp. III, 20 nov. 1920 (AAS 12 [1920] 575); PC 14; LMR II: 11

630 §2: c. 518 §1; SCRIS Decr. *Dum canonicarum legum,* 8 dec. 1970, 3 (AAS 63 [1971] 318)
630 §3: c. 520 §1; SCRIS Decr. *Dum canonicarum legum,* 8 dec. 1970, 4b, d (AAS 63 [1971] 318)
630 §4: c. 518 §§2 et 3
630 §5: c. 530 §§1 et 2

trust, to whom they can freely and on their own initiative open their minds. Superiors, however, are forbidden to induce the members in any way to make a manifestation of conscience to them.

adeant, quibus animum suum libere ac sponte aperire possunt. Vetantur autem Superiores eos quoquo modo inducere ad conscientiae manifestationem sibi peragendam.

ART. 2. *Chapters*

ART. 2. *De Capitulis*

CAN. 631 §1. The general chapter, which holds supreme authority in the institute according to the norm of the constitutions, is to be composed in such a way that, representing the entire institute, it becomes a true sign of its unity in charity. It is for the general chapter principally: to protect the patrimony of the institute mentioned in can. 578, promote suitable renewal according to that patrimony, elect the supreme moderator, treat affairs of greater importance, and issue norms which all are bound to obey.

CAN. 631 §1. Capitulum generale, quod supremam auctoritatem ad normam constitutionum in instituto obtinet, ita efformetur ut totum institutum repraesentans, verum signum eiusdem unitatis in caritate evadat. Eius praecipue est: patrimonium instituti, de quo in can. 578, tueri et accommodatam renovationem iuxta ipsum promovere, Moderatorem supremum eligere, maiora negotia tractare, necnon normas edicere, quibus omnes parere tenentur.

§2. The constitutions are to define the composition and extent of the power of a chapter; proper law is to determine further the order to be observed in the celebration of the chapter, especially in what pertains to elections and the manner of handling affairs.

§2. Compositio et ambitus potestatis capituli definiantur in constitutionibus; ius proprium ulterius determinet ordinem servandum in celebratione capituli, praesertim quod ad electiones et rerum agendarum rationes attinet.

§3. According to the norms determined in proper law, not only provinces and local communities, but also any member can freely send wishes and suggestions to a general chapter.

§3. Iuxta normas in iure proprio determinatas, non modo provinciae et communitates locales, sed etiam quilibet sodalis optata sua et suggestiones capitulo generali libere mittere potest.

CAN. 632 Proper law is to determine accurately what is to pertain to other chapters of the institute and to other similar assemblies, namely, what pertains to their nature, authority, composition, way of proceeding and time of celebration.

CAN. 632 Ius proprium accurate determinet quae pertineant ad alia instituti capitula et ad alias similes coadunationes, nempe ad eorum naturam, auctoritatem, compositionem, modum procedendi et tempus celebrationis.

631 §1: MG: 568–570; PC 14; ES II: 1–3, 18, 19; SCRIS *Index articulorum pro redigendis Constitutionibus* (1978): «De Capitulo Generali»

    631 §2: PC 4

631 §3: PC 4, 14; ES II: 4

    632: SCRIS *Index articulorum pro redigendis Constitutionibus* (1978): «Modus exercendi auctoritatem in Religionibus»

CAN. 633 §1. Organs of participation or consultation are to fulfill faithfully the function entrusted to them according to the norm of universal and proper law and to express in their own way the concern and participation of all the members for the good of the entire institute or community.

§2. In establishing and using these means of participation and consultation, wise discretion is to be observed and their procedures are to conform to the character and purpose of the institute.

ART. 3. *Temporal Goods and Their Administration*

CAN. 634 §1. As juridic persons by the law itself, institutes, provinces, and houses are capable of acquiring, possessing, administering, and alienating temporal goods unless this capacity is excluded or restricted in the constitutions.

§2. Nevertheless, they are to avoid any appearance of excess, immoderate wealth, and accumulation of goods.

CAN. 635 §1. Since the temporal goods of religious institutes are ecclesiastical, they are governed by the prescripts of Book V, *The Temporal Goods of the Church*, unless other provision is expressly made.

§2. Nevertheless, each institute is to establish suitable norms concerning the use and administration of goods, by which the poverty proper to it is to be fostered, protected, and expressed.

CAN. 636 §1. In each institute and likewise in each province which is governed by a major superior, there is to be a finance officer, distinct

CAN. 633 §1. Organa participationis vel consultationis munus sibi commissum fideliter expleant ad normam iuris universalis et proprii, eademque suo modo curam et participationem omnium sodalium pro bono totius instituti vel communitatis exprimant.

§2. In his mediis participationis et consultationis instituendis et adhibendis sapiens servetur discretio, atque modus eorum agendi indoli et fini instituti sit conformis.

ART. 3. *De Bonis Temporalibus Eorumque Administratione*

CAN. 634 §1. Instituta, provinciae et domus, utpote personae iuridicae ipso iure, capaces sunt acquirendi, possidendi, administrandi et alienandi bona temporalia, nisi haec capacitas in constitutionibus excludatur vel coarctetur.

§2. Vitent tamen quamlibet speciem luxus, immoderati lucri et bonorum cumulationis.

CAN. 635 §1. Bona temporalia institutorum religiosorum, utpote ecclesiastica, reguntur praescriptis Libri V *De bonis Ecclesiae temporalibus*, nisi aliud expresse caveatur.

§2. Quodlibet tamen institutum aptas normas statuat de usu et administratione bonorum, quibus paupertas sibi propria foveatur, defendatur et exprimatur.

CAN. 636 §1. In quolibet instituto et similiter in qualibet provincia quae a Superiore maiore regitur, habeatur oeconomus, a

633 §1: PC 14; ES II: 18
633 §2: ES II: 4, 12, 13
634 §1: cc. 531, 1495 §2; PC 13
634 §2: PC 13; PO 17

635 §1: c. 1497 §1
635 §2: c. 532 §1; PC 13; ES II: 23
636 §1: c. 516 §§2 et 3

from the major superior and constituted according to the norm of proper law, who is to manage the administration of goods under the direction of the respective superior. Insofar as possible, a finance officer distinct from the local superior is to be designated even in local communities.

§2. At the time and in the manner established by proper law, finance officers and other administrators are to render an account of their administration to the competent authority.

CAN. 637 The autonomous monasteries mentioned in can. 615 must render an account of their administration to the local ordinary once a year. Moreover, the local ordinary has the right to be informed about the financial reports of a religious house of diocesan right.

CAN. 638 §1. Within the scope of universal law, it belongs to proper law to determine acts which exceed the limit and manner of ordinary administration and to establish what is necessary to place an act of extraordinary administration validly.

§2. In addition to superiors, the officials who are designated for this in proper law also validly incur expenses and perform juridic acts of ordinary administration within the limits of their function.

§3. For the validity of alienation and of any other affair in which the patrimonial condition of a juridic person can worsen, the written permission of the competent superior with the consent of the council is required. Nevertheless, if it concerns an affair which exceeds the amount defined by the Holy See for each region, or things given to the Church by vow, or

Superiore maiore distinctus et ad normam iuris proprii constitutus, qui administrationem bonorum gerat sub directione respectivi Superioris. Etiam in communitatibus localibus instituatur, quantum fieri potest, oeconomus a Superiore locali distinctus.

§2. Tempore et modo iure proprio statutis, oeconomi et alii administratores auctoritati competenti peractae administrationis rationem reddant.

CAN. 637 Monasteria sui iuris, de quibus in can. 615, Ordinario loci rationem administrationis reddere debent semel in anno; loci Ordinario insuper ius esto cognoscendi de rationibus oeconomicis domus religiosae iuris dioecesani.

CAN. 638 §1. Ad ius proprium pertinet, intra ambitum iuris universalis, determinare actus qui finem et modum ordinariae administrationis excedant, atque ea statuere quae ad valide ponendum actum extraordinariae administrationis necessaria sunt.

§2. Expensas et actus iuridicos ordinariae administrationis valide, praeter Superiores, faciunt, intra fines sui muneris, officiales quoque, qui in iure proprio ad hoc designantur.

§3. Ad validitatem alienationis et cuiuslibet negotii in quo condicio patrimonialis personae iuridicae peior fieri potest, requiritur licentia in scripto data Superioris competentis cum consensu sui consilii. Si tamen agatur de negotio quod summam a Sancta Sede pro cuiusque regione definitam superet, itemque de rebus ex voto Ecclesiae donatis aut de re-

---

636 §2: cc. 516 §2, 1523, 5°
637: cc. 535 §1, 1°, 535 §3, 1°, 1519 §1
638 §1: c. 1527 §1
638 §2: c. 532 §2
638 §3: cc. 534 §1, 1533; SCConc Resol., 12 iul. 1919

(AAS 11 [1919] 416–419); PM 32; CA 9; SCR Decr. *Religionum laicalium*, 31 maii 1966, n. 2 (AAS 59 [1967] 362); SCpC Litt. circ., 11 apr. 1971 (AAS 63 [1971] 315–317)

things precious for artistic or historical reasons, the permission of the Holy See itself is also required.

§4. For the autonomous monasteries mentioned in can. 615 and for institutes of diocesan right, it is also necessary to have the written consent of the local ordinary.

CAN. 639 §1. If a juridic person has contracted debts and obligations even with the permission of the superiors, it is bound to answer for them.

§2. If a member has entered into a contract concerning his or her own goods with the permission of the superior, the member must answer for it, but if the business of the institute was conducted by mandate of the superior, the institute must answer.

§3. If a religious has entered into a contract without any permission of superiors, he or she must answer, but not the juridic person.

§4. It is a fixed rule, however, that an action can always be brought against one who has profited from the contract entered into.

§5. Religious superiors are to take care that they do not permit debts to be contracted unless it is certain that the interest on the debt can be paid off from ordinary income and that the capital sum can be paid off through legitimate amortization within a period that is not too long.

CAN. 640 Taking into account local conditions, institutes are to strive to give, as it were, a collective witness of charity and poverty and are to contribute according to their ability something from their own goods to provide for the needs of the Church and the support of the poor.

bus pretiosis artis vel historiae causa, requiritur insuper ipsius Sanctae Sedis licentia.

§4. Pro monasteriis sui iuris, de quibus in can. 615, et institutis iuris dioecesani accedat necesse est consensus Ordinarii loci in scriptis praestitus.

CAN. 639 §1. Si persona iuridica debita et obligationes contraxerit etiam cum Superiorum licentia, ipsa tenetur de eisdem respondere.

§2. Si sodalis cum licentia Superioris contraxerit de suis bonis, ipse respondere debet, si vero de mandato Superioris negotium instituti gesserit, institutum respondere debet.

§3. Si contraxerit religiosus sine ulla Superiorum licentia, ipse respondere debet, non autem persona iuridica.

§4. Firmum tamen esto, contra eum, in cuius rem aliquid ex inito contractu versum est, semper posse actionem institui.

§5. Caveant Superiores religiosi ne debita contrahenda permittant, nisi certo constet ex consuetis reditibus posse debiti foenus solvi et intra tempus non nimis longum per legitimam amortizationem reddi summam capitalem.

CAN. 640 Instituta, ratione habita singulorum locorum, testimonium caritatis et paupertatis quasi collectivum reddere satagant et pro viribus ex propriis bonis aliquid conferant ad Ecclesiae necessitatibus et egenorum sustentationi subveniendum.

638 §4: cc. 533 §1, 1°, 534 §1
639 §1: c. 536 §1
639 §2: c. 536 §2
639 §3: c. 536 §3

639 §4: c. 536 §4
639 §5: c. 536 §5
640: c. 537; PC 13; PO 17

CHAPTER III. The Admission of Candidates and the Formation of Members

ART. 1. *Admission to the Novitiate*

CAN. 641 The right to admit candidates to the novitiate belongs to major superiors according to the norm of proper law.

CAN. 642 With vigilant care, superiors are only to admit those who, besides the required age, have the health, suitable character, and sufficient qualities of maturity to embrace the proper life of the institute. This health, character, and maturity are to be verified even by using experts, if necessary, without prejudice to the prescript of can. 220.

CAN. 643 §1. The following are admitted to the novitiate invalidly:

1° one who has not yet completed seventeen years of age;

2° a spouse, while the marriage continues to exist;

3° one who is currently bound by a sacred bond to some institute of consecrated life or is incorporated in some society of apostolic life, without prejudice to the prescript of can. 684;

4° one who enters the institute induced by force, grave fear, or malice, or the one whom a superior, induced in the same way, has received;

5° one who has concealed his or her incorporation in some institute of consecrated life or in some society of apostolic life.

§2. Proper law can establish other impediments even for validity of admission or can attach conditions.

CAPUT III. De Candidatorum Admissione et de Sodalium Institutione

ART. 1. *De Admissione In Novitiatum*

CAN. 641 Ius candidatos admittendi ad novitiatum pertinet ad Superiores maiores ad normam iuris proprii.

CAN. 642 Superiores vigilanti cura eos tantum admittant qui, praeter aetatem requisitam, habeant valetudinem, aptam indolem et sufficientes maturitatis qualitates ad vitam instituti propriam amplectendam; quae valetudo, indoles et maturitas comprobentur adhibitis etiam, si opus fuerit, peritis, firmo praescripto can. 220.

CAN. 643 §1. Invalide ad novitiatum admittitur:

1° qui decimum septimum aetatis annum nondum compleverit;

2° coniux, durante matrimonio;

3° qui sacro vinculo cum aliquo instituto vitae consecratae actu obstringitur vel in aliqua societate vitae apostolicae incorporatus est, salvo praescripto can. 684;

4° qui institutum ingreditur vi, metu gravi aut dolo inductus, vel is quem Superior eodem modo inductus recipit;

5° qui celaverit suam incorporationem in aliquo instituto vitae consecratae aut in aliqua societate vitae apostolicae.

§2. Ius proprium potest alia impedimenta etiam ad validitatem admissionis constituere vel condiciones apponere.

641: c. 543

642: SCSO Notif., *Nimia facilitate,* 1956; Ssap II, III; SCong 31, 33, 34; SCR Instr. *Religiosorum institutio,* 2 feb. 1961, nn. 14–17, 31; SCSO Monitum *Cum compertum,* 15 iul. 1961, 4, (AAS 53 [1961] 571); PC 12; OT 11; RC 11: II–III, 12, 14; RFS 11, 39; PAULUS PP. VI, Enc. *Sacerdotalis caelibatus,* 24 iun. 1967, 63, 65, 71

(AAS 59 [1967] 682, 683, 685, 686); RH 21

643 §1, 1°: c. 542, 1°; RC 4
643 §1, 2°: c. 542, 1°
643 §1, 3°: c. 542, 1°
643 §1, 4°: c. 542, 1°
643 §1, 5°: c. 542, 1°
643 §2: c. 542

CAN. 644 Superiors are not to admit to the novitiate secular clerics without consulting their proper ordinary nor those who, burdened by debts, cannot repay them.

CAN. 645 §1. Before candidates are admitted to the novitiate, they must show proof of baptism, confirmation, and free status.

§2. If it concerns the admission of clerics or those who had been admitted in another institute of consecrated life, in a society of apostolic life, or in a seminary, there is additionally required the testimony of, respectively, the local ordinary, the major superior of the institute or society, or the rector of the seminary.

§3. Proper law can require other proof about the requisite suitability of candidates and freedom from impediments.

§4. Superiors can also seek other information, even under secrecy, if it seems necessary to them.

ART. 2. *The Novitiate and Formation of Novices*

CAN. 646 The novitiate, through which life in an institute is begun, is arranged so that the novices better understand their divine vocation, and indeed one which is proper to the institute, experience the manner of living of the institute, and form their mind and heart in its spirit, and so that their intention and suitability are tested.

CAN. 647 §1. The erection, transfer, and suppression of a novitiate house are to be done

CAN. 644 Superiores ad novitiatum ne admittant clericos saeculares inconsulto proprio ipsorum Ordinario, nec aere alieno gravatos qui ad solvendum pares non sint.

CAN. 645 §1. Candidati, antequam ad novitiatum admittantur, testimonium baptismatis et confirmationis necnon status liberi exhibere debent.

§2. Si agatur de admittendis clericis iisve qui in aliud institutum vitae consecratae, in societatem vitae apostolicae vel in seminarium admissi fuerint, requiritur insuper testimonium respective Ordinarii loci vel Superioris maioris instituti, vel societatis, vel rectoris seminarii.

§3. Ius proprium exigere potest alia testimonia de requisita idoneitate candidatorum et de immunitate ab impedimentis.

§4. Superiores alias quoque informationes, etiam sub secreto, petere possunt, si ipsis necessarium visum fuerit.

ART. 2. *De Novitiatu et Novitiorum Institutione*

CAN. 646 Novitiatus, quo vita in instituto incipitur, ad hoc ordinatur, ut novitii vocationem divinam, et quidem instituti propriam, melius agnoscant, vivendi modum instituti experiantur eiusque spiritu mentem et cor informent, atque ipsorum propositum et idoneitas comprobentur.

CAN. 647 §1. Domus novitiatus erectio, translatio et suppressio fiant per decretum

---

644: c. 542, 2°
645 §1: c. 544 §1
645 §2: c. 544 §§3 et 4; SCR-SCSSU Decr.*Consiliis initis*, 25 iul. 1941 (AAS 33 [1941] 371); SCR Instr. *Religiosorum institutio*, 2 feb. 1961, 45
645 §3: cc. 542, 544 §6

645 §4: cc. 544 §6, 545 §4; SCR Instr. *Quantum Religiones*, 1 dec. 1931, 6 (AAS 24 [1932] 76); RFS 41
646: c. 565 §1; SCRIS Decr. *Sacra Congregatio*, 7 iul. 1956, 6 §1; ES II: 33; RC 4, 5, 13: I–II
647 §1: CA 18; SCRIS Decr. *Religionum laicalium*, 31 maii 1966, 7 (AAS 59 [1967] 363); RC 16: I

through written decree of the supreme moderator of the institute with the consent of the council.

§2. To be valid, a novitiate must be made in a house properly designated for this purpose. In particular cases and as an exception, by grant of the supreme moderator with the consent of the council, a candidate can make the novitiate in another house of the institute under the direction of some approved religious who acts in the place of the director of novices.

§3. A major superior can permit a group of novices to reside for a certain period of time in another house of the institute designated by the superior.

CAN. 648 §1. To be valid, a novitiate must include twelve months spent in the community itself of the novitiate, without prejudice to the prescript of can. 647, §3.

§2. To complete the formation of novices, in addition to the period mentioned in §1, the constitutions can establish one or more periods of apostolic exercises to be spent outside the community of the novitiate.

§3. The novitiate is not to last longer than two years.

CAN. 649 §1. Without prejudice to the prescripts of can. 647, §3 and can. 648, §2, an absence from the novitiate house which lasts more than three months, either continuous or interrupted, renders the novitiate invalid. An absence which lasts more than fifteen days must be made up.

§2. With the permission of the competent major superior, first profession can be anticipated, but not by more than fifteen days.

scripto datum supremi Moderatoris instituti de consensu sui consilii.

§2. Novitiatus, ut validus sit, peragi debet in domo ad hoc rite designata. In casibus particularibus et ad modum exceptionis, ex concessione Moderatoris supremi de consensu sui consilii, candidatus novitiatum peragere potest in alia instituti domo, sub moderamine alicuius probati religiosi, qui vices magistri novitiorum gerat.

§3. Superior maior permittere potest ut novitiorum coetus, per certa temporis spatia, in alia instituti domo, a se designata, commoretur.

CAN. 648 §1. Novitiatus, ut validus sit, duodecim menses in ipsa novitiatus communitate peragendos complecti debet, firmo praescripto can. 647, §3.

§2. Ad novitiorum institutionem perficiendam, constitutiones, praeter tempus de quo in §1, unum vel plura exercitationis apostolicae tempora extra novitiatus communitatem peragenda statuere possunt.

§3. Novitiatus ultra biennium ne extendatur.

CAN. 649 §1. Salvis praescriptis can. 647, §3 et can. 648, §2, absentia a domo novitiatus quae tres menses, sive continuos sive intermissos, superet, novitiatum invalidum reddit. Absentia quae quindecim dies superet, suppleri debet.

§2. De venia competentis Superioris maioris, prima professio anticipari potest, non ultra quindecim dies.

647 §2: c. 555 §1, 3°; RC 15, 16: I; 19
647 §3: c. 556 §4; RC 16: II
648 §1: c. 555 §1, 2°; RC 15: II; 21
648 §2: RC 23: I; 24: I–II; 25 I; 31: I–II

648 §3: RC 24: I
649 §1: c. 556 §§1 et 2; RC 22: I–II
649 §2: cc. 555 §1, 2°, 572 §1, 3°; RC 26

CAN. 650 §1. The scope of the novitiate demands that novices be formed under the guidance of a director according to the program of formation defined in proper law.

§2. Governance of the novices is reserved to one director under the authority of the major superiors.

CAN. 651 §1. The director of novices is to be a member of the institute who has professed perpetual vows and has been legitimately designated.

§2. If necessary, the director can be given assistants who are subject to the director in regard to the supervision of the novices and the program of formation.

§3. Members who are carefully prepared and who, not impeded by other duties, can carry out this function fruitfully and in a stable manner are to be placed in charge of the formation of novices.

CAN. 652 §1. It is for the director and assistants to discern and test the vocation of the novices and to form them gradually to lead correctly the life of perfection proper to the institute.

§2. Novices are to be led to cultivate human and Christian virtues; through prayer and self-denial they are to be introduced to a fuller way of perfection; they are to be taught to contemplate the mystery of salvation and to read and meditate on the sacred scriptures; they are to be prepared to cultivate the worship of God in the sacred liturgy; they are to learn a manner of leading a life consecrated to God and humanity in Christ through the evangelical counsels;

CAN. 650 §1. Scopus novitiatus exigit ut novitii sub directione magistri efformentur iuxta rationem institutionis iure proprio definiendam.

§2. Regimen novitiorum, sub auctoritate Superiorum maiorum, uni magistro reservatur.

CAN. 651 §1. Novitiorum magister sit sodalis instituti qui vota perpetua professus sit et legitime designatus.

§2. Magistro, si opus fuerit, cooperatores dari possunt, qui ei subsint quoad moderamen novitiatus et institutionis rationem.

§3. Novitiorum institutioni praeficiantur sodales sedulo praeparati qui, aliis oneribus non impediti, munus suum fructuose et stabili modo absolvere possint.

CAN. 652 §1. Magistri eiusque cooperatorum est novitiorum vocationem discernere et comprobare, eosque gradatim ad vitam perfectionis instituti propriam rite ducendam efformare.

§2. Novitii ad virtutes humanas et christianas excolendas adducantur; per orationem et sui abnegationem in pleniorem perfectionis viam introducantur; ad mysterium salutis contemplandum et sacras Scripturas legendas et meditandas instruantur; ad Dei cultum in sacra liturgia excolendum praeparentur; rationem addiscant vitam ducendi Deo hominibusque in Christo per consilia evangelica consecratam; de instituti indole et spiritu,

650 §1: cc. 559 §1, 561 §1, 565 §1; RC 30, 31: I
650 §2: c. 561 §§1 et 2; RC 30
651 §1: cc. 559 §1, 560; AIE 3°
651 §2: c. 559 §2; RC 30
651 §3: cc. 554 §3, 559 §3; Ssap III; SCong 24; 25 §4; 26 §2; 28, 7°; SCR Instr. *Religiosorum institutio*, 2 feb.

1961, 33, 2; PC 18d; OT 5; RFS 30, 31, 37
652 §1: cc. 562, 565 §1; RC 13, 15: II–III; RFS 40; LMR II: 11
652 §2: cc. 561 §1, 562, 565 §1; SCR Instr. *Plures exstant*, 3 nov. 1921, I (AAS 13 [1921] 539); Ssap III; PC 6; OT 8–11; RC 15: II–IV; 31: II; RFS 48–55; SFS

they are to be instructed regarding the character and spirit, the purpose and discipline, the history and life of the institute; and they are to be imbued with love for the Church and its sacred pastors.

§3. Conscious of their own responsibility, the novices are to collaborate actively with their director in such a way that they faithfully respond to the grace of a divine vocation.

§4. Members of the institute are to take care that they cooperate for their part in the work of formation of the novices through example of life and prayer.

§5. The time of the novitiate mentioned in can. 648, §1 is to be devoted solely to the task of formation and consequently novices are not to be occupied with studies and functions which do not directly serve this formation.

CAN. 653   §1. A novice can freely leave an institute; moreover, the competent authority of the institute can dismiss a novice.

§2. At the end of the novitiate, if judged suitable, a novice is to be admitted to temporary profession; otherwise the novice is to be dismissed. If there is doubt about the suitability of a novice, the major superior can extend the time of probation according to the norm of proper law, but not beyond six months.

ART. 3. Religious Profession

CAN. 654   By religious profession, members assume the observance of the three evangelical counsels by public vow, are consecrated to God through the ministry of the Church, and are incorporated into the institute with the rights and duties defined by law.

fine et disciplina, historia et vita edoceantur atque amore erga Ecclesiam eiusque sacros Pastores imbuantur.

§3. Novitii, propriae responsabilitatis conscii, ita cum magistro suo active collaborent ut gratiae divinae vocationis fideliter respondeant.

§4. Curent instituti sodales, ut in opere institutionis novitiorum pro parte sua cooperentur vitae exemplo et oratione.

§5. Tempus novitiatus, de quo in can. 648, §1, in opus formationis proprie impendatur, ideoque novitii ne occupentur in studiis et muniis, quae huic formationi non directe inserviunt.

CAN. 653   §1. Novitius institutum libere deserere potest; competens autem instituti auctoritas potest eum dimittere.

§2. Exacto novitiatu, si idoneus iudicetur, novitius ad professionem temporariam admittatur, secus dimittatur; si dubium supersit de eius idoneitate, potest probationis tempus a Superiore maiore ad normam iuris proprii, non tamen ultra sex menses prorogari.

ART. 3. *De Professione Religiosa*

CAN. 654   Professione religiosa sodales tria consilia evangelica observanda voto publico assumunt, Deo per Ecclesiae ministerium consecrantur et instituto incorporantur cum iuribus et officiis iure definitis.

652 §3: SCR Instr. *Religiosorum institutio,* 2 feb. 1961, 20; RC 32: I–II; RFS 39, 40

652 §4: c. 544 §3; PC 24; OT 2; RC 5, 35e; MR 18

652 §5: c. 565 §3; SCR Instr. *Plures exstant,* 3 nov. 1921, II (AAS 13 [1921] 539); SCong 36 §1, 2°; RC 29, 30

653 §1: c. 571 §1

653 §2: c. 571 §2; SCR Decl., 30 dec. 1922 (AAS 15 [1923] 156–158)

654: cc. 487, 488, 1°; LG 44, 45; RC 7, 34, 36

CAN. 655 Temporary profession is to be made for a period defined in proper law; it is not to be less than three years nor longer than six.

CAN. 656 For the validity of temporary profession it is required that:

1° the person who is to make it has completed at least eighteen years of age;

2° the novitiate has been validly completed;

3° admission has been given freely by the competent superior with the vote of the council according to the norm of law;

4° the profession is expressed and made without force, grave fear, or malice;

5° the profession is received by a legitimate superior personally or through another.

CAN. 657 §1. When the period for which profession was made has elapsed, a religious who freely petitions and is judged suitable is to be admitted to renewal of profession or to perpetual profession; otherwise, the religious is to depart.

§2. If it seems opportune, however, the competent superior can extend the period of temporary profession according to proper law, but in such a way that the total period in which the member is bound by temporary vows does not exceed nine years.

§3. Perpetual profession can be anticipated for a just cause, but not by more than three months.

CAN. 658 In addition to the conditions mentioned in can. 656, nn. 3, 4, and 5 and others imposed by proper law, the following are required for the validity of perpetual profession:

CAN. 655 Professio temporaria ad tempus iure proprio definitum emittatur, quod neque triennio brevius neque sexennio longius sit.

CAN. 656 Ad validitatem professionis temporariae requiritur ut:

1° qui eam emissurus est, decimum saltem octavum aetatis annum compleverit;

2° novitiatus valide peractus sit;

3° habeatur admissio a competenti Superiore cum voto sui consilii ad normam iuris libere facta;

4° sit expressa et absque vi, metu gravi aut dolo emissa;

5° a legitimo Superiore per se vel per alium recipiatur.

CAN. 657 §1. Expleto tempore ad quod professio emissa fuerit, religiosus, qui sponte petat et idoneus iudicetur, ad renovationem professionis vel ad professionem perpetuam admittatur, secus discedat.

§2. Si opportunum vero videatur, periodus professionis temporariae a competenti Superiore, iuxta ius proprium, prorogari potest, ita tamen ut totum tempus, quo sodalis votis temporariis abstringitur, non superet novennium.

§3. Professio perpetua anticipari potest ex iusta causa, non tamen ultra trimestre.

CAN. 658 Praeter condiciones de quibus in can. 656, nn. 3, 4 et 5 aliasque iure proprio appositas, ad validitatem professionis perpetuae requiritur:

655: c. 574 §§1 et 2; SCR Resp., 15 iul. 1919 (AAS 11 [1919] 321–322); CI Resp. I, 1 mar. 1921 (AAS 13 [1921] 177); RC 37, I

656, 1°: c. 572 §1, 1°; RC 4
656, 2°: c. 572 §1, 3°
656, 3°: cc. 543, 572 §1, 2°, 575 §2

656, 4°: c. 572 §1, 4°, 5°
656, 5°: c. 572 §1, 6°; CI Resp. III, 1 mar. 1921 (AAS 13 [1921] 178)
657 §1: cc. 575 §1, 577 §1
657 §2: c. 574 §2; RC 37, I
657 §3: cc. 555 §1, 2°, 572 §1, 3°, 577 §2; RC 26

1° the completion of at least twenty-one years of age;

2° previous temporary profession of at least three years, without prejudice to the prescript of can. 657, §3.

ART. 4. *The Formation of Religious*

CAN. **659** §1. In individual institutes the formation of all the members is to be continued after first profession so that they lead the proper life of the institute more fully and carry out its mission more suitably.

§2. Therefore, proper law must define the program of this formation and its duration, attentive to the needs of the Church and the conditions of people and times, insofar as the purpose and character of the institute require it.

§3. Universal law and the program of studies proper to the institute govern the formation of members who are preparing to receive holy orders.

CAN. **660** §1. Formation is to be systematic, adapted to the capacity of the members, spiritual and apostolic, doctrinal and at the same time practical. Suitable degrees, both ecclesiastical and civil, are also to be obtained when appropriate.

§2. During the time of this formation, offices and tasks which may impede it are not to be entrusted to the members.

CAN. **661** Through their entire life, religious are to continue diligently their spiritual, doctrinal, and practical formation. Superiors,

ART. 4. *De Religiosorum Institutione*

CAN. **659** §1. In singulis institutis, post primam professionem omnium sodalium institutio perficiatur ad vitam instituti propriam plenius ducendam et ad eius missionem aptius prosequendam.

§2. Quapropter ius proprium rationem definire debet huius institutionis eiusdemque durationis, attentis Ecclesiae necessitatibus atque hominum temporumque condicionibus, prout a fine et indole instituti exigitur.

§3. Institutio sodalium, qui ad sacros ordines suscipiendos praeparantur, iure universali regitur et propria instituti ratione studiorum.

CAN. **660** §1. Institutio sit systematica, captui sodalium accommodata, spiritualis et apostolica, doctrinalis simul ac practica, titulis etiam congruentibus, tam ecclesiasticis quam civilibus, pro opportunitate obtentis.

§2. Perdurante tempore huius institutionis, sodalibus officia et opera ne committantur, quae eam impediant.

CAN. **661** Per totam vitam religiosi formationem suam spiritualem, doctrinalem et practicam sedulo prosequantur; Superiores

658, 1°: c. 573

658, 2°: cc. 572 §2, 574 §1; SCR Resp., 15 iul. 1919 (AAS 11 [1919] 321–322); CI Resp. I, 1 mar. 1921 (AAS 13 [1921] 177)

659 §1: SCong 8 §2; PC 18; OT 22; PO 19; ES II: 33, 35; RC 4, 10: I; RFS 100

659 §2: PC 18; ES, II, 38; RFS 101

659 §3: cc. 587–591; Ssap IV; SCong 40–46; OT;

ES II: 34, 35; REU 73 §2; 77, 2°; RFS

660 §1: Ssap III, IV; PC 18; ES II: 33, 36; RFS 3; MR 31, 32

660 §2: c. 589 §2; SCong 26 §2; 40 §§ 6 et 7; SCR Instr. *Religiosorum institutio*, 2 feb. 1961, 49; PC 18

661: c. 129; Ssap IV; SCong 50–53; CD 16; PC 18; PO 19; ES II: 19; RFS 100; MR 24–3

moreover, are to provide them with the resources and time for this.

CHAPTER IV. The Obligations and Rights of Institutes and Their Members

CAN. 662 Religious are to have as the supreme rule of life the following of Christ proposed in the gospel and expressed in the constitutions of their own institute.

CAN. 663 §1. The first and foremost duty of all religious is to be the contemplation of divine things and assiduous union with God in prayer.

§2. Members are to make every effort to participate in the eucharistic sacrifice daily, to receive the most sacred Body of Christ, and to adore the Lord himself present in the sacrament.

§3. They are to devote themselves to the reading of sacred scripture and mental prayer, to celebrate worthily the liturgy of the hours according to the prescripts of proper law, without prejudice to the obligation for clerics mentioned in can. 276, §2, n. 3, and to perform other exercises of piety.

§4. With special veneration, they are to honor the Virgin Mother of God, the example and protector of all consecrated life, also through the marian rosary.

§5. They are to observe faithfully an annual period of sacred retreat.

CAN. 664 Religious are to strive after con-

autem eis adiumenta et tempus ad hoc procurent.

CAPUT IV. De Institutorum Eorumque Sodalium Obligationibus et Iuribus

CAN. 662 Religiosi sequelam Christi in Evangelio propositam et in constitutionibus proprii instituti expressam tamquam supremam vitae regulam habeant.

CAN. 663 §1. Rerum divinarum contemplatio et assidua cum Deo in oratione unio omnium religiosorum primum et praecipuum sit officium.

§2. Sodales cotidie pro viribus Sacrificium eucharisticum participent, sanctissimum Corpus Christi recipiant et ipsum Dominum in Sacramento praesentem adorent.

§3. Lectioni sacrae Scripturae et orationi mentali vacent, iuxta iuris proprii praescripta liturgiam horarum digne celebrent, firma pro clericis obligatione de qua in can. 276, §2, n. 3, et alia pietatis exercitia peragant.

§4. Speciali cultu Virginem Deiparam, omnis vitae consecratae exemplum et tutamen, etiam per mariale rosarium prosequantur.

§5. Annua sacri recessus tempora fideliter servent.

CAN. 664 In animi erga Deum conver-

662: c. 593; LG 46; PC 1–2a; PO 18; ES II: 16; ET 12

663 §1: CD 33; PC 2, 5, 6; PO 18; RC 5; VS V; ET 42, 43, 45; MR 16, 24; LMR II: 1

663 §2: cc. 125, 2°, 595 §1, 2° et §2, 610 §2; PC 6; PO 18; ET 47, 48; MF 771; LMR II: 9

663 §3: cc. 125, 2°, 595 §1, 2°, 610 §§1 et 3; PC 6; OT 8; DV 25; PO 18; ES II: 21; SCR Rescr., 17 aug. 1967, 1; VS II; ET 42, 43, 45; MR 24; LMR II: 8, 12

663 §4: c. 125, 2°; LG 65; OT 8; PAULUS PP. VI, Adh. Ap. *Signum magnum,* 13 maii 1967, II (AAS 59 [1967] 471); ET 56; PAULUS PP. VI, Adh. Ap. *Marialis cultus,* 2 feb. 1974, 21, 49 (AAS 66 [1974] 132–133, 158–159); LMR II: 13

663 §5: cc. 126, 595 §1, 1°; PO 18; ET 35

664: cc. 125, 1°, 595 §1, 3°; PO 18; Paen. IIIc; SCRIS Decr. *Dum canonicarum legum,* 8 dec. 1970, 3 (AAS 63 [1971] 318); LMR II: 10

version of the soul toward God, to examine their conscience, even daily, and to approach the sacrament of penance frequently.

CAN. 665 §1. Observing common life, religious are to live in their own religious house and are not to be absent from it except with the permission of their superior. If it concerns a lengthy absence from the house, however, the major superior, with the consent of the council and for a just cause, can permit a member to live outside a house of the institute, but not for more than a year, except for the purpose of caring for ill health, of studies, or of exercising an apostolate in the name of the institute.

§2. A member who is absent from a religious house illegitimately with the intention of withdrawing from the power of the superiors is to be sought out solicitously by them and is to be helped to return to and persevere in his or her vocation.

CAN. 666 In the use of means of social communication, necessary discretion is to be observed and those things are to be avoided which are harmful to one's vocation and dangerous to the chastity of a consecrated person.

CAN. 667 §1. In all houses, cloister adapted to the character and mission of the institute is to be observed according to the determinations of proper law, with some part of a religious house always reserved to the members alone.

§2. A stricter discipline of cloister must be observed in monasteries ordered to contemplative life.

§3. Monasteries of nuns which are ordered

sione insistant religiosi, conscientiam etiam cotidie examinent et ad paenitentiae sacramentum frequenter accedant.

CAN. 665 §1. Religiosi in propria domo religiosa habitent vitam communem servantes, nec ab ea discedant nisi de licentia sui Superioris. Si autem agatur de diuturna a domo absentia, Superior maior, de consensu sui consilii atque iusta de causa, sodali concedere potest ut extra domum instituti degere possit, non tamen ultra annum, nisi causa infirmitatis curandae, ratione studiorum aut apostolatus exercendi nomine instituti.

§2. Sodalis, qui e domo religiosa illegitime abest cum animo sese subducendi a potestate Superiorum, sollicite ab eisdem quaeratur et adiuvetur ut redeat et in sua vocatione perseveret.

CAN. 666 In usu mediorum communicationis socialis servetur necessaria discretio atque vitentur quae sunt vocationi propriae nociva et castitati personae consecratae periculosa.

CAN. 667 §1. In omnibus domibus clausura indoli et missioni instituti accommodata servetur secundum determinationes proprii iuris, aliqua parte domus religiosae solis sodalibus semper reservata.

§2. Strictior disciplina clausuram in monasteriis ad vitam contemplativam ordinatis servanda est.

§3. Monasteria monialium, quae integre

665 §1: cc. 594 §1, 606; CA 15; PC 15; SCR Decr. *Religionum laicalium*, 31 maii 1966, 4 (AAS 59 [1967] 362); ES II: 25

665 §2: cc. 616 §1, 644, 645, 2385, 2386, 2389

666: SCS Notif., 10 iul. 1957; SCR Litt. circ., 6 aug. 1957; IM 9, 10; SCS Instr., 15 iul. 1964; PC 12; ES I: 25 §2a, b; CICS Instr. *Communio et progressio*, 21

maii 1971, 64–70 (AAS 63 [1971] 617–620); ET 46; LMR II: 14

667 §1: c. 604 §§1 et 2; SCR Rescr., 17 aug. 1967, 3; ET 46

667 §2: cc. 597–599; PC 16; ES II: 30; VS VII: 1, 2

667 §3: cc. 597 §1, 600–603; CI Resp. III, I mar. 1921 (AAS 13 [1921] 177); SCR Instr. *Nuper edito*, 6 feb.

entirely to contemplative life must observe *papal* cloister, that is, cloister according to the norms given by the Apostolic See. Other monasteries of nuns are to observe a cloister adapted to their proper character and defined in the constitutions.

§4. For a just cause, a diocesan bishop has the faculty of entering the cloister of monasteries of nuns which are in his diocese and, for a grave cause and with the consent of the superior, of permitting others to be admitted to the cloister and the nuns to leave it for a truly necessary period of time.

CAN. 668 §1. Before first profession, members are to cede the administration of their goods to whomever they prefer and, unless the constitutions state otherwise, are to make disposition freely for their use and revenue. Moreover, at least before perpetual profession, they are to make a will which is to be valid also in civil law.

§2. To change these dispositions for a just cause and to place any act regarding temporal goods, they need the permission of the superior competent according to the norm of proper law.

§3. Whatever a religious acquires through personal effort or by reason of the institute, the religious acquires for the institute. Whatever accrues to a religious in any way by reason of pension, subsidy, or insurance is acquired for the institute unless proper law states otherwise.

ad vitam contemplativam ordinantur, clausuram *papalem*, iuxta normas scilicet ab Apostolica Sede datas, observare debent. Cetera monialium monasteria clausuram propriae indoli accommodatam et in constitutionibus definitam servent.

§4. Episcopus dioecesanus facultatem habet ingrediendi, iusta de causa, intra clausuram monasteriorum monialium, quae sita sunt in sua dioecesi, atque permittendi, gravi de causa et assentiente Antistita, ut alii in clauseram admittantur, ac moniales ex ipsa egrediantur ad tempus vere necessarium.

CAN. 668 §1. Sodales ante primam professionem suorum bonorum administrationem cedant cui maluerint et, nisi constitutiones aliud ferant, de eorum usu et usufructu libere disponant. Testamentum autem, quod etiam in iure civili sit validum, saltem ante professionem perpetuam condant.

§2. Ad has dispositiones iusta de causa mutandas et ad quemlibet actum ponendum circa bona temporalia, licentia Superioris competentis ad normam iuris proprii indigent.

§3. Quidquid religiosus propria acquirit industria vel ratione instituti, acquirit instituto. Quae e ratione pensionis, subventionis vel assecurationis quoquo modo obveniunt, instituto acquiruntur, nisi aliud iure proprio statuatur.

1924 (AAS 16 [1924] 96–101); SCR Instr. *Inter cetera,* 25 mar. 1956 (AAS 48 [1956] 512–526); SpC IV; SCR Instr. *Inter praeclara,* 23 nov. 1950. I–XVI (AAS 43 [1951] 37–41); PC 7, 16; ES II: 30–32; VS VII: 1–17

667 §4: cc. 600, 1° et 4°, 601; PM 34; SCRIS Decl., 2 ian. 1970

668 § 1: cc. 569 §§1 et 3, 580 §1; CI Resp. 9, 16 oct. 1919 (AAS 11 [1919] 478); SCR Resp., 26 mar. 1957;

SCR Resp., 1 mar. 1958; AIE 6

668 §2: cc. 580 §3, 583, 2°; CA 17; SCR Decr. *Religionum laicalium,* 31 maii 1966, 6 (AAS 59 [1967] 363); SCRIS Decr. *Cum superiores generales,* 27 nov. 1969 (AAS 61 [1969] 738–739)

668 §3: cc. 580 §§1 et 2, 582, 594 §2; SCR Resp., 16 mar. 1922 (AAS 14 [1922] 196–197); PC 13; ES II: 23; ET 21

§4. A person who must renounce fully his or her goods due to the nature of the institute is to make that renunciation before perpetual profession in a form valid, as far as possible, even in civil law; it is to take effect from the day of profession. A perpetually professed religious who wishes to renounce his or her goods either partially or totally according to the norm of proper law and with the permission of the supreme moderator is to do the same.

§5. A professed religious who has renounced his or her goods fully due to the nature of the institute loses the capacity of acquiring and possessing and therefore invalidly places acts contrary to the vow of poverty. Moreover, whatever accrues to the professed after renunciation belongs to the institute according to the norm of proper law.

CAN. 669 §1. Religious are to wear the habit of the institute, made according to the norm of proper law, as a sign of their consecration and as a witness of poverty.

§2. Clerical religious of an institute which does not have a proper habit are to wear clerical dress according to the norm of can. 284.

CAN. 670 An institute must supply the members with all those things which are necessary to achieve the purpose of their vocation, according to the norm of the constitutions.

CAN. 671 A religious is not to accept functions and offices outside the institute without the permission of a legitimate superior.

CAN. 672 Religious are bound by the pre-

§4. Qui ex instituti natura plene bonis suis renuntiare debet, illam renuntiationem, forma, quantum fieri potest, etiam iure civili valida, ante professionem perpetuam faciat a die emissae professionis valituram. Idem faciat professus a votis perpetuis, qui ad normam iuris proprii bonis suis pro parte vel totaliter de licentia supremi Moderatoris renuntiare velit.

§5. Professus, qui ob instituti naturam plene bonis suis renuntiaverit, capacitatem acquirendi et possidendi amittit, ideoque actus voto paupertatis contrarios invalide ponit. Quae autem et post renuntiationem obveniunt, instituto cedunt ad normam iuris proprii.

CAN. 669 §1. Religiosi habitum instituti deferant, ad normam iuris proprii confectum, in signum suae consecrationis et in testimonium paupertatis.

§2. Religiosi clerici instituti, quod proprium non habet habitum, vestem clericalem ad normam can. 284 assumant.

CAN. 670 Institutum debet sodalibus suppeditare omnia quae ad normam constitutionum necessaria sunt ad suae vocationis finem assequendum.

CAN. 671 Religiosus munera et officia extra proprium institutum ne recipiat absque licentia legitimi Superioris.

Can. 672 Religiosi adstringuntur prae-

668 §4: c. 581; CA 16; ES II: 24; SCR Decr. *Religionum laicalium*, 31 maii 1966, 6 (AAS 59 [1967] 363)
668 §5: cc. 579, 582, 1°
669 §1: c. 596; SCR Notif., 6 feb. 1965; PC 17; SCR Rescr., 17 aug. 1967, 2; SCRIS Normae, 8 iun. 1970; ET 22; SCRIS Notif., 25 feb. 1972; SCRIS Notif., mar. 1974; SCRIS Resp., 5 dec. 1974; SCRIS Notif., 12 nov. 1976; SCGE Litt. circ., 25 ian. 1977; SCRIS Ep., 4 mar.

1977
669 §2: cc. 136 §1, 188, 7°, 2379; SCRIS Notif., 25 feb. 1972; SCRIS Notif., mar. 1974; SCE Litt. circ., 27 ian. 1976; SCRIS Notif. 12 nov. 1976
670: LG 43; PC 18; ET 26
671: CD 35, 2; ET 20, 26
672: c. 592; SCR Resp., 15 iul. 1919 (AAS 11 [1919] 321–323); SCR Litt. circ., 10 feb. 1924; SCR Litt., 29

scripts of cann. 277, 285, 286, 287, and 289, and religious clerics additionally by the prescripts of can. 279, §2; in lay institutes of pontifical right, the proper major superior can grant the permission mentioned in can. 255, §4.

CHAPTER V. The Apostolate of Institutes

CAN. 673 The apostolate of all religious consists first of all in the witness of their consecrated life, which they are bound to foster by prayer and penance.

CAN. 674 Institutes which are entirely ordered to contemplation always hold a distinguished place in the mystical Body of Christ: for they offer an extraordinary sacrifice of praise to God, illumine the people of God with the richest fruits of holiness, move it by their example, and extend it with hidden apostolic fruitfulness. For this reason, members of these institutes cannot be summoned to furnish assistance in the various pastoral ministries however much the need of the active apostolate urges it.

CAN. 675 §1. Apostolic action belongs to the very nature of institutes dedicated to works of the apostolate. Accordingly, the whole life of the members is to be imbued with an apostolic spirit; indeed the whole apostolic action is to be informed by a religious spirit.

§2. Apostolic action is to proceed always from an intimate union with God and is to confirm and foster this union.

§3. Apostolic action, to be exercised in the name and by the mandate of the Church, is to be carried out in the communion of the Church.

scriptis cann. 277, 285, 286, 287 et 289, et religiosi clerici insuper praescriptis can. 279, §2; in institutis laicalibus iuris pontificii, licentia de qua in can. 255, §4, concedi potest a proprio Superiore maiore.

CAPUT V. De Apostolatu Institutorum

CAN. 673 Omnium religiosorum apostolatus primum in eorum vitae consecratae testimonio consistit, quod oratione et paenitentia fovere tenentur.

CAN. 674 Instituta, quae integre ad contemplationem ordinantur in Corpore Christi mystico praeclaram semper partem obtinent: Deo enim eximium laudis sacrificium offerunt, populum Dei uberrimis sanctitatis fructibus collustrant eumque exemplo movent necnon arcana fecunditate apostolica dilatant. Qua de causa, quantumvis actuosi apostolatus urgeat necessitas, sodales horum institutorum advocari nequeunt ut in variis ministeriis pastoralibus operam adiutricem praestent.

CAN. 675 §1. In institutis operibus apostolatus deditis, apostolica actio ad ipsam eorundem naturam pertinet. Proinde, tota vita sodalium spiritu apostolico imbuatur, tota vero actio apostolica spiritu religioso informetur.

§2. Actio apostolica ex intima cum Deo unione semper procedat eandemque confirmet et foveat.

§3. Actio apostolica, nomine et mandato Ecclesiae exercenda, in eius communione peragatur.

apr. 1946; SCR Litt. circ., 2 maii 1951; SCR Decr. *Militare servitium*, 30 iul. 1957 (AAS 49 [1957] 871–874); LMR I

673: LG 42, 44, 46; CD 33; PC 5, 6; AG 11, 12; MR 14; LMR II: 26

674: LG 46; CD 35, 1; PC 7, 9
675 §1: LG 12; PC 8
675 §2: PC 8
675 §3: CD 33–35; PC 8; AA 20d, 23; ES I: 23–40; DCG 129

CAN. 676 Lay institutes, whether of men or of women, participate in the pastoral function of the Church through spiritual and corporal works of mercy and offer the most diverse services to people. Therefore, they are to persevere faithfully in the grace of their vocation.

CAN. 677 §1. Superiors and members are to retain faithfully the mission and works proper to the institute. Nevertheless, attentive to the necessities of times and places, they are to accommodate them prudently, even employing new and opportune means.

§2. Moreover, if they have associations of the Christian faithful joined to them, institutes are to assist them with special care so that they are imbued with the genuine spirit of their family.

CAN. 678 §1. Religious are subject to the power of bishops whom they are bound to follow with devoted submission and reverence in those matters which regard the care of souls, the public exercise of divine worship, and other works of the apostolate.

§2. In exercising an external apostolate, religious are also subject to their proper superiors and must remain faithful to the discipline of the institute. The bishops themselves are not to fail to urge this obligation if the case warrants it.

§3. In organizing the works of the apostolate of religious, diocesan bishops and religious superiors must proceed through mutual consultation.

CAN. 679 When a most grave cause demands it, a diocesan bishop can prohibit a member of a religious institute from residing in the diocese if his or her major superior, after

CAN. 676 Laicalia instituta, tum virorum tum mulierum, per misericordiae opera spiritualia et corporalia munus pastorale Ecclesiae participant hominibusque diversissima praestant servitia; quare in suae vocationis gratia fideliter permaneant.

CAN. 677 §1. Superiores et sodales missionem et opera instituti propria fideliter retineant; ea tamen, attentis temporum et locorum necessitatibus, prudenter accommodent, novis etiam et opportunis mediis adhibitis.

§2. Instituta autem, si quas habeant associationes christifidelium sibi coniunctas, speciali cura adiuvent, ut genuino spiritu suae familiae imbuantur.

CAN. 678 §1. Religiosi subsunt potestati Episcoporum, quos devoto obsequio ac reverentia prosequi tenentur, in iis quae curam animarum, exercitium publicum cultus divini et alia apostolatus opera respiciunt.

§2. In apostolatu externo exercendo religiosi propriis quoque Superioribus subsunt et disciplinae instituti fideles permanere debent; quam obligationem ipsi Episcopi, si casus ferat, urgere ne omittant.

§3. In operibus apostolatus religiosorum ordinandis Episcopi dioecesani et Superiores religiosi collatis consiliis procedant oportet.

CAN. 679 Episcopus dioecesanus, urgente gravissima causa, sodali instituti religiosi prohibere potest quominus in dioecesi commoretur, si eius Superior maior monitus

676: LG 46; PC 10
677 §1: PC 20; ES I: 28
677 §2: cc. 702–706; AA 25; ES I: 35; MR 59
678 §1: cc. 344, 500 §§1 et 2, 512 §2, 2°, 608 §1, 618 §2, 619; MG: 570–571; LG 45; CD 34, 35: 1, 3, 4; PC 6; ES I: 23 §1, 24, 25 §1; 26, 29, 35–36

678 §2: LG 44, 45; CD 35: 2; PC 14; ES I: 25, 26, 29 §1; MR 28; 33–35, 46, 52
678 §3: CD 35: 6, 36; AG 32, 33; ES I: 24, 30, 31, 39 §1; ES II: 43; DPME 207, b, c, e; MR 21, 62–66; LMR II: 23
679: cc. 618 §2, 2°, 619; PM 39

having been informed, has neglected to make provision; moreover, the matter is to be referred immediately to the Holy See.

CAN. 680 Among the various institutes and also between them and the secular clergy, there is to be fostered an ordered cooperation and a coordination under the direction of the diocesan bishop of all the works and apostolic activities, without prejudice to the character and purpose of individual institutes and the laws of the foundation.

CAN. 681 §1. Works which a diocesan bishop entrusts to religious are subject to the authority and direction of the same bishop, without prejudice to the right of religious superiors according to the norm of can. 678, §§2 and 3.

§2. In these cases, the diocesan bishop and the competent superior of the institute are to draw up a written agreement which, among other things, is to define expressly and accurately those things which pertain to the work to be accomplished, the members to be devoted to it, and economic matters.

CAN. 682 §1. If it concerns conferring an ecclesiastical office in a diocese upon some religious, the diocesan bishop appoints the religious, with the competent superior making the presentation, or at least assenting to the appointment.

§2. A religious can be removed from the office entrusted to him or her at the discretion either of the entrusting authority after having informed the religious superior or of the superior after having informed the one entrusting; neither requires the consent of the other.

CAN. 683 §1. At the time of pastoral visi-

prospicere neglexerit, re tamen ad Sanctam Sedem statim delata.

CAN. 680 Inter varia instituta, et etiam inter eadem et clerum saecularem, ordinata foveatur cooperatio necnon, sub moderamine Episcopi dioecesani, omnium operum et actionum apostolicarum coordinatio, salvis indole, fine singulorum institutorum et legibus fundationis.

CAN. 681 §1. Opera quae ab Episcopo dioecesano committuntur religiosis, eiusdem Episcopi auctoritati et directioni subsunt, firmo iure Superiorum religiosorum ad normam can. 678, §§2 et 3.

§2. In his casibus ineatur conventio scripta inter Episcopum dioecesanum et competentem instituti Superiorem, qua, inter alia, expresse et accurate definiantur quae ad opus explendum, ad sodales eidem addicendos et ad res oeconomicas spectent.

CAN. 682 §1. Si de officio ecclesiastico in dioecesi alicui sodali religioso conferendo agatur, ab Episcopo dioecesano religiosus nominatur, praesentante vel saltem assentiente competenti Superiore.

§2. Religiosus ab officio commisso amoveri potest ad nutum sive auctoritatis committentis, monito Superiore religioso, sive Superioris, monito committente, non requisito alterius consensu.

CAN. 683 §1. Ecclesias et oratoria,

680: c. 608 §§1 et 2; SCR Normae, 26 mar. 1956, 4 (AAS 48 [1956] 296); Ssap I; CD 35: 5, 6; AG 33; ES, I, 28; ES II: 43; ES III: 21; MR 36, 37, 59; LMR I: 21, 22

681 §1: cc. 608 §1, 631 §1; AG 32; ES I: 25 §1; 29 §2; 30 §1; 31

681 §2: ES I: 30 §1, 31, 33 §§1 et 2; MR 56 b, 57

682 §1: cc. 455 §1, 456, 529; ES I: 30 §2, 31, 32, 33 §§1 et 2; NM 57c, 58

682 §2: cc. 454 §5, 631 §2; ES I: 32; MR 58

683 §1: cc. 344 §§1 et 2, 512 §2, 2°, 1382; CI Resp., 8 apr. 1924; CD 35: 4; ES I: 25 §1, 38, 39 §2

tation and also in the case of necessity, the diocesan bishop, either personally or through another, can visit churches and oratories which the Christian faithful habitually attend, schools, and other works of religion or charity, whether spiritual or temporal, entrusted to religious, but not schools which are open exclusively to the institute's own students.

§2. If by chance he has discovered abuses and the religious superior has been warned in vain, he himself can make provision on his own authority.

quibus christifideles habitualiter accedunt, scholas aliaque opera religionis vel caritatis sive spiritualis sive temporalis religiosis commissa, Episcopus dioecesanus visitare potest, sive per se sive per alium, tempore visitationis pastoralis et etiam in casu necessitatis; non vero scholas, quae exclusive pateant propriis instituti alumnis.

§2. Quod si forte abusus deprehenderit, frustra Superiore religioso monito, propria auctoritate ipse per se providere potest.

CHAPTER VI. Separation of Members from the Institute

ART. 1. *Transfer to Another Institute*

CAN. 684 §1. A member in perpetual vows cannot transfer from one religious institute to another except by a grant of the supreme moderator of each institute and with the consent of their respective councils.

§2. After completing a probation which is to last at least three years, the member can be admitted to perpetual profession in the new institute. If the member refuses to make this profession or is not admitted to make it by competent superiors, however, the member is to return to the original institute unless an indult of secularization has been obtained.

§3. For a religious to transfer from an autonomous monastery to another of the same institute or federation or confederation, the consent of the major superior of each monastery and of the chapter of the receiving monastery is required and is sufficient, without prejudice to other requirements established by proper law; a new profession is not required.

CAPUT VI. De Separatione Sodalium Ab Instituto

ART. 1. *De Transitu ad Aliud Institutum*

CAN. 684 §1. Sodalis a votis perpetuis nequit a proprio ad aliud institutum religiosum transire, nisi ex concessione supremi Moderatoris utriusque instituti et de consensu sui cuiusque consilii.

§2. Sodalis, post peractam probationem quae ad tres saltem annos protrahenda est, ad professionem perpetuam in novo instituto admitti potest. Si autem sodalis hanc professionem emittere renaut vel ad eam emittendam a competentibus Superioribus non admittatur, ad pristinum institutum redeat, nisi indultum saecularizationis obtinuerit.

§3. Ut religiosus a monasterio sui iuris ad aliud eiusdem instituti vel foederationis aut confoederationis transire possit, requiritur et sufficit consensus Superioris maioris utriusque monasterii et capituli monasterii recipientis, salvis aliis requisitis iure proprio statutis; nova professio non requiritur.

683 §2: cc. 618 §2, 2°, 619; ES I: 25 §1; 38
684 §1: c. 632

684 §2: cc. 633 §§1 et 2, 634
684 §3: cc. 632, 633 §3

§4. Proper law is to determine the time and manner of the probation which must precede the profession of a member in the new institute.

§5. For a transfer to be made to a secular institute or a society of apostolic life or from them to a religious institute, permission of the Holy See is required, whose mandates must be observed.

CAN. 685 §1. Until a person makes profession in the new institute, the rights and obligations which the member had in the former institute are suspended although the vows remain. Nevertheless, from the beginning of probation, the member is bound to the observance of the proper law of the new institute.

§2. Through profession in the new institute, the member is incorporated into it while the preceding vows, rights, and obligations cease.

ART. 2. *Departure from An Institute*

CAN. 686 §1. With the consent of the council, the supreme moderator for a grave cause can grant an indult of exclaustration to a member professed by perpetual vows, but not for more than three years, and if it concerns a cleric, with the prior consent of the ordinary of the place in which he must reside. To extend an indult or to grant it for more than three years is reserved to the Holy See, or to the diocesan bishop if it concerns institutes of diocesan right.

§2. It is only for the Apostolic See to grant an indult of exclaustration for nuns.

§3. At the petition of the supreme moderator with the consent of the council, exclaustration can be imposed by the Holy See on a member

§4. Ius proprium determinet tempus et modum probationis, quae professioni sodalis in novo instituto praemittenda est.

§5. Ut ad institutum saeculare aut ad societatem vitae apostolicae vel ex illis ad institutum religiosum fiat transitus, requiritur licentia Sanctae Sedis, cuius mandatis standum est.

CAN. 685 §1. Usque ad emissionem professionis in novo instituto, manentibus votis, iura et obligationes quae sodalis in priore instituto habebat, suspenduntur; ab incepta tamen probatione, ipse ad observantiam iuris proprii novi instituti tenetur.

§2. Per professionem in novo instituto sodalis eidem incorporatur, cessantibus votis, iuribus et obligationibus praecedentibus.

ART. 2. *De Egressu Ab Instituto*

CAN. 686 §1. Supremus Moderator, de consensu sui consilii, sodali a votis perpetuis professo, gravi de causa concedere potest indultum exclaustrationis, non tamen ultra triennium, praevio consensu Ordinarii loci in quo commorari debet, si agitur de clerico. Indultum prorogare vel illud ultra triennium concedere Sanctae Sedi vel, si de institutis iuris dioecesani agitur, Episcopo dioecesano reservatur.

§2. Pro monialibus indultum exclaustrationis concedere unius Apostolicae Sedis est.

§3. Petente supremo Moderatore de consensu sui consilii, exclaustratio imponi potest a Sancta Sede pro sodale instituti iuris pon-

684 §4: c. 634
684 §5: c. 681
685 §1: c. 633 §1
685 §2: cc. 635, 636

686 §1: c. 638
686 §2: c. 638
686 §3: SCRIS Normae, 19 ian. 1974

of an institute of pontifical right, or by a diocesan bishop on a member of an institute of diocesan right, for grave causes, with equity and charity observed.

tificii vel ab Episcopo dioecesano pro sodale instituti iuris dioecesani, ob graves causas, servata aequitate et caritate.

CAN. 687 An exclaustrated member is considered freed from the obligations which cannot be reconciled with the new condition of his or her life, yet remains dependent upon and under the care of superiors and also of the local ordinary, especially if the member is a cleric. The member can wear the habit of the institute unless the indult determines otherwise. Nevertheless, the member lacks active and passive voice.

CAN. 687 Sodalis exclaustratus exoneratus habetur ab obligationibus, quae cum nova suae vitae condicione componi nequeunt, itemque sub dependentia et cura manet suorum Superiorum et etiam Ordinarii loci, praesertim si de clerico agitur. Habitum instituti deferre potest, nisi aliud indulto statuatur. Voce tamen activa et passiva caret.

CAN. 688 §1. A person who wishes to leave an institute can depart from it when the time of profession has been completed.

§2. During the time of temporary profession, a person who asks to leave the institute for a grave cause can obtain an indult of departure from the supreme moderator with the consent of the council in an institute of pontifical right. In institutes of diocesan right and in the monasteries mentioned in can. 615, however, the bishop of the house of assignment must confirm the indult for it to be valid.

CAN. 688 §1. Qui expleto professionis tempore ab instituto egredi voluerit, illud derelinquere potest.

§2. Qui perdurante professione temporaria, gravi de causa, petit ut institutum derelinquat, indultum discedendi consequi potest in instituto iuris pontificii a supremo Moderatore de consensu sui consilii; in institutis autem iuris dioecesani et in monasteriis, de quibus in can. 615, indultum, ut valeat, confirmari debet ab Episcopo domus assignationis.

CAN. 689 §1. If there are just causes, the competent major superior, after having heard the council, can exclude a member from making a subsequent profession when the period of temporary profession has been completed.

§2. Physical or psychic illness, even contracted after profession, which in the judgment of experts renders the member mentioned in §1 unsuited to lead the life of the institute consti-

CAN. 689 §1. Sodalis, expleta professione temporaria, si iustae causae affuerint, a competenti Superiore maiore, audito suo consilio, a subsequenti professione emittenda excludi potest.

§2. Infirmitas physica vel psychica, etiam post professionem contracta, quae, de iudicio peritorum, sodalem, de quo in §1, reddit ineptum ad vitam in instituto ducendam,

687: c. 639; CI Resp. III, 12 nov. 1922 (AAS 14 [1922] 602)

688 §1: c. 637

688 §2: c. 638; CA 14: SCR Decr. *Religionum laicalium*, 31 maii 1966, I, 3 (AAS 59 [1967] 362–364); SCRIS Decr. *Cum superiores generales*, 27 nov. 1969 (AAS 61 [1969] 738–739)

689 §1: c. 637

689 §2: c. 637; SCRIS Decr. *Dum canonicarum legum*, 8 dec. 1970, 5 (AAS 63 [1971] 319)

tutes a cause for not admitting the member to renew profession or to make perpetual profession, unless the illness had been contracted through the negligence of the institute or through work performed in the institute.

§3. If, however, a religious becomes insane during the period of temporary vows, even though unable to make a new profession, the religious cannot be dismissed from the institute.

CAN. 690 §1. The supreme moderator with the consent of the council can readmit without the burden of repeating the novitiate one who had legitimately left the institute after completing the novitiate or after profession. Moreover, it will be for the same moderator to determine an appropriate probation prior to temporary profession and the time of vows to precede perpetual profession, according to the norm of cann. 655 and 657.

§2. The superior of an autonomous monastery with the consent of the council possesses the same faculty.

CAN. 691 §1. A perpetually professed religious is not to request an indult of departure from an institute except for the gravest of causes considered before the Lord. The religious is to present a petition to the supreme moderator of the institute who is to transmit it along with a personal opinion and the opinion of the council to the competent authority.

§2. In institutes of pontifical right, an indult of this type is reserved to the Apostolic See. In institutes of diocesan right, however, the bishop of the diocese in which the house of assignment is situated can also grant it.

CAN. 692 Unless it has been rejected by the member in the act of notification, an indult

causam constituit eum non admittendi ad professionem renovandam vel ad perpetuam emittendam, nisi ob neglegentiam instituti vel ob laborem in instituto peractum infirmitas contracta fuerit.

§3. Si vero religiosus, perdurantibus votis temporariis, amens evaserit, etsi novam professionem emittere non valeat, ab instituto tamen dimitti non potest.

CAN. 690 §1. Qui, expleto novitiatu vel post professionem, legitime ab instituto egressus fuerit, a Moderatore supremo de consensu sui consilii rursus admitti potest sine onere repetendi novitiatum; eiusdem autem Moderatoris erit determinare congruam probationem praeviam professioni temporariae et tempus votorum ante professionem perpetuam praemittendum, ad normam cann. 655 et 657.

§2. Eadem facultate gaudet Superior monasterii sui iuris cum consensu sui consilii.

CAN. 691 §1. Professus a votis perpetuis indultum discedendi ab instituto ne petat, nisi ob gravissimas causas coram Domino perpensas; petitionem suam deferat supremo instituti Moderatori, qui eam una cum voto suo suique consilii auctoritati competenti transmittat.

§2. Huiusmodi indultum in institutis iuris pontificii Sedi Apostolicae reservatur; in institutis vero iuris dioecesani, id etiam Episcopus dioecesis, in qua domus assignationis sita est, concedere potest.

CAN. 692 Indultum discedendi legitime concessum et sodali notificatum, nisi in actu

689 §3: SCR Resp., 5 feb. 1925 (AAS 17 [1925] 107)   [1939] 321)
690 §1: c. 640 §2; RC 38, I, II   692: c. 640 § 1; CI Resp. III, 1, 12 feb. 1922 (AAS 14
691 §2: c. 638; CI Resp. II, 24 iul. 1939 (AAS 31   [1922] 662)

of departure granted legitimately and made known to the member entails by the law itself dispensation from the vows and from all the obligations arising from profession.

CAN. 693 If a member is a cleric, an indult is not granted before he finds a bishop who incardinates him in the diocese or at least receives him experimentally. If he is received experimentally, he is incardinated into the diocese by the law itself after five years have passed, unless the bishop has refused him.

ART. 3. *Dismissal of Members*

CAN. 694 §1. A member must be held as *ipso facto* dismissed from an institute who:

1° has defected notoriously from the Catholic faith;

2° has contracted marriage or attempted it, even only civilly.

§2. In these cases, after the proofs have been collected, the major superior with the council is to issue without any delay a declaration of fact so that the dismissal is established juridically.

CAN. 695 §1. A member must be dismissed for the delicts mentioned in cann. 1397, 1398, and 1395, unless in the delicts mentioned in can. 1395, §2, the superior decides that dismissal is not completely necessary and that correction of the member, restitution of justice, and reparation of scandal can be resolved sufficiently in another way.

§2. In these cases, after the proofs regarding the facts and imputability have been collected, the major superior is to make known the accusation and proofs to the member to be dis-

notificationis ab ipso sodale reiectum fuerit, ipso iure secumfert dispensationem a votis necnon ab omnibus obligationibus ex professione ortis.

CAN. 693 Si sodalis sit clericus, indultum non conceditur priusquam inveniat Episcopum qui eum in dioecesi incardinet vel saltem ad experimentum recipiat. Si ad experimentum recipiatur, transacto quinquennio, ipso iure dioecesi incardinatur, nisi Episcopus eum recusaverit.

ART. 3. *De Dimissione Sodalium*

CAN. 694 §1. Ipso facto dimissus ab instituto habendus est sodalis qui:

1° a fide catholica notorie defecerit;

2° matrimonium contraxerit vel, etiam civiliter tantum, attentaverit.

§2. His in casibus Superior maior cum suo consilio, nulla mora interposita, collectis probationibus, declarationem facti emittat, ut iuridice constet de dimissione.

CAN. 695 §1. Sodalis dimitti debet ob delicta de quibus in cann. 1397, 1398 et 1395, nisi in delictis, de quibus in can. 1395, §2, Superior censeat dimissionem non esse omnino necessariam et emendationi sodalis atque restitutioni iustitiae et reparationi scandali satis alio modo consuli posse.

§2. Hisce in casibus, Superior maior, collectis probationibus circa facta et imputabilitatem, sodali dimittendo accusationem atque probationes significet, data eidem facultate

693: c. 641; CI Resp. 2, 27 iul. 1942 (AAS 34 [1942] 241); ES I: 3 §5; SA Sententia, 20 maii 1978
694 §1, 1°: c. 646 §1, 1°
694 §1, 2°: c. 646 §1, 3°
694 §2: c. 646 §2; CI Resp. III, 30 iul. 1934 (AAS 26 [1934] 494)
695 §2: cc. 647 §2, 3°, 650 §3; SCRIS Rescr., 25 nov. 1969, 5; 9 §1; 14 §3; SCRIS Decr. *Processus iudicialis*, 2 mar. 1974 (AAS 66 [1974] 215–216); SCRIS Litt. circ., 1975, II, III

missed, giving the member the opportunity for self-defense. All the acts, signed by the major superior and a notary, together with the responses of the member, put in writing and signed by that member, are to be transmitted to the supreme moderator.

CAN. 696 §1. A member can also be dismissed for other causes provided that they are grave, external, imputable, and juridically proven such as: habitual neglect of the obligations of consecrated life; repeated violations of the sacred bonds; stubborn disobedience to the legitimate prescripts of superiors in a grave matter; grave scandal arising from the culpable behavior of the member; stubborn upholding or diffusion of doctrines condemned by the magisterium of the Church; public adherence to ideologies infected by materialism or atheism; the illegitimate absence mentioned in can. 665, §2, lasting six months; other causes of similar gravity which the proper law of the institute may determine.

§2. For the dismissal of a member in temporary vows, even causes of lesser gravity established in proper law are sufficient.

CAN. 697 In the cases mentioned in can. 696, if the major superior, after having heard the council, has decided that a process of dismissal must be begun:

1° the major superior is to collect or complete the proofs;

2° the major superior is to warn the member in writing or before two witnesses with an explicit threat of subsequent dismissal unless the member reforms, with the cause for dismissal clearly indicated and full opportunity for self-defense given to the member; if the warning oc-

sese defendendi. Acta omnia a Superiore maiore et a notario subscripta, una cum responsionibus sodalis scripto redactis et ab ipso sodale subscriptis, supremo Moderatori transmittantur.

CAN. 696 §1. Sodalis dimitti etiam potest ob alias causas, dummodo sint graves, externae, imputabiles et iuridice comprobatae, uti sunt: habitualis neglectus obligationum vitae consecratae; iteratae violationes sacrorum vinculorum; pertinax inoboedientia legitimis praescriptis Superiorum in materia gravi; grave scandalum ex culpabili modo agendi sodalis ortum; pertinax sustentatio vel diffusio doctrinarum ab Ecclesiae magisterio damnatarum; publica adhaesio ideologiis materialismo vel atheismo infectis; illegitima absentia, de qua in can. 665, §2, per semestre protracta; aliae causae similis gravitatis iure proprio instituti forte determinatae.

§2. Ad dimissionem sodalis a votis temporariis, etiam causae minoris gravitatis in iure proprio statutae sufficiunt.

CAN. 697 In casibus de quibus in can. 696, si Superior maior, audito suo consilio, censuerit processum dimissionis esse inchoandum:

1° probationes colligat vel compleat;

2° sodalem scripto vel coram duobus testibus moneat cum explicita comminatione subsecuturae dimissionis nisi resipiscat, clare significata causa dimissionis et data sodali plena facultate sese defendendi; quod si monitio incassum cedat, ad alteram moni-

696 §1: cc. 647 §2, 1° et 3°, 651 §1, 656, 2389
696 §2: cc. 575 §1, 647 §2; CI Resp. I, 2°, 1 mar. 1921 (AAS 13 [1921] 177)

697: cc. 649, 650 §§1 et 3, 654, 656, 660, 661 §3, 663, 664 §2

curs in vain, however, the superior is to proceed to another warning after an intervening space of at least fifteen days;

3° if this warning also occurs in vain and the major superior with the council decides that incorrigibility is sufficiently evident and that the defenses of the member are insufficient, after fifteen days have elapsed from the last warning without effect, the major superior is to transmit to the supreme moderator all the acts, signed personally and by a notary, along with the signed responses of the member.

CAN. 698 In all the cases mentioned in cann. 695 and 696, the right of the member to communicate with and to offer defenses directly to the supreme moderator always remains intact.

CAN. 699 §1. The supreme moderator with the council, which must consist of at least four members for validity, is to proceed collegially to the accurate consideration of the proofs, arguments, and defenses; if it has been decided through secret ballot, the supreme moderator is to issue a decree of dismissal with the reasons in law and in fact expressed at least summarily for validity.

§2. In the autonomous monasteries mentioned in can. 615, it belongs to the diocesan bishop, to whom the superior is to submit the acts examined by the council, to decide on dismissal.

CAN. 700 A decree of dismissal does not have effect unless it has been confirmed by the Holy See, to which the decree and all the acts must be transmitted; if it concerns an institute of diocesan right, confirmation belongs to the

tionem, spatio saltem quindecim dierum interposito, procedat;

3° si haec quoque monitio incassum ceciderit et Superior maior cum suo consilio censuerit de incorrigibilitate satis constare et defensiones sodalis insufficientes esse, post quindecim dies ab ultima monitione frustra elapsos, acta omnia ab ipso Superiore maiore et a notario subscripta una cum responsionibus sodalis ab ipso sodale subscriptis supremo Moderatori transmittat.

CAN. 698 In omnibus casibus, de quibus in cann. 695 et 696, firmum semper manet ius sodalis cum supremo Moderatore communicandi et illi directe suas defensiones exhibendi.

CAN. 699 §1. Supremus Moderator cum suo consilio, quod ad validitatem saltem quattuor membris constare debet, collegialiter procedat ad probationes, argumenta et defensiones accurate perpendenda, et si per secretam suffragationem id decisum fuerit, decretum dimissionis ferat, expressis ad validitatem saltem summarie motivis in iure et in facto.

§2. In monasteriis sui iuris, de quibus in can. 615, dimissionem decernere pertinet ad Episcopum dioecesanum, cui Superior acta a consilio suo recognita submittat.

CAN. 700 Decretum dimissionis vim non habet, nisi a Sancta Sede confirmatum fuerit, cui decretum et acta omnia transmittenda sunt; si agatur de instituto iuris dioecesani, confirmatio spectat ad Episcopum dioe-

698: c. 650 §3
699 §1: cc. 650 §§1 et 2, 2°, 655 §1, 665, 666
699 §2: cc. 647 §1, 652 §2
700: cc. 647 §2, 4°, 650 §2, 2°, 666; SCR Decl., 20

iul. 1923 (AAS 15 [1923] 457–458), SCRIS Decr. *Processus iudicialis*, 2 mar. 1974 (AAS 66 [1974] 215–216); SCRIS Litt. circ., 1975, II, III

bishop of the diocese where the house to which the religious has been attached is situated. To be valid, however, the decree must indicate the right which the dismissed possesses to make recourse to the competent authority within ten days from receiving notification. The recourse has suspensive effect.

CAN. 701 By legitimate dismissal, vows as well as the rights and obligations deriving from profession cease *ipso facto*. Nevertheless, if the member is a cleric, he cannot exercise sacred orders until he finds a bishop who receives him into the diocese after an appropriate probation according to the norm of can. 693 or at least permits him to exercise sacred orders.

CAN. 702 §1. Those who depart from a religious institute legitimately or have been dismissed from it legitimately can request nothing from the institute for any work done in it.

§2. Nevertheless, the institute is to observe equity and the charity of the gospel toward a member who is separated from it.

CAN. 703 In the case of grave external scandal or of most grave imminent harm to the institute, a member can be expelled immediately from a religious house by the major superior or, if there is danger in delay, by the local superior with the consent of the council. If it is necessary, the major superior is to take care to begin a process of dismissal according to the norm of law or is to refer the matter to the Apostolic See.

CAN. 704 In the report referred to in can. 592, §1, which is to be sent to the Apostolic See, mention is to be made of members who have been separated from the institute in any way.

cesis ubi sita est domus, cui religiosus adscriptus est. Decretum vero, ut valeat, indicare debet ius, quo dimissus gaudet, recurrendi intra decem dies a recepta notificatione ad auctoritatem competentem. Recursus effectum habet suspensivum.

CAN. 701 Legitima dimissione ipso facto cessant vota necnon iura et obligationes ex professione promanantia. Si tamen sodalis sit clericus, sacros ordines exercere nequit, donec Episcopum inveniat qui eum post congruam probationem in dioecesi, ad normam can. 693, recipiat vel saltem exercitium sacrorum ordinum permittat.

CAN. 702 §1. Qui ex instituto religioso legitime egrediantur vel ab eo legitime dimissi fuerint, nihil ab eodem repetere possunt ob quamlibet operam in eo praestitam.

§2. Institutum tamen aequitatem et evangelicam caritatem servet erga sodalem, qui ab eo separatur.

CAN. 703 In casu gravis scandali exterioris vel gravissimi nocumenti instituto imminentis, sodalis statim a Superiore maiore vel, si periculum sit in mora, a Superiore locali cum consensu sui consilii e domo religiosa eici potest. Superior maior, si opus sit, dimissionis processum ad normam iuris instituendum curet, aut rem Sedi Apostolicae deferat.

CAN. 704 De sodalibus, qui ab instituto sunt quoquo modo separati, fiat mentio in relatione Sedi Apostolicae mittenda, de qua in can. 592, §1.

701: cc. 641, 648, 672 §2; ES I: 3 §5
702 §1: c. 643 §1
702 §2: c. 643 §2; SCDF Normae, 13 ian. 1971, VI, 5 (AAS 63 [1971] 308); SCRIS Decl., 25 ian. 1974;

SCRIS Litt. circ., 1975, IV
703: cc. 653, 668
704: SCR Normae, 9 dec. 1948, 248–264

CHAPTER VII. **Religious Raised to the Episcopate**

CAN. 705 A religious raised to the episcopate remains a member of his institute but is subject only to the Roman Pontiff by virtue of the vow of obedience and is not bound by obligations which he himself prudently judges cannot be reconciled with his condition.

CAN. 706 The religious mentioned above:

1° if he has lost the right of ownership of goods through profession, has the use, revenue, and administration of goods which accrue to him; a diocesan bishop and the others mentioned in can. 381, §2, however, acquire property on behalf of the particular church; others, on behalf of the institute or the Holy See insofar as the institute is capable or not of possession;

2° if he has not lost the right of ownership of goods through profession, recovers the use, revenue, and administration of the goods which he had; those things which accrue to him afterwards he fully acquires for himself;

3° in either case, however, must dispose of goods according to the intention of the donors when they do not accrue to him personally.

CAN. 707 §1. A retired religious bishop can choose a place of residence even outside the houses of his institute, unless the Apostolic See has provided otherwise.

§2. If he has served some diocese, can. 402, §2 is to be observed with respect to his appropriate and worthy support, unless his own institute wishes to provide such support; otherwise the Apostolic See is to provide in another manner.

CAPUT VII. **De Religiosis ad Episcopatum Evectis**

CAN. 705 Religiosus ad episcopatum evectus instituti sui sodalis remanet, sed vi voti oboedientiae uni Romano Pontifici obnoxius est, et obligationibus non adstringitur, quas ipse prudenter iudicet cum sua condicione componi non posse.

CAN. 706 Religiosus de quo supra:

1° si per professionem dominium bonorum amiserit, bonorum quae ipsi obveniant habet usum, usumfructum et administrationem; proprietatem vero Episcopus dioecesanus aliique, de quibus in can. 381, §2, acquirunt Ecclesiae particulari; ceteri, instituto vel Sanctae Sedi, prout institutum capax est possidendi vel minus;

2° si per professionem dominium bonorum non amiserit, bonorum, quae habebat, recuperat usum, usumfructum et administrationem; quae postea ipsi obveniant, sibi plene acquirit;

3° in utroque autem casu de bonis, quae ipsi obveniant non intuitu personae, disponere debet secundum offerentium voluntatem.

CAN. 707 §1. Religiosus Episcopus emeritus habitationis sedem sibi eligere potest etiam extra domos sui instituti, nisi aliud a Sede Apostolica provisum fuerit.

§2. Quoad eius congruam et dignam sustentationem, si cuidam dioecesi inserviverit, servetur can. 402, §2, nisi institutum proprium talem sustentationem providere voluerit; secus Sedes Apostolica aliter provideat.

705: c. 627 §§1 et 2
706, 1°: c. 628, 1°
706, 2°: c. 628, 2°

706, 3°: c. 628, 3°
707 §1: c. 629
707 §2: ES I: 11

CHAPTER VIII. Conferences of Major Superiors

CAN. 708 Major superiors can be associated usefully in conferences or councils so that by common efforts they work to achieve more fully the purpose of the individual institutes, always without prejudice to their autonomy, character, and proper spirit, or to transact common affairs, or to establish appropriate coordination and cooperation with the conferences of bishops and also with individual bishops.

CAN. 709 Conferences of major superiors are to have their own statutes approved by the Holy See, by which alone they can be erected even as a juridic person and under whose supreme direction they remain.

TITLE III. Secular Institutes

CAN. 710 A secular institute is an institute of consecrated life in which the Christian faithful, living in the world, strive for the perfection of charity and seek to contribute to the sanctification of the world, especially from within.

CAN. 711 The consecration of a member of a secular institute does not change the member's proper canonical condition among the people of God, whether lay or clerical, with due regard for the prescripts of the law which refer to institutes of consecrated life.

CAN. 712 Without prejudice to the pre-

CAPUT VIII. De Conferentiis Superiorum Maiorum

CAN. 708 Superiores maiores utiliter in conferentiis seu consiliis consociari possunt ut, collatis viribus, allaborent sive ad finem singulorum institutorum plenius assequendum, salvis semper eorum autonomia, indole proprioque spiritu, sive ad communia negotia pertractanda, sive ad congruam coordinationem et cooperationem cum Episcoporum conferentiis et etiam cum singulis Episcopis instaurandam.

CAN. 709 Conferentiae Superiorum maiorum sua habeant statuta a Sancta Sede approbata, a qua unice, etiam in personam iuridicam, erigi possunt et sub cuius supremo moderamine manent.

TITULUS III. De Institutis Saecularibus

CAN. 710 Institutum saeculare est institutum vitae consecratae, in quo christifideles in saeculo viventes ad caritatis perfectionem contendunt atque ad mundi sanctificationem praesertim ab intus conferre student.

CAN. 711 Instituti saecularis sodalis vi suae consecrationis propriam in populo Dei canonicam condicionem, sive laicalem sive clericalem, non mutat, servatis iuris praescriptis quae instituta vitae consecratae respiciunt.

CAN. 712 Firmis praescriptis cann.

708: CD 35: 5, 6; PC 22, 23; AG 33; ES II: 42, 43; ES III, 16, 21; MR 61–66; PA 21

709: PC 23; REU 73 §5; MR 61

710: PME I, III §2; PF V; CSan 10; PC 11; PAULUS PP. VI, All., 26 sep. 1970 (AAS 62 [1970] 619, 620, 622, 623)

711: PF II; CSan 7d; LG 36; AA 2; PAULUS PP. VI, All., 26 sep. 1970 (AAS 62 [1970] 619)

712: PME III §§2 et 3; PF II; CSan 7; SCR Resp., 19 maii 1949, I; PC 11; REU 74; PAULUS PP. VI, All., 2 feb. 1972, A et B (AAS 64 [1972] 207, 209, 210)

scripts of cann. 598–601, the constitutions are to establish the sacred bonds by which the evangelical counsels are assumed in the institute and are to define the obligations which these same bonds bring about; the proper secularity of the institute, however, is always to be preserved in its way of life.

CAN. 713 §1. Members of these institutes express and exercise their own consecration in apostolic activity, and like leaven they strive to imbue all things with the spirit of the gospel for the strengthening and growth of the Body of Christ.

§2. In the world and from the world, lay members participate in the evangelizing function of the Church whether through the witness of a Christian life and of fidelity toward their own consecration, or through the assistance they offer to order temporal things according to God and to inform the world by the power of the gospel. They also cooperate in the service of the ecclesial community according to their own secular way of life.

§3. Through the witness of consecrated life especially in the *presbyterium,* clerical members help their brothers by a particular apostolic charity, and by their sacred ministry among the people of God they bring about the sanctification of the world.

CAN. 714 Members are to lead their lives in the ordinary conditions of the world according to the norm of the constitutions, whether alone, or in their own families, or in a group living as brothers or sisters.

CAN. 715 §1. Clerical members incardi-

598–601, constitutiones statuant vincula sacra, quibus evangelica consilia in instituto assumuntur, et definiant obligationes quas eadem vincula inducunt, servata tamen in vitae ratione semper propria instituti saecularitate.

CAN. 713 §1. Sodales horum institutorum propriam consecrationem in actuositate apostolica exprimunt et exercent, iidemque, ad instar fermenti, omnia spiritu evangelico imbuere satagunt ad robur et incrementum Corporis Christi.

§2. Sodales laici, munus Ecclesiae evangelizandi, in saeculo et ex saeculo, participant sive per testimonium vitae christianae et fidelitatis erga suam consecrationem, sive per adiutricem quam praebent operam ad ordinandas secundum Deum res temporales atque ad mundum virtute Evangelii informandum. Suam etiam cooperationem, iuxta propriam vitae rationem saecularem, in communitatis ecclesialis servitium offerunt.

§3. Sodales clerici per vitae consecratae testimonium, praesertim in presbyterio, peculiari caritate apostolica confratribus adiutorio sunt, et in populo Dei mundi sanctificationem suo sacro ministerio perficiunt.

CAN. 714 Sodales vitam in ordinariis mundi condicionibus vel soli, vel in sua quisque familia, vel in vitae fraternae coetu, ad normam constitutionum ducant.

CAN. 715 §1. Sodales clerici in dioecesi

713 §1: PME I–III; PF II, III
713 §2: CSan 7d; LG 31, 33, 36; PC 11; AA 2; AG 40; EN 70
713 §3: Pius PP. XII, All., 8 dec. 1950 (AAS 43 [1951] 29); PO 3, 9, et passim; Paulus PP. VI, All., 2

feb. 1972 (AAS 64 [1972] 210, 211)
714: PME III §4; CSan 7; PC 11
715 §1: CSan 10b; SCR Resp. *Estne institutum,* 1952; CD 28; Paulus PP. VI, All., 2 feb. 1972 (AAS 64 [1972] 211)

nated in a diocese are subject to the diocesan bishop, without prejudice to those things which regard consecrated life in their own institute.

§2. Those who are incardinated in an institute according to the norm of can. 266, §3, however, are subject to the bishop like religious if they are appointed to the proper works of the institute or to the governance of the institute.

CAN. 716 §1. All members are to participate actively in the life of the institute according to proper law.

§2. Members of the same institute are to preserve communion among themselves, caring solicitously for a spirit of unity and a genuine relationship as brothers or sisters.

CAN. 717 §1. The constitutions are to prescribe the proper manner of governance; they are to define the time during which the moderators hold their office and the manner by which they are designated.

§2. No one is to be designated as supreme moderator who is not incorporated definitively.

§3. Those who have been placed in charge of the governance of an institute are to take care that its unity of spirit is preserved and that the active participation of the members is promoted.

CAN. 718 The administration of the goods of an institute, which must express and foster evangelical poverty, is governed by the norms of Book V, *The Temporal Goods of the Church*, and by the proper law of the institute. Likewise, proper law is to define the obligations of the institute, especially financial ones, towards members who carry on work for it.

incardinati ab Episcopo dioecesano dependent, salvis iis quae vitam consecratam in proprio instituto respiciunt.

§2. Qui vero ad normam can. 266, §3 instituto incardinantur, si ad opera instituti propria vel ad regimen instituti destinentur, ad instar religiosorum ab Episcopo dependent.

CAN. 716 §1. Sodales omnes vitam instituti, secundum ius proprium, actuose participent.

§2. Eiusdem instituti sodales communionem inter se servent, sollicite curantes spiritus unitatem et genuinam fraternitatem.

CAN. 717 §1. Constitutiones proprium regiminis modum praescribant, tempus quo Moderatores suo officio fungantur et modum quo iidem designantur definiant.

§2. Nemo in Moderatore supremum designetur, qui non sit definitive incorporatus.

§3. Qui regimini instituti praepositi sunt, curent ut eiusdem spiritus unitas servetur et actuosa sodalium participatio promoveatur.

CAN. 718 Administratio bonorum instituti, quae paupertatem evangelicam exprimere et fovere debet, regitur normis Libri V *De bonis Ecclesiae temporalibus* necnon iure proprio instituti. Item ius proprium definiat obligationes praesertim oeconomicas instituti erga sodales, qui pro ipso operam impendunt.

715 §2: PF III; CSan 8; SCR Resp. *Regimen internum*, 1952; CD 35: 1, 4
716 §1: PME III §3, 2°; PF II; CSan 7b, 10b
716 §2: PME II §1, 2°; III §4; PF III; CSan 7d; PC 15

717 §1: PME IX; PF IV; CSan 3
717 §2: c. 504; AIE 3
717 §3: PC 14; ES II: 18
718: éc. 532 §1, 1497 §1; PME III §3, 2°; PF III; CSan 7b; PC 13; ES II: 23

CAN. 719 §1. For members to respond faithfully to their vocation and for their apostolic action to proceed from their union with Christ, they are to devote themselves diligently to prayer, to give themselves in a fitting way to the reading of sacred scripture, to observe an annual period of spiritual retreat, and to perform other spiritual exercises according to proper law.

§2. The celebration of the Eucharist, daily if possible, is to be the source and strength of their whole consecrated life.

§3. They are to approach freely the sacrament of penance which they are to receive frequently.

§4. They are to obtain freely necessary direction of conscience and to seek counsel of this kind even from the moderators, if they wish.

CAN. 720 The right of admission into the institute, either for probation or for the assumption of sacred bonds, whether temporary or perpetual or definitive, belongs to the major moderators with their council, according to the norm of the constitutions.

CAN. 721 §1. A person is admitted to initial probation invalidly:

1° who has not yet attained the age of majority;

2° who is bound currently by a sacred bond in some institute of consecrated life or is incorporated in a society of apostolic life;

3° a spouse, while the marriage continues to exist.

§2. The constitutions can establish other impediments to admission even for validity or can attach conditions.

§3. Moreover, to be received, the person

CAN. 719 §1. Sodales, ut vocationi suae fideliter respondeant eorumque actio apostolica ex ipsa unione cum Christo procedat, sedulo orationi vacent, sacrarum Scripturarum lectioni apto modo incumbant, annua recessus tempora servent atque alia spiritualia exercitia iuxta ius proprium peragant.

§2. Eucharistiae celebratio, quantum fieri potest cotidiana, sit totius eorum vitae consecratae fons et robur.

§3. Libere ad sacramentum paenitentiae accedant, quod frequenter recipiant.

§4. Necessarium conscientiae moderamen libere obtineant atque huius generis consilia a suis etiam Moderatoribus, si velint, requirant.

CAN. 720 Ius admittendi in institutum, vel ad probationem vel ad sacra vincula sive temporaria sive perpetua aut definitiva assumenda, ad Moderatores maiores cum suo consilio ad normam constitutionum pertinet.

CAN. 721 §1. Invalide admittitur ad initialem probationem:

1° qui maiorem aetatem nondum attigerit;

2° qui sacro vinculo in aliquo instituto vitae consecratae actu obstringitur, aut in societate vitae apostolicae incorporatus est;

3° coniux durante matrimonio.

§2. Constitutiones possunt alia admissionis impedimenta etiam ad validitatem statuere vel condiciones apponere.

§3. Praeterea, ut quis recipiatur, habeat

---

719 §1: PME III §2; CD 33; PC 2e, 5, 6, 11; DV 25; ET 35
   719 §2: c. 595 §1, 2°; MF 753–774; PC 6
   719 §3: c. 595 §1, 3°; Paen. IIIc

719 §4: LMR II: 11
720: c. 543
721 §1: c. 542, 1°
721 §3: Ssap II, III; SCong 31, 33, 34; PC 12

must have the maturity necessary to lead rightly the proper life of the institute.

CAN. 722 §1. Initial probation is to be ordered in a way that the candidates understand more fittingly their own divine vocation, and indeed, the one proper to the institute, and that they are trained in the spirit and way of life of the institute.

§2. Candidates are properly to be formed to lead a life according to the evangelical counsels and are to be taught to transform their whole life into the apostolate, employing those forms of evangelization which better respond to the purpose, spirit, and character of the institute.

§3. The constitutions are to define the manner and length of this probation before first taking on sacred bonds in the institute; the length is not to be less than two years.

CAN. 723 §1. When the period of initial probation has elapsed, a candidate who is judged suitable is to assume the three evangelical counsels strengthened by a sacred bond or is to depart from the institute.

§2. This first incorporation is to be temporary according to the norm of the constitutions; it is not to be less than five years.

§3. When the period of this incorporation has elapsed, the member who is judged suitable is to be admitted to perpetual incorporation or to definitive incorporation, that is, with temporary bonds that are always to be renewed.

§4. Definitive incorporation is equivalent to perpetual incorporation with regard to the specific juridic effects established in the constitutions.

CAN. 724 §1. Formation after the first as-

oportet maturitatem, quae ad vitam instituti propriam recte ducendam est necessaria.

CAN. 722 §1. Probatio initialis eo ordinetur, ut candidati suam divinam vocationem et quidem instituti propriam aptius cognoscant iidemque in spiritu et vivendi modo instituti exerceantur.

§2. Ad vitam secundum evangelica consilia ducendam candidati rite instituantur atque ad eandem integre in apostolatum convertendam edoceantur, eas adhibentes evangelizationis formas, quae instituti fini, spiritui et indoli magis respondeant.

§3. Huius probationis modus et tempus ante sacra vincula in instituto primum suscipienda, biennio non brevius, in constitutionibus definiantur.

CAN. 723 §1. Elapso probationis initialis tempore, candidatus qui idoneus iudicetur, tria consilia evangelica, sacro vinculo firmata, assumat vel ab instituto discedat.

§2. Quae prima incorporatio, quinquennio non brevior, ad normam constitutionum temporaria sit.

§3. Huius incorporationis tempore elapso, sodalis, qui idoneus iudicetur, admittatur ad incorporationem perpetuam vel definitivam, vinculis scilicet temporariis semper renovandis.

§4. Incorporatio definitiva, quoad certos effectus iuridicos in constitutionibus statuendos, perpetuae aequiparatur.

CAN. 724 §1. Institutio post vincula

---

722 §1: c. 565 §1; SCong 6 §1; ES II: 33
722 §2: c. 565 §1; PME; PF III; Ssap III
723 §1: cc. 571 §2, 574 §1; SCong 7 §1, 1°
723 §2: c. 574 §1; SCong 7 §1, 2°

723 §3: cc. 488, 1°, 575 §1, 577 §1; PME III §3; SCong 8 §1, 1°
723 §4: SCong 8 §1, 2°
724 §1: SCong 8 §1, 3°; PC 18; ES II: 33, 35

sumption of sacred bonds is to be continued without interruption according to the constitutions.

§2. Members are to be formed in divine and human things at the same time; moreover, moderators of the institute are to have a serious concern for the continued spiritual formation of the members.

CAN. 725 An institute can associate to itself by some bond determined in the constitutions other members of the Christian faithful who are to strive for evangelical perfection according to the spirit of the institute and are to participate in its mission.

CAN. 726 §1. When the period of temporary incorporation has elapsed, a member is able to leave the institute freely or the major moderator, after having heard the council, can exclude a member for a just cause from the renewal of the sacred bonds.

§2. For a grave cause, a temporarily incorporated member who freely petitions it is able to obtain an indult of departure from the supreme moderator with the consent of the council.

CAN. 727 §1. After having considered the matter seriously before the Lord, a perpetually incorporated member who wishes to leave the institute is to seek an indult of departure from the Apostolic See through the supreme moderator if the institute is of pontifical right; otherwise the member may also seek it from the diocesan bishop, as it is defined in the constitutions.

§2. If it concerns a cleric incardinated in the institute, the prescript of can. 693 is to be observed.

sacra primum assumpta iugiter secundum constitutiones est protrahenda.

§2. Sodales in rebus divinis et humanis pari gressu instituantur; de continua vero eorum spirituali formatione seriam habeant curam instituti Moderatores.

CAN. 725 Institutum sibi associare potest, aliquo vinculo in constitutionibus determinato, alios christifideles, qui ad evangelicam perfectionem secundum spiritum instituti contendant eiusdemque missionem participent.

CAN. 726 §1. Elapso tempore incorporationis temporariae, sodalis institutum libere derelinquere valet vel a sacrorum vinculorum renovatione iusta de causa a Moderatore maiore, audito suo consilio, excludi potest.

§2. Sodalis temporariae incorporationis id sponte petens, indultum discedendi a supremo Moderatore de consensu sui consilii gravi de causa obtinere valet.

CAN. 727 §1. Sodalis perpetue incorporatus, qui institutum derelinquere velit, indultum discedendi, re coram Domino serio perpensa, a Sede Apostolica per Moderatorem supremum petat, si institutum est iuris pontificii; secus etiam ab Episcopo dioecesano, prout in constitutionibus definitur.

§2. Si agatur de clerico instituto incardinato, servetur praescriptum can. 693.

724 §2: Ssap IV; SCong 50–53; PC 11; ES II: 19
725: c. 500 §3; CSan 7a, 9a; AA 4
726 §1: c. 637; SCRIS Decr. *Dum canonicarum legum*, 8 dec. 1970, 3 (AAS 63 [1971] 318)
726 §2: CA 14; SCR Decr. *Religionum laicalium*, 31 maii 1966, I, 3 (AAS 59 [1967] 362–364); SCRIS Decr. *Cum superiores generales*, 27 nov. 1969 (AAS 61 [1969] 738–739)
727 §1: c. 638

CAN. 728 When an indult of departure has been granted legitimately, all the bonds as well as the rights and obligations deriving from incorporation cease.

CAN. 729 A member is dismissed from an institute according to the norm of cann. 694 and 695; moreover, the constitutions are to determine other causes for dismissal provided that they are proportionately grave, external, imputable, and juridically proven, and the method of proceeding established in cann. 697–700 is to be observed. The prescript of can. 701 applies to one dismissed.

CAN. 730 In order for a member of a secular institute to transfer to another secular institute, the prescripts of cann. 684, §§1, 2, 4, and 685 are to be observed; moreover, for transfer to be made to a religious institute or to a society of apostolic life or from them to a secular institute, the permission of the Apostolic See is required, whose mandates must be observed.

SECTION II. Societies of Apostolic Life

CAN. 731 §1. Societies of apostolic life resemble institutes of consecrated life; their members, without religious vows, pursue the apostolic purpose proper to the society and, leading a life in common as brothers or sisters according to their proper manner of life, strive for the perfection of charity through the observance of the constitutions.

§2. Among these are societies in which members assume the evangelical counsels by some bond defined in the constitutions.

CAN. 728 Indulto discedendi legitime concesso, cessant omnia vincula necnon iura et obligationes ab incorporatione promanantia.

CAN. 729 Sodalis ab instituto dimittitur ad normam cann. 694 et 695; constitutiones praeterea determinent alias causas dimissionis, dummodo sint proportionate graves, externae, imputabiles et iuridice comprobatae, atque modus procedendi servetur in cann. 697–700 statutus. Dimisso applicatur praescriptum can. 701.

CAN. 730 Ut sodalis instituti saecularis ad aliud institutum saeculare transeat, serventur praescripta cann. 694, §§1, 2, 4 et 685; ut vero ad institutum religiosum vel ad societatem vitae apostolicae aut ex illis ad institutum saeculare fiat transitus, licentia requiritur Sedis Apostolicae, cuius mandatis standum est.

SECTIO II. *De Societatibus Vitae Apostolicae*

CAN. 731 §1. Institutis vitae consecratae accedunt societates vitae apostolicae, quarum sodales, sine votis religiosis, finem apostolicum societatis proprium prosequuntur et, vitam fraternam in communi ducentes, secundum propriam vitae rationem, per observantiam constitutionum ad perfectionem caritatis tendunt.

§2. Inter has sunt societates in quibus sodales, aliquo vinculo constitutionibus definito, consilia evangelica assumunt.

728: c. 640 §1
731 §1: c. 673 §1

731 §2: PC 1, 12–14

CAN. 732 Those things which are established in cann. 578–597 and 606 apply to societies of apostolic life, without prejudice, however, to the nature of each society; moreover, cann. 598–602 apply to the societies mentioned in can. 731, §2.

CAN. 733 §1. The competent authority of the society erects a house and establishes a local community with the previous written consent of the diocesan bishop, who must also be consulted concerning its suppression.

§2. Consent to erect a house entails the right to have at least an oratory in which the Most Holy Eucharist is to be celebrated and reserved.

CAN. 734 The constitutions determine the governance of a society, with cann. 617–633 observed according to the nature of each society.

CAN. 735 §1. The proper law of each society determines the admission, probation, incorporation, and formation of members.

§2. In what pertains to admission into a society, the conditions established in cann. 642–645 are to be observed.

§3. Proper law must determine the manner of probation and formation, especially doctrinal, spiritual, and apostolic, adapted to the purpose and character of the society, in such a way that the members, recognizing their divine vocation, are suitably prepared for the mission and life of the society.

CAN. 736 §1. In clerical societies, clerics are incardinated in the society itself unless the constitutions establish otherwise.

CAN. 732 Quae in cann. 578–597 et 606 statuuntur, societatibus vitae apostolicae applicantur, salva tamen uniuscuiusque societatis natura; societatibus vero, de quibus in can. 731, §2, etiam cann. 598–602 applicantur.

CAN. 733 §1. Domus erigitur et communitas localis constituitur a competenti auctoritate societatis, praevio consensu Episcopi dioecesani in scriptis dato, qui etiam consuli debet, cum agitur de eius suppressione.

§2. Consensus ad erigendam domum secumfert ius habendi saltem oratorium, in quo sanctissima Eucharistia celebretur et asservetur.

CAN. 734 Regimen societatis a constitutionibus determinatur, servatis, iuxta naturam uniuscuiusque societatis, cann. 617–633.

CAN. 735 §1. Sodalium admissio, probatio, incorporatio et institutio determinantur iure proprio cuiusque societatis.

§2. Ad admissionem in societatem quod attinet, serventur condiciones in cann. 642–645 statutae.

§3. Ius proprium determinare debet rationem probationis et institutionis fini et indoli societatis accommodatam, praesertim doctrinalem, spiritualem et apostolicam, ita ut sodales vocationem divinam agnoscentes ad missionem et vitam societatis apte praeparentur.

CAN. 736 §1. In societatibus clericalibus clerici ipsi societati incardinantur, nisi aliter ferant constitutiones.

733 §1: cc. 497 §1, 498, 674, 1501; ES I: 34; AIE 2°
733 §2: cc. 497 §2, 1162 §4
734: c. 675
735 §1: c. 677; SCR Decl., 30 dec. 1922 (AAS 15 [1923] 156–158)

735 §3: Ssap III, IV; PC 18; RC 1, 2, 5; ES I: 33–36; RFS III; MR 31, 32
736 §1: cc. 115, 585; SCPF Ind., 12 iun. 1923; SCPF Resp., 30 maii 1932, SCConc Resol., 15 iul. 1933 (AAS 26 [1934] 234–236); CI Resp., 24 iul. 1946

§2. In those things which belong to the program of studies and to the reception of orders, the norms for secular clerics are to be observed, without prejudice to §1.

CAN. 737 Incorporation entails on the part of the members the obligations and rights defined in the constitutions and on the part of the society concern for leading the members to the purpose of their proper vocation according to the constitutions.

CAN. 738 §1. All members are subject to their proper moderators according to the norm of the constitutions in those matters which regard the internal life and discipline of the society.

§2. They are also subject to the diocesan bishop in those matters which regard public worship, the care of souls, and other works of the apostolate, with attention to cann. 679–683.

§3. The constitutions or particular agreements define the relations of a member incardinated in a diocese with his own bishop.

CAN. 739 In addition to the obligations to which members as members are subject according to the constitutions, they are bound by the common obligations of clerics unless it is otherwise evident from the nature of the thing or the context.

CAN. 740 Members must live in a house or in a legitimately established community and must observe common life according to the norm of proper law, which also governs absences from the house or community.

CAN. 741 §1. Societies and, unless the constitutions determine otherwise, their parts and

§2. In iis quae ad rationem studiorum et ad ordines suscipiendos pertinent, serventur normae clericorum saecularium, firma tamen §1.

CAN. 737 Incorporatio secumfert ex parte sodalium obligationes et iura in constitutionibus definita, ex parte autem societatis, curam sodales ad finem propriae vocationis perducendi, iuxta constitutiones.

CAN. 738 §1. Sodales omnes subsunt propriis Moderatoribus ad normam constitutionum in iis quae vitam internam et disciplinam societatis respiciunt.

§2. Subsunt quoque Episcopo dioecesano in iis quae cultum publicum, curam animarum aliaque apostolatus opera respiciunt, attentis cann. 679–683.

§3. Relationes sodalis dioecesi incardinati cum Episcopo proprio constitutionibus vel particularibus conventionibus definiuntur.

CAN. 739 Sodales, praeter obligationes quibus, uti sodales, obnoxii sunt secundum constitutiones, communibus obligationibus clericorum abstringuntur, nisi ex natura rei vel ex contextu sermonis aliud constet.

CAN. 740 Sodales habitare debent in domo vel in communitate legitime constituta et servare vitam communem, ad normam iuris proprii, quo quidem etiam absentiae a domo vel communitate reguntur.

CAN. 741 §1. Societates et, nisi aliter ferant constitutiones, earum partes et domus,

736 §2: cc. 587–591, 678; Ssap IV; SCong 40–46, 50; OT; ES II: 34, 35; RFS 2

738 §1: CD 35: 2; PC 14; MR 28, 33–35, 46, 52

738 §2: cc. 344, 500 §§1 et 2, 512 §2, 2°, 608 §1, 618 §2, 619; MG: 570–571; LG 45; CD 34, 35: 1, 3, 4; PC 6;

ES I: 23 §1, 24, 25 §1, 26, 29, 35–36

739: c. 679 §1

740: c. 673 §1; CI Resp. VI, 2–3 iun. 1918 (AAS 10 [1918] 347); CA 15; PC 15; ES II: 25–29

741 §1: c. 676 §§1 et 2

houses are juridic persons and, as such, capable of acquiring, possessing, administering, and alienating temporal goods according to the norm of the prescripts of Book V, *The Temporal Goods of the Church*, of cann. 636, 638, and 639, and of proper law.

§2. According to the norm of proper law, members are also capable of acquiring, possessing, administering, and disposing of temporal goods, but whatever comes to them on behalf of the society is acquired by the society.

CAN. 742 The constitutions of each society govern the departure and dismissal of a member not yet definitively incorporated.

CAN. 743 Without prejudice to the prescript of can. 693, a definitively incorporated member can obtain an indult of departure from the society from the supreme moderator with the consent of the council, unless it is reserved to the Holy See according to the constitutions; with the indult, the rights and obligations deriving from incorporation cease.

CAN. 744 §1. It is equally reserved to the supreme moderator with the consent of the council to grant permission for a definitively incorporated member to transfer to another society of apostolic life; the rights and obligations proper to the society are suspended in the meantime, without prejudice to the right of returning before definitive incorporation in the new society.

§2. Transfer to an institute of consecrated life or from one to a society of apostolic life requires the permission of the Holy See, whose mandates must be observed.

CAN. 745 The supreme moderator with

personae sunt iuridicae et, qua tales, capaces bona temporalia acquirendi, possidendi, administrandi et alienandi, ad normam praescriptorum Libri V *De bonis Ecclesiae temporalibus*, cann. 636, 638 et 639, necnon iuris proprii.

§2. Sodales capaces quoque sunt, ad normam iuris proprii, bona temporalia acquirendi, possidendi, administrandi de iisque disponendi, sed quidquid ipsis intuitu societatis obveniat, societati acquiritur.

CAN. 742 Egressus et dimissio sodalis nondum definitive incorporati reguntur constitutionibus cuiusque societatis.

CAN. 743 Indultum discedendi a societate, cessantibus iuribus et obligationibus ex incorporatione promanantibus, firmo praescripto can. 693, sodalis definitive incorporatus a supremo Moderatore cum consensu eius consilii obtinere potest, nisi id iuxta constitutiones Sanctae Sedi reservetur.

CAN. 744 §1. Supremo quoque Moderatori cum concensu sui consilii pariter reservatur licentiam concedere sodali definitive incorporato ad aliam societatem vitae apostolicae transeundi, suspensis interim iuribus et obligationibus propriae societatis, firmo tamen iure redeundi ante definitivam incorporationem in novam societatem.

§2. Ut transitus fiat ad institutum vitae consecratae vel ex eo ad societatem vitae apostolicae, licentia requiritur Sanctae Sedis, cuius mandatis standum est.

CAN. 745 Supremus Moderator cum

741 §2: cc. 580 §§1 et 2, 594 §2, 676 §3; PC 13
742: CA 14
743: cc. 638, 640 §1, 641; SCConc Resol., 15 iul. 1933 (AAS 26 [1934] 234–236); CI Resp. 2, 27 iul. 1942

(AAS 34 [1942] 241)
744: c. 681
745: CA 15

the consent of the council can grant an indult to live outside the society to a definitively incorporated member, but not for more than three years; the rights and obligations which cannot be reconciled with the new condition of the member are suspended, but the member remains under the care of the moderators. If it concerns a cleric, moreover, the consent of the ordinary of the place in which he must reside is required, under whose care and dependence he also remains.

CAN. 746 For the dismissal of a definitively incorporated member, cann. 694–704 are to be observed with appropriate adaptations.

concensu sui consilii sodali definitive incorporato concedere potest indultum vivendi extra societatem, non tamen ultra triennium, suspensis iuribus et obligationibus quae cum ipsius nova condicione componi non possunt; permanet tamen sub cura Moderatorum. Si agitur de clerico, requiritur praeterea consensus Ordinarii loci in quo commorari debet, sub cuius cura et dependentia etiam manet.

CAN. 746 Ad dismissionem sodalis definitive incorporati serventur, congrua congruis referendo, cann. 694–704.

746: c. 681; CI Resp. II, 1 mar. 1921 (AAS 13 [1921] 177)

BOOK III. THE TEACHING FUNCTION OF THE CHURCH

LIBER III. DE ECCLESIAE MUNERE DOCENDI

CAN. 747 §1. The Church, to which Christ the Lord has entrusted the deposit of faith so that with the assistance of the Holy Spirit it might protect the revealed truth reverently, examine it more closely, and proclaim and expound it faithfully, has the duty and innate right, independent of any human power whatsoever, to preach the gospel to all peoples, also using the means of social communication proper to it.

§2. It belongs to the Church always and everywhere to announce moral principles, even about the social order, and to render judgment concerning any human affairs insofar as the fundamental rights of the human person or the salvation of souls requires it.

CAN. 748 §1. All persons are bound to seek the truth in those things which regard God and his Church and by virtue of divine law are bound by the obligation and possess the right of embracing and observing the truth which they have come to know.

§2. No one is ever permitted to coerce persons to embrace the Catholic faith against their conscience.

CAN. 749 §1. By virtue of his office, the Supreme Pontiff possesses infallibility in teaching

CAN. 747 §1. Ecclesiae, cui Christus Dominus fidei depositum concredidit ut ipsa, Spiritu Sancto assistente, veritatem revelatam sancte custodiret, intimius perscrutaretur, fideliter annuntiaret atque exponeret, officium est et ius nativum, etiam mediis communicationis socialis sibi propriis adhibitis, a qualibet humana potestate independens, omnibus gentibus Evangelium praedicandi.

§2. Ecclesiae competit semper et ubique principia moralia etiam de ordine sociali annuntiare, necnon iudicium ferre de quibuslibet rebus humanis, quatenus personae humanae iura fundamentalia aut animarum salus id exigat.

CAN. 748 §1. Omnes homines veritatem in iis, quae Deum eiusque Ecclesiam respiciunt, quaerere tenentur eamque cognitam amplectendi ac servandi obligatione vi legis divinae adstringuntur et iure gaudent.

§2. Homines ad amplectendam fidem catholicam contra ipsorum conscientiam per coactionem adducere nemini umquam fas est.

CAN. 749 §1. Infallibilitate in magisterio, vi muneris sui gaudet Summus Pontifex

747 §1: c. 1322; Pius PP. XII, Enc. *Mystici Corporis Christi*, 29 iun. 1943 (AAS 35 [1943] 193–248); Ioannes XXIII, All., 11 oct. 1962 (AAS 54 [1962] 790); IM 3; LG 24, 25; CD 19; DV 7–10; DH 13; Paulus PP. VI, Hom., 7 dec. 1965 (AAS 58 [1966] 51–59); Paulus PP. VI, Adh. AP. *Quinque iam anni*, 8 dec. 1970, I (AAS 63 [1971] 98–100); SE Decl., 25 oct. 1974, 4; EN 6–15; RH 19

747 §2: Pius PP. XI, Enc. *Firmissimam constantiam*, 28 mar. 1937 (AAS 29 [1937] 196); Ioannes PP. XXIII, Enc. *Mater et Magistra*, 15 maii 1961, passim

(AAS 53 [1961] 401–464); Ioannes PP. XXIII, Enc. *Pacem in terris*, 11 apr. 1963 (AAS 55 [1963] 301); CD 12; DH 15; GS 76, 89; HV 4; SE *Convenientes ex universo*, 30 nov. 1971 (AAS 67 [1971] 923–942)

748 §1: c. 1322 §2; Ioannes XXIII, Enc. *Ad Petri Cathedram*, 29 iun. 1959 (AAS 51 [1959] 497–531); DH 1

748 §2: c. 1351; Sec Notif. *Se réferant*, 25 ian. 1942; DH 2, 4; AG 13

749 §1: LG 25

when as the supreme pastor and teacher of all the Christian faithful, who strengthens his brothers and sisters in the faith, he proclaims by definitive act that a doctrine of faith or morals is to be held.

§2. The college of bishops also possesses infallibility in teaching when the bishops gathered together in an ecumenical council exercise the magisterium as teachers and judges of faith and morals who declare for the universal Church that a doctrine of faith or morals is to be held definitively; or when dispersed throughout the world but preserving the bond of communion among themselves and with the successor of Peter and teaching authentically together with the Roman Pontiff matters of faith or morals, they agree that a particular proposition is to be held definitively.

§3. No doctrine is understood as defined infallibly unless this is manifestly evident.

CAN. 750 §1. A person must believe with divine and Catholic faith all those things contained in the word of God, written or handed on, that is, in the one deposit of faith entrusted to the Church, and at the same time proposed as divinely revealed either by the solemn magisterium of the Church or by its ordinary and universal magisterium which is manifested by the common adherence of the Christian faithful under the leadership of the sacred magisterium; therefore all are bound to avoid any doctrines whatsoever contrary to them.

§2. Each and every thing which is proposed definitively by the magisterium of the Church concerning the doctrine of faith and morals,

quando ut supremus omnium christifidelium Pastor et Doctor, cuius est fratres suos in fide confirmare, doctrinam de fide vel de moribus tenendam definitivo actu proclamat.

§2. Infallibilitate in magisterio pollet quoque Collegium Episcoporum quando magisterium exercent Episcopi in Concilio Oecumenico coadunati, qui, ut fidei et morum doctores et iudices, pro universa Ecclesia doctrinam de fide vel de moribus definitive tenendam declarant; aut quando per orbem dispersi, communionis nexum inter se et cum Petri successore servantes, una cum eodem Romano Pontifice authentice res fidei vel morum docentes, in unam sententiam tamquam definitive tenendam conveniunt.

§3. Infallibiliter definita nulla intellegitur doctrina, nisi id manifesto constiterit.

CAN. 750 §1. Fide divina et catholica ea omnia credenda sunt quae verbo Dei scripto vel tradito, uno scilicet fidei deposito Ecclesiae commisso, continentur, et insimul ut divinitus revelata proponuntur sive ab Ecclesiae magisterio sollemni, sive ab eius magisterio ordinario et universali, quod quidem communi adhaesione christifidelium sub ductu sacri magisterii manifestatur; tenentur igitur omnes quascumque devitare doctrinas iisdem contrarias.

§2 . Firmiter etiam amplectenda ac retinenda sunt omnia et singula quae circa doctrinam de fide vel moribus ab Ecclesiae mag-

749 §2: LG 25

749 §3: c. 1323 §3; SCpC Instr. *Inter ea,* 4 nov. 1969, 9 (AAS 62 [1970] 126–127)

750 §1: c. 1323 §1; Pius PP. XII, Const. Ap. *Munificentissimus Dominus,* 1 nov. 1950 (AAS 42 [1950]

753–771); LG 25; DV 5, 10; SCDF Ep. *Cum Oecumenicum,* 24 iul. 1966 (AAS 58 [1966] 659–661); SE Decl., 28 oct. 1967; SCDF Decl., 24 iun. 1973, 2–5 (AAS 65 [1973] 398–404)

that is, each and every thing which is required to safeguard reverently and to expound faithfully the same deposit of faith, is also to be firmly embraced and retained; therefore, one who rejects those propositions which are to be held definitively is opposed to the doctrine of the Catholic Church.

CAN. 751 Heresy is the obstinate denial or obstinate doubt after the reception of baptism of some truth which is to be believed by divine and Catholic faith; apostasy is the total repudiation of the Christian faith; schism is the refusal of submission to the Supreme Pontiff or of communion with the members of the Church subject to him.

CAN. 752 Although not an assent of faith, a religious submission of the intellect and will must be given to a doctrine which the Supreme Pontiff or the college of bishops declares concerning faith or morals when they exercise the authentic magisterium, even if they do not intend to proclaim it by definitive act; therefore, the Christian faithful are to take care to avoid those things which do not agree with it.

CAN. 753 Although the bishops who are in communion with the head and members of the college, whether individually or joined together in conferences of bishops or in particular councils, do not possess infallibility in teaching, they are authentic teachers and instructors of the faith for the Christian faithful entrusted to their care; the Christian faithful are bound to adhere with religious submission of mind to the authentic magisterium of their bishops.

isterio definitive proponunter, scilicet quae ad idem fidei depositum sancte custodiendum et fideliter exponendum requiruntur; ideoque doctrinae Ecclesiae catholicae adversatur qui easdem propositiones definitive tenendas recusat.

CAN. 751 Dicitur haeresis, pertinax, post receptum baptismum, alicuius veritatis fide divina et catholica credendae denegatio, aut de eadem pertinax dubitatio; apostasia, fidei christianae ex toto repudiatio; schisma, subiectionis Summo Pontifici aut communionis cum Ecclesiae membris eidem subditis detrectatio.

CAN. 752 Non quidem fidei assensus, religiosum tamen intellectus et voluntatis obsequium praestandum est doctrinae, quam sive Summus Pontifex sive Collegium Episcoporum de fide vel de moribus enuntiant, cum magisterium authenticum exercent, etsi definitivo actu eandem proclamare non intendant; christifideles ergo devitare curent quae cum eadem non congruant.

CAN. 753 Episcopi, qui sunt in communione cum Collegii capite et membris, sive singuli sive in conferentiis Episcoporum aut in conciliis particularibus congregati, licet infallibilitate in docendo non polleant, christifidelium suae curae commissorum authentici sunt fidei doctores et magistri; cui authentico magisterio suorum Episcoporum christifideles religioso animi obsequio adhaerere tenentur.

751: c. 1325 §2

752: Pius PP. XII, Enc. *Humani generis,* 12 aug. 1950 (AAS 42 [1950] 567–568; LG 25; Vaticanum II, Notif. *Quaesitum est,* 15 nov. 1965 (AAS 58 [1966] 836); SCDF Ep., 24 iul. 1966 (AAS 58 [1966] 659–661); SE Decl., 28 oct. 1967, 2; SCpC Instr. *Inter ea,* 4 nov.

1969, 9 (AAS 62 [1970] 126–127); SCDF Decl., 24 iun. 1973, 2–5 (AAS 65 [1973] 398–404)

753: c. 1326; Pius PP. XII, All., 31 maii 1954 (AAS 46 [1954] 313–317); LG 25; SCDF Ep., 24 iul. 1966 (AAS 58 [1966] 659–661); SE Decl., 28 oct. 1967

CAN. 754 All the Christian faithful are obliged to observe the constitutions and decrees which the legitimate authority of the Church issues in order to propose doctrine and to proscribe erroneous opinions, particularly those which the Roman Pontiff or the college of bishops puts forth.

CAN. 755 §1. It is above all for the entire college of bishops and the Apostolic See to foster and direct among Catholics the ecumenical movement whose purpose is the restoration among all Christians of the unity which the Church is bound to promote by the will of Christ.

§2. It is likewise for the bishops and, according to the norm of law, the conferences of bishops to promote this same unity and to impart practical norms according to the various needs and opportunities of the circumstances; they are to be attentive to the prescripts issued by the supreme authority of the Church.

CAN. 754 Omnes christifideles obligatione tenentur servandi constitutiones et decreta, quae ad doctrinam proponendam et erroneas opiniones proscribendas fert legitima Ecclesiae auctoritas, speciali vero ratione, quae edit Romanus Pontifex vel Collegium Episcoporum.

CAN. 755 §1. Totius Collegii Episcoporum et Sedis Apostolicae imprimis est fovere et dirigere motum oecumenicum apud catholicos, cuius finis est unitatis redintegratio inter universos christianos, ad quam promovendam Ecclesia ex voluntate Christi tenetur.

§2. Episcoporum item est, et, ad normam iuris, Episcoporum conferentiarum, eandem unitatem promovere atque pro variis adiunctorum necessitatibus vel opportunitatibus, normas practicas impertire, attentis praescriptis a suprema Ecclesiae auctoritate latis.

TITLE I. The Ministry of the Divine Word

TITULUS I. De Divini Verbi Ministerio

CAN. 756 §1. With respect to the universal Church, the function of proclaiming the gospel has been entrusted principally to the Roman Pontiff and the college of bishops.

§2. With respect to the particular church entrusted to him, an individual bishop, who is the

CAN. 756 §1. Quoad universam Ecclesiam munus Evangelii annuntiandi praecipue Romano Pontifici et Collegio Episcoporum commissum est.

§2. Quoad Ecclesiam particularem sibi concreditam illud munus exercent singuli

754: c. 1324; Pius PP. XII, Enc. *Humani generis*, 12 aug. 1950 (AAS 42 [1950] 561–578); SCDF Ep., 24 iul. 1966 (AAS 58 [1966] 659–661); SE Decl., 28 oct. 1967

755 §1: Pius PP. XI, Enc. *Mortalium animos*, 6 ian. 1928 (AAS 20 [1928] 5–16); LG 13–15; OE 24–30; UR 4, 8, 9; AA 13, 14; AG 15, 36; SCDF Ep., 24 iul. 1966, 10 (AAS 58 [1966] 661); DO I; SE *Convenientes ex universo*, 30 nov. 1971 (AAS 63 [1971] 938)

755 §2: SCSO Instr. *Ecclesia catholica*, 20 dec.

1949 (AAS 42 [1950] 142–147); UR 4, 8, 9; SCDF Ep., 24 iul. 1966, 10 (AAS 58 [1966] 661); DO I, 2–7; DO II, 64–66; SCUF Instr. *En mars*, 15 aug. 1970; DPME 48; SCUF Normae, 22 feb. 1975

756 §1: c. 1327 §1; Pius PP. XII, All., 31 maii 1954, (AAS 46 [1954] 313–317); LG 23, 25; CD 3; AG 29; SE Decl., 28 oct. 1967; SE Decl., 22 oct. 1969, III; Paulus PP. VI, Adh. Ap. *Quinque iam anni*, 8 dec. 1970, (AAS 63 [1971] 97–107); EN 67; PA

756 §2: c. 1327 §2; Benedictus PP. XV, Enc. *Hu-*

moderator of the entire ministry of the word within it, exercises that function; sometimes several bishops fulfill this function jointly with respect to different churches at once, according to the norm of law.

CAN. 757 It is proper for presbyters, who are co-workers of the bishops, to proclaim the gospel of God; this duty binds especially pastors and others to whom the care of souls is entrusted with respect to the people committed to them. It is also for deacons to serve the people of God in the ministry of the word in communion with the bishop and his *presbyterium*.

CAN. 758 By virtue of their consecration to God, members of institutes of consecrated life give witness to the gospel in a special way and the bishop appropriately calls upon them as a help in proclaiming the gospel.

CAN. 759 By virtue of baptism and confirmation, lay members of the Christian faithful are witnesses of the gospel message by word and the example of a Christian life; they can also be called upon to cooperate with the bishop and presbyters in the exercise of the ministry of the word.

CAN. 760 The mystery of Christ is to be set forth completely and faithfully in the ministry of the word, which must be based upon sacred scripture, tradition, liturgy, the magisterium, and the life of the Church.

Episcopi, qui quidem totius ministerii verbi in eadem sunt moderatores; quandoque vero aliqui Episcopi coniunctim illud explent quoad diversas simul Ecclesias, ad normam iuris.

CAN. 757 Presbyterorum, qui quidem Episcoporum cooperatores sunt, proprium est Evangelium Dei annuntiare; praesertim hoc officio tenentur, quoad populum sibi commissum, parochi aliique quibus cura animarum concreditur; diaconorum etiam est in ministerio verbi populo Dei, in communione cum Episcopo eiusque presbyterio, inservire.

CAN. 758 Sodales institutorum vitae consecratae, vi propriae Deo consecrationis, peculiari modo Evangelii testimonium reddunt, iidemque in Evangelio annuntiando ab Episcopo in auxilium convenienter assumuntur.

CAN. 759 Christifideles laici, vi baptismatis et confirmationis, verbo et vitae christianae exemplo evangelici nuntii sunt testes; vocari etiam possunt ut in exercitio ministerii verbi cum Episcopo et presbyteris cooperentur.

CAN. 760 In ministerio verbi, quod sacra Scriptura, Traditione, liturgia, magisterio vitaque Ecclesiae innitatur oportet, Christi mysterium integre ac fideliter proponatur.

mani generis, 15 iun. 1917 (AAS 9 [1917] 305–317); SCC Normae, 28 iun. 1917, 1 (AAS 9 [1917] 328–334); LG 23; CD 3; PAULUS PP. VI, Adh. Ap. *Quinque iam anni*, 8 dec. 1970, (AAS 63 [1971] 97–107); SE Decl., 22 oct. 1969, III; DPME 55–61; EN 68

757: c. 1327 §2; SCC Normae, 28 iun. 1917, 1 (AAS 9 [1917] 328–334); LG 28, 29; CD 30; PO 4; SE Decl., 30 nov. 1971, II/I 1 (AAS 63 [1971] 898–922); SDO 22, 6°; DPME 62; EN 68; PA

758: c. 1327 §2; SCC Normae, 28 iun. 1917, 1 (AAS

9 [1917] 328–334); LG 44; CD 33; PC 8–11; DPME 62; EN 69; MR 4; PA passim

759: c. 1327 §2; PIUS PP. XII, All., 31 maii 1954, (AAS 46 [1954] 316–317); LG 33, 35; AA passim; AG 41; DPME 62; EN 70–73; PA 7

760: BENEDICTUS PP. XV, Enc. *Humani generis*, 15 iun. 1917 (AAS 9 [1917] 305–317); EcS III; DCG 38; SE Decl., 30 nov. 1971, II/I 1c (AAS 63 [1971] 898–922); EN 25–39; RH 19; CT 6, 21, 30

CAN. 761 The various means available are to be used to proclaim Christian doctrine: first of all preaching and catechetical instruction, which always hold the principal place, but also the presentation of doctrine in schools, academies, conferences, and meetings of every type and its diffusion through public declarations in the press or in other instruments of social communication by legitimate authority on the occasion of certain events.

CAN. 761 Varia media ad doctrinam christianam annuntiandam adhibeantur quae praesto sunt, imprimis praedicatio atque catechetica institutio, quae quidem semper principem locum tenent, sed et propositio doctrinae in scholis, in academiis, conferentiis et coadunationibus omnis generis, necnon eiusdem diffusio per declarationes publicas a legitima auctoritate occasione quorundam eventuum factas prelo aliisque instrumentis communicationis socialis.

CHAPTER I. The Preaching of the Word of God

CAPUT I. De Verbi Dei Praedicatione

CAN. 762 Sacred ministers, among whose principal duties is the proclamation of the gospel of God to all, are to hold the function of preaching in esteem since the people of God are first brought together by the word of the living God, which it is certainly right to require from the mouth of priests.

CAN. 762 Cum Dei populus primum coadunetur verbo Dei vivi, quod ex ore sacerdotum omnino fas est requirere, munus praedicationis magni habeant sacri ministri, inter quorum praecipua officia sit Evangelium Dei omnibus annuntiare.

CAN. 763 Bishops have the right to preach the word of God everywhere, including in churches and oratories of religious institutes of pontifical right, unless the local bishop has expressly forbidden it in particular cases.

CAN. 763 Episcopis ius est ubique, non exclusis ecclesiis et oratoriis institutorum religiosorum iuris pontificii, Dei verbum praedicare, nisi Episcopus loci in casibus particularibus expresse renuerit.

CAN. 764 Without prejudice to the prescript of can. 765, presbyters and deacons possess the faculty of preaching everywhere; this faculty is to be exercised with at least the presumed consent of the rector of the church, unless the competent ordinary has restricted or taken away the faculty or particular law requires express permission.

CAN. 764 Salvo praescripto can. 765, facultate ubique praedicandi, de consensu saltem praesumpto rectoris ecclesiae exercenda, gaudent presbyteri et diaconi, nisi ab Ordinario competenti eadem facultas restricta fuerit aut sublata, aut lege particulari licentia expressa requiratur.

CAN. 765 Preaching to religious in their

CAN. 765 Ad praedicandum religiosis

761: EcS 648; IM 13, 14; CD 13; SE Decl., 28 oct. 1967; DCG 116–124; CT 46–5
762: LG 25; PO 4; DPME 55; EN 42
763: cc. 349 §1, 1°, 1343 §1; PM II, 1

764: cc. 1337, 1338 §3, 1340–1342; SCC Normae, 28 iun. 1917, II et IV (AAS 9 [1917] 330–331, 333)
765: c. 1338 §2

churches or oratories requires the permission of the superior competent according to the norm of the constitutions.

CAN. 766 Lay persons can be permitted to preach in a church or oratory, if necessity requires it in certain circumstances or it seems advantageous in particular cases, according to the prescripts of the conference of bishops and without prejudice to can. 767, §1.

CAN. 767 §1. Among the forms of preaching, the homily, which is part of the liturgy itself and is reserved to a priest or deacon, is preeminent; in the homily the mysteries of faith and the norms of Christian life are to be explained from the sacred text during the course of the liturgical year.

§2. A homily must be given at all Masses on Sundays and holy days of obligation which are celebrated with a congregation, and it cannot be omitted except for a grave cause.

§3. It is strongly recommended that if there is a sufficient congregation, a homily is to be given even at Masses celebrated during the week, especially during the time of Advent and Lent or on the occasion of some feast day or a sorrowful event.

§4. It is for the pastor or rector of a church to take care that these prescripts are observed conscientiously.

CAN. 768 §1. Those who proclaim the divine word are to propose first of all to the Chris-

in eorum ecclesiis vel oratoriis licentia requiritur Superioris ad normam constitutionum competentis.

CAN. 766 Ad praedicandum in ecclesia vel oratorio admitti possunt laici, si certis in adiunctis necessitas id requirat aut in casibus particularibus utilitas id suadeat, iuxta Episcoporum conferentiae praescripta, et salvo can. 767, §1.

CAN. 767 §1. Inter praedicationis formas eminet homilia, quae est pars ipsius liturgiae et sacerdoti aut diacono reservatur; in eadem per anni liturgici cursum ex textu sacro fidei mysteria et normae vitae christianae exponantur.

§2. In omnibus Missis diebus dominicis et festis de praecepto, quae concursu populi celebrantur, homilia habenda est nec omitti potest nisi gravi de causa.

§3. Valde commendatur ut, si sufficiens detur populi concursus, homilia habeatur etiam in Missis quae infra hebdomadam, praesertim tempore adventus et quadragesimae aut occasione alicuius festi vel luctuosi eventus, celebrentur.

§4. Parochi aut ecclesiae rectoris est curare ut haec praescripta religiose serventur.

CAN. 768 §1. Divini verbi praecones christifidelibus imprimis proponant, quae ad

---

766: c. 1342; Pius PP. XII, All., 31 maii 1954 (AAS 46 [1954] 316); IOe 37

767 §1: MD 529; SC 35, 52; IOe 54–56; DV 24; PO 4; SCCD Instr. *Actio pastoralis*, 15 maii 1969, 6 (AAS 61 [1969] 809); IGMR 41, 42, 165; SCCD Instr. *Liturgicae instaurationes*, 15 sep. 1970, 2 (AAS 62 [1970] 695–696); CIV Resp., 11 ian. 1971 (AAS 63 [1971] 329); SCpC Rescr., 20 nov. 1973; DPME 59, 64; EN 43; CT 48; ID 3

767 §2: cc. 1344 §1, 1345; SC 52; Paulus PP. VI, Litt. Ap. *Sacram Liturgiam*, 25 ian. 1964, III (AAS 56 [1964] 141); IOe 53; IGMR 42; DPME 64; CT 48

767 §3: c. 1346 §1; SC 49; Paulus PP. VI, Litt. Ap. *Sacram Liturgiam*, 25 ian. 1964, III (AAS 56 [1964] 141); IOe 53; IGMR 42; DPME 64; CT 48

768 §1: c. 1347 §1; SCC Normae, 28 iun. 1917, III (AAS 9 [1917] 331–333); CD 12; EN 27

tian faithful those things which one must believe and do for the glory of God and the salvation of humanity.

§2. They are also to impart to the faithful the doctrine which the magisterium of the Church sets forth concerning the dignity and freedom of the human person, the unity and stability of the family and its duties, the obligations which people have from being joined together in society, and the ordering of temporal affairs according to the plan established by God.

CAN. 769 Christian doctrine is to be set forth in a way accommodated to the condition of the listeners and in a manner adapted to the needs of the times.

CAN. 770 At certain times according to the prescripts of the diocesan bishop, pastors are to arrange for those types of preaching which are called spiritual exercises and sacred missions or for other forms of preaching adapted to needs.

CAN. 771 §1. Pastors of souls, especially bishops and pastors, are to be concerned that the word of God is also proclaimed to those of the faithful who because of the condition of their life do not have sufficient common and ordinary pastoral care or lack it completely.

§2. They are also to make provision that the message of the gospel reaches non-believers living in the territory since the care of souls must also extend to them no less than to the faithful.

CAN. 772 §1. In the exercise of preaching,

Dei gloriam hominumque salutem credere et facere oportet.

§2. Impertiant quoque fidelibus doctrinam, quam Ecclesiae magisterium proponit de personae humanae dignitate et libertate, de familiae unitate et stabilitate eiusque muniis, de obligationibus quae ad homines in societate coniunctos pertinent, necnon de rebus temporalibus iuxta ordinem a Deo statutum componendis.

CAN. 769 Doctrina christiana proponatur modo auditorum condicioni accommodato atque ratione temporum necessitatibus aptata.

CAN. 770 Parochi certis temporibus, iuxta Episcopi dioecesani praescripta, illas ordinent praedicationes, quas exercitia spiritualia et sacras missiones vocant, vel alias formas necessitatibus aptatas.

CAN. 771 §1. Solliciti sint animarum pastores, praesertim Episcopi et parochi, ut Dei verbum iis quoque fidelibus nuntietur, qui ob vitae suae condicionem communi et ordinaria cura pastorali non satis fruantur aut eadem penitus careant.

§2. Provideant quoque, ut Evangelii nuntium perveniat ad non credentes in territorio degentes, quippe quos, non secus ac fideles, animarum cura complecti debeat.

CAN. 772 §1. Ad exercitium praedica-

768 §2: CD 12; GS 41, 42; CIP Decl., 10 dec. 1974, 70–77; EN 29

769: c. 1347 §2; CD 13; PO 4; GS 4; EN 40, 63

770: c. 1349; SCConc Ind., 25 ian. 1927; SCConc Ind., 3 mar. 1938; SCConc Rescr., 2 feb. 1960

771 §1: Pius PP. XII, Const. Ap. *Exsul Familia*, 1 aug. 1952, 32–49 (AAS 44 [1952] 699–702); CD 18; SCpC Instr. *Peregrinans in terra*, 30 apr. 1969, II, 3 B

c (AAS 61 [1969] 375–376); SCE Instr. *Nemo est*, 22 aug. 1969 (AAS 61 [1969] 614–643); DPME 58, 71; EN 52, 56

771 §2: c. 1350 §1; SC 9; LG 16; CD 13; AG 10, 20; DPME 71, 160; EN 55, 58

772 §1: c. 1345; SCC Normae, 28 iun. 1917, 1 (AAS 9 [1917] 328–334); DPME 64

moreover, all are to observe the norms issued by the diocesan bishop.

§2. In giving a radio or television talk on Christian doctrine, the prescripts established by the conference of bishops are to be observed.

CHAPTER II. Catechetical Instruction

CAN. 773 It is a proper and grave duty especially of pastors of souls to take care of the catechesis of the Christian people so that the living faith of the faithful becomes manifest and active through doctrinal instruction and the experience of Christian life.

CAN. 774 §1. Under the direction of legitimate ecclesiastical authority, solicitude for catechesis belongs to all members of the Church according to each one's role.

§2. Parents above others are obliged to form their children by word and example in faith and in the practice of Christian life; sponsors and those who take the place of parents are bound by an equal obligation.

CAN. 775 §1. Having observed the prescripts issued by the Apostolic See, it is for the diocesan bishop to issue norms for catechetics, to make provision that suitable instruments of catechesis are available, even by preparing a cat-

tionis quod attinet, ab omnibus praeterea serventur normae ab Episcopo dioecesano latae.

§2. Ad sermonem de doctrina christiana faciendum via radiophonica aut televisifica, serventur praescripta ab Episcoporum conferentia statuta.

CAPUT II. **De Catechetica Institutione**

CAN. 773 Proprium et grave officium pastorum praesertim animarum est catechesim populi christiani curare, ut fidelium fides, per doctrinae institutionem et vitae christianae experientiam, viva fiat explicita atque operosa.

CAN. 774 §1. Sollicitudo catechesis, sub moderamine legitimae ecclesiasticae auctoritatis, ad omnia Ecclesiae membra pro sua cuiusque parte pertinet.

§2. Prae ceteris parentes obligatione tenentur verbo et exemplo filios in fide et vitae christianae praxi efformandi; pari obligatione adstringuntur, qui parentum locum tenent atque patrini.

CAN. 775 §1. Servatis praescriptis ab Apostolica Sede latis, Episcopi dioecesani est normas de re catechetica edicere itemque prospicere ut apta catechesis instrumenta praesto sint, catechismum etiam

772 §2: IM 13; DPME 65
773: c. 1329; CD 14; GE 4; DCG; EN 44; SE Nuntius, 28 oct. 1977; RH 19; CT 1, 14–16, 24, 62–64
774 §1: DCG 9, 17; SE Nuntius, 28 oct. 1977; CT 16, 63–70
774 §2: cc. 769, 1135, 1335, 1372 §2; Pius PP. XI, Enc. *Divini illius Magistri*, 31 dec. 1929 (AAS 22 [1930] 59–62); Pius PP. XII, All., 23 mar. 1952 (AAS 44 [1952] 270); Ioannes PP. XXIII, All., 3 maii 1959; LG 11, 35; GE 3, 6–8; AA 11, 30; GS 48; Paulus PP. VI, All., 4

maii 1970; DCG 78–81; EN 71; Paulus PP. VI, All., 28 dec. 1975; CT 68
775 §1: cc. 1329, 1336; SCConc Litt. circ., 31 maii 1920 (AAS 12 [1920] 299–300); SCConc Litt. circ., 24 iun. 1924 (AAS 16 [1924] 332–333); SCConc Litt. circ., 28 aug. 1924; SCConc Litt. circ., 21 iun. 1930 (AAS 22 [1930] 395–409); SCConc Decr. *Provido sane*, 12 ian. 1935 (AAS 27 [1935] 148–154); LG 25, 27; CD 2, 13, 14; GE 2; DCG 106, 108, 109, 116–126, 129; DPME 64, CT 63

echism if it seems opportune, and to foster and coordinate catechetical endeavors.

§2. If it seems useful, it is for the conference of bishops to take care that catechisms are issued for its territory, with the previous approval of the Apostolic See.

§3. The conference of bishops can establish a catechetical office whose primary function is to assist individual dioceses in catechetical matters.

CAN. 776   By virtue of his function, a pastor is bound to take care of the catechetical formation of adults, youth, and children, to which purpose he is to use the help of the clerics attached to the parish, of members of institutes of consecrated life and of societies of apostolic life, taking into account the character of each institute, and of lay members of the Christian faithful, especially of catechists. None of these are to refuse to offer their help willingly unless they are legitimately impeded. The pastor is to promote and foster the function of parents in the family catechesis mentioned in can. 774, §2.

CAN. 777   Attentive to the norms established by the diocesan bishop, a pastor is to take care in a special way:

1° that suitable catechesis is imparted for the celebration of the sacraments;

2° that through catechetical instruction imparted for an appropriate period of time children are prepared properly for the first reception of the sacraments of penance and the Most

parando, si opportunum id videatur, necnon incepta catechetica fovere atque coordinare.

§2. Episcoporum conferentiae est, si utile videatur, curare ut catechismi pro suo territorio, praevia Sedis Apostolicae approbatione, edantur.

§3. Apud Episcoporum conferentiam institui potest officium catecheticum, cuius praecipuum munus sit singulis dioecesibus in re catechetica auxilium praebere.

CAN. 776   Parochus, vi sui muneris, catecheticam efformationem adultorum, iuvenum et puerorum curare tenetur, quem in finem sociam sibi operam adhibeat clericorum paroeciae addictorum, sodalium institutorum vitae consecratae necnon societatum vitae apostolicae, habita ratione indolis uniuscuiusque instituti, necnon christifidelium laicorum, praesertim catechistarum; hi omnes, nisi legitime impediti, operam suam libenter praestare ne renuant. Munus parentum, in catechesi familiari, de quo in can. 774, §2, promoveat et foveat.

CAN. 777   Peculiari modo parochus, attentis normis ab Episcopo dioecesano statutis, curet:

1° ut apta catechesis impertiatur pro sacramentorum celebratione;

2° ut pueri, ope catecheticae institutionis per congruum tempus impertitae, rite praeparentur ad primam receptionem sacramentorum paenitentiae et sanctissimae

---

775 §2: AG 31; DCG 46, 119, 134; CT 50; EP 4, 1
775 §3: SCConc Normae, 12 dec. 1929; DCG 128
776: cc. 1330–1334; SCConc Litt. circ., 31 maii 1920 (AAS 12 [1920] 299–300); Pius PP. XI, m. p. *Orbem catholicum*, 29 iun. 1923 (AAS 15 [1923] 327–329); SCConc Litt. circ., 24 iun. 1924 (AAS 16 [1924] 332–333); SCConc Decr. *Provido sane*, 12 ian. 1935, I–III, 4 (AAS 27 [1935] 150–151); Pius PP. XII, All., 6

feb. 1940; IOANNES PP. XXIII, All., 10 feb. 1959; PAULUS PP. VI, All., 12 feb. 1964; LG 28, 29; CD 30, 35; PC 8; AA 3, 10; PO 4–9; EN 68–71; CT 64–67
777, 1°: SCConc Litt. circ., 23 apr. 1924 (AAS 16 [1924] 287–289); SC 14; GE 4; DCG 25, 56–59; OICA Prae. 4–7; CT 23
777, 2°: c. 1330; CD 30; EMys 14; DCG 79–81, 91, et Addendum; OICA 306–309; CT 37

Holy Eucharist and for the sacrament of confirmation;

3° that having received first communion, these children are enriched more fully and deeply through catechetical formation;

4° that catechetical instruction is given also to those who are physically or mentally impeded, insofar as their condition permits;

5° that the faith of youth and adults is strengthened, enlightened, and developed through various means and endeavors.

CAN. 778 Religious superiors and superiors of societies of apostolic life are to take care that catechetical instruction is imparted diligently in their churches, schools, and other works entrusted to them in any way.

CAN. 779 Catechetical instruction is to be given by using all helps, teaching aids, and instruments of social communication which seem more effective so that the faithful, in a manner adapted to their character, capabilities and age, and conditions of life, are able to learn Catholic doctrine more fully and put it into practice more suitably.

CAN. 780 Local ordinaries are to take care that catechists are duly prepared to fulfill their function properly, namely, that continuing formation is made available to them, that they understand the doctrine of the Church appropri-

Eucharistiae necnon ad sacramentum confirmationis;

3° ut iidem, prima communione recepta, uberius ac profundius catechetica efformatione excolantur;

4° ut catechetica institutio iis etiam tradatur, quantum eorum condicio sinat, qui corpore vel mente sint praepediti;

5° ut iuvenum et adultorum fides, variis formis et inceptis, muniatur, illuminetur atque evolvatur.

CAN. 778 Curent Superiores religiosi et societatum vitae apostolicae ut in suis ecclesiis, scholis aliisve operibus sibi quoquo modo concreditis, catechetica institutio sedulo impertiatur.

CAN. 779 Institutio catechetica tradatur omnibus adhibitis auxiliis, subsidiis didacticis et communicationis socialis instrumentis, quae efficaciora videantur ut fideles, ratione eorum indoli, facultatibus et aetati necnon vitae condicionibus aptata, plenius catholicam doctrinam ediscere eamque aptius in praxim deducere valeant.

CAN. 780 Curent locorum Ordinarii ut catechistae ad munus suum rite explendum debite praeparentur, ut nempe continua formatio ipsis praebeatur, iidemque Ecclesiae doctrinam apte cognoscant atque normas

777, 3°: c. 1331; CT 38–40, 42, 45

777, 4°: DCG 91; CT 41

777, 5°: c. 1332; SCConc Decr. *Provido sane*, 12 ian. 1935, II (AAS 27 [1935] 150); DCG 92–97; OICA 19, 20, 98–132; CT 39–45

778: cc. 509 §2, 2°; 1334; 1381; SCR Instr. *Quantum homini*, 25 nov. 1929 (AAS 22 [1930] 28–29); SCSSU Litt. circ., 20 nov. 1939; CD 35; ES I, 37; EN 69; CT 65

779: SCConc Litt. circ., 23 apr. 1924 (AAS 16 [1924] 288); SCConc Litt. circ., 21 iun. 1930 (AAS 22 [1930] 398–399); PIUS PP. XII, All., 14 oct. 1950; IOANNES PP. XXIII, Enc. *Princeps Pastorum*, 28 nov.

1959 (AAS 51 [1959] 851); SCConc Litt. circ., 4 iun. 1964; IM 3, 6, 13, 14, 17; CD 13, 14; AG 26; DCG 116–124; CICS Instr. *Communio et progressio*, 23 maii 1971, 126–134 (AAS 63 [1971] 638–640); EN 40, 45; CT 17, 22, 31, 46, 51, 55

780: PIUS PP. XII, Ep., 14 sep. 1951 (AAS 43 [1951] 778–779); Ssap 364; IOANNES PP. XXIII, Enc. *Princeps Pastorum*, 28 nov. 1959 (AAS 51 [1959] 855); SCSSU Instr. *Mentre in ogni parte*, 3 sep. 1963; CD 14; DV 25; AG 15, 17; DCG 108–115; EN 73; SE Nuntius, 28 oct. 1977, 14; CT 15, 63, 66, 71

ately, and that they learn in theory and in practice the methods proper to the teaching disciplines.

disciplinis paedagogicis proprias theoretice ac practice addiscant.

TITLE II. The Missionary Action of the Church

TITULUS II. De Actione Ecclesiae Missionali

CAN. 781   Since the whole Church is by its nature missionary and the work of evangelization must be held as a fundamental duty of the people of God, all the Christian faithful, conscious of their responsibility, are to assume their part in missionary work.

CAN. 782   §1. The Roman Pontiff and the college of bishops have the supreme direction and coordination of endeavors and actions which belong to missionary work and missionary cooperation.

§2. As sponsors of the universal Church and of all the churches, individual bishops are to have special solicitude for missionary work, especially by initiating, fostering, and sustaining missionary endeavors in their own particular churches.

CAN. 783   Since by virtue of their consecration members of institutes of consecrated life dedicate themselves to the service of the Church, they are obliged to engage in missionary action in a special way and in a manner proper to their institute.

CAN. 781   Cum tota Ecclesia natura sua sit missionaria et opus evangelizationis habendum sit fundamentale officium populi Dei, christifideles omnes, propriae responsabilitatis conscii, partem suam in opere missionali assumant.

CAN. 782   §1. Suprema directio et coordinatio inceptorum et actionum, quae ad opus missionale atque ad cooperationem missionariam pertinent, competit Romano Pontifici et Collegio Episcoporum.

§2. Singuli Episcopi, utpote Ecclesiae universae atque omnium Ecclesiarum sponsores, operis missionalis peculiarem sollicitudinem habeant, praesertim incepta missionalia in propria Ecclesia particulari suscitando, fovendo ac sustinendo.

CAN. 783   Sodales institutorum vitae consecratae, cum vi ipsius consecrationis sese servitio Ecclesiae dedicent, obligatione tenentur ad operam, ratione suo instituto propria, speciali modo in actione missionali navandam.

781: PAULUS PP. VI, All., 6 nov. 1964 (AAS 56 [1964] 998–999); LG 23; AG 2, 35, 39; SCGE Litt. circ., 17 maii 1970; PAULUS PP. VI, All., 11 ian. 1975, (AAS 67 [1975] 103–108); PAULUS PP. VI, Nuntius, 14 apr. 1976 (AAS 68 [1976] 341–347); EN 9–15, 50–56; PAULUS PP. VI, Nuntius, 14 maii 1978 (AAS 70 [1978] 345–349); PA 3–7, 22

782 §1: c. 1350 §2; LG 23; AG 6, 29; REU 82; SCGE Instr. *Quo aptius*, 24 feb. 1969 (AAS 61 [1969] 276–281); PA 3–7, 19

782 §2: BENEDICTUS PP. XV, Enc. *Maximum il-*

lud, 30 nov. 1919 (AAS 11 [1919] 451–454); PIUS PP. XI, Enc. *Rerum Ecclesiae*, 28 feb. 1926 (AAS 18 [1926] 67); PIUS PP. XII, Enc. *Evangelii Praecones*, 2 iun. 1951 (AAS 43 [1951] 497–528); PIUS PP. XII, Enc. *Fidei donum*, 21 apr. 1957 (AAS 49 [1957] 237); LG 23, 24; CD 6; AG 6, 38; ES III, 3–11; SCGE Normae, 24 apr. 1971; PAULUS PP. VI, Nuntius, 22 oct. 1972 (AAS 64 [1972] 729); DPME 46; PA 4

783: LG 44; PC 20; AG 15, 18, 23, 27; ES III, 10–12; MR 19; PA 6; EN 69

CAN. 784 Missionaries, that is, those whom competent ecclesiastical authority sends to carry out missionary work, can be chosen from among natives or non-natives, whether secular clerics, members of institutes of consecrated life or of societies of apostolic life, or other lay members of the Christian faithful.

CAN. 785 §1. Catechists are to be used in carrying out missionary work; catechists are lay members of the Christian faithful, duly instructed and outstanding in Christian life, who devote themselves to setting forth the teaching of the gospel and to organizing liturgies and works of charity under the direction of a missionary.

§2. Catechists are to be formed in schools designated for this purpose or, where such schools are lacking, under the direction of missionaries.

CAN. 786 The Church accomplishes the specifically missionary action which implants the Church among peoples or groups where it has not yet taken root especially by sending heralds of the gospel until the young churches are established fully, that is, when they are provided with the proper resources and sufficient means to be able to carry out the work of evangelization themselves.

CAN. 787 §1. By the witness of their life and word, missionaries are to establish a sincere dialogue with those who do not believe in Christ so that, in a manner adapted to their own temperament and culture, avenues are opened enabling them to understand the message of the gospel.

CAN. 784 Missionarii, qui scilicet a competenti auctoritate ecclesiastica ad opus missionale explendum mittuntur, eligi possunt autochthoni vel non, sive clerici saeculares, sive institutorum vitae consecratae vel societatis vitae apostolicae sodales, sive alii christifideles laici.

CAN. 785 §1. In opere missionali peragendo assumantur catechistae, christifideles nempe laici debite instructi et vita christiana praestantes, qui, sub moderamine missionarii, doctrinae evangelicae proponendae et liturgicis exercitiis caritatisque operibus ordinandis sese impendant.

§2. Catechistae efformentur in scholis ad hoc destinatis vel, ubi desint, sub moderamine missionariorum.

CAN. 786 Actio proprie missionalis, qua Ecclesia implantatur in populis vel coetibus ubi nondum radicata est, ab Ecclesia absolvitur praesertim mittendo Evangelii praecones donec novellae Ecclesiae plene constituantur, cum scilicet instructae sint propriis viribus et sufficientibus mediis, quibus opus evangelizandi per se ipsae peragere valeant.

CAN. 787 §1. Missionarii, vitae ac verbi testimonio, dialogum sincerum cum non credentibus in Christum instituant, ut ipsis, ratione eorundem ingenio et culturae aptata, aperiantur viae quibus ad evangelicum nuntium cognoscendum adduci valeant.

784: AG 23; PA 3, 7; SCGE Litt. circ., 17 maii 1970, II, B

785 §1: SCPF Litt., 20 maii 1923 (AAS 15 [1923] 369–372); Ioannes PP. XXIII, Enc. *Princeps Pastorum,* 28 nov. 1959 (AAS 51 [1959] 855); AG 17, 26, 35; SCGE Decl., apr. 1970

785 §2: AG 17, 26, 35

786: SCPF Instr. *Quo efficacius,* 6 ian. 1920; LG 17; AG 6 et passim; SCGE Litt. circ., 17 maii 1970; SCGE Litt. circ., 17 maii 1970, III

787 §1: AG 11, 12; SPNC Instr. *Documentum quod,* 28 aug. 1968 (AAS 60 [1968] 692–704); EN 51–53

§2. Missionaries are to take care that they teach the truths of faith to those whom they consider prepared to receive the gospel message so that they can be admitted to receive baptism when they freely request it.

CAN. 788 §1. When the period of the pre-catechumenate has been completed, those who have made known their intention to embrace faith in Christ are to be admitted to the cate-chumenate in liturgical ceremonies and their names are to be inscribed in the book designated for this purpose.

§2. Through instruction and the first experience of Christian life, catechumens are to be initiated suitably into the mystery of salvation and introduced into the life of the faith, the liturgy, the charity of the people of God, and the apostolate.

§3. It is for the conference of bishops to issue statutes which regulate the catechumenate by determining what things must be expected of the catechumens and by defining what prerogatives are to be recognized as theirs.

CAN. 789 Neophytes are to be formed through suitable instruction to understand the gospel truth more deeply and to fulfill the duties assumed through baptism; they are to be imbued with a sincere love for Christ and his Church.

CAN. 790 §1. It is for the diocesan bishop in the territories of a mission:

1° to promote, direct, and coordinate endeavors and works which pertain to missionary action;

§2. Curent ut quos ad evangelicum nuntium recipiendum aestiment paratos, veritates fidei edoceant, ita quidem ut ipsi ad baptismum recipiendum, libere id petentes, admitti possint.

CAN. 788 §1. Qui voluntatem amplectendi fidem in Christum manifestaverint, expleto tempore praecatechumenatus, liturgicis caerimoniis admittantur ad catechumenatum, atque eorum nomina scribantur in libro ad hoc destinato.

§2. Catechumeni, per vitae christianae institutionem et tirocinium, apte initientur mysterio salutis atque introducantur in vitam fidei, liturgiae et caritatis populi Dei atque apostolatus.

§3. Conferentiae Episcoporum est statuta edere quibus catechumenatus ordinetur, determinando quaenam a catechumenis sint praestanda, atque definiendo quaenam eis agnoscantur praerogativae.

CAN. 789 Neophyti, apta institutione ad veritatem evangelicam penitius cognoscendam et officia per baptismum suscepta implenda efformentur; sincero amore erga Christum eiusque Ecclesiam imbuantur.

CAN. 790 §1. Episcopi dioecesani in territoriis missionis est:

1° promovere, moderari et coordinare incepta et opera, quae ad actionem missionalem spectant;

---

787 §2: AG 13

788 §1: SRC Decr. *Ordo baptismi*, 16 apr. 1962 (AAS 54 [1962] 310–315); SC 64; AG 13, 14; DCG 130; OICA 7, 17; DPME 72

788 §2: SRC Decr. *Ordo baptismi*, 16 apr. 1962 (AAS 54 [1962] 310–315); AG 14; OICA 19, 98

788 §3: SRC Resp., 8 mar. 1919 (AAS 11 [1919] 144); AG 14; OICA 12, 20, 64, 65

789: AG 15; OICA 7, 37–40

790 §1, 1°: AG 30; SCGE Instr. *Relationes in territoriis*, 24 feb. 1969, 13b (AAS 61 [1969] 285)

2° to take care that appropriate agreements are entered into with moderators of institutes which dedicate themselves to missionary work and that relations with them result in the good of the mission.

§2. All missionaries, even religious and their assistants living in his jurisdiction, are subject to the prescripts issued by the diocesan bishop mentioned in §1, n. 1.

CAN. 791 To foster missionary cooperation in individual dioceses:

1° missionary vocations are to be promoted;

2° a priest is to be designated to promote effectively endeavors for the missions, especially the *Pontifical Missionary Works;*

3° an annual day for the missions is to be celebrated;

4° a suitable offering for the missions is to be contributed each year and sent to the Holy See.

CAN. 792 Conferences of bishops are to establish and promote works by which those who come to their territory from mission lands for the sake of work or study are received as brothers and sisters and assisted with adequate pastoral care.

2° curare ut debitae ineantur conventiones cum Moderatoribus institutorum quae operi missionali se dedicant, utque relationes cum iisdem in bonum cedant missionis.

§2. Praescriptis ab Episcopo dioecesano de quibus in §1, n. 1 editis, subsunt omnes missionarii, etiam religiosi eorumque auxiliares in eius dicione degentes.

CAN. 791 In singulis dioecesibus ad cooperationem missionalem fovendam:

1° promoveantur vocationes missionales;

2° sacerdos deputetur ad incepta pro missionibus efficaciter promovenda, praesertim *Pontificia Opera Missionalia;*

3° celebretur dies annualis pro missionibus;

4° solvatur quotannis congrua pro missionibus stips, Sanctae Sedi transmittenda.

CAN. 792 Episcoporum conferentiae opera instituant ac promoveant, quibus ii qui e terris missionum laboris aut studii causa ad earundem territorium accedant, fraterne recipiantur et congruenti pastorali cura adiuventur.

790 §1, 2°: SCPF Instr. *Quum huic,* 8 dec. 1929 (AAS 22 [1930] 111–115); AG 32; SCGE Instr. *Relationes in territoriis,* 24 feb. 1969, 14c (AAS 61 [1969] 286); SCGE *Schema contractuum 1969*

790 §2: c. 296 §1; AG 30; SCGE Instr. *Relationes in territoriis,* 24 feb. 1969, 14d (AAS 61 [1969] 285)

791, 1°: ES III, 5, 6; DPME 46

791, 2°: ES III, 4; SCGE *Statuta Pontificalium Operum Missionalium,* 26 iun. 1980, 6; SCGE Instr. *Quo aptius,* 24 feb. 1969, A 2, 3 (AAS 61 [1969] 277); DPME 46

791, 3°: SCPF Instr. *Plurimis abhinc,* 29 iun. 1952, 6 (AAS 44 [1952] 549–551); ES III, 3

791, 4°: SRC Rescr. *Il consiglio,* 14 apr. 1926 (AAS 19 [1927] 23–24); SCPF Instr. *Plurimis abhinc,* 29 iun. 1952, 4, 6 (AAS 44 [1952] 549–551); ES III, 8; PA 19; SCGE Instr. *Quo aptius,* 24 feb. 1969, A 2, 3 (AAS 61 [1969] 277)

792: Pius PP. XII, Enc. *Fidei donum,* 21 apr. 1957 (AAS 49 [1957] 245); Ioannes PP. XXIII, Enc. *Princeps Pastorum,* 28 nov. 1959 (AAS 51 [1959] 861–862); AG 38; ES III, 23

TITLE III. **Catholic Education**

CAN. 793 §1. Parents and those who take their place are bound by the obligation and possess the right of educating their offspring. Catholic parents also have the duty and right of choosing those means and institutions through which they can provide more suitably for the Catholic education of their children, according to local circumstances.

§2. Parents also have the right to that assistance, to be furnished by civil society, which they need to secure the Catholic education of their children.

CAN. 794 §1. The duty and right of educating belongs in a special way to the Church, to which has been divinely entrusted the mission of assisting persons so that they are able to reach the fullness of the Christian life.

§2. Pastors of souls have the duty of arranging everything so that all the faithful have a Catholic education.

CAN. 795 Since true education must strive for complete formation of the human person that looks to his or her final end as well as to the common good of societies, children and youth are to be nurtured in such a way that they are able to develop their physical, moral, and intellectual talents harmoniously, acquire a more perfect sense of responsibility and right use of freedom, and are formed to participate actively in social life.

TITULUS III. **De Educatione Catholica**

CAN. 793 §1. Parentes, necnon qui eorum locum tenent, obligatione adstringuntur et iure gaudent prolem educandi; parentes catholici officium quoque et ius habent ea eligendi media et instituta quibus, iuxta locorum adiuncta, catholicae filiorum educationi aptius prospicere queant.

§2. Parentibus ius est etiam iis fruendi auxiliis a societate civili praestandis, quibus in catholica educatione filiorum procuranda indigeant.

CAN. 794 §1. Singulari ratione officium et ius educandi spectat ad Ecclesiam, cui divinitus missio concredita est homines adiuvandi, ut ad christianae vitae plenitudinem pervenire valeant.

§2. Animarum pastoribus officium est omnia disponendi, ut educatione catholica omnes fideles fruantur.

CAN. 795 Cum vera educatio integram persequi debeat personae humanae formationem, spectantem ad finem eius ultimum et simul ad bonum commune societatum, pueri et iuvenes ita excolantur ut suas dotes physicas, morales et intellectuales harmonice evolvere valeant, perfectiorem responsabilitatis sensum libertatisque rectum usum acquirant et ad vitam socialem active participandam conformentur.

793 §1: c. 1372 §2; Pius PP. XI, Enc. *Divini illius Magistri,* 31 dec. 1929, 59–60 (AAS 22 [1930] 49–86); Pius PP. XI, Enc. *Mit brennender Sorge,* 14 mar. 1937, 164–165 (AAS 29 [1937] 145–167); Pius PP. XII, All., 8 sept. 1946; GE 3, 6; CIP Decl., 10 dec. 1974, 38, 5°

793 §2: GE 6, 7; SCIC Instr. *La Scuola Cattolica,* 19 mar. 1977, 81, 82

794 §1: Pius PP. XI, Enc. *Divini illius Magistri,* 31 dec. 1929, 59s (AAS 22 [1930] 49–86); Pius PP. XI,

Enc. *Mit brennender Sorge,* 14 mar. 1937, 164s (AAS 29 [1937] 145–167); Pius PP. XII, All., 8 Sept. 1946; GE Intro., 3

794 §2: Pius PP. XI, Enc. *Divini illius Magistri,* 31 dec. 1929, 53–59 (AAS 22 [1930] 49–86); GE 3, 4

795: Pius PP. XI, Enc. *Divini illius Magistri,* 31 dec. 1929, 50, 69–71, 83–85 (AAS 22 [1930] 49–86); GE 1; Paulus PP. VI, Ep. *A maintes reprises,* 8 dec. 1970; CIP Decl., 10 dec. 1974

CHAPTER I. **Schools**

CAN. 796 §1. Among the means to foster education, the Christian faithful are to hold schools in esteem; schools are the principal assistance to parents in fulfilling the function of education.

§2. Parents must cooperate closely with the teachers of the schools to which they entrust their children to be educated; moreover, teachers in fulfilling their duty are to collaborate very closely with parents, who are to be heard willingly and for whom associations or meetings are to be established and highly esteemed.

CAN. 797 Parents must possess a true freedom in choosing schools; therefore, the Christian faithful must be concerned that civil society recognizes this freedom for parents and even supports it with subsidies; distributive justice is to be observed.

CAN. 798 Parents are to entrust their children to those schools which provide a Catholic education. If they are unable to do this, they are obliged to take care that suitable Catholic education is provided for their children outside the schools.

CAN. 799 The Christian faithful are to strive so that in civil society the laws which regulate the formation of youth also provide for their religious and moral education in the schools themselves, according to the conscience of the parents.

CAN. 800 §1. The Church has the right to

CAPUT I. **De Scholis**

CAN. 796 §1. Inter media ad excolendam educationem christifideles magni faciant scholas, quae quidem parentibus, in munere educationis implendo, praecipuo auxilio sunt.

§2. Cum magistris scholarum, quibus filios educandos concredant, parentes arcte cooperentur oportet; magistri vero in officio suo persolvendo intime collaborent cum parentibus, qui quidem libenter audiendi sunt eorumque consociationes vel conventus instaurentur atque magni existimentur.

CAN. 797 Parentes in scholis eligendis vera libertate gaudeant oportet; quare christifideles solliciti esse debent ut societas civilis hanc libertatem parentibus agnoscat atque, servata iustitia distributiva, etiam subsidiis tueatur.

CAN. 798 Parentes filios concredant illis scholis in quibus educationi catholicae provideatur; quod si facere non valeant, obligatione tenentur curandi, ut extra scholas debitae eorundem educationi catholicae prospiciatur.

CAN. 799 Christifideles enitantur ut in societate civili leges quae iuvenum formationem ordinant, educationi eorum religiosae et morali quoque, iuxta parentum conscientiam, in ipsis scholis prospiciant.

CAN. 800 §1. Ecclesiae ius est scholas

796 §1: Pius PP. XI, Enc. *Divini illius Magistri,* 31 dec. 1929, 76 (AAS 22 [1930] 49–86); Pius PP. XII, All., 31 dec. 1956; GE 5

796 §2: Pius PP. XII, All., 5 ian. 1954; GE 7; SCIC Instr. *La Scuola Cattolica,* 19 mar. 1977, 73

797: Pius PP. XI, Enc. *Divini illius Magistri,* 31 dec. 1929, 60, 63–64 (AAS 22 [1930] 49–86); GE 6

798: c. 1374; GE 8; AA 30; SCIC Instr. *La Scuola Cattolica,* 19 mar. 1977, 73

799: GE 7

800 §1: c. 1375; Benedictus PP. XV, Ep. Ap. *Communes litteras,* 10 apr. 1919 (AAS 11 [1919] 172); Pius PP. XI, Enc. *Divini illius Magistri,* 31 dec. 1929 (AAS 22 [1930] 49–86); SCSSU Normae, 28 iul. 1948, 2; Ioannes PP. XXIII, Nuntius, 30 dec. 1959 (AAS 52 [1960] 57–59); GE 8

establish and direct schools of any discipline, type, and level.

§2. The Christian faithful are to foster Catholic schools, assisting in their establishment and maintenance according to their means.

CAN. 801 Religious institutes whose proper mission is education, retaining their mission faithfully, are also to strive to devote themselves to Catholic education through their schools, established with the consent of the diocesan bishop.

CAN. 802 §1. If schools which offer an education imbued with a Christian spirit are not available, it is for the diocesan bishop to take care that they are established.

§2. Where it is expedient, the diocesan bishop is to make provision for the establishment of professional schools, technical schools, and other schools required by special needs.

CAN. 803 §1. A Catholic school is understood as one which a competent ecclesiastical authority or a public ecclesiastical juridic person directs or which ecclesiastical authority recognizes as such through a written document.

§2. The instruction and education in a Catholic school must be grounded in the principles of Catholic doctrine; teachers are to be outstanding in correct doctrine and integrity of life.

§3. Even if it is in fact Catholic, no school is to bear the name *Catholic school* without the consent of competent ecclesiastical authority.

cuiusvis disciplinae, generis et gradus condendi ac moderandi.

§2. Christifideles scholas catholicas foveant, pro viribus adiutricem operam conferentes ad easdem condendas et sustentandas.

CAN. 801 Instituta religiosa quibus missio educationis propria est, fideliter hanc suam missionem retinentes, satagant educationi catholicae etiam per suas scholas, consentiente Episcopo dioecesano conditas, sese impendere.

CAN. 802 §1. Si praesto non sint scholae in quibus educatio tradatur christiano spiritu imbuta, Episcopi dioecesani est curare ut condantur.

§2. Ubi id expediat, Episcopus dioecesanus provideat ut scholae quoque condantur professionales et technicae necnon aliae quae specialibus necessitatibus requirantur.

CAN. 803 §1. Schola catholica ea intellegitur quam auctoritas ecclesiastica competens aut persona iuridica ecclesiastica publica moderatur, aut auctoritas ecclesiastica documento scripto uti talem agnoscit.

§2. Institutio et educatio in schola catholica principiis doctrinae catholicae nitatur oportet; magistri recta doctrina et vitae probitate praestent.

§3. Nulla schola, etsi reapse catholica, nomen *scholae catholicae* gerat, nisi de consensu competentis auctoritatis ecclesiasticae.

800 §2: c. 1379 §3; GE 8, 9; SCIC Instr. *La Scuola Cattolica,* 19 mar. 1977

801: Pius PP. XI, Ep. *Procuratores generales,* 31 mar. 1954 (AAS 46 [1954] 202–205); CD 35: 4; ES I, 39 §1; SCIC Decl., 1 feb. 1971 (AAS 63 [1971] 250–251); SCIC Instr. *La Scuola Cattolica,* 19 mar. 1977, 74–76, 89

802 §1: c. 1379 §1

802 §2: GE 9; DPME 66

803 §1: SCIC Instr. *La Scuola Cattolica,* 19 mar. 1977, 33–37, 71

803 §2: Pius PP. XI, Enc. *Divini illius Magistri,* 31 dec. 1929, 77–79 (AAS 22 [1930] 49–86); Pius PP. XII, All., 14 sep. 1958 (AAS 50 [1958] 696–700); GE 8, 9; AA 30; SCIC Instr. *La Scuola Cattolica,* 19 mar. 1977, 33–37, 43, 49, 71, 73, 78

803 §3: AA 24

CAN. 804 §1. The Catholic religious instruction and education which are imparted in any schools whatsoever or are provided through the various instruments of social communication are subject to the authority of the Church. It is for the conference of bishops to issue general norms about this field of action and for the diocesan bishop to regulate and watch over it.

§2. The local ordinary is to be concerned that those who are designated teachers of religious instruction in schools, even in non-Catholic ones, are outstanding in correct doctrine, the witness of a Christian life, and teaching skill.

CAN. 805 For his own diocese, the local ordinary has the right to appoint or approve teachers of religion and even to remove them or demand that they be removed if a reason of religion or morals requires it.

CAN. 806 §1. The diocesan bishop has the right to watch over and visit the Catholic schools in his territory, even those which members of religious institutes have founded or direct. He also issues prescripts which pertain to the general regulation of Catholic schools; these prescripts are valid also for schools which these religious direct, without prejudice, however, to their autonomy regarding the internal direction of their schools.

§2. Directors of Catholic schools are to take care under the watchfulness of the local ordinary that the instruction which is given in them is at least as academically distinguished as that in the other schools of the area.

CAN. 804 §1. Ecclesiae auctoritati subicitur institutio et educatio religiosa catholica quae in quibuslibet scholis impertitur aut variis communicationis socialis instrumentis procuratur; Episcoporum conferentiae est de hoc actionis campo normas generales edicere, atque Episcopi dioecesani est eundem ordinare et in eum invigilare.

§2. Loci Ordinarius sollicitus sit, ut qui ad religionis institutionem in scholis, etiam non catholicis, deputentur magistri recta doctrina, vitae christianae testimonio atque arte paedagogica sint praestantes.

CAN. 805 Loci Ordinario pro sua dioecesi ius est nominandi aut approbandi magistros religionis, itemque, si religionis morumve ratio id requirat, amovendi aut exigendi ut amoveantur.

CAN. 806 §1. Episcopo dioecesano competit ius invigilandi et invisendi scholas catholicas in suo territorio sitas, eas etiam quae ab institutorum religiosorum sodalibus conditae sint aut dirigantur; eidem item competit praescripta edere quae ad generalem attinent ordinationem scholarum catholicarum: quae praescripta valent de scholis quoque quae ab iisdem sodalibus diriguntur, salva quidem eorundem quoad internum earum scholarum moderamen autonomia.

§2. Curent scholarum catholicarum Moderatores, advigilante loci Ordinario, ut institutio quae in iisdem traditur pari saltem gradu ac in aliis scholis regionis, ratione scientifica sit praestans.

804 §1: c. 1381 §§1 et 2; SCConc Normae, 28 aug. 1924; SCConc Litt. circ., 21 iun. 1930 (AAS 22 [1930] 395–400); Pius PP. XII, Enc. *Humani generis,* 12 aug. 1950 (AAS 42 [1950] 561–578, 577); SCIC Instr. *La Scuola Cattolica,* 19 mar. 1977, 73

804 §2: SCConc Litt. circ., 28 ian. 1924; SCConc Resp., 26 iul. 1948; SCR Resp., 26 ian. 1959; AA 30;

SCIC Instr. *La Scuola Cattolica,* 19 mar. 1977, 43, 78

805: c. 1381 §3; SCConc Litt. circ., 28 ian. 1924

806 §1: c. 1382; SCSSU Litt. circ., 2 aug. 1939; SCR Resp., 26 ian. 1959; CD 35: 4; ES I, 39 §§1 et 2; DPME 66

806 §2: SCSSU Normae, 28 iul. 1948, 2°; Pius PP. XII, All. 13 sep. 1951

CHAPTER II. **Catholic Universities and Other Institutes of Higher Studies**

CAN. 807 The Church has the right to erect and direct universities, which contribute to a more profound human culture, the fuller development of the human person, and the fulfillment of the teaching function of the Church.

CAN. 808 Even if it is in fact Catholic, no university is to bear the title or name of *Catholic university* without the consent of competent ecclesiastical authority.

CAN. 809 If it is possible and expedient, conferences of bishops are to take care that there are universities or at least faculties suitably spread through their territory, in which the various disciplines are studied and taught, with their academic autonomy preserved and in light of Catholic doctrine.

CAN. 810 §1. The authority competent according to the statutes has the duty to make provision so that teachers are appointed in Catholic universities who besides their scientific and pedagogical qualifications are outstanding in integrity of doctrine and probity of life and that they are removed from their function when they lack these requirements; the manner of proceeding defined in the statutes is to be observed.

§2. The conferences of bishops and diocesan bishops concerned have the duty and right of being watchful so that the principles of Catholic doctrine are observed faithfully in these same universities.

CAPUT II. **De Catholicis Universitatibus Aliisque Studiorum Superiorum Institutis**

CAN. 807 Ius est Ecclesiae erigendi et moderandi studiorum universitates, quae quidem ad altiorem hominum culturam et pleniorem personae humanae promotionem necnon ad ipsius Ecclesiae munus docendi implendum conferant.

CAN. 808 Nulla studiorum universitas, etsi reapse catholica, titulum seu nomen *universitatis catholicae* gerat, nisi de consensu competentis auctoritatis ecclesiasticae.

CAN. 809 Episcoporum conferentiae curent ut habeantur, si fieri possit et expediat, studiorum universitates aut saltem facultates, in ipsarum territorio apte distributae, in quibus variae disciplinae, servata quidem earum scientifica autonomia, investigentur et tradantur, doctrinae catholicae ratione habita.

CAN. 810 §1. Auctoritati iuxta statuta competenti officium est providendi ut in universitatibus catholicis nominentur docentes qui, praeterquam idoneitate scientifica et paedagogica, doctrinae integritate et vitae probitate praestent utque, deficientibus his requisitis, servato modo procedendi in statutis definito, a munere removeantur.

§2. Episcoporum conferentiae et Episcopi dioecesani, quorum interest, officium habent et ius invigilandi, ut in iisdem universitatibus principia doctrinae catholicae fideliter serventur.

807: c. 1375; DSD introductio; SCSSU Decl., 17 nov. 1959 (AAS 51 [1959] 920); GE 8, 10; PAULUS PP. VI, All., 13 maii 1972 (AAS 64 [1972] 360–370); SCIC Ep., 23 apr. 1973; SCh prooemium, II, 1
  808: AA 24
  809: c. 1379 §2; GE 10; SCh 25 §3, 26

810 §1: c. 1381 §3; PIUS PP. XI, Const. Ap. *Deus scientiarum Dominus*, 24 maii 1931, 21, 22 (AAS 23 [1931] 251)
  810 §2: cc. 1381 §1, 2317; DPME 68; SCIC Ep., 23 apr. 1973

CAN. 811 §1. The competent ecclesiastical authority is to take care that in Catholic universities a faculty or institute or at least a chair of theology is erected in which classes are also given for lay students.

§2. In individual Catholic universities, there are to be classes which especially treat those theological questions which are connected to the disciplines of their faculties.

CAN. 812 Those who teach theological disciplines in any institutes of higher studies whatsoever must have a mandate from the competent ecclesiastical authority.

CAN. 813 The diocesan bishop is to have earnest pastoral care for students, even by erecting a parish or at least by designating priests stably for this, and is to make provision that at universities, even non-Catholic ones, there are Catholic university centers which give assistance, especially spiritual assistance, to youth.

CAN. 814 The prescripts established for universities apply equally to other institutes of higher learning.

CHAPTER III. Ecclesiastical Universities and Faculties

CAN. 815 Ecclesiastical universities or faculties, which are to investigate the sacred disciplines or those connected to the sacred and to instruct students scientifically in the same disciplines, are proper to the Church by virtue of its function to announce the revealed truth.

CAN. 811 §1. Curet auctoritas ecclesiastica competens ut in universitatibus catholicis erigatur facultas aut institutum aut saltem cathedra theologiae, in qua lectiones laicis quoque studentibus tradantur.

§2. In singulis universitatibus catholicis lectiones habeantur, in quibus eae praecipue tractentur quaestiones theologicae, quae cum disciplinis earundem facultatum sunt conexae.

CAN. 812 Qui in studiorum superiorum institutis quibuslibet disciplinas tradunt theologicas, auctoritatis ecclesiasticae competentis mandatum habeant oportet.

CAN. 813 Episcopus dioecesanus impensam habeat curam pastoralem studentium, etiam per paroeciae erectionem, vel saltem per sacerdotes ad hoc stabiliter deputatos, et provideat ut apud universitates, etiam non catholicas, centra habeantur universitaria catholica, quae iuventuti adiutorio sint, praesertim spirituali.

CAN. 814 Quae de universitatibus statuuntur praescripta, pari ratione applicantur aliis studiorum superiorum institutis.

CAPUT III. De Universitatibus et Facultatibus Ecclesiasticis

CAN. 815 Ecclesiae, vi muneris sui veritatem revelatam nuntiandi, propriae sunt universitates vel facultates ecclesiasticae ad disciplinas sacras vel cum sacris conexas pervestigandas, atque studentes in iisdem disciplinis scientifice instituendos.

811 §1: GE 10
811 §2: GE 10; GS 62
812: SCh 27 §1
813: GE 10; AG 38; DPME 68; SCIC Litt. circ., iun. 1976

814: SCh 85–87
815: DSD; SCSSU Ordinationes, 12 iun. 1931 (AAS 23 [1931] 263–284); SCIC Normae, 20 maii 1968; SCh 1–3; SCIC Ordinationes, 29 apr. 1979 (AAS 71 [1979] 500–521)

CAN. 816 §1. Ecclesiastical universities and faculties can be established only through erection by the Apostolic See or with its approval; their higher direction also pertains to it.

§2. Individual ecclesiastical universities and faculties must have their own statutes and plan of studies approved by the Apostolic See.

CAN. 817 No university or faculty which has not been erected or approved by the Apostolic See is able to confer academic degrees which have canonical effects in the Church.

CAN. 818 The prescripts established for Catholic universities in cann. 810, 812, and 813 are also valid for ecclesiastical universities and faculties.

CAN. 819 To the extent that the good of a diocese, a religious institute, or even the universal Church itself requires it, diocesan bishops or the competent superiors of the institutes must send to ecclesiastical universities or faculties youth, clerics, and members, who are outstanding in character, virtue, and talent.

CAN. 820 The moderators and professors of ecclesiastical universities and faculties are to take care that the various faculties of the university offer mutual assistance as their subject matter allows and that there is mutual cooper-

CAN. 816 §1. Universitates et facultates ecclesiasticae constitui tantum possunt erectione ab Apostolica Sede facta aut approbatione ab eadem concessa; eidem competit etiam earundem superius moderamen.

§2. Singulae universitates et facultates ecclesiasticae sua habere debent statuta et studiorum rationem ab Apostolica Sede approbata.

CAN. 817 Gradus academicos, qui effectus canonicos in Ecclesia habeant, nulla universitas vel facultas conferre valet, quae non sit ab Apostolica Sede erecta vel approbata.

CAN. 818 Quae de universitatibus catholicis in cann. 810, 812 et 813 statuuntur praescripta, de universitatibus facultatibusque ecclesiasticis quoque valent.

CAN. 819 Quatenus dioecesis aut instituti religiosi immo vel ipsius Ecclesiae universae bonum id requirat, debent Episcopi dioecesani aut institutorum Superiores competentes ad universitates vel facultates ecclesiasticas mittere iuvenes et clericos et sodales indole, virtute et ingenio praestantes.

CAN. 820 Curent universitatum et facultatum ecclesiasticarum Moderatores ac professores ut variae universitatis facultates mutuam sibi, prout obiectum siverit, praestent operam, utque inter propriam universi-

816 §1: c. 1376 §1; DSD 4; SCSSU Ordinationes, 12 iun. 1931, 1 (AAS 23 [1931] 263–284); SCh 5

816 §2: c. 1376 §2; DSD 5; SCSSU Ordinationes, 12 iun. 1931, 3 (AAS 23 [1931] 263–284); SCh 7; SCIC Ordinationes, 29 apr. 1979, 6 (AAS 71 [1979] 500–521)

817: c. 1377; DSD 6–10; SCSSU Ordinationes, 12 iun. 1931, 2 (AAS 23 [1931] 263–284); SCh 6, 9; SCIC Ordinationes, 29 apr. 1979, 7 (AAS 71 [1979] 500–521)

818: DSD 14, 19–22; SCSSU Ordinationes, 12 iun. 1931, 5 (AAS 23 [1931] 263–284); SCIC Normae, 20

maii 1968, 17–22; SCh 22–30; SCIC Ordinationes, 29 apr. 1979, 1, 64 (AAS 71 [1979] 500, 517)

819: c. 1380; SCC Decr. *Nemo de sacro,* 30 apr. 1918 (AAS 10 [1918] 237–238); Sec Litt. circ., 18 nov. 1920; SCSSU Litt. circ., 15 aug. 1931; SCSSU Normae *Nessun sacerdote,* 20 aug. 1942; SCSSU Normae, 1 nov. 1950; SCSSU Ep., 18 ian. 1958; OT 18; GE 10; AG 16; RFS 82–85; SCIC Normae, 22 apr. 1971; DPME 195

820: GE 12; GS 62; SCIC Normae, 20 maii 1968, 64; SCh 64; SCIC Ordinationes, 29 apr. 1979, 49 (AAS 71 [1979] 500–521)

ation between their own university or faculty and other universities and faculties, even non-ecclesiastical ones, by which they work together for the greater advance of knowledge through common effort, meetings, coordinated scientific research, and other means.

CAN. 821 The conference of bishops and the diocesan bishop are to make provision so that where possible, higher institutes of the religious sciences are established, namely, those which teach the theological disciplines and other disciplines which pertain to Christian culture.

tatem vel facultatem et alias universitates et facultates, etiam non ecclesiasticas, mutua habeatur cooperatio, qua nempe eaedem coniuncta opera, conventibus, investigationibus scientificis coordinatis aliisque mediis, ad maius scientiarum incrementum conspirent.

CAN. 821 Provideant Episcoporum conferentia atque Episcopus dioecesanus ut, ubi fieri possit, condantur instituta superiora scientiarum religiosarum, in quibus nempe edoceantur disciplinae theologicae aliaeque quae ad culturam christianam pertineant.

TITLE IV. Instruments of Social Communication and Books in Particular

TITULUS IV. De Instrumentis Communicationis Socialis et in Specie de Libris

CAN. 822 §1. The pastors of the Church, using a right proper to the Church in fulfilling their function, are to endeavor to make use of the instruments of social communication.

§2. These same pastors are to take care to teach the faithful that they are bound by the duty of cooperating so that a human and Christian spirit enlivens the use of instruments of social communication.

§3. All the Christian faithful, especially those who in any way have a role in the regulation or use of the same instruments, are to be concerned to offer assistance in pastoral action so that the Church exercises its function effectively through these instruments.

CAN. 823 §1. In order to preserve the integrity of the truths of faith and morals, the pas-

CAN. 822 §1. Ecclesiae pastores, in suo munere explendo iure Ecclesiae proprio utentes, instrumenta communicationis socialis adhibere satagant.

§2. Iisdem pastoribus curae sit fideles edocere se officio teneri cooperandi ut instrumentorum communicationis socialis usus humano christianoque spiritu vivificetur.

§3. Omnes christifideles, ii praesertim qui quoquo modo in eorundem instrumentorum ordinatione aut usu partem habent, solliciti sint operam adiutricem actioni pastorali praestare, ita ut Ecclesia etiam his instrumentis munus suum efficaciter exerceat.

CAN. 823 §1. Ut veritatum fidei morumque integritas servetur, officium et ius est

821: GE 10; DPME 69, 70

822: Pius PP. XII, Enc. *Miranda prorsus*, 8 sep. 1957 (AAS 49 [1957] 765–805); Ioannes PP. XXIII, Ep. *Nostra Patris*, 29 iun. 1961 (AAS 53 [1961] 491–495);

IM 1–3, 13, 16; CICS Instr. *Communio et progressio*, 23 iun. 1971 (AAS 63 [1971] 593–656); DPME 74

823 §1: c. 1384 §1; SCC Ep., 14 iun. 1938; SCSO Instr. *Cum in pravis*, 17 apr. 1943 (AAS 35 [1943]

tors of the Church have the duty and right to be watchful so that no harm is done to the faith or morals of the Christian faithful through writings or the use of instruments of social communication. They also have the duty and right to demand that writings to be published by the Christian faithful which touch upon faith or morals be submitted to their judgment and have the duty and right to condemn writings which harm correct faith or good morals.

§2. Bishops, individually or gathered in particular councils or conferences of bishops, have the duty and right mentioned in §1 with regard to the Christian faithful entrusted to their care; the supreme authority of the Church, however, has this duty and right with regard to the entire people of God.

CAN. 824 §1. Unless it is established otherwise, the local ordinary whose permission or approval to publish books must be sought according to the canons of this title is the proper local ordinary of the author or the ordinary of the place where the books are published.

§2. Those things established regarding books in the canons of this title must be applied to any writings whatsoever which are destined for public distribution, unless it is otherwise evident.

CAN. 825 §1. Books of the sacred scriptures cannot be published unless the Apostolic See or the conference of bishops has approved them. For the publication of their translations

Ecclesiae pastoribus invigilandi, ne scriptis aut usu instrumentorum communicationis socialis christifidelium fidei aut moribus detrimentum afferatur; item exigendi, ut quae scripta fidem moresve tangant a christifidelibus edenda suo iudicio subiciantur; necnon reprobandi scripta quae rectae fidei aut bonis moribus noceant.

§2. Officium et ius, de quibus in §1, competunt Episcopis, tum singulis tum in conciliis particularibus vel Episcoporum conferentiis adunatis quoad christifideles suae curae commissos, supremae autem Ecclesiae auctoritati quoad universum Dei populum.

CAN. 824 §1. Nisi aliud statuatur, loci Ordinarius, cuius licentia aut approbatio ad libros edendos iuxta canones huius tituli est petenda, est loci Ordinarius proprius auctoris aut Ordinarius loci in quo libri publici iuris fient.

§2. Quae in canonibus huius tituli statuuntur de libris, quibuslibet scriptis divulgationi publicae destinatis applicanda sunt, nisi aliud constet.

CAN. 825 §1. Libri sacrarum Scripturarum edi non possunt nisi ab Apostolica Sede aut ab Episcoporum conferentia approbati sint; itemque ut eorundem versiones in

144–145); Pius PP. XII, Enc. *Humani generis*, 12 aug. 1950 (AAS 42 [1950] 561–578, 577–578); SCSO Monitum, 28 feb. 1962; SCDF Notif., 14 iun. 1966 (AAS 58 [1966] 455); SCDF Decr. *Post editam*, 15 nov. 1966 (AAS 58 [1966] 1186); SPNC Instr. *Documentum quod*, 28 aug. 1968, in fine (AAS 60 [1968] 692–704); DPME 73; EP prooemium

823 §2: SCSO Monitum, 15 mar. 1923 (AAS 15 [1923] 152; SCSO Instr. *Cum in pravis*, 17 apr. 1943 (AAS 35 [1943] 144–145); Pius PP. XII, Enc. *Humani*

generis, 12 aug. 1950 (AAS 42 [1950] 561–578, 577–578); SCDF Instr. *Litteris apostolicis*, 23 feb. 1967; DPME 73; EP prooemium

824 §1: c. 1385 §2; EP 1, 1°

824 §2: c. 1384 §2; SCSO Monitum, 1 mar. 1962; EP 1, 2°

825 §1: cc. 1385 §1, 1°, 1391; CI Resp., 20 maii 1923, VIII (AAS 16 [1924] 115); Commissio Biblica, Resp., 22 aug. 1943 (AAS 35 [1943] 270–271); DV 22, 25; EP 2, 1°

into the vernacular, it is also required that they be approved by the same authority and provided with necessary and sufficient annotations.

§2. With the permission of the conference of bishops, Catholic members of the Christian faithful in collaboration with separated brothers and sisters can prepare and publish translations of the sacred scriptures provided with appropriate annotations.

CAN. 826 §1. The prescripts of can. 838 are to be observed concerning liturgical books.

§2. To reprint liturgical books, their translations into the vernacular, or their parts, an attestation of the ordinary of the place where they are published must establish their agreement with the approved edition.

§3. Books of prayers for the public or private use of the faithful are not to be published without the permission of the local ordinary.

CAN. 827 §1. To be published, catechisms and other writings pertaining to catechetical instruction or their translations require the approval of the local ordinary, without prejudice to the prescript of can. 775, §2.

§2. Books which regard questions pertaining to sacred scripture, theology, canon law, ecclesiastical history, and religious or moral disciplines cannot be used as texts on which instruction is based in elementary, middle, or higher schools unless they have been published with the approval of competent ecclesiastical

linguam vernaculam edi possint, requiritur ut ab eadem auctoritate sint approbatae atque insimul necessariis et sufficientibus explicationibus sint instructae.

§2. Versiones sacrarum Scripturarum convenientibus explicationibus instructas, communi etiam cum fratribus seiunctis opera, parare atque edere possunt christifideles catholici de licentia Episcoporum conferentiae.

CAN. 826 §1. Ad libros liturgicos quod attinet, serventur praescripta can. 838.

§2. Ut iterum edantur libri liturgici necnon eorum versiones in linguam vernaculam eorumve partes, constare debet de concordantia cum editione approbata ex attestatione Ordinarii loci in quo publici iuris fiunt.

§3. Libri precum pro publico vel privato fidelium usu ne edantur nisi de licentia loci Ordinarii.

CAN. 827 §1. Catechismi necnon alia scripta ad institutionem catecheticam pertinentia eorumve versiones, ut edantur, approbatione egent loci Ordinarii, firmo praescripto can. 775, §2.

§2. Nisi cum approbatione competentis auctoritatis ecclesiasticae editi sint aut ab ea postea approbati, in scholis, sive elementaris sive mediis sive superioribus, uti textus, quibus institutio nititur, adhiberi non possunt libri qui quaestiones respiciunt ad sacram Scripturam, ad theologiam, ius canonicum,

825 §2: DV 22; EP 2, 2°

826 §1: c. 1257; SC 22 §2, 36, 39, 40; IOe 21, 40; OE 5; UR 15; CONSILIUM AD EXSEQUENDAM CONSTITUTIONEM DE SACRA LITURGIA Litt. circ., 30 iun. 1965; AG 22; GS 58; SCCD Resp., 11 iun. 1970; EP 3; SCSCD Ep., 5 iun. 1976

826 §2: c. 1390; SRC Decr. *Cum, nostra aetate,* 27 ian. 1966, 9 (AAS 58 [1966] 170); CONSILIUM AD EXSEQUEDAM CONSTITUTIONEM DE SACRA LITURGIA Ep.

circ., 21 iun. 1967, 6; SCCD Instr. *Liturgicae instaurationes,* 15 sep. 1970, 11 (AAS 62 [1970] 702–703); SCDF Decl., 25 ian. 1974 (AAS 66 [1974] 661); EP 3, 2°

826 §3: c. 1385 §1, 2°; SCSO Decr. *Supremae huic,* 17 apr. 1942 (AAS 34 [1942] 149); EP 3, 3°

827 §1: c. 1385 §1, 2°; DCG 134; EP 4, 1°; SCDF Resp., 25 iun. 1980, I (AAS 72 [1980] 756)

827 §2: c. 1385 §1, 2°; EP 4, 2°

authority or have been approved by it subsequently.

§3. It is recommended that books dealing with the matters mentioned in §2, although not used as texts in instruction, as well as writings which especially concern religion or good morals are submitted to the judgment of the local ordinary.

§4. Books or other writings dealing with questions of religion or morals cannot be exhibited, sold, or distributed in churches or oratories unless they have been published with the permission of competent ecclesiastical authority or approved by it subsequently.

CAN. 828 It is not permitted to reprint collections of decrees or acts published by some ecclesiastical authority unless the prior permission of the same authority has been obtained and the conditions prescribed by it have been observed.

CAN. 829 The approval or permission to publish some work is valid for the original text but not for new editions or translations of the same.

CAN. 830 §1. The conference of bishops can compile a list of censors outstanding in knowledge, correct doctrine, and prudence to be available to diocesan curias or can also establish a commission of censors which local ordinaries can consult; the right of each local ordinary to entrust judgment regarding books to persons he approves, however, remains intact.

§2. In fulfilling this office, laying aside any favoritism, the censor is to consider only the doctrine of the Church concerning faith and morals

historiam ecclesiasticam, et ad religiosas aut morales disciplinas pertinentes.

§3. Commendatur ut libri materias de quibus in §2 tractantes, licet non adhibeantur uti textus in institutione tradenda, itemque scripta in quibus aliquid habetur quod religionis aut morum honestatis peculiariter intersit, iudicio subiciantur loci Ordinarii.

§4. In ecclesiis oratoriisve exponi, vendi aut dari non possunt libri vel alia scripta de quaestionibus religionis aut morum tractantia, nisi cum licentia competentis auctoritatis ecclesiasticae edita sint aut ab ea postea approbata.

CAN. 828 Collectiones decretorum aut actorum ab aliqua auctoritate ecclesiastica editas, iterum edere non licet, nisi impetrata prius eiusdem auctoritatis licentia et servatis condicionibus ab eadem praescriptis.

CAN. 829 Approbatio vel licentia alicuius operis edendi pro textu originali valet, non vero pro eiusdem novis editionibus vel translationibus.

CAN. 830 §1. Integro manente iure uniuscuiusque loci Ordinarii committendi personis sibi probatis iudicium de libris, ab Episcoporum conferentia confici potest elenchus censorum, scientia, recta doctrina et prudentia praestantium, qui curiis dioecesanis praesto sint, aut constitui etiam potest commissio censorum, quam loci Ordinarii consulere possint.

§2. Censor, in suo obeundo officio, omni personarum acceptione seposita, prae oculis tantummodo habeat Ecclesiae de fide et

827 §3: c. 1385 §1, 2°; EP 5, 1°; SCDF Resp., 25 iun. 1980, II (AAS 72 [1980] 756)
827 §4: EP 4, 4°
828: c. 1389
829: c. 1392 §1

830 §1: c. 1393 §1; SCSO Decr. *Supremae huic,* 17 apr. 1942 (AAS 34 [1942] 149); Pius PP. XII, All., 13 feb. 1955 (AAS 48 [1956] 127–135); EP 6, 1°
830 §2: c. 1393 §2; Ioannes PP. XXIII, All., 18 nov. 1959 (AAS 51 [1959] 867–868); EP 6, 2°

as it is proposed by the ecclesiastical magisterium.

§3. A censor must give his or her opinion in writing; if it is favorable, the ordinary, according to his own prudent judgment, is to grant permission for publication to take place, with his name and the time and place of the permission granted expressed. If he does not grant permission, the ordinary is to communicate the reasons for the denial to the author of the work.

CAN. 831 §1. Except for a just and reasonable cause, the Christian faithful are not to write anything for newspapers, magazines, or periodicals which are accustomed to attack openly the Catholic religion or good morals; clerics and members of religious institutes, however, are to do so only with the permission of the local ordinary.

§2. It is for the conference of bishops to establish norms concerning the requirements for clerics and members of religious institutes to take part on radio or television in dealing with questions of Catholic doctrine or morals.

CAN. 832 Members of religious institutes also need permission of their major superior according to the norm of the constitutions in order to publish writings dealing with questions of religion or morals.

TITLE V. The Profession of Faith

CAN. 833 The following are obliged personally to make a profession of faith according to the formula approved by the Apostolic See:

moribus doctrinam, uti a magisterio ecclesiastico proponitur.

§3. Censor sententiam suam scripto dare debet; quae si faverit, Ordinarius pro suo prudenti iudicio licentiam concedat ut editio fiat, expresso suo nomine necnon tempore ac loco concessae licentiae; quod si eam non concedat, rationes denegationis cum operis scriptore Ordinarius communicet.

CAN. 831 §1. In diariis, libellis aut foliis periodicis quae religionem catholicam aut bonos mores manifesto impetere solent, ne quidpiam conscribant christifideles, nisi iusta et rationabili de causa; clerici autem et institutorum religiosorum sodales, tantummodo de licentia loci Ordinarii.

§2. Episcoporum conferentiae est normas statuere de requisitis ut clericis atque sodalibus institutorum religiosorum partem habere liceat in tractandis via radiophonica aut televisifica quaestionibus, quae ad doctrinam catholicam aut mores attineant.

CAN. 832 Institutorum religiosorum sodales ut scripta quaestiones religionis morumve tractantia edere possint, licentia quoque egent sui Superioris maioris ad normam constitutionum.

TITULUS V. De Fidei Professione

CAN. 833 Obligatione emittendi personaliter professionem fidei, secundum formulam a Sede Apostolica probatam, tenentur:

830 §3: cc. 1393 §4, 1394 §2; EP 6, 3°
831 §1: c. 1386 §2; Sec Resp., 3 nov. 1928; EP 5, 2°
832: c. 1385 §3

833: c. 1406; CI Resp., 25 iul. 1926, III (AAS 18 [1926] 393); SCPF Rescr., 12 nov. 1966; SCDF *Formula professionis fidei* (AAS 59 [1967] 1058); Sec *Re-*

1° in the presence of the president or his delegate, all those who attend with either a deliberative or consultative vote an ecumenical or particular council, a synod of bishops, and a diocesan synod; the president, however, makes it in the presence of the council or synod;

2° those promoted to the cardinalatial dignity, according to the statutes of the sacred college;

3° in the presence of the one delegated by the Apostolic See, all those promoted to the episcopate as well as those who are equivalent to a diocesan bishop;

4° in the presence of the college of consultors, the diocesan administrator;

5° in the presence of the diocesan bishop or his delegate, vicars general, episcopal vicars, and judicial vicars;

6° in the presence of the local ordinary or his delegate and at the beginning of their function, pastors, the rector of a seminary, and teachers of theology and philosophy in seminaries; those to be promoted to the order of the diaconate;

7° in the presence of the grand chancellor or, in his absence, in the presence of the local ordinary or their delegates, the rector of an ecclesiastical or Catholic university, when the rector's function begins; in the presence of the rector if he is a priest or in the presence of the local ordinary or their delegates, teachers in any universities whatsoever who teach disciplines pertaining to faith or morals, when they begin their function;

8° Superiors in clerical religious institutes and societies of apostolic life, according to the norm of the constitutions.

1° coram praeside eiusve delegato, omnes qui Concilio Oecumenico vel particulari, synodo Episcoporum atque synodo dioecesanae intersunt cum voto sive deliberativo sive consultivo; praeses autem coram Concilio aut synodo;

2° promoti ad cardinalitiam dignitatem iuxta sacri Collegii statuta;

3° coram delegato ab Apostolica Sede, omnes promoti ad episcopatum, itemque qui Episcopo dioecesano aequiparantur;

4° coram collegio consultorum, Administrator dioecesanus;

5° coram Episcopo dioecesano eiusve delegato, Vicarii generales et Vicarii episcopales necnon Vicarii iudiciales;

6° coram loci Ordinario eiusve delegato, parochi, rector, magistri theologiae et philosophiae in seminariis, initio suscepti muneris; promovendi ad ordinem diaconatus;

7° coram Magno Cancellario eoque deficiente coram Ordinario loci eorumve delegatis, rector universitatis ecclesiasticae vel catholicae, initio suscepti muneris; coram rectore, si sit sacerdos, vel coram loci Ordinario eorumve delegatis, docentes qui disciplinas ad fidem vel mores pertinentes in quibusvis universitatibus tradunt, initio suscepti muneris;

8° Superiores in institutis religiosis et societatibus vitae apostolicae clericalibus, ad normam constitutionum.

---

golamento generale della Curia Romana, 22 feb. 1968, 12 (AAS 60 [1968] 135); SCh 27 §1; SCIC Ordinationes, 29 apr. 1979, 8, 4° (AAS 71 [1979] 500–521)

BOOK IV. THE SANCTIFYING FUNCTION OF THE CHURCH

LIBER IV. DE ECCLESIAE MUNERE SANCTIFICANDI

CAN. 834 §1. The Church fulfills its sanctifying function in a particular way through the sacred liturgy, which is an exercise of the priestly function of Jesus Christ. In the sacred liturgy the sanctification of humanity is signified through sensible signs and effected in a manner proper to each sign. In the sacred liturgy, the whole public worship of God is carried out by the Head and members of the mystical Body of Jesus Christ.

§2. Such worship takes place when it is carried out in the name of the Church by persons legitimately designated and through acts approved by the authority of the Church.

CAN. 835 §1. The bishops in the first place exercise the sanctifying function; they are the high priests, the principal dispensers of the mysteries of God, and the directors, promoters, and guardians of the entire liturgical life in the church entrusted to them.

§2. Presbyters also exercise this function; sharing in the priesthood of Christ and as his ministers under the authority of the bishop, they are consecrated to celebrate divine worship and to sanctify the people.

§3. Deacons have a part in the celebration of divine worship according to the norm of the prescripts of the law.

§4. The other members of the Christian faithful also have their own part in the function of sanctifying by participating actively in their own way in liturgical celebrations, especially the Eucharist. Parents share in a particular way in

CAN. 834 §1. Munus sanctificandi Ecclesia peculiari modo adimplet per sacram liturgiam, quae quidem habetur ut Iesu Christi muneris sacerdotalis exercitatio, in qua hominum sanctificatio per signa sensibilia significatur ac modo singulis proprio efficitur, atque a mystico Iesu Christi Corpore, Capite nempe et membris, integer cultus Dei publicus exercetur.

§2. Huiusmodi cultus tunc habetur, cum defertur nomine Ecclesiae a personis legitime deputatis et per actus ab Ecclesiae auctoritate probatos.

CAN. 835 §1. Munus sanctificandi exercent imprimis Episcopi, qui sunt magni sacerdotes, mysteriorum Dei praecipui dispensatores atque totius vitae liturgicae in Ecclesia sibi commissa moderatores, promotores atque custodes.

§2. Illud quoque exercent presbyteri, qui nempe, et ipsi Christi sacerdotii participes, ut eius ministri sub Episcopi auctoritate, ad cultum divinum celebrandum et populum sanctificandum consecrantur.

§3. Diaconi in divino cultu celebrando partem habent, ad normam iuris praescriptorum.

§4. In munere sanctificandi propriam sibi partem habent ceteri quoque christifideles actuose liturgicas celebrationes, eucharisticam praesertim, suo modo participando; peculiari modo idem munus participant par-

834 §1: MD 522, 528, 529; SC 7
834 §2: c. 1256; MD 555; SRC Instr. *De musica sacra*, 3 sep. 1958, 1 (AAS 50 [1958] 632); LG 11
835: LG cap. V

835 §1: SC 41; LG 26, 41; CD 11, 15
835 §2: LG 28, 41; CD 15; PO 5; IGMR 59
835 §3: LG 29, 41
835 §4: SC 26–31; LG 41; GS 48; MQ 530

this function by leading a conjugal life in a Christian spirit and by seeing to the Christian education of their children.

CAN. 836 Since Christian worship, in which the common priesthood of the Christian faithful is carried out, is a work which proceeds from faith and is based on it, sacred ministers are to take care to arouse and enlighten this faith diligently, especially through the ministry of the word, which gives birth to and nourishes the faith.

CAN. 837 §1. Liturgical actions are not private actions but celebrations of the Church itself which is *the sacrament of unity,* that is, a holy people gathered and ordered under the bishops. Liturgical actions therefore belong to the whole body of the Church and manifest and affect it; they touch its individual members in different ways, however, according to the diversity of orders, functions, and actual participation.

§2. Inasmuch as liturgical actions by their nature entail a common celebration, they are to be celebrated with the presence and active participation of the Christian faithful where possible.

CAN. 838 §1. The direction of the sacred liturgy depends solely on the authority of the Church which resides in the Apostolic See and, according to the norm of law, the diocesan bishop.

§2. It is for the Apostolic See to order the sacred liturgy of the universal Church, publish liturgical books and review their translations in vernacular languages, and exercise vigilance that liturgical regulations are observed faithfully everywhere.

entes vitam coniugalem spiritu christiano ducendo et educationem christianam filiorum procurando.

CAN. 836 Cum cultus christianus, in quo sacerdotium commune christifidelium exercetur, opus sit quod a fide procedit et eadem innititur, ministri sacri eandem excitare et illustrare sedulo curent, ministerio praesertim verbi, quo fides nascitur et nutritur.

CAN. 837 §1. Actiones liturgicae non sunt actiones privatae, sed celebrationes Ecclesiae ipsius, quae est «unitatis sacramentum», scilicet plebs sancta sub Episcopis adunata et ordinata; quare ad universum corpus Ecclesiae pertinent illudque manifestant et afficiunt; singula vero membra ipsius attingunt diverso modo, pro diversitate ordinum, munerum et actualis participationis.

§2. Actiones liturgicae, quatenus suapte natura celebrationem communem secumferant, ubi id fieri potest, cum frequentia et actuosa participatione christifidelium celebrentur.

CAN. 838 §1. Sacrae liturgiae moderatio ab Ecclesiae auctoritate unice pendet: quae quidem est penes Apostolicam Sedem et, ad normam iuris, penes Episcopum dioecesanum.

§2. Apostolicae Sedis est sacram liturgiam Ecclesiae universae ordinare, libros liturgicos edere eorumque versiones in linguas vernaculas recognoscere, necnon advigilare ut ordinationes liturgicae ubique fideliter observentur.

836: MD 536; SC 9–11, 33–36, 59; LG 10, 11, 28, 34; CD 30; DCG 57; DPME 55; 59
  837 §1: MD 538, 555; SC 26–32; MF 761–762
  837 §2: SC 14, 26, 27, 48
  838 §1: cc. 1257, 1260; MD 544; SCSO Monitum,

14 feb. 1958 (AAS 50 [1958] 114); SCSO Monitum, 24 iul. 1958 (AAS 50 [1958] 536); SC 22 §1; IOe 22: PAULUS PP. VI, m.p. *Sacram Liturgiam,* 25 ian. 1964, XI (AAS 56 [1964] 144).
  838 §2: c. 1257; SC 36; IOe 21

§3. It pertains to the conferences of bishops to prepare and publish, after the prior review of the Holy See, translations of liturgical books in vernacular languages, adapted appropriately within the limits defined in the liturgical books themselves.

§4. Within the limits of his competence, it pertains to the diocesan bishop in the Church entrusted to him to issue liturgical norms which bind everyone.

CAN. 839 §1. The Church carries out the function of sanctifying also by other means, both by prayers in which it asks God to sanctify the Christian faithful in truth, and by works of penance and charity which greatly help to root and strengthen the kingdom of Christ in souls and contribute to the salvation of the world.

§2. Local ordinaries are to take care that the prayers and pious and sacred exercises of the Christian people are fully in keeping with the norms of the Church.

§3. Ad Episcoporum conferentias spectat versiones librorum liturgicorum in linguas vernaculas, convenienter intra limites in ipsis libris liturgicis definitos aptatas, parare, easque edere, praevia recognitione Sanctae Sedis.

§4. Ad Episcopum dioecesanum in Ecclesia sibi commissa pertinet, intra limites suae competentiae, normas de re liturgica dare, quibus omnes tenentur.

CAN. 839 §1. Aliis quoque mediis munus sanctificationis peragit Ecclesia, sive orationibus, quibus Deum deprecatur ut christifideles sanctificati sint in veritate, sive paenitentiae et caritatis operibus, quae quidem magnopere ad Regnum Christi in animis radicandum et roborandum adiuvant et ad mundi salutem conferunt.

§2. Curent locorum Ordinarii ut orationes necnon pia et sacra exercitia populi christiani normis Ecclesiae plene congruant.

838 §3: SC 22 §2; 36 §§3 et 4; 39; 40; IOe 40; OE 5; UR 15; Consilium ad exsequendam Constitutionem de Sacra Liturgia Litt. circ., 30 iun. 1965; AG 22; GS 58; EP 3; SCCD Resp., 11 iun. 1970; SCSCD Ep., 5 iun. 1976

838 §4: c. 1261 §2; SC 22; IOe 22; LG 26; CD 15, 35; SRC Instr. *Tres abhinc annos,* 4 maii 1967 (AAS 59 [1967] 442–448); SCCD Instr. *Liturgicae instaurationes,* 5 sep. 1970 (AAS 62 [1970] 694)

839 §1: MD 583–587; SC 12, 13; LG 12

839 §2: cc. 1259–1261; SCSO Decr. *Iam olim,* 26 maii 1937 (AAS 29 [1937] 304–305); SCSO Decr. *Quaesitum est,* 18 iun. 1938 (AAS 30 [1938] 226–227); SCSO Decr. *In generali,* 12 dec. 1939 (AAS 32 [1940] 24); MD 587; SC 13

PART I. THE SACRAMENTS

PARS I. DE SACRAMENTIS

CAN. 840 The sacraments of the New Testament were instituted by Christ the Lord and entrusted to the Church. As actions of Christ and the Church, they are signs and means which express and strengthen the faith, render worship to God, and effect the sanctification of humanity and thus contribute in the greatest way to establish, strengthen, and manifest ecclesiastical communion. Accordingly, in the celebration of the sacraments the sacred ministers and the other members of the Christian faithful must use the greatest veneration and necessary diligence.

CAN. 841 Since the sacraments are the same for the whole Church and belong to the divine deposit, it is only for the supreme authority of the Church to approve or define the requirements for their validity; it is for the same or another competent authority according to the norm of can. 838 §§3 and 4 to decide what pertains to their licit celebration, administration, and reception and to the order to be observed in their celebration.

CAN. 842 §1. A person who has not received baptism cannot be admitted validly to the other sacraments.

§2. The sacraments of baptism, confirmation, and the Most Holy Eucharist are interrelated in such a way that they are required for full Christian initiation.

CAN. 840 Sacramenta Novi Testamenti, a Christo Domino instituta et Ecclesiae concredita, utpote actiones Christi et Ecclesiae, signa exstant ac media quibus fides exprimitur et roboratur, cultus Deo redditur et hominum sanctificatio efficitur, atque ideo ad communionem ecclesiasticam inducendam, firmandam et manifestandam summopere conferunt; quapropter in iis celebrandis summa veneratione debitaque diligentia uti debent tum sacri ministri tum ceteri christifideles.

CAN. 841 Cum sacramenta eadem sint pro universa Ecclesia et ad divinum depositum pertineant, unius supremae Ecclesiae auctoritatis est probare vel definire quae ad eorum validitatem sunt requisita, atque eiusdem aliusve auctoritatis competentis, ad normam can. 838, §§3 et 4, est decernere quae ad eorum celebrationem, administrationem et receptionem licitam necnon ad ordinem in eorum celebratione servandum spectant.

CAN. 842 §1. Ad cetera sacramenta valide admitti nequit, qui baptismum non recepit.

§2. Sacramenta baptismi, confirmationis et sanctissimae Eucharistiae ita inter se coalescunt, ut ad plenam initiationem christianam requirantur.

840: c. 731 §1; SC 6, 7, 14, 26–28, 59; LG 7, 14; UT 911
841: c. 733 §1; MD 539
842 §1: c. 737 §1

842 §2: SC 71; OBP Prae. gen., 2; PAULUS PP. VI, Const. Ap. *Divinae consortium naturae*, 15 aug. 1971 (AAS 63 [1971] 657); OICA Prae., 34 et 36

CAN. 843 §1. Sacred ministers cannot deny the sacraments to those who seek them at appropriate times, are properly disposed, and are not prohibited by law from receiving them.

§2. Pastors of souls and other members of the Christian faithful, according to their respective ecclesiastical function, have the duty to take care that those who seek the sacraments are prepared to receive them by proper evangelization and catechetical instruction, attentive to the norms issued by competent authority.

CAN. 844 §1. Catholic ministers administer the sacraments licitly to Catholic members of the Christian faithful alone, who likewise receive them licitly from Catholic ministers alone, without prejudice to the prescripts of §§2, 3, and 4 of this canon, and can. 861, §2.

§2. Whenever necessity requires it or true spiritual advantage suggests it, and provided that danger of error or of indifferentism is avoided, the Christian faithful for whom it is physically or morally impossible to approach a Catholic minister are permitted to receive the sacraments of penance, Eucharist, and anointing of the sick from non-Catholic ministers in whose Churches these sacraments are valid.

§3. Catholic ministers administer the sacraments of penance, Eucharist, and anointing of the sick licitly to members of Eastern Churches which do not have full communion with the Catholic Church if they seek such on their own accord and are properly disposed. This is also valid for members of other Churches which in the judgment of the Apostolic See are in the same condition in regard to the sacraments as these Eastern Churches.

CAN. 843 §1. Ministri sacri denegare non possunt sacramenta iis qui opportune eadem petant, rite sint dispositi, nec iure ab iis recipiendis prohibeantur.

§2. Animarum pastores ceterique christifideles, pro suo quisque ecclesiastico munere, officium habent curandi ut qui sacramenta petunt debita evangelizatione necnon catechetica institutione ad eadem recipienda praeparentur, attentis normis a competenti auctoritate editis.

CAN. 844 §1. Ministri catholici sacramenta licite administrant solis christifidelibus catholicis, qui pariter eadem a solis ministris catholicis licite recipiunt, salvis huius canonis §§2, 3 et 4, atque can. 861, §2 praescriptis.

§2. Quoties necessitas id postulet aut vera spiritualis utilitas id suadeat, et dummodo periculum vitetur erroris vel indifferentismi, licet christifidelibus quibus physice aut moraliter impossibile sit accedere ad ministrum catholicum, sacramenta paenitentiae, Eucharistiae et unctionis infirmorum recipere a ministris non catholicis, in quorum Ecclesia valida exsistunt praedicta sacramenta.

§3. Ministri catholici licite sacramenta paenitentiae, Eucharistiae et unctionis infirmorum administrant membris Ecclesiarum orientalium quae plenam cum Ecclesia catholica communionem non habent, si sponte id petant et rite sint disposita; quod etiam valet quoad membra aliarum Ecclesiarum, quae iudicio Sedis Apostolicae, ad sacramenta quod attinet, in pari condicione ac praedictae Ecclesiae orientales versantur.

843 §1: cc. 467, 468, 682
843 §2: SC 19; PO 4; DCG; UT 911, 921
844 §1: c. 731 §2; UR 8
844 §2: SCSO Resp., 15 nov. 1941; OE 27; DO I, 43,

46, 55–59; SCUF Decl., 7 ian. 1970, 6 (AAS 62 [1970] 184–188); SCUF Communicatio, 17 oct. 1973, 9 (AAS 65 [1973] 616–619)
844 §3: OE 27; UR 15; DO I: 46

§4. If the danger of death is present or if, in the judgment of the diocesan bishop or conference of bishops, some other grave necessity urges it, Catholic ministers administer these same sacraments licitly also to other Christians not having full communion with the Catholic Church, who cannot approach a minister of their own community and who seek such on their own accord, provided that they manifest Catholic faith in respect to these sacraments and are properly disposed.

§5. For the cases mentioned in §§2, 3, and 4, the diocesan bishop or conference of bishops is not to issue general norms except after consultation at least with the local competent authority of the interested non-Catholic Church or community.

CAN. 845 §1. Since the sacraments of baptism, confirmation, and orders imprint a character, they cannot be repeated.

§2. If after completing a diligent inquiry a prudent doubt still exists whether the sacraments mentioned in §1 were actually or validly conferred, they are to be conferred conditionally.

CAN. 846 §1. In celebrating the sacraments the liturgical books approved by competent authority are to be observed faithfully; accordingly, no one is to add, omit, or alter anything in them on one's own authority.

§2. The minister is to celebrate the sacraments according to the minister's own rite.

CAN. 847 §1. In administering the sacra-

§4. Si adsit periculum mortis aut, iudicio Episcopi dioecesani aut Episcoporum conferentiae, alia urgeat gravis necessitas, ministri catholici licite eadem sacramenta administrant ceteris quoque christianis plenam communionem cum Ecclesia catholica non habentibus, qui ad suae communitatis ministrum accedere nequeant atque sponte id petant, dummodo quoad eadem sacramenta fidem catholicam manifestent et rite sint dispositi.

§5. Pro casibus de quibus in §§2, 3 et 4, Episcopus dioecesanus aut Episcoporum conferentia generales normas ne ferant, nisi post consultationem cum auctoritate competenti saltem locali Ecclesiae vel communitatis non catholicae, cuius interest.

CAN. 845 §1. Sacramenta baptismi, confirmationis et ordinis, quippe quae characterem imprimant, iterari nequeunt.

§2. Si, diligenti inquisitione peracta, prudens adhuc dubium supersit num sacramenta de quibus in §1 revera aut valide collata fuerint, sub condicione conferantur.

CAN. 846 §1. In sacramentis celebrandis fideliter serventur libri liturgici a competenti auctoritate probati; quapropter nemo in iisdem quidpiam proprio marte addat, demat aut mutet.

§2. Minister sacramenta celebret secundum proprium ritum.

CAN. 847 §1. In administrandis sacra-

844 §4: DO I: 55; SCUF Instr. *In quibus rerum,* 1 iun. 1972, 6 (AAS 64 [1972] 518–525)

844 §5: DO I: 42

845 §1: c. 732; OBP Prae. gen., 4; OC 2; OICA appendix, 7

845 §2: OICA appendix, 7; OD 1: 9–18

846 §1: c. 733 §1; SCSO Monitum, 24 iul. 1958 (AAS 50 [1958] 536); SCC Decr. *Privilegia et gratias,* 8 aug. 1959 (AAS 51 [1959] 915–918); SC 22 §3; 63; SRC

Instr. *Tres abhinc annos,* 4 maii 1967 (AAS 59 [1967] 442–443); SCCD Instr. *Liturgicae instaurationes,* 5 sep. 1970 (AAS 62 [1970] 693); ID 4, 5

846 §2: c. 733 §2; SC 4; OE 3, 6; SRC *Ritus servandus in concelebratione Missae et ritus Communionis sub utraque specie,* Prae. 7 (1965)

847 §1: cc. 734, 735; PAULUS PP. VI, Const. Ap. *Sacram Unctionem infirmorum,* 30 nov. 1972 (AAS 65 [1973] 5–9); *Ordo Benedicendi Oleum Catechu-*

ments in which holy oils must be used, the minister must use oils pressed from olives or other plants and, without prejudice to the prescript of can. 999, n. 2, consecrated or blessed recently by a bishop; he is not to use old oils unless it is necessary.

§2. The pastor is to obtain the holy oils from his own bishop and is to preserve them diligently with proper care.

CAN. 848 The minister is to seek nothing for the administration of the sacraments beyond the offerings defined by competent authority, always taking care that the needy are not deprived of the assistance of the sacraments because of poverty.

TITLE I. Baptism

CAN. 849 Baptism, the gateway to the sacraments and necessary for salvation by actual reception or at least by desire, is validly conferred only by a washing of true water with the proper form of words. Through baptism men and women are freed from sin, are reborn as children of God, and, configured to Christ by an indelible character, are incorporated into the Church.

CHAPTER I. The Celebration of Baptism

CAN. 850 Baptism is administered according to the order prescribed in the approved liturgical books, except in case of urgent necessity when only those things required for the validity of the sacrament must be observed.

mentis, in quibus sacra olea adhibenda sunt, minister uti debet oleis ex olivis aut aliis ex plantis expressis atque, salvo praescripto can. 999, n. 2, ab Episcopo consecratis vel benedictis, et quidem recenter; veteribus ne utatur, nisi adsit necessitas.

§2. Parochus olea sacra a proprio Episcopo impetret eaque decenti custodia diligentur asservet.

CAN. 848 Minister, praeter oblationes a competenti auctoritate definitas, pro sacramentorum administratione nihil petat, cauto semper ne egentes priventur auxilio sacramentorum ratione paupertatis.

TITULUS I. De Baptismo

CAN. 849 Baptismus, ianua sacramentorum, in re vel saltem in voto ad salutem necessarius, quo homines a peccatis liberantur, in Dei filios regenerantur atque indelebili charactere Christo configurati Ecclesiae incorporantur, valide confertur tantummodo per lavacrum aquae verae cum debita verborum forma.

CAPUT I. De Baptismi Celebratione

CAN. 850 Baptismus ministratur secundum ordinem in probatis liturgicis libris praescriptum, excepto casu necessitatis urgentis, in quo ea tantum observari debent, quae ad validitatem sacramenti requiruntur.

menorum et Infirmorum et Conficiendi Chrisma, 3 dec. 1970, 3, 4

847 §2: *Ordo Benedicendi Oleum Catechumenorum et Infirmorum et Conficiendi Chrisma*, 3 dec. 1970, 28

848: c. 736; IOe 22; UT 921

849: cc. 87, 737 §1; LG 11, 16, 40; AG 14; PO 5; OBP Prae. gen., 1–6, 18, 21, 23

850: c. 737 §2; OBP Prae. gen. 23, Prae. 21, 22, cap. V; OICA cap. III

CAN. 851   The celebration of baptism must be prepared properly; consequently:

1° an adult who intends to receive baptism is to be admitted to the catechumenate and is to be led insofar as possible through the various stages to sacramental initiation, according to the order of initiation adapted by the conference of bishops and the special norms issued by it;

2° the parents of an infant to be baptized and those who are to undertake the function of sponsor are to be instructed properly on the meaning of this sacrament and the obligations attached to it. The pastor personally or through others is to take care that the parents are properly instructed through both pastoral advice and common prayer, bringing several families together and, where possible, visiting them.

CAN. 852   §1. The prescripts of the canons on adult baptism are to be applied to all those who, no longer infants, have attained the use of reason.

§2. A person who is not responsible for oneself *(non sui compos)* is also regarded as an infant with respect to baptism.

CAN. 853   Apart from a case of necessity, the water to be used in conferring baptism must be blessed according to the prescripts of the liturgical books.

CAN. 854   Baptism is to be conferred either by immersion or by pouring; the prescripts of the conference of bishops are to be observed.

CAN. 855   Parents, sponsors, and the pas-

CAN. 851   Baptismi celebratio debite praeparetur oportet; itaque:

1° adultus, qui baptismum recipere intendit, ad catechumenatum admittatur et, quatenus fieri potest, per varios gradus ad initiationem sacramentalem perducatur, secundum ordinem initiationis ab Episcoporum conferentia aptatum et peculiares normas ab eadem editas;

2° infantis baptizandi parentes, itemque qui munus patrini sunt suscepturi, de significatione huius sacramenti deque obligationibus cum eo cohaerentibus rite edoceantur; parochus per se vel per alios curet ut ita pastoralibus monitionibus, immo et communi precatione, debite parentes instruantur, plures adunando familias atque, ubi fieri possit, eas visitando.

CAN. 852   §1. Quae in canonibus de baptismo adulti habentur praescripta, applicantur omnibus qui, infantia egressi, rationis usum assecuti sunt.

§2. Infanti assimilatur, etiam ad baptismum quod attinet, qui non est sui compos.

CAN. 853   Aqua in baptismo conferendo adhibenda, extra casum necessitatis, benedicta sit oportet, secundum librorum liturgicorum praescripta.

CAN. 854   Baptismus conferatur sive per immersionem sive per infusionem, servatis Episcoporum conferentiae praescriptis.

CAN. 855   Curent parentes, patrini et

851: SC 64, 67; LG 14; CD 14; AG 14; SRC Decr. *Ordo Baptismi Adultorum per Gradus Catechumenatus Dispositus,* 16 apr. 1962 (AAS 54 [1962] 310); OBP Prae. gen., 12–14; Prae., 5, 1; DCG 96a, c; OICA Prae., cap. I, II; SCDF Instr. *Pastoralis actio,* 20 oct. 1980, 27–33 (AAS 72 [1980] 1150–1155)
852 §1: OICA cap. V; OC 11

852 §2: c. 745 §2, 1°
853: c. 757; SC 70; OBP Prae. gen., 21; Prae., 18, 28; OICA Prae., 28, 29, cap. I, 208, 210
854: c. 758; OBP Prae. gen., 22, 30, Prae., 18; OICA 32, 220
855: c. 761; OICA 26, 88, 203–205

tor are to take care that a name foreign to Christian sensibility is not given.

CAN. 856 Although baptism can be celebrated on any day, it is nevertheless recommended that it be celebrated ordinarily on Sunday or, if possible, at the Easter Vigil.

CAN. 857 §1. Apart from a case of necessity, the proper place of baptism is a church or oratory.

§2. As a rule an adult is to be baptized in his or her parish church and an infant in the parish church of the parents unless a just cause suggests otherwise.

CAN. 858 §1. Every parish church is to have a baptismal font, without prejudice to the cumulative right already acquired by other churches.

§2. After having heard the local pastor, the local ordinary can permit or order for the convenience of the faithful that there also be a baptismal font in another church or oratory within the boundaries of the parish.

CAN. 859 If because of distance or other circumstances the one to be baptized cannot go or be brought to the parish church or to the other church or oratory mentioned in can. 858, §2 without grave inconvenience, baptism can and must be conferred in another nearer church or oratory, or even in another fitting place.

CAN. 860 §1. Apart from a case of necessity, baptism is not to be conferred in private houses, unless the local ordinary has permitted it for a grave cause.

§2. Except in a case of necessity or for some

parochus ne imponatur nomen a sensu christiano alienum.

CAN. 856 Licet baptismus quolibet die celebrari possit, commendatur tamen ut ordinarie die dominica aut, si fieri possit, in vigilia Paschatis, celebretur.

CAN. 857 §1. Extra casum necessitatis, proprius baptismi locus est ecclesia aut oratorium.

§2. Pro regula habeatur ut adultus baptizetur in propria ecclesia paroeciali, infans vero in ecclesia paroeciali parentum propria, nisi iusta causa aliud suadeat.

CAN. 858 §1. Quaevis ecclesia paroecialis baptismalem fontem habeat, salvo iure cumulativo aliis ecclesiis eam quaesito.

§2. Loci Ordinarius, audito loci parocho, potest ad fidelium commoditatem permittere aut iubere, ut fons baptismalis habeatur etiam in alia ecclesia aut oratorio intra paroeciae fines.

CAN. 859 Si ad ecclesiam paroecialem aut ad aliam ecclesiam vel oratorium, de quo in can. 858, §2, baptizandus, propter locorum distantiam aliave adiuncta, sine gravi incommodo accedere vel transferri nequeat, baptismus conferri potest et debet in alia propinquiore ecclesia vel oratorio, aut etiam alio in loco decenti.

CAN. 860 §1. Praeter casum necessitatis, baptismus ne conferatur in domibus privatis, nisi loci Ordinarius gravi de causa id permiserit.

§2. In valetudinariis, nisi aliter Episcopus

856: c. 772; OBP Prae. gen., 6, Prae. 9, 29; DPME 86a; OICA 49, 55, 59, 244, 343

857 §1: c. 773; OBP Prae. gen. 24–26, Prae., 10–13

857 §2: SCCD Resp., 19 aug. 1970; OBP Prae. 10

858 §1: c. 774 §1; CI Resp., 12 nov. 1922, IV (AAS 14 [1922] 662); OBP Prae. 10

858 §2: c. 774 §2; OBP Prae. 11

859: c. 775

860 §1: c. 776; SCDS Resp., 22 iul. 1925 (AAS 17 [1925] 452); OBP Prae. 12

860 §2: OBP Prae. 13

other compelling pastoral reason, baptism is not to be celebrated in hospitals unless the diocesan bishop has established otherwise.

CHAPTER II. The Minister of Baptism

CAN. 861   §1. The ordinary minister of baptism is a bishop, a presbyter, or a deacon, without prejudice to the prescript of can. 530, n. 1.

§2. When an ordinary minister is absent or impeded, a catechist or another person designated for this function by the local ordinary, or in a case of necessity any person with the right intention, confers baptism licitly. Pastors of souls, especially the pastor of a parish, are to be concerned that the Christian faithful are taught the correct way to baptize.

CAN. 862   Except in a case of necessity, no one is permitted to confer baptism in the territory of another without the required permission, not even upon his own subjects.

CAN. 863   The baptism of adults, at least of those who have completed their fourteenth year, is to be deferred to the diocesan bishop so that he himself administers it if he has judged it expedient.

CHAPTER III. Those to be Baptized

CAN. 864   Every person not yet baptized and only such a person is capable of baptism.

CAN. 865   §1. For an adult to be baptized, the person must have manifested the intention to receive baptism, have been instructed sufficiently about the truths of the faith and Christian obligations, and have been tested in the

dioecesanus statuerit, baptismus ne celebretur, nisi in casu necessitatis vel alia ratione pastorali cogente.

CAPUT II. De Baptismi Ministro

CAN. 861   §1. Minister ordinarius baptismi est Episcopus, presbyter et diaconus, firmo praescripto can. 530, n. 1.

§2. Absente aut impedito ministro ordinario, licite baptismum confert catechista aliusve ad hoc munus ab Ordinario loci deputatus, immo, in casu necessitatis, quilibet homo debita intentione motus; solliciti sint animarum pastores, praesertim parochus, ut christifideles de recto baptizandi modo edoceantur.

CAN. 862   Excepto casu necessitatis, nemini licet, sine debita licentia, in alieno territorio baptismum conferre, ne suis quidem subditis.

CAN. 863   Baptismus adultorum, saltem eorum qui aetatem quattuordecim annorum expleverunt, ad Episcopum dioecesanum deferatur ut, si id expedire iudicaverit, ab ipso administretur.

CAPUT III. De Baptizandis

CAN. 864   Baptismi capax est omnis et solus homo nondum baptizatus.

CAN. 865   §1. Ut adultus baptizari possit, oportet voluntatem baptismum recipiendi manifestaverit, de fidei veritatibus obligationibusque christianis sufficienter sit instructus atque in vita christiana per catechumenatum

---

861 §1: cc. 738, 741; LG 26, 29; PO 5; SDO 22, 1; OBP Prae. gen. 11

861 §2: c. 742; OBP Prae. gen. 16, 17, cap. IV et V; OICA cap. III

862: c. 739

863: c. 744; OICA 44

864: c. 745 §1

865 §1: c. 752 §1; SCSO et SCPF Resp., 19 feb. 1938; OICA 20, 49, 62

Christian life through the catechumenate. The adult is also to be urged to have sorrow for personal sins.

§2. An adult in danger of death can be baptized if, having some knowledge of the principal truths of the faith, the person has manifested in any way at all the intention to receive baptism and promises to observe the commandments of the Christian religion.

CAN. 866   Unless there is a grave reason to the contrary, an adult who is baptized is to be confirmed immediately after baptism and is to participate in the eucharistic celebration also by receiving communion

CAN. 867   §1. Parents are obliged to take care that infants are baptized in the first few weeks; as soon as possible after the birth or even before it, they are to go to the pastor to request the sacrament for their child and to be prepared properly for it.

§2. An infant in danger of death is to be baptized without delay.

CAN. 868   §1. For an infant to be baptized licitly:

1° the parents or at least one of them or the person who legitimately takes their place must consent;

2° there must be a founded hope that the infant will be brought up in the Catholic religion; if such hope is altogether lacking, the baptism is to be delayed according to the prescripts of particular law after the parents have been advised about the reason.

§2. An infant of Catholic parents or even of

sit probatus; admoneatur etiam ut de peccatis suis doleat.

§2. Adultus, qui in periculo mortis versatur, baptizari potest si, aliquam de praecipuis fidei veritatibus cognitionem habens, quovis modo intentionem suam baptismum recipiendi manifestaverit et promittat se christianae religionis mandata esse servaturum.

CAN. 866   Adultus qui baptizatur, nisi gravis obstet ratio, statim post baptismum confirmetur atque celebrationem eucharisticam, communionem etiam recipiendo, participet.

CAN. 867   §1. Parentes obligatione tenentur curandi ut infantes intra priores hebdomadas baptizentur; quam primum post nativitatem, immo iam ante eam, parochum adeant ut sacramentum pro filio petant et debite ad illud praeparentur.

§2. Si infans in periculo mortis versetur, sine ulla mora baptizetur.

CAN. 868   §1. Ut infans licite baptizetur, oportet:

1° parentes, saltem eorum unus aut qui legitime eorundem locum tenet, consentiant;

2° spes habeatur fundata eum in religione catholica educatum iri; quae si prorsus deficiat, baptismus secundum praescripta iuris particularis differatur, monitis de ratione parentibus.

§2. Infans parentum catholicorum, immo

865 §2: c. 752 §2; OICA 279
866: OICA 34
867 §1: c. 770; SCSO Monitum, 18 feb. 1958 (AAS 50 [1958] 114); OBP Prae. 8: 2 et 3; 25; SCDF Instr. *Pastoralis actio*, 20 oct. 1980 (AAS 72 [1980] 1137–1156)
867 §2: c. 771; OBP Prae. 8, 1

868 §1, 1°: c. 750 §2, 1°; SCSO Resp., 20 mar. 1933; OBP Prae. 5
868 §1, 2°: c. 750 §2; OBP Prae. 3; SCDF Resp., 13 iul. 1970; SCDF Instr. *Pastoralis actio*, 20 oct. 1980, 30, 31 (AAS 72 [1980] 1154–1155)
868 §2: c. 750 §1; OBP Prae. 8, 1

non-Catholic parents is baptized licitly in danger of death even against the will of the parents.

CAN. 869 §1. If there is a doubt whether a person has been baptized or whether baptism was conferred validly and the doubt remains after a serious investigation, baptism is to be conferred conditionally.

§2. Those baptized in a non-Catholic ecclesial community must not be baptized conditionally unless, after an examination of the matter and the form of the words used in the conferral of baptism and a consideration of the intention of the baptized adult and the minister of the baptism, a serious reason exists to doubt the validity of the baptism.

§3. If in the cases mentioned in §§1 and 2 the conferral or validity of the baptism remains doubtful, baptism is not to be conferred until after the doctrine of the sacrament of baptism is explained to the person to be baptized, if an adult, and the reasons of the doubtful validity of the baptism are explained to the person or, in the case of an infant, to the parents.

CAN. 870 An abandoned infant or a foundling is to be baptized unless after diligent investigation the baptism of the infant is established.

CAN. 871 If aborted fetuses are alive, they are to be baptized insofar as possible.

CHAPTER IV. **Sponsors**

CAN. 872 Insofar as possible, a person to be baptized is to be given a sponsor who assists an adult in Christian initiation or together with the parents presents an infant for baptism. A

et non catholicorum, in periculo mortis licite baptizatur, etiam invitis parentibus.

CAN. 869 §1. Si dubitetur num quis baptizatus fuerit, aut baptismi valide collatus fuerit, dubio quidem post seriam investigationem permanente, baptismus eidem sub condicione conferatur.

§2. Baptizati in communitate ecclesiali non catholica non sunt sub condicione baptizandi, nisi, inspecta materia et verborum forma in baptismo collato adhibitis necnon attenta intentione baptizati adulti et ministri baptizantis, seria ratio adsit de baptismi validitate dubitandi.

§3. Quod si, in casibus de quibus in §§1 et 2, dubia remaneat baptismi collatio aut validitas, baptismus ne conferatur nisi postquam baptizando, si sit adultus, doctrina de baptismi sacramento exponatur, atque eidem aut, si de infante agitur, eius parentibus rationes dubiae validitatis baptismi celebrati declarentur.

CAN. 870 Infans expositus aut inventus, nisi re diligenter investigata de eius baptismo constet, baptizetur.

CAN. 871 Fetus abortivi, si vivant, quatenus fieri potest, baptizentur.

CAPUT IV. **De Patrinis**

CAN. 872 Baptizando, quantum fieri potest, detur patrinus, cuius est baptizando adulto in initiatione christiana adstare, et baptizandum infantem una cum parentibus

869 §1: c. 749
869 §2: cc. 750, 751; SCSO Resp., 15 nov. 1941; SCSO Resp., 28 dec. 1948 (AAS 41 [1949] 650); DO I: 12–14; OICA appendix, 7
869 §3: DO I: 15, 18

870: c. 749
871: cc. 746, 747
872: c. 762; SCDS Instr. *Ex responsionibus datis*, 25 nov. 1925 (AAS 18 [1926] 44–47); OBP Prae. gen. 8; OICA 42, 43, 135–137, 236

sponsor also helps the baptized person to lead a Christian life in keeping with baptism and to fulfill faithfully the obligations inherent in it.

CAN. 873 There is to be only one male sponsor or one female sponsor or one of each.

CAN. 874 §1. To be permitted to take on the function of sponsor a person must:

1° be designated by the one to be baptized, by the parents or the person who takes their place, or in their absence by the pastor or minister and have the aptitude and intention of fulfilling this function;

2° have completed the sixteenth year of age, unless the diocesan bishop has established another age, or the pastor or minister has granted an exception for a just cause;

3° be a Catholic who has been confirmed and has already received the most holy sacrament of the Eucharist and who leads a life of faith in keeping with the function to be taken on;

4° not be bound by any canonical penalty legitimately imposed or declared;

5° not be the father or mother of the one to be baptized.

§2. A baptized person who belongs to a non-Catholic ecclesial community is not to participate except together with a Catholic sponsor and then only as a witness of the baptism.

CHAPTER V. The Proof and Registration of the Conferral of Baptism

CAN. 875 A person who administers baptism is to take care that, unless a sponsor is present, there is at least a witness who can attest to the conferral of the baptism.

ad baptismum praesentare itemque operam dare ut baptizatus vitam christianam baptismo congruam ducat obligationesque eidem inhaerentes fideliter adimpleat.

CAN. 873 Patrinus unus tantum vel matrina una vel etiam unus et una assumantur.

CAN. 874 §1. Ut quis ad munus patrini suscipiendum admittatur, oportet:

1° ab ipso baptizando eiusve parentibus aut ab eo qui eorum locum tenet aut, his deficientibus, a parocho vel ministro sit designatus atque aptitudinem et intentionem habeat hoc munus gerendi;

2° decimum sextum aetatis annum expleverit, nisi alia aetas ab Episcopo dioecesano statuta fuerit vel exceptio iusta de causa parocho aut ministro admittenda videatur;

3° sit catholicus, confirmatus et sanctissimum Eucharistiae sacramentum iam receperit, idemque vitam ducat fidei de muneri suscipiendo congruam;

4° nulla poena canonica legitime irrogata vel declarata sit innodatus;

5° non sit pater aut mater baptizandi.

§2. Baptizatus ad communitatem ecclesialem non catholicam pertinens, nonnisi una cum patrino catholico, et quidem ut testis tantum baptismi, admittatur.

CAPUT V. De Collati Baptismi Probatione et Adnotatione

CAN. 875 Qui baptismum administrat curet ut, nisi adsit patrinus, habeatur saltem testis quo collatio baptismi probari possit.

873: c. 764; OBP Prae. 6
874 §1: c. 765; OBP Prae. gen. 10; OICA 43

874 §2: DO I: 48, 57; OBP Prae. gen. 10, 3
875: c. 779

CAN. 876 To prove the conferral of baptism, if prejudicial to no one, the declaration of one witness beyond all exception is sufficient or the oath of the one baptized if the person received baptism as an adult.

CAN. 877 §1. The pastor of the place where the baptism is celebrated must carefully and without any delay record in the baptismal register the names of the baptized, with mention made of the minister, parents, sponsors, witnesses, if any, the place and date of the conferral of the baptism, and the date and place of birth.

§2. If it concerns a child born to an unmarried mother, the name of the mother must be inserted, if her maternity is established publicly or if she seeks it willingly in writing or before two witnesses. Moreover, the name of the father must be inscribed if a public document or his own declaration before the pastor and two witnesses proves his paternity; in other cases, the name of the baptized is inscribed with no mention of the name of the father or the parents.

§3. If it concerns an adopted child, the names of those adopting are to be inscribed and, at least if it is done in the civil records of the region, also the names of the natural parents according to the norm of §§1 and 2, with due regard for the prescripts of the conference of bishops.

CAN. 878 If the baptism was not administered by the pastor or in his presence, the minister of baptism, whoever it is, must inform the pastor of the parish in which it was administered of the conferral of the baptism, so that he records the baptism according to the norm of can. 877, §1.

CAN. 876 Ad collatum baptismum comprobandum, si nemini fiat praeiudicium, sufficit declaratio unius testis omni exceptione maioris, aut ipsius baptizati iusiurandum, si ipse in aetate adulta baptismum receperit.

CAN. 877 §1. Parochus loci, in quo baptismus celebratur, debet nomina baptizatorum, mentione facta de ministro, parentibus, patrinis necnon, si adsint, testibus, de loco ac die collati baptismi, in baptizatorum libro sedulo et sine ulla mora referre, simul indicatis die et loco nativitatis.

§2. Si de filio agatur e matre non nupta nato, matris nomen inserendum est, si publice de eius maternitate constet aut ipsa sponte sua, scripto vel coram duobus testibus, id petat; item nomen patris inscribendum est, si eius paternitas probatur aliquo publico documento aut ipsius declaratione coram parocho et duobus testibus facta; in ceteris casibus, inscribatur baptizatus, nulla facta de patris aut parentum nomine indicatione.

§3. Si de filio adoptivo agitur, inscribantur nomina adoptantium necnon, saltem si ita fiat in actu civili regionis, parentum naturalium ad normam §§1 et 2, attentis Episcoporum conferentiae praescriptis.

CAN. 878 Si baptismus neque a parocho neque eo praesente administratus fuerit, minister baptismi, quicumque est, de collato baptismo certiorem facere debet parochum paroeciae in qua baptismus administratus est, ut baptismum adnotet ad normam can. 877, §1.

876: c. 779
877 §1: c. 777 §1; SCConc Resp., 31 ian. 1927; SCDS Normae, 2 oct. 1941: OBP Prae. gen. 29

877 §2: c. 777 §2; CI Resp., 14 iul. 1922 (AAS 14 [1922] 528)
878: c. 778; SCConc Resp., 31 ian. 1927

TITLE II. The Sacrament of Confirmation

CAN. 879 The sacrament of confirmation strengthens the baptized and obliges them more firmly to be witnesses of Christ by word and deed and to spread and defend the faith. It imprints a character, enriches by the gift of the Holy Spirit the baptized continuing on the path of Christian initiation, and binds them more perfectly to the Church.

CHAPTER I. The Celebration of Confirmation

CAN. 880 §1. The sacrament of confirmation is conferred by the anointing of chrism on the forehead, which is done by the imposition of the hand and through the words prescribed in the approved liturgical books.

§2. The chrism to be used in the sacrament of confirmation must be consecrated by a bishop even if a presbyter administers the sacrament.

CAN. 881 It is desirable to celebrate the sacrament of confirmation in a church and during Mass; for a just and reasonable cause, however, it can be celebrated outside Mass and in any worthy place.

CHAPTER II. The Minister of Confirmation

CAN. 882 The ordinary minister of confirmation is a bishop; a presbyter provided with

TITULUS II. De Sacramento Confirmationis

CAN. 879 Sacramentum confirmationis, quod characterem imprimit et quo baptizati, iter initiationis christianae prosequentes, Spiritus Sancti dono ditantur atque perfectius Ecclesiae vinculantur, eosdem roborat arctiusque obligat ut verbo et opere testes sint Christi fidemque diffundant et defendant.

CAPUT I. De Confirmationis Celebratione

CAN. 880 §1. Sacramentum confirmationis confertur per unctionem chrismatis in fronte, quae fit manus impositione atque per verba in probatis liturgicis libris praescripta.

§2. Chrisma in sacramento confirmationis adhibendum debet esse ab Episcopo consecratum, etiamsi sacramentum a presbytero ministretur.

CAN. 881 Expedit ut confirmationis sacramentum in ecclesia, et quidem intra Missam, celebretur; ex causa tamen iusta et rationabili, extra Missam et quolibet loco digno celebrari potest.

CAPUT II. De Confirmationis Ministro

CAN. 882 Confirmationis minister ordinarius est Episcopus; valide hoc sacramen-

879: *Rituale Romanum*, 1952, tit. III, cap. I; LG 11; AG 36; PO 5; Paulus PP. VI, Const. Ap. *Divinae consortium naturae*, 15 aug. 1971 (AAS 63 [1971] 660); OC 1, 2; OBP Prae. gen. 2

880 §1: c. 780, 781 §2; Paulus PP. VI, Const. Ap. *Divinae consortium naturae*, 15 aug. 1971 (AAS 63 [1971] 657, 664); CIV Resp., 6 iun. 1972 (AAS 64 [1972] 526); OC 9

880 §2: c. 781 §1; *Ordo Benedicendi Oleum Catechumenorum et Infirmorum et Conficiendi Chrisma*, 3 dec. 1970, Prae. 6; OC 10

881: c. 791; SC 71; OC 11, 13

882: c. 782 §§1 et 2; Pius PP. XI, Facul., 30 apr. 1929, 3 (AAS 21 [1929] 555); SCDS Instr. *Sacramenti Confirmationis*, 20 maii 1934 (AAS 27 [1935] 11, 12); SCDS Decr. *Spiritus Sancti Munera*, 14 sep. 1946

this faculty in virtue of universal law or the special grant of the competent authority also confers this sacrament validly.

CAN. 883 The following possess the faculty of administering confirmation by the law itself:

1° within the boundaries of their jurisdiction, those who are equivalent in law to a diocesan bishop;

2° as regards the person in question, the presbyter who by virtue of office or mandate of the diocesan bishop baptizes one who is no longer an infant or admits one already baptized into the full communion of the Catholic Church;

3° as regards those who are in danger of death, the pastor or indeed any presbyter.

CAN. 884 §1. The diocesan bishop is to administer confirmation personally or is to take care that another bishop administers it. If necessity requires it, he can grant the faculty to one or more specific presbyters, who are to administer this sacrament.

§2. For a grave cause the bishop and even the presbyter endowed with the faculty of confirming in virtue of the law or the special grant of the competent authority can in single cases also associate presbyters with themselves to administer the sacrament.

CAN. 885 §1. The diocesan bishop is obliged to take care that the sacrament of confirmation is conferred on subjects who properly and reasonably seek it.

tum confert presbyter quoque hac facultate vi iuris universalis aut peculiaris concessionis competentis auctoritatis instructus.

CAN. 883 Ipso iure facultate confirmationem ministrandi gaudent:

1° intra fines suae dicionis, qui iure Episcopo dioecesano aequiparantur;

2° quoad personam de qua agitur, presbyter qui, vi officii vel mandati Episcopi dioecesani, infantia egressum baptizat aut iam baptizatum in plenam Ecclesiae catholicae communionem admittit;

3° quoad eos qui in periculo mortis versantur, parochus, immo quilibet presbyter.

CAN. 884 §1. Episcopus dioecesanus confirmationem administret per se ipse aut curet ut per alium Episcopum administretur; quod si necessitas id requirat, facultatem concedere potest uni vel pluribus determinatis presbyteris, qui hoc sacramentum adminstrent.

§2. Gravi de causa, Episcopus itemque presbyter, vi iuris aut peculiaris concessionis competentis auctoritatis facultate confirmandi donatus, possunt in singulis casibus presbyteros, ut et ipsi sacramentum administrent, sibi sociare.

CAN. 885 §1. Episcopus dioecesanus obligatione tenetur curandi ut sacramentum confirmationis subditis rite et rationabiliter petentibus conferatur.

(AAS 38 [1946] 349–358); *Rituale Romanum,* 1952, tit. III, cap. III; LG 26; OE 13, 14; OC 7; DPME 87c

883, 1°: c. 782 §3; OC 7

883, 2°: OC 8; OICA Prae. 46, appendix 8; CIV Resp., 21 dec. 1979 (AAS 72 [1980] 105, 106); Resp., 25 apr. 1975 (AAS 67 [1975] 348)

883, 3°: SCDS Instr., 20 maii 1934 (AAS 27 [1935] 11, 12); SCDS Decr. *Spiritus Sancti munera,* 14 sep. 1946 (AAS 38 [1946] 349–358); SCDS Resp., 6 mar.

1947; SCPF Decr. *Post latum a,* 18 dec. 1947 (AAS 40 [1948] 41); SCC Decl., 7 oct. 1953, I (AAS 45 [1953] 758); PM 13; SCE Instr. *Nemo est,* 22 aug. 1969, 38, 39 §4a (AAS 61 [1969] 633–634); OC 7c; OUI 31

884 §2: SCDS Decr. *Spiritus Sancti munera,* 14 sep. 1946 (AAS 38 [1946] 349–354); SCDS Relatio, 1 iul. 1957 (AAS 49 [1957] 943, 944); OC 8

885 §1: c. 785 §1

§2. A presbyter who possesses this faculty must use it for the sake of those in whose favor the faculty was granted.

CAN. 886 §1. A bishop in his diocese legitimately administers the sacrament of confirmation even to faithful who are not his subjects, unless their own ordinary expressly prohibits it.

§2. To administer confirmation licitly in another diocese, a bishop needs at least the reasonably presumed permission of the diocesan bishop unless it concerns his own subjects.

CAN. 887 A presbyter who possesses the faculty of administering confirmation also confers this sacrament licitly on externs in the territory assigned to him unless their proper ordinary prohibits it; he cannot confer it validly on anyone in another territory, without prejudice to the prescript of can. 883, n. 3.

CAN. 888 Within the territory in which they are able to confer confirmation, ministers can administer it even in exempt places.

CHAPTER III. Those to be Confirmed

CAN. 889 §1. Every baptized person not yet confirmed and only such a person is capable of receiving confirmation.

§2. To receive confirmation licitly outside the danger of death requires that a person who has the use of reason be suitably instructed, properly disposed, and able to renew the baptismal promises.

CAN. 890 The faithful are obliged to receive this sacrament at the proper time. Parents and pastors of souls, especially pastors of parishes, are to take care that the faithful are

§2. Presbyter, qui hac facultate gaudet, eadem uti debet erga eos in quorum favorem facultas concessa est.

CAN. 886 §1. Episcopus in sua dioecesi sacramentum confirmationis legitime administrat etiam fidelibus non subditis, nisi obstet expressa proprii ipsorum Ordinarii prohibitio.

§2. Ut in aliena dioecesi confirmationem licite administret, Episcopus indiget, nisi agatur de suis subditis, licentia saltem rationabiliter praesumpta Episcopi dioecesani.

CAN. 887 Presbyter facultate confirmationem ministrandi gaudens, in territorio sibi designato hoc sacramentum extraneis quoque licite confert, nisi obstet proprii eorum Ordinarii vetitum; illud vero in alieno territorio nemini valide confert, salvo praescripto can. 883, n. 3.

CAN. 888 Intra territorium in quo confirmationem conferre valent, ministri in locis quoque exemptis eam ministrare possunt.

CAPUT III. De Confirmandis

CAN. 889 §1. Confirmationis recipiendae capax est omnis et solus baptizatus, nondum confirmatus.

§2. Extra periculum mortis, ut quis licite confirmationem recipiat, requiritur, si rationis usu polleat, ut sit apte institutus, rite dispositus et promissiones baptismales renovare valeat.

CAN. 890 Fideles tenentur obligatione hoc sacramentum tempestive recipiendi; curent parentes, animarum pastores, praesertim parochi, ut fideles ad illud recipiendum

885 §2: c. 785 §2
886 §1: c. 783 §1
886 §2: c. 783 §2
887: c. 784; SCEO Decr. *Cum, ex canone,* 1 maii 1948 (AAS 40 [1948] 423)
888: c. 792

889 §1: c. 786; *Rituale Romanum*, 1952, tit. III, cap. I; OC 12
889 §2: c. 786; *Rituale Romanum*, 1952, tit. III, cap. III; OC 11
890: c. 787; OC 3

properly instructed to receive the sacrament and come to it at the appropriate time.

CAN. 891 The sacrament of confirmation is to be conferred on the faithful at about the age of discretion unless the conference of bishops has determined another age, or there is danger of death, or in the judgment of the minister a grave cause suggests otherwise.

rite instruantur et opportuno tempore accedant.

CAN. 891 Sacramentum confirmationis conferatur fidelibus circa aetatem discretionis, nisi Episcoporum conferentia aliam aetatem determinaverit, aut adsit periculum mortis vel, de iudicio ministri, gravis causa aliud suadeat.

CHAPTER IV. **Sponsors**

CAN. 892 Insofar as possible, there is to be a sponsor for the person to be confirmed; the sponsor is to take care that the confirmed person behaves as a true witness of Christ and faithfully fulfills the obligations inherent in this sacrament.

CAN. 893 §1. To perform the function of sponsor, a person must fulfill the conditions mentioned in can. 874.

§2. It is desirable to choose as sponsor the one who undertook the same function in baptism.

CAPUT IV. **De Patrinis**

CAN. 892 Confirmando, quantum id fieri potest, adsit patrinus, cuius est curare ut confirmatus tamquam verus Christi testis se gerat obligationesque eidem sacramento inhaerentes fideliter adimpleat.

CAN. 893 §1. Ut quis patrini munere fungatur, condiciones adimpleat oportet, de quibus in can. 874.

§2. Expedit ut tamquam patrinus assumatur qui idem munus in baptismo suscepit.

CHAPTER V. **The Proof and Registration of the Conferral of Confirmation**

CAN. 894 To prove the conferral of confirmation the prescripts of can. 876 are to be observed.

CAN. 895 The names of those confirmed with mention made of the minister, the parents

CAPUT V. **De Collatae Confirmationis Probatione et Adnotatione**

CAN. 894 Ad collatam confirmationem probandam serventur praescripta can. 876.

CAN. 895 Nomina confirmatorum, facta mentione ministri, parentum et patrinorum,

891: c. 788; CI Resp. II, 16 iun. 1931 (AAS 23 [1931] 353); SCDS Instr. *Plures petitiones,* 30 iun. 1932 (AAS 24 [1932] 271, 272); SCDS Instr. *Sacramenti Confirmationis,* 20 maii 1934 (AAS 27 [1935] 11–22); SCDS Decr. *Spiritus Sancti Munera,* 14 sep. 1946 (AAS 38 [1946] 349–358); *Rituale Romanum,* 1952, tit. III. cap. II; CI Resp. III, 26 mar. 1952 (AAS 44 [1952] 496); OC 11, 12

892: c. 793; SCDS Instr., 25 nov. 1925 (AAS 18

[1926] 44–47); *Rituale Romanum,* 1952, tit. III, cap. I; OC 5

893 §1: c. 795; OC 6; SCCD Documentorum explanatio (*Notitiae* 11 [1975] 61, 62)

893 §2: c. 796; OC 5; OICA 299; SCCD Documentorum explanatio (*Notitiae* 11 [1975] 61, 62)

894: *Rituale Romanum,* 1952, tit. III, cap. I

895: c. 798; OC 14

and sponsors, and the place and date of the conferral of confirmation are to be recorded in the confirmation register of the diocesan curia or, where the conference of bishops or the diocesan bishop has prescribed it, in a register kept in the parish archive. The pastor must inform the pastor of the place of baptism about the conferral of confirmation so that a notation is made in the baptismal register according to the norm of can. 535, §2.

CAN. 896 If the pastor of the place was not present, the minister either personally or through another is to inform him as soon as possible of the conferral of confirmation.

loci et diei collatae confirmationis in librum confirmatorum Curiae dioecesanae adnotentur, vel, ubi id praescripserit Episcoporum conferentia aut Episcopus dioecesanus, in librum in archivo paroeciali conservandum; parochus debet de collata confirmatione monere parochum loci baptismi, ut adnotatio fiat in libro baptizatorum, ad normam can. 535, §2.

CAN. 896 Si parochus loci praesens non fuerit, eundem de collata confirmatione minister per se vel per alium quam primum certiorem faciat.

TITLE III. The Most Holy Eucharist

CAN. 897 The most August sacrament is the Most Holy Eucharist in which Christ the Lord himself is contained, offered, and received and by which the Church continually lives and grows. The eucharistic sacrifice, the memorial of the death and resurrection of the Lord, in which the sacrifice of the cross is perpetuated through the ages is the summit and source of all worship and Christian life, which signifies and effects the unity of the People of God and brings about the building up of the body of Christ. Indeed, the other sacraments and all the ecclesiastical works of the apostolate are closely connected with the Most Holy Eucharist and ordered to it.

TITULUS III. De Sanctissima Eucharistia

CAN. 897 Augustissimum Sacramentum est sanctissima Eucharistia, in qua ipsemet Christus Dominus continetur, offertur ac sumitur, et qua continuo vivit et crescit Ecclesia. Sacrificium eucharisticum, memoriale mortis et resurrectionis Domini, in quo Sacrificium crucis in saecula perpetuatur, totius cultus et vitae christianae est culmen et fons, quo significatur et efficitur unitas populi Dei et corporis Christi aedificatio perficitur. Cetera enim sacramenta et omnia ecclesiastica apostolatus opera cum sanctissima Eucharistia cohaerent et ad eam ordinantur.

896: c. 799; OC 15

897: c. 801; SC 10, 47; LG 3, 11, 17, 26; PAULUS PP. VI, Ep. Ap. *Investigabiles divitias Christi*, 6 feb. 1965 (AAS 57 [1965] 301); MF 753, 774; CD 30; AG 14; PO 5; EMys 1, 3, 6, 10; IGMR 7; SCUF Instr. *In quibus*, 1 iun. 1972, 2, 3 (AAS 64 [1972] 519–522); PAULUS PP. VI, Adh. Ap. *Marialis cultus*, 2 feb. 1974, 20 (AAS 66 [1974] 131–132); SCIC Instr. *In ecclesiastica futurorum*, 3 iun. 1979, 22; IOANNES PAULUS PP. II, Ep. Ap. *Patres Ecclesiae*, 2 ian. 1980 (AAS 72 [1980] 18)

CAN. 898 The Christian faithful are to hold the Most Holy Eucharist in highest honor, taking an active part in the celebration of the most august sacrifice, receiving this sacrament most devoutly and frequently, and worshiping it with the highest adoration. In explaining the doctrine about this sacrament, pastors of souls are to teach the faithful diligently about this obligation.

CAN. 898 Christifideles maximo in honore sanctissimam Eucharistiam habeant, actuosam in celebratione augustissimi Sacrificii partem habentes, devotissime et frequenter hoc sacramentum recipientes, atque summa cum adoratione idem colentes; animarum pastores doctrinam de hoc sacramento illustrantes, fideles hanc obligationem sedulo edoceant.

CHAPTER I. The Eucharistic Celebration

CAPUT I. De Eucharistica Celebratione

CAN. 899 §1. The eucharistic celebration is the action of Christ himself and the Church. In it, Christ the Lord, through the ministry of the priest, offers himself, substantially present under the species of bread and wine, to God the Father and gives himself as spiritual food to the faithful united with his offering.

CAN. 899 §1. Eucharistica celebratio actio est ipsius Christi et Ecclesiae, in qua Christus Dominus, ministerio sacerdotis, semetipsum, sub speciebus panis et vini substantialiter praesentem, Deo Patri offert atque fidelibus in sua oblatione sociatis se praebet ut cibum spiritualem.

§2. In the eucharistic gathering the people of God are called together with the bishop or, under his authority, a presbyter presiding and acting in the person of Christ. All the faithful who are present, whether clerics or laity, unite together by participating in their own way according to the diversity of orders and liturgical functions.

§2. In eucharistica Synaxi populus Dei in unum convocatur, Episcopo aut, sub eius auctoritate, presbytero praeside, personam Christi gerente, atque omnes qui intersunt fideles, sive clerici sive laici, suo quisque modo pro ordinum et liturgicorum munerum diversitate, participando concurrunt.

§3. The eucharistic celebration is to be organized in such a way that all those participating receive from it the many fruits for which Christ the Lord instituted the eucharistic sacrifice.

§3. Celebratio eucharistica ita ordinetur, ut omnes participantes exinde plurimos capiant fructus, ad quos obtinendos Christus Dominus Sacrificium eucharisticum instituit.

898: c. 863; SC 48; PO 5; MF 754, 755; EMys 12, 15
899 §1: PO 13; MF 761, 762; EMys 3; IGMR 1, 4

899 §2: SC 14, 26, 33; PO 5; IGMR 2, 7, 58, 59
899 §3: SC 47; IGMR 2

ART. 1. *The Minister of the Most Holy Eucharist*

CAN. 900 §1. The minister who is able to confect the sacrament of the Eucharist in the person of Christ is a validly ordained priest alone.

§2. A priest not impeded by canon law celebrates the Eucharist licitly; the provisions of the following canons are to be observed.

CAN. 901 A priest is free to apply the Mass for anyone, living or dead.

CAN. 902 Unless the welfare of the Christian faithful requires or suggests otherwise, priests can concelebrate the Eucharist. They are completely free to celebrate the Eucharist individually, however, but not while a concelebration is taking place in the same church or oratory.

CAN. 903 A priest is to be permitted to celebrate even if the rector of the church does not know him, provided that either he presents a letter of introduction from his ordinary or superior, issued at least within the year, or it can be judged prudently that he is not impeded from celebrating.

CAN. 904 Remembering always that in the mystery of the eucharistic sacrifice the work of redemption is exercised continually, priests are to celebrate frequently; indeed, daily celebration is recommended earnestly since, even if the faithful cannot be present, it is the act of Christ and the Church in which priests fulfill their principal function.

ART. 1. *De Sanctissimae Eucharistiae Ministro*

CAN. 900 §1. Minister, qui in persona Christi sacramentum Eucharistiae conficere valet, est solus sacerdos valide ordinatus.

§2. Licite Eucharistiam celebrat sacerdos lege canonica non impeditus, servatis praescriptis canonum qui sequuntur.

CAN. 901 Integrum est sacerdoti Missam applicare pro quibusvis, tum vivis tum defunctis.

CAN. 902 Nisi utilitas christifidelium aliud requirat aut suadeat, sacerdotes Eucharistiam concelebrare possunt, integra tamen pro singulis libertate manente Eucharistiam individuali modo celebrandi, non vero eo tempore, quo in eadem ecclesia aut oratorio concelebratio habetur.

CAN. 903 Sacerdos ad celebrandum admittatur etiamsi rectori ecclesiae sit ignotus, dummodo aut litteras commendatitias sui Ordinarii vel sui Superioris, saltem intra annum datas, exhibeat, aut prudenter existimari possit eundem a celebratione non esse impeditum.

CAN. 904 Sacerdotes, memoria semper tenentes in mysterio Sacrificii eucharistici opus redemptionis continuo exerceri, frequenter celebrent; immo enixe commendatur celebratio cotidiana, quae quidem, etiam si praesentia fidelium haberi non possit, actus est Christi et Ecclesiae, in quo peragendo munus suum praecipuum sacerdotes adimplent.

900 §1: c. 802; LG 10, 26, 28; EMys 42, 43; IGMR 59, 60; SCDF Decl., 15 feb. 1975 (AAS 67 [1975] 203–204)

901: c. 809; SCDF Decr. *Accidit,* 11 iun. 1976 (AAS 68 [1976] 621)

902: SC 57; SRC Decr. *Ecclesiae semper,* 7 mar. 1965 (AAS 57 [1965] 410–412); EMys 47; IGMR 153–158; SCCD Decl. *In celebratione Missae,* 7 aug. 1972 (AAS 64 [1972] 561–563)

903: c. 804 §§1 et 2

904: c. 805; SC 2, 27; LG 3, 28; AG 39; PO 2, 5, 13; MF 761, 762; EMys 44; IGMR 4

CAN. 905 §1. A priest is not permitted to celebrate the Eucharist more than once a day except in cases where the law permits him to celebrate or concelebrate more than once on the same day.

§2. If there is a shortage of priests, the local ordinary can allow priests to celebrate twice a day for a just cause, or if pastoral necessity requires it, even three times on Sundays and holy days of obligation.

CAN. 906 Except for a just and reasonable cause, a priest is not to celebrate the eucharistic sacrifice without the participation of at least some member of the faithful.

CAN. 907 In the eucharistic celebration deacons and lay persons are not permitted to offer prayers, especially the eucharistic prayer, or to perform actions which are proper to the celebrating priest.

CAN. 908 Catholic priests are forbidden to concelebrate the Eucharist with priests or ministers of Churches or ecclesial communities which do not have full communion with the Catholic Church.

CAN. 909 A priest is not to neglect to prepare himself properly through prayer for the celebration of the eucharistic sacrifice and to offer thanks to God at its completion.

CAN. 910 §1. The ordinary minister of

CAN. 905 §1. Exceptis casibus in quibus ad normam iuris licitum est pluries eadem die Eucharistiam celebrare aut concelebrare, non licet sacerdoti plus semel in die celebrare.

§2. Si sacerdotum penuria habeatur, concedere potest loci Ordinarius ut sacerdotes, iusta de causa, bis in die, immo, necessitate pastorali id postulante, etiam ter in diebus dominicis et festis de praecepto, celebrent.

CAN. 906 Nisi iusta et rationabili de causa, sacerdos Sacrificium eucharisticum ne celebret sine participatione alicuius saltem fidelis.

CAN. 907 In celebratione eucharistica diaconis et laicis non licet orationes, speciatim precem eucharisticam, proferre vel actionibus fungi, quae sacerdotis celebrantis sunt propriae.

CAN. 908 Sacerdotibus catholicis vetitum est una cum sacerdotibus vel ministris Ecclesiarum communitatumve ecclesialium plenam communionem cum Ecclesia catholica non habentium, Eucharistiam concelebrare.

CAN. 909 Sacerdos ne omittat ad eucharistici Sacrificii celebrationem oratione debite se praeparare, eoque expleto Deo gratias agere.

CAN. 910 §1. Minister ordinarius

905 §1: c. 806 §1; SRC Resp., 26 ian. 1920 (AAS 12 [1920] 122); SRC Instr., 12 iun. 1921 (AAS 13 [1921] 154–155); SC 57; EMys 47; IGMR 158

905 §2: c. 806 §2; PM 2

906: c. 813; SRC Resp. *Dubia*, 4 aug. 1922 (AAS 14 [1922] 505); SCDS Instr. *Quam plurimum*, 1 oct. 1949 (AAS 41 [1949] 506–508); SRC Instr. *De musica sacra*, 3 sep. 1958, 14c et 31 (AAS 50 [1958] 636, 642); MF 761, 762; SC 27; IGMR 211

907: SRC *Dubia*, 4 aug. 1922 (AAS 14 [1922] 505); SRC Instr. *De musica sacra*, 3 sep. 1958, 14c et 31 (AAS 50 [1958] 636, 642); SC 28; SRC Instr. *Musicam*

sacram, 5 mar. 1967, 14 (AAS 59 [1967] 304); IGMR 10–12; SCCD Instr. *Liturgicae instaurationes*, 5 sep. 1970, 4 (AAS 62 [1970] 698); SCCD Litt. circ. *Eucharistiae participationem*, 27 apr. 1973, 8 (AAS 65 [1973] 343); ID Introductio et 4

908: SUCF Decl., 7 ian. 1970 (AAS 62 [1970] 184–188)

909: c. 810; MD 566–568; EMys 38

910 §1: cc. 845 §§1 et 2, 848, 849; CI Resp., 13 iul. 1930, II (AAS 22 [1930] 365); *Rituale Romanum*, 1925 et 1952, tit. V; LG 29; EMys 31; SDO 22, 3; CEM 17

holy communion is a bishop, presbyter, or deacon.

§2. The extraordinary minister of holy communion is an acolyte or another member of the Christian faithful designated according to the norm of can. 230, §3.

CAN. 911 §1. The pastor, parochial vicars, chaplains, and, with regard to all those dwelling in the house, the superior of a community in clerical religious institutes and societies of apostolic life have the duty and right of bringing the Most Holy Eucharist as Viaticum to the sick.

§2. In the case of necessity or with at least the presumed permission of the pastor, chaplain, or superior, who must be notified afterwards, any priest or other minister of holy communion must do this.

ART. 2. *Participation in the Most Holy Eucharist*

CAN. 912 Any baptized person not prohibited by law can and must be admitted to holy communion.

CAN. 913 §1. The administration of the Most Holy Eucharist to children requires that they have sufficient knowledge and careful preparation so that they understand the mystery of Christ according to their capacity and are able to receive the body of Christ with faith and devotion.

§2. The Most Holy Eucharist, however, can

sacrae communionis est Episcopus, presbyter et diaconus.

§2. Extraordinarius sacrae communionis minister est acolythus necnon alius christifidelis ad normam can. 230, §3 deputatus.

CAN. 911 §1. Officium et ius sanctissimam Eucharistiam per modum Viatici ad infirmos deferendi habent parochus et vicarii paroeciales, cappellani, necnon Superior communitatis in clericalibus institutis religiosis aut societatibus vitae apostolicae quoad omnes in domo versantes.

§2. In casu necessitatis aut de licentia saltem praesumpta parochi, cappellani vel Superioris, cui postea notitiam dari oportet, hoc facere debet quilibet sacerdos vel alius sacrae communionis minister.

ART. 2. *De Sanctissima Eucharistia Participanda*

CAN. 912 Quilibet baptizatus, qui iure non prohibeatur, admitti potest et debet ad sacram communionem.

CAN. 913 §1. Ut sanctissima Eucharistia ministrari possit pueris, requiritur ut ipsi sufficienti cognitione et accurata praeparatione gaudeant, ita ut mysterium Christi pro suo captu percipiant et Corpus Domini cum fide et devotione sumere valeant.

§2. Pueris tamen in periculo mortis ver-

910 §2: MQ VI; SCDS Instr. *Fidei custos*, 30 apr. 1969; IC 1; CEM 17; IOANNES PAULUS PP. II, Ep. *Dominicae cenae*, 24 feb. 1980, 11 (AAS 72 [1980] 142); ID 10

911 §1: cc. 397, 3°, 514 §§1–3, 848, 850; CI Resp. I, 16 iun. 1931 (AAS 23 [1931] 353; OUI 29

911 §2: LG 29; SDO 22, 3; OUI 29; IC 265

912: c. 853

913 §1: c. 854 §§3 et 4; CI Resp., 22 feb. 1920; SCDS Instr., 30 iun. 1932 (AAS 24 [1932] 272); PO 5; EMys 14; DCG Addendum: De primo accessu ad sacramenta paenitentiae et Eucharistiae (AAS 64 [1972] 155); SCCD *Directorium de Missis cum pueris*, 12 (AAS 66 [1974] 33–34)

913 §2: c. 854 §2

be administered to children in danger of death if they can distinguish the body of Christ from ordinary food and receive communion reverently.

CAN. 914 It is primarily the duty of parents and those who take the place of parents, as well as the duty of pastors, to take care that children who have reached the use of reason are prepared properly and, after they have made sacramental confession, are refreshed with this divine food as soon as possible. It is for the pastor to exercise vigilance so that children who have not attained the use of reason or whom he judges are not sufficiently disposed do not approach holy communion.

CAN. 915 Those who have been excommunicated or interdicted after the imposition or declaration of the penalty and others obstinately persevering in manifest grave sin are not to be admitted to holy communion.

CAN. 916 A person who is conscious of grave sin is not to celebrate Mass or receive the body of the Lord without previous sacramental confession unless there is a grave reason and there is no opportunity to confess; in this case the person is to remember the obligation to make an act of perfect contrition which includes the resolution of confessing as soon as possible.

CAN. 917 A person who has already received the Most Holy Eucharist can receive it a second time on the same day only within the eucharistic celebration in which the person participates, without prejudice to the prescript of can. 921, §2.

santibus sanctissima Eucharistia ministrari potest, si Corpus Christi a communi cibo discernere et communionem reverenter suscipere possint.

CAN. 914 Parentum imprimis atque eorum qui parentum locum tenent necnon parochi officium est curandi ut pueri usum rationis assecuti debite praeparentur et quam primum, praemissa sacramentali confessione, hoc divino cibo reficiantur; parochi etiam est advigilare ne ad sacram Synaxim accedant pueri, qui rationis usum non sint adepti aut quos non sufficienter dispositos iudicaverit.

CAN. 915 Ad sacram communionem ne admittantur excommunicati et interdicti post irrogationem vel declarationem poenae alique in manifesto gravi peccato obstinate perseverantes.

CAN. 916 Qui conscius est peccati gravis, sine praemissa sacramentali confessione Missam ne celebret neve Corpori Domini communicet, nisi adsit gravis ratio et deficiat opportunitas confitendi; quo in casu meminerit se obligatione teneri ad eliciendum actum perfectae contritionis, qui includit propositum quam primum confitendi.

CAN. 917 Qui sanctissimam Eucharistiam iam recepit, potest eam iterum eadem die suscipere solummodo intra eucharisticam celebrationem cui participat, salvo praescripto can. 921, §2.

914: c. 854 §§4 et 5; CI Resp., 22 feb. 1920; EMys 14, 35; DCG Addendum: De primo accessu ad sacramenta paenitentiae et Eucharistiae (AAS 64 [1972] 155); SCDS et SCpC Decl., 24 maii 1973 (AAS 65 [1973] 410); SCSCD et SCpC Resp., 20 maii [1967] 442–448]; EMys 28; IC 2

915: c. 855

916: cc. 807, 856; EMys 35; SCDF *Normae Pastorales,* 16 iun. 1972, prooemium et VI (AAS 64 [1972] 510, 512); CEM 23

917: cc. 857, 858; IOe 60; SRC Instr. *Tres abhinc annos,* 4 maii 1967, 14 (AAS 59 [1967] 442–448); EMys 28; IC 2

CAN. 918 It is highly recommended that the faithful receive holy communion during the eucharistic celebration itself. It is to be administered outside the Mass, however, to those who request it for a just cause, with the liturgical rites being observed.

CAN. 919 §1. A person who is to receive the Most Holy Eucharist is to abstain for at least one hour before holy communion from any food and drink, except for only water and medicine.

§2. A priest who celebrates the Most Holy Eucharist two or three times on the same day can take something before the second or third celebration even if there is less than one hour between them.

§3. The elderly, the infirm, and those who care for them can receive the Most Holy Eucharist even if they have eaten something within the preceding hour.

CAN. 920 §1. After being initiated into the Most Holy Eucharist, each of the faithful is obliged to receive holy communion at least once a year.

§2. This precept must be fulfilled during the Easter season unless it is fulfilled for a just cause at another time during the year.

CAN. 921 §1. The Christian faithful who are in danger of death from any cause are to be

CAN. 918 Maxime commendatur ut fideles in ipsa eucharistica celebratione sacram communionem recipiant; ipsis tamen iusta de causa petentibus extra Missam ministretur, servatis liturgicis ritibus.

CAN. 919 §1. Sanctissimam Eucharistiam recepturus per spatium saltem unius horae ante sacram communionem abstineat a quocumque cibo et potu, excepta tantummodo aqua atque medicina.

§2. Sacerdos, qui eadem die bis aut ter sanctissimam Eucharistiam celebrat, aliquid sumere potest ante secundam aut tertiam celebrationem, etiamsi non intercesserit spatium unius horae.

§3. Aetate provecti et infirmitate quadam laborantes necnon eorum curae addicti, sanctissimam Eucharistiam accipere possunt, etiamsi intra horam antecedentem aliquid sumpserint.

CAN. 920 §1. Omnis fidelis, postquam ad sanctissimam Eucharistiam initiatus sit, obligatione tenetur semel saltem in anno, sacram communionem recipiendi.

§2. Hoc praeceptum impleri debet tempore paschali, nisi iusta de causa alio tempore intra annum adimpleatur.

CAN. 921 §1. Christifideles qui versantur in periculo mortis, quavis ex causa proce-

918: c. 863; MD 564–566; SRC Decr. *Novum rubricarum,* 26 iul. 1960, 502 (AAS 52 [1960] 680); SC 55; PM I: 4, II: b; CA I, 1; EMys 31, 33; IGMR prooemium (13); CEM 14

919 §1: SCSO Litterae, 22 mar. 1923 (AAS 15 [1923] 151–152); SCSO Normae, 1 iul. 1931; Pius PP. XII, Const. Ap. *Christus Dominus,* 6 ian. 1953 (AAS 45 [1953] 15–24); SCSO Instr., 6 ian. 1953 (AAS 45 [1953] 47–53); SRC Decr. *Romana,* 3 iun. 1953 (AAS 46 [1954] 68–71); Pius PP. XII, m.p., *Sacram communionem,* 19 mar. 1957 (AAS 49 [1957] 177–178); Paulus PP. VI, Rescr., 21 nov. 1964 (AAS 57 [1965] 186); EM

IX, 20; SCCD Instr. *Actio pastoralis,* 15 maii 1969, 10d (AAS 61 [1969] 810); IC 3; CEM 24

919 §2: PM I, 3; SCE *Index facultatum,* 1 ian. 1968 34

919 §3: c. 858 §2; CI Resp., 24 nov. 1927; Pius PP. XII, Const. Ap. *Christus Dominus,* 6 ian. 1953 (AAS 45 [1953] 15–24); Pius PP. XII, m. p., *Sacram communionem,* 19 mar. 1957, 4 (AAS 49 [1957] 177–178); IC 3; CEM 24

920: cc. 859–861; CI Resp., 3 ian. 1918; SCConc Ind. part., 18 nov. 1924

921 §1: c. 864 §1; EMys 39; OUI 27, 29; DPME 89

nourished by holy communion in the form of Viaticum.

§2. Even if they have been nourished by holy communion on the same day, however, those in danger of death are strongly urged to receive communion again.

§3. While the danger of death lasts, it is recommended that holy communion be administered often, but on separate days.

CAN. 922 Holy Viaticum for the sick is not to be delayed too long; those who have the care of souls are to be zealous and vigilant that the sick are nourished by Viaticum while fully conscious.

CAN. 923 The Christian faithful can participate in the eucharistic sacrifice and receive holy communion in any Catholic rite, without prejudice to the prescript of can. 844.

ART. 3. *The Rites and Ceremonies of the Eucharistic Celebration*

CAN. 924 §1. The most holy eucharistic sacrifice must be offered with bread and with wine in which a little water must be mixed.

§2. The bread must be only wheat and recently made so that there is no danger of spoiling.

§3. The wine must be natural from the fruit of the vine and not spoiled.

CAN. 925 Holy communion is to be given

denti, sacra communione per modum Viatici reficiantur.

§2. Etiamsi eadem die sacra communione refecti fuerint, valde tamen suadetur ut qui in vitae discrimen adducti sint, denuo communicent.

§3. Perdurante mortis periculo, commendatur ut sacra communio pluries, distinctis diebus, administretur.

CAN. 922 Sanctum Viaticum infirmis ne nimium differatur; qui animarum curam gerunt sedulo advigilent, ut eodem infirmi plene sui compotes reficiantur.

CAN. 923 Christifideles Sacrificium eucharisticum participare et sacram communionem suscipere possunt quolibet ritu catholico, firmo praescripto can. 844.

ART. 3. *De Ritibus et Caeremoniis Eucharisticae Celebrationis*

CAN. 924 §1. Sacrosanctum eucharisticum Sacrificium offerri debet ex pane et vino, cui modica aqua miscenda est.

§2. Panis debet esse mere triticeus et recenter confectus, ita ut nullum sit periculum corruptionis.

§3. Vinum debet esse naturale de gemine vitis et non corruptum.

CAN. 925 Sacra communio conferatur

921 §2: c. 864 §2; EMys 39
921 §3: c. 864 §3
922: c. 865; EMys 39
923: c. 866 §1; SCEO Resol., 26 ian. 1925
924 §1: c. 814; IGMR 281; ID 8
924 §2: c. 815 §1; SCDS Resp. 7 dec. 1918; SCDS Instr. *Dominus salvator noster*, 26 mar. 1929 (AAS 11 [1929] 631–642); *Rituale Romanum*, 1952, tit. V c. I, 7; IGMR 282, 285; SCCD Instr. *Liturgicae instaurationes*, 5 sep. 1970, 5 (AAS 62 [1980] 700); ID 8
924 §3: c. 815 §2; SCSO Resp., 2 aug. 1922; IGMR 284

925: c. 852; SC 55; *Ritus servandus in concelebratione Missae et ritus communionis sub utraque specie*, 1965; EMys 32, 41; SCCD Instr. *Actio pastoralis*, 15 maii 1969, 7 (AAS 61 [1969] 806–811); SCCD Instr. *Memoriale Domini*, 29 maii 1969 (AAS 61 [1969] 541–545); IGMR prooemium (14), 240–242; SCCD Instr. *Sacramentali communione*, 29 iun. 1970 (AAS 62 [1970] 664–666); SCCD Instr. *Liturgicae instaurationes*, 5 sep. 1970, 6 (AAS 62 [1970] 700); OUI 95; ID 12

under the form of bread alone, or under both species according to the norm of the liturgical laws, or even under the form of wine alone in a case of necessity.

CAN. 926 According to the ancient tradition of the Latin Church, the priest is to use unleavened bread in the eucharistic celebration whenever he offers it.

CAN. 927 It is absolutely forbidden, even in extreme urgent necessity, to consecrate one matter without the other or even both outside the eucharistic celebration.

CAN. 928 The eucharistic celebration is to be carried out in the Latin language or in another language provided that the liturgical texts have been legitimately approved.

CAN. 929 In celebrating and administering the Eucharist, priests and deacons are to wear the sacred vestments prescribed by the rubrics.

CAN. 930 §1. If an infirm or elderly priest is unable to stand, he can celebrate the eucharistic sacrifice while seated, but not before the people except with the permission of the local ordinary; the liturgical laws are to be observed.

§2. A blind or otherwise infirm priest licitly celebrates the eucharistic sacrifice by using any

sub sola specie panis aut, ad normam legum liturgicarum, sub utraque specie; in casu autem necessitatis, etiam sub sola specie vini.

CAN. 926 In eucharistica celebratione secundum antiquam Ecclesiae latinae traditionem sacerdos adhibeat panem azymum ubicumque litat.

CAN. 927 Nefas est, urgente etiam extrema necessitate, alteram materiam sine altera, aut etiam utramque extra eucharisticam celebrationem, consecrare.

CAN. 928 Eucharistica celebratio peragatur lingua latina aut alia lingua, dummodo textus liturgici legitime approbati fuerint.

CAN. 929 Sacerdotes et diaconi in Eucharistia celebranda et ministranda sacra ornamenta rubricis praescripta deferant.

CAN. 930 §1. Sacerdos infirmus aut aetate provectus, si stare nequeat, Sacrificium eucharisticum celebrare potest sedens, servatis quidem legibus liturgicis, non tamen coram populo, nisi de licentia loci Ordinarii.

§2. Sacerdos caecus aliave infirmitate laborans licite eucharisticum Sacrificium cel-

926: c. 816; SCCD Instr. *Actio pastoralis*, 15 maii 1969, 10d (AAS 61 [1969] 810); IGMR 282; SCCD Instr. *Liturgicae instaurationes*, 5 sep. 1970, 5 (AAS 62 [1970] 698)

927: c. 817

928: c. 819; SC 36, 54; IOe 57; SRC Resp. ad dubia: Ad n. 57 (*Notitiae* [1965] 185–186), 98; SRC Instr. *In edicendis normis*, 23 nov. 1965, 17–18 (AAS 57 [1965] 1012); SRC Instr. *Musicam sacram*, 5 mar. 1967, 47, 48 (AAS 59 [1967] 314); SRC Instr. *Tres abhinc annos*, 4 maii 1967, 2, 28 (AAS 59 [1967] 443, 448); IGMR 11–13; SCCD Notif., 14 ian. 1971, 1 (AAS 63 [1971] 713–714); IOANNES PAULUS PP. II. Litt. *Dominici cenae*, 24 feb. 1980, 10 (AAS 72 [1980] 134–137).

929: cc. 811 §1, 818; SRC Instr. *Praeter calicem*, 28 ian. 1920; SRC Resp., Dubium, 9 dec. 1925 (AAS 18

[1926] 58–59); SRC Decl., 20 aug. 1957 (AAS 49 [1957] 762); IOANNES PP. XXIII, m.p. *Rubricarum instructum*, 25 iul. 1960 (AAS 52 [1960] 593–595); SRC Decr. gen. *Novum rubricarum*, 26 iul. 1960, 117–137 (AAS 52 [1960] 617–621); SRC *Ritus servandus in concelebratione Missae*, 7 mar. 1965, 12 (AAS 57 [1965] 412); SRC Instr. *Tres abhinc annos*, 4 maii 1967, 25–27 (AAS 59 [1967] 447–448); SRC Instr. *Pontificales ritus*, 21 iun. 1968, 5, 6 (AAS 60 [1968] 408); SCCD Instr. *Actio pastoralis*, 15 maii 1969, 11b (AAS 61 [1969] 811); IGMR 298–300, 302; CEM 24; IOANNES PAULUS PP. II, Litt. *Dominici cenae*, 24 feb. 1980, 12 (AAS 72 [1980] 144–145)

930 §1: PM I, 10; CA I, 5

930 §2: PM I, 5 et 6; CA I, 2; SRC Instr. *Tres abhinc annos*, 4 maii 1967, 18 (AAS 59 [1967] 446)

approved text of the Mass with the assistance, if needed, of another priest, deacon, or even a properly instructed lay person.

ebrat, adhibendo textum quemlibet Missae ex probatis, adstante, si casus ferat, alio sacerdote vel diacono, aut etiam laico rite instructo, qui eundem adiuvet.

ART. 4. *The Time and Place of the Celebration of the Eucharist*

ART. 4. *De Tempore et Loco Celebrationis Eucharistiae*

CAN. 931 The celebration and distribution of the Eucharist can be done at any day and hour except those which the liturgical norms exclude.

CAN. 931 Eucharistiae celebratio et distributio fieri potest qualibet die et hora, iis exceptis, quae secundum liturgicas normas excluduntur.

CAN. 932 §1. The eucharistic celebration is to be carried out in a sacred place unless in a particular case necessity requires otherwise; in such a case the celebration must be done in a decent place.

CAN. 932 §1. Celebratio eucharistica peragatur in loco sacro, nisi in casu particulari necessitas aliud postulet; quo in casu, in loco honesto celebratio fieri debet.

§2. The eucharistic sacrifice must be carried out on a dedicated or blessed altar; outside a sacred place a suitable table can be used, always with a cloth and a corporal.

§2. Sacrificium eucharisticum peragendum est super altare dedicatum vel benedictum; extra locum sacrum adhiberi potest mensa conveniens, retentis semper tobalea et corporali.

CAN. 933 For a just cause and with the express permission of the local ordinary, a priest is permitted to celebrate the Eucharist in the place of worship of some Church or ecclesial community which does not have full communion with the Catholic Church so long as there is no scandal.

CAN. 933 Iusta de causa et de licentia expressa Ordinarii loci licet sacerdoti Eucharistiam celebrare in templo alicuius Ecclesiae aut communitatis ecclesialis plenam communionem cum Ecclesia catholica non habentium, remoto scandalo.

931: cc. 820, 821, 867; SCDS Resp., 22 apr. 1924, (AAS 17 [1925] 100–106); Pius PP. XII, Const. Ap. *Christus Dominus*, IV, 6 ian. 1953 (AAS 45 [1953] 22–23); SCSO Decr., 31 maii 1953 (AAS 45 [1953] 426); CI Resp., 5 mar. 1954; SCSO Monitum, 22 mar. 1955 (AAS 46 [1957] 218); SRC Decr. gen. *Maxima redemptionis*, 16 nov. 1955 (AAS 47 [1955] 838–841); SRC Ordinationes et Decl., 1 feb. 1957 (AAS 49 [1957] 91–95); Pius PP. XII, m.p. *Sacram communionem*, 19 mar. 1957, 1 (AAS 49 [1957] 178); PM I, 4; CA I, 1; SCE *Index facultatum*, 1 ian. 1968, 27

932 §1: c. 822 §§1 et 4; PM I 7 et 8; CA I, 4; SCCD Instr. *Actio pastoralis*, 15 maii 1969, 3, 4 (AAS 61

[1969] 808); IGMR 253, 260, SCDF Instr. *Liturgicae instaurationes*, 5 sep. 1970, 9 (AAS 62 [1970] 701–702); DPME 85; SCCD *Directorium de Missis cum pueris*, 1 nov. 1973, 25 (AAS 66 [1974] 38)

932 §2: c. 822; CI Resp. 12, 16 oct. 1919 (AAS 11 [1919] 478); SCDS Litt., 26 iul. 1924 (AAS 16 [1924] 370–371); SCDS Resp. *Romana et aliarum*, 3 maii 1926 (AAS 18 [1926] 388–391); SCDS Instr. *Dominus salvator noster*, 26 mar. 1929 (AAS 11 [1929] 631–642); SRC Decr., 12 mar. 1947; SCDS Instr. *Quam plurimum*, 1 oct. 1949 (AAS 41 [1949] 501–506); CI Resp. IV, 26 mar. 1952 (AAS 44 [1952] 497); IGMR 260

933: c. 823 §1

CHAPTER II. The Reservation and Veneration of the Most Holy Eucharist

CAN. 934 §1. The Most Holy Eucharist:

1° must be reserved in the cathedral church or its equivalent, in every parish church, and in a church or oratory connected to the house of a religious institute or society of apostolic life;

2° can be reserved in the chapel of the bishop and, with the permission of the local ordinary, in other churches, oratories, and chapels.

§2. In sacred places where the Most Holy Eucharist is reserved, there must always be someone responsible for it and, insofar as possible, a priest is to celebrate Mass there at least twice a month.

CAN. 935 No one is permitted to keep the Eucharist on one's person or to carry it around, unless pastoral necessity urges it and the prescripts of the diocesan bishop are observed.

CAN. 936 In the house of a religious institute or some other pious house, the Most Holy Eucharist is to be reserved only in the church or principal oratory attached to the house. For a just cause, however, the ordinary can also permit it to be reserved in another oratory of the same house.

CAN. 937 Unless there is a grave reason to the contrary, the church in which the Most Holy Eucharist is reserved is to be open to the faithful for at least some hours every day so that they can pray before the Most Blessed Sacrament.

CAN. 938 §1. The Most Holy Eucharist is

CAPUT II. De Sanctissima Eucharistia Asservanda et Veneranda

CAN. 934 §1. Sanctissima Eucharistia:

1° asservari debet in ecclesia cathedrali aut eidem aequiparata, in qualibet ecclesia paroeciali necnon in ecclesia vel oratorio domui instituti religiosi aut societatis vitae apostolicae adnexo;

2° asservari potest in sacello Episcopi et, de licentia Ordinarii loci, in aliis ecclesiis, oratoriis et sacellis.

§2. In locis sacris ubi sanctissima Eucharistia asservatur, adesse semper debet qui eius curam habeat et, quantum fieri potest, sacerdos saltem bis in mense Missam ibi celebret.

CAN. 935 Nemini licet sanctissimam Eucharistiam apud se retinere aut secum in itinere deferre, nisi necessitate pastorali urgente et servatis Episcopi dioecesani praescriptis.

CAN. 936 In domo instituti religiosi aliave pia domo, sanctissima Eucharistia asservetur tantummodo in ecclesia aut in oratorio principali domui adnexo; potest tamen iusta de causa Ordinarius permittere, ut etiam in alio oratorio eiusdem domus asservetur.

CAN. 937 Nisi gravis obstet ratio, ecclesia in qua sanctissima Eucharistia asservatur, per aliquot saltem horas cotidie fidelibus pateat, ut coram sanctissimo Sacramento orationi vacare possint.

CAN. 938 §1. Sanctissima Eucharistia

934: c. 1265; CI Resp., 7, 20 maii 1923 (AAS 41 [1949] 508–511); PM II, 5
  935: c. 1265 §3
  936: c. 1267; CI Resp. 5, 2–3 iun. 1918 (AAS 10 [1918].346–347)

937: c. 1266; EMys 51; CEM 8
  938 §1: c. 1268 §1; IOe 95; EMys 52; IGMR 277; CEM 10

to be reserved habitually in only one tabernacle of a church or oratory.

§2. The tabernacle in which the Most Holy Eucharist is reserved is to be situated in some part of the church or oratory which is distinguished, conspicuous, beautifully decorated, and suitable for prayer.

§3. The tabernacle in which the Most Holy Eucharist is reserved habitually is to be immovable, made of solid and opaque material, and locked in such a way that the danger of profanation is avoided as much as possible.

§4. For a grave cause, it is permitted to reserve the Most Holy Eucharist in some other fitting and more secure place, especially at night.

§5. The person responsible for the church or oratory is to take care that the key of the tabernacle in which the Most Holy Eucharist is reserved is safeguarded most diligently.

CAN. 939 Consecrated hosts in a quantity sufficient for the needs of the faithful are to be kept in a pyx or small vessel; they are to be renewed frequently and the older hosts consumed properly.

CAN. 940 A special lamp which indicates and honors the presence of Christ is to shine continuously before a tabernacle in which the Most Holy Eucharist is reserved.

CAN. 941 §1. In churches or oratories

habitualiter in uno tantum ecclesiae vel oratorii tabernaculo asservetur.

§2. Tabernaculum, in quo sanctissima Eucharistia asservatur, situm sit in aliqua ecclesiae vel oratorii parte insigni, conspicua, decore ornata, ad orationem apta.

§3. Tabernaculum, in quo habitualiter sanctissima Eucharistia asservatur, sit inamovibile, materia solida non transparenti confectum, et ita clausum ut quam maxime periculum profanationis vitetur.

§4. Gravi de causa, licet sanctissimam Eucharistiam, nocturno praesertim tempore, alio in loco tutiore et decoro asservare.

§5. Qui ecclesiae vel oratorii curam habet, prospiciat ut clavis tabernaculi, in quo sanctissima Eucharistia asservatur, diligentissime custodiatur.

CAN. 939 Hostiae consecratae quantitate fidelium necessitatibus sufficienti in pyxide seu vasculo serventur, et frequenter, veteribus rite consumptis, renoventur.

CAN. 940 Coram tabernaculo, in quo sanctissima Eucharistia asservatur, peculiaris perenniter luceat lampas, qua indicetur et honoretur Christi praesentia.

CAN. 941 §1. In ecclesiis aut oratoriis

938 §2: c. 1268 §2; IOe 95; MF 35; EMys 53; CEM 9; IGMR 276, 277; SCIC Instr. *In ecclesiasticam futurorum*, 3 iun. 1979, 27; ID 24

938 §3: c. 1269 §§1 et 2; SCDS Instr. *De sanctissima Eucharistia sedulo custodienda*, 26 maii 1938 (AAS 30 [1938] 198–207); SCDS Monitum, 10 feb. 1941 (AAS 33 [1941] 57); SCDS Ep., 15 sep. 1943 (AAS 35 [1943] 282–285); SRC Decr. *Urbis et Orbis*, 1 iun. 1957 (AAS 49 [1957] 425–426); IOe 95; EMys 54; IGMR 277; CEM 10; ID 25

938 §4: c. 1269 §3; SCDS Ep., 15 sep. 1943 (AAS 35 [1943] 282–285)

938 §5: c. 1269 §4; CEM 10

939: cc. 1270, 1272; SCDS Resp., 7 dec. 1918 (AAS 11 [1918] 8); SCDS Instr. *Dominus salvator noster*, 26 mar. 1929 (AAS 11 [1929] 631–642); *Rituale Romanum*, 1952, tit. V, c. I, 7; IGMR 285; CEM 7

940: c. 1271; SRC Decr. *Urbis et Orbis*, 13 mar. 1942 (AAS [1942] 112); SRC Decr. *Urbis et Orbis*, 18 aug. 1949 (AAS [1949] 476–477); SRC Decr. *Plures locorum Ordinarii*, 13 dec. 1957 (AAS [1958] 50–51); EMys 57; CEM 11; ID 25

941 §1: c. 1274 §1; CI Resp. X, 14 iul. 1922 (AAS 14 [1922] 529); CI Resp. 3, 6 mar. 1927 (AAS 19 [1927] 161); EMys 60, 62–66; CEM 82–90

where it is permitted to reserve the Most Holy Eucharist, there can be expositions with the pyx or the monstrance; the norms prescribed in the liturgical books are to be observed.

§2. Exposition of the Most Blessed Sacrament is not to be held in the same area of the church or oratory during the celebration of Mass.

CAN. 942   It is recommended that in these churches and oratories an annual solemn exposition of the Most Blessed Sacrament be held for an appropriate period of time, even if not continuous, so that the local community more profoundly meditates on and adores the eucharistic mystery. Such an exposition is to be held, however, only if a suitable gathering of the faithful is foreseen and the established norms are observed.

CAN. 943   The minister of exposition of the Most Blessed Sacrament and of eucharistic benediction is a priest or deacon; in special circumstances, the minister of exposition and reposition alone without benediction is the acolyte, extraordinary minister of holy communion, or someone else designated by the local ordinary; the prescripts of the diocesan bishop are to be observed.

CAN. 944   §1. When it can be done in the judgment of the diocesan bishop, a procession through the public streets is to be held as a public witness of veneration toward the Most Holy Eucharist, especially on the solemnity of the Body and Blood of Christ.

§2. It is for the diocesan bishop to establish regulations which provide for the participation in and the dignity of processions.

quibus datum est asservare sanctissimam Eucharistiam, fieri possunt expositiones sive cum pyxide sive cum ostensorio, servatis normis in libris liturgicis praescriptis.

§2. Celebratione Missae durante, ne habeatur in eadem ecclesiae vel oratorii aula sanctissimi Sacramenti expositio.

CAN. 942   Commendatur ut in iisdem ecclesiis et oratoriis quotannis fiat sollemnis sanctissimi Sacramenti expositio per congruum tempus, etsi non continuum, protracta, ut communitas localis eucharisticum mysterium impensius meditetur et adoret; huiusmodi tamen expositio fiat tantum si congruus praevideatur fidelium concursus et servatis normis statutis.

CAN. 943   Minister expositionis sanctissimi Sacramenti et benedictionis eucharisticae est sacerdos vel diaconus; in peculiaribus adiunctis, solius expositionis et repositionis, sine tamen benedictione, est acolythus, minister extraordinarius sacrae communionis aliusve ab Ordinario loci deputatus, servatis Episcopi dioecesani praescriptis.

CAN. 944   §1. Ubi de iudico Episcopi dioecesani fieri potest, in publicum erga sanctissimam Eucharistiam venerationis testimonium, habeatur, praesertim in sollemnitate Corporis et Sanguinis Christi, processio per vias publicas ducta.

§2. Episcopi dioecesani est de processionibus statuere ordinationes, quibus earum participationi et dignitati prospiciatur.

941 §2: EMys 61; CEM 83
942: c. 1275; EMys 63; CEM 86
943: c. 1274 §2; SDO V, 3; MQ VI; CEM 91
944 §1: c. 1291; EMys 59; CEM 101–104

944 §2: c. 1295; SRC Resp., 28 oct. 1922 (AAS 16 [1924] 103–104); SRC Resp., 24 aug. 1933; SRC Resp., 25 aug. 1938; EMys 59; CEM 101

CHAPTER III. **The Offering Given for the Celebration of Mass**

CAPUT III. **De Oblata ad Missae Celebrationem Stipe**

CAN. 945 §1. In accord with the approved practice of the Church, any priest celebrating or concelebrating is permitted to receive an offering to apply the Mass for a specific intention.

CAN. 945 §1. Secundum probatum Ecclesiae morem, sacerdoti cuilibet Missam celebranti aut concelebranti licet stipem oblatam recipere, ut iuxta certam intentionem Missam applicet.

§2. It is recommended earnestly to priests that they celebrate Mass for the intention of the Christian faithful, especially the needy, even if they have not received an offering.

§2. Enixe commendatur sacerdotibus ut, etiam nulla recepta stipe, Missam ad intentionem christifidelium praecipue egentium celebrent.

CAN. 946 The Christian faithful who give an offering to apply the Mass for their intention contribute to the good of the Church and by that offering share its concern to support its ministers and works.

CAN. 946 Christifideles stipem offerentes, ut ad suam intentionem Missa applicetur, ad bonum conferunt Ecclesiae atque eius curam in ministris operibusque sustinendis ea oblatione participant.

CAN. 947 Any appearance of trafficking or trading is to be excluded entirely from the offering for Masses.

CAN. 947 A stipe Missarum quaelibet etiam species negotiationis vel mercaturae omnino arceatur.

CAN. 948 Separate Masses are to be applied for the intentions of those for whom a single offering, although small, has been given and accepted.

CAN. 948 Distinctae applicandae sunt Missae ad eorum intentiones pro quibus singulis stips, licet exigua, oblata et acceptata est.

CAN. 949 A person obliged to celebrate and apply Mass for the intention of those who gave an offering is bound by the obligation even if the offerings received have been lost through no fault of his own.

CAN. 949 Qui obligatione gravatur Missam celebrandi et applicandi ad intentionem eorum qui stipem obtulerunt, eadem obligatione tenetur, etiamsi sine ipsius culpa stipes perceptae perierint.

CAN. 950 If a sum of money is offered for the application of Masses without an indication of the number of Masses to be celebrated, the number is to be computed on the basis of the offering established in the place where the donor resides, unless the intention of the donor

CAN. 950 Si pecuniae summa offertur pro Missarum applicatione, non indicato Missarum celebrandarum numero, hic supputetur attenta stipe statuta in loco quo oblator commoratur, nisi aliam fuisse eius intentionem legitime praesumi debeat.

---

945 §1: c. 824 §1; PAULUS PP. VI, m. p. *Firma in traditione*, 13 iun. 1974 (AAS 66 [1974] 308); Sec Normae, 17 iun. 1974

946: PAULUS PP. VI, m. p. *Firma in traditione*, 13 iun. 1974 (AAS 66 [1974] 308); Sec Normae, 17 iun. 1974

947: c. 827; SCConc Causa, 10 ian. 1920 (AAS 12

[1920] 70); SCConc Causa, 16 apr. 1921 (AAS 13 [1921] 532–533)

948: c. 828; SCConc Causa, 9 iul. 1921 (AAS 13 [1921] 502–504)

949: c. 829

950: c. 830

must be presumed legitimately to have been different.

CAN. 951 §1. A priest who celebrates several Masses on the same day can apply each to the intention for which the offering was given, but subject to the rule that, except on Christmas, he is to keep the offering for only one Mass and transfer the others to the purposes prescribed by the ordinary, while allowing for some recompense by reason of an extrinsic title.

§2. A priest who concelebrates a second Mass on the same day cannot accept an offering for it under any title.

CAN. 952 §1. It is for the provincial council or a meeting of the bishops of the province to define by decree for the entire province the offering to be given for the celebration and application of Mass, and a priest is not permitted to seek a larger sum. Nevertheless, he is permitted to accept for the application of a Mass a voluntary offering which is larger or even smaller than the one defined.

§2. Where there is no such decree, the custom in force in the diocese is to be observed.

§3. Members of all religious institutes must also observe the same decree or local custom mentioned in §§1 and 2.

CAN. 953 No one is permitted to accept more offerings for Masses to be applied by himself than he can satisfy within a year.

CAN. 954 If in certain churches or oratories more Masses are asked to be celebrated than

CAN. 951 §1. Sacerdos plures eadem die Missas celebrans, singulas applicare potest ad intentionem pro qua stips oblata est, ea tamen lege ut, praeterquam in die Nativitatis Domini, stipem pro una tantum Missa faciat suam, ceteras vero in fines ab Ordinario praescriptos concredat, admissa quidem aliqua retributione ex titulo extrinseco.

§2. Sacerdos alteram Missam eadem die concelebrans, nullo titulo pro ea stipem recipere potest.

CAN. 952 §1. Concilii provincialis aut conventus Episcoporum provinciae est pro universa provincia per decretum definire quaenam pro celebratione et applicatione Missae sit offerenda stips, nec licet sacerdoti summam maiorem expetere; ipsi tamen fas est stipem sponte oblatam definita maiorem pro Missae applicatione accipere, et etiam minorem.

§2. Ubi desit tale decretum, servetur consuetudo in dioecesi vigens.

§3. Sodales quoque institutorum religiosorum quorumlibet stare debent eidem decreto aut consuetudini loci, de quibus in §§1 et 2.

CAN. 953 Nemini licet tot stipes Missarum per se applicandarum accipere, quibus intra annum satisfacere non potest.

CAN. 954 Si certis in ecclesiis aut oratoriis Missae petuntur celebrandae numero

951 §1: c. 824 §2; SCConc Causa, 10 nov. 1917 (AAS 10 [1918] 368–373); SCConc Causa, 8 maii 1920 (AAS 12 [1920] 536–549); CI Resp., 13 dec. 1923 (AAS 16 [1924] 116); SCConc Resol., 13 nov. 1937 (AAS 30 [1938] 101–103); Paulus PP. VI, m.p. *Firma in traditione*, IIIª, 13 iun. 1974 (AAS 66 [1974] 308); Sec Normae, 17 iun. 1974
951 §2: SCCD Decl. *In celebratione Missae*, 7 aug. 1972 (AAS 64 [1972] 563); Paulus PP. VI, m.p. *Firma*

in traditione, IIIª, 13 iun. 1974 (AAS 66 [1974] 308); Sec Normae, 17 iun. 1974
952 §1: c. 831; SCConc Resol., 15 iun. 1918 (AAS 10 [1918] 504–507)
952 §2: c. 831 §2
952 §3: c. 831 §3
953: c. 835
954: c. 836

can be celebrated there, it is permitted for them to be celebrated elsewhere unless the donors have expressly indicated a contrary intention.

CAN. 955 §1. A person who intends to entrust to others the celebration of Masses to be applied is to entrust their celebration as soon as possible to priests acceptable to him, provided that he is certain that they are above suspicion. He must transfer the entire offering received unless it is certain that the excess over the sum fixed in the diocese was given for him personally. He is also obliged to see to the celebration of the Masses until he learns that the obligation has been accepted and the offering received.

§2. The time within which Masses must be celebrated begins on the day the priest who is to celebrate them received them unless it is otherwise evident.

§3. Those who entrust to others Masses to be celebrated are to record in a book without delay both the Masses which they received and those which they transferred to others, as well as their offerings.

§4. Every priest must note accurately the Masses which he accepted to celebrate and those which he has satisfied.

CAN. 956 Each and every administrator of pious causes or those obliged in any way to see to the celebration of Masses, whether clerics or laity, are to hand over to their ordinaries according to the method defined by the latter the Mass obligations which have not been satisfied within a year.

CAN. 957 The duty and right of exercising

plures quam ut ibidem celebrari possint, earundem celebratio alibi fieri licet, nisi contrariam voluntatem oblatores expresse manifestaverint.

CAN. 955 §1. Qui celebrationem Missarum applicandarum aliis committere intendat, earum celebrationem quam primum sacerdotibus sibi acceptis committat, dummodo ipsi constet eos esse omni exceptione maiores; integram stipem receptam transmittere debet, nisi certo constet excessum supra summam in dioecesi debitam datum esse intuitu personae; obligatione etiam tenetur Missarum celebrationem curandi, donec tum susceptae obligationis tum receptae stipis testimonium acceperit.

§2. Tempus intra quod Missae celebrandae sunt initium habet a die quo sacerdos easdem celebraturus recepit, nisi aliud constet.

§3. Qui aliis Missas celebrandas committunt, sine mora in librum referant tum Missas quas acceperunt, tum eas, quas aliis tradiderunt, notatis etiam earundem stipibus.

§4. Quilibet sacerdos accurate notare debet Missas quas celebrandas acceperit, quibusque satisfecerit.

CAN. 956 Omnes et singuli administratores causarum piarum aut quoquo modo obligati ad Missarum celebrationem curandam, sive clerici sive laici, onera Missarum quibus intra annum non fuerit satisfactum suis Ordinariis tradant, secundum modum ab his definiendum.

CAN. 957 Officium et ius advigilandi ut

955 §1: cc. 837–840; SCConc Causa, 19 feb. 1921 (AAS 13 [1921] 228–230); SCConc Causa, 16 apr. 1921 (AAS 13 [1921] 532–534)
955 §2: c. 837

955 §3: c. 844 §1
955 §4: c. 844 §2
956: c. 841 §1
957: c. 842

vigilance that Mass obligations are fulfilled belong to the local ordinary in churches of secular clergy and to the superiors in churches of religious institutes or societies of apostolic life.

CAN. 958 §1. The pastor and the rector of a church or other pious place which regularly receives offerings for Masses are to have a special book in which they note accurately the number of Masses to be celebrated, the intention, the offering given, and their celebration.

§2. The ordinary is obliged to examine these books each year either personally or through others.

TITLE IV. The Sacrament of Penance

CAN. 959 In the sacrament of penance the faithful who confess their sins to a legitimate minister, are sorry for them, and intend to reform themselves obtain from God through the absolution imparted by the same minister forgiveness for the sins they have committed after baptism and, at the same, time are reconciled with the Church which they have wounded by sinning.

CHAPTER I. The Celebration of the Sacrament

CAN. 960 Individual and integral confession and absolution constitute the only ordinary means by which a member of the faithful conscious of grave sin is reconciled with God and the Church. Only physical or moral impos-

Missarum onera adimpleantur, in ecclesiis cleri saecularis pertinet ad loci Ordinarium, in ecclesiis institutorum religiosorum aut societatum vitae apostolicae ad eorum Superiores.

CAN. 958 §1. Parochus necnon rector ecclesiae aliusve pii loci, in quibus stipes Missarum recipi solent, peculiarem habeant librum, in quo accurate adnotent Missarum celebrandarum numerum, intentionem, stipem oblatam, necnon celebrationem peractam.

§2. Ordinarius obligatione tenetur singulis annis huiusmodi libros per se aut per alios recognoscendi.

TITULUS IV. De Sacramento Paenitentiae

CAN. 959 In sacramento paenitentiae fideles peccata legitimo ministro confitentes, de iisdem contriti atque propositum sese emendandi habentes, per absolutionem ab eodem ministro impertitam, veniam peccatorum quae post baptismum commiserint a Deo obtinent, simulque reconciliantur cum Ecclesia, quam peccando vulneraverunt.

CAPUT I. De Celebratione Sacramenti

CAN. 960 Individualis et integra confessio atque absolutio unicum constituunt modum ordinarium, quo fidelis peccati gravis sibi conscius cum Deo et Ecclesia reconciliatur; solummodo impossibilitas physica vel

---

958 §1: c. 843 §1
958 §2: c. 843 §2

960: SC 72; SCDF *Normae Pastorales*, 16 iun. 1972,
I (AAS 64 [1972] 510); OP 31

sibility excuses from confession of this type; in such a case reconciliation can be obtained by other means.

CAN. 961 §1. Absolution cannot be imparted in a general manner to many penitents at once without previous individual confession unless:

1° danger of death is imminent and there is insufficient time for the priest or priests to hear the confessions of the individual penitents;

2° there is grave necessity, that is, when in view of the number of penitents, there are not enough confessors available to hear the confessions of individuals properly within a suitable period of time in such a way that the penitents are forced to be deprived for a long while of sacramental grace or holy communion through no fault of their own. Sufficient necessity is not considered to exist when confessors cannot be present due only to the large number of penitents such as can occur on some great feast or pilgrimage.

§2. It belongs to the diocesan bishop to judge whether the conditions required according to the norm of §1, n. 2 are present. He can determine the cases of such necessity, attentive to the criteria agreed upon with the other members of the conference of bishops.

CAN. 962 §1. For a member of the Christian faithful validly to receive sacramental abso-

moralis ab huiusmodi confessione excusat, quo in casu aliis quoque modis reconciliatio haberi potest.

CAN. 961 §1. Absolutio pluribus insimul paenitentibus sine praevia individuali confessione, generali modo impertiri non potest, nisi:

1° immineat periculum mortis et tempus non suppetat sacerdoti vel sacerdotibus ad audiendas singulorum paenitentium confessiones;

2° adsit gravis necessitas, videlicet quando, attento paenitentium numero, confessariorum copia praesto non est ad rite audiendas singulorum confessiones intra congruum tempus, ita ut paenitentes, sine propria culpa, gratia sacramentali aut sacra communione diu carere cogantur; necessitas vero non censetur sufficiens, cum confessarii praesto esse non possunt, ratione solius magni concursus paenitentium, qualis haberi potest in magna aliqua festivitate aut peregrinatione.

§2. Iudicium ferre an dentur condiciones ad normam §1, n. 2 requisitae, pertinet ad Episcopum dioecesanum, qui, attentis criteriis cum ceteris membris Episcoporum conferentiae concordatis, casus talis necessitatis determinare potest.

CAN. 962 §1. Ut christifidelis sacramentali absolutione una simul pluribus data

961 §1, 1°: SPA Facul., 30 aug. 1939, 2–3; SCC *Index facultatum,* 8 dec. 1939, 14b (AAS 31 [1939] 712); SPA Instr. *Ut dubia,* 25 mar. 1944, I (AAS 36 [1944] 155–156); SCDF *Normae Pastorales,* 16 iun. 1972, II (AAS 64 [1972] 511); OP 31

961 §1, 2°: SCDS Ind., 22 apr. 1940; SPA Resp., 10 dec. 1940 (AAS 32 [1940] 571); SPA Instr. *Ut dubia,* 25 mar. 1944, II (AAS 36 [1944] 156); SCDF *Normae Pastorales,* 16 iun. 1972, III (AAS 64 [1972] 511); OP 31;

SCDF Resp., 20 ian. 1978; PAULUS PP. VI, All., 20 apr. 1978 (AAS 70 [1978] 330–331); IOANNES PAULUS PP. II, All., 30 ian. 1981 (AAS 73 [1981] 203)

961 §2: SCDF *Normae Pastorales,* 16 iun. 1972, V (AAS 64 [1972] 512); OP 32

962 §1: SPA Ind., 30 aug. 1939, 2; SPA Resp., 10 dec. 1940; SPA Instr. *Ut dubia,* 25 mar. 1944, IV (AAS 36 [1944] 156); SCDF *Normae Pastorales,* 16 iun. 1972, VI (AAS 64 [1972] 512); OP 33

lution given to many at one time, it is required not only that the person is properly disposed but also at the same time intends to confess within a suitable period of time each grave sin which at the present time cannot be so confessed.

§2. Insofar as it can be done even on the occasion of the reception of general absolution, the Christian faithful are to be instructed about the requirements of the norm of §1. An exhortation that each person take care to make an act of contrition is to precede general absolution even in the case of danger of death, if there is time.

CAN. 963 Without prejudice to the obligation mentioned in can. 989, a person whose grave sins are remitted by general absolution is to approach individual confession as soon as possible, given the opportunity, before receiving another general absolution, unless a just cause intervenes.

CAN. 964 §1. The proper place to hear sacramental confessions is a church or oratory.

§2. The conference of bishops is to establish norms regarding the confessional; it is to take care, however, that there are always confessionals with a fixed grate between the penitent and the confessor in an open place so that the faithful who wish to can use them freely.

§3. Confessions are not to be heard outside a confessional without a just cause.

valide fruatur, requiritur non tantum ut sit apte dispositus, sed ut insimul sibi proponat singillatim debito tempore confiteri peccata gravia, quae in praesens ita confiteri nequit.

§2. Christifideles, quantum fieri potest etiam occasione absolutionis generalis recipiendae, de requisitis ad normam §1 edoceantur et absolutioni generali, in casu quoque periculi mortis, si tempus suppetat, praemittatur exhortatio ut actum contritionis quisque elicere curet.

CAN. 963 Firma manente obligatione de qua in can. 989, is, cui generali absolutione gravia peccata remittuntur, ad confessionem individualem quam primum, occasione data, accedat, antequam aliam recipiat absolutionem generalem, nisi iusta causa interveniat.

CAN. 964 §1. Ad sacramentales confessiones excipiendas locus proprius est ecclesia aut oratorium.

§2. Ad sedem confessionalem quod attinet, normae ab Episcoporum conferentia statuantur, cauto tamen ut semper habeantur in loco patenti sedes confessionales crate fixa inter paenitentem et confessarium instructae, quibus libere uti possint fideles, qui id desiderent.

§3. Confessiones extra sedem confessionalem ne excipiantur, nisi iusta de causa.

962 §2: SPA Instr. *Ut dubia*, 25 mar. 1944, V (AAS 36 [1944] 155–156); SCDF *Normae Pastorales*, 16 iun. 1972, VIII (AAS 64 [1972] 513); OP 33

963: SPA Instr. *Ut dubia*, 25 mar. 1944, IVb (AAS 36 [1944] 156); SCDF *Normae Pastorales*, 16 iun. 1972,

VII (AAS 64 [1972] 512–513); OP 34; IOANNES PAULUS PP. II, All., 30 ian. 1981 (AAS 73 [1981] 201–204)

964 §1: c. 908; OP 12, 38b

964 §2: c. 909 §2; OP 38b

964 §3: c. 910

CHAPTER II. **The Minister of the Sacrament of Penance**

CAN. 965 A priest alone is the minister of the sacrament of penance.

CAN. 966 §1. The valid absolution of sins requires that the minister have, in addition to the power of orders, the faculty of exercising it for the faithful to whom he imparts absolution.

§2. A priest can be given this faculty either by the law itself or by a grant made by the competent authority according to the norm of can. 969.

CAN. 967 §1. In addition to the Roman Pontiff, cardinals have the faculty of hearing the confessions of the Christian faithful everywhere in the world by the law itself. Bishops likewise have this faculty and use it licitly everywhere unless the diocesan bishop has denied it in a particular case.

§2. Those who possess the faculty of hearing confessions habitually whether by virtue of office or by virtue of the grant of an ordinary of the place of incardination or of the place in which they have a domicile can exercise that faculty everywhere unless the local ordinary has denied it in a particular case, without prejudice to the prescripts of can. 974, §§2 and 3.

§3. Those who are provided with the faculty of hearing confessions by reason of office or grant of a competent superior according to the norm of cann. 968, §2 and 969, §2 possess the same faculty everywhere by the law itself as regards members and others living day and night in the house of the institute or society; they also use the faculty licitly unless some major superior has denied it in a particular case as regards his own subjects.

CAPUT II. **De Sacramenti Paenitentiae Ministro**

CAN. 965 Minister sacramenti paenitentiae est solus sacerdos.

CAN. 966 §1. Ad validam peccatorum absolutionem requiritur ut minister, praeterquam potestate ordinis, facultate gaudeat eandem in fideles, quibus absolutionem impertitur, exercendi.

§2. Hac facultate donari potest sacerdos, sive ipso iure sive concessione ab auctoritate competenti facta ad normam can. 969.

CAN. 967 §1. Praeter Romanum Pontificem, facultate christifidelium ubique terrarum confessiones excipiendi ipso iure gaudent Cardinales; itemque Episcopi, qui eadem et licite ubique utuntur, nisi Episcopus dioecesanus in casu particulari renuerit.

§2. Qui facultate confessiones habitualiter excipiendi gaudent sive vi officii sive vi concessionis Ordinarii loci incardinationis aut loci in quo domicilium habent, eandem facultatem ubique exercere possunt, nisi loci Ordinarius in casu particulari renuerit, firmis praescriptis can. 974, §§2 et 3.

§3. Ipso iure eadem facultate ubique potiuntur erga sodales aliosque in domo instituti aut societatis diu noctuque degentes, qui vi officii aut concessionis Superioris competentis ad normam cann. 968, §2 et 969, §2 facultate confessiones excipiendi sunt instructi; qui quidem eadem et licite utuntur, nisi aliquis Superior maior quoad proprios subditos in casu particulari renuerit.

965: c. 871; PO 5; OP 9a
966 §1: c. 872; OP 9b

967 §1: c. 873 §1; PM II, 2
967 §2: cc. 514, 875

CAN. 968 §1. In virtue of office, a local ordinary, canon penitentiary, a pastor, and those who take the place of a pastor possess the faculty of hearing confessions, each within his jurisdiction.

§2. In virtue of their office, superiors of religious institutes or societies of apostolic life that are clerical and of pontifical right, who have executive power of governance according to the norm of their constitutions, possess the faculty of hearing the confessions of their subjects and of others living day and night in the house, without prejudice to the prescript of can. 630, §4.

CAN. 969 §1. The local ordinary alone is competent to confer upon any presbyters whatsoever the faculty to hear the confessions of any of the faithful. Presbyters who are members of religious institutes, however, are not to use the faculty without at least the presumed permission of their superior.

§2. The superior of a religious institute or society of apostolic life mentioned in can. 968, §2 is competent to confer upon any presbyters whatsoever the faculty to hear the confessions of their subjects and of others living day and night in the house.

CAN. 970 The faculty to hear confessions is not to be granted except to presbyters who are found to be suitable through an examination or whose suitability is otherwise evident.

CAN. 971 The local ordinary is not to grant the faculty of hearing confessions habitually to a presbyter, even one having a domicile or quasi-domicile in his jurisdiction, unless he has first heard the ordinary of the same presbyter insofar as possible.

CAN. 972 The competent authority men-

CAN. 968 §1. Vi officii pro sua quisque dicione facultate ad confessiones excipiendas gaudent loci Ordinarius, canonicus paenitentiarius, itemque parochus aliique qui loco parochi sunt.

§2. Vi officii facultate gaudent confessiones excipiendi suorum subditorum aliorumque, in domo diu noctuque degentium, Superiores instituti religiosi aut societatis vitae apostolicae, si sint clericales iuris pontificii, ad normam constitutionem potestate regiminis exsecutiva fruentes, firmo tamen praescripto can. 630, §4.

CAN. 969 §1. Solus loci Ordinarius competens est qui facultatem ad confessiones quorumlibet fidelium excipiendas conferat presbyteris quibuslibet; presbyteri autem, qui sodales sunt institutorum religiosorum, eadem ne utantur sine licentia saltem praesumpta sui Superioris.

§2. Superior instituti religiosi aut societatis vitae apostolicae, de quo in can. 968, §2, competens est qui facultatem ad excipiendas confessiones suorum subditorum aliorumque in domo diu noctuque degentium presbyteris quibuslibet conferat.

CAN. 970 Facultas ad confessiones excipiendas ne concedatur nisi presbyteris qui idonei per examen reperti fuerint, aut de eorum idoneitate aliunde constet.

CAN. 971 Facultatem ad excipiendas habitualiter confessiones loci Ordinarius presbytero, etsi domicilium vel quasi-domicilium in sua dicione habenti, ne concedat, nisi prius, quantum fieri potest, audito eiusdem presbyteri Ordinario.

CAN. 972 Facultas ad confessiones

968 §1: c. 873 §§1–2
969 §1: c. 874 §1
969 §2: c. 875

970: c. 877
971: c. 874 §1
972: c. 878

tioned in can. 969 can grant the faculty to hear confessions for either an indefinite or a definite period of time.

CAN. 973   The faculty to hear confessions habitually is to be granted in writing.

CAN. 974   §1. The local ordinary and the competent superior are not to revoke the faculty to hear confessions habitually except for a grave cause.

§2. When the faculty to hear confessions has been revoked by the local ordinary who granted it as mentioned in can. 967, §2, a presbyter loses the faculty everywhere. If some other local ordinary has revoked the faculty, the presbyter loses it only in the territory of the one who revokes it.

§3. Any local ordinary who has revoked the faculty of some presbyter to hear confessions is to inform the proper ordinary of incardination of the presbyter or, if he is a member of a religious institute, his competent superior.

§4. If the proper major superior of a presbyter has revoked the faculty to hear confessions, the presbyter loses the faulty to hear the confessions of members of the institute everywhere. If some other competent superior has revoked the faculty, however, the presbyter loses it only with regard to the subjects in the jurisdiction of that superior.

CAN. 975   Besides by revocation, the faculty mentioned in can. 967, §2 ceases by loss of office, excardination, or loss of domicile.

CAN. 976   Even though a priest lacks the faculty to hear confessions, he absolves validly and licitly any penitents whatsoever in danger

excipiendas a competenti auctoritate, de qua in can. 969, concedi potest ad tempus sive indeterminatum sive determinatum.

CAN. 973   Facultas ad confessiones habitualiter excipiendas scripto concedatur.

CAN. 974   §1. Loci Ordinarius, itemque Superior competens, facultatem ad confessiones excipiendas habitualiter concessam ne revocet nisi gravem ob causam.

§2. Revocata facultate ad confessiones excipiendas a loci Ordinario qui eam concessit, de quo in can. 967, §2, presbyter eandem facultatem ubique amittit; revocata eadem facultate ab alio loci Ordinario, eandem amittit tantum in territorio revocantis.

§3. Quilibet loci Ordinarius, qui alicui presbytero revocaverit facultatem ad confessiones excipiendas, certiorem reddat Ordinarium qui ratione incardinationis est presbyteri proprius, aut, si agatur de sodali instituti religiosi, eiusdem competentem Superiorem.

§4. Revocata facultate ad confessiones excipiendas a proprio Superiore maiore, facultatem ad excipiendas confessiones ubique erga sodales instituti amittit presbyter; revocata autem eadem facultate ab alio Superiore competenti, eandem amittit erga solos in eiusdem dicione subditos.

CAN. 975   Praeterquam revocatione, facultas de qua in can. 967, §2 cessat amissione officii vel excardinatione aut amissione domicilii.

CAN. 976   Quilibet sacerdos, licet ad confessiones excipiendas facultate careat, quoslibet paenitentes in periculo mortis ver-

---

973: c. 879 §1
974 §1: c. 880 §1

975: cc. 873 §3, 967
976: c. 882

of death from any censures and sins, even if an approved priest is present.

CAN. 977 The absolution of an accomplice in a sin against the sixth commandment of the Decalogue is invalid except in danger of death.

CAN. 978 §1. In hearing confessions the priest is to remember that he is equally a judge and a physician and has been established by God as a minister of divine justice and mercy, so that he has regard for the divine honor and the salvation of souls.

§2. In administering the sacrament, the confessor as a minister of the Church is to adhere faithfully to the doctrine of the magisterium and the norms issued by competent authority.

CAN. 979 In posing questions, the priest is to proceed with prudence and discretion, attentive to the condition and age of the penitent, and is to refrain from asking the name of an accomplice.

CAN. 980 If the confessor has no doubt about the disposition of the penitent, and the penitent seeks absolution, absolution is to be neither refused nor deferred.

CAN. 981 The confessor is to impose salutary and suitable penances in accord with the quality and number of sins, taking into account the condition of the penitent. The penitent is obliged to fulfill these personally.

CAN. 982 Whoever confesses to have denounced falsely an innocent confessor to ecclesiastical authority concerning the crime of solicitation to sin against the sixth commandment of the Decalogue is not to be absolved unless the

santes valide et licite absolvit a quibusvis censuris et peccatis, etiamsi praesens sit sacerdos approbatus.

CAN. 977 Absolutio complicis in peccato contra sextum Decalogi praeceptum invalida est, praeterquam in periculo mortis.

CAN. 978 §1. Meminerit sacerdos in audiendis confessionibus se iudicis pariter et medici personam sustinere ac divinae iustitiae simul et misericordiae ministrum a Deo constitutum esse, ut honori divino et animarum saluti consulat.

§2. Confessarius, utpote minister Ecclesiae, in administrando sacramento, doctrinae Magisterii et normis a competenti auctoritate latis fideliter adhaereat.

CAN. 979 Sacerdos in quaestionibus ponendis cum prudentia et discretione procedat, attenta quidem condicione et aetate paenitentis, abstineatque a nomine complicis inquirendo.

CAN. 980 Si confessario dubium non est de paenitentis dispositione et hic absolutionem petat, absolutio ne denegetur nec differatur.

CAN. 981 Pro qualitate et numero peccatorum, habita tamen ratione paenitentis condicionis, salutares et convenientes satisfactiones confessarius iniungat; quas paenitens per se ipse implendi obligatione tenetur.

CAN. 982 Qui confitetur se falso confessarium innocentem apud auctoritatem ecclesiasticam denuntiasse de crimine sollicitationis ad peccatum contra sextum Decalogi praeceptum, ne absolvatur nisi prius falsam

977: cc. 882, 884, 2367
978 §1: c. 888 §1; OP 10 a, c
978 §2: OP 10 a
979: c. 888 §2; SCSO Instr. *Ecclesia numquam*, 16 maii 1943; OP 10 a

980: c. 886
981: c. 887; PAULUS PP. VI, Const. Ap. *Indulgentiarum doctrina*, 1 ian. 1967, 2–3 (AAS 59 [1967] 6–8); OP 6 c
982: c. 894

person has first formally retracted the false denunciation and is prepared to repair damages if there are any.

CAN. 983 §1. The sacramental seal is inviolable; therefore it is absolutely forbidden for a confessor to betray in any way a penitent in words or in any manner and for any reason.

§2. The interpreter, if there is one, and all others who in any way have knowledge of sins from confession are also obliged to observe secrecy.

CAN. 984 §1. A confessor is prohibited completely from using knowledge acquired from confession to the detriment of the penitent even when any danger of revelation is excluded.

§2. A person who has been placed in authority cannot use in any manner for external governance the knowledge about sins which he has received in confession at any time.

CAN. 985 The director of novices and his associate and the rector of a seminary or other institute of education are not to hear the sacramental confessions of their students residing in the same house unless the students freely request it in particular cases.

CAN. 986 §1. All to whom the care of souls has been entrusted in virtue of some function are obliged to make provision so that the confessions of the faithful entrusted to them are heard when they reasonably seek to be heard and that they have the opportunity to approach individual confession on days and at times established for their convenience.

§2. In urgent necessity, any confessor is obliged to hear the confessions of the Christian

denuntiationem formaliter retractaverit et paratus sit ad damna, si quae habeantur, reparanda.

CAN. 983 §1. Sacramentale sigillum inviolabile est; quare nefas est confessario verbis vel alio quovis modo et quavis de causa aliquatenus prodere paenitentem.

§2. Obligatione secretum servandi tenentur quoque interpres, si detur, necnon omnes alii ad quos ex confessione notitia peccatorum quoquo modo pervenerit.

CAN. 984 §1. Omnino confessario prohibetur scientiae ex confessione acquisitae usus cum paenitentis gravamine, etiam quovis revelationis periculo excluso.

§2. Qui in auctoritate est constitutus, notitia quam de peccatis in confessione quovis tempore excepta habuerit, ad exteriorem gubernationem nullo modo uti potest.

CAN. 985 Magister novitiorum eiusque socius, rector seminarii aliusve instituti educationis sacramentales confessiones suorum alumnorum in eadem domo commorantium ne audiant, nisi alumni in casibus particularibus sponte id petant.

CAN. 986 §1. Omnis, cui animarum cura vi muneris est demandata, obligatione tenetur providendi ut audiantur confessiones fidelium sibi commissorum, qui rationabiliter audiri petant, utque iisdem opportunitas praebeatur ad confessionem individualem, diebus ac horis in eorum commodum statutis, accedendi.

§2. Urgente necessitate, quilibet confessarius obligatione tenetur confessiones chris-

983 §1: c. 889; OP 10 d
984 §1: c. 890 §1; SCSO Instr., 15 iun. 1915; SPA Monitum, 1 feb. 1935 (AAS 27 [1935] 62)
984 §2: c. 890 §2
985: c. 891

986 §1: c. 892 §1; CD 30; PO 13; OP 10 b, 13; SCDF *Normae Pastorales*, 16 iun. 1972, IV, IX, XII (AAS 64 [1972] 512–514); PAULUS PP. VI, All., 20 apr. 1978 (AAS 70 [1978] 328–332)
986 §2: c. 892 §2

faithful, and in danger of death, any priest is so obliged.

tifidelium excipiendi, et in periculo mortis quilibet sacerdos.

CHAPTER III. **The Penitent**

CAN. 987 To receive the salvific remedy of the sacrament of penance, a member of the Christian faithful must be disposed in such a way that, rejecting sins committed and having a purpose of amendment, the person is turned back to God.

CAN. 988 §1. A member of the Christian faithful is obliged to confess in kind and number all grave sins committed after baptism and not yet remitted directly through the keys of the Church nor acknowledged in individual confession, of which the person has knowledge after diligent examination of conscience.

§2. It is recommended to the Christian faithful that they also confess venial sins.

CAN. 989 After having reached the age of discretion, each member of the faithful is obliged to confess faithfully his or her grave sins at least once a year.

CAN. 990 No one is prohibited from confessing through an interpreter as long as abuses and scandals are avoided and without prejudice to the prescript of can. 983, §2.

CAN. 991 Every member of the Christian faithful is free to confess sins to a legitimately approved confessor of his or her choice, even to one of another rite.

CAPUT III. **De Ipso Paenitente**

CAN. 987 Christifidelis, ut sacramenti paenitentiae remedium percipiat salutiferum, ita dispositus sit oportet ut, peccata quae commiserit repudians et propositum sese emendandi habens, ad Deum convertatur.

CAN. 988 §1. Christifidelis obligatione tenetur in specie et numero confitendi omnia peccata gravia post baptismum perpetrata et nondum per claves Ecclesiae directe remissa neque in confessione individuali accusata, quorum post diligentem sui discussionem conscientiam habeat.

§2. Commendatur christifidelibus ut etiam peccata venialia confiteantur.

CAN. 989 Omnis fidelis, postquam ad annos discretionis pervenerit, obligatione tenetur peccata sua gravia, saltem semel in anno, fideliter confitendi.

CAN. 990 Nemo prohibetur quominus per interpretem confiteatur, vitatis quidem abusibus et scandalis atque firmo praescripto can. 983, §2.

CAN. 991 Cuivis christifideli integrum est confessario legitime approbato etiam alius ritus, cui maluerit, peccata confiteri.

987: OP 6 a, 11; PAULUS PP. VI, Const. Ap. *Paenitemini,* 17 feb. 1966, I (AAS 58 [1966] 179)

988 §1: c. 901; OP 7 a

988 §2: c. 902; SCDF Ep. *Cum Oecumenicum Concilium,* 24 iul. 1966, 7 (AAS 58 [1966] 660); SCDF *Normae Pastorales,* 16 iun. 1972, XII (AAS 64 [1972] 514); OP 7 b; PAULUS PP. VI, Adh. Ap. *Gaudete in Domino,* 9 aug. 1975 (AAS 67 [1975] 311–312);

IOANNES PAULUS II, All., 30 ian. 1981 (AAS 73 [1981] 204)

989: c. 906; DCG Addendum; SCDS et SCpC Decl., 24 maii 1973 (AAS 65 [1973] 410); SCDF *Normae Pastorales,* 16 iun. 1972, VII (AAS 64 [1972] 512–513)

990: c. 903; CD 30

991: c. 905; OE 16

CHAPTER IV. **Indulgences**

CAN. 992 An indulgence is the remission before God of temporal punishment for sins whose guilt is already forgiven, which a properly disposed member of the Christian faithful gains under certain and defined conditions by the assistance of the Church which as minister of redemption dispenses and applies authoritatively the treasury of the satisfactions of Christ and the saints.

CAN. 993 An indulgence is partial or plenary insofar as it partially or totally frees from the temporal punishment due to sins.

CAN. 994 Any member of the faithful can gain partial or plenary indulgences for oneself or apply them to the dead by way of suffrage.

CAN. 995 §1. In addition to the supreme authority of the Church, only those to whom this power is acknowledged in the law or granted by the Roman Pontiff can bestow indulgences.

§2. No authority below the Roman Pontiff can entrust the power of granting indulgences to others unless the Apostolic See has given this expressly to the person.

CAN. 996 §1. To be capable of gaining indulgences, a person must be baptized, not excommunicated, and in the state of grace at least at the end of the prescribed works.

CAPUT IV. **De Indulgentiis**

CAN. 992 Indulgentia est remisso coram Deo poenae temporalis pro peccatis, ad culpam quod attinet iam deletis, quam christifidelis, apte dispositus et certis ac definitis condicionibus, consequitur ope Ecclesiae quae, ut ministra redemptionis, thesaurum satisfactionum Christi et Sanctorum auctoritative dispensat et applicat.

CAN. 993 Indulgentia est partialis aut plenaria, prout a poena temporali pro peccatis debita liberat ex parte aut ex toto.

CAN. 994 Quivis fidelis potest indulgentias sive partiales sive plenarias, aut sibi ipsi lucrari, aut defunctis applicare ad modum suffragii.

CAN. 995 §1. Praeter supremam Ecclesiae auctoritatem ii tantum possunt indulgentias elargiri, quibus haec potestas iure agnoscitur aut a Romano Pontifice conceditur.

§2. Nulla auctoritas infra Romanum Pontificem potest potestatem concedendi indulgentias aliis committere, nisi id ei a Sede Apostolica expresse fuerit indultum.

CAN. 996 §1. Ut quis capax sit lucrandi indulgentias debet esse baptizatus, non excommunicatus, in statu gratiae saltem in fine operum praescriptorum.

992: c. 911; PAULUS PP. VI, Const. Ap. *Indulgentiarum doctrina,* 1 ian. 1967, Normae 1 (AAS 59 [1967] 21); SPA Decr. *In Constitutione,* 29 iun. 1968, Normae de Indulgentiis, 1 (AAS 60 [1968] 414)

993: PAULUS PP. VI, Const. Ap. *Indulgentiarum doctrina,* 1 ian. 1967, Normae 2 (AAS 59 [1967] 21); SPA Decr. *In Constitutione,* 29 iun. 1968, Normae de Indulgentiis, 2 (AAS 60 [1968] 414)

994: PAULUS PP. VI, Const. Ap. *Indulgentiarum doctrina,* 1 ian. 1967, Normae 3 (AAS 59 [1967] 21);

SPA Decr. *In Constitutione,* 29 iun. 1968, Normae de Indulgentiis, 4 (AAS 60 [1968] 414)

995 §1: c. 912; SPA Decr. *In Constitutione,* 29 iun. 1968, Normae de Indulgentiis, 8 (AAS 60 [1968] 415)

995 §2: c. 913; SPA Decr. *In Constitutione,* 29 iun. 1968, Normae de Indulgentiis, 10, 1° (AAS 60 [1968] 415)

996 §1: cc. 925 §1, 2262; SPA Decr. *In Constitutione,* 29 iun. 1968, Normae de Indulgentiis, 22 §1 (AAS 60 [1968] 417)

§2. To gain indulgences, however, a capable subject must have at least the general intention of acquiring them and must fulfill the enjoined works in the established time and the proper method, according to the tenor of the grant.

CAN. 997 As regards the granting and use of indulgences, the other prescripts contained in the special laws of the Church must also be observed.

TITLE V. The Sacrament of the Anointing of the Sick

CAN. 998 The anointing of the sick, by which the Church commends the faithful who are dangerously ill to the suffering and glorified Lord in order that he relieve and save them, is conferred by anointing them with oil and pronouncing the words prescribed in the liturgical books.

CHAPTER I. The Celebration of the Sacrament

CAN. 999 In addition to a bishop, the following can bless the oil to be used in the anointing of the sick:

1° those equivalent to a diocesan bishop by law;

2° any presbyter in a case of necessity, but only in the actual celebration of the sacrament.

CAN. 1000 §1. The anointings with the

§2. Ut vero subiectum capax eas lucretur, habere debet intentionem saltem generalem eas acquirendi et opera iniuncta implere statuto tempore ac debito modo, secundum concessionis tenorem.

CAN. 997 Ad indulgentiarum concessionem et usum quod attinet, servanda sunt insuper cetera praescripta quae in peculiaribus Ecclesiae legibus continentur.

TITULUS V. De Sacramento Unctionis Infirmorum

CAN. 998 Unctio infirmorum, qua Ecclesia fideles periculose aegrotantes Domino patienti et glorificato, ut eos allevet et salvet, commendat, confertur eos liniendo olio atque verba proferendo in liturgicis libris praescripta.

CAPUT I. De Sacramenti Celebratione

CAN. 999 Praeter Episcopum, oleum in unctione infirmorum adhibendum benedicere possunt:

1° qui iure Episcopo dioecesano aequiparantur;

2° in casu necessitatis, quilibet presbyter in ipsa tamen celebratione sacramenti.

CAN. 1000 §1. Unctiones verbis, ordine

996 §2: c. 925 §2; SPA Decr. *In Constitutione,* 29 iun. 1968, Normae de Indulgentiis, 22 §2 (AAS 60 [1968] 417)

997: SPA Decr. *In Constitutione,* 29 iun. 1968, Normae de Indulgentiis (AAS 60 [1968] 414–419)

998: c. 937; SC 73; LG 11; PO 5; PAULUS PP. VI, Const. Ap. *Sacram unctionem Infirmorum,* 30 nov. 1972 (AAS 65 [1973] 5–9); OUI 5, 6

999: c. 945; OUI 21; *Ordo Benedicendi Oleum Catechumenorum et Infirmorum et Conficiendi Chrisma,* 3 dec. 1970, 8

1000 §1: c. 947 §1, *Rituale Romanum,* ed. typica 1925, Tit. VI, c. 2, 11; SC 75; OUI 23, 24

words, order, and manner prescribed in the liturgical books are to be performed carefully. In a case of necessity, however, a single anointing on the forehead or even on some other part of the body is sufficient, while the entire formula is said.

§2. The minister is to perform the anointings with his own hand, unless a grave reason warrants the use of an instrument.

CAN. 1001   Pastors of souls and those close to the sick are to take care that the sick are consoled by this sacrament at the appropriate time.

CAN. 1002   The communal celebration of the anointing of the sick for many of the sick at once, who have been suitably prepared and are properly disposed, can be performed according to the prescripts of the diocesan bishop.

CHAPTER II. **The Minister of the Anointing of the Sick**

CAN. 1003   §1. Every priest and a priest alone validly administers the anointing of the sick.

§2. All priests to whom the care of souls has been entrusted have the duty and right of administering the anointing of the sick for the faithful entrusted to their pastoral office. For a reasonable cause, any other priest can administer this sacrament with at least the presumed consent of the priest mentioned above.

§3. Any priest is permitted to carry blessed oil with him so that he is able to administer the sacrament of the anointing of the sick in a case of necessity.

et modo praescriptis in liturgicis libris, accurate peragantur; in casu tamen necessitatis, sufficit unctio unica in fronte vel etiam in alia corporis parte, integra formula prolata.

§2. Unctiones peragat minister propria manu, nisi gravis ratio usum instrumenti suadeat.

CAN. 1001   Curent animarum pastores et infirmorum propinqui, ut tempore opportuno infirmi hoc sacramento subleventur.

CAN. 1002   Celebratio communis unctionis infirmorum, pro pluribus infirmis simul, qui apte sint praeparati et rite dispositi, iuxta Episcopi dioecesani praescripta peragi potest.

CAPUT II. **De Ministro Unctionis Infirmorum**

CAN. 1003   §1. Unctionem infirmorum valide administrat omnis et solus sacerdos.

§2. Officium et ius unctionis infirmorum ministrandi habent omnes sacerdotes, quibus demandata est cura animarum, erga fideles suo pastorali officio commissos; ex rationabili causa, quilibet alius sacerdos hoc sacramentum ministrare potest de consensu saltem praesumpto sacerdotis de quo supra.

§3. Cuilibet sacerdoti licet oleum benedictum secumferre ut, in casu necessitatis, sacramentum unctionis infirmorum ministrare valeat.

1000 §2: c. 947 §4
1001: c. 944; SC 73; OUI, 13, 43
1002: OUI 17, 83
1003 §1: cc. 938 §1, 939; OUI 16

1003 §2: cc. 938 §2, 939; OUI 16, 18
1003 §3: SRC Decr. *Pientissima Mater*, 4 feb. 1965 (AAS 57 [1965] 409); SCpC Directorium *Peregrinans in terra*, 30 apr. 1969, II, B, b (AAS 61 [1969] 375)

CHAPTER III. **Those on Whom the Anointing of the Sick is to be Conferred**

CAPUT III. **De Iis Quibus Unctio Infirmorum Conferenda Sit**

CAN. 1004 §1. The anointing of the sick can be administered to a member of the faithful who, having reached the use of reason, begins to be in danger due to sickness or old age.

§2. This sacrament can be repeated if the sick person, having recovered, again becomes gravely ill or if the condition becomes more grave during the same illness.

CAN. 1005 This sacrament is to be administered in a case of doubt whether the sick person has attained the use of reason, is dangerously ill, or is dead.

CAN. 1006 This sacrament is to be conferred on the sick who at least implicitly requested it when they were in control of their faculties.

CAN. 1007 The anointing of the sick is not to be conferred upon those who persevere obstinately in manifest grave sin.

CAN. 1004 §1. Unctio infirmorum ministrari potest fideli qui, adepto rationis usu, ob infirmitatem vel senium in periculo incipit versari.

§2. Hoc sacramentum iterari potest, si infirmus, postquam convaluerit, denuo in gravem infirmitatem inciderit aut si, eadem infirmitate perdurante, discrimen factum gravius sit.

CAN. 1005 In dubio utrum infirmus rationis usum attigerit, an periculose aegrotet vel mortuus sit, hoc sacramentum ministretur.

CAN. 1006 Infirmis qui, cum suae mentis compotes essent, hoc sacramentum implicite saltem petierint, conferatur.

CAN. 1007 Unctio infirmorum ne conferatur illis, qui in manifesto gravi peccato obstinate perseverent.

TITLE VI. **Orders**

TITULUS VI. **De Ordine**

CAN. 1008 By divine institution, the sacrament of orders establishes some among the Christian faithful as sacred ministers through an indelible character which marks them. They are consecrated and designated, each according to his grade, to nourish the people of God, fulfilling in the person of Christ the Head the functions of teaching, sanctifying, and governing.

CAN. 1008 Sacramento ordinis ex divina institutione inter christifideles quidam, charactere indelebili quo signantur, constituuntur sacri ministri, qui nempe consecrantur et deputantur ut, pro suo quisque gradu, in persona Christi Capitis munera docendi, sanctificandi et regendi adimplentes, Dei populum pascant.

1004 §1: c. 940; Pius PP. XII, Ep. *Explorata res*, 2 feb. 1923; SC 73; OUI 8, 10, 11, 12
 1004 §2: OUI 9
 1005: c. 941; OUI 15, 135; Paulus PP. VI, Hom., 5 oct. 1975

1006: c. 943; OUI 14
1007: c. 942
1008: c. 948; LG 10, 11, 20, 27; PO 2, 5, 7, 12, 18; Paulus PP. VI, Const. Ap. *Pontificalis Romani*, 18 iun. 1968 (AAS 60 [1968] 370–371)

CAN. 1009 §1. The orders are the episcopate, the presbyterate, and the diaconate.

§2. They are conferred by the imposition of hands and the consecratory prayer which the liturgical books prescribe for the individual grades.

CAN. 1009 §1. Ordines sunt episcopatus, presbyteratus et diaconatus.

§2. Conferuntur manuum impositione et precatione consecratoria, quam pro singulis gradibus libri liturgici praescribunt.

CHAPTER I. The Celebration and Minister of Ordination

CAPUT I. De Ordinationis Celebratione et Ministro

CAN. 1010 Ordination is to be celebrated within the solemnities of the Mass on a Sunday or holy day of obligation. For pastoral reasons it can take place also on other days, even weekdays.

CAN. 1010 Ordinatio intra Missarum sollemnia celebretur, die dominico vel festo de praecepto, sed ob rationes pastorales aliis etiam diebus, ferialibus non exceptis, fieri potest.

CAN. 1011 §1. Ordination generally is to be celebrated in the cathedral church; for pastoral reasons, however, it can be celebrated in another church or oratory.

§2. Clerics and other members of the Christian faithful must be invited to the ordination so that as large an assembly as possible is present at the celebration.

CAN. 1011 §1. Ordinatio generaliter in cathedrali ecclesia celebretur; ob rationes tamen pastorales in alia ecclesia aut oratorio celebrari potest.

§2. Ad ordinationem invitandi sunt clerici aliique christifideles, ut quam maxima frequentia celebrationi intersint.

CAN. 1012 The minister of sacred ordination is a consecrated bishop.

CAN. 1012 Sacrae ordinationis minister est Episcopus consecratus.

CAN. 1013 No bishop is permitted to consecrate anyone a bishop unless it is first evident that there is a pontifical mandate.

CAN. 1013 Nulli Episcopo licet quemquam consecrare in Episcopum, nisi prius constet de pontificio mandato.

CAN. 1014 Unless the Apostolic See has granted a dispensation, the principal bishop consecrator in an episcopal consecration is to

CAN. 1014 Nisi Sedis Apostolicae dispensatio intercesserit, Episcopus consecrator principalis in consecratione episcopali duos

---

1009 §1: c. 949; LG 28, 29; PO 1; PIUS PP. XII, Const. Ap. *Sacramentum Ordinis*, 30 nov. 1947 (AAS 40 [1948] 5); SDO 18; PAULUS PP. VI, Const. Ap. *Pontificalis Romani*, 18 iun. 1968 (AAS 60 [1968] 370–371)

1009 §2: LG 21, 29; PIUS PP. XII, Const. Ap. *Sacramentum Ordinis*, 30 nov. 1947 (AAS 40 [1948] 6–7); PAULUS PP. VI, Const. Ap. *Pontificalis Romani*, 18 iun. 1968 (AAS 60 [1968] 372–373); PONTIFICALE ROMANUM [1968]: *De Ordinatione Diaconorum*, 20–21; *De Ordinatione Presbyterorum*, 20–22; *De Ordinatione Episcopi*, 24–26

1010: c. 1006; SCDS Ind., 18 maii 1940; PM 18; PONTIFICALE ROMANUM [1968]: *De Ordinatione Di-*

aconorum, 1; *De Ordinatione Presbyterorum*, 1; *De Ordinatione Episcopi*, 1

1011 §1: c. 1009 §§1 et 2; PM 18; DPME 87 d

1011 §2: c. 1009 §1; PONTIFICALE ROMANUM [1968]: *De Ordinatione Diaconorum*, 1; *De Ordinatione Presbyterorum*, 1; *De Ordinatione Episcopi*, 1

1012: c. 951; LG 21, 26; PO 5; PAULUS PP. VI, Const. Ap. *Pontificalis Romani*, 18 iun. 1968 (AAS 60 [1968] 372–373); DPME 77

1013: c. 953; CD 20; ES I, 10; PAULUS PP. VI, Const. Ap. *Pontificalis Romani*, 18 iun. 1968 (AAS 60 [1968] 372–373)

1014: c. 954; PIUS PP. XII, Const. Ap. *Episcopali*

be joined by at least two consecrating bishops; it is especially appropriate, however, that all the bishops present consecrate the elect together with the bishops mentioned.

CAN. 1015 §1. Each person is to be ordained to the presbyterate or the diaconate by his proper bishop or with legitimate dimissorial letters from him.

§2. If not impeded by a just cause, the proper bishop is to ordain his own subjects personally; without an apostolic indult, however, he cannot ordain licitly a subject of an Eastern rite.

§3. The person who can give dimissorial letters to receive orders can himself also confer the same orders personally if he possesses the episcopal character.

CAN. 1016 As regards the diaconal ordination of those who intend to be enrolled in the secular clergy, the proper bishop is the bishop of the diocese in which the candidate has a domicile or the bishop of the diocese to which the candidate is determined to devote himself. As regards the presbyteral ordination of secular clerics, it is the bishop of the diocese in which the candidate was incardinated through the diaconate.

CAN. 1017 A bishop cannot confer orders outside his own jurisdiction without the permission of the diocesan bishop.

CAN. 1018 §1. The following can give dimissorial letters for secular clergy:

1° the proper bishop mentioned in can. 1016;

2° an apostolic administrator and, with the

saltem Episcopos consecrantes sibi adiungat; valde convenit autem, ut una cum iisdem omnes Episcopi praesentes electum consecrent.

CAN. 1015 §1. Unusquisque ad presbyteratum et ad diaconatum a proprio Episcopo ordinetur aut cum legitimis eiusdem litteris dimissoriis.

§2. Episcopus proprius, iusta de causa non impeditus, per se ipse suos subditos ordinet; sed subditum orientalis ritus, sine apostolico indulto, licite ordinare non potest.

§3. Qui potest litteras dimissorias ad ordines recipiendos dare, potest quoque eosdem ordines per se ipse conferre, si charactere episcopali polleat.

CAN. 1016 Episcopus proprius, quod attinet ad ordinationem diaconalem eorum qui clero saeculari se adscribi intendant, est Episcopus dioecesis, in qua promovendus habet domicilium, aut dioecesis cui promovendus sese devovere statuit; quod attinet ad ordinationem presbyteralem clericorum saecularium, est Episcopus dioecesis, cui promovendus per diaconatum est incardinatus.

CAN. 1017 Episcopus extra propriam dicionem nonnisi cum licentia Episcopi dioecesani ordines conferre potest.

CAN. 1018 §1. Litteras dimissorias pro saecularibus dare possunt:

1° Episcopus proprius, de quo in can. 1016;

2° Administrator apostolicus atque, de

consecratione, 30 nov. 1944 (AAS 37 [1945] 131–132; SC 76; IOe 69; LG 21, 24; PONTIFICALE ROMANUM [1968]: *De Ordinatione Episcopi*, 2, 23, 24
1015 §1: c. 955 §1; CI Resp. I, 17 feb. 1930 (AAS 22 [1930] 195)
1015 §2: c. 955 §2: CI Resp. I, I, 24 iul. 1939 (AAS 31 [1939] 321); OE 1–5

1015 §3: c. 959
1016: c. 956
1017: c. 1008; CD 11
1018: c. 958

consent of the college of consultors, a diocesan administrator; with the consent of the council mentioned in can. 495, §2, an apostolic pro-vicar and an apostolic pro-prefect.

§2. A diocesan administrator, apostolic pro-vicar, and apostolic pro-prefect are not to grant dimissorial letters to those who have been denied admission to orders by the diocesan bishop, the apostolic vicar, or the apostolic prefect.

CAN. 1019 §1. The major superior of a clerical religious institute of pontifical right or of a clerical society of apostolic life of pontifical right is competent to grant dimissorial letters for the diaconate and the presbyterate to their subjects who are enrolled perpetually or definitively in the institute or society according to their constitutions.

§2. The law for secular clerics governs the ordination of all other candidates of any institute or society; any other indult granted to superiors is revoked.

CAN. 1020 Dimissorial letters are not to be granted unless all the testimonials and documents required by law according to the norm of cann. 1050 and 1051 have been obtained beforehand.

CAN. 1021 Dimissorial letters can be sent to any bishop in communion with the Apostolic See except to a bishop of a rite different from the rite of the candidate unless there is an apostolic indult.

CAN. 1022 After the ordaining bishop has received legitimate dimissorial letters, he is not to proceed to the ordination unless it is clearly evident that the letters are authentic.

CAN. 1023 Dimissorial letters can be lim-

consensu collegii consultorum, Administrator dioecesanus; de consensu consilii, de quo in can. 495, §2, Pro-vicarius et Pro-praefectus apostolicus.

§2. Administrator dioecesanus, Pro-vicarius et Pro-praefectus apostolicus litteras dimissorias ne iis concedant, quibus ab Episcopo dioecesano aut a Vicario vel Praefecto apostolico accessus ad ordines denegatus fuerit.

CAN. 1019 §1. Superiori maiori instituti religiosi clericalis iuris pontificii aut societatis clericalis vitae apostolicae iuris pontificii competit ut suis subditis, iuxta constitutiones perpetuo vel definitive instituto aut societati adscriptis, concedat litteras dimissorias ad diaconatum et ad presbyteratum.

§2. Ordinatio ceterorum omnium alumnorum cuiusvis instituti aut societatis regitur iure clericorum saecularium, revocato quolibet indulto Superioribus concesso.

CAN. 1020 Litterae dimissoriae ne concedantur, nisi habitis antea omnibus testimoniis et documentis, quae iure exiguntur ad normam cann. 1050 et 1051.

CAN. 1021 Litterae dimissoriae mitti possunt ad quemlibet Episcopum communionem cum Sede Apostolica habentem, excepto tantum, citra apostolicum indultum, Episcopo ritus diversi a ritu promovendi.

CAN. 1022 Episcopus ordinans, acceptis legitimis litteris dimissoriis, ad ordinationem ne procedat, nisi de germana litterarum fide plane constet.

CAN. 1023 Litterae dimissoriae pos-

1019: c. 964 §§2 et 4; CA I, 11
1020: c. 960 §1
1021: c. 961; LG 22

1022: c. 962
1023: cc. 46, 963

ited or revoked by the one who granted them or by his successor, but once granted they do not lapse when the authority of the one who granted them ceases.

sunt ab ipso concedente aut ab eius successore limitibus circumscribi aut revocari, sed semel concessae non extinguuntur resoluto iure concedentis.

CHAPTER II. Those to be Ordained

CAPUT II. **De Ordinandis**

CAN. 1024 A baptized male alone receives sacred ordination validly.

CAN. 1024 Sacram ordinationem valide recipit solus vir baptizatus.

CAN. 1025 §1. To confer the presbyteral or diaconal orders licitly, it is required that the candidate, having completed the period of probation according to the norm of law, is endowed in the judgment of his own bishop or of the competent major superior with the necessary qualities, is prevented by no irregularity and no impediment, and has fulfilled the prerequisites according to the norm of cann. 1033–1039. Moreover, the documents mentioned in can. 1050 are to be obtained and the investigation mentioned in can. 1051 is to be completed.

CAN. 1025 §1. Ad licite ordines presbyteratus vel diaconatus conferendos requiritur ut candidatus, probatione ad normam iuris peracta, debitis qualitatibus, iudicio proprii Episcopi aut Superioris maioris competentis, praeditus sit, nulla detineatur irregularitate nulloque impedimento, atque praerequisita, ad normam cann. 1033–1039 adimpleverit; praeterea documenta habeantur, de quibus in can. 1050, atque scrutinium peractum sit, de quo in can. 1051.

§2. Furthermore, it is required that he is considered in the judgment of the same legitimate superior as useful for the ministry of the Church.

§2. Insuper requiritur ut, iudicio eiusdem legitimi Superioris, ad Ecclesiae ministerium utilis habeatur.

§3. The bishop ordaining his own subject who is destined to the service of another diocese must be sure that the one to be ordained is going to be attached to this other diocese.

§3. Episcopo ordinanti proprium subditum, qui servitio alius dioecesis destinetur, constare debet ordinandum huic dioecesi addictum iri.

ART. 1. *Requirements in Those to be Ordained*

ART. 1. *De Requisitis in Ordinandis*

CAN. 1026 A person must possess due freedom in order to be ordained. It is absolutely forbidden to force anyone in any way or for any reason to receive orders or to deter one who is canonically suitable from receiving them.

CAN. 1026 Ut quis ordinetur debita libertate gaudeat oportet; nefas eat quemquam, quovis modo, ob quamlibet causam ad ordines recipiendos cogere, vel canonice idoneum ab iisdem recipiendis averte.

1024: c. 968; PO 2; PAULUS PP. VI, Ep. ad Archiepiscopum Cantuariensem: I, 30 nov. 1975 (AAS 68 [1976] 599–600); II, 23 mar. 1976 (AAS 68 [1976] 600–601); SCDF Decl. *Inter insigniores,* 15 oct. 1976 (AAS 69 [1977] 98–99)

1025 §1: cc. 968, 973 §3, 974 §1; SDO I–III
1025 §2: c. 969 §1
1025 §3: c. 969 §2; OT 20
1026: c. 971; OT 6; SCDS Decr. *Ut locorum Ordinarii,* 9 iun. 1931 (AAS 23 [1931] 459–473)

CAN. 1027 Those aspiring to the diaconate and presbyterate are to be formed by careful preparation, according to the norm of law.

CAN. 1028 The diocesan bishop or the competent superior is to take care that before candidates are promoted to any order, they are instructed properly about those things which belong to the order and its obligations.

CAN. 1029 Only those are to be promoted to orders who, in the prudent judgment of their own bishop or of the competent major superior, all things considered, have integral faith, are moved by the right intention, have the requisite knowledge, possess a good reputation, and are endowed with integral morals and proven virtues and the other physical and psychic qualities in keeping with the order to be received.

CAN. 1030 Only for a canonical cause, even if occult, can the proper bishop or competent major superior forbid admission to the presbyterate to deacons subject to him who are destined to the presbyterate, without prejudice to recourse according to the norm of law.

CAN. 1031 §1. The presbyterate is not to be conferred except on those who have completed the twenty-fifth year of age and possess sufficient maturity; an interval of at least six months is to be observed between the diaconate and the presbyterate. Those destined to the presbyterate are to be admitted to the order of deacon only after completing the twenty-third year of age.

§2. A candidate for the permanent diaconate

CAN. 1027 Aspirantes ad diaconatum et presbyteratum accurata praeparatione efformentur, ad normam iuris.

CAN. 1028 Curet Episcopus dioecesanus aut Superior competens ut candidati, antequam ad ordinem aliquem promoveantur, rite edoceantur de iis, quae ad ordinem eiusque obligationes pertinent.

CAN. 1029 Ad ordines ii soli promoveantur qui, prudenti iudicio Episcopi proprii aut Superioris maioris competentis, omnibus perpensis, integram habent fidem, recta moventur intentione, debita pollent scientia, bona gaudent existimatione, integris moribus probatisque virtutibus atque aliis qualitatibus physicis et psychicis ordini recipiendo congruentibus sunt praediti.

CAN. 1030 Nonnisi ex causa canonica, licet occulta, proprius Episcopus vel Superior maior competens diaconis ad presbyteratum destinatis, sibi subditis, ascensum ad presbyteratum interdicere potest, salvo recursu ad normam iuris.

CAN. 1031 §1. Presbyteratus ne conferatur nisi iis qui aetatis annum vigesimum quintum expleverint et sufficienti gaudeant maturitate, servato insuper intervallo sex saltem mensium inter diaconatum et presbyteratum; qui ad presbyteratum destinantur, ad diaconatus ordinem tantummodo post expletum aetatis annum vigesimum tertium admittantur.

§2. Candidatus ad diaconatum perma-

1027: c. 972; SC 129; OT 6–11, 19, 20; PO 18, 19; SDO 6, 9, 14, 15, 26; RFS

1028: SCDS Instr. *Quam ingens,* 27 dec. 1930 (AAS 23 [1931] 120–129); SRC Instr. *Quantum religionis,* 1 dec. 1931 (AAS 24 [1932] 74–81); OT 9–12, 19–21; SDO 14

1029: cc. 968 §1, 973 §3, 974 §1; SCDS Instr. *Quam ingens,* 27 dec. 1930 (AAS 23 [1931] 120–127); SRC

Instr. *Quantum religionis,* 1 dec. 1931 (AAS 24 [1932] 74–81); SC 9; LG 41; OT 6, 8–12; PO 12, 15–19; SDO 8, 11–13; RFS 11; AP I, b

1030: c. 970; SCDS Instr. *Quam ingens,* 27 dec. 1930 (AAS 23 [1931] 120–129); SRC Instr. *Quantum religionis,* 1 dec. 1931 (AAS 24 [1932] 74–81); Ssap 2

1031 §1: c. 975; OT 12

1031 §2: OT 12; SDO 5, 12

who is not married is not to be admitted to the diaconate until after completing at least the twenty-fifth year of age; one who is married, not until after completing at least the thirty-fifth year of age and with the consent of his wife.

§3. The conference of bishops is free to establish norms which require an older age for the presbyterate and the permanent diaconate.

§4. A dispensation of more than a year from the age required according to the norm of §§1 and 2 is reserved to the Apostolic See.

CAN. 1032 §1. Those aspiring to the presbyterate can be promoted to the diaconate only after they have completed the fifth year of the curriculum of philosophical and theological studies.

§2. After a deacon has completed the curriculum of studies and before he is promoted to the presbyterate, he is to take part in pastoral care, exercising the diaconal order, for a suitable time defined by the bishop or competent major superior.

§3. A person aspiring to the permanent diaconate is not to be promoted to this order unless he has completed the time of formation.

ART. 2. *The Prerequisites for Ordination*

CAN. 1033 A person is promoted licitly to orders only if he has received the sacrament of confirmation.

CAN. 1034 §1. A person aspiring to the diaconate or presbyterate is not to be ordained

nentem qui non sit uxoratus ad eundem diaconatum ne admittatur, nisi post expletum vigesimum quintum saltem aetatis annum; qui matrimonio coniunctus est, nonnisi post expletum trigesimum quintum saltem aetatis annum, atque de uxoris consensu.

§3. Integrum est Episcoporum conferentiis normam statuere, qua provectior ad presbyteratum et ad diaconatum permanentem requiratur aetas.

§4.Dispensatio ultra annum super aetate requisita ad normam §§1 et 2 Apostolicae Sedi reservatur.

CAN. 1032 §1.Aspirantes ad presbyteratum promoveri possunt ad diaconatum solummodo post expletum quintum curriculi studiorum philosophico-theologicorum annum.

§2. Post expletum studiorum curriculum, diaconus per tempus congruum, ab Episcopo vel a Superiore maiore competenti definiendum, in cura pastorali partem habeat, diaconalem exercens ordinem, antequam ad presbyteratum promoveatur.

§3. Aspirans ad diaconatum permanentem, ad hunc ordinem ne promoveatur nisi post expletum formationis tempus.

ART. 2. *De Praerequisitis ad Ordinationem*

CAN. 1033 Licite ad ordines promovetur tantum qui recepit sacrae confirmationis sacramentum.

CAN. 1034 §1. Ad diaconatum vel presbyteratum aspirans ne ordinetur, nisi

1031 §3: SDO 5, 12; RFS 43
1031 §4: PM 15; CA I, 6; EM IX, 6; CI Resp. II, 19 iul. 1970 (AAS 62 [1970] 571)
1032 §1: c. 976 §2; EM IX, 7; AP VII, a
1032 §2: OT 12; RFS 42 c, 63

1032 §3: SDO 6, 8–10; AP VII, b
1033: cc. 974 §1, 1°, 993, 1°; LG 11
1034 §1: AP I, a; PONTIFICALE ROMANUM, *Admissione inter candidatos ad Diaconatum et Presbyteratum,* [1972], III, 1

unless he has first been enrolled among the candidates through the liturgical rite of admission by the authority mentioned in cann. 1016 and 1019; his petition is previously to have been written in his own hand, signed, and accepted in writing by the same authority.

§2. A person who has been received into a clerical institute through vows is not bound to obtain this admission.

CAN. 1035 §1. Before anyone is promoted to the permanent or transitional diaconate, he is required to have received the ministries of lector and acolyte and to have exercised them for a suitable period of time.

§2. There is to be an interval of at least six months between the conferral of the ministry of acolyte and the diaconate.

CAN. 1036 In order to be promoted to the order of diaconate or of presbyterate, the candidate is to present to his bishop or competent major superior a declaration written in his own hand and signed in which he attests that he will receive the sacred order of his own accord and freely and will devote himself perpetually to the ecclesiastical ministry and at the same time asks to be admitted to the order to be received.

CAN. 1037 An unmarried candidate for the permanent diaconate and a candidate for the presbyterate are not to be admitted to the order of diaconate unless they have assumed the obligation of celibacy in the prescribed rite publicly before God and the Church or have made perpetual vows in a religious institute.

CAN. 1038 A deacon who refuses to be

prius per liturgicum admissionis ritum ab auctoritate, de qua in cann. 1016 et 1019, adscriptionem inter candidatos obtinuerit post praeviam suam petitionem propria manu exaratam et subscriptam, atque ab eadem auctoritate in scriptis acceptatam.

§2. Ad eandem admissionem obtinendam non tenetur, qui per vota in clericale institutum cooptatus est.

CAN. 1035 §1. Antequam quis ad diaconatum sive permanentem sive transeuntem promoveatur, requiritur ut ministeria lectoris et acolythi receperit et per congruum tempus exercuerit.

§2. Inter acolythatus et diaconatus collationem intervallum intercedat sex saltem mensium.

CAN. 1036 Candidatus, ut ad ordinem diaconatus aut presbyteratus promoveri possit, Episcopo proprio aut Superiori maiori competenti declarationem tradat propria manu exaratam et subscriptam, qua testificetur se sponte ac libere sacrum ordinem suscepturum atque se ministerio ecclesiastico perpetuo mancipaturum esse, insimul petens ut ad ordinem recipiendum admittatur.

CAN. 1037 Promovendus ad diaconatum permanentem qui non sit uxoratus, itemque promovendus ad presbyteratum, ad ordinem diaconatus ne admittantur, nisi ritu praescripto publice coram Deo et Ecclesia obligationem caelibatus assumpserint, aut vota perpetua in instituto religioso emiserint.

CAN. 1038 Diaconus, qui ad presbyter-

1034 §2: AP I, a; PONTIFICALE ROMANUM, *Admissione inter candidatos ad Diaconatum et Presbyteratum*, [1972], III, 1

  1035 §1: AP II; MQ XI
  1035 §2: c. 978; AP IV
  1036: c. 992; SCDS Instr. *Quam ingens*, 27 dec.

1930 §3, 1 (AAS 23 [1931] 125); SRC Instr. *Quantum religionis*, 1 dec. 1931, 17 (AAS 24 [1932] 80–81); SRC Instr. *Religiosorum institutio*, 2 feb. 1961; AP V

  1037: DO 16; AP VI; PONTIFICALE ROMANUM, *De sacro caelibatu amplectendo*, 3 dec 1972, 1
  1038: c. 973 §2

promoted to the presbyterate cannot be prohibited from the exercise of the order received unless he is prevented by a canonical impediment or another grave cause to be evaluated in the judgment of the diocesan bishop or competent major superior.

CAN. 1039 All candidates for any order are to make a spiritual retreat for at least five days in a place and manner determined by the ordinary. Before the bishop proceeds to ordination, he must be certain that the candidates properly made this retreat.

ART. 3. *Irregularities and Other Impediments*

CAN. 1040 Those affected by any impediment, whether perpetual, which is called an irregularity, or simple, are prevented from receiving orders. The only impediments incurred, however, are those contained in the following canons.

CAN. 1041 The following are irregular for receiving orders:

1° a person who labors under some form of amentia or other psychic illness due to which, after experts have been consulted, he is judged unqualified to fulfill the ministry properly;

2° a person who has committed the delict of apostasy, heresy, or schism;

3° a person who has attempted marriage, even only civilly, while either impeded personally from entering marriage by a matrimonial bond, sacred orders, or a public perpetual vow of chastity, or with a woman bound by a valid marriage or restricted by the same type of vow;

4° a person who has committed voluntary

atum promoveri renuat, ab ordinis recepti exercitio prohiberi non potest, nisi impedimento detineatur canonico aliave gravi causa, de iudicio Episcopi dioecesani aut Superioris maioris competentis aestimanda.

CAN. 1039 Omnes, qui ad aliquem ordinem promovendi sunt, exercitiis spiritualibus vacent per quinque saltem dies, loco et modo ab Ordinario determinatis; Episcopus, antequam ad ordinationem procedat, certior factus sit oportet candidatos rite iisdem exercitiis vacasse.

ART. 3. *De Irregularitatibus Aliisque Impedimentis*

CAN. 1040 A recipiendis ordinibus arcentur qui quovis impedimento afficiuntur sive perpetuo, quod venit nomine irregularitatis, sive simplici; nullum autem impedimentum contrahitur, quod in canonibus qui sequuntur non contineatur.

CAN. 1041 Ad recipiendos ordines sunt irregulares:

1° qui aliqua forma laborat amentiae aliusve psychicae infirmitatis, qua, consultis peritis, inhabilis iudicatur ad ministerium rite implendum;

2° qui delictum apostasiae, haeresis aut schismatis commiserit;

3° qui matrimonium etiam civile tantum attentaverit, vel ipsemet vinculo matrimoniali aut ordine sacro aut voto publico perpetuo castitatis a matrimonio ineundo impeditus, vel cum muliere matrimonio valido coniuncta aut eodem voto adstricta;

4° qui voluntarium homicidium perpe-

1039: c. 1001 §§1 et 4
1040: cc. 968, 983
1041, 1°: c. 984, 3°

1041, 2°: c. 985, 1°
1041, 3°: c. 985, 3°
1041, 4°: c. 985, 4°

homicide or procured a completed abortion and all those who positively cooperated in either;

5° a person who has mutilated himself or another gravely and maliciously or who has attempted suicide;

6° a person who has placed an act of orders reserved to those in the order of episcopate or presbyterate while either lacking that order or prohibited from its exercise by some declared or imposed canonical penalty.

CAN. 1042 The following are simply impeded from receiving orders:

1° a man who has a wife, unless he is legitimately destined to the permanent diaconate;

2° a person who exercises an office or administration forbidden to clerics according to the norm of cann. 285 and 286 for which he must render an account, until he becomes free by having relinquished the office or administration and rendered the account;

3° a neophyte unless he has been proven sufficiently in the judgment of the ordinary.

CAN. 1043 If the Christian faithful are aware of impediments to sacred orders, they are obliged to reveal them to the ordinary or pastor before the ordination.

CAN. 1044 §1. The following are irregular for the exercise of orders received:

1° a person who has received orders illegitimately while affected by an irregularity to receive them;

2° a person who has committed a delict mentioned in can. 1041, n. 2, if the delict is public;

3° a person who has committed a delict mentioned in can. 1041, nn. 3, 4, 5, 6.

traverit aut abortum procuraverit, effectu secuto, omnesque positive cooperantes;

5° qui seipsum vel alium graviter et dolose mutilaverit vel sibi vitam adimere tentaverit;

6° qui actum ordinis posuerit constitutis in ordine episcopatus vel presbyteratus reservatum, vel eodem carens, vel ab eius exercitio poena aliqua canonica declarata vel irrogata prohibitus.

CAN. 1042 Sunt a recipiendis ordinibus simpliciter impediti:

1° vir uxorem habens, nisi ad diaconatum permanentem legitime destinetur;

2° qui officium vel administrationem gerit clericis ad normam cann. 285 et 286 vetitam cuius rationem reddere debet, donec, depositis officio et administratione atque rationibus redditis, liber factus sit;

3° neophytus, nisi, iudicio Ordinarii, sufficienter probatus fuerit.

CAN. 1043 Christifideles obligatione tenentur impedimenta ad sacros ordines, si qua norint, Ordinario vel parocho ante ordinationem revelandi.

CAN. 1044 §1. Ad exercendos ordines receptos sunt irregulares:

1° qui irregularitate ad ordines recipiendos dum afficiebatur, illegitime ordines recepit;

2° qui delictum commisit, de quo in can. 1041, n. 2, si delictum est publicum;

3° qui delictum commisit, de quibus in can. 1041, nn. 3, 4, 5, 6.

1041, 5°: c. 985, 5°
1041, 6°: c. 985, 7°
1042, 1°: c. 987, 2°; SDO 11, 13
1042, 2°: c. 987, 3°
1042, 3°: c. 987, 6°

1043: c. 999
1044 §1: c. 968 §2
1044 §1, 1°: c. 985 §1
1044 §1, 2°: c. 985 §§3–5 et 7

§2. The following are impeded from the exercise of orders:

1° a person who has received orders illegitimately while prevented by an impediment from receiving them;

2° a person who is affected by amentia or some other psychic illness mentioned in can. 1041, n. 1 until the ordinary, after consulting an expert, permits the exercise of the order.

CAN. 1045 Ignorance of the irregularities and impediments does not exempt from them.

CAN. 1046 Irregularities and impediments are multiplied if they arise from different causes. They are not multiplied, however, if they arise from the repetition of the same cause unless it is a question of the irregularity for voluntary homicide or for having procured a completed abortion.

CAN. 1047 §1. Dispensation from all irregularities is reserved to the Apostolic See alone if the fact on which they are based has been brought to the judicial forum.

§2. Dispensation from the following irregularities and impediments to receive orders is also reserved to the Apostolic See:

1° irregularities from the public delicts mentioned in can. 1041, nn. 2 and 3;

2° the irregularity from the delict mentioned in can. 1041, n. 4, whether public or occult;

3° the impediment mentioned in can. 1042, n. 1.

§3. Dispensation in public cases from the irregularities from exercising an order received mentioned in can. 1041, n. 3, and even in occult cases from the irregularities mentioned in can. 1041, n. 4 is also reserved to the Apostolic See.

§2. Ab ordinibus exercendis impediuntur:

1° qui impedimento ad ordines recipiendos detentus, illegitime ordines recepit;

2° qui amentia aliave infirmitate psychica de qua in can. 1041, n. 1 afficitur, donec Ordinarius, consulto perito, eiusdem ordinis exercitium permiserit.

CAN. 1045 Ignorantia irregularitatum atque impedimentorum ab eisdem non eximit.

CAN. 1046 Irregularitates et impedimenta multiplicantur ex diversis eorundem causis, non autem ex repetita eadem causa, nisi agatur de irregularitate ex homicidio voluntario aut ex procurato abortu, effectu secuto.

CAN. 1047 §1. Uni Apostolicae Sedi reservatur dispensatio ab omnibus irregularitatibus, si factum quo innituntur ad forum iudiciale deductum fuerit.

§2. Eidem etiam reservatur dispensatio ab irregularitatibus et impedimentis ad ordines recipiendos, quae sequuntur:

1° ab irregularitatibus ex delictis publicis, de quibus in can. 1041, nn. 2 et 3;

2° ab irregularitate ex delicto publico sive occulto, de quo in can. 1041, n. 4;

3° ab impedimento, de quo in can. 1042, n. 1.

§3. Apostolicae Sedi etiam reservatur dispensatio ab irregularitatibus ad exercitium ordinis suscepti, de quibus in can. 1041, n. 3, in casibus publicis tantum, atque in eodem canone, n. 4, etiam in casibus occultis.

1044 §2: c. 984 §3
1045: c. 988
1046: c. 989

1047 §1: c. 990 §1
1047 §2: EM IX, 9
1047 §3: PM 17; CA I

§4. An ordinary is able to dispense from irregularities and impediments not reserved to the Holy See.

CAN. 1048 In more urgent occult cases, if the ordinary or, when it concerns the irregularities mentioned in can. 1041, nn. 3 and 4, the Penitentiary cannot be approached and if there is imminent danger of grave harm or infamy, a person impeded by an irregularity from exercising an order can exercise it, but without prejudice to the obligation which remains of making recourse as soon as possible to the ordinary or the Penitentiary, omitting the name and through a confessor.

CAN. 1049 §1. Petitions to obtain a dispensation from irregularities or impediments must indicate all the irregularities and impediments. Nevertheless, a general dispensation is valid even for those omitted in good faith, except for the irregularities mentioned in can. 1041, n. 4, and for others brought to the judicial forum, but not for those omitted in bad faith.

§2. If it is a question of the irregularity from voluntary homicide or a procured abortion, the number of the delicts also must be mentioned for the validity of the dispensation.

§3. A general dispensation from irregularities and impediments to receive orders is valid for all the orders.

ART. 4. *The Required Documents and Investigation*

CAN. 1050 For a person to be promoted to sacred orders, the following documents are required:

1° a testimonial that studies have been properly completed according to the norm of can. 1032;

§4. Ab irregularitatibus et impedimentis Sanctae Sedi non reservatis dispensare valet Ordinarius.

CAN. 1048 In casibus occultis urgentioribus, si adiri nequeat Ordinarius aut cum de irregularitatibus agatur de quibus in can. 1041, nn. 3 et 4, Paenitentiaria, et si periculum immineat gravis damni aut infamiae, potest qui irregularitate ab ordine exercendo impeditur eundem exercere, firmo tamen manente onere quam primum recurrendi ad Ordinarium aut Paenitentiariam, reticito nomine et per confessarium.

CAN. 1049 §1. In precibus ad obtinendam irregularitatum et impedimentorum dispensationem, omnes irregularitates et impedimenta indicanda sunt; attamen, dispensatio generalis valet etiam pro reticitis bona fide, exceptis irregularitatibus de quibus in can. 1041, n. 4, aliisve ad forum iudiciale deductis, non autem pro reticitis mala fide.

§2. Si agatur de irregularitate ex voluntario homicidio aut ex procurato abortu, etiam numerus delictorum ad validitatem dispensationis exprimendus est.

§3. Dispensatio generalis ab irregularitatibus et impedimentis ad ordines recipiendos valet pro omnibus ordinibus.

ART. 4. *De Documentis Requisitis et de Scrutinio*

CAN. 1050 Ut quis ad sacros ordines promoveri possit, sequentia requiruntur documenta:

1° testimonium de studiis rite peractis ad normam can. 1032;

1048: c. 990 §2; EM IX, 10
1049: c. 991 §§1 et 3

1050: c. 993, 1° et 2°; SDO 11

2° for those to be ordained to the presbyterate, a testimonial that the diaconate was received;

3° for candidates to the diaconate, a testimonial that baptism, confirmation and the ministries mentioned in can. 1035 were received; likewise, a testimonial that the declaration mentioned in can. 1036 was made, and if the one to be ordained to the permanent diaconate is a married candidate, testimonials that the marriage was celebrated and the wife consents.

CAN. 1051 The following prescripts regarding the investigation about the qualities required in the one to be ordained are to be observed:

1° there is to be a testimonial of the rector of the seminary or house of formation about the qualities required to receive the order, that is, about the sound doctrine of the candidate, his genuine piety, good morals, and aptitude to exercise the ministry, as well as, after a properly executed inquiry, about his state of physical and psychic health;

2° in order to conduct the investigation properly, the diocesan bishop or major superior can employ other means which seem useful to him according to the circumstances of time and place, such as testimonial letters, public announcements, or other sources of information.

CAN. 1052 §1. For a bishop conferring ordination by his own right to proceed to the ordination, he must be sure that the documents mentioned in can. 1050 are at hand and that, after the investigation has been conducted ac-

2° si agatur de ordinandis ad presbyteratum, testimonium recepti diaconatus;

3° si agatur de promovendis ad diaconatum, testimonium recepti baptismi et confirmationis, atque receptorum ministeriorum de quibus in can. 1035; item testimonium factae declarationis de qua in can. 1036, necnon, si ordinandus qui promovendus est ad diaconatum permanentem sit uxoratus, testimonia celebrati matrimonii et consensus uxoris.

CAN. 1051 Ad scrutinium de qualitatibus in ordinando requisitis quod attinet, serventur praescripta quae sequuntur:

1° habeatur testimonium rectoris seminarii vel domus formationis de qualitatibus ad ordinem recipiendum requisitis, scilicet de candidati recta doctrina, genuina pietate, bonis moribus, aptitudine ad ministerium exercendum; itemque, rite peracta inquisitione, de eius statu valetudinis physicae et psychicae;

2° Episcopus dioecesanus aut Superior maior, ut scutinium rite peragatur, potest alia adhibere media quae sibi, pro temporis et loci adiunctis, utilia videantur, uti sunt litterae testimoniales, publicationes vel aliae informationes.

CAN. 1052 §1. Ut Episcopus ordinationem iure proprio conferens ad eam procedere possit, ipsi constare debet documenta, de quibus in can. 1050, praesto esse atque, scrutinio ad normam iuris peracto,

1051: cc. 993, 30; 1000; SCDS Instr. *Quam ingens,* 27 dec. 1930, (AAS 23 [1931] 120–129); SRC Instr. *Quantum religionis,* 1 dec. 1931, (AAS 24 [1932] 74–81); Pius PP. XI, Enc. *Ad catholici Sacerdotii,* 20 dec. 1935, III (AAS 28 [1936] 41); pius PP. XII, Adh. Ap. *Mentis nostrae,* 23 sep. 1950, III (AAS 42 [1950] 684); SCSO Monitum *Cum compertum,* 15 iun. 1961 (AAS 53

[1961] 571); Paulus PP. VI, Ep. Ap. *Summi Dei Verbum,* 4 nov. 1963 (AAS 55 [1963] 987–988); OT 6, 12; Paulus PP. VI, Enc. *Sacerdotalis coelibatus,* 24 iun. 1967, 63, 71 (AAS 59 [1967] 682, 685); RC 5, 11, 23, 24; RFS 39, 41, 42

1052 §1: Pius PP. XI, Enc. *Ad catholici Sacerdotii,* 20 dec. 1935, (AAS 28 [1936] 39); RFS 41

cording to the norm of law, positive arguments have proven the suitability of the candidate.

§2. For a bishop to proceed to the ordination of someone who is not his subject, it is sufficient that the dimissorial letters mention that the same documents are at hand, that the investigation has been performed according to the norm of the law, and that the suitability of the candidate has been established. Moreover, if the candidate is a member of a religious institute or a society of apostolic life, the same letters must also attest that he has been received definitively into the institute or society and is a subject of the superior who gives the letters.

§3. If, all these notwithstanding, the bishop doubts for specific reasons whether a candidate is suitable to receive orders, he is not to promote him.

CHAPTER III. The Notation and Testimonial of Ordination Conferred

CAN. 1053 §1. After an ordination has taken place, the names of those ordained and of the ordaining minister and the place and date of the ordination are to be noted in a special register to be kept carefully in the curia of the place of ordination; all the documents of individual ordinations are to be preserved carefully.

§2. The ordaining bishop is to give to each of the ordained an authentic testimonial of the reception of ordination; if a bishop other than their own promoted them with dimissorial letters, they are to show the testimonial to their own ordinary for notation of the ordination in a special register to be kept in the archive.

CAN. 1054 The local ordinary if it concerns seculars, or the competent major superi-

idoneitatem candidati positivis argumentis esse probatam.

§2. Ut Episcopus ad ordinationem procedat alieni subditi, sufficit ut litterae dimissoriae referant eadem documenta praesto esse, scrutinium ad normam iuris esse peractum atque de idoneitate candidati constare; quod si promovendus sit sodalis instituti religiosi aut societatis vitae apostolicae, eaedem litterae insuper testari debent ipsum in institutum vel societatem definitive cooptatum fuisse et esse subditum Superioris qui dat litteras.

§3. Si, his omnibus non obstantibus, ob certas rationes Episcopus dubitat num candidatus sit idoneus ad ordines recipiendos, eundem ne promoveat.

CAPUT III. De Adnotatione ac Testimonio Peractae Ordinationis

CAN. 1053 §1. Expleta ordinatione, nomina singulorum ordinatorum ac ministri ordinantis, locus et dies ordinationis notentur in peculiari libro apud curiam loci ordinationis diligenter custodiendo, et omnia singularum ordinationum documenta accurate serventur.

§2. Singulis ordinatis det Episcopus ordinans authenticum ordinationis receptae testimonium; qui, si ab Episcopo extraneo cum litteris dimissoriis promoti fuerint, illud proprio Ordinario exhibeant pro ordinationis adnotatione in speciali libro in archivo servando.

CAN. 1054 Loci Ordinarius, si agatur de saecularibus, aut Superior maior compe-

or if it concerns his own subjects, is to send notice of each ordination celebrated to the pastor of the place of baptism, who is to record it in his baptismal register according to the norm of can. 535, §2.

tens, si agatur de ipsius subditis, notitiam uniuscuiusque celebratae ordinationis transmittat ad parochum loci baptismi, qui id adnotet in suo baptizatorum libro, ad normam can. 535, §2.

TITLE VII. Marriage

CAN. 1055 §1. The matrimonial covenant, by which a man and a woman establish between themselves a partnership of the whole of life and which is ordered by its nature to the good of the spouses and the procreation and education of offspring, has been raised by Christ the Lord to the dignity of a sacrament between the baptized.

§2. For this reason, a valid matrimonial contract cannot exist between the baptized without it being by that fact a sacrament.

CAN. 1056 The essential properties of marriage are unity and indissolubility, which in Christian marriage obtain a special firmness by reason of the sacrament.

CAN. 1057 §1. The consent of the parties, legitimately manifested between persons qualified by law, makes marriage; no human power is able to supply this consent.

§2. Matrimonial consent is an act of the will by which a man and a woman mutually give and accept each other through an irrevocable covenant in order to establish marriage.

CAN. 1058 All persons who are not prohibited by law can contract marriage.

TITULUS VII. De Matrimonio

CAN. 1055 §1. Matrimoniale foedus, quo vir et mulier inter se totius vitae consortium constituunt, indole sua naturali ad bonum coniugum atque ad prolis generationem et educationem ordinatum, a Christo Domino ad sacramenti dignitatem inter baptizatos evectum est.

§2. Quare inter baptizatos nequit matrimonialis contractus validus consistere, quin sit eo ipso sacramentum.

CAN. 1056 Essentiales matrimonii proprietates sunt unitas et indissolubilitas, quae in matrimonio christiano ratione sacramenti peculiarem obtinent firmitatem.

CAN. 1057 §1. Matrimonium facit partium consensus inter personas iure habiles legitime manifestatus, qui nulla humana potestate suppleri valet.

§2. Consensus matrimonialis est actus voluntatis, quo vir et mulier foedere irrevocabili sese mutuo tradunt et accipiunt ad constituendum matrimonium.

CAN. 1058 Omnes possunt matrimonium contrahere, qui iure non prohibentur.

1055 §1: cc. 1012 §1, 1013 §1; CC 543–556, 581–584 et passim; Pius PP. XII, All., 3 oct. 1941 (AAS 33 [1941] 421–426); SCSO Decr. *De matrimonii finibus*, 1 apr. 1944 (AAS 36 [1944] 103); Pius PP. XII, All., 29 oct. 1951, IV; LG 11, 41; AA 11; GS 48; HV 8; OCM 1, 2; DCG 59; Paulus PP. VI, All., 9 feb. 1976 (AAS 68 [1976] 204–208)

1055 §2: c. 1012 §2; CC 554

1056: c. 1013 §2; CC 546–556, et passim; GS 48; HV 25; OCM 2

1057 §1: c. 1081 §1; CC 541; GS 48; Paulus PP. VI, All., 9 feb. 1976 (AAS 68 [1976] 204–208)

1057 §2: c. 1081 §2; HV 8

1058: c. 1035; SCSO Resp., 27 ian. 1949; SCSO Resp., 22 dec. 1949; Ioannes PP. XXIII, Enc. *Pacem in terris*, 11 apr. 1963, I (AAS 55 [1963] 259–269)

CAN. 1059 Even if only one party is Catholic, the marriage of Catholics is governed not only by divine law but also by canon law, without prejudice to the competence of civil authority concerning the merely civil effects of the same marriage.

CAN. 1060 Marriage possesses the favor of law; therefore, in a case of doubt, the validity of a marriage must be upheld until the contrary is proven.

CAN. 1061 §1. A valid marriage between the baptized is called *ratum tantum* if it has not been consummated; it is called *ratum et consummatum* if the spouses have performed between themselves in a human fashion a conjugal act which is suitable in itself for the procreation of offspring, to which marriage is ordered by its nature and by which the spouses become one flesh.

§2. After a marriage has been celebrated, if the spouses have lived together consummation is presumed until the contrary is proven.

§3. An invalid marriage is called putative if at least one party celebrated it in good faith, until both parties become certain of its nullity.

CAN. 1062 §1. A promise of marriage, whether unilateral or bilateral, which is called an engagement, is governed by the particular law established by the conference of bishops, after it has considered any existing customs and civil laws.

§2. A promise to marry does not give rise to an action to seek the celebration of marriage; an

CAN. 1059 Matrimonium catholicorum, etsi una tantum pars sit catholica, regitur iure non solum divino, sed etiam canonico, salva competentia civilis potestatis circa mere civiles eiusdem matrimonii effectus.

CAN. 1060 Matrimonium gaudet favore iuris; quare in dubio standum est pro valore matrimonii, donec contrarium probetur.

CAN. 1061 §1. Matrimonium inter baptizatos validum dicitur ratum tantum, si non est consummatum; ratum et consummatum, si coniuges inter se humano modo posuerunt coniugalem actum per se aptum ad prolis generationem, ad quem natura sua ordinatur matrimonium, et quo coniuges fiunt una caro.

§2. Celebrato matrimonio, si coniuges cohabitaverint, praesumitur consummatio, donec contrarium probetur.

§3. Matrimonium invalidum dicitur putativum, si bona fide ab una saltem parte celebratum fuerit, donec utraque pars de eiusdem nullitate certa evadat.

CAN. 1062 §1. Matrimonii promissio sive unilateralis sive bilateralis, quam sponsalia vocant, regitur iure particulari, quod ab Episcoporum conferentia, habita ratione consuetudinum et legum civilium, si quae sint, statutum fuit.

§2. Ex matrimonii promissione non datur actio ad petendam matrimonii celebra-

---

1059: c. 1016; CC 577–583; UR 16
1060: c. 1014; Pius PP. XII, All., 3 oct. 1941 (AAS 33 [1941] 421–426); CI Resp. III, 26 iun. 1947 (AAS 39 [1947] 374)
  1061 §1: c. 1015 §1; GS 49
  1061 §2: c. 1015 §2

1061 §3: c. 1015 §4; CI Resp. II, 26 iun. 1947 (AAS 39 [1947] 374)
  1062 §1: c. 1017 §1
  1062 §2: c. 1017 §3; CI Resp. IV, 1–2, 2–3 iun. 1947 (AAS 39 [1947] 345)

action to repair damages, however, does arise if warranted.

CHAPTER I. Pastoral Care and Those Things Which Must Precede the Celebration of Marriage

CAN. 1063 Pastors of souls are obliged to take care that their ecclesiastical community offers the Christian faithful the assistance by which the matrimonial state is preserved in a Christian spirit and advances in perfection. This assistance must be offered especially by:

1° preaching, catechesis adapted to minors, youth, and adults, and even the use of instruments of social communication, by which the Christian faithful are instructed about the meaning of Christian marriage and about the function of Christian spouses and parents;

2° personal preparation to enter marriage, which disposes the spouses to the holiness and duties of their new state;

3° a fruitful liturgical celebration of marriage which is to show that the spouses signify and share in the mystery of the unity and fruitful love between Christ and the Church;

4° help offered to those who are married, so that faithfully preserving and protecting the conjugal covenant, they daily come to lead holier and fuller lives in their family.

CAN. 1064 It is for the local ordinary to take care that such assistance is organized fittingly, after he has also heard men and women proven by experience and expertise if it seems opportune.

CAN. 1065 §1. Catholics who have not yet

CAPUT I. **De Cura Pastorali et de Iis Quae Matrimonii Celebrationi Praemitti Debent**

CAN. 1063 Pastores animarum obligatione tenentur curandi ut propria ecclesiastica communitas christifidelibus assistentiam praebeat, qua status matrimonialis in spiritu christiano servetur et in perfectione progrediatur. Haec assistentia imprimis praebenda est:

1° praedicatione, catechesi minoribus, iuvenibus et adultis aptata, immo usu instrumentorum communicationis socialis, quibus christifideles de significatione matrimonii christiani deque munere coniugum ac parentum christianorum instituantur;

2° praeparatione personali ad matrimonium ineundum, qua sponsi ad novi sui status sanctitatem et officia disponantur;

3° fructuosa liturgica matrimonii celebratione, qua eluceat coniuges mysterium unitatis et fecundi amoris inter Christum et Ecclesiam significare atque participare;

4° auxilio coniugatis praestito, ut ipsi, foedus coniugale fideliter servantes atque tuentes, ad sanctiorem in dies plenioremque in familia vitam ducendam perveniant.

CAN. 1064 Ordinarii loci est curare ut debite ordinetur eadem assistentia, auditis etiam, si opportunum videatur, viris et mulieribus experientia et peritia probatis.

CAN. 1065 §1. Catholici, qui sacramen-

tionem; datur tamen ad reparationem damnorum, si qua debeatur.

1063, 1°: cc. 1018, 1033; GS 47, 52
1063, 2°: cc. 1018, 1033; CC 3; GS 52; OCM Prae. 5
1063, 3°: cc. 1018, 1033; SC 19, 59, 77; OCM Prae. 6

1063, 4°: cc. 1018, 1033; LG 41; GS 52
1065 §1: c. 1021 §2

received the sacrament of confirmation are to receive it before they are admitted to marriage if it can be done without grave inconvenience.

§2. To receive the sacrament of marriage fruitfully, spouses are urged especially to approach the sacraments of penance and of the Most Holy Eucharist.

CAN. 1066   Before a marriage is celebrated, it must be evident that nothing stands in the way of its valid and licit celebration.

CAN. 1067   The conference of bishops is to establish norms about the examination of spouses and about the marriage banns or other opportune means to accomplish the investigations necessary before marriage. After these norms have been diligently observed, the pastor can proceed to assist at the marriage.

CAN. 1068   In danger of death and if other proofs cannot be obtained, the affirmation of the contracting parties, even sworn if the case warrants it, that they are baptized and are prevented by no impediment is sufficient unless there are indications to the contrary.

CAN. 1069   All the faithful are obliged to reveal any impediments they know about to the pastor or local ordinary before the celebration of the marriage.

CAN. 1070   If someone other than the pastor who is to assist at marriage has conducted the investigations, the person is to notify the pastor about the results as soon as possible through an authentic document.

tum confirmationis nondum receperint, illud, antequam ad matrimonium admittantur, recipiant, si id fieri possit sine gravi incommodo.

§2. Ut fructuose sacramentum matrimonii recipiatur, enixe sponsis commendatur, ut ad sacramenta paenitentiae et sanctissimae Eucharistiae accedant.

CAN. 1066   Antequam matrimonium celebretur, constare debet nihil eius validae ac licitae celebrationi obsistere.

CAN. 1067   Episcoporum conferentia statuat normas de examine sponsorum, necnon de publicationibus matrimonialibus alisve opportunis mediis ad investigationes peragendas, quae ante matrimonium necessaria sunt, quibus diligenter observatis, parochus procedere possit ad matrimonio assistendum.

CAN. 1068   In periculo mortis, si aliae probationes haberi nequeant, sufficit, nisi contraria adsint indicia, affirmatio contrahentium, si casus ferat etiam iurata, se baptizatos esse et nullo detineri impedimento.

CAN. 1069   Omnes fideles obligatione tenentur impedimenta, si quae norint, parocho aut loci Ordinario, ante matrimonii celebrationem, revelandi.

CAN. 1070   Si alius quam parochus, cuius est assistere matrimonio, investigationes peregerit, de harum exitu quam primum per authenticum documentum eundem parochum certiorem reddat.

1065 §2: c. 1033; OCM Prae. 7

1066: c. 1019 §1; SCDS Instr. *Iterum conquesti,* 4 iul. 1921 (AAS 13 [1921] 348–349); SCDS Instr. *Sacrosanctum matrimonii,* 29 iun. 1941 (AAS 33 [1941] 297–318)

1067: c. 1020; SCDS Instr. *Sacrosanctum matrimonii,* 29 iun. 1941 (AAS 33 [1941] 297–318)

1068: c. 1919 §2; SCDS Instr. *Iterum conquesti,* 4 iul. 1921, 4 (AAS 13 [1921] 348–349)

1069: c. 1027

1070: c. 1029; SCDS Instr. *Iterum conquesti,* 4 iul. 1921, 2 (AAS 13 [1921] 348–349)

CAN. 1071 §1. Except in a case of necessity, a person is not to assist without the permission of the local ordinary at:

1° a marriage of transients;

2° a marriage which cannot be recognized or celebrated according to the norm of civil law;

3° a marriage of a person who is bound by natural obligations toward another party or children arising from a previous union;

4° a marriage of a person who has notoriously rejected the Catholic faith;

5° a marriage of a person who is under a censure;

6° a marriage of a minor child when the parents are unaware or reasonably opposed;

7° a marriage to be entered into through a proxy as mentioned in can. 1105.

§2. The local ordinary is not to grant permission to assist at the marriage of a person who has notoriously rejected the Catholic faith unless the norms mentioned in can. 1125 have been observed with necessary adaptation.

CAN. 1072 Pastors of souls are to take care to dissuade youth from the celebration of marriage before the age at which a person usually enters marriage according to the accepted practices of the region.

CHAPTER II. Diriment Impediments in General

CAN. 1073 A diriment impediment renders a person unqualified to contract marriage validly.

CAN. 1074 An impediment which can be

CAN. 1071 §1. Excepto casu necessitatis, sine licentia Ordinarii loci ne quis assistat:

1° matrimonio vagorum;

2° matrimonio quod ad normam legis civilis agnosci vel celebrari nequeat;

3° matrimonio eius qui obligationibus teneatur naturalibus erga aliam partem filiosve ex praecedenti unione ortis;

4° matrimonio eius qui notorie catholicam fidem abiecerit;

5° matrimonio eius qui censura innodatus sit;

6° matrimonio filii familias minoris, insciis aut rationabiliter invitis parentibus;

7° matrimonio per procuratorem ineundo, de quo in can. 1105.

§2. Ordinarius loci licentiam assistendi matrimonio eius qui notorie catholicam fidem abiecerit ne concedat, nisi servatis normis de quibus in can. 1125, congrua congruis referendo.

CAN. 1072 Curent animarum pastores a matrimonii celebratione avertere iuvenes ante aetatem, qua secundum regionis receptos mores matrimonium iniri solet.

CAPUT II. De Impedimentis Dirimentibus in Genere

CAN. 1073 Impedimentum dirimens personam inhabilem reddit ad matrimonium valide contrahendum.

CAN. 1074 Publicum censetur impedi-

1071 §1, 1°: c. 1032; SCDS Instr. *Iterum conquesti,* 4 iul. 1921, 4 (AAS 13 [1921] 348–349)

1071 §1, 4°: c. 1065; SCSO Decl., 11 aug. 1949 (AAS 41 [1949] 427–428)

1071 §1, 5°: c. 1066

1071 §1, 6°: c. 1034

1071 §1, 7°: c. 1091

1071 §2: c. 1065 §2

1072: c. 1067 §2

1073: c. 1036 §2

1074: c. 1037; CI Resp. II, 25 iun. 1932 (AAS 24 [1932] 284); SCDS Resp. 3, 1 apr. 1957

proven in the external forum is considered to be public; otherwise it is occult.

CAN. 1075 §1. It is only for the supreme authority of the Church to declare authentically when divine law prohibits or nullifies marriage.

§2. Only the supreme authority has the right to establish other impediments for the baptized.

CAN. 1076 A custom which introduces a new impediment or is contrary to existing impediments is reprobated.

CAN. 1077 §1. In a special case, the local ordinary can prohibit marriage for his own subjects residing anywhere and for all actually present in his own territory but only for a time, for a grave cause, and for as long as the cause continues.

§2. Only the supreme authority of the Church can add a nullifying clause to a prohibition.

CAN. 1078 §1. The local ordinary can dispense his own subjects residing anywhere and all actually present in his own territory from all impediments of ecclesiastical law except those whose dispensation is reserved to the Apostolic See.

§2. Impediments whose dispensation is reserved to the Apostolic See are:

1° the impediment arising from sacred orders or from a public perpetual vow of chastity in a religious institute of pontifical right;

2° the impediment of crime mentioned in can. 1090.

§3. A dispensation is never given from the impediment of consanguinity in the direct line or in the second degree of the collateral line.

mentum, quod probari in foro externo potest; secus est occultum.

CAN. 1075 §1. Supremae tantum Ecclesiae auctoritatis est authentice declarare quandonam ius divinum matrimonium prohibeat vel dirimat.

§2. Uni quoque supremae auctoritati ius est alia impedimenta pro baptizatis constituere.

CAN. 1076 Consuetudo novum impedimentum inducens aut impedimentis exsistentibus contraria reprobatur.

CAN. 1077 §1. Ordinarius loci propriis subditis ubique commorantibus et omnibus in proprio territorio actu degentibus vetare potest matrimonium in casu peculiari, sed ad tempus tantum, gravi de causa eaque perdurante.

§2. Vetito clausulam dirimentem una suprema Ecclesiae auctoritas addere potest.

CAN. 1078 §1. Ordinarius loci proprios subditos ubique commorantes et omnes in proprio territorio actu degentes ab omnibus impedimentis iuris ecclesiastici dispensare potest, exceptis iis, quorum dispensatio Sedi Apostolicae reservatur.

§2. Impedimenta quorum dispensatio Sedi Apostolicae reservatur sunt:

1° impedimentum ortum ex sacris ordinibus aut ex voto publico perpetuo castitatis in instituto religioso iuris pontificii;

2° impedimentum criminis de quo in can. 1090.

§3. Numquam datur dispensatio ab impedimento consanguinitatis in linea recta aut in secundo gradu linea collateralis.

1075 §1: c. 1038 §1
1075 §2: c. 1038 §2
1076: c. 1041
1077 §1: c. 1039 §1; SCSO Resp., 14 feb. 1962
1077 §2: c. 1039 §2

1078 §1: c. 1040; SCDS Instr. *Sat frequentes*, 1 aug. 1931 (AAS 23 [1931] 413–415); PM I, 19, 20; CD 8b; EM IX
1078 §2: EM IX, 12, 13
1078 §3: c. 1076 §3

CAN. 1079 §1. In urgent danger of death, the local ordinary can dispense his own subjects residing anywhere and all actually present in his territory both from the form to be observed in the celebration of marriage and from each and every impediment of ecclesiastical law, whether public or occult, except the impediment arising from the sacred order of presbyterate.

§2. In the same circumstances mentioned in §1, but only for cases in which the local ordinary cannot be reached, the pastor, the properly delegated sacred minister, and the priest or deacon who assists at marriage according to the norm of can. 1116, §2 possess the same power of dispensing.

§3. In danger of death a confessor possesses the power of dispensing from occult impediments for the internal forum, whether within or outside the act of sacramental confession.

§4. In the case mentioned in §2, the local ordinary is not considered accessible if he can be reached only through telegraph or telephone.

CAN. 1080 §1. Whenever an impediment is discovered after everything has already been prepared for the wedding, and the marriage cannot be delayed without probable danger of grave harm until a dispensation is obtained from the competent authority, the local ordinary and, provided that the case is occult, all those mentioned in can. 1079, §§2–3 when the conditions prescribed therein have been observed possess the power of dispensing from all impediments except those mentioned in can. 1078, §2, n. 1.

CAN. 1079 §1. Urgente mortis periculo, loci Ordinarius potest tum super forma in matrimonii celebratione servanda, tum super omnibus et singulis impedimentis iuris ecclesiastici sive publicis sive occultis, dispensare proprios subditos ubique commorantes et omnes in proprio territorio actu degentes, excepto impedimento orto ex sacro ordine presbyteratus.

§2. In eisdem rerum adiunctis, de quibus in §1, sed solum pro casibus in quibus ne loci quidem Ordinarius adiri possit, eadem dispensandi potestate pollet tum parochus, tum minister sacer rite delegatus, tum sacerdos vel diaconus qui matrimonio, ad normam can. 1116, §2, assistit.

§3. In periculo mortis confessarius gaudet potestate dispensandi ab impedimentis occultis pro foro interno sive intra sive extra actum sacramentalis confessionis.

§4. In casu de quo in §2, loci Ordinarius censetur adiri non posse, si tantum per telegraphum vel telephonum id fieri possit.

CAN. 1080 §1. Quoties impedimentum detegatur cum iam omnia sunt parata ad nuptias, nec matrimonium sine probabili gravis mali periculo differri possit usquedum a competenti auctoritate dispensatio obtineatur, potestate gaudent dispensandi ab omnibus impedimentis, iis exceptis de quibus in can. 1078, §2, n. 1, loci Ordinarius et, dummodo casus sit occultus, omnes de quibus in can. 1079, §§2–3, servatis condicionibus ibidem praescriptis.

1079 §1: c. 1043; PM 20, 21
1079 §2: c. 1044; LG 29; SDO V, 22, 4; CIV Resp., 26 mar. 1968 (AAS 60 [1968] 363); Sec Resp., 21 maii 1968; CIV Resp., 4 apr. 1969 (AAS 61 [1969] 348)
1079 §4: CI Resp. V, 12 nov. 1922

1080 §1: c. 1045 §§1 et 3; CI Resp. IV, 1 mar. 1921 (AAS 13 [1921] 178); CI Resp. III, 28 dec. 1927 (AAS 20 [1928] 61); CI Resp. I, 27 iul. 1942 (AAS 34 [1942] 241)

§2. This power is valid even to convalidate a marriage if there is the same danger in delay and there is insufficient time to make recourse to the Apostolic See or to the local ordinary concerning impediments from which he is able to dispense.

CAN. 1081 The pastor or the priest or deacon mentioned in can. 1079, §2 is to notify the local ordinary immediately about a dispensation granted for the external forum; it is also to be noted in the marriage register.

CAN. 1082 Unless a rescript of the Penitentiary provides otherwise, a dispensation from an occult impediment granted in the non-sacramental internal forum is to be noted in a book which must be kept in the secret archive of the curia; no other dispensation for the external forum is necessary if afterwards the occult impediment becomes public.

CHAPTER III. Specific Diriment Impediments

CAN. 1083 §1. A man before he has completed his sixteenth year of age and a woman before she has completed her fourteenth year of age cannot enter into a valid marriage.

§2. The conference of bishops is free to establish a higher age for the licit celebration of marriage.

CAN. 1084 §1. Antecedent and perpetual impotence to have intercourse, whether on the part of the man or the woman, whether absolute or relative, nullifies marriage by its very nature.

§2. If the impediment of impotence is doubt-

§2. Haec potestas valet etiam ad matrimonium convalidandum, si idem periculum sit in mora nec tempus suppetat recurrendi ad Sedem Apostolicam vel ad loci Ordinarium, quod attinet ad impedimenta a quibus dispensare valet.

CAN. 1081 Parochus aut sacerdos vel diaconus, de quibus in can. 1079, §2, de concessa dispensatione pro foro externo Ordinarium loci statim certiorem faciat; eaque adnotetur in libro matrimoniorum.

CAN. 1082 Nisi aliud ferat Paenitentiariae rescriptum, dispensatio in foro interno non sacramentali concessa super impedimento occulto adnotetur in libro, qui in secreto curiae archivo asservandus est, nec alia dispensatio pro foro externo est necessaria, si postea occultum impedimentum publicum evaserit.

CAPUT III. De Impedimentis Dirimentibus in Specie

CAN. 1083 §1. Vir ante decimum sertum aetatis annum completum, mulier ante decimum quartum item completum, matrimonium validum inire non possunt.

§2. Integrum est Episcoporum conferentiae aetatem superiorem ad licitam matrimonii celebrationem statuere.

CAN. 1084 §1. Impotentia coeundi antecedens et perpetua, sive ex parte viri sive ex parte mulieris, sive absoluta sive relativa, matrimonium ex ipsa eius natura dirimit.

§2. Si impedimentum impotentiae dubi-

1080 §2: c. 1045 §2; SCDF Resp., 18 dec. 1968
1081: c. 1946; LG 29; SDO V, 22, 4; CIV Resp., 26 mar. 1968 (AAS 60 [1968] 363); Sec Resp., 21 maii 1968; CIV Resp., 4 apr. 1969 (AAS 61 [1969] 348)
1082: c. 1047
1083 §1: c. 1067 §1

1084 §1: c. 1068 §1; SCDF Decr., 13 maii 1977 (AAS 69 [1977] 426)
1084 §2: c. 1068 §2; SCSO Resp., 16 feb. 1935; SCSO Resp., 28 sep. 1957; SCSO Resp., 28 ian. 1964; SCSO Resp., 25 mar. 1964

ful, whether by a doubt about the law or a doubt about a fact, a marriage must not be impeded nor, while the doubt remains, declared null.

§3. Sterility neither prohibits nor nullifies marriage, without prejudice to the prescript of can. 1098.

CAN. 1085 §1. A person bound by the bond of a prior marriage, even if it was not consummated, invalidly attempts marriage.

§2. Even if the prior marriage is invalid or dissolved for any reason, it is not on that account permitted to contract another before the nullity or dissolution of the prior marriage is established legitimately and certainly.

CAN. 1086 §1. A marriage between two persons, one of whom has been baptized in the Catholic Church or received into it and has not defected from it by a formal act and the other of whom is not baptized, is invalid.

§2. A person is not to be dispensed from this impediment unless the conditions mentioned in cann. 1125 and 1126 have been fulfilled.

§3. If at the time the marriage was contracted one party was commonly held to have been baptized or the baptism was doubtful, the validity of the marriage must be presumed according to the norm of can. 1060 until it is proven with certainty that one party was baptized but the other was not.

CAN. 1087 Those in sacred orders invalidly attempt marriage.

CAN. 1088 Those bound by a public perpetual vow of chastity in a religious institute invalidly attempt marriage.

CAN. 1089 No marriage can exist between a man and a woman who has been abducted or

um sit, sive dubio iuris sive dubio facti, matrimonium non est impediendum nec, stante dubio, nullum declarandum.

§3. Sterilitas matrimonium nec prohibet nec dirimit, firmo praescripto can. 1098.

CAN. 1085 §1. Invalide matrimonium attentat qui vinculo tenetur prioris matrimonii, quamquam non consummati.

§2. Quamvis prius matrimonium sit irritum aut solutum qualibet ex causa, non ideo licet aliud contrahere, antequam de prioris nullitate aut solutione legitime et certo constiterit.

CAN. 1086 §1. Matrimonium inter duas personas, quarum altera sit baptizata in Ecclesia catholica vel in eandem recepta nec actu formali ab ea defecerit, et altera non baptizata, invalidum est.

§2. Ab hoc impedimento ne dispensetur, nisi impletis condicionibus de quibus in cann. 1125 et 1126.

§3. Si pars tempore contracti matrimonii tamquam baptizata communiter habebatur aut eius baptismus erat dubius, praesumenda est, ad normam can. 1060, validitas matrimonii, donec certo probetur alteram partem baptizatam esse, alteram vero non baptizatam.

CAN. 1087 Invalide matrimonium attentant, qui in sacris ordinibus sunt constituti.

CAN. 1088 Invalide matrimonium attentant, qui voto publico perpetuo castitatis in instituto religioso adstricti sunt.

CAN. 1089 Inter virum et mulierem abductam vel saltem retentam intuitu matri-

1084 §3: c. 1068 §3
1085 §1: c. 1069 §1
1085 §2: c. 1069 §2
1086 §1: c. 1070 §1; SCPF Resp., 26 feb. 1924;
MM 2

1086 §2: c. 1071
1086 §3: c. 1070 §2
1087: c. 1072
1088: c. 1073
1089: c. 1074 §§1 et 2

at least detained with a view of contracting marriage with her unless the woman chooses marriage of her own accord after she has been separated from the captor and established in a safe and free place.

CAN. 1090 §1. Anyone who with a view to entering marriage with a certain person has brought about the death of that person's spouse or of one's own spouse invalidly attempts this marriage.

§2. Those who have brought about the death of a spouse by mutual physical or moral cooperation also invalidly attempt a marriage together.

CAN. 1091 §1. In the direct line of consanguinity marriage is invalid between all ancestors and descendants, both legitimate and natural.

§2. In the collateral line marriage is invalid up to and including the fourth degree.

§3. The impediment of consanguinity is not multiplied.

§4. A marriage is never permitted if doubt exists whether the partners are related by consanguinity in any degree of the direct line or in the second degree of the collateral line.

CAN. 1092 Affinity in the direct line in any degree invalidates a marriage.

CAN. 1093 The impediment of public propriety arises from an invalid marriage after the establishment of common life or from notorious or public concubinage. It nullifies marriage in the first degree of the direct line between the man and the blood relatives of the woman, and vice versa.

monii cum ea contrahendi nullum matrimonium consistere potest, nisi postea mulier a raptore separata et in loco tuto ac libero constituta, matrimonium sponte eligat.

CAN. 1090 §1. Qui intuitu matrimonii cum certa persona ineundi, huius coniugi vel proprio coniugi mortem intulerit, invalide hoc matrimonium attentat.

§2. Invalide quoque matrimonium inter se attentant qui mutua opera physica vel morali mortem coniugi intulerunt.

CAN. 1091 §1. In linea recta consanguinitatis matrimonium irritum est inter omnes ascendentes et descendentes tum legitimos tum naturales.

§2. In linea collaterali irritum est usque ad quartum gradum inclusive.

§3. Impedimentum consanguinitatis non multiplicatur.

§4. Numquam matrimonium permittatur, si quod subest dubium num partes sint consanguineae in aliquo gradu lineae rectae aut in secundo gradu lineae collateralis.

CAN. 1092 Affinitas in linea recta dirimit matrimonium in quolibet gradu.

CAN. 1093 Impedimentum publicae honestatis oritur ex matrimonio invalido post instauratam vitam communem aut ex notorio vel publico concubinatu; et nuptias dirimit in primo gradu lineae rectae inter virum et consanguineas mulieris, ac vice versa.

1090 §1: c. 1075, 2°
1090 §2: c. 1075, 3°
1091 §1: c. 1076 §1
1091 §2: c. 1076 §2
1091 §3: c. 1076 §3

1092: c. 1077 §1; CI Resp. IV, 5, 2–3 iun. 1918 (AAS 10 [1918] 346); SCSO Resp., 31 ian. 1957 (AAS 49 [1957] 77)
1093: c. 1078; CI Resp. II, 12 mar. 1929 (AAS 21 [1927] 170)

CAN. 1094 Those who are related in the direct line or in the second degree of the collateral line by a legal relationship arising from adoption cannot contract marriage together validly.

CAN. 1094 Matrimonium inter se valide contrahere nequeunt qui cognatione legali ex adoptione orta, in linea recta aut in secundo gradu lineae collateralis, coniuncti sunt.

CAPUT IV. **De Consensu Matrimoniali**

CHAPTER IV. **Matrimonial Consent**

CAN. 1095 The following are incapable of contracting marriage:

1° those who lack the sufficient use of reason;

2° those who suffer from a grave defect of discretion of judgment concerning the essential matrimonial rights and duties mutually to be handed over and accepted;

3° those who are not able to assume the essential obligations of marriage for causes of a psychic nature.

CAN. 1096 §1. For matrimonial consent to exist, the contracting parties must be at least not ignorant that marriage is a permanent partnership between a man and a woman ordered to the procreation of offspring by means of some sexual cooperation.

§2. This ignorance is not presumed after puberty.

CAN. 1095 Sunt incapaces matrimonii contrahendi:

1° qui sufficienti rationis usu carent;

2° qui laborant gravi defectu discretionis iudicii circa iura et officia matrimonialia essentialia mutuo tradenda et accepta;

3° qui ob causas naturae psychicae obligationes matrimonii essentiales assumere non valent.

CAN. 1096 §1. Ut consensus matrimonialis haberi possit, necesse est ut contrahentes saltem non ignorent matrimonium esse consortium permanens inter virum et mulierem ordinatum ad prolem, cooperatione aliqua sexuali, procreandam.

§2. Haec ignorantia post pubertatem non praesumitur.

1094: c. 1080

1095, 1°: SRR Decisio coram Julien, 30 iul. 1932 (SRRD 24 [1932] 364–382); SRR Decisio coram Grazioli, 1 iul. 1933 (SRRD 25 [1933] 403–419); SRR Decisio coram Wynen, 25 feb. 1943; SRR Decisio coram Canestri, 16 iul. 1943; SRR Decisio coram Heard, 4 dec. 1943 (SRRD 35 [1943] 885–903); SRR Decisio coram Felici, 22 maii 1956; SRR Decisio coram Felici, 3 dec. 1957; SRR Decisio coram Sabattani, 24 feb. 1961; SRR Decisio coram De Jorio, 18 dec. 1961; SRR Decisio coram Mattioli, 4 apr. 1966; SRR Decisio coram Pompedda, 3 iul. 1979

1095, 2°: SRR Decisio coram Wynen, 25 feb. 1941; SRR Decisio coram Wynen, 25 feb. 1943; SRR Decisio coram Felici, 3 dec. 1957; SRR Decisio coram Sabattani, 24 feb. 1961; SRR Decisio coram Pinto, 4 feb. 1974

1095, 3°: SRR Decisio coram Sabattani, 21 iun. 1957; SRR Decisio coram Pinna, 4 apr. 1963; SRR Decisio coram Anné, 17 ian. 1967; SRR Decisio coram Lefebvre, 2 dec. 1967 (SRRD 59 [1967] 803); SRR Decisio coram De Jorio, 20 dec. 1967 (SRRD 59 [1967] 869–879); SRR Decisio coram Anné, 2 feb. 1969; SRR Decisio coram Serrano, 3 apr. 1973; SRR Decisio coram Raad, 14 apr. 1975; SRR Decisio coram Pinto, 14 apr. 1975; SA Decisio coram Staffa, 29 nov. 1975; SRR Decisio coram Anné, 4 dec. 1975; SRR Decisio coram Lefebvre, 31 ian. 1976; SRR Decisio coram Serrano, 9 iul. 1976; SRR Decisio coram Pinto, 15 iul. 1977; SRR Decisio coram Masala, 10 maii 1978; SRR Decisio coram Huot, 7 iun. 1979; SRR Decisio coram Ferraro, 6 feb. 1979

1096 §1: c. 1082 §1
1096 §2: c. 1082 §2

CAN. 1097 §1. Error concerning the person renders a marriage invalid.

§2. Error concerning a quality of the person does not render a marriage invalid even if it is the cause for the contract, unless this quality is directly and principally intended.

CAN. 1098 A person contracts invalidly who enters into a marriage deceived by malice, perpetrated to obtain consent, concerning some quality of the other partner which by its very nature can gravely disturb the partnership of conjugal life.

CAN. 1099 Error concerning the unity or indissolubility or sacramental dignity of marriage does not vitiate matrimonial consent provided that it does not determine the will.

CAN. 1100 The knowledge or opinion of the nullity of a marriage does not necessarily exclude matrimonial consent.

CAN. 1101 §1. The internal consent of the mind is presumed to conform to the words and signs used in celebrating the marriage.

§2. If, however, either or both of the parties by a positive act of the will exclude marriage itself, some essential element of marriage, or some essential property of marriage, the party contracts invalidly.

CAN. 1102 §1. A marriage subject to a condition about the future cannot be contracted validly.

§2. A marriage entered into subject to a condition about the past or the present is valid or

CAN. 1097 §1. Error in persona invalidum reddit matrimonium.

§2. Error in qualitate personae, etsi det causam contractui, matrimonium irritum non reddit, nisi haec qualitas directe et principaliter intendatur.

CAN. 1098 Qui matrimonium init deceptus dolo, ad obtinendum consensum patrato, circa aliquam alterius partis qualitatem, quae suapte natura consortium vitae coniugalis graviter perturbare potest, invalide contrahit.

CAN. 1099 Error circa matrimonii unitatem vel indissolubilitatem aut sacramentalem dignitatem, dummodo non determinet voluntatem, non vitiat consensum matrimonialem.

CAN. 1100 Scientia aut opinio nullitatis matrimonii consensum matrimonialem non necessario excludit.

CAN. 1101 §1. Internus animi consensus praesumitur conformis verbis vel signis in celebrando matrimonio adhibitis.

§2. At si alterutra vel utraque pars positivo voluntatis actu excludat matrimonium ipsum vel matrimonii essentiale aliquod elementum, vel essentialem aliquam proprietatem, invalide contrahit.

CAN. 1102 §1. Matrimonium sub condicione de futuro valide contrahi nequit.

§2. Matrimonium sub condicione de praeterito vel de praesenti initum est

---

1097 §1: c. 1083 §1

1097 §2: c. 1083 §2

1099: c. 1084; SRR Decisio coram Felici, 13 iul. 1954; SRR Decisio coram Felici, 17 dec. 1957; SRR Decisio coram Filipiak, 23 mar. 1956; SRR Decisio coram Sabattani, 12 nov. 1964; SRR Decisio coram Ewers, 24 feb. 1968; SRR Decisio coram Ewers, 16 maii 1968; SRR Decisio coram Anné, 11 mar. 1975

1100: c. 1085

1101 §1: c. 1086 §1

1101 §2: c. 1086 §2; SRR Decisio coram Anné, 8 nov. 1963 (SRRD 55 [1963] 764); SRR Decisio coram Lefebvre, 19 feb. 1965 (SRRD 57 [1965] 176)

1102 §1: c. 1092, 1°–3°; CAl 83

1102 §2: c. 1092, 4°

not insofar as that which is subject to the condition exists or not.

§3. The condition mentioned in §2, however, cannot be placed licitly without the written permission of the local ordinary.

CAN. 1103   A marriage is invalid if entered into because of force or grave fear from without, even if unintentionally inflicted, so that a person is compelled to choose marriage in order to be free from it.

CAN. 1104   §1. To contract a marriage validly the contracting parties must be present together, either in person or by proxy.

§2. Those being married are to express matrimonial consent in words or, if they cannot speak, through equivalent signs.

CAN. 1105   §1. To enter into a marriage validly by proxy it is required that:

1° there is a special mandate to contract with a specific person;

2° the proxy is designated by the one mandating and fulfills this function personally.

§2. To be valid the mandate must be signed by the one mandating and by the pastor or ordinary of the place where the mandate is given, or by a priest delegated by either of them, or at least by two witnesses, or it must be made by means of a document which is authentic according to the norm of civil law.

§3. If the one mandating cannot write, this is to be noted in the mandate itself and another witness is to be added who also signs the document; otherwise, the mandate is invalid.

§4. If the one mandating revokes the man-

validum vel non, prout id quod condicioni subest, exsistit vel non.

§3. Condicio autem, de qua in §2, licite apponi nequit, nisi cum licentia Ordinarii loci scripto data.

CAN. 1103   Invalidum est matrimonium initum ob vim vel metum gravem ab extrinseco, etiam haud consulto incussum, a quo ut quis se liberet, eligere cogatur matrimonium.

CAN. 1104   §1. Ad matrimonium valide contrahendum necesse est ut contrahentes sint praesentes una simul sive per se ipsi, sive per procuratorem.

§2. Sponsi consensum matrimonialem verbis exprimant; si vero loqui non possunt, signis aequipollentibus.

CAN. 1105   §1. Ad matrimonium per procuratorem valide ineundum requiritur:

1° ut adsit mandatum speciale ad contrahendum cum certa persona;

2° ut procurator ab ipso mandante designetur, et munere suo per se ipse fungatur.

§2. Mandatum, ut valeat, subscribendum est a mandante et praeterea a parocho vel Ordinario loci in quo mandatum datur, aut a sacerdote ab alterutro delegato, aut a duobus saltem testibus; aut confici debet per documentum ad normam iuris civilis authenticum.

§3. Si mandans scribere nequeat, id in ipso mandato adnotetur et alius testis addatur qui scripturam ipse quoque subsignet; secus mandatum irritum est.

§4. Si mandans, antequam procurator

1103: c. 1087

1104 §1: c. 1088 §1; SCSO Resp., 18 maii 1949 (AAS 41 [1949] 427)

1104 §2: c. 1088 §2

1105 §1, 1°: c. 1089 §1, 4°; CI Resp., 31 maii 1948 (AAS 40 [1948] 302)

1105 §2: c. 1089 §1; SCDS Litt. circ., 1 maii 1932; SCDS Litt. circ., 10 sep. 1941

1105 §3: c. 1089 §2

1105 §4: c. 1089 §3

date or develops amentia before the proxy contracts in his or her name, the marriage is invalid even if the proxy or the other contracting party does not know this.

CAN. 1106 A marriage can be contracted through an interpreter; the pastor is not to assist at it, however, unless he is certain of the trustworthiness of the interpreter.

CAN. 1107 Even if a marriage was entered into invalidly by reason of an impediment or a defect of form, the consent given is presumed to persist until its revocation is established.

CHAPTER V. The Form of the Celebration of Marriage

CAN. 1108 §1. Only those marriages are valid which are contracted before the local ordinary, pastor, or a priest or deacon delegated by either of them, who assist, and before two witnesses according to the rules expressed in the following canons and without prejudice to the exceptions mentioned in cann. 144, 1112, §1, 1116, and 1127, §§1–2.

§2. The person who assists at a marriage is understood to be only that person who is present, asks for the manifestation of the consent of the contracting parties, and receives it in the name of the Church.

CAN. 1109 Unless the local ordinary and pastor have been excommunicated, interdicted, or suspended from office or declared such through a sentence or decree, by virtue of their office and within the confines of their territory

eius nomine contrahat, mandatum revocaverit aut in amentiam inciderit, invalidum est matrimonium, licet sive procurator sive altera pars contrahens haec ignoraverit.

CAN. 1106 Matrimonium per interpretem contrahi potest; cui tamen parochus ne assistat, nisi de interpretis fide sibi constet.

CAN. 1107 Etsi matrimonium invalide ratione impedimenti vel defectus formae initum fuerit, consensus praestitus praesumitur perseverare, donec de eius revocatione constiterit.

CAPUT V. De Forma Celebrationis Matrimonii

CAN. 1108 §1. Ea tantum matrimonia valida sunt, quae contrahuntur coram loci Ordinario aut parocho aut sacerdote vel diacono ab alterutro delegato qui assistant, necnon coram duobus testibus, secundum tamen regulas expressas in canonibus qui sequuntur, et salvis exceptionibus de quibus in cann. 144, 1112, §1, 1116 et 1127, §§1–2.

§2. Assistens matrimonio intellegitur tantum qui praesens exquirit manifestationem contrahentium consensus eamque nomine Ecclesiae recipit.

CAN. 1109 Loci Ordinarius et parochus, nisi per sententiam vel per decretum fuerint excommunicati vel interdicti vel suspensi ab officio aut tales declarati, vi officii, intra fines sui territorii, valide matrimoniis as-

---

1106: cc. 1090, 1091

1107: c. 1093

1108 §1: c. 1094; CI Resp. V, 25 mar. 1952 (AAS 44 [1952] 497); SCC Decl. II, 7 oct. 1953 (AAS 45 [1953] 758–759); LG 29; SDO 22, 4; CIV Resp. 2, 26 mar. 1968 (AAS 60 [1968] 363); Sec Resp., 21 maii 1968

1108 §2: c. 1095 §1, 3°; CI Resp. 11, 10 mar. 1928 (AAS 20 [1928] 120); SC 77; SCDF Resp., 28 nov. 1975

1109: cc. 1095 §1, 1° et 2°; 1099 §1, 3°; CAl 88 §3; CI pro CIC Orientali Resp. 5 et 6, 3 maii 1953 (AAS 45 [1953] 313)

they assist validly at the marriages not only of their subjects but also of those who are not their subjects provided that one of them is of the Latin rite.

CAN. 1110   By virtue of office, a personal ordinary and a personal pastor assist validly only at marriages where at least one of the parties is a subject within the confines of their jurisdiction.

CAN. 1111   §1. As long as they hold office validly, the local ordinary and the pastor can delegate to priests and deacons the faculty, even a general one, of assisting at marriages within the limits of their territory.

§2. To be valid, the delegation of the faculty to assist at marriages must be given to specific persons expressly. If it concerns special delegation, it must be given for a specific marriage; if it concerns general delegation, it must be given in writing.

CAN. 1112   §1. Where there is a lack of priests and deacons, the diocesan bishop can delegate lay persons to assist at marriages, with the previous favorable vote of the conference of bishops and after he has obtained the permission of the Holy See.

§2. A suitable lay person is to be selected, who is capable of giving instruction to those preparing to be married and able to perform the matrimonial liturgy properly.

CAN. 1113   Before special delegation is granted, all those things which the law has established to prove free status are to be fulfilled.

sistunt non tantum subditorum, sed etiam non subditorum, dummodo eorum alteruter sit ritus latini.

CAN. 1110   Ordinarius et parochus personalis vi officii matrimonio solummodo eorum valide assistunt, quorum saltem alteruter subditus sit intra fines suae dicionis.

CAN. 1111   §1. Loci Ordinarius et parochus, quamdiu valide officio funguntur, possunt facultatem intra fines sui territorii matrimoniis assistendi, etiam generalem, sacerdotibus et diaconis delegare.

§2. Ut valida sit delegatio facultatis assistendi matrimoniis, determinatis personis expresse dari debet; si agitur de delegatione speciali, ad determinatum matrimonium danda est; si vero agitur de delegatione generali, scripto est concedenda.

CAN. 1112   §1. Ubi desunt sacerdotes et diaconi, potest Episcopus dioecesanus, praevio voto favorabili Episcoporum conferentiae et obtenta licentia Sanctae Sedis, delegare laicos, qui matrimoniis assistant.

§2. Laicus seligatur idoneus, ad institutionem nupturientibus tradendam capax et qui liturgiae matrimoniali rite peragendae aptus sit.

CAN. 1113   Antequam delegatio concedatur specialis, omnia provideantur, quae ius statuit ad libertatem status comprobandam.

1110: SCC Instr. *Sollemne semper,* 23 apr. 1951, VI et X (AAS 43 [1951] 563–564); PIUS PP. XII, Const. Ap. *Exsul Familia,* 35, 36 et 39 (AAS 44 [1952] 700); SCC Instr. *Per instructionem,* 20 oct. 1956, 98–109 (AAS 49 [1957] 158–159); SCE Instr. *Nemo est,* 22 aug. 1969, 38 et 39 (AAS 61 [1969] 633–634)

1111 §1: c. 1095 §2; CI Resp. V et VI, 20 maii 1923 (AAS 10 [1924] 114–115); LG 29; SDO 22, 4; CIV Resp., 26 mar. 1968 (AAS 60 [1968] 363); Sec Resp.,

21 maii 1968; CIV Resp., 4 apr. 1969 (AAS 61 [1969] 348)

1111 §2: c. 1096 §1; CI Resp. VI, 20 maii 1923 (AAS 10 [1924] 115); CI Resp. IV, 28 dec. 1927 (AAS 20 [1927] 61–62)

1112: SCDS Instr. *Ad Sanctam Sedem,* 7 dec. 1971; SCDS Instr. *Sacramentalem indolem,* 15 maii 1974; SCCD Normae, dec. 1974

1113: c. 1096 §2

CAN. 1114 The person assisting at marriage acts illicitly unless the person has made certain of the free status of the contracting parties according to the norm of law and, if possible, of the permission of the pastor whenever the person assists in virtue of general delegation.

CAN. 1115 Marriages are to be celebrated in a parish where either of the contracting parties has a domicile, quasi-domicile, or month long residence or, if it concerns transients, in the parish where they actually reside. With the permission of the proper ordinary or proper pastor, marriages can be celebrated elsewhere.

CAN. 1116 §1. If a person competent to assist according to the norm of law cannot be present or approached without grave inconvenience, those who intend to enter into a true marriage can contract it validly and licitly before witnesses only:

1° in danger of death;

2° outside the danger of death provided that it is prudently foreseen that the situation will continue for a month.

§2. In either case, if some other priest or deacon who can be present is available, he must be called and be present at the celebration of the marriage together with the witnesses, without prejudice to the validity of the marriage before witnesses only.

CAN. 1117 The form established above must be observed if at least one of the parties contracting marriage was baptized in the Catholic Church or received into it and has not

CAN. 1114 Assistens matrimonio illicite agit, nisi ipsi constiterit de libero statu contrahentium ad normam iuris atque, si fieri potest, de licentia parochi, quoties vi delegationis generalis assistit.

CAN. 1115 Matrimonia celebrentur in paroecia ubi alterutra pars contrahentium habet domicilium vel quasi-domicilium vel menstruam commorationem, aut, si de vagis agitur, in paroecia ubi actu commorantur; cum licentia proprii Ordinarii aut parochi proprii, alibi celebrari possunt.

CAN. 1116 §1. Si haberi vel adiri nequeat sine gravi incommodo assistens ad normam iuris competens, qui intendunt verum matrimonium inire, illud valide ac licite coram solis testibus contrahere possunt:

1° in mortis periculo;

2° extra mortis periculum, dummodo prudenter praevideatur earum rerum condicionem esse per mensem duraturam.

§2. In utroque casu, si praesto sit alius sacerdos vel diaconus qui adesse possit, vocari et, una cum testibus, matrimonii celebrationi adesse debet, salva coniugii validitate coram solis testibus.

CAN. 1117 Statuta superius forma servanda est, si saltem alterutra pars matrimonium contrahentium in Ecclesia catholica baptizata vel in eandem recepta sit neque

1114: c. 1097 §1, 1° et 3°; SCDS Instr., 4 iul. 1921 (AAS 13 [1921] 348–349)

1115: c. 1097 §1, 2°

1116, §1: c. 1098, 1°; CI Resp. VIII, 10 nov. 1925 (AAS 17 [1925] 583); CI Resp. I, 10 mar. 1928 (AAS 20 [1928] 120); CI Resp. I, 25 iul. 1931 (AAS 23 [1931] 388); SCDS Resp., 24 apr. 1935; CI Resp. 2, 3 maii 1945 (AAS 37 [1945] 149); SCDS Instr. *Ad Sanctam Sedem*, 7 dec. 1971

1116 §2: c. 1098, 2°; LG 29; SDO 22, 4; CIV Resp., 26 mar. 1968 (AAS 60 [1968] 363); Sec Resp., 21 maii 1968; CIV Resp., 4 apr. 1969 (AAS 61 [1969] 348)

1117: c. 1099 §1

defected from it by a formal act, without prejudice to the prescripts of can. 1127, §2.

CAN. 1118 §1. A marriage between Catholics or between a Catholic party and a non-Catholic baptized party is to be celebrated in a parish church. It can be celebrated in another church or oratory with the permission of the local ordinary or pastor.

§2. The local ordinary can permit a marriage to be celebrated in another suitable place.

§3. A marriage between a Catholic party and a non-baptized party can be celebrated in a church or in another suitable place.

CAN. 1119 Outside the case of necessity, the rites prescribed in the liturgical books approved by the Church or received by legitimate customs are to be observed in the celebration of a marriage.

CAN. 1120 The conference of bishops can produce its own rite of marriage, to be reviewed by the Holy See, in keeping with the usages of places and peoples which are adapted to the Christian spirit; nevertheless, the law remains in effect that the person who assists at the marriage is present, asks for the manifestation of consent of the contracting parties, and receives it.

CAN. 1121 §1. After a marriage has been celebrated, the pastor of the place of the celebration or the person who takes his place, even if neither assisted at the marriage, is to note as soon as possible in the marriage register the names of the spouses, the person who assisted, and the witnesses, and the place and date of the celebration of the marriage according to the method prescribed by the conference of bishops or the diocesan bishop.

actu formali ab ea defecerit, salvis praescriptis can. 1127, §2.

CAN. 1118 §1. Matrimonium inter catholicos vel inter partem catholicam et partem non catholicam baptizatam celebretur in ecclesia paroeciali; in alia ecclesia aut oratorio celebrari poterit de licentia Ordinarii loci vel parochi.

§2. Matrimonium in alio convenienti loco celebrari Ordinarius loci permittere potest.

§3. Matrimonium inter partem catholicam et partem non baptizatam in ecclesia vel in alio convenienti loco celebrari poterit.

CAN. 1119 Extra casum necessitatis, in matrimonii celebratione serventur ritus in libris liturgicis, ab Ecclesia probatis, praescripti aut legitimis consuetudinibus recepti.

CAN. 1120 Episcoporum conferentia exarare potest ritum proprium matrimonii, a Sancta Sede recognoscendum, congruentem locorum et populorum usibus ad spiritum christianum aptatis, firma tamen lege ut assistens matrimonio praesens requirat manifestationem consensus contrahentium eamque recipiat.

CAN. 1121 §1. Celebrato matrimonio, parochus loci celebrationis vel qui eius vices gerit, etsi neuter eidem astiterit, quam primum adnotet in matrimoniorum regestis nomina coniugum, assistentis ac testium, locum et diem celebrationis matrimonii, iuxta modum ab Episcoporum conferentia aut ab Episcopo dioecesano praescriptum.

1118 §1: c. 1109 §§1 et 3
1118 §2: c. 1109 §§1 et 2
1118 §3: c. 1109 §§1 et 3; OCM cap. III
1119: c. 1100; SC 78; SCR Resp. V. 6 nov. 1925
(AAS 18 [1926] 22–23)

1120: SC 77, 78; OCM 17
1121 §1: c. 1103 §1

§2. Whenever a marriage is contracted according to the norm of can. 1116, a priest or deacon, if he was present at the celebration, or otherwise the witnesses *in solidum* with the contracting parties are bound to inform as soon as possible the pastor or local ordinary about the marriage entered into.

§3. For a marriage contracted with a dispensation from canonical form, the local ordinary who granted the dispensation is to take care that the dispensation and celebration are inscribed in the marriage registers of both the curia and the proper parish of the Catholic party whose pastor conducted the investigation about the free status. The Catholic spouse is bound to notify as soon as possible the same ordinary and pastor about the marriage celebrated and also to indicate the place of the celebration and the public form observed.

CAN. 1122 §1. The contracted marriage is to be noted also in the baptismal registers in which the baptism of the spouses has been recorded.

§2. If a spouse did not contract marriage in the parish in which the person was baptized, the pastor of the place of the celebration is to send notice of the marriage which has been entered into as soon as possible to the pastor of the place of the conferral of baptism.

CAN. 1123 Whenever a marriage is either convalidated in the external forum, declared null, or legitimately dissolved other than by death, the pastor of the place of the celebration of the marriage must be informed so that a notation is properly made in the marriage and baptismal registers.

§2. Quoties matrimonium ad normam can. 1116 contrahitur, sacerdos vel diaconus, si celebrationi adfuerit, secus testes tenentur in solidum cum contrahentibus parochum aut Ordinarium loci de inito coniugio quam primum certiorem reddere.

§3. Ad matrimonium quod attinet cum dispensatione a forma canonica contractum, loci Ordinarius, qui dispensationem concessit, curet ut inscribatur dispensatio et celebratio in libro matrimoniorum tum curiae tum paroeciae propriae partis catholicae, cuius parochus inquisitiones de statu libero peregit; de celebrato matrimonio eundem Ordinarium et parochum quam primum certiorem reddere tenetur coniux catholicus, indicans etiam locum celebrationis necnon formam publicam servatam.

CAN. 1122 §1. Matrimonium contractum adnotetur etiam in regestis baptizatorum, in quibus baptismus coniugum inscriptus est.

§2. Si coniux matrimonium contraxerit non in paroecia in qua baptizatus est, parochus loci celebrationis notitiam initi coniugii ad parochum loci collati baptismi quam primum transmittat.

CAN. 1123 Quoties matrimonium vel convalidatur pro foro externo, vel nullum declaratur, vel legitime praeterquam morte solvitur, parochus loci celebrationis matrimonii certior fieri debet, ut adnotatio in regestis matrimoniorum et baptizatorum rite fiat.

1121 §2: c. 1103 §3
1121 §3: MM 10

1122 §1: c. 1103 §2
1122 §2: c. 1103 §2

CHAPTER VI. Mixed Marriages

CAN. 1124   Without express permission of the competent authority, a marriage is prohibited between two baptized persons of whom one is baptized in the Catholic Church or received into it after baptism and has not defected from it by a formal act and the other of whom is enrolled in a Church or ecclesial community not in full communion with the Catholic Church.

CAN. 1125   The local ordinary can grant a permission of this kind if there is a just and reasonable cause. He is not to grant it unless the following conditions have been fulfilled:

1° the Catholic party is to declare that he or she is prepared to remove dangers of defecting from the faith and is to make a sincere promise to do all in his or her power so that all offspring are baptized and brought up in the Catholic Church;

2° the other party is to be informed at an appropriate time about the promises which the Catholic party is to make, in such a way that it is certain that he or she is truly aware of the promise and obligation of the Catholic party;

3° both parties are to be instructed about the purposes and essential properties of marriage which neither of the contracting parties is to exclude.

CAN. 1126   It is for the conference of bishops to establish the method in which these declarations and promises, which are always required, must be made and to define the manner in which they are to be established in the external forum and the non-Catholic party informed about them.

CAN. 1127   §1. The prescripts of can. 1108

CAPUT VI. De Matrimoniis Mixtis

CAN. 1124   Matrimonium inter duas personas baptizatas, quarum altera sit in Ecclesia catholica baptizata vel in eandem post baptismum recepta, quaeque nec ab ea actu formali defecerit, altera vero Ecclesiae vel communitati ecclesiali plenam communionem cum Ecclesia catholica non habenti adscripta, sine expressa auctoritatis competentis licentia prohibitum est.

CAN. 1125   Huiusmodi licentiam concedere potest Ordinarius loci, si iusta et rationabilis causa habeatur; eam ne concedat, nisi impletis condicionibus quae sequuntur:

1° pars catholica declaret se paratam esse pericula a fide deficiendi removere atque sinceram promissionem praestet se omnia pro viribus facturam esse, ut universa proles in Ecclesia catholica baptizetur et educetur;

2° de his promissionibus a parte catholica faciendis altera pars tempestive certior fiat, adeo ut constet ipsam vere consciam esse promissionis et obligationis partis catholicae;

3° ambae partes edoceantur de finibus et proprietatibus essentialibus matrimonii, a neutro contrahente excludendis.

CAN. 1126   Episcoporum conferentiae est tum modum statuere, quo hae declarationes et promissiones, quae semper requiruntur, faciendae sint, tum rationem definire, qua de ipsis et in foro externo constet et pars non catholica certior reddatur.

CAN. 1127   §1. Ad formam quod attinet

1124: c. 1060; MS; MM 1
1125: c. 1061 §§1 et 2; MS I et II; MM 1; Sec Litt., 15 apr. 1970

1126: MM 7
1127 §1: OE 18; SCEO Decr. *Crescens matrimoniorum,* 22 feb. 1967 (AAS 59 [1967] 165–166)

are to be observed for the form to be used in a mixed marriage. Nevertheless, if a Catholic party contracts marriage with a non-Catholic party of an Eastern rite, the canonical form of the celebration must be observed for liceity only; for validity, however, the presence of a sacred minister is required and the other requirements of law are to be observed.

§2. If grave difficulties hinder the observance of canonical form, the local ordinary of the Catholic party has the right of dispensing from the form in individual cases, after having consulted the ordinary of the place in which the marriage is celebrated and with some public form of celebration for validity. It is for the conference of bishops to establish norms by which the aforementioned dispensation is to be granted in a uniform manner.

§3. It is forbidden to have another religious celebration of the same marriage to give or renew matrimonial consent before or after the canonical celebration according to the norm of §1. Likewise, there is not to be a religious celebration in which the Catholic who is assisting and a non-Catholic minister together, using their own rites, ask for the consent of the parties.

CAN. 1128 Local ordinaries and other pastors of souls are to take care that the Catholic spouse and the children born of a mixed marriage do not lack the spiritual help to fulfill their obligations and are to help spouses foster the unity of conjugal and family life.

CAN. 1129 The prescripts of cann. 1127 and 1128 must be applied also to marriages which the

in matrimonio mixto adhibendam, serventur praescripta can. 1108; si tamen pars catholica matrimonium contrahit cum parte non catholica ritus orientalis, forma canonica celebrationis servanda est ad liceitatem tantum; ad validitatem autem requiritur interventus ministri sacri, servatis aliis de iure servandis.

§2. Si graves difficultates formae canonicae servandae obstent, Ordinario loci partis catholicae ius est ab eadem in singulis casibus dispensandi, consulto tamen Ordinario loci in quo matrimonium celebratur, et salva ad validitatem aliqua publica forma celebrationis; Episcoporum conferentiae est normas statuere, quibus praedicta dispensatio concordi ratione concedatur.

§3. Vetatur ne, ante vel post canonicam celebrationem ad normam §1, alia habeatur eiusdem matrimonii celebratio religiosa ad matrimonialem consensum praestandum vel renovandum; item ne fiat celebratio religiosa, in qua assistens catholicus et minister non catholicus insimul, suum quisque ritum peragens, partium consensum exquirant.

CAN. 1128 Locorum Ordinarii aliique animarum pastores curent, ne coniugi catholico et filiis e matrimonio mixto natis auxilium spirituale desit ad eorum obligationes adimplendas atque coniuges adiuvent ad vitae coniugalis et familiaris fovendam unitatem.

CAN. 1129 Praescripta cann. 1127 et 1128 applicanda sunt quoque matrimoniis,

---

1127 §2: MS III; MM 9; Sec. Litt., 15 apr. 1970; SCDF Resp., 13 iul. 1971; CIV Resp. I, 11 feb. 1972 (AAS 64 [1972] 397)

1127 §3: cc. 1063 §§1 et 2, 1102 §1; SCSO Resp., 26 nov. 1919; SCSO Resp., 6 iul. 1928; SCEO Resp., 26

oct. 1964; SCSO Resp., 9 feb. 1965; SCDF Resp., 16 iun. 1966; MS V; MM 13

1128: MS VI; MM 14; Sec Litt., 15 apr. 1970

1129: c. 1971; MS; MM

impediment of disparity of cult mentioned in can. 1086, §1 impedes.

CHAPTER VII. Marriage Celebrated Secretly

CAN. 1130 For a grave and urgent cause, the local ordinary can permit a marriage to be celebrated secretly.

CAN. 1131 Permission to celebrate a marriage secretly entails the following:

1° the investigations which must be conducted before the marriage are done secretly;

2° the local ordinary, the one assisting, the witnesses, and the spouses observe secrecy about the marriage celebrated.

CAN. 1132 The obligation of observing the secrecy mentioned in can. 1131, n. 2 ceases on the part of the local ordinary if grave scandal or grave harm to the holiness of marriage is imminent due to the observance of the secret; this is to be made known to the parties before the celebration of the marriage.

CAN. 1133 A marriage celebrated secretly is to be noted only in a special register to be kept in the secret archive of the curia.

CHAPTER VIII. The Effects of Marriage

CAN. 1134 From a valid marriage there arises between the spouses a bond which by its nature is perpetual and exclusive. Moreover, a special sacrament strengthens and, as it were, consecrates the spouses in a Christian marriage for the duties and dignity of their state.

CAN. 1135 Each spouse has an equal duty

quibus obstat impedimentum disparitatis cultus, de quo in can. 1086, §1.

CAPUT VII. **De Matrimonio Secreto Celebrando**

CAN. 1130 Ex gravi et urgenti causa loci Ordinarius permittere potest, ut matrimonium secreto celebretur.

CAN. 1131 Permissio matrimonium secreto celebrandi secumfert:

1° ut secreto fiant investigationes quae ante matrimonium peragendae sunt;

2° ut secretum de matrimonio celebrato servetur ab Ordinario loci, assistente, testibus, coniugibus.

CAN. 1132 Obligatio secretum servandi, de qua in can. 1131, n. 2, ex parte Ordinarii loci cessat si grave scandalum aut gravis erga matrimonii sanctitatem iniuria ex secreti observantia immineat, idque notum fiat partibus ante matrimonii celebrationem.

CAN. 1133 Matrimonium secreto celebratum in peculiari tantummodo regesto, servando in secreto curiae archivo, adnotetur.

CAPUT VIII. **De Matrimonii Effectibus**

CAN. 1134 Ex valido matrimonio enascitur inter coniuges vinculum natura sua perpetuum et exclusivum; in matrimonio praeterea christiano coniuges ad sui status officia et dignitatem peculiari sacramento roborantur et veluti consecrantur.

CAN. 1135 Utrique coniugi aequum of-

1130: c. 1104
1131: c. 1105
1132: c. 1106
1133: c. 1107

1134: c. 1110; LG 41; GS 48; HV 25
1135: c. 1111; SRR Decisio coram Anné, 8 nov. 1963; HV 9, 10; SRR Decisio coram Serrano, 3 apr. 1973

and right to those things which belong to the partnership of conjugal life.

CAN. 1136 Parents have the most grave duty and the primary right to take care as best they can for the physical, social, cultural, moral, and religious education of their offspring.

CAN. 1137 The children conceived or born of a valid or putative marriage are legitimate.

CAN. 1138 §1. The father is he whom a lawful marriage indicates unless clear evidence proves the contrary.

§2. Children born at least 180 days after the day when the marriage was celebrated or within 300 days from the day of the dissolution of conjugal life are presumed to be legitimate.

CAN. 1139 Illegitimate children are legitimated by the subsequent valid or putative marriage of their parents or by a rescript of the Holy See.

CAN. 1140 As regards canonical effects, legitimated children are equal in all things to legitimate ones unless the law has expressly provided otherwise.

CHAPTER IX. **The Separation of Spouses**

ART. 1. *Dissolution of the Bond*

CAN. 1141 A marriage that is *ratum et consummatum* can be dissolved by no human power and by no cause, except death.

CAN. 1142 For a just cause, the Roman

---

ficium et ius est ad ea quae pertinent ad consortium vitae coniugalis.

CAN. 1136 Parentes officium gravissimum et ius primarium habent prolis educationem tum physicam, socialem et culturalem, tum moralem et religiosam pro viribus curandi.

CAN. 1137 Legitimi sunt filii concepti aut nati ex matrimonio valido vel putativo.

CAN. 1138 §1. Pater is est, quem iustae nuptiae demonstrant, nisi evidentibus argumentis contrarium probetur.

§2. Legitimi praesumuntur filii, qui nati sunt saltem post dies 180 a die celebrati matrimonii, vel infra dies 300 a die dissolutae vitae coniugalis.

CAN. 1139 Filii illegitimi legitimantur per subsequens matrimonium parentum sive validum sive putativum, vel per rescriptum Sanctae Sedis.

CAN. 1140 Filii legitimati, ad effectus canonicos quod attinet, in omnibus aequiparantur legitimis, nisi aliud expresse iure cautum fuerit.

CAPUT IX. **De Separatione Coniugum**

ART. 1. *De Dissolutione Vinculi*

CAN. 1141 Matrimonium ratum et consummatum nulla humana potestate nullaque causa, praeterquam morte, dissolvi potest.

CAN. 1142 Matrimonium non consum-

1136: cc. 1113, 1372 §2; Pius PP. XI, Enc. *Divini Illius Magistri*, 31 dec. 1929, 59–60 (AAS 22 [1930] 49–86); Pius PP. XI, Enc. *Mit brennender Sorge*, 14 mar. 1937, 164–165 (AAS 29 [1937] 145–167); Pius PP. XII, All., 8 sept. 1946; LG 11; GE 3, 6; GS 48; CIP Decl. *Il dinamismo della fede*, 10 dec. 1974, n. 38, 5°

1137: c. 1114

1138 §1: c. 1115 §1

1138 §2: c. 1115 §2

1139: c. 1116; CI Resp. II, 6 dec. 1930 (AAS 23 [1931] 25)

1140: c. 1117

1141: c. 1118; CC 552; Pius PP. XII, All., 3 oct. 1941 (AAS 33 [1941] 424–425); Pius PP. XII, All., 6 oct. 1946 (AAS 38 [1946] 396); GS 48

1142: c. 1119

Pontiff can dissolve a non-consummated marriage between baptized persons or between a baptized party and a non-baptized party at the request of both parties or of one of them, even if the other party is unwilling.

CAN. 1143 §1. A marriage entered into by two non-baptized persons is dissolved by means of the pauline privilege in favor of the faith of the party who has received baptism by the very fact that a new marriage is contracted by the same party, provided that the non-baptized party departs.

§2. The non-baptized party is considered to depart if he or she does not wish to cohabit with the baptized party or to cohabit peacefully without affront to the Creator unless the baptized party, after baptism was received, has given the other a just cause for departing.

CAN. 1144 §1. For the baptized party to contract a new marriage validly, the non-baptized party must always be interrogated whether:

1° he or she also wishes to receive baptism;

2° he or she at least wishes to cohabit peacefully with the baptized party without affront to the Creator.

§2. This interrogation must be done after baptism. For a grave cause, however, the local ordinary can permit the interrogation to be done before baptism or can even dispense from the interrogation either before or after baptism provided that it is evident at least by a summary and extrajudicial process that it cannot be done or would be useless.

CAN. 1145 §1. The interrogation is regularly to be done on the authority of the local ordinary of the converted party. This ordinary

matum inter baptizatos vel inter partem baptizatam et partem non baptizatam a Romano Pontifice dissolvi potest iusta de causa, utraque parte rogante vel alterutra, etsi altera pars sit invita.

CAN. 1143 §1. Matrimonium initum a duobus non baptizatis solvitur ex privilegio paulino in favorem fidei partis quae baptismum recepit ipso facto quo novum matrimonium ab eadem parte contrahitur, dummodo pars non baptizata discedat.

§2. Discedere censetur pars non baptizata, si nolit cum parte baptizata cohabitare vel cohabitare pacifice sine contumelia Creatoris, nisi haec post baptismum receptum iustam illi dederit discedendi causam.

CAN. 1144 §1. Ut pars baptizata novum matrimonium valide contrahat, pars non baptizata semper interpellari debet an:

1° velit et ipsa baptismum recipere;

2° saltem velit cum parte baptizata pacifice cohabitare, sine contumelia Creatoris.

§2. Haec interpellatio post baptismum fieri debet; at loci Ordinarius, gravi de causa, permittere potest ut interpellatio ante baptismum fiat, immo et ab interpellatione dispensare, sive ante sive post baptismum, dummodo constet modo procedendi saltem summario et extraiudiciali eam fieri non posse aut fore inutilem.

CAN. 1145 §1. Interpellatio fiat regulariter de auctoritate loci Ordinarii partis conversae; a quo Ordinario concedendae sunt

1143 §1: cc. 1120, 1126
1143 §2: cc. 1123, 1124
1144 §1: c. 1121 §1

1144 §2: c. 1121 §2; PM I, 23
1145 §1: c. 1122 §1

must grant the other spouse a period of time to respond if the spouse seeks it, after having been advised, however, that his or her silence will be considered a negative response if the period passes without effect.

§2. Even an interrogation made privately by the converted party is valid and indeed licit if the form prescribed above cannot be observed.

§3. In either case, the fact that the interrogation was done and its outcome must be established legitimately in the external forum.

CAN. 1146 The baptized party has the right to contract a new marriage with a Catholic party:

1° if the other party responded negatively to the interrogation or if the interrogation had been omitted legitimately;

2° if the non-baptized party, already interrogated or not, at first persevered in peaceful cohabitation without affront to the Creator but then departed without a just cause, without prejudice to the prescripts of cann. 1144 and 1145.

CAN. 1147 For a grave cause, however, the local ordinary can allow a baptized party who uses the pauline privilege to contract marriage with a non-Catholic party, whether baptized or not baptized; the prescripts of the canons about mixed marriages are also to be observed.

CAN. 1148 §1. When he receives baptism in the Catholic Church, a non-baptized man who has several non-baptized wives at the same time can retain one of them after the others have been dismissed, if it is hard for him to remain with the first one. The same is valid for a non-baptized woman who has several non-baptized husbands at the same time.

§2. In the cases mentioned in §1, marriage

alteri coniugi, si quidem eas petierit, induciae ad respondendum, eodem tamen monito ut, si induciae inutiliter praeterlabantur, eius silentium pro responsione negativa habeatur.

§2. Interpellatio etiam privatim facta ab ipsa parte conversa valet, immo est licita, si forma superius praescripta servari nequeat.

§3. In utroque casu de interpellatione facta deque eiusdem exitu in foro externo legitime constare debet.

CAN. 1146 Pars baptizata ius habet novas nuptias contrahendi cum parte catholica:

1° si altera pars negative interpellationi responderit, aut si interpellatio legitime omissa fuerit;

2° si pars non baptizata, sive iam interpellata sive non, prius perseverans in pacifica cohabitatione sine contumelia Creatoris, postea sine iusta causa discesserit, firmis praescriptis cann. 1144 et 1145.

CAN. 1147 Ordinarius loci tamen, gravi de causa, concedere potest ut pars baptizata, utens privilegio paulino, contrahat matrimonium cum parte non catholica sive baptizata sive non baptizata, servatis etiam praescriptis canonum de matrimoniis mixtis.

CAN. 1148 §1. Non baptizatus, qui plures uxores non baptizatas simul habeat, recepto in Ecclesia catholica baptismo, si durum ei sit cum earum prima permanere, unam ex illis, ceteris dimissis, retinere potest. Idem valet de muliere non baptizata, quae plures maritos non baptizatos simul habeat.

§2. In casibus de quibus in §1, matrimo-

1145 §2: c. 1122 §2
1145 §3: c. 1122 §2
1146: cc. 1123, 1124
1147: PM I, 20

1148 §1: c. 1125; CI Resp. 1, 26 ian. 1919; CI Resp., 3 aug. 1919; SCSO Resp., 30 iun. 1937
1148 §2: SCSO Resp., 30 iun. 1937

must be contracted in legitimate form after baptism has been received, and the prescripts about mixed marriages, if necessary, and other matters required by the law are to be observed.

§3. Keeping in mind the moral, social, and economic conditions of places and of persons, the local ordinary is to take care that the needs of the first wife and the others dismissed are sufficiently provided for according to the norms of justice, Christian charity, and natural equity.

CAN. 1149 A non-baptized person who, after having received baptism in the Catholic Church, cannot restore cohabitation with a non-baptized spouse by reason of captivity or persecution can contract another marriage even if the other party has received baptism in the meantime, without prejudice to the prescript of can. 1141.

CAN. 1150 In a doubtful matter the privilege of faith possesses the favor of the law.

ART. 2. *Separation with the Bond Remaining*

CAN. 1151 Spouses have the duty and right to preserve conjugal living unless a legitimate cause excuses them.

CAN. 1152 §1. Although it is earnestly recommended that a spouse, moved by Christian charity and concerned for the good of the family, not refuse forgiveness to an adulterous partner and not disrupt conjugal life, nevertheless, if the spouse did not condone the fault of the other expressly or tacitly, the spouse has the right to sever conjugal living unless the spouse consented to the adultery, gave cause for it, or also committed adultery.

§2. Tacit condonation exists if the innocent

nium, recepto baptismo, forma legitima contrahendum est, servatis etiam, si opus sit, praescriptis de matrimoniis mixtis et aliis de iure servandis.

§3. Ordinarius loci, prae oculis habita condicione morali, sociali, oeconomica locorum et personarum, curet ut primae uxoris ceterarumque dimissarum necessitatibus satis provisum sit, iuxta normas iustitiae, christianae caritatis et naturalis aequitatis.

CAN. 1149 Non baptizatus qui, recepto in Ecclesia catholica baptismo, cum coniuge non baptizato ratione captivitatis vel persecutionis cohabitationem restaurare nequeat, aliud matrimonium contrahere potest, etiamsi altera pars baptismum interea receperit, firmo praescripto can. 1141.

CAN. 1150 In re dubia privilegium fidei gaudet favore iuris.

ART. 2. *De Separatione Manente Vinculo*

CAN. 1151 Coniuges habent officium et ius servandi convictum coniugalem, nisi legitima causa eos excuset.

CAN. 1152 §1. Licet enixe commendetur ut coniux, caritate christiana motus et boni familiae sollicitus, veniam non abnuat comparti adulterae atque vitam coniugalem non disrumpat, si tamen eiusdem culpam expresse aut tacite non condonaverit, ius ipsi est solvendi coniugalem convictum, nisi in adulterium consenserit aut eidem causam dederit aut ipse quoque adulterium commiserit.

§2. Tacita condonatio habetur si coniux

1149: c. 1125
1150: c. 1127; SCSO Resp., 10 iun. 1937
1151: c. 1128

1152 §1: c. 1129 §1
1152 §2: c. 1129 §2

spouse has had marital relations voluntarily with the other spouse after having become certain of the adultery. It is presumed, moreover, if the spouse observed conjugal living for six months and did not make recourse to the ecclesiastical or civil authority.

§3. If the innocent spouse has severed conjugal living voluntarily, the spouse is to introduce a cause for separation within six months to the competent ecclesiastical authority which, after having investigated all the circumstances, is to consider carefully whether the innocent spouse can be moved to forgive the fault and not to prolong the separation permanently.

CAN. 1153 §1. If either of the spouses causes grave mental or physical danger to the other spouse or to the offspring or otherwise renders common life too difficult, that spouse gives the other a legitimate cause for leaving, either by decree of the local ordinary or even on his or her own authority if there is danger in delay.

§2. In all cases, when the cause for the separation ceases, conjugal living must be restored unless ecclesiastical authority has established otherwise.

CAN. 1154 After the separation of the spouses has taken place, the adequate support and education of the children must always be suitably provided.

CAN. 1155 The innocent spouse laudably can readmit the other spouse to conjugal life; in this case the innocent spouse renounces the right to separate.

innocens, postquam de adulterio certior factus est, sponte cum altero coniuge maritali affectu conversatus fuerit; praesumitur vero, si per sex menses coniugalem convictum servaverit, neque recursum apud auctoritatem ecclesiasticam vel civilem fecerit.

§3. Si coniux innocens sponte convictum coniugalem solverit, intra sex menses causam separationis deferat ad competentem auctoritatem ecclesiasticam, quae, omnibus inspectis adiunctis, perpendat si coniux innocens adduci possit ad culpam condonandam et ad separationem in perpetuum non protrahendam.

CAN. 1153 §1. Si alteruter coniugum grave seu animi seu corporis periculum alteri aut proli facessat, vel aliter vitam communem nimis duram reddat, alteri legitimam praebet causam discedendi, decreto Ordinarii loci et, si periculum sit in mora, etiam propria auctoritate.

§2. In omnibus casibus, causa separationis cessante, coniugalis convictus restaurandus est, nisi ab auctoritate ecclesiastica aliter statuatur.

CAN. 1154 Instituta separatione coniugum, opportune semper cavendum est debitae filiorum sustentationi et educationi.

CAN. 1155 Coniux innocens laudabiliter alterum coniugem ad vitam coniugalem rursus admittere potest, quo in casu iuri separationis renuntiat.

1152 §3: c. 1130
1153 §1: c. 1131 §1; CI Resp. III, 25 iun. 1932 (AAS 24 [1932] 284)

1153 §2: c. 1131 §2
1154: c. 1132
1155: c. 1130

CHAPTER X. **The Convalidation of Marriage**

ART. 1. *Simple Convalidation*

CAN. 1156 §1. To convalidate a marriage which is invalid because of a diriment impediment, it is required that the impediment ceases or is dispensed and that at least the party conscious of the impediment renews consent.

§2. Ecclesiastical law requires this renewal for the validity of the convalidation even if each party gave consent at the beginning and did not revoke it afterwards.

CAN. 1157 The renewal of consent must be a new act of the will concerning a marriage which the renewing party knows or thinks was null from the beginning.

CAN. 1158 §1. If the impediment is public, both parties must renew the consent in canonical form, without prejudice to the prescript of can. 1127, §2.

§2. If the impediment cannot be proven, it is sufficient that the party conscious of the impediment renews the consent privately and in secret, provided that the other perseveres in the consent offered; if the impediment is known to both parties, both are to renew the consent.

CAN. 1159 §1. A marriage which is invalid because of a defect of consent is convalidated if the party who did not consent now consents, provided that the consent given by the other party perseveres.

§2. If the defect of consent cannot be proven, it is sufficient that the party who did not consent gives consent privately and in secret.

CAPUT X. **De Matrimonii Convalidatione**

ART. 1. *De Convalidatione Simplici*

CAN. 1156 §1. Ad convalidandum matrimonium irritum ob impedimentum dirimens, requiritur ut cesset impedimentum vel ab eodem dispensetur, et consensum renovet saltem pars impedimenti conscia.

§2. Haec renovatio iure ecclesiastico requiritur ad validitatem convalidationis, etiamsi initio utraque pars consensum praestiterit nec postea revocaverit.

CAN. 1157 Renovatio consensus debet esse novus voluntatis actus in matrimonium, quod pars renovans scit aut opinatur ab initio nullum fuisse.

CAN. 1158 §1. Si impedimentum sit publicum, consensus ab utraque parte renovandus est forma canonica, salvo praescripto can. 1127, §2.

§2. Si impedimentum probari nequeat, satis est ut consensus renovetur privatim et secreto, et quidem a parte impedimenti conscia, dummodo altera in consensu praestito perseveret, aut ab utraque parte, si impedimentum sit utrique parti notum.

CAN. 1159 §1. Matrimonium irritum ob defectum consensus convalidatur, si pars quae non consenserat, iam consentiat, dummodo consensus ab altera parte praestitus perseveret.

§2. Si defectus consensus probari nequeat, satis est ut pars, quae non consenserat, privatim et secreto consensum praestet.

1156 §1: c. 1133 §1; SCSO Resp., 19 iul. 1955
1156 §2: c. 1133 §2
1157: c. 1134
1158 §1: c. 1135 §1

1158 §2: c. 1135 §§2 et 3
1159 §1: c. 1136 §1
1159 §2: c. 1136 §2

§3. If the defect of consent can be proven, the consent must be given in canonical form.

CAN. 1160 A marriage which is null because of defect of form must be contracted anew in canonical form in order to become valid, without prejudice to the prescript of can. 1127, §2.

ART. 2. *Radical Sanation*

CAN. 1161 §1. The radical sanation of an invalid marriage is its convalidation without the renewal of consent, which is granted by competent authority and entails the dispensation from an impediment, if there is one, and from canonical form, if it was not observed, and the retroactivity of canonical effects.

§2. Convalidation occurs at the moment of the granting of the favor. Retroactivity, however, is understood to extend to the moment of the celebration of the marriage unless other provision is expressly made.

§3. A radical sanation is not to be granted unless it is probable that the parties wish to persevere in conjugal life.

CAN. 1162 §1. A marriage cannot be radically sanated if consent is lacking in either or both of the parties, whether the consent was lacking from the beginning or, though present in the beginning, was revoked afterwards.

§2. If this consent was indeed lacking from the beginning but was given afterwards, the sanation can be granted from the moment the consent was given.

§3. Si defectus consensus probari potest, necesse est ut consensus forma canonica praestetur.

CAN. 1160 Matrimonium nullum ob defectum formae, ut validum fiat, contrahi denuo debet forma canonica, salvo praescripto can. 1127, §2.

ART. 2. *De Sanatione in Radice*

CAN. 1161 §1. Matrimonii irriti sanatio in radice est eiusdem, sine renovatione consensus, convalidatio, a competenti auctoritate concessa, secumferens dispensationem ab impedimento, si adsit, atque a forma canonica, si servata non fuerit, necnon retrotractionem effectuum canonicorum ad praeteritum.

§2. Convalidatio fit a momento concessionis gratiae; retrotractio vero intelligitur facta ad momentum celebrationis matrimonii, nisi aliud expresse caveatur.

§3. Sanatio in radice ne concedatur, nisi probabile sit partes in vita coniugali perseverare velle.

CAN. 1162 §1. Si in utraque vel alterutra parte deficiat consensus, matrimonium nequit sanari in radice, sive consensus ab initio defuerit, sive, ab initio praestitus, postea fuerit revocatus.

§2. Quod si consensus ab initio quidem defuerat, sed postea praestitus est, sanatio concedi potest a momento praestiti consensus.

1159 §3: c. 1136 §3
1160: c. 1137
1161 §1: c. 1138 §1

1161 §2: c. 1138 §2
1162 §1: c. 1140 §1
1162 §2: c. 1140 §2

CAN. 1163 §1. A marriage which is invalid because of an impediment or a defect of legitimate form can be sanated provided that the consent of each party perseveres.

§2. A marriage which is invalid because of an impediment of natural law or of divine positive law can be sanated only after the impediment has ceased.

CAN. 1164 A sanation can be granted validly even if either or both of the parties do not know of it; nevertheless, it is not to be granted except for a grave cause.

CAN. 1165 §1. The Apostolic See can grant a radical sanation.

§2. The diocesan bishop can grant a radical sanation in individual cases even if there are several reasons for nullity in the same marriage, after the conditions mentioned in can. 1125 for the sanation of a mixed marriage have been fulfilled. He cannot grant one, however, if there is an impediment whose dispensation is reserved to the Apostolic See according to the norm of can. 1078, §2, or if it concerns an impediment of natural law or divine positive law which has now ceased.

CAN. 1163 §1. Matrimonium irritum ob impedimentum vel ob defectum legitimae formae sanari potest, dummodo consensus utriusque partis perseveret.

§2. Matrimonium irritum ob impedimentum iuris naturalis aut divini positivi sanari potest solummodo postquam impedimentum cessavit.

CAN. 1164 Sanatio valide concedi potest etiam alterutra vel utraque parte inscia; ne autem concedatur nisi ob gravem causam.

CAN. 1165 §1. Sanatio in radice concedi potest ab Apostolica Sede.

§2. Concedi potest ab Episcopo dioecesano in singulis casibus, etiam si plures nullitatis rationes in eodem matrimonio concurrant, impletis condicionibus, de quibus in can. 1125, pro sanatione matrimonii mixti; concedi autem ab eodem nequit, si adsit impedimentum cuius dispensatio Sedi Apostolicae reservatur ad normam can. 1078, §2, aut agatur de impedimento iuris naturalis aut divini positivi quod iam cessavit.

1163 §1: c. 1139 §1
1163 §2: EM IX, 18 b
1164: c. 1138 §3

1165 §1: c. 1141; SCDS Resp., 10 mar. 1937
1165 §2: PM 21, 22; EM IX, 18 a et b

PART II. OTHER ACTS OF DIVINE WORSHIP

PARS II. DE CETERIS ACTIBUS CULTUS DIVINI

TITLE I. Sacramentals

CAN. 1166 Sacramentals are sacred signs by which effects, especially spiritual effects, are signified in some imitation of the sacraments and are obtained through the intercession of the Church.

CAN. 1167 §1. The Apostolic See alone can establish new sacramentals, authentically interpret those already received, or abolish or change any of them.

§2. In confecting or administering sacramentals, the rites and formulas approved by the authority of the Church are to be observed carefully.

CAN. 1168 The minister of sacramentals is a cleric who has been provided with the requisite power. According to the norm of the liturgical books and to the judgment of the local ordinary lay persons who possess the appropriate qualities can also administer some sacramentals.

CAN. 1169 §1. Those marked with the episcopal character and presbyters permitted by law or legitimate grant can perform consecrations and dedications validly.

TITULUS I. De Sacramentalibus

CAN. 1166 Sacramentalia sunt signa sacra, quibus, ad aliquam sacramentorum imitationem, effectus praesertim spirituales significantur et ex Ecclesiae impetratione obtinentur.

CAN. 1167 §1. Nova sacramentalia constituere aut recepta authentice interpretari, ex eis aliqua abolere aut mutare, sola potest Sedes Apostolica.

§2. In sacramentalibus conficiendis seu administrandis accurate serventur ritus et formulae ab Ecclesiae auctoritate probata.

CAN. 1168 Sacramentalium minister est clericus debita potestate instructus; quaedam sacramentalia, ad normam librorum liturgicorum, de iudicio loci Ordinarii, a laicis quoque, congruis qualitatibus praeditis, administrari possunt.

CAN. 1169 §1. Consecrationes et dedicationes valide peragere possunt qui charactere episcopali insigniti sunt, necnon presbyteri quibus iure vel legitima concessione id permittitur.

1166: c. 1144; SC 60
1167 §1: c. 1145; SC 63, 79
1168: SCConc Facul., 18 oct. 1927; SC 79; LG 29; SDO 22; OEx 19; OICA 48, 66
1169 §1: c. 1147 §1; CI Resp. I, 29 ian. 1931 (AAS 23

[1931] 110); SRC Resp., 14 apr. 1950; *Ordo Consecrationis Virginum*, 31 maii 1970, 6; *Ordo Benedicendi Oleum Catechumenorum et Infirmorum et Conficiendi Chrisma*, 3 dec. 1970, 6; SCCD Resp., mar. 1971; ODE cap. II, 6; cap. IV, 12

§2. Any presbyter can impart blessings except those reserved to the Roman Pontiff or bishops.

§3. A deacon can impart only those blessings expressly permitted by law.

CAN. 1170 Blessings, which are to be imparted first of all to Catholics, can also be given to catechumens and even to non-Catholics unless there is a prohibition of the Church to the contrary.

CAN. 1171 Sacred objects, which are designated for divine worship by dedication or blessing, are to be treated reverently and are not to be employed for profane or inappropriate use even if they are owned by private persons.

CAN. 1172 §1. No one can perform exorcisms legitimately upon the possessed unless he has obtained special and express permission from the local ordinary.

§2. The local ordinary is to give this permission only to a presbyter who has piety, knowledge, prudence, and integrity of life.

TITLE II. **The Liturgy of the Hours**

CAN. 1173 Fulfilling the priestly function of Christ, the Church celebrates the liturgy of the hours. In the liturgy of the hours, the Church, hearing God speaking to his people

§2. Benedictiones, exceptis iis quae Romano Pontifici aut Episcopis reservantur, impertire potest quilibet presbyter.

§3. Diaconus illas tantum benedictiones impertire potest, quae ipsi expresse iure permittuntur.

CAN. 1170 Benedictiones, imprimis impertiendae catholicis, dari possunt catechumenis quoque, immo, nisi obstet Ecclesiae prohibitio, etiam non catholicis.

CAN. 1171 Res sacrae, quae dedicatione vel benedictione ad divinum cultum destinatae sunt, reverenter tractentur nec ad usum profanum vel non proprium adhibeantur, etiamsi in dominio sint privatorum.

CAN. 1172 §1. Nemo exorcismos in obsessos proferre legitime potest, nisi ab Ordinario loci peculiarem et expressam licentiam obtinuerit.

§2. Haec licentia ab Ordinario loco concedatur tantummodo presbytero pietate, scientia, prudentia ac vitae integritate praedito.

TITULUS II. **De Liturgia Horarum**

CAN. 1173 Ecclesia, sacerdotale munus Christi adimplens, liturgiam horarum celebrat, qua Deum ad populum suum loquentem audiens et memoriam mysterii

1169 §2: c. 1147 §§2 et 3; SC 79; *Ordo Benedictionis Abbatis*, 9 nov. 1970, Prae., 2; *Ordo Benedictionis Abbatissae*, 9 nov. 1970, Prae., 2; *Ordo Benedicendi Oleum Catechumenorum et Infirmorum et Conficiendi Chrisma*, 3 dec. 1970, 7, 8; ODE cap. V, 2; cap. VI, 4; cap. VII, 3

1169 §3: c. 1147 §4; LG 29; SDO 22; CIV Resp., 13 nov. 1974 (AAS 66 [1974] 667)

1170: c. 1149; SRC Resp. Vicario Apostolico Gabonensi, 8 mar. 1919 (AAS 11 [1919] 144); OICA 18, 102
1171: c. 1150
1172 §1: c. 1151 §1
1172 §2: c. 1151 §2
1173: MD III; SC 83, 84; PAULUS PP. VI, Const. Ap. *Laudis canticum*, 1 nov. 1970, 8 (AAS 63 [1971] 531–532); IGLH 6, 7

and recalling the mystery of salvation, praises him without ceasing by song and prayer and intercedes for the salvation of the whole world.

CAN. 1174 §1. Clerics are obliged to carry out the liturgy of the hours according to the norm of can. 276, §2, n. 3; members of institutes of consecrated life and societies of apostolic life, however, are bound according to the norm of their constitutions.

§2. Other members of the Christian faithful, according to circumstances, are also earnestly invited to participate in the liturgy of the hours as an action of the Church.

CAN. 1175 In carrying out the liturgy of the hours, the true time for each hour is to be observed insofar as possible.

salutis agens, Ipsum sine intermissione, cantu et oratione, laudat atque interpellat pro totius mundi salute.

CAN. 1174 §1. Obligatione liturgiae horarum persolvendae adstringuntur clerici, ad normam can. 276, §2, n. 3; sodales vero institutorum vitae consecratae necnon societatum vitae apostolicae, ad normam suarum constitutionum.

§2. Ad participandam liturgiam horarum, utpote actionem Ecclesiae, etiam ceteri christifideles, pro adiunctis, enixe invitantur.

CAN. 1175 In liturgia horarum persolvenda, quantum fieri potest, verum tempus servetur uniuscuiusque horae.

TITLE III. Ecclesiastical Funerals

CAN. 1176 §1. Deceased members of the Christian faithful must be given ecclesiastical funerals according to the norm of law.

§2. Ecclesiastical funerals, by which the Church seeks spiritual support for the deceased, honors their bodies, and at the same time brings the solace of hope to the living, must be celebrated according to the norm of the liturgical laws.

TITULUS III. De Exequiis Ecclesiasticis

CAN. 1176 §1. Christifideles defuncti exequiis ecclesiasticis ad normam iuris donandi sunt.

§2. Exequiae ecclesiasticae, quibus Ecclesia defunctis spiritualem opem impetrat eorumque corpora honorat ac simul vivis spei solacium affert, celebrandae sunt ad normam legum liturgicarum.

1174 §1: cc. 135, 413 §§1 et 2; 610 §§1 et 3; 679 §1; MD III; *Rubricae Breviarii et Missalis Romani*, 26 iul. 1960, 149–157 (AAS 52 [1960] 623–625); SC 95–98; Paulus PP. VI, m.p. *Sacram Liturgiam*, 25 ian. 1964, VI–IX (AAS 56 [1964] 142–143); IOe 78; Paulus PP. VI, Ep. *Sacrificium laudis*, 15 aug. 1966; ES II, 20; Paulus PP. VI, Const. Ap. *Laudis canticum*, 1 nov. 1970, 1, 8 (AAS 63 [1971] 529, 534); IGLH 20–26, 28–32; SCCD Notif., 6 aug. 1972 (*Notitiae*, 8 [1972] 254–258)

1174 §2: MD III; SC 100; Paulus PP. VI, Const. Ap. *Laudis canticum*, 1 nov. 1970, 1, 8 (AAS 63 [1971]

529, 534); SCCD Decr. *Cum editio*, 2 feb. 1971; IGLH 21–23, 27, 32, 33, 40, 254

1175: SRC Decl., 28 dec. 1960; Ioannes PP. XXIII, Facul., 17 ian. 1961; SC 88, 89, 94; Paulus PP. VI, Const. Ap. *Laudis canticum*, 1 nov. 1970, 2 (AAS 63 [1971] 529); IGLH 38, 39, 75, 77, 84, 95

1176 §1: c. 1239 §3; SCConc Rescr., 12 ian. 1924 (AAS 16 [1924] 189)

1176 §2: c. 1215; SCConc Rescr., 12 ian. 1924 (AAS 16 [1924] 189–190); SCCD Decr. *Ritibus exsequiarum*, 15 aug. 1969; IGMR 335; OEx 1–3

§3. The Church earnestly recommends that the pious custom of burying the bodies of the deceased be observed; nevertheless, the Church does not prohibit cremation unless it was chosen for reasons contrary to Christian doctrine.

CHAPTER I. The Celebration of Funerals

CAN. 1177 §1. A funeral for any deceased member of the faithful must generally be celebrated in his or her parish church.

§2. Any member of the faithful or those competent to take care of the funeral of a deceased member of the faithful are permitted to choose another church for the funeral rite with the consent of the person who governs it and after notification of the proper pastor of the deceased.

§3. If a death occurred outside the person's own parish, and the body was not transferred to it nor another church legitimately chosen for the funeral rite, the funeral is to be celebrated in the church of the parish where the death occurred unless particular law has designated another church.

CAN. 1178 The funeral of a diocesan bish-

§3. Enixe commendat Ecclesia, ut pia consuetudo defunctorum corpora sepeliendi servetur; non tamen prohibet cremationem, nisi ob rationes christianae doctrinae contrarias electa fuerit.

CAPUT I. **De Exequiarum Celebratione**

CAN. 1177 §1. Exequiae pro quolibet fideli defuncto generatim in propriae paroeciae ecclesia celebrari debent.

§2. Fas est autem cuilibet fideli, vel iis quibus fidelis defuncti exequias curare competit, aliam ecclesiam funeris eligere de consensu eius, qui eam regit, et monito defuncti parocho proprio.

§3. Si extra propriam paroeciam mors acciderit, neque cadaver ad eam translatum fuerit, neque aliqua ecclesia funeris legitime electa, exequiae celebrentur in ecclesia paroeciae ubi mors accidit, nisi alia iure particulari designata sit.

CAN. 1178 Exequiae Episcopi dioece-

1176 §3: c. 1203; SCConc Resp., 16 ian. 1920; SCSO Resp., 23 feb. 1926; SCSO Instr. *Cadaverum cremationis*, 19 iun. 1926 (AAS 18 [1926] 282–283); SCSO Instr. *De cadaverum crematione*, 5 iul. 1963 (AAS 56 [1964] 822–823); SCPF Resp., 7 mar. 1967; OEx 15; SCSCD Resp., ian. 1977

1177 §1: cc. 1215, 1216, 1230 §§1–5, 7; SCConc Resol., 21 apr. 1917 (AAS 10 [1918] 138–144); SCConc Resol., 2 iun. 1917 (AAS 10 [1918] 326–331); CI Resp., 16 oct. 1919, 15 (AAS 11 [1919] 479); SCConc Resol., 9 iul. 1921 (AAS 13 [1921] 534–537); SCConc Resol., 9 iun. 1923 (AAS 17 [1925] 508–510); SCConc Resol., 12 ian. 1924 (AAS 16 [1924] 189–190); SCConc Resol., 24 maii et 15 nov. 1930 (AAS 25 [1933] 157); SCConc Resol., 4 iul. 1936 (AAS 29 [1937] 475); SCConc Resol., 9 dec. 1939 (AAS 32 [1940] 75–76); SCConc Resol., 5 iul. 1941 (AAS 34 [1942] 101–103)

1177 §2: cc. 1219–1221, 1223–1229 §§1 et 2; SCConc Resol., 9 iul. 1921 (AAS 13 [1921] 535–537); SCConc Resol., 12 nov. 1927 (AAS 20 [1928] 142–145); SCConc Resol., 15 nov. 1930 (AAS 25 [1933] 155–157); SCConc Resol., 4 iul. 1936 (AAS 29 [1937] 475); SCConc Resol., 9 dec. 1939 (AAS 32 [1940] 75–76); CI Resp., 4 ian. 1941 (AAS 34 [1942] 101–103)

1177 §3: cc. 1216 §2, 1218, 1230 §§1 et 7; SCConc Resol., 21 apr. 1917 (AAS 10 [1918] 138–144); SCConc Resol., 2 iun. 1917 (AAS 10 [1918] 326–331); SCConc Resol., 9 iun. 1923 (AAS 17 [1925] 508–510); SCConc Resol., 9 dec. 1939 (AAS 32 [1940] 75–76)

1178: cc. 1219 §2, 1230 §6; SCConc Resol., 9 dec. 1939 (AAS 32 [1940] 76)

op is to be celebrated in his own cathedral church unless he has chosen another church.

CAN. 1179 The funerals of religious or members of a society of apostolic life are generally to be celebrated in their own church or oratory by the superior if the institute or society is clerical; otherwise by the chaplain.

CAN. 1180 §1. If a parish has its own cemetery, the deceased members of the faithful must be buried in it unless the deceased or those competent to take care of the burial of the deceased have chosen another cemetery legitimately.

§2. Everyone, however, is permitted to choose the cemetery of burial unless prohibited by law.

CAN. 1181 Regarding offerings on the occasion of funeral rites, the prescripts of can. 1264 are to be observed, with the caution, however, that there is to be no favoritism toward persons in funerals and that the poor are not deprived of fitting funerals.

CAN. 1182 When the burial has been completed, a record is to be made in the register of deaths according to the norm of particular law.

CHAPTER II. **Those To Whom Ecclesiastical Funerals Must Be Granted or Denied**

CAN. 1183 §1. When it concerns funerals, catechumens must be counted among the Christian faithful.

---

sani in propria ecclesia cathedrali celebrentur, nisi ipse aliam ecclesiam elegerit.

CAN. 1179 Exequiae religiosorum aut sodalium societatis vitae apostolicae generatim celebrentur in propria ecclesia aut oratorio a Superiore, si institutum aut societas sint clericalia, secus a cappellano.

CAN. 1180 §1. Si paroecia proprium habeat coemeterium, in eo tumulandi sunt fideles defuncti, nisi aliud coemeterium legitime electum fuerit ab ipso defuncto vel ab iis quibus defuncti sepulturam curare competit.

§2. Omnibus autem licet, nisi iure prohibeantur, eligere coemeterium sepulturae.

CAN. 1181 Ad oblationes occasione funerum quod attinet, serventur praescripta can. 1264, cauto tamen ne ulla fiat in exequiis personarum acceptio neve pauperes debitis exequiis priventur.

CAN. 1182 Expleta tumulatione, inscriptio in librum defunctorum fiat ad normam iuris particularis.

CAPUT II. **De Iis Quibus Exequiae Ecclesiasticae Concedendae Sunt aut Denegandae**

CAN. 1183 §1. Ad exequias quod attinet, christifidelibus catechumeni accensendi sunt.

1179: cc. 1221, 1222, 1230 §5; CI Resp. IV, 20 iul. 1929 (AAS 21 [1929] 573); CI Resp. 2, 31 ian. 1942 (AAS 34 [1942] 50)

1180 §1: cc. 1228, 1231; SCConc Resol., 2 iun. 1917 (AAS 10 [1918] 326–331); SCConc Resol., 9 iul. 1921 (AAS 13 [1921] 535–537); SCConc Resol., 12 nov. 1927 (AAS 20 [1928] 142–145); SCConc Resol., 4 iul. 1936 (AAS 29 [1937] 475)

1180 §2: cc. 1223, 1224, 1226–1229; SCConc Resol., 2 iun. 1917 (AAS 10 [1918] 326–331); SCConc Resol., 9 iul. 1921 (AAS 13 [1921] 535–537); SCConc Resol., 12 nov. 1927 (AAS 20 [1928] 142–145)

1181: cc. 1234–1237; SCConc Resol., 9 iul. 1921, (AAS 13 [1921] 535–537); SCConc Resol., 9 iun. 1923 (AAS 17 [1925] 508–510); CI Resp. II, 6 mar. 1927 (AAS 19 [1927] 161); SCConc Resol., 24 maii et 15 nov. 1930 (AAS 25 [1933] 157); SCConc Resol., 5 iul. 1941 (AAS 34 [1942] 101–103); SCConc Resp., 30 iul. 1953; SC 32; OEx 20

1182: c. 1238

1183 §1: c. 1239 §2; OICA 18

§2. The local ordinary can permit children whom the parents intended to baptize but who died before baptism to be given ecclesiastical funerals.

§3. In the prudent judgment of the local ordinary, ecclesiastical funerals can be granted to baptized persons who are enrolled in a non-Catholic Church or ecclesial community unless their intention is evidently to the contrary and provided that their own minister is not available.

CAN. 1184 §1. Unless they gave some signs of repentance before death, the following must be deprived of ecclesiastical funerals:

1° notorious apostates, heretics, and schismatics;

2° those who chose the cremation of their bodies for reasons contrary to Christian faith;

3° other manifest sinners who cannot be granted ecclesiastical funerals without public scandal of the faithful.

§2. If any doubt occurs, the local ordinary is to be consulted, and his judgment must be followed.

CAN. 1185 Any funeral Mass must also be denied a person who is excluded from ecclesiastical funerals.

§2. Ordinarius loci permittere potest ut parvuli, quos parentes baptizare intendebant quique autem ante baptismum mortui sunt, exequiis ecclesiasticis donentur.

§3. Baptizatis alicui Ecclesiae aut communitati ecclesiali non catholicae adscriptis, exequiae ecclesiasticae concedi possunt de prudenti Ordinarii loci iudicio, nisi constet de contraria eorum voluntate et dummodo minister proprius haberi nequeat.

CAN. 1184 §1. Exequiis ecclesiasticis privandi sunt, nisi ante mortem aliqua dederint paenitentiae signa:

1° notorii apostatae, haeretici et schismatici;

2° qui proprii corporis cremationem elegerint ob rationes fidei christianae adversas;

3° alii peccatores manifesti, quibus exequiae ecclesiasticae non sine publico fidelium scandalo concedi possunt.

§2. Occurrente aliquo dubio, consulatur loci Ordinarius, cuius iudicio standum est.

CAN. 1185 Excluso ab ecclesiasticis exequiis deneganda quoque est quaelibet Missa exequialis.

1183 §2: c. 1239 §2; O Ex 82

1183 §3: c. 1240 §1, 1°; SCPF Resp., 31 maii et 29 iul. 1922; SCSO Resp., 15 nov. 1941; SCDF Decr. *Accidit in diversis*, 11 iun. 1976 (AAS 68 [1976] 621–622)

1184 §1, 1°: c. 1240 §1, 1°; SCPF Resp. 2, 31 maii et 29 iul. 1922; SCSO Resp., 15 nov. 1941

1184 §1, 2°: c. 1240 §1, 5°; SCConc Resp., 16 ian. 1920; CI Resp. X, 10 dec. 1925 (AAS 17 [1925] 583); SCSO Resp., 23 feb. 1926; SCSO Instr. *Cadaverum*

cremationis, 19 iun. 1926 (AAS 18 [1926] 282–283); SCSO Instr. *De cadaverum crematione*, 5 iul. 1963 (AAS 56 [1964] 822–823); OEx 15

1184 §1, 3°: c. 1240 §1, 6°; SCDF Decr. *Patres Sacrae*, 20 sep. 1973 (AAS 65 [1975] 500)

1184 §2: c. 1240 §2; SCSO Resp., 15 nov. 1941; SCDF Decr. *Patres Sacrae*, 20 sep. 1973 (AAS 65 [1975] 500)

1185: c. 1241

TITLE IV. **The Veneration of the Saints, Sacred Images, and Relics**

TITULUS IV. **De Cultu Sanctorum, Sacrarum Imaginum et Reliquiarum**

CAN. 1186 To foster the sanctification of the people of God, the Church commends to the special and filial reverence of the Christian faithful the Blessed Mary ever Virgin, Mother of God, whom Christ established as the mother of all people, and promotes the true and authentic veneration of the other saints whose example instructs the Christian faithful and whose intercession sustains them.

CAN. 1187 It is permitted to reverence through public veneration only those servants of God whom the authority of the Church has recorded in the list of the saints or the blessed.

CAN. 1188 The practice of displaying sacred images in churches for the reverence of the faithful is to remain in effect. Nevertheless, they are to be exhibited in moderate number and in suitable order so that the Christian people are not confused nor occasion given for inappropriate devotion.

CAN. 1189 If they are in need of repair, precious images, that is, those distinguished by age, art, or veneration, which are exhibited in churches or oratories for the reverence of the faithful are never to be restored without the

CAN. 1186 Ad sanctificationem populi Dei fovendam, Ecclesia peculiari et filiali christifidelium venerationi commendat Beatam Mariam semper Virginem, Dei Matrem, quam Christus hominum omnium Matrem constituit, atque verum et authenticum promovet cultum aliorum Sanctorum, quorum quidem exemplo christifideles aedificantur et intercessione sustentantur.

CAN. 1187 Cultu publico eos tantum Dei servos venerari licet, qui auctoritate Ecclesiae in album Sanctorum vel Beatorum relati sint.

CAN. 1188 Firma maneat praxis in ecclesiis sacras imagines fidelium venerationi proponendi; attamen moderato numero et congruo ordine exponantur, ne populi christiani admiratio excitetur, neve devotioni minus rectae ansa praebeatur.

CAN. 1189 Imagines pretiosae, idest vetustate, arte, aut cultu praestantes, in ecclesiis vel oratoriis fidelium venerationi expositae, si quando reparatione indigeant, numquam restaurentur sine data scripto li-

---

1186: cc. 1255, 1276, 1278; MD III; Pius PP. XII, Const. Ap. *Munificentissimus Deus*, 1 nov. 1950 (AAS 42 [1950] 753–771); Pius PP. XII, Enc. *Fulgens corona*, 8 sep. 1953 (AAS 45 [1953] 577–592); Pius PP. XII, Enc. *Ad Caeli Reginam*, 11 oct. 1954 (AAS 46 [1954] 625–640); SC 103, 104, 111; LG 49–69; Paulus PP. VI, Enc. *Mense maio*, 29 apr. 1965 (AAS 57 [1965] 353–358); Paulus PP. VI, Enc. *Christi Matri*, 15 sep. 1965 (AAS 58 [1966] 745–749); Paulus PP. VI, Adh. Ap. *Signum magnum*, 13 maii 1967 (AAS 59 [1967] 465–475); Paulus PP. VI, Litt. Ap. *Mysterii paschalis*, 14 feb. 1969, II (AAS 61 [1969] 224–226); SRC Nor-

mae, 21 mar. 1969, cap. II; SCCD Instr. *Calendaria particularia*, 24 iun. 1970 (AAS 62 [1970] 651–663); SCCD Normae, 19 mar. 1973 (AAS 65 [1973] 276–279); Paulus PP. VI, Adh. Ap. *Marialis cultus*, 2 feb. 1974 (AAS 66 [1974] 113–168)

1187: c. 1277

1188: cc. 1276, 1279; MD III: SCSO Instr. *Sacrae artis*, 30 iun. 1952 (AAS 44 [1952] 542–546); SC 111, 125; LG 65, 66; IGMR 278; SCCD Normae, 25 mar. 1973 (AAS 65 [1973] 280–281)

1189: c. 1280; SCpC Litt. circ., 11 apr. 1971 (AAS 63 [1971] 315–317)

written permission of the ordinary; he is to consult experts before he grants permission.

CAN. 1190 §1. It is absolutely forbidden to sell sacred relics.

§2. Relics of great significance and other relics honored with great reverence by the people cannot be alienated validly in any manner or transferred permanently without the permission of the Apostolic See.

§3. The prescript of §2 is valid also for images which are honored in some church with great reverence by the people.

centia ab Ordinario; qui, antequam eam concedat, peritos consulat.

CAN. 1190 §1. Sacras reliquias vendere nefas est.

§2. Insignes reliquiae itemque aliae, quae magna populi veneratione honorantur, nequeunt quoquo modo valide alienari neque perpetuo transferri sine Apostolicae Sedis licentia.

§3. Praescriptum §2 valet etiam pro imaginibus, quae in aliqua ecclesia magna populi veneratione honorantur.

TITLE V. **A Vow and An Oath**

CHAPTER I. **A Vow**

CAN. 1191 §1. A vow, that is, a deliberate and free promise made to God about a possible and better good, must be fulfilled by reason of the virtue of religion.

§2. Unless they are prohibited by law, all who possess suitable use of reason are capable of making a vow.

§3. A vow made out of grave and unjust fear or malice is null by the law itself.

CAN. 1192 §1. A vow is *public* if a legitimate superior accepts it in the name of the Church; otherwise, it is *private*.

§2. A vow is *solemn* if the Church has recognized it as such; otherwise, it is *simple*.

§3. A vow is *personal* if the person making the vow promises an action; *real* if the person

TITULUS V. **De Voto et Iureiurando**

CAPUT I. **De Voto**

CAN. 1191 §1. Votum, idest promissio deliberata ac libera Deo facta de bono possibili et meliore, ex virtute religionis impleri debet.

§2. Nisi iure prohibeantur, omnes congruenti rationis usu pollentes, sunt voti capaces.

§3. Votum metu gravi et iniusto vel dolo emissum ipso iure nullum est.

CAN. 1192 §1. Votum est *publicum*, si nomine Ecclesiae a legitimo Superiore acceptetur; secus *privatum*.

§2. *Sollemne*, si ab Ecclesia uti tale fuerit agnitum; secus *simplex*.

§3. *Personale*, quo actio voventis promittitur; *reale*, quo promittitur res aliqua; *mixt-*

1190 §1: c. 1289 §1
1190 §2: c. 1281
1190 §3: c. 1281 §1; SC 126
1191 §1: c. 1307 §1
1191 §2: c. 1307 §2

1191 §3: c. 1307 §3
1192 §1: c. 1308 §1; PME 119; SC 80; LG 44, 45;
Ordo professionis religiosae, 2 feb. 1970, 2
1192 §2: c. 1308 §2; SCR Rescr., 8 iul. 1974
1192 §3: c. 1308 §4

making the vow promises some thing; *mixed* if it shares the nature of a personal and a real vow.

CAN. 1193 By its nature a vow obliges only the person who makes it.

CAN. 1194 A vow ceases by the lapse of the time designated to fulfill the obligation, by a substantial change of the matter promised, by the absence of a condition on which the vow depends, by the absence of the purpose of the vow, by dispensation, or by commutation.

CAN. 1195 The person who has power over the matter of the vow can suspend the obligation of the vow for as long a time as the fulfillment of the vow brings disadvantage to that person.

CAN. 1196 In addition to the Roman Pontiff, the following can dispense from private vows for a just cause provided that a dispensation does not injure a right acquired by others:

1° the local ordinary and the pastor with regard to all their subjects and even travelers;

2° the superior of a religious institute or society of apostolic life if it is clerical and of pontifical right with regard to members, novices, and persons who live day and night in a house of the institute or society;

3° those to whom the Apostolic See or the local ordinary has delegated the power of dispensing.

CAN. 1197 The person who makes a private vow can commute the work promised by the vow into a better or equal good; however, one who has the power of dispensing according to the norm of can. 1196 can commute it into a lesser good.

um, quod personalis et realis naturam participat.

CAN. 1193 Votum non obligat, ratione sui, nisi emittentem.

CAN. 1194 Cessat votum lapsu temporis ad finiendam obligationem appositi, mutatione substantiali materiae promissae, deficiente condicione a qua votum pendet aut eiusdem causa finali, dispensatione, commutatione.

CAN. 1195 Qui potestatem in voti materiam habet, potest voti obligationem tamdiu suspendere, quamdiu voti adimpletio sibi praeiudicium afferat.

CAN. 1196 Praeter Romanum Pontificem, vota privata possunt iusta de causa dispensare, dummodo dispensatio ne laedat ius aliis quaesitum:

1° loci Ordinarius et parochus, quod attinet ad omnes ipsorum subditos atque etiam peregrinos;

2° Superior instituti religiosi aut societatis vitae apostolicae, si sint clericalia iuris pontificii, quod attinet ad sodales, novitios atque personas, quae diu noctuque in domo instituti aut societatis degunt;

3° ii quibus ab Apostolica Sede vel ab Ordinario loci delegata fuerit dispensandi potestas.

CAN. 1197 Opus voto privato promissum potest in maius vel in aequale bonum ab ipso vovente commutari; in minus vero bonum, ab illo cui potestas est dispensandi ad normam can. 1196.

1193: c. 1310; SCpC Resp., 18 ian. 1936 (AAS 29 [1937] 343–345)
1194: c. 1311
1195: c. 1312
1196, 1°: c. 1313, 1°
1196, 2°: c. 1313, 2°
1196, 3°: c. 1313, 3°
1197: c. 1314

CAN. 1198 Vows made before religious profession are suspended while the person who made the vow remains in the religious institute.

CHAPTER II. An Oath

CAN. 1199 §1. An oath, that is, the invocation of the divine name in witness to the truth, cannot be taken unless in truth, in judgment, and in justice.

§2. An oath which the canons require or permit cannot be taken validly through a proxy.

CAN. 1200 §1. A person who freely swears to do something is bound by a special obligation of religion to fulfill what he or she affirmed by oath.

§2. An oath extorted by malice, force, or grave fear is null by the law itself.

CAN. 1201 §1. A promissory oath follows the nature and conditions of the act to which it is attached.

§2. If an oath is added to an act which directly tends toward the harm of others or toward the disadvantage of the public good or of eternal salvation, then the act is not reinforced by the oath.

CAN. 1202 The obligation arising from a promissory oath ceases:

1° if it is remitted by the person for whose benefit the oath was made;

2° if the matter sworn to is substantially changed or if, after the circumstances have changed, it becomes either evil or entirely indifferent or, finally, impedes a greater good;

CAN. 1198 Vota ante professionem religiosam emissa suspenduntur, donec vovens in instituto religioso permanserit.

CAPUT II. De Iureiurando

CAN. 1199 §1. Iusiurandum, idest invocatio Nominis divini in testem veritatis, praestari nequit, nisi in veritate, in iudicio et in iustitia.

§2. Iusiurandum quod canones exigunt vel admittunt, per procuratorem praestari valide nequit.

CAN. 1200 §1. Qui libere iurat se aliquid facturum, peculiari religionis obligatione tenetur implendi, quod iureiurando firmaverit.

§2. Iusiurandum dolo, vi aut metu gravi extortum, ipso iure nullum est.

CAN. 1201 §1. Iusiurandum promissorium sequitur naturam et condiciones actus cui adicitur.

§2. Si actui directe vergenti in damnum aliorum aut in praeiudicium boni publici vel salutis aeternae iusiurandum adiciatur, nullam exinde actus consequitur firmitatem.

CAN. 1202 Obligatio iureiurando promissorio inducta desinit:

1° si remittatur ab eo in cuius commodum iusiurandum emissum fuerat;

2° si res iurata substantialiter mutetur, aut, mutatis adiunctis, fiat vel mala vel omnino indifferens, vel denique maius bonum impediat;

1198: c. 1315
1199 §1: c. 1316 §1
1199 §2: c. 1316 §2
1200 §1: c. 1317 §1
1200 §2: c. 1317 §2

1201 §1: c. 1318 §1
1201 §2: cc. 1317 §3, 1318 §2
1202, 1°: c. 1319, 1°
1202, 2°: c. 1319, 2°

3° if the purpose or a condition under which the oath may have been taken ceases;

4° by dispensation or commutation, according to the norm of can. 1203.

CAN. 1203 Those who can suspend, dispense, or commute a vow have the same power in the same manner over a promissory oath; but if the dispensation from the oath tends to the disadvantage of others who refuse to remit the obligation of the oath, only the Apostolic See can dispense the oath.

CAN. 1204 An oath must be interpreted strictly according to the law and according to the intention of the person taking the oath or, if that person acts out of malice, according to the intention of the person to whom the oath is made.

3° deficiente causa finali aut condicione sub qua forte iusiurandum datum est;

4° dispensatione, commutatione, ad normam can. 1203.

CAN. 1203 Qui suspendere, dispensare, commutare possunt votum, eandem potestatem eademque ratione habent circa iusiurandum promissorium; sed si iurisiurandi dispensatio vergat in praeiudicium aliorum qui obligationem remittere recusent, una Apostolica Sedes potest iusiurandum dispensare.

CAN. 1204 Iusiurandum stricte est interpretandum secundum ius et secundum intentionem iurantis aut, si hic dolo agat, secundum intentionem illius cui iusiurandum praestatur.

1202, 3°: c. 1319, 3°
1202, 4°: c. 1319, 4°

1203: c. 1320
1204: c. 1321

PART III. SACRED PLACES AND TIMES

PARS III. DE LOCIS ET TEMPORIBUS SACRIS

TITLE I. Sacred Places

TITULUS I. De Locis Sacris

CAN. 1205 Sacred places are those which are designated for divine worship or for the burial of the faithful by a dedication or a blessing which the liturgical books prescribe for this purpose.

CAN. 1206 The dedication of any place belongs to the diocesan bishop and to those equivalent to him by law; they can entrust the function of carrying out a dedication in their territory to any bishop or, in exceptional cases, to a presbyter.

CAN. 1207 Sacred places are blessed by the ordinary; the blessing of churches, however, is reserved to the diocesan bishop. Either of them, moreover, can delegate another priest for this purpose.

CAN. 1208 When the dedication or blessing of a church or the blessing of a cemetery has been completed, a document is to be drawn up, one copy of which is to be kept in the diocesan curia and another in the archive of the church.

CAN. 1209 The dedication or blessing of any place is sufficiently proven by one witness who is above suspicion, provided that no harm is done to anyone.

CAN. 1210 Only those things which serve

CAN. 1205 Loca sacra ea sunt quae divino cultui fideliumve sepulturae deputantur dedicatione vel benedictione, quam liturgici libri ad hoc praescribunt.

CAN. 1206 Dedicatio alicuius loci spectat ad Episcopum dioecesanum et ad eos qui ipsi iure aequiparantur; iidem possunt cuilibet Episcopo vel, in casibus exceptionalibus, presbytero munus committere dedicationem peragendi in suo territorio.

CAN. 1207 Loca sacra benedicuntur ab Ordinario; benedictio tamen ecclesiarum reservatur Episcopo dioecesano; uterque vero potest alium sacerdotem ad hoc delegare.

CAN. 1208 De peracta dedicatione vel benedictione ecclesiae, itemque de benedictione coemeterii redigatur documentum, cuius alterum exemplar in curia dioecesana, alterum in ecclesiae archivo servetur.

CAN. 1209 Dedicatio vel benedictio alicuius loci, modo nemini damnum fiat, satis probatur etiam per unum testem omni exceptione maiorem.

CAN. 1210 In loco sacro ea tantum ad-

1205: c. 1154; IGMR 255, 265; ODE cap. II, 6; cap. IV, 12; cap. V, 1 et 2; cap. VI, 1 et 4

1206: cc. 1155, 1157; CI Resp. I, 29 ian. 1931 (AAS 23 [1931] 110); ODE cap. II, 6; cap. IV, 12

1207: cc. 1156, 1157, 1163; CI Resp. I, 29 ian. 1931 (AAS 23 [1931] 110); ODE cap. V, 2; cap. VI, 4

1208: c. 1158; ODE cap. II, 25
1209: c. 1159 §1
1210: cc. 1164 §2, 1165 §2, 1171, 1178; MD III; SCSO Instr. *Sacrae artis,* 30 iun. 1952 (AAS 44 [1952] 542–546); SRC Instr. *De musica sacra,* 3 sep. 1958, 55 (AAS 50 [1958] 648); SC 124–128; SCCD Instr. *Litur-*

the exercise or promotion of worship, piety, or religion are permitted in a sacred place; anything not consonant with the holiness of the place is forbidden. In an individual case, however, the ordinary can permit other uses which are not contrary to the holiness of the place.

CAN. 1211 Sacred places are violated by gravely injurious actions done in them with scandal to the faithful, actions which, in the judgment of the local ordinary, are so grave and contrary to the holiness of the place that it is not permitted to carry on worship in them until the damage is repaired by a penitential rite according to the norm of the liturgical books.

CAN. 1212 Sacred places lose their dedication or blessing if they have been destroyed in large part, or have been turned over permanently to profane use by decree of the competent ordinary or in fact.

CAN. 1213 The ecclesiastical authority freely exercises its powers and functions in sacred places.

CHAPTER I. Churches

CAN. 1214 By the term church is understood a sacred building designated for divine worship to which the faithful have the right of entry for the exercise, especially the public exercise, of divine worship.

CAN. 1215 §1. No church is to be built without the express written consent of the diocesan bishop.

§2. The diocesan bishop is not to give consent unless, after having heard the presbyteral council and the rectors of the neighboring

mittantur quae cultui, pietati, religioni exercendis vel promovendis inserviunt, ac vetatur quidquid a loci sanctitate absonum sit. Ordinarius vero per modum actus alios usus, sanctitati tamen loci non contrarios, permittere potest.

CAN. 1211 Loca sacra violantur per actiones graviter iniuriosas cum scandalo fidelium ibi positas, quae, de iudicio Ordinarii loci, ita graves et sanctitati loci contrariae sunt ut non liceat in eis cultum exercere, donec ritu paenitentiali ad normam librorum liturgicorum iniuria reparetur.

CAN. 1212 Dedicationem vel benedictionem amittunt loca sacra, si magna ex parte destructa fuerint, vel ad usus profanos permanenter decreto competentis Ordinarii vel de facto reducta.

CAN. 1213 Potestates suas et munera auctoritas ecclesiastica in locis sacris libere exercet.

CAPUT I. De Ecclesiis

CAN. 1214 Ecclesiae nomine intellegitur aedes sacra divino cultui destinata, ad quam fidelibus ius est adeundi ad divinum cultum praesertim publice exercendum.

CAN. 1215 §1. Nulla ecclesia aedificetur sine expresso Episcopi dioecesani consensu scriptis dato.

§2. Episcopus dioecesanus consensum ne praebeat nisi, audito consilio presbyterali et vicinarum ecclesiarum rectoribus, censeat

gicae instaurationes, 5 sep. 1970, 10 (AAS 62 [1970]
694); IGMR 254
    1211: cc. 1172–1177
    1212: c. 1170

1213: cc. 1160, 1179
1214: c. 1161
1215 §1: c. 1162 §1; SAr 544
1215 §2: c. 1162 §§2 et 3; SAr 544

churches, he judges that the new church can serve the good of souls and that the means necessary for building the church and for divine worship will not be lacking.

§3. Although religious institutes have received from the diocesan bishop consent to establish a new house in the diocese or the city, they must also obtain his permission before building a church in a certain and determined place.

CAN. 1216 In the building and repair of churches, the principles and norms of the liturgy and of sacred art are to be observed, after the advice of experts has been taken into account.

CAN. 1217 §1. After construction has been completed properly, a new church is to be dedicated or at least blessed as soon as possible; the laws of the sacred liturgy are to be observed.

§2. Churches, especially cathedrals and parish churches, are to be dedicated by the solemn rite.

CAN. 1218 Each church is to have its own title which cannot be changed after the church has been dedicated.

CAN. 1219 In a church that has legitimately been dedicated or blessed, all acts of divine worship can be performed, without prejudice to parochial rights.

CAN. 1220 §1. All those responsible are to take care that in churches such cleanliness and beauty are preserved as befit a house of God and that whatever is inappropriate to the holiness of the place is excluded.

§2. Ordinary care for preservation and fitting

novam ecclesiam bono animarum inservire posse, et media ad ecclesiae aedificationem et ad cultum divinum necessaria non esse defutura.

§3. Etiam instituta religiosa, licet consensum constituendae novae domus in dioecesi vel civitate ab Episcopo dioecesano rettulerint, antequam tamen ecclesiam in certo ac determinato loco aedificent, eiusdem licentiam obtinere debent.

CAN. 1216 In ecclesiarum aedificatione et refectione, adhibito peritorum consilio, serventur principia et normae liturgiae et artis sacrae.

CAN. 1217 §1. Aedificatione rite peracta, nova ecclesia quam primum dedicetur aut saltem benedicatur, sacrae liturgiae legibus servatis.

§2. Sollemni ritu dedicentur ecclesiae, praesertim cathedrales et paroeciales.

CAN. 1218 Unaquaeque ecclesia suum habeat titulum qui, peracta ecclesiae dedicatione, mutari nequit.

CAN. 1219 In ecclesia legitime dedicata vel benedicta omnes actus cultus divini perfici possunt, salvis iuribus paroecialibus.

CAN. 1220 §1. Curent omnes ad quos res pertinet, ut in ecclesiis illa munditia ac decor serventur, quae domum Dei addeceant, et ab iisdem arceatur quidquid a sanctitate loci absonum sit.

§2. Ad bona sacra et pretiosa tuenda or-

1215 §3: c. 1162 §4

1216: c. 1164 §1; MD IV; SAr 542–546; SC 123–128; IOe 13 c, 90–99; EMys 24, 52–56; IGMR 253, 254, 256–280; CEM 6, 9, 10; ODE cap. II, 3

1217 §1: c. 1165 §§1, 2 et 4, 1166, 1167; IGMR 255; ODE cap. II, III et V

1217 §2: c. 1165 §3; IGMR 255; ODE cap. V, 1

1218: c. 1168; SCCD Normae, 19 mar. 1973 (AAS 65 [1973] 276–279); ODE cap. II, 4

1219: c. 1171

1220 §1: c. 1178; MD IV; SAr 542–546; SC 122, 124; PO 5; EMys 24; IGMR 253; ODE cap. II, 3

1220 §2: cc. 1182 §1, 1184, 1186; SCConc Instr. *In applicatione,* 25 iun. 1930 (AAS 22 [1930] 410–417); SC 126; SCpC Litt. circ., 11 apr. 1971 (AAS 63 [1971] 315–317)

means of security are to be used to protect sacred and precious goods.

CAN. 1221 Entry to a church is to be free and gratuitous during the time of sacred celebrations.

CAN. 1222 §1. If a church cannot be used in any way for divine worship and there is no possibility of repairing it, the diocesan bishop can relegate it to profane but not sordid use.

§2. Where other grave causes suggest that a church no longer be used for divine worship, the diocesan bishop, after having heard the presbyteral council, can relegate it to profane but not sordid use, with the consent of those who legitimately claim rights for themselves in the church and provided that the good of souls suffers no detriment thereby.

CHAPTER II. **Oratories and Private Chapels**

CAN. 1223 By the term oratory is understood a place for divine worship designated by permission of the ordinary for the benefit of some community or group of the faithful who gather in it and to which other members of the faithful can also come with the consent of the competent superior.

CAN. 1224 §1. The ordinary is not to grant the permission required to establish an oratory unless he has first visited the place destined for the oratory personally or through another and has found it properly prepared.

§2. After permission has been given, however, an oratory cannot be converted to profane use without the authority of the same ordinary.

dinaria conservationis cura et opportuna securitatis media adhibeantur.

CAN. 1221 Ingressus in ecclesiam tempore sacrarum celebrationum sit liber et gratuitus.

CAN. 1222 §1. Si qua ecclesia nullo modo ad cultum divinum adhiberi queat et possibilitas non detur eam reficiendi, in usum profanum non sordidum ab Episcopo dioecesano redigi potest.

§2. Ubi aliae graves causae suadeant ut aliqua ecclesia ad divinum cultum amplius non adhibeatur, eam Episcopus dioecesanus, audito consilio presbyterali, in usum profanum non sordidum redigere potest, de consensu eorum qui iura in eadem sibi legitime vindicent, et dummodo animarum bonum nullum inde detrimentum capiat.

CAPUT II. **De Oratoriis et de Sacellis Privatis**

CAN. 1223 Oratorii nomine intelligitur locus divino cultui, in commodum alicuius communitatis vel coetus fidelium eo convenientium de licentia Ordinarii destinatus, ad quem etiam alii fideles de consensu Superioris competentis accedere possunt.

CAN. 1224 §1. Ordinarius licentiam ad constituendum oratorium requisitam ne concedat, nisi prius per se vel per alium locum ad oratorium destinatum visitaverit et decenter instructum reppererit.

§2. Data autem licentia, oratorium ad usus profanos converti nequit sine eiusdem Ordinarii auctoritate.

1221: c. 1181
1222 §1: c. 1187
1222 §2: SCpC Litt. circ., 11 apr. 1971, 6 (AAS 63 [1971] 317)

1223: c. 1188; DPME 90 a, 180
1224 §1: c. 1192 §§1 et 2; DPME 180
1224 §2: c. 1192 §3

CAN. 1225 All sacred celebrations can be performed in legitimately established oratories except those which the law or a prescript of the local ordinary excludes or the liturgical norms prohibit.

CAN. 1226 By the term private chapel is understood a place for divine worship designated by permission of the local ordinary for the benefit of one or more physical persons.

CAN. 1227 Bishops can establish a private chapel for themselves which possesses the same rights as an oratory.

CAN. 1228 Without prejudice to the prescript of can. 1227, the permission of the local ordinary is required for Mass or other sacred celebrations to take place in any private chapel.

CAN. 1229 It is fitting for oratories and private chapels to be blessed according to the rite prescribed in the liturgical books. They must, however, be reserved for divine worship alone and free from all domestic uses.

CHAPTER III. **Shrines**

CAN. 1230 By the term shrine is understood a church or other sacred place to which numerous members of the faithful make pilgrimage for a special reason of piety, with the approval of the local ordinary.

CAN. 1231 For a shrine to be called a national shrine, the conference of bishops must give its approval; for it to be called an international shrine, the approval of the Holy See is required.

CAN. 1232 §1. The local ordinary is competent to approve the statutes of a diocesan

CAN. 1225 In oratoriis legitime constitutis omnes celebrationes sacrae peragi possunt, nisi quae iure aut Ordinarii loci praescripto excipiantur, aut obstent normae liturgicae.

CAN. 1226 Nomine sacelli privati intellegitur locus divino cultui, in commodum unius vel plurium personarum physicarum, de licentia Ordinarii loci destinatus.

CAN. 1227 Episcopi sacellum privatum sibi constituere possunt, quod iisdem iuribus ac oratorium gaudet.

CAN. 1228 Firmo praescripto can. 1227, ad Missam aliasve sacras celebrationes in aliquo sacello privato peragendas requiritur Ordinarii loci licentia.

CAN. 1229 Oratoria et sacella privata benedici convenit secundum ritum in libris liturgicis praescriptum; debent autem esse divino tantum cultui reservata et ab omnibus domesticis usibus libera.

CAPUT III. **De Sanctuariis**

CAN. 1230 Sanctuarii nomine intelleguntur ecclesia vel alius locus sacer ad quos, ob peculiarem pietatis causam, fideles frequentes, approbante Ordinario loci, peregrinantur.

CAN. 1231 Ut sanctuarium dici possit nationale, accedere debet approbatio Episcoporum conferentiae; ut dici possit internationale, requiritur approbatio Sanctae Sedis.

CAN. 1232 §1. Ad approbanda statuta sanctuarii dioecesani, competens est Ordi-

1225: cc. 1191, 1193
1226: cc. 1188 §2, 3°; 1190; SCDS Instr. *Quam plurimum*, 1 oct. 1949, 1–19 (AAS 41 [1949] 493–501)
1227: c. 1189; PM II, 5
1228: cc. 1194, 1195

1229: c. 1196; ODE cap. V, 1
1230: SCConc Decr. *Inter publicas*, 11 feb. 1936 (AAS 28 [1936] 167–168); SCS Resp., 8 feb. 1956
1232: SCC Decr. *Pompeiana Praelatura*, 21 mar. 1942 (AAS 34 [1942] 203–204); PAULUS PP. VI,

shrine; the conference of bishops for the statutes of a national shrine; the Holy See alone for the statutes of an international shrine.

§2. The statutes are to determine especially the purpose, the authority of the rector, and the ownership and administration of goods.

CAN. 1233 Certain privileges can be granted to shrines whenever local circumstances, the large number of pilgrims, and especially the good of the faithful seem to suggest it.

CAN. 1234 §1. At shrines the means of salvation are to be supplied more abundantly to the faithful by the diligent proclamation of the word of God, the suitable promotion of liturgical life especially through the celebration of the Eucharist and of penance, and the cultivation of approved forms of popular piety.

§2. Votive offerings of popular art and piety are to be kept on display in the shrines or nearby places and guarded securely.

CHAPTER IV. **Altars**

CAN. 1235 §1. An altar, or a table upon which the eucharistic sacrifice is celebrated, is called *fixed* if it is so constructed that it adheres to the floor and thus cannot be moved; it is called *movable* if it can be removed.

§2. It is desirable to have a fixed altar in every church, but a fixed or a movable altar in other places designated for sacred celebrations.

narius loci; ad statuta sanctuarii nationalis, Episcoporum conferentia; ad statuta sanctuarii internationalis, sola Sancta Sedes.

§2. In statutis determinentur praesertim finis, auctoritas rectoris, dominium et administratio bonorum.

CAN. 1233 Sanctuariis quaedam privilegia concedi poterunt, quoties locorum circumstantiae, peregrinantium frequentia et praesertim fidelium bonum id suadere videantur.

CAN. 1234 §1. In sanctuariis abundantius fidelibus suppeditentur media salutis, verbum Dei sedulo annuntiando, vitam liturgicam praesertim per Eucharistiae et paenitentiae celebrationem apte fovendo, necnon probatas pietatis popularis formas colendo.

§2. Votiva artis popularis et pietatis documenta in sanctuariis aut locis adiacentibus spectabilia serventur atque secure custodiantur.

CAPUT IV. **De Altaribus**

CAN. 1235 §1. Altare, seu mensa super quam Sacrificium eucharisticum celebratur, *fixum* dicitur, si ita exstruatur ut cum pavimento cohaereat ideoque amoveri nequeat; *mobile* vero, si transferri possit.

§2. Expedit in omni ecclesia altare fixum inesse; ceteris vero in locis, sacris celebrationibus destinatis, altare fixum vel mobile.

Const. *Laurentanae Almae*, 24 iun. 1965 (AAS 58 [1966] 265–268); SCR Resp., 18 iun. 1966; PAULUS PP. VI, m. p. *Inclita toto*, 8 aug. 1969 (AAS 61 [1969] 533–535).

1233: SCConc Facul., 8 feb. 1940; SRC Rescr., 9 feb. 1967 (AAS 59 [1967] 181–182); SCC *Directorium quoad turismum*, 30 apr. 1969, II, B, d

1234 §1: SCConc Decr. *Inter publicas*, 11 feb. 1936 (AAS 28 [1936] 167–168); PAULUS PP. VI, Const. *Lau-*

rentanae Almae, 24 iun. 1965 (AAS 58 [1966] 266); DPME 90 b, 180

1234 §2: SC 124; PAULUS PP. VI, Const. *Laurentanae Almae*, 24 iun. 1965 (AAS 58 [1966] 266); SCpC Litt. circ., 11 apr. 1971, 6 (AAS 63 [1971] 317)

1235 §1: c. 1197 §1; EMys 24; IGMR 259–261, 264; ODE cap. IV, 3, 6

1235 §2: c. 1197 §2; IGMR 262; ODE cap. IV, 6

CAN. 1236 §1. According to the traditional practice of the Church, the table of a fixed altar is to be of stone, and indeed of a single natural stone. Nevertheless, another worthy and
solid material can also be used in the judgment
of the conference of bishops. The supports or
base, however, can be made of any material.

§2. A movable altar can be constructed of
any solid material suitable for liturgical use.

CAN. 1237 §1. Fixed altars must be dedicated, and movable altars must be dedicated or
blessed, according to the rites prescribed in the
liturgical books.

§2. The ancient tradition of placing relics of
martyrs or other saints under a fixed altar is to
be preserved, according to the norms given in
the liturgical books.

CAN. 1238 §1. An altar loses its dedication
or blessing according to the norm of can. 1212.

§2. Altars, whether fixed or movable, do not
lose their dedication or blessing if the church or
other sacred place is relegated to profane uses.

CAN. 1239 §1. An altar, whether fixed or
movable, must be reserved for divine worship
alone, to the absolute exclusion of any profane
use.

§2. A body is not to be buried beneath an altar; otherwise, it is not permitted to celebrate
Mass on the altar.

CAN. 1236 §1. Iuxta traditum Ecclesiae
morem mensa altaris fixi sit lapidea, et quidem ex unico lapide naturali; attamen etiam
alia materia digna et solida, de iudicio Episcoporum conferentiae, adhiberi potest. Stip-
ites vero seu basis ex qualibet materia confici possunt.

§2. Altare mobile ex qualibet materia
solida, usui liturgico congruenti, extrui potest.

CAN. 1237 §1. Altaria fixa dedicanda
sunt, mobilia vero dedicanda aut benedicenda, iuxta ritus in liturgicis libris praescriptos.

§2. Antiqua traditio Martyrum aliorumve
Sanctorum reliquias sub altari fixo condendi
servetur, iuxta normas in libris liturgicis traditas.

CAN. 1238 §1. Altare dedicationem vel
benedictionem amittit ad normam can. 1212.

§2. Per reductionem ecclesiae vel alius
loci sacri ad usus profanos, altaria sive fixa
sive mobilia non amittunt dedicationem vel
benedictionem.

CAN. 1239 §1. Altare tum fixum tum
mobile divino dumtaxat cultui reservandum
est, quolibet profano usu prorsus excluso.

§2. Subtus altare nullum sit reconditum
cadaver; secus Missam super illud celebrare
non licet.

1236 §1: c. 1198 §§1–3; SRC Resp., 17 oct. 1931; SRC
Ind., 7 nov. 1951; IGMR 263; ODE cap. IV, 9

1236 §2: IGMR 264; ODE cap. VI, 2

1237 §1: cc. 1197 §1, 1° et 2°; 1199 §§1–3; SRC *Ritus
... brevior consecrationis altaris immobilis...*,
(AAS 12 [1920] 449); SRC *Ritus... brevior in consecratione altarium...*, (AAS 12 [1920] 450–453); IGMR
265; ODE cap. IV, 2; VI, 1

1237 §2: c. 1198 §4; IGMR 266: ODE cap. II, 5, 14;
cap. IV, 5, 11; cap. VI, 3

1238 §1: c. 1200 §§1–3

1238 §2: c. 1200 §4

1239 §1: c. 1202 §1

1239 §2: c. 1202 §2; SRC Resp., 25 oct. 1933; SRC
Resp., 25 oct. 1942

CHAPTER V. **Cemeteries**

CAN. 1240 §1. Where possible, the Church is to have its own cemeteries or at least areas in civil cemeteries that are designated for the deceased members of the faithful and properly blessed.

§2. If this cannot be achieved, however, then individual graves are to be properly blessed.

CAN. 1241 §1. Parishes and religious institutes can have their own cemetery.

§2. Other juridic persons or families can also have a special cemetery or tomb, to be blessed according to the judgment of the local ordinary.

CAN. 1242 Bodies are not to be buried in churches unless it is a question of burying in their own church the Roman Pontiff, cardinals, or diocesan bishops, including retired ones.

CAN. 1243 Particular law is to establish appropriate norms about the discipline to be observed in cemeteries, especially with regard to protecting and fostering their sacred character.

TITLE II. **Sacred Times**

CAN. 1244 §1. It is only for the supreme ecclesiastical authority to establish, transfer, and suppress feast days and days of penance common to the universal Church, without prejudice to the prescript of can. 1246, §2.

CAPUT V. **De Coemeteriis**

CAN. 1240 §1. Coemeteria Ecclesiae propria, ubi fieri potest, habeantur, vel saltem spatia in coemeteriis civilibus fidelibus defunctis destinata, rite benedicenda.

§2. Si vero hoc obtineri nequeat, toties quoties singuli tumuli rite benedicantur.

CAN. 1241 §1. Paroeciae et instituta religiosa coemeterium proprium habere possunt.

§2. Etiam aliae personae iuridicae vel familiae habere possunt peculiare coemeterium seu sepulcrum, de iudicio Ordinarii loci benedicendum.

CAN. 1242 In ecclesiis cadavera ne sepeliantur, nisi agatur de Romano Pontifice aut Cardinalibus vel Episcopis dioecesanis etiam emeritis in propria ecclesia sepeliendis.

CAN. 1243 Opportunae normae de disciplina in coemeteriis servanda, praesertim ad eorum indolem sacram tuendam et fovendam quod attinet, iure particulari statuantur.

TITULUS II. **De Temporibus Sacris**

CAN. 1244 §1. Dies festos itemque dies paenitentiae, universae Ecclesiae communes, constituere, transferre, abolere, unius est supremae ecclesiasticae auctoritatis, firmo praescripto can. 1246, §2.

1240 §1: cc. 1205 §1, 1206 §§1 et 2; SCSO Resp., 13 feb. 1936; IOe 77

1240 §2: c. 1206 §3

1241 §1: c. 1208 §§1 et 2; SCConc Resol., 12 nov. 1927 (AAS 20 [1928] 142–145)

1241 §2: cc. 1208 §3, 1209; SCConc Resol., 12 nov. 1927 (AAS 20 [1928] 142–145)

1242: c. 1205 §2; CI Resp. 15, 16 oct. 1919 (AAS 11 [1919] 479); SCConc Resol., 10 dec. 1927 (AAS 20 [1928] 261–264)

1243: cc. 1209–1211

1244 §1: cc. 1243, 1244 §1: SCPF Ind., 15 mar. 1951, 3 et 4

§2. Diocesan bishops can decree special feast days or days of penance for their dioceses or places, but only in individual instances.

CAN. 1245 Without prejudice to the right of diocesan bishops mentioned in can. 87, for a just cause and according to the prescripts of the diocesan bishop, a pastor can grant in individual cases a dispensation from the obligation of observing a feast day or a day of penance or can grant a commutation of the obligation into other pious works. A superior of a religious institute or society of apostolic life, if they are clerical and of pontifical right, can also do this in regard to his own subjects and others living in the house day and night.

CHAPTER I. Feast Days

CAN. 1246 §1. Sunday, on which by apostolic tradition the paschal mystery is celebrated, must be observed in the universal Church as the primordial holy day of obligation. The following days must also be observed: the Nativity of our Lord Jesus Christ, the Epiphany, the Ascension, the Body and Blood of Christ, Holy Mary the Mother of God, her Immaculate Conception, her Assumption, Saint Joseph, Saint Peter and Saint Paul the Apostles, and All Saints.

§2. With the prior approval of the Apostolic See, however, the conference of bishops can suppress some of the holy days of obligation or transfer them to a Sunday.

§2. Episcopi dioecesani peculiares suis dioecesibus seu locis dies festos aut dies paenitentiae possunt, per modum tantum actus, indicere.

CAN. 1245 Firmo iure Episcoporum dioecesanorum de quo in can. 87, parochus, iusta de causa et secundum Episcopi dioecesani praescripta, singulis in casibus concedere potest dispensationem ab oligatione servandi diem festum vel diem paenitentiae aut commutationem eiusdem in alia pia opera; idque potest etiam Superior instituti religiosi aut societatis vitae apostolicae, si sint clericalia iuris pontificii, quoad proprios subditos aliosque in domo diu noctuque degentes.

CAPUT I. De Diebus Festis

CAN. 1246 §1. Dies dominica in qua mysterium paschale celebratur, ex apostolica traditione, in universa Ecclesia uti primordialis dies festus de praecepto servanda est. Itemque servari debent dies Nativitatis Domini Nostri Iesu Christi, Epiphaniae, Ascensionis et sanctissimi Corporis et Sanguinis Christi, Sanctae Dei Genetricis Mariae, eiusdem Immaculatae Conceptionis et Assumptionis, sancti Ioseph, sanctorum Petri et Pauli Apostolorum, omnium denique Sanctorum.

§2. Episcoporum conferentia tamen potest, praevia Apostolicae Sedis approbatione, quosdam ex diebus festis de praecepto abolere vel ad diem dominicam transferre.

1244 §2: c. 1244 §2

1245: c. 1245; CI Resp. III, 12 mar. 1929 (AAS 21 [1929] 170); SCNE Ind., 19 dec. 1941 (AAS 33 [1941] 516–517); SCConc Ind., 22 ian. 1946 (AAS 38 [1947] 27); Paen. VII

1246 §1: c. 1247 §1; SC 102, 106–108; EMys 25; PAULUS PP. VI, m. p. *Mysterii paschalis,* 14 feb. 1969,

I (AAS 61 [1969] 223); SRC Normae, 21 mar. 1969, 4, 5; DPME 86; PAULUS PP. VI, Adh. Ap. *Marialis cultus,* 2 feb. 1974, 20 (AAS 66 [1974] 131–132); PAULUS PP. VI, Ep., 4 aug. 1977; SCIC Instr. *In ecclesiasticam futurorum,* 3 iun. 1979, 32

1246 §2: c. 1247 §§2 et 3; SCConc Ind., 18 nov. 1958; SRC Normae, 21 mar. 1969, 7

CAN. 1247 On Sundays and other holy days of obligation, the faithful are obliged to participate in the Mass. Moreover, they are to abstain from those works and affairs which hinder the worship to be rendered to God, the joy proper to the Lord's day, or the suitable relaxation of mind and body.

CAN. 1248 §1. A person who assists at a Mass celebrated anywhere in a Catholic rite either on the feast day itself or in the evening of the preceding day satisfies the obligation of participating in the Mass.

§2. If participation in the eucharistic celebration becomes impossible because of the absence of a sacred minister or for another grave cause, it is strongly recommended that the faithful take part in a liturgy of the word if such a liturgy is celebrated in a parish church or other sacred place according to the prescripts of the diocesan bishop or that they devote themselves to prayer for a suitable time alone, as a family, or, as the occasion permits, in groups of families.

CHAPTER II. **Days of Penance**

CAN. 1249 The divine law binds all the Christian faithful to do penance each in his or her own way. In order for all to be united among themselves by some common observance of penance, however, penitential days are prescribed on which the Christian faithful devote themselves in a special way to prayer, perform works of piety and charity, and deny

CAN. 1247 Die dominica aliisque diebus festis de praecepto fideles obligatione tenentur Missam participandi; abstineant insuper ab illis operibus et negotiis quae cultum Deo reddendum, laetitiam diei Domini propriam, aut debitam mentis ac corporis relaxationem impediant.

CAN. 1248 §1. Praecepto de Missa participanda satisfacit qui Missae assistit ubicumque celebratur ritu catholico vel ipso die festo vel vespere diei praecedentis.

§2. Si deficiente ministro sacro aliave gravi de causa participatio eucharisticae celebrationis impossibilis evadat, valde commendatur ut fideles in liturgia Verbi, si quae sit in ecclesia paroeciali aliove sacro loco, iuxta Episcopi dioecesani praescripta celebrata, partem habeant, aut orationi per debitum tempus personaliter aut in familia vel pro opportunitate in familiarum coetibus vacent.

CAPUT II. **De Diebus Paenitentiae**

CAN. 1249 Omnes christifideles, suo quisque modo, paenitentiam agere ex lege divina tenentur; ut vero cuncti communi quadam paenitentiae observatione inter se coniungantur, dies paenitentiales praescribuntur, in quibus christifideles speciali modo orationi vacent, opera pietatis et caritatis exerceant, se ipsos abnegent, proprias obliga-

---

1247: c. 1248; SCPF Resp., 2 dec. 1922; SCConc Instr. *Saepe numero,* 14 iul. 1941 (AAS 33 [1941] 389–391); SCConc Litt. circ., 25 mar. 1952 (AAS 44 [1952] 232–233); SC 106; SCPF Resp., 14 feb. 1966; EMys 25; DPME 86 a

1248 §1: c. 1249; CI Resp. IV, 25 mar. 1952, (AAS 44 [1952] 497); Sancta Sedes Decl., 7 ian. 1954; SCConc Rescr., 2 iul. 1964; SCConc Rescr., 15 maii

1965; SRC Ep., 25 sep. 1965; SCConc Rescr., 19 oct. 1965; SCConc Rescr., 2 feb. 1966; SCPF Rescr., 14 feb. 1966; SCPF Rescr., 5 maii 1966; EMys 28; SRC Normae, 21 mar. 1969, 3; SCCD Rescr., maii 1967

1248 §2: SC 35, 4; IOe 37; PAULUS PP. VI, All., 26 mar. 1977, 2 (AAS 69 [1977] 465)

1249: cc. 1250, 1251; SC 5; Paen. I–III; SCConc Rescr., 22 apr. 1966; SCConc Rescr., 24 feb. 1967

themselves by fulfilling their own obligations more faithfully and especially by observing fast and abstinence, according to the norm of the following canons.

CAN. 1250 The penitential days and times in the universal Church are every Friday of the whole year and the season of Lent.

CAN. 1251 Abstinence from eating meat or some other food according to the prescripts of the conference of bishops is to be observed on every Friday of the year unless a Friday occurs on a day listed as a solemnity. Abstinence and fasting, however, are to be observed on Ash Wednesday and Good Friday.

CAN. 1252 The law of abstinence binds those who have completed their fourteenth year of age. The law of fasting, however, binds all those who have attained their majority until the beginning of their sixtieth year. Nevertheless, pastors of souls and parents are to take care that minors not bound by the law of fast and abstinence are also educated in a genuine sense of penance.

CAN. 1253 The conference of bishops can determine more precisely the observance of fast and abstinence as well as substitute other forms of penance, especially works of charity and exercises of piety, in whole or in part, for abstinence and fast.

tiones fidelius adimplendo et praesertim ieiunium et abstinentiam, ad normam canonum qui sequuntur, observando.

CAN. 1250 Dies et tempora paenitentialia in universa Ecclesia sunt singulae feriae sextae totius anni et tempus quadragesimae.

CAN. 1251 Abstinentia a carnis comestione vel ab alio cibo iuxta conferentiae Episcoporum praescripta, servetur singulis anni sextis feriis, nisi cum aliquo die inter sollemnitates recensito occurrant; abstinentia vero et ieiunium, feria quarta Cinerum et feria sexta in Passione et Morte Domini Nostri Iesu Christi.

CAN. 1252 Lege abstinentiae tenentur qui decimum quartum aetatis annum expleverint; lege vero ieiunii adstringuntur omnes aetate maiores usque ad annum inceptum sexagesimum. Curent tamen animarum pastores et parentes ut etiam ii qui, ratione minoris aetatis ad legem ieiunii et abstinentiae non tenentur, ad genuinum paenitentiae sensum informentur.

CAN. 1253 Episcoporum conferentia potest pressius determinare observantiam ieiunii et abstinentiae, necnon alias formas paenitentiae, praesertim opera caritatis et exercitationes pietatis, ex toto vel ex parte pro abstinentia et ieiunio substituere.

1250: c. 1252; SCConc Decr. *Pia mater Ecclesia*, 29 ian. 1917 (AAS 9 [1917] 84); CI Resp., 3 ian. 1918; SCConc Decr. *Plures ex America*, 10 nov. 1919 (AAS 11 [1919] 462); SCPF Ind., 27 apr. 1920; SCConc Ind., 20 dec. 1940 (AAS 33 [1941] 24); SCConc Decr. *Cum adversa*, 28 ian. 1949 (AAS 41 [1949] 31–32); SC 110; Paen. III, II §§1 et 2

1251: c. 1252; SCConc Decr. *Pia mater Ecclesia*, 29 ian. 1917 (AAS 9 [1917] 84); CI Resp., 17 feb. 1918 (AAS 10 [1918] 170); SCConc Decr. *Plures ex America*, 10 nov. 1919 (AAS 11 [1919] 462); SCPF Ind., 27 apr. 1920; CI Resp., 24 nov. 1918 (AAS 12 [1920] 576–577);

SCConc Ind., 14 feb. 1922; SCConc Resp., 17 oct. 1923; SCConc Ind., 20 dec. 1940; SCNE Ind., 19 dec. 1941 (AAS 33 [1941] 516–517); SCConc Ind., 22 ian. 1946 (AAS 38 [1946] 27); SCConc Decr. *Cum adversa*, 28 ian. 1949 (AAS 41 [1949] 32–33); SC 110; Paen. III, II §§2 et 3; III §§1 et 2; SRC Normae, 21 mar. 1969, 20

1252: c. 1254; CI Resp., 13 ian. 1918; Paen. III, IV

1253: SCPF Ind., 27 apr. 1920; SCConc Ind., 14 feb. 1922; SCConc Ind., 15 sep. 1931; SCConc Ind., 20 dec. 1940; SCConc Ind., 22 ian. 1946 (AAS 38 [1946] 27); LG 26; Paen. III, VI

BOOK V. THE TEMPORAL GOODS OF THE CHURCH

LIBER V. DE BONIS ECCLESIAE TEMPORALIBUS

CAN. 1254 §1. To pursue its proper purposes, the Catholic Church by innate right is able to acquire, retain, administer, and alienate temporal goods independently from civil power.

§2. The proper purposes are principally: to order divine worship, to care for the decent support of the clergy and other ministers, and to exercise works of the sacred apostolate and of charity, especially toward the needy.

CAN. 1255 The universal Church and the Apostolic See, the particular churches, as well as any other juridic person, public or private, are subjects capable of acquiring, retaining, administering, and alienating temporal goods according to the norm of law.

CAN. 1256 Under the supreme authority of the Roman Pontiff, ownership of goods belongs to that juridic person which has acquired them legitimately.

CAN. 1257 §1. All temporal goods which belong to the universal Church, the Apostolic See, or other public juridic persons in the Church are ecclesiastical goods and are governed by the following canons and their own statutes.

§2. The temporal goods of a private juridic person are governed by its own statutes but not by these canons unless other provision is expressly made.

CAN. 1258 In the following canons, the term Church signifies not only the universal

CAN. 1254 §1. Ecclesia catholica bona temporalia iure nativo, independenter a civili potestate, acquirere, retinere, administrare et alienare valet ad fines sibi proprios prosequendos.

§2. Fines vero proprii praecipue sunt: cultus divinus ordinandus, honesta cleri aliorumque ministrorum sustentatio procuranda, opera sacri apostolatus et caritatis, praesertim erga egenos, exercenda.

CAN. 1255 Ecclesia universa atque Apostolica Sedes, Ecclesiae particulares necnon alia quaevis persona iuridica, sive publica sive privata, subiecta sunt capacia bona temporalia acquirendi, retinendi, administrandi et alienandi ad normam iuris.

CAN. 1256 Dominium bonorum, sub suprema auctoritate Romani Pontificis, ad eam pertinet iuridicam personam, quae eadem bona legitime acquisiverit.

CAN. 1257 §1. Bona temporalia omnia quae ad Ecclesiam universam, Apostolicam Sedem aliasve in Ecclesia personas iuridicas publicas pertinent, sunt bona ecclesiastica et reguntur canonibus qui sequuntur, necnon propriis statutis.

§2. Bona temporalia personae iuridicae privatae reguntur propriis statutis, non autem hisce canonibus, nisi expresse aliud caveatur.

CAN. 1258 In canonibus qui sequuntur nomine Ecclesiae significatur non solum Ec-

---

1254 §1: c. 1495 §1; Benedictus PP. XV, Ep., 12 mar. 1919 (AAS 11 [1919] 123); LG 8; CD 28; DH 13, 14; GS 76

1254 §2: c. 1496; AA 8; PO 17; GS 42; DPME 117; 124–130; 133–137

1255: c. 1495 §2; Concordato fra la Santa Sede e l'Italia, 11 feb. 1929, art. 30 (AAS 21 [1929] 289); CI Resp., 23 iun. 1953; PC 13; DPME 123, 127,133,134

1256: c. 1499 §2

1257 §1: c. 1497 §1

1258: c. 1498

Church or the Apostolic See but also any public juridic person in the Church unless it is otherwise apparent from the context or the nature of the matter.

clesia universa aut Sedes Apostolica, sed etiam quaelibet persona iuridica publica in Ecclesia, nisi ex contextu sermonis vel ex natura rei aliud appareat.

TITLE I. **The Acquisition of Goods**

CAN. 1259 The Church can acquire temporal goods by every just means of natural or positive law permitted to others.

CAN. 1260 The Church has an innate right to require from the Christian faithful those things which are necessary for the purposes proper to it.

CAN. 1261 §1. The Christian faithful are free to give temporal goods for the benefit of the Church.

§2. The diocesan bishop is bound to admonish the faithful of the obligation mentioned in can. 222, §1 and in an appropriate manner to urge its observance.

CAN. 1262 The faithful are to give support to the Church by responding to appeals and according to the norms issued by the conference of bishops.

CAN. 1263 After the diocesan bishop has heard the finance council and the presbyteral council, he has the right to impose a moderate tax for the needs of the diocese upon public juridic persons subject to his governance; this tax is to be proportionate to their income. He is

TITULUS I. **De Acquisitione Bonorum**

CAN. 1259 Ecclesia acquirere bona temporalia potest omnibus iustis modis sive naturalis sive positivi, quibus aliis licet.

CAN. 1260 Ecclesiae nativum ius est exigendi a christifidelibus, quae ad fines sibi proprios sint necessaria.

CAN. 1261 §1. Integrum est christifidelibus bona temporalia in favorem Ecclesiae conferre.

§2. Episcopus dioecesanus fideles de obligatione, de qua in can. 222, §1, monere tenetur et opportuno modo eam urgere.

CAN. 1262 Fideles subsidia Ecclesiae conferant per subventiones rogatas et iuxta normas ab Episcoporum conferentia latas.

CAN. 1263 Ius est Episcopo dioecesano, auditis consilio a rebus oeconomicis et consilio presbyterali, pro dioecesis necessitatibus, personis iuridicis publicis suo regimini subiectis moderatum tributum, earum redditibus proportionatum, imponendi; ceteris

1259: c. 1499 §1; SA Sententia, 12 dec. 1972

1260: c. 1496; CONCORDATO fra Sua Santità il Papa Pio XI e lo Stato Bavarese, 29 mar. 1924, art. 10 §5 (AAS 17 [1925] 50)

1261 §1: c. 1513

1261 §2: CD 6, 17; PO 20; GS 88; DPME 117, 124–129, 133, 134

1263: cc. 1504, 1506; SCConc Resol., 20 aug. 1917 (AAS 9 [1917] 497–502); SCConc Resol., 13 mar. 1920 (AAS 12 [1920] 444–447); SCConc Rescr., 9 ian. 1951; SCConc Rescr., 3 mar. 1955; SCConc Ind., 23 iul. 1955; SCConc Rescr., 15 ian. 1960

permitted only to impose an extraordinary and moderate exaction upon other physical and juridic persons in case of grave necessity and under the same conditions, without prejudice to particular laws and customs which attribute greater rights to him.

CAN. 1264   Unless the law has provided otherwise, it is for a meeting of the bishops of a province:

1° to fix the fees for acts of executive power granting a favor or for the execution of rescripts of the Apostolic See, to be approved by the Apostolic See itself;

2° to set a limit on the offerings on the occasion of the administration of sacraments and sacramentals.

CAN. 1265   §1. Without prejudice to the right of religious mendicants, any private person, whether physical or juridic, is forbidden to beg for alms for any pious or ecclesiastical institute or purpose without the written permission of that person's own ordinary and of the local ordinary.

§2. The conference of bishops can establish norms for begging for alms which all must observe, including those who by their foundation are called and are mendicants.

CAN. 1266   In all churches and oratories which are, in fact, habitually open to the Christian faithful, including those which belong to religious institutes, the local ordinary can order the taking up of a special collection for specific parochial, diocesan, national, or universal projects; this collection must be diligently sent afterwards to the diocesan curia.

personis physicis et iuridicis ipsi licet tantum, in casu gravis necessitatis et sub iisdem condicionibus, extraordinariam et moderatam exactionem imponere, salvis legibus et consuetudinibus particularibus quae eidem potiora iura tribuant.

CAN. 1264   Nisi aliud iure cautum sit, conventus Episcoporum provinciae est:

1° praefinire taxas pro actibus potestatis exsecutivae gratiosae vel pro exsecutione rescriptorum Sedis Apostolicae, ab ipsa Sede Apostolica approbandas;

2° definire oblationes occasione ministrationis sacramentorum et sacramentalium.

CAN. 1265   §1. Salvo iure religiosorum mendicantium, vetatur persona quaevis privata, sive physica sive iuridica, sine proprii Ordinarii et Ordinarii loci licentia, in scriptis data, stipem cogere pro quolibet pio aut ecclesiastico instituto vel fine.

§2. Episcoporum conferentia potest normas de stipe quaeritanda statuere, quae ab omnibus servari debent, iis non exclusis, qui ex institutione mendicantes vocantur et sunt.

CAN. 1266   In omnibus ecclesiis et oratoriis, etiam ad instituta religiosa pertinentibus, quae de facto habitualiter christifidelibus pateant, Ordinarius loci praecipere potest ut specialis stips colligatur pro determinatis inceptis paroecialibus, dioecesanis, nationalibus vel universalibus, ad curiam dioecesanam postea sedulo mittenda.

1264: c. 1507 §1; SCConc Resol., 11 dec. 1920 (AAS 13 [1921] 350–352)

1265 §1: c. 1503; CI Resp., 16 oct. 1919, n. 10 (AAS 11 [1919] 478); SCEO Decr. *Saepenumero Apostolica Sedes*, 7 ian. 1930 (AAS 20 [1930] 108–110); SCEO

Decr. *Sacrae Congregationi*, 20 iul. 1937 (AAS 29 [1937] 342–343)

1265 §2: c. 1624; ES I, 27

1266: c. 1505; ES III, 8

CAN. 1267   §1. Unless the contrary is established, offerings given to superiors or administrators of any ecclesiastical juridic person, even a private one, are presumed given to the juridic person itself.

§2. The offerings mentioned in §1 cannot be refused except for a just cause and, in matters of greater importance if it concerns a public juridic person, with the permission of the ordinary; the permission of the same ordinary is required to accept offerings burdened by a modal obligation or condition, without prejudice to the prescript of can. 1295.

§3. Offerings given by the faithful for a certain purpose can be applied only for that same purpose.

CAN. 1268   The Church recognizes prescription as a means of acquiring temporal goods and freeing oneself from them, according to the norm of cann. 197–199.

CAN. 1269   If sacred objects are privately owned, private persons can acquire them through prescription, but it is not permitted to employ them for profane uses unless they have lost their dedication or blessing; if they belong to a public ecclesiastical juridic person, however, only another public ecclesiastical juridic person can acquire them.

CAN. 1270   If they belong to the Apostolic See, immovable property, precious movable objects, and personal or real rights and actions are prescribed by a period of a hundred years; if they belong to another public ecclesiastical juridic person, they are prescribed by a period of thirty years.

CAN. 1271   By reason of the bond of unity and charity and according to the resources of

CAN. 1267 §1. Nisi contrarium constet, oblationes quae fiunt Superioribus vel administratoribus cuiusvis personae iuridicae ecclesiasticae, etiam privatae, praesumuntur ipsi personae iuridicae factae.

§2. Oblationes, de quibus in §1, repudiari nequeunt nisi iusta de causa et, in rebus maioris momenti, de licentia Ordinarii, si agitur de persona iuridica publica; eiusdem Ordinarii licentia requiritur ut acceptentur quae onere modali vel condicione gravantur, firmo praescripto can. 1295.

§3. Oblationes a fidelibus ad certum finem factae, nonnisi ad eundem finem destinari possunt.

CAN. 1268   Praescriptionem, tamquam acquirendi et se liberandi modum, Ecclesia pro bonis temporalibus recipit, ad normam cann. 197–199.

CAN. 1269   Res sacrae, si in domino privatorum sunt, praescriptione acquiri a privatis personis possunt, sed eas adhibere ad usus profanos non licet, nisi dedicationem vel benedictionem amiserint; si vero ad personam iuridicam ecclesiasticam publicam pertinent, tantum ab alia persona iuridica ecclesiastica publica acquiri possunt.

CAN. 1270   Res immobiles, mobiles pretiosae, iura et actiones sive personales sive reales, quae pertinent ad Sedem Apostolicam, spatio centum annorum praescribuntur; quae ad aliam personam iuridicam publicam ecclesiasticam pertinent, spatio triginta annorum.

CAN. 1271   Episcopi, ratione vinculi unitatis et caritatis, pro suae dioecesis facul-

1267 §1: c. 1536 §1
1267 §2: c. 1536 §2
1268: cc. 1508, 1509

1269: c. 1510
1270: c. 1511
1271: LG 23; DPME 46–49, 138

their dioceses, bishops are to assist in procuring those means which the Apostolic See needs, according to the conditions of the times, so that it is able to offer service properly to the universal Church.

CAN. 1272   In regions where benefices properly so called still exist, it is for the conference of bishops, through appropriate norms agreed to and approved by the Apostolic See, to direct the governance of such benefices in such a way that the income and even, insofar as possible, the endowment itself of the benefices are gradually transferred to the institute mentioned in can. 1274, §1.

tatibus, conferant ad media procuranda, quibus Sedes Apostolica secundum temporum condiciones indiget, ut servitium erga Ecclesiam universam rite praestare valeat.

CAN. 1272   In regionibus ubi beneficia proprie dicta adhuc exsistunt, Episcoporum conferentiae est, opportunis normis cum Apostolica Sede concordatis et ab ea approbatis, huiusmodi beneficiorum regimen moderari, ita ut reditus, immo quatenus possibile sit ipsa dos beneficiorum ad institutum, de quo in can. 1274, §1, paulatim deferatur.

TITLE II. The Administration of Goods

CAN. 1273   By virtue of his primacy of governance, the Roman Pontiff is the supreme administrator and steward of all ecclesiastical goods.

CAN. 1274   §1. Each diocese is to have a special institute which is to collect goods or offerings for the purpose of providing, according to the norm of can. 281, for the support of clerics who offer service for the benefit of the diocese, unless provision is made for them in another way.

§2. Where social provision for the benefit of clergy has not yet been suitably arranged, the conference of bishops is to take care that there is an institute which provides sufficiently for the social security of clerics.

TITULUS II. De Administratione Bonorum

CAN. 1273   Romanus Pontifex, vi primatus regiminis, est omnium bonorum ecclesiasticorum supremus administrator et dispensator.

CAN. 1274   §1. Habeatur in singulis dioecesibus speciale institutum, quod bona vel oblationes colligat eum in finem ut sustentationi clericorum, qui in favorem dioecesis servitium praestant, ad normam can. 281 provideatur, nisi aliter eisdem provisum sit.

§2. Ubi praevidentia socialis in favorem cleri nondum apte ordinata est, curet Episcoporum conferentia ut habeatur institutum, quo securitati sociali clericorum satis provideatur.

1272: CI Resp. 24 nov. 1920 (AAS 12 [1920] 577); CD 28; PO 20, 21; ES I, 8, 18, 21; PAULUS PP. VI, m.p. *Ad hoc usque tempus*, III (AAS 61 [1969] 226–227); CIV Resp., 3 iul. 1969 (AAS 61 [1969] 551)
1273: c. 1518
1274 §1: SCConc Litt. circ., 25 feb. 1950; SCConc

Decl., 17 dec. 1951 (AAS 41 [1952] 44); LG 13, 23; CD 6, 21, 31; PC 13: AG 17, 38; PO 8, 20, 21; ES I, 8, 11, 20: ES III, 8, 19; SDO IV, 19–21; DPME 117, 134–138
1274 §2: SCConc Litt. circ., 1 iul. 1941; SCConc Regolamento della Cassa di Sovvenzioni per il Clero secolare d'Italia, 15 iun. 1943

§3. Insofar as necessary, each diocese is to establish a common fund through which bishops are able to satisfy obligations towards other persons who serve the Church and meet the various needs of the diocese and through which the richer dioceses can also assist the poorer ones.

§4. According to different local circumstances, the purposes mentioned in §§2 and 3 can be obtained more suitably through a federation of diocesan institutes, through a cooperative endeavor, or even through an appropriate association established for various dioceses or for the entire territory of the conference of bishops.

§5. If possible, these institutes are to be established in such a way that they also have recognition in civil law.

CAN. 1275 An aggregate of goods which come from different dioceses is administered according to the norms appropriately agreed upon by the bishops concerned.

CAN. 1276 §1. It is for the ordinary to exercise careful vigilance over the administration of all the goods which belong to public juridic persons subject to him, without prejudice to legitimate titles which attribute more significant rights to him.

§2. With due regard for rights, legitimate customs, and circumstances, ordinaries are to take care of the ordering of the entire matter of the administration of ecclesiastical goods by issuing special instructions within the limits of universal and particular law.

CAN. 1277 The diocesan bishop must hear

§3. In singulis dioecesibus constituatur, quatenus opus sit, massa communis qua valeant Episcopi obligationibus erga alias personas Ecclesiae deservientes satisfacere variisque dioecesis necessitatibus occurrere, quaque etiam dioeceses divitiores possint pauperioribus subvenire.

§4. Pro diversis locorum adiunctis, fines de quibus in §§2 et 3 aptius obtineri possunt per instituta dioecesana inter se foederata, vel per cooperationem aut etiam per convenientem consociationem pro variis dioecesibus, immo et pro toto territorio ipsius Episcoporum conferentiae constitutam.

§5. Haec instituta, si fieri possit, ita constituenda sunt, ut efficaciam quoque in iure civili obtineant.

CAN. 1275 Massa bonorum ex diversis dioecesibus provenientium administratur secundum normas ab Episcopis, quorum interest, opportune concordatas.

CAN. 1276 §1. Ordinarii est sedulo advigilare administrationi omnium bonorum, quae ad personas iuridicas publicas sibi subiectas pertinent, salvis legitimis titulis quibus eidem Ordinario potiora iura tribuantur.

§2. Habita ratione iurium, legitimarum consuetudinum et circumstantiarum, Ordinarii, editis peculiaribus instructionibus intra fines iuris universalis et particularis, universum administrationis bonorum ecclesiasticorum negotium ordinandum curent.

CAN. 1277 Episcopus dioecesanus

1275: DPME 138

1276 §1: c. 1519 §1; SRR Decisio, 28 feb. 1919 (AAS 12 [1920] 85–91)

1276 §2: c. 1519 §2; SCConc Litt. circ., 20 iun. 1929 (AAS 21 [1929] 384–399); SCC Normae, 30 iun. 1934

(AAS 27 [1934] 551–556); SCConc Litt. circ., 24 maii 1939 (AAS 31 [1939] 266–268); SCConc Litt. circ., 10 sep. 1960

1277: c. 1520 §3; AA 10; AG 41; PO 17; ES I, 8

the finance council and college of consultors to place acts of administration which are more important in light of the economic condition of the diocese. In addition to the cases specially expressed in universal law or the charter of a foundation, however, he needs the consent of the finance council and of the college of consultors to place acts of extraordinary administration. It is for the conference of bishops to define which acts are to be considered of extraordinary administration.

CAN. 1278 In addition to the functions mentioned in can. 494, §§3 and 4, the diocesan bishop can entrust to the finance officer the functions mentioned in cann. 1276, §1 and 1279, §2.

CAN. 1279 §1. The administration of ecclesiastical goods pertains to the one who immediately governs the person to which the goods belong unless particular law, statutes, or legitimate custom determine otherwise and without prejudice to the right of the ordinary to intervene in case of negligence by an administrator.

§2. In the administration of the goods of a public juridic person which does not have its own administrators by law, the charter of the foundation, or its own statutes, the ordinary to whom it is subject is to appoint suitable persons for three years; the same persons can be reappointed by the ordinary.

CAN. 1280 Each juridic person is to have its own finance council or at least two counselors who, according to the norm of the statutes, are to assist the administrator in fulfilling his or her function.

CAN. 1281 §1. Without prejudice to the

quod attinet ad actus administrationis ponendos, qui, attento statu oeconomico dioecesis, sunt maioris momenti, consilium a rebus oeconomicis et collegium consultorum audire debet; eiusdem tamen consilii atque etiam collegii consultorum consensu eget, praeterquam in casibus iure universali vel tabulis fundationis specialiter expressis, ad ponendos actus extraordinariae administrationis. Conferentiae autem Episcoporum est definire quinam actus habendi sint extraordinariae administrationis.

CAN. 1278 Praeter munera de quibus in can. 494, §§3 et 4, oeconomo committi possunt ab Episcopo dioecesano munera de quibus in cann. 1276, §1 et 1279, §2.

CAN. 1279 §1. Administratio bonorum ecclesiasticorum ei competit, qui immediate regit personam ad quam eadem bona pertinent, nisi aliud ferant ius particulare, statuta aut legitima consuetudo, et salvo iure Ordinarii interveniendi in casu neglegentiae administratoris.

§2. In administratione bonorum personae iuridicae publicae, quae ex iure vel tabulis fundationis aut propriis statutis suos non habeat administratores, Ordinarius, cui eadem subiecta est, personas idoneas ad triennium assumat; eaedem ab Ordinario iterum nominari possunt.

CAN. 1280 Quaevis persona iuridica suum habeat consilium a rebus oeconomics vel saltem duos consiliarios, qui administratorem, ad normam statutorum, in munere adimplendo adiuvent.

CAN. 1281 §1. Firmis statutorum prae-

1279 §1: c. 1182 §2
1279 §2: c. 1521 §1

1281 §1: c. 1527 §1

prescripts of the statutes, administrators invalidly place acts which exceed the limits and manner of ordinary administration unless they have first obtained a written faculty from the ordinary.

§2. The statutes are to define the acts which exceed the limit and manner of ordinary administration; if the statutes are silent in this regard, however, the diocesan bishop is competent to determine such acts for the persons subject to him, after having heard the finance council.

§3. Unless and to the extent that it is to its own advantage, a juridic person is not bound to answer for acts invalidly placed by its administrators. A juridic person itself, however, will answer for acts illegitimately but validly placed by its administrators, without prejudice to its right of action or recourse against the administrators who have damaged it.

CAN. 1282 All clerics or lay persons who take part in the administration of ecclesiastical goods by a legitimate title are bound to fulfill their functions in the name of the Church according to the norm of law.

CAN. 1283 Before administrators begin their function:

1° they must take an oath before the ordinary or his delegate that they will administer well and faithfully;

2° they are to prepare and sign an accurate and clear inventory of immovable property, movable objects, whether precious or of some cultural value, or other goods, with their description and appraisal; any inventory already done is to be reviewed;

3° one copy of this inventory is to be preserved in the archive of the administration and

scriptis, administratores invalide ponunt actus qui fines modumque ordinariae administrationis excedunt, nisi prius ab Ordinario facultatem scripto datam obtinuerint.

§2. In statutis definiantur actus qui finem et modum ordinariae administrationis excedunt; si vero de hac re sileant statuta, competit Episcopo dioecesano, audito consilio a rebus oeconomicis, huiusmodi actus pro personis sibi subiectis determinare.

§3. Nisi quando et quatenus in rem suam versum sit, persona iuridica non tenetur respondere de actibus ab administratoribus invalide positis; de actibus autem ab administratoribus illegitime sed valide positis respondebit ipsa persona iuridica, salva eius actione seu recursu adversus administratores qui damna eidem intulerint.

CAN. 1282 Omnes, sive clerici sive laici, qui legitimo titulo partes habent in administratione bonorum ecclesiasticorum, munera sua adimplere tenentur nomine Ecclesiae, ad normam iuris.

CAN. 1283 Antequam administratores suum munus ineant:

1° debent se bene et fideliter administraturos coram Ordinario vel eius delegato iureiurando spondere;

2° accuratum ac distinctum inventarium, ab ipsis subscribendum, rerum immobilium, rerum mobilium sive pretiosarum sive utcumque ad bona culturalia pertinentium aliarumve cum descriptione atque aestimatione earundem redigatur, redactumque recognoscatur;

3° huius inventarii alterum exemplar conservetur in tabulario administrationis, al-

---

1281 §3: c. 1527 §2
1282: c. 1521 §2; PO 17

1283: c. 1522

another in the archive of the curia; any change which the patrimony happens to undergo is to be noted in each copy.

CAN. 1284 §1. All administrators are bound to fulfill their function with the diligence of a good householder.

§2. Consequently they must:

1° exercise vigilance so that the goods entrusted to their care are in no way lost or damaged, taking out insurance policies for this purpose insofar as necessary;

2° take care that the ownership of ecclesiastical goods is protected by civilly valid methods;

3° observe the prescripts of both canon and civil law or those imposed by a founder, a donor, or legitimate authority, and especially be on guard so that no damage comes to the Church from the non-observance of civil laws;

4° collect the return of goods and the income accurately and on time, protect what is collected, and use them according to the intention of the founder or legitimate norms;

5° pay at the stated time the interest due on a loan or mortgage and take care that the capital debt itself is repaid in a timely manner;

6° with the consent of the ordinary, invest the money which is left over after expenses and can be usefully set aside for the purposes of the juridic person;

7° keep well organized books of receipts and expenditures;

8° draw up a report of the administration at the end of each year;

9° organize correctly and protect in a suitable and proper archive the documents and records on which the property rights of the Church or

terum in archivo curiae; et in utroque quaelibet immutatio adnotetur, quam patrimonium subire contingat.

CAN. 1284 §1. Omnes administratores diligentia boni patrisfamilias suum munus implere tenentur.

§2. Exinde debent:

1° vigilare ne bona suae curae concredita quoquo modo pereant aut detrimentum capiant, initis in hunc finem, quatenus opus sit, contractibus assecurationis;

2° curare ut proprietas bonorum ecclesiasticorum modis civiliter validis in tuto ponatur;

3° praescripta servare iuris tam canonici quam civilis, aut quae a fundatore vel donatore vel legitima auctoritate imposita sint, ac praesertim cavere ne ex legum civilium inobservantia damnum Ecclesiae obveniat;

4° reditus bonorum ac proventus accurate et iusto tempore exigere exactosque tuto servare et secundum fundatoris mentem aut legitimas normas impendere;

5° foenus vel mutui vel hypothecae causa solvendum, statuto tempore solvere, ipsamque debiti summam capitalem opportune reddendam curare;

6° pecuniam, quae de expensis supersit et utiliter collocari possit, de consensu Ordinarii in fines personae iuridicae occupare;

7° accepti et expensi libros bene ordinatos habere;

8° rationem administrationis singulis exeuntibus annis componere;

9° documenta et instrumenta, quibus Ecclesiae aut instituti iura in bona nituntur, rite ordinare et in archivo convenienti et apto

the institute are based, and deposit authentic copies of them in the archive of the curia when it can be done conveniently.

§3. It is strongly recommended that administrators prepare budgets of incomes and expenditures each year; it is left to particular law, however, to require them and to determine more precisely the ways in which they are to be presented.

CAN. 1285 Within the limits of ordinary administration only, administrators are permitted to make donations for purposes of piety or Christian charity from movable goods which do not belong to the stable patrimony.

CAN. 1286 Administrators of goods:

1° in the employment of workers are to observe meticulously also the civil laws concerning labor and social policy, according to the principles handed on by the Church;

2° are to pay a just and decent wage to employees so that they are able to provide fittingly for their own needs and those of their dependents.

CAN. 1287 §1. Both clerical and lay administrators of any ecclesiastical goods whatever which have not been legitimately exempted from the power of governance of the diocesan bishop are bound by their office to present an annual report to the local ordinary who is to present it for examination by the finance council; any contrary custom is reprobated.

§2. According to norms to be determined by particular law, administrators are to render an account to the faithful concerning the goods offered by the faithful to the Church.

custodire; authentica vero eorum exemplaria, ubi commode fieri potest, in archivo curiae deponere.

§3. Provisiones accepti et expensi, ut ab administratoribus quotannis componantur, enixe commendatur; iuri autem particulari relinquitur eas praecipere et pressius determinare modos quibus exhibendae sint.

CAN. 1285 Intra limites dumtaxat ordinariae administrationis fas est administratoribus de bonis mobilibus, quae ad patrimonium stabile non pertinent, donationes ad fines pietatis aut christianae caritatis facere.

CAN. 1286 Administratores bonorum:

1° in operarum locatione leges etiam civiles, quae ad laborem et vitam socialem attinent, adamussim servent, iuxta principia ab Ecclesia tradita;

2° iis, qui operam ex condicto praestant, iustam et honestam mercedem tribuant, ita ut iidem suis et suorum necessitatibus convenienter providere valeant.

CAN. 1287 §1. Reprobata contraria consuetudine, administratores tam clerici quam laici quorumvis bonorum ecclesiasticorum, quae ab Episcopi dioecesani potestate regiminis non sint legitime subducta, singulis annis officio tenentur rationes Ordinario loci exhibendi, qui eas consilio a rebus oeconomicis examinandas committat.

§2. De bonis, quae a fidelibus Ecclesiae offeruntur, administratores rationes fidelibus reddant iuxta normas iure particulari statuendas.

1285: c. 1535
1286: c. 1524; Pius PP. XI, Enc. *Quadragesimo anno* (AAS 23 [1931] 200–201); Pius PP. XI, Enc. *Divini Redemptoris* (AAS 29 [1937] 92); Pius PP. XII, Radiomessagio per Natale 1942 (AAS 35 [1943] 20;

Pius PP. XII, Discorso, 13 iun. 1943 (AAS 35 [1943] 172; Ioannes PP. XXIII, Enc. *Mater et Magistra* (AAS 53 [1961] 419); AA 22; GS 67
1287 §1: c. 1525 §1; SCRIS Decl., 30 sep. 1972
1287 §2: c. 1525 §2

CAN. 1288 Administrators are neither to initiate nor to contest litigation in a civil forum in the name of a public juridic person unless they have obtained the written permission of their own ordinary.

CAN. 1289 Even if not bound to administration by the title of an ecclesiastical office, administrators cannot relinquish their function on their own initiative; if the Church is harmed from an arbitrary withdrawal, moreover, they are bound to restitution.

CAN. 1288 Administratores litem nomine personae iuridicae publicae ne inchoent neve contestentur in foro civili, nisi licentiam scripto datam Ordinarii proprii obtinuerint.

CAN. 1289 Quamvis ad administrationem non teneantur titulo officii ecclesiastici, administratores munus susceptum arbitratu suo dimittere nequeunt; quod si ex arbitraria dismissione damnum Ecclesiae obveniat, ad restitutionem tenentur.

TITLE III. Contracts and Especially Alienation

TITULUS III. De Contractibus ac Praesertim de Alienatione

CAN. 1290 The general and particular provisions which the civil law in a territory has established for contracts and their disposition are to be observed with the same effects in canon law insofar as the matters are subject to the power of governance of the Church unless the provisions are contrary to divine law or canon law provides otherwise, and without prejudice to the prescript of can. 1547.

CAN. 1291 The permission of the authority competent according to the norm of law is required for the valid alienation of goods which constitute by legitimate designation the stable patrimony of a public juridic person and whose value exceeds the sum defined by law.

CAN. 1292 §1. Without prejudice to the

CAN. 1290 Quae ius civile in territorio statuit de contractibus tam in genere quam in specie et de solutionibus, eadem iure canonico quoad res potestati regiminis Ecclesiae subiectas iisdem cum effectibus serventur, nisi iuri divino contraria sint aut aliud iure canonico caveatur, et firmo praescripto can. 1547.

CAN. 1291 Ad valide alienanda bona, quae personae iuridicae publicae ex legitima assignatione patrimonium stabile constituunt et quorum valor summam iure definitam excedit, requiritur licentia auctoritatis ad normam iuris competentis.

CAN. 1292 §1. Salvo praescripto can.

1288: c. 1526
1289: c. 1528
1290: c. 1529
1291: c. 1530 §1, 3°; SCConc Resol., 17 maii 1919 (AAS 11 [1919] 382–387); SCConc Resol., 12 iul. 1919 (AAS 11 [1919] 416–419); CI Resp., 24 nov. 1920 (AAS 12 [1920] 577); SCConc Litt. circ., 20 iun. 1929, art. 41 (AAS 21 [1929] 384–399); SCIC Decl. (Prot. 427/70/

15), 2 ian. 1974; SCIC-SCRIS Decl. (Prot. 300/74), 7 oct. 1974
1292 §1: c. 1532 §3; SCConc Resol., 17 maii 1919 (AAS 11 [1919] 382–387); SCConc Resol., 12 iul. 1919 (AAS 11 [1919] 416–419); CI Resp., 24 nov. 1920 (AAS 12 [1920] 577); SCConc Resp., 14 ian. 1922 (AAS 14 [1922] 160–161); PM I, 32

prescript of can. 638, §3, when the value of the goods whose alienation is proposed falls within the minimum and maximum amounts to be defined by the conference of bishops for its own region, the competent authority is determined by the statutes of juridic persons if they are not subject to the diocesan bishop; otherwise, the competent authority is the diocesan bishop with the consent of the finance council, the college of consultors, and those concerned. The diocesan bishop himself also needs their consent to alienate the goods of the diocese.

§2. The permission of the Holy See is also required for the valid alienation of goods whose value exceeds the maximum amount, goods given to the Church by vow, or goods precious for artistic or historical reasons.

§3. If the asset to be alienated is divisible, the parts already alienated must be mentioned when seeking permission for the alienation; otherwise the permission is invalid.

§4. Those who by advice or consent must take part in alienating goods are not to offer advice or consent unless they have first been thoroughly informed both of the economic state of the juridic person whose goods are proposed for alienation and of previous alienations.

CAN. 1293 §1. The alienation of goods whose value exceeds the defined minimum amount also requires the following:

1° a just cause, such as urgent necessity, evi-

638, §3, cum valor bonorum, quorum alienatio proponitur, continetur intra summam minimam et summam maximam ab Episcoporum conferentia pro sua cuiusque regione definiendas, auctoritas competens, si agatur de personis iuridicis Episcopo dioecesano non subiectis, propriis determinatur statutis; secus, auctoritas competens est Episcopus dioecesanus cum consensu consilii a rebus oeconomicis et collegii consultorum necnon eorum quorum interest. Eorundem quoque consensu eget ipse Episcopus dioecesanus ad bona dioecesis alienanda.

§2. Si tamen agatur de rebus quarum valor summam maximam excedit, vel de rebus ex voto Ecclesiae donatis, vel de rebus pretiosis artis vel historiae causa, ad validitatem alienationis requiritur insuper licentia Sanctae Sedis.

§3. Si res alienanda sit divisibilis, in petenda licentia pro alienatione exprimi debent partes antea alienatae; secus licentia irrita est.

§4. Ii, qui in alienandis bonis consilio vel consensu partem habere debent, ne praebeant consilium vel consensum nisi prius exacte fuerint edocti tam de statu oeconomico personae iuridicae cuius bona alienanda proponuntur, quam de alienationibus iam peractis.

CAN. 1293 §1. Ad alienanda bona, quorum valor summam minimam definitam excedit, requiritur insuper:

1° iusta causa, veluti urgens necessitas,

1292 §2: c. 1532 §1; SCConc Resol., 12 iul. 1919 (AAS 11 [1919] 416–419); CI Resp. V, 20 iul. 1929 (AAS 21 [1929] 574); SCConc Normae, 24 maii 1939 (AAS 31 [1939] 266–268); SCConc Ep., 1 iul. 1941; SCConc Decr. *Cum mutata nummorum,* 13 iul. 1951 (AAS 43 [1951] 602–603); SCC Notif., 25 iul. 1952; SCC Notif., 18 oct. 1952; SCC Facul., 27 apr. 1953; SCC Notif., 28 iun. 1958; SCpC Litt. circ., 11 apr. 1971 (AAS 63 [1971] 315–316); Sancta Sedes Notif., 1978

1292 §3: c. 1532 §4; SCPF Resp., 10 iul. 1920

1293 §1: c. 1530 §1; SCpC Litt. circ., 11 apr. 1971 (AAS 63 [1971] 315–317)

dent advantage, piety, charity, or some other grave pastoral reason;

2° a written appraisal by experts of the asset to be alienated.

§2. Other precautions prescribed by legitimate authority are also to be observed to avoid harm to the Church.

CAN. 1294 §1. An asset ordinarily must not be alienated for a price less than that indicated in the appraisal.

§2. The money received from the alienation is either to be invested carefully for the advantage of the Church or to be expended prudently according to the purposes of the alienation.

CAN. 1295 The requirements of cann. 1291–1294, to which the statutes of juridic persons must also conform, must be observed not only in alienation but also in any transaction which can worsen the patrimonial condition of a juridic person.

CAN. 1296 Whenever ecclesiastical goods have been alienated without the required canonical formalities but the alienation is valid civilly, it is for the competent authority, after having considered everything thoroughly, to decide whether and what type of action, namely, personal or real, is to be instituted by whom and against whom in order to vindicate the rights of the Church.

CAN. 1297 Attentive to local circumstances, it is for the conference of bishops to establish norms for the leasing of Church goods, especially regarding the permission to be obtained from competent ecclesiastical authority.

CAN. 1298 Unless an asset is of little val-

evidens utilitas, pietas, caritas vel gravis alia ratio pastoralis;

2° aestimatio rei alienandae a peritis scripto facta.

§2. Aliae quoque cautelae a legitima auctoritate praescriptae serventur, ut Ecclesiae damnum vitetur.

CAN. 1294 §1. Res alienari minore pretio ordinarie non debet, quam quod in aestimatione indicatur.

§2. Pecunia ex alienatione percepta vel in commodum Ecclesiae caute collocetur vel, iuxta alienationis fines, prudenter erogetur.

CAN. 1295 Requisita ad normam cann. 1291–1294, quibus etiam statuta personarum iuridicarum conformanda sunt, servari debent non solum in alienatione, sed etiam in quolibet negotio, quo condicio patrimonialis personae iuridicae peior fieri possit.

CAN. 1296 Si quando bona ecclesiastica sine debitis quidem sollemnitatibus canonicis alienata fuerint, sed alienatio sit civiliter valida, auctoritatis competentis est decernere, omnibus mature perpensis, an et qualis actio, personalis scilicet vel realis, a quonam et contra quemnam instituenda sit ad Ecclesiae iura vindicanda.

CAN. 1297 Conferentiae Episcoporum est, attentis locorum adiunctis, normas statuere de bonis Ecclesiae locandis, praesertim de licentia a competenti auctoritate ecclesiastica obtinenda.

CAN. 1298 Nisi res sit minimi momenti,

1293 §2: c. 1530 §2
1294 §1: c. 1531 §1
1294 §2: c. 1531 §3; CI Resp. (Praesidis), 17 feb. 1920; SCConc Decl., 17 dec. 1951 (AAS 44 [1952] 44)
1295: c. 1533; SCConc Normae, 24 maii 1939 (AAS 31 [1939] 266–268)

1296: c. 1534 §1
1297: c. 1541
1298: c. 1540

ue, ecclesiastical goods are not to be sold or leased to the administrators of these goods or to their relatives up to the fourth degree of consanguinity or affinity without the special written permission of competent authority.

bona ecclesiastica propriis administratoribus eorumve propinquis usque ad quartum consanguinitatis vel affinitatis gradum non sunt vendenda aut locanda sine speciali competentis auctoritatis licentia scripto data.

TITLE IV. Pious Wills in General and Pious Foundations

TITULUS IV. De Piis Voluntatibus in Genere et de Piis Fundationibus

CAN. 1299 §1. A person who by natural law and canon law is able freely to dispose of his or her goods can bestow goods for pious causes either through an act *inter vivos* or through an act *mortis causa.*

§2. In dispositions *mortis causa* for the good of the Church, the formalities of civil law are to be observed if possible; if they have been omitted, the heirs must be admonished regarding the obligation, to which they are bound, of fulfilling the intention of the testator.

CAN. 1300 The legitimately accepted wills of the faithful who give or leave their resources for pious causes, whether through an act *inter vivos* or through an act *mortis causa,* are to be fulfilled most diligently even regarding the manner of administration and distribution of goods, without prejudice to the prescript of can. 1301, §3.

CAN. 1301 §1. The ordinary is the executor of all pious wills whether *mortis causa* or *inter vivos.*

§2. By this right, the ordinary can and must exercise vigilance, even through visitation, so

CAN. 1299 §1. Qui ex iure naturae et canonico libere valet de suis bonis statuere, potest ad causas pias, sive per actum inter vivos sive per actum mortis causa, bona relinquere.

§2. In dispositionibus mortis causa in bonum Ecclesiae serventur, si fieri possit, sollemnitates iuris civilis; quae si omissae fuerint, heredes moneri debent de obligatione, qua tenentur, adimplendi testatoris voluntatem.

CAN. 1300 Voluntates fidelium facultates suas in pias causas donantium vel relinquentium, sive per actum inter vivos sive per actum mortis causa, legitime acceptatae, diligentissime impleantur etiam circa modum administrationis et erogationis bonorum, firmo praescripto can. 1301, §3.

CAN. 1301 §1. Ordinarius omnium piarum voluntatum tam mortis causa quam inter vivos exsecutor est.

§2. Hoc ex iure Ordinarius vigilare potest ac debet, etiam per visitationem, ut piae

1299 §1: c. 1513 §1; SCConc Resol., 23 apr. 1927 (AAS 20 [1928] 362–364)
1299 §2: c. 1513 §2; CI Resp., 17 feb. 1930
1300: c. 1514

1301 §1: c. 1515 §1
1301 §2: c. 1515 §2; CI Resp. IV, 25 iul. 1926 (AAS 18 [1926] 393)

that pious wills are fulfilled, and other executors are bound to render him an account after they have performed their function.

§3. Stipulations contrary to this right of an ordinary attached to last wills and testaments are to be considered non-existent.

CAN. 1302 §1. A person who has accepted goods in trust for pious causes either through an act *inter vivos* or by a last will and testament must inform the ordinary of the trust and indicate to him all its movable and immovable goods with the obligations attached to them. If the donor has expressly and entirely prohibited this, however, the person is not to accept the trust.

§2. The ordinary must demand that goods held in trust are safeguarded and also exercise vigilance for the execution of the pious will according to the norm of can. 1301.

§3. When goods held in trust have been entrusted to a member of a religious institute or society of apostolic life and if the goods have also been designated for some place or diocese or for the assistance of their inhabitants or pious causes, the ordinary mentioned in §§1 and 2 is the local ordinary; otherwise, it is the major superior in a clerical institute of pontifical right and in clerical societies of apostolic life of pontifical right or the proper ordinary of the member in other religious institutes.

CAN. 1303 §1. In law, the term pious foundations includes:

1° *autonomous pious foundations,* that is, aggregates of things *(universitates rerum)* destined for the purposes mentioned in can. 114, §2 and erected as a juridic person by competent ecclesiastical authority;

voluntates impleantur, eique ceteri exsecutores, perfuncti munere, reddere rationem tenentur.

§3. Clausulae huic Ordinarii iuri contrariae, ultimis voluntatibus adiectae, tamquam non appositae habeantur.

CAN. 1302 §1. Qui bona ad pias causas sive per actum inter vivos sive ex testamento fiduciarie accepit, debet de sua fiducia Ordinarium certiorem reddere, eique omnia istiusmodi bona mobilia vel immobilia cum oneribus adiunctis indicare; quod si donator id expresse et omnino prohibuerit, fiduciam ne acceptet.

§2. Ordinarius debet exigere ut bona fiduciaria in tuto collocentur, itemque vigilare pro exsecutione piae voluntatis ad normam can. 1301.

§3. Bonis fiduciariis alicui sodali instituti religiosi aut societatis vitae apostolicae commissis, si quidem bona sint attributa loco seu dioecesi eorumve incolis aut piis causis iuvandis, Ordinarius, de quo in §§1 et 2, est loci Ordinarius; secus est Superior maior in instituto clericali iuris pontificii et in clericalibus societatibus vitae apostolicae iuris pontificii, aut Ordinarius eiusdem sodalis proprius in aliis institutis religiosis.

CAN. 1303 §1. Nomine piarum fundationum in iure veniunt:

1° *piae fundationes autonomae,* scilicet universitates rerum ad fines de quibus in can. 114, §2 destinatae et a competenti auctoritate ecclesiastica in personam iuridicam erectae;

1301 §3: c. 1515 §3
1302 §1: c. 1516 §1
1302 §2: c. 1516 §2

1302 §3: c. 1516 §3
1303 §1: c. 1544 §1

2° *non-autonomous pious foundations*, that is, temporal goods given in some way to a public juridic person with the obligation for a long time, to be determined by particular law, of celebrating Masses and performing other specified ecclesiastical functions or of otherwise pursuing the purposes mentioned in can. 114, §2, from the annual revenues.

§2. If the goods of a non-autonomous pious foundation have been entrusted to a juridic person subject to a diocesan bishop, they must be remanded to the institute mentioned in can. 1274, §1 when the time is completed unless some other intention of the founder had been expressly manifested; otherwise, they accrue to the juridic person itself.

CAN. 1304 §1. For a juridic person to be able to accept a foundation validly, the written permission of the ordinary is required. He is not to grant this permission before he has legitimately determined that the juridic person can satisfy both the new obligation to be undertaken and those already undertaken; most especially he is to be on guard so that the revenues completely respond to the attached obligations, according to the practice of each place or region.

§2. Particular law is to define additional conditions for the establishment and acceptance of foundations.

CAN. 1305 Money and movable goods assigned to an endowment are to be deposited immediately in a safe place approved by the ordinary so that the money or value of the movable goods is protected; as soon as possible, these are to be invested cautiously and usefully for the benefit of the foundation, with express and specific mention made of the obligation;

2° *piae fundationes non autonomae*, scilicet bona temporalia alicui personae iuridicae publicae quoquo modo data cum onere in diuturnum tempus, iure particulari determinandum, ex reditibus annuis Missas celebrandi aliasque praefinitas functiones ecclesiasticas peragendi, aut fines de quibus in can. 114, §2 aliter persequendi.

§2. Bona piae fundationis non autonomae, si concredita fuerint personae iuridicae Episcopo dioecesano subiectae, expleto tempore, ad institutum de quo in can. 1274, §1 destinari debent, nisi alia fuerit fundatoris voluntas expresse manifestata; secus ipsi personae iuridicae cedunt.

CAN. 1304 §1. Ut fundatio a persona iuridica valide acceptari possit, requiritur licentia Ordinarii in scriptis data; qui eam ne praebeat, antequam legitime compererit personam iuridicam tum novo oneri suscipiendo, tum iam susceptis satisfacere posse; maximeque caveat ut reditus omnino respondeant oneribus adiunctis, secundum cuiusque loci vel regionis morem.

§2. Ulteriores condiciones ad constitutionem et acceptationem fundationum quod attinet, iure particulari definiantur.

CAN. 1305 Pecunia et bona mobilia, dotationis nomine assignata, statim in loco tuto ab Ordinario approbando deponantur eum in finem, et eadem pecunia vel bonorum mobilium pretium custodiantur et quam primum caute et utiliter secundum prudens eiusdem Ordinarii iudicium, auditis et iis quorum interest et proprio a rebus oeco-

this investment is to be made according to the prudent judgment of the ordinary, after he has heard those concerned and his own finance council.

CAN. 1306   §1. Foundations, even if made orally, are to be put in writing.

§2. One copy of the charter is to be preserved safely in the archive of the curia and another copy in the archive of the juridic person to which the foundation belongs.

CAN. 1307   §1. A list of the obligations incumbent upon pious foundations is to be composed and displayed in an accessible place so that the obligations to be fulfilled are not forgotten; the prescripts of cann. 1300–1302 and 1287 are to be observed.

§2. In addition to the book mentioned in can. 958, §1, another book is to be maintained and kept by the pastor or rector in which the individual obligations, their fulfillment, and the offerings are noted.

CAN. 1308   §1. A reduction of the obligations of Masses, to be made only for a just and necessary cause, is reserved to the Apostolic See, without prejudice to the following prescripts.

§2. If it is expressly provided for in the charters of the foundations, the ordinary is able to reduce the Mass obligations because of diminished revenues.

§3. With regard to Masses independently founded in legacies or in any other way, the diocesan bishop has the power, because of diminished revenues and for as long as the cause

nomicis consilio, collocentur in commodum eiusdem fundationis cum expressa et individua mentione oneris.

CAN. 1306   §1. Fundationes, etiam viva voce factae, scripto consignentur.

§2. Alterum tabularum exemplar in curiae archivo, alterum in archivo personae iuridicae ad quam fundatio spectat, tuto asserventur.

CAN. 1307   §1. Servatis praescriptis cann. 1300–1302 et 1287, onerum ex piis fundationibus incumbentium tabella conficiatur, quae in loco patenti exponatur, ne obligationes adimplendae in oblivionem cadant.

§2. Praeter librum de quo in can. 958, §1, alter liber retineatur et apud parochum vel rectorem servetur, in quo singula onera eorumque adimpletio et eleemosynae adnotentur.

CAN. 1308   §1. Reductio onerum Missarum, ex iusta tantum et necessaria causa facienda, reservatur Sedi Apostolicae, salvis praescriptis quae sequuntur.

§2. Si in tabulis fundationum id expresse caveatur, Ordinarius ob imminutos reditus onera Missarum reducere valet.

§3. Episcopo dioecesano competit potestas reducendi ob deminutionem redituum, quamdiu causa perduret, ad rationem eleemosynae in dioecesi legitime vigentis,

1306 §1: c. 1548 §1
1306 §2: c. 1548 §2
1307 §1: c. 1549 §2
1307 §2: c. 1549 §2
1308 §1: c. 1551 §1; CI Resp. XI, 14 iul. 1922 (AAS 14 [1922] 529); SCConc Resol., 21 maii 1927 (AAS 21 [1929] 116–119); SCConc Decr. *Cum haec Sacra*, 1 aug.

1941; SCConc Decr. *Cum extraordinaria rerum*, 30 iun. 1949 (AAS 41 [1949] 374); PM I, 11, 12; CIV Resp. I, 1 iul. 1971 (AAS 63 [1971] 860); Sec Notif., 29 nov. 1971 (AAS 63 [1971] 841); PAULUS PP. VI, m.p. *Firma in traditione*, 13 iun. 1974 (AAS 66 [1974] 308–311); Sec Normae, 17 iun. 1974

exists, to reduce the obligations to the level of offering legitimately established in the diocese, provided that there is no one obliged to increase the offering who can effectively be made to do so.

§4. The diocesan bishop also has the power to reduce the obligations or legacies of Masses binding an ecclesiastical institute if the revenue has become insufficient to pursue appropriately the proper purpose of the institute.

§5. The supreme moderator of a clerical religious institute of pontifical right possesses the same powers mentioned in §§3 and 4.

CAN. 1309 The authorities mentioned in can. 1308 also have the power to transfer, for an appropriate cause, the obligations of Masses to days, churches, or altars different from those determined in the foundations.

CAN. 1310 §1. The ordinary, only for a just and necessary cause, can reduce, moderate, or commute the wills of the faithful for pious causes if the founder has expressly entrusted this power to him.

§2. If through no fault of the administrators the fulfillment of the imposed obligations has become impossible because of diminished revenues or some other cause, the ordinary can equitably lessen these obligations, after having heard those concerned and his own finance council and with the intention of the founder preserved as much as possible; this does not hold for the reduction of Masses, which is governed by the prescripts of can. 1308.

§3. In other cases, recourse is to be made to the Apostolic See.

Missas legatorum vel quoquo modo fundatas, quae sint per se stantia, dummodo nemo sit qui obligatione teneatur et utiliter cogi possit ad eleemosynae augmentum faciendum.

§4. Eidem competit potestas reducendi onera seu legata Missarum gravantia institutum ecclesiasticum, si reditus insufficientes evaserint ad finem proprium eiusdem instituti congruenter consequendum.

§5. Iisdem potestatibus, de quibus in §§3 et 4, gaudet supremus Moderator instituti religiosi clericalis iuris pontificii.

CAN. 1309 Iisdem auctoritatibus, de quibus in can. 1308, potestas insuper competit transferendi, congrua de causa, onera Missarum in dies, ecclesias vel altaria diversa ab illis, quae in fundationibus sunt statuta.

CAN. 1310 §1. Fidelium voluntatum pro piis causis reductio, moderatio, commutatio, si fundator potestatem hanc Ordinario expresse concesserit, potest ab eodem fieri ex iusta tantum et necessaria causa.

§2. Si exsecutio onerum impositorum, ob imminutos reditus aliamve causam, nulla administratorum culpa, impossibilis evaserit, Ordinarius, auditis iis quorum interest et proprio consilio a rebus oeconomicis atque servata, meliore quo fieri potest modo, fundatoris voluntate, poterit eadem onera aeque imminuere, excepta Missarum reductione, quae praescriptis can. 1308 regitur.

§3. In ceteris casibus recurrendum est ad Sedem Apostolicam.

1309: SA Decisio, 6 apr. 1920 (AAS 12 [1920] 252–259); PAULUS PP. VI, m.p. *Firma in traditione,* III, c, 13 iun. 1974 (AAS 66 [1974] 308–311); Sec Normae, 17 iun. 1974

1310 §1: c. 1517 §1; CI Resp. IX, 14 iul. 1922 (AAS 14 [1922] 529)
1310 §2: c. 1517 §2; PM I, 11, 12

BOOK VI. SANCTIONS IN THE CHURCH

LIBER VI. DE SANCTIONIBUS IN ECCLESIA

PART I. DELICTS AND PENALTIES IN GENERAL

PARS I. DE DELICTIS ET POENIS IN GENERE

TITLE I. The Punishment of Delicts in General

TITULUS I. De Delictorum Punitione Generatim

CAN. 1311 The Church has the innate and proper right to coerce offending members of the Christian faithful with penal sanctions.

CAN. 1312 §1. The following are penal sanctions in the Church:

1° medicinal penalties, or censures, which are listed in cann. 1331–1333;

2° expiatory penalties mentioned in can. 1336.

§2. The law can establish other expiatory penalties which deprive a member of the Christian faithful of some spiritual or temporal good and which are consistent with the supernatural purpose of the Church.

§3. Penal remedies and penances are also used; the former especially to prevent delicts, the latter to substitute for or to increase a penalty.

CAN. 1311 Nativum et proprium Ecclesiae ius est christifideles delinquentes poenalibus sanctionibus coercere.

CAN. 1312 §1. Sanctiones poenales in Ecclesia sunt:

1° poenae medicinales seu censurae, qua in cann. 1331–1333 recensentur;

2° poenae expiatoriae, de quibus in can. 1336.

§2. Lex alias poenas expiatorias constituere potest, quae christifidelem aliquo bono spirituali vel temporali privent et supernaturali Ecclesiae fini sint consentaneae.

§3. Praeterea remedia poenalia et paenitentiae adhibentur, illa quidem praesertim ad delicta praecavenda, hae potius ad poenam substituendam vel augendam.

TITLE II. Penal Law and Penal Precept

TITULUS II. De Lege Poenali ac de Praecepto Poenali

CAN. 1313 §1. If a law is changed after a delict has been committed, the law more favorable to the accused is to be applied.

CAN. 1313 §1. Si post delictum commissum lex mutetur, applicanda est lex reo favorabilior.

1311: c. 2214 §1; LG 8; GS 76; Paulus PP. VI., All., 4 oct. 1969, (AAS 61 [1969] 711); Paulus PP. VI, All., 4 aug. 1976; Princ. 9

1312 §1: S. Augustinus, *De civitate Dei*, 21, 13; cc. 2216, 1° et 2°, 2241, 2286; Pius PP. XII, All., 3 oct. 1953 (AAS 45 [1953] 742–743); Pius PP. XII, All., 5 feb. 1955 (AAS 47 [1955] 81); Pius PP. XII, All., 26 maii 1957

(AAS 49 [1957] 407–408); Paulus PP. VI, All., 4 oct. 1969 (AAS 61 [1969] 711)

1312 §2: c. 2215; LG 9; Princ. 3; Pius PP. XII, All. 5 dec. 1954 (AAS 47 [1955] 67–68); Pius PP. XII, All. 5 feb. 1955 (AAS 47 [1955] 78)

1312 §3: cc. 2216, 3°, 2223 §3, 3°, 2307, 2312

1313 §1: cc. 19, 2219 §1; 2226 §2

§2. If a later law abolishes a law or at least the penalty, the penalty immediately ceases.

CAN. 1314   Generally, a penalty is *ferendae sententiae,* so that it does not bind the guilty party until after it has been imposed; if the law or precept expressly establishes it, however, a penalty is *latae sententiae,* so that it is incurred ipso facto when the delict is committed.

CAN. 1315   §1. A person who has legislative power can also issue penal laws; within the limits of his competence by reason of territory or of persons, moreover, he can by his own laws also strengthen with an appropriate penalty a divine law or an ecclesiastical law issued by a higher authority.

§2. The law itself can determine a penalty, or its determination can be left to the prudent appraisal of a judge.

§3. Particular law also can add other penalties to those established by universal law for some delict; however, this is not to be done except for very grave necessity. If universal law threatens an indeterminate or facultative penalty, particular law can also establish a determinate or obligatory one in its place.

CAN. 1316   Insofar as possible, diocesan bishops are to take care that if penal laws must be issued, they are uniform in the same city or region.

CAN. 1317   Penalties are to be established only insofar as they are truly necessary to provide more suitably for ecclesiastical discipline. Particular law, however, cannot establish a penalty of dismissal from the clerical state.

CAN. 1318   A legislator is not to threaten

§2. Quod si lex posterior tollat legem vel saltem poenam, haec statim cessat.

CAN. 1314   Poena plerumque est ferendae sententiae, ita ut reum non teneat, nisi postquam irrogata sit; est autem latae sententiae, ita ut in eam incurratur ipso facto commissi delicti, si lex vel praeceptum id expresse statuat.

CAN. 1315   §1. Qui legislativam habet potestatem, potest etiam poenales leges ferre; potest autem suis legibus etiam legem divinam vel legem ecclesiasticam, a superiore auctoritate latam, congrua poena munire, servatis suae competentiae limitibus ratione territorii vel personarum.

§2. Lex ipsa potest poenam determinare vel prudenti iudicis aestimatione determinandam relinquere.

§3. Lex particularis potest etiam poenis universali lege constitutis in aliquod delictum alias addere; id autem ne faciat, nisi ex gravissima necessitate. Quod si lex universalis indeterminatam vel facultativam poenam comminetur, lex particularis potest etiam in illius locum poenam determinatam vel obligatoriam constituere.

CAN. 1316   Curent Episcopi dioecesani ut, quatenus fieri potest, in eadem civitate vel regione uniformes ferantur, si quae ferendae sint, poenales leges.

CAN. 1317   Poenae eatenus constituantur, quatenus vere necessariae sint ad aptius providendum ecclesiasticae disciplinae. Dimissio autem e statu clericali lege particulari constitui nequit.

CAN. 1318   Latae sententiae poenas ne

1313 §2: c. 2226 §3
1314: c. 2217 §1, 2° et §2; PIUS PP. XII, All., 5 dec. 1954 (AAS 47 [1955] 64); Princ. 9
1315 §1: cc. 2220 §1; 2221
1315 §2: c. 2217 §1, 1°

1315 §3: c. 2221
1316: LG 27; CD 36, 37
1317: cc. 2214 §2, 2303 §3, 2305 §2; LG 27
1318: c. 2241 §1; Princ. 9

latae sententiae penalties except possibly for certain singularly malicious delicts which either can result in graver scandal or cannot be punished effectively by *ferendae sententiae* penalties; he is not, however, to establish censures, especially excommunication, except with the greatest moderation and only for graver delicts.

CAN. 1319 §1. Insofar as a person can impose precepts in the external forum in virtue of the power of governance, the person can also threaten determinate penalties by precept, except perpetual expiatory penalties.

§2. A penal precept is not to be issued unless the matter has been considered thoroughly and those things established in cann. 1317 and 1318 about particular laws have been observed.

CAN. 1320 The local ordinary can coerce religious with penalties in all those matters in which they are subject to him.

comminetur legislator, nisi forte in singularia quaedam delicta dolosa, quae vel graviori esse possint scandalo vel efficaciter puniri poenis ferendae sententiae non possint; censuras autem, praesertim excommunicationem, ne constituat, nisi maxima cum moderatione et in sola delicta graviora.

CAN. 1319 §1. Quatenus quis potest vi potestatis regiminis in foro externo praecepta imponere, eatenus potest etiam poenas determinatas, exceptis expiatoriis perpetuis, per praeceptum comminari.

§2. Praeceptum poenale ne feratur, nisi re mature perpensa, et iis servatis, quae in cann. 1317 et 1318 de legibus particularibus statuuntur.

CAN. 1320 In omnibus in quibus religiosi subsunt Ordinario loci, possunt ab eodem poenis coerceri.

TITLE III. The Subject Liable to Penal Sanctions

TITULUS III. De Subiecto Poenalibus Sanctionibus Obnoxio

CAN. 1321 §1. No one is punished unless the external violation of a law or precept, committed by the person, is gravely imputable by reason of malice or negligence.

§2. A penalty established by a law or precept binds the person who has deliberately violated the law or precept; however, a person who violated a law or precept by omitting necessary diligence is not punished unless the law or precept provides otherwise.

CAN. 1321 §1. Nemo punitur, nisi externa legis vel praecepti violatio, ab eo commissa, sit graviter imputabilis ex dolo vel ex culpa.

§2. Poena lege vel praecepto statuta is tenetur, qui legem vel praeceptum deliberate violavit; qui vero id egit ex omissione debitae diligentiae, non punitur, nisi lex vel praeceptum aliter caveat.

1319: c. 2220 §1

1320: cc. 619, 631; Pius PP. XII, All., 8 dec. 1950, I (AAS 43 [1951] 28); CD 35; ES I, 25; MR 44

1321 §1: cc. 2195 §1, 2199, 2200 §1, 2218 §2, 2228; Pius PP. XII, All., 3 oct. 1953 (AAS 45 [1953] 737, 741); Pius PP. XII, All., 5 dec. 1954 (AAS 47 [1955] 62);

Pius PP. XII, All., 26 maii 1957 (AAS 49 [1957] 406)

1321 §2: cc. 2199, 2200 §1, 2203 §1, 2226 §1, 2228; Pius PP. XII, All., 3 oct. 1953 (AAS 45 [1953] 741–743); Pius PP. XII, All., 5 dec. 1954 (AAS 47 [1955] 62); Pius PP. XII, All., 26 maii 1957 (AAS 49 [1957] 406)

§3. When an external violation has occurred, imputability is presumed unless it is otherwise apparent.

CAN. 1322 Those who habitually lack the use of reason are considered to be incapable of a delict, even if they violated a law or precept while seemingly sane.

CAN. 1323 The following are not subject to a penalty when they have violated a law or precept:

1° a person who has not yet completed the sixteenth year of age;

2° a person who without negligence was ignorant that he or she violated a law or precept; inadvertence and error are equivalent to ignorance;

3° a person who acted due to physical force or a chance occurrence which the person could not foresee or, if foreseen, avoid;

4° a person who acted coerced by grave fear, even if only relatively grave, or due to necessity or grave inconvenience unless the act is intrinsically evil or tends to the harm of souls;

5° a person who acted with due moderation against an unjust aggressor for the sake of legitimate self-defense or defense of another;

6° a person who lacked the use of reason, without prejudice to the prescripts of cann. 1324, §1, n. 2 and 1325;

7° a person who without negligence thought that one of the circumstances mentioned in nn. 4 or 5 was present.

CAN. 1324 §1. The perpetrator of a violation is not exempt from a penalty, but the

§3. Posita externa violatione, imputabilitas praesumitur, nisi aliud appareat.

CAN. 1322 Qui habitualiter rationis usu carent, etsi legem vel praeceptum violaverint dum sani videbantur, delicti incapaces habentur.

CAN. 1323 Nulli poenae est obnoxius qui, cum legem vel praeceptum violavit:

1° sextum decimum aetatis annum nondum explevit;

2° sine culpa ignoravit se legem vel praeceptum violare; ignorantiae autem inadvertentia et error aequiparantur;

3° egit ex vi physica vel ex casu fortuito, quem praevidere vel cui praeviso occurrere non potuit;

4° metu gravi, quamvis relative tantum, coactus egit, aut ex necessitate vel gravi incommodo, nisi tamen actus sit intrinsece malus aut vergat in animarum damnum;

5° legitimae tutelae causa contra iniustum sui vel alterius aggressorem egit, debitum servans moderamen;

6° rationis usu carebat, firmis praescriptis cann. 1324, §1, n. 2 et 1325;

7° sine culpa putavit aliquam adesse ex circumstantiis, de quibus in nn. 4 vel 5.

CAN. 1324 §1. Violationis auctor non eximitur a poena, sed poena lege vel prae-

1321 §3: c. 2200 §2; Pius PP. XII, All., 3 oct. 1953 (AAS 45 [1953] 741)

1322: c. 2201 §2; Pius PP. XII, All., 5 dec. 1954 (AAS 47 [1955] 61)

1323: cc. 2201 §1, 2202, 2203 §2, 2204, 2205 §§1–4, 2230; CI Resp., 30 dec. 1937 (AAS 30 [1938] 73); Pius

PP. XII, All., 3 oct. 1953 (AAS 45 [1953] 737); Pius PP. XII, All., 5 dec. 1954 (AAS 47 [1955] 61); Pius PP. XII, All., 26 maii 1957 (AAS 49 [1957] 405)

1324 §1: cc. 2199, 2201 §§3 et 4, 2202 §2, 2204, 2205 §§2 et 4, 2206, 2218 §1, 2229 §2 et §3, 2° et 3°, 2230; CI Resp., 30 dec. 1937 (AAS 30 [1938] 73); Pius PP. XII,

penalty established by law or precept must be tempered or a penance employed in its place if the delict was committed:

1° by a person who had only the imperfect use of reason;

2° by a person who lacked the use of reason because of drunkenness or another similar culpable disturbance of mind;

3° from grave heat of passion which did not precede and hinder all deliberation of mind and consent of will and provided that the passion itself had not been stimulated or fostered voluntarily;

4° by a minor who has completed the age of sixteen years;

5° by a person who was coerced by grave fear, even if only relatively grave, or due to necessity or grave inconvenience if the delict is intrinsically evil or tends to the harm of souls;

6° by a person who acted without due moderation against an unjust aggressor for the sake of legitimate self-defense or defense of another;

7° against someone who gravely and unjustly provokes the person;

8° by a person who thought in culpable error that one of the circumstances mentioned in can. 1323, nn. 4 or 5 was present;

9° by a person who without negligence did not know that a penalty was attached to a law or precept;

10° by a person who acted without full imputability provided that the imputability was grave.

§2. A judge can act in the same manner if another circumstance is present which diminishes the gravity of a delict.

cepto statuta temperari debet vel in eius locum paenitentia adhiberi, si delictum patratum sit:

1° ab eo, qui rationis usum imperfectum tantum habuerit;

2° ab eo qui rationis usu carebat propter ebrietatem aliamve similem mentis perturbationem, quae culpabilis fuerit;

3° ex gravi passionis aestu, qui non omnem tamen mentis deliberationem et voluntatis consensum praecesserit et impedierit, et dummodo passio ipsa ne fuerit voluntarie excitata vel nutrita;

4° a minore, qui aetatem sedecim annorum explevit;

5° ab eo, qui metu gravi, quamvis relative tantum, coactus est, aut ex necessitate vel gravi incommodo, si delictum sit intrinsece malum vel in animarum damnum vergat;

6° ab eo, qui legitimae tutelae causa contra iniustum sui vel alterius aggressorem egit, nec tamen debitum servavit moderamen;

7° adversus aliquem graviter et iniuste provocantem;

8° ab eo, qui per errorem, ex sua tamen culpa, putavit aliquam adesse ex circumstantiis, de quibus in can. 1323, nn. 4 vel 5;

9° ab eo, qui sine culpa ignoravit poenam legi vel praecepto esse adnexam;

10° ab eo, qui egit sine plena imputabilitate, dummodo haec gravis permanserit.

§2. Idem potest iudex facere, si qua alia adsit circumstantia, quae delicti gravitatem deminuat.

All., 3 oct. 1953 (AAS 45 [1953] 737); Pius PP. XII, All., 5 dec. 1954 (AAS 47 [1955] 61); Pius PP. XII, All., 26 maii 1957 (Aas 49 [1957] 405)

1324 §2: c. 2223 §3, 3°; Pius PP. XII, All., 3 oct. 1953 (AAS 45 [1953] 737); Pius PP. XII, All., 5 dec. 1954 (AAS 47 [1955] 61); Pius PP. XII, All., 26 maii 1957 (AAS 49 [1957] 405)

§3. In the circumstances mentioned in §1, the accused is not bound by a *latae sententiae* penalty.

CAN. 1325 Crass, supine, or affected ignorance can never be considered in applying the prescripts of cann. 1323 and 1324; likewise drunkenness or other disturbances of mind cannot be considered if they are sought deliberately in order to commit or excuse a delict, nor can passion which is voluntarily stimulated or fostered.

CAN. 1326 §1. A judge can punish the following more gravely than the law or precept has established:

1° a person who after a condemnation or after the declaration of a penalty continues so to offend that from the circumstances the obstinate ill will of the person can prudently be inferred;

2° a person who has been established in some dignity or who has abused a position of authority or office in order to commit the delict;

3° an accused person who, when a penalty has been established against a delict based on negligence, foresaw the event and nonetheless omitted precautions to avoid it, which any diligent person would have employed.

§2. If the penalty established in the cases mentioned in §1 is *latae sententiae*, another penalty or a penance can be added.

CAN. 1327 Particular law can establish other exempting, mitigating, or aggravating circumstances besides the cases in cann. 1323–1326, either by general norm or for individual delicts. Likewise, circumstances can be established in a precept which exempt from, mitigate, or increase a penalty established by the precept.

CAN. 1328 §1. A person who has done or

§3. In circumstantiis, de quibus in §1, reus poena latae sententiae non tenetur.

CAN. 1325 Ignorantia crassa vel supina vel affectata numquam considerari potest in applicandis praescriptis cann. 1323 et 1324; item ebrietas aliaeve mentis perturbationes, si sint de industria ad delictum patrandum vel excusandum quaesitae, et passio, quae voluntarie excitata vel nutrita sit.

CAN. 1326 §1. Iudex gravius punire potest quam lex vel praeceptum statuit:

1° eum, qui post condemnationem vel poenae declarationem ita delinquere pergit, ut ex adiunctis prudenter eius pertinacia in mala voluntate conici possit;

2° eum, qui in dignitate aliqua constitutus est, vel qui auctoritate aut officio abusus est ad delictum patrandum;

3° reum, qui, cum poena in delictum culposum constituta sit, eventum praevidit et nihilominus cautiones ad eum vitandum omisit, quas diligens quilibet adhibuisset.

§2. In casibus, de quibus in §1, si poena constituta sit latae sententiae, alia poena addi potest vel paenitentia.

CAN. 1327 Lex particularis potest alias circumstantias eximentes, attenuantes vel aggravantes, praeter casus in cann. 1323–1326, statuere, sive generali norma, sive pro singulis delictis. Item in praecepto possunt circumstantiae statui, quae a poena praecepto constituta eximant, vel eam attenuent vel aggravent.

CAN. 1328 §1. Qui aliquid ad delictum

omitted something in order to commit a delict and yet, contrary to his or her intent, did not commit the delict is not bound by the penalty established for a completed delict unless the law or precept provides otherwise.

§2. If the acts or omissions are by their nature conducive to the execution of the delict, however, their perpetrator can be subjected to a penance or penal remedy unless the perpetrator voluntarily ceased from carrying out the delict which had been initiated. If scandal or some other grave damage or danger resulted, however, the perpetrator, even if he or she voluntarily desisted, can be punished with a just penalty, although one lesser than that established for a completed delict.

CAN. 1329 §1. If *ferendae sententiae* penalties are established for the principal perpetrator, those who conspire together to commit a delict and are not expressly named in a law or precept are subject to the same penalties or to others of the same or lesser gravity.

§2. Accomplices who are not named in a law or precept incur a *latae sententiae* penalty attached to a delict if without their assistance the delict would not have been committed, and the penalty is of such a nature that it can affect them; otherwise, they can be punished by *ferendae sententiae* penalties.

CAN. 1330 A delict which consists in a declaration or in another manifestation of will, doctrine, or knowledge must not be considered completed if no one perceives the declaration or manifestation.

patrandum egit vel omisit, nec tamen, praeter suam voluntatem, delictum consummavit, non tenetur poena in delictum consummatum statuta, nisi lex vel praeceptum aliter caveat.

§2. Quod si actus vel omissiones natura sua ad delicti exsecutionem conducant, auctor potest paenitentiae vel remedio poenali subici, nisi sponte ab incepta delicti exsecutione destiterit. Si autem scandalum aliudve grave damnum vel periculum evenerit, auctor, etsi sponte destiterit, iusta potest poena puniri, leviore tamen quam quae in delictum consummatum constituta est.

CAN. 1329 §1. Qui communi delinquendi consilio in delictum concurrunt, neque in lege vel praecepto expresse nominantur, si poenae ferendae sententiae in auctorem principalem constitutae sint, iisdem poenis subiciuntur vel aliis eiusdem vel minoris gravitatis.

§2. In poenam latae sententiae delicto adnexam incurrunt complices, qui in lege vel praecepto non nominantur, si sine eorum opera delictum patratum non esset, et poena sit talis naturae, ut ipsos afficere possit; secus poenis ferendae sententiae puniri possunt.

CAN. 1330 Delictum quod in declaratione consistat vel in alia voluntatis vel doctrinae vel scientiae manifestatione, tamquam non consummatum censendum est, si nemo eam declarationem vel manifestationem percipiat.

1328 §2: cc. 2212 §2, 2213 §§2 et 3, 2235
1329 §1: cc. 2209, 2211, 2230, 2231

1329 §2: cc. 2209 §§3 et 4, 2211, 2230, 2231

TITLE IV. Penalties and Other Punishments

CHAPTER I. Censures

CAN. 1331 §1. An excommunicated person is forbidden:

1° to have any ministerial participation in celebrating the sacrifice of the Eucharist or any other ceremonies of worship whatsoever;

2° to celebrate the sacraments or sacramentals and to receive the sacraments;

3° to exercise any ecclesiastical offices, ministries, or functions whatsoever or to place acts of governance.

§2. If the excommunication has been imposed or declared, the offender:

1° who wishes to act against the prescript of §1, n. 1 must be prevented from doing so, or the liturgical action must be stopped unless a grave cause precludes this;

2° invalidly places acts of governance which are illicit according to the norm of §1, n. 3;

3° is forbidden to benefit from privileges previously granted;

4° cannot acquire validly a dignity, office, or other function in the Church;

5° does not appropriate the benefits of a dignity, office, any function, or pension, which the offender has in the Church.

CAN. 1332 The prohibitions mentioned in can. 1331, §1, nn. 1 and 2 bind an interdicted person. If the interdict has been imposed or declared, however, the prescript of can. 1331, §2, n. 1 must be observed.

CAN. 1333 §1. Suspension, which can affect only clerics, prohibits:

TITULUS IV. De Poenis Aliisque Punitionibus

CAPUT I. De Censuris

CAN. 1331 §1. Excommunicatus vetatur:

1° ullam habere participationem ministerialem in celebrandis Eucharistiae Sacrificio vel quibuslibet aliis cultus caerimoniis;

2° sacramenta vel sacramentalia celebrare et sacramenta recipere;

3° ecclesiasticis officiis vel ministeriis vel muneribus quibuslibet fungi vel actus regiminis ponere.

§2. Quod si excommunicatio irrogata vel declarata sit, reus:

1° si agere velit contra praescriptum §1, n. 1, est arcendus aut a liturgica actione est cessandum, nisi gravis obstet causa;

2° invalide ponit actus regiminis, qui ad normam §1, n. 3, sunt illiciti;

3° vetatur frui privilegiis antea concessis;

4° nequit valide consequi dignitatem, officium aliudve munus in Ecclesia;

5° fructus dignitatis, officii, muneris cuiuslibet, pensionis, quam quidem habeat in Ecclesia, non facit suos.

CAN. 1332 Interdictus tenetur vetitis, de quibus in can. 1331, §1, nn. 1 et 2; quod si interdictum irrogatum vel declaratum sit, praescriptum can. 1331, §2, n. 1 servandum est.

CAN. 1333 §1. Suspensio, quae clericos tantum afficere potest, vetat:

1331 §1: cc. 2255–2267
1331 §2: cc. 2259 §2, 2260, 2261 §3, 2263, 2264, 2265 §2, 2266, 2267

1332: cc. 2255, 2256, 2268–2277
1333 §1: cc. 2255, 2256, 2278–2285

1° either all or some acts of the power of orders;

2° either all or some acts of the power of governance;

3° the exercise of either all or some of the rights or functions attached to an office.

§2. A law or precept can establish that a suspended person cannot place acts of governance validly after a condemnatory or declaratory sentence.

§3. A prohibition never affects:

1° the offices or the power of governance which are not under the power of the superior who establishes the penalty;

2° the right of residence which the offender may have by reason of office;

3° the right to administer goods which may pertain to the office of the person suspended if the penalty is *latae sententiae.*

§4. A suspension prohibiting a person from receiving benefits, a stipend, pensions, or any other such thing entails the obligation of making restitution for whatever has been received illegitimately, even if in good faith.

CAN. 1334   §1. Within the limits established by the preceding canon, either the law or precept itself or the sentence or decree which imposes the penalty defines the extent of a suspension.

§2. A law, but not a precept, can establish a *latae sententiae* suspension without additional determination or limitation; such a penalty has all the effects listed in can. 1333, §1.

CAN. 1335   If a censure prohibits the celebration of sacraments or sacramentals or the placing of an act of governance, the prohibition

1° vel omnes vel aliquos actus potestatis ordinis;

2° vel omnes vel aliquos actus potestatis regiminis;

3° exercitium vel omnium vel aliquorum iurium vel munerum officio inhaerentium.

§2. In lege vel praecepto statui potest, ut post sententiam condemnatoriam vel declaratoriam actus regiminis suspensus valide ponere nequeat.

§3. Vetitum numquam afficit:

1° officia vel regiminis potestatem, quae non sint sub potestate Superioris poenam constituentis;

2° ius habitandi, si quod reus ratione officii habeat;

3° ius administrandi bona, quae ad ipsius suspensi officium forte pertineant, si poena sit latae sententiae.

§4. Suspensio vetans fructus, stipendium, pensiones aliave eiusmodi percipere, obligationem secumfert restituendi quidquid illegitime, quamvis bona fide, perceptum sit.

CAN. 1334 §1. Suspensionis ambitus, intra limites canone praecedenti statutos, aut ipsa lege vel praecepto definitur, aut sententia vel decreto quo poena irrogatur.

§2. Lex, non autem praeceptum, potest latae sententiae suspensionem, nulla addita determinatione vel limitatione, constituere; eiusmodi autem poena omnes effectus habet, qui in can. 1333, §1 recensentur.

CAN. 1335   Si censura vetet celebrare sacramenta vel sacramentalia vel ponere actum regiminis, vetitum suspenditur, quoties

1333 §2: c. 2284
1333 §3: cc. 2279, 2280 §1, 2282
1333 §4: c. 2280 §2

1334 §1: c. 2278 §2
1334 §2: cc. 2281, 2282
1335: cc. 2261 §§2 et 3, 2275, 2°, 2284

is suspended whenever it is necessary to care for the faithful in danger of death. If a *latae sententiae* censure has not been declared, the prohibition is also suspended whenever a member of the faithful requests a sacrament or sacramental or an act of governance; a person is permitted to request this for any just cause.

CHAPTER II. Expiatory Penalties

CAN. 1336 §1. In addition to other penalties which the law may have established, the following are expiatory penalties which can affect an offender either perpetually, for a prescribed time, or for an indeterminate time:

1° a prohibition or an order concerning residence in a certain place or territory;

2° privation of a power, office, function, right, privilege, faculty, favor, title, or insignia, even merely honorary;

3° a prohibition against exercising those things listed under n. 2, or a prohibition against exercising them in a certain place or outside a certain place; these prohibitions are never under pain of nullity;

4° a penal transfer to another office;

5° dismissal from the clerical state.

§2. Only those expiatory penalties listed in §1, n. 3 can be *latae sententiae*.

CAN. 1337 §1. A prohibition against residing in a certain place or territory can affect both clerics and religious; however, the order to reside in a certain place or territory can affect secular clerics and, within the limits of the constitutions, religious.

§2. To impose an order to reside in a certain place or territory requires the consent of the or-

id necessarium sit ad consulendum fidelibus in mortis periculo constitutis; quod si censura latae sententiae non sit declarata, vetitum praeterea suspenditur, quoties fidelis petit sacramentum vel sacramentale vel actum regiminis; id autem petere ex qualibet iusta causa licet.

CAPUT II. De Poenis Expiatoriis

CAN. 1336 §1. Poenae expiatoriae, quae delinquentem afficere possunt aut in perpetuum aut in tempus praefinitum aut in tempus indeterminatum, praeter alias, quas forte lex constituerit, hae sunt:

1° prohibitio vel praescriptio commorandi in certo loco vel territorio;

2° privatio potestatis, officii, muneris, iuris, privilegii, facultatis, gratiae, tituli, insignis, etiam mere honorifici;

3° prohibitio ea exercendi, quae sub n. 2 recensentur, vel prohibitio ea in certo loco vel extra certum locum exercendi; quae prohibitiones numquam sunt sub poena nullitatis;

4° translatio poenalis ad aliud officium;

5° dimissio e statu clericali.

§2. Latae sententiae eae tantum poenae expiatoriae esse possunt, quae in §1, n. 3. recensentur.

CAN. 1337 §1. Prohibitio commorandi in certo loco vel territorio sive clericos sive religiosos afficere potest; praescriptio autem commorandi, clericos saeculares et, intra limites constitutionem, religiosos.

§2. Ut praescriptio commorandi in certo loco vel territorio irrogetur, accedat oportet

---

1336 §1: cc. 2286–2305
1337 §1: cc. 619, 2302; CD 35; ES I, 25; MR 44

1337 §2: c. 2301

dinary of that place unless it is a question of a house designated for clerics doing penance or being rehabilitated even from outside the diocese.

CAN. 1338 §1. The privations and prohibitions listed in can. 1336, §1, nn. 2 and 3, never affect powers, offices, functions, rights, privileges, faculties, favors, titles, or insignia which are not subject to the power of the superior who establishes the penalty.

§2. Privation of the power of orders is not possible but only a prohibition against exercising it or some of its acts; likewise, privation of academic degrees is not possible.

§3. The norm given in can. 1335 for censures must be observed for the prohibitions listed in can. 1336, §1, n. 3.

CHAPTER III. **Penal Remedies and Penances**

CAN. 1339 §1. An ordinary, personally or through another, can warn a person who is in the proximate occasion of committing a delict or upon whom, after investigation, grave suspicion of having committed a delict has fallen.

§2. He can also rebuke a person whose behavior causes scandal or a grave disturbance of order, in a manner accommodated to the special conditions of the person and the deed.

§3. The warning or rebuke must always be established at least by some document which is to be kept in the secret archive of the curia.

CAN. 1340 §1. A penance, which can be imposed in the external forum, is the perfor-

consensus Ordinarii illius loci, nisi agatur de domo extradioecesanis quoque clericis paenitentibus vel emendandis destinata.

CAN. 1338 §1. Privationes et prohibitiones, quae in can. 1336, §1, nn. 2 et 3 recensentur, numquam afficiunt potestates, officia, munera, iura, privilegia, facultates, gratias, titulos, insignia, quae non sint sub potestate Superioris poenam constituentis.

§2. Potestatis ordinis privatio dari nequit, sed tantum prohibitio eam vel aliquos eius actus exercendi; item dari nequit privatio graduum academicorum.

§3. De prohibitionibus, quae in can. 1336, §1, n. 3 indicantur, norma servanda est, quae de censuris datur in can. 1335.

CAPUT III. **De Remediis Poenalibus et Paenitentiis**

CAN. 1339 §1. Eum, qui versatur in proxima delinquendi occasione, vel in quem, ex investigatione peracta, gravis cadit suspicio delicti commissi, Ordinarius per se vel per alium monere potest.

§2. Eum vero, ex cuius conversatione scandalum vel gravis ordinis perturbatio oriatur, etiam corripere potest, modo peculiaribus personae et facti condicionibus accommodato.

§3. De monitione et correptione constare semper debet saltem ex aliquo documento, quod in secreto curiae archivo servetur.

CAN. 1340 §1. Paenitentia, quae imponi potest in foro externo, est aliquod reli-

---

1338 §1: c. 201 §1
1338 §2: cc. 211 §1, 2296 §2
1338 §3: cc. 2261 §2, 2275, 2°, 2284
1339 §1: cc. 2306, 1°, 2307, 2309 §§1, 2 et 6

1339 §2: cc. 2306, 2°, 2308, 2309
1339 §3: c. 2309 §5
1340 §1: cc. 2312 §1, 2313 §1

mance of some work of religion, piety, or charity.

§2. A public penance is never to be imposed for an occult transgression.

§3. According to his own prudent judgment, an ordinary can add penances to the penal remedy of warning or rebuke.

TITLE V. The Application of Penalties

CAN. 1341 An ordinary is to take care to initiate a judicial or administrative process to impose or declare penalties only after he has ascertained that fraternal correction or rebuke or other means of pastoral solicitude cannot sufficiently repair the scandal, restore justice, reform the offender.

CAN. 1342 §1. Whenever just causes preclude a judicial process, a penalty can be imposed or declared by extrajudicial decree; penal remedies and penances, however, can be applied by decree in any case whatsoever.

§2. Perpetual penalties cannot be imposed or declared by decree, nor can penalties be so applied when the law or precept establishing them prohibits their application by decree.

§3. What a law or precept states about the imposition or declaration of a penalty by a judge in a trial must be applied to a superior who imposes or declares a penalty by extrajudicial decree unless it is otherwise evident or un-

gionis vel pietatis vel caritatis opus peragendum.

§2. Ob transgressionem occultam numquam publica imponatur paenitentia.

§3. Paenitentias Ordinarius pro sua prudentia addere potest poenali remedio monitionis vel correptionis.

TITULUS V. De Poenis Applicandis

CAN. 1341 Ordinarius proceduram iudicialem vel administrativam ad poenas irrogandas vel declarandas tunc tantum promovendam curet, cum perspexerit neque fraterna correctione neque correptione neque aliis pastoralis sollicitudinis viis satis posse scandalum reparari, iustitiam restitui, reum emendari.

CAN. 1342 §1. Quoties iustae obstent causae ne iudicialis processus fiat, poena irrogari vel declarari potest per decretum extra iudicium; remedia poenalia autem et paenitentiae applicari possunt per decretum in quolibet casu.

§2. Per decretum irrogari vel declarari non possunt poenae perpetuae, neque poenae quas lex vel praeceptum eas constituens vetet per decretum applicare.

§3. Quae in lege vel praecepto dicuntur de iudice, quod attinet ad poenam irrogandam vel declarandam in iudicio, applicanda sunt ad Superiorem, qui per decretum extra iudicium poenam irroget vel declaret, nisi

1340 §2: c. 2312 §2
1340 §3: c. 2313 §2
1341: c. 2214 §2; Pius PP. XII, All., 5 dec. 1954 (AAS 47 [1955] 68–70); Pius PP. XII, All., 5 feb. 1955 (AAS 47 [1955] 73)

1342 §2: c. 1933 §§2 et 4
1342 §3: Pius PP. XII, All., 5 dec. 1954 (AAS 47 [1955] 66)

less it concerns prescripts which pertain only to procedural matters.

CAN. 1343 If the law or precept gives the judge the power to apply or not apply a penalty, the judge can also temper the penalty or impose a penance in its place, according to his own conscience and prudence.

CAN. 1344 Even if the law uses preceptive words, the judge can, according to his own conscience and prudence:

1° defer the imposition of the penalty to a more opportune time if it is foreseen that greater evils will result from an overly hasty punishment of the offender;

2° abstain from imposing a penalty, impose a lighter penalty, or employ a penance if the offender has reformed and repaired the scandal or if the offender has been or, it is foreseen, will be punished sufficiently by civil authority;

3° suspend the obligation of observing an expiatory penalty if it is the first offense of an offender who has lived a praiseworthy life and if the need to repair scandal is not pressing, but in such a way that if the offender commits an offense again within the time determined by the judge, the person is to pay the penalty due for each delict unless in the interim the time for the prescription of a penal action has elapsed for the first delict.

CAN. 1345 Whenever the offender had only the imperfect use of reason or committed the delict from fear, necessity, the heat of passion, or mental disturbance from drunkenness or something similar, the judge can also abstain

aliter constet neque agatur de praescriptis quae ad procedendi tantum rationem attineant.

CAN. 1343 Si lex vel praeceptum iudici det potestatem applicandi vel non applicandi poenam, iudex potest etiam, pro sua conscientia et prudentia, poenam temperare vel in eius locum paenitentiam imponere.

CAN. 1344 Etiamsi lex utatur verbis praeceptivis, iudex pro sua conscientia et prudentia potest:

1° poenae irrogationem in tempus magis opportunum differre, si ex praepropera rei punitione maiora mala eventura praevideantur;

2° a poena irroganda abstinere vel poenam mitiorem irrogare aut paenitentiam adhibere, si reus emendatus sit et scandalum reparaverit, aut si ipse satis a civili auctoritate punitus sit vel punitum iri praevideatur;

3° si reus primum post vitam laudabiliter peractam deliquerit neque necessitas urgeat reparandi scandalum, obligationem servandi poenam expiatoriam suspendere, ita tamen ut, si reus intra tempus ab ipso iudice determinatum rursus deliquerit, poenam utrique delicto debitam luat, nisi interim tempus decurrerit ad actionis poenalis pro priore delicto praescriptionem.

CAN. 1345 Quoties delinquens vel usum rationis imperfectum tantum habuerit, vel delictum ex metu vel necessitate vel passionis aestu vel in ebrietate aliave simili mentis perturbatione patraverit, iudex potest

---

1343: c. 2223 §2; Pius PP. XII, All., 5 dec 1954 (AAS 47 [1955] 66)

1344: cc. 2223 §3, 1° et 2°, 2288; Pius PP. XII, All., 5 dec. 1954 (AAS 47 [1955] 66); Pius PP. XII, All., 5 feb. 1955 (AAS 47 [1955] 75)

1345: cc. 2218 §1, 2223 §3, 3°; Pius PP. XII, All., 5 dec. 1954 (AAS 47 [1955] 66); Pius PP. XII. All., 26 maii 1957 (AAS 49 [1957] 405)

from imposing any penalty if he thinks that re-form of the person can be better accomplished in another way.

CAN. 1346 Whenever the offender has committed several delicts, it is left to the prudent decision of the judge to moderate the penalties within equitable limits if the sum of the *ferendae sententiae* penalties appears excessive.

CAN. 1347 §1. A censure cannot be imposed validly unless the offender has been warned at least once beforehand to withdraw from contumacy and has been given a suitable time for repentance.

§2. An offender who has truly repented of the delict and has also made suitable reparation for damages and scandal or at least has seriously promised to do so must be considered to have withdrawn from contumacy.

CAN. 1348 When an accused is acquitted of an accusation or when no penalty is imposed, the ordinary can provide for the welfare of the person and for the public good through appropriate warnings and other means of pastoral solicitude or even through penal remedies if the matter warrants it.

CAN. 1349 If a penalty is indeterminate and the law does not provide otherwise, the judge is not to impose graver penalties, especially censures, unless the seriousness of the case clearly demands it; he cannot, however, impose perpetual penalties.

CAN. 1350 §1. Unless it concerns dismissal from the clerical state, when penalties are imposed on a cleric, provision must always be made so that he does not lack those things necessary for his decent support.

etiam a qualibet punitione irroganda abstinere, si censeat aliter posse melius consuli eius emendationi.

CAN. 1346 Quoties reus plura delicta patraverit, si nimius videatur poenarum ferendae sententiae cumulus, prudenti iudicis arbitrio relinquitur poenas intra aequos terminos moderari.

CAN. 1347 §1. Censura irrogari valide nequit, nisi antea reus semel saltem monitus sit ut a contumacia recedat, dato congruo ad resipiscentiam tempore.

§2. A contumacia recessisse dicendus est reus, quem delicti vere paenituerit, quique praeterea congruam damnorum et scandali reparationem dederit vel saltem serio promiserit.

CAN. 1348 Cum reus ab accusatione absolvitur vel nulla poena ei irrogatur, Ordinarius potest opportunis monitis aliisque pastoralis sollicitudinis viis, vel etiam, si res ferat, poenalibus remediis eius utilitati et publico bono consulere.

CAN. 1349 Si poena sit indeterminata neque aliud lex caveat, iudex poenas graviores, praesertim censuras, ne irroget, nisi casus gravitas id omnino postulet; perpetuas autem poenas irrogare non potest.

CAN. 1350 §1. In poenis clerico irrogandis semper cavendum est, ne iis quae ad honestam sustentationem sunt necessaria ipse careat, nisi agatur de dimissione e statu clericali.

1346: c. 2224 §2; PIUS PP. XII. All., 5 dec. 1954 (AAS 47 [1955] 66)

1347 §1: c. 2233 §3; CI Resp. XV, 14 iul. 1922 (AAS 14 [1922] 530)

1347 §2: c. 2242 §3: PIUS PP. XII, All., 5 feb. 1955

(AAS 47 [1955] 73, 82); PAULUS PP. VI, All., 4 oct. 1969 (AAS 61 [1969] 711)

1348: cc. 2223 §3, 3°, 2229 §4

1349: c. 2223 §1

1350 §1: cc. 122, 1923 §1, 2299 §3

§2. In the best manner possible, however, the ordinary is to take care to provide for a person dismissed from the clerical state who is truly in need because of the penalty.

CAN. 1351   Unless other provision is expressly made, a penalty binds the offender everywhere, even when the authority of the one who established or imposed the penalty has lapsed.

CAN. 1352   §1. If a penalty prohibits the reception of the sacraments or sacramentals, the prohibition is suspended as long as the offender is in danger of death.

§2. The obligation to observe an undeclared *latae sententiae* penalty which is not notorious in the place where the offender is present, is suspended totally or partially whenever the offender cannot observe it without danger of grave scandal or infamy.

CAN. 1353   An appeal or recourse from judicial sentences or from decrees, which impose or declare a penalty, has a suspensive effect.

§2. Dimisso autem e statu clericali, qui propter poenam vere indigeat, Ordinarius meliore quo fieri potest modo providere curet.

CAN. 1351   Poena reum ubique tenet, etiam resoluto iure eius qui poenam constituit vel irrogavit, nisi aliud expresse caveatur.

CAN. 1352   §1. Si poena vetet recipere sacramenta vel sacramentalia, vetitum suspenditur, quamdiu reus in mortis periculo versatur.

§2. Obligatio servandi poenam latae sententiae, quae neque declarata sit neque sit notoria in loco ubi delinquens versatur, eatenus ex toto vel ex parte suspenditur, quatenus reus eam servare nequeat sine periculo gravis scandali vel infamiae.

CAN. 1353   Appellatio vel recursus a sententiis iudicialibus vel a decretis, quae poenam quamlibet irrogent vel declarent, habent effectum suspensivum.

TITLE VI. The Cessation of Penalties

TITULUS VI. De Poenarum Cessatione

CAN. 1354   §1. In addition to the persons listed in cann. 1355–1356, all who can dispense from a law which includes a penalty or who can exempt from a precept which threatens a penalty can also remit that penalty.

§2. Moreover, a law or precept which establishes a penalty can also give the power of remission to others.

CAN. 1354   §1. Praeter eos, qui in cann. 1355–1356 recensentur, omnes, qui a lege, quae poena munita est, dispensare possunt vel a praecepto poenam comminanti eximere, possunt etiam eam poenam remittere.

§2. Potest praeterea lex vel praeceptum, poenam constituens, aliis quoque potestatem facere remittendi.

1350 §2: c. 2303 §2
1351: c. 2226 §4
1352 §1: c. 2252
1352 §2: cc. 2232 §1, 2290 §1
1353: cc. 2243, 2287

1354 §1: c. 2236 §2; Pius PP. XII, All., 5 feb. 1955 (AAS 47 [1955] 80)
1354 §2: c. 2236 §1; Pius PP. XII, All., 5 feb. 1955 (AAS 47 [1955] 80)

§3. If the Apostolic See has reserved the remission of a penalty to itself or to others, the reservation must be interpreted strictly.

CAN. 1355 §1. Provided that the penalty has not been reserved to the Apostolic See, the following can remit an imposed or declared penalty established by law:

1° the ordinary who initiated the trial to impose or declare a penalty or who personally or through another imposed or declared it by decree;

2° the ordinary of the place where the offender is present, after the ordinary mentioned under n. 1 has been consulted unless this is impossible because of extraordinary circumstances.

§2. If the penalty has not been reserved to the Apostolic See, an ordinary can remit a *latae sententiae* penalty established by law but not yet declared for his subjects and those who are present in his territory or who committed the offense there; any bishop can also do this in the act of sacramental confession.

CAN. 1356 §1. The following can remit a *ferendae sententiae* or *latae sententiae* penalty established by a precept not issued by the Apostolic See:

1° the ordinary of the place where the offender is present;

2° if the penalty has been imposed or declared, the ordinary who initiated the trial to impose or declare the penalty or who personally or through another imposed or declared it by decree.

§2. The author of the precept must be consulted before remission is made unless this is impossible because of extraordinary circumstances.

CAN. 1357 §1. Without prejudice to the

§3. Si Apostolica Sedes poenae remissionem sibi vel aliis reservaverit, reservatio stricte est interpretanda.

CAN. 1355 §1. Poenam lege constitutam, si sit irrogata vel declarata, remittere possunt, dummodo non sit Apostolicae Sedi reservata:

1° Ordinarius, qui iudicium ad poenam irrogandam vel declarandam promovit vel decreto eam per se vel per alium irrogavit vel declaravit;

2° Ordinarius loci in quo delinquens versatur, consulto tamen, nisi propter extraordinarias circumstantias impossible sit, Ordinario, de quo sub n. 1.

§2. Poenam latae sententiae nondum declaratam lege constitutam, si Sedi Apostolicae non sit reservata, potest Ordinarius remittere suis subditis et iis qui in ipsius territorio versantur vel ibi deliquerint, et etiam quilibet Episcopus in actu tamen sacramentalis confessionis.

CAN. 1356 §1. Poenam ferendae vel latae sententiae constitutam praecepto quod non sit ab Apostolica Sede latum, remittere possunt:

1° Ordinarius loci, in quo delinquens versatur;

2° si poena sit irrogata vel declarata, etiam Ordinarius qui iudicium ad poenam irrogandam vel declarandam promovit vel decreto eam per se vel alium irrogavit vel declaravit.

§2. Antequam remissio fiat, consulendus est, nisi propter extraordinarias circumstantias impossibile sit, praecepti auctor.

CAN. 1357 §1. Firmis praescriptis cann.

1354 §3: c. 2246 §2; Pius PP. XII, All., 5 feb. 1955 (AAS 47 [1955] 80)
  1355 §1: cc. 2236 §1, 2237 §1, 2245, 2253 §3

1355 §2: c. 2237 §2
1356 §1: cc. 2236 §1, 2245 §2, 2253, 2° et 3 °
1357 §1: c. 2254 §1

prescripts of cann. 508 and 976, a confessor can remit in the internal sacramental forum an undeclared *latae sententiae* censure of excommunication or interdict if it is burdensome for the penitent to remain in the state of grave sin during the time necessary for the competent superior to make provision.

§2. In granting the remission, the confessor is to impose on the penitent, under the penalty of reincidence, the obligation of making recourse within a month to the competent superior or to a priest endowed with the faculty and the obligation of obeying his mandates; in the meantime he is to impose a suitable penance and, insofar as it is demanded, reparation of any scandal and damage; however, recourse can also be made through the confessor, without mention of the name.

§3. After they have recovered, those for whom an imposed or declared censure or one reserved to the Apostolic See has been remitted according to the norm of can. 976 are also obliged to make recourse.

CAN. 1358 §1. Remission of a censure cannot be granted unless the offender has withdrawn from contumacy according to the norm of can. 1347, §2; it cannot be denied, however, to a person who withdraws from contumacy.

§2. The person who remits a censure can make provision according to the norm of can. 1348 or can even impose a penance.

CAN. 1359 If several penalties bind a person, a remission is valid only for the penalties expressed in it; a general remission, however, takes away all penalties except those which the offender in bad faith omitted in the petition.

508 et 976, censuram latae sententiae excommunicationis vel interdicti non declaratam confessarius remittere potest in foro interno sacramentali, si paenitenti durum sit in statu gravis peccati permanere per tempus necessarium ut Superior competens provideat.

§2. In remissione concedenda confessarius paenitenti onus iniungat recurrendi intra mensem sub poena reincidentiae ad Superiorem competentem vel ad sacerdotem facultate praeditum, et standi huius mandatis; interim imponat congruam paenitentiam et, quatenus urgeat, scandali et damni reparationem; recursus autem fieri potest etiam per confessarium, sine nominis mentione.

§3. Eodem onere recurrendi tenentur, postquam convaluerint, ii quibus ad normam can. 976 remissa est censura irrogata vel declarata vel Sedi Apostolicae reservata.

CAN. 1358 §1. Remissio censurae dari non potest nisi delinquenti qui a contumacia, ad normam can. 1347, §2, recesserit; recedenti autem denegari nequit.

§2. Qui censuram remittit, potest ad normam can. 1348 providere vel etiam paenitentiam imponere.

CAN. 1359 Si quis pluribus poenis detineatur, remissio valet tantummodo pro poenis in ipsa expressis; generalis autem remissio omnes aufert poenas, iis exceptis quas in petitione reus mala fide reticuerit.

1357 §2: c. 2254 §§1 et 3; CI Resp. VIII, 12 nov. 1922 (AAS 14 [1922] 663)

1357 §3: c. 2252; CI Resp. VIII, 12 nov. 1922 (AAS 14 [1922] 663)

1358: c. 2248 §2; Pius PP. XII, All., 5 feb. 1955 (AAS 47 [1955] 73)

1359: c. 2249 §2

CAN. 1360 The remission of a penalty extorted by grave fear is invalid.

CAN. 1361 §1. A remission can also be given conditionally or to a person who is absent.

§2. A remission in the external forum is to be given in writing unless a grave cause suggests otherwise.

§3. Care is to be taken that the petition of remission or the remission itself is not divulged except insofar as it is either useful to protect the reputation of the offender or necessary to repair scandal.

CAN. 1362 §1. Prescription extinguishes a criminal action after three years unless it concerns:

1° delicts reserved to the Congregation for the Doctrine of the Faith;

2° an action arising from the delicts mentioned in cann. 1394, 1395, 1397, and 1398, which have a prescription of five years;

3° delicts which are not punished in the common law if particular law has established another period for prescription.

§2. Prescription runs from the day on which the delict was committed or, if the delict is continuous or habitual, from the day on which it ceased.

CAN. 1363 §1. Prescription extinguishes an action to execute a penalty if the offender is not notified of the executive decree of the judge mentioned in can. 1651 within the time limits mentioned in can. 1362; these limits are to be computed from the day on which the condemnatory sentence became a *res iudicata*.

§2. Having observed what is required, the same is valid if the penalty was imposed by extrajudicial decree.

CAN. 1360 Poenae remissio metu gravi extorta irrita est.

CAN. 1361 §1. Remissio dari potest etiam absenti vel sub condicione.

§2. Remissio in foro externo detur scripto, nisi gravis causa aliud suadeat.

§3. Caveatur ne remissionis petitio vel ipsa remissio divulgetur, nisi quatenus id vel utile sit ad rei famam tuendam vel necessarium ad scandalum reparandum.

CAN. 1362 §1. Actio criminalis praescriptione extinguitur triennio, nisi agatur:

1° de delictis Congregationi pro Doctrina Fidei reservatis;

2° de actione ob delicta de quibus in cann. 1394, 1395, 1397, 1398, quae quinquennio praescribitur;

3° de delictis quae non sunt iure communi punita, si lex particularis alium praescriptionis terminum statuerit.

§2. Praescriptio decurrit ex die quo delictum patratum est, vel, si delictum sit permanens vel habituale, ex die quo cessavit.

CAN. 1363 §1. Si intra terminos de quibus in can. 1362, ex die quo sententia condemnatoria in rem iudicatam transierit computandos, non sit reo notificatum exsecutorium iudicis decretum de quo in can. 1651, actio ad poenam exsequendam praescriptione extinguitur.

§2. Idem valet, servatis servandis, si poena per decretum extra iudicium irrogata sit.

1360: c. 2238
1361 §1: c. 2239 §1
1361 §2: c. 2239 §2

1362 §1: cc. 1703, 2240; REU 29, 31, 32, 35, 36
1362 §2: c. 1705
1363: cc. 1703, 1918, 2240

PART II. PENALTIES FOR INDIVIDUAL DELICTS

PARS II. DE POENIS IN SINGULA DELICTA

TITLE I. Delicts Against Religion and the Unity of the Church

TITULUS I. De Delictis Contra Religionem et Ecclesiae Unitatem

CAN. 1364 §1. Without prejudice to the prescript of can. 194, §1, n. 2, an apostate from the faith, a heretic, or a schismatic incurs a *latae sententiae* excommunication; in addition, a cleric can be punished with the penalties mentioned in can. 1336, §1, nn. 1, 2, and 3.

§2. If contumacy of long duration or the gravity of scandal demands it, other penalties can be added, including dismissal from the clerical state.

CAN. 1365 A person guilty of prohibited participation in sacred rites *(communicatio in sacris)* is to be punished with a just penalty.

CAN. 1366 Parents or those who take the place of parents who hand over their children to be baptized or educated in a non-Catholic religion are to be punished with a censure or other just penalty.

CAN. 1367 A person who throws away the consecrated species or takes or retains them for a sacrilegious purpose incurs a *latae sententiae* excommunication reserved to the Apostolic See; moreover, a cleric can be punished with another penalty, not excluding dismissal from the clerical state.

CAN. 1364 §1. Apostata a fide, haereticus vel schismaticus in excommunicationem latae sententiae incurrit, firmo praescripto can. 194, §1, n. 2; clericus praeterea potest poenis, de quibus in can. 1336, §1, nn. 1, 2 et 3, puniri.

§2. Si diuturna contumacia vel scandali gravitas postulet, aliae poenae addi possunt, non excepta dimissione e statu clericali.

CAN. 1365 Reus vetitae communicationis in sacris iusta poena puniatur.

CAN. 1366 Parentes vel parentum locum tenentes, qui liberos in religione acatholica baptizandos vel educandos tradunt, censura aliave iusta poena puniantur.

CAN. 1367 Qui species consecratas abicit aut in sacrilegum finem abducit vel retinet, in excommunicationem latae sententiae Sedi Apostolicae reservatam incurrit; clericus praeterea alia poena, non exclusa dimissione e statu clericali, puniri potest.

1364 §1: c. 2314 §1; CI Resp., 30 iul. 1934, I (AAS 26 [1934] 494); SCSO Decr. *Quaesitum est*, 1 iul. 1949, 4 (AAS 41 [1949] 334); DO 19, 20
   1364 §2: c. 2314 §1, 2° et 3°

1365: cc. 1258, 2316; UR 8; DO 38, 42–63
1366: c. 2319 §1, 3° et 4°; MM 15
1367: c. 2320; SCSO Decr. *Cum ex expresso*, 21 iul. 1934 (AAS 26 [1934] 550)

CAN. 1368 A person who commits perjury while asserting or promising something before ecclesiastical authority is to be punished with a just penalty.

CAN. 1369 A person who in a public show or speech, in published writing, or in other uses of the instruments of social communication utters blasphemy, gravely injures good morals, expresses insults, or excites hatred or contempt against religion or the Church is to be punished with a just penalty.

TITLE II. Delicts Against Ecclesiastical Authorities and the Freedom of the Church

CAN. 1370 §1. A person who uses physical force against the Roman Pontiff incurs a *latae sententiae* excommunication reserved to the Apostolic See; if he is a cleric, another penalty, not excluding dismissal from the clerical state, can be added according to the gravity of the delict.

§2. A person who does this against a bishop incurs a *latae sententiae* interdict and, if he is a cleric, also a *latae sententiae* suspension.

§3. A person who uses physical force against a cleric or religious out of contempt for the faith, the Church, ecclesiastical power, or the ministry is to be punished with a just penalty.

CAN. 1371 The following are to be punished with a just penalty:

1° in addition to the case mentioned in can. 1364, §1, a person who teaches a doctrine con-

CAN. 1368 Si quis, asserens vel promittens aliquid coram ecclesiastica auctoritate, periurium committit, iusta poena puniatur.

CAN. 1369 Qui in publico spectaculo vel concione, vel in scripto publice evulgato, vel aliter instrumentis communicationis socialis utens, blasphemiam profert, aut bonos mores graviter laedit, aut in religionem vel Ecclesiam iniurias exprimit vel odium contemptumve excitat, iusta poena puniatur.

TITULUS II. De Delictis Contra Ecclesiasticas Auctoritates et Ecclesiae Libertatem

CAN. 1370 §1. Qui vim physicam in Romanum Pontificem adhibet, in excommunicationem latae sententiae Sedi Apostolicae reservatam incurrit, cui, si clericus sit, alia poena, non exclusa dimissione e statu clericali, pro delicti gravitate addi potest.

§2. Qui id agit in eum qui episcopali charactere pollet, in interdictum latae sententiae et, si sit clericus, etiam in suspensionem latae sententiae incurrit.

§3. Qui vim physicam in clericum vel religiosum adhibet in fidei vel Ecclesiae vel ecclesiasticae potestatis vel ministerii contemptum, iusta poena puniatur.

CAN. 1371 Iusta poena puniatur:

1° qui, praeter casum de quo in can. 1364, § 1, doctrinam a Romano Pontifice vel

---

1368: cc. 1743 §3, 1755 §3, 1794, 2323
1369: cc. 2323, 2344
1370 §1: c. 2343 §1; SCSO Decr. *Cum ex expresso,* 21 iul. 1934 (AAS 26 [1934] 550)

1370 §2: c. 2343 §3
1370 §3: c. 2343 §4
1371: cc. 2317, 2331 §1

demned by the Roman Pontiff or an ecumenical council or who obstinately rejects the doctrine mentioned in can. 750, §2 or in can. 752 and who does not retract after having been admonished by the Apostolic See or an ordinary;

2° a person who otherwise does not obey a legitimate precept or prohibition of the Apostolic See, an ordinary, or a superior and who persists in disobedience after a warning.

CAN. 1372   A person who makes recourse against an act of the Roman Pontiff to an ecumenical council or the college of bishops is to be punished with a censure.

CAN. 1373   A person who publicly incites among subjects animosities or hatred against the Apostolic See or an ordinary because of some act of power or ecclesiastical ministry or provokes subjects to disobey them is to be punished by an interdict or other just penalties.

CAN. 1374   A person who joins an association which plots against the Church is to be punished with a just penalty; however, a person who promotes or directs an association of this kind is to be punished with an interdict.

CAN. 1375   Those who impede the freedom of ministry, of election, or of ecclesiastical power or the legitimate use of sacred goods or other ecclesiastical goods or who greatly intimidate an elector, one elected, or one who exercises ecclesiastical power or ministry can be punished with a just penalty.

CAN. 1376   A person who profanes a movable or immovable sacred object is to be punished with a just penalty.

CAN. 1377   A person who alienates ecclesi-

a Concilio Oecumenico damnatam docet vel doctrinam, de qua in can. 750, § 2 vel in can. 752, pertinaciter respuit, et ab Apostolica Sede vel ab Ordinario admonitus non retractat;

2° qui aliter Sedi Apostolicae, Ordinario, vel Superiori legitime praecipienti vel prohibenti non obtemperat, et post monitum in inoboedientia persistit.

CAN. 1372   Qui contra Romani Pontificis actum ad Concilium Oecumenicum vel ad Episcoporum collegium recurrit censura puniatur.

CAN. 1373   Qui publice aut subditorum simultates vel odia adversus Sedem Apostolicam vel Ordinarium excitat propter aliquem potestatis vel ministerii ecclesiastici actum, aut subditos ad inoboedientiam in eos provocat, interdicto vel aliis iustis poenis puniatur.

CAN. 1374   Qui nomen dat consociationi, quae contra Ecclesiam machinatur, iusta poena puniatur; qui autem eiusmodi consociationem promovet vel moderatur, interdicto puniatur.

CAN. 1375   Qui impediunt libertatem ministerii vel electionis vel potestatis ecclesiasticae aut legitimum bonorum sacrorum aliorumve ecclesiasticorum bonorum usum, aut perterrent electorem vel electum vel eum qui potestatem vel ministerium ecclesiasticum exercuit, iusta poena puniri possunt.

CAN. 1376   Qui rem sacram, mobilem vel immobilem, profanat, iusta poena puniatur.

CAN. 1377   Qui sine praescripta licentia

1372: c. 2332
1373: cc. 2331 §2, 2344; SCConc Decr. *Catholica Ecclesia*, 29 iun. 1950 (AAS 42 [1950] 601–602)
1374: c. 2335; SCDF Litt., 18 iul. 1974; SCDF Decl., 26 feb. 1975; SCDF Decl., 17 feb. 1981 (AAS 73 [1981] 240–241)

1375: cc. 2334, 2337, 2345, 2346, 2390; CI Resp. V, 25 iul. 1926 (AAS 18 [1926] 394); SCConc Decr. *Catholica Ecclesia*, 29 iun. 1950 (AAS 42 [1950] 601–602)
1376: cc. 2325, 2328, 2329
1377: c. 2347

astical goods without the prescribed permission is to be punished with a just penalty.

bona ecclesiastica alienat, iusta poena puniatur.

TITLE III. Usurpation of Ecclesiastical Functions and Delicts in Their Exercise

TITULUS III. **De Munerum Ecclesiasticorum Usurpatione deque Delictis in Iis Exercendis**

CAN. 1378 §1. A priest who acts against the prescript of can. 977 incurs a *latae sententiae* excommunication reserved to the Apostolic See.

§2. The following incur a *latae sententiae* penalty of interdict or, if a cleric, a *latae sententiae* penalty of suspension:

1° a person who attempts the liturgical action of the Eucharistic sacrifice though not promoted to the sacerdotal order;

2° apart from the case mentioned in §1, a person who, though unable to give sacramental absolution validly, attempts to impart it or who hears sacramental confession.

§3. In the cases mentioned in §2, other penalties, not excluding excommunication, can be added according to the gravity of the delict.

CAN. 1379 In addition to the cases mentioned in can. 1378, a person who simulates the administration of a sacrament is to be punished with a just penalty.

CAN. 1380 A person who celebrates or receives a sacrament through simony is to be punished with an interdict or suspension.

CAN. 1381 §1. Whoever usurps an ecclesiastical office is to be punished with a just penalty.

CAN. 1378 §1. Sacerdos qui contra praescriptum can. 977 agit, in excommunicationem latae sententiae Sedi Apostolicae reservatam incurrit.

§2. In poenam latae sententiae interdicti vel, si sit clericus, suspensionis incurrit:

1° qui ad ordinem sacerdotalem non promotus liturgicam eucharistici Sacrificii actionem attentat;

2° qui, praeter casum de quo in §1, cum sacramentalem absolutionem dare valide nequeat, eam impertire attentat, vel sacramentalem confessionem audit.

§3. In casibus de quibus in §2, pro delicti gravitate, aliae poenae, non exclusa excommunicatione, addi possunt.

CAN. 1379 Qui, praeter casus de quibus in can. 1378, sacramentum se administrare simulat, iusta poena puniatur.

CAN. 1380 Qui per simoniam sacramentum celebrat vel recipit, interdicto vel suspensione puniatur.

CAN. 1381 §1. Quicumque officium ecclesiasticum usurpat, iusta poena puniatur.

1378 §1: c. 2367 §1; SCSO Decr. *Cum ex expresso*, 21 iul. 1934 (AAS 26 [1934] 550); SCSO Decr. *In plenario*, 16 nov. 1934 (AAS 26 [1934] 634)
1378 §2: cc. 2322, 1°, 2366

1378 §3: c. 2322, 1°
1380: c. 2371
1381 §1: c. 2394; SCConc Decr. *Catholica Ecclesia*, 29 iun. 1950 (AAS 42 [1950] 601–602)

§2. Illegitimate retention of a function after its privation or cessation is equivalent to usurpation.

CAN. 1382 A bishop who consecrates someone a bishop without a pontifical mandate and the person who receives the consecration from him incur a *latae sententiae* excommunication reserved to the Apostolic See.

CAN. 1383 A bishop who, contrary to the prescript of can. 1015, ordains without legitimate dimissorial letters someone who is not his subject is prohibited for a year from conferring the order. The person who has received the ordination, however, is ipso facto suspended from the order received.

CAN. 1384 In addition to the cases mentioned in cann. 1378–1383, a person who illegitimately performs a priestly function or another sacred ministry can be punished with a just penalty.

CAN. 1385 A person who illegitimately makes a profit from a Mass offering is to be punished with a censure or another just penalty.

CAN. 1386 A person who gives or promises something so that someone who exercises a function in the Church will do or omit something illegitimately is to be punished with a just penalty; likewise, the one who accepts such gifts or promises.

CAN. 1387 A priest who in the act, on the occasion, or under the pretext of confession solicits a penitent to sin against the sixth commandment of the Decalogue is to be punished,

§2. Usurpationi aequiparatur illegitima, post privationem vel cessationem a munere, eiusdem retentio.

CAN. 1382 Episcopus qui sine pontificio mandato aliquem consecrat in Episcopum, itemque qui ab eo consecrationem recipit, in excommunicationem latae sententiae Sedi Apostolicae reservatam incurrunt.

CAN. 1383 Episcopus qui, contra praescriptum can. 1015, alienum subditum sine legitimis litteris dimissoriis ordinavit, prohibetur per annum ordinem conferre. Qui vero ordinationem recepit, est ipso facto a recepto ordine suspensus.

CAN. 1384 Qui, praeter casus, de quibus in cann. 1378–1383, sacerdotale munus vel aliud sacrum ministerium illegitime exsequitur, iusta poena puniri potest.

CAN. 1385 Qui quaestum illegitime facit ex Missae stipe, censura vel alia iusta poena puniatur.

CAN. 1386 Qui quidvis donat vel pollicetur ut quis, munus in Ecclesia exercens, illegitime quid agat vel omittat, iusta poena puniatur; item qui ea dona vel pollicitationes acceptat.

CAN. 1387 Sacerdos, qui in actu vel occasione vel praetextu confessionis paenitentem ad peccatum contra sextum Decalogi praeceptum sollicitat, pro delicti gravitate,

1381 §2: c. 2401: SCConc Decr. *Catholica Ecclesia*, 29 iun. 1950 (AAS 42 [1950] 601–602)

1382: c. 2370; SCSO Decr. *Suprema Sacra*, 9 apr. 1951 (AAS 43 [1951] 217–218); SCDF Decr. *Episcopi qui alios*, 17 sep. 1976 (AAS 68 [1976] 623)

1383: cc. 2373, 1°, 2374; SCDF Decr. *Episcopi qui alios*, 17 sep. 1976 (AAS 68 [1976] 623)

1384: c. 2322, 2°
1385: c. 2324
1386: c. 2407
1387: c. 2368 §1

according to the gravity of the delict, by suspension, prohibitions, and privations; in graver cases he is to be dismissed from the clerical state.

CAN. 1388 §1. A confessor who directly violates the sacramental seal incurs a *latae sententiae* excommunication reserved to the Apostolic See; one who does so only indirectly is to be punished according to the gravity of the delict.

§2. An interpreter and the others mentioned in can. 983, §2 who violate the secret are to be punished with a just penalty, not excluding excommunication.

CAN. 1389 §1. A person who abuses an ecclesiastical power or function is to be punished according to the gravity of the act or omission, not excluding privation of office, unless a law or precept has already established the penalty for this abuse.

§2. A person who through culpable negligence illegitimately places or omits an act of ecclesiastical power, ministry, or function with harm to another is to be punished with a just penalty.

suspensione, prohibitionibus, privationibus puniatur, et in casibus gravioribus dimittatur e statu clericali.

CAN. 1388 §1. Confessarius, qui sacramentale sigillum directe violat, in excommunicationem latae sententiae Sedi Apostolicae reservatam incurrit; qui vero indirecte tantum, pro delicti gravitate puniatur.

§2. Interpres aliique, de quibus in can. 983, §2, qui secretum violant, iusta poena puniantur, non exclusa excommunicatione.

CAN. 1389 §1. Ecclesiastica potestate vel munere abutens pro actus vel omissionis gravitate puniatur, non exclusa officii privatione, nisi in eum abusum iam poena sit lege vel praecepto constituta.

§2. Qui vero, ex culpabili neglegentia, ecclesiasticae potestatis vel ministerii vel muneris actum illegitime cum damno alieno ponit vel omittit, iusta poena puniatur.

TITLE IV. The Crime of Falsehood

TITULUS IV. De Crimine Falsi

CAN. 1390 §1. A person who falsely denounces before an ecclesiastical superior a confessor for the delict mentioned in can. 1387 incurs a *latae sententiae* interdict and, if he is a cleric, also a suspension.

§2. A person who offers an ecclesiastical superior any other calumnious denunciation of a delict or who otherwise injures the good reputation of another can be punished with a just penalty, not excluding a censure.

CAN. 1390 §1. Qui confessarium de delicto, de quo in can. 1387, apud ecclesiasticum Superiorem falso denuntiat, in interdictum latae sententiae incurrit et, si sit clericus, etiam in suspensionem.

§2. Qui aliam ecclesiastico Superiori calumniosam praebet delicti denuntiationem, vel aliter alterius bonam famam laedit, iusta poena, non exclusa censura, puniri potest.

1388 §1: c. 2369 §1; SCSO Decr. *Cum ex expresso,* 21 iul. 1934 (AAS 26 [1934] 550)

1388 §2: c. 2369 §2; SCDF Decl., 23 mar. 1973 (AAS 65 [1973] 678)

1389 §1: CI Resp. VI, 2–3 iun. 1918 (AAS 10 [1918] 347)

1390 §1: c. 2363

1390 §2: c. 2355

§3. A calumniator can also be forced to make suitable reparation.

CAN. 1391   The following can be punished with a just penalty according to the gravity of the delict:

1° a person who produces a false public ecclesiastical document, who changes, destroys, or conceals an authentic one, or who uses a false or altered one;

2° a person who uses another false or altered document in an ecclesiastical matter;

3° a person who asserts a falsehood in a public ecclesiastical document.

§3. Calumniator potest cogi etiam ad congruam satisfactionem praestandam.

CAN. 1391   Iusta poena pro delicti gravitate puniri potest:

1° qui ecclesiasticum documentum publicum falsum conficit, vel verum mutat, destruit, occultat, vel falso vel mutato utitur;

2° qui alio falso vel mutato documento utitur in re ecclesiastica;

3° qui in publico ecclesiastico documento falsum asserit.

TITLE V. Delicts Against Special Obligations

TITULUS V. De Delictis Contra Speciales Obligationes

CAN. 1392   Clerics or religious who exercise a trade or business contrary to the prescripts of the canons are to be punished according to the gravity of the delict.

CAN. 1393   A person who violates obligations imposed by a penalty can be punished with a just penalty.

CAN. 1394   §1. Without prejudice to the prescript of can. 194, §1, n. 3, a cleric who attempts marriage, even if only civilly, incurs a *latae sententiae* suspension. If he does not repent after being warned and continues to give scandal, he can be punished gradually by privations or even by dismissal from the clerical state.

§2. A perpetually professed religious who is not a cleric and who attempts marriage, even if only civilly, incurs a *latae sententiae* interdict, without prejudice to the prescript of can. 694.

CAN. 1392   Clerici vel religiosi mercaturam vel negotiationem contra canonum praescripta exercentes pro delicti gravitate puniantur.

CAN. 1393   Qui obligationes sibi ex poena impositas violat, iusta poena puniri potest.

CAN. 1394   §1. Firmo praescripto can. 194, §1, n. 3, clericus matrimonium, etiam civiliter tantum, attentans, in suspensionem latae sententiae incurrit; quod si monitus non resipuerit et scandalum dare perrexerit, gradatim privationibus ac vel etiam dimissione e statu clericali puniri potest.

§2. Religiosus a votis perpetuis, qui non sit clericus, matrimonium etiam civiliter tantum attentans, in interdictum latae sententiae incurrit, firmo praescripto can. 694.

1390 §3: c. 2355
1391: cc. 2360, 2362
1392: c. 2380; SCConc Decr. *Catholica Ecclesia,* 29 iun. 1950 (AAS 42 [1950] 601–602)

1394 §1: c. 2388; SPA Decr. *Lex sacri coelibatus,* 18 apr. 1936 (AAS 28 [1936] 42–43); SPA Decl., 4 maii 1937 (AAS 29 [1937] 283–284)
1394 §2: c. 2388

CAN. 1395 §1. A cleric who lives in concubinage, other than the case mentioned in can. 1394, and a cleric who persists with scandal in another external sin against the sixth commandment of the Decalogue is to be punished by a suspension. If he persists in the delict after a warning, other penalties can gradually be added, including dismissal from the clerical state.

§2. A cleric who in another way has committed an offense against the sixth commandment of the Decalogue, if the delict was committed by force or threats or publicly or with a minor below the age of sixteen years, is to be punished with just penalties, not excluding dismissal from the clerical state if the case so warrants.

CAN. 1396 A person who gravely violates the obligation of residence which binds by reason of ecclesiastical office is to be punished by a just penalty, not excluding, after a warning, even privation from office.

CAN. 1395 §1. Clericus concubinarius, praeter casum de quo in can. 1394, et clericus in alio peccato externo contra sextum Decalogi praeceptum cum scandalo permanens, suspensione puniantur, cui, persistente post monitionem delicto, aliae poenae gradatim addi possunt usque ad dimissionem e statu clericali.

§2. Clericus qui aliter contra sextum Decalogi praeceptum deliquerit, si quidem delictum vi vel minis vel publice vel cum minore infra aetatem sedecim annorum patratum sit, iustis poenis puniatur, non exclusa, si casus ferat, dimissione e statu clericali.

CAN. 1396 Qui graviter violat residentiae obligationem cui ratione ecclesiastici officii tenetur, iusta poena puniatur, non exclusa, post monitionem, officii privatione.

TITLE VI. Delicts Against Human Life and Freedom

TITULUS VI. De Delictis Contra Hominis Vitam et Libertatem

CAN. 1397 A person who commits a homicide or who kidnaps, detains, mutilates, or gravely wounds a person by force or fraud is to be punished with the privations and prohibitions mentioned in can. 1336 according to the gravity of the delict. Homicide against the persons mentioned in can. 1370, however, is to be punished by the penalties established there.

CAN. 1398 A person who procures a com-

CAN. 1397 Qui homicidium patrat, vel hominem vi aut fraude rapit vel detinet vel mutilat vel graviter vulnerat, privationibus et prohibitionibus, de quibus in can. 1336, pro delicti gravitate puniatur; homicidium autem in personas de quibus in can. 1370, poenis ibi statutis punitur.

CAN. 1398 Qui abortum procurat, ef-

1395 §1: c. 2359 §§1 et 3
1395 §2: c. 2359 §2
1396: c. 2381; SCConc Resol., 10 iul. 1920 (AAS 12 [1920] 357); SCConc Resp., 23 apr. 1927 (AAS 19 [1927] 415)

1397: cc. 2343 §1, 2354; SCSO Decr. *Cum ex expresso*, 21 iul. 1934 (AAS 26 [1934] 550)
1398: c. 2350 §1; Pius PP. XII, All., 21 maii 1948; Pius PP. XII, All., 27 nov. 1951; GS 27, 51; Paulus PP. VI, All., 9 dec. 1972 (AAS 64 [1972] 776–779); SCDF

pleted abortion incurs a *latae sententiae* excommunication.

fectu secuto, in excommunicationem latae sententiae incurrit.

TITLE VII. General Norm

CAN. 1399 In addition to the cases established here or in other laws, the external violation of a divine or canonical law can be punished by a just penalty only when the special gravity of the violation demands punishment and there is an urgent need to prevent or repair scandals.

TITULUS VII. Norma Generalis

CAN. 1399 Praeter casus hac vel aliis legibus statutos, divinae vel canonicae legis externa violatio tunc tantum potest iusta quidem poena puniri, cum specialis violationis gravitas punitionem postulat, et necessitas urget scandala praeveniendi vel reparandi.

Decl., 18 nov. 1974 (AAS 66 [1974] 730–747); PAULUS PP. VI, All., 23 apr. 1977 (AAS 69 [1977] 281– 283)

1399: c. 2222 §1; PIUS PP. XII, All., 5 dec. 1955 (AAS 47 [1955] 64)

BOOK VII. PROCESSES

LIBER VII. DE PROCESSIBUS

PART I. TRIALS IN GENERAL

PARS I. DE IUDICIIS IN GENERE

CAN. 1400 §1. The object of a trial is:

1° the pursuit or vindication of the rights of physical or juridic persons, or the declaration of juridic facts;

2° the imposition or declaration of a penalty for delicts.

§2. Nevertheless, controversies arising from an act of administrative power can be brought only before the superior or an administrative tribunal.

CAN. 1401 By proper and exclusive right the Church adjudicates:

1° cases which regard spiritual matters or those connected to spiritual matters;

2° the violation of ecclesiastical laws and all those matters in which there is a question of sin, in what pertains to the determination of culpability and the imposition of ecclesiastical penalties.

CAN. 1402 The following canons govern all tribunals of the Church, without prejudice to the norms of the tribunals of the Apostolic See.

CAN. 1403 §1. Special pontifical law governs the causes of canonization of the servants of God.

§2. The prescripts of this Code, however, apply to these causes whenever the special pontif-

CAN. 1400 §1. Obiectum iudicii sunt:

1° personarum physicarum vel iuridicarum iura persequenda aut vindicanda, vel facta iuridica declaranda;

2° delicta, quod spectat ad poenam irrogandam vel declarandam.

§2. Attamen controversiae ortae ex actu potestatis administrativae deferri possunt solummodo ad Superiorem vel ad tribunal administrativum.

CAN. 1401 Ecclesia iure proprio et exclusivo cognoscit:

1° de causis quae respiciunt res spirituales et spiritualibus adnexas;

2° de violatione legum ecclesiasticarum deque omnibus in quibus inest ratio peccati, quod attinet ad culpae definitionem et poenarum ecclesiasticarum irrogationem.

CAN. 1402 Omnia Ecclesiae tribunalia reguntur canonibus qui sequuntur, salvis normis tribunalium Apostolicae Sedis.

CAN. 1403 §1. Causae canonizationis Servorum Dei reguntur peculiari lege pontificia.

§2. Iisdem causis applicantur praeterea praescripta huius Codicis, quoties in eadem

1400 §1: c. 1522 §2

1400 §2: c. 1601; CI Resp., 22 maii 1923 (AAS 16 [1924] 251); REU 106

1401: c. 1553 §1, 1° et 2°; SCConc Resol., 11 dec. 1920 (AAS 13 [1921] 262–268)

1402: c. 1555 §§1 et 2; REU 108, 110

1403 §1: cc. 1999–2141; Paulus PP. VI, m.p. *Sanc-*

titas clarior, 19 feb. 1969 (AAS 61 [1969] 149–153); Paulus PP. VI, Const. Ap. *Sacra Rituum Congregatio,* 8 maii 1969 (AAS 61 [1969] 297–305); Sacra Congregatio pro Causis Sanctorum, Decr. *Ne ob diuturnum,* 3 apr. 1970 (AAS 62 [1970] 554–555); Sacra Congregatio pro Causis Sanctorum, Notif., 16 dec. 1972

ical law refers to the universal law, or norms are involved which also affect these causes by the very nature of the matter.

lege ad ius universale remissio fit vel de normis agitur quae, ex ipsa rei natura, easdem quoque causas afficiunt.

TITLE I. The Competent Forum

TITULUS I. De Foro Competenti

CAN. 1404 The First See is judged by no one.

CAN. 1405 §1. It is solely the right of the Roman Pontiff himself to judge in the cases mentioned in can. 1401:

1° those who hold the highest civil office of a state;

2° cardinals;

3° legates of the Apostolic See and, in penal cases, bishops;

4° other cases which he has called to his own judgment.

§2. A judge cannot review an act or instrument confirmed specifically *(in forma specifica)* by the Roman Pontiff without his prior mandate.

§3. Judgment of the following is reserved to the Roman Rota:

1° bishops in contentious matters, without prejudice to the prescript of can. 1419, §2;

2° an abbot primate or abbot superior of a monastic congregation and a supreme moderator of religious institutes of pontifical right;

3° dioceses or other physical or juridic ecclesiastical persons which do not have a superior below the Roman Pontiff.

CAN. 1406 §1. If the prescript of can. 1404 is violated, the acts and decisions are considered as not to have been placed.

CAN. 1404 Prima Sedes a nemine iudicatur.

CAN. 1405 §1. Ipsius Romani Pontificis dumtaxat ius est iudicandi in causis de quibus in can. 1401:

1° eos qui supremum tenent civitatis magistratum;

2° Patres Cardinales;

3° Legatos Sedis Apostolicae, et in causis poenalibus Episcopos;

4° alias causas quas ipse ad suum advocaverit iudicium.

§2. Iudex de actu vel instrumento a Romano Pontifice in forma specifica confirmato videre non potest, nisi ipsius praecesserit mandatum.

§3. Rotae Romanae reservatur iudicare:

1° Episcopos in contentiosis, firmo praescripto can. 1419, §2;

2° Abbatem primatem, vel Abbatem superiorem congregationis monasticae, et supremum Moderatorem institutorum religiosorum iuris pontificii;

3° dioeceses aliasve personas ecclesiasticas, sive physicas sive iuridicas, quae Superiorem infra Romanum Pontificem non habent.

CAN. 1406 §1. Violato praescripto can. 1404, acta et decisiones pro infectis habentur.

1404: c. 1556
1405 §1: c. 1557 §§1 et 3; PrM 2 §§1 et 3

1405 §2: c. 1557 §2

§2. In the cases mentioned in can. 1405, the incompetence of other judges is absolute.

CAN. 1407 §1. No one can be brought to trial in first instance except before an ecclesiastical judge who is competent by reason of one of the titles determined in cann. 1408–1414.

§2. The incompetence of a judge supported by none of these titles is called relative.

§3. The petitioner follows the forum of the respondent. If the respondent has more than one forum, the choice of forum is granted to the petitioner.

CAN. 1408 Anyone can be brought to trial before the tribunal of domicile or quasi-domicile.

CAN. 1409 §1. A transient has a forum in the place of his or her actual residence.

§2. A person whose domicile, quasi-domicile, and place of residence are unknown can be brought to trial in the forum of the petitioner provided that no other legitimate forum is available.

CAN. 1410 By reason of the location of an object, a party can be brought to trial before the tribunal of the place where the object in dispute is located whenever the action is directed against the object or concerns damages.

CAN. 1411 §1. By reason of a contract, a party can be brought to trial before the tribunal of the place where the contract was entered into or must be fulfilled unless the parties agree to choose some other tribunal.

§2. If the case concerns obligations which originate from another title, a party can be

§2. In causis, de quibus in can. 1405, aliorum iudicum incompetentia est absoluta.

CAN. 1407 §1. Nemo in prima instantia conveniri potest, nisi coram iudice ecclesiastico qui competens sit ob unum ex titulis qui in cann. 1408–1414 determinantur.

§2. Incompetentia iudicis, cui nullus ex his titulis suffragatur, dicitur relativa.

§3. Actor sequitur forum partis conventae; quod si pars conventa multiplex forum habet, optio fori actori conceditur.

CAN. 1408 Quilibet conveniri potest coram tribunali domicilii vel quasi-domicilii.

CAN. 1409 §1. Vagus forum habet in loco ubi actu commoratur.

§2. Is, cuius neque domicilium aut quasi-domicilium neque locus commorationis nota sint, conveniri potest in foro actoris, dummodo aliud forum legitimum non suppetat.

CAN. 1410 Ratione rei sitae, pars conveniri potest coram tribunali loci, ubi res litigiosa sita est, quoties actio in rem directa sit, aut de spolio agatur.

CAN. 1411 §1. Ratione contractus pars conveniri potest coram tribunali loci in quo contractus initus est vel adimpleri debet, nisi partes concorditer aliud tribunal elegerint.

§2. Si causa versetur circa obligationes quae ex alio titulo proveniant, pars conveniri

1406 §2: c. 1558
1407 §1: c. 1559 §1
1407 §2: c. 1559 §2
1407 §3: c. 1559 §3
1408: c. 1561 §1

1409: c. 1563
1410: c. 1564
1411 §1: c. 1565; CI Resp., XII, 14 iul. 1922 (AAS 14 [1922] 529)

brought to trial before the tribunal of the place where the obligation either originated or must be fulfilled.

CAN. 1412   In penal cases the accused, even if absent, can be brought to trial before the tribunal of the place where the delict was committed.

CAN. 1413   A party can be brought to trial:

1° in cases which concern administration, before the tribunal of the place where the administration was conducted;

2° in cases which regard inheritances or pious legacies, before the tribunal of the last domicile, quasi-domicile, or place of residence, according to the norm of cann. 1408–1409, of the one whose inheritance or pious legacy is at issue unless it concerns the mere execution of the legacy, which must be examined according to the ordinary norms of competence.

CAN. 1414   By reason of connection, interconnected cases must be adjudicated by one and the same tribunal in the same process unless a prescript of law prevents this.

CAN. 1415   By reason of prevention, if two or more tribunals are equally competent, the right of adjudicating the case belongs to the one which legitimately cited the respondent first.

CAN. 1416   The appellate tribunal resolves conflicts of competence between tribunals subject to it; if the tribunals are not subject to the same appellate tribunal, the Apostolic Signatura resolves conflicts of competence.

potest coram tribunali loci, in quo obligatio vel orta est vel est adimplenda.

CAN. 1412   In causis poenalibus accusatus, licet absens, conveniri potest coram tribunali loci, in quo delictum patratum est.

CAN. 1413   Pars conveniri potest:

1° in causis quae circa administrationem versantur, coram tribunali loci ubi administratio gesta est;

2° in causis quae respiciunt hereditates vel legata pia, coram tribunali ultimi domicilii vel quasi-domicilii vel commorationis, ad normam cann. 1408–1409, illius de cuius hereditate vel legato pio agitur, nisi agatur de mera exsecutione legati, quae videnda est secundum ordinarias competentiae normas.

CAN. 1414   Ratione conexionis, ab uno eodemque tribunali et in eodem processu cognoscendae sunt causae inter se conexae, nisi legis praescriptum obstet.

CAN. 1415   Ratione praeventionis, si duo vel plura tribunalia aeque competentia sunt, ei ius est causam cognoscendi, quod prius partem conventam legitime citaverit.

CAN. 1416   Conflictus competentiae inter tribunalia eidem tribunali appellationis subiecta, ab hoc tribunali solvuntur; a Signatura Apostolica, si eidem tribunali appellationis non subsunt.

1412: c. 1566
1413: c. 1560, 3° et 4 °
1414: c. 1567

1415: c. 1568; PrM 11
1416: c. 1612; PrM 10

TITLE II. Different Grades and Kinds of Tribunals

TITULUS II. **De Variis Tribunalium Gradibus et Speciebus**

CAN. 1417   §1. By reason of the primacy of the Roman Pontiff, any member of the faithful is free to bring or introduce his or her own contentious or penal case to the Holy See for adjudication in any grade of a trial and at any stage of the litigation.

§2. Recourse brought to the Apostolic See, however, does not suspend the exercise of jurisdiction by a judge who has already begun to adjudicate a case except in the case of an appeal. For this reason, the judge can prosecute a trial even to the definitive sentence unless the Apostolic See has informed the judge that it has called the case to itself.

CAN. 1418   Any tribunal has the right to call upon the assistance of another tribunal to instruct a case or to communicate acts.

CAN. 1417   §1. Ob primatum Romani Pontificis integrum est cuilibet fideli causam suam sive contentiosam sive poenalem, in quovis iudicii gradu et in quovis litis statu, cognoscendam ad Sanctam Sedem deferre vel apud eandem introducere.

§2. Provocatio tamen ad Sedem Apostolicam interposita non suspendit, praeter casum appellationis, exercitium iurisdictionis in iudice qui causam iam cognoscere coepit; quique idcirco poterit iudicium prosequi usque ad definitivam sententiam, nisi Sedes Apostolica iudici significaverit se causam advocasse.

CAN. 1418   Quodlibet tribunal ius habet in auxilium vocandi aliud tribunal ad causam instruendam vel ad actus intimandos.

CHAPTER I. The Tribunal of First Instance

ART. 1. *The Judge*

CAN. 1419   §1. In each diocese and for all cases not expressly excepted by law, the judge of first instance is the diocesan bishop, who can exercise judicial power personally or through others according to the following canons.

§2. If a case concerns the rights or temporal goods of a juridic person represented by the bishop, the appellate tribunal judges in first instance.

CAPUT I. **De Tribunali Primae Instantiae**

ART. 1. *De Iudice*

CAN. 1419   §1. In unaquaque dioecesi et pro omnibus causis iure expresse non exceptis, iudex primae instantiae est Episcopus dioecesanus, qui iudicialem potestatem exercere potest per se ipse vel per alios, secundum canones qui sequuntur.

§2. Si vero agatur de iuribus aut bonis temporalibus personae iuridicae ab Episcopo repraesentatae, iudicat in primo gradu tribunal appellationis.

1417 §1: c. 1559 §1
1417 §2: c. 1559 §2; SA Litt. circ., 13 dec. 1977
1418: c. 1570 §2

1419 §1: c. 1572 §1; LG 27; SA Litt., 24 iul. 1972, n. 1
1419 §2: c. 1572 §2 CI Resp. III, 29 apr. 1940

CAN. 1420 §1. Each diocesan bishop is bound to appoint a judicial vicar, or officialis, with ordinary power to judge, distinct from the vicar general unless the small size of the diocese or the small number of cases suggests otherwise.

§2. The judicial vicar constitutes one tribunal with the bishop but cannot judge cases which the bishop reserves to himself.

§3. The judicial vicar can be given assistants who are called adjutant judicial vicars, or vice-officiales.

§4. Both the judicial vicar and adjutant judicial vicars must be priests, of unimpaired reputation, doctors or at least licensed in canon law, and not less than thirty years of age.

§5. When the see is vacant, they do not cease from their function and cannot be removed by the diocesan administrator; when the new bishop arrives, however, they need confirmation.

CAN. 1421 §1. In a diocese, the bishop is to appoint diocesan judges, who are to be clerics.

§2. The conference of bishops can also permit the appointment of lay persons as judges; when it is necessary, one of them can be selected to form a college.

§3. Judges are to be of unimpaired reputation and doctors or at least licensed in canon law.

CAN. 1422 The judicial vicar, adjutant judicial vicars, and other judges are appointed for a definite time, without prejudice to the prescript of can. 1420, §5 and cannot be removed except for a legitimate and grave cause.

CAN. 1420 §1. Quilibet Episcopus dioecesanus tenetur Vicarium iudicialem seu Officialem constituere cum potestate ordinaria iudicandi, a Vicario generali distinctum, nisi parvitas dioecesis aut paucitas causarum aliud suadeat.

§2. Vicarius iudicialis unum constituit tribunal cum Episcopo, sed nequit iudicare causas quas Episcopus sibi reservat.

§3. Vicario iudiciali dari possunt adiutores, quibus nomen est Vicariorum iudicialium adiunctorum seu Vice-officialium.

§4. Tum Vicarius iudicialis tum Vicarii iudiciales adiuncti esse debent sacerdotes, integrae famae, in iure canonico doctores vel saltem licentiati, annos nati non minus triginta.

§5. Ipsi, sede vacante, a munere non cessant nec ab Administratore dioecesano amoveri possunt; adveniente autem novo Episcopo, indigent confirmatione.

CAN. 1421 §1. In dioecesi constituantur ab Episcopo iudices dioecesani, qui sint clerici.

§2. Episcoporum conferentia permittere potest ut etiam laici iudices constituantur, e quibus, suadente necessitate, unus assumi potest ad collegium efformandum.

§3. Iudices sint integrae famae et in iure canonico doctores vel saltem licentiati.

CAN. 1422 Vicarius iudicialis, Vicarii iudiciales adiuncti et ceteri iudices nominantur ad definitum tempus, firmo praescripto can. 1420, §5, nec removeri possunt nisi ex legitima gravique causa.

1420 §1: c. 1573; SCPF Decl., 7 apr. 1927; SA Litt., 24 iul. 1972, n. 2

1420 §2: c. 1573 §; SA Litt., 24 iul. 1972, n. 2

1420 §3: c. 1573 §3

1420 §4: c. 1573 §4; PrM 21

1420 §5: c. 1573 §5

1421 §1: c. 1574 §1; CM V §1; SA Decr., 9 aug. 1972

1421 §2: c. 1574 §1: CM V §1

1421 §3: c. 1574 §1; PrM 21; CM VII

1422: cc. 588, 1574 §2

CAN. 1423 §1. With the approval of the Apostolic See, several diocesan bishops can agree to establish a single tribunal of first instance for their dioceses in place of the diocesan tribunals mentioned in cann. 1419–1421. In this case, the group of bishops or a bishop they designate has all the powers which a diocesan bishop has over his own tribunal.

§2. The tribunals mentioned in §1 can be established either for any cases whatsoever or only for certain types of cases.

CAN. 1424 In any trial, a single judge can employ two assessors who consult with him; they are to be clerics or lay persons of upright life.

CAN. 1425 §1. With every contrary custom reprobated, the following cases are reserved to a collegiate tribunal of three judges:

1° contentious cases: a) concerning the bond of sacred ordination; b) concerning the bond of marriage, without prejudice to the prescripts of cann. 1686 and 1688;

2° penal cases: a) concerning delicts which can entail the penalty of dismissal from the clerical state; b) concerning the imposition or declaration of an excommunication.

§2. The bishop can entrust more difficult cases or those of greater importance to the judgment of three or five judges.

§3. Unless the bishop establishes otherwise in individual cases, the judicial vicar is to assign the judges in order by turn to adjudicate individual cases.

CAN. 1423 §1. Plures dioecesani Episcopi, probante Sede Apostolica, possunt concordes, in locum tribunalium dioecesanorum de quibus in cann. 1419–1421, unicum constituere in suis dioecesibus tribunal primae instantiae; quo in casu ipsorum Episcoporum coetui vel Episcopo ab eisdem designato omnes competunt potestates, quas Episcopus dioecesanus habet circa suum tribunal.

§2. Tribunalia, de quibus in §1, constitui possunt vel ad causas quaslibet vel ad aliqua tantum causarum genera.

CAN. 1424 Unicus iudex in quolibet iudicio duos assessores, clericos vel laicos probatae vitae, sibi consulentes asciscere potest.

CAN. 1425 §1. Reprobata contraria consuetudine, tribunali collegiali trium iudicum reservantur:

1° causae contentiosae: *a)* de vinculo sacrae ordinationis; *b)* de vinculo matrimonii, firmis praescriptis cann. 1686 et 1688;

2° causae poenales: *a)* de delictis quae poenam dimissionis e statu clericali secumferre possunt; *b)* de irroganda vel declaranda excommunicatione.

§2. Episcopus causas difficiliores vel maioris momenti committere potest iudicio trium vel quinque iudicum.

§3. Vicarius iudicialis ad singulas causas cognoscendas iudices ex ordine per turnum advocet, nisi Episcopus in singulis casibus aliter statuerit.

1423 §1: Pius PP. XI, m.p. *Qua cura,* 8 aug. 1938, I (AAS 30 [1938] 410); SCDS Normae, 10 iul. 1940 (AAS 32 [1940] 304–308); SA Normae, 25 mar. 1968, 18, 6°; SA Normae, 28 dec. 1970, 1 §1 (AAS 63 [1971] 486–492)

1423 §2: Pius PP. XI, m.p. *Qua cura,* 8 aug. 1938, I (AAS 30 [1938] 410)

1424: c. 1575; CM V §2, VI et VII; Sec Rescr., 1 oct. 1974

1425 §1: c. 1576 §1; PrM 13
1425 §2: c. 1576 §2
1425 §3: c. 1576 §3; CI Resp. I, 28 iul. 1932 (AAS 24 [1932] 314)

§4. If it happens that a collegiate tribunal cannot be established in the first instance of a trial, the conference of bishops can permit the bishop, for as long as the impossibility continues, to entrust cases to a single clerical judge who is to employ an assessor and auditor where possible.

§5. The judicial vicar is not to substitute judges once they have been assigned except for a most grave cause expressed in a decree.

CAN. 1426 §1. A collegiate tribunal must proceed collegially and render its sentences by majority vote.

§2. The judicial vicar or an adjutant judicial vicar must preside over a collegiate tribunal insofar as possible.

CAN. 1427 §1. If there is a controversy between religious or houses of the same clerical religious institute of pontifical right, the judge of first instance is the provincial superior unless the constitutions provide otherwise; if it is an autonomous monastery, the local abbot judges in first instance.

§2. Without prejudice to a different prescript of the constitutions, if a contentious matter arises between two provinces, the supreme moderator will judge in first instance either personally or through a delegate; if the controversy is between two monasteries, the abbot superior of the monastic congregation will judge in first instance.

§3. Finally, if the controversy arises between physical or juridic religious persons of different religious institutes or of the same clerical institute of diocesan right or of the same lay institute, or between a religious and a secular cleric

§4. In primo iudicii gradu, si forte collegium constitui nequeat, Episcoporum conferentia, quamdiu huiusmodi impossibilitas perduret, permittere potest ut Episcopus causas unico iudici clerico committat, qui, ubi fieri possit, assessorem et auditorem sibi asciscat.

§5. Iudices semel designatos ne subroget Vicarius iudicialis, nisi ex gravissima causa in decreto exprimenda.

CAN. 1426 §1. Tribunal collegiale collegialiter procedere debet, et per maiorem suffragiorum partem sententias ferre.

§2. Eidem praeesse debet, quatenus fieri potest, Vicarius iudicialis vel Vicarius iudicialis adiunctus.

CAN. 1427 §1. Si controversia sit inter religiosos vel domos eiusdem instituti religiosi clericalis iuris pontificii, iudex primae instantiae, nisi aliud in constitutionibus caveatur, est Superior provincialis, aut, si monasterium sit sui iuris, Abbas localis.

§2. Salvo diverso constitutionum praescripto, si res contentiosa agatur inter duas provincias, in prima instantia iudicabit per se ipse vel per delegatum supremus Moderator; si inter duo monasteria, Abbas superior congregationis monasticae.

§3. Si demum controversia enascatur inter religiosas personas physicas vel iuridicas diversorum institutorum religiosorum, aut etiam eiusdem instituti clericalis iuris dioecesani vel laicalis, aut inter personam reli-

---

1425 §4: CPEN Normae, 28 apr. 1970, 3; SCGE Formula facultatum, 1 ian. 1971, 20; CM V §2; Sec Normae, 1 nov. 1974, 2

1426 §1: c. 1577 §1; NSRR 139; PrM 14 §1

1426 §2: c. 1577 §2; PrM 14 §2
1427 §1: c. 1579 §1; CA I, 13
1427 §2: c. 1579 §2
1427 §3: c. 1579 §3

or lay person or a non-religious juridic person, the diocesan tribunal judges in first instance.

ART. 2. *Auditors and Relators*

CAN. 1428 §1. The judge or the president of a collegiate tribunal can designate an auditor, selected either from the judges of the tribunal or from persons the bishop approves for this function, to instruct the case.

§2. The bishop can approve for the function of auditor clerics or lay persons outstanding for their good character, prudence, and doctrine.

§3. It is for the auditor, according to the mandate of the judge, only to collect the proofs and hand those collected over to the judge. Unless the mandate of the judge prevents it, however, the auditor can in the meantime decide what proofs are to be collected and in what manner if a question may arise about this while the auditor exercises his or her function.

CAN. 1429 The president of a collegiate tribunal must designate one of the judges of the college as the *ponens* or *relator* who is to report about the case at the meeting of the judges and put the sentence into writing. For a just cause the president can substitute another in place of the original *relator*.

ART. 3. *The Promoter of Justice, The Defender of the Bond, and The Notary*

CAN. 1430 A promoter of justice is to be appointed in a diocese for contentious cases which can endanger the public good and for

ART. 2. *De Auditoribus et Relatoribus*

CAN. 1428 §1. Iudex vel tribunalis collegialis praeses possunt auditorem designare ad causae instructionem peragendam, eum seligentes aut ex tribunalis iudicibus aut ex personis ab Episcopo ad hoc munus approbatis.

§2. Episcopus potest ad auditoris munus approbare clericos vel laicos, qui bonis moribus, prudentia et doctrina fulgeant.

§3. Auditoris est, secundum iudicis mandatum, probationes tantum colligere easque collectas iudici tradere; potest autem, nisi iudicis mandatum obstet, interim decidere quae et quomodo probationes colligendae sint, si forte de hac re quaestio oriatur, dum ipse munus suum exercet.

CAN. 1429 Tribunalis collegialis praeses debet unum ex iudicibus collegii ponentem seu relatorem designare, qui in coetu iudicum de causa referat et sententias in scriptis redigat; in ipsius locum idem praeses alium ex iusta causa substituere potest.

ART. 3. *De Promotore Iustitiae, Vinculi Defensore et Notario*

CAN. 1430 Ad causas contentiosas, in quibus bonum publicum in discrimen vocari potest, et ad causas poenales constituatur in

---

1428 §1: c. 1580; PrM 23 §1; CM VI, VII
1428 §2: Sec Rescr., 1 oct. 1974
1428 §3: c. 1582, PrM 24

1429: c. 1584; PrM 22 §1
1430: c. 1586; NSRR 24 §1; PrM 16 §1

penal cases; the promoter of justice is bound by office to provide for the public good.

CAN. 1431 §1. In contentious cases, it is for the diocesan bishop to judge whether or not the public good can be endangered unless the intervention of the promoter of justice is prescribed by law or is clearly necessary from the nature of the matter.

§2. If the promoter of justice has intervened in a previous instance, such intervention is presumed necessary in a further instance.

CAN. 1432 A defender of the bond is to be appointed in a diocese for cases concerning the nullity of sacred ordination or the nullity or dissolution of a marriage; the defender of the bond is bound by office to propose and explain everything which reasonably can be brought forth against nullity or dissolution.

CAN. 1433 If the promoter of justice or defender of the bond was not cited in cases which require their presence, the acts are invalid unless they actually took part even if not cited or, after they have inspected the acts, at least were able to fulfill their function before the sentence.

CAN. 1434 Unless other provision is expressly made:

1° whenever the law requires the judge to hear either both or one of the parties, the promoter of justice and the defender of the bond must also be heard if they take part in the trial;

2° whenever the request of a party is required in order for the judge to be able to decide something, the request of the promoter of justice or defender of the bond who takes part in the trial has the same force.

dioecesi promotor iustitiae, qui officio tenetur providendi bono publico.

CAN. 1431 §1. In causis contentiosis, Episcopi dioecesani est iudicare utrum bonum publicum in discrimen vocari possit necne, nisi interventus promotoris iustitiae lege praecipiatur vel ex natura rei evidenter necessarius sit.

§2. Si in praecedenti instantia intervenerit promotor iustitiae, in ulteriore gradu huius interventus praesumitur necessarius.

CAN. 1432 Ad causas, in quibus agitur de nullitate sacrae ordinationis aut de nullitate vel solutione matrimonii, constituatur in dioecesi defensor vinculi, qui officio tenetur proponendi et exponendi omnia quae rationabiliter adduci possint adversus nullitatem vel solutionem.

CAN. 1433 In causis in quibus promotoris iustitiae aut defensoris vinculi praesentia requiritur, iis non citatis, acta irrita sunt, nisi ipsi, etsi non citati, revera interfuerint, aut saltem ante sententiam, actis inspectis, munere suo fungi potuerint.

CAN. 1434 Nisi aliud expresse caveatur:

1° quoties lex praecipit ut iudex partes earumve alteram audiat, etiam promotor iustitiae et vinculi defensor, si iudicio intersint, audiendi sunt;

2° quoties instantia partis requiritur ut iudex aliquid decernere possit, instantia promotoris iustitiae vel vinculi defensoris, qui iudicio intersint, eandem vim habet.

1431 §1: c. 1586; PrM 16 §1; 38 §2

1431 §2: SA 15 mar. 1921 (AAS 13 [1921] 269); NSRR 27 §2

1432: cc. 1586, 1968, 1969; PrM 15, 70–72; SCDS Litt., 15 ian. 1937; PIUS PP. XII, All., 2 oct. 1944, 2 b

(AAS 36 [1944] 284); IOANNES PAULUS PP. II, All., 14 feb. 1980 (AAS 72 [1980] 172–178)

1433: c. 1587; SA 15 mar. 1921 (AAS 13 [1921] 269); PrM 15 §2

1434: SN can. 64

CAN. 1435 It is for the bishop to appoint the promoter of justice and defender of the bond; they are to be clerics or lay persons, of unimpaired reputation, doctors or licensed in canon law, and proven in prudence and zeal for justice.

CAN. 1436 §1. The same person can hold the office of promoter of justice and defender of the bond but not in the same case.

§2. The promoter and the defender can be appointed for all cases or for individual cases; however, the bishop can remove them for a just cause.

CAN. 1437 §1. A notary is to take part in any process, so much so that the acts are null if the notary has not signed them.

§2. Acts which notaries prepare warrant public trust.

CHAPTER II. The Tribunal of Second Instance

CAN. 1438 Without prejudice to the prescript of can. 1444, §1, n. 1:

1° from the tribunal of a suffragan bishop, appeal is made to the metropolitan tribunal, without prejudice to the prescript of can. 1439;

2° in cases tried in first instance before the metropolitan, appeal is made to the tribunal which the metropolitan has designated in a stable manner with the approval of the Apostolic See;

3° for cases tried before a provincial superior, the tribunal of second instance is under the authority of the supreme moderator; for cases tried before the local abbot, the tribunal of second instance is under the authority of the abbot superior of the monastic congregation.

CAN. 1435 Episcopi est promotorem iustitiae et vinculi defensorem nominare, qui sint clerici vel laici, integrae famae, in iure canonico doctores vel licentiati, ac prudentia et iustitiae zelo probati.

CAN. 1436 §1. Eadem persona, non autem in eadem causa, officium promotoris iustitiae et defensoris vinculi gerere potest.

§2. Promotor et defensor constitui possunt tum ad universitatem causarum tum ad singulas causas; possunt autem ab Episcopo, iusta de causa, removeri.

CAN. 1437 §1. Cuilibet processui intersit notarius, adeo ut nulla habeantur acta, si non fuerint ab eo subscripta.

§2. Acta, quae notarii conficiunt, publicam fidem faciunt.

CAPUT II. De Tribunali Secundae Instantiae

CAN. 1438 Firmo praescripto can. 1444, §1, n. 1:

1° a tribunali Episcopi suffraganei appellatur ad tribunal Metropolitae, salvo praescripto can. 1439;

2° in causis in prima instantia pertractatis coram Metropolita fit appellatio ad tribunal quod ipse, probante Sede Apostolica, stabiliter designaverit;

3° pro causis coram Superiore provinciali actis tribunal secundae instantiae est penes supremum Moderatorem; pro causis actis coram Abbate locali, penes Abbatem superiorem congregationis monasticae.

1435: c. 1598 §1; PrM 21; Paulus PP. VI, Rescr., 26 mar. 1976; SA Decl., 12 nov. 1977
1436 §1: c. 1588 §1
1436 §2: cc. 1588 §2, 1590 §2

1437 §1: c. 1585 §1; PrM 17
1437 §2: c. 1593; PrM 18 §3
1438: c. 1594 §§1, 2 et 4; CD 40; ES I, 42

CAN. 1439 §1. If a single tribunal of first instance has been established for several dioceses according to the norm of can. 1423, the conference of bishops must establish a tribunal of second instance with the approval of the Apostolic See unless the dioceses are all suffragans of the same archdiocese.

§2. With the approval of the Apostolic See, a conference of bishops can establish one or more tribunals of second instance in addition to the cases mentioned in §1.

§3. Over the tribunals of second instance mentioned in §§1–2, the conference of bishops or the bishop it designates has all the powers which a diocesan bishop has over his own tribunal.

CAN. 1440 If competence by reason of grade according to the norm of cann. 1438 and 1439 is not observed, the incompetence of the judge is absolute.

CAN. 1441 The tribunal of second instance must be established in the same way as the tribunal of first instance. Nevertheless, if a single judge rendered a sentence in the first instance of the trial according to can. 1425, §4, the tribunal of second instance is to proceed collegially.

CHAPTER III. The Tribunals of the Apostolic See

CAN. 1442 The Roman Pontiff is the supreme judge for the entire Catholic world; he

CAN. 1439 §1. Si quod tribunal primae instantiae unicum pro pluribus dioecesibus, ad normam can. 1423, constitutum sit, Episcoporum conferentia debet tribunal secundae instantiae, probante Sede Apostolica, constituere, nisi dioeceses sint omnes eiusdem archdioecesis suffraganeae.

§2. Episcoporum conferentia potest, probante Sede Apostolica, unum vel plura tribunalia secundae instantiae constituere, etiam praeter casus de quibus in §1.

§3. Quod attinet ad tribunalia secundae instantiae, de quibus in §§1–2, Episcoporum conferentia vel Episcopus ab ea designatus omnes habent potestates, quae Episcopo dioecesano competunt circa suum tribunal.

CAN. 1440 Si competentia ratione gradus, ad normam cann. 1438 et 1439 non servetur, incompetentia iudicis est absoluta.

CAN. 1441 Tribunal secundae instantiae eodem modo quo tribunal primae instantiae constitui debet. Si tamen in primo iudicii gradu, secundum can. 1425, §4, iudex unicus sententiam tulit, tribunal secundae instantiae collegialiter procedat.

CAPUT III. De Apostolicae Sedis Tribunalibus

CAN. 1442 Romanus Pontifex pro toto orbe catholico iudex est supremus, qui vel

1439 §1: Pius PP. XI, m.p. *Qua cura,* 8 aug. 1938, II (AAS 30 [1938] 410–413); SCDS Decr. *Excellentissimi Ordinarii,* 20 dec. 1940 (AAS 33 [1941] 363–364); SCDS Decr. *Per decretum,* 25 mar. 1952 (AAS 44 [1952] 281–282); SCDS Decr. *Excellentissimi Ordinarii,* 31 dec. 1956 (AAS 49 [1957] 163–169); REU 105; SA Normae, 28 dec. 1970, 2 §1 (AAS 63 [1971] 486–488); SA Rescr., 2 ian. 1971

1439 §2: SA Normae, 28 dec. 1970, 2 §3 (AAS 63 [1971] 486–488)

1439 §3: SA Normae, 28 dec. 1970, 4 (AAS 63 [1971] 486–488)

1441: cc. 1595, 1596; Pius PP. XII, m.p. *Apostolico Hispaniarum Nuntio,* 7 apr. 1947, art. 1 (AAS 39 [1947] 155–163)

1442: c. 1597

renders judicial decisions personally, through the ordinary tribunals of the Apostolic See, or through judges he has delegated.

CAN. 1443 The Roman Rota is the ordinary tribunal established by the Roman Pontiff to receive appeals.

CAN. 1444 §1. The Roman Rota judges:

1° in second instance, cases which have been adjudicated by the ordinary tribunals of first instance and brought before the Holy See through legitimate appeal;

2° in third or further instance, cases which the Roman Rota or any other tribunals have already adjudicated unless the matter is a *res iudicata*.

§2. This tribunal also judges in first instance the cases mentioned in can. 1405, §3 and others which the Roman Pontiff, either *motu proprio* or at the request of the parties, has called to his own tribunal and entrusted to the Roman Rota; unless the rescript entrusting the function provides otherwise, the Rota also judges these cases in second and further instance.

CAN. 1445 §1. The supreme tribunal of the Apostolic Signatura adjudicates:

1° complaints of nullity, petitions for *restitutio in integrum* and other recourses against rotal sentences;

2° recourses in cases concerning the status of persons which the Roman Rota refused to admit to a new examination;

3° exceptions of suspicion and other cases against the auditors of the Roman Rota for acts done in the exercise of their function;

4° conflicts of competence mentioned in can. 1416.

per se ipse ius dicit, vel per ordinaria Sedis Apostolicae tribunalia, vel per iudices a se delegatos.

CAN. 1443 Tribunal ordinarium a Romano Pontifice constitutum appellationibus recipiendis est Rota Romana.

CAN. 1444 §1. Rota Romana iudicat:

1° in secunda instantia, causas quae ab ordinariis tribunalibus primae instantiae diiudicatae fuerint et ad Sanctam Sedem per appellationem legitimam deferantur;

2° in tertia vel ulteriore instantia, causas ab ipsa Rota Romana et ab aliis quibusvis tribunalibus iam cognitas, nisi res iudicata habeatur.

§2. Hoc tribunal iudicat etiam in prima instantia causas de quibus in can. 1405, §3, aliasve quas Romanus Pontifex sive motu proprio, sive ad instantiam partium ad suum tribunal advocaverit et Rotae Romanae commiserit; easque, nisi aliud cautum sit in commissi muneris rescripto, ipsa Rota iudicat etiam in secunda et ulteriore instantia.

CAN. 1445 §1. Supremum Signaturae Apostolicae Tribunal cognoscit:

1° querelas nullitatis et petitiones restitutionis in integrum et alios recursus contra sententias rotales;

2° recursus in causis de statu personarum, quas ad novum examen Rota Romana admittere renuit;

3° exceptiones suspicionis aliasque causas contra Auditores Rotae Romanae propter acta in exercitio ipsorum muneris;

4° conflictus competentiae de quibus in can. 1416.

1443: c. 1598 §1; NSRR 1; REU 109; SRR *Nuove Norme*, 25 maii 1969, art. 1 §1

1444 §1: c. 1599 §1; PrM 216 §1; REU 109; NSRR 27 §2; PAULUS PP. VI, Const. Ap. *Vicariae potestatis*, 6 ian. 1977, art 20 et 22 (AAS 69 [1977] 17)

1444 §2: c. 1599 §2

1445 §1: c. 1603 §1; SA Decisio, 25 nov. 1922; NSSA 17 §2; 19 §1; 20 §1; 21 §1

§2. This tribunal deals with conflicts which have arisen from an act of ecclesiastical administrative power and are brought before it legitimately, with other administrative controversies which the Roman Pontiff or the dicasteries of the Roman Curia bring before it, and with a conflict of competence among these dicasteries.

§3. Furthermore it is for this supreme tribunal:

1° to watch over the correct administration of justice and discipline advocates or procurators if necessary;

2° to extend the competence of tribunals;

3° to promote and approve the erection of the tribunals mentioned in cann. 1423 and 1439.

TITLE III. The Discipline To Be Observed in Tribunals

CHAPTER I. The Duty of Judges and Ministers of the Tribunal

CAN. 1446 §1. All the Christian faithful, and especially bishops, are to strive diligently to avoid litigation among the people of God as much as possible, without prejudice to justice, and to resolve litigation peacefully as soon as possible.

§2. Whenever the judge perceives some hope of a favorable outcome at the start of litigation or even at any other time, the judge is not to neglect to encourage and assist the parties to collaborate in seeking an equitable solution to the controversy and to indicate to them suitable

§2. Ipsum Tribunal videt de contentionibus ortis ex actu potestatis administrativae ecclesiasticae ad eam legitime delatis, de aliis controversiis administrativis quae a Romano Pontifice vel a Romanae Curiae dicasteriis ipsi deferantur, et de conflictu competentiae inter eadem dicasteria.

§3. Supremi huius Tribunalis praeterea est:

1° rectae administrationi iustitiae invigilare et in advocatos vel procuratores, si opus sit, animadvertere;

2° tribunalium competentiam prorogare;

3° promovere et approbare erectionem tribunalium, de quibus in cann. 1423 et 1439.

TITULUS III. De Disciplina in Tribunalibus Servanda

CAPUT I. De Officio Iudicum et Tribunalis Ministrorum

CAN. 1446 §1. Christifideles omnes, in primis autem Episcopi, sedulo annitantur ut, salva iustitia, lites in populo Dei, quantum fieri possit, vitentur et pacifice quam primum componantur.

§2. Iudex in limine litis, et etiam quolibet alio momento, quotiescumque spem aliquam boni exitus perspicit, partes hortari et adiuvare ne omittat, ut de aequa controversiae solutione quaerenda communi consilio curent, viasque ad hoc propositum idoneas

1445 §2: REU 106, 107; NSSA 96; SA Decisio, 10 maii 1968; SA Decisio, 21 maii 1968; SA Decisio, 24 mar. 1969; SA Decl., 9 nov. 1970; SA Decisio, 15 dec. 1970

1445 §3: REU 105; NSSA 17 §1, 18; SA Decl., 22 oct.

1970; SA Rescr., 2 ian. 1971; SA Rescr., 26 mar. 1974; SA Rescr., 20 feb. 1976

1446 §1: c. 1925 §1; NSRR 75 §1
1446 §2: c. 1925 §2

means to this end, even by using reputable persons for mediation.

§3. If the litigation concerns the private good of the parties, the judge is to discern whether the controversy can be concluded advantageously by an agreement or the judgment of arbitrators according to the norm of cann. 1713–1716.

CAN. 1447 A person who has taken part in a case as a judge, promoter of justice, defender of the bond, procurator, advocate, witness, or expert cannot later in another instance validly decide the same case as judge or perform the function of assessor.

CAN. 1448 §1. A judge is not to undertake the adjudication of a case in which the judge is involved by reason of consanguinity or affinity in any degree of the direct line and up to the fourth degree of the collateral line or by reason of trusteeship, guardianship, close acquaintance, great animosity, the making of a profit, or the avoidance of a loss.

§2. In these circumstances the promoter of justice, the defender of the bond, the assessor, and the auditor must abstain from their office.

CAN. 1449 §1. If in the cases mentioned in can. 1448 the judge does not withdraw, a party can lodge an objection against the judge.

§2. The judicial vicar deals with the objection; if the objection is lodged against him, the bishop who presides over the tribunal deals with it.

§3. If the bishop is the judge and the objection is lodged against him, he is to abstain from judging.

§4. If the objection is lodged against the pro-

ipsis indicet, gravibus quoque hominibus ad mediationem adhibitis.

§3. Quod si circa privatum partium bonum lis versetur, dispiciat iudex num transactione vel arbitrorum iudicio, ad normam cann. 1713–1716, controversia finem habere utiliter possit.

CAN. 1447 Qui causae interfuit tamquam iudex, promotor iustitiae, defensor vinculi, procurator, advocatus, testis aut peritus, nequit postea valide eandem causam in alia instantia tamquam iudex definire aut in eadem munus assessoris sustinere.

CAN. 1448 §1. Iudex cognoscendam ne suscipiat causam, in qua ratione consanguinitatis vel affinitatis in quolibet gradu lineae rectae et usque ad quartum gradum lineae collateralis, vel ratione tutelae et curatelae, intimae vitae consuetudinis, magnae simultatis, vel lucri faciendi aut damni vitandi, aliquid ipsius intersit.

§2. In iisdem adiunctis ab officio suo abstinere debent iustitiae promotor, defensor vinculi, assessor et auditor.

CAN. 1449 §1. In casibus, de quibus in can. 1448, nisi iudex ipse abstineat, pars potest eum recusare.

§2. De recusatione videt Vicarius iudicialis; si ipse recusetur, videt Episcopus qui tribunali praeest.

§3. Si Episcopus sit iudex et contra eum recusatio opponatur, ipse abstineat a iudicando.

§4. Si recusatio opponatur contra pro-

1446 §3: c. 1925 §§1 et 3
1447: cc. 1571, 1613 §1
1448 §1: c. 1613 §1; PrM 30 §1
1448 §2: c. 1613 §2; PrM 30 §2
1449 §1: c. 1614 §1; PrM 31 §1; CIV Resp. I, 1 iul. 1976 (AAS 68 [1976] 635)

1449 §2: c. 1614 §1; PrM 31 §1
1449 §3: c. 1614 §2; PrM 31 §2
1449 §4: c. 1614 §3; PrM 31 §3

moter of justice, the defender of the bond, or other officials of the tribunal, the president in a collegiate tribunal or the single judge deals with this exception.

CAN. 1450   If the objection is accepted, the persons must be changed but not the grade of the trial.

CAN. 1451   §1. The question of an objection must be decided as promptly as possible (*expeditissime*) after the parties have been heard as well as the promoter of justice or defender of the bond, if they take part in the trial and are not the ones against whom the objection has been lodged.

§2. Acts placed by a judge before an objection is lodged are valid; nevertheless, those acts placed after the objection has been lodged must be rescinded if a party requests it within ten days from the acceptance of the objection.

CAN. 1452   §1. In a matter which concerns private persons alone, a judge can proceed only at the request of a party. Once a case has been legitimately introduced, however, the judge can and must proceed even *ex officio* in penal cases and other cases which regard the public good of the Church or the salvation of souls.

§2. Furthermore, the judge can supply for the negligence of the parties in furnishing proofs or in lodging exceptions whenever the judge considers it necessary in order to avoid a gravely unjust judgment, without prejudice to the prescripts of can. 1600.

CAN. 1453   Without prejudice to justice, judges and tribunals are to take care that all cases are completed as soon as possible and that in a tribunal of first instance they are not pro-

motorem iustitiae, defensorem vinculi aut alios tribunalis administros, de hac exceptione videt praeses in tribunali collegiali vel ipse iudex, si unicus sit.

CAN. 1450   Recusatione admissa, personae mutari debent, non vero iudicii gradus.

CAN. 1451   §1. Quaestio de recusatione expeditissime definienda est, auditis partibus, promotore iustitiae vel vinculi defensore, si intersint, neque ipsi recusati sint.

§2. Actus positi a iudice antequam recusetur, validi sunt; qui autem positi sunt post propositam recusationem, rescindi debent, si pars petat intra decem dies ab admissa recusatione.

CAN. 1452   §1. In negotio quod privatorum solummodo interest, iudex procedere potest dumtaxat ad instantiam partis. Causa autem legitime introducta, iudex procedere potest et debet etiam ex officio in causis poenalibus aliisque, quae publicum Ecclesiae bonum aut animarum salutem respiciunt.

§2. Potest autem praeterea iudex partium neglegentiam in probationibus afferendis vel in exceptionibus opponendis supplere, quoties id necessarium censeat ad vitandam graviter iniustam sententiam, firmis praescriptis can. 1600.

CAN. 1453   Iudices et tribunalia curent ut quam primum, salva iustitia, causae omnes terminentur, utque in tribunali primae instantiae ultra annum ne protrahantur, in tri-

longed beyond a year and in a tribunal of second instance beyond six months.

CAN. 1454 All who constitute a tribunal or assist it must take an oath to carry out their function correctly and faithfully.

CAN. 1455 §1. Judges and tribunal personnel are always bound to observe secrecy of office in a penal trial, as well as in a contentious trial if the revelation of some procedural act could bring disadvantage to the parties.

§2. They are also always bound to observe secrecy concerning the discussion among the judges in a collegiate tribunal before the sentence is passed and concerning the various votes and opinions expressed there, without prejudice to the prescript of can. 1609, §4.

§3. Whenever the nature of the case or the proofs is such that disclosure of the acts or proofs will endanger the reputation of others, provide opportunity for discord, or give rise to scandal or some other disadvantage, the judge can bind the witnesses, the experts, the parties, and their advocates or procurators by oath to observe secrecy.

CAN. 1456 The judge and all officials of the tribunal are prohibited from accepting any gifts on the occasion of their acting in a trial.

CAN. 1457 §1. The competent authority can punish with fitting penalties, not excluding privation from office, judges who refuse to render a judgment when they are certainly and manifestly competent, who declare themselves competent with no supporting prescript of law and adjudicate and decide cases, who violate the

bunali vero secundae instantiae, ultra sex menses.

CAN. 1454 Omnes qui tribunal constituunt aut eidem opem ferunt, iusiurandum de munere rite et fideliter implendo praestare debent.

CAN. 1455 §1. In iudicio poenali semper, in contentioso autem si ex revelatione alicuius actus processualis praeiudicium partibus obvenire possit, iudices et tribunalis auditores tenentur ad secretum officii servandum.

§2. Tenentur etiam semper ad secretum servandum de discussione quae inter iudices in tribunali collegiali ante ferendam sententiam habetur, tum etiam de variis suffragiis et opinionibus ibidem prolatis, firmo praescripto can. 1609, §4.

§3. Immo, quoties natura causae vel probationum talis sit ut ex actorum vel probationum evulgatione aliorum fama periclitetur, vel praebeatur ansa dissidiis, aut scandalum aliudve id genus incommodum oriatur, iudex poterit testes, peritos, partes earumque advocatos vel procuratores iureiurando astringere ad secretum servandum.

CAN. 1456 Iudex et omnes tribunalis administri, occasione agendi iudicii, dona quaevis acceptare prohibentur.

CAN. 1457 §1. Iudices qui, cum certe et evidenter competentes sint, ius reddere recusent, vel nullo suffragante iuris praescripto se competentes declarent atque causas cognoscant ac definiant, vel secreti legem violent, vel ex dolo aut gravi neglegentia aliud litigantibus damnum inferant, congruis poe-

---

1454: c. 1621; PrM 20
1455 §1: c. 1623 §1
1455 §2: c. 1623 §2; PrM 203 §2

1455 §3: c. 1623 §3; PrM 130 §1
1456: c. 1624
1457 §1: c. 1625 §§1 et 2

law of secrecy, or who inflict some other damage on the litigants out of malice or grave negligence.

§2. The ministers and personnel of a tribunal are subject to these same sanctions if they fail in their office as described above; the judge can also punish all of them.

CHAPTER II. The Order of Adjudication

CAN. 1458 Cases are to be adjudicated in the order in which they were presented and inscribed in the register unless one of them requires speedier treatment than the others; this fact must be established through a special decree which gives the substantiating reasons.

CAN. 1459 §1. Defects which can render the sentence null can be introduced as exceptions at any stage or grade of the trial; the judge can likewise declare them *ex officio*.

§2. In addition to the cases mentioned in §1, dilatory exceptions, especially those which regard the persons and the manner of the trial, must be proposed before the joinder of the issue unless they emerged after the issue was already joined; they must be decided as soon as possible.

CAN. 1460 §1. If an exception is proposed against the competence of the judge, that judge must deal with the matter.

§2. In the case of an exception of relative incompetence, if the judge finds for competence, the decision does not admit of appeal; a complaint of nullity and *restitutio in integrum*, however, are not prohibited.

§3. If the judge finds for incompetence, however, the party who feels injured can appeal to the appellate tribunal within fifteen useful days.

nis a competenti auctoritate puniri possunt, non exclusa officii privatione.

§2. Iisdem sanctionibus subsunt tribunalis ministri et adiutores, si officio suo, ut supra, defuerint; quos omnes etiam iudex punire potest.

CAPUT II. De Ordine Cognitionum

CAN. 1458 Causae cognoscendae sunt eo ordine quo fuerunt propositae et in albo inscriptae, nisi ex iis aliqua celerem prae ceteris expeditionem exigat, quod quidem peculiari decreto, rationibus suffulto, statuendum est.

CAN. 1459 §1. Vitia, quibus sententiae nullitas haberi potest, in quolibet iudicii statu vel gradu excipi possunt itemque a iudice ex officio declarari.

§2. Praeter casus de quibus in §1, exceptiones dilatoriae, eae praesertim quae respiciunt personas et modum iudicii, proponendae sunt ante contestationem litis, nisi contestata iam lite emerserint, et quam primum definiendae.

CAN. 1460 §1. Si exceptio proponatur contra iudicis competentiam, hac de re ipse iudex videre debet.

§2. In casu exceptionis de incompetentia relativa, si iudex se competentem pronuntiet, eius decisio non admittit appellationem, at non prohibentur querela nullitatis et restitutio in integrum.

§3. Quod si iudex se incompetentem declaret, pars, quae se gravatam reputat, potest intra quindecim dies utiles provocare ad tribunal appellationis.

1457 §2: c. 1625 §3
1458: c. 1627
1459 §1: c. 1628 §2
1459 §2: c. 1628 §1; PrM 27 §§1 et 3

1460 §1: c. 1610 §1
1460 §2: c. 1610 §2; PrM 28 §1
1460 §3: c. 1610 §3; PrM 28 §2, 29

CAN. 1461 A judge who becomes aware of being absolutely incompetent at any stage of the case must declare the incompetence.

CAN. 1462 §1. Exceptions of *res iudicata,* of agreement, and other peremptory exceptions which are called *litis finitae* must be proposed and adjudicated before the joinder of the issue. A person who proposes them later must not be rejected but is liable for expenses unless the person proves that the presentation was not delayed maliciously.

§2. Other peremptory exceptions are to be proposed during the joinder of the issue and must be treated at the proper time according to the rules for incidental questions.

CAN. 1463 §1. Counterclaims cannot be proposed validly except within thirty days from the joinder of the issue.

§2. They are to be adjudicated, however, along with the original action, that is, in the same grade with it unless it is necessary to adjudicate them separately or the judge considers it more opportune to do so.

CAN. 1464 Questions concerning the provision for judicial expenses or a grant of gratuitous legal assistance which had been requested from the very beginning and other such questions as a rule must be dealt with before the joinder of the issue.

CHAPTER III. **Time Limits and Delays**

CAN. 1465 §1. *Fatalia legis,* that is, the time limits established by law for extinguishing rights, cannot be extended nor validly shortened unless the parties request it.

CAN. 1461 Iudex in quovis stadio causae se absolute incompetentem agnoscens, suam incompetentiam declarare debet.

CAN. 1462 §1. Exceptiones rei iudicatae, transactionis et aliae peremptoriae quae dicuntur *litis finitae,* proponi et cognosci debent ante contestationem litis; qui serius eas opposuerit, non est reiciendus, sed condemnetur ad expensas, nisi probet se oppositionem malitiose non distulisse.

§2. Aliae exceptiones peremptoriae proponantur in contestatione litis, et suo tempore tractandae sunt secundum regulas circa quaestiones incidentes.

CAN. 1463 §1. Actiones reconventionales proponi valide nequeunt, nisi intra triginta dies a lite contestata.

§2. Eaedem autem cognoscantur simul cum conventionali actione, hoc est pari gradu cum ea, nisi eas separatim cognoscere necessarium sit aut iudex id opportunius existimaverit.

CAN. 1464 Quaestiones de cautione pro expensis iudicialibus praestanda aut de concessione gratuiti patrocinii, quod statim ab initio postulatum fuerit, et aliae huiusmodi regulariter videndae sunt ante litis contestationem.

CAPUT III. **De Terminis et Dilationibus**

CAN. 1465 §1. Fatalia legis quae dicuntur, id est termini perimendis iuribus lege constituti, prorogari non possunt, neque valide, nisi petentibus partibus, coarctari.

1461: c. 1611; PrM 27 §2
1462 §1: c. 1629 §1
1462 §2: c. 1629 §2
1463 §1: c. 1630 §1

1463 §2: c. 1630 §1
1464: c. 1631
1465 §1: c. 1634 §1

§2. Before the judicial or conventional time limits lapse, however, the judge can extend them for a just cause after the parties have been heard or if they request it; the judge, however, can never shorten those limits validly unless the parties agree.

§3. Nevertheless, the judge is to take care that such an extension does not overly prolong the litigation.

CAN. 1466 When the law in no way establishes time limits for completing procedural acts, the judge must define them after having taken into consideration the nature of each act.

CAN. 1467 If the tribunal is closed on the day scheduled for a judicial act, the time limit is extended to the first day following which is not a holiday.

CHAPTER IV. **The Place of the Trial**

CAN. 1468 Insofar as possible, every tribunal is to be in an established location open during stated hours.

CAN. 1469 §1. A judge expelled by force from his territory or impeded from the exercise of jurisdiction there can exercise jurisdiction and render a sentence outside that territory; the diocesan bishop, however, is to be informed of this.

§2. In addition to the case mentioned in §1, for a just cause and after having heard the parties, the judge can also go outside the territory to acquire proofs. This is to be done, however, with the permission of the diocesan bishop of the place where the judge goes and in the location designated by that bishop.

§2. Termini autem iudiciales et conventionales, ante eorum lapsum, poterunt, iusta intercedente causa, a iudice, auditis vel petentibus partibus, prorogari, numquam autem, nisi partibus consentientibus, valide coarctari.

§3. Caveat tamen iudex ne nimis diuturna lis fiat ex prorogatione.

CAN. 1466 Ubi lex terminos haud statuat ad actus processuales peragendos, iudex illos praefinire debet, habita ratione naturae uniuscuiusque actus.

CAN. 1467 Si die ad actum iudicialem indicto vacaverit tribunal, terminus intellegitur prorogatus ad primum sequentem diem non feriatum.

CAPUT IV. **De Loco Iudicii**

CAN. 1468 Uniuscuiusque tribunalis sedes sit, quantum fieri potest, stabilis, quae statutis horis pateat.

CAN. 1469 §1. Iudex e territorio suo vi expulsus vel a iurisdictione ibi exercenda impeditus, potest extra territorium iurisdictionem suam exercere et sententiam ferre, certiore tamen hac de re facto Episcopo dioecesano.

§2. Praeter casum de quo in §1, iudex, ex iusta causa et auditis partibus, potest ad probationes acquirendas etiam extra proprium territorium se conferre, de licentia tamen Episcopi dioecesani loci adeundi et in sede ab eodem designata.

1465 §2: c. 1634 §2
1465 §3: c. 1634 §3
1467: c. 1635

1468: cc. 1636, 1638 §1
1469 §1: c. 1637

CHAPTER V. **Persons to be Admitted to the Court and the Manner of Preparing and Keeping the Acts**

CAN. 1470 §1. Unless particular law provides otherwise, while cases are being heard before the tribunal, only those persons are to be present in court whom the law or the judge has established as necessary to expedite the process.

§2. With appropriate penalties, the judge can call to task all those present at a trial who are gravely lacking in the respect and obedience due the tribunal; furthermore, the judge can also suspend advocates and procurators from the exercise of their function in ecclesiastical tribunals.

CAN. 1471 If a person to be questioned speaks a language unknown to the judge or the parties, an interpreter designated by the judge and under oath is to be used. The statements, however, are to be put into writing in the original language and a translation added. An interpreter is also to be used if a speech or hearing impaired person must be questioned unless the judge may prefer the person to answer the questions in writing.

CAN. 1472 §1. The judicial acts, both the acts of the case, that is, those regarding the merit of the question, and the acts of the process, that is, those pertaining to the procedure, must be put in writing.

§2. The individual pages of the acts are to be numbered and authenticated.

CAN. 1473 Whenever judicial acts require the signature of the parties or witnesses and the party or witness is unable or unwilling to sign, this is to be noted in the acts; the judge and the

CAPUT V. **De Personis in Aulam Admittendis et de Modo Conficiendi et Conservandi Acta**

CAN. 1470 §1. Nisi aliter lex particularis caveat, dum causae coram tribunali aguntur, ii tantummodo adsint in aula quos lex aut iudex ad processum expediendum necessarios esse statuerit.

§2. Omnes iudicio assistentes, qui reverentiae et oboedientiae tribunali debitae graviter defuerint, iudex potest congruis poenis ad officium reducere, advocatos praeterea et procuratores etiam a munere apud tribunalia ecclesiastica exercendo suspendere.

CAN. 1471 Si qua persona interroganda utatur lingua iudici vel partibus ignota, adhibeatur interpres iuratus a iudice designatus. Declarationes tamen scripto redigantur lingua originaria et translatio addatur. Interpres etiam adhibeatur si surdus vel mutus interrogari debet, nisi forte malit iudex quaestionibus a se datis scripto respondeatur.

CAN. 1472 §1. Acta iudicialia, tum quae meritum quaestionis respiciunt, seu acta causae, tum quae ad formam procedendi pertinent, seu acta processus, scripto redacta esse debent.

§2. Singula folia actorum numerentur et authenticitatis signo muniantur.

CAN. 1473 Quoties in actis iudicialibus partium aut testium subscriptio requiritur, si pars aut testis subscribere nequeat vel nolit, id in ipsis actis adnotetur, simulque iudex et

---

1470 §1: c. 1640 §1
1470 §2: c. 1640 §2
1471: c. 1641

1472 §1: c. 1642 §1
1472 §2: c. 1643 §1
1473: c. 1643 §3

notary are also to attest that the act was read to the party or the witness verbatim and that the party or the witness was either not able or unwilling to sign.

CAN. 1474 §1. In the case of an appeal, a copy of the acts authenticated by the attestation of a notary is to be sent to the higher tribunal.

§2. If the acts were written in a language unknown to the higher tribunal, they are to be translated into one known to that tribunal, with due precautions taken that the translation is a faithful one.

CAN. 1475 §1. When the trial has been completed, documents which belong to private persons must be returned; a copy of them, however, is to be retained.

§2. Without a mandate of the judge, notaries and the chancellor are forbidden to furnish a copy of the judicial acts and documents acquired in the process.

notarius fidem faciant actum ipsum de verbo ad verbum parti aut testi perlectum fuisse, et partem aut testem vel non potuisse vel noluisse subscribere.

CAN. 1474 §1. In casu appellationis, actorum exemplar, fide facta a notario de eius authenticitate, ad tribunal superius mittatur.

§2. Si acta exarata fuerint lingua tribunali superiori ignota, transferantur in aliam eidem tribunali cognitam, cautelis adhibitis, ut de fideli translatione constet.

CAN. 1475 §1. Iudicio expleto, documenta quae in privatorum dominio sunt, restitui debent, retento tamen eorum exemplari.

§2. Notarii et cancellarius sine iudicis mandato tradere prohibentur exemplar actorum iudicialium et documentorum, quae sunt processui acquisita.

TITLE IV. The Parties in a Case

CHAPTER I. The Petitioner and the Respondent

CAN. 1476 Anyone, whether baptized or not, can bring action in a trial; however, a party legitimately summoned must respond.

CAN. 1477 Even if the petitioner or respondent has appointed a procurator or advocate, they themselves are nevertheless always bound to be present at the trial according to the prescript of the law or of the judge.

TITULUS IV. De Partibus in Causa

CAPUT I. De Actore et de Parte Conventa

CAN. 1476 Quilibet, sive baptizatus sive non baptizatus, potest in iudicio agere; pars autem legitime conventa respondere debet.

CAN. 1477 Licet actor vel pars conventa procuratorem vel advocatum constituerit, semper tamen tenetur in iudicio ipsemet adesse ad praescriptum iuris vel iudicis.

1474 §1: c. 1644 §1
1474 §2: c. 1644 §2
1475 §1: c. 1645 §1
1475 §2: c. 1645 §3

1476: c. 1646; SCSO Resp., 27 ian. 1928 (AAS 20 [1928] 75); PrM 35 §3; CIV Resp., 8 ian. 1973 (AAS 65 [1973] 59); SA Decl., 31 oct. 1977
1477: c. 1647; PrM 45

CAN. 1478 §1. Minors and those who lack the use of reason can stand trial only through their parents, guardians, or curators, without prejudice to the prescript of §3.

§2. If the judge thinks that the rights of minors are in conflict with the rights of the parents, guardians, or curators or that the latter cannot adequately protect the rights of the former, then the minors are to stand trial through a guardian or curator appointed by the judge.

§3. Nevertheless, in spiritual cases and those connected with spiritual matters, if the minors have attained the use of reason, they can petition and respond without the consent of their parents or guardian. They can do so personally if they have completed their fourteenth year of age; otherwise, they do so through the curator appointed by the judge.

§4. Those deprived of the administration of goods and those of diminished mental capacity can stand trial personally only to answer for their own delicts or at the order of the judge; otherwise, they must petition and respond through their curators.

CAN. 1479 Whenever a guardian or curator appointed by civil authority is present, the ecclesiastical judge can admit the guardian or curator after having heard, if possible, the diocesan bishop of the person to whom the guardian or curator was given; if the guardian or curator is not present or does not seem admissible, the judge will appoint a guardian or curator for the case.

CAN. 1480 §1. Juridic persons stand trial through their legitimate representatives.

CAN. 1478 §1. Minores et ii, qui rationis usu destituti sunt, stare in iudicio tantummodo possunt per eorum parentes aut tutores vel curatores, salvo praescripto §3.

§2. Si iudex existimet minorum iura esse in conflictu cum iuribus parentum vel tutorum vel curatorum, aut hos non satis tueri posse ipsorum iura, tunc stent in iudicio per tutorem vel curatorem a iudice datum.

§3. Sed in causis spiritualibus et cum spiritualibus conexis, si minores usum rationis assecuti sint, agere et respondere queunt sine parentum vel tutoris consensu, et quidem per se ipsi, si aetatem quattuordecim annorum expleverint; secus per curatorem a iudice constitutum.

§4. Bonis interdicti, et ii qui minus firmae mentis sunt, stare in iudicio per se ipsi possunt tantummodo ut de propriis delictis respondeant, aut ad praescriptum iudicis; in ceteris agere et respondere debent per suos curatores.

CAN. 1479 Quoties adest tutor aut curator ab auctoritate civili constitutus, idem potest a iudice ecclesiastico admitti, audito, si fieri potest, Episcopo dioecesano eius cui datus est; quod si non adsit aut non videatur admittendus, ipse iudex tutorem aut curatorem pro causa designabit.

CAN. 1480 §1. Personae iuridicae in iudicio stant per suos legitimos repraesentantes.

1478 §1: c. 1648 §1
1478 §2: c. 1648 §2
1478 §3: c. 1648 §3
1478 §4: c. 1650

1479: c. 1651; PrM 78 §§1 et 2; CIC Resp. II, 25 ian. 1943 (AAS 35 [1943] 58)
1480 §1: c. 1649

§2. In a case of the lack of or negligence of the representative, however, the ordinary himself can stand trial personally or through another in the name of juridic persons subject to his authority.

CHAPTER II. Procurators for Litigation and Advocates

CAN. 1481 §1. A party can freely appoint an advocate and procurator; except for the cases established in §§2 and 3, however, the party can also petition and respond personally unless the judge has decided that the services of a procurator or advocate are necessary.

§2. In a penal trial, the accused must always have an advocate either appointed personally or assigned by the judge.

§3. In a contentious trial which involves minors or in a trial which affects the public good, with the exception of marriage cases, the judge is to appoint *ex officio* a defender for a party who does not have one.

CAN. 1482 §1. A person can appoint only one procurator who cannot substitute another unless the procurator has been given the expressed faculty to do so.

§2. If a person appoints several procurators for a just cause, however, they are to be designated in such a way that prevention is operative among them.

§3. Nevertheless, several advocates can be appointed together.

CAN. 1483 The procurator and advocate must have attained the age of majority and be of good reputation; moreover, the advocate

§2. In casu vero defectus vel neglegentiae repraesentantis, potest ipse Ordinarius per se vel per alium stare in iudicio nomine personarum iuridicarum, quae sub eius potestate sunt.

CAPUT II. De Procuratoribus ad Lites et Advocatis

CAN. 1481 §1. Pars libere potest advocatum et procuratorem sibi constituere; sed praeter casus in §§2 et 3 statutos, potest etiam per se ipsa agere et respondere, nisi iudex procuratoris vel advocati ministerium necessarium existimaverit.

§2. In iudicio poenali accusatus aut a se constitutum aut a iudice datum semper habere debet advocatum.

§3. In iudicio contentioso, si agatur de minoribus aut de iudicio in quo bonum publicum vertitur, exceptis causis matrimonialibus, iudex parti carenti defensorem ex officio constituat.

CAN. 1482 §1. Unicum sibi quisque potest constituere procuratorem, qui nequit alium sibimet substituere, nisi expressa facultas eidem facta fuerit.

§2. Quod si tamen, iusta causa suadente, plures ab eodem constituantur, hi ita designentur, ut detur inter ipsos locus praeventioni.

§3. Advocati autem plures simul constitui queunt.

CAN. 1483 Procurator et advocatus esse debent aetate maiores et bonae famae; advocatus debet praeterea esse catholicus,

---

1480 §2: c. 1653 §5
1481 §1: c. 1655 §3; PrM 43 §1, 44 §1
1481 §2: c. 1655 §1
1481 §3: c. 1655 §2
1482 §1: c. 1656 §1; PrM 47 §1

1482 §2: c. 1656 §2; PrM 47 §2
1482 §3: c. 1656 §3; PrM 47 §3
1483: cc. 1657 §§1 et 2, 1658 §§1 et 2, SA Decl., 15 dec. 1923 (AAS 16 [1924] 105); PrM 48 §§1, 2 et 4

must be a Catholic unless the diocesan bishop permits otherwise, a doctor in canon law or otherwise truly expert, and approved by the same bishop.

CAN. 1484 §1. Before the procurator and advocate undertake their function, they must present an authentic mandate to the tribunal.

§2. To prevent the extinction of a right, however, the judge can admit a procurator even if the mandate has not been presented, once a suitable guarantee has been furnished if the case warrants it; the act, however, lacks any force if the procurator does not correctly present the mandate within the peremptory time established by the judge.

CAN. 1485 Without a special mandate, a procurator cannot validly renounce an action, an instance, or judicial acts nor come to an agreement, make a bargain, enter into arbitration, or in general do those things for which the law requires a special mandate.

CAN. 1486 §1. For the removal of a procurator or advocate to take effect, they must be informed; if the issue has already been joined, the judge and the opposing party must also be informed about the removal.

§2. After the definitive sentence has been issued, the right and duty to appeal, if the mandating person does not refuse, remains with the procurator.

CAN. 1487 For a grave cause, the judge either *ex officio* or at the request of the party can remove the procurator and the advocate by decree.

CAN. 1488 §1. Both the procurator and the advocate are forbidden to resolve the litigation

nisi Episcopus dioecesanus aliter permittat, et doctor in iure canonico, vel alioquin vere peritus et ab eodem Episcopo approbatus.

CAN. 1484 §1. Procurator et advocatus antequam munus suscipiant, mandatum authenticum apud tribunal deponere debent.

§2. Ad iuris tamen extinctionem impediendam iudex potest procuratorem admittere etiam non exhibito mandato, praestita, si res ferat, idonea cautione; actus autem qualibet vi caret, si intra terminum peremptorium a iudice statuendum, procurator mandatum rite non exhibeat.

CAN. 1485 Nisi speciale mandatum habuerit, procurator non potest valide renuntiare actioni, instantiae vel actis iudicialibus, nec transigere, pacisci, compromittere in arbitros et generatim ea agere pro quibus ius requirit mandatum speciale.

CAN. 1486 §1. Ut procuratoris vel advocati remotio effectum sortiatur, necesse est ipsis intimetur, et, si lis iam contestata fuerit, iudex et adversa pars certiores facti sint de remotione.

§2. Lata definitiva sententia, ius et officium appellandi, si mandans non renuat, procuratori manet.

CAN. 1487 Tum procurator tum advocatus possunt a iudice, dato decreto, repelli sive ex officio sive ad instantiam partis, gravi tamen de causa.

CAN. 1488 §1. Vetatur uterque emere litem, aut sibi de immodico emolumento vel

---

1484 §1: cc. 1659 §1, 1661; PrM 49 §§1 et 4, 60
1484 §2: SN can. 177
1485: c. 1662; PrM 50
1486 §1: c. 1664 §1; PrM 52 §1

1486 §2: c. 1664 §2; PrM 52 §2
1487: c. 1663; PrM 51
1488 §1: c. 1665; PrM 54, 1°

by bribery or to make an agreement for an excessive profit or for a share in the object in dispute. If they do so, the agreement is null, and the judge can fine them. Moreover, the bishop who presides over the tribunal can suspend the advocate from office and even remove him or her from the list of advocates if it happens again.

§2. Advocates and procurators can be punished in the same way if in deceit of the law they withdraw cases from competent tribunals so that the cases will be decided more favorably by other tribunals.

CAN. 1489 Advocates and procurators who betray their office for gifts, promises, or any other reason are to be suspended from the exercise of legal assistance and punished with a fine or other suitable penalties.

CAN. 1490 As far as possible, legal representatives are to be appointed in a stable manner in each tribunal, who receive a stipend from the tribunal and are to exercise, especially in marriage cases, the function of advocate or procurator on behalf of parties who wish to select them.

rei litigiosae parte vindicata pacisci. Quae si fecerint, nulla est pactio, et a iudice poterunt poena pecuniaria mulctari. Advocatus praeterea tum ab officio suspendi, tum etiam, si recidivus sit, ab Episcopo, qui tribunali praeest, ex albo advocatorum expungi potest.

§2. Eodem modo puniri possunt advocati et procuratores qui a competentibus tribunalibus causas, in fraudem legis, subtrahunt ut ab aliis favorabilius definiantur.

CAN. 1489 Advocati ac procuratores qui ob dona aut pollicitationes aut quamlibet aliam rationem suum officium prodiderint, a patrocinio exercendo suspendantur, et mulcta pecuniaria aliisve congruis poenis plectantur.

CAN. 1490 In unoquoque tribunali, quatenus fieri possit, stabiles patroni constituantur, ab ipso tribunali stipendium recipientes, qui munus advocati vel procuratoris in causis praesertim matrimonialibus pro partibus quae eos seligere malint, exerceant.

TITLE V. Actions and Exceptions

CHAPTER I. Actions and Exceptions in General

CAN. 1491 Every right is protected not only by an action but also by an exception unless other provision is expressly made.

CAN. 1492 §1. Every action is extinguished by prescription according to the norm of law or

TITULUS V. De Actionibus et Exceptionibus

CAPUT I. De Actionibus et Exceptionibus in Genere

CAN. 1491 Quodlibet ius non solum actione munitur, nisi aliud expresse cautum sit, sed etiam exceptione.

CAN. 1492 §1. Quaevis actio extinguitur praescriptione ad normam iuris

by some other legitimate means, with the exception of actions concerning the status of persons, which are never extinguished.

§2. Without prejudice to the prescript of can. 1462, an exception is always available and is perpetual by its very nature.

CAN. 1493 A petitioner can bring a person to trial with several actions at once, either concerning the same or different matters, so long as the actions do not conflict among themselves and do not exceed the competence of the tribunal approached.

CAN. 1494 §1. The respondent can file a counterclaim against the petitioner before the same judge in the same trial either because of the connection of the case with the principal action or to remove or diminish the claim of the petitioner.

§2. A counterclaim to a counterclaim is not allowed.

CAN. 1495 The counterclaim must be presented to the judge before whom the first action was filed even if the judge was delegated for only one case or is otherwise relatively incompetent.

CHAPTER II. Specific Actions and Exceptions

CAN. 1496 §1. A person, who through at least probable arguments has shown a right over something held by another and the threat of damage unless the thing is placed in safekeeping, has the right to obtain its sequestration from the judge.

§2. In similar circumstances, a person can obtain an order to restrain another from the exercise of a right.

aliove legitimo modo, exceptis actionibus de statu personarum, quae numquam extinguuntur.

§2. Exceptio, salvo praescripto can. 1462, semper competit et est suapte natura perpetua.

CAN. 1493 Actor pluribus simul actionibus, quae tamen inter se non confligant, sive de eadem re sive de diversis, aliquem convenire potest, si aditi tribunalis competentiam non egrediantur.

CAN. 1494 §1. Pars conventa potest coram eodem iudice in eodem iudicio contra actorem vel propter causae nexum cum actione principali vel ad submovendam vel ad minuendam actoris petitionem, actionem reconventionalem instituere.

§2. Reconventio reconventionis non admittitur.

CAN. 1495 Actio reconventionalis proponenda est iudici coram quo actio prior instituta est, licet ad unam causam dumtaxat delegato vel alioquin relative incompetenti.

CAPUT II. De Actionibus et Exceptionibus in Specie

CAN. 1496 §1. Qui probabilibus saltem argumentis ostenderit super aliqua re ab alio detenta ius se habere, sibique damnum imminere nisi res ipsa custodienda tradatur, ius habet obtinendi a iudice eiusdem rei sequestrationem.

§2. In similibus rerum adiunctis obtinere potest, ut iuris excercitium alicui inhibeatur.

1492 §2: cc. 1629, 1667
1493: c. 1669 §1
1494 §1: c. 1690 §1
1494 §2: c. 1690 §2

1495: c. 1692
1496 §1: c. 1672 §1
1496 §2: c. 1672 §2

CAN. 1497 §1. Sequestration of a thing is also allowed as security for a loan provided that the right of the creditor is sufficiently evident.

§2. Sequestration can also be extended to the goods of the debtor which are discovered in the possession of others under any title and to the loans of the debtor.

CAN. 1498 Sequestration of a thing and restraint upon the exercise of a right can in no way be decreed if the harm which is feared can be repaired in another way and suitable security for its repair is offered.

CAN. 1499 A judge who grants the sequestration of a thing or a restraint upon the exercise of a right can first impose an obligation upon the person to compensate for damages if that person's right is not proven.

CAN. 1500 The prescripts of the civil law of the place where the object whose possession is in question is located are to be observed regarding the nature and force of a possessory action.

CAN. 1497 §1. Ad crediti quoque securitatem sequestratio rei admittitur, dummodo de creditoris iure satis constet.

§2. Sequestratio extendi potest etiam ad res debitoris quae quolibet titulo apud alias personas reperiantur, et ad debitoris credita.

CAN. 1498 Sequestratio rei et inhibitio exercitii iuris decerni nullatenus possunt, si damnum quod timetur possit aliter reparari et idonea cautio de eo reparando offeratur.

CAN. 1499 Iudex potest ei, cui sequestrationem rei vel inhibitionem exercitii iuris concedit, praeviam imponere cautionem de damnis, si ius suum non probaverit, resarciendis.

CAN. 1500 Ad naturam et vim actionis possessoriae quod attinet, serventur praescripta iuris civilis loci ubi sita est res de cuius possessione agitur.

1497 §1: c. 1673 §1
1497 §2: c. 1673 §2

1498: c. 1674
1499: SN can. 192

PART II. THE CONTENTIOUS TRIAL

PARS II. DE IUDICIO CONTENTIOSO

SECTION I. The Ordinary Contentious Trial

SECTIO I. De Iudicio Contentioso Ordinario

TITLE I. The Introduction of the Case

TITULUS I. De Causae Introductione

CHAPTER I. The Introductory *Libellus* of Litigation

CAPUT I. De Libello Litis Introductorio

CAN. 1501 A judge cannot adjudicate a case unless the party concerned or the promoter of justice has presented a petition according to the norm of the canons.

CAN. 1501 Iudex nullam causam cognoscere potest, nisi petitio, ad normam canonum, proposita sit ab eo cuius interest, vel a promotore iustitiae.

CAN. 1502 A person who wishes to bring another to trial must present to a competent judge a *libellus* which sets forth the object of the controversy and requests the services of the judge.

CAN. 1502 Qui aliquem convenire vult, debet libellum competenti iudici exhibere, in quo controversiae obiectum proponatur, et ministerium iudicis expostuletur.

CAN. 1503 §1. The judge can accept an oral petition whenever the petitioner is impeded from presenting a *libellus* or the case is easily investigated and of lesser importance.

CAN. 1503 §1. Petitionem oralem iudex admittere potest, quoties vel actor libellum exhibere impediatur vel causa sit facilis investigationis et minoris momenti.

§2. In either case, however, the judge is to order the notary to put the act into writing; the written record must be read to and approved by the petitioner and has all the legal effects of a *libellus* written by the petitioner.

§2. In utroque tamen casu iudex notarium iubeat scriptis actum redigere qui actori legendus est et ab eo probandus, quique locum tenet libelli ab actore scripti ad omnes iuris effectus.

CAN. 1504 The *libellus*, which introduces litigation, must:

CAN. 1504 Libellus, quo lis introducitur, debet:

1501: SN can. 226
1502: c. 1706; PrM 55 §2
1503 §1: c. 1707 §§1 et 2; PrM 56

1503 §2: c. 1707 §3; PrM 56
1504: c. 1708; PrM 57

1° express the judge before whom the case is introduced, what is being sought and by whom it is being sought;

2° indicate the right upon which the petitioner bases the case and, at least generally, the facts and proofs which will prove the allegations;

3° be signed by the petitioner or the petitioner's procurator, indicating the day, month, and year, and the address where the petitioner or procurator lives or where they say they reside for the purpose of receiving the acts;

4° indicate the domicile or quasi-domicile of the respondent.

CAN. 1505 §1. When a single judge or the president of a collegiate tribunal has seen that the matter is within his competence and the petitioner does not lack legitimate personal standing in the trial, he must accept or reject the *libellus* as soon as possible by decree.

§2. A *libellus* can be rejected only:

1° if the judge or tribunal is incompetent;

2° if without doubt it is evident that the petitioner lacks legitimate personal standing in the trial;

3° if the prescripts of can. 1504, nn. 1–3 have not been observed;

4° if it is certainly clear from the *libellus* itself that the petition lacks any basis and that there is no possibility that any such basis will appear through a process.

§3. If the *libellus* has been rejected because of defects which can be corrected, the petitioner can resubmit a new, correctly prepared *libellus* to the same judge.

§4. A party is always free within ten available days to make recourse with substantiating rea-

1° exprimere coram quo iudice causa introducatur, quid petatur et a quo petatur;

2° indicare quo iure innitatur actor et generatim saltem quibus factis et probationibus ad evincenda ea quae asseruntur;

3° subscribi ab actore vel eius procuratore, appositis die, mense et anno, necnon loco in quo actor vel eius procurator habitant, aut residere se dixerint actorum recipiendorum gratia;

4° indicare domicilium vel quasi-domicilium partis conventae.

CAN. 1505 §1. Iudex unicus vel tribunalis collegialis praeses, postquam viderint et rem esse suae competentiae et actori legitimam personam standi in iudicio non deesse, debent suo decreto quam primum libellum aut admittere aut reicere.

§2. Libellus reici potest tantum:

1° si iudex vel tribunal incompetens sit;

2° si sine dubio constet actori legitimam deesse personam standi in iudicio;

3° si non servata sint praescripta can. 1504, nn. 1–3;

4° si certo pateat ex ipso libello petitionem quolibet carere fundamento, neque fieri posse, ut aliquod ex processu fundamentum appareat.

§3. Si libellus reiectus fuerit ob vitia quae emendari possunt, actor novum libellum rite confectum potest eidem iudici denuo exhibere.

§4. Adversus libelli reiectionem integrum semper est parti intra tempus utile decem

1505 §1: c. 1709 §1; NSRR 60; PrM 61
1505 §2: PrM 64

1505 §3: c. 1709 §2; PrM 62
1505 §4: c. 1709 §3; PrM 66

sons against the rejection of a *libellus* either to the appellate tribunal or to the college if the *libellus* was rejected by the presiding judge; the question of the rejection is to be decided as promptly as possible *(expeditissime)*.

CAN. 1506 If within a month from the presentation of the *libellus* the judge has not issued a decree which accepts or rejects the *libellus* according to the norm of can. 1505, the interested party can insist that the judge fulfill his function. If the judge takes no action within ten days from the request, then the *libellus* is to be considered as accepted.

CHAPTER II. The Citation and Notification of Judicial Acts

CAN. 1507 §1. In the decree which accepts the *libellus* of the petitioner, the judge or the presiding judge must call the other parties to trial, that is, cite them to the joinder of the issue, establishing whether they must respond in writing or present themselves before the judge to come to agreement about the doubts. If from the written responses the judge perceives it necessary to convene the parties, the judge can establish that by a new decree.

§2. If the *libellus* is considered as accepted according to the norm of can. 1506, the decree of citation to the trial must be issued within twenty days from the request mentioned in that canon.

§3. If the litigating parties de facto present themselves before the judge to pursue the case, however, there is no need for a citation, but the notary is to note in the acts that the parties were present for the trial.

CAN. 1508 §1. The decree of citation to the

dierum recursum rationibus suffultum interponere vel ad tribunal appellationis vel ad collegium, si libellus reiectus fuerit a praeside; quaestio autem reiectionis expeditissime definienda est.

CAN. 1506 Si iudex intra mensem ab exhibito libello decretum non ediderit, quo libellum admittit vel reicit ad normam can. 1505, pars, cuius interest, instare potest ut iudex suo munere fungatur; quod si nihilominus iudex sileat, inutiliter lapsis decem diebus a facta instantia, libellus pro admisso habeatur.

CAPUT II. De Citatione et Denuntiatione Actorum Iudicialium

CAN. 1507 §1. In decreto, quo actoris libellus admittitur, debet iudex vel praeses ceteras partes in iudicium vocare seu citare ad litem contestandam, statuens utrum eae scripto respondere debeant an coram ipso se sistere ad dubia concordanda. Quod si ex scriptis responsionibus perspiciat necessitatem partes convocandi, id potest novo decreto statuere.

§2. Si libellus pro admisso habeatur ad normam can. 1506, decretum citationis in iudicium fieri debet intra viginti dies a facta instantia, de qua in eo canone.

§3. Quod si partes litigantes de facto coram iudice se sistant ad causam agendam, opus non est citatione, sed actuarius significet in actis partes iudicio adfuisse.

CAN. 1508 §1. Decretum citationis in

1506: c. 1710; PrM 67
1507 §1: c. 1711 §1; NSRR 65; PrM 74 §1, 75

1507 §3: c. 1711 §2; PrM 74 §2
1508 §1: c. 1712 §1: NSRR 65, 67; NSSA 37

trial must be communicated immediately to the respondent and at the same time to others who must appear.

§2. The *libellus* which introduces litigation is to be attached to the citation unless for grave causes the judge determines that the *libellus* must not be made known to the party before that party makes a deposition in the trial.

§3. If litigation is introduced against someone who does not have the free exercise of his or her rights or the free administration of the things in dispute, the citation must be communicated, as the case may be, to the guardian, curator, or special procurator, that is, the one who is bound to undertake the trial in the name of that person according to the norm of law.

CAN. 1509 §1. The notification of citations, decrees, sentences, and other judicial acts must be made through the public postal services or by some other very secure method according to the norms established in particular law.

§2. The fact of notification and its method must be evident in the acts.

CAN. 1510 A respondent who refuses to accept the document of citation or who prevents its delivery is considered to be legitimately cited.

CAN. 1511 If the citation was not communicated legitimately, the acts of the process are null, without prejudice to the prescript of can. 1507, §3.

CAN. 1512 When the citation has been communicated legitimately or the parties have appeared before the judge to pursue the case:

1° the matter ceases to be *res integra;*

iudicium debet statim parti conventae notificari, et simul ceteris, qui comparere debent, notum fieri.

§2. Citationi libellus litis introductorius adiungatur, nisi iudex propter graves causas censeat libellum significandum non esse parti, antequam haec deposuerit in iudicio.

§3. Si lis moveatur adversus eum qui non habet liberum exercitium suorum iurium, vel liberam administrationem rerum de quibus disceptatur, citatio denuntianda est, prout casus ferat, tutori, curatori, procuratori speciali, seu ei qui ipsius nomine iudicium suscipere tenetur ad normam iuris.

CAN. 1509 §1. Citationum, decretorum, sententiarum aliorumque iudicialium actorum notificatio facienda est per publicos tabellarios vel alio modo qui tutissimus sit, servatis normis lege particulari statutis.

§2. De facto notificationis et de eius modo constare debet in actis.

CAN. 1510 Conventus, qui citatoriam schedam recipere recuset, vel qui impedit quominus citatio ad se perveniat, legitime citatus habeatur.

CAN. 1511 Si citatio non fuerit legitime notificata, nulla sunt acta processus, salvo praescripto can. 1507, §3.

CAN. 1512 Cum citatio legitime notificata fuerit aut partes coram iudice steterint ad causam agendam:

1° res desinit esse integra;

1508 §2: c. 1712 §1
1508 §3: c. 1713; PrM 77; CI Resp. II, 25 ian. 1943 (AAS 35 [1943] 58)
1509 §1: cc. 1717, 1719, 1720, 1877; PrM 79, 80, 204; NSSA 27

1509 §2: c. 1722; NSRR 67; PrM 81; NSSA 27 §2
1510: c. 1718; NSRR 70 §1; PrM 82
1511: c. 1723; PrM 84
1512: c. 1725; NSRR 85; PrM 85

2° the case becomes proper to the otherwise competent judge or tribunal before which the action was initiated;

3° the jurisdiction of a delegated judge is fixed in such a way that it does not cease when the authority of the one delegating expires;

4° prescription is interrupted unless other provision is made;

5° the litigation begins to be pending; therefore, the principle *while litigation is pending, nothing is to be altered* immediately takes effect.

2° causa fit propria illius iudicis aut tribunalis ceteroquin competentis, coram quo actio instituta est;

3° in iudice delegato firma redditur iurisdictio, ita ut non expiret resoluto iure delegantis;

4° interrumpitur praescriptio, nisi aliud cautum sit;

5° lis pendere incipit; et ideo statim locum habet principium «*lite pendente, nihil innovetur*».

TITLE II. The Joinder of the Issue

TITULUS II. **De Litis Contestatione**

CAN. 1513 §1. The joinder of the issue *(contestatio litis)* occurs when the terms of the controversy, derived from the petitions and responses of the parties, are defined through a decree of the judge.

§2. The petitions and responses of the parties, besides those in the *libellus* which introduces the litigation, can be expressed either in a response to the citation or in the oral declarations made before the judge; in more difficult cases, however, the judge must convene the parties to resolve the doubt or doubts which must be answered in the sentence.

§3. The decree of the judge must be communicated to the parties; unless they have already agreed to the terms, the parties can make recourse to the judge within ten days in order to change them; a decree of the judge, however, must resolve the question as promptly as possible *(expeditissime)*.

CAN. 1513 §1. Contestatio litis habetur cum per iudicis decretum controversiae termini, ex partium petitionibus et responsionibus desumpti, definiuntur.

§2. Partium petitiones responsionesque, praeterquam in libello litis introductorio, possunt vel in responsione ad citationem exprimi vel in declarationibus ore coram iudice factis; in causis autem difficilioribus partes convocandae sunt a iudice ad dubium vel dubia concordanda, quibus in sententia respondendum sit.

§3. Decretum iudicis partibus notificandum est; quae, nisi iam consenserint, possunt intra decem dies ad ipsum iudicem recurrere, ut mutetur; quaestio autem expeditissime ipsius iudicis decreto dirimenda est.

1513 §1: cc. 1726, 1727, 1729 §3; NSRR 76 §§1 et 2; PrM 87, 92; NSSA 38; CPEN Rescr., 28 apr. 1970, nn. 10, 11

1513 §2: cc. 1728, 1729 §2
1513 §3: NSRR 73

CAN. 1514 Once established, the terms of the controversy cannot be changed validly except by a new decree, for a grave cause, at the request of a party, and after the other parties have been heard and their arguments considered.

CAN. 1515 After the issue has been joined, the possessor of the property of another ceases to be in good faith; therefore, if the possessor is sentenced to restore the property, the person must also return the profits made from the day of the joinder and repair any damages.

CAN. 1516 After the issue has been joined, the judge is to prescribe a suitable time for the parties to present and complete the proofs.

CAN. 1514 Controversiae termini semel statuti mutari valide nequeunt, nisi novo decreto, ex gravi causa, ad instantiam partis et auditis reliquis partibus earumque rationibus perpensis.

CAN. 1515 Lite contestata, possessor rei alienae desinit esse bonae fidei; ideoque, si damnatur ut rem restituat, fructus quoque a contestationis die reddere debet et damna sarcire.

CAN. 1516 Lite contestata, iudex congruum tempus partibus praestituat probationibus proponendis et explendis.

TITLE III. The Trial of the Litigation

TITULUS III. De Litis Instantia

CAN. 1517 A trial begins with the citation; it ends not only by the pronouncement of a definitive sentence but also by other methods defined by law.

CAN. 1518 If the litigating party dies, changes status, or ceases from the office in virtue of which action is taken:

1° if the case has not yet been concluded, the trial is suspended until the heir of the deceased, the successor, or an interested party resumes the litigation;

2° if the case has been concluded, the judge must proceed to the additional acts, after having cited the procurator, if there is one, or otherwise the heir of the deceased or the successor.

CAN. 1519 §1. If the guardian, curator, or procurator who is necessary according to the

CAN. 1517 Instantiae initium fit citatione; finis autem non solum pronuntiatione sententiae definitivae, sed etiam aliis modis iure praefinitis.

CAN. 1518 Si pars litigans moriatur aut statum mutet aut cesset ab officio cuius ratione agit:

1° causa nondum conclusa, instantia suspenditur donec heres defuncti aut successor aut is, cuius intersit, litem resumat;

2° causa conclusa, iudex procedere debet ad ulteriora, citato procuratore, si adsit, secus defuncti herede vel successore.

CAN. 1519 §1. Si a munere cesset tutor vel curator vel procurator, qui sit ad normam

1514: cc. 1729 §4, 1731, 1°; NSRR 76 §3; NSSA 42
1515: c. 1731, 3°
1516: c. 1731, 2°; NSRR 73

1517: c. 1732; NSRR 81; SN can. 254
1518: c. 1733; NSRR 79; PrM 222 §1
1519 §1: c. 1735, NSRR 80

norm of can. 1481, §§1 and 3 ceases from that function, the trial is suspended in the meantime.

§2. The judge, however, is to appoint another guardian or curator as soon as possible; the judge can appoint a procurator for the litigation if the party has neglected to do so within the brief time period established by the judge.

CAN. 1520 If the parties, without any impediment, propose no procedural act for six months, the trial is abated. Particular law can establish other terms of abatement.

CAN. 1521 Abatement takes effect by the law itself against all persons, including minors or those equivalent to minors, and must be declared *ex officio*, without prejudice to the right of seeking indemnity against guardians, curators, administrators, or procurators, who have not proved that they were not negligent.

CAN. 1522 Abatement extinguishes the acts of the process but not the acts of the case; indeed these acts can also have force in another trial provided that the case involves the same persons and the same issue; regarding those not party to the case, however, the acts have no force other than that of documents.

CAN. 1523 Each litigant is to bear the expenses of the abated trial which that litigant has incurred.

CAN. 1524 §1. The petitioner can renounce the trial at any stage or grade of the trial; likewise both the petitioner and the respondent can renounce either all or only some of the acts of the process.

§2. To renounce a trial, guardians and administrators of juridic persons need the coun-

can. 1481, §§1 et 3 necessarius, instantia interim suspenditur.

§2. Alium autem tutorem vel curatorem iudex quam primum constituat; procuratorem vero ad litem constituere potest, si pars neglexerit intra brevem terminum ab ipso iudice statutum.

CAN. 1520 Si nullus actus processualis, nullo obstante impedimento, ponatur a partibus per sex menses, instantia perimitur. Lex particularis alios peremptionis terminos statuere potest.

CAN. 1521 Peremptio obtinet ipso iure et adversus omnes, minores quoque aliosve minoribus aequiparatos, atque etiam ex officio declarari debet, salvo iure petendi indemnitatem adversus tutores, curatores, administratores, procuratores, qui culpa se caruisse non probaverint.

CAN. 1522 Peremptio exstinguit acta processus, non vero acta causae; immo haec vim habere possunt etiam in alia instantia, dummodo causa inter easdem personas et super eadem re intercedat; sed ad extraneos quod attinet, non aliam vim obtinent nisi documentorum.

CAN. 1523 Perempti iudicii expensas, quas quisque ex litigantibus fecerit, ipse ferat.

CAN. 1524 §1. In quolibet statu et gradu iudicii potest actor instantiae renuntiare; item tum actor tum pars conventa possunt processus actis renuntiare sive omnibus sive nonnullis tantum.

§2. Tutores et administratores personarum iuridicarum, ut renuntiare possint in-

1520: c. 1736; NSRR 81
1521: c. 1737; NSRR 82
1522: c. 1738

1523: c. 1739
1524 §1: c. 1740 §1
1524 §2: c. 1527 §1

sel or consent of those whose involvement is required to place acts which exceed the limits of ordinary administration.

§3. To be valid, a renunciation must be written and signed by the party or by a procurator of the party who has a special mandate to do so; it must be communicated to the other party, accepted or at least not challenged by that party, and accepted by the judge.

CAN. 1525 A renunciation accepted by the judge has the same effects for the acts renounced as the abatement of the trial; it also obliges the renouncing party to pay the expenses for the acts renounced.

stantiae, egent consilio vel consensu eorum, quorum concursus requiritur ad ponendos actus, qui ordinariae administrationis fines excedunt.

§3. Renuntiatio, ut valeat, peragenda est scripto, eademque a parte vel ab eius procuratore, speciali tamen mandato munito, debet subscribi, cum altera parte communicari, ab eaque acceptari vel saltem non impugnari, et a iudice admitti.

CAN. 1525 Renuntiatio a iudice admissa, pro actis quibus renuntiatum est, eosdem parit effectus ac peremptio instantiae, itemque obligat renuntiantem ad solvendas expensas actorum, quibus renuntiatum fuit.

TITLE IV. **Proofs**

CAN. 1526 §1. The burden of proof rests upon the person who makes the allegation.

§2. The following do not need proof:

1° matters presumed by the law itself;

2° facts alleged by one of the contending parties and admitted by the other unless the law or the judge nevertheless requires proof.

CAN. 1527 §1. Proofs of any kind which seem useful for adjudicating the case and are licit can be brought forward.

§2. If a party insists that a proof rejected by a judge be accepted, the judge is to decide the matter as promptly as possible *(expeditissime)*.

CAN. 1528 If a party or a witness refuses to appear before the judge to testify, it is permissible to hear them through a lay person designated by the judge or to require of them a declara-

TITULUS IV. **De Probationibus**

CAN. 1526 §1. Onus probandi incumbit ei qui asserit.

§2. Non indigent probatione:

1° quae ab ipsa lege praesumuntur;

2° facta ab uno ex contendentibus asserta et ab altero admissa, nisi iure vel a iudice probatio nihilominus exigatur.

CAN. 1527 §1. Probationes cuiuslibet generis, quae ad causam cognoscendam utiles videantur et sint licitae, adduci possunt.

§2. Si pars instet ut probatio a iudice reiecta admittatur, ipse iudex rem expeditissime definiat.

CAN. 1528 Si pars vel testis se sistere ad respondendum coram iudice renuant, licet eos audire etiam per laicum a iudice designatum aut requirere eorum declarationem

---

1524 §3: c. 1740 §2; NSRR 87–90
1525: c. 1741; NSRR 91
1526 §1: c. 1748 §1; PrM 94

1526 §2: c. 1747; PrM 93
1527 §1: c. 1749; PrM 95

tion either before a notary public or in any other legitimate manner.

CAN. 1529 Except for a grave cause, the judge is not to proceed to collect the proofs before the joinder of the issue.

CHAPTER I. The Declarations of the Parties

CAN. 1530 The judge can always question the parties to draw out the truth more effectively and indeed must do so at the request of a party or to prove a fact which the public interest requires to be placed beyond doubt.

CAN. 1531 §1. A party legitimately questioned must respond and must tell the whole truth.

§2. If a party refuses to respond, it is for the judge to decide what can be inferred from that refusal concerning the proof of the facts.

CAN. 1532 In cases where the public good is at stake, the judge is to administer an oath to the parties to tell the truth or at least to confirm the truth of what they have said unless a grave cause suggests otherwise; the same can be done in other cases according to the judge's own prudence.

CAN. 1533 The parties, the promoter of justice, and the defender of the bond can present the judge with items about which the party is to be questioned.

CAN. 1534 The provisions of cann. 1548, §2, n. 1, 1552, and 1558–1565 concerning witnesses are to be observed to the extent possible when questioning the parties.

CAN. 1535 A judicial confession is the

coram publico notario vel quovis alio legitimo modo.

CAN. 1529 Iudex ad probationes colligendas ne procedat ante litis contestationem nisi ob gravem causam.

CAPUT I. De Partium Declarationibus

CAN. 1530 Iudex ad veritatem aptius eruendam partes interrogare semper potest, immo debet, ad instantiam partis vel ad probandum factum quod publice interest extra dubium poni.

CAN. 1531 §1. Pars legitime interrogata respondere debet et veritatem integre fateri.

§2. Quod si respondere recusaverit, iudicis est aestimare quid ad factorum probationem exinde erui possit.

CAN. 1532 In casibus, in quibus bonum publicum in causa est, iudex partibus iusiurandum de veritate dicenda aut saltem de veritate dictorum deferat, nisi gravis causa aliud suadeat; in aliis casibus, potest pro sua prudentia.

CAN. 1533 Partes, promotor iustitiae et defensor vinculi possunt iudici exhibere articulos, super quibus pars interrogetur.

CAN. 1534 Circa partium interrogationem cum proportione serventur, quae in cann. 1548, §2, n. 1, 1552 et 1558–1565 de testibus statuuntur.

CAN. 1535 Assertio de aliquo facto,

1529: c. 1730; PrM 110
1530: c. 1742 §§1 et 2
1531 §1: c. 1743 §1; PrM 111; CPEN Rescr., 28 apr. 1970, 14
1531 §2: c. 1743 §2; PrM 112; CPEN Rescr., 28 apr. 1970, 14

1532: c. 1744; PrM 96 §1, 110; SN can. 266
1533: cc. 1745 §1, 1968, 1°; NSRR 93 §2, 99; PrM 70 §1, 1°; SA Resp. (Prot. 966/497/C.P.), 19 nov. 1947
1534: c. 1745 §2
1535: c. 1750

written or oral assertion of some fact against oneself before a competent judge by any party concerning the matter of the trial, whether made spontaneously or while being questioned by the judge.

CAN. 1536 §1. The judicial confession of one party relieves the other parties from the burden of proof if it concerns some private matter and the public good is not at stake.

§2. In cases which regard the public good, however, a judicial confession and declarations of the parties which are not confessions can have a probative force which the judge must evaluate together with the other circumstances of the case; the force of full proof cannot be attributed to them, however, unless other elements are present which thoroughly corroborate them.

CAN. 1537 After considering all the circumstances, it is for the judge to decide how much value must be accorded an extrajudicial confession introduced into the trial.

CAN. 1538 A confession or any other declaration of a party lacks any force if it is shown that it was made due to an error of fact or extorted by force or grave fear.

CHAPTER II. Proof Through Documents

CAN. 1539 In any kind of trial, proof by means of both public and private documents is allowed.

ART. 1. *The Nature and Trustworthiness of Documents*

CAN. 1540 §1. Public ecclesiastical documents are those which a public person has

scripto vel ore, coram iudice competenti, ab aliqua parte circa ipsam iudicii materiam, sive sponte sive iudice interrogante, contra se peracta, est confessio iudicialis.

CAN. 1536 §1. Confessio iudicialis unius partis, si agatur de negotio aliquo privato et in causa non sit bonum publicum, ceteras relevat ab onere probandi.

§2. In causis autem quae respiciunt bonum publicum, confessio iudicialis et partium declarationes, quae non sint confessiones, vim probandi habere possunt, a iudice aestimandam una cum ceteris causae adiunctis, at vis plenae probationis ipsis tribui nequit, nisi alia accedant elementa quae eas omnino corroborent.

CAN. 1537 Quoad extraiudicialem confessionem in iudicium deductam, iudicis est, perpensis omnibus adiunctis, aestimare quanti ea sit facienda.

CAN. 1538 Confessio vel alia quaevis partis declaratio qualibet vi caret, si constet eam ex errore facti esse prolatam, aut vi vel metu gravi extortam.

CAPUT II. De Probatione Per Documenta

CAN. 1539 In quolibet iudicii genere admittitur probatio per documenta tum publica tum privata.

ART. 1. *De Natura et Fide Documentorum*

CAN. 1540 §1. Documenta publica ecclesiastica ea sunt, quae persona publica

---

1536 §1: c. 1751
1536 §2: SCSO Instr., 12 nov. 1947; SCSO Instr., 21 iun. 1951; SA Rescr., 10 nov. 1970, 1; SA Rescr., 2 ian. 1971, II, 1

1537: c. 1753; PrM 116
1538: c. 1752
1539: c. 1812; PrM 155
1540 §1: c. 1813 §1; PrM 156 §1

drawn up in the exercise of that person's function in the Church, after the solemnities prescribed by law have been observed.

§2. Public civil documents are those which the laws of each place consider to be such.

§3. Other documents are private.

CAN. 1541 Unless contrary and evident arguments prove otherwise, public documents are to be trusted concerning everything which they directly and principally affirm.

CAN. 1542 A private document, whether acknowledged by a party or approved by the judge, has the same force of proof against the author or signatory and those deriving a case from them as an extrajudicial confession. It has the same force against those who are not parties to the case as declarations of the parties which are not confessions, according to the norm of can. 1536, §2.

CAN. 1543 If the documents are shown to have been erased, emended, falsified, or otherwise defective, it is for the judge to decide what value, if any, must be afforded them.

ART. 2. *The Presentation of Documents*

CAN. 1544 Documents do not have probative force in a trial unless they are originals or authentic copies and deposited at the tribunal chancery so that the judge and the opposing party can examine them.

CAN. 1545 The judge can order a document common to both parties to be presented in the process.

CAN. 1546 §1. Even if documents are common, no one is bound to present those which

in exercitio sui muneris in Ecclesia confecit, servatis sollemnitatibus iure praescriptis.

§2. Documenta publica civilia ea sunt, quae secundum uniuscuiusque loci leges talia iure censentur.

§3. Cetera documenta sunt privata.

CAN. 1541 Nisi contrariis et evidentibus argumentis aliud evincatur, documenta publica fidem faciunt de omnibus quae directe et principaliter in iis affirmantur.

CAN. 1542 Documentum privatum, sive agnitum a parte sive recognitum a iudice, eandem probandi vim habet adversus auctorem vel subscriptorem et causam ab iis habentes, ac confessio extra iudicium facta; adversus extraneos eandem vim habet ac partium declarationes quae non sint confessiones, ad normam can. 1536, §2.

CAN. 1543 Si abrasa, correcta, interpolata aliove vitio documenta infecta demonstrentur, iudicis est aestimare an et quanti huiusmodi documenta sint facienda.

ART. 2. *De Productione Documentorum*

CAN. 1544 Documenta vim probandi in iudicio non habent, nisi originalia sint aut in exemplari authentico exhibita et penes tribunalis cancellariam deposita, ut a iudice et ab adversario examinari possint.

CAN. 1545 Iudex praecipere potest ut documentum utrique parti commune exhibeatur in processu.

CAN. 1546 §1. Nemo exhibere tenetur documenta, etsi communia, quae communi-

---

1540 §2: c. 1813 §2; PrM 156 §2
1540 §3: c. 1813 §3; PrM 156 §3
1541: cc. 1814–1816
1542: c. 1817

1543: c. 1818
1544: cc. 1819, 1820; PrM 159, 160
1545: c. 1822
1546 §1: c. 1823 §1

cannot be communicated without danger of harm according to the norm of can. 1548, §2, n. 2 or without danger of violating an obligation to observe secrecy.

§2. Nonetheless, if at least some small part of a document can be transcribed and presented in copy without the above-mentioned disadvantages, the judge can decree that it be produced.

CHAPTER III. **Witnesses and Testimonies**

CAN. 1547 Proof by means of witnesses is allowed under the direction of the judge in cases of any kind.

CAN. 1548 §1. When the judge questions witnesses legitimately, they must tell the truth.

§2. Without prejudice to the prescript of can. 1550, §2, n. 2, the following are exempted from the obligation to respond:

1° clerics regarding what has been made known to them by reason of sacred ministry; civil officials, physicians, midwives, advocates, notaries, and others bound by professional secrecy even by reason of having given advice, regarding those matters subject to this secrecy;

2° those who fear that from their own testimony ill repute, dangerous hardships, or other grave evils will befall them, their spouses, or persons related to them by consanguinity or affinity.

ART. 1. *Those Who Can Be Witnesses*

CAN. 1549 All persons can be witnesses unless the law expressly excludes them in whole or in part.

cari nequeunt sine periculo damni ad normam can. 1548, §2, n. 2 aut sine periculo violationis secreti servandi.

§2. Attamen si qua saltem documenti particula describi possit et in exemplari exhiberi sine memoratis incommodis, iudex decernere potest ut eadem producatur.

CAPUT III. **De Testibus et Attestationibus**

CAN. 1547 Probatio per testes in quibuslibet causis admittitur, sub iudicis moderatione.

CAN. 1548 §1. Testes iudici legitime interroganti veritatem fateri debent.

§2. Salvo praescripto can. 1550, §2, n. 2, ab obligatione respondendi eximuntur:

1° clerici, quod attinet ad ea quae ipsis manifestata sunt ratione sacri ministerii; civitatum magistratus, medici, obstetrices, advocati, notarii aliique qui ad secretum officii etiam ratione praestiti consilii tenentur, quod attinet ad negotia huic secreto obnoxia;

2° qui ex testificatione sua sibi aut coniugi aut proximis consanguineis vel affinibus infamiam, periculosas vexationes, aliave mala gravia obventura timent.

ART. 1. *Qui Testes Esse Possint*

CAN. 1549 Omnes possunt esse testes, nisi expresse iure repellantur vel in totum vel ex parte.

1546 §2: c. 1823 §2
1547: c. 1754
1548 §1: c. 1755 §1; PrM 121 §1

1548 §2: c. 1755 §2; PrM 121 §2
1549: c. 1756; PrM 118

CAN. 1550 §1. Minors below the four-teenth year of age and those of limited mental capacity are not allowed to give testimony; they can, however, be heard by a decree of the judge which declares such a hearing expedient.

§2. The following are considered incapable:

1° the parties in the case or those who stand for the parties at the trial, the judge and the judge's assistants, the advocate, and others who assist or have assisted the parties in the same case;

2° priests regarding all matters which they have come to know from sacramental confession even if the penitent seeks their disclosure; moreover, matters heard by anyone and in any way on the occasion of confession cannot be accepted even as an indication of the truth.

ART. 2. *The Introduction and Exclusion of Witnesses*

CAN. 1551 The party who has introduced a witness can renounce the examination of that witness; the opposing party, however, can request that the witness be examined nevertheless.

CAN. 1552 §1. When proof through witnesses is requested, their names and domicile are to be communicated to the tribunal.

§2. The items of discussion about which questioning of the witnesses is sought are to be presented within the time period set by the judge; otherwise, the request is to be considered as abandoned.

CAN. 1553 It is for the judge to curb an excessive number of witnesses.

CAN. 1554 Before the witnesses are examined, their names are to be communicated to

CAN. 1550 §1. Ne admittantur ad testimonium ferendum minores infra decimum quartum aetatis annum et mente debiles; audiri tamen poterunt ex decreto iudicis, quo id expedire declaretur.

§2. Incapaces habentur:

1° qui partes sunt in causa, aut partium nomine in iudicio consistunt, iudex eiusve assistentes, advocatus aliique qui partibus in eadem causa assistunt vel astiterunt;

2° sacerdotes, quod attinet ad ea omnia quae ipsis ex confessione sacramentali innotuerunt, etsi poenitens eorum manifestationem petierit; immo audita a quovis et quoquo modo occasione confessionis, ne ut indicium quidem veritatis recipi possunt.

ART. 2. *De Inducendis et Excludendis Testibus*

CAN. 1551 Pars, quae testem induxit, potest eius examini renuntiare; sed adversa pars postulare potest ut nihilominus testis examinetur.

CAN. 1552 §1. Cum probatio per testes postulatur, eorum nomina et domicilium tribunali indicentur.

§2. Exhibeantur, intra terminum a iudice praestitutum, articuli argumentorum super quibus petitur testium interrogatio; alioquin petitio censeatur deserta.

CAN. 1553 Iudicis est nimiam multitudinem testium refrenare.

CAN. 1554 Antequam testes examinentur, eorum nomina cum partibus commu-

---

1550 §1: cc. 1757 §1, 1758: PrM 119 §1, 120
1550 §2: cc. 1757 §3, 1974; PrM 119 §3, 122
1551: c. 1759 §4; PrM 132 §1
1552 §1: c. 1761 §1; PrM 125 §1

1552 §2: c. 1761; CI Resp. IV, 12 mar. 1929; PrM 125 §2
1553: c. 1762; PrM 123 §2
1554: c. 1763; PrM 126

the parties; if in the prudent judgment of the judge, however, that cannot be done without grave difficulty, it is to be done at least before the publication of the testimonies.

CAN. 1555 Without prejudice to the prescript of can. 1550, a party can request the exclusion of a witness if a just cause for the exclusion is shown before the questioning of the witness.

CAN. 1556 The citation of a witness occurs through a decree of the judge legitimately communicated to the witness.

CAN. 1557 A witness who has been cited properly is to appear or to inform the judge of the reason for the absence.

ART. 3. *The Examination of Witnesses*

CAN. 1558 §1. Witnesses must be examined at the tribunal unless the judge deems otherwise.

§2. Cardinals, patriarchs, bishops, and those who possess a similar favor by civil law are to be heard in the place they select.

§3. The judge is to decide where to hear those for whom it is impossible or difficult to come to the tribunal because of distance, sickness, or some impediment, without prejudice to the prescripts of cann. 1418 and 1469, §2.

CAN. 1559 The parties cannot be present at the examination of the witnesses unless the judge has decided to admit them, especially when the matter concerns a private good. Their advocates or procurators, however, can be present unless the judge has decided that the examination must proceed in secret due to the circumstances of the matters and persons.

nicentur; quod si id, prudenti iudicis existimatione, fieri sine gravi difficultate nequeat, saltem ante testimoniorum publicationem fiat.

CAN. 1555 Firmo praescripto can. 1550, pars petere potest ut testis excludatur, si iusta exclusionis causa demonstretur ante testis excussionem.

CAN. 1556 Citatio testis fit decreto iudicis testi legitime notificato.

CAN. 1557 Testis rite citatus pareat aut causam suae absentiae iudici notam faciat.

ART. 3. *De Testium Examine*

CAN. 1558 §1. Testes sunt examini subiciendi in ipsa tribunalis sede, nisi aliud iudici videatur.

§2. Cardinales, Patriarchae, Episcopi et ii qui, suae civitatis iure, simili favore gaudent, audiantur in loco ab ipsis selecto.

§3. Iudex decernat ubi audiendi sint ii, quibus propter distantiam, morbum aliudve impedimentum impossibile vel difficile sit tribunalis sedem adire, firmis praescriptis cann. 1418 et 1469, §2.

CAN. 1559 Examini testium partes assistere nequeunt, nisi iudex, praesertim cum res est de bono privato, eas admittendas censuerit. Assistere tamen possunt earum advocati vel procuratores, nisi iudex propter rerum et personarum adiuncta censuerit secreto esse procedendum.

1555: c. 1764; PrM 131
1556: c. 1765
1557: c. 1766 §1; PrM 127 §1
1558 §1: c. 1770 §1
1558 §2: c. 1770 §2, 1°; PrM 98 §1

1558 §3: c. 1770 §2, 2°–4°; PrM 98 §2; SCDS Regulae, 7 maii 1923, 24 §1
1559: c. 1771; PrM 128; CPEN Rescr., 28 apr. 1970, 13

CAN. 1560 §1. Each witness must be examined separately.

§2. If witnesses disagree among themselves or with a party in a grave matter, the judge, after having removed discord and scandal insofar as possible, can have those who disagree meet together or confront one another.

CAN. 1561 The judge, the judge's delegate, or an auditor examines the witness; the examiner must have the assistance of a notary. Consequently, if the parties, the promoter of justice, the defender of the bond, or the advocates present at the examination have any questions to be put to the witness, they are to propose them not to the witness but to the judge or the one who takes the place of the judge, who is to ask the questions, unless particular law provides otherwise.

CAN. 1562 §1. The judge is to call to the attention of the witness the grave obligation to speak the whole truth and only the truth.

§2. The judge is to administer an oath to the witness according to can. 1532; a witness who refuses to take it, however, is to be heard without the oath.

CAN. 1563 The judge is first of all to establish the identity of the witness, then ask what relationship the witness has with the parties, and, when addressing specific questions to the witness concerning the case, also inquire about the sources of his or her knowledge and the precise time when the witness learned what he or she asserts.

CAN. 1564 The questions are to be brief, accommodated to the mental capacity of the person being questioned, not comprised of several points at the same time, not deceitful or de-

CAN. 1560 §1. Testes seorsim singuli examinandi sunt.

§2. Si testes inter se aut cum parte in re gravi dissentiant, iudex discrepantes inter se conferre seu comparare potest, remotis, quantum fieri poterit, dissidiis et scandalo.

CAN. 1561 Examen testis fit a iudice, vel ab eius delegato aut auditore, cui assistat oportet notarius; quapropter partes, vel promotor iustitiae, vel defensor vinculi, vel advocati qui examini intersint, si alias interrogationes testi faciendas habeant, has non testi, sed iudici vel eius locum tenenti proponant, ut eas ipse deferat, nisi aliter lex particularis caveat.

CAN. 1562 §1. Iudex testi in mentem revocet gravem obligationem dicendi totam et solam veritatem.

§2. Iudex testi deferat iuramentum iuxta can. 1532; quod si testis renuat illud emittere, iniuratus audiatur.

CAN. 1563 Iudex imprimis testis identitatem comprobet; exquirat quaenam sit ipsi cum partibus necessitudo et, cum ipsi interrogationes specificas circa causam defert, sciscitetur quoque fontes eius scientiae et quo definito tempore ea, quae asserit, cognoverit.

CAN. 1564 Interrogationes breves sunto, interrogandi captui accommodatae, non plura simul complectentes, non captiosae, non subdolae, non suggerentes respon-

1560 §1: c. 1772 §1
1560 §2: c. 1772 §§2 et 3; PrM 133
1561: c. 1773; SCDS Regulae, 7 maii 1923, 24 §1; PrM 101

1562 §1: c. 1767 §4; PrM 96 §2
1562 §2: c. 1767 §1; PrM 96 §1
1563: c. 1774; PrM 97, 99, 100
1564: c. 1775; PrM 102

ceptive or suggestive of a response, free from any kind of offense, and pertinent to the case being tried.

CAN. 1565 §1. Questions must not be communicated to the witnesses beforehand.

§2. Nonetheless, if the matters about which testimony must be given are so remote to memory that they cannot be affirmed with certainty unless previously recalled, the judge can advise the witness beforehand on some matters if the judge thinks this can be done without danger.

CAN. 1566 Witnesses are to give testimony orally and are not to read written materials unless they are computations and accounts; in this case, they can consult the notes which they brought with them.

CAN. 1567 §1. The notary is to write down the response immediately and must report the exact words of the testimony given, at least in what pertains to those points which touch directly upon the material of the trial.

§2. The use of a tape recorder can be allowed, provided that the responses are afterwards transcribed and, if possible, signed by the deponents.

CAN. 1568 The notary is to make mention in the acts of whether the oath was taken, excused, or refused, of the presence of the parties and other persons, of the questions added *ex officio*, and in general of everything worth remembering which may have occurred while the witnesses were being examined.

CAN. 1569 §1. At the end of the examination, what the notary has written down from the deposition must be read to the witness, or what has been recorded with the tape recorder dur-

sionem, remotae a cuiusvis offensione et pertinentes ad causam quae agitur.

CAN. 1565 §1. Interrogationes non sunt cum testibus antea communicandae.

§2. Attamen si ea quae testificanda sunt ita a memoria sint remota, ut nisi prius recolantur certo affirmari nequeant, poterit iudex nonnulla testem praemonere, si id sine periculo fieri posse censeat.

CAN. 1566 Testes ore testimonium dicant, et scriptum ne legant, nisi de calculo et rationibus agatur; hoc enim in casu, adnotationes, quas secum attulerint, consulere poterunt.

CAN. 1567 §1. Responsio statim redigenda est scripto a notario et referre debet ipsa editi testimonii verba, saltem quod attinet ad ea quae iudicii materiam directe attingunt.

§2. Admitti potest usus machinae magnetophonicae, dummodo dein responsiones scripto consignentur et subscribantur, si fieri potest, a deponentibus.

CAN. 1568 Notarius in actis mentionem faciat de praestito, remisso aut recusato iureiurando, de partium aliorumque praesentia, de interrogationibus ex officio additis et generatim de omnibus memoria dignis quae forte acciderint, cum testes excutiebantur.

CAN. 1569 §1. In fine examinis, testi legi debent quae notarius de eius depositione scripto redegit, vel ipsi audita facere quae ope magnetophonii de eius depositione

1565 §1: c. 1776 §1; PrM 103 §1 a
1565 §2: c. 1776 §2
1566: c. 1777; PrM 103 §1 b
1567 §1: c. 1778; PrM 103 §2, 129; SCDS Instr. *Dis-*

pensationis matrimonii, 7 mar. 1972 II d (AAS 64 [1972] 248)
1568: c. 1779
1569 §1: c. 1780 §1; PrM 104 §1

ing the deposition must be played, giving the witness the opportunity to add, suppress, correct, or change it.

§2. Finally, the witness, the judge, and the notary must sign the acts.

CAN. 1570 Although already examined, witnesses can be recalled for examination before the acts or testimonies are published, either at the request of a party or *ex officio*, if the judge decides it is necessary or useful, provided that there is no danger of collusion or corruption.

CAN. 1571 Both the expenses which the witnesses incurred and the income which they lost by giving testimony must be reimbursed to them according to the just assessment of the judge.

ART. 4. *The Trustworthiness of Testimonies*

CAN. 1572 In evaluating testimony, the judge, after having requested testimonial letters if necessary, is to consider the following:

1° what the condition or reputation of the person is;

2° whether the testimony derives from personal knowledge, especially from what has been seen or heard personally, or whether from opinion, rumor, or hearsay;

3° whether the witness is reliable and firmly consistent or inconsistent, uncertain, or vacillating;

4° whether the witness has co-witnesses to the testimony or is supported or not by other elements of proof.

CAN. 1573 The testimony of one witness

incisa sunt, data eidem testi facultate addendi, supprimendi, corrigendi, variandi.

§2. Denique actui subscribere debent testis, iudex et notarius.

CAN. 1570 Testes, quamvis iam excusi, poterunt parte postulante aut ex officio, antequam acta seu testificationes publici iuris fiant, denuo ad examen vocari, si iudex id necessarium vel utile ducat, dummodo collusionis vel corruptelae quodvis absit periculum.

CAN. 1571 Testibus, iuxta aequam iudicis taxationem, refundi debent tum expensae, quas fecerint, tum lucrum, quod amiserint, testificationis reddendae causa.

ART. 4. *De Testimoniorum Fide*

CAN. 1572 In aestimandis testimoniis iudex, requisitis, si opus sit, testimonialibus litteris, consideret:

1° quae condicio sit personae, quaeve honestas;

2° utrum de scientia propria, praesertim de visu et auditu proprio testificetur, an de sua opinione, de fama, aut de auditu ab aliis;

3° utrum testis constans sit et firmiter sibi cohaereat, an varius, incertus vel vacillans;

4° utrum testimonii contestes habeat, aliisve probationis elementis confirmetur necne.

CAN. 1573 Unius testis depositio ple-

1569 §2: c. 1780 §2: PrM 104 §2
1570: c. 1781; PrM 107, 135
1571: c. 1787; PrM 127 §3
1572: c. 1789; PrM 136, 138 §1; CPEN Rescr., 28

apr. 1970, 16; SCDS Instr. *Dispensationis matrimonii,* 7 mar. 1972, II b (AAS 64 [1972] 248)
1573: c. 1791 §1; PrM 136 §1; SA Rescr., 10 nov. 1970, 1; SA Rescr., 2 ian. 1971, II, 1

cannot produce full proof unless it concerns a qualified witness making a deposition concerning matters done *ex officio*, or unless the circumstances of things and persons suggest otherwise.

nam fidem facere non potest, nisi agatur de teste qualificato qui deponat de rebus ex officio gestis, aut rerum et personarum adiuncta aliud suadeant.

CHAPTER IV. Experts

CAPUT IV. **De Peritis**

CAN. 1574 The assistance of experts must be used whenever the prescript of a law or of the judge requires their examination and opinion based on the precepts of art or science in order to establish some fact or to discern the true nature of some matter.

CAN. 1575 After having heard the parties and their suggestions, it is for the judge to appoint the experts or, if the case warrants, to accept reports already drawn up by other experts.

CAN. 1576 Experts are excluded or can be objected to for the same reasons as a witness.

CAN. 1577 §1. Attentive to what the litigants may bring forward, the judge is to determine in a decree the individual items upon which the services of the expert must focus.

§2. The acts of the case and other documents and aids which the expert can need to fulfill his or her function correctly and faithfully must be turned over to the expert.

§3. After having heard the expert, the judge is to determine the time within which the expert must complete the examination and produce the report.

CAN. 1578 §1. Each of the experts is to prepare a report separate from the others unless the judge decrees that one report signed by the ex-

CAN. 1574 Peritorum opera utendum est quoties ex iuris vel iudicis praescripto eorum examen et votum, praeceptis artis vel scientiae innixum, requiruntur ad factum aliquod comprobandum vel ad veram alicuius rei naturam dignoscendam.

CAN. 1575 Iudicis est peritos nominare, auditis vel proponentibus partibus, aut, si casus ferat, relationes ab aliis peritis iam factas assumere.

CAN. 1576 Easdem ob causas quibus testis, etiam periti excluduntur aut recusari possunt.

CAN. 1577 §1. Iudex, attentis iis quae a litigantibus forte deducantur, singula capita decreto suo definiat circa quae periti opera versari debeat.

§2. Perito remittenda sunt acta causae aliaque documenta et subsidia quibus egere potest ad suum munus rite et fideliter exsequendum.

§3. Iudex, ipso perito audito, tempus praefiniat intra quod examen perficiendum est et relatio proferenda.

CAN. 1578 §1. Periti suam quisque relationem a ceteris distinctam conficiant, nisi iudex unam a singulis subscribendam fieri

1574: c. 1792; PrM 140 §1
1575: c. 1793; PrM 141
1576: cc. 1795 §2; 1796; PrM 142 §2 - 145
1577 §1: c. 1799 §1; PrM 147 §§1 et 3

1577 §2: c. 1800; PrM 147 §2
1577 §3: c. 1799 §2; PrM 147 §4
1578 §1: c. 1802; PrM 148

perts individually be drawn up; if this is done, differences of opinion, if there are any, are to be noted carefully.

§2. Experts must indicate clearly by what documents or other suitable means they gained certainty of the identity of the persons, things, or places, by what manner and method they proceeded in fulfilling the function entrusted to them, and above all on which arguments they based their conclusions.

§3. The judge can summon the expert to supply explanations which later seem necessary.

CAN. 1579 §1. The judge is to weigh carefully not only the conclusions of the experts, even if they are in agreement, but also the other circumstances of the case.

§2. When giving reasons for the decision, the judge must express what considerations prompted him or her to accept or reject the conclusions of the experts.

CAN. 1580 The judge must justly and equitably determine the expenses and fees to be paid to the experts, with due regard for particular law.

CAN. 1581 §1. The parties can designate private experts whom the judge must approve.

§2. If the judge allows them, the private experts can inspect the acts of the case insofar as necessary and attend the presentation of the expert testimony; moreover, they can always present their own report.

iubeat: quod si fiat, sententiarum discrimina, si qua fuerint, diligenter adnotentur.

§2. Periti debent indicare perspicue quibus documentis vel aliis idoneis modis certiores facti sint de personarum vel rerum vel locorum identitate, qua via et ratione processerint in explendo munere sibi demandato et quibus potissimum argumentis suae conclusiones nitantur.

§3. Peritus accersiri potest a iudice ut explicationes, quae ulterius necessariae videantur, suppeditet.

CAN. 1579 §1. Iudex non peritorum tantum conclusiones, etsi concordes, sed cetera quoque causae adiuncta attente perpendat.

§2. Cum reddit rationes decidendi, exprimere debet quibus motus argumentis peritorum conclusiones aut admiserit aut reiecerit.

CAN. 1580 Peritis solvenda sunt expensae et honoraria a iudice ex bono et aequo determinanda, servato iure particulari.

CAN. 1581 §1. Partes possunt peritos privatos, a iudice probandos, designare

§2. Hi, si iudex admittat, possunt acta causae, quatenus opus sit, inspicere, peritiae exsecutioni interesse; semper autem possunt suam relationem exhibere.

1578 §2: c. 1801 §3; PrM 148 §1
1578 §3: c. 1801 §2; PrM 152; SA Rescr., 10 nov. 1970, 2; SA Rescr., 2 ian. 1971, II, 2
1579 §1: c. 1804 §1; PrM 154 §1

1579 §2: c. 1804 §2; PrM 154 §2
1580: c. 1805
1581 §2: c. 1797 §2

CHAPTER V. **Judicial Examination and Inspection**

CAN. 1582 If, in order to decide a case, the judge considers it opportune to visit some place or to inspect some thing, the judge, after having heard the parties, is to order it by a decree describing in summary fashion those things which must be exhibited during the visit or inspection.

CAN. 1583 When the visit or inspection has been completed, a report about it is to be drafted.

CHAPTER VI. **Presumptions**

CAN. 1584 A presumption is a probable conjecture about an uncertain matter; a presumption of law is one which the law itself establishes; a human presumption is one which a judge formulates.

CAN. 1585 A person who has a favorable presumption of law is freed from the burden of proof, which then falls to the other party.

CAN. 1586 The judge is not to formulate presumptions which are not established by law unless they are directly based on a certain and determined fact connected with the matter in dispute.

TITLE V. **Incidental Cases**

CAN. 1587 An incidental case arises whenever, after the trial has begun through the citation, a question is proposed which nevertheless pertains to the case in such a way that it fre-

CAPUT V. **De Accessu et de Recognitione Iudicali**

CAN. 1582 Si ad definitionem causae iudex opportunum duxerit ad aliquem locum accedere vel aliquam rem inspicere, decreto id praestituat, quo ea quae in accessu praestanda sint, auditis partibus, summatim describat.

CAN. 1583 Peractae recognitionis instrumentum conficiatur.

CAPUT VI. **De Praesumptionibus**

CAN. 1584 Praesumptio est rei incertae probabilis coniectura; eaque alia est iuris, quae ab ipsa lege statuitur; alia hominis, quae a iudice conicitur.

CAN. 1585 Qui habet pro se iuris praesumptionem, liberatur ab onere probandi, quod recidit in partem adversam.

CAN. 1586 Praesumptiones, quae non statuuntur a iure, iudex ne coniciat, nisi ex facto certo et determinato, quod cum eo, de quo controversia est, directe cohaereat.

TITULUS V. **De Causis Incidentibus**

CAN. 1587 Causa incidens habetur quoties, incepto per citationem iudicio, quaestio proponitur quae, tametsi libello, quo lis introducitur, non contineatur ex-

1582: c. 1806; NSRR 100 §1
1583: c. 1811
1584: c. 1825 §1; PrM 170 §1

1585: c. 1827
1586: c. 1828; PrM 173
1587: c. 1837; PrM 187

quently must be resolved before the principal question, even if it was not expressly contained in the *libellus* which introduced the litigation.

CAN. 1588   An incidental case is proposed in writing or orally before the judge competent to decide the principal case, indicating the connection between this and the principal case.

CAN. 1589   §1. After having received the petition and heard the parties, the judge is to decide as promptly as possible *(expeditissime)* whether the proposed incidental question seems to have a foundation and a connection with the principal trial or rather must be rejected at the outset. If the judge admits the incidental question, the judge is to decide whether it is of such gravity that it must be resolved by an interlocutory sentence or by a decree.

§2. If the judge decides not to resolve the incidental question before the definitive sentence, however, the judge is to decree that the question will be considered when the principal case is decided.

CAN. 1590   §1. If the incidental question must be resolved by sentence, the norms for the oral contentious process are to be observed unless the judge decides otherwise due to the gravity of the matter.

§2. If the matter must be resolved by decree, however, the tribunal can entrust the matter to an auditor or the presiding judge.

CAN. 1591   Before the principal case is completed, the judge or the tribunal can revoke or reform the decree or interlocutory sentence for a just reason either at the request of a party or *ex officio* after the parties have been heard.

presse, nihilominus ita ad causam pertinet ut resolvi plerumque debeat ante quaestionem principalem.

CAN. 1588   Causa incidens proponitur scripto vel ore, indicato nexu qui intercedit inter ipsam et causam principalem, coram iudice competenti ad causam principalem definiendam.

CAN. 1589   §1. Iudex, recepta petitione et auditis partibus, expeditissime decernat utrum proposita incidens quaestio fundamentum habere videatur et nexum cum principali iudicio, an vero sit in limine reicienda; et, si eam admittat, utrum talis sit gravitatis, ut solvi debeat per sententiam interlocutoriam vel per decretum.

§2. Si vero iudicet quaestionem incidentem non esse resolvendam ante sententiam definitivam, decernat ut eiusdem ratio habeatur, cum causa principalis definietur.

CAN. 1590   §1. Si quaestio incidens solvi debeat per sententiam, serventur normae de processu contentioso orali, nisi, attenta rei gravitate, aliud iudici videatur.

§2. Si vero solvi debeat per decretum, tribunal potest rem committere auditori vel praesidi.

CAN. 1591   Antequam finiatur causa principalis, iudex vel tribunal potest decretum vel sententiam interlocutoriam, iusta intercedente ratione, revocare aut reformare, sive ad partis instantiam, sive ex officio, auditis partibus.

1588: c. 1838; NSRR 106
1589 §1: cc. 1839, 1840 §1; NSRR 109 §1, 110; PrM 189 §1, 190 §1
1589 §2: NSRR 109 §1; PrM 189 §2

1590 §1: c. 1840 §2; NSRR 111; PrM 191
1590 §2: c. 1840 §2; NSRR 112; PrM 192 §1
1591: c. 1841; NSRR 114 §2; PrM 195

CHAPTER I. **Parties Who Do Not Appear**

CAN. 1592 §1. If the cited respondent has neither appeared nor given a suitable excuse for being absent or has not responded according to the norm of can. 1507, §1, the judge, having observed what is required, is to declare the respondent absent from the trial and decree that the case is to proceed to the definitive sentence and its execution.

§2. Before issuing the decree mentioned in §1, the judge must be certain that a legitimately executed citation has reached the respondent within the useful time, even by issuing a new citation if necessary.

CAN. 1593 §1. If the respondent appears at the trial later or responds before a decision in the case, the respondent can offer conclusions and proofs, without prejudice to the prescript of can. 1600; the judge, however, is to take care that the trial is not prolonged intentionally through longer and unnecessary delays.

§2. Even if the respondent did not appear or respond before a decision in the case, the respondent can use challenges against the sentence; if the respondent proves that there was a legitimate impediment for being detained and there was no personal fault in its not being made known beforehand, the respondent can use a complaint of nullity.

CAN. 1594 If the petitioner has not appeared on the day and at the hour prescribed for the joinder of the issue and has not offered a suitable excuse:

1° the judge is to cite the petitioner again;

CAPUT I. **De Partibus Non Comparentibus**

CAN. 1592 §1. Si pars conventa citata non comparuerit nec idoneam absentiae excusationem attulerit aut non responderit ad normam can. 1507, §1, iudex eam a iudicio absentem declaret et decernat ut causa, servatis servandis, usque ad sententiam definitivam eiusque exsecutionem procedat.

§2. Antequam decretum, de quo in §1, feratur, debet, etiam per novam citationem, si opus fuerit, constare citationem, legitime factam, ad partem conventam tempore utili pervenisse.

CAN. 1593 §1. Si pars conventa dein in iudicio se sistat aut responsum dederit ante causae definitionem, conclusiones probationesque afferre potest, firmo praescripto can. 1600; caveat autem iudex, ne de industria in longiores et non necessarias moras iudicium protrahatur.

§2. Etsi non comparuerit aut responsum non dederit ante causae definitionem, impugnationibus uti potest adversus sententiam; quod si probet se legitimo impedimento fuisse detentam, quod sine sua culpa antea demonstrare non potuerit, querela nullitatis uti potest.

CAN. 1594 Si die et hora ad litis contestationem praestitutis actor neque comparuerit neque idoneam excusationem attulerit:

1° iudex eum citet iterum;

1592 §1: cc. 1842, 1843 §1, 1844; NSRR 69 §1, 70 §1; PrM 89 §§1 et 2

1592 §2: c. 1843 §1, 1° et §2; NSRR 69 §2; PrM 89 §2

1593 §1: c. 1846; NSRR 116

1593 §2: c. 1847

1594: c. 1849; NSRR 74; PrM 91 §1

2° if the petitioner does not comply with the new citation, the petitioner is presumed to have renounced the trial according to the norm of cann. 1524–1525;

3° if the petitioner later wishes to intervene in the process, can. 1593 is to be observed.

CAN. 1595 §1. A petitioner or respondent who is absent from the trial and has not given proof of a just impediment is obliged both to pay the expenses of the litigation which have accrued because of the absence and to indemnify the other party if necessary.

§2. If both the petitioner and the respondent were absent from the trial, they are obliged *in solidum* to pay the expenses of the litigation.

CHAPTER II. The Intervention of a Third Person in a Case

CAN. 1596 §1. A person who has an interest can be admitted to intervene in a case at any instance of the litigation, either as a party defending a right or in an accessory manner to help a litigant.

§2. To be admitted, the person must present a *libellus* to the judge before the conclusion of the case; in the *libellus* the person briefly is to demonstrate his or her right to intervene.

§3. A person who intervenes in a case must be admitted at that stage which the case has reached, with a brief and peremptory period of time assigned to the person to present proofs if the case has reached the probatory period.

CAN. 1597 After having heard the parties, the judge must summon to the trial a third person whose intervention seems necessary.

2° si actor novae citationi non paruerit, praesumitur instantiae renuntiasse ad normam cann. 1524–1525;

3° quod si postea in processu intervenire velit, servetur can. 1593.

CAN. 1595 §1. Pars absens a iudicio, sive actor sive pars conventa, quae iustum impedimentum non comprobaverit, tenetur obligatione tum solvendi litis expensas, quae ob ipsius absentiam factae sunt, tum etiam, si opus sit, indemnitatem alteri parti praestandi.

§2. Si tum actor tum pars conventa fuerint absentes a iudicio, ipsi obligatione expensas litis solvendi tenentur in solidum.

CAPUT II. De Interventu Tertii in Causa

CAN. 1596 §1. Is cuius interest admitti potest ad interveniendum in causa, in qualibet litis instantia, sive ut pars quae proprium ius defendit, sive accessorie ad aliquem litigantem adiuvandum.

§2. Sed ut admittatur, debet ante conclusionem in causa libellum iudici exhibere, in quo breviter suum ius interveniendi demonstret.

§3. Qui intervenit in causa, admittendus est in eo statu in quo causa reperitur, assignato eidem brevi ac peremptorio termino ad probationes suas exhibendas, si causa ad periodum probatoriam pervenerit.

CAN. 1597 Tertium, cuius interventus videatur necessarius, iudex, auditis partibus, debet in iudicium vocare.

1595 §1: c. 1851 §1; PrM 90
1595 §2: c. 1851 §2
1596 §1: c. 1852 §1; NSRR 160

1596 §2: c. 1852 §2; NSRR 117 §1
1596 §3: c. 1852 §3
1597: c. 1853; NSRR 118 §1

TITLE VI. The Publication of the Acts, the Conclusion of the Case, and the Discussion of the Case

CAN. 1598 §1. After the proofs have been collected, the judge by a decree must permit the parties and their advocates, under penalty of nullity, to inspect at the tribunal chancery the acts not yet known to them; furthermore, a copy of the acts can also be given to advocates who request one. In cases pertaining to the public good to avoid a most grave danger the judge can decree that a specific act must be shown to no one; the judge is to take care, however, that the right of defense always remains intact.

§2. To complete the proofs, the parties can propose additional proofs to the judge. When these proofs have been collected, it is again an occasion for the decree mentioned in §1 if the judge thinks it necessary.

CAN. 1599 §1. When everything pertaining to the production of proofs has been completed, the conclusion of the case is reached.

§2. This conclusion occurs whenever the parties declare that they have nothing else to add, the useful time prescribed by the judge to propose proofs has elapsed, or the judge declares that the case is instructed sufficiently.

§3. The judge is to issue a decree that the case has reached its conclusion, in whatever manner it has occurred.

CAN. 1600 §1. After the conclusion of the case, the judge can still summon the same or other witnesses or arrange for other proofs which were not requested earlier, only:

TITULUS VI. De Actorum Publicatione, de Conclusione in Causa et de Causae Discussione

CAN. 1598 §1. Acquisitis probationibus, iudex decreto partibus et earum advocatis permittere debet, sub poena nullitatis, ut acta nondum eis nota apud tribunalis cancellariam inspiciant; quin etiam advocatis id petentibus dari potest actorum exemplar; in causis vero ad bonum publicum spectantibus iudex ad gravissima pericula evitanda aliquod actum nemini manifestandum esse decernere potest, cauto tamen ut ius defensionis semper integrum maneat.

§2. Ad probationes complendas partes possunt alias iudici proponere; quibus acquisitis, si iudex necessarium duxerit, iterum est locus decreto de quo in §1.

CAN. 1599 §1. Expletis omnibus quae ad probationes producendas pertinent, ad conclusionem in causa devenitur.

§2. Haec conclusio habetur quoties aut partes declarent se nihil aliud adducendum habere, aut utile proponendis probationibus tempus a iudice praestitutum elapsum sit, aut iudex declaret se satis instructam causam habere.

§3. De peracta conclusione in causa, quocumque modo ea acciderit, iudex decretum ferat.

CAN. 1600 §1. Post conclusionem in causa iudex potest adhuc eosdem testes vel alios vocare aut alias probationes, quae antea non fuerint petitae, disponere tantummodo:

1598 §1: cc. 1858, 1859; NSRR 120; PrM 175 §§1 et 2; CPEN Rescr., 28 apr. 1970, 18

1598 §2: PrM 175 §§3 et 4; CPEN Rescr., 28 apr. 1970, 18

1599 §1: c. 1860 §1; NSRR 121; PrM 176
1599 §2: c. 1860 §2; PrM 177 §2
1599 §3: c. 1860 §3; PrM 177 §1
1600 §1: c. 1861 §1; NSRR 121; PrM 178 §1

1° in cases which concern the private good of the parties alone, if all the parties consent;

2° in other cases, after the parties have been heard and provided that there is a grave reason and any danger of fraud or subornation is eliminated;

3° in all cases whenever it is likely that the sentence will be unjust because of the reasons mentioned in can. 1645, §2, nn. 1–3 unless the new proof is allowed.

§2. The judge, moreover, can order or allow a document to be shown, which may have been unable to be shown earlier through no negligence of the interested person.

§3. New proofs are to be published according to can. 1598, §1.

CAN. 1601 After the conclusion of the case, the judge is to determine a suitable period of time to present defense briefs or observations.

CAN. 1602 §1. The defense briefs and the observations are to be written unless the judge, with the consent of the parties, considers a debate before a session of the tribunal to be sufficient.

§2. To print the defense briefs along with the principal documents requires the previous permission of the judge, without prejudice to the obligation of secrecy, if such exists.

§3. The regulations of the tribunal are to be observed regarding the length of the defense briefs, the number of copies, and other matters of this kind.

CAN. 1603 §1. When the defense briefs

1° in causis, in quibus agitur de solo privato partium bono, si omnes partes consentiant;

2° in ceteris causis, auditis partibus et dummodo gravis exstet ratio itemque quodlibet fraudis vel subornationis periculum removeatur;

3° in omnibus causis, quoties verisimile est, nisi probatio nova admittatur, sententiam iniustam futuram esse propter rationes, de quibus in can. 1645, §2, nn. 1–3.

§2. Potest autem iudex iubere vel admittere ut exhibeatur documentum, quod forte antea sine culpa eius, cuius interest, exhiberi non potuit.

§3. Novae probationes publicentur, servato can. 1598, §1.

CAN. 1601 Facta conclusione in causa, iudex congruum temporis spatium praestituat ad defensiones vel animadversiones exhibendas.

CAN. 1602 §1. Defensiones et animadversiones scriptae sint, nisi disputationem pro tribunali sedente iudex, consentientibus partibus, satis esse censeat.

§2. Si defensiones cum praecipuis documentis typis imprimantur, praevia iudicis licentia requiritur, salva secreti obligatione, si qua sit.

§3. Quoad extensionem defensionum, numerum exemplarium, aliaque huiusmodi adiuncta, servetur ordinatio tribunalis.

CAN. 1603 §1. Communicatis vicissim

1600 §2: c. 1861 §1; NSRR 121; PrM 178 §1
1600 §3: c. 1861 §2; NSRR 121; PrM 178 §3
1601: c. 1862; PrM 179 §1
1602 §1: c. 1863 §1; PrM 179 §2
1602 §2: c. 1863 §§3 et 4; NSRR 122 §1, 125 §1; PrM 179 §3

1602 §3: c. 1863 §§1 et 2, 1864; NSRR 124, 126 §1; PrM 179 §2, 182
1603 §1: c. 1865 §1; NSRR 126 §§3 et 4, 128 §1; PrM 180 §§1, 2 et 3

and observations have been communicated to each party, either party is permitted to present responses within the brief time period established by the judge.

§2. The parties are given this right only once unless the judge decides that it must be granted a second time for a grave cause; then, however, the grant made to one party is considered as given to the other also.

§3. The promoter of justice and the defender of the bond have the right to reply a second time to the responses of the parties.

CAN. 1604 §1. It is absolutely forbidden for information given to the judge by the parties, advocates, or even other persons to remain outside the acts of the case.

§2. If the discussion of the case has been done in writing, the judge can order a moderate oral debate to be held before a session of the tribunal in order to explain certain questions.

CAN. 1605 A notary is to be present at the oral debate mentioned in cann. 1602, §1 and 1604, §2 so that, if the judge orders it or a party requests it and the judge consents, the notary can immediately report in writing about what was discussed and concluded.

CAN. 1606 If the parties have neglected to prepare a defense brief within the time available to them or have entrusted themselves to the knowledge and conscience of the judge, and if from the acts and proofs the judge considers the matter fully examined, the judge can pronounce the sentence immediately, after having requested the observations of the promoter of justice and the defender of the bond if they are involved in the trial.

defensionibus atque animadversionibus, utrique parti responsiones exhibere licet, intra breve tempus a iudice praestitutum.

§2. Hoc ius partibus semel tantum esto, nisi iudici gravi ex causa iterum videatur concedendum; tunc autem concessio, uni parti facta, alteri quoque data censeatur.

§3. Promotor iustitiae et defensor vinculi ius habent iterum replicandi partium responsionibus.

CAN. 1604 §1. Omnino prohibentur partium vel advocatorum vel etiam aliorum informationes iudici datae, quae maneant extra acta causae.

§2. Si causae discussio scripto facta sit, iudex potest statuere ut moderata disputatio fiat ore pro tribunali sedente, ad quaestiones nonnullas illustrandas.

CAN. 1605 Disputationi orali, de qua in cann. 1602, §1 et 1604, §2, assistat notarius ad hoc ut, si iudex praecipiat aut pars postulet et iudex consentiat, de disceptatis et conclusis scripto statim referre possit.

CAN. 1606 Si partes parare sibi tempore utili defensionem neglexerint, aut se remittant iudicis scientiae et conscientiae, iudex, si ex actis et probatis rem habeat plane perspectam, poterit statim sententiam pronuntiare, requisitis tamen animadversionibus promotoris iustitiae et defensoris vinculi, si iudicio intersint.

1603 §2: c. 1865 §2; NSRR 128 §2; PrM 180 §4
1603 §3: PrM 183
1604 §1: c. 1866 §1; NSRR 132 §1; NSSA 53
1604 §2: c. 1866 §§2 et 3; NSRR 132 §1, 133 §§1 et 2; PrM 186 §§1–4; NSSA 31–33; 52

1605: c. 1866 §4; NSRR 133 §3; PrM 186 §5
1606: c. 1867; NSRR 71, 73 §1, 131; PrM 89 §4

TITLE VII. The Pronouncements of the Judge

CAN. 1607 When a case has been handled in a judicial manner, if it is the principal case, the judge decides it through the definitive sentence; if an incidental case, through an interlocutory sentence, without prejudice to the prescript of can. 1589, §1.

CAN. 1608 §1. For the pronouncement of any sentence, the judge must have moral certitude about the matter to be decided by the sentence.

§2. The judge must derive this certitude from the acts and the proofs.

§3. The judge, however, must appraise the proofs according to the judge's own conscience, without prejudice to the prescripts of law concerning the efficacy of certain proofs.

§4. A judge who was not able to arrive at this certitude is to pronounce that the right of the petitioner is not established and is to dismiss the respondent as absolved, unless it concerns a case which has the favor of law, in which case the judge must pronounce for that.

CAN. 1609 §1. In a collegiate tribunal the president of the college is to establish the date and time when the judges are to convene for deliberation; unless a special reason suggests otherwise, the meeting is to be held at the tribunal office.

TITULUS VII. De Iudicis Pronuntiationibus

CAN. 1607 Causa iudiciali modo pertractata, si sit principalis, definitur a iudice per sententiam definitivam; si sit incidens, per sententiam interlocutoriam, firmo praescripto can. 1589, §1.

CAN. 1608 §1. Ad pronuntiationem cuiuslibet sententiae requiritur in iudicis animo moralis certitudo circa rem sententia definiendam.

§2. Hanc certitudinem iudex haurire debet ex actis et probatis.

§3. Probationes autem aestimare iudex debet ex sua conscientia, firmis praescriptis legis de quarundam probationum efficacia.

§4. Iudex qui eam certitudinem adipisci non potuit, pronuntiet non constare de iure actoris et conventum absolutum dimittat, nisi agatur de causa iuris favore fruente, quo in casu pro ipsa pronuntiandum est.

CAN. 1609 §1. In tribunali collegiali, qua die et hora iudices ad deliberandum conveniant, collegii praeses statuat, et nisi peculiaris causa aliud suadeat, in ipsa tribunalis sede conventus habeatur.

1607: c. 1868; NSRR 135 §2; PrM 196 §1; Paulus PP. VI, All., 8 feb. 1973 (AAS 65 [1973] 100–103)

1608 §1: c. 1869; PrM 197; Pius PP. XII, All., 3 oct. 1941 (AAS 33 [1941] 421–426); Pius PP. XII, All., 1 oct. 1942 (AAS 34 [1942] 338–343); Pius PP. XII, All., 5 dec. 1954 (AAS 47 [1955] 64); CPEN Rescr., 28 apr. 1970, 21; Ioannes Paulus PP. II, All., 4 feb. 1980, 4–6 (AAS 72 [1980] 174–176)

1608 §2: c. 1869 §2; PrM 197 §2; Pius PP. XII, All., 5 dec. 1954 (AAS 47 [1955] 64); Ioannes Paulus PP. II, All., 4 feb. 1980, 5 (AAS 72 [1980] 175)

1608 §3: c. 1869 §3; PrM 197 §3; Pius PP. XII, All., 5 dec. 1954 (AAS 47 [1955] 64); Pius PP. XII, All., 1 oct. 1942, 4 (AAS 34 [1942] 341–342)

1608 §4: c. 1869 §4; PrM 197 §4; Pius PP. XII, All., 5 dec. 1954 (AAS 47 [1955] 64); Ioannes Paulus PP. II. All., 4 feb. 1980, 7–9 (AAS 72 [1980] 176–178)

1609 §1: c. 1871 §1; NSRR 135 §1; PrM 198 §1

§2. On the date assigned for the meeting, the individual judges are to submit their written conclusions on the merit of the case with the reasons in law and in fact which led them to their conclusions; these conclusions are to be added to the acts of the case and must be kept secret.

§3. After the invocation of the Divine Name, the individual judges are to present their conclusions in order of precedence, always beginning, however, with the *ponens* or *relator* of the case. A discussion then follows under the leadership of the tribunal president, especially to determine what must be established in the dispositive part of the sentence.

§4. In the discussion each judge is permitted to withdraw from his or her original conclusion. The judge who is unwilling to assent to the decision of the others, however, can demand that his or her conclusions be transmitted to the higher tribunal if an appeal is made.

§5. If the judges are unwilling or unable to arrive at a sentence during the first discussion, the decision can be deferred to a new meeting, but not for more than a week, unless the instruction of the case must be completed according to the norm of can. 1600.

CAN. 1610 §1. If there is only one judge, he will write the sentence himself.

§2. In a collegiate tribunal, it is for the *ponens* or *relator* to write the sentence, selecting the reasons from those the individual judges brought forth during the discussion, unless a majority of the judges have already determined the reasons to be presented. The sentence must then be submitted for the approval of the individual judges.

§2. Assignata conventui die, singuli iudices scriptas afferant conclusiones suas in merito causae, et rationes tam in iure quam in facto, quibus ad conclusionem suam venerint; quae conclusiones actis causae adiungantur, secreto servandae.

§3. Post divini Nominis invocationem, prolatis ex ordine singulorum conclusionibus secundum praecedentiam, ita tamen ut semper a causae ponente seu relatore initium fiat, habeatur discussio sub tribunalis praesidis ductu, praesertim ut constabiliatur quid statuendum sit in parte dispositiva sententiae.

§4. In discussione autem fas unicuique est a pristina sua conclusione recedere. Iudex vero, qui ad decisionem aliorum accedere noluit, exigere potest ut, si fiat appellatio, suae conclusiones ad tribunal superius transmittantur.

§5. Quod si iudices in prima discussione ad sententiam devenire aut nolint aut nequeant, differri poterit decisio ad novum conventum, non tamen ultra hebdomadam, nisi ad normam can. 1600 complenda sit causae instructio.

CAN. 1610 §1. Si iudex sit unicus, ipse sententiam exarabit.

§2. In tribunali collegiali, ponentis seu relatoris est exarare sententiam, desumendo motiva ex iis quae singuli iudices in discussione attulerunt, nisi a maiore numero iudicum praefinita fuerint motiva praeferenda; sententia dein singulorum iudicum subicienda est approbationi.

1609 §2: c. 1871 §2; NSRR 136 §1; PrM 198 §2
1609 §3: c. 1871 §3; NSRR 137, 142 §1; PrM 198 §§3 et 6; NSSA 120–122 §1
1609 §4: c. 1871 §4; NSRR 138, 143 §4; PrM 198 §4, 203 §§1 et 2

1609 §5: c. 1871 §5; NSRR 140, 141; PrM 198 §5; NSSA 122 §1
1610 §1: c. 1872
1610 §2: c. 1873 §2; NSRR 143 §§2 et 3; PrM 200 §§2, 4 et 5; NSSA 121, 122 §§2 et 3

§3. The sentence must be issued no more than a month from the day on which the case was decided unless in a collegiate tribunal the judges set a longer period for a grave reason.

CAN. 1611   The sentence must:

1° decide the controversy deliberated before the tribunal with an appropriate response given to the individual doubts;

2° determine what obligations have arisen for the parties from the trial and how they must be fulfilled;

3° set forth the reasons or motives in law and in fact on which the dispositive part of the sentence is based;

4° determine the expenses of the litigation.

CAN. 1612   §1. After the invocation of the Divine Name, the sentence must express in order the judge or the tribunal, the petitioner, the respondent, and the procurator, with their names and domiciles correctly designated, and the promoter of justice and defender of the bond if they took part in the trial.

§2. Next, it must briefly relate the facts together with the conclusions of the parties and the formula of the doubts.

§3. The dispositive part of the sentence follows the above, preceded by the reasons on which it is based.

§4. It is to conclude with the indication of the date and the place where it was rendered, with the signature of the judge or, if it is a collegiate tribunal, of all the judges, and the notary.

CAN. 1613   The rules proposed above for a

§3. Sententia edenda est non ultra mensem a die quo causa definita est, nisi, in tribunali collegiali, iudices gravi ex ratione longius tempus praestituerint.

CAN. 1611   Sententia debet:

1° definire controversiam coram tribunali agitatam, data singulis dubiis congrua responsione;

2° determinare quae sint partium obligationes ex iudicio ortae et quomodo implendae sint;

3° exponere rationes seu motiva, tam in iure quam in facto, quibus dispositiva sententiae pars innititur;

4° statuere de litis expensis.

CAN. 1612   §1. Sententia, post divini Nominis invocationem, exprimat oportet ex ordine qui sit iudex aut tribunal; qui sit actor, pars conventa, procurator, nominibus et domiciliis rite designatis, promotor iustitiae, defensor vinculi, si partem in iudicio habuerint.

§2. Referre postea debet breviter facti speciem cum partium conclusionibus et formula dubiorum.

§3. Hisce subsequatur pars dispositiva sententiae, praemissis rationibus quibus innititur.

§4. Claudatur cum indicatione diei et loci in quibus prolata est et cum subscriptione iudicis vel, si tribunali collegiali agatur, omnium iudicum et notarii.

CAN. 1613   Regulae superius positae de

1610 §3: NSRR 143 §1; PrM 200 §1

1611, 1°: c. 1873 §1, 1°; NSSR 146; PrM 201 §1; NSSA 122 §1

1611, 2°: c. 1873 §1, 2°; NSRR 146 §2

1611, 3°: cc. 1605, 1873 §1, 3°; NSRR 143 §3; PrM 200 §3; NSSA 122 §§2 et 3

1611, 4°: c. 1873 §1, 4°; NSRR 144 §3, 147–149; PrM 200 §3; Paulus PP. VI, All., 11 ian. 1965 (AAS 57 [1965] 236)

1612 §1: c. 1874 §§1 et 2; NSRR 144 §1; PrM 202 §§1 et 2; Paulus PP. VI, All., 8 feb. 1973 (AAS 65 [1973] 102–103)

1612 §2: c. 1874 §3; NSRR 144 §2; PrM 202 §3

1612 §3: c. 1874 §4; NSRR 144 §2; PrM 202 §4; NSSA 122 §§2 et 3

1612 §4: c. 1874 §5; CI Resp. XIII, 14 iul. 1922 (AAS 14 [1922] 529); NSRR 144 §4; PrM 202 §5

1613: c. 1875; NSRR 139

definitive sentence are to be adapted for an interlocutory sentence.

CAN. 1614 The sentence is to be published as soon as possible, with an indication of the means by which it can be challenged. It has no force before publication even if the dispositive part was made known to the parties with the permission of the judge.

CAN. 1615 Publication or communication of the sentence can be done either by giving a copy of the sentence to the parties or their procurators or by sending them a copy according to the norm of can. 1509.

CAN. 1616 §1. If in the text of the sentence an error in calculations turns up, a material error occurs in transcribing the dispositive section or in relating the facts or the petitions of the parties, or the requirements of can. 1612, §4 are omitted, the tribunal which rendered the sentence must correct or complete it either at the request of a party or *ex officio*, but always after the parties have been heard and a decree appended to the bottom of the sentence.

§2. If any party objects, the incidental question is to be decided by a decree.

CAN. 1617 Other pronouncements of the judge besides the sentence are decrees, which have no force if they are not merely procedural unless they express the reasons at least in a summary fashion or refer to reasons expressed in another act.

CAN. 1618 An interlocutory sentence or a decree has the force of a definitive sentence if it prevents a trial or puts an end to a trial or some grade of a trial with respect to at least some party in the case.

sententia definitiva sententiae quoque interlocutoriae aptandae sunt.

CAN. 1614 Sententia quam primum publicetur, indicatis modis quibus impugnari potest; neque ante publicationem vim ullam habet, etiamsi dispositiva pars, iudice permittente, partibus significata sit.

CAN. 1615 Publicatio seu intimatio sententiae fieri potest vel tradendo exemplar sententiae partibus aut earum procuratoribus, vel eisdem transmittendo idem exemplar ad normam can. 1509.

CAN. 1616 §1. Si in sententiae textu vel error irrepserit in calculis, vel error materialis acciderit in transcribenda parte dispositiva aut in factis vel partium petitionibus referendis, vel omissa sint quae can. 1612, §4 requirit, sententia ab ipso tribunali, quod eam tulit, corrigi vel compleri debet sive ad partis instantiam sive ex officio, semper tamen auditis partibus et decreto ad calcem sententiae apposito.

§2. Si qua pars refragetur, quaestio incidens decreto definiatur.

CAN. 1617 Ceterae iudicis pronuntiationes, praeter sententiam, sunt decreta, quae si mere ordinatoria non sint, vim non habent, nisi saltem summarie motiva exprimant, vel ad motiva in alio actu expressa remittant.

CAN. 1618 Sententia interlocutoria vel decretum vim sententiae definitivae habent, si iudicium impediunt vel ipsi iudicio aut alicui ipsius gradui finem ponunt, quod attinet ad aliquam saltem partem in causa.

1614: c. 1876; NSRR 142 §2; PrM 199; PAULUS PP. VI, All., 11 ian. 1965 (AAS 57 [1965] 235); PAULUS PP. VI, All., 26 ian. 1966 (AAS 58 [1966] 155); NSSA 58 §1

1615: c. 1877; NSRR 151; PrM 204 §1; CI Resp. II, 25 ian. 1943 (AAS 35 [1943] 58)

1616 §1: c. 1878 §§1 et 2; NSRR 145; PrM 205 §2
1616 §2: c. 1878 §3; PrM 205 §3
1617: cc. 1840 §3, 1868 §2; NSRR 113, 135 §2; PrM 193, 196 §2; CIV (AAS 66 [1974] 463)
1618: PrM 214 §2

TITLE VIII. Challenge of the Sentence

CHAPTER I. Complaint of Nullity against the Sentence

CAN. 1619 Without prejudice to cann. 1622 and 1623, whenever a case involves the good of private persons, the sentence itself sanates the nullities of acts established by positive law which were not declared to the judge before the sentence even though they were known to the party proposing the complaint.

CAN. 1620 A sentence suffers from the defect of irremediable nullity if:

1° it was rendered by an absolutely incompetent judge;

2° it was rendered by a person who lacks the power of judging in the tribunal in which the case was decided;

3° a judge rendered a sentence coerced by force or grave fear;

4° the trial took place without the judicial petition mentioned in can. 1501 or was not instituted against some respondent;

5° it was rendered between parties, at least one of whom did not have standing in the trial;

6° someone acted in the name of another without a legitimate mandate;

7° the right of defense was denied to one or the other party;

8° it did not decide the controversy even partially.

CAN. 1621 The complaint of nullity mentioned in can. 1620 can be proposed by way of

TITULUS VIII. De Impugnatione Sententiae

CAPUT I. De Querela Nullitatis Contra Sententiam

CAN. 1619 Firmis cann. 1622 et 1623, nullitates actuum, positivo iure statutae, quae, cum essent notae parti querelam proponenti, non sint ante sententiam iudici denuntiatae, per ipsam sententiam sanantur, quoties agitur de causa ad privatorum bonum attinenti.

CAN. 1620 Sententia vitio insanabilis nullitatis laborat, si:

1° lata est a iudice absolute incompetenti;

2° lata est ab eo, qui careat potestate iudicandi in tribunali in quo causa definita est;

3° iudex vi vel metu gravi coactus sententiam tulit;

4° iudicium factum est sine iudiciali petitione, de qua in can. 1501, vel non institutum fuit adversus aliquam partem conventam;

5° lata est inter partes, quarum altera saltem non habeat personam standi in iudicio;

6° nomine alterius quis egit sine legitimo mandato;

7° ius defensionis alterutri parti denegatum fuit;

8° controversia ne ex parte quidem definita est.

CAN. 1621 Querela nullitatis, de qua in can. 1620, proponi potest per modum ex-

1619: NSSA 103; CPEN Rescr., 28 apr. 1970, 22
1620, 1°: c. 1892, 1°; PrM 207, 1°
1620, 3°: CPEN Rescr., 28 apr. 1970, 22 §3
1620, 4°: CPEN Rescr., 28 apr. 1970, 22 §1
1620, 5°: c. 1892, 2°; PrM 207, 2°; CI Resp., 4 ian. 1946 (AAS 38 [1946] 162)

1620, 6°: c. 1892, 3°; PrM 207, 3°
1620, 7°: CPEN Rescr., 28 apr. 1970, 22 §2; SA Litt. 30 dec. 1971, III, 8; SA Litt. circ. 24 iul. 1972, 5, c et d
1620, 8°: NSSA 122 §1; CPEN Rescr., 28 apr. 1970, 22 §4
1621: c. 1893; PrM 208

exception in perpetuity and also by way of action before the judge who rendered the sentence within ten years from the date of the publication of the sentence.

CAN. 1622 A sentence suffers from the defect of remediable nullity only if:

1° it was rendered by an illegitimate number of judges contrary to the prescript of can. 1425, §1;

2° it does not contain the motives or reasons for the decision;

3° it lacks the signatures prescribed by law;

4° it does not indicate the year, month, day, and place in which it was rendered;

5° it is based on a null judicial act whose nullity was not sanated according to the norm of can. 1619;

6° it was rendered against a party legitimately absent according to can. 1593, §2.

CAN. 1623 A complaint of nullity in the cases mentioned in can. 1622 can be proposed within three months from the notice of the publication of the sentence.

CAN. 1624 The judge who rendered the sentence deals with the complaint of nullity. If the party fears that the judge who rendered the sentence challenged by the complaint of nullity is prejudiced and therefore considers the judge suspect, the party can demand that another judge be substituted according to the norm of can. 1450.

CAN. 1625 A complaint of nullity can be proposed together with an appeal within the time established for an appeal.

CAN. 1626 §1. Not only the parties who

CAN. 1622 Sententia vitio sanabilis nullitatis dumtaxat laborat, si:

1° lata est a non legitimo numero iudicum, contra praescriptum can. 1425, §1;

2° motiva seu rationes decidendi non continet;

3° subscriptionibus caret iure praescriptis;

4° non refert indicationem anni, mensis, diei et loci in quo prolata fuit;

5° actu iudiciali nullo innititur, cuius nullitas non sit ad normam can. 1619 sanata;

6° lata est contra partem legitime absentem, iuxta can. 1593, §2.

CAN. 1623 Querela nullitatis in casibus, de quibus in can. 1622, proponi potest intra tres menses a notitia publicationis sententiae.

CAN. 1624 De querela nullitatis videt ipse iudex qui sententiam tulit; quod si pars vereatur ne iudex, qui sententiam querela nullitatis impugnatam tulit, praeoccupatum animum habeat ideoque eum suspectum existimet, exigere potest ut alius iudex in eius locum subrogetur ad normam can. 1450.

CAN. 1625 Querela nullitatis proponi potest una cum appellatione, intra terminum ad appellationem statutum.

CAN. 1626 §1. Querelam nullitatis in-

1622, 1°: c. 1892, 1°; PrM 207, 1°
1622, 2°: c. 1894, 2°; PrM 209, 2°
1622, 3°: c. 1894, 3°; CI Resp. XIII, 14 iul. 1922
(AAS 14 [1922] 529); PrM 209, 3°
1622, 4°: c. 1894, 4°; PrM 209, 4°

1623: c. 1895; PrM 210
1624: cc. 1893, 1895, 1896; PrM 208, 210, 211 §4
1625: c. 1895; PrM 210
1626 §1: c. 1897 §1; PrM 211 §1

consider themselves aggrieved can introduce a complaint of nullity but also the promoter of justice and the defender of the bond whenever they have the right to intervene.

§2. The judge can retract or emend *ex officio* a null sentence, which that judge has rendered, within the time limit for acting established by can. 1623 unless an appeal together with a complaint of nullity has been introduced in the meantime or the nullity has been sanated through the expiration of the time limit mentioned in can. 1623.

CAN. 1627 Cases concerning a complaint of nullity can be treated according to the norms for the oral contentious process.

CHAPTER II. **Appeal**

CAN. 1628 A party who considers himself or herself aggrieved by any sentence as well as the promoter of justice and the defender of the bond in cases which require their presence have the right to appeal the sentence to a higher judge, without prejudice to the prescript of can. 1629.

CAN. 1629 There is no appeal:

1° from a sentence of the Supreme Pontiff himself or the Apostolic Signatura;

2° from a sentence tainted by a defect of nullity, unless the appeal is joined with a complaint of nullity according to the norm of can. 1625;

3° from a sentence which has become a *res iudicata;*

4° from a decree of a judge or from an interlocutory sentence which does not have the force of a definitive sentence, unless it is joined with an appeal from a definitive sentence;

terponere possunt non solum partes, quae se gravatas putant, sed etiam promotor iustitiae aut defensor vinculi, quoties ipsis ius est interveniendi.

§2. Ipse iudex potest ex officio sententiam nullam a se latam retractare vel emendare intra terminum ad agendum can. 1623 statutum, nisi interea appellatio una cum querela nullitatis interposita fuerit, aut nullitas sanata sit per decursum termini de quo in can. 1623.

CAN. 1627 Causae de querela nullitatis secundum normas de processu contentioso orali tractari possunt.

CAPUT II. **De Appellatione**

CAN. 1628 Pars quae aliqua sententia se gravatam putat, itemque promotor iustitiae et defensor vinculi in causis in quibus eorum praesentia requiritur, ius habent a sententia appellandi ad iudicem superiorem, salvo praescripto can. 1629.

CAN. 1629 Non est locus appellationi:

1° a sententia ipsius Summi Pontificis vel Signaturae Apostolicae;

2° a sententia vitio nullitatis infecta, nisi cumuletur cum querela nullitatis ad normam can. 1625;

3° a sententia quae in rem iudicatam transiit;

4° a iudicis decreto vel a sententia interlocutoria, quae non habeant vim sententiae definitivae, nisi cumuletur cum appellatione a sententia definitiva;

1626 §2: c. 1897 §2; PrM 211 §2
1627: NSSA 31–33
1628: c. 1879; NSRR 154; PrM 212 §§1 et 2
1629, 1°: c. 1880, 1°; NSSA 58 §2, 77, 82

1629, 2°: c. 1880, 3°
1629, 3°: c. 1880, 4°; NSRR 161
1629, 4°: c. 1880, 6°; NSRR 114 §1; PrM 215 §1

5° from a sentence or a decree in a case where the law requires the matter to be decided as promptly as possible *(expeditissime)*.

CAN. 1630 §1. An appeal must be introduced before the judge who rendered the sentence within the peremptory period of fifteen useful days from the notice of the publication of the sentence.

§2. If an appeal is made orally, the notary is to put it in writing in the presence of the appellant.

CAN. 1631 If a question arises about the right to appeal, the appellate tribunal deals with it as promptly as possible *(expeditissime)* according to the norms of the oral contentious process.

CAN. 1632 §1. If the appeal does not indicate the tribunal to which it is directed, it is presumed to be made to the tribunal mentioned in cann. 1438 and 1439.

§2. If the other party has appealed to another appellate tribunal, the tribunal of higher grade deals with the case, without prejudice to can. 1415.

CAN. 1633 An appeal must be pursued before the appellate judge within a month from its introduction unless the judge from whom appeal is made has established a longer period for a party to pursue it.

CAN. 1634 §1. To pursue an appeal it is required and suffices that a party calls upon the services of a higher judge for an emendation of the challenged sentence, attaches a copy of this sentence, and indicates the reasons for the appeal.

5° a sententia vel a decreto in causa de qua ius cavet expeditissime rem esse definiendam.

CAN. 1630 §1. Appellatio interponi debet coram iudice a quo sententia prolata sit, intra peremptorium terminum quindecim dierum utilium a notitia publicationis sententiae.

§2. Si ore fiat, notarius eam scripto coram ipso appellante redigat.

CAN. 1631 Si quaestio oriatur de iure appellandi, de ea videat expeditissime tribunal appellationis iuxta normas processus contentiosi oralis.

CAN. 1632 §1. Si in appellatione non indicetur ad quod tribunal ipsa dirigatur, praesumitur facta tribunali de quo in cann. 1438 et 1439.

§2. Si alia pars ad aliud tribunal appellationis provocaverit, de causa videt tribunal quod superioris est gradus, salvo can. 1415.

CAN. 1633 Appellatio prosequenda est coram iudice *ad quem* dirigitur intra mensem ab eius interpositione, nisi iudex *a quo* longius tempus ad eam prosequendam parti praestituerit.

CAN. 1634 §1. Ad prosequendam appellationem requiritur et sufficit ut pars ministerium invocet iudicis superioris ad impugnatae sententiae emendationem, adiuncto exemplari huius sententiae et indicatis appellationis rationibus.

1629, 5°: c. 1880, 7°
1630 §1: c. 1881; NSRR 155, 156 §1; PrM 215 §1
1630 §2: c. 1882 §1
1631: NSRR 159 §§1 et 2; PrM 215 §2
1632 §2: PrM 216 §2

1633: c. 1883; NSRR 156 §1; PrM 215 §1; SN can. 409
1634 §1: c. 1884 §1; NSRR 157; PrM 215 §1; SN can. 410 §1

§2. If a party cannot obtain a copy of the challenged sentence from the tribunal from which appeal is made within the useful time, the time limits do not run in the meantime; the impediment must be made known to the appellate judge who is to bind the judge from whom appeal is made by a precept to fulfill that judge's duty as soon as possible.

§3. Meanwhile the judge from whom appeal is made must transmit the acts to the appellate judge according to the norm of can. 1474.

CAN. 1635 Once the deadline for appeal has passed without action either before the judge from whom the appeal is made or before the appellate judge, the appeal is considered abandoned.

CAN. 1636 §1. The appellant can renounce the appeal with the effects mentioned in can. 1525.

§2. If the defender of the bond or the promoter of justice has introduced the appeal, the defender of the bond or the promoter of justice of the appellate tribunal can renounce it, unless the law provides otherwise.

CAN. 1637 §1. An appeal made by the petitioner also benefits the respondent and vice versa.

§2. If there are several respondents or petitioners and the sentence is challenged by only one or against only one of them, the challenge is considered to be made by all of them and against all of them whenever the matter sought is indivisible or a joint obligation.

§3. If one party introduces an appeal against one ground of the sentence, the other party can

§2. Quod si pars exemplar impugnatae sententiae intra utile tempus a tribunali *a quo* obtinere nequeat, interim termini non decurrunt, et impedimentum significandum est iudici appellationis, qui iudicem *a quo* praecepto obstringat officio suo quam primum satisfaciendi.

§3. Interea iudex *a quo* debet acta ad normam can. 1474 iudici appellationis transmittere.

CAN. 1635 Inutiliter elapsis fatalibus appellatoriis sive coram iudice *a quo* sive coram iudice *ad quem*, deserta censetur appellatio.

CAN. 1636 §1. Appellans potest appellationi renuntiare cum effectibus, de quibus in can. 1525.

§2. Si appellatio proposita sit a vinculi defensore vel a promotore iustitiae, renuntiatio fieri potest, nisi lex aliter caveat, a vinculi defensore vel promotore iustitiae tribunalis appellationis.

CAN. 1637 §1. Appellatio facta ab actore prodest etiam convento, et vicissim.

§2. Si plures sunt conventi vel actores et ab uno vel contra unum tantum ex ipsis sententia impugnetur, impugnatio censetur ab omnibus et contra omnes facta, quoties res petita est individua aut obligatio solidalis.

§3. Si interponatur ab una parte super aliquo sententiae capite, pars adversa, etsi

1634 §2: c. 1884 §2; PrM 215 §2; SN can. 410 §2
1634 §3: c. 1890; CI Resp., 31 ian. 1942 (AAS 34 [1942] 50); SN can. 416
1635: c. 1886; NSRR 156 §2; SN can. 412
1636: c. 1889, 9°; PrM 41 §4, 221 §§2 et 3; SN can. 404, 9°; CM IX §2; SA Decisio, 16 nov. 1971

1637 §1: c. 1887 §1; PrM 212 §3; SN can. 413 §1
1637 §2: c. 1888; SN can. 414
1637 §3: c. 1887 §2; NSRR 161

appeal incidentally against other grounds within the peremptory period of fifteen days from the day on which the original appeal was made known to the latter, even if the deadline for an appeal has passed.

§4. Unless it is otherwise evident, an appeal is presumed to be made against all the grounds of a sentence.

CAN. 1638 An appeal suspends the execution of the sentence.

CAN. 1639 §1. Without prejudice to the prescript of can. 1683, a new cause for petitioning cannot be admitted at the appellate grade, not even by way of useful accumulation; consequently, the joinder of the issue can only address whether the prior sentence is to be confirmed or revised either totally or partially.

§2. New proofs, however, are admitted only according to the norm of can. 1600.

CAN. 1640 The appellate grade must proceed in the same manner as first instance with appropriate adjustments; immediately after the issue has been joined according to the norm of can. 1513, §1 and can. 1639, §1 and unless the proofs possibly must be completed, the discussion of the case is to take place and the sentence rendered.

TITLE IX. *Res Iudicata* and *Restitutio in Integrum*

CHAPTER I. *Res iudicata*

CAN. 1641 Without prejudice to the prescript of can. 1643, a *res iudicata* occurs:

fatalia appellationis fuerint transacta, potest super aliis capitibus incidenter appellare intra terminum peremptorium quindecim dierum a die, quo ipsi appellatio principalis notificata est.

§4. Nisi aliud constet, appellatio praesumitur facta contra omnia sententiae capita.

CAN. 1638 Appellatio exsecutionem sententiae suspendit.

CAN. 1639 §1. Salvo praescripto can. 1683, in gradu appellationis non potest admitti nova petendi causa, ne per modum quidem utilis cumulationis; ideoque litis contestatio in eo tantum versari potest, ut prior sententia vel confirmetur vel reformetur sive ex toto sive ex parte.

§2. Novae autem probationes admittuntur tantum ad normam can. 1600.

CAN. 1640 In gradu appellationis eodem modo, quo in prima instantia, congrua congruis referendo, procedendum est; sed, nisi forte complendae sint probationes, statim post litem ad normam can. 1513, §1 et can. 1639, §1 contestatam, ad causae discussionem deveniatur et ad sententiam.

TITULUS IX. **De re iudicata et de restitutione in integrum**

CAPUT I. **De re iudicata**

CAN. 1641 Firmo praescripto can. 1643, res iudicata habetur:

1637 §4: c. 1887 §3; SN can. 413 §3
1638: c. 1889 §2; SN can. 415 §2
1639 §1: c. 1891 §1; PrM 219 §1; SN can. 417 §1
1639 §2: c. 1891 §2; NSRR 160 §1

1640: c. 1595; NSRR 163; PrM 213; SN can. 417 §1; CPEN Rescr., 28 apr. 1970, 23 §1
1641: c. 1902; SN can. 429

1° if a second concordant sentence is rendered between the same parties over the same issue and on the same cause for petitioning;

2° if an appeal against the sentence has not been introduced within the useful time;

3° if at the appellate grade, the trial has been abated or renounced;

4° if a definitive sentence has been rendered from which there is no appeal according to the norm of can. 1629.

CAN. 1642   §1. A *res iudicata* possesses the stability of law and cannot be challenged directly except according to the norm of can. 1645, §1.

§2. It establishes the rights between the parties and permits an action for execution and an exception of *res iudicata* which the judge can also declare *ex officio* in order to prevent a new introduction of the same case.

CAN. 1643   Cases concerning the status of persons, including cases concerning the separation of spouses, never become *res iudicata*.

CAN. 1644   §1. If a second concordant sentence has been rendered in a case concerning the status of persons, recourse can be made at any time to the appellate tribunal if new and grave proofs or arguments are brought forward within the peremptory time limit of thirty days from the proposed challenge. Within a month from when the new proofs and arguments are brought forward, however, the appellate tribunal must establish by decree whether a new presentation of the case must be admitted or not.

§2. Recourse to a higher tribunal in order to obtain a new presentation of the case does not suspend the execution of the sentence unless ei-

1° si duplex intercesserit inter easdem partes sententia conformis de eodem petito et ex eadem causa petendi;

2° si appellatio adversus sententiam non fuerit intra tempus utile proposita;

3° si, in gradu appellationis, instantia perempta sit vel eidem renuntiatum fuerit;

4° si lata sit sententia definitiva, a qua non datur appellatio ad normam can. 1629.

CAN. 1642   §1. Res iudicata firmitate iuris gaudet nec impugnari potest directe, nisi ad normam can. 1645, §1.

§2. Eadem facit ius inter partes et dat actionem iudicati atque exceptionem rei iudicatae, quam iudex ex officio quoque declarare potest ad impediendam novam eiusdem causae introductionem.

CAN. 1643   Numquam transeunt in rem iudicatam causae de statu personarum, haud exceptis causis de coniugum separatione.

CAN. 1644   §1. Si duplex sententia conformis in causa de statu personarum prolata sit, potest quovis tempore ad tribunal appellationis provocari, novis iisque gravibus probationibus vel argumentis intra peremptorium terminum triginta dierum a proposita impugnatione allatis. Tribunal autem appellationis intra mensem ab exhibitis novis probationibus et argumentis debet decreto statuere utrum nova causae propositio admitti debeat necne.

§2. Provocatio ad superius tribunal ut nova causae propositio obtineatur, exsecutionem sententiae non suspendit, nisi aut lex

1642 §1: c. 1904 §1; SN can. 431 §1
1642 §2: c. 1904 §2; SN can. 431 §2
1643: cc. 1903, 1989; SRR Decisio, 20 iun. 1922 (AAS 14 [1922] 600–607); PrM 217 §1; CI Resp., 8 apr. 1941 (AAS 33 [1941] 173); SN can. 430

1644 §1: cc. 1903, 1989; PrM 217, 218 §2; SN can. 430; CM IX §1

ther the law provides otherwise or the appellate tribunal orders its suspension according to the norm of can. 1650, §3.

aliter caveat aut tribunal appellationis ad normam can. 1650, §3 suspensionem iubeat.

CHAPTER II. *Restitutio in integrum*

CAPUT II. **De restitutione in integrum**

CAN. 1645 §1. *Restitutio in integrum* is granted against a sentence which has become *res iudicata* provided that its injustice is clearly established.

§2. Injustice, however, is not considered to be established clearly unless:

1° the sentence is based on proofs which afterwards are discovered to be false in such a way that without those proofs the dispositive part of the sentence is not sustained;

2° documents have been revealed afterwards which undoubtedly prove new facts and demand a contrary decision;

3° the sentence was rendered due to the malice of one party resulting in harm to the other party;

4° a prescript of the law which is not merely procedural was clearly neglected;

5° the sentence is contrary to a previous decision which has become *res iudicata*.

CAN. 1646 §1. *Restitutio in integrum* for the reasons mentioned in can. 1645, §2, nn. 1–3 must be sought from the judge who rendered the sentence within three months computed from the day the person became aware of these same reasons.

§2. *Restitutio in integrum* for the reasons mentioned in can. 1645 §2, nn. 4 and 5 must be sought from the appellate tribunal within three months from the notice of the publication of

CAN. 1645 §1. Adversus sententiam quae transierit in rem iudicatam, dummodo de eius iniustitia manifesto constet, datur restitutio in integrum.

§2. De iniustitia autem manifesto constare non censetur, nisi:

1° sententia ita probationibus innitatur, quae postea falsae deprehensae sint, ut sine illis probationibus pars sententiae dispositiva non sustineatur;

2° postea detecta fuerint documenta, quae facta nova et contrariam decisionem exigentia indubitanter probent;

3° sententia ex dolo partis prolata fuerit in damnum alterius;

4° legis non mere processualis praescriptum evidenter neglectum fuerit;

5° sententia adversetur praecedenti decisioni, quae in rem iudicatam transierit.

CAN. 1646 §1. Restitutio in integrum propter motiva, de quibus in can. 1645, §2, nn. 1–3, petenda est a iudice qui sententiam tulit intra tres menses a die cognitionis eorundem motivorum computandos.

§2. Restitutio in integrum propter motiva, de quibus in can. 1645, §2, nn. 4 et 5, petenda est a tribunali appellationis, intra tres menses a notitia publicationis sententiae;

1645 §1: c. 1905 §1; SN can 432 §1
1645 §2: c. 1905 §2; SA Decisio, 6 apr. 1920 (AAS 12 [1920] 252–259); SN can. 432 §2

1646 §1: c. 1906; SN can. 433
1646 §2: c. 1906; SN can. 433

the sentence; if in the case mentioned in can. 1645, §2, n. 5 notice of the previous decision occurs later, however, the time limit runs from this notice.

§3. The time limits mentioned above do not run as long as the injured person is a minor.

CAN. 1647 §1. The petition for *restitutio in integrum* suspends the execution of a sentence if execution has not yet begun.

§2. If from probable indications there is a suspicion that a petition has been made in order to delay the execution, however, the judge can decree execution of the sentence, though with suitable guarantees to the one seeking the *restitutio* that there will be indemnity if the *restitutio in integrum* is granted.

CAN. 1648 If *restitutio in integrum* is granted, the judge must pronounce on the merits of the case.

TITLE X. Judicial Expenses and Gratuitous Legal Assistance

CAN. 1649 §1. The bishop who directs the tribunal is to establish norms concerning:

1° the requirement of the parties to pay or compensate judicial expenses;

2° the fees for the procurators, advocates, experts, and interpreters and the indemnity for the witnesses;

3° the grant of gratuitous legal assistance or reduction of the expenses;

4° the recovery of damages owed by a person who not only lost the trial but also entered into the litigation rashly;

quod si in casu, de quo in can. 1645, §2, n. 5, notitia praecedentis decisionis serius habeatur, terminus ab hac notitia decurrit.

§3. Termini de quibus supra non decurrunt, quamdiu laesus minoris sit aetatis.

CAN. 1647 §1. Petitio restitutionis in integrum sententiae exsecutionem nondum inceptam suspendit.

§2. Si tamen ex probabilibus indiciis suspicio sit petitionem factam esse ad moras exsecutioni nectendas, iudex decernere potest ut sententia exsecutioni demandetur, assignata tamen restitutionem petenti idonea cautione ut, si restituatur in integrum, indemnis fiat.

CAN. 1648 Concessa restitutione in integrum, iudex pronuntiare debet de merito causae.

TITULUS X. De Expensis Iudicialibus et de Gratuito Patrocinio

CAN. 1649 §1. Episcopus, cuius est tribunal moderari, statuat normas:

1° de partibus damnandis ad expensas iudiciales solvendas vel compensandas;

2° de procuratorum, advocatorum, peritorum et interpretum honorariis deque testium indemnitate;

3° de gratuito patrocinio vel expensarum deminutione concedendis;

4° de damnorum refectione quae debetur ab eo qui non solum in iudicio succubuit, sed temere litigavit;

1646 §3: c. 1687; SN can. 207
1647 §1: c. 1907 §1; SN can. 434 §1
1647 §2: c. 1907 §1; SN can. 434 §2

1649: cc. 1908–1912, 1914–1916; NSRR 164–180, 182–185; PrM 232–236 §§1 et 2, 237–240; SN cann. 435–439, 441–444

5° the deposit of money or the provision furnished for the payment of expenses and recovery of damages.

§2. There is no separate appeal from the determination of expenses, fees, and recovery of damages, but the party can make recourse within fifteen days to the same judge who can adjust the assessment.

TITLE XI. The Execution of the Sentence

CAN. 1650 §1. A sentence that has become a *res iudicata* can be executed, without prejudice to the prescript of can. 1647.

§2. The judge who rendered the sentence and, if an appeal has been proposed, also the appellate judge can order *ex officio* or at the request of a party a provisional execution of a sentence which has not yet become *res iudicata*, after having set suitable guarantees, if the case warrants, for provisions or payments ordered for necessary support; they can also do so if some other just cause urges it.

§3. If the sentence mentioned in §2 is challenged, the judge who must investigate the challenge can suspend the execution or subject it to a guarantee if the judge sees that the challenge is probably well founded and irreparable damage can arise from execution.

CAN. 1651 Execution cannot occur prior to the executory decree of the judge which declares that the sentence must be executed. This decree is to be included in the text of the sen-

5° de pecuniae deposito vel cautione praestanda circa expensas solvendas et damna reficienda.

§2. A pronuntiatione circa expensas, honoraria et damna reficienda non datur distincta appellatio, sed pars recurrere potest intra quindecim dies ad eundem iudicem, qui poterit taxationem emendare.

TITULUS XI. De Exsecutione Sententiae

CAN. 1650 §1. Sententia quae transiit in rem iudicatam, exsecutioni mandari potest, salvo praescripto can. 1647.

§2. Iudex qui sententiam tulit et, si appellatio proposita sit, etiam iudex appellationis, sententiae, quae nondum transierit in rem iudicatam, provisoriam exsecutionem iubere possunt ex officio vel ad instantiam partis, idoneis, si casus ferat, praestitis cautionibus, si agatur de provisionibus seu praestationibus ad necessariam sustentationem ordinatis, vel alia iusta causa urgeat.

§3. Quod si sententia, de qua in §2, impugnetur, iudex qui de impugnatione cognoscere debet, si videt hanc probabiliter fundatam esse et irreparabile damnum ex exsecutione oriri posse, potest vel exsecutionem ipsam suspendere vel eam cautioni subicere.

CAN. 1651 Non antea exsecutioni locus esse poterit, quam exsecutorium iudicis decretum habeatur, quo edicatur sententiam ipsam exsecutioni mandari debere; quod de-

1650 §1: c. 1917 §1; SN can. 445 §1
1650 §2: c. 1917 §1, 1°; SN can. 445 §2, 1°

1650 §3: c. 1917 §2, 2°; SN can. 445 §2, 2°
1651: c. 1918; SN can. 446

tence or issued separately according to the particular nature of the cases.

CAN. 1652 If the execution of a sentence requires a prior rendering of accounts, it is an incidental question which the same judge who rendered the sentence ordering the execution must decide.

CAN. 1653 §1. Unless particular law establishes otherwise, the bishop of the diocese in which the sentence was rendered in the first grade must execute the sentence personally or through another.

§2. If he refuses or neglects to do this, the execution of the sentence, either at the request of an interested party or even *ex officio,* pertains to the authority to whom the appellate tribunal is subject according to the norm of can. 1439, §3.

§3. Among religious the execution of the sentence pertains to the superior who rendered the sentence to be executed or the superior who delegated the judge.

CAN. 1654 §1. Unless the text of the sentence leaves it to the judgment of the executor, the executor must execute the sentence according to the obvious sense of the words.

§2. The executor is permitted to deal with exceptions concerning the manner and force of the execution but not concerning the merit of the case. If it is discovered from another source that the sentence is null or manifestly unjust according to the norm of cann. 1620, 1622, and 1645, the executor is to refrain from executing it and, after having informed the parties, is to refer the matter to the tribunal which rendered the sentence.

cretum pro diversa causarum natura vel in ipso sententiae tenore includatur vel separatim edatur.

CAN. 1652 Si sententiae exsecutio praeviam rationum redditionem exigat, quaestio incidens habetur, ab illo ipso iudice decidenda, qui tulit sententiam exsecutioni mandandam.

CAN. 1653 §1. Nisi lex particularis aliud statuat, sententiam exsecutioni mandare debet per se vel per alium Episcopus dioecesis, in qua sententia primi gradus lata est.

§2. Quod si hic renuat vel neglegat, parte cuius interest instante vel etiam ex officio, exsecutio spectat ad auctoritatem cui tribunal appellationis ad normam can. 1439, §3 subicitur.

§3. Inter religiosos exsecutio sententiae spectat ad Superiorem qui sententiam exsecutioni mandandam tulit aut iudicem delegavit.

CAN. 1654 §1. Exsecutor, nisi quid eius arbitrio in ipso sententiae tenore fuerit permissum, debet sententiam ipsam, secundum obvium verborum sensum, exsecutioni mandare.

§2. Licet ei videre de exceptionibus circa modum et vim exsecutionis, non autem de merito causae; quod si habeat aliunde compertum sententiam esse nullam vel manifeste iniustam ad normam cann. 1620, 1622, 1645, abstineat ab exsecutione, et rem ad tribunal a quo lata est sententia remittat, partibus certioribus factis.

1652: c. 1919; SN can. 447
1653 §1: c. 1920 §1; SN can. 448 §1
1653 §2: c. 1920 §2; SN can. 448 §2

1653 §3: c. 1920 §3; SN can. 448 §3
1654 §1: c. 1921 §1; SN can. 449 §1
1654 §2: c. 1921 §2; SN can. 449 §2

CAN. 1655 §1. In real actions, whenever the petitioner is awarded something, it must be handed over to the petitioner as soon as there is a *res iudicata*.

§2. In personal actions, when the guilty party is condemned to furnish a movable thing, to pay money, or to give or do something else, the judge in the text of the sentence or the executor according to his or her judgment and prudence is to establish a time limit to fulfill the obligation; this time limit, however, is not to be less than fifteen days nor more than six months.

CAN. 1655 §1. Quod attinet ad reales actiones, quoties adiudicata actori res aliqua est, haec actori tradenda est statim ac res iudicata habetur.

§2. Quod vero attinet ad actiones personales, cum reus damnatus est ad rem mobilem praestandam, vel ad solvendam pecuniam, vel ad aliud dandum aut faciendum, iudex in ipso tenore sententiae vel exsecutor pro suo arbitrio et prudentia terminum statuat ad implendam obligationem, qui tamen neque infra quindecim dies coarctetur neque sex menses excedat.

SECTION II. The Oral Contentious Process

SECTIO II. De Processu Contentioso Orali

CAN. 1656 §1. All cases not excluded by law can be treated in the oral contentious process mentioned in this section unless a party requests the ordinary contentious process.

§2. If the oral process is used outside of the cases permitted in law, the judicial acts are null.

CAN. 1657 The oral contentious process takes place in the first grade before a single judge according to the norm of can. 1424.

CAN. 1658 §1. In addition to the things enumerated in can. 1504, the *libellus* which introduces the litigation must:

1° set forth briefly, completely, and clearly the facts on which the requests of the petitioner are based;

2° indicate the proofs by which the petitioner intends to demonstrate the facts but which

CAN. 1656 §1. Processu contentioso orali, de quo in hac sectione, tractari possunt omnes causae a iure non exclusae, nisi pars processum contentiosum ordinarium petat.

§2. Si processus oralis adhibeatur extra casus iure permissos, actus iudiciales sunt nulli.

CAN. 1657 Processus contentiosus oralis fit in primo gradu coram iudice unico, ad normam can. 1424.

CAN. 1658 §1. Libellus quo lis introducitur, praeter ea quae in can. 1504 recensentur, debet:

1° facta quibus actoris petitiones innitantur, breviter, integre et perspicue exponere;

2° probationes quibus actor facta demonstrare intendit, quasque simul afferre

---

1655 §1: c. 1922 §1; SN can. 450 §1
1655 §2: c. 1922 §§2 et 3; SN can. 450 §§2 et 3
1656: SN cann. 453–467

1657: SN can. 453
1658: SN can. 456

cannot be presented at once, in such a way that the judge can collect them immediately.

§2. The documents on which the petition is based must be attached to the *libellus*, at least in an authentic copy.

CAN. 1659 §1. If the attempt at reconciliation according to the norm of can. 1446, §2 proved useless and the judge thinks that the *libellus* has some foundation, the judge is to order within three days by a decree appended to the bottom of the *libellus* that a copy of the petition be communicated to the respondent, giving to the latter the opportunity to send a written response to the tribunal chancery within fifteen days.

§2. This notification has the effect of the judicial citation mentioned in can. 1512.

CAN. 1660 If the exceptions of the respondent demand it, the judge is to establish a time limit for the petitioner to respond, in such a way that from the points brought forth by both of the parties the judge clarifies the object of the controversy.

CAN. 1661 §1. When the time limits mentioned in cann. 1659 and 1660 have elapsed, the judge, after an examination of the acts, is to determine the formula of the doubt. Next, the judge is to cite all those who must take part to a hearing which must be held within thirty days; the formula of the doubt is to be attached to the citation of the parties.

§2. In the citation the parties are to be informed that they can present a brief written statement to the tribunal to verify their claims at least three days before the hearing.

CAN. 1662 At the hearing the questions mentioned in cann. 1459–1464 are treated first.

nequit, ita indicare ut statim colligi a iudice possint.

§2. Libello adnecti debent, saltem in exemplari authentico, documenta quibus petitio innititur.

CAN. 1659 §1. Si conamen conciliationis ad normam can. 1446, §2 inutile cesserit, iudex, si aestimet libellum aliquo fundamento niti, intra tres dies, decreto ad calcem ipsius libelli apposito, praecipiat ut exemplar petitionis notificetur parti conventae, facta huic facultate mittendi, intra quindecim dies, ad cancellariam tribunalis scriptam responsionem.

§2. Haec notificatio effectus habet citationis iudicialis, de quibus in can. 1512.

CAN. 1660 Si exceptiones partis conventae id exigant, iudex parti actrici praefiniat terminum ad respondendum, ita ut ex allatis utriusque partis elementis ipse controversiae obiectum perspectum habeat.

CAN. 1661 §1. Elapsis terminis, de quibus in cann. 1659 et 1660, iudex; perspectis actis, formulam dubii determinet; dein ad audientiam, non ultra triginta dies celebrandam, omnes citet qui in ea interesse debent, addita pro partibus dubii formula.

§2. In citatione partes certiores fiant se posse, tres saltem ante audientiam dies, aliquod breve scriptum tribunali exhibere ad sua asserta comprobanda.

CAN. 1662 In audientia primum tractantur quaestiones de quibus in cann. 1459–1464.

1659: SN can. 457
1660: SN can. 458

1661 §1: SN can. 459
1661 §2: SN can. 460

CAN. 1663 §1. The proofs are collected at the hearing without prejudice to the prescript of can. 1418.

§2. A party and his or her advocate can be present at the examination of the other parties, the witnesses, and the experts.

CAN. 1664 The notary must put into writing the responses of the parties, the witnesses, and the experts and the petitions and exceptions of the advocates, but in a summary fashion and only in those matters pertaining to the substance of the dispute; the deponents must sign these acts.

CAN. 1665 The judge can admit proofs which are not brought forth or sought in the petition or response only according to the norm of can. 1452. After even one witness has been heard, however, the judge can only decide about new proofs according to the norm of can. 1600.

CAN. 1666 If all the proofs were not able to be collected during the hearing, a second hearing is to be scheduled.

CAN. 1667 When the proofs have been collected, the oral discussion takes place at the same hearing.

CAN. 1668 §1. Unless the discussion reveals that something must be supplied in the instruction of the case or something else turns up which prevents a proper pronouncement of the sentence, at the completion of the hearing the judge in private is to decide the case immediately; the dispositive part of the sentence is to be read at once before the parties who are present.

§2. The tribunal can defer the decision up to

CAN. 1663 §1. Probationes colliguntur in audientia, salvo praescripto can. 1418.

§2. Pars eiusque advocatus assistere possunt excussioni ceterarum partium, testium, et peritorum.

CAN. 1664 Responsiones partium, testium, peritorum, petitiones et exceptiones advocatorum, redigendae sunt scripto a notario, sed summatim et in iis tantummodo quae pertinent ad substantiam rei controversae, et a deponentibus subsignandae.

CAN. 1665 Probationes, quae non sint in petitione vel responsione allatae aut petitae, potest iudex admittere tantum ad normam can. 1452; postquam autem vel unus testis auditus est, iudex potest tantummodo ad normam can. 1600 novas probationes decernere.

CAN. 1666 Si in audientia probationes omnes colligi non potuerint, altera statuatur audientia.

CAN. 1667 Probationibus collectis, fit in eadem audientia discussio oralis.

CAN. 1668 §1. Nisi ex discussione aliquid supplendum in causae instructione comperiatur, vel aliud exsistat quod impediat sententiam rite proferri, iudex illico, expleta audientia, causam seorsum decidat; dispositiva sententiae pars statim coram partibus praesentibus legatur.

§2. Potest autem tribunal propter rei dif-

1663 §1: SN can. 461
1663 §2: SN can. 454
1665: SN can. 464
1666: SN can. 464

1667: SN can. 462
1668 §1: SN can. 467
1668 §2: SN can. 467

the fifth useful day because of the difficulty of the matter or for some other just cause.

§3. The complete text of the sentence with the reasons expressed is to be communicated to the parties as soon as possible, ordinarily in not more than fifteen days.

CAN. 1669 If the appellate tribunal discovers that the oral contentious process was used at a lower grade of a trial in cases excluded by law, it is to declare the nullity of the sentence and remit the case to the tribunal which rendered the sentence.

CAN. 1670 In other matters pertaining to the manner of proceeding, the prescripts of the canons for the ordinary contentious trial are to be observed. In order to expedite matters without prejudice to justice, however, the tribunal, by a decree expressing the reasons for its decision, can derogate from procedural norms which have not been established for validity.

ficultatem vel aliam iustam causam usque ad quintum utilem diem decisionem differre.

§3. Integer sententiae textus, motivis expressis, quam primum, ordinarie non ultra quindecim dies, partibus notificetur.

CAN. 1669 Si tribunal appellationis perspiciat in inferiore iudicii gradu processum contentiosum oralem esse adhibitum in casibus a iure exclusis, nullitatem sententiae declaret et causam remittat tribunali quod sententiam tulit.

CAN. 1670 In ceteris quae ad rationem procedendi attinent, serventur praescripta canonum de iudicio contentioso ordinario. Tribunal autem potest suo decreto, motivis praedito, normis processualibus, quae non sint ad validitatem statutae, derogare, ut celeritati, salva iustitia, consulat.

1668 §3: SN can. 466

PART III. CERTAIN SPECIAL
PROCESSES

TITLE I. **Marriage Processes**

CHAPTER I. **Cases to Declare the Nullity of Marriage**

ART. 1. *The Competent Forum*

CAN. 1671 Marriage cases of the baptized belong to the ecclesiastical judge by proper right.

CAN. 1672 Cases concerning the merely civil effects of marriage belong to the civil magistrate unless particular law establishes that an ecclesiastical judge can investigate and decide these cases if they are done in an incidental or accessory manner.

CAN. 1673 In cases concerning the nullity of marriage which are not reserved to the Apostolic See, the following are competent:

1° the tribunal of the place in which the marriage was celebrated;

2° the tribunal of the place in which the respondent has a domicile or quasi-domicile;

3° the tribunal of the place in which the pe-

TITULUS I. **De Processibus Matrimonialibus**

CAPUT I. **De Causis ad Matrimonii Nullitatem Declarandam**

ART. 1. *De Foro Competenti*

CAN. 1671 Causae matrimoniales baptizatorum iure proprio ad iudicem ecclesiasticum spectant.

CAN. 1672 Causae de effectibus matrimonii mere civilibus pertinent ad civilem magistratum, nisi ius particulare statuat easdem causas, si incidenter et accessorie agantur, posse a iudice ecclesiastico cognosci ac definiri.

CAN. 1673 In causis de matrimonii nullitate, quae non sint Sedi Apostolicae reservatae, competentia sunt:

1° tribunal loci in quo matrimonium celebratum est;

2° tribunal loci in quo pars conventa domicilium vel quasi-domicilium habet;

3° tribunal loci in quo pars actrix domi-

1671: c. 1960; PrM 1 §1; SN can. 468; CM I; CMat I

1672: c. 1961; PrM 1 §2; SN can. 469; CM II; CMat II

1673: cc. 1962, 1964; CI Resp. XIV, 14 iul. 1922 (AAS 14 [1922] 529–530); SCDS Instr., 22 dec. 1929

(AAS 22 [1930] 168–171); PrM 3, 5–8; SN cann. 470 et 472; CPEN Rescr., 28 apr. 1970, 7; SA Rescr., 2 ian. 1971; CM III, IV; SA Decr. *Instantia diei*, 6 apr. 1973; CMat III, IV; CPEN Rescr., 1 nov. 1974; CIV Resp., 14 feb. 1977 (AAS 69 [1977] 296); SA Decl., 12 apr. 1978

titioner has a domicile, provided that both parties live in the territory of the same conference
of bishops and the judicial vicar of the domicile
of the respondent gives consent after he has
heard the respondent;

4° the tribunal of the place in which in fact
most of the proofs must be collected, provided
that consent is given by the judicial vicar of the
domicile of the respondent, who is first to ask if
the respondent has any exception to make.

ART. 2. *The Right to Challenge a Marriage*

CAN. 1674 The following are qualified to
challenge a marriage:

1° the spouses;

2° the promoter of justice when nullity has
already become public, if the convalidation of
the marriage is not possible or expedient.

CAN. 1675 §1. A marriage which was not
accused while both spouses were living cannot
be accused after the death of either one or both
of the spouses unless the question of validity is
prejudicial to the resolution of another controversy either in the canonical forum or in the civil forum.

§2. If a spouse dies while the case is pending,
however, can. 1518 is to be observed.

ART. 3. *The Duty of the Judges*

CAN. 1676 Before accepting a case and
whenever there is hope of a favorable outcome,
a judge is to use pastoral means to induce the

---

cilium habet, dummodo utraque pars in territorio eiusdem Episcoporum conferentiae de-
gat et Vicarius iudicialis domicilii partis conventae, ipsa audita, consentiat;

4° tribunal loci in quo de facto colligendae sunt pleraeque probationes, dummodo
accedat consensus Vicarii iudicialis domicilii
partis conventae, qui prius ipsam interroget,
num quid excipiendum habeat.

ART. 2. *De Iure Impugnandi Matrimonium*

CAN. 1674 Habiles sunt ad matrimonium impugnandum:

1° coniuges;

2° promotor iustitiae, cum nullitas iam
divulgata est, si matrimonium convalidari
nequeat aut non expediat.

CAN. 1675 §1. Matrimonium quod,
utroque coniuge vivente, non fuit accusatum,
post mortem alterutrius vel utriusque coniugis accusari non potest, nisi quaestio de
validitate sit praeiudicialis ad aliam solvendam controversiam sive in foro canonico
sive in foro civili.

§2. Si autem coniux moriatur pendente
causa, servetur can. 1518.

ART. 3. *De Officio Iudicum*

CAN. 1676 Iudex, antequam causam
acceptet et quotiescumque spem boni exitus
perspicit, pastoralia media adhibeat, ut con-

1674: c. 1971; SCSO Resp., 27 ian. 1928 (AAS 20 [1928] 75); CI Resp. V, 12 mar. 1929 (AAS 21 [1929] 171); CI Resp. VI, 17 feb. 1930 (AAS 22 [1930] 196); CI Resp. II, 17 iul. 1933 (AAS 25 [1933] 345); PrM 35, 38, 39; SCSO Resp., 22 mar. 1939 (AAS 31 [1939] 131); SCSO Resp., 15 ian. 1940 (AAS 32 [1940] 52); CI Resp. III, 27 iul. 1942 (AAS 34 [1942] 241); CI Resp. I, 6 dec. 1943 (AAS 36 [1944] 94); CI Resp. III, 3 maii 1945 (AAS 37 [1945] 149); CI Resp. III, 4 ian. 1946 (AAS 38 [1946] 162); SN can. 478; CPEN Rescr., 28 apr. 1970, 8, 9; CIV Resp., 8 ian. 1973 (AAS 65 [1973] 59)

1675: c. 1972; PrM 42, 222; SN can. 479

1676: c. 1965; PrM 65; SN can. 473

spouses if possible to convalidate the marriage and restore conjugal living.

CAN. 1677 §1. When the *libellus* has been accepted, the presiding judge or the *ponens* is to proceed to the communication of the decree of citation according to the norm of can. 1508.

§2. When fifteen days have passed from the communication and unless either party has requested a session for the joinder of the issue, the presiding judge or the *ponens* is to establish the formula of the doubt or doubts within ten days by *ex officio* decree and is to notify the parties.

§3. The formula of the doubt not only is to ask whether the nullity of the marriage is established in the case but also must determine on what ground or grounds the validity of the marriage is to be challenged.

§4. Ten days after the communication of the decree, the presiding judge or the *ponens* is to arrange for the instruction of the case by a new decree if the parties have lodged no objection.

ART. 4. *Proofs*

CAN. 1678 §1. The defender of the bond, the legal representatives of the parties, and also the promoter of justice, if involved in the trial, have the following rights:

1° to be present at the examination of the parties, the witnesses, and the experts, without prejudice to the prescript of can. 1559;

2° to inspect the judicial acts, even those not yet published, and to review the documents presented by the parties.

§2. The parties cannot be present at the examination mentioned in §1, n. 1.

iuges, si fieri potest, ad matrimonium forte convalidandum et ad coniugalem convictum restaurandum inducantur.

CAN. 1677 §1. Libello accepto, praeses vel ponens procedat ad notificationem decreti citationis ad normam can. 1508.

§2. Transacto termino quindecim dierum a notificatione, praeses vel ponens, nisi alterutra pars sessionem ad litem contestandam petierit, intra decem dies formulam dubii vel dubiorum decreto suo statuat ex officio et partibus notificet.

§3. Formula dubii non tantum quaerat an constet de nullitate matrimonii in casu, sed determinare etiam debet quo capite vel quibus capitibus nuptiarum validitas impugnetur.

§4. Post decem dies a notificatione decreti, si partes nihil opposuerint, praeses vel ponens novo decreto causae instructionem disponat.

ART. 4. *De Probationibus*

CAN. 1678 §1. Defensori vinculi, partium patronis et, si in iudicio sit, etiam promotori iustitiae ius est:

1° examini partium, testium et peritorum adesse, salvo praescripto can. 1559;

2° acta iudicialia, etsi nondum publicata, invisere et documenta a partibus producta recognoscere.

§2. Examini, de quo in §1, n. 1, partes assistere nequeunt.

1677 §1: PrM 74–86
1677 §2: PrM 92; CPEN Rescr., 28 apr. 1970, 11
1677 §3: PrM 88
1678 §1: cc. 1968, 1969; PrM 70, 71, 128; SA Litt., 19

nov. 1947; SN cann. 476 et 477; CPEN Rescr., 28 apr. 1970, 13 et 15
1678 §2: PrM 128

CAN. 1679 Unless there are full proofs from elsewhere, in order to evaluate the depositions of the parties according to the norm of can. 1536, the judge, if possible, is to use witnesses to the credibility of those parties in addition to other indications and supporting factors.

CAN. 1680 In cases of impotence or defect of consent because of mental illness, the judge is to use the services of one or more experts unless it is clear from the circumstances that it would be useless to do so; in other cases the prescript of can. 1574 is to be observed.

ART. 5. *The Sentence and the Appeal*

CAN. 1681 Whenever, during the instruction of a case, a very probable doubt emerges that consummation of the marriage did not occur, after suspending the case of nullity with the consent of the parties, the tribunal can complete the instruction for a dispensation *super rato* and then transmit the acts to the Apostolic See together with a petition for a dispensation from either one or both of the spouses and the *votum* of the tribunal and the bishop.

CAN. 1682 §1. The sentence which first declared the nullity of the marriage is to be transmitted *ex officio* to the appellate tribunal within twenty days from the publication of the sentence, together with the appeals, if there are any, and the other acts of the trial.

§2. If a sentence in favor of the nullity of a

CAN. 1679 Nisi probationes aliunde plenae habeantur, iudex, ad partium depositiones ad normam can. 1536 aestimandas, testes de ipsarum partium credibilitate, si fieri potest, adhibeat, praeter alia indicia et adminicula.

CAN. 1680 In causis de impotentia vel de consensus defectu propter mentis morbum iudex unius periti vel plurium opera utatur, nisi ex adiunctis inutilis evidenter appareat; in ceteris causis servetur praescriptum can. 1574.

ART. 5. *De Sententia et Appellatione*

CAN. 1681 Quoties in instructione causae dubium valde probabile emerserit de non secuta matrimonii consummatione, tribunal potest, suspensa de consensu partium causa nullitatis, instructionem complere pro dispensatione super rato, ac tandem acta transmittere ad Sedem Apostolicam una cum petitione dispensationis ab alterutro vel utroque coniuge et cum voto tribunalis et Episcopi.

CAN. 1682 §1. Sententia, quae matrimonii nullitatem primum declaraverit, una cum appellationibus, si quae sint, et ceteris iudicii actis, intra viginti dies a sententiae publicatione ad tribunal appellationis ex officio transmittatur.

§2. Si sententia pro matrimonii nullitate

1679: c. 1975; PrM 137; SN can. 482

1680: cc. 1976–1982; PrM 139–154; SCSO Decr. *Qua singulari*, 12 iun. 1942 (AAS 34 [1942] 200–202); SN cann. 483–489; CPEN Rescr., 28 apr. 1970, 17; SA Rescr., 10 nov. 1970, 2 et 3; SA Rescr., 2 ian. 1971, II, 2 et 3

1681: cc. 1963 §2, 1985; SCDS Regulae, 7 maii 1923, 3, 4 (AAS 15 [1923] 392) SCEO Instr. *Quo facilius*, 10 iun. 1935, art. 4 (AAS 27 [1935] 334); PrM 206; SN cann. 471 et 492; SCEO Instr. *Instructionem quo*, 13 iul. 1953, art. 5; SRR Nuove norme, 27 maii 1969, Ap-

pendix II, 2; SCDS Instr. *Dispensationis matrimonii*, 7 mar. 1972, Ie (AAS 64 [1972] 246–247); SA Decr. *Precibus diei*, 6 apr. 1973; SRR Normae, 16 ian. 1982, Allegato I, 2 (AAS 74 [1982] 516)

1682 §1: c. 1986; PrM 212 §2; SN can. 493; CM VIII §1; CMat VIII §1

1682 §2: CM VIII §§2 et 3; CMat VIII §§2 et 3; CIV Resp., 31 oct. 1973 (AAS 65 [1973] 620); CIV Resp., 14 feb. 1974 (AAS 66 [1974] 463); CIV Resp., 1 iul. 1976 (AAS 68 [1976] 635)

marriage was given in the first grade of a trial, the appellate tribunal is either to confirm the decision at once by decree or to admit the case to an ordinary examination in a new grade, after having weighed carefully the observations of the defender of the bond and those of the parties if there are any.

CAN. 1683 If a new ground of nullity of the marriage is alleged at the appellate grade, the tribunal can admit it and judge it as if in first instance.

CAN. 1684 §1. After the sentence which first declared the nullity of the marriage has been confirmed at the appellate grade either by a decree or by a second sentence, the persons whose marriage has been declared null can contract a new marriage as soon as the decree or second sentence has been communicated to them unless a prohibition attached to the sentence or decree or established by the local ordinary has forbidden this.

§2. The prescripts of can. 1644 must be observed even if the sentence which declared the nullity of the marriage was confirmed not by a second sentence but by a decree.

CAN. 1685 As soon as the sentence is executed, the judicial vicar must notify the local ordinary of the place in which the marriage was celebrated. The local ordinary must take care that the declaration of the nullity of the marriage and any possible prohibitions are noted as soon as possible in the marriage and baptismal registers.

prolata sit in primo iudicii gradu, tribunal appellationis, perpensis animadversionibus defensoris vinculi et, si quae sint, etiam partium, suo decreto vel decisionem continenter confirmet vel ad ordinarium examen novi gradus causam admittat.

CAN. 1683 Si in gradu appellationis novum nullitatis matrimonii caput afferatur, tribunal potest, tamquam in prima instantia, illud admittere et de eo iudicare.

CAN. 1684 §1. Postquam sententia, quae matrimonii nullitatem primum declaravit, in gradu appellationis confirmata est vel decreto vel altera sententia, ii, quorum matrimonium declaratum est nullum, possunt novas nuptias contrahere statim ac decretum vel altera sententia ipsis notificata est, nisi vetito ipsi sententiae aut decreto apposito vel ab Ordinario loci statuto id prohibeatur.

§2. Praescripta can. 1644 servanda sunt, etiam si sententia, quae matrimonii nullitatem declaraverit, non altera sententia sed decreto confirmata sit.

CAN. 1685 Statim ac sententia facta est exsecutiva, Vicarius iudicialis debet eandem notificare Ordinario loci in quo matrimonium celebratum est. Is autem curare debet ut quam primum de decreta nullitate matrimonii et de vetitis forte statutis in matrimoniorum et baptizatorum libris mentio fiat.

1683: PrM 219 §2; SN can. 494; SRR Nuove norme, 27 maii 1969, App. II, 1; SRR Normae, 16 ian. 1982, Alleg. I, 1 (AAS 74 [1982] 516)

1684 §1: c. 1987; PrM 220; SN can. 495; CM VIII §3; CMat VIII §3
1685: c. 1988; PrM 224, 225; SN can. 496

ART. 6. *The Documentary Process*

ART. 6. *De Processu Documentali*

CAN. 1686 After receiving a petition proposed according to the norm of can. 1677, the judicial vicar or a judge designated by him can declare the nullity of a marriage by sentence if a document subject to no contradiction or exception clearly establishes the existence of a diriment impediment or a defect of legitimate form, provided that it is equally certain that no dispensation was given, or establishes the lack of a valid mandate of a proxy. In these cases, the formalities of the ordinary process are omitted except for the citation of the parties and the intervention of the defender of the bond.

CAN. 1687 §1. If the defender of the bond prudently thinks that either the flaws mentioned in can. 1686 or the lack of a dispensation are not certain, the defender of the bond must appeal against the declaration of nullity to the judge of second instance; the acts must be sent to the appellate judge who must be advised in writing that a documentary process is involved.

§2. The party who considers himself or herself aggrieved retains the right of appeal.

CAN. 1688 The judge of second instance, with the intervention of the defender of the bond and after having heard the parties, will decide in the same manner as that mentioned in can. 1686 whether the sentence must be confirmed or whether the case must rather proceed according to the ordinary method of law; in the latter event the judge remands the case to the tribunal of first instance.

CAN. 1686 Recepta petitione ad normam can. 1677 proposita, Vicarius iudicialis vel iudex ab ipso designatus potest, praetermissis sollemnitatibus ordinarii processus sed citatis partibus et cum interventu defensoris vinculi, matrimonii nullitatem sentential declarare, si ex documento, quod nulli contradictioni vel exceptioni sit obnoxium, certo constet de exsistentia impedimenti dirimentis vel de defectu legitimae formae, dummodo pari certitudine pateat dispensationem datam non esse, aut de defectu validi mandati procuratoris.

CAN. 1687 §1. Adversus hanc declarationem defensor vinculi, si prudenter existimaverit vel vitia de quibus in can. 1686 vel dispensationis defectum non esse certa, appellare debet ad iudicem secundae instantiae, ad quem acta sunt transmittenda quique scripto monendus est agi de processu documentali.

§2. Integrum manet parti, quae se gravatam putet, ius appellandi.

CAN. 1688 Iudex alterius instantiae, cum interventu defensoris vinculi et auditis partibus, decernet eodem modo, de quo in can. 1686, ultrum sententia sit confirmanda, an potius procedendum in causa sit iuxta ordinarium tramitem iuris; quo in casu eam remittit ad tribunal primae instantiae.

1686: c. 1990; CI Resp. 17, 16 oct. 1919 (AAS 11 [1919] 479); CI Resp. IV, 16 iun. 1931 (AAS 23 [1931] 353–354); PrM 226–228; CI Resp. I–III, 6 dec. 1943 (AAS 36 [1944] 94); SN can. 498; CM X, XI; SA Decr., 3 maii 1972; CMat X, XI

1687: c. 1991; PrM 229; SN can. 499; CI Resp. IV, 6 dec. 1943 (AAS 36 [1944] 94); CM XII; CMat XII
1688: c. 1992; PrM 230; CI Resp. IV, 6 dec. 1943 (AAS 36 [1944] 94); SN can. 500; CM XIII; CMat XIII

ART. 7. *General Norms*

CAN. 1689 In the sentence the parties are to be reminded of the moral and even civil obligations which may bind them both toward one another and toward their children to furnish support and education.

CAN. 1690 Cases for the declaration of the nullity of a marriage cannot be treated in an oral contentious process.

CAN. 1691 In other procedural matters, the canons on trials in general and on the ordinary contentious trial must be applied unless the nature of the matter precludes it; the special norms for cases concerning the status of persons and cases pertaining to the public good are to be observed.

CHAPTER II. Cases of Separation of Spouses

CAN. 1692 §1. Unless other provision is legitimately made in particular places, a decree of the diocesan bishop or a judicial sentence can decide the personal separation of baptized spouses according to the norm of the following canons.

§2. Where an ecclesiastical decision has no civil effects or if a civil sentence is not contrary to divine law, the bishop of the diocese of the residence of the spouses, after having weighed the special circumstances, can grant permission to approach the civil forum.

§3. If a case concerns only the merely civil effects of marriage, the judge, after having observed the prescript of §2, is to try to defer the case to the civil forum from the start.

CAN. 1693 §1. Unless a party or the promoter of justice requests the ordinary con-

ART. 7. *Normae Generales*

CAN. 1689 In sententia partes moneantur de obligationibus moralibus vel etiam civilibus, quibus forte teneantur, altera erga alteram et erga prolem, ad sustentationem et educationem praestandam.

CAN. 1690 Causae ad matrimonii nullitatem declarandam nequeunt processu contentioso orali tractari.

CAN. 1691 In ceteris quae ad rationem procedendi attinent, applicandi sunt, nisi rei natura obstet, canones de iudiciis in genere et de iudicio contentioso ordinario, servatis specialibus normis circa causas de statu personarum et causas ad bonum publicum spectantes.

CAPUT II. De Causis Separationis Coniugum

CAN. 1692 §1. Separatio personalis coniugum baptizatorum, nisi aliter pro locis particularibus legitime provisum sit, decerni potest Episcopi dioecesani decreto vel iudicis sententia ad normam canonum qui sequuntur.

§2. Ubi decisio ecclesiastica effectus civiles non sortitur, vel si sententia civilis praevidetur non contraria iuri divino, Episcopus dioecesis commorationis coniugum poterit, perpensis peculiaribus adiunctis, licentiam concedere adeundi forum civile.

§3. Si causa versetur etiam circa effectus mere civiles matrimonii, satagat iudex ut, servato praescripto §2, causa inde ab initio ad forum civile deferatur.

CAN. 1693 §1. Nisi qua pars vel promotor iustitiae processum contentiosum or-

1689: GE 3

1692: cc. 1130, 1131; CI Resp. III, 25 iun. 1932 (AAS 24 [1932] 284); CAI 119, 120

tentious process, the oral contentious process is to be used.

§2. If the ordinary contentious process has been used and an appeal is proposed, the tribunal of second grade, observing what is required, is to proceed according to the norm of can. 1682, §2.

CAN. 1694 The prescripts of can. 1673 are to be observed in what pertains to the competence of the tribunal.

CAN. 1695 Before accepting the case and whenever there is hope of a favorable outcome, the judge is to use pastoral means to reconcile the spouses and persuade them to restore conjugal living.

CAN. 1696 Cases concerning the separation of spouses also pertain to the public good; therefore the promoter of justice must always take part in them according to the norm of can. 1433.

dinarium petant, processus contentiosus oralis adhibeatur.

§2. Si processus contentiosus ordinarius adhibitus sit et appellatio proponatur, tribunal secundi gradus ad normam can. 1682, §2 procedat, servatis servandis.

CAN. 1694 Quod attinet ad tribunalis competentiam, serventur praescripta can. 1673.

CAN. 1695 Iudex, antequam causam acceptet et quotiescumque spem boni exitus perspicit, pastoralia media adhibeat, ut coniuges concilientur et ad coniugalem convictum restaurandum inducantur.

CAN. 1696 Causae de coniugum separatione ad publicum quoque bonum spectant; ideoque iis interesse semper debet promotor iustitiae, ad normam can. 1433.

CHAPTER III. **Process for the Dispensation of a Marriage *Ratum et non consummatum***

CAN. 1697 Only the spouses, or one of them even if the other is unwilling, have the right to petition for the favor of a dispensation from a marriage *ratum et non consummatum.*

CAN. 1698 §1. Only the Apostolic See adjudicates the fact of the non-consummation of a marriage and the existence of a just cause to grant a dispensation.

§2. Only the Roman Pontiff, however, grants the dispensation.

CAPUT III. **De Processu ad Dispensationem Super Matrimonio Rato et non consummato**

CAN. 1697 Soli coniuges, vel alteruter, quamvis altero invito, ius habent petendi gratiam dispensationis super matrimonio rato et non consummato.

CAN. 1698 §1. Una Sedes Apostolica cognoscit de facto inconsummationis matrimonii et de exsistentia iustae causae ad dispensationem concedendam.

§2. Dispensatio vero ab uno Romano Pontifice conceditur.

1697: cc. 1119, 1973; SCDS Regulae, 7 maii 1923, art. 5 §1 (AAS 15 [1923] 393); SCEO Instr. *Quo facilius,* 10 iun. 1935, 1 (AAS 27 [1935] 334); CAl 108; SN can. 480; SCEO Instr. *Instructionem quo,* 13 iul. 1953, 2; SCDS Instr. *Dispensationis matrimonii,* 7 mar. 1972, Ib (AAS 64 [1972] 246)

1698 §1: cc. 249 §3, 1119, 1962, 1963; SCDS Regu-

lae, 7 maii 1923, 1 et 2 (AAS 15 [1923] 392); CAl 108; SN cann. 470, 471; SCEO Instr. *Instructionem quo,* 13 iul. 1953, 1; CS 196 §3; REU 56; SCDS Instr. *Dispensationis matrimonii,* 7 mar. 1972, I (AAS 64 [1972] 245); Sec Rescr., 15 iul. 1973 (AAS 64 [1973] 602)

1698 §2: SCDS Regulae, 7 maii 1923, 102 (AAS 15 [1923] 413); SCEO Instr. *Quo facilius,* 10 iun. 1935, 1

CAN. 1699 §1. The person competent to accept a *libellus* seeking a dispensation is the diocesan bishop of the domicile or quasi-domicile of the petitioner, who must arrange for the instruction of the process if the petition is well founded.

§2. If the proposed case has special difficulties of the juridical or moral order, however, the diocesan bishop is to consult the Apostolic See.

§3. Recourse to the Apostolic See is available against a decree by which a bishop rejects a *libellus.*

CAN. 1700 §1. Without prejudice to the prescript of can. 1681, the bishop is to entrust the instruction of these processes either in a stable manner or in individual cases to his tribunal, that of another diocese, or a suitable priest.

§2. If a judicial petition to declare the nullity of the same marriage has been introduced, however, the instruction is to be entrusted to the same tribunal.

CAN. 1701 §1. The defender of the bond must always intervene in these processes.

§2. A legal representative is not admitted, but because of the difficulty of a case, a bishop can permit the petitioner or the respondent to have the assistance of a legal expert.

CAN. 1702 In the instruction each spouse is to be heard, and the canons on the collection

CAN. 1699 §1. Competens ad accipiendum libellum, quo petitur dispensatio, est Episcopus dioecesanus domicilii vel quasi-domicilii oratoris, qui, si constiterit de fundamento precum, processus instructionem disponere debet.

§2. Si tamen casus propositus speciales habeat difficultates ordinis iuridici vel moralis, Episcopus dioecesanus consulat Sedem Apostolicam.

§3. Adversus decretum quo Episcopus libellum reicit, patet recursus ad Sedem Apostolicam.

CAN. 1700 §1. Firmo praescripto can. 1681, horum processuum instructionem committat Episcopus, stabiliter vel in singulis casibus, tribunali suae vel alienae dioecesis aut idoneo sacerdoti.

§2. Quod si introducta sit petitio iudicialis ad declarandam nullitatem eiusdem matrimonii, instructio ad idem tribunal committatur.

CAN. 1701 §1. In his processibus semper intervenire debet vinculi defensor.

§2. Patronus non admittitur, sed, propter casus difficultatem, Episcopus permittere potest ut iurisperiti opera orator vel pars conventa iuvetur.

CAN. 1702 In instructione uterque coniux audiatur et serventur, quatenus fieri

(AAS 27 [1935] 334); CAl 108; SCEO Instr. *Instructionem quo,* 13 iul. 1953, 1

1699: SCDS Regulae, 7 maii 1923, 7–12 (AAS 15 [1923] 393–394); SCDS Rescr., 7 nov. 1970; SCDS Instr. *Dispensationis matrimonii,* 7 mar. 1972, I (AAS 64 [1972] 245)

1700: c. 1966; SCDS Regulae, 7 maii 1923, 13–19 (AAS 15 [1923] 394–395); SCEO Instr. *Quo facilius,* 10 iun. 1935, 5 et 6 (AAS 27 [1935] 334); SN can. 474; SCEO Instr. *Instructionem quo,* 13 iul. 1953, 6–7; SCDS Instr. *Dispensationis matrimonii,* 7 mar. 1972, II a (AAS 64 [1972] 248)

1701 §1: c. 1967; SCDS Regulae, 7 maii 1923, 27

(AAS 15 [1923] 398); SCEO Instr. *Quo facilius,* 10 iun. 1935, 5 (AAS 27 [1935] 334); SN can. 475; SCDS Litt., 15 ian. 1937; SCEO Instr. *Instructionem quo,* 13 iul. 1953, 6

1701 §2: SCDS Instr. *Dispensationis matrimonii,* 7 mar. 1972, IIe (AAS 64 [1972] 249–250)

1702: SCDS Regulae, 7 maii 1923, 20–96 (AAS 15 [1923] 396–411); SCDS Normae, 27 mar. 1929 (AAS 21 [1929] 490–493); SCEO Instr. *Quo facilius,* 10 iun. 1935, 8–25 (AAS 27 [1935] 335–339); SCEO Instr. *Instructionem quo,* 13 iul. 1953, 9–28; SCDS Instr. *Dispensationis matrimonii,* 7 mar. 1972, II a–d (AAS 64 [1972] 248–249)

of proofs in the ordinary contentious trial and in cases of the nullity of marriage are to be observed insofar as possible, provided that they can be reconciled with the character of these processes.

CAN. 1703   §1. There is no publication of the acts. If the judge perceives that the proofs brought forward seriously hinder the request of the petitioner or the exception of the respondent, however, he is prudently to inform the interested party.

§2. The judge can show a document introduced or a testimony received to a party who requests it and set a time to present observations.

CAN. 1704   §1. When the instruction has been completed, the instructor is to give all the acts along with a suitable report to the bishop, who is to prepare a *votum* on the veracity of the fact of the non-consummation, the just cause for the dispensation, and the suitability of the favor.

§2. If the instruction of the process has been entrusted to another tribunal according to the norm of can. 1700, the observations in favor of the bond are to be made in the same forum; the *votum* mentioned in §1, however, pertains to the entrusting bishop, to whom the instructor is to hand over a suitable report together with the acts.

CAN. 1705   §1. The bishop is to transmit to the Apostolic See all the acts together with his *votum* and the observations of the defender of the bond.

§2. If supplemental instruction is required in

possit, canones de probationibus colligendis in iudicio contentioso ordinario et in causis de matrimonii nullitate, dummodo cum horum processuum indole componi queant.

CAN. 1703   §1. Non fit publicatio actorum; iudex tamen, si conspiciat petitioni partis oratricis vel exceptioni partis conventae grave obstaculum obvenire ob adductas probationes, id parti cuius interest prudenter patefaciat.

§2. Parti instanti documentum allatum vel testimonium receptum iudex ostendere poterit et tempus praefinire ad deductiones exhibendas.

CAN. 1704   §1. Instructor, peracta instructione, omnia acta cum apta relatione deferat ad Episcopum, qui votum pro rei veritate promat tum super facto inconsummationis tum super iusta causa ad dispensandum et gratiae opportunitate.

§2. Si instructio processus commissa sit alieno tribunali ad normam can. 1700, animadversiones pro vinculo in eodem foro conficiantur, sed votum de quo in §1 spectat ad Episcopum committentem, cui instructor simul cum actis aptam relationem tradat.

CAN. 1705   §1. Acta omnia Episcopus una cum suo voto et animadversionibus defensoris vinculi transmittat ad Sedem Apostolicam.

§2. Si, iudicio Apostolicae Sedis, re-

1703: c. 1985; SCDS Regulae, 7 maii 1923, 97 (AAS 15 [1923] 412); SCEO Instr. *Instructionem quo*, 13 iul. 1953, 31; SN can. 492

1704: SCDS Regulae, 7 maii 1923, 98 (AAS 15 [1923] 412); SCEO Instr. *Quo facilius*, 10 iun. 1935, 27 (AAS 27 [1935] 340); SCDS Resp., 31 iul. 1941; SCEO Instr. *Instructionem quo*, 13 iul. 1953, 30; SCDS Instr. *Dispensationis matrimonii*, 7 mar. 1972, II f (AAS 64 [1972] 250)

1705 §1: c. 1985; SCDS Regulae, 7 maii 1923, 98 §2, 101 (AAS 15 [1923] 412); SCEO Instr. *Quo facilius*, 10 iun. 1935, 28 (AAS 27 [1935] 340); SN can. 492; SCEO Instr. *Instructionem quo*, 13 iul. 1953, 31; SCDS Instr. *Dispensationis matrimonii*, 7 mar. 1972, II g (AAS 64 [1972] 250–251)

1705 §2: SCDS Instr. *Dispensationis matrimonii*, 7 mar. 1972, I a (AAS 64 [1972] 245–246)

the judgment of the Apostolic See, this requirement will be communicated to the bishop with an indication of the points on which the instruction must be completed.

§3. If the Apostolic See replies that non-consummation has not been established from the materials presented, then the legal expert mentioned in can. 1701, §2 can inspect the acts of the process, though not the *votum* of the bishop, at the tribunal to consider whether any grave reason can be brought forth in order to resubmit the petition.

CAN. 1706 The Apostolic See transmits the rescript of the dispensation to the bishop who will notify the parties about the rescript and also as soon as possible will order the pastor both of the place where the marriage was contracted and of the place of baptism to note the granting of the dispensation in the marriage and baptismal registers.

CHAPTER IV. Process in the Presumed Death of a Spouse

CAN. 1707 §1. Whenever the death of a spouse cannot be proven by an authentic ecclesiastical or civil document, the other spouse is not considered free from the bond of marriage until after the diocesan bishop has issued a declaration of presumed death.

§2. The diocesan bishop is able to issue the declaration mentioned in §1 only if, after having carried out appropriate investigations, he attains moral certitude of the death of the spouse from the depositions of witnesses, from rumor, or

quiratur supplementum instructionis, id Episcopo significabitur, indicatis elementis circa quae instructio complenda est.

§3. Quod si Apostolica Sedes rescripserit ex deductis non constare de inconsummatione, tunc iurisperitus de quo in can. 1701, §2 potest acta processus, non vero votum Episcopi, invisere in sede tribunalis ad perpendendum num quid grave adduci possit ad petitionem denuo proponendam.

CAN. 1706 Rescriptum dispensationis a Sede Apostolica transmittitur ad Episcopum; is vero rescriptum partibus notificabit et praeterea parocho tum loci contracti matrimonii tum suscepti baptismi quam primum mandabit, ut in libris matrimoniorum et baptizatorum de concessa dispensatione mentio fiat.

CAPUT IV. De Processu Praesumptae Mortis Coniugis

CAN. 1707 §1. Quoties coniugis mors authentico documento ecclesiastico vel civili comprobari nequit, alter coniux a vinculo matrimonii solutus non habeatur, nisi post declarationem de morte praesumpta ab Episcopo dioecesano prolatam.

§2. Declarationem, de qua in §1, Episcopus dioecesanus tantummodo proferre valet si, peractis opportunis investigationibus, ex testium depositionibus, ex fama aut ex indiciis moralem certitudinem de coniugis

1706: SCDS Regulae, 7 maii 1923, 102–106 (AAS 15 [1923] 413); SCDS Instr. *Dispensationis matrimonii,* 7 mar. 1972, III (AAS 64 [1972] 251–252)

1707: cc. 1053, 1069 §2; SCDS Rescr., 18 nov. 1920

(AAS 14 [1922] 96–97); SCDS Instr., 1 iul. 1929, 48 (AAS 21 [1929] 360); SCDS Instr., 29 iun. 1941, 4 c (AAS 33 [1941] 300); CAI 43, 59 §2; CI Resp., 26 mar. 1952 (AAS 44 [1952] 496)

from evidence. The absence of a spouse alone, even for a long time, is not sufficient.

§3. The bishop is to consult the Apostolic See in uncertain and complicated cases.

obitu obtinuerit. Solo coniugis absentia, quamvis diuturna, non sufficit.

§3. In casibus incertis et implexis Episcopus Sedem Apostolicam consulat.

TITLE II. Cases for Declaring the Nullity of Sacred Ordination

TITULUS II. De Causis ad Sacrae Ordinationis Nullitatem Declarandam

CAN. 1708 The cleric himself, the ordinary to whom the cleric is subject, or the ordinary in whose diocese the cleric was ordained has the right to challenge the validity of sacred ordination.

CAN. 1708 Validitatem sacrae ordinationis ius habent accusandi sive ipse clericus sive Ordinarius, cui clericus subest vel in cuius dioecesi ordinatus est.

CAN. 1709 §1. The *libellus* must be sent to the competent congregation which will decide whether the congregation of the Roman Curia itself or a tribunal designated by it must handle the case.

§2. Once the *libellus* has been sent, the cleric is forbidden to exercise orders by the law itself.

CAN. 1709 §1. Libellus mitti debet ad competentem Congregationem, quae decernet utrum causa ab ipsa Curiae Romanae Congregatione an a tribunali ab ea designato sit agenda.

§2. Misso libello, clericus ordines exercere ipso iure vetatur.

CAN. 1710 If the congregation refers the case to a tribunal, the canons on trials in general and on the ordinary contentious trial are to be observed unless the nature of the matter precludes it and without prejudice to the prescripts of this title.

CAN. 1710 Si Congregatio causam ad tribunal remiserit, serventur, nisi rei natura obstet, canones de iudiciis in genere et de iudicio contentioso ordinario, salvis praescriptis huius tituli.

CAN. 1711 In these cases the defender of the bond possesses the same rights and is bound by the same duties as the defender of the marriage bond.

CAN. 1711 In his causis defensor vinculi iisdem gaudet iuribus iisdemque tenetur officiis, quibus defensor vinculi matrimonialis.

1708: c. 1994; SCDS Regulae, 9 iun. 1931, 3 (AAS 23 [1931] 458); SN can. 502

1709 §1: c. 1993 §1; COETUS S.R.E. CARD., Resp. II, 13 et 27 nov. 1922 (AAS 15 [1923] 39); SCDS Regulae, 9 iun. 1931, 1, 2, 4, 6 (AAS 23 [1931] 458–459); SN can. 501 §1; REU 57

1709 §2: c. 1997; SN can. 505

1710: cc. 1993 §2, 1995; SCDS Regulae, 9 iun. 1931, 7–70 (AAS 23 [1931] 459–472); SN cann. 501 §2, 503

1711: c. 1996; SCDS Regulae, 9 iun. 1931, 18–20 (AAS 23 [1931] 462); SN can. 504

CAN. 1712 After a second sentence has confirmed the nullity of sacred ordination, the cleric loses all rights proper to the clerical state and is freed from all obligations.

CAN. 1712 Post secundam sententiam, quae nullitatem sacrae ordinationis confirmavit, clericus omnia iura statui clericali propria amittit et ab omnibus obligationibus liberatur.

TITLE III. Methods of Avoiding Trials

TITULUS III. **De Modis Evitandi Iudicia**

CAN. 1713 In order to avoid judicial contentions an agreement or reconciliation is employed usefully, or the controversy can be committed to the judgment of one or more arbitrators.

CAN. 1713 Ad evitandas iudiciales contentiones transactio seu reconciliatio utiliter adhibetur, aut controversia iudicio unius vel plurium arbitrorum committi potest.

CAN. 1714 For an agreement, a compromise, and an arbitrated judgment, the norms selected by the parties or, if the parties have selected none, the law laid down by the conference of bishops, if there is such a law, or the civil law in force in the place where the agreement is entered into is to be observed.

CAN. 1714 De transactione, de compromisso, deque iudicio arbitrali serventur normae a partibus selectae vel, si partes nullas selegerint, lex ab Episcoporum conferentia lata, si qua sit, vel lex civilis vigens in loco ubi conventio initur.

CAN. 1715 §1. An agreement or compromise cannot be made validly concerning matters which pertain to the public good and other matters about which the parties cannot make disposition freely.

CAN. 1715 §1. Nequit transactio aut compromissum valide fieri circa ea quae ad bonum publicum pertinent, aliaque de quibus libere disponere partes non possunt.

§2. For temporal ecclesiastical goods, the formalities established by law for the alienation of ecclesiastical goods are to be observed whenever the matter demands it.

§2. Si agitur de bonis ecclesiasticis temporalibus, serventur, quoties materia id postulat, sollemnitates iure statutae pro rerum ecclesiasticarum alienatione.

CAN. 1716 §1. If the civil law does not recognize the force of an arbitrated sentence unless a judge confirms it, an arbitrated sentence in an ecclesiastical controversy, in order to have force

CAN. 1716 §1. Si lex civilis arbitrali sententiae vim non agnoscat, nisi a iudice confirmetur, sententia arbitralis de controversia ecclesiastica, ut vim habeat in foro

1712: c. 1998; SN can. 506
1713: cc. 1925, 1929; SN cann. 94, 98
1714: cc. 1926, 1930; SN cann. 96, 107

1715: cc. 1927, 1930; SN cann. 96, 99
1716: SN can. 120

in the canonical forum, needs the confirmation of an ecclesiastical judge of the place where it was rendered.

§2. If civil law permits the challenge of an arbitrated judgment before a civil judge, however, the same challenge can be proposed in the canonical forum before an ecclesiastical judge competent to judge the controversy in the first grade.

canonico, confirmatione indiget iudicis ecclesiastici loci, in quo lata est.

§2. Si autem lex civilis admittat sententiae arbitralis coram civili iudice impugnationem, in foro canonico eadem impugnatio proponi potest coram iudice ecclesiastico, qui in primo gradu competens est ad controversiam iudicandam.

PART IV. THE PENAL PROCESS

PARS IV. DE PROCESSU POENALI

CAPUT I. **De Praevia Investigatione**

CHAPTER I. **The Preliminary Investigation**

CAN. 1717 §1. Whenever an ordinary has knowledge, which at least seems true, of a delict, he is carefully to inquire personally or through another suitable person about the facts, circumstances, and imputability, unless such an inquiry seems entirely superfluous.

§2. Care must be taken so that the good name of anyone is not endangered from this investigation.

§3. The person who conducts the investigation has the same powers and obligations as an auditor in the process; the same person cannot act as a judge in the matter if a judicial process is initiated later.

CAN. 1718 §1. When it seems that sufficient evidence has been collected, the ordinary is to decide:

1° whether a process to inflict or declare a penalty can be initiated;

2° whether, attentive to can. 1341, this is expedient;

3° whether a judicial process must be used or, unless the law forbids it, whether the matter must proceed by way of extrajudicial decree.

§2. The ordinary is to revoke or change the decree mentioned in §1 whenever new evidence indicates to him that another decision is necessary.

CAN. 1717 §1. Quoties Ordinarius notitiam, saltem veri similem, habet de delicto, caute inquirat, per se vel per aliam idoneam personam, circa facta et circumstantias et circa imputabilitatem, nisi haec inquisitio omnino superflua videatur.

§2. Cavendum est ne ex hac investigatione bonum cuiusquam nomen in discrimen vocetur.

§3. Qui investigationem agit, easdem habet, quas auditor in processu, potestates et obligationes; idemque nequit, si postea iudicialis processus promoveatur, in eo iudicem agere.

CAN. 1718 §1. Cum satis collecta videantur elementa, decernat Ordinarius:

1° num processus ad poenam irrogandam vel declarandam promoveri possit;

2° num id, attento can. 1341, expediat;

3° utrum processus iudicialis sit adhibendus an, nisi lex vetet, sit procedendum per decretum extra iudicium.

§2. Ordinarius decretum, de quo in §1, revocet vel mutet, quoties ex novis elementis aliud sibi decernendum videatur.

§3. In issuing the decrees mentioned in §§1 and 2, the ordinary is to hear two judges or other experts of the law if he considers it prudent.

§4. Before he makes a decision according to the norm of §1 and in order to avoid useless trials, the ordinary is to examine carefully whether it is expedient for him or the investigator, with the consent of the parties, to resolve equitably the question of damages.

CAN. 1719 The acts of the investigation, the decrees of the ordinary which initiated and concluded the investigation, and everything which preceded the investigation are to be kept in the secret archive of the curia if they are not necessary for the penal process.

CHAPTER II. The Development of the Process

CAN. 1720 If the ordinary thinks that the matter must proceed by way of extrajudicial decree:

1° he is to inform the accused of the accusation and the proofs, giving an opportunity for self-defense, unless the accused neglected to appear after being properly summoned;

2° he is to weigh carefully all the proofs and arguments with two assessors;

3° if the delict is certainly established and a criminal action is not extinguished, he is to issue a decree according to the norm of cann. 1342–1350, setting forth the reasons in law and in fact at least briefly.

CAN. 1721 §1. If the ordinary has decreed that a judicial penal process must be initiated, he is to hand over the acts of the investigation to the promoter of justice who is to present a *libellus* of accusation to the judge according to the norm of cann. 1502 and 1504.

§3. In ferendis decretis, de quibus in §§1 et 2, audiat Ordinarius, si prudenter censeat, duos iudices aliosve iuris peritos.

§4. Antequam ad normam §1 decernat, consideret Ordinarius num, ad vitanda inutilia iudicia, expediat ut, partibus consentientibus, vel ipse vel investigator quaestionem de damnis ex bono et aequo dirimat.

CAN. 1719 Investigationis acta et Ordinarii decreta, quibus investigatio initur vel clauditur, eaque omnia quae investigationem praecedunt, si necessaria non sint ad poenalem processum, in secreto curiae archivo custodiantur.

CAPUT II. De Processus Evolutione

CAN. 1720 Si Ordinarius censuerit per decretum extra iudicium esse procedendum:

1° reo accusationem atque probationes, data facultate sese defendendi, significet, nisi reus, rite vocatus, comparere neglexerit;

2° probationes et argumenta omnia cum duobus assessoribus accurate perpendat;

3° si de delicto certo constet neque actio criminalis sit extincta, decretum ferat ad normam cann. 1342–1350, expositis, breviter saltem, rationibus in iure et in facto.

CAN. 1721 §1. Si Ordinarius decreverit processum poenalem iudicialem esse ineundum, acta investigationis promotori iustitiae tradat, qui accusationis libellum iudici ad normam cann. 1502 et 1504 exhibeat.

1719: c. 1946 §2, 1° et 2°
1720: cc. 1933 §4, 2225, 2233 §1

1721 §1: cc. 1934, 1954, 1955

§2. The promoter of justice appointed to the higher tribunal acts as the petitioner before that tribunal.

CAN. 1722 To prevent scandals, to protect the freedom of witnesses, and to guard the course of justice, the ordinary, after having heard the promoter of justice and cited the accused, at any stage of the process can exclude the accused from the sacred ministry or from some office and ecclesiastical function, can impose or forbid residence in some place or territory, or even can prohibit public participation in the Most Holy Eucharist. Once the cause ceases, all these measures must be revoked; they also end by the law itself when the penal process ceases.

CAN. 1723 §1. The judge who cites the accused must invite the accused to appoint an advocate according to the norm of can. 1481, §1 within the time limit set by the judge.

§2. If the accused does not make provision, the judge is to appoint an advocate before the joinder of the issue; this advocate will remain in this function as long as the accused does not appoint an advocate personally.

CAN. 1724 §1. At any grade of the trial the promoter of justice can renounce the trial at the command of or with the consent of the ordinary whose deliberation initiated the process.

§2. For validity the accused must accept the renunciation unless the accused was declared absent from the trial.

CAN. 1725 In the discussion of the case, whether done in written or oral form, the accused, either personally or through the advocate or procurator, always has the right to write or speak last.

§2. Coram tribunali superiore partes actoris gerit promotor iustitiae apud illud tribunal constitutus.

CAN. 1722 Ad scandala praevenienda, ad testium libertatem protegendam et ad iustitiae cursum tutandum, potest Ordinarius, audito promotore iustitiae et citato ipso accusato, in quolibet processus stadio accusatum a sacro ministerio vel ab aliquo officio et munere ecclesiastico arcere, ei imponere vel interdicere commorationem in aliquo loco vel territorio, vel etiam publicam sanctissimae Eucharistiae participationem prohibere; quae omnia, causa cessante, sunt revocanda, eaque ipso iure finem habent, cessante processu poenali.

CAN. 1723 §1. Iudex reum citans debet eum invitare ad advocatum, ad normam can. 1481, §1, intra terminum ab ipso iudice praefinitum, sibi constituendum.

§2. Quod si reus non providerit, iudex ante litis contestationem advocatum ipse nominet, tamdiu in munere mansurum quamdiu reus sibi advocatum non constituerit.

CAN. 1724 §1. In quolibet iudicii gradu renuntiatio instantiae fieri potest a promotore iustitiae, mandante vel consentiente Ordinario, ex cuius deliberatione processus promotus est.

§2. Renuntiatio, ut valeat, debet a reo acceptari, nisi ipse sit a iudicio absens declaratus.

CAN. 1725 In causae discussione, sive scripto haec fit sive ore, accusatus semper ius habeat ut ipse vel eius advocatus vel procurator postremus scribat vel loquatur.

1722: cc. 1956–1958
1723 §1: SN can. 536

1725: SN cann. 553, 570

CAN. 1726 If at any grade and stage of the penal trial it is evidently established that the accused did not commit the delict, the judge must declare this in a sentence and absolve the accused even if it is also established that criminal action has been extinguished.

CAN. 1727 §1. The accused can propose an appeal even if the sentence dismissed the accused only because the penalty was facultative or because the judge used the power mentioned in cann. 1344 and 1345.

§2. The promoter of justice can appeal whenever the promoter judges that the repair of scandal or the restoration of justice has not been provided for sufficiently.

CAN. 1728 §1. Without prejudice to the prescripts of the canons of this title and unless the nature of the matter precludes it, the canons on trials in general and on the ordinary contentious trial must be applied in a penal trial; the special norms for cases which pertain to the public good are also to be observed.

§2. The accused is not bound to confess the delict nor can an oath be administered to the accused.

CHAPTER III. **Action to Repair Damages**

CAN. 1729 §1. In the penal trial itself an injured party can bring a contentious action to repair damages incurred personally from the delict, according to the norm of can. 1596.

§2. The intervention of the injured party mentioned in §1 is not admitted later if it was not made in the first grade of the penal trial.

§3. The appeal in a case for damages is made according to the norm of cann. 1628–1640 even if an appeal cannot be made in the penal trial; if

CAN. 1726 In quolibet poenalis iudicii gradu et stadio, si evidenter constet delictum non esse a reo patratum, iudex debet id sententia declarare et reum absolvere, etiamsi simul constet actionem criminalem esse extinctam.

CAN. 1727 §1. Appellationem proponere potest reus, etiam si sententia ipsum ideo tantum dimiserit, quia poena erat facultativa, vel quia iudex potestate usus est, de qua in cann. 1344 et 1345.

§2. Promotor iustitiae appellare potest quoties censet scandali reparationi vel iustitiae restitutioni satis provisum non esse.

CAN. 1728 §1. Salvis praescriptis canonum huius tituli, in iudicio poenali applicandi sunt, nisi rei natura obstet, canones de iudiciis in genere et de iudicio contentioso ordinario, servatis specialibus normis de causis quae ad bonum publicum spectant.

§2. Accusatus ad confitendum delictum non tenetur, nec ipsi iusiurandum deferri potest.

CAPUT III. **De Actione ad Damna Reparanda**

CAN. 1729 §1. Pars laesa potest actionem contentiosam ad damna reparanda ex delicto sibi illata in ipso poenali iudicio exercere, ad normam can. 1596.

§2. Interventus partis laesae, de quo in §1, non amplius admittitur, si factus non sit in primo iudicii poenalis gradu.

§3. Appellatio in causa de damnis fit ad normam cann. 1628–1640, etiamsi appellatio in poenali iudicio fieri non possit; quod si

1728: c. 1959

both appeals are proposed, although by different parties, there is to be a single appellate trial, without prejudice to the prescript of can. 1730.

CAN. 1730 §1. To avoid excessive delays in the penal trial the judge can defer the judgment for damages until he has rendered the definitive sentence in the penal trial.

§2. After rendering the sentence in the penal trial, the judge who does this must adjudicate for damages even if the penal trial still is pending because of a proposed challenge or the accused has been absolved for a cause which does not remove the obligation to repair damages.

CAN. 1731 Even if the sentence rendered in a penal trial has become a *res iudicata,* it in no way establishes the right of the injured party unless this party has intervened according to the norm of can. 1729.

utraque appellatio, licet a diversis partibus, proponatur, unicum fiat iudicium appellationis, salvo praescripto can. 1730.

CAN. 1730 §1. Ad nimias poenalis iudicii moras vitandas potest iudex iudicium de damnis differre usque dum sententiam definitivam in iudicio poenali protulerit.

§2. Iudex, qui ita egerit, debet, postquam sententiam tulerit in poenali iudicio, de damnis cognoscere, etiamsi iudicium poenale propter propositam impugnationem adhuc pendeat, vel reus absolutus sit propter causam quae non auferat obligationem reparandi damna.

CAN. 1731 Sententia lata in poenali iudicio, etiamsi in rem iudicatam transierit, nullo modo ius facit erga partem laesam, nisi haec intervenerit ad normam can. 1729.

PART V. THE METHOD OF PROCEEDING IN ADMINISTRATIVE RECOURSE AND IN THE REMOVAL OR TRANSFER OF PASTORS

PARS V. DE RATIONE PROCEDENDI IN RECURSIBUS ADMINISTRATIVIS ATQUE IN PAROCHIS AMOVENDIS VEL TRANSFERENDIS

SECTION I. Recourse Against Administrative Decrees

SECTIO I. De Recursu Adversus Decreta Administrativa

CAN. 1732 What is established in the canons of this section concerning decrees must be applied to all singular administrative acts which are given in the external forum outside a trial excepting those which have been issued by the Roman Pontiff or an ecumenical council.

CAN. 1733 §1. Whenever a person considers himself or herself aggrieved by a decree, it is particularly desirable that the person and the author of the decree avoid any contention and take care to seek an equitable solution by common counsel, possibly using the mediation and effort of wise persons to avoid or settle the controversy in a suitable way.

§2. The conference of bishops can determine that each diocese establish in a stable manner an office or council whose function is to seek and suggest equitable solutions according to the norms determined by the conference. If the conference has not ordered this, however, the

CAN. 1732 Quae in canonibus huius sectionis de decretis statuuntur, eadem applicanda sunt ad omnes administrativos actus singulares, qui in foro externo extra iudicium dantur, iis exceptis, qui ab ipso Romano Pontifice vel ab ipso Concilio Oecumenico ferantur.

CAN. 1733 §1. Valde optandum est ut, quoties quis gravatum se decreto putet, vitetur inter ipsum et decreti auctorem contentio atque inter eos de aequa solutione quaerenda communi consilio curetur, gravibus quoque personis ad mediationem et studium forte adhibitis, ita ut per idoneam viam controversia praecaveatur vel dirimatur.

§2. Episcoporum conferentia statuere potest ut in unaquaque dioecesi officium quoddam vel consilium stabiliter constituatur, cui, secundum normas ab ipsa conferentia statuendas, munus sit aequas solutiones quaerere et suggerere; quod si confer-

bishop can establish a council or office of this kind.

§3. The office or council mentioned in §2 is especially to be of assistance when the revocation of a decree has been requested according to the norm of can. 1734 and the time limits for making recourse have not elapsed. If recourse has been proposed against a decree, however, the superior who deals with the recourse is to urge the person making recourse and the author of the decree to seek a solution of this kind whenever he sees hope of a favorable outcome.

CAN. 1734   §1. Before proposing recourse a person must seek the revocation or emendation of the decree in writing from its author. When this petition is proposed, by that very fact suspension of the execution of the decree is also understood to be requested.

§2. The petition must be made within the peremptory period of ten useful days from the legitimate notification of the decree.

§3. The norms of §§1 and 2 are not valid:

1° for recourse proposed to a bishop against decrees issued by authorities subject to him;

2° for recourse proposed against a decree which decides a hierarchical recourse unless the bishop gave the decision;

3° for recourse proposed according to the norm of cann. 57 and 1735.

CAN. 1735   If within thirty days after receiving the petition mentioned in can. 1734 the author of the decree communicates a new decree by which he either emends the earlier one or decides that the petition must be rejected, the time limits for making recourse run from the notification of the new decree. If the author makes no decision within the thirty days, however, the time limits run from the thirtieth day.

entia id non iusserit, potest Episcopus eiusmodi consilium vel officium constituere.

§3. Officium vel consilium, de quo in §2, tunc praecipue operam navet, cum revocatio decreti petita est ad normam can. 1734, neque termini ad recurrendum sunt elapsi; quod si adversus decretum recursus propositus sit, ipse Superior, qui de recursu videt, recurrentem et decreti auctorem hortetur, quotiescumque spem boni exitus perspicit, ad eiusmodi solutiones quaerendas.

CAN. 1734   §1. Antequam quis recursum proponat, debet decreti revocationem vel emendationem scripto ab ipsius auctore petere; qua petitione proposita, etiam suspensio exsecutionis eo ipso petita intellegitur.

§2. Petitio fieri debet intra peremptorium terminum decem dierum utilium a decreto legitime intimato.

§3. Normae §§1 et 2 non valent:

1° de recursu proponendo ad Episcopum adversus decreta lata ab auctoritatibus, quae ei subsunt;

2° de recursu proponendo adversus decretum, quo recursus hierarchicus deciditur, nisi decisio data sit ab Episcopo;

3° de recursibus proponendis ad normam cann. 57 et 1735.

CAN. 1735   Si intra triginta dies, ex quo petitio, de qua in can. 1734, ad auctorem decreti pervenit, is novum decretum intimet, quo vel prius emendet vel petitionem reiciendam esse decernat, termini ad recurrendum decurrunt ex novi decreti intimatione; si autem intra triginta dies nihil decernat, termini decurrunt ex tricesimo die.

CAN. 1736 §1. In those matters in which hierarchical recourse suspends the execution of a decree, the petition mentioned in can. 1734 also has the same effect.

§2. In other cases, if the author of the decree has not decreed the suspension of execution within ten days after receiving the petition mentioned in can. 1734, an interim suspension can be sought from his hierarchical superior who can decree a suspension only for grave reasons and always cautiously so that the salvation of souls suffers no harm.

§3. If the execution of the decree has been suspended according to the norm of §2 and recourse is proposed afterwards, the person who must deal with the recourse according to the norm of can. 1737, §3 is to decide whether the suspension must be confirmed or revoked.

§4. If no recourse is proposed against the decree within the established time limit, the interim suspension of the execution given according to the norm of §§1 or 2 ceases by that very fact.

CAN. 1737 §1. A person who claims to have been aggrieved by a decree can make recourse for any just reason to the hierarchical superior of the one who issued the decree. The recourse can be proposed before the author of the decree who must transmit it immediately to the competent hierarchical superior.

§2. Recourse must be proposed within the peremptory time limit of fifteen useful days which in the cases mentioned in can. 1734, §3 run from the day on which the decree was communicated; in other cases, however, they run according to the norm of can. 1735.

§3. Nevertheless, even in cases in which recourse does not suspend the execution of the decree by the law itself and suspension has not been decreed according to the norm of can.

CAN. 1736 §1. In iis materiis, in quibus recursus hierarchicus suspendit decreti exsecutionem, idem efficit etiam petitio, de qua in can. 1734.

§2. In ceteris casibus, nisi intra decem dies, ex quo petitio de qua in can. 1734 ad ipsum auctorem decreti pervenit, is exsecutionem suspendendam decreverit, potest suspensio interim peti ab eius Superiore hierarchico, qui eam decernere potest gravibus tantum de causis et cauto semper ne quid salus animarum detrimenti capiat.

§3. Suspensa decreti exsecutione ad normam §2, si postea recursus proponatur, is qui de recursu videre debet, ad normam can. 1737, §3 decernat utrum suspensio sit confirmanda an revocanda.

§4. Si nullus recursus intra statutum terminum adversus decretum proponatur, suspensio exsecutionis, ad normam §1 vel §2 interim effecta, eo ipso cessat.

CAN. 1737 §1. Qui se decreto gravatum esse contendit, potest ad Superiorem hierarchicum eius, qui decretum tulit, propter quodlibet iustum motivum recurrere; recursus proponi potest coram ipso decreti auctore, qui eum statim ad competentem Superiorem hierarchicum transmittere debet.

§2. Recursus proponendus est intra peremptorium terminum quindecim dierum utilium, qui in casibus de quibus in can. 1734, §3 decurrunt ex die quo decretum intimatum est, in ceteris autem casibus decurrunt ad normam can. 1735.

§3. Etiam in casibus, in quibus recursus non suspendit ipso iure decreti exsecutionem neque suspensio ad normam can. 1736, §2 decreta est, potest tamen gravi de

1736, §2, the superior can order the execution to be suspended for a grave cause, yet cautiously so that the salvation of souls suffers no harm.

CAN. 1738 The person making recourse always has the right to use an advocate or procurator, but useless delays are to be avoided; indeed, a legal representative is to be appointed *ex officio* if the person making recourse lacks one and the superior thinks it necessary. Nevertheless, the superior always can order the person making recourse to be present in order to be questioned.

CAN. 1739 The superior who deals with the recourse, as the case warrants, is permitted not only to confirm the decree or declare it invalid but also to rescind or revoke it or, if it seems more expedient to the superior, to emend, replace, or modify it.

causa Superior iubere ut exsecutio suspendatur, cauto tamen ne quid salus animarum detrimenti capiat.

CAN. 1738 Recurrens semper ius habet advocatum vel procuratorem adhibendi, vitatis inutilibus moris; immo vero patronus ex officio constituatur, si recurrens patrono careat et Superior id necessarium censeat; semper tamen potest Superior iubere ut recurrens ipse compareat ut interrogetur.

CAN. 1739 Superiori, qui de recursu videt, licet, prout casus ferat, non solum decretum confirmare vel irritum declarare, sed etiam rescindere, revocare, vel, si id Superiori magis expedire videatur, emendare, subrogare, ei obrogare.

SECTION II. The Procedure in the Removal or Transfer of Pastors

SECTIO II. De Procedura in Parochis Amovendis vel Transferendis

CHAPTER I. The Manner of Proceeding in the Removal of Pastors

CAPUT I. De Modo Procedendi in Amotione Parochorum

CAN. 1740 When the ministry of any pastor becomes harmful or at least ineffective for any cause, even through no grave personal negligence, the diocesan bishop can remove him from the parish.

CAN. 1741 The causes for which a pastor can be removed legitimately from his parish are especially the following:

1° a manner of acting which brings grave

CAN. 1740 Cum alicuius parochi ministerium ob aliquam causam, etiam citra gravem ipsius culpam, noxium aut saltem inefficax evadat, potest ipse ab Episcopo dioecesano a paroecia amoveri.

CAN. 1741 Causae, ob quas parochus a sua paroecia legitime amoveri potest, hae praesertim sunt:

1° modus agendi qui ecclesiasticae com-

1740: c. 2147 §1; CIV Resp., 7 iul. 1978 (AAS 70 [1978] 534)

1741: cc. 2147 §2, 2157 §1; CD 31; ES I, 20 §1

detriment or disturbance to ecclesiastical communion;

2° ineptitude or a permanent infirmity of mind or body which renders the pastor unable to fulfill his functions usefully;

3° loss of a good reputation among upright and responsible parishioners or an aversion to the pastor which it appears will not cease in a brief time;

4° grave neglect or violation of parochial duties which persists after a warning;

5° poor administration of temporal affairs with grave damage to the Church whenever another remedy to this harm cannot be found.

CAN. 1742 §1. If the instruction which was carried out has established the existence of one of the causes mentioned in can. 1740, the bishop is to discuss the matter with two pastors selected from the group established for this purpose in a stable manner by the presbyteral council at the proposal of the bishop. If the bishop then judges that removal must take place, he paternally is to persuade the pastor to resign within fifteen days, after having explained, for validity, the cause and arguments for the removal.

§2. The prescript of can. 682, §2 is to be observed for pastors who are members of a religious institute or a society of apostolic life.

CAN. 1743 A pastor can submit a resignation not only purely and simply but also conditionally, provided that the bishop can accept it legitimately and actually does accept it.

CAN. 1744 §1. If the pastor has not responded within the prescribed days, the bishop

munioni grave detrimentum vel perturbationem afferat;

2° imperitia aut permanens mentis vel corporis infirmitas, quae parochum suis muneribus utiliter obeundis imparem reddunt;

3° bonae existimationis amissio penes probos et graves paroecianos vel aversio in parochum, quae praevideantur non brevi cessaturae;

4° gravis neglectus vel violatio officiorum paroecialium quae post monitionem persistat;

5° mala rerum temporalium administratio cum gravi Ecclesiae damno, quoties huic malo aliud remedium afferri nequeat.

CAN. 1742 §1. Si ex instructione peracta constiterit adesse causam de qua in can. 1740, Episcopus rem discutiat cum duobus parochis, e coetu ad hoc stabiliter, a consilio presbyterali constituto, Episcopo proponente, selectis; quod si exinde censeat ad amotionem esse deveniendum, causa et argumentis ad validitatem indicatis, parocho paterne suadeat ut intra tempus quindecim dierum renuntiet.

§2. De parochis qui sunt sodales instituti religiosi aut societatis vitae apostolicae, servetur praescriptum can. 682, §2.

CAN. 1743 Renuntiatio a parocho fieri potest non solum pure et simpliciter, sed etiam sub condicione, dummodo haec ab Episcopo legitime acceptari possit et reapse acceptetur.

CAN. 1744 §1. Si parochus intra praestitutos dies non responderit, Episcopus

1742 §1: cc. 2148, 2158
1742 §2: c. 2157 §2
1743: c. 2150 §3; CI Resp., 20 maii 1923 (AAS 16 [1924] 116)

1744: c. 2149

is to repeat the invitation and extend the useful time to respond.

§2. If the bishop establishes that the pastor received the second invitation but did not respond even though not prevented by any impediment, or if the pastor refuses to resign without giving any reasons, the bishop is to issue a decree of removal.

CAN. 1745 If the pastor opposes the cause given and its reasons and alleges reasons which seem insufficient to the bishop, the bishop, in order to act validly, is:

1° to invite the pastor to organize his objections in a written report after he has inspected the acts, and offer any proofs he has to the contrary;

2° when any necessary instruction is completed, to consider the matter together with the same pastors mentioned in can. 1742, §1, unless others must be designated because those pastors are unavailable;

3° finally, to establish whether the pastor must be removed or not and promptly to issue a decree on the matter.

CAN. 1746 After the pastor has been removed, the bishop is to make provision either for an assignment to some other office, if he is suitable for this, or for a pension as the case warrants and circumstances permit.

CAN. 1747 §1. The removed pastor must refrain from exercising the function of pastor, vacate the rectory as soon as possible, and hand over everything belonging to the parish to the person to whom the bishop has entrusted the parish.

§2. If, however, the man is sick and cannot be transferred elsewhere from the rectory with-

iteret invitationem prorogando tempus utile ad respondendum.

§2. Si Episcopo constiterit parochum alteram invitationem recepisse, non autem respondisse etsi nullo impedimento detentum, aut si parochus renuntiationem nullis adductis motivis recuset, Episcopus decretum amotionis ferat.

CAN. 1745 Si vero parochus causam adductam eiusque rationes oppugnet, motiva allegans quae insufficientia Episcopo videantur, hic ut valide agat:

1° invitet illum ut, inspectis actis, suas impugnationes in relatione scripta colligat, immo probationes in contrarium, si quas habeat, afferat;

2° deinde, completa, si opus sit, instructione, una cum iisdem parochis de quibus in can. 1742, §1, nisi alii propter illorum impossibilitatem sint designandi, rem perpendat;

3° tandem statuat utrum parochus sit amovendus necne, et mox decretum de re ferat.

CAN. 1746 Amoto parocho, Episcopus consulat sive assignatione alius officii, si ad hoc idoneus sit, sive pensione, prout casus ferat et adiuncta permittant.

CAN. 1747 §1. Parochus amotus debet a parochi munere exercendo abstinere, quam primum liberam relinquere paroecialem domum, et omnia quae ad paroeciam pertinent ei tradere, cui Episcopus paroeciam commiserit.

§2. Si autem de infirmo agatur, qui e paroeciali domo sine incommodo nequeat

---

out inconvenience, the bishop is to leave him the use, even exclusive use, of the rectory while this necessity lasts.

§3. While recourse against a decree of removal is pending, the bishop cannot appoint a new pastor, but is to provide a parochial administrator in the meantime.

CHAPTER II. The Manner of Proceeding in the Transfer of Pastors

CAN. 1748 If the good of souls or the necessity or advantage of the Church demands that a pastor be transferred from a parish which he is governing usefully to another parish or another office, the bishop is to propose the transfer to him in writing and persuade him to consent to it out of love of God and souls.

CAN. 1749 If the pastor does not intend to submit to the counsel and persuasions of the bishop, he is to explain the reasons in writing.

CAN. 1750 Notwithstanding the reasons alleged, if the bishop decides not to withdraw from his proposal, he is to consider the reasons which favor or oppose the transfer with two pastors selected according to the norm of can. 1742, §1. If he then decides to implement the transfer, however, he is to repeat the paternal exhortations to the pastor.

CAN. 1751 §1. When this has been done, if the pastor still refuses and the bishop thinks that the transfer must be made, he is to issue a decree of transfer, establishing that the parish will be vacant after the lapse of a set time.

§2. If this period of time has passed without action, he is to declare the parish vacant.

alio transferri, Episcopus eidem relinquat eius usum etiam exclusivum, eadem necessitate durante.

§3. Pendente recursu adversus amotionis decretum, Episcopus non potest novum parochum nominare, sed per administratorem paroecialem interim provideat.

CAPUT II. De Modo Procedendi in Translatione Parochorum

CAN. 1748 Si bonum animarum vel Ecclesiae necessitas aut utilitas postulet, ut parochus a sua, quam utiliter regit, ad aliam paroeciam aut ad aliud officium transferatur, Episcopus eidem translationem scripto proponat ac suadeat ut pro Dei atque animarum amore consentiat.

CAN. 1749 Si parochus consilio ac suasionibus Episcopi obsequi non intendat, rationes in scriptis exponat.

CAN. 1750 Episcopus, si, non obstantibus allatis rationibus, iudicet a proposito non esse recedendum, cum duobus parochis ad normam can. 1742, §1 selectis, rationes perpendat quae translationi faveant vel obstent; quod si exinde translationem peragendam censeat, paternas exhortationes parocho iteret.

CAN. 1751 §1. His peractis, si adhuc et parochus renuat et Episcopus putet translationem esse faciendam, hic decretum translationis ferat, statuens paroeciam, elapso praefinito tempore, esse vacaturam.

§2. Hoc tempore inutiliter transacto, paroeciam vacantem declaret.

1747 §3: c. 2146 §3; SA Decisio, 1 nov. 1970; CIV Resp. III, 1 iul. 1971 (AAS 63 [1971] 860)
1748: c. 2162; ES I, 20 §2
1749: c. 2164
1750: cc. 2165, 2166
1751: c. 2167

CAN. **1752** In cases of transfer the pre-scripts of can. 1747 are to be applied, canonical equity is to be observed, and the salvation of souls, which must always be the supreme law in the Church, is to be kept before one's eyes.

CAN. **1752** In causis translationis applicentur praescripta canonis 1747, servata aequitate canonica et prae oculis habita salute animarum, quae in Ecclesia superma semper lex esse debet.

1752: Ivo Carnutensis, *Decretum* (PL 162, 74); S. Raymundus de Penaforte, *Summa de poenitentia et matrimoniis,* Introductio: S. Thoma de Aquino, *Quaestiones quodlibetales,* 12, 16, 2; Pius PP. XII, All., 24 iun. 1939 (AAS 31 [1939] 248); Pius PP. XII, All., 2 oct. 1944 (AAS 36 [1944] 288); Pius PP. XII, All., 17 oct. 1953 (AAS 45 [1953] 68); Paulus PP. VI, All., 8 feb. 1973 (AAS 65 [1973] 95–103); Paulus PP. VI, All., 17 sep. 1973: Paulus PP. VI, All., 4 feb. 1977 (AAS 69 [1977] 147–153).

INDEX

TABLES OF CORRESPONDING CANONS

APPENDICES

INDEX

References are to specific canons.

A

abatement of a trial if no procedural act is proposed for six months, 1520; particular law may establish other terms of, 1520; takes effect against all persons, 1521; extinguishes acts of the process but not acts of the case, 1522; each litigant bears own expenses of abated trial, 1523

abbot territorial abbot governs a territorial abbacy just like a diocesan bishop, 370; abbot primate is comparable to a major superior but with less power in universal law, 620; abbot primate or abbot superior of a monastic congregation is judged by Roman Rota, 1405, §3, 2°; local abbot judges a controversy of an autonomous monastery, 1427, §1; tribunal of the abbot superior of the monastic congregation is second instance for cases tried before the local abbot, 1438, 3°

abduction marriage impediment of, 1089; delict of, 1397

aborted fetus if alive is to be baptized, 871

abortion member of a religious institute must be dismissed for, 695, §1; member of a secular institute must be dismissed for, 729; member of a society of apostolic life must be dismissed for, 746; irregularity to receive orders, 1041, 4°; irregularity to exercise orders, 1044, §1, 3°; dispensation from the irregularity to receive orders, 1049; delict of, 1398

abrogation of agreements entered into by the Apostolic See with nations or other political societies, 3; of laws when this Code takes force, 6, §1; when a later law abrogates an earlier law, 20; of statutes of a chapter of canons, 505

absence travelers are not bound by particular laws of their territory when they are absent, 13, §2, 1°; power to dispense when absent from one's territory, 91; from an election, 166, §2; of the diocesan bishop, 395, §§2–4; the coadjutor and auxiliary with special faculty take the place of the diocesan bishop when he is absent, 405, §2; of the coadjutor and auxiliary bishop, 410; the diocesan bishop can appoint another vicar general or episcopal vicar when they are absent, 477, §2; of the pastor, 533, §§2–3, 549; of a religious superior from the house, 629; from a novitiate house, 649, §1; of a religious from a house, 665; illegitimate absence as a cause to dismiss a religious, 696, §1; of members of societies of apostolic life from the house or community, 740; remission of a penalty can be given to an absent person, 1361, §1; delict of violating the obligation of residence, 1396; in a trial, 1412, 1557, 1592–1595, 1622, 6°, 1724, §2; of a spouse is insufficient to presume death, 1707, §2

absolution *sacramental:* notion, 959; ordinary means of reconciliation, 960; general, 961–963; requires power of orders and faculty to exercise it, 966, §1; in danger of death, 976; of an accomplice in sin against the sixth commandment, 977, 1378, §1; not to be refused or deferred to a properly disposed penitent, 980; of one who falsely denounced a confessor, 982

delicts involving: absolution of an accomplice in sin against the sixth commandment , 1378, §1; attempting to impart absolution though unable to do so validly, 1378, §2, 2°

from penalties: by the canon penitentiary, 508, §1; by chaplains, 566, §2; in danger of death, 976; remission of penalties, 1354–1361

abstinence before receiving the Eucharist, 919; from works and affairs hindering worship, joy, and relaxation on Sundays and holydays of obligation, 1247; from imposing penalties, 1344, 2°, 1345; from judicial offices, 1448–1449

penitential: notion, 1249; on every Friday, unless it is a solemnity, and Ash Wednesday, 1251; binds persons who have reached their fourteenth year, 1252; more precise observance can be determined by conference of bishops, which can also substitute other forms of penance for, 1253

abuse of a privilege, 84; in associations of the Christian faithful, 305, §1; diocesan bishop is to exercise vigilance so abuses do not creep into ecclesiastical discipline, 392, §2; metropolitan is to inform the Supreme Pontiff of, 436, §1, 1°; pastor is to watch that abuses do not creep in the parish,

religious institutes, 634, §1; of secular institutes, 718; of societies of apostolic life, 741, §1; of relics and revered images, 1190; delict of alienating temporal goods without permission, 1377; and methods of avoiding trials, 1715, §2

alms   juridic persons sustained by alms are not subject to the seminary tax, 264, §2; an annual report of alms collected to be made in public associations, 319, §2; given to a church which is both parochial and capitular are presumed given to the parish, 510, §4; permission to beg for, 1265, §1; norms established by conference of bishops on begging for, 1265, §2

altar(s)   notion, 1235, §1; *fixed* or *moveable,* 1235, §1; in churches and other places designated for sacred celebrations, 1235, §2; material to construct, 1236; dedication or blessing, 1237, §1; relics under a fixed, 1237, §2; loss of dedication or blessing, 1238, 1212; to be reserved for divine worship alone, 1239, §1; a body not to be buried under, 1239, §2; eucharistic celebration to be carried out on, 932, §2; transfer of Mass obligations to altars different than mentioned in the foundations, 1309

All Saints   holyday of obligation, 1246, §1

amentia   irregularity for receiving orders, 1041, 1°; impediment to exercise orders, 1044, §2, 2°; developed by the one mandating a proxy for marriage, 1105, §4

anchoritic life   notion, 603

anointing of the sick   notion, 998; celebration of the sacrament, 999–1002; minister, 1003; recipients, 1004–1007; function especially entrusted to a pastor, 530, 3°; faculty of chaplains for, 566, §1; administration to and from non-Catholics, 844

anointing with chrism   in confirmation, 880, §1

apostasy   notion, 751; irregularity to receive orders, 1041, 2°, 1047, §2, 1°; irregularity to exercise orders received, 1044, §1, 2°; and deprivation of ecclesiastical funerals and funeral Mass, 1184, §1, 1°, 1185; delict of, 1364

apostolate   as a purpose of juridic persons, 114, §2; obligation of the Christian faithful to assist the, 222, §1; lay persons through baptism and confirmation are designated by God for the, 225, §1; formation of lay persons for the, 229, §1; formation of seminarians in the, 258; of associations, 298, §1; of associations related to institutes of consecrated life, 311; and moderators in public associations, 317, §4; of private associations, 323, §2; of lay associations, 329; diocesan bishop is to foster the, 394; and the conference of bishops, 447;

and the diocesan pastoral council, 512, §2, 514, §1; and exemption of institutes of consecrated life, 591; living outside a religious house to exercise the, 665, §1; of religious institutes, 673–683; and formation of members of secular institutes, 722, §2; and members of societies of apostolic life, 738, §2; and catechumens, 788, §2; is closely connected with the Eucharist and ordered to it, 897; as a principal and proper purpose of the Church, 1254, §2

apostolic administration   notion, 368, 371, §2; likened to a diocese, 368

apostolic administrator   notion, 371, §2; equivalent in law to a diocesan bishop, 381, §2; a local ordinary, 134, §2; can issue dimissorial letters, 1018, §1, 2°

apostolic blessing   to the dying is a function especially entrusted to a pastor, 530, 3°

apostolic prefect   notion, 371, §1; equivalent in law to a diocesan bishop, 381, §2; a local ordinary, 134, §2; has no obligation to make the *ad limina* visit, 400, §3; must appoint an apostolic pro-vicar after taking possession of the vicariate, 420; is to establish a council of at least three missionary presbyters, 495, §2, which has the functions of the college of consultors, 502, §4; can issue dimissorial letters for secular clergy, 1018

apostolic prefecture   notion, 368, 371, §1; likened to a diocese, 368

apostolic pro-prefect   governs a vacant apostolic prefecture, 420; a local ordinary, 134, §2; giving dimissorial letters, 1018

apostolic pro-vicar   governs a vacant apostolic prefecture, 420; a local ordinary, 134, §2; giving dimissorial letters, 1018

Apostolic See   notion, 361; and agreements with nations or other political societies, 3; acquired rights and privileges granted by the, 4; abrogation of universal or particular laws issued by the, 6, §1, 3°; rescripts granted by the, 68, 72; privileges granted by the, 84; a diocesan bishop cannot grant dispensation from laws reserved to the, 87, §1; grants permission to enroll in another Church *sui iuris,* 112, §1, 1°; has the character of a moral person by divine ordinance, 113, §1; executive power delegated by the, 137, §2

and the People of God: gives approval for erection of an interdiocesan seminary and its statutes, 237, §2; grants incardination in a secular institute, 266, §3; grants the loss of the clerical state to deacons and presbyters, 290, 3°; permits a cleric who lost the clerical state to be enrolled again among

grant a radical sanation, 1165, §1; establishes new sacramentals, authentically interprets those already received, abolishes or changes them, 1167, §1; gives permission for the valid alienation or permanent transfer of relics, 1190, §2; delegates the power to dispense from private vows, 1196, 3°; can dispense an oath, 1203; approves the conference of bishops suppressing some holydays or transferring them to a Sunday, 1246, §2

and the temporal goods of the Church: all temporal goods belonging to the Apostolic See are ecclesiastical goods, 1257, §1, 1258; approves the fees set by the provincial bishops for execution of rescripts of the, 1264, 1°; prescription of one hundred years for immoveable property, precious moveable objects, and personal or real rights and actions belonging to the, 1270; from diocesan resources, bishops procure the means needed by the, 1271; and benefices, 1272; and reduction of Mass obligations, 1308, §1, 1310, §3

and sanctions: remission of a penalty reserved to the, 1354, §3, 1355, 1356, §1, 1357, §3; delicts with penalties reserved to the, 1367, 1370, §1, 1378, §1, 1382, 1388, §1; delict of not retracting from teaching a condemned doctrine after being admonished by the, 1371, 1°; delict of not obeying a precept or prohibition of the, 1371, 2°; delict of inciting animosities or hatred against the, 1373

and processes: norms of the tribunals of the, 1402; Roman Pontiff judges legates of the, 1405, §1, 3°; power of a judge who has begun to adjudicate is not suspended by recourse to the, 1417, §2; gives approval for several diocesan bishops to establish a single tribunal of first instance and of second instance, 1423, §1, 1439, §§1–2; approves the tribunal designated by the metropolitan as his appellate tribunal, 1438, 2°; competence for marriage nullity cases not reserved to the, 1673; and the dispensation *super rato,* 1681, 1698, §1, 1699, §§2–3, 1705–1706; is consulted by a bishop in uncertain and complicated cases of presumed death of a spouse, 1707, §3

Apostolic Signatura governed by special norms, 1402; competency, 1416, 1445; no appeal from a sentence of the, 1629, 1°

apostolic vicar notion, 371, §1; equivalent in law to a diocesan bishop, 381, §2; a local ordinary, 134, §2; can make *ad limina* visit through a proxy, 400, §3; must appoint an apostolic pro-vicar after taking possession of the vicariate, 420; to establish a council of at least three missionary presbyters, 495, §2, which has the functions of the college of consultors, 502, §4; can issue dimissorial letters for secular clergy, 1018

apostolic vicariate notion, 368, 371, §1; likened to a diocese, 368

appeal no appeal or recourse is permitted against a sentence or decree of the Roman Pontiff, 333, §3, 1629, 1°; against privation of or removal from office, 143, §2

in processes: norms, 1628–1640; to the Apostolic See, 1417, §2; to the metropolitan tribunal from the tribunal of a suffragan bishop, 1438, 1°; from the metropolitan to a tribunal designated in a stable manner, 1438, 2°; Roman Rota is ordinary tribunal established by the Roman Pontiff to receive, 1443, 1444, §1, 1°; and exceptions proposed against the competence of a judge, 1460, §§2–3; copy of authenticated acts is to be sent to the higher tribunal on, 1474; the procurator has the right and duty to, 1486, §2; a dissenting judge can demand that his or her conclusions be transmitted to the higher court on, 1609, §4; a complaint of nullity can be proposed together with, 1625, 1626, §2; and a *res iudicata,* 1641, 2°–4°; from determination of expenses, fees, and recovery of damages, 1649, §2; and provisional execution of a sentence, 1650, §2; in the oral contentious process, 1669; in marriage nullity cases, 1682–1684; in documentary marriage nullity cases, 1687–1688; in cases of separation of spouses, 1693, §2; in the penal process, 1353, 1727, 1729, §3

appellate tribunal resolves conflicts of competence between tribunals subject to it, 1416; judges in first instance a case concerning rights or temporal goods of a juridic person represented by the bishop, 1419, §2; receives an appeal by a party who feels injured by a judge's finding for incompetence, 1460, §3; receives recourse against the rejection of a *libellus,* 1505, §4; deals with a question about the right to appeal, 1631; appeal being made to a different, 1632, §2; its defender of the bond or promoter of justice can renounce an appeal made by the defender of the bond or promoter of justice of the lower tribunal, 1636, §2; and appeal after a second concordant sentence in a case concerning the status of persons, 1644; and *restitutio in integrum,* 1646, §2; and execution of a sentence which is not being executed by the bishop of the diocese of first grade, 1653, §2; and the oral contentious process used at a lower grade, 1669; and marriage nullity cases, 1682–1684

appointment of guardians for minors, 98, §2; of legates of the Roman Pontiff, 362; of bishops by the Supreme Pontiff, 377, 403, §3; of those who exercise offices in the diocesan curia by the diocesan bishop, 470; of vicars general and episcopal vicars by the diocesan bishop, 475–476, 477, §1; of

archive *of an administration:* and the inventory of goods made before an administrator begins to function, 1283, 3°; and the documents and records on which property rights are based, 1284, §2, 9°

of churches (cathedral, collegial, parochial, and other): diocesan bishop is to take care that acts and documents are diligently preserved in, 491, §1; inspection or removal of documents in the, 491, §3; and a document attesting to its dedication or blessing, 1208

of a college or group electing: and the acts of the election, 173, §4

of the diocesan curia: notion, 486, §2; inventory or catalogue of documents in the, 486, §3; to be locked with limited access, 487, §1; copies of documents in the, 487, §2; removal of documents from the, 488; and the confirmation register, 895; and the ordination register, 1053; and a document attesting to the dedication or blessing of a church, or the blessing of a cemetery, 1208; and the inventory of goods made before an administrator begins to function, 1283, 3°; and the documents and records on which property rights are based, 1284, §2, 9°; and the charter of a foundation, 1306, §2

of the diocesan curia (secret): notion, 489, §1; and preservation of documents of criminal cases in matters of morals, 489, §2; to be locked with very limited access, 490, §§1–2; documents are not to be removed from the, 490, §3; and the book noting a dispensation from an occult marriage impediment in the non-sacramental internal forum, 1082; and the special register for marriages celebrated secretly, 1133; and a document of warning or rebuke, 1339, §3; and the preliminary investigation for the penal process, 1719

of the diocese (historical): diocesan bishop is to take care that it exists and its documents are diligently protected and systematically ordered, 491, §2; inspection or removal of documents in the, 491, §3

of a juridic person: and the charter of a foundation belonging to it, 1306, §2

of a parish: notion, 535, §4; and the confirmation register, 895

as promptly as possible (*expeditissime*) the question of an objection must be decided, 1451, §1; the question of a rejected *libellus* must be decided, 1505, §4; the judge must resolve the question of the joinder of the issue, 1513, §3; the judge is to decide on accepting a proof previously rejected, 1527, §2; the judge is to decide on a proposed incidental case, 1589, §1; there is no appeal from a sentence or decree in a case where the law requires the matter to be decided, 1629, 5°; the appellate tribunal deals with a question about the right to appeal, 1631

Ascension holyday of obligation, 1246, §1

Ash Wednesday day of abstinence and fasting, 1251

assessor(s) a single judge can employ two, 1424; assists single clerical judge where possible, 1425, §4; if one was earlier a judge, promoter of justice, defender of the bond, procurator, advocate, witness, or expert, that person cannot later be judge or assessor in the same case, 1447; must abstain from office in certain circumstances, 1448, §2; if the ordinary believes a penal process must proceed by extrajudicial decree, he is to weigh the proofs and arguments with two, 1720, 2°

associations of the Christian faithful common norms, 298–311; public associations, 312–320; private associations, 321–326; special norms for lay associations, 327–329; Christian faithful have the right to found and direct associations for charity and piety or the promotion of the Christian vocation in the world, 215; must take into account the good of the Church, rights of others, and duties toward others, 223, §1; lay persons joined in associations have the obligation and right to bring the divine message of salvation everywhere, 225, §1; clerics in, 278, §3; the pastor is to foster associations for the purpose of religion, 529, §2; joined to religious institutes, 677, §2; delict of joining, promoting, or moderating an association which plots against the Church, 1374

Assumption holyday of obligation, 1246, §1

auditor(s) notion, 1428; assist a single clerical judge where possible, 1425, §4; must abstain from office in certain circumstances, 1448, §2; examine witnesses, 1561; and resolution of incidental cases by decree, 1590, §2; the person who conducts the preliminary penal investigation has the same powers and obligations as, 1717, §3

of the Roman Rota: Apostolic Signatura adjudicates exceptions of suspicion and other cases against, 1445, §1, 3°

autonomous foundation notion, 115, §3

autonomous houses moderator is a major superior by law, 613, §2, 620; suppression of, 616, §3; term of superiors of, 624, §1

autonomous monasteries when to be entrusted to the special vigilance of the diocesan bishop, 615; suppression of an autonomous monastery of nuns, 616, §4; bishop presides at elections of superior, 625, §2; diocesan bishop has the right and duty to visit even with respect to religious discipline, 628, §2, 1°; must render an annual account of administration to the local ordinary, 637; the local ordinary must give written consent for some alienations, 638, §4; transfer to another of the same institute or federation or confederation, 684, §3; departure of members of, 688, §2; readmission of members of, 690, §2; dismissal of members from, 699, §2; in controversies local abbot judges in first instance, 1427, §1

autonomous pious foundations notion, 1303, §1, 1°

autonomy of private associations, 323; of an aggregated institute of consecrated life, 580; of individual institutes of consecrated life, 586, 708, 806, §1; academic autonomy is to be preserved in universities and faculties in light of Catholic doctrine, 809

aversion to a pastor which it appears will not cease in a brief time as cause for removal of a pastor, 1741, 3°

B

baptism notion, 849; in the Catholic Church makes one a subject of merely ecclesiastical laws, 11; incorporates one into the Church, 96, 204, §1; enrolls one in a ritual Church *sui iuris*, 111–112; baptized persons in the full communion of the Catholic Church, 205; calls one to lead a life in keeping with the gospel, 217, 759; designates lay persons for the apostolate, 225, §1; required for admission to the major seminary, 241, §2; required for admission to novitiate, 645, §1; and missionaries, 787, §2; and neophytes, 789; doorway to the sacraments, 842, §1, 889, 912, 1024, 1050, 3°, 1055; a sacrament of Christian initiation, 842, §2; imprints a character so cannot be repeated, 845, §1; conditional conferral, 845, §2, 869; to be administered according to approved liturgical books, 850, 853; of adults, 851, 1°, 852, §1, 883, 2°; of infants, 851, 2°, 852, §2; conferred by immersion or pouring, 854; a name foreign to Christian sensibility is not to be given at, 855; time of celebration, 856; place of, 857, 859–860; baptismal font, 858, 530, 6°; minister of, 861–863, 230, §3, 530, 1°; those to be baptized, 864–871; sponsors, 872–874, 851, 2°, 855; baptized non-Catholic witness, 874, §2; proof and registration of, 875–878, 535, §1, 1068; contents of baptismal register, 535, §2, 877, 895, 1054, 1122–1123, 1685, 1706; required to gain indulgences, 996, §1; marriage is a sacrament between the baptized, 1055–1056, 1061, §1,

1141–1142; power of the supreme authority to establish impediments for the baptized, 1075, §2; and impediment of disparity of cult, 1086; baptismal status of the partners and the place of Catholic marriages, 1118; and mixed marriages, 1124; of children born to a mixed marriage, 1125, 1°; dissolution of marriages of the unbaptized, 1143–1150; ecclesiastical funerals for unbaptized children, 1183, §2; ecclesiastical funerals for baptized non-Catholics, 1183, §3; delict of handing over children to baptism in a non-Catholic religion, 1366

baptismal certificate contents, 535, §2

baptismal font every parish church is to have a, 858, §1; in non-parochial churches and oratories, 858, §2; blessing of the baptismal font at Easter is a function especially entrusted to a pastor, 530, 6°

baptismal register each parish is to have its own, 535 §1; entries in the, 535, §2, 877, 895, 1054, 1122–1123, 1685, 1706

bargain a procurator needs a special mandate to make a, 1485

benediction, eucharistic minister is a priest or deacon, 943

benefices income and endowment to be gradually transferred to a special institute for the support of clerics, 1272

bishop of the Roman Church Roman Pontiff as, 331

bishop(s) govern the Church, 204, §2, 375, §1; successors of the Apostles, 330, 375, §1; communion with the Roman Pontiff, 204, §2, 333, §§1–2; assist the Roman Pontiff in exercising his office, 334; college of, 336; and ecumenical council, 337–341; synod of, 342–348; cardinals must be, 351, §1; *diocesan* or *titular*, 376; appointment of, 377; no future rights of appointment granted to civil authorities, 377, §5; suitability of a candidate for episcopacy, 378; episcopal consecration, 379, 1013–1014; must make profession of faith and take oath of fidelity to the Apostolic See before taking canonical possession, 380, 833, 3°; and particular councils, 443, §§1–2; conferences of, 447–459; religious, 705–707; private chapel with Eucharist reserved, 1227–1228, 934, §1, 2°; and remission of penalties in sacramental confession, 1355, §2; delict of violent force against, 1370, §2; delict of ordination of a bishop without pontifical mandate, 1382; judged by Roman Pontiff in penal cases, 1405, §1, 3°; judged by Roman Rota in contentious cases, 1405, §3, 1°; to be heard as a witness in a place he selects, 1558, §2

functions: teaching, 375, 753, 756, §2, 763; sanctify-

ordinary, 1277; can entrust special functions to the diocesan finance officer, 1278; determines acts which exceed ordinary administration for juridic persons subject to him, 1281, §2; alienation of goods whose value is between the minimum and maximum amounts, 1292, §1; and reduction of Mass obligations, 1308, §§3–4

sanctifying function: 387, 835, §1, 838, §§1, 4; issues norms on administration of penance, Eucharist, and anointing of the sick to non-Catholics, 844, §§4–5; can permit baptisms in hospitals, 860, §2; baptizes those who are fourteen and older, 863; can establish age for baptismal sponsors, 874, §1, 2°; and confirmation, 884, 885, §1, 886; presides at the Eucharist, 899, §2, 389; issues prescripts on carrying the Eucharist, 935; issues prescripts on eucharistic exposition, 943; makes judgments and regulations on eucharistic processions, 944; judges if conditions are present for general absolution, 961, §2; can deny other bishops the faculty to hear confessions licitly, 967, §1; issues prescripts on communal anointing of the sick, 1002; and ordination of presbyters and deacons, 1015–1016, 1028–1030, 1032, §2, 1051, 2°, 1052, §§1, 3; gives dimissorial letters, 1015, §1, 1018, §1, 1°; gives permission for another bishop to confer orders, 1017; judges if a transitional deacon is prohibited from exercising that order, 1038; and delegation of lay persons to assist at marriage, 1112, §1; and the marriage register, 1121, §1; and radical sanations, 1165, §2; and dedication of a sacred place, 1206; and blessing of churches, 1207; and permission to build a church, 1215; and relegation of a church to profane but not sordid use, 1222; decrees special feast days or days of penance, 1244, §2; issues prescripts on dispensation or commutation of sacred times, 1245; issues prescripts for the liturgy of the word when eucharistic celebration is impossible, 1248, §2

teaching function: preaches and oversees the ministry of the word, 386, 756, §2, 757–759; right to preach everywhere, 763; proclaiming the word to those in special circumstances, 771; issues norms on preaching, 772, §1; issues norms on catechesis, 775, §1, 777; and the missions, 790–791; and Catholic schools, 801–802, 804, §1 806, §1; and Catholic universities, ecclesiastical universities and faculties, 810, §2, 813, 818–819, 821

persons equivalent to: 381, §2

bishop(s), titular notion, 376; and particular councils, 443, §1, 3°, §2; and the conference of bishops, 450, 454, §2

blasphemy delict of uttering blasphemy in instruments of social communication, 1369

blessed list of the, 1187

blessing apostolic blessing is function especially entrusted to pastor, 530, 3°; nuptial blessing is function especially entrusted to pastor, 530, 4°; of baptismal font is function especially entrusted to pastor, 530, 6°; of holy oils, 847, §1, 999; of baptismal water, 853; imparted by a presbyter or deacon, 1169, §§2–3; given to catechumens and non-Catholics, 1170; of sacred objects, 1171; of sacred places, 1205, 1207; of a church, 1207–1208, 1217, §1, 1219; documents attesting to, 1208; proof by a witness, 1209; loss of blessing of sacred places, 1212; of oratories and private chapels, 1229; of altars, 1237, §1, 1238; of cemeteries and graves, 1240

blind celebration of Mass by a blind priest, 930, §2

body not to be buried beneath an altar, 1239, §2

Body and Blood of Christ diocesan bishop not to be absent on, 395, §3; public procession on, 944, §1; holyday of obligation, 1246, §1

bond of marriage impediment of, 1085, §1; a perpetual and exclusive bond arises from a valid marriage, 1134; dissolution of the, 1141–1150, 1697–1706; separation of spouses with bond remaining, 1151–1155

book(s) permission or approval of the local ordinary to publish, 824, §1, 829; of sacred scripture, 825; liturgical or prayer, 826, 838, §2–3; catechisms and books of catechetical instruction, 827, §1; on sacred scripture, theology, canon law, ecclesiastical history, and religious or moral disciplines, 827, §§2–4; reprinting collections of decrees or acts, 828; censors of, 830; writings which openly attack the Catholic religion or good morals, 831, §1; permission of religious to publish writings on religion or morals, 832

liturgical: Apostolic See publishes and reviews their translations, 838, §2; conference of bishops prepares and publishes translations of, 838, §3; to be observed in the celebration of the sacraments, 846, §1, 850, 853, 880, §1, 998, 1000, §1, 1009, §2, 1119; liturgy of the hours is to be carried out according to the proper and approved, 276, §2, 3°; to be observed in confecting or administering sacramentals, 1167, §2, 1168; to be observed in dedicating or blessing sacred places, 1205, 1211, 1229, 1237

for Mass offerings: those who entrust Masses to others are to maintain a book recording the Masses they received and transferred, and their offerings, 955, §3; a pastor or rector recording number of Masses to be celebrated, the intention, the offering, and their celebration, 958, §1; the ordinary examines annually, 958, §2

requiring priestly order cannot be conferred on one not yet a priest, 150; provision of an office entailing care of souls is not to be deferred, 151; a presbyter selected by all who have care of souls in each vicariate forane for the diocesan synod, 463, §1, 8°; religious are subject to the power of bishops in those matters which regard the, 678, §1; members of societies of apostolic life are subject to the diocesan bishop in those matters which regard the, 738, §2; pastors and those to whom the care of souls is entrusted are to proclaim the word of God, 757; pastors of souls proclaim the gospel to non-believers to whom the care of souls is also extended, 771, §2; Viaticum and those who have the, 922; provision for confessions by all to whom is entrusted the, 986, §1; anointing of the sick by all priests to whom is entrusted the, 1003, §2

catechetical instruction duty of pastors of souls, 773; all are to have solicitude for, 774, §1, 776; role of parents in, 774, §2; role of diocesan bishop, 775, §1, 386, §1; conference of bishops to issue a catechism, 775, §2; catechetical office to be established by conference of bishops, 775, §3; pastor and, 777, 528, §1; religious superiors and superiors of societies of apostolic life and, 778; means to impart, 779; catechists and, 780; publication of works on, 827, §1; and preparation to receive the sacraments, 843, §2; and preparation for marriage, 1063, 1°

catechetical office can be established by conference of bishops to assist dioceses in catechetical matters, 775, §3

catechetical skills formation of seminarians in, 256, §1

catechism prepared by the diocesan bishop, 775, §1; issued by the conference of bishops, 775, §2; requires approval of the local ordinary to be published, 827, §1

catechists notion, 785, §1; pastor is to use the help of catechists in catechetical formation, 776; local ordinaries are to take care that catechists are duly prepared, 780; formation of, 785, §2; and conferral of baptism, 861, §2

catechumenate admission to the, 788, §1, 851, 1°; book listing catechumens, 788, §1; formation of, 788, §2; statutes regulating the, 788, §3; tests one for Christian life in preparation for baptism, 865, §1

catechumen(s) notion, 206; formation of, 788, §2; blessings can be given to, 1170; funerals of, 1183, §1

Catholic (name) the name *Catholic* claimed by apostolic actions of the Christian faithful, 216; the name *Catholic* given to an apostolic undertaking

needs consent of competent authority, 300; the name *Catholic school* needs consent of competent authority, 803, §3; the name *Catholic university* needs consent of competent authority, 808

Catholic Church those baptized in the Catholic Church are bound by ecclesiastical laws, 11; has the status of a moral person by divine ordinance, 113, §1; the Church subsists in the, 204, §2; those fully in the communion of the, 205; the pontifical legate collaborates with bishops to foster relations between the Catholic Church and other Churches or ecclesial communities, 364, 6°; exists in and from the particular churches, 368; members of the diocesan pastoral council are to be in full communion with the, 512, §1; by innate right is able to acquire, retain, administer, and alienate temporal goods independently from civil power, 1254, §1

Catholic ministers administering sacraments to Catholics, 844, §1; unavailable to administer sacraments to Catholics, 844, §2; administering the sacraments of penance, Eucharist, and anointing of the sick to non-Catholics, 844, §§3–4

celibacy formation of permanent deacons who are married or celibate, 236, 2°; preparation of seminarians to observe, 247, §1; obligation of clerics, 277, §1; loss of clerical state does not entail a dispensation from, 291; evangelical counsel of chastity entails obligation of perfect continence in, 599; obligation to be assumed before ordination, 1037

cemetery choice of a, 1180; document attesting to the blessing of a, 1208; the Church is to have its own, or at least an area in civil cemeteries, 1240, §1; of a parish or religious institute, 1241, §1; of other juridic persons or families, 1241, §2; particular law about the discipline to be observed in, 1243

censor(s) list compiled by conference of bishops, 830, §1; right of local ordinary to entrust books to his own, 830, §1; function of, 830, §§2–3

censure(s) notion, 1312, §1, 1°, 1331–1335; a legislator is not to establish censures, especially excommunication, except with the greatest moderation and only for the graver delicts, 1318; excommunication, 1331; interdict, 1332; suspension, 1333–1334; suspension of the prohibition to celebrate sacraments or sacramentals and, 1335, 1338, §3; warning prior to imposing a, 1347, §1; unless the seriousness of the case clearly demands it, a judge is not to impose a, 1349; remission of, 1354–1361; prescription and, 1362–1363; marriage of a person under a, 1071, §1, 5°

ward spouses who depart, 1148, §3; moves a spouse to forgive an adulterous partner, 1152, §1; bishops assist the Apostolic See by reason of unity and, 1271; administrators are permitted to make donations for, 1285; as a just cause for alienation of goods, 1293, §1, 1°

chastity evangelical counsel of, 573, §2, 598, §1, 599; dangers to, 666; vow of chastity and the irregularity to receive orders, 1041, 3°; marriage impediment of vow of, 1078, §2, 1°, 1088

children place of origin of, 101; adopted, 110; ritual Church *sui iuris* of, 112, §1, 3°; education of, 226, §2, 528, §1, 795, 835, §4, 1136; catechetical instruction of, 774, §2, 776, 777, 2°–3°; baptism of, 877, §§2–3; participation in the Eucharist, 913; permission of the local ordinary to marry one with obligations toward children, 1071, §1, 3°; permission of the local ordinary for a minor child to marry if parents are unaware or reasonably opposed, 1071, §1, 6°; born of a mixed marriage, 1128; legitimate, 1137, 1138, §2; illegitimate, 1139; legitimated, 1139–1140; whose parents have separated, 1154; ecclesiastical funerals of unbaptized, 1183, §2; delict of handing over children to be baptized or educated in a non-Catholic religion, 1366; parties to be reminded of obligations toward children in the sentence, 1689

chrism and sacrament of confirmation, 880, §1; to be consecrated by a bishop, 880, §2

Christian initiation sacraments of, 842, §2, 866

Christian faithful notion, 204, §1; among them are clerics and lay persons, and from both groups some are consecrated, 207; obligations and rights of all the, 208–223; obligations and rights of the lay, 224–231; rules of order for meetings convoked by, 95, §1; power of governance and the lay, 129, §2; and prescription, 199, 3°, 7°; associations of, 215, 223, 225, §1, 298–329; bishop and, 383, §1, 387; and particular councils, 443, §4; and conference of bishops, 447; and diocesan synod, 460, 463, §1, 5°, §2; and diocesan finance council, 492, §1; and diocesan pastoral council, 512; and the parish, 515, §1, 518–519, 524; and the quasi-parish, 516, §1; pastor and the, 528–529; offering given by the Christian faithful when a certain parochial function is performed, 531; baptismal register to contain what pertains to canonical status of, 535, §2; pastor to sign and seal documents concerning the canonical status of, 535, §3; and parish pastoral council, 536, §1; and parish finance council, 537; local ordinary can order a rector to make the church available for certain groups of the, 560; to a chaplain is entrusted a community or group of

the, 564; and consecrated life, 573, §2, 574, §2, 603, §1; and members of secular institutes, 710, 725; and the teaching function of the Church, 752–754; lay Christian faithful witness the gospel message by word and example, 759; those who proclaim the word of God must propose to the Christian faithful what to believe and do for the glory of God and human salvation, 768, §1; lay Christian faithful assist in catechetical formation, 776; and missionary action of the Church, 781, 784, 785, §1; and Catholic education, 796, §1, 797, 799, 800, §2; role in social communication, 822, §3, 823; and collaboration with non-Catholics in scripture translations, 825, §2; writings of the, 831, §1; and the sanctifying function of the Church, 835, §4, 836, 837, §2; and the sacraments in general, 840, 843, §2, 844, §§1–2; to hold the Eucharist in the highest honor, 898; as extraordinary ministers of holy communion, 910, §2; and participation in the eucharistic sacrifice in any Catholic rite, 923; even without an offering it is recommended that priests celebrate Mass for the, 945, §2; who give an offering to apply a Mass, 946; and sacrament of penance, 962, 986, §2, 987–988, 991; to be invited to ordinations so the assembly is as large as possible, 1011, §2; to reveal impediments to sacred orders, 1043; and marriage preparation, 1063; and liturgy of the hours, 1174, §2; and veneration of the saints, 1186; and days of penance, 1249; and the acquisition of goods, 1260, 1621, §1; local ordinary can order special collections in churches and oratories habitually open to the, 1266; to avoid litigation, 1446, §1

Christmas diocesan bishop not to be absent on, 395, §3; priests keeping Mass offerings on, 951, §1; holyday of obligation, 1246, §1

Church *Latin:* the canons of this Code regard only the, 1; baptism into the, 111; and enrollment into or from another ritual Church *sui iuris*, 112; the titles of patriarch and primate entail no power of governance in the, 438; unleavened bread is used in the Eucharist in the, 926

particular: notion, 368; a bishop or equivalent figure is placed over, 134, §1; diocesan bishop provides offices in the, 157; the Christian faithful are to fulfill their duties toward their, 209, §2; seminarians to have solicitude for their, 257, §1; seminarians moving to another, 257, §2; incardination and excardination of clerics and the, 265–272; relation of a personal prelature to a, 297; Roman Pontiff has primacy of ordinary power over every, 333, §1; legates of the Roman Pontiff to, 362, 363, §1, 364; as a rule is limited to territory but can be distinguished by rite or some other reason, 372; erected by the supreme authority of the Church and has juridic personality, 373; divided into parishes, 374, §1, 515–516; diocésan bishop has ordinary, proper, and immediate power in, 381, §1; diocesan bishop governs with legislative, executive, and judicial power in, 391, §1; neighboring particular churches are brought together into ecclesiastical provinces, 431; if particular churches are more numerous, neighboring ecclesiastical provinces can be brought together into ecclesiastical regions, 433; and provincial councils, 440, §1, 443, §3, 1°, §5; and conferences of bishops, 448; celebration of a synod in a, 460, 461, §1; property acquired for the particular church by a religious bishop, 706, 1°; diocesan bishop is moderator of the entire ministry of the word in, 756, §2; diocesan bishop promotes missionary endeavor in his, 782, §2; diocesan bishop and liturgy in the, 835, §1, 838, §4; is capable of acquiring, retaining, administering, and alienating temporal goods, 1255

ritual: by baptism one is enrolled in a, 111; change of enrollment, 112, 535, §2; Christian faithful have the right to worship God according to their own, 214; can be erected in the same territory, 372, §2; diocesan bishop is to care for those of another through priests or an episcopal vicar, 383, §2, 476, 479, §2, 518; ordinaries of another rite in the conference of bishops, 450, §1; a minister celebrates sacraments according to the minister's own, 846, §2; Christian faithful can participate in the eucharistic sacrifice and receive communion in any Catholic, 923; one may confess to a priest of another, 991; a bishop needs apostolic indult to ordain licitly a subject of an Eastern, 1015, §2, 1021; assistance at marriage of persons of another, 1109; one satisfies the obligation of participating in Mass by assisting at a Mass celebrated anywhere in a Catholic, 1248, §1

Roman: Roman Pontiff is bishop of the, 331; cardinals of the, 349–359; pallium signifies power of metropolitan in his province in communion with the, 437, §1

suburbicarian: title assigned by Roman Pontiff to cardinals, 350, §1; those who hold title to a suburbicarian church recommend one from their group to be dean, 352, §2; cardinals have no power of governance in their, 357, §1

universal: Roman Pontiff and the, 331, 333, §1–2, 756, §1; when the Roman See is vacant or completely impeded, nothing is to be altered in the governance of the, 335; college of bishops and the, 336, 337, §§1, 3, 749, §2, 756, §1; synod of bishops

and the, 345; cardinals assist the Roman Pontiff in daily care of the, 349; and the Roman curia, 360; diocesan bishops protect the unity of the, 392, §1; Apostolic See orders the liturgy of the, 838, §2; feast days and days of penance common to the, 1244, §1, 1246, §1, 1250; is a subject capable of acquiring, retaining, administering, and alienating temporal goods, 1255; and ecclesiastical goods, 1257, §1; diocesan bishops assist the Apostolic See so it can offer service properly to the, 1271

church(es)   *building:* notion, 1214; pontifical legate can perform liturgical celebrations in all churches in his legation, 366, 2°; diocesan bishop frequently presides at eucharistic celebrations in, 389; metropolitans and, 436, §3, 437, §2; archive of the, 491, §1; rector of a, 556–563; of religious, 611, 3°, 683, §1, 763, 765, 936; lay persons can preach in a, 766; exhibition, sale, or distribution of books in, 827, §4; proper place for baptism, 857, 858, §1, 859; celebration of confirmation in a, 881; Eucharist reserved in, 934, §1; proper place to hear confessions, 964, §1; ordination to be celebrated in a, 1011, §1; marriage to be celebrated in a, 1118, §1; building and repair, 1215–1216; dedication or blessing of, 1217, 1219; unchangeable title of, 1218; care for, 1220, 555, §1, 3°; free and gratuitous entry during sacred celebrations, 1221; relegation to profane but not sordid use, 1222; burial of bodies in, 1242

cathedral: diocesan bishop takes canonical possession of the diocese in the, 382, §§3–4; diocesan bishop to preside frequently at the eucharistic celebration in, 389; metropolitan is to inform the diocesan bishop before performing pontificals in that bishop's, 436, §3; canons of the cathedral church take part in the diocesan synod, 463, §1, 3°; archive of the, 491, §1; chapter of canons in the, 503; canon penitentiary of the, 508, §1; conferral of canonries in the, 509, §1; Eucharist to be reserved in the, 934, §1, 1°; ordination generally is to be celebrated in the, 1011, §1; funeral of a diocesan bishop is to be in his own, 1178; to be dedicated by the solemn rite, 1217, §2

collegial: chapter of canons in the, 503; canon penitentiary of the, 508, §1; conferral of canonries in the, 509, §1

parish: archive of the, 491, §1; which at the same time is capitular, 510; pastor is to live in a rectory near the, 533, §1; as place of baptism for adults and infants, 857, §2, 859; to have a baptismal font, 858, §1; Eucharist to be reserved in the, 934, §1, 1°; marriage to be celebrated in, 1118, §1; generally one's funeral to be celebrated in, 1177, §1; to be dedicated by the solemn rite, 1217, §2

church-state relations   and the pontifical legate, 365

Churches (non-Catholic) pontifical legate is to collaborate with bishops to foster relations with other Churches or ecclesial communities, 364, 6°; diocesan bishop can invite as observers to the diocesan synod either ministers or members of Churches or ecclesial communities not in full communion, 463, §3; Catholic priests are forbidden to concelebrate the Eucharist with priests or ministers of Churches or ecclesial communities not in full communion, 908; the local ordinary may permit a priest to celebrate the Eucharist in the worship place of a Church or ecclesial community not in full communion, 933; without express permission of competent authority, marriage of a Catholic is forbidden with a baptized person of a Church or ecclesiastical community not in full communion, 1124; ecclesiastical funerals can be granted to baptized persons enrolled in a non-Catholic Church or ecclesial community, 1183, §3

citation and the ordinary contentious trial, 1507–1512; begins the trial, 1517; of witnesses, 1556–1557; incidental cases after the trial has begun through the, 1587; parties who do not appear after the, 1592, 1594, 1°–2°; and the oral contentious process, 1659, §2, 1661; in marriage nullity cases, 1677, §1, 1686

civil *authority:* and appointment of bishops, 377, §5; and the merely civil effects of marriage, 1059; and separation of spouses, 1152, §2; application of penalties by the Church and punishment by, 1344, 2°; guardian or curator appointed by, 1479

cemeteries: 1240, §1

documents: 1540, §2

effects of marriage: 1059, 1672, 1692, §§2–3

forum: administrators initiating or contesting litigation in the, 1288; and right to challenge marriage, 1675, §1; and separation of spouses, 1692, §§2–3

laws: to which the Church yields are to be observed, 22; on minors, 98, §2, 105, §1; on adoption, 110; on prescription, 197; on remuneration of lay persons, 231, §2; expertise of diocesan finance council members in, 492, §1; and wills of religious, 668, §1; and renunciation of goods by religious, 668, §4; on formation of youth, 799; on engagements, 1062, §1; not recognizing or permitting celebration of certain marriages, 1071, §1, 2°; and the mandate of a proxy for marriage, 1105, §2; and diocesan institutes for clergy, church workers, and diocesan needs, 1274, §5; to be observed in administration of goods, 1284, §2, 2°–3°; on labor and social policy, 1286, 1°; on contracts,

1290; on dispositions *mortis causa*, 1299, §2; on possessions, 1500; in agreements, compromises, and arbitrated judgments, 1714, 1716

magistrate: 1672

obligations in marriage: 1689

officials: Roman Pontiff judges cases of highest civil, 1405, §1, 1°; exempt as witnesses, 1548, §2, 1°

power: clerics are forbidden to assume public offices which entail exercise of, 285, §3; Catholic Church has innate right to acquire, retain, administer, and alienate temporal goods independently from, 1254, §1

sentence of separation of spouses: 1692, §2

society and Catholic education: 793, §2, 797, 799

clause clause prohibiting future customs contained in a canonical law, 26; derogating clause in an administrative act, 38; contrary clauses in a rescript, 61; the clause *ad beneplacitum nostrum* in a privilege, 81; attached clauses and cessation of delegated power, 142, §1; nullifying clause added to a marriage prohibition, 1077, §2

clerics notion, 207, §1; formation of, 232–264; enrollment, or incardination, of, 265–272; obligations and rights of, 273–289; loss of the clerical state, 290–293, 194, §1, 1°, 3°; and associations of the Christian faithful, 298, §1, 302; as companions of diocesan bishop during visitation, 396, §2; as members of diocesan synod, 463, §2; and chapters of canons, 507, §2; as members of diocesan pastoral council, 512, §1; vicars forane and, 555, §1, 2°, §2, 1°; rector of the church of a seminary or college governed by, 557, §3; clerical institute of consecrated life, 588, §2; admission of clerics to novitiate, 645, §2; religious who are, 663, §3, 669, §2, 672, 686, §1, 687, 701; members of secular institutes who are, 713, §3, 715, §1; members of societies of apostolic life who are, 736, §1, 739; assist the pastor in catechetical formation, 776; sent to ecclesiastical universities or faculties, 819; and instruments of social communication, 831; and eucharistic celebration, 899, §2, 956; to be invited to ordinations, 1011, §2; and impediment to receive orders, 1042, 2°; as minister of sacramentals, 1168; and the liturgy of the hours, 1174, §1; support of, 1274, §§1–2; as administrators of goods, 1282, 1287, §1; suspension affects only, 1333; penalties imposed on, 1337, 1350, §1; delict concerning, 1364, §1, 1367, 1370, 1390, §1, 1392, 1394–1395; as judges, 1421, §1; as assessors, 1424; as single judge, 1425, §4; as auditor, 1428, §2; as promoter of justice or defender of the bond, 1435; exempted as witnesses, 1548, §2, 1°; and cases for declaring the nullity of sacred ordination, 1708–1712

512, §1; celebration of sacraments of penance, Eucharist, and anointing of the sick with persons who are not in, 844, §§3–4; faculty of a presbyter to confirm a person being admitted into the, 883, 2°; Catholic priests are forbidden to concelebrate the Eucharist with priests or ministers of Churches or ecclesial communities which do not have, 908; the local ordinary can permit a priest to celebrate the Eucharist in worship place of some Church or ecclesial community which does not have, 933; mixed marriage is between a Catholic and a baptized person who is not in, 1124

hierarchical: and the college of bishops, 336; episcopal powers can be exercised only in, 375, §2

of the Church: to be promoted to an ecclesiastical office one must be in the, 149, §1; one is unqualified to vote who has defected notoriously from the, 171, §1, 4°; one is removed from an ecclesiastical office by the law itself who has publicly defected from the, 194, §1, 2°; the baptized who are joined by the bonds of profession of faith, the sacraments, and ecclesiastical governance are fully in the, 205; religious institutes carry out their apostolic action in the, 675, §3

with the Apostolic See: supreme moderator's report on institutes of consecrated life fosters, 592, §1; dimissorial letters can be sent to any bishop in, 1021

with the Church: the Christian faithful are always obliged to maintain, 209, §1

with the head of the college: bishops in hierarchical, 336; episcopal powers to be exercised in hierarchical, 375, §2; teaching authority of bishops in communion with the head and members of the college, 753

with the Roman Church: pallium signifies power which the metropolitan, in communion with the Roman Church, has in his province, 437, §1

commutation   of vows, 1194, 1197; of oaths, 1202, 4°, 1203; of the obligation to observe a feast day or day of penance, 1245; of the wills of the faithful for pious causes, 1310, §1

competence   of those who possess executive power to issue general executory decrees, 31, §1; of those who possess executive power to issue instructions, 34, §1; of those who possess executive power to issue a singular administrative act, 35; of those who possess executive power to grant dispensations, 85; to represent a juridic person and act in its name, 118; the Christian faithful have the right and even at times the duty to manifest their opinion according to their, 212, §3; of the Roman

Curia is defined in special law, 360; of the diocesan bishop in cases not assigned to the conference of bishops, 455, §4; of the vicar general and episcopal vicar in what pertains to habitual faculties and the execution of rescripts, 479, §3; of the diocesan bishop and liturgical norms, 838, §4; to grant dimissorial letters, 1019, §1; of civil authority over the merely civil effects of marriage, 1059; of one with legislative power to strengthen a divine law or an ecclesiastical law issued by a higher authority with an appropriate penalty, 1315, §1

in processes: of the Roman Pontiff, 1405, §§1–2; of the Roman Rota, 1405, §3, 1444; of a tribunal of domicile or quasi-domicile, 1408; of the tribunal of a transient, 1409, §1; of the tribunal of the petitioner, 1409, §2; of the tribunal of the place of an object, 1410; of the tribunal of the place of a contract, 1411; in penal cases, 1412; in cases concerning administration, 1413, 1°; in cases of inheritances or pious legacies, 1413, 2°; ordinary norms of competence apply in the execution of a legacy, 1413, 2°; appellate tribunal resolves conflicts of competence between tribunals subject to it, 1416; hierarchical, 1440; Apostolic Signatura adjudicates conflicts of competence of tribunals not subject to the same appellate tribunal, 1445, §1, 4°; Apostolic Signatura adjudicates conflicts of competence among the dicasteries of the Roman Curia, 1445, §2; Apostolic Signatura extends the competence of tribunals, 1445, §3; exception against the competence of a judge is to be adjudicated by that judge, 1460, §1; several actions can be brought at once by the same petitioner provided the actions do not exceed the limits of the competence of the tribunal approached, 1493; the judge must see that the matter is within his competence, 1505, §1; in marriage nullity cases, 1673; in matters of separation of spouses, 1694; in the process for the dispensation of a marriage *ratum et non consummatum*, 1699; in cases for declaring the nullity of sacred ordination, 1709

competent authority   to revoke general executory decrees, 33, §2; to revoke instructions, 34, §3; to add a derogating clause to an administrative act which injures an acquired right or is contrary to a law or approved custom, 38; to revoke an administrative act, 47; to issue a singular decree, 48, 57, §§1, 3; to revoke a singular decree, 58, §1; to issue a rescript, 59, §1, 64; to revoke a privilege, 79; to accept the renunciation of a privilege, 80, §1; to judge when circumstances of a privilege have changed, 83, §2; to constitute juridic persons, 114, §1; to grant juridic personality, 114, §3, 116, §2; to constitute public juridic persons, 116, §1; to approve statutes of an aggregate of persons or things, 117; to suppress a public juridic person, 120, §1; to judge when a private juridic person has ceased to exist, 120, §1; one being approached does not suspend the executive power of another, 139, §1; to constitute and confer an ecclesiastical office, 145, §2; to confer an ecclesiastical office, 147; to rescind the provision of an ecclesiastical office, 149, §2; to rescind an election, 166, §2; to confirm an election, 179, §§1–2; for postulation, 180, §1, 182, §§1, 3, 4, 183, §1; to communicate the loss of an office, 186; to prescribe when a prior office becomes vacant, 191, §1; to remove a person from office, 192, 194, §2, 195; to confer an office, 193, §2

and the People of God: to consent to the name *Catholic* being given to an apostolic undertaking, 216; to summon the Christian faithful to trial, 221, §2; to establish who other than its rector represents the seminary for certain affairs, 238, §2; and associations for secular clerics, 278, §2; to entrust functions to clerics, 278, §3; to judge if clerics are to have an active part in political parties and in governing labor unions, 287, §2; to erect, praise, or commend associations, 298, §2, 301; to review the statutes of a private association, 299, §3; to consent to an association assuming the name *Catholic,* 300; to recognize associations as clerical, 302; to exercise vigilance over associations, 305, §1; to erect public associations, 312, §1; to suppress a public association, 320, §3; to grant juridic personality to a private juridic person, 322, §1; to exercise vigilance over a private juridic person, 325, §1; to suppress a private association, 326, §1; to determine the power of an auxiliary bishop when the see is vacant, 409, §2; to erect institutes of consecrated life, 573, §2; to interpret the evangelical counsels, 576; to sanction the mind and designs of founders of institutes of consecrated life, 578; to aggregate one institute of consecrated life to another, 580; to divide an institute of consecrated life, to erect new parts, to join those erected, or to redefine boundaries of an institute of consecrated life, 581; to suppress parts of an institute of consecrated life, 585; to approve the fundamental code or constitutions of an institute of consecrated life, 587, §2; to establish norms for an institute of consecrated life which are collected into codes, 587, §4; to erect houses of a religious institute, 609, §1; to receive an account of administrators in religious institutes, 636, §2; to dismiss a novice, 653, §1; to receive a petition for an indult of departure from a religious institute, 691, §1; to receive recourse against the dismissal

of a religious, 700; to erect a house and establish a local community of a society of apostolic life, 733, §1; to send missionaries, 784; directs a Catholic school, 803, §1; to consent to a school bearing the name *Catholic school,* 803, §3; to consent to a university bearing the name *Catholic university,* 808; to appoint teachers in Catholic universities, 810, §1; is to take care that theology is taught in Catholic universities, 811, §1; to give a mandate to teach theological disciplines, 812; to approve textbooks on religious questions, 827, §2; to permit the publication of books or other writings on religious or moral questions, 827, §4

and the sanctifying function of the Church: to define what pertains to the licit celebration of sacraments, 841; to issue norms on preparation for the sacraments, 843, §2; of a non-Catholic Church or community to be consulted before general norms are issued on the sacraments being received from or given to its members, 844, §5; to approve liturgical books for celebrating the sacraments, 846, §1; to define offerings for the administration of the sacraments, 848; to grant a presbyter the faculty to confirm, 882, 884, §2; to grant the faculty to give absolution, 966, §2, 972; to issue norms on administration of the sacrament of penance, 978, §2; to dispense from marriage impediments, 1078–1080; to grant permission for mixed marriage, 1124; to be approached for separation of spouses, 1152, §3; to grant the radical sanation of marriage, 1161, §1

and the temporal goods of the Church: to give permission for alienation, 1291, 1292, §1; to decide action against canonically illicit but civilly valid alienation, 1296; to give permission for leasing church goods, 1297; to give permission for the sale or lease of ecclesiastical goods to their administrators or close relatives, 1298; to erect an *autonomous pious foundation,* 1303, §1, 1°

and processes: to punish judges, 1457, §1

competent forum for trials in general, 1404–1416; for marriage nullity cases, 1671–1673

complaint of nullity adjudicated by the Apostolic Signatura, 1445, §1, 1°; and an exception of relative incompetence, 1460, §2; and a respondent who is detained, 1593, §2; and cases involving the good of private persons, 1619; and irremediable nullity, 1620–1621; and remediable nullity, 1622–1623; the judge who rendered the sentence deals with the, 1624; can be proposed together with an appeal, 1625, 1629, 2°; can be introduced by the parties, the promoter of justice, and the defender of the bond, 1626, §1; power of a judge to retract or emend *ex officio* a null sentence,

1626, §2; can be treated according to the oral contentious process, 1627

compromise in elections, 174, §§1, 3, 175, 180, §2; as a method of avoiding trials, 1714, 1715, §1

computation of time notion, 200; continuous time, 201, §1; useful time, 201, §2; computation of a day, week, month, and year, 202, §1; a month and year in continuous time, 202, §2; computation of the initial day (*a quo*), 203, §1; computation of the final day (*ad quem*), 203, §2

concelebration priests are permitted to concelebrate but may celebrate individually though not while a concelebration is taking place in the same church or oratory, 902; law may permit a priest to celebrate or concelebrate more than once on the same day, 905, §1; forbidden with non-Catholic priests or ministers, 908; priest concelebrating is permitted to receive an offering for Mass, 945, §1; a priest who concelebrates a second Mass on the same day cannot accept an offering under any title, 951, §2

conclusion of the case notion, 1599; whether the judge proceeds if the litigant dies after the, 1518, 2°; a third party is to introduce a *libellus* before the, 1596, §2; new proofs after the, 1600; judge determines a suitable period of time to present defense briefs or observations after the, 1601

concordats pontifical legate deals with drafting and implementation of, 365, §1, 2°

concubinage marriage impediment of public propriety arises from notorious or public, 1093; delict of a cleric living in, 1395, §1

conditional conferral of sacraments baptism, confirmation, and orders are to be conferred conditionally if a prudent doubt exists about their conferral after a diligent inquiry, 845, §2; conditional conferral of baptism, 869

condition(s) and the power to issue general decrees, 30; in an administrative act, 39, 41–42; in a rescript of the Apostolic See, 68; the canonical condition of a physical person, 96–112, 208, 711; an act placed out of ignorance or error concerning what amounts to a condition *sine qua non* is invalid, 126; attached to a vote, 172, §2; attached to a compromise agreement, 174, §3, 175, 2°; the patrimonial condition of a juridic person, 638, §3, 1295; conditions on the validity of admission to novitiate, 643, §2; for religious profession, 656, 658; and marriage consent, 1102; to be fulfilled before permission is granted for a mixed marriage, 1125; attached to a vow, 1194; attached to an oath, 1201, §1, 1202, 3°; for the establishment and acceptance

of foundations, 1304, §2; attached to remission of a penalty, 1361, §1; in evaluating testimony a judge is to consider the condition of the person, 1572, 1°; a pastor can submit his resignation with, 1743

confederation(s) of public associations, 313; of institutes of consecrated life, 582; transfer from an autonomous monastery to another of the same, 684, §3; of societies of apostolic life, 732

conference of bishops notion, 447; composition, 448, 450; supreme authority of the Church erects, suppresses, and alters, 449, §1; possesses juridic personality, 449, §2; statutes, 451; officers, 452; plenary meetings, 453; deliberative or consultative vote of members, 454; legislative competence, 455; its president sends its acts and decrees to Apostolic See, 456; permanent council, 457; general secretariat, 458; relations between conferences of bishops, especially neighboring ones, 459; meetings of bishops of an ecclesiastical region does not normally have its powers, 434; teaching authority of, 753; catechetical office, 775, §3; and the competent forum for marriage nullity cases, 1673, 3°

issues norms on: age and qualifications for lay men to be admitted to the ministries of lector and acolyte, 230, §1; the permanent diaconate, 236, 276, §2, 3°; program for priestly formation, 242, §1; clerical garb, 284; the presbyteral council, 496; the functions of the college of consultors being entrusted to the cathedral chapter, 502, §3; appointment of pastors for a specific period, 522; parochial registers, 535, §1, 895, 1121, §1; suitable support and housing for a retired pastor, 538, §3; ecumenism, 755, §2; catechisms, 775, §2; the catechumenate, 788, §3, 851, 1°; Catholic religious instruction and education in schools and through instruments of social communication, 804, §1; requirements for clerics and religious on radio or television concerning Catholic doctrine or morals, 831, §2; the sacraments of penance, Eucharist, and anointing of the sick being given to or received from non-Catholics, 844, §§4–5; the conferral of baptism by immersion or pouring, 854; inscribing the names of the natural parents of an adopted child, 877, §3; the age to confer confirmation, 891; when the conditions for general absolution are present, 961, §2; the confessional, 964, §2; an older age for presbyterate and permanent diaconate, 1031, §3; the examination of spouses and marriage banns, 1067; the licit celebration of marriage at an older age, 1083, §2; the declarations and promises made by the Catholic in a mixed marriage, 1126; the dispensation from canonical form being granted in a uniform manner, 1127, §2; suppression or transfer of holydays

between ecclesiastical universities or faculties and other universities or faculties, 820; of the faithful to enliven instruments of social communication with a human and Christian spirit, 822, §2; through a federation of diocesan institutes in providing for the social security of clerics and common funds for church workers, 1274, §4

in abortion: and irregularity to receive orders, 1041, 4°; and irregularity to exercise orders, 1044, §1, 3°; dispensation from these irregularities, 1047–1049

coordination   by a bishop of apostolic works, 394, §1; by the diocesan bishop of all affairs belonging to diocesan administration, 473, §1; by the diocesan bishop of the pastoral action of his vicars general and episcopal vicars, 473, §2; by the vicar forane of pastoral activity, 555, §1, 1°; by the diocesan bishop of the works and apostolic activities of religious institutes, 680; of major superiors with the conference of bishops or individual bishops, 708; by the diocesan bishop of catechetical endeavors, 775, §1; by the Roman Pontiff and college of bishops, of missionary work and cooperation, 782, §1; by the diocesan bishop in mission territories of missionary endeavors and works, 790, §1, 1°; of scientific research between ecclesiastical universities or faculties and other universities or faculties, 820

corporal   to be used in the eucharistic sacrifice, 932, §2

correction   prudent correction of parishioners by the pastor, 529, §1; fraternal correction and the application of penalties, 1341; of testimony by witnesses, 1569, §1; of a sentence, 1616, §1

Council for the Public Affairs of the Church   part of the Roman Curia, 360; the term Apostolic See or Holy See includes the, 361

council *(concilium)* ecumenical: the college of bishops exercises its power solemnly in an, 337, §1; and the Roman Pontiff, 337–338; membership, 339; interrupted if the Apostolic See becomes vacant, 340; force of the decrees of an, 341; and infallibility, 749, §2; the profession of faith to be taken by those who attend an, 833, 1°; delict of teaching a doctrine condemned by an, 1371, 1°; delict of making recourse against an act of the Roman Pontiff to an, 1372; administrative recourse against decrees of an, 1732

particular: notion, 445; membership, 443, §§1–5; guests, 443, §6; obligation to attend and impediments to attendance, 444; promulgation of decrees, 446; teaching authority of bishops joined in a, 753; the profession of faith to be taken by those

who attend a, 833, 1°; local ordinary can dispense from the laws issued by a, 88

plenary: notion, 439; role of the conference of bishops in a, 441

provincial: notion, 440; role of the metropolitan, 442; its power in an ecclesiastical province, 432, §1; defines Mass offerings, 952, §1

council *(consilium)* participation of qualified lay persons in, 228, §2

finance (diocesan): notion, 492, §1; membership, 492, §§2–3; functions, 493; and the diocesan finance officer, 494; selects a temporary finance officer if the diocesan finance officer is elected diocesan administrator, 423, §2; examines annual financial reports of goods not exempted from governance of the diocesan bishop, 1287, §1; when to be heard by the diocesan bishop, 1263, 1277, 1281, §2, 1305, 1310, §2; when to give consent to the diocesan bishop, 1277, 1292, §1

finance (of a juridic person): notion, 1280; when to be heard, 1305, 1310, §2

finance (parish): notion, 537

episcopal: notion, 473, §4

missionary: notion, 495, §2; has the functions of the college of consultors, 502, §4

pastoral (diocesan): notion, 511; membership, 512; constituted for a period of time, 513, §1; ceases when the see is vacant, 513, §2; possesses a consultative vote only, 514, §1; diocesan bishop convokes, presides, and publicizes what it has done, 514, §1; to be convoked at least once a year, 514, §2; and participation in particular council, 443, §5; participates in the diocesan synod, 463, §1, 5°

pastoral (parish): notion, 536, §1; pastor presides, 536, §1; possesses a consultative vote only, 536, §2; diocesan bishop establishes norms for, 536, §2

presbyteral: notion, 495, §1; statutes, 496; membership and elections, 497–499; diocesan bishop convokes, presides, determines questions or receives proposals, 500, §1; consultative or deliberative vote, 500, §2; cannot act without the diocesan bishop who makes public its affairs, 500, §3; terms of members, 501, §1; ceases when the see is vacant, 501, §2; new diocesan bishop must establish within a year of taking possession, 501, §2; dissolution of, 501, §3; and participation in a provincial council, 443, §5; participates in the diocesan synod, 463, §1, 4°; establishes a group of pastors to be consulted by the diocesan bishop in the removal or transfer of pastors, 1742, §1, 1750; when to be heard by the diocesan bishop, 461, §1, 515, §2, 531, 536, §1, 1215, §2, 1222, §2, 1263

moderator in each parish, 526, §2; introducing a new marriage impediment or contrary to existing impediments, 1076; of administrators not presenting an annual report to the local ordinary, 1287, §1; on the cases reserved to a collegiate tribunal of three judges, 1425, §1

D

damage(s) obligation to repair damage illegitimately inflicted by a juridic act or any other act placed with malice or negligence, 128; before absolution one who has falsely denounced a confessor must retract and be prepared to repair, 982; a broken engagement gives rise to an action to repair, 1062, §2; repair of damage in a sacred place, 1211; resulting when the perpetrator of a delict withdrew from it, 1328, §2; withdrawn from contumacy and reparation of, 1347, §2; remission of a censure and reparation of, 1357, §2; one can be brought to trial before the tribunal of the place of a disputed object when the action concerns, 1410; punishment of judges who inflict damage on litigants, 1457, §1; and sequestration of a thing, 1496, §1, 1499; restoration of property and repair of any, 1515; bishop is to establish norms on recovery of, 1649, §1, 4°–5°, §2; judgment about irreparable damage arising from execution of a sentence, 1650, §3; and the penal process, 1718, §4, 1729–1731; a pastor can be removed legitimately for poor administration of temporal affairs with grave damage to the Church, 1741, 5°

danger of grave harm in delay and dispensations, 87, §2; in delay and expulsion of a religious, 703; of error or indifferentism to be avoided when Catholics receive sacraments of penance, Eucharist, and anointing of the sick from non-Catholic ministers, 844, §2; of spoiling the bread for the eucharistic sacrifice, 924, §2; of profanation of the Eucharist to be avoided, 938, §3; of revelation of a sinner from use of confessional knowledge, 984, §1; due to sickness or old age and anointing of the sick, 1004, §1; of grave harm and exercise of an order by one impeded, 1048; of grave harm until a marriage dispensation is obtained from competent authority, 1080; removing dangers of defecting from the faith and permission for mixed marriage, 1125, 1°; grave mental or physical danger and separation of spouses, 1153, §1; resulting when the perpetrator of a delict withdrew from it, 1328, §2; suspension of obligation to observe an undeclared *latae sententiae* penalty when one cannot observe it without danger of grave scandal or infamy, 1352, §2; one is not bound to present documents which cannot be communicated without

danger of harm or without danger of violating secrecy, 1546, §1; the judge can advise witnesses beforehand of remote issues if this can be done without danger, 1565, §2; the judge can recall witnesses if there is no danger of collusion or corruption, 1570; in cases of the public good the judge can decree that a specific act must be shown to no one to avoid a most grave, 1598, §1; after the conclusion of the case the judge can summon witnesses or gather proofs if danger of fraud or subornation is eliminated, 1600, §1, 2°

danger of death function especially entrusted to a pastor is administration of confirmation to those in, 530, 2°; administration of confirmation by a chaplain to those in, 566, §1; and Catholic ministers administering penance, Eucharist, and anointing of the sick to non-Catholics, 844, §4; baptism of an adult in, 865, §2; baptism of an infant in, 867, §2, 868, §2; confirmation in, 883, 3°, 889, §2, 891; administration of Eucharist to children in, 913, §2; Viaticum to the faithful in, 921; absolution in general manner in, 961, §1, 1°, 962, §2; penance in, 976–977, 986, §2; proof of freedom to marry in, 1068; marriage dispensations in, 1079, §§1, 3; celebration of marriage in, 1116, §1; censures and, 1335, 1352, §1

day computation in law, 202, §1

days of penance notion, 1249; the supreme ecclesiastical authority establishes, transfers, and suppresses universal, 1244, §1; diocesan bishops can decree, 1244, §2; dispensations from, 1245; Fridays of the whole year and the season of Lent as, 1250; abstinence and fasting on, 1251–1253

deacon(s) incardination of, 266; are invited to participate in the daily offering of Eucharist, 276, §2, 2°; and the liturgy of the hours, 276, §2, 3°; rescript of loss of the clerical state, 290, 3°; and participation in the exercise of pastoral care of a parish under the direction of a priest with the powers and faculties of a pastor, 517, §2; and ministry of the divine word, 757; profession of faith by those to be ordained, 833, 6°; and the celebration of divine worship, 835, §3; are not permitted to offer prayers proper to the celebrating priest in the eucharistic celebration, 907; the orders are episcopate, presbyterate, and diaconate, 1009, §1; ordination by proper bishop or with dimissorials, 1015, §1, 1016, 1019; licit ordination of, 1025; formation of, 1027, 1032; destined to the presbyterate, 1030; age requirement, 1031, §1; interval of at least six months between diaconate and presbyterate, 1031, §1; exercise of the diaconal order for a suitable time before promotion to the presbyterate, 1032, §2; enrollment among the candidates for ordination, 1034, §1; exercise of the ministry of lector and of acolyte for a suitable time before diaconal ordination, 1035, §1; interval of at least six months between conferral of ministry of acolyte and the diaconate, 1035, §2; handwritten declaration of candidate for ordination as, 1036; and assuming the obligation of celibacy, 1037; who refuse promotion to the presbyterate, 1038; required testimonials, 1050; and imparting blessings, 1169, §3

permanent: formation of, 235, 1032, §2; remuneration of, 281, §3; prescriptions of law not binding, 288; minimum age for ordination, 1031, §§2–3; marriage not a simple impediment for, 1042, 1°; required testimonials for ordination, 1050, 3°

presbyters or deacons: and dispensations, 89; in personal prelatures, 294; cooperation with the pastor of a parish, 519; and faculty to preach, 764; ordinary ministers of baptism, 861, §1; ordinary ministers of holy communion, 910, §1

dean(s) *cardinal:* holds the title of the Diocese of Ostia and the other church he already has as a title, 350, §4; role in the college of cardinals, 352; ordains as bishop one elected as Roman Pontiff if he needs to be ordained, 355, §1

of faculties of theology and of canon law: to be called to particular councils, 443, §3, 3°

vicars forane: 553–555

dead/death personal privilege extinguished with, 78, §2; before installation in office and new right of presentation, 161, §2; of a diocesan bishop and vacancy of an episcopal see, 416–417, 422; of a diocesan administrator, 430, §2; care of a pastor for those who are close to, 529, §1; death register, 535, §1, 1182; the vicar forane and the death of a pastor, 555, §3; evangelical counsel of obedience and following of Christ obedient unto, 601; the eucharistic sacrifice is the memorial of the death and resurrection of the Lord, 897; application of Mass for the dead, 901; gaining indulgences for the dead, 994; and the anointing of the sick, 1005; of a spouse brought about in order to marry, 1090; notation in the baptismal and marriage registers of a marriage dissolved by any reason other than, 1123; dissolves a *ratum et consummatum* marriage, 1141; and ecclesiastical funerals, 1176–1185; of a litigating party, 1518; accusing a marriage after a spouse's, 1675, §1; of a spouse while the case is pending, 1675, §2; process in the presumed death of a spouse, 1707

declaration(s) of a diocesan synod, 466–467; public

declarations of Christian doctrine in the press or other instruments of social communication, 761; by the supreme authority of the Church when the divine law prohibits or nullifies marriage, 1075, §1; of the Catholic in mixed marriages, 1125–1126; delicts consisting in, 1330; of a party or a witness in a trial, 1528; of the parties in a trial, 1530–1538; of the nullity of marriage, 1671–1691; of the presumed death of a spouse, 1707, §§1–2; of the nullity of sacred ordination, 1708–1712

decree(s) constituting juridic persons, 114, §1, 116, §2; constituting and conferring an ecclesiastical office, 145, §2; juridic personality of a private association acquired through, 322, §1; obligation to observe decrees of legitimate church authority, 754; reprinting of collections of, 828

administrative: recourse against, 1732–1739

extrajudicial: and imposition or declaration of a penalty, 1342, 1353, 1363; and separation of spouses, 1692, §1; and penal process, 1718, §1, 3°, §§2–3, 1720

general: notion, 29; authority competent to grant, 30

general executory: notion, 31 §1; competent authority to grant, 31, §1; promulgation and suspensive period of, 31, §2; who are obliged by, 32; do not derogate from laws, 33 §1; cessation of, 33, §2

of a bishop: rejecting a *libellus* for the dispensation of a *ratum et non consummatum* marriage, 1699, §3

of the college of bishops: have obligatory force when confirmed and promulgated by the Roman Pontiff, 341, §2

of the conference of bishops: in cases prescribed by universal law or by special mandate of the Apostolic See, 455, §§1–2; manner of promulgation and effective date, 455, §3; to be sent to the Apostolic See for review when its plenary meeting has ended, 456, 458, 1°; on admitting lay men on a stable basis to the ministries of lector and acolyte, 230, §1; permitting a diocesan bishop to appoint a pastor for a specific period, 522

of a diocesan synod: signed and published by the diocesan bishop, 466; communicated to the metropolitan and conference of bishops, 467

of an ecumenical council: have obligatory force when approved by the Roman Pontiff with the council fathers, confirmed by him, and promulgated at his order, 341, §1, 338, §1

of a judge: notion, 1617; and prescription, 1363, §1; permitting cases to be given speedier treatment, 1458; and acceptance or rejection of a *libellus*,

tory and, unless the contrary is indicated, for travelers in the territory, and for himself, 91; subject to strict interpretation, 92; cessation of a dispensation with successive application, 93

individual dispensations: and postulation, 180, §1, 182, §1; from the obligation of celibacy and loss of the clerical state, 291; from the method of taking canonical possession of a parish, 527, §2; from constitutions of an institute of consecrated life by a diocesan bishop, 595, §2; from religious vows, 692; from requirement of the principal bishop consecrator in an episcopal consecration being joined by at least two consecrating bishops, 1014; from the age requirement for ordination, 1031, §4; from irregularities or impediments to receive orders and to exercise orders, 1047, 1049; from marriage impediments, 1079–1082, 1686, 1687, §1; from canonical form of marriage, 1121, §3, 1127, §2; from interrogation in the pauline privilege, 1144, §2; and simple convalidation of marriage, 1156, §1; and radical sanation of marriage, 1161, §1, 1165, §2; from vows, 1194, 1196–1197; from oaths, 1202, 4°, 1203; from obligation of observing a feast day or day of precept, 1245; of a marriage *ratum et non consummatum*, 1697–1706, 1681

disposition administering the sacraments of penance, Eucharist, and anointing of the sick to non-Catholics who are properly disposed, 844, §§3–4; to receive the sacrament of penance, 962, §1, 980, 987; to receive an indulgence, 992; to receive the anointing of the sick, 1002

dissolution of a private juridic person, 120, §1; of an ecumenical council, 338, §1, 340; of a synod of bishops, 344, 6°, 347, §2; of a diocesan synod, 468, §1; of a presbyteral council, 501, §3; of a marriage, 1085, §2, 1123, 1138, §2, 1141–1150, 1432

division of an aggregate which possesses public juridic personality, 122; of a particular church into distinct parts or parishes, 374, §1; of an institute of consecrated life into parts, 581

doctorate or licentiate *in canon law:* requirement for the judicial vicar and adjutant judicial vicars, 1420, §4; requirement for judges, 1421, §3; requirement for the promoter of justice and defender of the bond, 1435; for the advocate, 1483

in canon law or theology: and the vicar general and episcopal vicar, 478, §1

in sacred scripture, theology, or canon law: and suitability to be a candidate for the episcopacy, 378, §1, 5°

doctrine instructors are to have a concern for the intimate unity and harmony of the entire, 254, §1;

clerics are to strive after solid, 279, §1; competent authority can suppress a private association if its activity causes grave harm to ecclesiastical, 326, §1; those promoted as cardinals are to be outstanding in, 351, §1; bishops are teachers of, 375, §1; qualification of diocesan administrator, 425, §2; qualification of vicar general and episcopal vicar, 478, §1; qualification of a canon, 509, §2; qualification of a pastor, 521, §2; a religious may be dismissed for stubborn upholding or diffusion of condemned, 696, §1; infallible of faith or morals, 749; all are bound to avoid any doctrines contrary to church teaching, 750; religious submission of intellect given to doctrines of the authentic magisterium, 752; all are bound to observe constitutions and decrees issued to propose, 754; teachers in Catholic universities are to be outstanding in integrity of, 810, §1; about baptism, 869, §3; about the Eucharist, 898; confessor is to adhere faithfully to, 978, §2; delicts consisting in a declaration of, 1330; delicts concerning, 1371, 1°; qualification of an auditor, 1428, §2

Catholic: to be imparted to seminarians, 252, §1; and catechetical instruction, 779; and instruction and education in a Catholic school, 803, §2; and universities or faculties, 809–810; and norms established by the conference of bishops on clerics and religious taking part on television or radio on matters of, 831, §2

Christian: lay persons have the obligation and right to acquire a knowledge of, 229, §1; associations of the Christian faithful to promote, 298, §1, 301, §1; and the diocesan bishop, 386, §1; various means available are to be used to proclaim, 761; to be set forth in a way accommodated to the condition of the listeners and adapted to the needs of the times, 769; prescripts of the conference of bishops to be observed in giving a radio or television talk on, 772, §2; cremation is permitted if not chosen for reasons contrary to, 1176, §3

of the Church: the Christian faithful have the right to follow a form of spiritual life consonant with the, 214; and the education of children, 226, §2; the lay Christian faithful are not to put forth their own opinion as the, 227; those who proclaim the divine word are to impart, 768, §2; local ordinaries are to take care that catechists understand appropriately the, 780; a censor is to consider only the, 830, §2

documentary process for marriage nullity cases, 1686–1688

documents containing general executory decrees, 33 §1; of the reception of baptism and confirmation

about one being deprived of ecclesiastical funerals, 1184, §2; formula of the, 1507, §1, 1513, §2, 1612, §2, 1661, §1, 1677, §§2–3; to be addressed in the sentence, 1611, 1°, 1612, §2; about consummation of marriage emerging during the instruction of a case to declare the nullity of marriage, 1681

drunkenness and being liable to penal sanctions, 1324, §1, 2°; 1325; and the application of penalties, 1345

E

Easter diocesan bishop not to be absent on, 395, §3; a function entrusted to pastor is blessing of baptismal font at, 530, 6°

Easter season after receiving first communion, each of the Christian faithful is obliged to receive it during the, 920, §2

Easter vigil baptism to be celebrated on Sunday or, if possible, at the Easter vigil, 856

Eastern Churches Catholics and members of non-Catholic Eastern Churches administering and receiving the sacraments of penance, Eucharist, and anointing of the sick, 844, §3

Eastern patriarchs who are cardinals belong to the episcopal order of cardinals, 350, §1; who are cardinals have their own patriarchal see as a title, 350, §3

Eastern rite a bishop can ordain a subject of an Eastern rite licitly only with apostolic mandate, 1015, §2; if a Catholic marries a non-Catholic of an Eastern rite, canonical form must be observed only for liceity, 1127, §1

ecclesial communities (not in full communion) pontifical legate is to collaborate with bishops to foster relations with other Churches or, 364, 6°; diocesan bishop can invite as observers to the diocesan synod either ministers or members of Churches or, 463, §3; conditional baptism of one baptized in, 869, §2; a baptized person belonging to a non-Catholic ecclesial community can be a witness of baptism, 874, §2; Catholic priests are forbidden to concelebrate the Eucharist with priests or ministers of Churches or, 908; the local ordinary may permit a priest to celebrate the Eucharist in the worship place of a Church or, 933; without express permission of competent authority, marriage of a Catholic is forbidden with a baptized person of a Church or, 1124; ecclesiastical funerals can be granted to baptized persons enrolled in a, 1183, §3

ecclesiastical communion baptism and, 96; one who has defected from cannot be received validly

into public associations, 316, §1; sacraments establish, strengthen, and manifest, 840; a pastor can be removed legitimately if his manner of acting brings grave detriment or disturbance to, 1741, 1°

ecclesiastical garb clergy are to wear suitable, 284

ecclesiastical goods notion, 1257, §1; vicar forane to see that they are administered carefully, 555, §1, 3°; Roman Pontiff is supreme administrator and steward of all, 1273; ordinaries are to take care of administration of, 1276, §2; to whom belongs the administration of, 1279; those who administer ecclesiastical goods are bound to fulfill their functions in the name of the Church, 1282; administrators are to take care that ownership of ecclesiastical goods is protected by civilly valid methods, 1284, §2, 2°; administrators of ecclesiastical goods are to present an annual report to the local ordinary, 1287, §1; alienation of ecclesiastical goods without required canonical formalities, 1296; those to whom ecclesiastical goods are not to be sold or leased, 1298; delict of impeding the legitimate use of, 1375; delict of alienating ecclesiastical goods without prescribed permission, 1377; formalities for alienation of ecclesiastical goods are to be observed in methods of avoiding trials, 1715, §2

ecclesiastical history formation of seminarians in, 252, §3, 253, §2; approval of text books on, 827, §2

ecumenical council college of bishops exercises power over the universal Church solemnly in an, 337, §1; Roman Pontiff alone convokes, presides over, transfers, suspends, dissolves, and approves decrees of an, 338, §1; Roman Pontiff determines matters to be treated in an, 338, §2; members of the college of bishops have duty and right to take part in an, 339, §1; others who are not bishops can be called to an, 339, §2; when the Apostolic See becomes vacant, is suspended until the new Supreme Pontiff continues or dissolves it, 340; Roman Pontiff approves, confirms, and promulgates decrees of an, 341, §1; infallibility of the college of bishops in an, 749, §2; profession of faith to be made by those who attend an, 833, 1°; delict of teaching a doctrine condemned by an, 1371, 1°; delict of making recourse against an act of the Roman Pontiff to an, 1372; recourse against singular administrative acts issued by an, 1732

ecumenism seminarians are to be so instructed that they have solicitude for, 256, §2; diocesan bishop is to foster, 383, §3; the college of bishops and the Apostolic See foster and direct the ecumenical movement among Catholics, 755, §1

education Christian faithful have a right to a Chris-

anointing of the sick from non-Catholic ministers, 844, §2; and marriage consent, 1097, 1099; and the subject of penal sanctions, 1323, 2°, 1324, §1, 8°; and confession or declaration of a party, 1538; in a sentence, 1616, §1

Eucharist/eucharistic notion, 897; to be the center of seminary life, 246, §1; clerics are to nurture their spiritual life from sacred scripture and the, 276, §2, 2°; the diocesan bishop gathers the people entrusted to him in the Holy Spirit through the gospel and the, 369; the diocesan bishop is frequently to preside at celebrations of the, 389; the pastor is to see that the Eucharist is the center of the parish assembly and is to work that the faithful frequently approach the, 528, §2; a function entrusted to the pastor is the more solemn eucharistic celebration on Sundays and holydays of obligation, 530, 7°; the vicar forane has the duty and right to see that sacred furnishings are maintained carefully, especially in the eucharistic celebration and custody of the, 555, §1, 3°; one needs the permission of the rector or superior of a church to celebrate the Eucharist in it, 561; each religious house is to have at least an oratory where the Eucharist is celebrated and reserved, 608; religious are to participate in the eucharistic sacrifice daily, receive the Body of Christ, and adore the Lord in the sacrament, 663, §2; the daily celebration of the Eucharist is to be the source and strength of consecrated life, 719, §2; the diocesan bishop's consent to erect a house for a society of apostolic life entails the right of at least an oratory where the Eucharist is celebrated and reserved, 733, §2; catechetical instruction to prepare for first reception of the, 777, 2°; all the Christian faithful are to participate in liturgical celebrations, especially of the, 835, §4; the sacraments of initiation are baptism, confirmation, and, 842, §2; reception of the Eucharist from and by non-Catholics, 844, §§2–3; unless there is a grave contrary reason, immediately after baptism an adult is to be confirmed and is to participate in the eucharistic celebration, 866; baptism and confirmation sponsors are to be confirmed and to have received the, 874, §1, 3°, 893, §1; the Christian faithful are to hold the Eucharist in highest honor, take an active part in its celebration, receive it devoutly and frequently, and worship it, 898; eucharistic celebration, 899; minister of the Eucharist, 900–911; participation in the Eucharist, 912–923; rites and ceremonies of the eucharistic celebration, 924–930; time and place of the celebration of the, 931–933; reservation and veneration of the, 934–944; offerings given for the cele-

bration of Mass, 945–958; before their wedding spouses are urged to approach the, 1065, §2; at shrines the means of salvation are to be supplied more abundantly also by the celebration of the, 1234, §1; an altar is the table on which the eucharistic sacrifice is celebrated, 1235, §1; when the eucharistic celebration is impossible, a liturgy of the word is strongly recommended, 1248, §2; an excommunicated person is forbidden to have any ministerial participation in celebrating the, 1331, §1, 1°; delict of attempting the eucharistic sacrifice though not a priest, 1378, §2, 1°

evangelical counsel(s) may be professed by clerics and lay persons by vows or other sacred bonds, 207, §2; life consecrated through the evangelical counsels is a stable form of living, 573, §1; members of institutes of consecrated life profess the evangelical counsels by vows or other sacred bonds, 573, §2; the state of those who profess the evangelical counsels in institutes belongs to the life and holiness of the Church and contributes to its salvific mission, 574, §1; are a divine gift which the Church received from the Lord, 575; competent church authority interprets the, 576; each institute defines how the evangelical counsels must be observed, 598, §1; all members of institutes of consecrated life must observe the evangelical counsels faithfully and fully, 598, §2; of chastity, 599; of poverty, 600; of obedience, 601; a hermit publicly professes the evangelical counsels in the hands of the diocesan bishop, 603, §2; novices are to learn a manner of living consecrated through the, 652, §2; by religious profession members assume the observance of the three evangelical counsels by public vow, 654; constitutions of secular institutes are to establish the sacred bonds by which the evangelical counsels are assumed, 712; candidates in secular institutes are to be formed to lead a life according to the, 722, §2; when initial probation in a secular institute is complete, a candidate may assume the three evangelical counsels by a sacred bond, 723, §1; among societies of apostolic life some assume the evangelical counsels by a bond defined in the constitutions, 731, §2

evangelization associations of the Christian faithful may exercise initiatives in, 298, §1; lay members of secular institutes participate in the evangelizing function of the Church, 713, §2; members of secular institutes are to employ the forms of evangelization which respond to the purpose, spirit, and character of the institute, 722, §2; is a fundamental duty of the people of God, so all are to assume their part in missionary work, 781; the Church sends heralds of the gospel until the young churches are able to carry on evangelization themselves, 786; pastors of souls and others are to take care that those who seek the sacraments are prepared to receive them by proper, 843, §2

examination of a presbyter to evidence his suitability to be a pastor, 521, §3; of conscience, 664, 988, §1; of presbyters to determine suitability to hear confessions, 970; of spouses before the wedding, 1067; of witnesses, 1558–1571; judicial examination and inspection, 1582–1583

excardination before incardination in another particular church one must obtain a letter of excardination from his diocesan bishop, 267, §1; takes effect when incardination in another particular church is obtained, 267, §2; a diocesan bishop may allow incardination after he has a legitimate document that excardination has been granted and has testimonials from the excardinating bishop, 269, 2°; excardination can be granted for just causes, 270; a diocesan administrator can grant excardination only after the episcopal see has been vacant for a year and with the consent of the college of consultors, 272; the habitual faculty to hear confessions ceases by, 975

exceptions laws which contain an exception from the law are subject to strict interpretation, 18; the Church receives prescription as in civil law, without prejudice to the code's, 197; as an exception one may make novitiate outside the novitiate house, 647, §2; the pastor or minister can grant exceptions to the age of a sponsor for baptism or confirmation, 874, §1, 2°, 893, §1; to canonical form, 1108, §1; the Apostolic Signatura adjudicates exceptions of suspicion and other cases against rotal auditors, 1445, §1, 3°; in processes, 1449, §4, 1452, §2, 1459, §2, 1460, §§1–2, 1462, 1491–1500, 1621, 1642, §2, 1654, §2, 1660, 1664, 1686, 1703, §1

exclaustration can be imposed on religious by the Holy See for pontifical institutes, or by the diocesan bishop for diocesan institutes, 686, §3; status of an exclaustrated member, 687

exclusion of a member of a secular institute from renewal of sacred bonds, 726, §1; from ecclesiastical funerals, 1185; of witnesses, 1551–1557; of an accused from the sacred ministry or from some office and ecclesiastical function, 1722

excommunication *sanction:* notion, 1331; and qualification to vote 171, §1, 3°; and reception into public associations, 316, §1; and admission to holy

communion, 915; and capability to receive indulgences, 996, §1; and assistance at marriage, 1109; to be established with greatest moderation and only for graver delicts, 1318; remission of, 1357, §1; and penal cases reserved to a collegiate tribunal, 1425, §1, 2°

individual delicts: being an apostate, heretic, or schismatic, 1364, §1; throwing away the consecrated species or taking or retaining them for a sacrilegious purpose, 1367; using physical force against the Roman Pontiff, 1370, §1; absolving an accomplice in sin against the sixth commandment, 1378, §1; attempting to celebrate Mass though not a priest, or attempting to give absolution or hear confessions, 1378, §3; bishop consecrating a bishop without a pontifical mandate, and the one so receiving episcopal consecration, 1382; directly violating the sacramental seal, 1388; procuring a completed abortion, 1398

execution/executor instructions and execution of laws, 34; of singular administrative acts, 37; of administrative acts, 41–45; of a singular decree, 54, §1, 58, §1; of rescripts, 62, 63, §3, 68–70, 479, §3, 1264, 1°; executive power and executing universal or particular laws for travelers, 136; of decisions made by the conference of bishops, 457; of a pious will, 1301, 1302, §2; of a delict, 1328, §2; of a legacy and trials, 1413, 2°; of a sentence, 1592, §2, 1638, 1644, §2, 1647, 1650–1655, 1685; and *restitutio in integrum*, 1642, §2; of an administrative decree, 1734, §1, 1736, 1737, §3

executive power notion, 134, §§1, 3, 135, §§1, 4; and general decrees, 30; and general executory decrees, 31, §1; and instructions, 34, §1; and singular administrative acts, 35; and dispensations, 85; scope of exercise, 136; delegation of, 137; interpretation of, 138; suspension of when another competent authority is approached, 139, §1; and several persons acting, 140; Church supplying, 144, §1; of the diocesan bishop, 391; of the vicar general and episcopal vicar, 479, §§1–2; of superiors in clerical religious institutes and societies of apostolic life, which are of pontifical right, 968, §2; fees for acts of executive power granting a favor, 1264, 1°

exempt dioceses as a rule are no longer to exist, 431, §2

exempt places ministers can administer confirmation within their territory even in, 888

exempt/exemption from universal laws not in force in a territory, 12, §2; of minors from the authority of parents or guardians, 98, §2; of a seminary from parochial governance, 262; from exercising functions and public civil offices foreign to the clerical state, 289, §2; of cardinals from the power of governance of the bishop in whose diocese they reside, 357, §2; of the seat of a pontifical legation from the power of the local ordinary except in celebrating marriages, 366, 1°; of institutes of consecrated life by the Supreme Pontiff, 591; and penal sanctions, 1327, 1354, §1; of witnesses, 1548, §2

exorcisms requires special and express permission from the local ordinary, 1172, §1; qualities of the priest to whom permission is given to perform, 1172, §2

expenses of the diocesan bishop's pastoral visitation, 398; to be reviewed annually by the diocesan finance council, 493; which the diocesan finance officer is to meet, 494, §§3–4; legitimately incurred by officials in religious institutes, 638, §2; administrators are to invest monies left over after, 1284, §2, 6°

judicial: 1462, §1, 1464, 1523, 1525, 1571, 1580, 1595, 1611, 4°, 1649

experts lay persons may assist pastors of the Church as, 228, §2; judgement of experts about illness of religious renewing profession or making perpetual profession, 689, §2; consultation of experts about amentia or other psychic weakness disqualifying one from receiving or exercising orders, 1041, 1°, 1044, §2, 2°; and restoring precious images, 1189; and building or restoring churches, 1216; and alienation of goods whose value exceeds the defined minimum, 1293, §1, 2°

judicial: 1447, 1455, §3, 1574–1581, 1649, §1, 3°, 1663, §2, 1664, 1678, §1, 1°, 1680, 1718, §3

expiatory penalties notion, 1312, §1, 2°, §2, 1336–1338; one who can impose precepts in the external forum by virtue of power of governance can threaten penalties by precept, except perpetual expiatory penalties, 1319, §1; judge can suspend the obligation of observing, 1344, 3°

expiration of rescripts issued by the Apostolic See, 72; of the mandate of the vicar general and episcopal vicar, 481, §1

exposition of the Most Blessed Sacrament place of, 941; recommended annual solemn exposition, 942; minister of, 943

expulsion immediate expulsion of a religious, 703; of a judge from his territory, 1469, §1

extraordinary minister of holy communion notion, 910, §2, 230, §3; and exposition and reposition of the Most Blessed Sacrament without benediction, 943

F

fact(s) doubt about a, 14; ignorance or error about a fact concerning oneself or another, 15, §2; positive and probable doubt of, 144, §1; in process of dismissal of a religious, 694, §2, 695, §2; on which irregularities are based, 1047, §1; doubt about a fact and impotence, 1084, §2; of a sacred place having been turned over permanently to profane use, 1212; an object of trial is to declare juridic, 1400, §1, 1°; *libellus* must indicate facts and proofs which will prove allegations, 1504, 2°; of notification about juridic acts and its method must be evident in the acts, 1509, §2; when facts agreed upon by the parties need proof, 1526, §2, 2°; judge must question the parties to prove a fact of public interest, 1530; what the refusal of a party to respond infers for the proof of the, 1531, §2; judicial confession is the assertion of a fact against oneself, 1535; the declaration of a party made due to error of fact lacks any force, 1538; experts to establish some, 1574; presumptions of a judge must be based on a certain and determined, 1586; a sentence must briefly relate the, 1612, §2; material error in relating the facts in a sentence, 1616, §1; *restitutio in integrum* when later documents undoubtedly prove new, 1645, §2, 2°; *libellus* in oral contentious process must set forth the facts and indicate how petitioner will demonstrate the, 1658, §1, 1°–2°; only the Apostolic See adjudicates the fact of non-consummation, 1698, §1, 1704, §1; careful inquiry about the facts during the preliminary investigation of the penal process, 1717, §1

faculties habitual, 132, 479, §3; and Church supplying executive power of governance, 144, §2; auxiliary bishop with special, 403, §2; coadjutor bishop has special, 403, §3; of an auxiliary bishop when the see is vacant, 409, §2; of the canon penitentiary, 508, §1; of a pastor, 510, §2, 517, §2; of a vicar forane, 555, §1; of chaplains, 566; of presbyters and deacons to preach, 764; to administer confirmation, 882–884, 885, §2, 887; to hear confessions, 966–976; to assist at marriage, 1109–1111; of administrators to exceed the limits and manner of ordinary administration, 1281, §1; expiatory penalty of privation of, 1336, §1, 2°, 1338, §1

faculties (academic) lay persons have the right to acquire fuller knowledge of sacred sciences taught in ecclesiastical universities and, 229, §2; teachers in seminaries are to have a doctorate or licentiate from a university or faculty recognized by the Holy See, 253, §1; the conference of bishops is to see that universities or at least faculties are suitably spread through their territory, 809; in Catholic universities a faculty or institute or at

favor(s)   a rescript grants a privilege, dispensation, or other, 59, §1; prescripts for rescripts are valid also for the oral grant of a permission or, 59, §2; subreption and a rescript of a favor given *motu proprio*, 63, §1; denied by any dicastery of the Roman Curia, 64; denied by one's ordinary, 65; rescript granting a favor entrusted to an executor, 70; no one is bound to use a rescript unless bound by another canonical obligation, 71; a favor granted in the internal forum to be proven in the external forum, 74; privileges and, 76, §1, 77, 80, §2; one with executive power may exercise it over travelers if it concerns granting, 136; clerics are to use exemptions from civil service granted in their, 289, §2; spiritual favors of an association of the Christian faithful, 306; a presbyter must use the faculty to confirm in favor of those for whom it is granted, 885, §2; provincial bishops are to fix fees for granting a, 1264, 1°; privation of favors as expiatory penalty, 1336, §1, 2°, 1338, §1; cardinals, patriarchs, bishops, and those who possess a similar favor by civil law are to be heard as witnesses in the place they select, 1558, §2; the bishop is to prepare a *votum* on the suitability of the, 1704, §1

favor of the faith   dissolution of marriage by means of the pauline privilege in, 1143, §1

favor of the law   marriage possesses, 1060; in a doubtful matter the privilege of faith possesses the, 1150; if a judge cannot arrive at moral certitude in a case which has the favor of law, the judge must pronounce for that, 1608, §4

fear, grave   juridic act placed out of grave fear is valid but may be rescinded, 125, §2; the vote of one coerced by grave fear is invalid, 172, §1, 1°; a resignation made out of grave fear is invalid, 188; novitiate is invalid when entered by, 643, §1, 4°; temporary profession is invalid when made with, 656, 4°; a marriage entered because of grave fear from without, 1103; a vow made out of grave and unjust fear is null, 1191, §3; an oath extorted by grave fear is null, 1200, §2; and penal sanctions, 1323, 4°, 1324, §1, 5°, 1345; remission of a penalty extorted by grave fear is invalid, 1360; a confession or declaration of party extorted by grave fear lacks force, 1538; a sentence rendered by a judge coerced by grave fear suffers irremediable nullity, 1620, 3°

feast days   supreme ecclesiastical authority establishes, transfers, and suppresses universal, 1244, §1; diocesan bishops can decree special, 1244, §2; dispensation from observing, 1245; listing of, 1246, §1; conference of bishops can suppress or

transfer, 1246, §2; Mass obligation on, 1248; when the diocesan bishop is not to be absent, 395, §3; a homily is strongly recommended on, 767, §3

federation(s)   of institutes of consecrated life, 582; transfer from an autonomous monastery to another of the same, 684, §3; of societies of apostolic life, 732; of diocesan institutes to assist the social security of clerics and obligations toward others who serve the Church, 1274, §4

fees   provincial bishops are to fix fees for acts of executive power granting a favor or for execution of rescripts of the Apostolic See, 1264, 1°; judge must determine fees for experts, 1580; bishop of tribunal to establish norms on fees for procurators, advocates, experts, and interpreters, and the indemnity for witnesses, 1649, §1, 2°; there is no separate appeal from the determination of these, 1649, §2

ferendae sententiae penalties   notion, 1314; *latae sententiae* penalties when delicts cannot be punished effectively by, 1318; and accomplices, 1329; judge to make a prudent decision when the sum appears excessive, 1346; remission of, 1356, §1

fetus   a living aborted fetus is to be baptized, 871

finance council   *diocesan:* notion, 492, §1; term of membership, 492, §2; qualifications of membership, 492, §§1, 3; preparation of annual budget and review of annual revenues and expenses, 493; to elect a temporary finance officer if the diocesan finance officer is elected diocesan administrator, 423, §2; and imposition of taxes in the diocese, 1263; diocesan bishop hears the finance council for more important acts of administration, 1277; diocesan bishop needs consent of the finance council to place acts of extraordinary administration, 1277; diocesan bishop hears the finance council before determining acts exceeding ordinary administration of persons subject to him, 1281, §2; examines annual reports of ecclesiastical goods not exempt from power of governance of the diocesan bishop, 1287, §1; gives consent for the diocesan bishop to alienate goods whose value is between the minimum and maximum amounts defined by the conference of bishops, 1292, §1; advises the ordinary on investment of goods for the benefit of an endowment, 1305; advises the ordinary on lessening obligations of pious causes, 1310, §2

of juridic persons: each is to have its own, or at least two counselors assisting the administrator, 1280

parish: 537

penalty prevents a diocesan bishop from exercising his function, 415; and a vacant see, 419; and a vacant apostolic vicariate or prefecture, 420; removal of diocesan administrator by the, 430, §2; can unite neighboring ecclesiastical provinces into ecclesiastical regions, 433, §1; can grant certain powers to an ecclesiastical region, 434; issues norms on canons, 506, §2; moderators of institutes of consecrated life are to promote knowledge of documents of the, 592, §2; suppression of the only house of a religious institute belongs to the, 616, §2; gives permission for alienation in an affair which exceeds the amount defined by the Holy See, 638, §3; a diocesan bishop prohibiting a religious from residing in his diocese if the superior has neglected to make provision is to be referred to the, 679; gives permission for transfer of a religious to a secular institute or a society of apostolic life, or from them to a religious institute, 684, §5; indult of exclaustration for more than three years is reserved to the, 686, §1; exclaustration can be imposed by the, 686, §3; confirms a decree of dismissal of a religious, 700; a religious bishop acquiring property on behalf of the, 706, 1°; approves statutes of conferences of major superiors, 709; an indult of departure for a definitively incorporated member of a society of apostolic life may be reserved to the, 743; transfer from a society of apostolic life to an institute of consecrated life or another society of apostolic life requires the permission of the, 744, §2

and the teaching function of the Church: in each diocese an annual offering for the missions is to be sent to the, 791, 4°

and the sanctifying function of the Church: gives prior review of translations of liturgical books, 838, §3; an ordinary can dispense from irregularities and impediments not reserved to the, 1047, §4; gives permission for a diocesan bishop to delegate lay persons to assist at marriages, 1112, §1; reviews a rite of marriage produced by the conference of bishops, 1120; illegitimate children are legitimated by rescript of the, 1139; gives approval for a shrine to be called international, 1231; approves statutes for an international shrine, 1232, §1

and the temporal goods of the Church: gives permission for valid alienation of goods whose value exceeds the maximum amount defined by the conference of bishops, goods given to the Church by vow, or goods precious for artistic or historic reasons, 1292, §2

and processes: any member of the faithful is free to bring or introduce for adjudication a con-

tentious or penal case to the, 1417, §1; Roman Rota judges in second instance cases brought through legitimate appeal before the, 1444, §1, 1°

Holy Spirit influences catechumens, 206, §1; bishop gathers the diocese in the, 369; bishops succeed to the place of the Apostles through the, 375, §1; those in consecrated life follow Christ more closely under the action of the, 573, §1; diocesan bishops are to discern new gifts of consecrated life given to the Church by the, 605; and the teaching function of the Church, 747, §1; in confirmation the baptized are enriched by the gift of the, 879

Holy Week diocesan bishop not to be absent during, 395, §3

holydays of obligation notion, 1246; obligation of the faithful on, 1247; Mass obligation on, 1248, §1; if Mass attendance is impossible on, 1248, §2; Mass for the people on, 388, §1, 534, §1; homilies to be given on, 528, §1, 767, §2; a function entrusted to a pastor is to celebrate the more solemn Mass on, 530, 7°; if pastoral necessity requires it, local ordinary may allow priests to celebrate three Masses on, 905, §2; ordinations to be celebrated within Mass on, 1010

homicide cause for dismissal of a religious, 695, §1; irregularity to receive orders, 1041, 4°; delict of, 1397

homily notion, 767, §1; to be given on Sundays and holydays of obligation, 767, §2, 528, §1; strongly recommended on weekdays, 767, §3; pastor or rector to see to observation of prescripts about the, 767, §4; seminarians are to be instructed in skills for the, 256, §1; diocesan bishop to see to observation of prescripts on the, 386, §1

hospitals special faculty to absolve from *latae sententiae* censures given to the chaplain in, 566, §2; baptism celebrated in, 860, §2

house for young candidates for diaconate, 236, 1°; for clerics doing penance or being rehabilitated, 1337, §2

autonomous: a religious house of canons regular or of monks is an, 613, §1; its moderator is a major superior by law, 613, §2; suppression of, 616, §3; those who govern, 620; its superiors normally govern for a certain and appropriate time unless constitutions determine otherwise, 624, §1

of a religious institute: permission for erection includes permission for a public association of the Christian faithful proper to the institute, 312, §2; chaplain appointed to a house of a lay religious institute, 567, §1; religious community must live

J

joinder of the issue notion, 1513; dilatory exceptions must be proposed before, 1459, §2; exceptions of *res iudicata*, agreement, and other peremptory exceptions called *litis finitae* must be proposed and adjudicated before, 1462, §1; other peremptory exceptions are to be proposed during, 1462, §2; judicial expenses or grant of gratuitous legal assistance to be dealt with before, 1464; and changing terms of controversy after, 1514; possessor ceases to be in good faith after, 1515; judge is to set time for proofs after, 1516; normally proofs not to be gathered before the, 1529; when the petitioner does not appear for the, 1594; of the appellate grade, 1639; judge determining the formula of the doubt in the oral contentious process, 1661, §1; in marriage nullity cases, 1677, §§2–3; judge to appoint an advocate, if the accused does not, in penal cases before the, 1723, §2

joy on Sundays and holydays the faithful must refrain from what hinders the joy proper to the Lord's day, 1247

judge(s) rescinding an act placed out of grave fear, unjustly inflicted, or out of malice, 125, §2; possesses judicial power, 135, §3; diocesan bishop governs with judicial power personally or through the judicial vicar and, 391, §2, 1419, §1; bishops as judges of faith and morals, 749, §2; confessor as, 978, §1; determining a penalty, 1315, §2; determining if a circumstance diminishes gravity of a delict, 1324, §2; punishing a person more gravely than law or precept establishes, 1326, §1; applying penalties, 1342, §3, 1343–1346, 1349; cessation of penalties, 1363, §1; Roman Pontiff as, 1405, §§1–2, 1406, §2, 1442; competence or incompetence of, 1406, §2, 1407, §§1–2, 1440, 1460–1461; recourse to the Apostolic See and jurisdiction of a, 1417, §2; in a case of temporal goods of a juridic person represented by the diocesan bishop, 1419, §2; judicial vicar, adjutant judicial vicar, and, 1420–1422; single, 1424, 1425, §4, 1441, 1449, §4, 1505, §1, 1610, §1, 1657; collegiate tribunal of, 1425–1426; in cases between religious or houses of the same clerical religious institute of pontifical right, or an autonomous monastery, 1427, §1; in cases between two provinces or two monasteries, 1427, §2; in cases between physical or juridic religious persons of different religious institutes or of the same clerical institute of diocesan right or of the same lay institute, or between a religious and a secular cleric or lay person or a non-religious juridic person, 1427, §3; and auditors, 1428; and relators, 1429; hearing the parties or acting at request of a party, 1434; duties of,

1446–1449, 1451–1453, 1455–1457; and counterclaims, 1463, §2; defining time limits, 1466; exercising jurisdiction out of his territory, 1469; admitting persons to the courtroom, 1470; designating an interpreter, 1471; and a person unwilling to sign a juridic act, 1473; permitting the chancellor and notary to furnish a copy of juridic acts and case documents, 1475, §2; requiring presence of parties in a trial, 1477; and rights of minors, 1478, §§2–4; admitting a guardian or curator appointed by civil law, 1479; party can appear personally before a, 1481, §1; in penal cases can assign an advocate, 1481, §2; appoints a defender for cases involving minors or affecting the public good, 1481, §3; admitting a procurator without mandate, 1484, §2; must be informed of removal of a procurator, 1486, §1; can remove procurator and advocate by decree, 1487; fining procurator and advocate who resolve litigation by bribery or agreement for excessive profit or share in disputed object, 1488, §1; respondent can file counterclaim against petitioner before same, 1494, §1, 1495; and sequestration of a thing, 1496, §1, 1499; and *libellus*, 1501–1506; and citation, 1507–1508, 1512; and joinder of the issue, 1513, 1516; if case is concluded and a party dies, judge must proceed to additional acts, 1518, 2°; appoints another guardian or curator if one ceases function, 1519, §2; accepting renunciation of a case, 1524, §3, 1525; and proofs, 1528–1537, 1542–1548, 1550, §2, 1°, 1552, §2, 1553–1554, 1557–1563, 1565, §2, 1569, §2, 1570–1575, 1577–1582, 1584; and incidental cases, 1588, 1589, §1, 1590, §1, 1591, 1592, §1, 1593, §1, 1594, §1, 1596, §2, 1597; and publication of the acts, 1598; and conclusion of the case, 1599, §§2–3, 1600; and discussion of the case, 1601–1606; pronouncements of, 1607–1610, 1612, 1614, 1617; and challenge of the sentence, 1619–1622, 1624, 1626, §2, 1628, 1630, §1, 1633–1635; and *res iudicata*, 1642, §2; and *restitutio in integrum*, 1646, §1, 1647, §2, 1648; and judicial expenses, 1649, §2; and execution of the sentence, 1650, §§2–3, 1652, 1653, §3, 1655, §2; and oral contentious process, 1658, §1, 2°, 1659, §1, 1660, 1661, §1, 1665, 1668, §1; and marriage nullity cases, 1671–1672, 1676, 1679–1680, 1686, 1687, §1, 1688; and cases of separation of spouses, 1692, §§1, 3, 1695; and the process for dispensation of a marriage *ratum et non consummatum*, 1703; and methods of avoiding trials, 1716; and the penal process, 1717, §3, 1718, §3, 1721, §1, 1723, 1726, 1727, §1, 1730

judicial act(s) chancellor and notaries establish authenticity for, 483, §1; if tribunal is closed on a day scheduled for a, 1467; must be put into writ-

the stubborn upholding or diffusion of doctrines condemned by the, 696, §1; and college of bishops, 749, §2; one must believe as divinely revealed what is proposed by, 750, §1; one must embrace and retain everything proposed by the, 750, §2; religious submission to be given to a doctrine of the, 752–753; the ministry of the word must be based on the, 760; preachers must impart the doctrine of the, 768, §2; censors are to consider only the doctrine proposed by the, 830, §2; confessors are to adhere faithfully to the doctrine of, 978, §2

major superior(s)   notion, 620, 636, §1; called to particular councils, 443, §3, 2°; moderator of a religious house of canons regular or monks is a, 613, §2; qualifications to be in constitutions, 623; confirms the election of other superiors, 625, §3; has right to admit candidates to novitiate, 641; gives testimony on one who had been admitted and departed, 645, §2; can permit a group of novices to reside outside novitiate, 647, §3; can permit first profession to be anticipated, 649, §2; oversees director of novices, 650, §2; can extend novice's period of probation, 653, §2; can permit a member to live outside a house of the institute, 665, §1; can permit lay members to manage goods entailing rendering an account, 672; permits transfer of a religious from one autonomous monastery to another of the same institute or federation, 684, §3; can refuse subsequent profession after temporary profession, 689, §1; and dismissal of members, 694, §2, 695, §2, 697, 703; gives permission for members to publish writings on religion or morals, 832

conferences of: 708–709

clerical: is an ordinary, 134, §1; can deny licit use of faculty to hear confessions in particular cases, 967, §3; can revoke a presbyter's faculty to hear confessions, 974, §4; grants dimissorial letters, 1019, §1; judges suitability of member for ordination, 1025, §1, 1029; can forbid only for a canonical cause admission to presbyterate of a deacon destined to it, 1030; defines the time of diaconal ministry before presbyteral ordination, 1032, §2; receives the written declaration of candidates for ordination, 1036; deacon refusing presbyteral ordination cannot be prohibited from exercising the diaconal order unless prevented by a grave cause to be evaluated by his, 1038; is to investigate the qualities of candidates for orders, 1051, 2°; sends notice of ordination to place of baptism, 1054; and goods accepted in trust for pious causes, 1302, §3

majority   reached when eighteen years are completed, 97, §1; a person who has reached majority has full exercise of rights, 98, §1; one cannot be admitted to initial probation in a secular institute who has not attained, 721, §1, 1°

malice   and rescripts, 67, §2, 69; and juridic acts, 125, §2, 128; and votes, 172, §1, 1°; and postulation, 182, §2; and resignation from office, 188; and admission to novitiate, 643, §1, 4°; and temporary profession, 656, 4°; and marriage consent, 1098; and vows, 1191, §3; and oaths, 1200, §2, 1204; and punishment for external violation of a penal law or precept, 1321, §1; and actions of judges, 1457, §1; and *restitutio in integrum*, 1645, §2, 3°

mandate(s)   executor of an administrative act must proceed according to, 42; and delegated power, 133, 140, §2, 141, 142, §1; to teach the sacred sciences, 229, §3; of a pontifical legate, 364, 8°, 367; of a vicar general and an episcopal vicar, 481, §1; of a parochial vicar, 548, §1; from a superior to a religious to enter into a contract, 639, §2; about apostolic action of religious, 675, §3; from the Holy See about transfer among religious institutes, secular institutes, and societies of apostolic life, 684, §5, 730, 744, §2; to teach theological disciplines in any institutes of higher studies whatsoever, 812; of a presbyter to confirm, 883, 2°; of a proxy to enter marriage, 1105; of one competent to remit a censure, 1357, §2; of the Roman Pontiff to review an act or instrument confirmed specifically by him, 1405, §2; of an auditor, 1428, §3; of a notary and chancellor to furnish copies of judicial acts and documents, 1475, §2; of a procurator and advocate, 1484, 1686; illegitimate mandate and null sentence, 1620, 6°

pontifical: to consecrate a bishop, 1013, 1382

special: of the vicar general and episcopal vicar, 134, §3, 479, §§1–2; given to a coadjutor bishop and an auxiliary with special faculties, 406, §1; from the Apostolic See to a conference of bishops, 455, §§1, 4; of a proxy to enter marriage, 1105, §1, 1°; of a procurator, 1485, 1524, §3

marriage   notion, 1055, §1; sacramentality, 1055, §2; essential properties, 1056; consent, 1057; who can marry, 1058; Catholic, 1059; possesses favor of the law, 1060; *ratum, ratum et consummatum*, putative, 1061; promise to marry, 1062; pastoral care and marriage preparation, 1063–1072; diriment impediments in general, 1073–1082; specific diriment impediments, 1083–1094; consent, 1095–1107; canonical form, 1108–1123, 543, §1; mixed, 1124–1129; celebrated secretly, 1130–1133; effects of, 1134–1140; dissolution of, 1141–1150; separation of

and anointing of the sick to non-Catholics under certain conditions, 844, §§3–4; to celebrate the sacraments according to their own rite, 846, §2; oils used by in administering the sacraments, 847, §1; and offerings for administering the sacraments, 848; of baptism, 861–863, 874, §1, 1°–2°, 877, §1, 878, 530, 1°; of confirmation, 882–888, 895–896; of Most Holy Eucharist, 900–911; of exposition of the Most Blessed Sacrament, 943; of penance, 959, 965–986; of anointing of the sick, 1000, §2, 1003; of ordination, 1012; of marriage, 1057, §1; of sacramentals, 1168–1169; of exorcism, 1172; support of as a proper purpose of the Church, 1254, §2

non-Catholic: as observers at diocesan synod, 463, §3; administering sacraments to Catholics, 844, §2; assisting with a Catholic minister at a marriage, using their own rituals, is not permitted, 1127, §3

ministry *of lector and of acolyte:* conference of bishops can permit lay men to be admitted on a stable basis to the, 230, §1; must be received prior to ordination to diaconate, 1035, §1

of the word: and lay persons, 230, §3, 759; and bishops, 386, §1, 392, §2, 756, §2; and the Roman Pontiff and college of bishops, 756, §1; and presbyters, 757; and deacons, 757; and members of institutes of consecrated life, 758; and lay persons, 759; to be based on sacred scripture, tradition, liturgy, the magisterium, and church life, 760; various means available for, 761

delicts against the: 1370, 1375, 1378–1389, 1392, 1394–1396

minor(s) notion, 97; subject to parents and guardians except in matters exempted, 98, §2; domicile and quasi-domicile, 105; marriage preparation adapted to, 1063, 1°; marriage of, 1071, §1, 6°, 1072; and the law of fast and abstinence, 1252; and being liable to sanctions, 1324, §1, 4°; delict of a cleric committing an offense against the sixth commandment with a minor below sixteen, 1395, §2; and processes, 1478, §§1–3, 1481, §3, 1521, 1550, §1, 1646, §3

missionary (action of the Church) the whole Church is by its nature missionary, 781; direction and coordination by Roman Pontiff and college of bishops, 782, §1; solicitude of individual bishops for, 782, §2; and members of institutes of consecrated life, 783; missionaries, 784, 786–787, 790, §2; catechists, 785; precatechumenate and catechumenate, 788; neophytes, 789; function of diocesan bishops in mission lands, 790, §1; missionary cooperation in all dioceses, 791; pastoral care of those from mission lands working or studying elsewhere, 792; formation of seminarians about, 256, §2; distribution of clergy, 257; missionary work of personal prelatures, 294, 297; diocesan bishop to foster missionary vocations, 385

mission, council of the to be established in apostolic vicariates and prefectures, 495, §2; has the functions of the college of consultors, 502, §4

missions, sacred according to prescripts of the diocesan bishop, pastors are to arrange for in their parishes, 770

missus specialis cardinal who is a special envoy of the Roman Pontiff with competence only as entrusted to him, 358

moderator(s) *major (of a secular institute):* admits members, 720; excludes one after temporary probation, 726, §1

of an autonomous house: of canons regular or monks, 613

of an autonomous monastery: notion, 615; election of, 625, §2; and dismissal, 699, §2

of associations of the Christian faithful: designation, 309

of public associations of the Christian faithful: designation, 317; removal, 318, §2; and suppression of the association, 320, §3

of private associations of the Christian faithful: designation, 324, §1

of lay associations: 329

of several priests to whom is entrusted in solidum the care of one or several parishes: 517, §1, 520, §1, 526, §2, 542, 3°, 543, §2, 3°, 544

of the curia: notion, 473, §2; normally to be a vicar general, 473, §3; chancellor is to inform him of juridic acts of the curia, 474; gives permission to enter diocesan archive, 487, §1; gives consent to remove documents from the curial archive, 488

supreme: notion, 622; and report on state and life of institutes sent to the Apostolic See, 592, §1; and suppression of an erected house, 616, §1; constitution for a certain period of time, 624, §1; election of, 625, §1, 631, §1; and novitiate house, 647, §§1–2; permission for renunciation of goods by a member of the institute, 668, §4; and transfer of a member to another religious institute, 684, §1; and exclaustration, 686, §§1, 3; and departure of a member, 688, §2, 691, §1; and readmission of members, 690, §1; and dismissal of members, 695, §2, 697, 3°, 698, 699, §1; in secular institutes, 717, §2, 726, §2, 727, §1; in societies of apostolic

being admonished by an, 1371, 1°; delict of not obeying one's, 1371, 2°; delict of inciting animosities or hatred against an, 1373

and processes: can stand trial in the name of juridic persons subject to him, 1480, §2; has right to challenge the validity of sacred ordination, 1708; and penal process, 1717, §1, 1718–1720, 1721, §1, 1724, §1

ordinary, local notion, 134, §2; can dispense from diocesan laws and those issued by a plenary or provincial council or conference of bishops, 88; of a transient, 107, §2

and the People of God: and relation to a personal prelature, 297; and associations of the Christian faithful, 305, §2, 311, 324, §2, 325, §2; does not govern the seat of a pontifical legation except in marriage matters, 366, 1°; is notified that pontifical legate will perform liturgical celebrations, 366, 2°; gives express consent for a diocesan bishop to perform pontifical functions outside his diocese, 390; places a pastor in possession and prescribes the time within which possession must be taken, 527, §§2–3; can permit a pastor to reside in a house shared by several presbyters, 533, §1; is to be informed when the pastor is absent for more than a week, 533, §2; is to be informed when a parish becomes vacant, 541, §2; can permit a parochial vicar to reside in a house shared by several presbyters, 550, §1; is to promote common life in the rectory between pastor and parochial vicars, 550, §2; judges if liturgical functions by a rector in his church harm parochial ministry, 559; can order a rector to celebrate particular functions in his church, 560; oversees the functions of the rector of a church, 562; can remove the rector of a church, 563; appoints a chaplain, 565, 567, §1; preserves and safeguards the autonomy of an institute of consecrated life, 586, §2; institutes of consecrated life can be exempted from his governance by the Supreme Pontiff, 591; approves ordinary confessors for religious institutes, 630, §3; receives an annual account of administration from autonomous monasteries, 637; has the right to be informed about financial reports of a religious house of diocesan right, 637; gives written consent for validity of alienation or any other affair which can worsen the condition of an autonomous monastery or religious institute of diocesan right, 638, §4; gives testimony on a candidate dismissed from a seminary now seeking admission to novitiate, 645, §2; gives consent for an exclaustrated religious cleric to reside in his jurisdiction, 686, §1; exclaustrated religious, especially clerics, are dependent on the, 687; gives consent

for a clerical member of a society of apostolic life, with an indult to live outside the society, to reside in his jurisdiction, 745

and the teaching function of the Church: takes care that catechists fulfill their function properly, 780; is to have concern for teachers of religion, 804, §2; appoints, approves, removes, or demands removal of teachers of religion, 805; sees that directors of Catholic schools provide academically distinguished instruction, 806, §2; gives permission or approval to publish books, 824, §1; attests that reprints and translations of liturgical books conform to the approved edition, 826, §2; gives permission to publish prayer books, 826, §3; approves publishing catechisms and books on catechetical instruction and their translations, 827, §1; may judge other books about faith, religion and morals which are not used as texts, 827, §3; and censors, 830, §1; gives permission for clerics and religious to write for newspapers, magazines, or periodicals accustomed to attack openly the Catholic faith or good morals, 831, §1; and profession of faith, 833, 6°–7°

and the sanctifying function of the Church: takes care that prayers and sacred exercises of the Christian people reflect church norms, 839, §2; can permit or order a baptismal font in a non-parochial church or oratory, 858, §2; for a grave cause may give permission for baptism in a private house, 860, §1; designates a person to perform baptism when the ordinary minister is absent or impeded, 861, §2; can allow priests to celebrate Mass twice a day for a just cause and, if pastoral necessity requires, three times on Sundays and holydays of obligation, 905, §2; can permit an infirm or elderly priest to celebrate Mass seated before the people, 930, §1; can permit a priest to celebrate the Eucharist in the place of worship of some non-Catholic church or ecclesial community, 933; can permit reservation of the Eucharist in non-parochial churches, oratories, and chapels, 934, §1, 2°; can designate one not a cleric to expose the Blessed Sacrament, 943; exercises vigilance over fulfillment of Mass obligations in churches of secular clerics, 957; grants faculty to hear confessions, 967, §2; possesses by office the faculty to hear confessions in his jurisdiction, 968, §1; is competent to confer the faculty to hear confessions on any presbyter, 969, §1; is to hear the ordinary of a presbyter before granting the habitual faculty to hear confessions, 971; is competent to revoke the faculty to hear confessions, 974; is to send notice of the ordination of his subjects to the pastor of the place of baptism, 1054; is

1215, §3; for a judge from another jurisdiction to acquire proofs, 1469, §2; for a couple to approach the civil forum for separation, 1692, §2

of the judge: to print defense briefs along with the principal documents, 1602, §2

of the local ordinary: to publish books, 824, §1, 826, §3; for clerics and religious to write in newspapers, magazines, or periodicals accustomed to attack openly the Catholic religion or good morals, 831, §1; for an elderly or infirm priest to celebrate Mass seated, 930, §1; for a priest to celebrate Mass in the place of worship of some non-Catholic Church or ecclesial community, 933; for the reservation of the Eucharist in non-parochial churches, oratories, and chapels, 934, §1, 2°; to assist at certain marriages, 1071; for a past or present condition to be attached licitly to marriage consent, 1102, §3; for the celebration of marriage in a non-parochial church or oratory, or another suitable place, 1118, §§1–2; for a mixed marriage, 1125; to perform exorcisms, 1172; to designate a private chapel, 1226; for Mass or other sacred celebrations in a private chapel, 1228; for a private person to beg for alms for any pious or ecclesiastical institute or purpose, 1265, §1

of the moderator of the curia and chancellor: to enter the diocesan archive, 487, §1

of the ordinary: to preach, if required by particular law, 764; to repair precious images, 1189; to designate an oratory, 1223–1224; to refuse offerings to ecclesiastical juridic persons, 1267, §2; for a juridic person to accept a foundation, 1304, §1

of the pastor: for one with general delegation to assist at a marriage, 1114; to celebrate marriage in a non-parochial church or oratory, 1118, §1

of the pastor, chaplain, or superior: to bring Viaticum in case of necessity, 911, §2

of the proper ordinary: for a cleric without a residential office to be absent from the diocese for a notable period, 283, §1; for a cleric to take on management of goods belonging to lay persons or secular offices that entail rendering accounts, 285, §4; for a cleric to volunteer for military service, 289, §1; to celebrate marriage outside the parish of either party, 1115; for a private person to beg for alms for any pious or ecclesiastical institute or purpose, 1265, §1; for administrators to initiate or contest civil litigation in the name of a juridic person, 1288

of the rector: for a person to celebrate the Eucharist, administer sacraments, or perform other sacred functions, 561

of the religious superior: for the validity of alien-ation or any other affair which can worsen the patrimonial condition of a juridic person, 638, §3; to contract debts and obligations, 639, §§1–3; for religious to be absent from their house, 665, §1; to change dispositions for the use and revenue of goods and to place any act regarding temporal goods, 668, §2; for a perpetually professed religious to renounce personal goods, 668, §4; for a religious to accept functions or offices outside the institute, 671; to take on the management of goods belonging to lay persons or secular offices which entail rendering accounts, 672; to preach to religious in their churches or oratories, 765; for religious to publish writings dealing with religion or morals, 832; for presbyters of religious institutes to use the faculty to hear confessions, 969, §1

of the supreme moderator: for a definitively incorporated member to transfer to another society of apostolic life, 744, §1

perpetuity of a privilege is presumed, 78, §1; of a juridic person, 120, §1; and incardination, 268, §2; of clerical continence, 277, §1; of a parish being entrusted to a clerical religious institute or clerical society of apostolic life, 520, §2; of religious profession, 657–658; of incorporation in secular institutes, 720, 723, §§3–4; of ecclesiastical service, 1036; of impediments to receive orders, called irregularities, 1040; of marriage impediment of impotence, 1084, §1; of the bond of marriage, 1134; of separation of spouses with the bond remaining, 1152, §3; and penalties, 1319, §1, 1336, §1, 1342, §2, 1349; and processes, 1492, §2, 1621

person(s) *juridic:* subjects in canon law of obligations and rights, 113, §2; constitution, 114; aggregates of persons or of things, 115–117; representatives of, 118; collegial acts of, 119; perpetual by nature, 120; extinction of, 120, 123; joining of juridic persons, 121; dividing of juridic persons, 122; capable of acquiring, retaining, administering, and alienating temporal goods, 1255; ownership of goods, 1256–1257; rendered by *Church* in Book V, 1258; stand trial through their legitimate representatives, 1480, §1

juridic (identified in the law): seminaries, 238, §1; particular churches, 373; ecclesiastical province, 432, §2; conference of bishops, 449, §2; parishes, 515, §3; Holy See may erect conferences of major superiors as, 709

moral: the Catholic Church and Apostolic See are moral persons by divine ordinance, 113, §1

physical: constituted in the Church by baptism with rights and duties proper to Christians, 96; majority, 97, §1, 98, §1; minor, 97, §1, 98, §2; in-

ed in individual dioceses to promote mission endeavors, 791, 2°; who teaches faith and morals in any university is to make profession of faith before the rector, 833, 7°; and eucharistic celebration, 899, §1, 900–909, 911, §2, 919, §2, 926, 930, 933, 934, §2, 945, 951, 952, §1, 955, §§1–2, 4; and sacrament of penance, 961, §1, 1°, 965, 966, §2, 976, 978, §1, 979, 986, §2; and anointing of the sick, 1003; and marriage, 1105, §2; and blessing of sacred places and churches, 1207; and remission of penalties, 1357, §2; and delict of absolution of an accomplice, 1378, §1; and delict of solicitation of a penitent, 1387; judicial vicar and adjutant judicial vicar must be, 1420, §4; is incapable of being a witness regarding confessional knowledge, 1550, §2, 2°; as instructor of petition for a dispensation of a marriage *ratum et non consummatum,* 1700, §1

primate the title entails no power of governance in the Latin Church apart from a prerogative of honor unless the contrary is clear from apostolic privilege or approved custom, 438

abbot: comparable to a major superior, 620; judgement of is reserved to the Roman Rota, 1405, §3, 2°

privacy right of the Christian faithful, 220

private association of the Christian faithful notion, 299; statutes, 304, §1; title or name of, 304, §2; if not established as a juridic person cannot be subject of obligations and rights, 310; Christian faithful guide and direct, 321; can acquire juridic personality, 322; and ecclesiastical authority, 323; moderator and officials of, 324, §1; spiritual advisor of, 324, §2; and goods, 325; cessation of, 326

privation notion, 196; and suspension of ordinary power, 143, §2; and loss of ecclesiastical office, 184, §1; of office of diocesan bishop, 416; as expiatory penalty, 1336, §1, 2°, 1338, §§1–2; of judges, 1457, §1

delicts: priest soliciting a penitent, 1387; person who abuses ecclesiastical power or office, 1389, §1; priest who, despite warnings, remains in an attempted marriage, 1394, §1; person who violates obligation of residence, 1396; person who commits homicide or who kidnaps, detains, mutilates, or gravely wounds a person by force or fraud, 1397

privilege of faith possesses favor of the law in a doubtful matter concerning dissolution of marriage, 1150

privileges notion: 76, §1; granted by a rescript, 59, §1, 75; centenary or immemorial possession induces presumption of, 76, §2; interpretation of, 77; presumed perpetual, 78, §1; cessation, 78, §§2–3, 79–83; deprivation of, 84; apostolic, 199, 2°, 312, §1, 3°, 317, §2, 328, 438; can be granted to shrines, 1233; and excommunication, 1331, §2, 3°; and expiatory penalties, 1336, §1, 2°, 1338, §1

revoked: accompanying the diocesan bishop in visitation, 396, §2; someone other than diocesan bishop conferring canonries, 509, §1; only one pastor per parish, 526, §2

probation and members of religious institutes, 684, §§2, 4, 685, §1, 690, §1, 701; and members of secular institutes, 720–722, 723, §1; and societies of apostolic life, 735, §§1, 3; before ordination to diaconate and presbyterate, 1025, §1

processes *in general:* object of a trial, 1400, §1; administrative controversies, 1400, §2; proper and exclusive right of the Church to judge, 1401–1402; canonization processes, 1403; competent forum, 1404–1416; different grades and kinds of tribunals, 1417–1445; discipline to be observed in a trial, 1446–1475; parties in a case, 1476–1490; actions and exceptions, 1491–1500

ordinary contentious trial: introduction of a case, 1501–1506; citation and notification of juridic acts, 1507–1512; joinder of the issue, 1513–1516; trial of the litigation, 1517–1525; proofs, 1526–1586; incidental cases, 1587–1597; publication of the acts, conclusion of the case, discussion of the case, 1598–1606; pronouncements of the judge, 1607–1618; challenge of the sentence, 1619–1640; *res iudicata* and *restitutio in integrum,* 1641–1648; judicial expenses and gratuitous legal assistance, 1649; execution of the sentence, 1650–1655

oral contentious process: 1656–1670

certain special processes: marriage processes, 1671–1707; cases for declaring the nullity of sacred ordination, 1708–1712; methods of avoiding trials, 1713–1716

penal process: preliminary investigation, 1717–1719; development of the process, 1720–1728; action to repair damage, 1729–1731

method of proceeding in administrative recourse and in the removal and transfer of pastors: recourse against administrative decrees, 1732–1739; procedure to remove pastors, 1740–1747; procedure to transfer pastors, 1748–1752

processions entrusted to pastor is the function of leading processions outside church, 530, 6°; through public streets with the Most Holy Eucharist according to norms set by diocesan bishop, 944

ties in a trial, 1532, 1536; judge can decree that a specific act not be shown in cases pertaining to the, 1598, §1; and marriage nullity cases, 1691; and cases of separation of spouses, 1696; agreement and compromise in matters pertaining to the, 1715, §1; and penal trials, 1728, §1

public impediment(s) to marriage can be proven in the external forum, 1074; of ecclesiastical law, except presbyterate, can be dispensed in danger of death, 1079, §§1–2, 4

public order travelers are bound by territorial laws regarding the, 13, §2, 2°

public postal service notification of citations, decrees, sentences, and other judicial acts must be made known through public postal service or another very secure method, 1509, §1

public propriety marriage impediment of, 1093

public vow notion, 1192, §1

publication of declarations and decrees of a diocesan synod, 466; of books/writings, 823, §1, 824, §1, 825, 826, §3, 827, 829, 830, §3, 832; of translations of liturgical books, 826, §2, 838, §3; of acts, 1598–1606, 1703, §1; of a sentence, 1614–1615, 1623, 1630, §1, 1646, §2, 1682, §1

purpose(s) of law and its interpretation, 17; of juridic persons, 114, 116, §1; of ecclesiastical office, 145, §1; of associations of the Christian faithful, 215, 299, §1, 301, §§1–2, 304, 313, 325, §1, 327, 529, §2; of seminary formation, 255; of association among clerics, 278, §§1, 3; of conference of bishops, 451; of institutes of consecrated life, 574, §2, 578, 588, §§2–3; of religious institutes, 607, §3, 633, §2, 652, §2, 659, §2, 670, 680; of secular institutes, 722, §2; of societies of apostolic life, 735, §3, 737; of ecumenical movement, 755, §1; of catechetical formation, 776; prescribed by the ordinary for offerings when more than one Mass a day is celebrated, 951, §1; of marriage, 1125, 3°; of shrines, 1232, §2; of temporal goods of the Church, 1254; of begging for alms, 1265, §1; of offerings given by the faithful are to be used for that purpose, 1267, §3; of an institute to provide for support of clerics, 1274, §§1, 4; of insurance policies, 1284, §2, 1°; excess funds invested for purposes of juridic person, 1284, §2, 6°; donations for purposes of piety or Christian charity, 1285; of alienation, 1294, §2; of autonomous pious foundations, 1303, §1, 1°; of non-autonomous pious foundations, 1303, §1, 2°; expiatory penalties consistent with the supernatural purpose of the Church, 1312, §2; delict of taking or retaining consecrated species for a sacrilegious, 1367

putative marriage notion, 1061, §3; and legitimacy, 1137, 1139

pyx reservation of consecrated hosts in a, 939; exposition of the Most Holy Eucharist with a, 941, §1

Q

qualification(s) of a person to place a juridic act, 124, §1; of one who has received sacred orders for the power of governance, 129, §1; of lay persons for ecclesiastical offices and functions, 228, §1; of lay persons to assist the pastors of the Church as experts and advisors, 228, §2; of lay persons to receive a mandate to teach, 229, §3; of those admitted to the major seminary, 241, §1; of seminarians to examine questions by their own research and with scientific methodology, 254, §2; by law of persons to consent to marriage, 1057, §1; of persons to challenge a marriage, 1674

quasi-domicile and subject of particular ecclesiastical laws, 12, §3; one is a temporary resident (*advena*) in a, 100; acquired by, 101, §1, 102, §2; parochial or diocesan, 102, §3; of members of religious institutes and societies of apostolic life, 103; of spouses, 104; of minors, 105; loss of, 106; determines proper pastor and ordinary, 107, §§1, 3; and convocation of electors, 166, §1; right of election in constituting the presbyteral council can be conferred on priests with a domicile or, 498, §2; and grant of faculty to hear confessions, 971; and parish of marriage, 1115; and competent forum, 1408, 1409, §2, 1413, 2°, 1673, 2°, 1699, §1; of respondent to be indicated in introductory *libellus*, 1504, 4°

quasi-parish notion, 516, §1; pastoral care is to be given to a community which cannot be erected as a parish or a, 516, §2

quinquennial report notion, 399

R

radical sanation of marriage notion, 1161, §§1–2; requirements, 1161, §3, 1162–1164; authority competent to grant, 1165

radio norms of the conference of bishops for clerics and religious to take part in radio programs dealing with religion or morals, 831, §2

ratum et consummatum valid marriage between parties who have performed between themselves the conjugal act in a human fashion, 1061, §1; can be dissolved by no human power and by no cause, except death, 1141

ratum et non consummatum/ratum tantum valid

marriage between the baptized not yet consummated, 1061, §1; process for the dispensation of, 1697–1706

rebuke penal remedy, 1339, §§2–3, 1340, §3, 1341

rescissory action and an act entered out of ignorance or error, 126

reconciliation and oral contentious process, 1659, §1; of spouses, 1695; as a method of avoiding trials, 1713

recourse concerning doubtful ecclesiastical laws, 17; to obtain a decree, 57, §§1–2; to the Holy See for dispensations, 87, §2; against privation of or removal from office, 143, §2; in elections, 166, §2; and dismissal from a public association, 316, §2; not possible against a sentence or decree of the Roman Pontiff, 333, §3; to the Holy See when an ecclesiastical penalty prevents a diocesan bishop from exercising his function, 415; against decree of dismissal from religious institute, 700; dispensation from some ecclesiastical marriage impediment with insufficient time to make recourse to the Apostolic See or local ordinary, 1080, §2; to ecclesiastical or civil authority over adultery, 1152, §2; against administrators who have exceeded the limits and manner of ordinary administration, 1281, §3; to Apostolic See to modify pious wills, 1310, §3; from judicial sentences or decrees, which impose or declare a penalty, 1353; to the Apostolic See concerning previous remission of a reserved censure, 1357, §§2–3; delict of making recourse against an act of Roman Pontiff, ecumenical council, or college of bishops, 1372; to the Apostolic See and jurisdiction of a judge who has begun to adjudicate, 1417, §2; to the Apostolic Signatura against rotal decisions, 1445, §1, 1°–2°; against a rejected *libellus*, 1505, §4; and the joinder of the issue, 1513, §3; after a second concordant sentence on the status of persons, 1644; against judicial assessment, 1649, §2; to the Apostolic See against a bishop's decree rejecting a *libellus* for a dispensation of a marriage *ratum et non consummatum*, 1699, §3; against administrative decrees, 1732–1739; by a pastor against a decree of removal, 1747, §3

rector of a church, 556–563, 570, 764, 767, §4, 903, 958, §1, 1215, §2, 1307, §2; of a seminary, 238, §2, 239, §§1, 3, 260–262, 443, §3, 4°, 463, §1, 6°, 645, §2, 833, 6°, 985, 1051, 1°; of an ecclesiastical or Catholic university, 443, §3, 3°, 833, 7°; of a shrine, 1232, §2

rectory pastor is to reside in, 533, §1; common life between pastor and parochial vicars is to be fos-

tered in, 550, §2; duty and right of vicar forane to see to proper care of, 555, §1, 3°; used by a removed pastor, 1747, §§1–2

register(s) baptismal, 535, §1, 877, 895, 1054, 1121, §1, 1123, 1685, 1706; marriage, 535, §1, 1081, 1121, §§1, 3, 1123, 1685, 1706; death, 535, §1, 1182; other parochial registers prescribed by conference of bishops or the diocesan bishop, 535, §1; the vicar forane is to see parochial registers are inscribed correctly and protected appropriately, 555, §1, 3°, §3; confirmation, 895; ordination, 1053; marriages celebrated secretly, 1133; for adjudication of cases, 1458

rejection of the Catholic faith and valid admission into public associations, 316, §1; and prior permission of the local ordinary to assist at marriage, 1071, §1, 4°, §2

relator (*ponens*) notion, 1429; and deliberation of a case, 1609, §3; and writing the sentence, 1610, §2, 1677; in marriage cases, 1677, §§1, 2, 4

relics forbidden sale of, 1190, §1; permission of the Apostolic See for alienation or permanent transfer of, 1190, §2; under a fixed altar, 1237, §2

religious institute notion, 607; and public associations of the Christian faithful, 303, 312, §2, 317, §2, 320, §2; visit of bishop, 397, §2; chaplain for a lay, 567; erection and suppression of houses, 608–616; superiors and councils, 617–630; chapters, 631–633; temporal goods and their administration, 634–640; apostolate of, 673–683; whose mission is education, 801; instruments of social communication and, 831–832; cemeteries of, 1241, §1; competent authority for resolution of controversies among, 1427

churches of: rectors of churches connected to a house of, 556; right of bishops to preach in, 763; Eucharist reserved in, 934, §1, 1°, 936; vigilance of superiors over Mass obligations in, 957; permission from diocesan bishop to build a, 1215, §3; special collections in, 1266

members: domicile, quasi-domicile of, 103; joining associations of the Christian faithful, 307, §3; and synod of bishops, 346, §§1–2; admission to novitiate, 641–645; novitiate and formation of novices, 646–653; religious profession, 535, §2, 654–658, 1037, 1088; formation of religious, 659–661, 819; obligations and rights, 662–672; transfer to another, 684–685; departure from, 686–693; dismissal from, 241, §3, 694–704; religious raised to the episcopate, 705–707; incardination and studies of clerics, 266, §2, 268, §2; active and passive election in constituting the presbyteral council, 498, §1, 2°; as pastors, 538, §2,

682, §2, 1742, §2; preaching to, 765; and catecheti-cal formation, 776; as missionaries, 784; and Mass offerings, 952, §3; dimissorial letters for ordina-tion, 1019, §1, 1052, §2; marriage impediment, 1078, §2, 1°, 1088; obligation to carry out the litur-gy of the hours, 1174, §1; funerals, 1179; suspen-sion of vows made before religious profession, 1198; goods held in trust, 1302, §3; local ordinary coercing with penalties, 1320; prohibition against residence, order to reside in a certain place, 1337, §1; delict of using physical force against, 1370, §3; delict of exercising a trade or business contrary to the canons, 1392; delict for perpetually professed attempting marriage, 1394, §1; competent author-ity to execute a sentence, 1653, §3

major superiors: called to particular councils with consultative vote, 443, §3, 2°

major superiors (clerical): as ordinaries, 134, §1

superiors: and diocesan synod, 463, §1, 9°

superiors (clerical): duty and right of bringing Vi-aticum, 911, §1; and faculty of hearing confes-sions, 968, §2, 969, 974, §§3–4; and power to dis-pense from private vows, 1196, 2°; and power to dispense from or commute obligation of feast days or days of penance, 1245

remission of a penalty authority competent for, 1354–1357; necessity that offender withdraw from contumacy, 1358, §1; person remitting imposing warnings, penal remedies, penances, 1358, §2; re-mission of several penalties, 1359; extorted by grave fear is invalid, 1360; remission given condi-tionally or to one absent, 1361, §1; external remis-sion to be in writing unless grave cause suggests otherwise, 1361, §2; petition of remission or the remission itself are not normally to be divulged, 1361, §3; and prescription, 1362–1363

removal *general:* suspension of ordinary power dur-ing appeal or recourse against, 143, §2; as loss of ecclesiastical office, 184, §1; to be by decree or by law, 192; from an office conferred for an in-definite or definite period of time, 193, §§1–2; from office conferred at prudent discretion of competent authority, 193, §3; to be communicat-ed in writing, 193, §4; by the law itself, 194; by de-cree, 195

of persons: of a teacher in a seminary, 253, §3; of moderator of a public juridic person, 318, §2; of diocesan administrator, 430, §2; of vicar general and episcopal vicar, 477, §1, 481, §1; of chancellor and other notaries, 485; of finance officer, 494, §2; of pastor, 538, §§1–2, 1740–1747; of parochial vic-ar, 552; of vicar forane, 554, §3; of rector of a church, 563; of chaplain, 572; of religious superi-

ors, 624, §3; of a religious from an ecclesiastical office in a diocese, 682, §2; of judicial vicar, adju-tant judicial vicar, and judges, 1422; of promoter of justice and defender of the bond, 1436, §2; of procurator or advocate, 1486, §1, 1487

remuneration and transfer of office, 191, §2; of lec-tors and acolytes, 230, 1; of lay persons devoted to special service of the Church, 231, §2; of teachers in a seminary, 263; of clerics, 281, §1; of married deacons, 281, §3; of bishop being transferred, 418, §2, 2°; of clerics fulfilling certain parochial func-tions, 531

renunciation of privilege, 80; of office, 161, §2; of temporal goods by religious, 668, §§4–5; of the right to separate from a spouse, 1155; of an action, an instance, or judicial acts by a procurator with a special mandate, 1485; of a trial by a petitioner, 1524–1525, 1594, 2°; of the examination of a wit-ness by the party proposing, 1551; of appeal by the appellant, 1636, §1, 1641, 3°; of the penal process by the promoter of justice, 1724, §1; of the penal process to be accepted by the accused, 1724, §2

reparation of damages, 57, §3, 128, 982, 1062, §2, 1347, §2, 1357, §2, 1515, 1729–1731; by calumniator, 1390, §3

repetition of sacraments of baptism, confirmation, orders which imprint a character, 845, §1; of anointing of the sick, 1004, §2

representative of a juridic person, 118, 1480; of sem-inary, 238, §2; of Roman Pontiff, 358, 363, §1; of the Apostolic See, 363, §2; of the diocese, 393; of the parish, 532, 543, §2, 3°; of parties in a trial, 1478–1479, 1481–1490, 1678, §1

reputation harm illegitimately done to, 220, 1390, §2, 1455, §3; of candidates for the episcopacy, 378, §1, 2°; of chancellor and notaries, 483, §2; and re-mission of a penalty, 1361, §3; of judicial vicar, ad-jutant judicial vicar, and judges, 1420, §4, 1421, §3; of promoter of justice and defender of the bond, 1435; disclosure of acts and, 1455, §3; of procura-tor and advocate, 1483; of witnesses, 1572, 1°; lost by a pastor, 1741, 3°

res integra when parties are cited the matter ceases being, 1512, 1°

res iudicata notion, 1641–1642; prescription and, 1363, §1; Roman Rota and, 1444, §1, 2°; exception of to be raised before joinder of issues, 1462, §1; appeal from a sentence, 1629, 3°; cases concerning status of persons, 1643–1644; exception to, 1645; execution of a sentence, 1650, §§1–2; real actions and, 1655, §1; penal sentence, 1731

rescripts notion, 59; as singular administrative act,

35, 38; can be requested by all not prohibited, 60; can be requested for another without the person's assent, 61; effective moment, 62; subreption, obreption, 63; denial among dicasteries of Roman Curia, 64; denial among local ordinaries, 65; errors in, 66; contrary rescripts, 67; of Apostolic See with no executor named, 68; for whose presentation no time is specified, 69; entrusted to an executor, 70; obligation to use, 71; extension of rescripts of Apostolic See by diocesan bishop, 72; revoked by contrary law, 73; proof in external forum of favor granted orally and used in internal forum, 74; containing a privilege or dispensation, 75, 76–93; habitual faculties to execute rescripts of Apostolic See granted to bishops, 479, §3; fees fixed by bishops of a province, 1264, 1°

issued by Apostolic See: loss of clerical state, 290, 3°; enrollment again among clerics, 293; dispensation from marriage impediments by Penitentiary, 1082; legitimization of children, 1139; dispensation of marriage *ratum et non consummatum*, 1706

reservation of the Eucharist required in cathedral churches, parish churches, 934, §1, 1°; in other churches, oratories, and chapels, 934, §1, 2°; in religious houses, 608, 934, §1, 1°, 936; care for and celebration of Eucharist in, 934, §2; churches to be open to the faithful at least some hours daily, 937; and tabernacle, 938; and consecrated hosts in pyx to be renewed frequently, 939; and special lamp honoring presence of Christ in, 940; and exposition, 941

residence and particular laws, 12, §3; and domicile, quasi-domicile, 100–107; and notice of convocation, 166, §1; of cardinals, 356–357; and diocesan bishop, 395, §1; of retired bishop, 402, §1; of coadjutor and auxiliary bishop, 410; of diocesan administrator, 429; of pastor, 533, §1; of priests to whom is entrusted *in solidum* the care of a parish, 543, §2, 1°; of parochial vicars, 550; of superiors, 629; of novices, 647, §§2–3; diocesan bishop's prohibition of a religious residing in his diocese, 679; of retired religious bishop, 707, §1; and members of societies of apostolic life living outside the society, 745; and parish of marriage, 1115; never affected by suspension, 1333, §3, 2°; and expiatory penalties, 1336, §1, 1°, 1337, §1; and delict of violating place of, 1396; and processes, 1409, 1413, 2°, 1504, 3°, 1722; and diocesan bishop competent to permit spouses to approach the civil forum for separation, 1692, §2

resident (*incola*) a person with a domicile, 100

resignation of a delegate, 142, §1; loss of ecclesiastical office by, 184, §1, 187–189; and title of emeritus, 185; of Roman Pontiff, 332, §2; of cardinals,

354; of pontifical legate, 367; of diocesan bishop, 401–402, 416; of coadjutor and auxiliary bishop, 411; of diocesan administrator, 430, §2; of vicar general and episcopal vicar, 481, §1; of pastor, 538, §§1, 3; and process to remove pastors, 1742, §1, 1743, 1744, §2

respondent competent forum, 1407, §3, 1415, 1673, 2°–4°; parties in a trial, 1476–1480; counterclaim, 1494, §1; introductory *libellus,* 1504, 4°; citation, 1508, §1, 1510; renunciation of the trial, 1524, §1; parties who do not appear, 1592–1593, 1595; pronouncements of the judge, 1608, §4, 1612, §1; complaint of nullity against sentence, 1620, 4°; appeal, 1637, §§1–2; oral contentious process, 1659, §1, 1660; in process for dispensation of marriage *ratum et non consummatum,* 1701, §2, 1703, §1

restitutio in integrum general norms, 1645–1648; against rotal sentences adjudicated by Apostolic Signatura, 1445, §1, 1°; and decision against exception of incompetence, 1460, §2

retired conference of bishops to see to suitable and decent support of, 402, §2; bishops called to particular councils, 443, §2; diocesan bishop must provide suitable support and housing for a retired pastor, 538, §3; religious bishops choosing their residence, 707, §1; burial in a church of a diocesan bishop who is, 1242

retreat, spiritual of seminarians, 246, §5; of clerics, 276, §2, 4°; of pastor, 533, §2; of members of religious institutes, 663, §5; of members of secular institutes, 719, §1; of candidates for ordination, 1039

retroactivity of authentic interpretation declaring the words of the law which are certain in themselves, 16, §2; and radical sanation of marriage, 1161, §1

revocation of acquired rights and privileges granted by the Apostolic See prior to the code, 4; of pre-existing ecclesiastical laws, 21; of customs, 28; of decrees, 33, §2; of instructions, 34, §3; of administrative acts, 47; of singular decrees, 58, §1; of rescripts, 73; of privileges, 79; of delegated power, 142, §1; of postulation, 182, §4; of resignation, 189, §4; of faculty to hear confessions, 974–975; of dimissorial letters, 1023; of marriage consent, 1107, 1156, §2, 1162, §1; of decree of interlocutory sentence, 1591; of acts in penal process, 1718, §2, 1722; of administrative decrees, 1733, §3, 1734, §1, 1736, §3, 1739

right(s) acquired, 4, 36, §1, 38, 121–123, 192, 326, §2, 562, 616, §1, 858, §1, 1196; exercise of, 18, 1496, §2, 1508, §3, 1499; injured, 50; of all the Christian faithful, 96, 208–223; of minors, 98, §2, 1478, §2;

persons own goods, 1256; is supreme administrator and steward of all ecclesiastical goods, 1273; delicts against, 1370, §1, 1371, 1°, 1372; and competent forum for processes, 1405, 1417, §1; as supreme judge for Catholic world, 1442; and Roman Rota, 1443, 1444, §2; and Apostolic Signatura, 1445, §2; and recourse against his singular administrative acts, 1732

Roman Rota notion, 1443; makes judgments on, 1405, §3, 1444; and judgments of Apostolic Signatura, 1445, §1, 1°–3°

rosary and seminarians, 246, §3; and religious, 663, §4

rubrics in celebrating and administering the Eucharist, clergy are to wear vestments prescribed by the, 929

rule of life of associations for secular clerics, 278, §2; of religious, 662

rules of order (*ordines*) to be observed in meetings and other celebrations, defining constitution, direction, and ways of proceeding, 95

S

sacrament of unity Church as, 837, §1

sacramental character baptism, 845, §1; confirmation, 845, §1, 879; orders, 845, §1, 1008

sacramental seal of penance is inviolable, 983, §1; delict of violating by confessor, interpreter, others, 1388

sacramentals notion, 1166; bishop to exercise vigilance over celebration of, 392, §2; Apostolic See and, 1167, §1; rites and formulas to be used, 1167, §2; ministers of, 1168; consecrations and dedications, 1169, §1; blessings, 1169, §2–3, 1170; sacred objects designated for divine worship, 1171; exorcisms, 1172; offerings for the administration of, 1264, 2°; censures and, 1331, §1, 2°, 1335, 1352, §1

sacraments notion, 840; reception of in another ritual Church *sui iuris*, 112, §2; and the full communion of the Church, 205; right of the Christian faithful to receive, 213; formation of clerics in celebration of, 256, §1; the diocesan bishop and, 387, 392, §2; pastor and, 528, §2, 529, §1, 530, 777, 1°–2°; permission of the rector of a church required to celebrate, 561; supreme authority of the Church and, 841; administration of, 843; administration to and from non-Catholics, 844; sacramental character imprinted, 845, §1; conditional celebration of, 845, §2; appropriate liturgical books and rite, 846; oils used in the administration of, 847; and sacramentals, 1166; offerings for the adminis-

tration of, 848, 1264, 2°; censures and, 1331, §1, 2°, 1335, 1352, §1; delict of simulating administration of, 1379; delict of celebrating or receiving through simony, 1380

individual sacraments: baptism, 204, §1, 205, 842, §1, 845, §1, 849–878; confirmation, 845, §1, 879–896; Holy Eucharist, 897–958; penance, 959–991; anointing of the sick, 998–1007; orders, 845, §1, 1008–1054; marriage, 1055–1165

of Christian initiation: 842, §2

sacred places notion, 1205; dedication of, 1206; blessing of, 1207; documentation of dedication or blessing, 1208; other proof of dedication or blessing, 1209; actions performed in, 1210–1211, 1213; loss of dedication or blessing, 1212; churches, 1214–1222; oratories, 1223–1225, 1229; private chapels, 1226–1229; shrines, 1230–1234; altars, 1235–1239; cemeteries, 1240–1243

sacred scripture instruction in seminaries, 252, §2, 253, §2; nourishing spiritual life of clerics, 276, §2, 2°; continuing formation of priests after ordination, 279, §1; formation of novices, 652, §2; devotion of religious to, 663, §3; secular institutes and, 719, §1; ministry of the word to be based in, 760; publications of, 825; text books on, 827, §2

sacred times supreme ecclesiastical authority and, 1244, §1; diocesan bishops and, 1244, §2; dispensations from, 1245; feast days, 1246–1248; days of penance, 1249–1253

Saint Joseph holyday of obligation, 1246, §1

Saint Peter and Saint Paul the Apostles holyday of obligation, 1246, §1

Saint Thomas as teacher of dogmatic theology, 252, §3

saints public veneration of, 1186–1190; relics of saints in fixed altars, 1237, §2

sanctifying function of the Church sacred liturgy and the, 834; exercised by bishops, presbyters, deacons, and others, 835–837; direction of the sacred liturgy, 838; other means of sanctification than sacred liturgy, 839; sacraments, 840–1165; sacramentals, 1166–1172; liturgy of the hours, 1173–1175; ecclesiastical funerals, 1176–1185; veneration of saints, sacred images, and relics, 1186–1190; vows, 1191–1198; oaths, 1199–1204; sacred places, 1205–1243; sacred times, 1244–1253

sanctions in the Church *delicts and penalties in general:* punishment of delicts in general, 1311–1312; penal law and penal precept, 1313–1320; subject liable to penal sanctions, 1321–1330; censures, 1331–1335; expiatory penalties, 1336–1338; penal

theology vicar forane is to see that clerics attending theological meetings, 555, §2, 1°; in Catholic universities, 811, §1; provision to be made by conference of bishops and by diocesan bishop to teach, 821; books on, 827, §2; profession of faith and teachers of, 833, 6°

dogmatic: and formation of seminarians, 252, §3, 253, §2

moral: and formation of seminarians, 252, §3, 253, §2

third orders notion, 303

time(s) computation of, 200–203; continuous, 201, §1; useful, 201, §2; to receive holy communion, 920, true time for liturgy of the hours, 1175; sacred, 1244–1253

time limits/periods *and administrative acts:* decrees, 57; privileges, 83

and religious institutes: renewal of vows, 607, §2; appointment/election of superiors, 623, 624 §1–2; residence of novices and, 647, §3, 648; temporary profession, 655, 657

and sacraments: to receive confirmation, 890; for celebration of Mass, 955, §2; of faculty to hear confessions, 972; for other party to respond to interrogation in pauline privilege, 1145, §1

and secular institutes: holding office, 717, §1

for formation of clerics: permanent deacons, 236; presbyters, 250

for prescription: 198, 1270, 1344, 3°, 1362–1363

in administrative recourse: 1734, §§2–3, 1735, 1736, §4, 1737, §2

in councils: for diocesan finance council, 492, §2; for members of presbyteral council, 501, §1, 502, §1; for diocesan pastoral council, 513, §1

in delicts and penalties: of expiatory penalties, 1336, §1; for repentance to precede imposition of a penalty, 1347, §1; for penal process, 1723, §1

in elections: 165, 166, §2, 177, §1, 179, §1; postulation, 182

in trials: for trials in first and second instances, 1453; time limits and delays, 1465–1467; for procurator to present mandate, 1484, §2; for presentations of proofs, 1516; to introduce witnesses, 1552, §2; within which expert must complete work and produce report, 1577, §3; for intervention of a third party in a case, 1596, §3; conclusion of the case, 1599, §2; to present defense briefs or observations, 1601; to respond to defense briefs and observations, 1603, §1; to pronounce judgment, 1606; to issue sentence, 1610, §3; for complaint of nullity, 1623, 1626, §2; for appeals, 1630, §1, 1633, 1634, §2, 1637, §3, 1641, 2°, 1668, §2; to challenge

sentence, 1644, §1; for *restitutio in integrum,* 1646; to execute sentence, 1655, §2; in oral contentious process, 1659, §1, 1660–1661; in marriage cases, 1677, §2, 1682, §1

of delegated power: 142

of ecclesiastical offices: for conferral of office, 153, §2; presentation for office, 159, 162; loss of office, 184, §1, 186; removal from office, 193, §1–2; to take canonical possession of a diocese, 382, §2; for appointment of diocesan finance officer, 494, §2; for appointment of pastor, 522, 538, §1; to take possession of a parish, 527, §3; for appointment of vicar forane, 554, §2; for appointment of judicial vicar, adjutant judicial vicar, and other judges, 1422; in removal of a pastor, 1742, §1, 1744, §1; in transfer of a pastor, 1751

of vows: 1194

title(s) of a church which cannot be changed after dedication, 1218; privation of as expiatory penalty, 1336, §1, 2°, 1338, §1

titular bishop(s) to whom the care of a diocese is not entrusted, 376

tomb families and juridic persons other than parishes and religious institutes can have a, 1241, §2

transfer loss of ecclesiastical office and, 184, §1, 190–191; of cardinals between orders, 350, §§5–6; of bishops, 416, 418; of pastors, 538, §1, 1748–1752; of superiors, 624, §3; of novitiate house, 647, §1; from one religious institute to another or to a secular institute or a society of apostolic life, 684–685; from one secular institute to another or to a religious institute or a society of apostolic life, 730; of member of a society of apostolic life to another or to an institute of consecrated life, 744, of relics, 1190, §2; of the Mass obligations of pious foundations, 1309; as expiatory penalty, 1336, §1, 4°

transient(s) (*vagus/i*) notion, 100; bound by universal and particular laws, 13, §3; place of origin of a child born to, 101, §2; proper pastor and ordinary, 107, §2; transient clerics not permitted, 265; permission of the local ordinary required for marriage of, 1071, §1, 1°; place of marriage, 1115; place of residence as competent forum, 1409, §1

translations of sacred scripture, 825; of liturgical books, 826, §2, 838, §§2–3; of catechisms and other writings pertaining to catechetical instruction, 827, §1; approval of permission to publish, 829; in processes, 1471, 1474, §2

traveler(s) (*peregrinus/i*) notion, 100; laws binding, 13, §2; and dispensations, 91, 1196, 1°; executive power over, 136

secular institute, 721, §§1–2; of consecrations and dedications, 1169, §1; of alienation of relics, 1190, §§2–3; of an oath through a proxy, 1199, §2; acts placed illegitimately but validly by administrators, 1281, §3; civil validity of ownership of temporal goods, 1284, §2, 2°; of alienation of temporal goods, 1291, 1292, §2, 1295–1296; of acceptance of a foundation by a juridic person, 1304, §1; and censures, 1331, §2, 4°, 1333, §2, 1347, §1

and the sacraments: requirements for validity of sacraments approved or defined by supreme authority of the Church, 841; requirement of baptism for valid reception of other sacraments, 842, §1; validity of sacraments in non-Catholic Churches, 844, §2; of baptism, 845, §2, 869; of confirmation, 845, §2, 882; of absolution of sins, 962, §1, 966, §1, 1378, §2, 2°; of anointing of the sick, 1003, §1; of ordination, 845, §2, 1024; of dispensation from irregularities, 1049; and sacramentality of marriage between the baptized, 1055, §2; and marriage preparation, 1066; and marriage impediments, 1073; of marriage presumed in case of doubtful baptism, 1086, §3; and canonical form, 1108–1111, 1116, §1, 1127, §§1–2; of the pauline privilege, 1144, §1; renewal of consent and valid convalidation, 1156, §2; of a radical sanation, 1164

and procedures: of a judge who had been involved with a case in an earlier instance, 1447; of juridic acts placed by a judge before an objection is lodged, 1451, §2; of counterclaims, 1463, §1; and *fatalia legis,* 1465, §§1–2; of a procurator's acts with a special mandate, 1485; of changing terms of a controversy, 1514; derogation in oral contentious process of procedural norms not required for validity, 1670; posthumous challenge of marriage validity, 1675, §1; grounds for challenging marriage validity, 1677, §3; of mandate of a proxy, 1686; right to challenge validity of ordination, 1708; of an agreement or compromise, 1715, §1; in procedure to remove a pastor, 1742, §1, 1745

value documents having historic value, 491, §2; of temporal goods being alienated. 1291–1294

Vatican City cardinals who preside over dicasteries and other permanent institutions of the Roman Curia and, 354

veneration vigilance of the diocesan bishop over veneration of the saints, 392, §2; to be observed in celebration of sacraments, 840; of the Eucharist, 934–944; of the Blessed Virgin Mary, 246, §3, 276, §2, 5°, 663, §4, 1186; of saints, sacred images, and relics, 1186–1190

vestments to be worn by priests and deacons in celebrating and administering the Eucharist, 929

Viaticum function entrusted to pastor, 530, 3°; faculty of chaplain to administer, 566, §1; duty and right of pastor, parochial vicars, chaplains, and superiors in clerical religious institutes and societies of apostolic life to administer, 911, 922; for those in danger of death, 921; not to be delayed too long, 922

vicar *apostolic:* notion, 371, §1; equivalent in law to a diocesan bishop, 381, §2; a local ordinary, 134, §2; can make *ad limina* visit through a proxy, 400, §3; must appoint an apostolic pro-vicar after taking possession of the vicariate, 420; is to establish a council of at least three missionary presbyters, 495, §2, which has the functions of the college of consultors, 502, §4; can issue dimissorial letters for secular clergy, 1018

general: notion, 475; a local ordinary, 134, §2; powers of, 134, §3, 391, §2; must be appointed in each diocese, 475; is freely appointed and removed by the diocesan bishop, 477; requirements, 478; must report to the diocesan bishop and act according to his intention and mind, 480; cessation and suspension of power, 481; favors denied by, 65, §§2–3; visitation of the diocese for legitimately impeded diocesan bishop, 396, §1; coadjutor/auxiliary bishop as, 406, 409, 406 and, 413, §1; force of his actions until he receives certain notice of death of diocesan bishop, 417; power after transfer of diocesan bishop is announced, 418, §2, 1°; the one who governs the diocese before designation of diocesan administrator has powers of, 426; must be called to particular councils with consultative vote, 443, §3, 1°; the diocesan synod and, 462, §2, 463, §1, 2°; one should be moderator of the curia, 473, §3; is a member of the episcopal council, 473, §4; profession of faith and, 833, 5°; distinct from the judicial vicar, 1420, §1

episcopal: notion, 476; a local ordinary, 134, §2; powers of, 134, §3, 391, §2; is freely appointed and removed by the diocesan bishop, 477; requirements, 478; must report to the diocesan bishop and act according to his intention and mind, 480; cessation and suspension of power, 481; favors denied by, 65, §§2–3; can be appointed for spiritual care of faithful of a different rite, 383, §2; visitation of the diocese for legitimately impeded diocesan bishop, 396, §1; auxiliary bishop as, 406, §2, 409, §2; impeded see and, 413, §1; force of his actions until he receives certain notice of death of diocesan bishop, 417; power after transfer of diocesan bishop is announced, 418, §2, 1°; must be called to particular councils with consultative vote, 443, §3, 1°; the diocesan synod and, 462, §2,

TABLES OF
CORRESPONDING CANONS

Code of Canon Law (CIC)
Code of Canons of the Eastern Churches (CCEO)

At times there is a literal correspondence among the canons of the 1983 Code of Canon Law (CIC) and the 1990 Code of Canons of the Eastern Churches (CCEO). At other times there is substantial correspondence among them even though there are notable differences terminologically. At still other times there is only a partial correspondence among the canons of the two codes. Finally, at times there is no correspondence among the canons of the CIC and the CCEO, and this is indicated by an "X" in the appropriate columns.*

CIC	CCEO	CIC	CCEO	CIC	CCEO	CIC	CCEO
1	1	18	1500	35	1510, §1	53	X
2	3	19	1501	36	1512, §§1–2	54	1511; 1520, §1
3	4	20	1502	37	1514	55	1520, §2
4	5	21	1503	38	1515	56	1520, §3
5	6, 2°	22	1504	39	1516	57	1518
6	2; 6, 1°	23	1506, §1	40	1521	58	1513, §5
7	1488	24	1506, §2; 1507,	41	1522, §1	59	1510, §2, 3°;
8	1489		§§1–2	42	1523		1527, §1
9	1494	25	1507, §1	43	1524	60	X
10	1495	26	1507, §§3–4	44	1525	61	1528
11	1490	27	1508	45	1526	62	1511
12	1491, §§1, 2, 3°	28	1509	46	1513, §2	63	1529
13	1491, §3, 1°–2°,	29	X	47	1513, §3	64	X
	§4	30	X	48	1510, §2, 1°	65	1530
14	1496	31	X	49	1510, §2, 2°	66	X
15	1497	32	X	50	1517, §1	67	X
16	1498	33	X	51	1514; 1519, §2	68	X
17	1499	34	X	52	X	69	X

*This table substantially reproduces Appendix 7, pages 873–897 from *Eastern Catholic Church Law, Revised and Augmented Edition* by Victor J. Pospishil (New York, New York, Saint Maron Publications, 1996), with minor corrections and editing by Francis J. Marini. A corresponding canon may agree identically, partially or substantially. "X" indicates that there is no corresponding canon. Reprinted with permission.

CIC	CCEO	CIC	CCEO	CIC	CCEO	CIC	CCEO
70	1522, §2	115	920; 923	160	x	205	8
71	x	116	x	161	x	206	9
72	x	117	922, §1	162	x	207	323, §2
73	x	118	x	163	x	208	11
74	1527, §2	119	924, 1° –2°;	164	x	209	12
75	x		956, §1	165	947, §1	210	13
76	1531	120	925; 927, §1	166	948	211	14
77	1512, §3	121	x	167	949	212	15
78	1532, §1; 1532,	122	929	168	950	213	16
	§2, 1°–2°, §3	123	930	169	951	214	17
79	x	124	931	170	952	215	18
80	1533	125	932	171	953; 1434, §3	216	19
81	x	126	933	172	954	217	20
82	1534	127	934	173	955, §1–§3, §5	218	21
83	1532, §2, 3°–4°	128	935	174	x	219	22
84	1535	129	979	175	x	220	23
85	1536, §1	130	980, §2	176	956	221	24
86	1537	131	981; 983, §1	177	957	222	25
87	1537; 1538	132	982	178	958	223	26
88	x	133	983, §2, §3	179	959; 960	224	400
89	x	134	984; 987	180	961	225	401; 406
90	1536, §1, §3	135	985	181	962	226	407; 627, §1
91	1539	136	986	182	963	227	402
92	1512, §4	137	988	183	964	228	408, §1, §2
93	1513, §4	138	989	184	965, §1, §2;	229	404
94	x	139	x		966	230	403, §2; 709,
95	x	140	990	185	965, §4		§2
96	x	141	x	186	965, §3	231	409
97	909, §1, §2	142	992	187	967	232	328
98	910	143	991	188	968	233	329
99	909, §3	144	994; 995	189	969; 970; 971	234	331, §1; 332, §1;
100	911	145	936, §1–§2	190	972		334, §3
101	x	146	938	191	973	235	331, §2
102	912	147	939	192	974, §1	236	354
103	913	148	936, §3	193	974, §2; 975	237	332, §2; 334, §1
104	914	149	940; 946	194	976	238	335
105	915	150	x	195	977	239	338, §1; 339, §1;
106	917	151	x	196	978		340, §1; 471,
107	916, §1–§3	152	942	197	1540		§2
108	918	153	943	198	1541	240	339, §2–§3
109	919	154	944	199	1542	241	342
110	x	155	945	200	1543	242	330, §1, §2;
111	29, §1; 30; 588	156	x	201	1544		536, §2
112	32, §1; 33; 34	157	x	202	1545	243	337, §2, §3
113	920	158	x	203	1546	244	346, §1
114	921, §1, §3	159	x	204	7	245	346, §2, 7°–8°

CIC	CCEO	CIC	CCEO	CIC	CCEO	CIC	CCEO
246	346, §2, 2°–6°	288	x	333	45	379	188, §1
247	355	289	383, 2°, 3°	334	46, §1	380	187, §1
248	347	290	394	335	47	381	178
249	x	291	396	336	49	382	188, §2; 189
250	348, §1	292	395	337	50	383	192, §1–§3;
251	349, §1	293	398	338	51		193, §2; 678,
252	350, §1–§2	294	x	339	52		§2
253	340, §1; 471, §2	295	x	340	53	384	192, §4–§5
254	x	296	x	341	54	385	195
255	352, §1	297	x	342	x	386	196
256	352, §2–§3	298	x	343	x	387	197
257	352, §3	299	573, §2	344	x	388	198
258	353	300	x	345	x	389	199, §3
259	336, §1; 356, §2	301	573, §1; 574	346	346, §2	390	200
260	338, §2	302	x	347	x	391	191
261	x	303	x	348	x	392	201
262	336, §2	304	576, §1	349	x	393	190
263	341, §1	305	577	350	x	394	203
264	341	306	x	351	x	395	204
265	357, §1	307	578	352	x	396	205, §1
266	358; 428	308	581	353	x	397	205, §2–§3
267	359; 364	309	x	354	x	398	x
268	360, §2; 428	310	x	355	x	399	206, §2
269	366, §1, 1°,	311	x	356	x	400	208, §2
	3°–4°	312	575, §1, 1°, 3°,	357	x	401	210, §1, §2
270	365, §1		§2	358	x	402	62; 211
271	360, §1; 361;	313	x	359	x	403	212
	362	314	576, §2	360	x	404	214
272	363, 2°	315	x	361	48	405	213, §1, §3; 215,
273	370	316	580	362	x		§1
274	371, §2	317	x	363	x	406	215, §1–§2
275	379; 381, §3	318	x	364	x	407	215, §3–§4
276	368; 369; 377;	319	582	365	x	408	216
	378	320	583, §1, §2, 2°	366	x	409	222; 224, §1, 1°,
277	373; 374	321	x	367	x		§3
278	391	322	x	368	x	410	217
279	372	323	x	369	177, §1	411	218
280	376	324	x	370	311, §1; 312	412	233, §1
281	390	325	x	371	311, §1; 312	413	233
282	385, §1	326	x	372	x	414	x
283	386, §1; 392	327	x	373	177, §2	415	x
284	387	328	x	374	x	416	219
285	382; 383, 1°;	329	x	375	x	417	224, §2
	385, §3	330	42	376	178; 179	418	223, 1°, 3°; 224,
286	385, §2	331	43	377	181, §2		§1, 1°
287	384	332	44	378	180	419	220, 2°; 221, 2°

CIC	CCEO	CIC	CCEO	CIC	CCEO	CIC	CCEO
420	X	460	235	503	X	546	301, §1
421	220, 3°; 221, 3°, 4°	461	236	504	X	547	301, §3
		462	237, §1	505	X	548	302, §1, §3
422	220, 1°; 221, 1°, 5°	463	238, §1, 1°–2°, 4°–7°, 9°– 10°; §2, §3	506	X	549	X
423	225			507	X	550	302, §4
424	X	464	239	508	X	551	X
425	227	465	240, §4	509	X	552	303
426	X	466	241	510	X	553	276, §1; 277, §1
427	220, 4°; 221, 5°; 229	467	242	511	272	554	277
		468	237	512	273, §1, §2, §4	555	278
428	228	469	243, §1	513	274	556	304
429	X	470	244, §1	514	273, §1; 275	557	305
430	231	471	244, §2	515	279; 280, §2, §3	558	306, §1
431	X	472	X			559	306, §2
432	X	473	X	516	X	560	307
433	X	474	X	517	287, §2	561	308
434	X	475	245	518	280, §1	562	309
435	80, 1°, 3°; 133, §1; 134, §1	476	246	519	281, §1	563	310
		477	247, §1	520	281, §2; 282	564	X
436	133, §1, 4°, 5°; 137; 221, 4°	478	247, §2–§3	521	281, §1; 285, §1	565	X
		479	248	522	284, §3, 4°	566	X
437	X	480	249	523	284, §1	567	X
438	X	481	224, §1; 251	524	285, §3	568	X
439	X	482	252	525	286	569	X
440	X	483	253	526	287	570	X
441	X	484	254	527	288	571	X
442	133, §1, 2°	485	255	528	289, §1, §2	572	X
443	X	486	256	529	289, §3	573	410
444	X	487	257	530	290, §2; 677, §1; 739, §2	574	410; 411
445	X	488	258			575	X
446	X	489	259	531	291	576	X
447	X	490	260	532	290, §1	577	X
448	X	491	261	533	292	578	426
449	X	492	263, §1	534	294	579	435; 506, §1; 566
450	X	493	263, §5	535	296		
451	X	494	262, §1–§4	536	295	580	X
452	X	495	264	537	295	581	508, §2
453	X	496	265	538	297; 1391, §2	582	439; 440, §1, §2
454	X	497	266	539	298		
455	X	498	267	540	299	583	X
456	X	499	268	541	300	584	438, §1, §2, §4; 507; 556
457	X	500	269	542	X		
458	X	501	270	543	X	585	438, §3; 508, §2
459	X	502	271, §1–§5	544	X		
				545	301, §1, §2	586	X

CIC	CCEO	CIC	CCEO	CIC	CCEO	CIC	CCEO
587	x	618	421	650	458; 459, §1; 524, §3; 525, §1	683	415, §2, §4; 554, §2; 638
588	505, §3; 554, §2	619	421			684	487, §1, §2; 488, §1–§3; 544, §1–§3; 545, §1–§3
589	434; 505, §1, §2, 1°, 3°; 554, §2; 563, §2	620	418, §1; 441, §3	651	458, §1; 524, §1, §2		
		621	508, §1; 566	652	459; 525, §1		
		622	x	653	461; 525, §1	685	488, 545, §1–§2
590	412, §1; 555; 564	623	442; 513; 557	654	462, §1; 469; 531	686	490; 491; 548
591	412, §2	624	444, §1, §2; 514; 557	655	526	687	491; 548, §2
592	419; 554, §2	625	443; 515, §1, §2; 557	656	464, 1°–3°; 527, 1°–3°	688	496; 546
593	413; 554, §2			657	x	689	547
594	413; 554, §2	626	445; 515, §3; 557	658	464, 4° 532	690	493, §2; 546, §1
595	414, §1, 1°, 2°, §3; 554, §2; 566	627	422, §1; 557	659	471; 536		
		628	414, §1, 3°; 420, §2, §3; 554, §2; 566	660	x	691	492; 549, §1, §2, 2°
596	441, §1, §2; 511; 557; 995			661	x		
		629	446	662	x	692	493, §1; 549, §3
597	448; 449; 450, 1°; 518; 559, §1; 568, §1	630	473, §2, 2°; 475; 539	663	473, §2, 1°, 3°; 538, §2	693	494; 549, §3
		631	512; 557			694	497; 551; 562, §3
598	426	632	x	664	473, §2, 2°; 474, §1; 538, §3		
599	x	633	x			695	x
600	x	634	423; 558, §1; 567, §1	665	478; 495; 550	696	500, §2, 1°; 551; 552, §2, 1°; 553; 562, §3
601	x			666	x		
602	x	635	424; 425; 558, §2; 567, §2	667	477, §1; 541	697	500, §2, 2°–4°; §3; 551; 553; 562, §3
603	481; 570			668	460; 467; 468, §1; 529, §3; 533; 540		
604	570	636	447; 516; 558, §3			698	x
605	571	637	x			699	500, §1; 553; 562, §3
606	1505	638	x	669	476; 540		
607	x	639	468, §2, §3; 529, §5; 533	670	x	700	500, §4; 501, §2, §3; 552, §3; 553; 562, §3
608	x			671	431, §1		
609	436, §2; 509, §1; 556; 566	640	x	672	427		
		641	453, §1; 519	673	x	701	502; 553; 562, §3
610	x	642	448; 453, §2	674	x		
611	437, §1; 509, §2; 556; 566; 556; 566	643	450, 4°–7°; 517, §1; 559, §1	675	x	703	503; 553; 562, §3
				676	x		
		644	452	677	x	704	x
612	437, §3; 509, §2; 556; 566	645	453, §3; 519	678	415, §1; 554, §2	705	431, §2, 1°
		646	459, §1; 525, §1	679	x	706	431, §3
613	418, §1; 433, §1	647	456, §2, §3; 522	680	x	707	62; 211; 431, §2, 2°
614	x			681	282, §2; 543		
615	x	648	457, §1, §3; 459, §2; 523	682	284, §2; 303; 431, §1; 1391, §2	708	x
616	438; 510; 556; 566					709	x
617	x	649	457, §2; 523, §1			710	563, §1

CIC	CCEO	CIC	CCEO	CIC	CCEO	CIC	CCEO
711	563, §1, 4°	756	x	800	631, §2	842	675, §2; 697
712	563, §1, 1°	757	x	801	x	843	381, §2
713	563, §1, 2°	758	x	802	635	844	671
714	563, §1, 3°	759	x	803	632; 639	845	672
715	x	760	x	804	636, §1; 639	846	668, §2; 674
716	x	761	x	805	636, §2	847	693
717	566	762	x	806	634, §3; 638, §1	848	x
718	576, §2	763	610, §1	807	640, §1	849	675, §1
719	x	764	610, §2–§3	808	642, §1	850	676
720	568, §1	765	612	809	x	851	686, §2
721	x	766	610, §4	810	x	852	681, §3
722	x	767	614, §1–§2, §4	811	643	853	x
723	x	768	616	812	644	854	x
724	x	769	626	813	645	855	x
725	x	770	615	814	640, §2	856	x
726	x	771	192, §1, §3	815	646	857	687, §1
727	x	772	609; 653	816	649; 650	858	x
728	x	773	617	817	648	859	x
729	568, §2	774	618	818	x	860	687, §2
730	x	775	621, §3; 622,	819	x	861	677
731	572		§2; 623, §1	820	x	862	x
732	x	776	624	821	x	863	x
733	x	777	x	822	651	864	679
734	x	778	x	823	652, §2	865	682
735	x	779	x	824	654; 662, §1	866	x
736	x	780	x	825	655, §1, §3	867	686, §1
737	x	781	584, §1	826	655, §1; 656,	868	681, §1; §4
738	x	782	x		§1; 657, §3	869	x
739	x	783	x	827	658; 659; 665,	870	681, §2
740	x	784	x		§1	871	680
741	x	785	x	828	666, §2	872	684
742	x	786	590	829	663, §1	873	x
743	x	787	x	830	664	874	685
744	562	788	587, §1, §3	831	660	875	688
745	x	789	x	832	662, §2	876	691
746	x	790	x	833	187, §2	877	689
747	595	791	585, §3	834	668, §1	878	690
748	586	792	x	835	x	879	692
749	597	793	627, §1–§2	836	x	880	693
750	598	794	628	837	673	881	x
751	x	795	629	838	657, §1, §2;	882	694
752	599	796	631, §1		668, §2	883	x
753	600	797	627, §3;	839	x	884	x
754	10	798	633, §3	840	667	885	x
755	902; 904, §1	799	x	841	669	886	696, §3

CIC	CCEO	CIC	CCEO	CIC	CCEO	CIC	CCEO
887	696, §3	932	705, §1; 707, §1	975	726, §3	1020	751
888	x	933	705, §2	976	725	1021	472; 537, §2;
889	x	934	714, §1	977	730		560; 752
890	695, §1	935	x	978	732, §2	1022	x
891	695, §1	936	714, §1	979	x	1023	753
892	x	937	x	980	x	1024	754
893	x	938	x	981	732, §1	1025	758, §2
894	x	939	x	982	731	1026	756
895	x	940	x	983	733	1027	758, §1, 4°
896	x	941	x	984	734, §1–§2	1028	x
897	698	942	x	985	734, §3	1029	758, §1, 2°
898	699, §3	943	x	986	735	1030	755
899	x	944	x	987	x	1031	758, §1, 6°; 759
900	699, §1	945	715; 716	988	x	1032	760
901	x	946	x	989	719	1033	758, §1, 1°
902	700	947	x	990	x	1034	x
903	703, §1	948	x	991	x	1035	x
904	378	949	x	992	x	1036	761
905	x	950	x	993	x	1037	x
906	x	951	x	994	x	1038	757
907	x	952	x	995	x	1039	772
908	702	953	x	996	x	1040	764
909	707, §1	954	x	997	x	1041	762, §1, 1°–6°
910	709	955	x	998	737, §1	1042	762, §1, 7°–8°
911	x	956	x	999	741	1043	771, §2
912	x	957	x	1000	742	1044	763
913	710	958	x	1001	738	1045	765
914	x	959	718	1002	x	1046	766
915	712	960	720, §1	1003	739	1047	767, §1–§2
916	711	961	720, §2, §3	1004	x	1048	767, §3
917	x	962	721	1005	x	1049	768
918	713, §1	963	x	1006	740	1050	769, §1, 1°–3°
919	713, §2	964	736, §1	1007	x	1051	769, §1, 4°–6°;
920	708; 881, §3	965	722, §1	1008	323, §1; 743		771, §3, §4
921	708	966	722, §3	1009	325; 744	1052	770
922	x	967	722, §2; §4;	1010	773	1053	774
923	x		723, §2; 724,	1011	773	1054	775
924	706		§2	1012	744	1055	776, §1–§2
925	x	968	723	1013	745	1056	776, §3
926	707, §1	969	724	1014	746, §1	1057	817
927	x	970	x	1015	747; 748, §2	1058	778
928	x	971	x	1016	748, §1	1059	780, §1
929	707, §1	972	x	1017	749	1060	779
930	x	973	x	1018	750	1061	x
931	707, §1	974	726, §1, §2	1019	472; 537, §1	1062	782

CIC	CCEO	CIC	CCEO	CIC	CCEO	CIC	CCEO
1063	783, §1, §3	1107	827	1152	863	1197	x
1064	x	1108	828	1153	864, §1, §3	1198	894
1065	783, §2	1109	829, §1	1154	865	1199	895
1066	785	1110	829, §2	1155	866	1200	x
1067	784	1111	830	1156	843	1201	x
1068	785, §2	1112	x	1157	844	1202	x
1069	786	1113	x	1158	845	1203	x
1070	787	1114	x	1159	846	1204	x
1071	789, 1°–3°,	1115	831, §1, 1°, 2°	1160	847	1205	x
	4°–6°	1116	832, §1, §2	1161	848; 849, §2	1206	x
1072	x	1117	834, §1	1162	851	1207	871, §2
1073	790, §1	1118	838, §1	1163	850	1208	871, §2
1074	791	1119	836	1164	849	1209	x
1075	792	1120	x	1165	852	1210	872, §1
1076	793	1121	841, §1, §3	1166	867, §1	1211	x
1077	794	1122	841, §2	1167	867, §2	1211	x
1078	795	1123	842	1168	x	1212	x
1079	796	1124	813	1169	x	1213	x
1080	797	1125	814	1170	x	1214	869
1081	798	1126	815	1171	x	1215	870
1082	799	1127	834; 839	1172	x	1216	x
1083	800	1128	816	1173	x	1217	871, §1
1084	801	1129	x	1174	377	1218	x
1085	802	1130	840, §1	1175	x	1219	x
1086	803	1131	840, §1	1176	875; 876, §3	1220	872
1087	804	1132	840, §2	1177	x	1221	x
1088	805	1133	840, §3	1178	x	1222	873
1089	806	1134	776, §2	1179	x	1223	x
1090	807	1135	777	1180	x	1224	x
1091	808	1136	627, §1	1181	878	1225	x
1092	809, §1	1137	x	1182	879	1226	x
1093	810	1138	x	1183	875; 876, §1, §2	1227	x
1094	812	1139	x	1184	877	1228	x
1095	818	1140	x	1185	x	1229	x
1096	819	1141	853	1186	884	1230	x
1097	820	1142	862	1187	885	1231	x
1098	821	1143	854	1188	886	1232	x
1099	822	1144	855	1189	887, §2	1233	x
1100	823	1145	856	1190	887, §1 888	1234	x
1101	824	1146	857	1191	889, §1–§3	1235	x
1102	826	1147	858	1192	889, §4	1236	x
1103	825	1148	859	1193	890	1237	x
1104	837, §1	1149	860	1194	891	1238	x
1105	837, §2	1150	861	1195	892	1239	x
1106	x	1151	x	1196	893, §3	1240	874, §2

CIC	CCEO	CIC	CCEO	CIC	CCEO	CIC	CCEO
1241	874, §4	1285	1029	1330	x	1373	1447, §1
1242	874, §3	1286	1030	1331	1434	1374	1448, §2
1243	x	1287	1031	1332	1431, §1	1375	1447, §2
1244	880, §1	1288	1032	1333	1432	1376	1441
1245	x	1289	1033	1334	1432, §1	1377	1449
1246	880, §3	1290	1034	1335	1435, §2	1378	1443; 1457
1247	881, §1, §4	1291	1035, §1, 3°	1336	1432, §2, §3	1379	1443
1248	881, §2	1292	1036, §1; 1038	1337	1429	1380	1461
1249	x	1293	1035, 1°, 2°, §2	1338	1430	1381	1462
1250	x	1294	x	1339	1427, §1	1382	1459, §1
1251	882	1295	1042	1340	x	1383	1459, §2
1252	x	1296	1040	1341	x	1384	1462
1253	x	1297	x	1342	1402, §2	1385	x
1254	1007	1298	1041	1343	x	1386	1463
1255	1009, §1	1299	1043	1344	1409, §1, 1°, 2°, 4°	1387	1458
1256	1008, §2	1300	1044			1388	1456
1257	1009, §2	1301	1045	1345	x	1389	1464
1258	x	1302	1046	1346	1409, §1, 3°	1390	1452; 1454
1259	1010	1303	1047	1347	1407, §1, §2	1391	1455
1260	1011	1304	1048, §2, §3	1348	x	1392	1466
1261	x	1305	1049	1349	1409, §2	1393	1467
1262	x	1306	1050	1350	1410	1394	1453, §2–§3
1263	1012	1307	1051	1351	1412, §4	1395	1453, §1
1264	1013, §1	1308	1052, §1–§5	1352	1435, §1	1396	x
1265	1015	1309	1053	1353	1319; 1471, §1; 1487, §2	1397	1450, §1; 1451
1266	1014	1310	1054			1398	1450, §2
1267	1016	1311	x	1354	1419; 1423, §2	1399	x
1268	1017	1312	x	1355	1420, §1, §3	1400	1055
1269	1018	1313	1412, §2–§3	1356	1420, §2, §3	1401	x
1270	1019	1314	1408	1357	x	1402	1056
1271	x	1315	1405, §1–§2	1358	1424	1403	1057
1272	x	1316	1405, §3	1359	1425	1404	1058
1273	1008, §1	1317	1405, §1	1360	1421	1405	1060, §1, 2°–4°, §2, §3; 1061
1274	1021	1318	x	1361	1422		
1275	x	1319	1406, §1	1362	1152, §2–§3		
1276	1022	1320	415, §4	1363	1153	1406	1072
1277	263, §4	1321	1414	1364	1436, §1; 1437	1407	1073
1278	x	1322	x	1365	1440	1408	1074
1279	1023	1323	1413, §1	1366	1439	1409	1075
1280	x	1324	1413, §2; 1415	1367	1442	1410	1076
1281	1024	1325	x	1368	1444	1411	1077
1282	x	1326	1416	1369	1448, §1	1412	1078
1283	1025–1026	1327	x	1370	1445	1413	1079
1284	1020, §1, §2; 1028	1328	1418	1371	1436, §2; 1446	1414	1081
		1329	1417	1372	x	1415	1082

CIC	CCEO	CIC	CCEO	CIC	CCEO	CIC	CCEO
1416	1083, §1–§2	1460	1119	1505	1188	1550	1231
1417	1059	1461	1120	1506	1189	1551	1232
1418	1071	1462	1121	1507	1190	1552	1233
1419	1066	1463	1122	1508	1191	1553	1234
1420	1086; 1088, §2, §3	1464	1123	1509	1192, §1–§2	1554	1235
		1465	1124	1510	1192, §3	1555	1236
1421	1087	1466	1125	1511	1193	1556	1237
1422	1088, §1	1467	1126	1512	1194	1557	1238
1423	1067, §1, §4	1468	1127	1513	1195	1558	1239
1424	1089	1469	1128	1514	1196	1559	1240
1425	1984; 1090, §2	1470	1129	1515	1197	1560	1241
1426	1185; 1090, §1	1471	1130	1516	1198	1561	1242
1427	1069	1472	1131	1517	x	1562	1243
1428	1093	1473	1132	1518	1199	1563	1244
1429	1091, §2–§4	1474	1315, §2	1519	1200	1564	1245
1430	1094	1475	1133	1520	1201	1565	1246
1431	1095	1476	1134	1521	1202	1566	1247
1432	1096	1477	1135	1522	1203	1567	1248
1433	1097	1478	1136	1523	1204	1568	1249
1434	1098	1479	1137	1524	1205	1569	1250
1435	1099	1480	1138, §1, §3	1525	1206	1570	1251
1436	1100	1481	1139	1526	1207	1571	1252
1437	1101	1482	1140	1527	1208	1572	1253
1438	1063, §3; 1064	1483	1141	1528	1209	1573	1254
1439	1067, §5	1484	1142	1529	1210	1574	1255
1440	1072	1485	1143	1530	1211	1575	1256
1441	1085, §3	1486	1144	1531	1212	1576	1257
1442	1059, §1	1487	1145	1532	1213	1577	1258
1443	1065	1488	1146	1533	1214	1578	1259
1444	x	1489	1147	1534	1215	1579	1260
1445	x	1490	1148	1535	1216	1580	1261
1446	1103	1491	1149	1536	1217	1581	1262
1447	1105	1492	1149; 1150	1537	1218	1582	1263
1448	1106	1493	1155	1538	1219	1583	1264
1449	1107	1494	1156	1539	1220	1584	x
1450	1108	1495	1157	1540	1221	1585	1266
1451	1109	1496	1158	1541	1222	1586	1265
1452	1110	1497	1159	1542	1223	1587	1267
1453	1111	1498	1160	1543	1224	1588	1268
1454	1112	1499	1161	1544	1225	1589	1269
1455	1113	1500	1162	1545	1226	1590	1270
1456	1114	1501	1104, §2	1546	1227	1591	1271
1457	1115	1502	1185	1547	1228	1592	1272
1458	1117	1503	1186	1548	1229	1593	1273
1459	1118	1504	1187	1549	1230	1594	1274

CIC	CCEO	CIC	CCEO	CIC	CCEO	CIC	CCEO
1595	1275	1635	1316	1675	1361	1715	1165; 1169
1596	1276	1636	1317	1676	1362	1716	1181, §1; 1182,
1597	1277	1637	1318	1677	1363		§1; 1183
1598	1281	1638	1319	1678	1364	1717	1468
1599	1282	1639	1320	1679	1365	1718	1469
1600	1283	1640	1321	1680	1366	1719	1470
1601	1284	1641	1322	1681	1367	1720	1486
1602	1285	1642	1323	1682	1368	1721	1472
1603	1286	1643	1324	1683	1369	1722	1473
1604	1287	1644	1325	1684	1370	1723	1474
1605	1288	1645	1326	1685	1371	1724	1475
1606	1289	1646	1327	1686	1372, §1	1725	1478
1607	1290	1647	1328	1687	1373	1726	1482
1608	1291	1648	1329	1688	1374	1727	1481
1609	1292	1649	1335; 1336	1689	1377	1728	1471
1610	1293	1650	1337	1690	1375	1729	1483
1611	1294	1651	1338	1691	1376	1730	1484
1612	1295	1652	1339	1692	1378	1731	1485
1613	1296	1653	1340	1693	1379	1732	996
1614	1297	1654	1341	1694	1380	1733	998
1615	1298	1655	1342	1695	1381	1734	999
1616	1299	1656	1343	1696	1382	1735	x
1617	1300	1657	x	1697	x	1736	1000
1618	1301	1658	1344	1698	x	1737	997, §1; 1001
1619	1302	1659	1345	1699	x	1738	1003
1620	1303, §1	1660	1346	1700	x	1739	1004
1621	1303, §2	1661	1347	1701	x	1740	1389
1622	1304, §1	1662	1348	1702	x	1741	1390
1623	1304, §2	1663	1349	1703	x	1742	1391
1624	1305	1664	1350	1704	x	1743	1392
1625	1306	1665	1351	1705	x	1744	1393
1626	1307	1666	1352	1706	x	1745	1394
1627	1308	1667	1353	1707	1383	1746	1395
1628	1309	1668	1354	1708	1385	1747	1396
1629	45, §3; 1310	1669	1355	1709	1386, §1, §3	1748	1397
1630	1311	1670	1356	1710	1386, §2	1749	1398
1631	1313	1671	1357	1711	x	1750	1399, §1
1632	x	1672	1358	1712	1387	1751	1399, §2, §3
1633	1314	1673	1359	1713	x	1752	1400
1634	1315	1674	1360	1714	1164		

Code of Canons of the Eastern Churches (CCEO)
Code of Canon Law (CIC)

At times there is a literal correspondence among the canons of the 1990 Code of Canons of the Eastern Churches (CCEO) and the 1983 Code of Canon Law (CIC). At other times there is substantial correspondence among them even though there are notable differences terminologically. At still other times there is only a partial correspondence among the canons of the two codes. Finally, at times there is no correspondence among the canons of the CIC and the CCEO, and this is indicated by an "X" in the appropriate columns.*

CCEO	CIC	CCEO	CIC	CCEO	CIC	CCEO	CIC
1	1	24	221	48	361	72	X
2	6, §2	25	222	49	336	73	X
3	2	26	223	50	337	74	X
4	3	27	X	51	338	75	X
5	4	28	X	52	339	76	X
6	5, §1; 6, §1, 2°,	29	111, §1	53	340	77	X
	4°	30	111, §2	54	341	78	X
7	204	31	X	55	X	79	X
8	205	32	112, §1, 1°	56	X	80	435
9	206	33	112, §1, 2°	57	X	81	X
10	754	34	112, §1, 3°	58	X	82	X
11	208	35	X	59	X	83	X
12	209	36	X	60	X	84	X
13	210	37	X	61	X	85	X
14	211	38	112, §2	62	X	86	X
15	212	39	X	63	X	87	X
16	213	40	X	64	X	88	X
17	214	41	X	65	X	89	X
18	215	42	330	66	X	90	X
19	216	43	331	67	X	91	X
20	217	44	332	68	X	92	X
21	218	45	333; 1629, 1°	69	X	93	X
22	219	46	334; 346	70	X	94	X
23	220	47	335	71	X	95	X

*This table substantially reproduces Appendix 7, pages 852–872 from *Eastern Catholic Church Law, Revised and Augmented Edition* by Victor J. Pospishil (New York, New York, Saint Maron Publications, 1996), with minor corrections and editing by Francis J. Marini. A corresponding canon may agree identically, partially or substantially. "X" indicates that there is no corresponding canon. Reprinted with permission.

CCEO	CIC	CCEO	CIC	CCEO	CIC	CCEO	CIC
96	x	141	x	187	380; 833, 3°	226	x
97	x	142	x	188	379; 382, §2	227	425
98	x	143	x	189	382, §1, §3	228	428
99	x	144	x	190	393	229	427, §1
100	x	145	x	191	391	230	x
101	x	146	x	192	383, §1, §3, §4; 384; 771	231	430
102	x	147	x			232	x
103	x	148	x	193	383, §2	233	412; 413
104	x	149	x	194	x	234	x
105	x	150	x	195	385	235	460
106	x	151	x	196	386	236	461, §1
107	x	152	x	197	387	237	462; 468
108	x	153	x	198	388, §1	238	463
109	x	154	x	199	389	239	464
110	x	155	x	200	390	240	465
111	x	156	x	201	392	241	466
112	x	157	x	202	x	242	467
113	x	158	x	203	394	243	469
114	x	159	x	204	395	244	470; 471
115	x	160	x	205	396, §1; 397	245	475, §1
116	x	161	x	206	399, §1	246	476
117	x	162	x	207	x	247	477, §1; 478
118	x	163	x	208	400, §1	248	479
119	x	164	x	209	x	249	480
120	x	165	x	210	401	250	x
121	x	166	x	211	402	251	481
122	x	167	x	212	403, §1, §3	252	482
123	x	168	x	213	405, §1	253	483
124	x	169	x	214	404	254	484
125	x	170	x	215	405, §2; 406; 407, §2–§3	255	485
126	x	171	x			256	486, §2, §3
127	x	172	x	216	408	257	487
128	x	173	x	217	410	258	488
129	x	174	x	218	411	259	489
130	x	175	x	219	416	260	490
131	x	176	x	220	419; 421; 422; 427, §2; 833	261	491, §1, §3
132	x	177	369; 373			262	494
133	435; 436, §1; 442, §1	178	376; 381, §1	221	419; 421; 422; 427, §2; 436, §1, 3°	263	492, §1, §3; 493; 1277
		179	376				
134	435	180	378, §1	222	409, §1	264	495, §1
135	x	181	377, §1	223	418	265	496
136	x	182	x	224	409, §2; 417; 418, §2, 1°; 481, §1	266	497
137	436, §2	183	x			267	498
138	436, §1	184	x			268	499
139	x	185	x	225	423	269	500
140	x	186	x			270	501

CCEO	CIC	CCEO	CIC	CCEO	CIC	CCEO	CIC
271	502, §1, §2	314	x	358	266, §1	398	293
272	511	315	x	359	267, §1	399	x
273	512; 514, §1	316	x	360	268, §1; 271,	400	224
274	513	317	x		§1, §2	401	225, §2
275	514, §1	318	x	361	271, §1	402	227
276	553, §1	319	x	362	271, §2, §3	403	230, §3
277	553, §2; 554	320	x	363	272	404	229
278	555	321	x	364	267, §2	405	x
279	515, §1	322	x	365	270	406	225, §1
280	515, §2, §3; 518	323	207, §1;	366	269	407	226, §1
281	519; 520, §1;		1008	367	x	408	228, §1, §2
	521, §1	324	x	368	276, §1	409	231
282	520; 681, §2	325	1009, §1	369	276, §2, 2°, 4°,	410	573; 574, §2
283	x	326	x		5°	411	574, §1
284	522; 523; 682,	327	x	370	273	412	590, §2; 591
	§1	328	232	371	274, §2	413	593; 594
285	521, §2; 524	329	233	372	279	414	595; 628, §2
286	525	330	242, §1	373	277, §1	415	678, §1; 683;
287	517, §1; 526	331	234, §1; 235, §1	374	277, §3		1320
288	527, §1	332	234, §1; 237, §1	375	x	416	x
289	528; 529, §1	333	x	376	280	417	x
290	530, 1°–2°,	334	237, §2	377	276, §2, 3°;	418	620
	4°–5°; 532	335	238		1174, §1	419	592, §1
291	531	336	259, §1; 262	378	276, §2, 2°;	420	628
292	533	337	239, §3; 243		904	421	618; 619
293	x	338	239, §1; 260	379	275, §1	422	627
294	534, §1	339	239, §2; 240	380	x	423	634, §1
295	536, §1; 537	340	239, §1; 253, §1	381	275, §2; 843,	424	635, §2
296	535	341	263; 264		§1	425	635, §1
297	538, §1, §3	342	241	382	285, §1–§2	426	578; 598, §2
298	539	343	x	383	285, §3; 289	427	x
299	540	344	234	384	287	428	266, §2; 268,
300	541	345	x	385	282; 285, §4;		§2
301	545; 546; 547	346	244; 245; 246		286	429	x
302	548; 550, §1, §3	347	248	386	283, §1	430	x
303	552	348	250	387	284	431	671; 682, §1;
304	556	349	251	388	x		705; 706
305	557	350	252, §1, §2	389	x	432	x
306	558; 559	351	x	390	281	433	613, §1
307	560	352	255; 256; 257,	391	278	434	589
308	561		§1	392	283, §2	435	579
309	562	353	258	393	x	436	609, §1
310	563	354	236	394	290	437	611, 2° 3°; 612
311	370; 371, §2	355	247, §2	395	292	438	584; 616, §1,
312	370; 371, §2	356	259, §2	396	291		§3
313	x	357	265	397	x	439	582

CCEO	CIC	CCEO	CIC	CCEO	CIC	CCEO	CIC
440	582	476	669, §1	519	641; 642; 645, §1, §2	554	x
441	596, §1, §2; 620	477	667, §1	520	646	555	590, §2
		478	665, §1	521	647, §1	556	x
442	623	479	x	522	647, §2, §3	557	x
443	625, §2	480	x	523	648; 649, §1	558	634, §1; 635, §1
444	624, §1; 625, §3	481	603	524	648, §3; 650, §2; 651, §1, §2	559	x
445	626	482	x			560	x
446	629	483	x			561	x
447	636, §1	484	x	525	650, §1; 652, §2, §5; 653; 668	562	x
448	597, §1; 642	485	x			563	710; 711; 712; 713, §1; 714
449	597, §2	486	x	526	655	564	590, §2
450	643, §1, 1°–4°	487	684, §3	527	656, 2°–5°	565	266, §3
451	x	488	684, §3, §4	528	x	566	717, §1
452	644	489	686, §1	529	639, §2, §3; 668, §2, §3	567	634, §1
453	641; 642; 645, §1, §3	490	686, §3			568	720; 729
		491	687	530	668, §1	569	x
454	x	492	691	531	654	570	603, §1; 604, §1
455	x	493	690, §1; 692	532	658, 2°		
456	647, §2	494	693	533	x	571	605
457	648, §1, §3; 649, §1	495	665, §2	534	x	572	731, §1
		496	668, §2	535	x	573	299, §2, §3; 301, §3
458	650, §2; 651, §1	497	694	536	659		
		498	703	537	1019; 1021	574	301, §1
459	646; 648, §2; 650, §1; 652, §5	499	x	538	630, §1; 663; 664	575	312, §1, 1°, 3°; 312, §2
		500	696, §1; 697, 2°–3°; 699, §1			576	304, §1; 314
460	x			539	630, §2–§3	577	305
461	648, §3; 653	501	700	540	669, §1	578	307
462	654	502	701	541	667, §1	579	x
463	x	503	702	542	x	580	316
464	656, 2°–5°	504	x	543	681, §1	581	308
465	x	505	588, §2; 589	544	684, §1	582	319, §1
466	x	506	579	545	684, §2, §4; 685	583	320, §1, §2
467	668, §4	507	584			584	781
468	639, §2–§4; 668, §3, §5	508	581; 585; 621	546	688; 690, §1547; 689	585	791, 2°
		509	609, §1			586	748, §2
469	654	510	616, §1–§2	548	686, §1, §3	587	788
470	x	511	596, §1–§2	549	690, §1; 691; 692; 693	588	111, §2
471	659	512	631, §1–§3			589	x
472	1019; 1021	513	623	550	665, §2	590	786
473	630, §2; 663, §1–§3, §5; 664	514	624	551	694; 696, §1; 697; 703	591	x
		515	625, §1, §3; 626			592	x
		516	636, §1	552	696, §1; 700	593	x
474	630, §1; 664	517	643, §1, 1°	553	699, §1	594	x
475	630, §2, §3	518	597, §2			595	747

CCEO	CIC	CCEO	CIC	CCEO	CIC	CCEO	CIC
596	x	639	803, §2; 804, §2	681	852, §2; 868; 870	722	965–967
597	749					723	967, §3; 968
598	750	640	807; 814	682	865	724	967, §3; 969
599	752	641	x	683	x	725	976
600	753	642	808	684	872	726	974, §1, §2, §4; 975
601	x	643	811, §1	685	874		
602	x	644	812	686	851, 2°; 867, §1	727	x
603	x	645	813	687	857, §2; 860, §1	728	x
604	x	646	815			729	x
605	x	647	x	688	875	730	977
606	x	648	817	689	877	731	982
607	x	649	816, §1	690	878	732	978, §1; 981
608	x	650	816, §2	691	876	733	983
609	772, §1	651	822, §1, §3	692	879	734	984–985
610	763; 764; 766	652	823	693	847, §1; 880, §2	735	986
611	x	653	772, §2			736	964, §1
612	765	654	824, §2	694	882	737	998
613	x	655	825	695	890; 891	738	1001
614	767, §1, §2, §4	656	826, §1, §3	696	886, §1; 887	739	530, 3°; 1003, §1-§2
615	770	657	826, §2, §3; 838, §2, §3	697	842, §2		
616	768			698	897	740	1006
617	773	658	827, §1–§2	699	898; 900, §1	741	999
618	774, §2	659	827, §3	700	902	742	1001, §1
619	x	660	831, §1	701	x	743	1008
620	x	661	x	702	908	744	1009, §2; 1012
621	775, §2	662	824, §1; 832	703	903		
622	775, §3	663	829	704	x	745	1013
623	775, §1	664	830	705	932, §2; 933	746	1014
624	776	665	827, §4	706	924	747	1015, §1
625	x	666	828	707	909; 924; 926; 929; 932, §1	748	1015, §2; 1016
626	769	667	840			749	1017
627	226, §2; 793; 797; 1136	668	834, §2; 838, §1; 846, §1	708	920; 921, §1	750	1018
				709	230, §3; 910	751	1020
628	794	669	841	710	913, §1	752	1021
629	795	670	x	711	916	753	1023
630	x	671	844	712	915	754	1024
631	796, §1; 800, §1	672	845	713	918; 919, §1	755	1030
		673	837, §2	714	934; 936	756	1026
632	803, §1	674	846	715	945, §1	757	1038
633	798	675	842, §1; 849	716	945, §2	758	1025, §1; 1027; 1029; 1031, §1; 1033
634	806, §2	676	850	717	x		
635	802	677	530, 1°; 861	718	959		
636	804, §1; 805	678	383, §2	719	989	759	1031
637	x	679	864	720	960; 961	760	1032, §1, §3
638	683; 806, §1	680	871	721	962	761	1036

CCEO	CIC	CCEO	CIC	CCEO	CIC	CCEO	CIC
762	1041; 1042, 2°, 3°	801	1084	844	1157	887	1189; 1190, §3
		802	1085	845	1158	888	1190
763	1044	803	1086	846	1159	889	1191; 1192, §1
764	1040	804	1087	847	1160	890	1193
765	1045	805	1088	848	1161, §1, §2	891	1194
766	1046	806	1089	849	1161, §3; 1164	892	1195
767	1047, §1, §2, 1°, 2°; §3, §4; 1048	807	1090	850	1163	893	1196, 1°, 2°
		808	1091	851	1162	894	1198
		809	1092	852	1165	895	1199, §1
768	1049	810	1093	853	1141	896	x
769	1050; 1051	811	x	854	1143	897	x
770	1052, §2–§3	812	1094	855	1144	898	x
771	1043; 1051, 2°	813	1124	856	1145	899	x
772	1039	814	1125	857	1146	900	x
773	1010; 1011	815	1126	858	1147	901	x
774	1053	816	1128	859	1148	902	755, §1
775	1054	817	1057	860	1149	903	x
776	1055; 1056; 1134	818	1095	861	1150	904	755, §2
		819	1096, §1	862	1142	905	x
777	1135	820	1097	863	1152	906	x
778	1058	821	1098	864	1153	907	x
779	1060	822	1099	865	1154	908	x
780	1059	823	1100	866	1155	909	97; 99
781	x	824	1101	867	1166; 1167	910	98
782	1062	825	1103	868	x	911	100
783	1063, 1°, 2°, 4°; 1065, §2; 1136	826	1102, §1	869	1214	912	102, §1, §2
		827	1107	870	1215, §1	913	103
		828	1108	871	1207; 1208; 1217, §2	914	104
784	1067	829	1109			915	105
785	1066; 1068	830	1111	872	1210; 1220	916	107
786	1069	831	1115	873	1222	917	106
787	1070	832	1116	874	1240; 1241, §1; 1242	918	108
788	x	833	x			919	109
789	1071, §1, 1°–4°, 6°; §2	834	1117; 1127, §1	875	1176, §1, §2; 1183	920	113, §2; 115, §2
		835	x			921	114, §1, §3; 117
790	1073	836	1119	877	1184, §1	922	117
791	1074	837	1104, §1; 1105, §1	878	1181	923	115, §2
792	1075, §2			879	1182	924	119, 2°, 3°
793	1076	838	1118, §1, §2	880	1244, §1; 1246	925	120, §2
794	1077	839	1127, §3	881	920, §1; 1247; 1248, §1	926	x
795	1078	840	1130; 1131; 1132; 1133			927	120, §1
796	1079			882	1251	928	x
797	1080	841	1121, §1, §3; 1122	883	x	929	122
798	1081			884	1186	930	123
799	1082	842	1123	885	1187	931	124
800	1083	843	1156	886	1188	932	125

CCEO	CIC	CCEO	CIC	CCEO	CIC	CCEO	CIC
933	126	976	194	1020	1284, §2, 2°	1062	x
934	127	977	195	1021	1274, §1, §2,	1063	1438, 1°
935	128	978	196, §1		§3	1064	1438, 1°, 2°
936	145; 148	979	129	1022	1276	1065	1443
937	x	980	130	1023	1279, §1	1066	1419
938	146	981	131, §1, §2	1024	1281	1067	1423, §1; 1439,
939	147	982	132	1025	1283, 1°, 2°		§1
940	149, §1, §2	983	131, §3; 133	1026	1283, 3°	1068	x
941	x	984	134, §1, §2	1027	x	1069	1427, §1, §3
942	152	985	135, §1, §2, §3	1028	1284	1070	x
943	153	986	136	1029	1285	1071	1418
944	154	987	134, §3	1030	1286	1072	1406, §2; 1440
945	155	988	137	1031	1287	1073	1407
946	149, §3	989	138	1032	1288	1074	1408
947	165	990	140	1033	1289	1075	1409
948	166	991	143	1034	1290	1076	1410
949	167	992	142	1035	1291; 1293, §1	1077	1411
950	168	993	x	1036	1292	1078	1412
951	169	994	144, §1	1037	x	1079	1413
952	170	995	144, §2; 596,	1038	1292, §3, §4	1080	x
953	171, §1, 1°, 2°,		§3	1039	x	1081	1414
	4°	996	1732	1040	1296	1082	1415
954	172	997	1737, §1	1041	1298	1083	1416
955	173	998	1733, §1, §3	1042	1295	1084	1425, §1, §2,
956	119, 1°; 176	999	1734	1043	1299		§4
957	177	1000	1736	1044	1300	1085	1426, §1; 1441
958	178	1001	1737, §2, §4	1045	1301	1086	1420, §1–§4
959	179, §1, §4	1002	x	1046	1302	1087	1421
960	179, §2; §5	1003	1738	1047	1303	1088	1420, §5; 1422
961	180, §1	1004	1739	1048	1304	1089	1424
962	181, §1	1005	x	1049	1305	1090	1425, §3, §5
963	182	1006	x	1050	1306, §2	1091	1426, §2; 1429
964	183	1007	1254	1051	1307	1092	x
965	184, §1, §2;	1008	1256; 1273	1052	1308	1093	1428
	185; 186	1009	1255; 1257, §1	1053	1309	1094	1430
966	184, §3	1010	1259	1054	1310	1095	1431
967	187	1011	1260	1055	1400	1096	1432
968	188	1012	1263	1056	1402	1097	1433
969	189, §1	1013	1264	1057	1403, §1	1098	1434
970	189, §2, §3, §4	1014	1266	1058	1404	1099	1435
971	189, §4	1015	1265, §1	1059	1417; 1442	1100	1436
972	190	1016	1267	1060	1405, §1, 1°, 3°,	1101	1437
973	191	1017	1268		4°, §2, §3, 1°,	1102	x
974	192, 193, §4	1018	1269		3°	1103	1446
975	193, §1, §2, §3	1019	1270	1061	1405, §3, 3°	1104	1501

CCEO	CIC	CCEO	CIC	CCEO	CIC	CCEO	CIC
1105	1447	1149	1491; 1492, §2	1194	1512	1239	1558
1106	1448	1150	1492, §1	1195	1513	1240	1559
1107	1449, §2, §3,	1151	x	1196	1514	1241	1560
	§4; 1450	1152	1362	1197	1515	1242	1561
1108	1450	1153	1363	1198	1516	1243	1562
1109	1451	1154	x	1199	1518	1244	1563
1110	1452	1155	1493	1200	1519	1245	1564
1111	1453	1156	1494	1201	1520	1246	1565
1112	1454	1157	1495	1202	1521	1247	1566
1113	1455	1158	1496	1203	1522	1248	1567
1114	1456	1159	1497	1204	1523	1249	1568
1115	1457	1160	1498	1205	1524	1250	1569
1116	x	1161	1499	1206	1525	1251	1570
1117	1458	1162	1500	1207	1526	1252	1571
1118	1459	1163	x	1208	1527	1253	1572
1119	1460	1164	1714	1209	1528	1254	1573
1120	1461	1165	1715	1210	1529	1255	1574
1121	1462	1166	x	1211	1530	1256	1575
1122	1463	1167	x	1212	1531	1257	1576
1123	1464	1168	x	1213	1532	1258	1577
1124	1465	1169	1715, §1	1214	1533	1259	1578
1125	1466	1170	x	1215	1534	1260	1579
1126	1467	1171	x	1216	1535	1261	1580
1127	1468	1172	x	1217	1536	1262	1581
1128	1469	1173	x	1218	1537	1263	1582
1129	1470	1174	x	1219	1538	1264	1583
1130	1471	1175	x	1220	1539	1265	1586
1131	1472	1176	x	1221	1540	1266	1585
1132	1473	1177	x	1222	1541	1267	1587
1133	1475	1178	x	1223	1542	1268	1588
1134	1476	1179	x	1224	1543	1269	1589
1135	1477	1180	x	1225	1544	1270	1590
1136	1478	1181	1716, §1	1226	1545	1271	1591
1137	1479	1182	1716, §2	1227	1546	1272	1592
1138	1480	1183	1716, §2	1228	1547	1273	1593
1139	1481	1184	x	1229	1548	1274	1594
1140	1482	1185	1502	1230	1549	1275	1595
1141	1483	1186	1503	1231	1550	1276	1596
1142	1484	1187	1504	1232	1551	1277	1597
1143	1485	1188	1505	1233	1552	1278	x
1144	1486	1189	1506	1234	1553	1279	x
1145	1487	1190	1507	1235	1554	1280	x
1146	1488	1191	1508	1236	1555	1281	1598
1147	1489	1192	1509; 1510	1237	1556	1282	1599
1148	1490	1193	1511	1238	1557	1283	1600

CCEO	CIC	CCEO	CIC	CCEO	CIC	CCEO	CIC
1284	1601	1328	1647	1373	1687	1415	1324, §1, §2; 1345
1285	1602	1329	1648	1374	1688	1416	1326, §1
1286	1603	1330	x	1375	1690	1417	1329, §1
1287	1604	1331	x	1376	1691	1418	1328
1288	1605	1332	x	1377	1689	1419	1354, §1, §2
1289	1606	1333	x	1378	1692	1420	1355, §1; 1356
1290	1607	1334	x	1379	1693	1421	1360
1291	1608	1335	1649, §1	1380	1694	1422	1361
1292	1609	1336	1649, §2	1381	1695	1423	1354, §3
1293	1610	1337	1650	1382	1696	1424	1358, §1
1294	1611	1338	1651	1383	1707	1425	1359
1295	1612	1339	1652	1384	x	1426	x
1296	1613	1340	1653	1385	1708	1427	1339, §3
1297	1614	1341	1654	1386	1709–1710	1428	x
1298	1615	1342	1655	1387	1712	1429	1337
1299	1616	1343	1656	1388	x	1430	1338
1300	1617	1344	1658	1389	1740	1431	1332
1301	1618	1345	1659	1390	1741	1432	1333, §1, §3, 1°, 2°, §4; 1334, §1; 1336, §1, 3°
1302	1619	1346	1660	1391	538, §2; 682, §2; 1742		
1303	1620–1621	1347	1661	1392	1743	1433	1336, §1, 5°
1304	1622–1623	1348	1662	1393	1744	1434	171, §1, 3°; 1331
1305	1624	1349	1663	1394	1745	1435	1352, §1; 1335
1306	1625	1350	1664	1395	1746	1436	1364; 1371, 1°
1307	1626	1351	1665	1396	1747	1437	1364
1308	1627	1352	1666	1397	1748	1438	x
1309	1628	1353	1667	1398	1749	1439	1366
1310	1629	1354	1668	1399	1750; 1751	1440	1365
1311	1630	1355	1669	1400	1752	1441	1376
1312	x	1356	1670	1401	x	1442	1367
1313	1631	1357	1671	1402	1342, §1, §2	1443	1378, §2 §3; 1379
1314	1633	1358	1672	1403	x		
1315	1634, §1, §3; 1474	1359	1673	1404	x	1444	1368
		1360	1674	1405	1315, §1, §3; 1316; 1317	1445	1370
1316	1635	1361	1675			1446	1371, 2°
1317	1636	1362	1676	1406	1319	1447	1373; 1375
1318	1637	1363	1677	1407	1347	1448	1369; 1374
1319	1353; 1638	1364	1678	1408	1314	1449	1377
1320	1639	1365	1679	1409	1344; 1346	1450	1397; 1398
1321	1640	1366	1680	1410	1350	1451	1397
1322	1641	1367	1681	1411	x	1452	1390, §3
1323	1642	1368	1682	1412	1313; 1351	1453	1394; 1395, §1
1324	1643	1369	1683	1413	1323, 1°; 1324, §1, 4°	1454	1390
1325	1644	1370	1684	1414	1321		
1326	1645	1371	1685				
1327	1646	1372	1686				

CCEO	CIC	CCEO	CIC	CCEO	CIC	CCEO	CIC
1455	1391	1478	1725	1501	19	1524	43
1456	1388	1479	x	1502	20	1525	44
1457	1378, §1	1480	x	1503	21	1526	45
1458	1387	1481	1727	1504	22	1527	59, §2; 74
1459	1382; 1383	1482	1726	1505	x	1528	61
1460	x	1483	1729	1506	23; 24, §1	1529	63, §1, §2
1461	1380	1484	1730	1507	24, §2; 25; 26	1530	65
1462	1381; 1384	1485	1731	1508	27	1531	76
1463	1386	1486	1720	1509	28	1532	78; 83
1464	1389	1487	1353	1510	35; 48; 59, §1	1533	80
1465	x	1488	7	1511	54, §1; 62	1534	82
1466	1392	1489	8	1512	36, §1; 77; 92	1535	84
1467	1393	1490	11	1513	46; 47; 58; 93	1536	85; 90
1468	1717	1491	12, §1, §3; 13	1514	37; 51	1537	86; 87, §1
1469	1718	1492	x	1515	38	1538	87
1470	1719	1493	x	1516	39	1539	91
1471	1728	1494	9	1517	50	1540	197
1472	1721	1495	10	1518	57, §1, §2	1541	198
1473	1722	1496	14	1519	51	1542	199
1474	1723	1497	15	1520	55; 56	1543	200
1475	1724	1498	16	1521	40	1544	201
1476	x	1499	17	1522	41; 70	1545	202
1477	x	1500	18	1523	42	1546	203

APPENDIX 1

NEW LAWS FOR THE CAUSES OF SAINTS

JOHN PAUL BISHOP
Divinus perfectionis Magister
Promulgated January 25, 1983

CONGREGATION FOR THE CAUSES OF SAINTS
Norms to be Observed in Inquiries
Made by Bishops in the Causes of the
Saints
Promulgated February 7, 1983

CONGREGATION FOR THE CAUSES OF SAINTS
General Decree on the Causes of the
Servants of God Whose Judgement is
Presently Pending at the Sacred
Congregation
Promulgated February 7, 1983

JOHN PAUL
BISHOP

IOANNES PAULUS
EPISCOPUS

Divinus perfectionis
Magister

Divinus perfectionis
Magister

Servant of the Servants of God For Posterity

Servus Servorum Dei Ad
Perpetuam Rei Memoriam

THE DIVINE TEACHER AND MODEL OF PERFEC-
TION, Christ Jesus, who together with the Father and the
Holy Spirit is proclaimed as "alone holy", loved the Church
as His bride and delivered Himself up for her so that He
might sanctify her and make her glorious in His sight. Thus
He gave the commandment to all His disciples to imitate
the perfection of the Father and He sends upon all the Holy
Spirit, who might inspire them from within to love God
with their whole heart and to love one another as He Himself loved them. As the Second Vatican Council teaches, the
followers of Christ, called and justified in the Lord Jesus
not according to their works but according to His own purpose and grace, through baptism sought in faith truly become sons of God and sharers in the divine nature, and
thus truly holy.[1]

In all times, God chooses from these many who, following more closely the example of Christ, give outstanding testimony to the Kingdom of heaven by shedding their
blood or by the heroic practice of virtues.

The Church, in turn, from the earliest beginnings of
Christianity has always believed that the Apostles and Martyrs are more closely joined to us in Christ and has vener-
ated them, together with the Blessed Virgin Mary and the
holy Angels, with special devotion, devoutly imploring the
aid of their intercession. To these were soon added others

DIVINUS PERFECTIONIS MAGISTER et exemplar, Christus Iesus, qui una cum Patre et Spiritu
Sancto "unus sanctus" celebratur, Ecclesiam
tamquam sponsam dilexit atque seipsum pro ea
tradidit, ut illam sanctificaret sibique ipse glo-
riosam exhiberet. Praecepto igitur dato omnibus
discipulis suis, ut perfectionem Patris imitaren-
tur, in omnes Spiritum Sanctum mittit, qui eos
intus moveat, ut Deum diligant ex toto corde,
utque invicem sese diligant, quemadmodum ille
eos dilexit. Christi asseclae—uti per Concilium
Vaticanum II monemur—non secundum opera
sua, sed secundum propositum et gratiam Eius
vocati atque in Iesu Domino iustificati, in fidei
baptismate vere filii Dei et consortes divinae
naturae, ideoque reapse sancti effecti sunt.[1]

Inter hos quovis tempore plures Deus eligit,
qui Christi exemplum proximius secuti, sanguinis
effusione aut heroico virtutum exercitio praeclarum Regni caelorum praebeant testimonium.

Ecclesia autem, quae inde a primaevis
christianae religionis temporibus Apostolos et
Martyres in Christo arctius nobis coniunctos
esse semper credidit, eos simul cum beata
Virgine Maria et sanctis Angelis peculiari
veneratione prosecuta est, eorumque inter-

*English translation prepared by the Congregation for the
Causes of Saints, Vatican City. All rights reserved.*

1. Dog. Const. *Lumen Gentium,* no. 40.

also who had imitated more closely the virginity and poverty of Christ and, finally, others whose outstanding practice of the Christian virtues and whose divine charisms commended them to the pious devotion of, and imitation by, the faithful.

When we consider the life of those who have faithfully followed Christ, we are inspired with a new reason to seek the City that is to come and we are most safely taught the path by which, amid the changing things of this world and in keeping with the state in life and condition proper to each of us, we can arrive at that perfect union with Christ, which is holiness. Surrounded as we are by such an array of witnesses, through whom God is present to us and speaks to us, we are powerfully drawn to reach His Kingdom in heaven.[2]

From time immemorial, the Apostolic See has accepted these signs and has listened to the voice of her Lord with the greatest reverence and docility. Faithful to the serious duty entrusted to her of teaching, sanctifying and governing the People of God, she proposes to the faithful for their imitation, veneration and invocation, men and women who are outstanding in the splendor of charity and other evangelical virtues and, after due investigations, she declares them, in the solemn act of canonization, to be Saints.

The instruction of causes of canonization, which Our Predecessor Sixtus V entrusted to the Congregation of Sacred Rites, which he himself had established,[3] was, with the passage of time, always improved by new norms. Worthy of special mention are those of Urban VIII,[4] which Prosper Lambertini (later Benedict XIV), drawing upon the experiences of time past, handed down to later generations in a work entitled *De Servorum Dei beatificatione et de Beatorum canonizatione.* This work served as the rule of the Sacred Congregation of Rites for almost two centuries. Finally, these norms were substantially incorporated into the *Code of Canon Law* promulgated in 1917.

cessionis auxilium pie imploravit. Quibus mox adnumerati sunt alii quoque qui Christi virginitatem et paupertatem pressius erant imitati, et tandem ceteri quos praeclarum virtutum christianarum exercitium ac divina charismata piae fidelium devotioni et imitationi commendabant.

Dum illorum vitam conspicimus, qui Christum fideliter sunt secuti, nova quadam ratione ad futuram Civitatem inquirendam incitamur et tutissime viam edocemur qua, inter mundanas varietates, secundum statum condicionemque unicuique propriam, ad perfectam cum Christo coniunctionem seu sanctitatem pervenire possumus. Nimirum tantam habentes impositam nubem testium, per quos Deus nobis fit praesens nosque alloquitur, ad Regnum suum in coelis adipiscendum magna virtute attrahimur.[2]

Quae signa et vocem Domini sui maxima cum reverentia et docilitate suscipiens, Sedes Apostolica, ab immemorabilibus temporibus, pro gravi munere sibi concredito docendi, sanctificandi atque regendi Populum Dei, fidelium imitationi, venerationi et invocationi proponit viros et mulieres caritatis aliarumque evangelicarum virtutum fulgore praestantes, eosque, post debitas pervestigationes peractas, in sollemni canonizationis actu Sanctos vel Sanctas esse declarat.

Causarum canonizationis instructio, quam Praedecessor Noster Xystus V Congregationi Sacrorum Rituum ab ipso conditae concredidit,[3] decursu temporum novis semper aucta fuit normis, praesertim Urbani VIII opera,[4] quas Prosper Lambertini (postea Benedictus XIV), experientias quoque transacti temporis colligens, posteris tradidit in opere quod *De Servorum Dei beatificatione et de Beatorum canonizatione* inscribitur, quodque regula exstitit per duo fere saecula apud Sacram Rituum Congregationem. Huiusmodi normae tandem substantialiter receptae fuerunt in *Codicem Iuris Canonici,* anno 1917 publici iuris factum.

---

2. Cf. *ibid.,* no. 50.

3. Apost. Const. *Immensa Aeterni Dei* of January 22, 1588. Cf. *Bullarium Romanum,* ed Taurinensis, t. VIII, pp. 985–999.

4. Apost. Letter *Caelestis Hierusalem cives* of July 5, 1634; *Urban VIII P.O.M. Decreta servanda in canonizatione et beatificatione Sanctorum* of March 12, 1642.

Since recent progress in the field of historical studies has shown the necessity of providing the competent Congregation with an apparatus better suited for its task so as to respond more adequately to the dictates of historical criticism, Our Predecessor of happy memory, Pius XI, in the Apostolic Letter *Già da qualche tempo*, issued *motu proprio* on February 6, 1930, established the "Historical Section" within the Sacred Congregation of Rites and entrusted it with the study of "historical" causes.[5] On January 4, 1939, the same Pontiff also ordered the publication of *Normae servandae in construendis processibus ordinariis super causis historicis*,[6] which made the "apostolic" process no longer necessary so that a single process would then be conducted with ordinary authority in "historical" causes.

In the Apostolic Letter *Sanctitas clarior*, given *motu proprio* on March 19, 1969,[7] Paul VI established that even in recent causes there would be only one cognitional process for gathering proofs, which the Bishop conducts with previous permission, nevertheless, from the Holy See.[8] The same Pontiff, in the Apostolic Constitution *Sacra Rituum Congregatio*[9] of May 8, 1969, established two new Dicasteries in place of the Sacred Congregation of Rites. To one he gave the responsibility of regulating divine Worship and to the other, that of dealing with the causes of saints; on that same occasion, he changed, somewhat, the procedure to be followed in these causes.

Most recent experience, finally, has shown us the appropriateness of revising further the manner of instructing causes and of so structuring the Congregation for the Causes of Saints that we might meet the needs of experts and the desires of Our Brother Bishops, who have often called for a simpler process while maintaining the soundness of the investigation in matter of such great import. In light of the doctrine of the Second Vatican Council on collegiality, We also think that the Bishops themselves should be more closely associated with the Holy See in dealing with the causes of saints.

Therefore, having abrogated all laws of any kind which

Cum vero maxime auctus historicarum disciplinarum progressus nostris temporibus necessitatem ostendisset aptiore laboris instrumento competentem Congregationem ditandi, ut postulatis artis criticae melius responderet, Decessor Noster f.r. Pius XI Apostolicis Litteris *Già da qualche tempo* motu proprio die 6 mensis februarii anno 1930 editis, "Sectionem historicam" apud Sacram Rituum Congregationem instituit, eique studium causarum "historicarum" concredidit.[5] Die autem 4 ianuarii anno 1939 idem Pontifex *Normas servandas in construendis processibus ordinariis super causis historicis*[6] edi iussit, quibus processum "apostolicum" reapse supervacaneum reddidit, ita ut in causis "historicis" exinde unicus processus auctoritate ordinaria factus sit.

Paulus VI autem, Litteris Apostolicis *Sanctitas clarior* motu proprio die 19 martii anno 1969 editis,[7] statuit, ut etiam in causis recentioribus unicus fieret processus cognitionalis seu ad colligendas probationes, quem Episcopus instruit praevia tamen venia Sanciae Sedis.[8] Idem Pontifex, Constitutione Apostolica *Sacra Rituum Congregatio*[9] diei 8 maii 1969, loco Sacrae Rituum Congregationis duo nova constituit Dicasteria, quorum uni munus concredidit Cultum divinum ordinandi, alteri vero causas sanctorum tractandi; eadem data occasione ordinem in iisdem procedendi aliquantum immutavit.

Post novissimas experientias, denique, Nobis peropportunum visum est instructionis causarum viam ac rationem ulterius recognoscere ipsamque Congregationem pro Causis Sanctorum ita ordinare, ut et doctorum exigentiis obviam fieremus, et desideriis Fratrum Nostrorum in episcopatu, qui pluries flagitaverunt ipsius rationis agilitatem, servata tamen soliditate investigationum in negotio tantae gravitatis. Putamus etiam, praelucente doctrina de collegialitate a Concilio Vaticano II proposita, valde convenire ut ipsi Episcopi magis Apostolicae Sedi socientur in causis sanctorum pertractandis.

In posterum, igitur, abrogatis ad rem quod

5. AAS 22 (1930), pp. 87–88.
6. AAS 31 (1939), pp. 174–175.
7. AAS 61 (1969), pp. 149–153.

8. *Ibid.*, nos. 3–4.
9. AAS 61 (1969), pp. 297–305.

pertain to this matter, we establish that these following norms are henceforth to be observed.

attinet omnibus legibus cuiusvis generis, has quae sequuntur statuimus normas servandas.

I. Inquiries to be Made By Bishops

1) It is the right of diocesan Bishops or Bishops of the Eastern Rite and others who have the same powers in law, within the limits of their own jurisdiction, either *ex officio* or upon the request of individual members of the faithful or of legitimate groups and their representatives, to inquire about the life, virtues or martyrdom and reputation of sanctity or martyrdom, alleged miracles, as well as, if it be the case, ancient cult of the Servant of God, whose canonization is sought.

2) In inquiries of this kind, the Bishop is to proceed according to the particular *Norms* to be published by the Sacred Congregation for the Causes of Saints. This is the order to be followed:

1. From the postulator of the cause, legitimately appointed by the petitioner, the Bishop is to seek out accurate information about the life of the Servant of God and likewise be thoroughly informed by the postulator of the reasons which seem to support promoting the cause of canonization.

2. If the Servant of God has published any writings, the Bishop is to see to it that they are examined by theological censors.

3. If the writings have been found to contain nothing contrary to faith and good morals, then the Bishop should order persons qualified for this task to collect other unpublished writings (letters, diaries, etc.) as well as all documents, which in any way pertain to the cause. After they have faithfully completed their task, they are to write a report on their investigations.

4. If the Bishop has prudently judged that, on the basis of all that has been done so far, the cause can proceed, he is to see to it that those witnesses proposed by the postulator and others to be called *ex officio* are duly examined.

If, indeed, it is urgent that witnesses be examined lest any proofs be lost, they are to be questioned even though the gathering of the documents has not yet been completed.

5. The inquiry into alleged miracles is to be conducted separately from the inquiry into virtues or martyrdom.

6. When the inquiries are complete, a transcript of all

I. De Inquisitionibus Ab Episcopis Faciendis

1) Episcopis dioecesanis vel Hierarchis ceterisque in iure aequiparatis, intra fines suae iurisdictionis, sive ex officio, sive ad instantiam singulorum fidelium vel legitimorum coetuum eorumque procuratorum, ius competit inquirendi circa vitam, virtutes vel martyrium ac famam sanctitatis vel martyrii, asserta miracula, necnon, si casus ferat, antiquum cultum Servi Dei, cuius canonizatio petitur.

2) In huiusmodi inquisitionibus Episcopus iuxta peculiares Normas a Sacra Congregatione pro Causis Sanctorum edendas procedat, hoc quidem ordine:

1° A postulatore causae, legitime ab actore nominato, accuratam informationem de Servi Dei vita exquirat, simulque ab eo edoceatur de rationibus quae causae canonizationis promovendae favere videantur.

2° Si Servus Dei scripta a se exarata publice edidit, Episcopus curet ut eadem a censoribus theologis examinentur.

3° Si nihil contra fidem bonosque mores in iisdem scriptis repertum fuerit, tunc Episcopus alia scripta inedita (epistulas, diaria etc.) necnon omnia documenta, quoquo modo causam respicientia, perquiri iubeat a personis ad hoc idoneis, quae, postquam munus suum fideliter expleverint, relationem de perquisitionibus factis componant.

4° Si ex hucusque factis Episcopus prudenter iudicaverit ad ulteriora procedi posse, curet ut testes a postulatore inducti aliique ex officio vocandi rite examinentur.

Si vero urgeat examen testium ne pereant probationes, ipsi interrogandi sunt etiam nondum completa perquisitione documentorum.

5° Inquisitio de assertis miraculis ab inquisitione de virtutibus vel de martyrio separatim fiat.

6° Inquisitionibus peractis, transumptum

the acts is to be sent in duplicate to the Sacred Congregation, together with a copy of the books of the Servant of God which were examined by the theological censors and their judgment as well.

Furthermore, the Bishop is to attach a declaration on the observance of the decrees of Urban VIII regarding the absence of cult.

II. The Sacred Congregation for the Causes of Saints

3) The Sacred Congregation for the Causes of Saints is presided over by a Cardinal Prefect, assisted by a Secretary. Its duty is to deal with those matters which pertain to the canonization of Servants of God by providing advice and guidelines to Bishops in the instruction of the causes, by studying the causes thoroughly and, finally, by casting its vote.

It is also the duty of the Congregation to decide those things which pertain to the authenticity and preservation of relics.

4) The duty of the Secretary is:

1. to handle business with those outside the Congregation, especially with Bishops who are instructing causes;

2. to take part in the discussions about the merit of a cause and to cast a vote in the meeting of the Cardinal and Bishop Members of the Congregation;

3. to draw up the report that is to be given to the Supreme Pontiff on how the Cardinals and Bishops voted.

5) The Secretary is assisted in fulfilling his duty by an Undersecretary, whose task is primarily to ascertain whether the rules of law have been followed in the instruction of the causes. The Secretary is also assisted by an appropriate number of minor Officials.

6) For the purpose of studying the causes there exists in the Sacred Congregation a College of Relators, presided over by a Relator General.

7) The individual Relators are:

1. to study the causes entrusted to them, together with collaborators from outside the Congregation, and to prepare the *Positions* on virtues or on martyrdom;

2. to prepare written explanations of an historical nature which may have been requested by the Consultors;

3. to be present as experts at the meeting of the theologians, although without the right to vote.

8) One of the Relators shall be especially selected to prepare the *Positions* on miracles. He will take part in the meetings of the physicians and of the theologians.

omnium actorum in duplici exemplari ad Sacram Congregationem mittatur, una cum exemplari librorum Servi Dei a censoribus theologis examinatorum eorumque iudicio.

Episcopus praeterea adiungat declarationem de observantia decretorum Urbani VIII super non cultu.

II. De Sacra Congregatione Pro Causis Sanctorum

3) Sacrae Congregationis pro Causis Sanctorum, cui praeest Cardinalis Praefectus, adiuvante Secretario, munus est, ut ea agat quae ad canonizationem Servorum Dei pertinent, et quidem tum Episcopis in causis instruendis consilio atque instructionibus assistendo, tum causis funditus studendo, tum denique vota ferendo.

Ad eamdem Congregationem spectat decernere de iis omnibus quae ad authenticitatem et conservationem reliquiarum referuntur.

4) Secretarii officium est:

1° relationes cum externis, praesertim cum Episcopis qui causas instruunt, curare;

2° discussiones de merito causae participare, votum ferendo in congregatione Patrum Cardinalium et Episcoporum;

3° relationem, Summo Pontifici tradendam, de votis Cardinalium et Episcoporum conficere.

5) In munere suo adimplendo Secretarius adiuvatur a Subsecretario, cui competit praesertim videre si legis praescripta in causarum instructione adimpleta fuerint, necnon a congruo numero Officialium minorum.

6) Pro studio causarum apud Sacram Congregationem adest Collegium Relatorum, cui praeest Relator generalis.

7) Singulorum Relatorum est:

1° una cum externis cooperatoribus causis sibi commissis studere atque Positiones super virtutibus vel super martyrio parare;

2° enodationes historicas, si quae a Consultoribus requisitae fuerint, scriptis exarare;

3° Congressui theologorum tamquam expertos adesse, sine tamen voto.

8) Inter Relatores unus aderit specialiter deputatus pro elucubratione Positionum super miraculis, qui intererit Coetui medicorum et Congressui theologorum.

9) The Relator General, who presides over the meeting of the historical Consultors, is to be aided in his study by some Assistants.

10) The Sacred Congregation is to have one Promotor of the Faith or Prelate Theologian. His responsibility is:

1. to preside over the meeting of the theologians, with the right to vote;

2. to prepare the report on the meeting itself;

3. to be present as an expert at the meeting of the Cardinals and Bishops, although without the right to vote.

If necessary for one or another cause, a Promotor of the Faith for that particular case can be nominated by the Cardinal Prefect.

11) Consultors are to be drawn from various parts of the world to deal with the causes of Saints. Some are to be experts in historical matters and others in theology, particularly in spiritual theology.

12) There is to be a board of medical experts in the Sacred Congregation whose responsibility is to examine healings which are proposed as miracles.

III. Procedure in the Sacred Congregation

13) When the Bishop has sent to Rome all the acts and documents pertaining to a cause, the procedure in the Sacred Congregation for the Causes of Saints is as follows:

1. First of all, the Undersecretary is to verify whether all the rules of law have been followed in the inquiries conducted by the Bishop. He is to report the result of his examination in the ordinary meeting of the Congregation.

2. If the meeting judges that the cause was conducted according to the norms of law, it decides to which Relator the cause is to be assigned; the Relator, then, together with a collaborator from outside the Congregation, will prepare the *Position* on virtues or on martyrdom according to the rules of critical hagiography.

3. In ancient causes and in those recent causes whose particular nature, in the judgment of the Relator General, should demand it, the published *Position* is to be examined by Consultors who are specially expert in that field so that they can cast their vote on its scientific value and whether it contains sufficient elements required for the scope for which the *Position* has been prepared.

9) Relator generalis, qui praesidet Coetui Consultorum historicorum, adiuvatur a nonnullis Adiutoribus a studiis.

10) Apud Sacram Congregationem unus adest Promotor fidei seu Praelatus theologus, cuius est:

1° Congressui theologorum praeesse, in quo votum fert;

2° relationem de ipso Congressu parare;

3° congregationi Patrum Cardinalium et Episcoporum tamquam expertum adesse, sine tamen voto.

Pro una aliave causa, si opus fuerit, a Cardinali Praefecto nominari poterit Promotor fidei ad casum.

11) Causis sanctorum tractandis praesto sunt Consultores ex diversis regionibus acciti, alii in re historica alii in theologia praesertim spirituali periti.

12) Pro examine sanationum, quae tamquam miracula proponuntur, habetur apud Sacram Congregationem coetus in arte medica peritorum.

III. De Modo Procedendi In Sacra Congregatione

13) Cum omnia acta et documenta causam respicientia Episcopus Romam miserit, in Sacra Congregatione pro Causis Sanctorum hoc modo procedatur:

1° Ante omnia Subsecretarius scrutatur utrum in inquisitionibus ab Episcopo factis omnia legis statuta servata sint, et de exitu examinis in Congressu ordinario referet.

2° Si Congressus iudicaverit causam instructam fuisse ad legis normas, statuet cuinam ex Relatoribus committenda sit; Relator vero una cum cooperatore externo Positionem super virtutibus vel super martyrio conficiet iuxta regulas artis criticae in hagiographia servandas.

3° In causis antiquis et in iis recentioribus, quarum peculiaris indoles de iudicio Relatoris generalis id postulaverit, edita Positio examini subicienda erit Consultorum in re speciatim peritorum, ut de eius valore scientifico necnon sufficientia ad effectum de quo agitur votum ferant.

In particular cases, the Sacred Congregation can also give the *Position* to other scholars, who are not part of the group of Consultors, for their examination.

4. The *Position* (together with the votes of the historical Consultors as well as any new explanations by the Relator, should they be necessary) is handed over to the theological Consultors, who are to cast their vote on the merit of the cause; their responsibility, together wth the Promotor of the Faith, is to study the cause in such a way that, before the *Position* is submitted for discussion in their special meeting, controversial theological questions, if there be any, may be examined thoroughly.

5. The definitive votes of the theological Consultors, together with the written conclusions of the Promotor of the Faith, are submitted to the judgment of the Cardinals and Bishops.

14) The Congregation examines cases of alleged miracles in the following way:

1. The Relator assigned to this task is to prepare a *Position* on alleged miracles. They are discussed in a meeting of experts (in the case of healings, in a meeting of physicians), whose votes and conclusions are set forth in an accurate report.

2. Then the miracles are to be discussed in the special meeting of the theologians and, finally, in that of the Cardinals and Bishops.

15) The results of the discussions of the Cardinals and Bishops are reported to the Supreme Pontiff, who alone has the right to declare that public cult may be given by the Church to Servants of God.

16) By a special decree, the Sacred Congregation itself will establish the procedure to be followed henceforth in the individual causes of canonization whose judgment is presently pending at the Sacred Congregation, in accordance, however, with the spirit of this new law.

17) All that which we have established in this Our Constitution is to take effect from this very day.

Moreover, we wish that these Our statutes and rules should be, now and hereafter, binding and effective and, insofar as is necessary, we abrogate the Apostolic Constitutions and Regulations published by Our Predecessors and all other rules, including those which are worthy of special mention and derogation.

Given in Rome, at Saint Peter's, on the 25th day of the month of January in the year 1983, the 5th of Our Pontificate.

John Paul II

In singulis casibus Sacra Congregatio potest Positionem etiam aliis viris doctis, in Consultorum numerum non relatis, examinandam tradere.

4° Positio (una cum votis scriptis Consultorum historicorum necnon novis enodationibus Relatoris, si quae necessariae sint) tradetur Consultoribus theologis, qui de merito causae votum ferent; quorum est, una cum Promotore fidei, causae ita studere, ut, antequam ad discussionem in Congressu peculiari deveniatur, quaestiones theologicae controversae, si quae sint, funditus examinentur.

5° Vota definitiva Consultorum theologorum, una cum conclusionibus a Promotore fidei exaratis, Cardinalibus atque Episcopis iudicaturis tradentur.

14) De assertis miraculis Congregatio cognoscit sequenti ratione:

1° Asserta miracula, super quibus a Relatore ad hoc deputato paratur Positio, expenduntur in coetu peritorum (si de sanationibus agitur, in coetu medicorum), quorum vota et conclusiones in accurata relatione exponuntur.

2° Deinde miracula discutienda sunt in peculiari Congressu theologorum, ac denique in congregatione Patrum Cardinalium et Episcoporum.

15) Sententiae Patrum Cardinalium et Episcoporum referuntur ad Summum Pontificem, cui uni competit ius decernendi cultum publicum ecelesiasticum Servis Dei praestandum.

16) In singulis canonizationis causis, quarum iudicium in praesens apud Sacram Congregationem pendeat, Sacra ipsa Congregatio peculiari decreto statuet modum ad ulteriora procedendi, servata tamen mente huius novae legis.

17) Quae Constitutione hac Nostra praescripsimus ab hoc ipso die vigere incipiunt.

Nostra haec autem statuta et praescripta nunc et in posterum firma et efficacia esse et fore volumus, non obstantibus, quatenus opus est, Constitutionibus et Ordinationibus Apostolicis a Decessoribus Nostris editis, ceterisque praescriptionibus etiam peculiari mentione et derogatione dignis.

Datum Romae, apud Sanctum Petrum, die xxv mensis Ianuarii anno MCMLXXXIII, Pontificatus Nostri quinto.

Ioannes Paulus PP. II

Norms to be Observed in Inquiries Made by Bishops in the Causes of Saints

Normae servandae in inquisitionibus ab episcopis faciendis in causis sanctorum

THE APOSTOLIC CONSTITUTION *Divinus perfectionis Magister* of January 25, 1983 set forth the procedure for the inquiries which henceforth are to be made by Bishops in the causes of saints and likewise entrusted to this Sacred Congregation the duty of publishing particular Norms for this purpose. The Sacred Congregation has developed the following norms, which the Supreme Pontiff directed to be examined by a Plenary Meeting of the Fathers who are Members of this Congregation, which was held on June 22nd and 23rd of 1981. After consulting all the heads of the Offices of the Roman Curia, the same Pontiff approved these norms and ordered them to be published.

1. *a)* The petitioner advances the cause of canonization. Any member of the People of God or any group of the faithful recognized by ecclesiastical authority can exercise this function.

b) The petitioner handles the cause through a legitimately appointed postulator.

2. a) The postulator is appointed by the petitioner by means of a mandate written according to the norm of law, with the approval of the Bishop.

b) While the cause is being handled at the Sacred Congregation, the postulator, provided that he be approved by the Congregation itself, must reside in Rome.

3. *a)* Priests, members of Institutes of consecrated life

CUM IN CONSTITUTIONE APOSTOLICA *Divinus perfectionis Magister* diei 25 Ianuarii anni 1983 statutus sit ordo procedendi in inquisitionibus quae in posterum ab Episcopis faciendae sunt in causis sanctorum, itemque Sacrae huic Congregationi munus concreditum sit peculiares ad hoc Normas edendi, eadem Sacra Congregatio sequentes confecit normas, quas Summus Pontifex a Plenario Coetu Patrum praefatae Congregationi praepositorum, diebus 22 et 23 mensis Iunii anno 1981 habito, examinari voluit et, auditis quoque omnibus Patribus Dicasteriis Romanae Curiae praepositis, ratas habuit et promulgari iussit.

1. *a)* Causam canonizationis actor promovet; quo munere quilibet e populo Dei aut christifidelium coetus ab ecclesiastica auctoritate admissus, fungi potest.

b) Actor causam agit per postulatorem legitime constitutum.

2. *a)* Postulator constituitur ab actore per procurationis mandatum ad normam iuris redactum, probante Episcopo.

b) Dum causa apud Sacram Congregationem tractatur, postulator, dummodo ab ipsa Congregatione sit approbatus, in Urbe fixam sedem habere debet.

3. *a)* Munere postulatoris fungi possunt sac-

and lay persons can exercise the function of postulator; all must be experts in theological, canonical and historical matters, as well as versed in the practice of the Sacred Congregation.

b) The first duty of the postulator is to conduct thorough investigations into the life of the Servant of God in question, in order to establish his reputation of sanctity and the importance of the cause for the Church, and then to report his findings to the Bishop.

c) The postulator is also entrusted with the duty of administrating those funds offered for the cause according to the norms issued by the Sacred Congregation.

4. Through a legitimate mandate and with the consent of the petitioners, the postulator has the right to appoint others in his place who are called vice-postulators.

5. *a)* The Bishop competent to instruct causes of canonization is the one in whose territory the Servant of God died, unless particular circumstances, recognized as such by the Sacred Congregation, suggest otherwise.

b) In the case of an alleged miracle, the competent Bishop is the one in whose territory the event took place.

6. *a)* The Bishop can instruct the cause either personally or through his delegate, who is to be a priest truly expert in theological and canonical matters, as well as in historical matters, in the case of ancient causes.

b) The priest who is chosen as the promotor of justice must have the same qualities.

c) All officials, who take part in the cause, must take an oath to fulfil faithfully their duty, and are bound to maintain secrecy.

7. A cause can be recent or ancient: it is called recent if the martyrdom or virtues of the Servant of God can be proved through the oral depositions of eye witnesses; it is ancient, however, when the proofs for martyrdom or virtues can be brought to light only from written sources.

8. Whoever intends to initiate a cause of canonization is to present to the competent Bishop, through the postulator, a written petition, requesting the instruction of the cause.

9. *a)* In recent causes, the petition must be presented no sooner than five years after the death of the Servant of God.

b) If, however, it is presented after thirty years, the Bishop may not proceed further unless, upon investigation, he is convinced that there was no fraud in the case or deceit on the part of the petitioners in delaying the initiation of the cause.

erdotes, membra Institutorum vitae consecratae et laici, qui omnes oportet sint periti in re theologica, canonica et historica, necnon in praxi Sacrae Congregationis versati.

b) Postulatoris imprimis est peragere investigationes circa vitam Servi Dei de quo agitur, ad eius famam sanctitatis et causae momentum ecclesiale dignoscenda, de eisque Episcopo referre.

c) Postulatori committitur etiam munus bona pro causa oblata administrandi iuxta normas a Sacra Congregatione traditas.

4. Postulatori ius competit substituendi sibi, per legitimum mandatum ac de consensu actorum, alios qui vice-postulatores dicuntur.

5. *a)* In causis canonizationis instruendis Episcopus competens ille est in cuius territorio Servus Dei supremum diem obiit, nisi peculiaria adiuncta, a Sacra Congregatione probata, aliud suadeant.

b) Si de asserto miraculo agitur, competens est Episcopus in cuius territorio factum evenit.

6. *a)* Episcopus causam instruere valet sive per se sive per suum delegatum, qui sit sacerdos in re teologica, canonica et historica quoque, si de causis antiquis agatur, vere peritus.

b) Iisdem qualitatibus pollere debet sacerdos qui in promotorem iustitiae eligitur.

c) Omnes officiales partem in causa habentes debent iuramentum de munere fideliter adimplendo praestare, et secreto tenentur.

7. Causa potest esse recentior aut antiqua; *recentior* dicitur, si martyrium vel virtutes Servi Dei per orales depositiones testium de visu probari possunt; *antiqua* vero, cum probationes de martyrio vel virtutibus dumtaxat ex fontibus scriptis erui possunt.

8. Quicumque causam canonizationis inchoare intendit, per postulatorem Episcopo competenti supplicem libellum exhibeat, quo causae instructio petatur.

9. *a)* In causis recentioribus, libellus exhiberi debet non ante quintum annum a morte Servi Dei.

b) Si vero exhibetur post annum tricesimum, Episcopus ad ulteriora procedere nequit nisi, inquisitione peracta, sibi persuasum habuerit nullam in casu adfuisse fraudem vel dolum ex parte actorum in protracta inchoatione causae.

10. The postulator must present together with the written petition:

1. in both recent and ancient causes, a biography of any historical import of the Servant of God, should such exist, or otherwise an accurate, chronologically arranged report on the life and deeds of the Servant of God, on his virtues or martyrdom, on his reputation of sanctity and of signs. Nor should anything be omitted which seems to be contrary or less favorable to the cause;[1]

2. an authentic copy of all the published writings of the Servant of God;

3. in recent causes only, a list of persons who can help bring to light the truth about the virtues or the martyrdom of the Servant of God, and about his reputation of sanctity or of signs. Those with contrary opinions must also be included.

11. *a)* Once the petition has been accepted, the Bishop is to consult with the Conference of Bishops, at least of the region, about the appropriateness of initiating the cause.

b) Furthermore, the Bishop is to publicize the petition of the postulator in his own diocese and, if he has judged it opportune, in other dioceses, with the permission of their respective Bishops, and to invite all the faithful to bring to his attention any useful information, which they might have to offer regarding the cause.

12. *a)* If a significant obstacle to the cause emerges from the information he has received, the Bishop is to notify the postulator about it so that he can remove that obstacle.

b) If the obstacle has not been removed and the Bishop has therefore judged that the cause should not be admitted, he is to advise the postulator, giving the reasons for his decision.

13. If the Bishop intends to initiate the cause, he is to seek the vote of two theological censors on the published writings of the Servant of God. These censors are to report whether anything is found in these same writings, contrary to faith and good morals.[2]

14. *a)* If the votes of the theological censors are favorable, the Bishop is to order that all the writings of the Servant of God, those not yet published as well as each and every historical document, either handwritten or printed, which in any way pertain to the cause, are to be gathered.[3]

b) When such a search is to be made, especially in the

10. Postulator una cum supplici libello exhibere debet:

1° in causis tam recentioribus quam antiquis, biographiam alicuius historici momenti de Servo Dei, si extat, vel, ea deficiente, accuratam relationem chronologice digestam de vita et gestis ipsius Servi Dei, de eius virtutibus vel martyrio, de sanctitatis et signorum fama, non omissis iis quae ipsi causae contraria vel minus favorabilia videntur;[1]

2° omnia scripta edita Servi Dei in authentico exemplari;

3° in causis recentioribus tantum, elenchum personarum quae ad eruendam veritatem circa virtutes vel martyrium Servi Dei, necnon circa sanctitatis vel signorum famam conferre possunt vel adversari.

11. *a)* Accepto libello, Episcopus coetum Episcoporum saltem regionis de opportunitate causae inchoandae consulat.

b) Insuper in sua et, si id opportunum duxerit, in aliis dioecesibus, de consensu eorundem Episcoporum, petitionem postulatoris publici iuris faciat, omnes christifideles invitando ut utiles notitias causam respicientes, si quas suppeditandas habeant, sibi deferant.

12. *a)* Si ex informationibus receptis obstaculum alicuius momenti contra causam emerserit, de eo Episcopus postulatorem certiorem faciat, ut illud removere possit.

b) Si obstaculum remotum non fuerit et Episcopus ideo iudicaverit causam non esse admittendam, postulatorem moneat, allatis de decisione rationibus.

13. Si Episcopus causam inchoare intendit, votum super scriptis editis Servi Dei a duobus censoribus theologis exquirat, qui referant num in iisdem scriptis aliquid habeatur, quod fidei ac bonis moribus adversetur.[2]

14. *a)* Si vota censorum theologorum favorabilia sunt, Episcopus mandat ut universa scripta Servi Dei nondum edita necnon omnia et singula historica documenta sive manuscripta sive typis edita, quoquo modo causam respicientia, colligantur.[3]

b) In huiusmodi requisitione facienda, prae-

---

1. Cfr. Apost. Const. *Divinus perfectionis Magister,* no. 2, 1.

2. Cfr. *ibid.,* no. 2, 2.
3. Cfr. *ibid.,* no. 2, 3.

case of ancient causes, experts in historical matters and in matters that pertain to archives, are to be employed.

c) After the task has been completed, the experts are to hand over to the Bishop an accurate and precise report together with the collected writings. In this report, they are to indicate and testify that they fulfilled their duty properly; to include a list of the writings and documents; to give a judgment on their authenticity and their value as well as on the personality of the Servant of God, as it appears from the same writings and documents.

15. a) Once the report has been accepted, the Bishop is to hand over to the promotor of justice or to another expert everything gathered up to that point so that he might formulate the interrogatories most effective in searching out and discovering the truth about the life of the Servant of God, his virtues or martyrdom, his reputation of holiness or of martyrdom.

b) In ancient causes, however, the interrogatories are only to consider the reputation of sanctity or martyrdom existing until the present as well as, if it be the case, the cult given to the Servant of God in more recent times.

c) In the meantime, the Bishop is to send to the Sacred Congregation for the Causes of Saints a brief report on the life of the Servant of God and the relevance of the cause, in order to ascertain whether there is any obstacle on the part of the Holy See to the cause.

16. *a)* Then the Bishop or his delegate is to examine the witnesses proposed by the postulator and others to be questioned *ex officio.* A Notary is to be employed to transcribe the deposition of the witness, which is to be confirmed by the witness himself at the end of his testimony.

If, indeed, it is urgent that witnesses be examined lest any proofs be lost, they are to be questioned even though the gathering of the documents has not yet been completed.[4]

b) The promotor of justice is to be present at the examination of the witnesses. If, however, he was not present, the acts are to be submitted afterwards for his examination so that he can make his observations and propose anything which he judges to be necessary and opportune.

c) First of all, the witnesses are to be examined according to the interrogatories; the Bishop or his delegate, however, should not fail to propose to the witnesses other necessary or useful questions so that their statements may be put in a clearer light or any difficulties which may have emerged may be plainly resolved and explained.

sertim cum de causis antiquis agatur, periti in re historica et archivistica adhibeantur.

c) Munere expleto, periti una cum scriptis collectis diligentem et distinctam relationem Episcopo tradant, in qua referant et fidem faciant de officio bene adimpleto, elenchum scriptorum et documentorum includant, iudicium de eorum authenticitate et valore promant necnon de personalitate Servi Dei, uti ex ipsis scriptis et documentis eruitur.

15. a) Relatione accepta, Episcopus omnia usque ad illud tempus acquisita promotori iustitiae vel alii viro perito tradat, ut interrogatoria conficiat quae apta sint ad verum indagandum et inveniendum de Servi Dei vita, virtutibus vel martyrio, fama sanctitatis vel martyrii.

b) In causis antiquis vero interrogatoria dumtaxat famam sanctitatis vel martyrii adhuc vigentem necnon, si casus ferat, cultum recentioribus temporibus Servo Dei praestitum respiciant.

c) Interim Episcopus brevem de Servi Dei vita ac de causae pondere notitiam ad Sacram Congregationem pro Causis Sanctorum transmittat, ad videndum utrum ex parte Sanctae Sedis aliquid causae obsit.

16. a) Deinde Episcopus vel delegatus testes a postulatore inductos et alios ex officio interrogandos examinet, adhibito notario qui verba deponentis transcribat, in fine ab eodem confirmanda.

Si vero urgeat examen testium ne pereant probationes, ipsi interrogandi sunt etiam nondum completa perquisitione documentorum.[4]

b) Examini testium adsit promotor iustitiae; quodsi idem non interfuerit, acta postea eius examini subiciantur, ut ipsemet animadvertere ac proponere possit quae necessaria et opportuna iudicaverit.

c) Testes imprimis iuxta interrogatoria examinentur; Episcopus autem vel delegatus ne omittat alias necessarias vel utiles interrogationes testibus proponere, ut quae ab ipsis dicta sint in clariore luce ponantur vel difficultates, quae emerserint, plane solvantur et explanentur.

---

4. Cfr. *ibid.,* no. 2, 4.

17. The witnesses must be eye witnesses; if the case warrants it, second-hand witnesses may be added. All, however, must be trustworthy.

18. Blood relatives and relatives through marriage of the Servant of God are the first witnesses to be proposed as well as other friends and acquaintances.

19. In order to prove the martyrdom or the practice of virtues and the reputation of signs of the Servant of God who belonged to any Institute of consecrated life, a significant number of the proposed witnesses must be from outside the Institute unless, on account of the particular life of the Servant of God, this should prove impossible.

20. Those who are not to be allowed to testify are:

1. a priest, with regard to all those things which were made known to him through the sacrament of Penance.

2. regular confessors of the Servant of God or spiritual directors, with regard also to all those things which they learned from the Servant of God in the forum of conscience outside the sacrament of Penance;

3. the postulator of the cause, during his term as postulator.

21. *a)* The Bishop or his delegate is to call some witnesses *ex officio*, who can contribute to completing the inquiry, if it be the case, particularly if they are opposed to the cause;

b) The Bishop or his delegate is also to call as *ex officio* witnesses those experts who conducted the investigations of the documents and wrote the relative report. They must declare under oath: 1.- that they conducted all the investigations and that they gathered all those things which pertain to the cause; 2.- that they neither changed nor destroyed any document or text.

22. *a)* In the case of miraculous healings, the physicians who treated the patient are to be called as witnesses.

b) If they refuse to appear before the Bishop or his delegate, the aforementioned is to see to it that they write a report, sworn if possible, about the disease and its progress, which is to be inserted into the acts, or at least their opinion is to be heard by a third party, who is then to be examined.

23. In their testimony, which is to be sworn to under oath, the witnesses must indicate the source of their knowledge of the things they assert; otherwise, their testimony is to be considered of no value.

24. If any witness prefers to give to the Bishop or his delegate a previously prepared written statement, either together with his deposition or in addition to it, such a writ-

17. Testes debent esse de visu, quibus addi possunt, si casus ferat, nonnulli testes de auditu a videntibus; omnes autem sint fide digni.

18. Tamquam testes imprimis inducantur consanguinei et affines Servi Dei aliique, qui cum eodem familiaritatem aut consuetudinem habuerint.

19. Ad probandum martyrium aut virtutum exercitium et signorum famam Servi Dei qui pertinuerit ad aliquod Institutum vitae consecratae, notabilis pars testium inductorum debent esse extranei, nisi, ob peculiarem Servi Dei vitam, id impossibile evadat.

20. Ne admittantur ad testificandum:

1° sacerdos, quod attinet ad ea omnia quae ei ex confessione sacramentali innotuerunt;

2° habituales Servi Dei confessarii vel spiritus directores, quod attinet etiam ad ea omnia quae a Servo Dei in foro conscientiae extrasacramentali acceperint;

3° postulator in causa, durante munere.

21. *a)* Episcopus vel delegatus aliquos testes ex officio vocet, qui ad inquisitionem perficiendam, si casus ferat, contribuere valeant, praesertim si ipsi causae contrarii sunt.

b) Vocandi sunt tamquam testes ex officio viri periti qui pervestigationes documentorum fecerunt et relationem de ipsis exararunt, iidemque sub iuramento declarare debent: 1° se omnes investigationes peregisse ac omnia collegisse quae causam respiciant; 2° nullum documentum aut textum se adulterasse vel mutilasse.

22. *a)* Medici a curatione, cum de miris sanationibus agitur, tamquam testes sunt inducendi.

b) Quod si renuerint se Episcopo vel delegato sistere, is curet ut scriptam sub iuramento, si fieri potest, relationem de morbo eiusque progressione conficiant actis inserendam, vel saltem eorum sententia per interpositam personam excipiatur, deinde examini subiciendam.

23. Testes in sua testificatione, iuramento firmanda, propriae scientiae fontem indicare debent circa ea quae asserunt; secus eorum testimonium nihili faciendum est.

24. Si quis testis maluerit scriptum aliquod a seipso antea exaratum Episcopo vel delegato tradere sive una cum depositione sive praeter

ten statement is to be accepted, provided the witness himself shall have proved by an oath that he himself wrote it and that its contents are true. It is also to be made part of the acts of the cause.

25. *a)* In whatever way the witnesses provide their information, the Bishop or his delegate is carefully to see to it that he always authenticates it with his signature and his seal.

b) The documents and written testimony, whether gathered by the experts or handed over by others, are to be authenticated by the signature and seal of any notary or public official, who attests to its authenticity.

26. *a)* If inquiries regarding documents or witnesses must be made in another diocese, the Bishop or his delegate is to send a letter to the competent Bishop, who is to act according to the norm of these statutes.

b) The acts of this type of inquiry are to be kept in the archive of the Chancery, while a copy, made according to the norm of nos. 29 and 30, is to be sent to the Bishop, who requested the inquiry.

27. *a)* The Bishop or his delegate is to take the greatest care that in gathering the proofs nothing is omitted which in any way pertains to the cause, recognizing for sure that the positive outcome of a cause depends to a great extent on its good instruction.

b) Once all the proofs have been gathered, the promotor of justice is to inspect all the acts and documents so that, should he deem it necessary, he may request further inquiries.

c) The postulator is also entitled to inspect the acts so that, if it be the case, the proofs may be completed through new witnesses or documents.

28. *a)* Before the inquiry is concluded, the Bishop or his delegate is to inspect carefully the tomb of the Servant of God, the room in which he lived or died and, if there be any, other places where someone can display signs of cult in his honor. He is also to make a declaration on the observance of the decrees of Urban VIII regarding the absence of cult.[5]

b) A report is to be drawn up about everything which has been done and it is to be inserted into the acts.

29. *a)* Once the instruction has been completed, the Bishop or his delegate is to order that a transcript be made

eam, huiusmodi scriptum recipiatur, dummodo ipse testis iuramento probaverit se illud scripsisse et vera in eo esse contenta, idemque ad acta causae accenseatur.

25. *a)* Quocumque modo testes suas notitias tradiderint, curet diligenter Episcopus vel delegatus ut illas authenticas reddat semper sua subsignatione et proprio sigillo.

b) Documenta et testimonia scripta, sive a peritis collecta sive ab aliis tradita, authentica declarentur per appositionem nominis et sigilli alicuius notarii vel publici officialis fidem facientis.

26. *a)* Si inquisitiones circa documenta vel testes in alia dioecesi fieri debent, Episcopus vel delegatus litteras ad Episcopum competentem mittat, qui ad normam horum statutorum agat.

b) Acta huiusmodi inquisitionis in archivo Curiae serventur, sed exemplar ad normam nn. 29–30 confectum ad Episcopum rogantem mittatur.

27. *a)* Episcopus vel delegatus summa diligentia et industria curet ut in probationibus colligendis nihil omittatur, quod quoquo modo ad causam pertineat, pro certo habens felicem exitum causae ex bona eius instructione magna ex parte dependere.

b) Collectis igitur omnibus probationibus, promotor iustitiae omnia acta et documenta inspiciat ut, si ipsi necessarium videatur, ulteriores inquisitiones petere possit.

c) Postulatori quoque facultas danda est acta inspiciendi ut, si casus ferat, per novos testes aut documenta probationes compleri possint.

28. *a)* Antequam absolvatur inquisitio, Episcopus vel delegatus diligenter inspiciat sepulcrum Servi Dei, cubiculum in quo habitavit vel obiit et, si quae sint, alia loca ubi cultus signa in eius honorem quis exhibere possit, et declarationem faciat de observantia decretorum Urbani VIII super non cultu.[5]

b) De omnibus peractis relatio conficiatur actis inserenda.

29. *a)* Instructoriis actis absolutis, Episcopus vel delegatus statuat ut transumptum confi-

5. Cfr. *ibid.*, no. 2, 6.

unless, in light of proven circumstances, he has already permitted this to be done during the instruction itself.

b) The transcript is to be transcribed from the original acts and made in duplicate.

30. *a)* Once the transcript has been finished, a comparison is to be made with the original and the notary is at least to initial each page and stamp them with his seal.

b) The original, closed and secured with seals, is to be kept in the archive of the Chancery.

31. *a)* The transcript of the inquiry and attached documents in duplicate, duly wrapped and secured with seals, are to be sent by a secure means to the Sacred Congregation, together with a copy of the books of the Servant of God which were examined by the theological censors and their judgment.[6]

b) If a translation of the acts and documents into a language accepted at the Sacred Congregation is necessary, two copies of the translation are to be prepared and declared authentic. These are then to be sent to Rome.

c) Furthermore, the Bishop or his delegate is to send to the Cardinal Prefect a letter testifying to the trustworthiness of the witnesses and the legitimacy of the acts.

32. The inquiry on miracles is to be instructed separately from the inquiry on virtues or martyrdom and is to be conducted according to the norms which follow.[7]

33. *a)* Once the Bishop competent according to norm no. 5b has accepted the petition of the postulator together with a brief but accurate report on the alleged miracle as well as those documents which pertain to the case, he is to ask for the judgment of one or two experts.

b) If he has then decided to instruct a judicial inquiry, he is to examine all the witnesses either personally or through his delegate, according to the norms established above in nos. 15 a, 16–18 and 21–24.

34. *a)* In the case of a cure from some disease, the Bishop or his delegate is to seek help from a physician, who is to propose questions to the witnesses in order to clarify matters according to necessity and circumstances.

b) If the person healed is still alive, he is to be examined by experts so that the duration of the healing can be ascertained.

35. A transcript of the inquiry together with attached documents is to be sent to the Sacred Congregation according to what is laid down in nos. 29–31.

ciatur, nisi, attentis probatis circumstantiis, durante ipsa instructione iam fieri permiserit.

b) Transumptum ex actis originalibus transcribatur atque duplici exemplari fiat.

30. *a)* Absoluta transumpti confectione, collatio cum archetypo fiat, et notarius singulas paginas siglis saltem subscribat et suo sigillo muniat.

b) Archetypum clausum sigillisque munitum in archivo Curiae asservetur.

31. *a)* Transumptum inquisitionis et adnexa documenta in duplici exemplari ad Sacram Congregationem rite clausa, et sigillis munita tute mittantur, una cum exemplari librorum Servi Dei a censoribus theologis examinatorum eorumque iudicio.[6]

b) Si versio actorum atque documentorum in linguam apud Sacram Congregationem admissam necessaria sit, duo exemplaria versionis exarentur et authentica declarentur, Romam una cum transumpto mittenda.

c) Episcopus vel delegatus insuper litteras de fide testibus adhibenda et de legitimitate actorum ad Cardinalem Praefectum mittat.

32. Inquisitio super miraculis separatim instruenda est ab inquisitione super virtutibus vel martyrio et fiat iuxta normas quae sequuntur.[7]

33. *a)* Episcopus competens ad normam n. 5 b, accepto postulatoris libello una cum brevi sed accurata relatione de asserto miraculo necnon documentis illud respicientibus, iudicium exquirat ab uno vel duobus peritis.

b) Deinde si inquisitionem iuridicam instruere statuerit, per se vel per suum delegatum omnes testes examinet, iuxta normas supra nn. 15 a, 16–18 et 21–24 statutas.

34. *a)* Si de sanatione alicuius morbi agatur, Episcopus vel delegatus auxilium quaerat a medico, qui interrogationes testibus proponat ad res clarius illustrandas iuxta necessitatem et circumstantias.

b) Si sanatus adhuc vivat, eius inspectio a peritis fiat, ut constare possit de duratione sanationis.

35. Inquisitionis transumptum una cum adnexis documentis ad Sacram Congregationem mittatur, iuxta statuta in nn. 29–31.

---

6. *Ibid.*

7. *Ibid.*, no. 2, 5.

36. Any solemn celebrations or panegyric speeches about Servants of God whose sanctity of life is still being legitimately examined are prohibited in Churches.

Furthermore, one must also refrain, even outside of Church, from any acts which could mislead the faithful into thinking that the inquiry conducted by the Bishop into the life of the Servant of God and his virtues or martyrdom carries with it the certitude that the Servant of God will be one day canonized.

His Holiness Pope John Paul II, in an Audience granted to the undersigned Cardinal Prefect of the Congregation on the 7th day of February in the year 1983, approved and ratified these norms, ordering that they be published and take effect from this very day, and are to be duly and conscientiously observed by all Bishops who instruct causes of canonization and by all others whom they concern, notwithstanding anything to the contrary, even those things worthy of special mention.

Given in Rome, from the Offices of the Sacred Congregation for the Causes of Saints, on the 7th day of the month of February in the year 1983.

PIETRO Cardinal PALAZZINI, *Prefect*
+Traian Crisan,
Titular Archbishop of Drivasto,
Secretary

36. De Servis Dei, quorum sanctitas vitae adhuc legitimo examini subiecta est, quaelibet sollemnia vel panegyricae orationes in ecclesiis prohibentur.

Sed etiam extra ecclesiam abstinendum est ab iis actis quibus fideles induci possint ad falso putandum inquisitionem ab Episcopo factam de Servi Dei vita et virtutibus vel martyrio certitudinem secum ferre futurae eiusdem Servi Dei canonizationis.

Quas normas SS.mus D. N. Ioannes Paulus divina Providentia Papa II, in Audientia die 7 februarii a. 1983 infrascripto Congregationis Cardinali Praefecto concessa, approbare et ratas habere dignatus est, mandans ut eae publici iuris fiant et ab hoc ipso die vigere incipiant, ab omnibus Episcopis qui causas canonizationis instruunt, et a ceteris ad quos spectat, rite et religiose servandae, contrariis quibuscumque, etiam speciali mentione dignis, minime obstantibus.

Datum Romae, ex Aedibus Sacrae Congregationis pro Causis Sanctorum, die 7 mensis februarii a. 1983.

PETRUS Card. PALAZZINI, *Praefectus*
+Traianus Crisan,
Archiep. tit. Drivastensis,
a Secretis

CONGREGATION FOR THE CAUSES OF SAINTS

CONGREGATIO PRO CAUSIS SANCTORUM

General Decree on the Causes of the Servants of God Whose Judgment is Presently Pending at the Sacred Congregation

Decretum Generale de servorum Dei causis, quarum iudicium in praesens apud Sacram Congregationem pendet

THE APOSTOLIC CONSTITUTION *Divinus perfectionis Magister* of January 25, 1983, n. 16, established that the causes of the Servants of God, whose judgment is presently pending at the Sacred Congregation for the Causes of Saints, are henceforth to proceed according to the spirit of this new law. Furthermore, it gives to this same Congregation the responsibility of establishing by a special decree the rules for handling these causes from this moment on.

In the desire to fulfill its responsibility, the Sacred Congregation has divided these causes into four categories and has established the following rules:

1) As regards "recent" causes, in which the *Position* on virtues or on martyrdom has already been published, the *Position* is to be passed on to the theological Consultors for their vote in accordance with the norm of the new law.

2) As regards those causes, in which the Observations of the Promotor of the Faith or the Response of the Patron

CIRCA SERVORUM DEI CAUSAS, quarum iudicium in praesens apud Sacram Congregationem pro Causis Sanctorum pendet, in Constitutione Apostolica *Divinus perfectionis Magister* diei 25 ianuarii a. 1983, n. 16, statutum est, ne ad ulteriora procedatur nisi servata mente huius novae legis, atque insuper ipsi Sacrae Congregationi munus demandatur peculiari decreto ordinem statuendi, quo in huiusmodi causis in posterum sit procedendum.

Cui quidem muneri satisfacere sibi proponens, Sacra Congregatio huiusmodi causas in quattuor genera dividens, statuit quae sequuntur:

1) Quoad causas "recentiores", in quibus Positio super virtutibus vel super martyrio iam typis edita est, eadem Consultoribus theologis pro voto tradatur, ad normam novae legis discutienda.

2) Ad eas vero causas quod attinet, in quibus Animadversiones Promotoris fidei vel Re-

are being prepared, every care is to be taken that all the documents **that pertain to** the cause are critically examined and, if the case require it, be added to the Response.

3) In other "recent" causes, once the writings of the Servant of God have been examined, one may not proceed further unless, under the guidance of the Relator of the Cause, the *Position* on virtues or on martyrdom has first been prepared according to the critical method, after those documents **which** in any way pertain to the cause have been gathered and studied.

4) As regards "historical" causes, in which the *Position* on virtues or on martyrdom, compiled by the Historical-hagiographical Office, has already been published, that *Position*, together with the votes of the Consultors of the same Office, is to be passed to the theological Consultors for their vote according to the norm of the new law, together with any explanations, which the Relator General may judge to be necessary.

The Supreme Pontiff, John Paul II, in an Audience granted to the undersigned Cardinal Prefect of the Congregation on the 7th day of February in the year 1983, approved all the above and ordered them to be observed from this day forward.

Given in Rome, from the Offices of the Sacred Congregation for the Causes of Saints, on the 7th day of February in the year 1983.

> PIETRO Cardinal PALAZZINI, *Prefect*
> +Traian Crisan,
> Titular Archbishop of Drivasto,
> *Secretary*

sponsio Patroni sint in statu confectionis, omnino curetur, ut omnia documenta causam respicientia critice examinentur et, quatenus casus ferat, Responsioni addantur.

3) In ceteris causis "recentioribus", examinatis scriptis Servi Dei, ad ulteriora ne procedatur, nisi Positio super virtutibus vel super martyrio methodo critica, sub ductu Relatoris causae, parata fuerit, praevia inquisitione documentorum quae quoquo modo causam respiciant.

4) Quoad causas "historicas", de quibus adest iam typis edita Positio super virtutibus vel super martyrio ab Officio historico-hagiographico concinnata, eadem, una cum votis Consultorum huius Officii, Consultoribus theologis pro voto tradatur ad normam novae legis, additis tamen explanationibus, si quae de iudicio Relatoris generalis necessariae sint.

Quae omnia Summus Pontifex Ioannes Paulus II, in Audientia infrascripto Congregationis Cardinali Praefecto die 7 februarii a. 1983 concessa, rata habuit et ab hoc ipso die servari mandavit.

Datum Romae, ex Aedibus Sacrae Congregationis pro Causis Sanctorum, die 7 februarii a. 1983.

> PETRUS Card. PALAZZINI, *Praefectus*
> +Traianus Crisan,
> Archiep. tit. Drivastensis,
> *a Secretis*

APPENDIX 2

PASTOR BONUS

JOHN PAUL II

Apostolic Constitution on the Roman Curia

Promulgated June 28, 1988

TABLE OF CONTENTS

Introduction

JOHN PAUL, BISHOP

SERVANT OF THE SERVANTS
OF GOD
FOR AN
EVERLASTING MEMORIAL

IOANNES PAULUS EPISCOPUS

SERVUS
SERVORUM DEI
AD PERPETUAM REI
MEMORIAM

Introduction

1. THE GOOD SHEPHERD, the Lord Christ Jesus (cf. Jn 10: 11–14), conferred on the bishops, the successors of the Apostles, and in a singular way on the bishop of Rome, the successor of Peter, the mission of making disciples in all nations and of preaching the Gospel to every creature. And so the Church was established, the people of God, and the task of its shepherds or pastors was indeed to be that service "which is called very expressively in Sacred Scripture a *diaconia* or ministry."[1]

The main thrust of this service or *diaconia* is for *more and more communion or fellowship to be generated* in the whole body of the Church, and for this communion to thrive and produce good results. As the insight of the Second Vatican Council has taught us, we come, with the gentle prompting of the Holy Spirit, to see the meaning of the mystery of the Church in the manifold patterns within this communion: for the Spirit will guide "the Church in the way of all truth (cf. Jn 16:13) and [unify] her in communion and in the work of ministry, he bestows upon her varied hierarchic and charismatic gifts [. . .]. Constantly he renews her and leads her to perfect union with her Spouse."[2] Wherefore, as the same Council affirms, "fully incorporated into the Church are those who, possessing the Spirit of Christ, accept all the means of salvation given to the Church together with her entire organization, and who— by the bonds constituted by the profession of faith, the

1. PASTOR BONUS Dominus Christus Iesus (cf. *Io* 10, 11.14) missionem discipulos faciendi in omnibus gentibus atque praedicandi Evangelium omni creaturae Apostolorum successoribus Episcopis, et singulari ratione Romano Episcopo, Petri successori, ita contulit, ut Ecclesia, Dei Populus, constitueretur atque eiusmodi Populi sui Pastorum munus esset revera servitium, quod «in Sacris Litteris "diaconia" seu ministerium significanter nuncupatur».[1]

Hoc servitium seu *diaconia* eo praesertim tendit, ut in universo ecclesiali corpore *communio magis magisque instauretur*, vigeat atque perpulchros fructus edere pergat. Etenim, sicut Concilium Vaticanum II luculenter docuit, Ecclesiae mysterium per multiplices huiusmodi communionis rationes significatur, Spiritus Sancti suavissimo instinctu: etenim Spiritus «Ecclesiam, quam in omnem veritatem inducit (cf. *Io* 16,13) et in communione et ministratione unificat, diversis donis hierarchicis et charismaticis instruit ac dirigit ... eamque perpetuo renovat et ad consummatam cum Sponso suo unionem perducit».[2] Quam ob rem, ut idem Concilium asseverat, «illi plene Ecclesiae societati incorporantur, qui Spiritum Christi habentes, integram eius ordinationem omniaque media salutis in ea instituta

1. *LG* 24.   2. Ibid., 4.

sacraments, ecclesiastical government, and communion—are joined in the visible structure of the Church of Christ, who rules her through the Supreme Pontiff and the bishops."[3]

Not only has this notion of communion been explained in the documents of the Second Vatican Council in general, especially in the Dogmatic Constitution on the Church, but it also received attention from the Fathers attending the 1985 and 1987 General Assemblies of the Synod of Bishops. Into this definition of the Church comes a convergence of the actual mystery of the Church,[4] the orders or constituent elements of the messianic people of God,[5] and the hierarchical constitution of the Church itself.[6] To describe it all in one broad expression, we take the words of the Dogmatic Constitution *Lumen gentium* just mentioned and say that "the Church, in Christ, is in the nature of sacrament—a sign and instrument, that is, of communion with God and of unity among the whole of humankind."[7] That is why this sacred communion thrives in the whole Church of Christ, as our predecessor Paul VI so well described it, "which lives and acts in the various Christian communities, namely, in the particular Churches dispersed throughout the whole world."[8]

2. When one thinks about this communion, which is the force, as it were, that glues the whole Church together, then the hierarchical constitution of the Church unfolds and comes into effect. It was endowed by the Lord himself with *a primatial and collegial nature at the same time* when he constituted the apostles "in the form of a college or permanent assembly, at the head of which he placed Peter, chosen from amongst them."[9] Here we are looking at that special concept whereby the pastors of the Church share in the threefold task of Christ—to teach, to sanctify, and to govern: and just as the apostles acted with Peter, so do the bishops together with the bishop of Rome. To use the words of the Second Vatican Council once more: "In that way, then, with priests and deacons as helpers, the bishops received the charge of the community, presiding in God's stead over the flock of which they are the shepherds in that they are teachers of doctrine, ministers of sacred worship and holders of office in government. Moreover, just as the

accipiunt, et in eiusdem compage visibili cum Christo, eam per Summum Pontificem atque Episcopos regente, iunguntur, vinculis nempe professionis fidei, sacramentorum et ecclesiastici regiminis ac communionis».[3]

Cuiusmodi communionis notionem non modo Concilii Vaticani II documenta in universum edisseruerunt, ac praesertim Constitutio dogmatica de Ecclesia, sed ad illam animum intenderunt etiam Synodi Patres, qui anno MCM-LXXXV, itemque duos post annos Generales Synodi Episcoporum Coetus celebraverunt: quam in Ecclesiae definitionem coeunt sive ipsum Ecclesiae Mysterium,[4] sive messianici Populi Dei ordines,[5] sive hierarchica ipsius Ecclesiae constitutio.[6] Quae omnia ut una comprehensione describamus, verba sumentes ex eadem memorata Constitutione, Ecclesia est «in Christo veluti sacramentum seu signum et instrumentum intimae cum Deo unionis totiusque generis humani unitatis».[7] Quam ob rem, huiusmodi sacra communio in tota Christi Ecclesia viget, «quae—ut perbelle scripsit Paulus VI, Decessor noster—vivit et agit in variis communitatibus christianis, Ecclesiis scilicet particularibus, per omnem terrarum orbem dispersis».[8]

2. Habita igitur ratione huius communionis, universam Ecclesiam veluti conglutinantis, etiam hierarchica eiusdem Ecclesiae constitutio explicatur atque ad effectum deducitur: quae *collegiali simul ac primatiali* natura ab ipso Domino praedita est, cum «Apostolos ad modum collegii seu coetus stabilis instituit, cui ex iisdem electum Petrum praefecit».[9] Hic praesertim agitur de speciali illa ratione, qua Ecclesiae Pastores triplex Christi munus participant, docendi scilicet, sanctificandi atque gubernandi: et sicut Apostoli id una cum Petro egerunt, ita haud dissimili modo id Episcopi agunt simul cum Romano Episcopo. Ut Concilii Vaticani II verbis denuo utamur, «Episcopi igitur communitatis ministerium cum adiutoribus presbyteris et diaconis susceperunt, loco Dei praesidentes gregi, cuius sunt Pastores, ut doctrinae magistri, sacri cultus sacerdotes, gu-

---

3. Ibid., 14.
4. Ibid., ch. 1.
5. Ibid., ch. 2.
6. Ibid., ch. 3.

7. Ibid., 1.
8. Ap. Const. *Vicariae potestatis*, 6 January 1977, *AAS* 69 (1977) 6; *CLD* 8 (1973–1977) 255; cf. *LG* 15.
9. *LG* 19.

office which the Lord confided to Peter alone, as first of the apostles, destined to be transmitted to his successors, is a permanent one, so also endures the office, which the apostles received, of shepherding the Church, a charge destined to be exercised without interruption by the sacred order of bishops."[10] And so it comes about that "this college"—the college of bishops joined together with the bishop of Rome—"in so far as it is composed of many members, is the expression of the multifariousness and universality of the people of God; and of the unity of the flock of Christ, in so far as it is assembled under one head."[11]

The power and authority of the bishops bears the mark of *diaconia or stewardship*, fitting the example of Jesus Christ himself who "came not to be served, but to serve and to give his life as a ransom for many" (Mk 10:45). Therefore the power that is found in the Church is to be understood as the power of being a servant and is to be exercised in that way; before anything else it is the authority of a shepherd.

This applies to each and every bishop in his own particular Church; but all the more does it apply to the bishop of Rome, whose Petrine ministry works for the good and benefit of the universal Church. The Roman Church has charge over the "whole body of charity"[12] and so it is the servant of love. It is largely from this principle that those great words of old have come—"The servant of the servants of God"—, by which Peter's successor is known and defined.

That is why the Roman Pontiff has also taken pains to deal carefully with the business of particular Churches, referred to him by the bishops or in some other way come to his attention, in order to encourage his brothers in the faith (cf. Lk 22:32), by means of this wider experience and by virtue of his office as Vicar of Christ and pastor of the whole Church. For he was convinced that the reciprocal communion between the bishop of Rome and the bishops throughout the world, bonded in unity, charity, and peace, brought the greatest advantage in promoting and defending the unity of faith and discipline in the whole Church.[13]

3. In the light of the foregoing, it is understood that the *diaconia* peculiar to Peter and his successors is necessarily

bernationis ministri. Sicut autem permanet munus a Domino singulariter Petro, primo Apostolorum, concessum et successoribus eius transmittendum, ita permanet munus Apostolorum pascendi Ecclesiam, ab ordine sacrato Episcoporum iugiter exercendum».[10] Itaque fit ut «Collegium hoc»—Episcoporum dicimus cum Romano Pontifice coniunctorum—«quatenus ex multis compositum, varietatem et universalitatem Populi Dei, quatenus vero sub uno capite collectum, unitatem gregis Christi» exprimat.[11]

Episcoporum autem potestas atque auctoritas *diaconiae* notam prae se fert, ad ipsius Iesu Christi exemplum accommodatam, qui «non venit, ut ministraretur ei, sed ut ministraret et daret animam suam redemptionem pro multis» (*Mc* 10, 45). Potestas ergo, quae in Ecclesia datur, potissimum secundum serviendi normam et intellegenda et exercenda est, ita ut huiusmodi auctoritas pastorali nota in primis polleat.

Id vero ad singulos Episcopos in propria cuiusque particulari Ecclesia spectat; attamen tanto magis ad Romanum Episcopum pertinet, cuius ministerium Petrianum in universalis Ecclesiae bonum utilitatemque procurandam incumbit: Romana enim Ecclesia praesidet «universo caritatis coetui»,[12] ideoque caritati inservit. Ex hoc potissimum principio processerunt vetusta illa verba «Servus Servorum Dei», quibus Petri Successor denominatur atque definitur.

Quam ob causam, Romanus Pontifex Ecclesiarum etiam particularium negotia, ab Episcopis ad se delata aut utcumque cognita, diligenter perpendere curavit, ut, pleniore rerum experientia exinde adepta, vi muneris sui, Vicarii scilicet Christi totiusque Ecclesiae Pastoris, fratres suos in fide confirmaret (cf. *Lc* 22, 32). Id enim persuasum sibi habebat mutuam inter Episcopos in universo orbe constitutos et Romanum Episcopum communionem, in vinculo unitatis, caritatis et pacis, maximum afferre emolumentum unitati fidei necnon disciplinae in cuncta Ecclesia promovendae atque tuendae.[13]

3. Quibus praemissis, sic intellegitur *diaconia*, quae Petri eiusque successorum propria est,

10. Ibid., 20.
11. Ibid., 22.
12. St. Ignatius of Antioch, *To the Romans*, introd., *Pa-* *tres apostolici*, ed. F. X. Funk, vol. I, ed. 2ᵃ adaucta et emendata, Tubingae, H. Laupp, 1901, p. 252.
13. Cf. *LG* 22–23, 25.

related to the *diaconia* of the other apostles and their successors, whose sole purpose is to build up the Church in this world.

From ancient times, this essential and interdependent relation of the Petrine ministry with the task and ministry of the other apostles has demanded something of a visible sign, not just by way of a symbol but something existing in reality, and it must still demand it. Deeply conscious of the burden of apostolic toil, our predecessors have given clear and thoughtful expression to this need, as we see, for example, in the words of Innocent III who wrote to the bishops and prelates of France in 1198 when he was sending a legate to them: "Although the Lord has given us the fullness of power in the Church, a power that makes us owe something to all Christians, still we cannot stretch the limits of human nature. Since we cannot deal personally with every single concern—the law of human condition does not suffer it—we are sometimes constrained to use certain brothers of ours as extensions of our own body, to take care of things we would rather deal with in person if the convenience of the Church allowed it."[14]

This gives some insight into the nature of that institution that Peter's successor has used in exercising his mission for the good of the universal Church, and some understanding of the procedures by which the institution itself has had to carry out its task: we mean the Roman Curia, which from ancient times has been labouring to lend its help in the Petrine ministry.

For the Roman Curia came into existence for this purpose, that the fruitful communion we mentioned might be strengthened and make ever more bountiful progress, rendering more effective the task of pastor of the Church which Christ entrusted to Peter and his successors, a task that has been growing and expanding from day to day. Our predecessor Sixtus V, in the Apostolic Constitution *Immensa aeterni Dei*, admitted as much: "The Roman Pontiff, whom Christ the Lord constituted as visible head of his body, the Church, and appointed for the care of all the Churches, calls and rallies unto himself many collaborators for this immense responsibility [. . .]; so that he, the hold-

ut necessario referatur ad aliorum apostolorum, eorumque successorum, diaconiam, quae ad aedificandam Ecclesiam in hoc mundo unice intendit.

Haec necessaria ministerii Petriani ratio ac necessitudo cum ceterorum apostolorum munere ac ministerio quoddam signum iam antiquitus postulavit, atque postulare debet, quod non modo ad instar symboli, sed etiam in rerum veritate exstaret. Hanc quidem necessitatem Decessores Nostri, apostolici laboris gravitate perculsi, dilucide impenseque senserunt, sicuti, exempli gratia, Innocentii III verba testantur, qui anno MCXCVIII ad Galliae Episcopos praelatosque haec scripsit, cum ad ipsos suum quendam Legatum mitteret: «Licet commissa nobis a Domino potestatis ecclesiastice plenitudo universis Christi fidelibus nos constituerit debitores, statum tamen et ordinem conditionis humanae non possumus ampliare ... Quia vero lex humane conditionis non patitur nec possumus in persona propria gerere sollicitudines universas, interdum per fratres nostros, qui sunt membra corporis nostri, ea cogimur exercere, que, si commoditas ecclesie sustineret, personaliter libentius impleremus».[14]

Inde quidem perspiciuntur atque intelleguntur sive natura illius instituti, quo Petri successor usus est in sua exercenda missione in universalis Ecclesiae bonum, sive agendi ratio, qua ipsum institutum commissa munera ad effectum deduceret oportuit: Romanam Curiam dicimus, quae in ministerii Petriani adiutorium ab antiquis temporibus adlaborat praestandum.

Nam ut illa, quam diximus, frugifera communio firmior exstaret atque uberius usque proficeret, Romana Curia ad id exorta est, ut scilicet efficacius redderetur muneris exercitium Pastoris Ecclesiae, quod Petro eiusque successoribus ab ipso Christo traditum est, quodque in dies crevit ac dilatatum est. Enimvero Decessor Noster Xystus V in Constitutione apostolica «Immensa aeterni Dei» fatebatur: «Romanus Pontifex, quem Christus Dominus Corporis sui, quod est Ecclesia, visibile caput constituit omniumque Ecclesiarum sollicitudinem gerere voluit,

14. *Die Register Innocenz' III.*, 1, *Pontifikatsjahr 1198/99*, bearb. von. O. Hageneder und A. Haidacher, Graz, Köln, H. Böhlaus, 1964, pp. 515–516.

er of the key of all this power, may share the huge mass of business and responsibilities among them—i.e., the cardinals—and the other authorities of the Roman Curia, and by God's helping grace avoid breaking under the strain."[15]

4. Right from the most ancient times, as a matter of fact, if we may sketch out a few lines of history, the Roman Pontiffs, in the course of their service directed to the welfare of the whole Church, have engaged the help of institutions or individual men selected from that *Church of Rome* which our predecessor Gregory the Great has called the *Church of the Blessed Apostle Peter*.[16]

At first they used the services of priests or deacons belonging to the Church of Rome to function as legates, to be sent on various missions, or to represent the bishops of Rome at ecumenical councils.

When matters of particular importance were to be dealt with, the bishops of Rome called on the help of Roman synods or councils to which they summoned bishops working in the ecclesiastical province of Rome. These councils not only dealt with questions pertaining to doctrine and the magisterium, but also functioned like tribunals, judging cases of bishops referred to the Roman Pontiff.

From the time when the cardinals began to take on a special importance in the Roman Church, especially in the election of the Pope—a function reserved to them from 1059—, the Roman Pontiffs made more and more use of their services, with the result that the Roman synods and councils gradually lost their importance until they ceased entirely.

So it came about that, especially after the thirteenth century, the Supreme Pontiff was carrying out all the business of the Church together with the cardinals gathered in consistory. Thus temporary instruments, the councils or synods of Rome, were replaced by another instrument, a permanent one, always available to the Pope.

It was our predecessor Sixtus V who gave the Roman Curia its formal organization through the above-quoted

multos sibi tam immensi oneris adiutores advocat atque adsciscit … ut partita inter eos (sc. Cardinales) aliosque Romanae Curiae magistratus ingenti curarum negotiorumque mole, ipse tantae potestatis clavum tenens, divina gratia adiutrice, non succumbat».[15]

4. Revera, ut iam quaedam historiae lineamenta proponamus, Romani Pontifices, iam inde a remotissimis temporibus, in suo ministerio ad universae Ecclesiae bonum procurandum sive singulos viros sive instituta adhibuerunt, qui ex *Romana Ecclesia* deligebantur, siquidem eadem *Ecclesia Beati Petri apostoli* a Decessore Nostro Gregorio Magno nuncupata est.[16]

Primum enim presbyterorum diaconorumve, ad eandem Ecclesiam pertinentium, opera usi sunt, qui vel legati munere fungerentur, vel pluribus missionibus interessent, vel Romanorum Pontificum partes in Oecumenicis Conciliis agerent.

Cum autem peculiaris momenti res tractandae erant, Romani Pontifices in auxilium vocaverunt Synodos vel Concilia Romana, ad quae Episcopi, in ecclesiastica provincia Romana suo munere fungentes, arcessebantur; haec vero non modo quaestiones ad doctrinam et magisterium spectantes agebant, sed etiam ad tribunalium instar procedebant, in quibus Episcoporum causae, ad Romanum Pontificem delatae, iudicabantur.

Ex quo autem tempore Cardinales speciale momentum in Romana Ecclesia adsumere coeperunt, praesertim in Papae electione, quae inde ab anno MLIX ipsis reservata est, iidem Romani Pontifices Patrum Cardinalium collata opera magis magisque usi sunt, ita ut Romanae Synodi vel Concilii munus gradatim deminueretur, donec reapse cessaret.

Quare evenit ut, praesertim post saeculum XIII, Summus Pontifex omnia Ecclesiae negotia una cum Cardinalibus, in Consistorium coadunatis, ageret. Ita factum est, ut instrumentis non stabilibus, videlicet Conciliis seu Romanis Synodis, stabile aliud succederet, quod Romano Pontifici semper praesto esset.

Decessor Noster Xystus V, per iam commemoratam Constitutionem Apostolicam «Im-

---

15. *Prooemium*, par. 1.

16. *Reg.* XIII, 42, II, p. 405, 12.

Apostolic Constitution *Immensa aeterni Dei*, on 22 January 1588, the 1587th year from the Incarnation of Our Lord Jesus Christ. He set up fifteen dicasteries, so that the single College of Cardinals would be replaced by several colleges consisting of certain cardinals whose authority would be confined to a clearly defined field and to a definite subject matter. In this way, the Supreme Pontiffs could enjoy maximum benefit from these collegial counsels. Consequently, the consistory's own original role and importance were greatly diminished.

As the centuries passed and historical outlooks and world conditions were transformed, certain changes and refinements were brought in, especially when the commissions of cardinals were set up in the nineteenth century to give the Pope assistance beyond that of the other dicasteries of the Roman Curia. Then on 29 June 1908, our predecessor Saint Pius X promulgated the Apostolic Constitution *Sapienti consilio*, in which, referring to the plan of collecting the laws of the Church into a Code of Canon Law, he wrote: "It has seemed most fitting to start from the Roman Curia so that, structured in a suitable way that everyone can understand, the Curia may more easily and effectively lend its help to the Roman Pontiff and the Church."[17] Here are the principal effects of that reform: the Sacred Roman Rota, which had ceased to function in 1870, was reestablished to deal with judicial cases, while the Congregations lost their judicial competence and became purely administrative organs. The principle was also established whereby the Congregations would enjoy their own rights, deferring to nobody else, so that each individual matter was to be dealt with by its own dicastery, and not by several ones at the same time.

This reform by Pius X, later confirmed and completed in the Code of Canon Law promulgated in 1917 by our predecessor Benedict XV, remained fairly unchanged until 1967, not long after the Second Vatican Council in which the Church delved more deeply into the mystery of its own being and gained a more lively vision of its mission.

mensa aeterni Dei», die XXII mensis Ianuarii anno MDLXXXVIII—qui fuit MDLXXXVII ab Incarnatione D.N.I.C.—Romanae Curiae compagem eius formalem dedit seriem XV Dicasteriorum instituendo, eo consilio ut uni Cardinalium Collegio plura subrogarentur collegia, e quibusdam Cardinalibus exstantia, quorum tamen auctoritas ad definitum quendam campum certamque materiam restringeretur; quam ob rem Summi Pontifices huiusmodi collegialium consiliorum viribus maxime frui poterant. Consistorii ideo nativum munus propriumque momentum valde deminuta sunt.

Volventibus tamen saeculis ac rationibus historicis rerumque condicionibus mutantibus, temperamenta quaedam atque immutationes accesserunt, praesertim cum saeculo XIX Cardinalium Commissiones institutae sunt, quarum esset Summo Pontifici adiutricem operam praeter alia Romanae Curiae Dicasteria conferre. Denique, opera et iussu S. Pii X, Decessoris Nostri, edita est Constitutio apostolica *Sapienti consilio*, die XXIX mensis Iunii anno MCMVIII, in qua, respectu etiam propositi ecclesiasticas leges in Codicem Iuris Canonici colligendi, haec Ipse scripsit: «Maxime opportunum visum est a Romana Curia ducere initium, ut ipsa, modo apto et omnibus perspicuo ordinata, Romano Pontifici Ecclesiaeque operam suam praestare facilius valeat et suppetias ferre perfectius».[17] Cuius reformationis hi praecipui fuerunt effectus: Sacra Romana Rota, quae anno MDCCCLXX munere cessaverat, ea ratione restituta est, ut iudicialia negotia ageret, dum Congregationes, amissa iudiciorum competentia, administrationis instrumenta unice fierent. Praeterea, principium instauratum est, quo Congregationes suo proprio iure, nemini alii attribuendo, gauderent, scilicet ut singulae res a suo quaeque Dicasterio, non vero simul a pluribus, tractari deberent.

Quae quidem Pii X reformatio, postea in Codice Iuris Canonici anno MCMXVII a Benedicto XV, Decessore Nostro, promulgato, sancita et completa, fere immutata permansit usque ad annum MCMLXVII, non multo post Concilium Oecumenicum Vaticanum II peractum, in quo Ecclesia altius sui ipsius mysterium exploravit suumque vividius prospectavit officium.

17. *AAS* 1 (1909) 8.

5. This growing self-awareness of the Church was bound of itself, and in keeping with our times, to produce a certain updating of the Roman Curia. While the Fathers of the Council acknowledged that the Curia had hitherto rendered outstanding assistance to the Roman Pontiff and the pastors of the Church, at the same time they expressed the desire that the dicasteries of the Curia should undergo a reorganization better suited to the needs of the times and of different regions and rites.[18] Our predecessor Paul VI quickly complied with the wishes of the Council and put into effect the reorganization of the Curia with the promulgation of the Apostolic Constitution *Regimini Ecclesiae universae* on 15 August 1967.

Through this Constitution, Paul VI laid down more detailed specifications for the structure, competence, and procedures of the already existing dicasteries, and established new ones to support specific pastoral initiatives, while the other dicasteries would carry on their work of jurisdiction or governance. The composition of the Curia came to reflect more clearly the multiform image of the universal Church. Among other things, the Curia coopted diocesan bishops as members and at the same time saw to the internal coordination of the dicasteries by periodic meetings of the cardinals who presided over them, to pool ideas and consider common problems. To provide better protection of the principal rights of the faithful, the Second Section was created in the Tribunal of the Apostolic Signatura.

Fully aware that the reform of such ancient institutions needed more careful study, Paul VI ordered the new system to be reexamined more deeply five years after the promulgation of the Constitution, and for a new look to be taken at the question whether it really conformed to the demands of the Second Vatican Council and answered the needs of the Christian people and civil society. As far as necessary, it should be recast in an even more suitable form. To carry out this task, a special group of prelates was set up, chaired by a cardinal, and this Commission worked hard at the project, up to the death of that Pontiff.

5. Huiusmodi itaque Ecclesiae de seipsa aucta cognitio sponte novam quandam Romanae Curiae aptationem, nostrae aetati congruentem, secum ferre debuit. Siquidem Sacrosanti Concilii Patres ipsam Romano Pontifici atque Ecclesiae Pastoribus eximium hucusque praebuisse auxilium agnoverunt, simulque ut eiusdem Romanae Curiae Dicasteria novae ordinationi, temporum, regionum ritumque necessitatibus magis aptatae, subicerentur optaverunt.[18] Hisce igitur Concilii optatis satisfaciens, Paulus VI, Decessor Noster, novam Curiae ordinationem ad effectum alacriter adduxit, data Constitutione apostolica «Regimini Ecclesiae universae», die XV mensis Augusti anno MCMLXVII.

Equidem per hanc Constitutionem Summus ille Pontifex Romanae Curiae structuram, competentiam ac procedendi rationem Dicasteriorum iam exsistentium accuratius determinavit, novaque constituit, quorum esset particularia in Ecclesia pastoralia incepta promovere, dum cetera in iurisdictionis vel gubernationis officia incumbere pergerent; quam ob rem factum est, ut compositio Curiae multiformem universalis Ecclesiae imaginem clarius referret. Inter alia, dioecesanos Episcopos in ipsam accessivit, simulque internae coordinationi Dicasteriorum prospexit per periodicos conventus eorundem Cardinalium moderatorum ad communia problemata collatis consiliis perpendenda. Sectionem Alteram apud Tribunal Signaturae Apostolicae induxit, ad summa eaque principalia fidelium iura aptius tuenda.

Verumtamen, cum antiquorum institutorum reformationem maturiore studio egere plane novisset, idem Summus Pontifex iussit ut, quinque exactis annis a Constitutionis promulgatione, innovatus rerum ordo altius expenderetur, pariterque inspiceretur utrum Concilii Vaticani II postulatis reapse congrueret et christiani populi civilisque societatis necessitatibus responderet, atque, quantum res postularet, in aptiorem reduceretur formam. Cui muneri adimplendo Commissio, seu peculiare Praelatorum corpus, Cardinali praeside, destinata est, ipsaque usque ad eiusdem Pontificis obitum operam actuose navavit.

18. Cf. *CD* 9.

6. When by the inscrutable design of Providence we were called to the task of being the shepherd of the universal Church, from the very beginning of our pontificate we took steps not only to seek advice from the dicasteries on this grave matter, but also to ask the opinion of the whole College of Cardinals. These cardinals, twice gathered in general consistory, addressed the question and gave their advice on the ways and means to be followed in the organization of the Roman Curia. It was necessary to consult the cardinals first in this important matter, for they are joined to the ministry of the bishop of Rome by a close and most special bond and they "are also available to [him], either acting collegially, when they are summoned together to deal with questions of major importance, or acting individually, that is, in the offices which they hold in assisting [him] especially in the daily care of the universal Church."[19]

A very broad consultation, as we mentioned above, was again carried out, as was only fitting, among the dicasteries of the Roman Curia. The result of this general consultation was the "Draft of a special law concerning the Roman Curia," worked out over close to two years by a commission of prelates under the chairmanship of a cardinal. This draft was examined by the individual cardinals, the patriarchs of the Oriental Churches, the conferences of bishops through their presidents, the dicasteries of the Roman Curia, and was discussed at the plenary meeting of cardinals in 1985. As to the conferences of bishops, it was essential that we be thoroughly briefed about their true general feeling on the needs of the particular Churches and what they wanted and expected in this regard from the Roman Curia. In gaining a clear awareness of all this, we had strong and most timely help from the 1985 extraordinary Synod of Bishops, as we have mentioned above.

Then, taking into account the observations and suggestions that had been gathered in the course of these extensive consultations, and bearing in mind the considered judgement of certain private individuals, a commission of cardinals, which had been set up for this express purpose, prepared a particular law for the Roman Curia in harmony with the new Code of Canon Law.

19. C. 349.

6. Cum inscrutabili Providentiae consilio ad universalis Ecclesiae pascendae munus vocati simus, iam a Pontificatus primordiis sategimus non solum de re tam gravi Dicasteriorum mentem exquirere, verum etiam ab universo Cardinalium Collegio iudicium postulare. Qui Patres Cardinales, in generali Consistorio bis congregati, rei incubuerunt atque consilia praebuerunt de itinere rationibusque persequendis in Romanae Curiae ordinatione. Cardinales enim cum Romani Episcopi ministerio arctissimo ac singulari vinculo coniunguntur, eidemque «adsunt sive collegialiter agendo, cum ad quaestiones maioris momenti tractandas in unum convocantur, sive ut singuli, scilicet variis officiis, quibus funguntur, eidem ... operam praestando in cura praesertim cotidiana universae Ecclesiae»:[19] ii igitur in primis sciscitandi erant in tanti momenti causa.

Perampla sententiarum rogatio, quam supra memoravimus, apud Romanae Curiae Dicasteria, ut aequum erat, iterum facta est. Generalis consultationis fructus illud exstitit «Schema Legis peculiaris de Curia Romana», cui apparando incubuit Praelatorum Commissio, Patre Cardinali praeside, duos fere annos adlaborans, quodque singulorum Cardinalium, Ecclesiarum Orientalium Patriarcharum, Episcoporum Conferentiarum per earum Praesides, et Romanae Curiae Dicasteriorum examini subiectum est, atque in plenario Cardinalium Coetu anno MCMLXXXV excussum. Quod attinet ad Episcoporum Conferentias, oportebat ut de Ecclesiarum particularium necessitatibus atque de earum hac in materie exspectationibus optatisque ad Romanam Curiam pertinentibus per vere universalem sententiam certiores fieremus; quae omnia ut plane nosceremus, occasionem potissimum praebuit peropportunam extraordinaria Synodus pariter anno MCMLXXXV celebrata, sicut iam mentionem fecimus.

Denique Commissio Patrum Cardinalium ad hunc finem specialiter condita, ratione habita animadversionum et consiliorum ex multiplicibus consultationibus acceptorum, atque sententia etiam privatorum quorundam virorum cognita, Legem peculiarem pro Curia Romana apparavit, novo *Codici Iuris Canonici* congruenter aptatam.

It is this particular law that we wish to promulgate by means of this Apostolic Constitution, at the end of the fourth centenary of the afore-mentioned Apostolic Constitution *Immensa aeterni Dei* of Sixtus V, eighty years after the Apostolic Constitution *Sapienti consilio* of Saint Pius X, and scarcely twenty years after the coming into force of the Apostolic Constitution of Paul VI *Regimini Ecclesiae universae,* with which our own is closely linked, since both in some way derive from the Second Vatican Council and both originate from the same inspiration and intent.

7. In harmony with the Second Vatican Council, this inspiration and intent establish and express the steadfast activity of the renewed Curia, as in these words of the Council: "In exercising his supreme, full and immediate authority over the universal Church, the Roman Pontiff employs the various departments of the Roman Curia, which act in his name and by his authority for the good of the Churches and in service of the sacred pastors."[20]

Consequently, it is evident that the function of the Roman Curia, though not belonging to the essential constitution of the Church willed by God, has nevertheless *a truly ecclesial character* because it draws its existence and competence from the pastor of the universal Church. For the Curia exists and operates only insofar as it has a relation to the Petrine ministry and is based on it. But just as the ministry of Peter as the "servant of the servants of God" is exercised in relationship with both the whole Church and the bishops of the entire Church, similarly the Roman Curia, as the servant of Peter's successor, looks only to help the whole Church and its bishops.

This clearly shows that the principal *characteristic* of each and every dicastery of the Roman Curia is that of being *ministerial,* as the already-quoted words of the Decree *Christus Dominus* declare and especially these: "The Roman Pontiff *employs the various departments of the Roman Curia.*"[21] These words clearly show the Curia's instrumental nature, described as a kind of agent in the hands of the Pontiff, with the result that it is endowed with no force and no power apart from what it receives from the same Supreme Pastor. Paul VI himself, in 1963, two years before he promulgated the Decree *Christus Dominus,* defined the Roman Curia "as an instrument of immediate adhesion and

Quam quidem peculiarem Legem hac praesenti Constitutione apostolica promulgare volumus, dum quartum nuper exspiravit saeculum a commemorata Constitutione apostolica «Immensa aeterni Dei» Xysti V, atque octogesimus recurrit annus a S. Pii X Constitutione apostolica «Sapienti consilio», viginti denique vix expletis annis ex quo Constitutio apostolica Pauli VI «Regimini Ecclesiae universae» vim suam exserere coepit, quacum haec Nostra arcte coniungitur, quippe quod utraque a Concilio Vaticano II, eadem ducente cogitatione et mente, originem quodammodo ducat.

7. Hae mens atque cogitatio, Concilio Vaticano II congruentes, renovatae Romanae Curiae actuositatem firmant et exprimunt. Quae quidem hisce Concilii enuntiatur verbis: «In exercenda suprema, plena et immediata potestate in universam Ecclesiam, Romanus Pontifex utitur Romanae Curiae Dicasteriis, quae proinde nomine et auctoritate illius munus suum explent in bonum Ecclesiarum et in servitium Sacrorum Pastorum».[20]

Patet igitur Romanae Curiae munus, etsi ad propriam Ecclesiae constitutionem, iure divino conditam, non pertinet, *indolem* tamen *vere ecclesialem* habere, quatenus ab universalis Ecclesiae Pastore suam et exsistentiam et competentiam trahat. Ea enim in tantum exstat atque adlaborat, in quantum ad ministerium Petrianum refertur in eoque fundatur. Quoniam autem Petri ministerium, utpote «servi servorum Dei», sive erga universam Ecclesiam sive erga totius Ecclesiae Episcopos exercetur, Romana etiam Curia, Petri successori inserviens, ad universam Ecclesiam atque ad Episcopos iuvandos pariter spectat.

Plane inde elucet praecipuam notam omnium singulorumque Romanae Curiae Dicasteriorum esse eius *indolem ministerialem,* sicut iam prolata verba e Decreto «Christus Dominus» declarant, et haec praesertim: «Romanus Pontifex *utitur Romanae Curiae Dicasteriis».*[21] Perspicue enim indoles instrumentalis Curiae his indicatur, et ipsa veluti instrumentum in manibus Pontificis quodammodo describitur, ita ut nulla vi nullaque potestate polleat praeter eas quas ab eodem Summo Pastore recipit. Ipse enim Paulus VI, iam duobus annis antequam Decretum *Christus*

20. *CD* 9.

21. Ibid.

perfect obedience," an instrument the Pope uses to fulfill his universal mission. This notion is taken up throughout the Apostolic Constitution *Regimini Ecclesiae universae.*

This instrumental and ministerial characteristic seems indeed to define most appropriately the nature and role of this worthy and venerable institution. Its nature and role consist entirely in that the more exactly and loyally the institution strives to dedicate itself to the will of the Supreme Pontiff, the more valuable and effective is the help it gives him.

8. Beyond this ministerial character, the Second Vatican Council further highlighted what we may call the *vicarious character* of the Roman Curia, because, as we have already said, it does not operate by its own right or on its own initiative. It receives its power from the Roman Pontiff and exercises it within its own essential and innate dependence on the Pontiff. It is of the nature of this power that it always joins its own action to the will of the one from whom the power springs. It must display a faithful and harmonious interpretation of his will and manifest, as it were, an identity with that will, for the good of the Churches and service to the bishops. From this character the Roman Curia draws its energy and strength, and in it too finds the boundaries of its duties and its code of behaviour.

The fullness of this power resides in the head, in the very person of the Vicar of Christ, who imparts it to the dicasteries of the Curia according to the competence and scope of each one. Since, as we said earlier, the Petrine function of the Roman Pontiff by its very nature relates to the office of the college of his brother bishops and aims at building up and making firm and expanding the whole Church as well as each and every particular Church, this same *diaconia* of the Curia, which he uses in carrying out his own personal office, necessarily relates in the same way to the personal office of the bishops, whether as members of the college of bishops or as pastors of the particular Churches.

For this reason, not only is the Roman Curia far from being a *barrier or screen* blocking personal communications and dealings between bishops and the Roman Pontiff, or restricting them with conditions, but, on the contrary, it is itself the facilitator for communion and the sharing of concerns, and must be ever more so.

Dominus promulgaretur, scilicet anno MCMLXIII, Romanam Curiam definivit instrumentum immediatae adhaesionis et absolutae oboedientiae, quo Summus Pontifex ad suam universalem missionem explendam utitur. Quae notio in Constitutione apostolica «Regimini Ecclesiae universae» passim usurpata est.

Haec indoles ministerialis vel instrumentalis aptissime revera videtur huius valde benemeriti venerandique instituti naturam definire eiusque actionem significare, quae totae in eo consistunt ut auxilium Summo Pontifici eo validius et efficacius praestet, quo magis conformiter ac fidelius eius voluntati sese praebere nitatur.

8. Praeter hanc indolem ministerialem, a Concilio Vaticano II *character*, ut ita dicamus, *vicarius* Romanae Curiae in luce ulterius ponitur, quandoquidem ipsa, ut iam diximus, non proprio iure neque proprio marte operatur: potestatem enim a Romano Pontifice acceptam exercet essentiali quadam et nativa cum Ipso necessitudine, quia huiusmodi potestatis proprium est ut agendi studium cum voluntate illius, a quo oritur, semper coniungat, ea quidem ratione ut eiusdem voluntatis fidelem interpretationem, consonantiam, immo quasi aequalitatem prae se ferat atque manifestet, in Ecclesiarum bonum atque in Episcoporum servitium. Ex huiusmodi indole Romana Curia vim roburque haurit, pariterque officiorum suorum limites ac normarum codicem invenit.

Huius autem potestatis plenitudo in capite seu in ipsa Christi Vicarii persona insidet, qui propterea Curiae Dicasteriis eam committit pro singulorum competentia atque ambitu. Quoniam autem Romani Pontificis munus Petrianum, sicut diximus, ad fratrum Episcoporum Collegii munus suapte natura refertur, ad id simul spectans ut universa Ecclesia singulaeque particulares Ecclesiae aedificentur, constabiliantur atque dilatentur, eadem Curiae *diaconia*, qua Ipse in suo personali munere exercendo utitur, necessario pariter refertur ad personale Episcoporum munus, sive utpote Episcopalis Collegii membrorum, sive utpote particularium Ecclesiarum Pastorum.

Quam ob causam non modo longe abest ut Romana Curia personales rationes ac necessitudines inter Episcopos atque Summum Pontificem quoddam veluti *diaphragma* impediat vel condicionibus obstringat, sed contra ipsa est,

9. By reason of its *diaconia* connected with the Petrine ministry, one concludes, on one hand, that the Roman Curia is closely bound to the bishops of the whole world, and, on the other, that those pastors and their Churches are the first and principal beneficiaries of the work of the dicasteries. This is proved even by the composition of the Curia.

For the Roman Curia is composed of nearly all the cardinals who, by definition, belong to the Roman Church,[22] and they closely assist the Supreme Pontiff in governing the universal Church. When important matters are to be dealt with, they are all called together into regular or special consistories.[23] So they come to have a strong awareness of the needs of all of God's people, and they labour for the good of the whole Church.

In addition to this, most of the heads of the individual dicasteries have the character and grace of the episcopate, pertaining to the one College of Bishops, and so are inspired by the same solicitude for the whole Church as are all bishops in hierarchical communion with their head, the bishop of Rome.

Furthermore, as some diocesan bishops are coopted onto the dicasteries as members and are "better able to inform the Supreme Pontiff on the thinking, the hopes and the needs of all the Churches,"[24] so the collegial spirit between the bishops and their head works through the Roman Curia and finds *concrete* application, and this is extended to the whole Mystical Body which "is a corporate body of Churches."[25]

This collegial spirit is also fostered between the various dicasteries. All the cardinals in charge of dicasteries, or their representatives, when specific questions are to be addressed, meet periodically in order to brief one another on the more important matters and provide mutual assistance in finding solutions, thus providing unity of thought and action in the Roman Curia.

Apart from these bishops, the business of the dicaster-

atque magis magisque sit oportet, communionis atque sollicitudinum participationis administra.

9. Ratione igitur suae diaconiae, cum ministerio Petriano coniunctae, eruendum est tum Romanam Curiam cum totius orbis Episcopis arctissime coniungi, tum eosdem Pastores eorumque Ecclesias primos principalioresque esse veluti beneficiarios operis Dicasteriorum. Quod eiusdem Curiae etiam compositione probatur.

Etenim Romanam Curiam omnes fere componunt Patres Cardinales, ad Romanam Ecclesiam proprio nomine pertinentes,[22] qui proxime Summum Pontificem in universali Ecclesia gubernanda adiuvant, quique insuper cuncti sive in ordinaria sive in extraordinaria Consistoria convocantur, cum graviora negotia tractanda id suadeant;[23] quo igitur fit ut, necessitates totius Populi Dei plenius cognoscentes, Ecclesiae universae bono prospicere pergant.

Huc etiam accedit quod singulis Dicasteriis praepositi episcopali charactere et gratia plerumque pollent, ad unumque Episcoporum Collegium pertinent, itemque eadem etiam erga universam Ecclesiam sollicitudine urgentur, qua omnes Episcopi, in communione hierarchica cum Romano Episcopo suo Capite, devinciuntur.

Cum insuper inter Dicasteriorum membra aliqui cooptentur dioecesani Episcopi, «qui mentem, optata ac necessitates omnium Ecclesiarum Summo Pontifici plenius referre valeant»,[24] per Romanam Curiam collegialis affectus, qui inter Episcopos eorumque Caput intercedit, ad *concretam* applicationem perducitur, idemque ad totum mysticum Corpus extenditur, «quod est etiam corpus Ecclesiarum»[25].

Qui quidem collegialis affectus inter varia quoque Dicasteria colitur. Omnes enim Cardinales Dicasteriis praepositi certis temporibus inter se conveniunt, vel ipsorum partes agentes cum peculiares quaestiones tractandae sint, ut collatis consiliis de potioribus quaestionibus certiores fiant ad illasque solvendas mutuum adiutorium conferant atque ideo agendi cogitandique unitatem in Romana Curia provideant.

Praeter hos episcopali potestate praeditos

---

22. Cf. Ap. Const. *Vicariae potestatis*, 6 January 1977, *AAS* 69 (1977) 6; *CLD* 8 (1973–1977) 255.
    23. Cf. *C.I.C.* 353.

24. *CD* 10.
25. *LG* 23.

ies employs a number of collaborators who are of value and service to the Petrine ministry by work that is neither light nor easy and is often obscure.

The Roman Curia calls into its service diocesan priests from all over the world, who by their sharing in the ministerial priesthood are closely united with the bishops, male religious, most of whom are priests, and female religious, all of whom in their various ways lead their lives according to the evangelical counsels, furthering the good of the Church, and bearing special witness for Christ before the world, and lay men and women who by virtue of baptism and confirmation are fulfilling their own apostolic role. By this coalition of many forces, all ranks within the Church join in the ministry of the Supreme Pontiff and more effectively help him by carrying out the pastoral work of the Roman Curia. This kind of service by all ranks in the Church clearly has no equal in civil society and their labour is given with the intent of truly serving and of following and imitating the *diaconia* of Christ himself.

10. From this comes to light that the ministry of the Roman Curia is strongly imbued with a certain note of *collegiality,* even if the Curia itself is not to be compared to any kind of college. This is true whether the Curia be considered in itself or in its relations with the bishops of the whole Church, or because of its purposes and the corresponding spirit of charity in which that ministry has to be conducted. This collegiality enables it to work for the college of bishops and equips it with suitable means for doing so. Even more, it expresses the solicitude that the bishops have for the whole Church, inasmuch as bishops share this kind of care and zeal "with Peter and under Peter."

This comes out most strikingly and takes on a symbolic force when, as we have already said above, the bishops are called to collaborate in the individual dicasteries. Moreover, each and every bishop still has the inviolable right and duty to approach the successor of Saint Peter, especially by means of the visits *ad limina Apostolorum.*

These visits have a special meaning all of their own, in keeping with the ecclesiological and pastoral principles explained above. Indeed, they are first of all an opportunity of the greatest importance, and they constitute, as it were, the centre of the highest ministry committed to the Su-

viros ad Dicasteriorum navitatem plurimi requiruntur operis adiutores, qui suo labore, haud raro abscondito neque levi vel facili, ministerio Petriano inserviant ac prosint.

Etenim in Romanam Curiam advocantur sive dioecesani ex universo terrarum orbe presbyteri, qui sacerdotii ministerialis participes, cum Episcopis arcte coniunguntur; sive Religiosi, e quibus maxima pars sunt presbyteri, atque Religiosae Sodales, qui vitam suam ad Evangelii consilia diversimode componunt, ad Ecclesiae bonum augendum atque ad singulare Christi testimonium coram mundo praestandum; sive laici viri atque mulieres, qui ob Baptismi atque Confirmationis virtutem proprio apostolico munere funguntur. Quae plurium virium conspiratio efficit ut omnes Ecclesiae ordines in pastoralem Romanae Curiae operam continuandam efficacius usque adiuvent Summum Pontificem, cum Ipsius ministerio coniuncti. Exinde etiam patet, huiusmodi omnium Ecclesiae ordinum servitium nihil simile in civili societate invenire, atque ipsorum laborem cum animo vere serviendi praestandum esse, ad ipsius Christi diaconiam sequendam atque imitandam.

10. Clare inde elucet Romanae Curiae ministerium, sive in semet ipso consideretur, sive ob ipsius rationes cum universae Ecclesiae Episcopis, sive ob fines, ad quos contendit atque ob concordem caritatis affectum, quo ducatur oportet, quadam *collegialitatis* nota pollere, etiamsi ipsa Curia nulli sit comparanda cuiuslibet naturae collegio; quae nota eam ad inserviendum Episcoporum Collegio informat mediisque ad id idoneis instruit. Quin immo, ipsorum etiam Episcoporum sollicitudinem pro universa Ecclesia exprimit, siquidem Episcopi huiusmodi curam atque sedulitatem «cum Petro et sub Petro» participant.

Quod sane maxime excellit et symbolicam vim prae se fert, cum Episcopi—ut iam supra diximus—vocantur ut singulis Dicasteriis sociam operam praebeant. Praeterea omnibus et singulis Episcopis integrum ius manet et officium ipsum Beati Petri Successorem adeundi, potissimum per visitationes «ad Apostolorum limina».

Hae visitationes, ob supra exposita ecclesiologica et pastoralia principia, propriam peculiaremque significationem accipiunt. Sunt enim in primis maximi momenti opportunitas, et veluti centrum constituunt supremi illius ministerii,

preme Pontiff. For then the pastor of the universal Church talks and communicates with the pastors of the particular Churches, who have come to him in order to see Cephas (cf. Gal 1:18), to deal with him concerning the problems of their dioceses, face to face and in private, and so to share with him the solicitude for all the Churches (cf. 2 Cor 11:28). For these reasons, communion and unity in the innermost life of the Church is fostered to the highest degree through the *ad limina* visits.

These visits also allow the bishops a frequent and convenient way to contact the appropriate dicasteries of the Roman Curia, pondering and exploring plans concerning doctrine and pastoral action, apostolic initiatives, and any difficulties obstructing their mission to work for the eternal salvation of the people committed to them.

11. Thus since the zealous activity of the Roman Curia, united to the Petrine ministry and based on it, is dedicated to the good both the whole Church and the particular Churches, the Curia is in the first place being called on to fulfill that *ministry of unity* which has been entrusted in a singular way to the Roman Pontiff insofar as he has been set up by God's will as the permanent and visible foundation of the Church. Hence unity in the Church is a precious treasure to be preserved, defended, protected, and promoted, to be for ever exalted with the devoted cooperation of all, and most indeed by those who each in their turn *are the visible source and foundation of unity in their own particular Churches.*[26]

Therefore the cooperation which the Roman Curia brings to the Supreme Pontiff is rooted in this ministry of unity. This unity is in the first place the *unity of faith,* governed and constituted by the sacred deposit of which Peter's successor is the chief guardian and protector and through which indeed he receives his highest responsibility, that of strengthening his brothers. The unity is likewise the *unity of discipline,* the general discipline of the Church, which constitutes a system of norms and patterns of behaviour, gives shapes to the fundamental structure of the Church, safeguards the means of salvation and their correct administration, together with the ordered structure of the people of God.

Church government safeguards this unity and cares for it at all times. So far from suffering harm from the differ-

26. Cf. ibid., 23.

ences of life and behaviour among various persons and cultures, what with the immense variety of gifts poured out by the Holy Spirit, this same unity actually grows richer year by year, so long as there are no isolationist or centripetal attempts and so long as everything is brought together into the higher structure of the one Church. Our predecessor John Paul I brought this principle to mind quite admirably when he addressed the cardinals about the agencies of the Roman Curia: "[They] provide the Vicar of Christ with the concrete means of giving the apostolic service that he owes the entire Church. Consequently, they guarantee an organic articulation of legitimate autonomies, while maintaining an indispensable respect for that unity of discipline and faith for which Christ prayed on the very eve of his passion."[27]

And so it is that the highest ministry of unity in the universal Church has much respect for lawful customs, for the mores of peoples and for that authority which belongs by divine right to the pastors of the particular Churches. Clearly however, whenever serious reasons demand it, the Roman Pontiff cannot fail to intervene in order to protect unity in faith, in charity, or in discipline.

12. Consequently, since the mission of the Roman Curia is ecclesial, it claims the cooperation of the whole Church to which it is directed. For no one in the Church is cut off from others and each one indeed makes up the one and the same body with all others.

This kind of cooperation is carried out through that communion we spoke of at the beginning, namely of life, charity, and truth, for which the messianic people is set up by Christ Our Lord, taken up by Christ as an instrument of redemption, and sent out to the whole world as the light of the world and the salt of the earth.[28] Therefore, just as it is the duty of the Roman Curia to communicate with all the Churches, so the pastors of the particular Churches, governing these Churches "as vicars and legates of Christ,"[29] must take steps to communicate with the Roman Curia, so that, dealing thus with each other in all trust, they and the successor of Peter may come to be bound together ever so strongly.

This mutual communication between the centre of the

sis exsistendi et agendi modis pro varietate personarum et culturarum nedum detrimentum patiatur per donorum immensam varietatem, quae Spiritus Sanctus profundit, perenniter ditescit, dummodo ne exinde nisus sese separandi insularum ad instar vel fugae a centro exoriantur, sed omnia in altiorem unius Ecclesiae structuram componantur. Quod principium Decessor Noster Ioannes Paulus I optime commemoravit, cum Patres Cardinales allocutus haec de Romanae Curiae institutis asseveravit: eadem «Christi Vicario id praestant ut apostolico ministerio, cuius Ipse universae Ecclesiae debitor est, certe ac definite fungi possit, atque hac ratione provident ut legitim agendi libertates sese organico modo explicent, servato tamen necessario obsequio erga illam disciplinae immo etiam fidei unitatem, ad Ecclesiae naturam pertinentem, pro qua Christus antequam pateretur oravit».[27]

Quo fit ut supremum unitatis ministerium universalis Ecclesiae legitimas consuetudines, populorum mores atque potestatem, quae iure divino ad Ecclesiarum particularium Pastores pertinet, vereatur. Ipse tamen Romanus Pontifex, uti patet, praetermittere non valet quin manus apponat quotiescumque graves rationes pro tuenda unitate in fide, in caritate vel in disciplina id postulent.

12. Munus itaque Romanae Curiae ecclesiale cum sit, cooperationem totius Ecclesiae, ad quam dirigitur, requirit. Nemo enim in Ecclesia ab aliis est seiunctus, immo quisque cum ceteris omnibus unum idemque efficit corpus.

Cuiusmodi cooperatio per illam communionem agitur, e qua exordium sumpsimus, scilicet vitae, caritatis et veritatis, in quam Populus messianicus a Christo Domino est constitutus, ab Eoque ut redemptionis instrumentum assumitur et tamquam lux mundi et sal terrae ad universum mundum mittitur.[28] Sicut ergo Romanae Curiae est cum omnibus Ecclesiis communicare, ita Pastores Ecclesiarum particularium, quas ipsi «ut vicarii et legati Christi regunt»,[29] cum Romana Curia communicare satagant oportet, ut per haec fidentia commercia, firmiore vinculo cum Petri Successore obstringantur.

Quae inter Ecclesiae centrum eiusque, ut ita

---

27. Allocution to the college of cardinals, 30 August 1978, *AAS* 70 (1978) 703; *The Pope Speaks* 23 (1978) 318–319.

28. Cf. *LG* 9.

29. Ibid., 27.

Church and the periphery does not enlarge the scope of anyone's authority but promotes *communion* in the highest degree, in the manner of a living body that is constituted and activated precisely by the interplay of all its members. This was well expressed by our predecessor Paul VI: "It is obvious, in fact, that along with the movement toward the centre and heart of the Church, there must be another corresponding movement, spreading from the centre to the periphery and carrying, so to speak, to each and all of the local Churches, to each and all of the pastors and the faithful, the presence and testimony of that treasure of truth and grace of which Christ has made Us the partaker, depository and dispenser."[30]

All of this means that the ministry of salvation offers more effectively to this one and same people of God, a ministry, we repeat, which before anything else demands mutual help between the pastors of the particular Churches and the pastor of the whole Church, so that all may bring their efforts together and strive to fulfill that supreme law which is the salvation of souls.

History shows that when the Roman Pontiffs established the Roman Curia and adapted it to new conditions in the Church and in the world, they intended nothing other than to work all the better for this salvation of souls. With full justification did Paul VI visualise the Roman Curia as another cenacle or upper room of Jerusalem totally dedicated to the Church.[31] We ourselves have proclaimed to all who work there that the only possible code of action is to set the norm for the Church and to deliver eager service to the Church.[32] Indeed, in this new legislation on the Roman Curia it has been our will to insist that the dicasteries should approach all questions "by a pastoral route and with a pastoral sense of judgement, aiming at justice and the good of the Church and above all at the salvation of souls."[33]

13. Now as we are about to promulgate this Apostolic Constitution, laying down the new physionomy of the Roman Curia, we wish to bring together the ideas and intentions that have guided us.

dicamus, peripheriam mutua communicatio, dum nullius extollit auctoritatis fastigium, *communionem* inter omnes maximopere promovet, ad instar viventis cuiusdam corporis, quod ex mutuis omnium membrorum rationibus constat atque operatur. Quod feliciter expressit Paulus VI Decessor Noster: «Liquet enim motui ad centrum ac veluti ad cor Ecclesiae respondere opus esse alium motum, qui a medio ad extrema feratur atque quadam ratione omnes et singulas Ecclesias, cunctos et singulos Pastores ac fideles attingat, ita ut ille significetur et ostendatur thesaurus veritatis, gratiae et unitatis, cuius Christus Dominus ac Redemptor Nos effecit participes, custodes ac dispensatores».[30]

Quae omnia eo pertinent, ut uni eidemque Populo Dei efficacius praebeatur ministerium salutis; ministerium dicimus, quod praeprimis postulat mutuum inter particularium Ecclesiarum Pastores et universae Ecclesiae Pastorem adiutorium, ita ut omnes collatis viribus adnitantur adimplere supremam eam legem, quae est salus animarum.

Nihil omnino aliud, quam ut huic saluti animarum uberius usque consulerent, Summi Pontifices voluerunt, sive Romanam Curiam condendo, sive novis Ecclesiae mundique condicionibus ipsam aptando, sicut e rerum historia patet. Iure igitur merito Paulus VI Romanam Curiam, veluti alterum Hierosolymitanum cenaculum, et sanctae Ecclesiae prorsus debitam sibi effingebat.[31] Nosmetipsi idcirco ediximus omnibus, qui in ipsa operam dant, unicam agendi rationem esse et normam Ecclesiae et erga Ecclesiam alacre praestare servitium.[32] Immo in hac nova de Romana Curia Lege statuere voluimus, ut quaestiones omnes a Dicasteriis tractentur «viis ... ac iudiciis pastoralibus, animo intento tum ad iustitiam et Ecclesiae bonum tum praesertim ad animarum salutem».[33]

13. Iam igitur promulgaturi hanc Constitutionem apostolicam, qua nova Romanae Curiae lineamenta impertiuntur, placet nunc Nobis consilia atque proposita complecti, quibus ducti sumus.

---

30. M.P. *Sollicitudo omnium Ecclesiarum,* 24 June 1969, *AAS* 61 (1969) 475; *The Pope Speaks* 14 (1969) 261.

31. Allocution to the participants in the spiritual exercises held at the Apostolic Palace, 17 March 1973, *Insegnamenti di Paolo VI* 11 (1973) 257.

32. Cf. Allocution to the Roman Curia, 28 June 1986, *Insegnamenti di Giovanni Paolo II* 9 (1986), part 1, 1954; *Origins* 16 (1986–1987) 192.

33. Art. 15.

First of all we wanted the image and features of this Curia to respond to the demands of our time, bearing in mind the changes that have been made by us or our predecessor Paul VI after the publication of the Apostolic Constitution *Regimini Ecclesiae universae.*

Then it was our duty to fulfill and complete that renewal of the laws of the Church which was brought in by the publication of the new Code of Canon Law or which is to be brought into effect by the revision of the Oriental canonical legislation.

Then we had in mind that the traditional dicasteries and organs of the Roman Curia be made more suitable for the purposes they were meant for, that is, their share in governance, jurisdiction, and administration. For this reason, their areas of competence have been distributed more aptly among them and more distinctly delineated.

Then with an eye to what experience has taught in recent years and to the never ending demands of Church society, we reexamined the juridical figure and reason of existence of those organs which are rightly called "postconciliar," changing on occasion their shape and organization. We did this in order to make the work of those institutions more and more useful and beneficial, that is, supporting special pastoral activity and research in the Church which, at an ever accelerating pace, are filling pastors with concern and which with the same urgency demand timely and well thought out answers.

Finally, new and more stable measures have been devised to promote mutual cooperation between dicasteries, so that their manner of working may intrinsically bear the stamp of unity.

In a word, our whole steadfast approach has been to make sure that the structure and working methods of the Roman Curia increasingly correspond to the ecclesiology spelled out by the Second Vatican Council, be ever more clearly suitable for achieving the pastoral purposes of its own constitution, and more and more fit to meet the needs of Church and civil society.

Voluimus in primis ut eiusdem Curiae imago et facies novis responderet nostri temporis postulatis, ratione mutationum habita, quae post editam Constitutionem apostolicam «Regimini Ecclesiae universae» sive a Decessore Nostro Paulo VI sive a Nobis factae sunt.

Deinde Nostrum fuit ut Ecclesiae legum renovatio, quae per evulgatum novum Codicem Iuris Canonici inducta est, vel quae in eo est posita ut ad effectum deducatur in recognoscendo Codice Iuris Canonici Orientalis, aliquo modo expleretur atque conficeretur.

Tum in animo habuimus ut antiquitus recepta Romanae Curiae Dicasteria et Instituta magis idonea redderentur ad ipsorum fines consequendos, ad quos instituta sunt, scilicet ad participanda regiminis, iurisdictionis atque negotiorum exsecutionis munera; qua de re factum est ut horum Dicasteriorum agendi provinciae inter ipsa aptius distribuerentur ac distinctius designarentur.

Deinde, prae oculis habentes quae rerum usus hisce annis docuit quaeque semper novis ecclesialis societatis postulatis requiruntur, cogitavimus iuridicam figuram rationemque iterum considerare illorum institutorum, quae merito «post-conciliaria» appellantur, eorum forte conformationem ordinationemque mutando. Quod eo consilio fecimus, ut magis magisque utile fructuosumque ipsorum institutorum munus redderetur, scilicet in Ecclesia promovendi peculiaria pastoralia opera atque rerum studium, quae augescente in dies celeritate Pastorum sollicitudinem occupant eademque tempestivas securasque responsiones postulant.

Denique nova et etiam stabilia incepta ad mutuam operam inter Dicasteria consociandam excogitata sunt, quorum ope quaedam agendi ratio habeatur unitatis notam suapte natura prae se ferens.

Quae ut uno comprehendamus verbo, curae Nobis fuit continenter procedere ut Romanae Curiae constitutio atque agendi ratio tum ecclesiologicae illi rationi, a Concilio Vaticano II pertractatae, magis magisque responderent, tum ad ipsius constitutionis pastorales propositos fines obtinendos clariore usque modo idonea evaderent, tum ecclesialis civilisque societatis necessitatibus aptius in dies obviam irent.

It is indeed our conviction that now, at the beginning of the third millennium after the birth of Christ, the zeal of the Roman Curia in no small measure contributes to the fact that the Church might remain faithful to the mystery of her origin,[34] since the Holy Spirit keeps her ever young by the power of the Gospel.[35]

14. Having given thought to all these matters with the help of expert advisors, sustained by the wise counsel and collegial spirit of the cardinals and bishops, having diligently studied the nature and mission of the Roman Curia, we have commanded that this Apostolic Constitution be drawn up, led by the hope that this venerable institution, so necessary to the government of the Church, may respond to that new pastoral impulse by which all the faithful are moved, laity, priests and particularly bishops, especially now after the Second Vatican Council, to listen ever more deeply and follow what the Spirit is saying to the Churches (cf. Rev 2:7).

Just as all the pastors of the Church, and among them in a special way the bishop of Rome, are keenly aware that they are "Christ's servants, stewards entrusted with the mysteries of God" (1 Cor 4:1) and seek above all to be utterly loyal helpers whom the Eternal Father may easily use to carry out the work of salvation in the world, so also the Roman Curia has this strong desire, in each and every sphere of its important work, to be filled with the same spirit and the same inspiration; the Spirit, we say, of the Son of Man, of Christ the only begotten of the Father, who "has come to save what was lost" (Mt 18:11) and whose single and all-embracing wish is that all men "may have life and have it to the full" (Jn 10:10).

Therefore, with the help of God's grace and of the Most Blessed Virgin Mary, the Mother of the Church, we establish and decree the following norms for the Roman Curia.

I. GENERAL NORMS

Notion of Roman Curia

Art. 1. The Roman Curia is the complex of dicasteries and institutes which help the Roman Pontiff in the exercise

Siquidem persuasum Nobis est Romanae Curiae navitatem haud paulum conferre, ut Ecclesia, tertio post Christum natum adventante millennio, ortus sui mysterio fidelis perseveret,[34] cum Spiritus Sanctus virtute Evangelii eam iuvenescere faci.[35]

14. Hisce omnibus attentis, opera peritorum virorum adhibita, sapienti consilio et collegiali affectu suffulti Patrum Cardinalium et Episcoporum, diligenter perspectis Romanae Curiae natura et munere, hanc Apostolicam Constitutionem exarari iussimus, spe ducti ut veneranda haec et regimini Ecclesiae necessaria institutio, novo illi pastorali instinctui respondeat, quo praesertim post celebratum Concilium Vaticanum II fideles omnes, laici, presbyteri et praesertim Episcopi aguntur, quo penitius usque audiant atque sequantur ea quae Spiritus dicat Ecclesiis (cf. Ap 2, 7).

Quemadmodum enim omnes Ecclesiae Pastores, atque inter ipsos speciali modo Romanus Episcopus, persentiunt se esse «ministros Christi et dispensatores mysteriorum Dei» (*1 Cor* 4,1), atque cupiunt se praeprimis adiutores praebere fidelissimos, quibus Aeternus Pater facile utatur ad salutis opus in mundo prosequendum, ita Romana Curia, in singulis quibusque exercitatis suae magni momenti navitatis orbibus, peroptat ut ipsa quoque eodem Spiritu eodemque afflatu pervadatur: Spiritum dicimus Filii hominis, Christi Unigeniti Patris, qui «venit ... salvare quod perierat» (*Mt* 18,11), cuiusque unicum amplissimumque optatum perpetuo eo contendit, ut omnes homines «vitam habeant et abundantius habeant» (*Io* l0,10).

Propterea, opitulante Dei gratia ac favente Beatissimae Virginis Mariae, Ecclesiae Matris, auxilio, normas de Romana Curia quae sequuntur statuimus atque decernimus.

I. NORMAE GENERALES

De Curiae Romanae Notione

Art. 1. Curia Romana complexus est Dicasteriorum et Institutorum, quae Romano Pontifici

---

34. Cf. Enc. *Dominum et vivificantem* 66, 18 May 1986, *AAS* 78 (1986) 896–897; *Origins* 16 (1986–1987) 99.

35. Cf. *LG* 4.

of his supreme pastoral office for the good and service of the whole Church and of the particular Churches. It thus strengthens the unity of the faith and the communion of the people of God and promotes the mission proper to the Church in the world.

Structure of the Dicasteries

Art. 2. §1. By the word "dicasteries" are understood the Secretariat of State, Congregations, Tribunals, Councils and Offices, namely the Apostolic Camera, the Administration of the Patrimony of the Apostolic See, and the Prefecture for the Economic Affairs of the Holy See.

§2. The dicasteries are juridically equal among themselves.

§3. Among the institutes of the Roman Curia are the Prefecture of the Papal Household and the Office for the Liturgical Celebrations of the Supreme Pontiff.

Art. 3. §1. Unless they have a different structure in virtue of their specific nature or some special law, the dicasteries are composed of the cardinal prefect or the presiding archbishop, a body of cardinals and of some bishops, assisted by a secretary, consultors, senior administrators, and a suitable number of officials.

§2. According to the specific nature of certain dicasteries, clerics and other faithful can be added to the body of cardinals and bishops.

§3. Strictly speaking, the members of a congregation are the cardinals and the bishops.

Art. 4. The prefect or president acts as moderator of the dicastery, directs it and acts in its name.

The secretary, with the help of the undersecretary, assists the prefect or president in managing the business of the dicastery as well as its human resources.

Art. 5 §1. The prefect or president, the members of the body mentioned in art. 3, §1, the secretary, and the other senior administrators, as well as the consultors, are appointed by the Supreme Pontiff for a five-year term.

§2. Once they have completed seventy-five years of age, cardinal prefects are asked to submit their resignation to the Roman Pontiff, who, after considering all factors, will make the decision. Other moderators and secretaries cease from office, having completed seventy-five years of age; members, when they have completed eighty years of age; those who are attached to any dicastery by reason of their office cease to be members when their office ceases.

De Dicasteriorum Structura

Art. 2. §1. Dicasteriorum nomine intelleguntur: Secretaria Status, Congregationes, Tribunalia, Consilia et Officia, scilicet Camera Apostolica, Administratio Patrimonii Sedis Apostolicae, Praefectura Rerum Oeconomicarum Sanctae Sedis.

§2. Dicasteria sunt inter se iuridice paria.

§3. Institutis autem Curiae Romanae accedunt Praefectura Pontificalis Domus et Officium de Liturgicis Celebrationibus Summi Pontificis.

Art. 3. §1. Dicasteria, nisi ob peculiarem ipsorum naturam aut specialem legem aliam habeant structuram, constant ex Cardinali Praefecto vel Archiepiscopo Praeside, coetu Patrum Cardinalium et quorundam Episcoporum, adiuvante Secretario. Iisdem adsunt Consultores et operam praestant Administri maiores atque congruus Officialium numerus.

§2. Iuxta peculiarem naturam quorundam Dicasteriorum, ipsorum coetui adscribi possunt clerici necnon alii Christifideles.

§3. Congregationis autem Membra proprie dicta sunt Cardinales et Episcopi.

Art. 4. Praefectus vel Praeses Dicasterium moderatur, id dirigit eiusdemque personam gerit.

Secretarius, cooperante Subsecretario, Praefectum vel Praesidem in Dicasterii negotiis personisque moderandis, adiuvat.

Art. 5. §1. Praefectus vel Praeses, Membra coetus, Secretarius ceterique Administri maiores necnon Consultores a Summo Pontifice ad quinquennium nominantur.

§2. Expleto septuagesimo quinto aetatis anno, Cardinales praepositi rogantur ut officii renuntiationem exhibeant Romano Pontifici, qui, omnibus perpensis, providebit. Ceteri Moderatores necnon Secretarii, expleto septuagesimo quinto aetatis anno, a munere cessant; Membra, octogesimo anno expleto; qui tamen ratione muneris alicui Dicasterio adscripti sunt, cessante munere, desinunt esse Membra.

Art. 6. On the death of the Supreme Pontiff, all moderators and members of the dicasteries cease from their office. The camerlengo of the Roman Church and the major penitentiary are excepted, who expedite ordinary business and refer to the College of Cardinals those things which would have been referred to the Supreme Pontiff.

The secretaries see to the ordinary operations of the dicasteries, taking care of ordinary business only; they need to be confirmed in office by the Supreme Pontiff within three months of his election.

Art. 7. The members of the body mentioned in art. 3, §1, are taken from among the cardinals living in Rome or outside the city, to whom are added some bishops, especially diocesan ones, insofar as they have special expertise in the matters being dealt with; also, depending on the nature of the dicastery, some clerics and other Christian faithful, with this proviso that matters requiring the exercise of power of governance be reserved to those in holy orders.

Art. 8. Consultors also are appointed from among clerics or other Christian faithful outstanding for their knowledge and prudence, taking into consideration, as much as possible, the international character of the Church.

Art. 9. Officials are taken from among the Christian faithful, clergy or laity, noted for their virtue, prudence, and experience, and for the necessary knowledge attested by suitable academic degrees, and selected as far as possible from the various regions of the world, so that the Curia may express the universal character of the Church. The suitability of the applicants should be evaluated by test or other appropriate means, according to the circumstances.

Particular Churches, moderators of institutes of consecrated life and of societies of apostolic life will not fail to render assistance to the Apostolic See by allowing their Christian faithful or their members to be available for service at the Roman Curia.

Art. 10. Each dicastery is to have its own archive where incoming documents and copies of documents sent out are kept safe and in good order in a system of "protocol" organized according to modern methods.

Procedure

Art. 11. §1. Matters of major importance are reserved to the general meeting, according to the nature of each dicastery.

§2. All members must be called in due time to the plenary sessions, held as far as possible once a year, to deal

Art. 6. Occurrente morte Summi Pontificis, omnes Dicasteriorum Moderatores et Membra a munere cessant. Excipiuntur Romanae Ecclesiae Camerarius et Paenitentiarius Maior, qui ordinaria negotia expediunt, ea Cardinalium Collegio proponentes, quae ad Summum Pontificem essent referenda.

Secretarii ordinario moderamini Dicasteriorum prospiciunt, negotia tantum ordinaria curantes; ipsi vero indigent confirmatione Summi Pontificis, intra tres ab Eius electione menses.

Art. 7. Membra coetus sumuntur ex Cardinalibus sive in Urbe sive extra Urbem commorantibus, quibus accedunt, quatenus peculiari peritia in rebus, de quibus agitur, pollent, nonnulli Episcopi, praesertim dioecesani, necnon, iuxta Dicasterii naturam, quidam clerici et alii Christifideles, hac tamen lege, ut ea, quae exercitium potestatis regiminis requirunt, reserventur iis qui ordine sacro insigniti sunt.

Art. 8. Consultores quoque nominantur ex clericis vel ceteris Christifidelibus scientia et prudentia praestantibus, ratione universalitatis, quantum fieri potest, servata.

Art. 9. Officiales assumuntur ex Christifidelibus, clericis vel laicis, commendatis virtute, prudentia, usu rerum, debita scientia, aptis studiorum titulis comprobata, ex variis orbis regionibus, quantum fieri potest, selectis, ita ut Curia indolem universalem Ecclesiae exprimat. Candidatorum idoneitas experimentis aliisve congruentibus modis pro opportunitate comprobetur.

Ecclesiae particulares, Moderatores Institutorum vitae consecratae et Societatum vitae apostolicae ne omittant adiutricem operam Apostolicae Sedi praebere, sinentes ut eorum fideles aut sodales, si opus fuerit, in Romanam Curiam arcessantur.

Art. 10. Unumquodque Dicasterium proprium habet archivum, in quo documenta recepta atque exemplaria eorum, quae missa sunt, in «protocollum» relata, ordinate, tuto et secundum hodierni temporis rationes custodiantur.

De Agendi Ratione

Art. 11. §1. Negotia maioris momenti coetui generali, iuxta cuiusque Dicasterii naturam, reservantur.

§2. Ad plenarias sessiones, semel in anno, quantum fieri potest, celebrandas, pro quaes-

with questions involving general principles, and for other questions which the prefect or president may have deemed to require treatment. For ordinary sessions it is sufficient to convoke members who reside in Rome.

§3. The secretary participates in all sessions with the right to vote.

Art. 12. Consultors and those who are equivalent to them are to make a diligent study of the matter in hand and to present their considered opinion, usually in writing.

So far as opportunity allows and depending on the nature of each dicastery, consultors can be called together to examine questions in a collegial fashion and, as the case may be, present a common position.

For individual cases, others can be called in for consultation who, although not numbered among the consultors, are qualified by their special expertise in the matter to be treated.

Art. 13. Depending on their own proper field of competence, the dicasteries deal with those matters which, because of their special importance, either by their nature or by law, are reserved to the Apostolic See and those which exceed the competence of individual bishops and their groupings, as well as those matters committed to them by the Supreme Pontiff. The dicasteries study the major problems of the present age, so that the Church's pastoral action may be more effectively promoted and suitably coordinated, with due regard to relations with the particular Churches. The dicasteries promote initiatives for the good of the universal Church. Finally, they review matters that the Christian faithful, exercising their own right, bring to the attention of the Apostolic See.

Art. 14. The competence of dicasteries is defined on the basis of subject matter, unless otherwise expressly provided for.

Art. 15. Questions are to be dealt with according to law, be it universal law or the special law of the Roman Curia, and according to the norms of each dicastery, yet with pastoral means and criteria, attentive both to justice and the good of the Church and, especially, to the salvation of souls.

Art. 16. Apart from the official Latin language, it is acceptable to approach the Roman Curia in any of the languages widely known today.

For the convenience of the dicasteries, a centre is being established for translating documents into other languages.

tionibus naturam principii generalis habentibus aliisque, quas Praefectus vel Praeses tractandas censuerit, omnia Membra tempestive convocari debent. Ad ordinarias autem sessiones sufficit ut convocentur Membra in Urbe versantia.

§3. Omnes coetus sessiones Secretarius cum iure suffragium ferendi participat.

Art. 12. Consultorum atque eorum qui ipsis assimilantur est studio rei propositae diligenter incumbere suamque sententiam, pro more scriptam, de ea exarare.

Pro opportunitate atque iuxta cuiusque Dicasterii naturam, Consultores convocari possunt ut collegialiter quaestiones propositas examinent et, si casus ferat, sententiam communem proferant.

Singulis in casibus alii ad consulendum vocari possunt, qui, etsi in Consultorum numerum non sunt relati, peculiari tamen peritia rei pertractandae commendentur.

Art. 13. Dicasteria, secundum uniuscuiusque propriam competentiam, negotia tractant, quae ob peculiare suum momentum, natura sua aut iure, Sedi Apostolicae reservantur, atque ea quae fines competentiae singulorum Episcoporum eorumve coetuum excedunt, necnon ea quae ipsis a Summo Pontifice committuntur; in studium incumbunt problematum graviorum vigentis aetatis, ut actio pastoralis Ecclesiae efficacius promoveatur apteque coordinetur, debita servata relatione cum Ecclesiis particularibus; promovent incepta pro bono Ecclesiae universalis; ea denique cognoscunt, quae Christifideles, iure proprio utentes, ad Sedem Apostolicam deferunt.

Art. 14. Dicasteriorum competentia definitur ratione materiae nisi aliter expresse cautum sit.

Art. 15. Quaestiones tractandae sunt ad tramitem iuris, sive universalis sive peculiaris Romanae Curiae, atque iuxta normas uniuscuiusque Dicasterii, viis tamen ac iudiciis pastoralibus, animo intento tum ad iustitiam et Ecclesiae bonum tum praesertim ad animarum salutem.

Art. 16. Romanam Curiam fas est adire, praeterquam officiali Latino sermone, cunctis etiam sermonibus hodie latius cognitis.

In commodum omnium Dicasteriorum «Centrum» constituitur pro documentis in alias linguas vertendis.

Art. 17. General documents prepared by one dicastery will be communicated to other interested dicasteries, so that the text may be improved with any corrections that may be suggested, and, through common consultation, it may even be proceeded in a coordinated manner to their implementation.

Art. 18. Decisions of major importance are to be submitted for the approval of the Supreme Pontiff, except decisions for which special faculties have been granted to the moderators of the dicasteries as well as the sentences of the Tribunal of the Roman Rota and the Supreme Tribunal of the Apostolic Signatura within the limits of their proper competence.

The dicasteries cannot issue laws or general decrees having the force of law or derogate from the prescriptions of current universal law, unless in individual cases and with the specific approval of the Supreme Pontiff.

It is of the utmost importance that nothing grave and extraordinary be transacted unless the Supreme Pontiff be previously informed by the moderators of the dicasteries.

Art. 19. §1. Hierarchical recourses are received by whichever dicastery has competence in that subject matter, without prejudice to art. 21, §1.

§2. Questions, however, which are to be dealt with judicially are sent to the competent tribunals, without prejudice to arts. 52–53.

Art. 20. Conflicts of competence arising between dicasteries are to be submitted to the Supreme Tribunal of the Apostolic Signatura, unless it pleases the Supreme Pontiff to deal with them otherwise.

Art. 21. §1. Matters touching the competence of more than one dicastery are to be examined together by the dicasteries concerned.

To enable them to exchange advice, a meeting will be called by the moderator of the dicastery which has begun to deal with the matter, either on his own initiative or at the request of another dicastery concerned. However, if the subject matter demands it, it may be referred to a plenary session of the dicasteries concerned.

The meeting will be chaired by the moderator of the dicastery who called the meeting or by its secretary, if only the secretaries are meeting.

§2. Where needed, permanent interdicasterial commissions will be set up to deal with matters requiring mutual and frequent consultation.

Art. 17. Quae ab uno Dicasterio praeparantur documenta generalia cum aliis communicentur Dicasteriis, quorum interest, ut textus emendationibus forte propositis perfici possit et, collatis consiliis, etiam ad eorum exsecutionem concordius procedatur.

Art. 18. Summi Pontificis approbationi subiciendae sunt decisiones maioris momenti, exceptis iis pro quibus Dicasteriorum Moderatoribus speciales facultates tributae sunt exceptisque sententiis Tribunalis Rotae Romanae et Supremi Tribunalis Signaturae Apostolicae intra limites propriae competentiae latis.

Dicasteria leges aut decreta generalia vim legis habentia ferre non possunt nec iuris universalis vigentis praescriptis derogare, nisi singulis in casibus atque de specifica approbatione Summi Pontificis.

Hoc autem sollemne sit ut nihil grave et extraordinarium agatur, nisi a Moderatoribus Dicasteriorum Summo Pontifici fuerit antea significatum.

Art. 19. §1. Recursus hierarchici a Dicasterio recipiuntur, quod competens sit ratione materiae, firmo praescripto art. 21 §1.

§2. Quaestiones vero, quae iudicialiter sunt cognoscendae, remittuntur ad competentia Tribunalia, firmo praescripto artt. 52 et 53.

Art. 20. Conflictus competentiae inter Dicasteria, si qui oriantur, Supremo Tribunali Signaturae Apostolicae subiciantur, nisi Summo Pontifici aliter prospiciendum placuerit.

Art. 21. §1. Negotia, quae plurium Dicasteriorum competentiam attingunt, a Dicasteriis, quorum interest, simul examinentur.

Ut consilia conferantur, a Moderatore Dicasterii, quod res agere coepit, conventus convocetur, sive ex officio sive rogatu alius Dicasterii, cuius interest. Si tamen subiecta materia id postulet, res deferatur ad plenariam sessionem Dicasteriorum, quorum interest.

Conventui praeest Dicasterii Moderator, qui eundem coëgit, vel eiusdem Secretarius, si soli Secretarii conveniant.

§2. Ubi opus fuerit opportune commissiones «interdicasteriales» permanentes, ad negotia tractanda, quae mutua crebraque consultatione egeant, constituantur.

Meetings of Cardinals

Art. 22. By mandate of the Supreme Pontiff, the cardinals in charge of dicasteries meet together several times a year to examine more important questions, coordinate their activities, so that they may be able to exchange information and take counsel.

Art. 23. More serious business of a general character can be usefully dealt with, if the Supreme Pontiff so decides, by the cardinals assembled in plenary consistory according to proper law.

Council of Cardinals for the Study of Organizational and Economic Questions of the Apostolic See

Art. 24. The Council of Cardinals for the Study of Organizational and Economic Questions of the Apostolic See consists of fifteen cardinals who head particular Churches from various parts of the world and are appointed by the Supreme Pontiff for a five-year term of office.

Art. 25. §1. The Council is convened by the cardinal secretary of state, usually twice a year, to consider those economic and organizational questions which relate to the administration of the Holy See, with the assistance, as needed, of experts in these affairs.

§2. The Council also considers the activities of the special institute which is erected and located within the State of Vatican City in order to safeguard and administer economic goods placed in its care with the purpose of supporting works of religion and charity. This institute is governed by a special law.

Relations with Particular Churches

Art. 26. §1. Close relations are to be fostered with particular Churches and groupings of bishops, seeking out their advice when preparing documents of major importance that have a general character.

§2. As far as possible, documents of a general character or having a special bearing on their particular Churches should be communicated to the bishops before they are made public.

§3. Questions brought before the dicasteries are to be diligently examined and, without delay, an answer or, at least, a written acknowledgement of receipt, insofar as this is necessary, should be sent.

De Cardinalium Adunationibus

Art. 22. De mandato Summi Pontificis pluries in anno Cardinales, qui Dicasteriis praesunt, in unum conveniunt, ut graviores quaestiones examinentur, labores coordinentur, utque notitiae inter eos communicari et consilia capi possint.

Art. 23. Graviora indolis generalis negotia utiliter tractari possunt, si Summo Pontifici placuerit, a Cardinalibus in Consistorio plenario iuxta legem propriam adunatis.

De Coetu Cardinalium Ad Consulendum Rebus Organicis et Oeconomicis Apostolicae Sedis

Art. 24. Coetus ex quindecim Cardinalibus constat, totidem Praesulibus Ecclesiarum particularium e variis orbis partibus, a Romano Pontifice ad quinquennium nominatis.

Art. 25. §1. Coetus ex solito bis in anno convocatur a Cardinali Secretario Status ad res oeconomicas et organicas quoad Sanctae Sedis administrationem perpendendas, auxiliantibus, quatenus opus fuerit, harum rerum peritis.

§2. Idem cognoscit etiam de navitate peculiaris Instituti, quod erectum est et collocatum intra Statum Civitatis Vaticanae, ad bona oeconomica sibi commissa custodienda atque administranda, quae ad opera religionis et caritatis sustinenda inserviunt; quod peculiari lege regitur.

De Rationibus cum Ecclesiis Particularibus

Art. 26. §1. Crebrae relationes foveantur cum Ecclesiis particularibus coetibusque Episcoporum, eorum consilium exquirendo, cum agitur de apparandis documentis maioris momenti, indolem generalem habentibus.

§2. Quantum fieri potest, antequam publici iuris fiant, communicentur cum Episcopis dioecesanis documenta generalia aut quae earundem Ecclesiarum particularium speciali modo intersint.

§3. Quaestiones Dicasteriis propositae, diligenter examinentur atque sine mora responsio aut saltem syngraphum rei acceptae, quatenus opus fuerit, mittatur.

Art. 27. Dicasteries should not omit to consult with papal legates regarding business affecting the particular Churches where the legates are serving, nor should they omit to communicate to the legates the results of their deliberations.

Ad limina Visits

Art. 28. In keeping with a venerable tradition and the prescriptions of law, bishops presiding over particular Churches visit the tombs of the Apostles at predetermined times and on that occasion present to the Roman Pontiff a report on the state of their diocese.

Art. 29. These kinds of visits have a special importance in the life of the Church, marking as they do the summit of the relationship between the pastors of each particular Church with the Roman Pontiff. For he meets his brother bishops, and deals with them about matters concerning the good of the Churches and the bishops' role as shepherds, and he confirms and supports them in faith and charity. This strengthens the bonds of hierarchical communion and openly manifests the catholicity of the Church and the unity of the episcopal college.

Art. 30. The *ad limina* visits also concern the dicasteries of the Roman Curia. For through these visits a helpful dialogue between the bishops and the Apostolic See is increased and deepened, information is shared, advice and timely suggestions are brought forward for the greater good and progress of the Churches and for the observance of the common discipline of the Church.

Art. 31. These visits are to be prepared very carefully and appropriately so that they proceed well and enjoy a successful outcome in their three principal stages—namely, the pilgrimage to the tombs of the Princes of the Apostles and their veneration, the meeting with the Supreme Pontiff, and the meetings at the dicasteries of the Roman Curia.

Art. 32. For this purpose, the report on the state of the diocese should be sent to the Holy See six months before the time set for the visit. It is to be examined with all diligence by the competent dicasteries, and their remarks are to be shared with a special committee convened for this purpose so that a brief synthesis of these may be drawn up and be readily at hand in the meetings.

De Visitationibus ad Limina

Art. 27. Dicasteria consulere ne omittant Pontificios Legatos circa negotia, quae ad Ecclesias particulares, ubi munus exercent, attineant, necnon cum iisdem Legatis captas deliberationes communicare.

Art. 28. Iuxta venerandam traditionem et iuris praescriptum, Episcopi, qui Ecclesiis particularibus praesunt, Apostolorum limina, statutis temporibus, petunt eaque occasione relationem super dioecesis statu Romano Pontifici exhibent.

Art. 29. Huiusmodi visitationes peculiare in vita Ecclesiae habent momentum, quippe quae veluti culmen efficiant relationum cuiusvis Ecclesiae particularis Pastorum cum Romano Pontifice. Ipse enim, suos in Episcopatu fratres coram admittens, cum illis de rebus agit, quae ad bonum Ecclesiarum et ad Episcoporum pascendi munus pertinent, ipsosque in fide et caritate confirmat atque sustinet; quo quidem modo vincula hierarchicae communionis roborantur et catholicitas Ecclesiae necnon Episcoporum collegii unitas veluti palam ostenditur.

Art. 30. Visitationes ad limina Dicasteria quoque Curiae Romanae respiciunt. Per has enim dialogus proficuus inter Episcopos et Apostolicam Sedem augetur ac profundior fit, mutuae informationes dantur, consilia et opportunae suggestiones ad maius bonum et profectum Ecclesiarum necnon ad disciplinam Ecclesiae communem servandam afferuntur.

Art. 31. Sedula cura apteque visitationes parentur ita ut tres principales gradus quibus constant, videlicet ad Apostolorum Principum sepulcra peregrinatio eorumque veneratio, congressio cum Summo Pontifice, atque colloquia apud Romanae Curiae Dicasteria, feliciter procedant prosperumque habeant exitum.

Art. 32. Hunc in finem, relatio super dioecesis statu Sanctae Sedi sex mensibus ante tempus pro visitatione statutum mittatur. A Dicasteriis, quibus competit, omni cum diligentia examinetur eorumque animadversiones cum peculiari coetu ad hoc constituto communicentur ut brevis synthesis de his omnibus conficiatur, quae in colloquiis prae oculis habenda sit.

Pastoral Character of the Activity of the Roman Curia

Art. 33. The activity of all who work at the Roman Curia and the other institutes of the Holy See is a true ecclesial service, marked with a pastoral character, that all must discharge with a deep sense of duty as well as in a spirit of service, as it is a sharing in the world-wide mission of the bishop of Rome.

Art. 34. Each individual dicastery pursues its own end, yet dicasteries cooperate with one another. Therefore, all who are working in the Roman Curia are to do so in such a way that their work may come together and be forged into one. Accordingly, all must always be prepared to offer their services wherever needed.

Art. 35. Although any work performed within the institutes of the Holy See is a sharing in the apostolic action, priests are to apply themselves as best they can to the care of souls, without prejudice however to their own office.

Central Labour Office

Art. 36. According to its own terms of reference, the Central Labour Office deals with working conditions within the Roman Curia and related questions.

Regulations

Art. 37. To this Apostolic Constitution is added an *Ordo servandus* or common norms setting forth the ways and means of transacting business in the Curia itself, without prejudice to the norms of this Constitution.

Art. 38. Each dicastery is to have its own *Ordo servandus* or special norms setting forth the ways and means of transacting business within it.

The *Ordo servandus* of each dicastery shall be made public in the usual manner of the Apostolic See.

II. SECRETARIAT OF STATE

Art. 39. The Secretariat of State provides close assistance to the Supreme Pontiff in the exercise of his supreme office.

Art. 40. The Secretariat is presided over by the Cardi-

De Indole Pastorali Actuositatis

Art. 33. Eorum omnium actuositas, qui apud Romanam Curiam ceteraque Sanctae Sedis instituta operantur, verum ecclesiale est servitium, indole pastorali signatum, prouti in universali Romani Pontificis missione participatio, summa cum officii conscientia atque cum animo serviendi ab omnibus praestandum.

Art. 34. Singula Dicasteria proprios fines persequuntur, ea tamen inter se conspirant; quare omnes in Romana Curia operantes id efficere debent, ut eorum operositas in unum confluat et temperetur. Omnes igitur parati semper sint ad propriam operam praestandam ubicumque necesse fuerit.

Art. 35. Etsi quaevis opera in Sanctae Sedis Institutis praestita cooperatio est in actione apostolica, sacerdotes pro viribus in curam animarum, sine praeiudicio tamen proprii officii, actuose incumbant.

De Officio Centrali Laboris

Art. 36. De laboris exercitio in Curia Romana atque de quaestionibus cum eo connexis videt, iuxta suam competentiam, *Officium Centrale Laboris.*

De Ordinibus

Art. 37. Huic Constitutioni Apostolicae accedit *Ordo servandus* seu normae communes, quibus disciplina et modus tractandi negotia in Curia ipsa praestituitur, firmis manentibus normis generalibus huius Constitutionis.

Art. 38. Unicuique Dicasterio proprius sit *Ordo servandus* seu normae speciales, quibus disciplina et negotia tractandi rationes praestituantur.

Ordo servandus uniuscuiusque Dicasterii suetis Apostolicae Sedis formis publici iuris fiat.

II. SECRETARIA STATUS

Art. 39. Secretaria Status proxime iuvat Summum Pontificem in Eius supremo munere exercendo.

Art. 40. Eidem praeest Cardinalis Secretar-

nal Secretary of State. It is composed of two sections, the First being the *Section for General Affairs*, under the direct control of the substitute, with the help of the assessor; the Second being the *Section for Relations with States*, under the direction of its own secretary, with the help of the under-secretary. Attached to this latter section is a council of cardinals and some bishops.

First Section

Art. 41. §1. It is the task of the First Section in a special way to expedite the business concerning the daily service of the Supreme Pontiff; to deal with those matters which arise outside the ordinary competence of the dicasteries of the Roman Curia and of the other institutes of the Apostolic See; to foster relations with those dicasteries and co-ordinate their work, without prejudice to their autonomy; to supervise the office and work of the legates of the Holy See, especially as concerns the particular Churches. This section deals with everything concerning the ambassadors of States to the Holy See.

§2. In consultation with other competent dicasteries, this section takes care of matters concerning the presence and activity of the Holy See in international organizations, without prejudice to art. 46. It does the same concerning Catholic international organizations.

Art. 42. It is also the task of the First Section:

1° to draw up and dispatch apostolic constitutions, decretal letters, apostolic letters, epistles, and other documents entrusted to it by the Supreme Pontiff;

2° to prepare the appropriate documents concerning appointments to be made or approved by the Supreme Pontiff in the Roman Curia and in the other institutes depending on the Holy See;

3° to guard the leaden seal and the Fisherman's ring.

Art. 43. It is likewise within the competence of this Section:

1° to prepare for publication the acts and public documents of the Holy See in the periodical entitled *Acta Apostolicae Sedis;*

2° through its special office commonly known as the *Press Office,* to publish official announcements of acts of the Supreme Pontiff or of the activities of the Holy See;

3° in consultation with the Second Section, to oversee

Sectio Prior

Art. 41. §1. Ad priorem sectionem pertinet peculiari modo operam navare expediendis negotiis, quae Summi Pontificis cotidianum servitium respiciunt; ea agere, quae extra ordinariam Dicasteriorum Romanae Curiae aliorumque Apostolicae Sedis Institutorum competentiam tractanda obveniant; rationes cum iisdem Dicasteriis fovere sine praeiudicio eorum autonomiae et labores coordinare; Legatorum Sanctae Sedis officium eorumque operam, praesertim ad Ecclesias particulares quod attinet, moderari. Ipsius est omnia explere, quae Legatos Civitatum apud Sanctam Sedem respiciunt.

§2. Collatis consiliis cum aliis competentibus Dicasteriis, eadem curat quae Sanctae Sedis praesentiam et navitatem apud Internationalia Instituta respiciunt, firmo praescripto art. 46. Idem agit quod ad Institutiones Internationales Catholicas pertinet.

Art. 42. Eiusdem etiam est:

1° componere et mittere Constitutiones Apostolicas, Litteras Decretales, Litteras Apostolicas, Epistulas aliaque documenta a Summo Pontifice ipsi commissa;

2° omnia explere acta, quae nominationes a Summo Pontifice peragendas vel probandas respiciunt in Romana Curia in aliisque Institutis, a Sancta Sede pendentibus;

3° custodire sigillum plumbeum et anulum Piscatoris.

Art. 43. Ad hanc sectionem pariter pertinet:

1° editionem curare actorum et documentorum publicorum Sanctae Sedis in commentario, quod inscribitur *Acta Apostolicae Sedis;*

2° officialia nuntia, quae sive acta Summi Pontificis sive Sanctae Sedis navitatem respiciunt, publici facere iuris per peculiare officium sibi subiectum, vulgo *Sala Stampa* appellatum;

3° invigilare, collatis consiliis cum Altera

the newspaper called *L'Osservatore Romano*, the Vatican Radio Station, and the Vatican Television Centre.

Art. 44. Through the *Central Statistical Office*, it collects, organizes, and publishes all data, set down according to statistical standards, concerning the life of the whole Church throughout the world.

Second Section

Art. 45. The Section for Relations with States has the special task of dealing with heads of government.

Art. 46. The Section for Relations with States has within its competence:

1° to foster relations, especially those of a diplomatic nature, with States and other subjects of public international law, and to deal with matters of common interest, promoting the good of the Church and of civil society by means of concordats and other agreements of this kind, if the case arises, while respecting the considered opinions of the groupings of bishops that may be affected;

2° in consultation with the competent dicasteries of the Roman Curia, to represent the Holy See at international organizations and meetings concerning questions of a public nature;

3° within the scope of its competence, to deal with what pertains to the papal legates.

Art. 47. §1. In special circumstances and by mandate of the Supreme Pontiff, and in consultation with the competent dicasteries of the Roman Curia, this Section takes action for the provision of particular Churches, and for the constitution of and changes to these Churches and their groupings.

§2. In other cases, especially where a concordat is in force, and without prejudice to art. 78, this Section has competence to transact business with civil governments.

III. CONGREGATIONS

Congregation for the Doctrine of the Faith

Art. 48. The proper duty of the Congregation for the Doctrine of the Faith is to promote and safeguard the doctrine on faith and morals in the whole Catholic world; so

Sectione, ephemeridi vulgo *L'Osservatore Romano* appellatae, Stationi Radiophonicae Vaticanae atque Centro Televisifico Vaticano.

Art. 44. Per Officium rationarii vulgo *Statistica* appellatum colligit, ordine componit atque palam edit omnia indicia, ad rationarii normas exarata, quae Ecclesiae universae vitam per terrarum orbem respiciunt.

Sectio Altera

Art. 45. Alterius sectionis de rationibus cum Civitatibus peculiare munus est in ea incumbere, quae cum rerum publicarum Moderatoribus agenda sunt.

Art. 46. Eidem competit:

1° rationes praesertim diplomaticas cum Civitatibus aliisque publici iuris societatibus fovere atque communia negotia tractare, ut bonum Ecclesiae civilisque societatis promoveatur, ope, si casus ferat, concordatorum aliarumque huiusmodi conventionum, et ratione habita sententiae Episcoporum coetuum, quorum intersit;

2° apud Internationalia Instituta et conventus de indolis publicae quaestionibus Sanctae Sedis partes gerere, collatis consiliis cum competentibus Romanae Curiae Dicasteriis;

3° agere, in propria laborum provincia, quae ad Legatos Pontificios attinent.

Art. 47. §1. In peculiaribus rerum adiunctis, de mandato Summi Pontificis, haec sectio, collatis consiliis cum competentibus Curiae Romanae Dicasteriis, ea explet quae ad Ecclesiarum particularium provisionem necnon ad earum earumque coetuum constitutionem aut immutationem spectant.

§2. Ceteris in casibus, praesertim ubi regimen concordatarium viget, eidem competit, firmo praescripto art. 78, ea absolvere, quae cum civilibus guberniis agenda sunt.

III. CONGREGATIONES

Congregatio de Doctrina Fidei

Art. 48. Proprium Congregationis de Doctrina Fidei munus est doctrinam de fide et moribus in universo catholico orbe promovere atque tu-

it has competence in things that touch this matter in any way.

Art. 49. Fulfilling its duty of promoting doctrine, the Congregation fosters studies so that the understanding of the faith may grow and a response in the light of the faith may be given to new questions arising from the progress of the sciences or human culture.

Art. 50. It helps the bishops, individually or in groups, in carrying out their office as authentic teachers and doctors of the faith, an office that carries with it the duty of promoting and guarding the integrity of that faith.

Art. 51. To safeguard the truth of faith and the integrity of morals, the Congregation takes care lest faith or morals suffer harm through errors that have been spread in any way whatever.

Wherefore:

1° it has the duty of requiring that books and other writings touching faith or morals, being published by the Christian faithful, be subjected to prior examination by the competent authority;

2° it examines carefully writings and opinions that seem to be contrary or dangerous to true faith, and, if it is established that they are opposed to the teaching of the Church, reproves them in due time, having given authors full opportunity to explain their minds, and having forewarned the Ordinary concerned; it brings suitable remedies to bear, if this be opportune.

3° finally, it takes good care lest errors or dangerous doctrines, which may have been spread among the Christian people, do not go without apt rebuttal.

Art. 52. The Congregation examines offences against the faith and more serious ones both in behaviour or in the celebration of the sacraments which have been reported to it and, if need be, proceeds to the declaration or imposition of canonical sanctions in accordance with the norms of common or proper law.

Art. 53. It is to examine whatever concerns the privilege of the faith, both in law and in fact.

Art. 54. Documents being published by other dicasteries of the Roman Curia, insofar as they touch on the doctrine of faith or morals, are to be subjected to its prior judgement.

Art. 55. Established within the Congregation for the Doctrine of the Faith are the Pontifical Biblical Commission and the International Theological Commission, which

Art. 49. Munus promovendae doctrinae adimplens, ipsa studia fovet ut fidei intellectus crescat ac novis quaestionibus ex scientiarum humanive cultus progressu enatis responsio sub luce fidei praeberi possit.

Art. 50. Episcopis, sive singulis sive in coetibus adunatis, auxilio est in exercitio muneris, quo ipsi authentici fidei magistri atque doctores constituuntur, quoque officio integritatem eiusdem fidei custodiendi ac promovendi tenentur.

Art. 51. Ad veritatem fidei morumque integritatem tuendam, curam impendit, ne fides aut mores per errores quomodocumque vulgatos detrimentum patiantur.

Quapropter:

1° ipsi officium est exigendi, ut libri aliaque scripta a Christifidelibus edenda, quae fidem moresque respiciant, praevio competentis auctoritatis examini subiciantur;

2° scripta atque sententias, quae rectae fidei contraria atque insidiosa videantur, excutit, atque, si constiterit ea Ecclesiae doctrinae esse opposita, eadem, data auctori facultate suam mentem plene explicandi, tempestive reprobat, praemonito Ordinario, cuius interest, atque congrua remedia, si opportunum fuerit, adhibet;

3° curat, denique, ne erroneis ac periculosis doctrinis, forte in populum christianum diffusis, apta confutatio desit.

Art. 52. Delicta contra fidem necnon graviora delicta tum contra mores tum in sacramentorum celebratione commissa, quae ipsi delata fuerint, cognoscit atque, ubi opus fuerit, ad canonicas sanctiones declarandas aut irrogandas ad normam iuris, sive communis sive proprii, procedit.

Art. 53. Eiusdem pariter est cognoscere, tum in iure tum in facto, quae privilegium fidei respiciunt.

Art. 54. Praevio eius iudicio subiciuntur documenta, ab aliis Curiae Romanae Dicasteriis edenda, quatenus doctrinam de fide vel moribus attingunt.

Art. 55. Apud Congregationem de Doctrina Fidei constitutae sunt Pontifica Commissio Biblica et Commissio Theologica Internationalis,

act according to their own approved norms and are presided over by the cardinal prefect of this Congregation.

quae iuxta proprias probatas normas agunt quibusque praeest Cardinalis eiusdem Congregationis Praefectus.

Congregation for the Oriental Churches

Art. 56. The Congregation for the Oriental Churches considers those matters, whether concerning persons or things, affecting the Catholic Oriental Churches.

Art. 57. §1. The patriarchs and major archbishops of the Oriental Churches, and the president of the Council for Promoting Christian Unity, are *ipso iure* members of this Congregation.

§2. The consultors and officials are to be selected in such a way as to reflect as far as possible the diversity of rites.

Art. 58. §1. The competence of this Congregation extends to all matters which are proper to the Oriental Churches and which are to be referred to the Apostolic See, whether concerning the structure and organization of the Churches, the exercise of the office of teaching, sanctifying and governing, or the status, rights, and obligations of persons. It also handles everything that has to be done concerning quinquennial reports and the *ad limina* visits in accordance with arts. 31–32.

§2. This however does not infringe on the proper and exclusive competence of the Congregations for the Doctrine of the Faith and for the Causes of Saints, of the Apostolic Penitentiary, the Supreme Tribunal of the Apostolic Signatura or the Tribunal of the Roman Rota, as well as of the Congregation for Divine Worship and the Discipline of the Sacraments for what pertains to dispensation from a marriage *ratum et non consummatum*.

In matters which also affect the faithful of the Latin Church, the Congregation will proceed, if the matter is sufficiently important, in consultation with the dicastery that has competence in the same matter for the faithful of the Latin Church.

Art. 59. The Congregation pays careful attention to communities of Oriental Christian faithful living within the territories of the Latin Church, and attends to their spiritual needs by providing visitators and even a hierarchy of their own, so far as possible and where numbers and circumstances demand it, in consultation with the Congregation competent for the establishment of particular Churches in that region.

Congregatio pro Ecclesiis Orientalibus

Art. 56. Congregatio ea cognoscit, quae, sive quoad personas sive quoad res, Ecclesias Orientales Catholicas respiciunt.

Art. 57. §1. Eiusdem ipso iure Membra sunt Patriarchae et Archiepiscopi Maiores Ecclesiarum Orientalium necnon Praeses Consilii ad Unitatem Christianorum fovendam.

§2. Consultores et Officiales ita seligantur, ut diversitatis rituum, quantum fieri potest, ratio habeatur.

Art. 58. §1. Huius Congregationis competentia ad omnia extenditur negotia, quae Ecclesiis Orientalibus sunt propria, quaeque ad Sedem Apostolicam deferenda sunt, sive quoad Ecclesiarum structuram et ordinationem, sive quoad munerum docendi, sanctificandi et regendi exercitium, sive quoad personas, earundem statum, iura ac obligationes. Omnia quoque explet, quae de relationibus quinquennalibus ac visitationibus ad limina ad normam artt. 31, 32 agenda sunt.

§2. Integra tamen manet propria atque exclusiva competentia Congregationum de Doctrina Fidei et de Causis Sanctorum, Paenitentiariae Apostolicae, Supremi Tribunalis Signaturae Apostolicae et Tribunalis Rotae Romanae, necnon Congregationis de Cultu Divino et Disciplina Sacramentorum ad dispensationem pro matrimonio rato et non consummato quod attinet.

In negotiis, quae Ecclesiae Latinae fideles quoque attingunt, Congregatio procedat, si rei momentum id postulet, collatis consiliis cum Dicasterio in eadem materia pro fidelibus Latinae Ecclesiae competenti.

Art. 59. Congregatio sedula cura item prosequitur communitates Christifidelium orientalium in circumscriptionibus territorialibus Ecclesiae Latinae versantium, eorumque necessitatibus spiritualibus per Visitatores, immo, ubi numerus fidelium atque adiuncta id exigant, quatenus fieri possit, etiam per propriam Hierarchiam consulit, collatis consiliis cum Congregatione pro consti-

Art. 60. In regions where Oriental rites have been preponderant from ancient times, apostolic and missionary activity depends solely on this Congregation, even if it is carried out by missionaries of the Latin Church.

Art. 61. The Congregation proceeds in collaboration with the Council for Promoting Christian Unity in matters which may concern relations with non-Catholic Oriental Churches and with the Council for Inter-Religious Dialogue in matters within the scope of this Council.

Congregation for Divine Worship and the Discipline of the Sacraments

Art. 62. The Congregation for Divine Worship and the Discipline of the Sacraments does whatever pertains to the Apostolic See concerning the regulation and promotion of the sacred liturgy, primarily of the sacraments, without prejudice to the competence of the Congregation for the Doctrine of the Faith.

Art. 63. It fosters and safeguards the regulation of the administration of the sacraments, especially regarding their valid and licit celebration. It grants favours and dispensations not contained in the faculties of diocesan bishops in this subject matter.

Art. 64. §1. By effective and suitable means, the Congregation promotes liturgical pastoral activity, especially regarding the celebration of the Eucharist; it gives support to the diocesan bishops so that the Christian faithful may share more and more actively in the sacred liturgy.

§2. It sees to the drawing up and revision of liturgical texts. It reviews particular calendars and proper texts for the Mass and the Divine Office for particular Churches and institutes which enjoy that right.

§3. It grants the *recognitio* to translations of liturgical books and their adaptations that have been lawfully prepared by conferences of bishops.

Art. 65. The Congregation fosters commissions or institutes for promoting the liturgical apostolate or sacred music, song or art, and it maintains relations with them. In accordance with the law, it erects associations which have an international character or approves or grants the *recognitio* to their statutes. Finally, it contributes to the progress

tutione Ecclesiarum particularium in eodem territorio competenti.

Art. 60. Actio apostolica et missionalis in regionibus, in quibus ritus orientales ab antiqua aetate praeponderant, ex hac Congregatione unice pendet, etiamsi a missionariis Latinae Ecclesiae peragatur.

Art. 61. Congregatio mutua ratione procedit cum Consilio ad Unitatem Christianorum Fovendam, in iis quae relationes cum Ecclesiis Orientalibus non catholicis respicere possunt necnon cum Consilio pro Dialogo Inter Religiones, in materia quae ambitum eius tangit

Congregatio de Cultu Divino et Disciplina Sacramentorum

Art. 62. Congregatio ea agit quae, salva competentia Congregationis de Doctrina Fidei, ad Sedem Apostolicam pertinent quoad moderationem ac promotionem sacrae liturgiae, in primis Sacramentorum.

Art. 63. Sacramentorum disciplinam, praesertim quod attinet ad eorum validam et licitam celebrationem, fovet atque tuetur; gratias insuper atque dispensationes concedit, quae ad Episcoporum dioecesanorum facultates hac in regione non pertinent.

Art. 64. §1. Congregatio actionem pastoralem liturgicam, peculiari ratione ad Eucharisticam celebrationem quod attinet, efficacibus ac congruis mediis promovet; Episcopis dioecesanis adest, ut Christifideles sacram liturgiam magis in dies actuose participent.

§2. Textibus liturgicis conficiendis aut emendandis prospicit; recognoscit calendaria peculiaria atque Propria Missarum et Officiorum Ecclesiarum particularium necnon Institutorum, quae hoc iure fruuntur.

§3. Versiones librorum liturgicorum eorumque aptationes ab Episcoporum Conferentiis legitime paratas recognoscit.

Art. 65. Commissionibus vel Institutis ad apostolatum liturgicum vel musicam vel cantum vel artem sacram promovenda conditis favet et cum iis rationes habet; huiuscemodi consociationes, quae indolem internationalem prae se ferant, ad normam iuris erigit vel eorum statuta

of liturgical life by encouraging meetings from various regions.

Art. 66. The Congregation provides attentive supervision so that liturgical norms are accurately observed, abuses avoided, and that they be eradicated where they are found to exist.

Art. 67. This Congregation examines the fact of non-consummation in a marriage and the existence of a just cause for granting a dispensation. It receives all the acts together with the *votum* of the bishop and the remarks of the defender of the bond, weighs them according to its own special procedure, and, if the case warrants it, submits a petition to the Supreme Pontiff requesting the dispensation.

Art. 68. It is also competent to examine, in accordance with the law, cases concerning the nullity of sacred ordination.

Art. 69. This Congregation has competence concerning the cult of sacred relics, the confirmation of heavenly patrons and the granting of the title of minor basilica.

Art. 70. The Congregation gives assistance to bishops so that, in addition to liturgical worship, the prayers and pious exercises of the Christian people, in full harmony with the norms of the Church, may be fostered and held in high esteem.

Congregation for the Causes of Saints

Art. 71. The Congregation for the Causes of Saints deals with everything which, according to the established way, leads to the canonization of the servants of God.

Art. 72. §1. With special norms and timely advice, it assists diocesan bishops, who have competence to instruct the cause.

§2. It considers causes that have already been instructed, inquiring whether everything has been carried out in accordance with the law. It thoroughly examines the causes that have thus been reviewed, in order to judge whether everything required is present for a favorable recommendation to be submitted to the Supreme Pontiff, according to the previously established classification of causes.

Art. 73. The Congregation also is competent to examine what is necessary for the granting of the title of doctor to saints, after having received the recommendation of the Congregation for the Doctrine of the Faith concerning outstanding teaching.

Art. 74. Moreover, it has competence to decide every-

approbat ac recognoscit; conventus denique ex variis regionibus ad vitam liturgicam provehendam fovet.

Art. 66. Attente invigilat ut ordinationes liturgicae adamussim serventur, abusus praecaveantur iidemque, ubi deprehendantur, exstirpentur.

Art. 67. Huius Congregationis est cognoscere de facto inconsummationis matrimonii et de exsistentia iustae causae ad dispensationem concedendam. Ideoque acta omnia cum voto Episcopi et animadversionibus Defensoris Vinculi accipit et, iuxta peculiarem procedendi modum, perpendit atque, si casus ferat, Summo Pontifici petitionem ad dispensationem impetrandam subicit.

Art. 68. Ipsa competens quoque est in causis de nullitate sacrae ordinationis cognoscendis ad normam iuris.

Art. 69. Competens est quoad cultum sacrarum reliquiarum, confirmationem caelestium Patronorum et Basilicae minoris titulum concedendum.

Art. 70. Congregatio adiuvat Episcopos ut, praeter liturgicum cultum, preces necnon pia populi christiani exercitia, normis Ecclesiae plene congruentia, foveantur et in honore habeantur.

Congregatio de Causis Sanctorum

Art. 71. Congregatio ea omnia tractat, quae, secundum statutum iter, ad Servorum Dei canonizationem perducunt.

Art. 72. §1. Episcopis dioecesanis, quibus causae instructio competit, peculiaribus normis necnon opportunis consiliis adest.

§2. Causas iam instructas perpendit, inquirens utrum omnia ad normam legis peracta sint. Causas ita recognitas funditus perscrutatur ad iudicium ferendum utrum constet de omnibus quae requiruntur, ut Summo Pontifici vota favorabilia subiciantur, secundum ante constitutos gradus causarum.

Art. 73. Ad Congregationem praeterea spectat cognoscere de Doctoris titulo Sanctis decernendo, praehabito voto Congregationis de Doctrina Fidei ad eminentem doctrinam quod attinet.

Art. 74. Eius insuper est de iis omnibus de-

thing concerning the authentication of holy relics and their preservation.

Congregation for Bishops

Art. 75. The Congregation for Bishops examines what pertains to the establishment and provision of particular Churches and to the exercise of the episcopal office in the Latin Church, without prejudice to the competence of the Congregation for the Evangelization of Peoples.

Art. 76. This Congregation deals with everything concerning the constitution, division, union, suppression, and other changes of particular Churches and of their groupings. It also erects military ordinariates for the pastoral care of the armed forces.

Art. 77. It deals with everything concerning the appointment of bishops, even titular ones, and generally with the provision of particular Churches.

Art. 78. Whenever it is a matter of dealing with civil governments, either in establishing or modifying particular Churches and their groupings or in the provision of these Churches, this Congregation must procede only after consultation with the Section for Relations with States of the Secretariat of State.

Art. 79. Furthermore, the Congregation applies itself to matters relating to the correct exercise of the pastoral function of the bishops, by offering them every kind of assistance. For it is part of its duty to initiate general apostolic visitations where needed, in agreement with the dicasteries concerned and, in the same manner, to evaluate their results and to propose to the Supreme Pontiff the appropriate actions to be taken.

Art. 80. This Congregation has competence over everything involving the Holy See in the matter of personal prelatures.

Art. 81. For the particular Churches assigned to its care, the Congregation takes care of everything with respect to the *ad limina* visits; so it studies the quinquennial reports, submitted in accordance with art. 32. It is available to the bishops who come to Rome, especially to see that suitable arrangements are made for the meeting with the Supreme Pontiff and for other meetings and pilgrimages. When the visit is completed, it communicates in writing to the diocesan bishops the conclusions concerning their dioceses.

Art. 82. The Congregation deals with matters pertain-

cernere, quae ad sacras reliquias authenticas declarandas easdemque conservandas pertinent.

Congregatio pro Episcopis

Art. 75. Congregatio ea cognoscit quae Ecclesiarum particularium constitutionem et provisionem necnon episcopalis muneris exercitium respiciunt in Ecclesia Latina, salva competentia Congregationis pro Gentium Evangelizatione.

Art. 76. Huius Congregationis est ea omnia agere, quae ad Ecclesiarum particularium earumque coetuum constitutionem, divisionem, unionem, suppressionem ceterasque immutationes spectant. Eius quoque est Ordinariatus Castrenses pro pastorali cura militum erigere.

Art. 77. Omnia agit quae attinent ad Episcoporum, etiam titularium, nominationem, et generatim ad provisionem Ecclesiarum particularium.

Art. 78. Quotiescumque cum rerum publicarum Moderatoribus tractandum est sive ad Ecclesiarum particularium earumque coetuum constitutionem aut immutationem, sive ad earum provisionem quod attinet, nonnisi collatis consiliis cum Sectione de rationibus cum Civitatibus Secretariae Status procedat.

Art. 79. Congregatio in ea insuper incumbit, quae rectum muneris pastoralis Episcoporum exercitium respiciunt, eis omnimodam operam praebendo; eius enim est, si opus fuerit, communi sententia cum Dicasteriis, quorum interest, visitationes apostolicas generales indicere earumque exitus, pari procedendi modo, perpendere et, quae inde opportune decernenda sint, Summo Pontifici proponere.

Art. 80. Ad hanc Congregationem pertinent ea omnia, quae ad Sanctam Sedem spectant circa Praelaturas personales.

Art. 81. Pro Ecclesiis particularibus suae curae concreditis Congregatio omnia procurat quae visitationes ad limina respiciunt; ideoque relationes quinquennales ad normam art. 32 perpendit. Episcopis Romam adeuntibus adest, praesertim ut sive congressio cum Summo Pontifice sive alia colloquia et peregrinationes apte disponantur. Expleta visitatione, conclusiones, eorum dioeceses respicientes, cum Episcopis dioecesanis scripto communicat.

Art. 82. Congregatio ea absolvit, quae ad

ing to the celebration of particular councils as well as the erection of conferences of bishops and the *recognitio* of their statutes. It receives the acts of these bodies and, in consultation with the dicasteries concerned, it examines the decrees which require the *recognitio* of the Apostolic See.

Pontifical Commission for Latin America

Art. 83. §1. The function of the Pontifical Commission for Latin America is to be available to the particular Churches in Latin America, by counsel and by action, taking a keen interest in the questions that affect the life and progress of those Churches; and especially to help the Churches themselves in the solution of those questions, or to be helpful to those dicasteries of the Curia that are involved by reason of their competence.

§2. It is also to foster relations between the national and international ecclesiastical institutes that work for the regions of Latin America and the dicasteries of the Roman Curia.

Art. 84. §1. The president of the Commission is the prefect of the Congregation for Bishops, assisted by a bishop as vice-president.

They have as counselors some bishops either from the Roman Curia or selected from the Churches of Latin America.

§2. The members of the Commission are selected either from the dicasteries of the Roman Curia or from the *Consejo episcopal latinoamericano*, whether they be from among the bishops of Latin America or from the institutes mentioned in the preceding article.

§3. The Commission has its own staff.

Congregation for the Evangelization of Peoples

Art. 85. It pertains to the Congregation for the Evangelization of Peoples to direct and coordinate throughout the world the actual work of spreading the Gospel as well as missionary cooperation, without prejudice to the competence of the Congregation for the Oriental Churches.

Art. 86. The Congregation promotes research in mission theology, spirituality and pastoral work; it likewise proposes principles, norms, and procedures, fitting the needs of time and place, by which evangelization is carried out.

Art. 87. The Congregation strives to bring the people of

---

celebrationem Conciliorum particularium necnon ad Episcoporum Conferentiarum erectionem atque earundem statutorum recognitionem attinent; acta huiusmodi coetuum recipit atque decreta, quae recognitione egent, collatis consiliis cum Dicasteriis, quorum interest, recognoscit.

Pontificia Commissio pro America Latina

Art. 83. §1. Commissionis munus est Ecclesiis particularibus in America Latina tum consilio tum opere adesse, studio quoque incumbere quaestionibus, quae vitam ac profectum ipsarum Ecclesiarum respiciunt, praesertim ut sive Curiae Dicasteriis, quorum ratione competentiae interest, sive ipsis Ecclesiis in huiusmodi quaestionibus solvendis, auxilio sit.

§2. Ipsius quoque est fovere rationes inter ecclesiastica instituta internationalia et nationalia, quae pro Americae Latinae Regionibus adlaborant, et Curiae Romanae Dicasteria.

Art. 84. §1. Praeses Commissionis est Praefectus Congregationis pro Episcopis, qui ab Episcopo vices Praesidis agente adiuvatur.

Ipsis adsunt tamquam Consiliarii nonnulli Episcopi sive ex Curia Romana sive ex Americae Latinae Ecclesiis adlecti.

§2. Commissionis Membra sive ex Curiae Romanae Dicasteriis sive ex Consilio Episcopali Latino-Americano tum ex Episcopis Regionum Americae Latinae tum ex Institutis, de quibus in praecedenti articulo, seliguntur.

§3. Commissio proprios habet Administros.

Congregatio pro Gentium Evangelizatione

Art. 85. Ad Congregationem spectat dirigere et coordinare ubique terrarum ipsum opus gentium evangelizationis et cooperationem missionariam, salva Congregationis pro Ecclesiis Orientalibus competentia.

Art. 86. Congregatio promovet investigationes theologiae, spiritualitatis ac rei pastoralis missionariae, pariterque proponit principia, normas necnon operandi rationes, necessitatibus temporum locorumque accomodata, quibus evangelizatio peragatur.

Art. 87. Congregatio adnititur ut Populus

God, well aware of their duty and filled with missionary spirit, to cooperate effectively in the missionary task by their prayers and the witness of their lives, by their active work and contributions.

Art. 88. §1. It takes steps to awaken missionary vocations, whether clerical, religious, or lay, and advises on a suitable distribution of missionaries.

§2. In the territories subject to it, it also cares for the education of the secular clergy and of catechists, without prejudice to the competence of the Congregation of Seminaries and Educational Institutions[36] concerning the general programme of studies, as well as what pertains to the universities and other institutes of higher education.

Art. 89. Within its competence are mission territories, the evangelization of which is committed to suitable institutes and societies and to particular Churches. For these territories it deals with everything pertaining to the establishment and change of ecclesiastical circumscriptions and to the provision of these Churches, and it carries out the other functions that the Congregation for Bishops fulfills within the scope of its competence.

Art. 90. §1. With regard to members of institutes of consecrated life, whether these are erected in the mission territories or are just working there, the Congregation enjoys competence in matters touching those members as missionaries, individually and collectively, without prejudice to art. 21, §1.

§2. Those societies of apostolic life that were founded for the missions are subject to this Congregation.

Art. 91. To foster missionary cooperation, even through the effective collection and equal distribution of subsidies, the Congregation chiefly uses the Pontifical Missionary Works, namely, the Society for the Propagation of the Faith, the Society of St. Peter the Apostle, and the Holy Childhood Association, as well as the Pontifical Missionary Union of the Clergy.

Art. 92. Through a special office, the Congregation administers its own funds and other resources destined for the missions, with full accountability to the Prefecture for the Economic Affairs of the Holy See.

Dei, spiritu missionario imbutus atque sui officii conscius, precibus, testimonio vitae, actuositate et subsidiis ad opus missionale efficaciter collaboret.

Art. 88. §1. Vocationes missionarias sive clericales sive religiosas sive laicales suscitandas curat atque missionariorum aptae distributioni consulit.

§2. In territoriis sibi subiectis, ipsa pariter curat cleri saecularis atque catechistarum institutionem, salva competentia Congregationis de Seminariis atque Studiorum Institutis, ad generalem studiorum rationem necnon ad Universitates ceteraque studiorum superiorum Instituta quod attinet.

Art. 89. Eidem subsunt territoria missionum, quarum evangelizationem idoneis Institutis, Societatibus necnon Ecclesiis particularibus committit, et pro quibus ea omnia agit, quae sive ad circumscriptiones ecclesiasticas erigendas vel immutandas, sive ad Ecclesiarum provisionem pertinent ceteraque absolvit, quae Congregatio pro Episcopis intra suae competentiae ambitum exercet.

Art. 90. §1. Quod vero attinet ad sodales Institutorum vitae consecratae, in territoriis missionum erectorum aut ibi laborantium, Congregatio competentia gaudet in iis, quae ipsos qua missionarios sive singulos sive simul sumptos attingunt, firmo praescripto art. 21 §1.

§2. Huic Congregationi subiciuntur Societates vitae apostolicae pro missionibus erectae.

Art. 91. Ad cooperationem missionalem fovendam, etiam per efficacem collectionem et aequam distributionem subsidiorum, ipsa utitur praesertim Pontificiis Operibus Missionalibus, videlicet eis quae a Propagatione Fidei, a S. Petro Apostolo, a S. Infantia nomen ducunt atque Pontificia Unione Missionali Cleri.

Art. 92. Congregatio proprium aerarium aliaque bona missionibus destinata per peculiare officium administrat, firmo onere reddendi debitam rationem Praefecturae Rerum Oeconomicarum Sanctae Sedis.

36. See note * between art. 111 and art. 112.

Congregation for the Clergy

Art. 93. Without prejudice to the right of bishops and their conferences, the Congregation for the Clergy examines matters regarding priests and deacons of the secular clergy, with regard to their persons and pastoral ministry, and with regard to resources available to them for the exercise of this ministry; and in all these matters the Congregation offers timely assistance to the bishops.

Art. 94. It has the function of promoting the religious education of the Christian faithful of all ages and conditions; it issues timely norms so that catechetical instruction is correctly conducted; it gives great attention so that catechetical formation is properly given; and, with the assent of the Congregation for the Doctrine of the Faith, it grants the prescribed approval of the Holy See for catechisms and other writings pertaining to catechetical instruction. It is available to catechetical offices and international initiatives on religious education, coordinates their activities and, where necessary, lends assistance.

Art. 95. §1. The Congregation is competent concerning the life, conduct, rights, and obligations of clergy.

§2. It advises on a more suitable distribution of priests.

§3. It fosters the ongoing education of clergy, especially concerning their sanctification and the effective exercise of their pastoral ministry, most of all in the fitting preaching of the Word of God.

Art. 96. This Congregation deals with everything that has to do with the clerical state as such for all clergy, including religious, in consultation with the dicasteries involved when the matter so requires.

Art. 97. The Congregation deals with those matters that are within the competence of the Holy See:
1° both those concerning presbyteral councils, colleges of consultors, chapters of canons, pastoral councils, parishes, churches, shrines, or those concerning clerical associations, or ecclesiastical archives and records;

2° and those concerning Mass obligations as well as pious wills in general and pious foundations.

Art. 98. The Congregation carries out everything that pertains to the Holy See regarding the regulation of ecclesiastical goods, and especially their correct administration;

Congregatio pro Clericis

Art. 93. Congregatio, firmo iure Episcoporum eorumque Conferentiarum, ea cognoscit, quae presbyteros et diaconos Cleri saecularis respiciunt tum quoad personas, tum quoad pastorale ministerium, tum quoad res, quae ad hoc exercendum iis praesto sunt, atque in hisce omnibus opportuna auxilia Episcopis praebet.

Art. 94. Institutionem religiosam Christifidelium cuiuscumque aetatis et condicionis pro suo munere promovendam curat; opportunas normas praebet, ut lectiones catecheseos recta ratione tradantur; catecheticae institutioni rite impertiendae invigilat; praescriptam Sanctae Sedis approbationem pro catechismis aliisque scriptis ad institutionem catecheticam pertinentibus, de assensu Congregationis de Doctrina Fidei, concedit; officiis catecheticis atque inceptis ad religiosam institutionem spectantibus et indolem internationalem prae se ferentibus adest, eorum navitatem coordinat iisque auxilia, si opus fuerit praestat.

Art. 95. §1. Competens est ad clericorum vitam, disciplinam, iura atque obligationes quod spectat.

§2. Aptiori presbyterorum distributioni consulit.

§3. Permanentem clericorum formationem fovet, praesertim quod attinet ad ipsorum sanctificationem et ad pastorale ministerium fructuose exercendum, potissimum circa dignam verbi Dei praedicationem.

Art. 96. Huius Congregationis est tractare ea omnia, quae ad statum clericalem qua talem attinent, pro omnibus clericis, religiosis non exceptis, collatis consiliis cum Dicasteriis quorum interest, ubi res id requirat.

Art. 97. Congregatio ea agit, quae Sanctae Sedi competunt:
1° sive circa consilia presbyteralia, consultorum coetus, canonicorum capitula, consilia pastoralia, paroecias, ecclesias, sanctuaria, sive circa clericorum consociationes, sive circa ecclesiastica archiva seu tabularia;

2° circa onera Missarum necnon pias voluntates in genere et pias fundationes.

Art. 98. Congregatio ea omnia exercet, quae ad bonorum ecclesiasticorum moderamen ad Sanctam Sedem pertinent, et praesertim ad rec-

it grants the necessary approvals and *recognitiones,* and it further sees to it that serious thought is given to the support and social security of the clergy.

Pontifical Commission for Preserving the Patrimony of Art and History

Art. 99. At the Congregation for the Clergy there exists the Pontifical Commission for Preserving the Patrimony of Art and History that has the duty of acting as curator for the artistic and historical patrimony of the whole Church.

Art. 100. To this patrimony belong, in the first place, all works of every kind of art of the past, works that must be kept and preserved with the greatest care. Those works whose proper use has ceased are to be kept in a suitable manner in museums of the Church or elsewhere.

Art. 101. §1. Outstanding among valuable historical objects are all documents and materials referring and testifying to pastoral life and care, as well as to the rights and obligations of dioceses, parishes, churches, and other juridical persons in the Church.

§2. This historical patrimony is to be kept in archives or also in libraries and everywhere entrusted to competent curators lest testimonies of this kind be lost.

Art. 102. The Commission lends its assistance to particular Churches and conferences of bishops and together with them, where the case arises, sees to the setting up of museums, archives, and libraries, and ensures that the entire patrimony of art and history in the whole territory is properly collected and safeguarded and made available to all who have an interest in it.

Art. 103. In consultation with the Congregation for Seminaries and Educational Institutions and the Congregation for Divine Worship and the Discipline of the Sacraments, the Commission has the task of striving to make the people of God more and more aware of the need and importance of conserving the artistic and historical patrimony of the Church.

Art. 104. The president of the Commission is the cardinal prefect of the Congregation for the Clergy, assisted by the secretary of the Commission. Moreover, the Commission has its own staff.

Pontificia Commissio de Patrimonio Artis et Historiae Conservando

tam eorundem bonorum administrationem atque necessarias approbationes vel recognitiones concedit; praeterea prospicit ut clericorum sustentationi ac sociali securitati consulatur.

Art. 99. Apud Congregationem pro Clericis Commissio exstat, cuius officium est curae patrimonii historiae et artis totius Ecclesiae praeesse.

Art. 100. Ad hoc patrimonium pertinent imprimis omnia cuiusvis artis opera temporis praeteriti, quae summa diligentia custodiri et conservari oportet. Ea autem quorum usus proprius cessaverit, apto modo in Ecclesiae musaeis vel aliis in locis spectabilia asserventur.

Art. 101. §1. Inter bona historica eminent omnia documenta et instrumenta, quae vitam et curam pastoralem necnon iura et obligationes dioecesium, paroeciarum, ecclesiarum aliarumque personarum iuridicarum in Ecclesia conditarum respiciunt et testificantur.

§2. Hoc patrimonium historicum in tabulariis seu archivis vel etiam bibliothecis custodiatur, quae ubique competentibus curatoribus committantur, ne huiusmodi testimonia pereant.

Art. 102. Commissio Ecclesiis particularibus et Episcoporum coetibus adiutorium praebet et una cum iis, si casus ferat, agit, ut musaea, tabularia et bibliothecae constituantur atque collectio et custodia totius patrimonii artis et historiae in toto territorio apte ad effectum adducatur et omnibus, quorum interest, praesto sit.

Art. 103. Eiusdem Commissionis est, collatis consiliis cum Congregationibus de Seminariis atque Studiorum Institutis et de Cultu Divino et Disciplina Sacramentorum, adlaborare ut Populus Dei magis magisque conscius fiat momenti et necessitatis patrimonium historiae et artis Ecclesiae conservandi.

Art. 104. Eidem praeest Cardinalis Praefectus Congregationis pro Clericis, eiusdem commissionis Secretario adiuvante. Commissio praeterea proprios habet administros.

Congregation for Institutes of Consecrated Life and for Societies of Apostolic Life

Art. 105. The principal function of the Congregation for Institutes of Consecrated Life and for Societies of Apostolic Life is to promote and supervise in the whole Latin Church the practice of the evangelical counsels as they are lived in approved forms of consecrated life and, at the same time, the work of societies of apostolic life.

Art. 106. §1. The Congregation erects and approves religious and secular institutes and societies of apostolic life, or passes judgement on the suitability of their erection by the diocesan bishop. It also suppresses such institutes and societies if necessary.

§2. The Congregation is also competent to establish, or, if need be, to rescind, the unions or federations of institutes and societies.

Art. 107. The Congregation for its part takes care that institutes of consecrated life and societies of apostolic life grow and flourish according to the spirit of their founders and healthy traditions, faithfully follow their proper purpose and truly benefit the salvific mission of the Church.

Art. 108. §1. It deals with everything which, in accordance with the law, belongs to the Holy See concerning the life and work of the institutes and societies, especially the approval of their constitutions, their manner of government and apostolate, the recruitment and training as well as the rights and obligations of members, dispensation from vows and the dismissal of members, and the administration of goods.

§2. However, the organization of philosophical and theological studies and other academic subjects comes within the competence of the Congregation for Seminaries and Institutes of Studies.

Art. 109. It is the function of this Congregation to establish conferences of major superiors of men and women religious, to grant approval to their statutes and to give great attention in order that their activities are directed to achieving their true purpose.

Art. 110. The Congregation has competence also regarding eremetical life, the order of virgins and their associations as well as other forms of consecrated life.

Art. 111. Its competence also embraces the third orders and associations of the faithful which are erected with the intention that, after a period of preparation, they may eventually become institutes of consecrated life or societies of apostolic life.

Congregatio pro Institutis Vitae Consecratae et Societatibus Vitae Apostolicae

Art. 105. Congregationis munus praecipuum est praxim consiliorum evangelicorum, prout in probatis formis vitae consecratae exercetur, et insimul actuositatem Societatum vitae apostolicae in universa Ecclesia Latina promovere et moderari.

Art. 106. §1. Congregatio proinde Instituta religiosa et saecularia necnon Societates vitae apostolicae erigit, approbat aut iudicium fert de opportunitate eorum erectionis ab Episcopo dioecesano faciendae. Ipsi quoque pertinet huiusmodi Instituta et Societates, si necesse fuerit, supprimere.

§2. Eidem etiam competit Institutorum et Societatum uniones vel foederationes constituere aut, si oportuerit, rescindere.

Art. 107. Congregatio pro sua parte curat, ut Instituta vitae consecratae ac Societates vitae apostolicae secundum spiritum Fundatorum et sanas traditiones crescant et floreant, finem proprium fideliter persequantur atque salvificae missioni Ecclesiae reapse prosint.

Art. 108. §1. Ea omnia absolvit, quae ad normam iuris pertinent ad Sanctam Sedem de vita et industria Institutorum et Societatum praesertim de constitutionum approbatione, regimine et apostolatu, sodalium cooptatione et institutione, eorum iuribus et obligationibus, votorum dispensatione et sodalium dimissione atque etiam bonorum administratione.

§2. Ad ordinationem autem studiorum philosophiae et theologiae necnon ad studia academica quod attinet competens est Congregatio de Seminariis atque Studiorum Institutis.

Art. 109. Eiusdem Congregationis est Conferentias Superiorum maiorum religiosorum religiosarumque erigere, earundem statuta approbare necnon invigilare ut ipsarum actio ad fines proprios assequendos ordinetur.

Art. 110. Congregationi etiam subiciuntur vita eremitica, ordo virginum harumque consociationes ceteraeque formae vitae consecratae.

Art. 111. Ipsius competentia amplectitur quoque Tertios Ordines necnon consociationes fidelium, quae eo animo eriguntur ut, praevia praeparatione, Instituta vitae consecratae vel Societates vitae apostolicae aliquando evadant.

Congregation of Seminaries and
Educational Institutions[37]

Art. 112. The Congregation of Seminaries and Educational Institutions gives practical expression to the concern of the Apostolic See for the training of those who are called to holy orders, and for the promotion and organization of Catholic education.

Art. 113. §1. It is available to the bishops so that in their Churches vocations to the sacred ministry may be cultivated to the highest degree, and seminaries may be established and conducted in accordance with the law, where students may be suitably trained, receiving a solid formation that is human and spiritual, doctrinal and pastoral.

§2. It gives great attention that the way of life and government of the seminaries be in full harmony with the programme of priestly education, and that the superiors and teachers, by the example of their life and sound doctrine, contribute their utmost to the formation of the personality of the sacred ministers.

§3. It is also its responsibility to erect interdiocesan seminaries and to approve their statutes.

Art. 114. The Congregation makes every effort to see that the fundamental principles of Catholic education as set out by the magisterium of the Church be ever more deeply researched, championed, and known by the people of God.

It also takes care that in this matter the Christian faithful may be able to fulfill their duties and also strive to bring civil society to recognize and protect their rights.

Art. 115. The Congregation sets the norms by which Catholic schools are governed. It is available to diocesan bishops so that, wherever possible, Catholic schools be established and fostered with the utmost care, and that in every school appropriate undertakings bring catechetical instruction and pastoral care to the Christian pupils.

Art. 116. §1. The Congregation labours to ensure that there be in the Church a sufficient number of ecclesiastical and Catholic universities as well as other educational institutions in which the sacred disciplines may be pursued in

Congregatio de Seminariis atque
Studiorum Institutis

Art. 112. Congregatio exprimit atque exercet Sedis Apostolicae sollicitudinem circa eorum formationem, qui ad sacros ordines vocantur, necnon circa promotionem et ordinationem institutionis catholicae.

Art. 113. §1. Episcopis adest, ut in eorum Ecclesiis vocationes ad sacra ministeria quam maxime colantur atque in Seminariis, ad normam iuris constituendis ac gerendis, alumni solida formatione tum humana ac spirituali, tum doctrinali et pastorali apte edoceantur.

§2. Sedulo invigilat ut seminariorum convictus regimenque rationi institutionis sacerdotalis plene respondeant atque superiores ac magistri exemplo vitae ac recta doctrina ad formandas personas sacrorum ministrorum quam maxime conferant.

§3. Eius praeterea est seminaria interdioecesana erigere eorumque statuta approbare.

Art. 114. Congregatio adnititur, ut fundamentalia principia de catholica educatione prout ab Ecclesiae Magisterio proponuntur altius usque investigentur, vindicentur atque a Populo Dei cognoscantur.

Ea pariter curat, ut in hac materia Christifideles sua officia implere possint ac dent operam et nitantur ut etiam civilis societas ipsorum iura agnoscat atque tueatur.

Art. 115. Congregatio normas statuit, quibus schola catholica regatur; Episcopis dioecesanis adest, ut scholae catholicae, ubi fieri potest, constituantur, et summa sollicitudine foveantur utque in omnibus scholis educatio catechetica et pastoralis cura alumnis Christifidelibus per opportuna incepta praebeantur.

Art. 116. §1. Congregatio vires impendit, ut Universitatum ecclesiasticarum et catholicarum ceterorumque studiorum Institutorum sufficiens copia in Ecclesia habeatur, in quibus sacrae dis-

---

37. The Congregation for Catholic Education (of Seminaries and Educational Institutions) is the name used since the coming into force of *Pastor bonus* on 1 March 1989. The name given by the Apostolic Constitution, the Congregation of Seminaries and Educational Institutions, was never officially used and was modified by a letter of the Secretariat of State of 26 February 1989 (prot. no. 236.026), which can be read in Tarcisio BERTONE, "La Congregazione per l'educazione cattolica (dei seminari e degli istituti di studio),"

in Piero Antonio BONNET and Carlo GULLO (eds.), *La Curia romana nella Cost. ap. "Pastor bonus,"* Studi giuridici, XXI, Annali di dottrina e giurisprudenza canonica, 13, Città del Vaticano, Libreria Editrice Vaticana, 1990, pp. 387–388. Since the Latin name of the Congregation was never formally amended in the official text of *Pastor bonus*, the translation of the document cannot use the current name of the dicastery.

depth, studies in the humanities and the sciences may be promoted, with due regard for Christian truth, so that the Christian faithful may be suitably trained to fulfill their own tasks.

§2. It erects or approves ecclesiastical universities and institutions, ratifies their statutes, exercises the highest supervision on them and pays great attention so that the integrity of the Catholic faith is preserved in teaching doctrine.

§3. With regard to Catholic universities, it deals with those matters that are within the competence of the Holy See.

§4. It fosters cooperation and mutual help between universities and their associations and serves as a resource for them.

ciplinae altius investigentur necnon humanitatis scientiaeque cultus, habita christianae veritatis ratione, promoveatur et Christifideles ad propria munera implenda apte formentur.

§2. Universitates et Instituta ecclesiastica erigit aut approbat, eorum statuta rata habet, supremam moderationem in eis exercet atque invigilat, ut catholicae fidei integritas in tradendis doctrinis servetur.

§3. Ad Universitates Catholicas quod attinet, ea agit quae Sanctae Sedi competunt.

§4. Cooperationem mutuumque adiutorium inter Studiorum Universitates earumque consociationes fovet iisdemque praesidio est.

IV. TRIBUNALS

Apostolic Penitentiary

Art. 117. The competence of the Apostolic Penitentiary regards the internal forum and indulgences.

Art. 118. For the internal forum, whether sacramental or non-sacramental, it grants absolutions, dispensations, commutations, validations, condonations, and other favours.

Art. 119. The Apostolic Penitentiary sees to it that in the patriarchal basilicas of Rome there be a sufficient number of penitentiaries supplied with the appropriate faculties.

Art. 120. This dicastery is charged with the granting and use of indulgences, without prejudice to the right of the Congregation for the Doctrine of the Faith to review what concerns dogmatic teaching about them.

IV. TRIBUNALIA

Paenitentiaria Apostolica

Art. 117. Paenitentiariae Apostolicae competentia ad ea se refert, quae forum internum necnon indulgentias respiciunt.

Art. 118. Pro foro interno, tum sacramentali tum non sacramentali, absolutiones, dispensationes, commutationes, sanationes, condonationes aliasque gratias eadem largitur.

Art. 119. Ipsa prospicit ut in Patriarchalibus Urbis Basilicis Paenitentiarii sufficienti numero habeantur, opportunis facultatibus praediti.

Art. 120. Eidem Dicasterio committuntur ea, quae spectant ad concessionem et usum indulgentiarum, salvo iure Congregationis de Doctrina Fidei ea videndi, quae doctrinam dogmaticam circa easdem respiciunt.

Supreme Tribunal of the Apostolic Signatura

Art. 121. The Apostolic Signatura functions as the supreme tribunal and also ensures that justice in the Church is correctly administered.

Art. 122. This Tribunal adjudicates:

1° complaints of nullity and petitions for total reinstatement against sentences of the Roman Rota;

2° in cases concerning the status of persons, recourses when the Roman Rota has denied a new examination of the case;

Supremum Tribunal Signaturae Apostolicae

Art. 121. Hoc Dicasterium, praeter munus, quod exercet, Supremi Tribunalis, consulit ut iustitia in Ecclesia recte administretur.

Art. 122. Ipsum cognoscit:

1° querelas nullitatis et petitiones restitutionis in integrum contra sententias Rotae Romanae;

2° recursus, in causis de statu personarum, adversus denegatum a Rota Romana novum causae examen;

3° exceptions of suspicion and other proceedings against judges of the Roman Rota arising from the exercise of their functions;

4° conflicts of competence between tribunals which are not subject to the same appellate tribunal.

Art. 123. §1. The Signatura adjudicates recourses lodged within the peremptory limit of thirty useful days against singular administrative acts whether issued by the dicasteries of the Roman Curia or approved by them, whenever it is contended that the impugned act violated some law either in the decision-making process or in the procedure used.

§2. In these cases, in addition to the judgement regarding illegality of the act, it can also adjudicate, at the request of the plaintiff, the reparation of damages incurred through the unlawful act.

§3. The Signatura also adjudicates other administrative controversies referred to it by the Roman Pontiff or by dicasteries of the Roman Curia, as well as conflicts of competence between these dicasteries.

Art. 124. The Signatura also has the responsibility:

1° to exercise vigilance over the correct administration of justice, and, if need be, to censure advocates and procurators;

2° to deal with petitions presented to the Apostolic See for obtaining the commission of a case to the Roman Rota or some other favour relative to the administration of justice;

3° to prorogate the competence of lower tribunals;

4° to grant its approval to tribunals for appeals reserved to the Holy See, and to promote and approve the erection of interdiocesan tribunals.

Art. 125. The Apostolic Signatura is governed by its own law.

Tribunal of the Roman Rota

Art. 126. The Roman Rota is a court of higher instance at the Apostolic See, usually at the appellate stage, with the purpose of safeguarding rights within the Church; it fosters unity of jurisprudence, and, by virtue of its own decisions, provides assistance to lower tribunals.

Art. 127. The judges of this Tribunal constitute a college.

3° exceptiones suspicionis aliasque causas contra Iudices Rotae Romanae propter acta in exercitio ipsorum muneris;

4° conflictus competentiae inter tribunalia, quae non subiciuntur eidem tribunali appellationis.

Art. 123. §1. Praeterea cognoscit de recursibus, intra terminum peremptorium triginta dierum utilium interpositis, adversus actus administrativos singulares sive a Dicasteriis Curiae Romanae latos sive ab ipsis probatos, quoties contendatur num actus impugnatus legem aliquam in decernendo vel in procedendo violaverit.

§2. In his casibus, praeter iudicium de illegitimitate, cognoscere etiam potest, si recurrens id postulet, de reparatione damnorum actu illegitimo illatorum.

§3. Cognoscit etiam de aliis controversiis administrativis, quae a Romano Pontifice vel a Romanae Curiae Dicasteriis ipsi deferantur necnon de conflictibus competentiae inter eadem Dicasteria.

Art. 124. Ipsius quoque est:

1° rectae administrationi iustitiae invigilare et in advocatos vel procuratores, si opus sit, animadvertere;

2° videre de petitionibus Sedi Apostolicae porrectis ad obtinendam causae commissionem apud Rotam Romanam, vel aliam gratiam relative ad iustitiam administrandam;

3° tribunalium inferiorum competentiam prorogare;

4° approbationem Tribunalis quoad appellationem Sanctae Sedi reservatam concedere necnon promovere et approbare erectionem tribunalium interdioecesanorum.

Art. 125. Signatura Apostolica lege propria regitur.

Tribunal Rotae Romanae

Art. 126. Hoc Tribunal instantiae superioris partes apud Apostolicam Sedem pro more in gradu appellationis agit ad iura in Ecclesia tutanda, unitati iurisprudentiae consulit et, per proprias sententias, tribunalibus inferioribus auxilio est.

Art. 127. Huius Tribunalis Iudices, probata

Persons of proven doctrine and experience, they have been selected by the Supreme Pontiff from various parts of the world. The Tribunal is presided over by a dean, likewise appointed by the Supreme Pontiff from among the judges and for a specific term of office.

Art. 128. This Tribunal adjudicates:

1° in second instance, cases that have been decided by ordinary tribunals of the first instance and are being referred to the Holy See by legitimate appeal;

2° in third or further instance, cases already decided by the same Apostolic Tribunal and by any other tribunals, unless they have become a *res iudicata.*

Art. 129. §1. The Tribunal, however, judges the following in first instance:

1° bishops in contentious matters, unless it deals with the rights or temporal goods of a juridical person represented by the bishop;

2° abbots primate or abbots superior of a monastic congregation and supreme moderators of religious institutes of pontifical right;

3° dioceses or other ecclesiastical persons, whether physical or juridical, which have no superior below the Roman Pontiff;

4° cases which the Supreme Pontiff commits to this Tribunal.

§2. It deals with the same cases even in second and further instances, unless other provisions are made.

Art. 130. The Tribunal of the Roman Rota is governed by its own law.

V. PONTIFICAL COUNCILS

Pontifical Council for the Laity

Art. 131. The Pontifical Council for the Laity is competent in those matters pertaining to the Apostolic See in promoting and coordinating the apostolate of the laity and, generally, in those matters respecting the Christian life of laypeople as such.

Art. 132. The president is assisted by an Advisory Board of cardinals and bishops. Figuring especially among the members of the Council are certain Christian faithful engaged in various fields of activity.

Art. 133. §1. The Council is to urge and support laypeo-

---

doctrina et experientia pollentes atque e variis terrarum orbis partibus a Summo Pontifice selecti, collegium constituunt; eidem Tribunali praeest Decanus ad certum tempus a Summo Pontifice ex ipsis Iudicibus pariter nominatus.

Art. 128. Hoc Tribunal iudicat:

1° in secunda instantia, causas ab ordinariis tribunalibus primae instantiae diiudicatas, quae ad Sanctam Sedem per appellationem legitimam deferuntur;

2° in tertia vel ulteriore instantia, causas ab eodem Tribunali Apostolico et ab aliis quibusvis tribunalibus iam cognitas, nisi in rem iudicatam transierint.

Art. 129. §1. Idem vero in prima instantia iudicat:

1° Episcopos in contentiosis, modo ne agatur de iuribus aut bonis temporalibus personae iuridicae ab Episcopo repraesentatae;

2° Abbates primates, vel Abbates superiores congregationis monasticae et supremos Moderatores Institutorum religiosorum iuris pontificii;

3° dioeceses ceterasve personas ecclesiasticas, sive physicas sive iuridicas, quae superiorem infra Romanum Pontificem non habent;

4° causas quas Romanus Pontifex eidem Tribunali commiserit.

§2. Easdem causas, nisi aliter cautum sit, etiam in secunda et ulteriore instantia agit.

Art. 130. Tribunal Rotae Romanae lege propria regitur.

V. PONTIFICIA CONSILIA

Pontificium Consilium Pro Laicis

Art. 131. Consilium competens est in iis, quae ad Sedem Apostolicam pertinent in laicorum apostolatu promovendo et coordinando atque, universim, in iis, quae vitam christianam laicorum qua talium respiciunt.

Art. 132. Praesidi adest Coetus praesidialis ex Cardinalibus et Episcopis constans; inter membra Consilii potissimum adnumerantur Christifideles in variis actuositatis provinciis versantes.

Art. 133. §1. Eius est incitare et sustinere

ple to participate in the life and mission of the Church in their own way, as individuals or in associations, especially so that they may carry out their special responsibility of filling the realm of temporal things with the spirit of the Gospel.

§2. It fosters joint action among laypeople in catechetical instruction, in liturgical and sacramental life as well as in works of mercy, charity, and social development.

§3. The Council attends to and organizes international conferences and other projects concerning the apostolate of the laity.

Art. 134. Within the parameters of its own competence, the Council performs all activities respecting lay associations of the Christian faithful; it erects associations of an international character and provides approval or *recognitio* for their statutes, saving the competence of the Secretariat of State. As for secular third orders, the Council deals only with those matters concerning their apostolic activities.

Pontifical Council for Promoting Christian Unity

Art. 135. It is the function of the Pontifical Council for Promoting Christian Unity to engage in ecumenical work through timely initiatives and activities, labouring to restore unity among Christians.

Art. 136. §1. It sees that the decrees of the Second Vatican Council pertaining to ecumenism are put into practice.

It deals with the correct interpretation of the principles of ecumenism and enjoins that they be carried out.

§2. It fosters, brings together, and coordinates national and international Catholic organizations promoting Christian unity, and supervises their undertakings.

§3. After prior consultation with the Supreme Pontiff, the Council maintains relations with Christians of Churches and ecclesial communities that do not yet have full communion with the Catholic Church, and especially organizes dialogue and meetings to promote unity with them, with the help of theological experts of sound doctrine. As often as may seem opportune, the Council deputes Catholic observers to Christian meetings, and it invites observers from other Churches and ecclesial communities to Catholic meetings.

laicos ut vitam et missionem Ecclesiae modo sibi proprio participent, sive singuli, sive in consociationibus, praesertim ut ipsorum peculiare officium impleant rerum temporalium ordinem spiritu evangelico imbuendi.

§2. Laicorum cooperationem fovet in cathechetica institutione, in vita liturgica et sacramentali atque in operibus misericordiae, caritatis et promotionis socialis.

§3. Idem prosequitur et moderatur conventus internationales aliaque incepta, quae ad apostolatum laicorum attinent.

Art. 134. Consilium ea omnia intra ambitum propriae competentiae agit, quae ad consociationes laicales Christifidelium spectant; eas vero, quae internationalem indolem habent, erigit earumque statuta approbat vel recognoscit, salva competentia Secretariae Status; quoad Tertios Ordines saeculares ea tantum curat, quae ad eorum apostolicam operositatem pertinent.

Pontificium Consilium ad Unitatem Christianorum Fovendam

Art. 135. Consilii munus est per opportuna incepta et navitates operi oecumenico incumbere ad unitatem inter christianos redintegrandam.

Art. 136. §1. Curat ut decreta Concilii Vaticani II, quae ad rem oecumenicam pertinent, ad usum traducantur.

Agit de recta interpretatione principiorum de oecumenismo eaque exsecutioni mandat.

§2. Coetus catholicos tum nationales tum internationales christianorum unitatem promoventes fovet, colligit atque coordinat eorumque inceptis invigilat.

§3. Rebus ad Summum Pontificem prius delatis, rationes curat cum fratribus Ecclesiarum et communitatum ecclesialium, plenam communionem cum Ecclesia catholica nondum habentium, ac praesertim dialogum et colloquia ad unitatem cum ipsis fovendam instituit, peritis doctrina theologica probe instructis opem ferentibus. Observatores catholicos deputat pro conventibus christianis atque invitat aliarum Ecclesiarum et communitatum ecclesialium observatores ad conventus catholicos, quoties id opportunum videatur.

Art. 137. §1. Since the Council often deals with matters which by their very nature touch on questions of faith, it must proceed in close connection with the Congregation for the Doctrine of the Faith, especially if declarations and public documents have to be issued.

§2. In dealing with important matters concerning the separated Oriental Churches, the Council must first hear the Congregation for the Oriental Churches.

Art. 138. Within the Council there exists a Commission to study and deal with matters concerning the Jews from a religious perspective, the Commission for Religious Relations with the Jews; the president of the Council presides over the Commission.

Pontifical Council for the Family

Art. 139. The Pontifical Council for the Family promotes the pastoral care of families, protects their rights and dignity in the Church and in civil society, so that they may ever be more able to fulfill their duties.

Art. 140. The president is assisted by an advisory board of bishops. Figuring above all among the members of the Council are laypeople, both men and women, especially married ones, from all over the world.

Art. 141. §1. The Council works for a deeper understanding of the Church's teaching on the family and for its spread through suitable catechesis. It encourages studies in the spirituality of marriage and the family.

§2. It works together with the bishops and their conferences to ensure the accurate recognition of the human and social conditions of the family institution everywhere and to ensure a strong general awareness of initiatives that help pastoral work for families.

§3. The Council strives to ensure that the rights of the family be acknowledged and defended even in the social and political realm. It also supports and coordinates initiatives to protect human life from the first moment of conception and to encourage responsible procreation.

§4. Without prejudice to art. 133, it follows the activities of institutes and associations which seek to work for the good of the family.

Art. 137. §1. Cum materia ab hoc Dicasterio tractanda suapte natura saepe quaestiones fidei tangat, ipsum oportet procedat arcta coniunctione cum Congregatione de Doctrina Fidei, praesertim cum agitur de publicis documentis aut declarationibus edendis.

§2. In gerendis autem maioris momenti negotiis, quae Ecclesias seiunctas Orientis respiciunt, prius audiat oportet Congregationem pro Ecclesiis Orientalibus.

Art. 138. Apud Consilium exstat Commissio ad res investigandas atque tractandas, quae Iudaeos sub respectu religioso attingunt; eam eiusdem Consilii Praeses moderatur.

Pontificium Consilium Pro Familia

Art. 139. Consilium pastoralem familiarum curam promovet, earumque iura dignitatemque in Ecclesia et in civili societate fovet, ut ipsae munera sibi propria aptius usque implere valeant.

Art. 140. Praesidi adest Coetus praesidialis, ex Episcopis constans; in Consilium potissimum cooptantur laici viri mulieresque, praesertim coniugio iuncti, ex variis terrarum orbis partibus.

Art. 141. §1. Consilium Ecclesiae doctrinam de familia penitus cognoscendam et apta catechesi divulgandam curat; studia praecipue de matrimonii ac familiae spiritualitate fovet.

§2. Idem satagit ut, conspirans cum Episcopis eorumque Conferentiis, humanae socialesque instituti familiaris in variis regionibus condiciones accurate cognoscantur, pariterque incepta, quae rem pastoralem familiarem adiuvant, in communem perferantur notitiam.

§3. Adnititur ut iura familiae, etiam in vita sociali et politica, agnoscantur et defendantur; incepta quoque ad humanam vitam inde a conceptione tuendam et ad procreationem responsabilem fovendam sustinet atque coordinat.

§4. Firmo praescripto art. 133, navitatem persequitur institutorum atque consociationum, quibus propositum est familiae bono inservire.

Pontifical Council for Justice and Peace

Art. 142. The goal of the Pontifical Council for Justice and Peace is to promote justice and peace in this world in accordance with the Gospel and the social teaching of the Church.

Art. 143. §1. The Council makes a thorough study of the social teaching of the Church and takes pains to see that this teaching is widely spread and put into practice among people and communities, especially regarding the relations between workers and management, relations that must come to be more and more imbued with the spirit of the Gospel.

§2. It collects information and research on justice and peace, about human development and violations of human rights; it ponders all this, and, when the occasion offers, shares its conclusions with the groupings of bishops. It cultivates relationships with Catholic international organizations and other institutions, even ones outside the Catholic Church, which sincerely strive to achieve peace and justice in the world.

§3. It works to form among peoples a mentality which fosters peace, especially on the occasion of World Peace Day.

Art. 144. The Council has a special relationship with the Secretariat Pontifical of State, especially whenever matters of peace and justice have to be dealt with in public by documents or announcements.

Pontifical Council *Cor Unum*

Art. 145. The Pontifical Council *Cor Unum* shows the solicitude of the Catholic Church for the needy, in order that human fraternity may be fostered and that the charity of Christ be made manifest.

Art. 146. It is the function of the Council:

1° to stimulate the Christian faithful as participants in the mission of the Church, to give witness to evangelical charity and to support them in this concern;

2° to foster and coordinate the initiatives of Catholic organizations that labour to help peoples in need, especially those who go to the rescue in the more urgent crises and disasters, and to facilitate their relations with public international organizations operating in the same field of assistance and good works;

Pontificium Consilium de Iustitia et Pace

Art. 142. Consilium eo spectat, ut iustitia et pax in mundo secundum Evangelium et socialem Ecclesiae doctrinam promoveantur.

Art. 143. §1. Socialem Ecclesiae doctrinam altius pervestigat, data opera ut ipsa late diffundatur et apud homines communitatesque in usum vitae deducatur, praesertim quod spectat ad rationes inter opifices et conductores operis, spiritu Evangelii magis magisque imbuendas.

§2. Notitias et inquisitiones de iustitia et pace, de populorum progressione et de hominum iurium laesionibus in unum colligit, perpendit atque exinde deductas conclusiones pro opportunitate cum Episcoporum coetibus communicat; rationes fovet cum catholicis internationalibus consociationibus aliisque institutis etiam extra Ecclesiam catholicam exstantibus, quae ad iustitiae pacisque bona in mundo consequenda sincere contendunt.

§3. Operam impendit ut inter populos sentiendi ratio de pace fovenda formetur, praesertim occasione oblata *Diei Pacis in mundo provehendae.*

Art. 144. Peculiares necessitudines cum Secretaria Status habet, praesertim quotiescumque per documenta vel per enuntiationes in rebus de iustitia et pace publice agendum est.

Pontificium Consilium «Cor Unum»

Art. 145. Consilium Ecclesiae Catholicae sollicitudinem erga egentes ostendit, ut humana fraternitas foveatur et caritas Christi manifestetur.

Art. 146. Consilii munus est:

1° Christifideles incitare ad evangelicae caritatis testimonium praebendum, utpote ipsam Ecclesiae missionem participantes, eosque in hac cura sustinere;

2° incepta catholicorum institutorum fovere et coordinare, quae egentibus populis adiuvandis incumbunt, ea praesertim quae urgentioribus angustiis et calamitatibus succurrunt, facilioresque reddere institutorum catholicorum necessitudines cum publicis internationalibus con-

3° to give serious attention and promote plans and undertakings for joint action and neighbourly help serving human progress.

Art. 147. The president of this Council is the same as the president of the Pontifical Council for Justice and Peace, who sees to it that the activities of both dicasteries are closely coordinated.

Art. 148. To ensure that the objectives of the Council are more effectively achieved, among members of the Council are also men and women representing Catholic charitable organizations.

Pontifical Council for the Pastoral Care of Migrants and Itinerant People

Art. 149. The Pontifical Council for the Pastoral Care of Migrants and Itinerant People brings the pastoral concern of the Church to bear on the special needs of those who have been forced to leave their native land or who do not have one. It also sees to it that these matters are considered with the attention they deserve.

Art. 150. §1. The Council works to see that in the particular Churches refugees and exiles, migrants, nomads, and circus workers receive effective and special spiritual care, even, if necessary, by means of suitable pastoral structures.

§2. It likewise fosters pastoral solicitude in these same Churches for sailors, at sea and in port, especially through the Apostleship of the Sea, over which it exercises ultimate direction.

§3. The Council has the same concern for those who work in airports or airplanes.

§4. It tries to ensure that the Christian people come to an awareness of the needs of these people and effectively demonstrate their own brotherly attitude towards them, especially on the occasion of World Migration Day.

Art. 151. The Council works to ensure that journeys which Christians undertake for reasons of piety, study, or recreation, contribute to their moral and religious formation, and it is available to the particular Churches in order that all who are away from home receive suitable spiritual care.

siliis, quae in eodem beneficentiae et progressionis campo operantur;

3° consilia atque mutuae navitatis fraternique auxilii opera studio prosequi atque promovere, quae humano profectui inserviunt.

Art. 147. Huius Consilii Praeses idem est ac Praeses Pontificii Consilii pro Iustitia et Pace, qui curat ut utriusque Instituti actuositas arcta coniunctione procedat.

Art. 148. Inter Consilii membra viri etiam et mulieres cooptantur, qui catholicorum beneficentiae institutorum veluti partes agant quo efficacius proposita Consilii ad effectum deducantur.

Pontificium Consilium de Spirituali Migrantium atque Itinerantium Cura

Art. 149. Consilium pastoralem Ecclesiae sollicitudinem convertit ad peculiares necessitates eorum, qui patrium solum relinquere coacti sint vel eo penitus careant; itemque quaestiones, ad haec attinentes, accommodato studio perpendendas curat.

Art. 150. §1. Consilium dat operam, ut in Ecclesiis particularibus efficax propriaque cura spiritualis, etiam, si res ferat, per congruas pastorales structuras, praebeatur sive profugis et exsulibus, sive migrantibus, nomadibus et circensem artem exercentibus.

§2. Fovet pariter apud easdem Ecclesias pastoralem sollicitudinem pro maritimis sive navigantibus sive in portibus, praesertim per Opus Apostolatus Maris, cuius supremam moderationem exercet.

§3. Eandem sollicitudinem adhibet iis, qui in aëroportibus vel in ipsis aëronavibus officia exercent vel opus faciunt.

§4. Adnititur, ut populus christianus, praesertim occasione oblata celebrationis *Diei universalis pro migrantibus atque exsulibus*, conscientiam eorum necessitatum sibi comparet atque proprium fraternum animum erga eos efficaciter manifestet.

Art. 151. Adlaborat ut itinera pietatis causa vel studio discendi vel ad relaxationem suscepta ad moralem religiosamque Christifidelium formationem conferant atque Ecclesiis particularibus adest ut omnes, qui exinde extra proprium domicilium versantur, apta animarum cura frui possint.

Pontifical Council for the Pastoral Assistance to Health Care Workers

Art. 152. The Pontifical Council for the Pastoral Assistance to Health Care Workers shows the solicitude of the Church for the sick by helping those who serve the sick and suffering, so that their apostolate of mercy may ever more respond to people's needs.

Art. 153. §1. The Council is to spread the Church's teaching on the spiritual and moral aspects of illness as well as the meaning of human suffering.

§2. It lends its assistance to the particular Churches to ensure that health care workers receive spiritual help in carrying out their work according to Christian teachings, and especially that in turn the pastoral workers in this field may never lack the help they need to carry out their work.

§3. The Council fosters studies and actions which international Catholic organizations or other institutions undertake in this field.

§4. With keen interest it follows new health care developments in law and science so that these may be duly taken into account in the pastoral work of the Church.

Pontifical Council for the Interpretation of Legislative Texts

Art. 154. The function of the Pontifical Council for the Interpretation of Legislative Texts consists mainly in interpreting the laws of the Church.

Art. 155. With regard to the universal laws of the Church, the Council is competent to publish authentic interpretations which are confirmed by pontifical authority, after having heard in questions of major importance the views of the dicasteries concerned by the subject matter.

Art. 156. This Council is at the service of the other Roman dicasteries to assist them in order to ensure that general executory decrees and instructions which they are going to publish are in conformity with the prescriptions of the law currently in force and that they are drawn up in a correct juridical form.

Art. 157. Moreover, the general decrees of the conferences of bishops are to be submitted to this Council by the dicastery which is competent to grant them the *recognitio*, in order that they be examined from a juridical perspective.

Art. 158. At the request of those interested, this Coun-

Pontificium Consilium de Apostolatu pro Valetudinis Administris

Art. 152. Consilium sollicitudinem Ecclesiae pro infirmis ostendit adiuvando eos qui ministerium implent erga aegrotantes dolentesque, ut misericordiae apostolatus, quem exercent, novis postulationibus aptius usque respondeat.

Art. 153. §1. Consilii est Ecclesiae doctrinam diffundere circa spirituales et morales infirmitatis aspectus necnon humani doloris significationem.

§2. Ecclesiis particularibus adiutricem operam praebet, ut valetudinis administri spirituali cura iuventur in sua navitate secundum christianam doctrinam explenda, ac praeterea ne iis, qui in hoc ambitu pastoralem actionem gerunt, apta subsidia ad proprium exsequendum opus desint.

§3. Idem studii actionisque operi favet, quod sive Consociationes Internationales Catholicae sive alia instituta in hoc campo variis modis navant.

§4. Intento animo novitates in legibus et scientiis circa valetudinem prosequitur eo consilio, ut in opera pastorali Ecclesiae earum opportuna ratio habeatur.

Pontificium Consilium de Legum Textibus Interpretandis

Art. 154. Consilii munus in legibus Ecclesiae interpretandis praesertim consistit.

Art. 155. Consilio competit Ecclesiae legum universalium interpretationem authenticam pontificia auctoritate firmatam proferre, auditis in rebus maioris momenti Dicasteriis, ad quae res ratione materiae pertinet.

Art. 156. Hoc Consilium ceteris Romanis Dicasteriis praesto est ad illa iuvanda eo proposito ut decreta generalia exsecutoria et instructiones ab iisdem edendae iuris vigentis praescriptis congruant et recta forma iuridica exarentur.

Art. 157. Eidem insuper subicienda sunt a Dicasterio competenti pro recognitione decreta generalia Episcoporum coetuum ut examinentur ratione habita iuridica.

Art. 158. Iis quorum interest postulantibus,

cil determines whether particular laws and general decrees issued by legislators below the level of the supreme authority are in agreement or not with the universal laws of the Church.

Pontifical Council for Inter-Religious Dialogue

Art. 159. The Pontifical Council for Inter-Religious Dialogue fosters and supervises relations with members and groups of non-Christian religions as well as with those who are in any way endowed with religious feeling.

Art. 160. The Council fosters suitable dialogue with adherents of other religions, as well as other forms of relations. It promotes timely studies and conferences to develop mutual information and esteem, so that human dignity and the spiritual and moral riches of people may ever grow. The Council sees to the formation of those who engage in this kind of dialogue.

Art. 161. When the subject matter so requires, the Council must proceed in the exercise of its own function in consultation with the Congregation for the Doctrine of the Faith, and, if need be, with the Congregations for the Oriental Churches and for the Evangelization of Peoples.

Art. 162. This Council has a Commission, under the direction of the president of the Council, for fostering relations with Muslims from a religious perspective.

Pontifical Council for Dialogue with Non-Believers

Art. 163. The Pontifical Council for Dialogue with Non-Believers shows the pastoral solicitude of the Church for those who do not believe in God or who profess no religion.

Art. 164. It promotes the study of atheism and of the lack of faith and religion, looking into their causes and their consequences with regard to the Christian faith, so that suitable assistance may be given to pastoral action through the work especially of Catholic educational institutions.

Art. 165. The Council sets up dialogue with atheists and unbelievers whenever they agree to sincere cooperation, and it is represented by true specialists at conferences on this matter.

Pontificium Consilium pro Dialogo inter Religiones

Art. 159. Consilium fovet et moderatur rationes cum membris coetibusque religionum, quae christiano nomine non censentur, necnon cum iis, qui sensu religioso quocumque modo potiuntur.

Art. 160. Consilium operam dat, ut dialogus cum asseclis aliarum religionum apte conseratur, aliasque rationes cum ipsis fovet; opportuna studia et conventus promovet ut mutua notitia atque aestimatio habeantur, necnon hominis dignitas eiusque spiritualia et moralia bona consociata opera provehantur; formationi eorum consulit, qui in huiusmodi dialogum incumbunt.

Art. 161. Cum subiecta materia id requirit, in proprio munere exercendo collatis consiliis procedat oportet cum Congregatione de Doctrina Fidei, et, si opus fuerit, cum Congregationibus pro Ecclesiis Orientalibus et pro Gentium Evangelizatione.

Art. 162. Apud Consilium exstat Commissio ad rationes cum Musulmanis sub religioso respectu fovendas, moderante eiusdem Consilii Praeside.

Pontificium Consilium pro Dialogo cum Non Credentibus

Art. 163. Consilium pastoralem Ecclesiae sollicitudinem manifestat erga eos qui Deo non credunt vel nullam religionem profitentur.

Art. 164. Studium promovet atheismi necnon fidei religionisque defectus, eorum causas atque consecutiones inquirendo ad christianam fidem quod attinet, eo proposito, ut apta auxilia pastorali actioni comparentur, operam potissimum ferentibus catholicis studiorum Institutis.

Art. 165. Dialogum instituit cum atheis et non credentibus, quoties hi sincerae cooperationi assentiantur; studiorum de hac materia coetibus per vere peritos interest.

Pontifical Council for Culture

Art. 166. The Pontifical Council for Culture fosters relations between the Holy See and the realm of human culture, especially by promoting communication with various contemporary institutions of learning and teaching, so that secular culture may be more and more open to the Gospel, and specialists in the sciences, literature, and the arts may feel themselves called by the Church to truth, goodness, and beauty.

Art. 167. The Council has its own special structure. The president is assisted by an advisory board and another board, composed of specialists of various disciplines from several parts of the world.

Art. 168. The Council on its own undertakes suitable projects with respect to culture. It follows through on those which are undertaken by various institutes of the Church, and, so far as necessary, lends them assistance. In consultation with the Secretariat of State, it shows interest in measures adopted by countries and international agencies in support of human culture and, as appropriate, it is present in the principal organizations in the field of culture and fosters conferences.

Pontifical Council for Social Communications

Art. 169. §1. The Pontifical Council for Social Communications is involved in questions respecting the means of social communication, so that, also by these means, human progress and the news of salvation may benefit secular culture and mores.

§2. In carrying out its functions, the Council must proceed in close connection with the Secretariat of State.

Art. 170. §1. The chief task of this Council is to arouse the Church and the Christian faithful, in a timely and suitable way, to take part in the many forms of social communication, and to sustain their action. It takes pains to see that newspapers and periodicals, as well as films and radio or television broadcasts, are more and more imbued with a human and Christian spirit.

§2. With special solicitude the Council looks to Catholic newspapers and periodicals, as well as radio and television stations, that they may truly live up to their nature and function, by transmitting especially the teaching of the

Pontificium Consilium de Cultura

Art. 166. Consilium rationes fovet inter Sanctam Sedem et humani cultus provinciam, praesertim colloquium cum variis nostri temporis Institutis scientiae et doctrinae provehendo, ut civilis cultus magis magisque Evangelio aperiatur atque scientiarum, litterarum, artiumque cultores se ad veritatem, bonitatem et pulchritudinem ab Ecclesia vocari sentiant.

Art. 167. Consilium structuram habet peculiarem, in qua, una cum Praeside, adsunt Coetus praesidialis aliusque coetus cultorum variarum disciplinarum ex pluribus orbis terrarum regionibus.

Art. 168. Consilium apta incepta ad culturam attinentia per se suscipit; ea, quae a variis Ecclesiae Institutis capiuntur, persequitur atque ipsis, quatenus opus fuerit, adiutricem operam praebet. Collatis autem consiliis cum Secretaria Status attendit ad agendi rationes, quas ad humanum cultum fovendum Civitates et internationalia Consilia susceperint, atque in culturae ambitu praecipuis coetibus pro opportunitate interest et congressiones fovet.

Pontificium Consilium de Communicationibus Socialibus

Art. 169. §1. Consilium in quaestionibus ad communicationis socialis instrumenta attinentibus versatur, eo consilio ut etiam per ea salutis nuntium et humana progressio ad civilem cultum moresque fovendos provehantur.

§2. In suis muneribus explendis arcta coniunctione cum Secretaria Status procedat oportet.

Art. 170. §1. Consilium in praecipuum munus incumbit tempestive accommodateque suscitandi ac sustinendi Ecclesiae et Christifidelium actionem in multiplicibus socialis communicationis formis; operam dandi ut sive diaria aliaque periodica scripta, sive cinematographica spectacula, sive radiophonicae ac televisificae emissiones humano et christiano spiritu magis magisque imbuantur.

§2. Peculiari sollicitudine prosequitur catholicas ephemerides, periodicas scriptiones, stationes radiophonicas atque televisificas, ut propriae indoli ac muneri reapse respondeant,

Church as it is laid out by the Church's magisterium, and by spreading religious news accurately and faithfully.

§3. It fosters relations with Catholic associations active in social communications.

§4. It takes steps to make the Christian people aware, especially on the occasion offered by World Communications Day, of the duty of each and every person to make sure that the media be of service to the Church's pastoral mission.

praesertim Ecclesiae doctrinam, prout a Magisterio proponitur, evulgando, atque religiosos nuntios recte fideliterque diffundendo.

§3. Necessitudinem fovet cum catholicis consociationibus, quae communicationibus socialibus dant operam.

§4. Curat ut populus christianus, praesertim occasione data celebrationis *Diei communicationum socialium* conscius fiat officii, quo unusquisque tenetur, adlaborandi ut huiusmodi instrumenta pastorali Ecclesiae missioni praesto sunt.

VI. ADMINISTRATIVE SERVICES

Apostolic Camera

Art. 171. §1. The Apostolic Camera, presided over by the cardinal camerlengo of the Holy Roman Church, assisted by the vice-camerlengo and the other prelates of the Camera, chiefly exercises the functions assigned to it by the special law on the vacancy of the Apostolic See.

§2. When the Apostolic See falls vacant, it is the right and the duty of the cardinal camerlengo of the Holy Roman Church, personally or through his delegate, to request, from all administrations dependent on the Holy See, reports on their patrimonial and economic status as well as information on any extraordinary business that may at that time be under way, and, from the Prefecture for the Economic Affairs of the Holy See he shall request a financial statement on income and expenditures of the previous year and the budgetary estimates for the following year. He is in duty bound to submit these reports and estimates to the College of Cardinals.

VI. OFFICIA

Camera Apostolica

Art. 171. §1. Camera Apostolica, cui praeficitur Cardinalis Sanctae Romanae Ecclesiae Camerarius, iuvante Vice-Camerario una cum ceteris Praelatis Cameralibus, munera praesertim gerit, quae ipsi peculiari lege de vacante Sede Apostolica tribuuntur.

§2. Sede Apostolica vacante, Cardinali Sanctae Romanae Ecclesiae Camerario ius est et officium, etiam per suum delegatum, ab omnibus Administrationibus, quae e Sancta Sede pendent, relationes exposcere de earum statu patrimoniali et oeconomico itemque notitias de extraordinariis negotiis, quae tunc forte aguntur, et a Praefectura Rerum Oeconomicarum Sanctae Sedis generales computationes accepti et expensi anni superioris nec non praevias aestimationes pro anno subsequente; has autem relationes et computationes Cardinalium Collegio subiciendi officio tenetur.

Administration of the Patrimony of the Apostolic See

Art. 172. It is the function of the Administration of the Patrimony of the Apostolic See to administer the properties owned by the Holy See in order to underwrite the expenses needed for the Roman Curia to function.

Art. 173. This Council is presided over by a cardinal assisted by a board of cardinals; and it is composed of two sections, the Ordinary Section and the Extraordinary, under the control of the prelate secretary.

Administratio Patrimonii Sedis Apostolicae

Art. 172. Huic officio competit bona Sanctae Sedis propria administrare, quae eo destinantur, ut sumptus ad Curiae Romanae munera explenda necessarii suppeditentur.

Art. 173. Eidem Cardinalis praeest, cui Patrum Cardinalium coetus adest, idemque duabus sectionibus, Ordinaria atque Extraordinaria, constat, sub moderamine Praelati Secretarii.

Art. 174. The Ordinary Section administers the properties entrusted to its care, calling in the advice of experts if needed; it examines matters concerning the juridical and economic status of the employees of the Holy See; it supervises institutions under its fiscal responsibility; it sees to the provision of all that is required to carry out the ordinary business and specific aims of the dicasteries; it maintains records of income and expenditures, prepares the accounts of the money received and paid out for the past year, and draws up the estimates for the year to come.

Art. 175. The Extraordinary Section administers its own moveable goods and acts as a guardian for moveable goods entrusted to it by other institutes of the Holy See.

Prefecture for the Economic Affairs of the Holy See

Art. 176. The Prefecture for the Economic Affairs of the Holy See has the function of supervising and governing the temporal goods of the administrations that are dependent on the Holy See, or of which the Holy See has charge, whatever the autonomy these administrations may happen to enjoy.

Art. 177. The Prefecture is presided over by a cardinal assisted by a board of cardinals, with the collaboration of the prelate secretary and the general accountant.

Art. 178. §1. It studies the reports on the patrimonial and economic status of the Holy See, as well as the statements of income and expenditures for the previous year and the budget estimates for the following year of the administrations mentioned in art. 176, by inspecting books and documents, if need be.

§2. The Prefecture compiles the Holy See's consolidated financial statement of the previous year's expenditures as well as the consolidated estimates of the next year's expenditures, and submits these at specific times to higher authority for approval.

Art. 179. §1. The Prefecture supervises financial undertakings of the administrations and expresses its opinion concerning projects of major importance.

§2. It inquires into damages inflicted in whatever manner on the patrimony of the Holy See, and, if need be, lodges penal or civil actions to the competent tribunals.

Art. 174. Sectio Ordinaria bona administrat, quorum cura ipsi credita est, in consilium vocatis, si opus fuerit, etiam peritis; et perpendit quae ad statum iuridicum-oeconomicum ministrorum Sanctae Sedis attinent; institutis sub ipsius administratoria moderatione exstantibus invigilat; prospicit ut omnia apparentur, quae ordinaria Dicasteriorum navitas ad proprios fines assequendos requirit; rationes accepti et expensi habet atque pecuniae dandae et recipiendae sive computationem pro anno elapso sive pro subsequenti anno aestimationem conficit.

Art. 175. Extraordinaria Sectio peculiaria bona mobilia administrat, et mobilium bonorum procurationem agit, quae a ceteris Sanctae Sedis Institutis eidem committuntur.

Praefectura Rerum Oeconomicarum Sanctae Sedis

Art. 176. Praefecturae munus competit moderandi et gubernandi bonorum administrationes, quae a Sancta Sede pendent vel quibus ipsa praeest, quaecumque est autonomia qua forte gaudeant.

Art. 177. Eidem praeest Cardinalis, cui adest coetus Cardinalium, iuvantibus Praelato Secretario et Ratiocinatore Generali.

Art. 178. §1. Perpendit sive relationes de statu patrimoniali et oeconomico sive rationes accepti atque expensi tum annualium sumptuum praeviam tum subsequentem administrationum de quibus agit art. 176, libros et documenta, si opus fuerit, inspiciendo.

§2. Generalem computationem, sive ad praeviam sumptuum aestimationem sive ad rationem expensae pecuniae Sanctae Sedis quod attinet, apparat, eandemque tempore statuto Superiori Auctoritati approbandam subicit.

Art. 179. §1. Nummariis administrationum inceptis invigilat; sententiam de operum maioris momenti adumbrationibus fert.

§2. Cognoscit de damnis patrimonio Sanctae Sedis quomodocumque illatis, ad actiones poenales vel civiles, si opus fuerit, competentibus tribunalibus proponendas.

VII. OTHER INSTITUTES OF THE ROMAN CURIA

Prefecture of the Papal Household

Art. 180. The Prefecture of the Papal Household looks after the internal organization of the papal household, and supervises everything concerning the conduct and service of all clerics and laypersons who make up the papal chapel and family.

Art. 181. §1. It is at the service of the Supreme Pontiff, both in the Apostolic Palace and when he travels in Rome or in Italy.

§2. Apart from the strictly liturgical aspect, which is handled by the Office for the Liturgical Celebrations of the Supreme Pontiff, the Prefecture sees to the planning and carrying out of papal ceremonies and determines the order of precedence.

§3. It arranges public and private audiences with the Pontiff, in consultation with the Secretariat of State whenever circumstances so demand and under whose direction it arranges the procedures to be followed when the Roman Pontiff meets in a solemn audience with heads of State, ambassadors, members of governments, public authorities, and other distinguished persons.

Office for the Liturgical Celebrations of the Supreme Pontiff

Art. 182. §1. The Office for the Liturgical Celebrations of the Supreme Pontiff is to prepare all that is necessary for the liturgical and other sacred celebrations performed by the Supreme Pontiff or in his name and supervise them according to the current prescriptions of liturgical law.

§2. The master of papal liturgical celebrations is appointed by the Supreme Pontiff to a five-year term of office; papal masters of ceremonies who assist him in sacred celebrations are likewise appointed by the secretary of state to a term of the same length.

VIII. ADVOCATES

Art. 183. Apart from the advocates of the Roman Rota and the advocates for the causes of saints, there is a roster of advocates who, at the request of interested parties, are qualified to represent them in their cases at the Supreme Tribunal of the Apostolic Signatura and to offer assistance in hierarchical recourses lodged before dicasteries of the Roman Curia.

VII. CETERA CURIAE ROMANAE INSTITUTA

Praefectura Pontificalis Domus

Art. 180. Praefectura ordinem internum ad Pontificalem Domum spectantem respicit, atque iis omnibus sive clericis sive laicis moderatur, ad disciplinam et servitium quod attinet, qui Cappellam et Familiam Pontificiam constituunt.

Art. 181. §1. Summo Pontifici adest sive in Palatio Apostolico sive cum Ipse in Urbem vel in Italiam iter facit.

§2. Ordinationi et processui studet Caeremoniarum Pontificalium, extra partem stricte liturgicam, quae ab Officio Liturgicis Celebrationibus Summi Pontificis praeposito absolvitur; praecedentiae ordinem attribuit.

§3. Admissiones publicas privatasque coram Pontifice disponit, collatis consiliis, quoties rerum natura id postulet, cum Secretaria Status, qua moderante ea ordinat, quae servanda sunt, cum ab ipso Romano Pontifice coram sollemniter admittuntur supremi populorum Moderatores, Nationum Legati, Civitatum Ministri, Publicae Auctoritates ceteraeque personae dignitate insignes.

Officium de Liturgicis Celebrationibus Summi Pontificis

Art. 182. §1. Ipsius est ea quae necessaria sunt ad liturgicas aliasque sacras celebrationes, quae a Summo Pontifice aut Eius nomine peraguntur, parare easque, iuxta vigentia iuris liturgici praescripta, moderari.

§2. Magister pontificiarum Celebrationum Liturgicarum a Summo Pontifice ad quinquennium nominatur; caeremoniarii pontificii, qui eum in sacris celebrationibus adiuvant, a Secretario Status pariter ad idem tempus nominantur.

VIII. ADVOCATI

Art. 183. Praeter Romanae Rotae Advocatos et Advocatos pro causis Sanctorum, Album adest Advocatorum, qui habiles sunt, rogatu eorum quorum interest, ut patrocinium causarum apud Supremum Signaturae Apostolicae Tribunal suscipiant necnon, in recursibus hierarchicis apud Dicasteria Curiae Romanae, operam suam praestent.

Art. 184. Candidates can be inscribed in the roster by the cardinal secretary of state, after he has consulted a commission stably constituted for this purpose. Candidates must be qualified by a suitable preparation attested by appropriate academic degrees, and at the same time be recommended by their example of a Christian life, honourable character, and expertise. Should any of this cease to be the case at a later date, the advocate shall be struck from the roster.

Art. 185. §1. The body called "Advocates of the Holy See" is composed mainly of advocates listed in the roster of advocates, and its members are able to undertake the representation of cases in civil or ecclesiastical tribunals in the name of the Holy See or the dicasteries of the Roman Curia.

§2. They are appointed by the cardinal secretary of state to a five-year term of office on the recommendation of the commission mentioned in art. 184; for serious reasons, they may be removed from office. Once they have completed seventy-five years of age, they cease their office.

IX. INSTITUTIONS CONNECTED WITH THE HOLY SEE

Art. 186. There are certain institutes, some of ancient origin and some not long established, which do not belong to the Roman Curia in a strict sense but nevertheless provide useful or necessary services to the Supreme Pontiff himself, to the Curia and the whole Church, and are in some way connected with the Apostolic See.

Art. 187. Among such institutes are the Vatican Secret Archives, where documents of the Church's governance are preserved first of all so that they may be available to the Holy See itself and to the Curia as they carry out their own work, but then also, by papal permission, so that they may be available to everyone engaged in historical research and serve as a source of information on all areas of secular history that have been closely connected with the life of the Church in centuries gone by.

Art. 188. In the Vatican Apostolic Library, established by the Supreme Pontiffs, the Church has a remarkable instrument for fostering, guarding, and spreading culture. In its various sections, it offers to scholars researching truth a treasure of every kind of art and knowledge.

Art. 184. A Cardinali Secretario Status, audita commissione stabiliter ad hoc constituta, candidati in Albo inscribi possunt, qui congrua praeparatione, aptis titulis academicis comprobata, simulque vitae christianae exemplo, morum honestate ac rerum agendarum peritia commendentur. Quibus requisitis forte postea deficientibus, ex Albo expungendi sunt.

Art. 185. §1. Ex Advocatis praesertim in Albo adscriptis Corpus Sanctae Sedis Advocatorum constituitur, qui patrocinium causarum, nomine Sanctae Sedis vel Curiae Romanae Dicasteriorum, apud ecclesiastica vel civilia tribunalia suscipere valent.

§2. A Cardinali Secretario Status, audita commissione, de qua in art. 184, ad quinquennium nominantur; graves tamen ob causas, a munere removeri possunt. Expleto septuagesimo quinto aetatis anno, a munere cessant.

IX. INSTITUTIONES SANCTAE SEDI ADHAERENTES

Art. 186. Sunt Instituta quaedam, sive antiquae originis sive novae constitutionis, quae, quamvis ad Curiam Romanam sensu proprio non pertineant, nihilominus ipsi Summo Pontifici, Curiae et Ecclesiae universae servitia necessaria aut utilia praestant et cum Apostolica Sede aliquo modo cohaerent.

Art. 187. Inter huiusmodi Instituta eminet Tabularium seu Archivum Secretum Vaticanum, in quo documenta regiminis Ecclesiae adservantur, ut imprimis ipsi Sanctae Sedi et Curiae in proprio opere perficiendo praesto sunt deinde vero, ex ipsa concessione Pontificia, omnibus historiae explorandae studiosis, atque fontes cognitionis evadere possint omnium historiae profanae quoque regionum, quae cum vita Ecclesiae saeculis praeteritis arcte cohaerent.

Art. 188. Instrumentum insuper insigne Ecclesiae ad culturam fovendam, servandam, divulgandam a Summis Pontificibus constituta est Bibliotheca Apostolica Vaticana, quae thesauros omne genus scientiae et artis in suis variis sectionibus viris doctis veritatem investigantibus praebet.

Art. 189. To seek the truth and to spread it in the various areas of divine and human sciences there have arisen within the Roman Church various academies, as they are called, outstanding among which is the Pontifical Academy of Sciences.

Art. 190. In their constitution and administration, all these institutions of the Roman Church are governed by their own laws.

Art. 191. Of more recent origin, though partly based on examples of the past, are the Vatican Polyglot Press; the Vatican Publishing House and its bookstore; the daily, weekly and monthly newspapers, among which *L'Osservatore Romano* stands out; Vatican Radio; the Vatican Television Centre. These institutes, according to their own regulations, come within the competence of the Secretariat of State or of other agencies of the Roman Curia.

Art. 192. The Fabric of Saint Peter's deals, according to its own regulations, with matters concerning the Basilica of the Prince of the Apostles, with respect to the preservation and decoration of the building and behaviour among the employees and pilgrims who come into the church. Where necessary, the superiors of the Fabric act in harmony with the Chapter of that basilica.

Art. 193. The Office of Papal Charities carries on the work of aid of the Supreme Pontiff toward the poor and is subject directly to him.

We decree the present Apostolic Constitution to be firm, valid, and effective now and henceforth, that it shall receive its full and integral effects from the first day of the month of March of 1989, and that it must in each and everything and in any manner whatsoever be fully observed by all those to whom it applies or in any way shall apply, anything to the contrary notwithstanding, even if it is worthy of most special mention.

Given in Rome, at Saint Peter's, in the presence of the cardinals assembled in consistory, on the vigil of the solemnity of the Holy Apostles Peter and Paul, 28 June in the Marian Year 1988, the tenth of Our pontificate.

John Paul II

Art. 189. Ad veritatem inquirendam et diffundendam in variis scientiae divinae et humanae regionibus ortae sunt in sinu Ecclesiae Romanae variae, quae vocantur, Academiae, inter quas eminet Scientiarum Academia Pontificia.

Art. 190. Hae omnes Institutiones Ecclesiae Romanae reguntur propriis legibus constitutionis et administrationis.

Art. 191. Recentioris originis sunt, quamvis ex parte exemplis praeteritis inhaereant, Typographia Polyglotta Vaticana, Officina libraria editoria Vaticana, Ephemerides diurnae, hebdomadariae, menstruae, inter quas eminet *L'Osservatore Romano*, Statio Radiophonica Vaticana et Centrum Televisificum Vaticanum. Haec Instituta subiciuntur Secretariae Status aut aliis Curiae Romanae officiis iuxta proprias leges.

Art. 192. Fabrica Sancti Petri curare perget ea quae ad Basilicam Principis Apostolorum pertinent sive quoad conservationem et decorem aedificii sive quoad disciplinam internam custodum et peregrinorum, qui visendi causa templum ingrediuntur, iuxta proprias leges. In omnibus, quae id exigunt, Superiores Fabricae concorditer agant cum Capitulo eiusdem Basilicae.

Art. 193. Eleemosynaria Apostolica opus adiumenti pro Summo Pontifice exercet erga pauperes ac pendet directe ex Ipso.

Decernimus praesentem Constitutionem apostolicam firmam, validam et efficacem esse ac fore, suosque plenos et integros effectus sortiri atque obtinere a die 1 mensis Martii 1989 et ab illis ad quos spectat aut quomodolibet spectabit in omnibus et per omnia plenissime observari, contrariis quibusvis, etiam specialissima mentione dignis, non obstantibus.

Datum Romae, apud Sanctum Petrum, coram Patribus Cardinalibus in Consistorio adunatis, in pervigilio sollemnitatis Sanctorum Apostolorum Petri et Pauli, die XXVIII mensis Iunii Anno Mariali MCMLXXXVIII, Pontificatus Nostri decimo.

Ioannes Paulus PP. II

APPENDIX I

The Pastoral Significance of the Visit
ad limina Apostolorum

(cf. arts. 28–32)

That pastoral ideal which occupied the dominant place in the drafting of the Apostolic Constitution on the Roman Curia, has had the effect of attributing greater significance to visits *ad limina Apostolorum* by bishops, bringing a more adequate light to bear on the pastoral importance which the visits have gained in the present life of the Church.

1. These visits, as we know, take place when the bishops, joined as they are to the Apostolic See with the bond of communion and presiding in charity and service over the particular Churches throughout the world, set out at certain appointed times for Rome to visit the tombs of the Apostles.

On the one hand, these visits give the bishops an opportunity to sharpen their awareness of their responsibilities as successors of the Apostles and to feel more intensely their sense of hierarchical communion with the successor of Peter. On the other hand, the visits in some way constitute the highest and most central point in that universal ministry that the Holy Father is carrying out when he embraces his brother bishops, the pastors of the particular Churches, and takes up with them the business of sustaining their mission in the Church.

2. These *ad limina* visits bring into full view this movement or life-blood between the particular Churches and the Church as a whole that theologians call *perichoresis*. The process may be compared to the diastolic-systolic movements within the human body when the blood is carried to the outer limbs and from there flows back to the heart.

Some trace and example of a first *ad limina* visit is found in Paul's letter to the Galatians, in which the Apostle tells the story of his conversion and the journey he undertook among the pagans. Although he knew that he had been called and instructed personally by Christ who had conquered death, he wrote these words: "[Then] did I go up to Jerusalem to meet Cephas. I stayed fifteen days with him" (Gal 1:18). "It was not until fourteen years later that I travelled up to Jerusalem again [. . .] I expounded the whole gospel that I preach the gentiles, to make quite sure

ADNEXUM I

De pastorali momento Visitationis
«ad limina Apostolorum»,

de qua in articulis a 28 ad 32

Pastoralis illa ratio, quae in recognoscenda Apostolica Constitutione de Curia Romana primas partes habuit, id etiam effecit, ut Episcoporum Visitationi «ad limina Apostolorum» maior usque significatio attribueretur, eiusque pastorale momentum aptiore in lumine collocaretur, quod in Ecclesiae vita nostro tempore hae Visitationes consecutae sunt.

1. Sicuti cognitum est, ipsae fiunt, cum omnes Episcopi, qui, cum Apostolica Sede communionis vinculo coniuncti, per terrarum orbem Ecclesiis particularibus in caritate atque in ministerio praesunt, Romam ad Apostolorum limina visitanda statis temporibus petunt.

Ipsae enim Visitationes hinc occasionem praebent Episcopis officiorum suorum conscientiam, qua utpote Apostolorum successores premuntur, augendi et hierarchicae communionis cum Petri successore sensum alendi; hinc centrum et quodammodo caput universalis illius ministerii constituunt, quod Beatissimus Pater exercet, cum particularium Ecclesiarum Pastores, suos in episcopatu fratres, complectitur, cum iisque de rebus agit, quae ad ipsorum ecclesialem missionem sustinendam attinent.

2. Per Visitationes «ad limina» motus ille vel vitalis cursus, inter universam Ecclesiam atque particulares Ecclesias intercedens, fit aliquomodo adspectabilis, qui a theologis definitur veluti quaedam *perichoresis*, vel motibus comparatur, quibus humani corporis sanguis a corde ad extrema usque membra dilatatur atque ab istis ad cor refluit.

Primae cuiusdam Visitationis «ad limina» vestigium atque exemplar in Pauli epistola ad Galatas invenitur, in qua Apostolus suam conversionem atque iter ad paganos a se susceptum narrat, haec verba scribens, etiamsi ipse sciebat se a Christo mortis victore immediate vocatum atque edoctum esse: «Deinde . . . veni Hierosolymam videre Petrum, et mansi apud eum diebus quindecim» (1, 18); «deinde post annos quattuordecim iterum ascendi Hierosolymam . . .

that the efforts I was making and had already made should not be fruitless" (Gal 2: 1–2).

3. The natural result of this meeting with Peter's successor, first guardian of the deposit of truth passed on by the Apostles, is to strengthen unity in the same faith, hope and charity, and more and more to recognize and treasure that immense heritage of spiritual and moral wealth that the whole Church, joined with the bishop of Rome by the bond of communion, has spread throughout the world.

During the *ad limina* visit, two men stand face to face together, namely the bishop of a certain particular Church and the bishop of Rome, who is also the successor of Peter. Both carry on their shoulders the burden of office, which they cannot relieve themselves from, but they are not at all divided one from the other, for both of them in their own way represent, and must represent, the sum total of the faithful, the whole of the Church, and the sum total of the bishops, which together constitute the only "we and us" in the body of Christ. It is in their communion that the faithful under their care communicate with one another, and likewise the universal Church and particular Churches communicate with each other.

4. For all these reasons, the *ad limina* visits express *that pastoral solicitude* which thrives in the universal Church. Here we see the meeting of the pastors of the Church, joined together in a collegial unity that is based on apostolic succession. In this College, each and every one of the bishops displays that solicitude of Jesus Christ, the Good Shepherd, which all have received by way of inheritance.

This indeed is the highest ideal of the apostolate that has to be carried out in the Church and which concerns the bishops together with the successor of Peter. For each one of them stands at the centre of all the apostolate, in all its forms, that is carried out in each particular Church, joined at the same time in the universal dimension of the Church as a whole. All this apostolate, again in all its forms, demands and includes the work and help of all those who are building the Body of Christ in the Church, be it universal or particular: the priests, men and women religious consecrated to God, and the laypeople.

et contuli cum illis evangelium, quod praedico in gentibus . . . ne forte in vacuum currerem aut cucurrissem» (2, 2).

3. Congressio cum Petri successore, qui veritatis depositum ab Apostolis traditum primus custodit, eo tendit, ut unitas in eadem fide, spe et caritate confirmetur, atque immensum illud spiritualium moraliumque bonorum patrimonium magis magisque cognoscatur atque existimetur, quod universa Ecclesia, cum Romano Episcopo communionis vinculo coniuncta, per terrarum orbem diffudit.

Dum Visitatio «ad limina» agitur, duo coram inter se congrediuntur viri, scilicet Ecclesiae cuiusdam particularis Episcopus atque Romae Episcopus idemque Petri successor, qui ambo suorum officiorum onus, cui derogari non licet, sustinent, sed alter ab altero minime seiunguntur: ambo enim proprio modo repraesentant, atque repraesentare debent, summam Ecclesiae, summam fidelium, summamque Episcoporum, quae quodammodo unicum «nos» in Christi corpore constituunt. In ipsorum enim communione fideles ipsis concrediti inter se communicant, atque universalis Ecclesia Ecclesiaeque particulares inter se pariter communicant.

4. Hasce omnes ob causas, Visitationes «ad limina» *pastoralem illam sollicitudinem* exprimunt, quae in universali viget Ecclesia. Agitur enim de Ecclesiae Pastorum congressione, qui collegiali unitate, in Apostolorum successione fundata, inter se uniuntur. Nam in hoc Collegio omnes et singuli Episcopi ipsius Iesu Christi, Pastoris boni, sollicitudinem manifestant, quam hereditate quadam acceperunt.

Hic sane consistit summa apostolatus ratio, qui in Ecclesia agendus est, quique ad Episcopos una cum Petri Successore maxime pertinet. Etenim unusquisque eorum centrum totius apostolatus, undequaque absoluti, constituit, qui in singulis Ecclesiis particularibus exercetur, cum universali Ecclesiae amplitudine coniunctis. Totus huiusmodi apostolatus, undequaque absolutus, omnium eorum operam atque adiumentum postulat atque complectitur, qui in Ecclesia sive universali sive particulari Christi corpus aedificant, nempe: presbyterorum, religiosorum virorum ac mulierum Deo consecratarum, atque laicorum.

5. Now if the *ad limina* visits are conceived and viewed in this way, they come to be a *specific moment of that communion* which so profoundly determines the nature and essence of the Church, as it was admirably indicated in the Dogmatic Constitution on the Church, especially in chapters II and III. Given that society nowadays is leaning towards a closer sense of communion, and the Church experiences herself as "a sign and instrument [. . .] of communion with God and of unity among the whole of humankind," (*Lumen gentium*, 1) it seems utterly necessary that a permanent communication between particular Churches and the Apostolic See should be promoted and built up, especially by sharing pastoral solicitude regarding questions, experiences, problems, projects and ideas about life and action.

When pastors converge on Rome and meet together, there comes to pass a remarkable and most beautiful sharing of gifts from among all those riches in the Church, be they universal or local and particular, in accordance with that principle of catholicity by which "each part contributes its own gifts to other parts and to the whole Church, so that the whole and each of the parts are strengthened by the common sharing of all things and by the common effort to attain to fullness in unity." (*Lumen gentium*, 13)

Furthermore and in the same way, *ad limina* visits aim not only at a direct sharing of information but also and especially to an increase and strengthening of a *collegial structure* in the body of the Church, bringing about a remarkable unity in variety.

This communication in the Church is a two-way movement. On the one hand, the bishops converge towards the centre and the visible foundation of unity. We are referring to that unity which, when it comes to full bloom, casts its benefits on their own groupings or conferences, through each pastor's responsibilities and awareness of his functions and of their fulfilment, or through the *collegial spirit* of all the pastors. On the other hand, there is the commission "which the Lord confided to Peter alone, as the first of the apostles" (*Lumen gentium*, 20) which serves the ecclesial community and the spread of her mission, in such a way that nothing is left untried that may lead to the advancement and preservation of the unity of the faith and the common discipline of the whole Church, and all become

5. Quodsi Visitationes «ad limina» singulari hac ratione considerantur, eae fiunt etiam *peculiare momentum illius communionis,* quae Ecclesiae naturam atque essentiam tam alte confingit, sicut Constitutio dogmatica de Ecclesia optime significavit, praesertim in capitibus II et III. Dum enim hodierno tempore et hominum societas ad mutuam solidioremque communionem inclinatur, et Ecclesia sentit se esse «signum et instrumentum intimae cum Deo unionis totiusque generis humani unitatis» (*Lumen gentium,* 1), prorsus necessarium videtur ut continens communicatio inter particulares Ecclesias et Apostolicam Sedem promoveatur atque augeatur, praesertim per pastoralem sollicitudinem inter se participandam quoad quaestiones, rerum usum, problemata proposita atque navitatis vitaeque consilia.

Quando Pastores Romam conveniunt et inter se congrediuntur, peculiaris ac pulcherrima donorum communicatio fit inter omnia bona quae sive particularia atque localia sive universalia in Ecclesia sunt, secundum illius catholicitatis principium, vi cuius «singulae partes propria dona ceteris partibus et toti Ecclesiae afferunt, ita ut totum et singulae partes augeantur ex omnibus invicem communicantibus et ad plenitudinem in unitate conspirantibus» (*Lumen gentium,* 13).

Eadem pariter ratione Visitationes «ad limina» eo tendunt non modo ut nuntia invicem directo tradantur atque recipiantur sed praesertim etiam ut *collegialis conformatio* in Ecclesiae corpore augescat ac solidetur, per quam peculiaris unitas in varietate efficitur.

Huius autem ecclesialis communicationis motus est duplex. Hinc Episcopi versus centrum et adspectabile unitatis fundamentum coëunt: illam dicimus unitatem, quae sive per uniuscuiusque Pastoris officia et muneris conscientiam atque exercitium, sive per *collegialem* omnium Pastorum *affectum,* in proprios coetus vel Conferentias efflorescit; hinc munus habetur «a Domino singulariter Petro, primo Apostolorum, concessum» (*Lumen gentium,* 20), quod ecclesiali communitati atque missionali propagationi inservit, ita ut nil inexpertum relinquatur quod ad fidei unitatem et communem universae Ecclesiae disciplinam provehendam atque custodien-

more and more aware that the responsibility of proclaiming the Gospel everywhere throughout the world falls chiefly on the body of the pastors.

6. From all the principles established above to describe this most important process, one may deduce in what way that apostolic custom of "seeing Peter" is to be understood and put into practice.

First of all the *ad limina* visit has a *sacred meaning* in that the bishops with religious veneration pay a visit to the tombs of Peter and Paul, the Princes of the Apostles, shepherds and pillars of the Church of Rome.

Then the *ad limina* visit has a *personal meaning* because each individual bishop meets the successor of Peter and talks to him *face to face.*

Finally, the visit has a *curial meaning,* that is, a *hallmark of community,* because the bishops enter into conversation with the moderators of the dicasteries, councils, and offices of the Roman Curia. The Curia, after all, is a certain "community" that is closely joined with the Roman Pontiff in that area of the Petrine ministry which involves solicitude for all the Churches (cf. 2 Cor 11:28).

In the course of the *ad limina* visit, the access that the bishops have to the dicasteries is of a two-fold nature:

—First, it gives them access to each individual agency of the Roman Curia, especially to questions that the agencies are dealing with directly according to their competence, questions that have been referred by law to those agencies because of their expertise and experience.

—Second, bishops coming from all over the world, where each of the particular Churches can be found, are introduced to questions of common pastoral solicitude for the universal Church.

Bearing in mind this specific point of view, the Congregation for Bishops, in consultation with the other interested Congregations, is preparing a "Directory" for publication so that the *ad limina* visits can receive long- and short-term preparation and thus proceed smoothly.

7. Each and every bishop—by the very nature of that

dam conducat, pariterque ut omnes magis magisque conscii fiant, Evangelii ubique terrarum nuntiandi curam in Pastorum corpus potissimum recidere.

6. Ex omnibus principiis, quae supra statuta sunt ad huiusmodi maximi ponderis rerum ordinem describendum, plane deducitur qua ratione apostolicus ille mos «videndi Petrum» intellegatur atque in rem deducatur oporteat.

Primum enim Visitatio «ad limina» *sacram significationem* accipit, dum Sanctorum Petri et Pauli, Apostolorum Principum, Romanae Ecclesiae pastorum atque columnarum, sepulcra ab Episcopis invisuntur ac veneratione coluntur.

Deinde Visitatio «ad limina» *significationem personalem* indicat, quoniam singuli Episcopi cum Petri successore congrediuntur atque *os ad os* cum illo loquuntur.

Denique *significatio curialis,* id est *communitatis notam* prae se ferens habetur, cum Episcopi etiam apud Romanae Curia Dicasteria, Consilia et Officia in colloquium cum eorum Moderatoribus veniunt, quandoquidem Curia quandam efficit «communitatem», quae cum Romano Pontifice arctius coniungitur in ministerii Petriani regione, quae sollicitudinem omnium Ecclesiarum (cf. 2 *Cor* 11, 28) respicit.

Aditus, quem Episcopi ad Dicasteria habent, dum Visitationem «ad limina» agunt, duplici ratione notantur:

— ipsis accessus praebetur ad singulas Romanae Curiae compages, immo ad quaestiones, quas illae directo tractant secundum singulas cuiusque rerum provincias, quae illarum iuri tributae sunt, propria adhibita peritia atque exercitatione;

— Episcopi praeterea totius terrarum orbis ambitu, in quo singulae Ecclesiae particulares exstant, in communis pastoralis sollicitudinis quaestiones introducuntur, quae universalem Ecclesiam respiciunt.

Specialem huiusmodi rerum conspectum prae oculis habens Congregatio pro Episcopis, collatis consiliis cum Congregationibus, ad quas id etiam pertinet, «Directorium» edendum curat, per quod Visitationes «ad limina» sive quoad praeteritum sive quoad proximum tempus apte accomodeque apparentur atque procedant.

7. Singuli Episcopi. ratione et vi naturae il-

"ministry" that has been entrusted to him—is called and invited to visit the "tombs of the Apostles" at certain appointed times.

However, since the bishops living within each territory, nation or region, have already gathered together and now form conferences of bishops—collegial unions with an excellent, broad theoretical basis (cf. *Lumen gentium,* 23)—it is highly appropriate that the *ad limina* visits should proceed according to this collegial principle, for that carries much significance within the Church.

The institutes of the Apostolic See, and especially the nunciatures and apostolic delegations as well as the dicasteries of the Roman Curia, are most willing to offer assistance in order to ensure that *ad limina* visits be made possible, are suitably prepared and proceed well.

To sum up: the institution of the *ad limina* visit is an instrument of the utmost value, commanding respect because it is an ancient custom and has outstanding pastoral importance. Truly, these visits express the catholicity of the Church and the unity and communion of the College of Bishops, qualities rooted in the successor of Peter and signified by those holy places where the Princes of the Apostles underwent martyrdom, qualities of a theological, pastoral, social, and religious import known to all.

This institution therefore is to be favored and promoted in every possible way, especially at this moment of the history of salvation in which the teachings and magisterium of the Second Vatican Ecumenical Council shine out with ever brighter light.

APPENDIX II

The Collaborators of the Apostolic See as a Work Community

(cf. arts. 33–36)

1. The principal feature characterizing the revision of the Apostolic Constitution *Regimini Ecclesiae universae,* so that it might be adapted to the needs that arose after its promulgation, was certainly to emphasize the pastoral nature of the Roman Curia. Viewed in this way, the true char-

lius «ministerii» ipsis commissi. vocantur atque invitantur ut «limina Apostolorum» statis temporibus visitent.

Quoniam autem Episcopi in singulis territoriis, nationibus vel regionibus degentes iam sese simul collegerunt atque Episcopales Conferentias nunc constituunt. quae collegialis unio peramplis optimisque rationibus fundatur (cf. *Lumen gentium,* 23). maximopere congruit ut Visitationes «ad limina» secundum huiusmodi collegiale principium procedant: id enim eloquentissimam sane ecclesialem significationem praebet.

Singula quaeque Apostolicae Sedis instituta, ac praesertim Nuntiaturae ac Delegationes Apostolicae, praeter Romanae Curiae Dicasteria, parata sunt adiutricem operam libentissime navare, ut Visitationes «ad limina» facile habeantur, apte comparentur et bene procedant.

Etenim, ut omnia pressius comprehendamus, quae supra explicata sunt, Visitationis «ad limina» institutum, auctoritate sane grave ob moris antiquitatem atque ob praeclarum pastorale momentum, summae utilitatis instrumentum est, per quod sive Ecclesiae catholicitas sive Episcoporum Collegii unitas atque communio, in Petri successore fundatae, atque per illa sanctissima loca, in quibus Apostolorum Principes martyrium subierunt, significatae, re et veritate exprimuntur; quarum theologicum, pastorale, sociale religiosumquc pondus nemo est qui ignoret.

Idem propterea institutum summis viribus praedicandum atque fovendum est, praesertim hoc historiae salutis tempore, quo Concilii Oecumenici Vaticani II doctrina et magisterium maiore usque lumine splendent.

ADNEXUM II

De Apostolicae Sedis adiutoribus uti Laboris Communitate

de qua in articulis a 33 ad 36

1. Praecipua nota, cuius gratia Constitutio Apostolica a verbis incipiens *Regimini Ecclesiae universae* recognita est, ut necessitatibus accommodaretur, quae post ipsam promulgatam exortae erant, haec sane fuit: scilicet ut pastoralis

acter of the functions fulfilled in the midst, as it were, of the Apostolic See shines bright and clear, so that they provide the Supreme Pontiff with suitable instruments to carry out the mission entrusted to him by Christ Our Lord.

Through that unique ministry which he offers to the Church, the Supreme Pontiff strengthens his brothers in the faith (Lk 22:32)—the pastors, namely, and the Christian faithful of the universal Church—looking only to nourish and guard that Church communion in which "there are also particular Churches that retain their own traditions, without prejudice to the Chair of Peter which presides over the whole assembly of charity (cf. S. Ignatius M., *Ad Rom.*, pref., Funk, I, p. 252), and protects their legitimate variety and at the same time keeps watch to ensure that individual differences, so far from being harmful to unity, actually serve its cause." (*Lumen gentium*, 13)

2. By constant toil, this Petrine ministry reaches out to the whole world and claims the help of persons and other means throughout the Church. Help it does receive in a direct and privileged manner from all those who are called to perform various functions in the Roman Curia and in the various institutions which compose the structure of the Holy See, be they in holy orders as bishops and priests, or men and women consecrated to God in the religious families and secular institutes, or Christian lay men and women.

Out of this diversity emerge certain quite remarkable contours and the considerable importance of these duties, which have absolutely no equivalent at any other level of civil society, with which by its very nature indeed the Roman Curia cannot be compared. On this foundation stands that leading idea of the work community constituted by all those who, being well nourished with the one and the same faith and charity and "united, heart and soul" (Acts 4:32), make up those structures of collaboration just mentioned. Therefore those who under whatever title and in any manner help in the universal mission of the Supreme Pontiff to foster the Church community, have a further call to set up a communion of purpose, of undertakings, and of rules of behaviour, that deserves the name of *community* more than does any other form of grouping.

Curiae Romanae natura aequo in lumine collocaretur, atque ex hoc rerum prospectu propria niteret indoles illorum munerum, quae in Apostolica Sede veluti in proprio centro versantur ut eadem apta instrumenta praebeant ad Summi Pontificis missionem, ipsi a Christo Domino concreditam, exercendam.

Per illud enim ministerium, quod Summus Pontifex Ecclesiae praestat, fratres in fide Ipse confirmat (cfr. *Lc* 22, 32), scilicet Pastores et Christi fideles universalis Ecclesiae, ad id unice spectans ut ecclesiastica communio alatur atque protegatur: illam dicimus communionem, in qua «legitime adsunt Ecclesiae particulares, propriis traditionibus fruentes, integro manente primatu Petri Cathedrae, quae universo caritatis coetui praesidet[36], legitimas varietates tuetur et simul invigilat ut particularia, nedum unitati noceant, ei potius inserviant» (cfr. S. Ignatii M. *Ad Rom.*, Praef.: Funk, I, p. 252), (*Lumen Gentium*, 13).

2. Huic ministerio Petriano, quod in universum terrarum orbem assiduo labore protenditur, atque hominum et instrumentorum opem in tota Ecclesia requirit, adiutricem operam directa, immo nobiliore ratione ii omnes praestant, qui, variis muneribus addicti, in Romana Curia necnon in variis institutis adlaborant, quibus Apostolicae Sedis compositio ad agendum formatur: sive in episcopali vel in sacerdotali ordine constituti, sive qua Religiosarum Familiarum atque Institutorum Saecularium Deo consecrati viri et mulieres, sive utpote fideles utriusque sexus e laicorum ordine ad haec officia exercenda vocati.

Quam ob rem huiusmodi compositione peculiaria quaedam rerum lineamenta et grave officiorum momentum exoriuntur, quae nil prorsus aequale habent in ullo alio civilis societatis ambitu, cum qua Romana Curia suapte natura omnimodo comparari nequit: hic propterea principalis innititur ratio illius laboris communitatis ab iis omnibus constitutae, qui, una eademque fide caritateque nutriti veluti «cor unum et anima una» (*Act* 4, 32), illas memoratas adiutricis operae conformationes efficiunt. Ii igitur qui cooperando Romano Pontifici ecclesialem communitatem promoventi universalem Eius missionem quovis titulo vel modo adiuvant, etiam ad consiliorum propositorumque consuetudinem atque

3. The letter of Pope John Paul II of 20 November 1982 on the meaning of work performed for the Apostolic See, took pains to elaborate on the characteristics of this work community. The letter outlined its nature, unique and yet endowed with a variety of functions. All those who share in the "single, incessant activity of the Apostolic See," (n. 1); become in some way brothers. From this consideration the letter went on to conclude that those who shared in this work should be aware "of that specific character of their positions. In any case, such a consciousness has ever been the tradition and pride of those who have chosen to dedicate themselves to that noble service." *(ib.).* The letter adds: "This consideration applies to clerics and religious and to laity as well; both to those who occupy posts of high responsibility and to office and manual workers to whom auxiliary functions are assigned" *(ib.).*

The same letter points out the special nature of the Apostolic See, which, to preserve the exercise of spiritual freedom and its true and visible immunity, (cfr. n. 2) constitutes a sovereign State in its own right and yet "does not possess all ordinary characteristics of a political community," *(ib.)* different from all others. The practical results of this condition are seen in the operation of its affairs, especially as regards its economic organization. In the Apostolic See there is a total absence of a taxation system that other states have by right, and it has no economic activity producing goods and income. The "prime basis of sustenance of the Apostolic See is the spontaneous offerings" *(ib.),* by reason of a certain universal interdependence emanating from the Catholic family and elsewhere, which to a marvellous degree expresses that communion of charity over which the Apostolic See presides in the world and by which it lives.

From this basic condition flow certain consequences on the practical level and in the behaviour among the staff of the Holy See—"the spirit of thrift," "a readiness always to take account of the real but limited financial possibilities of the Holy See and their source," "a profound trust in Providence." (cfn. n. 3) And, over and above all these qualities, "those who work for the Holy See must therefore

vitae normarum constabiliendam communionem vocantur, cui *communitatis* appellatio melius quam ceteris omnibus consortionibus competit.

3. Epistula Summi Pontificis Ioannis Pauli II de laboris significatione, qui Apostolicae Sedi praebetur, die xx mensis Novembris MCM-LXXXII in huiusmodi laboris communitatis proprietatibus illustrandis immorata est. Eius unicam, at diversis muneribus praeditam delineavit naturam, per quam ii omnes hac ratione efficiuntur quodammodo fratres, qui «unicam et continuam participant actionem Apostolicae Sedis» (n. 1); ex hac vero consideratione illata est necessitas, ut istiusmodi laboris participes conscii sint «huius peculiaris indolis munium suorum; quae conscientia ceteroqui sollemne semper fuit et laus iis, qui nobili huic servitio se dedere voluerunt» *(ib.).* Epistula insuper addidit: «Haec animadversio tum ecclesiasticos, tum religiosos et laicos contingit; tum qui partes magnae rationis agunt, tum officiales et operosis artibus destinatos, quibus ministeria auxiliaria delegantur»[41].

Illic pariter propria commemorata est natura Sedis Apostolicae, quae, etsi Civitatem sui iuris constituit ut spiritualis eiusdem Sanctae Sedis libertatis exercitium ipsiusque vera et visibilis immunitas (cfn. n. 2) serventur, est «Status nulli alii Civitatum formae comparandus»[43], ab iisque diversus; atque huiusmodi condicionis delineati sunt in rerum ordine exitus, praesertim ad oeconomicam rationem quod attinet: etenim Apostolicae Sedi omnino desunt sive tributa, quae ex aliorum Civitatum iuribus manant, sive nummaria navitas reditus bonaque producens. Quam ob causam fit ut «caput primarium sustentationis Sedis Apostolicae efficiatur *ex donationibus voluntariis*» *(ib.),* ratione universalis cuiusdam necessitudinis a catholicorum hominum familia, immo aliunde etiam exhibitae, quae illam caritatis communionem mirum in modum exprimit, cui Apostolica Sedes in mundo praesidet et ex qua vivit.

Ex hac condicione quaedam consequuntur in rerum usu et in cotidiana agendi ratione eorum, qui cum Sancta Sede adiutricem operam coniungunt: nempe «spiritus parsimoniae»[45], «studium semper animadvertendi veram atque eximiam rationem nummariam eiusdem Sedis Apostolicae necnon nummariae rei originem»,

have the profound conviction that their work above all entails an ecclesial responsibility to live in a spirit of authentic faith, and that the juridical-administrative aspects of their relationship with the Apostolic See stand in a particular light" (n.5).

4. The remuneration owed to the clerical and lay staff at the Holy See, according to their personal conditions of life, is regulated by the major principles of the social teachings of the Church, which have been made quite clear by the magisterium of the Popes from the time of the publication of Leo XIII's Encyclical Letter *Rerum novarum* up to John Paul II's Encyclicals *Laborem exercens* and *Sollicitudo rei socialis.*

While labouring under a grave lack of economic means, the Holy See makes every effort to measure up to the heavy obligations to which it is held with regard to its workers—even granting them certain benefit packages—but subject to that basic situation which is peculiar to the Apostolic See and has been explained in the Pope's Letter, the fact, namely, that the Holy See cannot be compared to any other form of State, since it is deprived of the ordinary means of generating income, except the income that comes from universal charity. However the Holy See is conscious of the fact—and the same Apostolic Letter makes this clear—that the active cooperation of everybody, and especially of the lay members of the staff, is necessary so that regulations and interrelations may be protected, as well as those *rights and duties* that arise out of "social justice" when it is correctly applied to the relations between worker and employer. (cfr. n. 4). On this subject, the Apostolic Letter has pointed out the help that workers associations can give in this respect, like the "Associazione Dipendenti Laici Vaticani," recently founded through productive talks among the various administrative levels to promote the spirit of solicitude and justice. The Apostolic Letter however has cautioned us to beware lest this kind of group distort the leading ideal that must govern the work community of the See of Peter. The letter says: "However, a lapse of this type of organization into the field of extremist conflict and class struggle does not correspond to the Church's social teaching. Nor should such associations have a political character or openly or covertly serve partisan interests or other interests with quite different goals." (n. 4).

«magna Providentia fiducia» (cfr. n. 3): atque, praeter omnes hasce dotes, ii qui «Sanctae Sedi serviunt persuasissimum habere debent laborem suum exigere ecclesialem obligationem vivendi ex spiritu verae fidei, ac partes iuridiciales et ad administrationem pertinentes necessitudinis cum Sede Apostolica, in luce peculiari consistere» (n. 5).

4. Laboris remuneratio, quae Sanctae Sedis cooperatoribus sive ecclesiasticis sive laicis debetur secundum proprias eorum vitae condiciones, principalibus doctrinae socialis Ecclesiae normis regitur, a Summorum Pontificum magisterio absolutissime declaratis, iam inde ab editis Litteris Encyclicis Leonis XIII a verbis *Rerum novarum* incipientibus usque ad Ioannis Pauli II Litteras Encyclicas *Laborem exercens* et *Sollicitudo rei socialis* appellatas.

Sancta Sedes, quamquam oeconomicorum bonorum penuria laborat, gravibus oneribus omnimode respondere nititur, quibus erga suos cooperatores tenetur. illis etiam quaedam rei cotidianae beneficia praestando. ratione tamen habita illius condicionis, Apostolicae Sedi propriae et in Summi Pontificis Epistula explanatae, qua ipsa nulli alii Civitatum formae aequanda est, cum communibus facultatibus redituum comparandorum privetur, nisi eorum qui ab universali caritate manant. Attamen Sancta Sedes sibi est conscia. atque eadem Epistula de hoc perspicue agit. actuosam sociam omnium operam, peculiari autem modo laicorum administrorum, necessariam esse ut rationes et normae, *iura atque officia* protegantur, quae ex «iustitia sociali», recte ad rem deducenda, in necessitudinibus operatorem inter et conductorem oriuntur[47]. Ad quae respiciendo, Epistula operam memoravit quam, ad hunc finem spectando, operatorum Societates praestare possunt, sicut «Consociatio Laicorum Vaticanorum Administrorum», tunc temporis recens orta ad sollicitudinis et iustitiae spiritum promovendum per frugiferum inter varios officiorum ordines colloquium. Epistula vero monuit cavendum esse, ne huiusmodi instituta principale consilium detorquerent, quo communitas laboris Petri Sedi praestandi regatur oportet, hisce verbis: «Non est tamen secundum Ecclesiae socialem doctrinam eiusmodi societates ad conflictationem

5. At the same time the Supreme Pontiff declared his firm conviction that associations of this kind—like the one mentioned above—"set forward work problems and develop continuous and constructive dialogue with the competent organisms [and] will not fail to take account in every case of the particular character of the Apostolic See." (n. 4).

Now since the lay staff of Vatican City had very much at heart that there be an ever more suitable fine-tuning of working conditions and of everything touching the labour question, the Supreme Pontiff provided that "suitable executive documents" be prepared "for forthering a work community according to the principles set forth by means of suitable norms and structures" (cfr. *ib.*).

The outcome of the Pope's concern is now "The Labour Office of the Apostolic See" (L.A.A.S.), which is established by an Apostolic Letter given *motu proprio* together with the document specifying in detail the membership of the Labour Office, its authority, its functions, its regulatory and advisory organs as well as its proper norms to facilitate a fair, rapid, and efficient process; furthermore, as it has been just newly set up, this Office needs a reasonable period of time to operate *ad experimentum* so that its regulations and procedures may be confirmed and its true and objective importance reviewed. This *motu proprio* and the regulations of the new Labour Office are being published at the same time, together with the promulgation of the Apostolic Constitution on the renewal of the Roman Curia.

6. The chief purpose of the Labour Office—apart from the practical ends for which it was brought into existence—is to promote and preserve a work community among the various levels of staff of the Apostolic See, especially the laypeople. The spirit of this community should be characteristic of all who have been called to the privilege and responsibility of serving the Petrine ministry.

praeter modum vergere aut ad ordinum inter ipsos dimicationem; nec nota politica insignes esse debent aut servire, aperte vel clam, causae alicuius factionis aut aliorum entium proposita spectantium valde diversae naturae» (n. 4).

5. Eodem autem tempore Summus Pontifex suam certam declaravit fidem, eiusmodi Consociationes—cuiusmodi est illa, quae supra commemorata est—«in ineundis quaestionibus ad laborem pertinentibus et in utiliter atque continuo disserendo cum Institutis competentibus, ante oculos esse habituras quoquo modo peculiarem Sedis Apostolicae naturam» (n. 4).

Quoniam autem laicis Civitatis Vaticanae administris cordi praesertim fuit, ut operum conformatio et omnia ad laboris quaestionem attinentia aptius usque temperarentur, Summus Pontifex disposuit ut «opportuna instrumenta exsecutoria» appararentur «ut, per accommodatas normas et structuras, foveatur profectus communitatis laboris iuxta exposita principia» (cfr. ib.).

Huic Supremi Ecclesiae Pastoris sollicitudini nunc respondet institutio «Officii Laboris apud Apostolicam Sedem» (compendiariis litteris U.l.S.A. appellati), quod per Litteras Apostolicas Motu Proprio datas promulgatur una cum instrumento, quo eiusdem Officii describuntur ac singillatim exponuntur compositio, auctoritas, munera, regendi et consulendi organa cum propriis normis ad aequum, efficacem celeremque ipsius processum fovendum; idem praeterea Officium, cum nunc noviter erectum sit, accommodum navitatis tempus «ad experimentum» exigit, ut sive collata praecepta agendique modi comprobentur, sive eius momentum re et veritate recognoscatur. Quae Apostolicae Litterae Motu Proprio datae atque novi Officii Laboris disciplina simul in vulgus eduntur una cum promulgata Constitutione Apostolica de Curiae Romanae renovatione[51].

6. Laboris Officii praecipuus praevalensque finis—praeter alios, ad quorum assecutionem idem ad rem effectum est—huc potissimum spectat ut in variis adiutorum Sedis Apostolicae ordinibus, laicorum praesertim, illa promoveatur ac servetur laboris communitas, cuius nota omnes insigniri debent, qui ad honorem onusque inserviendi ministerio Petriano vocati sunt.

Again and again it is to be explained that these workers are in duty bound to foster and cultivate within themselves a special awareness of the Church, an awareness making them ever more fitted to fulfill the functions entrusted to them, no matter what these may be. These functions are not mere give and take arrangements—a certain labour given and a certain wage received—, as may happen in institutions in civil society; they constitute rather a service offered to Christ himself "who came not to be served but to serve" (Mt 20:28).

Therefore all the workers of the Holy See, clergy and laity, out of a sense of honour and sincerely conscious of their own duty before God and themselves, must resolve that their lives as priests and lay faithful shall be lived at an exemplary level, as is proposed by God's commandments, by the laws of the Church and by the pronouncements of the Second Vatican Council, especially in *Lumen gentium, Presbyterorum ordinis,* and *Apostolicam actuositatem.* However, this is a free decision, by which with full awareness certain responsibilities are taken on, the force of which is felt not only on the individuals but also on their families and even on the actual work community composed of all the collaborators of the Holy See.

"Well may we be asked 'of whose spirit we are' (cf. Lk 9:55 *Vulg.*)": thus the Pope writes at the end of the Apostolic Letter. So each and all, in searching their own sincerity as human beings and as Christians, are bound to be faithful to those promises, and to keep those bonds that they freely accepted when they were chosen to labour at the Holy See.

7. To keep in view the principles and norms indicated by the Pope in the afore-mentioned Apostolic Letter to the cardinal secretary of state, the full text is printed below. In fact, this document must be considered as the foundation and sign of the whole pattern of interdependence in order to maintain full cooperation and understanding within the work community at the service of the Apostolic See.

Iterum iterumque explicandum est, hosce adiutores ad peculiarem Ecclesiae conscientiam in se ipsis fovendam atque colendam teneri, quae eos ad munera sibi commissa adimplenda, quantacumque sint, aptiores usque reddat: munera dicimus, quae prorsus non sunt cuiusdam dati et accepti rationes, sicut illae, quae cum institutis in civili societate exstantibus intercedere possunt, sed ministerium efficiunt ipsi Christo praebitum, qui «non venit ministrari, sed ministrare» (*Mt* 20, 28).

Omnes ergo Sanctae cooperatores, sive ecclesiastici sive laici, velut ob honoris laudem comparandam, atque sincero animo proprii muneris coram Deo et hominibus conscii, sibi proponere debent ut suam sacerdotum et Christi fidelium vitam in exempli modum agant, sicut a Dei mandatis, ab ecclesiasticis legibus et ab actis Concilii Vaticani II, praesertim illis quae a verbis incipiunt *Lumen gentium, Presbyterorum ordinis* atque *Apostolicam actuositatem,* proponitur. Attamen hoc liberum est consilium, quo plena conscientia quaedam assumuntur onera, quorum momentum non modo in singulos, sed etiam in illorum familias, immo in ipsum laboris communitatis ambitum recidit, quem Sanctae Sedis cooperatores efficiunt.

«Quaerendum nobis est "cuius spiritus simus" (cfr. *Lc* 9, 55 *Vulg.*)»: ita Summus Pontifex in extrema Epistula scribit; ideo singuli atque omnes, propriam qua hominum et qua christianorum sinceritatem quaerendo, tenentur ad illa promissa vinculaque fideliter servanda, quibus libera voluntate obstricti sunt cum ad operam Sanctae Sedi praestandam sunt adlecti.

7. Quo praesentior consiliorum et normarum ratio habeatur, quae Summus Pontifex per memoratem Epistulam, ad Cardinalem a Publicis Ecclesiae negotiis missam, de laboris significatione Apostolicae Sedi praebendi significavit, ipsius integrum exemplum infra editur[52]: ea enim fundamentum et signum habenda est omnis illius necessitudinis, quae intra laboris communitatis ambitum, Apostolicae Sedi adiutricem operam navantis, ad simul agendum atque ad consensionem tuendam habeatur oportet.

LETTER OF THE
SUPREME PONTIFF JOHN PAUL II

The Meaning of Work Performed by
the Apostolic See

Addressed to the Venerable Brother
Agostino Cardinal Casaroli
Secretary of State

1. The Apostolic See, in exercising its mission, has recourse to the valid and precious work of the particular community made up of those men and women, priests, religious and laity who devote their efforts in their dicasteries and offices to the service of the universal Church.

Charges and duties are assigned to the members of this community; each of those charges and duties has its own purpose and dignity, in consideration both of the objective content and value of the work done and of the person who accomplishes it.

This concept of community, applied to those who aid the bishop of Rome in his ministry as pastor of the universal Church, permits us first of all to define the unitary character of functions which are nonetheless diverse among themselves. All persons called to perform them really participate in the single, incessant activity of the Apostolic See; that is, in that "concern for all the Churches" (cf. 2 Cor. 11:28) which enlivened the apostles' service from the earliest times and is the prerogative today in outstanding measure of the successors of St. Peter in the Roman See. It is very important that those who are associated in any way with the Apostolic See's activity should have a consciousness of that specific character of their positions. In any case, such a consciousness has ever been the tradition and pride of those who have chosen to dedicate themselves to that noble service.

This consideration applies to clerics and religious and to laity as well, both to those who hold posts of high responsibility, and to office and manual workers to whom auxiliary functions are assigned. It applies to persons attached to the service of the same Apostolic See more directly, inasmuch as they work in those organisms which are altogether known in fact under the name of "Holy See;" and it applies to those who are in the service of the Vatican City State, which is so closely linked with the Apostolic See.

In the recent Encyclical *Laborem exercens,* I recalled the principal truths of the "gospel of labour" and Catholic doc-

EPISTULA SUMMI PONTIFICIS
IOANNIS PAULI II

De laboris significatione
qui Apostolicae Sedi praebetur

Venerabili Fratri
Augustino S.R.E. Cardinali Casaroli
Status Secretario

1. APOSTOLICA SEDES, in suo munere exercendo, efficaci et perutili opera utitur peculiaris communitatis ex iis constantis—viris et mulieribus, sacerdotibus, religiosis, laicis—qui, in eius dicasteriis et officiis, Ecclesiae universae operam navant.

Huius communitatis membris negotia mandata sunt et munia, quorum quodque suum spectat propositum suamque dignitatem habet, ratione habita tum rerum substantiae momentique explicati laboris, tum personae quae illum exsequitur.

Ex hac communitatis notione adhibita pro iis qui Romanum Episcopum adiuvant in suo Pastoris universalis Ecclesiae ministerio, Nobis licet ante omnia definire unicam in *diversis muneribus naturam.* Omnes enim qui ad haec explenda vocantur, unicam et continuam participant actionem Apostolicae Sedis, eam videlicet «sollicitudinem omnium Ecclesiarum» (cfr. 2 Cor 11, 28), quae inde a priscis temporibus servitium Apostolorum incitabat, quaeque hodie praecipua est praerogativa Successorum Sancti Petri in sede Romana. Multum interest quotquot Sedis Apostolicae operum quoquo modo participes sunt, huius peculiaris indolis munium suorum sibi esse conscios; quae conscientia ceteroqui sollemne semper fuit et laus iis, qui nobili huic servitio se dedere voluerunt.

Haec animadversio tum ecclesiasticos et religiosos tum laicos contingit, tum qui partes magnae rationis agunt, tum officiales et operosis artibus destinatos, quibus ministeria auxiliaria delegantur. Contingit prorsus eos et qui recte proximeque Apostolicae Sedi serviunt, utpote cum suam navent operam apud ea Corpora, cui nomen est «Sancta Sedes», et qui in ministeriis sunt Vaticanae Civitatis, quae Apostolicae Sedi tam arcte coniungitur.

In recentibus Litteris Encyclicis a verbis «Laborem exercens» incipientibus praecipuas

trine on human work, a doctrine always alive in the Church's tradition. There is need for the life of that singular community which operates *sub umbra Petri*—in Peter's shadow—, in such immediate contact with the Apostolic See, to conform itself to these truths.

2. In order to apply these principles to reality, their objective significance must be borne in mind, together with the specific nature of the Apostolic See. This latter does not have the general form of true states even though, as I noted above, the entity described as the Vatican City State is closely linked with it; for true states are subjects of the political sovereignty of particular societies. On the other hand, the Vatican City State is sovereign, yet does not possess all ordinary characteristics of a political community. It is an atypical state. It exists as a fitting means of guaranteeing the exercise of the spiritual liberty of the Apostolic See; that is, as the means of assuring real and visible independence of the same in its activity of government for the sake of the universal Church, as well as of its pastoral work directed toward the whole human race. It does not possess a proper society for the service of which it was established nor does it base itself upon forms of social action which usually determine the structure and organization of every other state. Furthermore, the persons who aid the Apostolic See or even cooperate in government of the Vatican City State are with few exceptions not citizens of this state. Nor, consequently, do they have the rights and duties (those to do with taxation in particular) which ordinarily arise from belonging to a state.

The Apostolic See does not develop nor can it develop economic activity proper to a state, since it transcends the narrow confines of the Vatican City State in a much more important respect and extends its mission to the whole of the earth. Production of economic goods and enrichment by way of revenues are foreign to its institutional purposes. Besides the revenues of the Vatican City State and the limited income afforded by what remains of the funds obtained on the occasion of the Lateran Pacts as indemnity for the Papal States. and ecclesiastical goods passed to the Italian State, the prime basis of sustenance of the Apostolic See is the spontaneous offerings provided by Catholics throughout the world and by other men of good will. This corresponds to a tradition having its origin in the Gospel and the teachings of the apostles. This tradition has taken on various forms over the centuries in relation to the eco-

commemoravimus veritates de «evangelio laboris» deque doctrina catholica ad laborem humanum pertinente, semper sane in Ecclesiae traditions valida. Ad has veritates oportet se conformet peculiaris haec communitas quae *sub umbra Petri* operatur, tam cum Sede Apostolica coniuncte.

2. Ut apte haec principia rebus ipsis inserantur, necesse est reminisci eorum veram significationem et simul *propriam* Sedis Apostolicae *naturam*. Haec—etsi, ut iam supra diximus, ei tam arcte coniungitur ens Vaticanae Civitatis Status dictum—indole caret germanorum Statuum, qui in certas societates publice dominantur. Ceterum Vaticanae Civitatis Status sui iuris est, sed non omnes habet peculiares communitatis politicae notas. Hic Status nulli alii Civitatum formae comparandus est: exsistit enim ut convenienter tueatur Sedis Apostolicae spiritualis libertatis exercitium, id est tamquam instrumentum, quo tuta reddatur eiusdem Sedis vera et visibilis libertas tum in regimine exercendo pro Ecclesia universa, tum etiam in actione pastorali explicanda pro toto genere humano; propriam non habet societatem pro cuius servitio constitutus sit, nec in formis actionis socialis consistit, quae efficiunt plerumque cuiusvis alterius Status structuram et ordinationem. Praeterea, qui Sedem Apostolicam adiuvant, vel Vaticanae Civitatis Status regimini cooperantur, ipsius cives non sunt, perpaucis exceptis, nec igitur iura et onera habent (praesertim vectigalia), quae fere ex eo oriuntur, quod quis in dicione est alicuius Status.

Sedes Apostolica—cum ob valde maioris momenti causas fines angustos transcendat Vaticanae Civitatis Statum, adeo ut in omnem orbem terrarum munus suum extendat—operositatem oeconomicam Status cuiuslibet propriam nec explet nec potest explere; ab eius institutionis proposito et fructus bonorum oeconomicorum et redituum amplificatio excluduntur. Praeter proventus Vaticanae Civitatis Status proprios et exiguos reditus—constantes ex eo quod reliquum est pecuniarum occasions Pactionum Lateranensium obtentarum uti compensationem Statuum Pontificiorum et bonorum ecclesiasticorum, quae Statui Italico obvenerant—caput primarium sustentationis Sedis Apostolicae efficitur *ex donationibus voluntariis catholicorum totius*

nomic structures prevailing in various eras. In conformity with that tradition it must be affirmed that the Apostolic See may and ought to make use of the spontaneous contributions of the faithful and other people of good will, without having recourse to other means which might appear to be less respectful of the character proper to the Apostolic See.

3. The above-mentioned material contributions are the expression of a constant and moving solidarity with the Apostolic See and the activity carried out by it. My profound gratitude goes out to such great solidarity. It ought to be with a sense of responsibility commensurate with the nature of the contributions on the part of the Apostolic See itself, its individual organs and the persons working in them. That is to say that the contributions are to be used solely and always according to the dispositions and will of those offering them: for the general intention which is maintenance of the Apostolic See and the generality of its activities or for particular purposes (missionary, charitable, etc.), when these have been expressly mentioned.

Responsibility and loyalty toward those who show their solidarity with the Apostolic See through their aid and share its pastoral concern in some way are expressed in scrupulous fidelity to all tasks and duties assigned, as well as in the zeal, hard work and professional spirit which ought to distinguish whoever participates in the same Apostolic See's activities. Right intention must likewise be always cultivated, so as to exert watchful administration—in terms of their purposes—over both material goods which are offered and over what is acquired or conserved by means of such goods. This includes safeguarding and enhancing the See of Peter's precious inheritance in the religious-cultural and artistic fields.

In making use of means allocated for these ends, the Apostolic See and those directly collaborating with it must be distinguished not only by a spirit of thrift, but also by readiness always to take account of the real but limited financial possibilities of the Holy See and their source. Obviously such interior dispositions of mind ought to be well assimilated, becoming ingrained in the minds of religious and clerics through their training. But neither should they

mundi et, forte, aliorum hominum bonae voluntatis. Hoc consentaneum est traditioni quae ab Evangelio proficiscitur (cfr. Lc 10, 7) et ab Apostolorum doctrina (cfr. 1 Cor 9, 11. 14). Secundum hanc traditionem—quae multiformis per saecula fuit ad structuras oeconomicas quod attinet diversis temporibus praevalentes—affirmandum est Sedem Apostolicam posse et debere collationibus ultroneis frui fidelium aliorumque hominum bonae voluntatis, cum non oporteat aliis fruatur opibus, quae videri possint eius singulari naturae minus convenientes.

3. *Collationes* quas supra commemoravimus constantem et animum moventem necessitudinem cum Apostolica Sede cumque eius opera significant. Tantae necessitudini, quam gratissimo animo prosequimur, ipsa Apostolica Sedes, singula eius Corpora et qui in his laborant respondere debent officii conscientia exaequata collationum naturae, quae solum et semper adhibendae sunt iuxta intentiones et voluntates largitorum: vel pro proposito generali Sedem Apostolicam eiusque operum summam sustentandi; vel pro specialibus consiliis (missionalibus, beneficis, etc.), cum haec denuntiata sint.

Officii conscientia et probitas erga eos qui, auxilio suo, Sedem Apostolicam adiuvant et quodam modo pastoralem eius sollicitudinem communicant, ostenduntur per integram fidelitatem erga officia et munera delegata, sicut et per diligentiam, sedulitatem et per habitum professionis, unde discernendi sunt quicumque eiusdem Sedis Apostolicae navitatem participant. Oportet insuper recte animatos esse, ut prudenter administrentur, ex iis ad quae spectant, et bona corporea quae offeruntur, et ea omnia quae his bonis illa Sedes comparat vel servat, additis tutela et auctu praestantis hereditatis Sedis Petri in regionibus religioso-culturalibus et artis.

In usu opum haec proposita contingentium, Sedes Apostolica et qui cum ea directe et proxime cooperantur, eminere debent non solum *spiritu parsimoniae*, verum etiam *studio semper animadvertendi* veram atque exiguam rationem nummariam eiusdem Sedis Apostolicae necnon nummariae rei originem. Eiusmodi interiores habitus, ut par est, insiti esse debebunt per eo-

be lacking from the minds of laity who through their free choice accept working for and with the Apostolic See.

Moreover, all those who have particular responsibilities in running organisms, offices and services of the Apostolic See, as well as those employed in various functions, will know how to join this spirit of thrift with constant application to making the various activities ever more effective. This can be done through organization of work based, on the one hand, on full respect for persons and the valid contribution made by each according to his proper abilities and functions and, on the other hand, upon use of appropriate structures and technical means, so that the activity engaged in corresponds more and more to the demands of service to the universal Church. Recourse shall be had to everything that experience, science and technology teach; efforts will be made in this way to use human and financial resources with greater effectiveness by avoiding waste, self-interest and pursuit of unjustified privileges, and at the same time by promoting good human relations in every sector and the true and rightful interests of the Apostolic See.

Along with such commitment should go a profound trust in Providence, which, through the offerings of good people, will not allow a lack of the means to pursue the Apostolic See's proper ends. Should a lack of means impede accomplishment of some fundamental objective, a special appeal may be made to the generosity of the people of God, informing them of needs which are not sufficiently well known. In the normal way, however, it is fitting to be content with what bishops, priests, religious institutes and faithful offer spontaneously, since they themselves can see or discern rightful needs.

4. Many of those working with the Apostolic See are clerics. Since they live in celibacy, they have no families to their charge. They deserve remuneration proportional to the tasks performed and capable of assuring them a decent manner of living and means to carry out the duties of their state, including responsibilities which they may have in certain cases toward parents or other family members dependent on them. Nor should the demands of orderly social relationships be neglected, particularly and above all their obligation to assist the needy. This obligation is more impelling for clerics and religious than for the laity, by reason of their evangelical vocation.

rum aptam formationem, in religiosorum et ecclesiasticorum animis; sed, ne laicis quidem deesse debent, qui libero assensu suo comprobaverunt se cum et pro Sede Apostolica laborare.

Insuper, ii omnes, quibus peculiaria onera iniuncta sunt in regendis Corporibus, officiis et ministeriis Sedis Apostolicae, sicut et variis muneribus addicti, hunc parsimoniae spiritum cum constante cura coniungent ut numerosa negotia efficientiora reddantur per congruam dispositionem laboris, positi hinc in plena observantia personarum et praesentis auxilii, quod quisque fert pro suis facultatibus, et muniis; hinc in usu structurarum et instrumentorum technicorum aptorum, quo opera explicata melius in dies servitii Ecclesiae universae necessitatibus respondeat. Omnia adhibentes quae experientia, scientia et technologia docent, omnes curabunt ut bona humana et nummaria maiore cum efficacia tractentur, profusionem vitando et conquisitionem utilitatum singularium, privilegiorum non excusatorum, simul bonas necessitudines humanas provehendo in omni parte et iustum Sedis Apostolicae commodum.

Ad has curas adiungenda est magna *Providentiae fiducia*, quae per bonorum donationes non sinet opes deficere, quibus Sedis Apostolicae proposita possint obtineri. Si opum penuria impediat quominus aliquod fondamentale consilium ad effectum adducatur, speciali modo compellanda erit munificentia populi Dei, eum certiorem faciendo de non satis notis necessitatibus. Plerumque tamen oportebit acquiescere in iis, quae Episcopi, sacerdotes, Instituta religiosa et fideles sponte offerunt, quoniam ipsi iustas necessitates videre vel perspicere sciunt.

4. Inter eos qui Sedi Apostolicae cooperantur multi sunt ecclesiastici, quibus in caelibatu viventibus impensa pro familiis non est praestanda. Merces ad eos spectat muneribus quae explent conveniens talisque, quae decoram sustentationem provideat et sinat eos status sui officia exsequi simulque iis satisfacere oneribus, quibus interdum gravari possunt, subveniendi videlicet parentibus suis vel aliis propinquis, qui eis sustinendi sunt. Nec neglegenda sunt ea, quae rectus eorum usus socialis postulat, praesertim et ante omnia officium succurrendi indigentibus: quod officium, ob eorum evangeli-

Remuneration of the lay employees of the Apostolic See should also correspond to the tasks performed, taking into consideration at the same time their responsibility to support their families. Study should therefore be devoted, in a spirit of lively concern and justice, to ascertaining their objective material needs and those of their families, including needs regarding education of their children and suitable provision for old age, so as to meet those needs properly. The fundamental guidelines in this sector are to be found in Catholic teaching on remuneration for work. Immediate indications for the evaluation of circumstances can be obtained from examining experiences and programs of the society—in particular, the Italian society—to which almost all lay employees of the Apostolic See belong and in which they at any rate live.

A valid collaborative function may be performed by workers' associations such as the Association of Vatican Lay Employees, which recently came into existence, in promoting that spirit of concern and justice, through representing those working within the Apostolic See. Such associations take on a specific character within the Apostolic See. They are an initiative in conformity with the Church's social teaching, for the Church sees them as one instrument for better assuring social justice in relations between worker and employer. However, a lapse of this type of organization into the field of extremist conflict and class struggle does not correspond to the Church's social teaching. Nor should such associations have a political or openly or covertly serve partisan interests or other interests with quite different goals.

I express confidence that associations such as that now existing and just mentioned will perform a useful function in the work community, operating in solid harmony with the Apostolic See, by taking inspiration from the principles of the Church's social teaching. I am likewise certain that as they set forward work problems and develop continuous and constructive dialogue with the competent organisms they will not fail to take account in every case of the particular character of the Apostolic See, as pointed out in the initial part of this letter.

In relation to what has been expounded, Your Emi-

cam vocationem, magis ecclesiasticos et religiosos impellit, quam laicos.

Merces etiam laicorum, qui Sedi Apostolicae serviunt, consentanea esse debet muniis explicatis, onere simul considerato, ab eis suscepto, sustinendi familias suas. Magnae curae et iustitiae spiritu igitur videndum est quae sint eorum verae materiales necessitates et familiarum, non exceptis iis quae ad filiorum educationem et ad oeconomicam cautionem ad senectuti cavendum pertinent, ut eisdem convenienter consuli possit. Hac in re normae fundamentales in catholica doctrina inveniuntur de *remuneratione laboris*. Normae proximae ad adiuncta iudicanda possunt ex observationis experientiarum et consiliorum civilis societatis depromi, et praesertim societatis Italicae, ex qua conducuntur et in qua, quoquo modo, omnes fere vivunt laici qui Sedi Apostolicae serviunt.

Ad hunc sollicitudinis et iustitiae spiritum fovendum, vice fungentes eorum qui intra Sedem Apostolicam laborant, poterunt suum praestare officium operatorum Societates, sicut Consociatio Laicorum Vaticanorum Administrorum recenter orta, quae intra Sedem Apostolicam indole propria praeditae sunt, inceptum sunt doctrinae sociali Ecclesiae congruens, quae eas iudicat aptum subsidium esse ad tutam reddendam *iustitiam socialem* in necessitudinibus operatorem inter et conductorem. Non est tamen secundum Ecclesiae socialem doctrinam eiusmodi societates ad conflictationem praeter modum vergere aut ad ordinum inter ipsos dimicationem; nec nota politica insignes esse debent aut servire, aperte vel clam, causae alicuius factionis aut aliorum entium proposita spectantium valde diversae naturae.

Confidimus eiusmodi Consociationes, sicut ea est quam supra memoravimus—doctrinae socialis Ecclesiae principia sequentes—utile opus esse explicaturas in communitate laboris concorditer operante cum Sede Apostolica. Pro certo etiam habemus easdem, in ineundis quaestionibus ad laborem pertinentibus et in utiliter atque continuo disserendo cum Institutis competentibus, ante oculos esse habituras quoquo modo peculiarem Sedis Apostolicae naturam, sicut dictum est in prima huius Epistulae parte.

Quod ad ea attinet, quae exposuimus, Emi-

nence will wish to prepare suitable executive documents for furthering a work community according to the principles set forth by means of suitable norms and structures.

5. I emphasized in the Encyclical *Laborem exercens* that the worker's personal dignity requires expression in a particular relationship with the work entrusted to him. This relationship is objectively realizable in various ways according to the kind of work undertaken. It is realized subjectively when the worker lives it as "his own," even though he is working "for wages." Since the work in question here is performed within the Apostolic See and is therefore marked by the characteristics already mentioned, such a relationship calls for heartfelt sharing in that "concern for all the Churches" which is proper to the Chair of Peter.

Those who work for the Holy See must therefore have the profound conviction that their work above all entails an ecclesial responsibility to live in a spirit of authentic faith, and that the juridical-administrative aspects of their relationship with the Apostolic See stand in a particular light.

The Second Vatican Council provided us with copious teaching on the way in which all Christians, clerics, religious and laity can and ought to make such ecclesial concern their own.

So it seems necessary for all, especially those working with the Apostolic See, to deepen personal consciousness above all of the universal apostolic commitment of Christians and that arising from each one's specific vocation: that of the bishop, of the priest, of religious, of the laity. The answers to the present difficulties in the field of human labor are to be sought in the sphere of social justice. But they must also be sought in the area of an interior relationship with the work that each is called upon to perform. It seems evident that work—of whatever kind—carried out in the employment of the Apostolic See requires this in a quite special measure.

Besides the deepened interior relationship, this work calls for reciprocal respect, if it is to be advantageous and serene, based on human and Christian brotherhood by all and for all concerned. Only when it is allied with such brotherhood (that is, with love of man in truth), can justice manifest itself as true justice. We must try to find "of what spirit we are" (cf. Lk. 9:55, Vulg.).

nentia Tua opportuna instrumenta exsecutoria praeparabit ut, per accommodatas normas et structuras, foveatur profectus communitatis laboris iuxta exposita principia.

5. In Litteris Encyclicis a verbis «Laborem exercens» incipientibus monuimus dignitatem operatoris propriam exprimendam esse per specialem necessitudinem cum labore ei concredito. Ad hanc necessitudinem—quae ipsa per se multis modis fieri potest pro suscepti laboris genere—pervenitur subiective cum operator, quamvis operam exerceat «remuneratam», eam tamen exercet ut «propriam». Cum hic agatur de labore in ambitu Sedis Apostolicae exanclato ideoque fundamentali proprietate insignito, quae est supra memorata, haec necessitudo ardentem illam participationem postulat «sollicitudinis omnium Ecclesiarum», quae propria est Cathedrae Petri.

Qui itaque Sanctae Sedi serviunt persuasissimum habere debent laborem suum exigere ecclesialem obligationem vivendi ex spiritu verae fidei, ac partes iuridiciales et ad administrationem pertinentes necessitudinis cum Sede Apostolica, in luce peculiari consistere.

Concilium Vaticanum II multa nos docuit de ratione, qua omnes christiani, ecclesiastici, religiosi et laici, possunt—et debent—hanc ecclesialem sollicitudinem ad se revocare.

Oportere igitur videtur ut, praesertim ab iis qui Sedi Apostolicae cooperantur, *personalis* exacuatur conscientia, imprimis christianorum sedulitatis universalis simulque vocationis propriae cuiusque, sive episcopi, sive sacerdotis, sive religiosi, sive laici. Responsiones enim ad hodiernas difficultates in laboris humani provincia quaerendae sunt in finibus iustitiae socialis; sed sunt etiam quaerendae in interiore congruentia cum labore, quem quisque debet perficere. Patere videtur laborem—qualiscumque is est—sub potestate Sedis Apostolicae explicatum, id modo omnino singulari postulare.

Praeter altiorem congruentiam interiorem, hic labor, ut sit utilis et serenus, poscit mutuam observantiam, fraterna sodalitate nisam humana et christiana, ab omnibus et pro omnibus qui in illum incumbunt. Tum solum iustitia potest se aperire uti veram iustitiam, cum huic *fraternae sodalitati* coniungitur (id est amori erga

These latter questions have hardly been touched on here. They cannot be adequately formulated in administrative-juridical terms. This does not exempt us, however, from the search and effort necessary for making operative precisely within the circle of the Apostolic See that spirit of human work which comes from our Lord Jesus Christ.

As I entrust these thoughts, Most Reverend Cardinal, to your attentive consideration, I call down an abundance of the gifts of divine assistance upon the future commitment which putting them into practice requires. At the same time I impart my benediction to you from my heart and willingly extend it to all those who offer their meritorious service to the Apostolic See.

From the Vatican, 20 November 1982.

John Paul II

hominem in veritate praebito). Quaerendum nobis est «cuius spiritus simus» (cf. Lc 9, 55 Vulg.).

Hae quaestiones, quas postremo memoravimus, non possunt aeque enuntiari verbis iuridicialibus et ad administrationem pertinentibus. Hoc tamen non eximit inquisitione et nisu necessariis—et quidem in Sedis Apostolicae ambitu—ad efficientem reddendum illum humani laboris spiritum, qui a Domino nostro Iesu Christo proficiscitur.

Dum tibi, Venerabilis Frater, has cogitationes considerandas propronimus, pro futuro studio quod eaedem postulant, ut ad effectum adducantur, dona invocamus auxilii divini copiosa, tibique ex pectore Nostram impertimus Benedictionem, quam libenter etiam concedimus iis omnibus, qui bene meritam operam suam Sedi Apostolicae insumunt.

Ex Aedibus Vaticanis, die xx mensis Novembris, anno MCMLXXXII.

Ioannes Paulus PP. II

Code of Canon Law was designed and composed in Minion and Hiroshige Sans by Kachergis Book Design, Pittsboro, North Carolina; and printed on 50-pound Westminster Trade Book Natural and bound in Pearl Linen by Hamilton Printing Company, Rensselaer, New York.